# 62nd Annual Meeting of the Association for Computational Linguistics (ACL 2024)

System Demonstrations

Bangkok, Thailand
11-16 August 2024

ISBN: 979-8-3313-0150-7

**Printed from e-media with permission by:**

Curran Associates, Inc.
57 Morehouse Lane
Red Hook, NY 12571

CURRAN ASSOCIATES INC. proceedings.com

**Some format issues inherent in the e-media version may also appear in this print version.**



Printed with permission by Curran Associates, Inc. (2024)

For permission requests, please contact the Association for Computational Linguistics at the address below.

Association for Computational Linguistics
209 N. Eighth Street
Stroudsburg, Pennsylvania 18360

Phone: 1-570-476-8006
Fax: 1-570-476-0860

acl@aclweb.org

**Additional copies of this publication are available from:**

Curran Associates, Inc.
57 Morehouse Lane
Red Hook, NY 12571 USA
Phone: 845-758-0400
Fax: 845-758-2633
Email: curran@proceedings.com
Web: www.proceedings.com

ACL 2024

# 62nd Annual Meeting of the Association for Computational Linguistics (ACL 2024)

## Proceedings of the Conference

August 11-16, 2024

Order copies of this and other ACL proceedings from:

Association for Computational Linguistics (ACL)
317 Sidney Baker St. S
Suite 400 - 134
Kerrville, TX 78028
USA
Tel: +1-855-225-1962
acl@aclweb.org

# Introduction

The ACL 2024 System Demonstration Track (SDT) invites submissions to the Demonstration Program. The SDT at ACL 2024 is a venue for papers describing system demonstrations, ranging from early prototypes to mature production-ready systems. Publicly available open-source or open-access systems are of special interest.

All accepted demos are published in a companion volume of the conference proceedings. We expect at least one of the authors to present a live demo during a demo session at ACL 2024, with an accompanying poster.

Submissions will undergo a single-blind reviewing process. Therefore, papers may include author and affiliation information, and freely make references to previously published material, and URLs.

Following past years, we are incorporating ethical considerations in the review process. Authors will be allowed extra unlimited space after the main content for a broader impact statement or other discussion of ethics. Please review the ethics policy before submitting.

# Organizing Committee

**System Demonstration Chairs**

Yixin Cao, Singapore Management University
Yang Feng, Chinese Academy of Science
Deyi Xiong, Tianjin University

# Program Committee

Yixin Cao, Singapore Management University
Yang Feng, Chinese Academy of Sciences
Deyi Xiong, Tianjin University

# Table of Contents

# Program

**Monday, August 12, 2024**

11:00 - 12:30 *Demo Presentations A*

14:00 - 15:30 *Demo Presentations B*

16:00 - 17:30 *Demo Presentations C*

**Tuesday, August 13, 2024**

10:30 - 12:00 *Demo Presentations D*

16:00 - 17:30 *Demo Presentations E*

**Wednesday, August 14, 2024**

10:30 - 12:00 *Demo Presentations F*

# *PAI-Diffusion*: Constructing and Serving a Family of Open Chinese Diffusion Models for Text-to-image Synthesis on the Cloud

**Chengyu Wang[1], Zhongjie Duan[1,2], Bingyan Liu[1,3], Xinyi Zou[1], Cen Chen[2], Kui Jia[3], Jun Huang[1*]**

[1] Alibaba Group, Hangzhou, China

[2] East China Normal University, Shanghai, China

[3] South China University of Technology, Guangzhou, China

{chengyu.wcy,zouxinyi.zxy,huangjun.hj}@alibaba-inc.com

eeliubingyan@mail.scut.edu.cn,zjduan@stu.ecnu.edu.cn

cenchen@dase.ecnu.edu.cn,kuijia@gmail.com

## Abstract

Text-to-image synthesis for the Chinese language poses unique challenges due to its large vocabulary size, and intricate character relationships. While existing diffusion models have shown promise in generating images from textual descriptions, they often neglect domain-specific contexts and lack robustness in handling the Chinese language. This paper introduces *PAI-Diffusion*, a comprehensive framework that addresses these limitations. *PAI-Diffusion* incorporates both general and domain-specific Chinese diffusion models, enabling the generation of contextually relevant images. It explores the potential of using LoRA and ControlNet for fine-grained image style transfer and image editing, empowering users with enhanced control over image generation. Moreover, *PAI-Diffusion* seamlessly integrates with Alibaba Cloud's Platform for AI, providing accessible and scalable solutions. All the Chinese diffusion model checkpoints, LoRAs, and ControlNets, including domain-specific ones, are publicly available. A user-friendly Chinese WebUI and the *diffusers-api* elastic inference toolkit, also open-sourced, further facilitate the easy deployment of *PAI-Diffusion* models in various local and cloud environments, making it a valuable resource for Chinese text-to-image synthesis. [1]

## 1 Introduction

Recently, diffusion models (Rombach et al., 2022; Saharia et al., 2022) have emerged to address the challenges of generating realistic and high-quality images from textual descriptions. This research area has obtained widespread attention, driven by the increasing demand for automated image synthesis in various applications, such as art design, virtual reality, etc (Cao et al., 2023; Sun et al., 2023).

In the community, Stable Diffusion[2] has gained significant popularity due to its ability to generate high-quality images that align well with textual descriptions. However, when it comes to handling the Chinese language, similar models encounter certain challenges that hinder its performance. From the linguistic aspect, Chinese is a morphologically rich language with a large vocabulary size and complex inter-dependencies between characters. Furthermore, Chinese characters often have multiple meanings and can be combined to form compound words, making it challenging to establish accurate and consistent mappings between textual descriptions and visual representations (Liu et al., 2022).

Previously, in the literature, several works have been proposed to make specialized adaptations of diffusion models to improve the performance of text-to-image synthesis for Chinese (Wang et al., 2022c; Chen et al., 2023; Hu et al., 2023). Yet, there are still some notable drawbacks that need to be addressed. i) Many existing models focus on generating images based on generic textual descriptions, neglecting the ability to generate images in specific domains or contexts. ii) For the Chinese language, the potential of using LoRA (Hu et al., 2022) and ControlNet (Zhang and Agrawala, 2023) for fine-grained image style transfer and image editing have not been fully explored. iii) The lack of support for cloud-based product integration is another important drawback. Given the increasing popularity of cloud-based services and the demand for scalable and accessible text-to-image solutions, it is crucial to develop models and solutions that can be easily integrated into cloud platforms or deployed as cloud-based services.

In this work, we formally present *PAI-Diffusion*, which consists of a family of open Chinese diffusion models, together with user-friendly toolkits to serve these models on the cloud. Major features of *PAI-Diffusion* include the following:

*Corresponding author.

[1]Video presentation: https://atp-modelzoo-sh.oss-cn-shanghai.aliyuncs.com/release/conf_demo/acl_demo_2024.mov.

[2]https://stability.ai/stablediffusion



*Proceedings of the 62nd Annual Meeting of the Association for Computational Linguistics (Volume 3: System Demonstrations)*, pages 1–8
August 11-16, 2024 

- *PAI-Diffusion* incorporates both general and domain-specific Chinese diffusion models, specifically allowing for the generation of images that are tailored to specific contexts or domains (such as Chinese cuisine, poetry and paintings). This enables users to create visually compelling and relevant images for various domain-specific applications.

- *PAI-Diffusion* explores the potential of using LoRA and ControlNet for fine-grained style transfer and image editing, with a variety of corresponding Chinese models released. This empowers users with greater control over the generated images, enabling them to manipulate fine-grained semantic attributes and modify visual features based on their preferences.

- *PAI-Diffusion* extends our previous work (Liu et al., 2023) and ensures seamless integration with our Platform for AI (PAI) of Alibaba Cloud[3], providing users with accessible and scalable solutions. By integrating with cloud products, *PAI-Diffusion* enables users to harness the power of cloud computing and enjoy the benefits of user-friendly and resource-efficient systems. For designers, our Chinese WebUI toolkit largely extends the Stable Diffusion WebUI[4] to enrich its abilities to address the issues of the Chinese language. For application developers, our elastic inference toolkit *diffusers-api* makes it easy to deploy these models as RESTful web services. It further supports our compiler performance optimization tool named *PAI-Blade* (Zhu et al., 2021). When the functionality is enabled, the image generation speed is improved by 2-3 times compared to native PyTorch implementation, while maintaining the effectiveness.

To realize our promise for the *openness* of our research, we have taken the following actions to contribute *PAI-Diffusion* to the community:

- All the diffusion models, LoRAs and ControlNets of *PAI-Diffusion*, including domain-specific ones, have been released in our organizational Hugging Face repository[5]. Users can easily download and fine-tune all the models in order to support their own domain-specific applications.

- Our Chinese WebUI and *diffusers-api* toolkits have also been made publicly available[6], so that *PAI-Diffusion* models are easy to be deployed in other environments beyond the Alibaba Cloud ecosystem, for both designers and application developers.

- All our models and codes are released under the Apache License (Version 2.0) to support both academic and commercial use.

## 2 Models

We introduce the models of *PAI-Diffusion*, a family of open Chinese diffusion models designed to address the challenges of generating high-quality images from Chinese textual descriptions.

### 2.1 Model Zoo

The model zoo of *PAI-Diffusion* consists of a collection of over ten open-source models, including base diffusion models, together with their corresponding LoRAs and ControlNets. A summary of these models is presented in Table 1, with a few cases of generated images presented in Figure 1. Readers can also find these models from our organizational Hugging Face repository described previously. Note that the list of models is not static. More new models will be added to the repository when they are ready to be released.

### 2.2 Model Architecture

To ensure full compatibility with the open-source community, our model architectures generally follow the *de facto* standard practice of Stable Diffusion (Rombach et al., 2022) where a CLIP-based text encoder, a U-Net and a VAE model are leveraged to obtain text embeddings, generate image embeddings in the latent diffusion space and decode the image for output, respectively. Particularly, the architectures of the U-Nets and VAEs of our large and xlarge diffusion models are in line with Stable Diffusion 1.5 and 2.1, respectively. Note that the difference between "large" and "xlarge" models is the size of generated images, rather than the number of parameters.

[3] https://www.alibabacloud.com/product/machine-learning

[4] https://github.com/AUTOMATIC1111/stable-diffusion-webui

[5] https://huggingface.co/alibaba-pai

[6] The Chinese WebUI extension is released under the EasyNLP (Wang et al., 2022a,b) framework: https://github.com/alibaba/EasyNLP/tree/master/diffusion/chinese_sd_webui The *diffusers-api* repository: https://github.com/alibaba/diffusers-api

Figure 1: Some examples of the generated images by *PAI-Diffusion* models. Prompts are originally in Chinese and have been manually translated into English for reference.

| Model Name | #Parameters | Image Size (Default) | Domain |
|---|---|---|---|
| pai-diffusion-general-large-zh | 1.04B | 512×512 | General purpose |
| -controlnet-canny | 361M | 512×512 | General purpose |
| -controlnet-depth | 361M | 512×512 | General purpose |
| pai-diffusion-general-xlarge-zh | 1.04B | 768×768 | General purpose |
| pai-diffusion-artist-large-zh | 1.04B | 512×512 | Artistic pictures |
| -controlnet-canny | 361M | 512×512 | Artistic pictures |
| -controlnet-depth | 361M | 512×512 | Artistic pictures |
| -lora-poem | 25.5M | 512×512 | Paintings for Chinese poems |
| -lora-2.5d | 25.5M | 512×512 | 2.5D-style arts |
| pai-diffusion-artist-xlarge-zh | 1.04B | 768×768 | Artistic pictures |
| pai-diffusion-food-large-zh | 1.04B | 512×512 | Chinese cuisines |
| pai-diffusion-anime-large-zh | 1.04B | 768×512 | Cartoon characters (anime) |

Table 1: A summary of Chinese diffusion models, LoRAs and ControlNets released by us.

As for the Chinese language, we follow our previous work (Liu et al., 2023) to employ both 100 million text-image pairs from Wukong (Gu et al., 2022) and the largest Chinese KG available to us, i.e., OpenKG[7] as our knowledge source to pre-train a Chinese knowledge-enhanced CLIP model that better understand the morphologically rich semantics of the Chinese language. The resources for training general-purpose models are also the same as in (Liu et al., 2023). For more details, we refer our readers to the original paper.

We have also collected a variety of domain-specific datasets to produce domain-specific diffusion models or LoRAs, depending on the volume of the corresponding datasets. Such domains include artistic pictures, paintings for Chinese poems, 2.5D-style arts, Chinese cuisines and cartoon characters. Note that we try our best to ensure that our models are built on legally and ethically sourced data. We specifically filter out any images that may have the probability to exhibit some degree of ethical bias. We obtain the permission to use in-house datasets (such as Chinese cuisine) to train and release the corresponding models.

ControlNet (Zhang and Agrawala, 2023) operates by incorporating a set of control vectors that encode specific image attributes or features. These control vectors are then incorporated into the residual blocks of the diffusion models. Furthermore, ControlNet allows for interactive image editing, enabling users to iteratively refine and modify the generated images, based on our WebUI toolkit. To enable fine-grained control, *PAI-Diffusion* integrates several ControlNets with Chinese diffusion models, facilitating the modification and customization of generated images based on user preferences. Currently, we have released the ControlNets based on canny edge detection (Canny, 1986) and Midas depth maps (Ranftl et al., 2022). Users can train their own ControlNets, using the same methods as ControlNet for Stable Diffusion.

### 2.3 Applications

*PAI-Diffusion* opens up a wide range of applications for the Chinese language. Here, we highlight some potential applications of *PAI-Diffusion*.

#### 2.3.1 Artistic Creations and Design

Diffusion models revolutionize the way sketch images are transformed into captivating artworks. With our models, users can witness their sketch images come to life based on the image-to-image pipeline. Examples can be found in Figure 2. We can see that our models empower artists to explore their creative boundaries and produce truly unique and mesmerizing artistic creations.

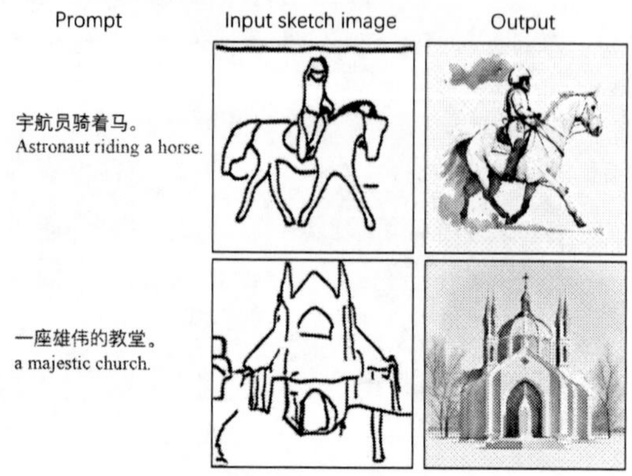


Figure 2: Two examples of artistic creations from sketch images using the image-to-image pipeline.

#### 2.3.2 Cultural Preservation and Heritage

Our models present an elegant approach to restoring ancient Chinese paintings through image inpainting techniques. By harnessing the power of diffusion, these applications enable the recreation of missing or damaged areas in the paintings, seamlessly blending them with the original artwork (with examples shown in Figure 3). Through the application, ancient Chinese paintings once damaged or fragmented can be revitalized, allowing future generations to appreciate the cultural significance of invaluable artistic treasures.

#### 2.3.3 Visual Reality Generation

Diffusion models offer a cutting-edge approach to creating immersive virtual reality experiences. Take traditional Chinese garden architecture as an example (see Figure 4). Our model blends various elements such as architecture, house and furniture to generate virtual scenes reminiscent of ancient Chinese gardens. Such applications serve as a valuable tool for people to experience and appreciate the beauty of ancient Chinese culture regardless of their physical location.

#### 2.3.4 Others

Apart from the three examples, our models can be harnessed in other domains such as fashion design, interior decor, and even product development. For

[7] http://openkg.cn/

Figure 3: Two examples of the restoration of ancient Chinese paintings via image in-painting.

instance, our model can create harmonious and visually stunning environments for interior decor. In fashion design, our diffusion models can be applied to blend both traditional and contemporary styles, creating unique and captivating clothing designs. We do not further elaborate.

## 3 Toolkits

*PAI-Diffusion* provides user-friendly toolkits that facilitate the deployment and usage of diffusion models for Chinese text-to-image synthesis. In this section, we briefly introduce our two toolkits.

### 3.1 Chinese WebUI Toolkit

The Chinese WebUI toolkit is an extension to the Stable Diffusion WebUI specifically developed to support our Chinese models. It offers a web-based graphical interface that allows users (especially designers without programming expertise) to interact with the diffusion models easily. The toolkit provides a seamless user experience, enabling users to perform image synthesizing and editing. Snapshots of the toolkit are shown in Figure 6. Additionally, our toolkit offers two modes: *single-node* mode and *cluster* mode (shown in Figure 5), providing users with options based on their specific requirements and resources, introduced as follows:

Figure 4: Four examples of scene generation for Chinese garden architecture using the text-to-image pipeline.

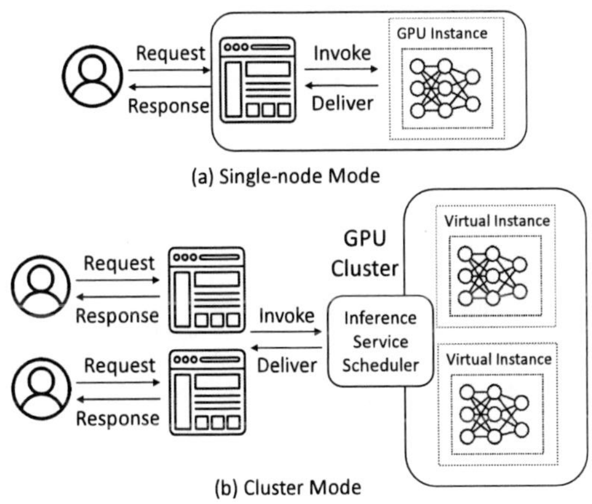


Figure 5: The system architectures of two modes to deploy our Chinese WebUI toolkit online.

- **Single-node**: It is suitable for scenarios when users want to quickly set up and use the toolkit with exclusive computational resources. It is particularly useful for individual users or small-scale deployments.
- **Cluster**: Leveraging the elastic inference service of PAI, the cluster is geared towards users who require high scalability and performance. In this mode, the toolkit utilizes a cluster of nodes to handle the workload, enabling parallel processing and efficient utilization of resources. It ensures efficient scaling and responsiveness, making it suitable for enterprise-level deployments or applications that require extensive computational power.

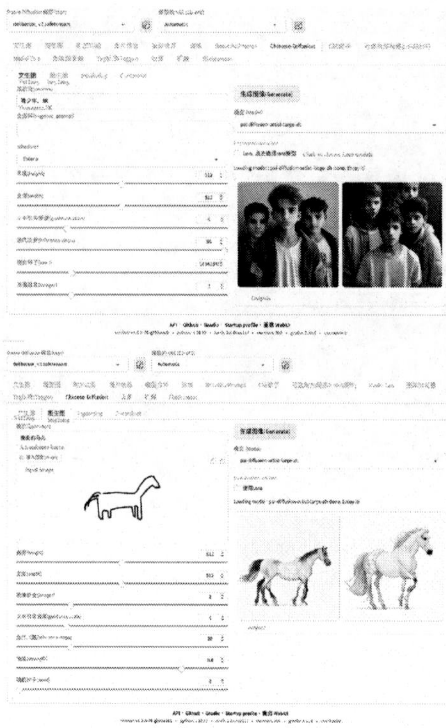

Figure 6: The snapshots of Chinese WebUI for text-to-image and image-to-image synthesis.

## 3.2 The *diffusers-api* Toolkit

The *diffusers-api* toolkit is built upon the Hugging Face *diffusers* library[8] that provides a cloud service implementation for *PAI-Diffusion* models based on the PAI elastic inference service.[9] Especially, we implement several inference pipelines customized for our Chinese models. Users can take advantage of a number of functions when sending HTTP requests, including text-to-image synthesis, image-to-image synthesis, image in-painting, image editing, etc. Below we show a sample request body for calling the *diffusers-api* service, with Chinese prompts manually translated into English for better understanding:

```
{
 "task_id": "001",
 "prompt": "romantic starry sky",
 "negative_prompt": "noise, low-quality",
 "func_name" : "t2i",
 "steps": 25,
 "image_num": 1,
 "width": 512,
 "height": 512,
 "use_base64": True
}
```

| Settings | PyTorch Native | *diffusers-api* |
|---|---|---|
| Inference time (s) | 6.34 | **2.96** |
| GPU memory (GB) | 6.94 | **5.56** |

Table 2: The performance of *diffusers-api* for online deployment of our diffusion model.

where "`func_name`" refers to the specific functionality that the user wish to use ("`t2i`" refers to text-to-image in this case). We release the source code of *diffusers-api* to provide users with the ability to quickly develop customized API services. This allows for easier implementation of any desired functionality, tailored to specific requirements. For example, users can build and customize their own schedulers (Duan et al., 2023).

In addition, *diffusers-api* leverages the AI compiler *PAI-Blade* (Zhu et al., 2021) for inference optimization. It significantly reduces the end-to-end latency of the inference processes and the GPU memory consumption, which ensures improved performance and efficiency in generating high-quality images, without any precision loss in computation. To verify the correctness of our argument, we have deployed our Chinese diffusion model (the large version) online using an NVIDIA A10 GPU with 50 sampling steps for inference. The generated image size is fixed to 512×512. We repeat the experiments in 20 times and report the averaged results in Table 2, which clearly prove the correctness of our claim.

## 4 Conclusion

This paper presents *PAI-Diffusion* to address the challenges in Chinese text-to-image synthesis. *PAI-Diffusion* integrates both general and domain-specific Chinese diffusion models, LoRAs and ControlNets, enabling the generation of contextually relevant images. Moreover, *PAI-Diffusion* ensures seamless integration with our cloud platform, offering accessible and scalable solutions. The release of models further encourages collaboration and innovation in the field. The public availability of Chinese WebUI and *diffusers-api* toolkits simplifies deployment in various environments. Our advancements pave the way for further research and development in Chinese text-to-image synthesis and relevant applications.

[8]`https://github.com/huggingface/diffusers`

[9]Note that *diffusers-api* is also compatible with original Stable Diffusion, which is not the focus of this paper.

## Acknowledgements

The authors would like to thank other members of the Platform for AI (PAI) team of Alibaba Cloud for the help of this work. This work was in part supported by the National Natural Science Foundation of China under grant number 62202170, Fundamental Research Funds for the Central Universities under grant number YBNLTS2023-014, Alibaba Group through Alibaba Innovative Research Program, and Alibaba Cloud through Research Talent Program with South China University of Technology.

## Limitations

There are still some limitations that should be acknowledged. The effectiveness of our models heavily relies on accurate mappings between textual descriptions and visual representations. While efforts have been made to include a variety of domain-specific models, there may still be domains or contexts for which specialized models are not available. This limitation restricts the full potential in generating highly relevant and specific images for a wide range of applications. We suggest that users should further fine-tune our models if necessary.

## Ethical Considerations

It is important to consider the ethical implications associated with its use and deployment. Diffusion models like *PAI-Diffusion* learn from large datasets, which may inadvertently contain biases present in the data. It is crucial to be aware of and mitigate any biases that may be perpetuated in the generated images. In addition, *PAI-Diffusion* has the potential to be misused for unethical purposes, such as generating inappropriate or harmful contents. Therefore, users should be encouraged to adhere to ethical standards and abide by terms and regulations when utilizing *PAI-Diffusion* models.

## References

John F. Canny. 1986. A computational approach to edge detection. *IEEE Trans. Pattern Anal. Mach. Intell.*, 8(6):679–698.

Shidong Cao, Wenhao Chai, Shengyu Hao, Yanting Zhang, Hangyue Chen, and Gaoang Wang. 2023. Difffashion: Reference-based fashion design with structure-aware transfer by diffusion models. *CoRR*, abs/2302.06826.

Zhongzhi Chen, Guang Liu, Bo-Wen Zhang, Qinghong Yang, and Ledell Wu. 2023. Altclip: Altering the language encoder in CLIP for extended language capabilities. In *ACL (Findings)*, pages 8666–8682. Association for Computational Linguistics.

Zhongjie Duan, Chengyu Wang, Cen Chen, Jun Huang, and Weining Qian. 2023. Optimal linear subspace search: Learning to construct fast and high-quality schedulers for diffusion models. *CoRR*, abs/2305.14677.

Jiaxi Gu, Xiaojun Meng, Guansong Lu, Lu Hou, Minzhe Niu, Hang Xu, Xiaodan Liang, Wei Zhang, Xin Jiang, and Chunjing Xu. 2022. Wukong: 100 million large-scale chinese cross-modal pre-training dataset and A foundation framework. *CoRR*, abs/2202.06767.

Edward J. Hu, Yelong Shen, Phillip Wallis, Zeyuan Allen-Zhu, Yuanzhi Li, Shean Wang, Lu Wang, and Weizhu Chen. 2022. Lora: Low-rank adaptation of large language models. In *ICLR*. OpenReview.net.

Jinyi Hu, Xu Han, Xiaoyuan Yi, Yutong Chen, Wenhao Li, Zhiyuan Liu, and Maosong Sun. 2023. Efficient cross-lingual transfer for chinese stable diffusion with images as pivots. *CoRR*, abs/2305.11540.

Bingyan Liu, Weifeng Lin, Zhongjie Duan, Chengyu Wang, Ziheng Wu, Zhang Zipeng, Kui Jia, Lianwen Jin, Cen Chen, and Jun Huang. 2023. Rapid diffusion: Building domain-specific text-to-image synthesizers with fast inference speed. In *ACL*, pages 295–304. Association for Computational Linguistics.

Tingting Liu, Chengyu Wang, Xiangru Zhu, Lei Li, Minghui Qiu, Jun Huang, Ming Gao, and Yanghua Xiao. 2022. ARTIST: A transformer-based chinese text-to-image synthesizer digesting linguistic and world knowledge. In *EMNLP (Findings)*, pages 881–888. Association for Computational Linguistics.

René Ranftl, Katrin Lasinger, David Hafner, Konrad Schindler, and Vladlen Koltun. 2022. Towards robust monocular depth estimation: Mixing datasets for zero-shot cross-dataset transfer. *IEEE Trans. Pattern Anal. Mach. Intell.*, 44(3):1623–1637.

Robin Rombach, Andreas Blattmann, Dominik Lorenz, Patrick Esser, and Björn Ommer. 2022. High-resolution image synthesis with latent diffusion models. In *IEEE/CVF Conference on Computer Vision and Pattern Recognition*, pages 10674–10685. IEEE.

Chitwan Saharia, William Chan, Saurabh Saxena, Lala Li, Jay Whang, Emily L. Denton, Seyed Kamyar Seyed Ghasemipour, Raphael Gontijo Lopes, Burcu Karagol Ayan, Tim Salimans, Jonathan Ho, David J. Fleet, and Mohammad Norouzi. 2022. Photorealistic text-to-image diffusion models with deep language understanding. In *NeurIPS*.

Shiqi Sun, Shancheng Fang, Qian He, and Wei Liu. 2023. Design booster: A text-guided diffusion model for image translation with spatial layout preservation. *CoRR*, abs/2302.02284.

Chengyu Wang, Minghui Qiu, and Jun Huang. 2022a. Building natural language processing applications with easynlp. In *CIKM*, pages 5100–5101. ACM.

Chengyu Wang, Minghui Qiu, Taolin Zhang, Tingting Liu, Lei Li, Jianing Wang, Ming Wang, Jun Huang, and Wei Lin. 2022b. Easynlp: A comprehensive and easy-to-use toolkit for natural language processing. In *EMNLP*, pages 22–29. Association for Computational Linguistics.

Junjie Wang, Yuxiang Zhang, Lin Zhang, Ping Yang, Xinyu Gao, Ziwei Wu, Xiaoqun Dong, Junqing He, Jianheng Zhuo, Qi Yang, Yongfeng Huang, Xiayu Li, Yanghan Wu, Junyu Lu, Xinyu Zhu, Weifeng Chen, Ting Han, Kunhao Pan, Rui Wang, Hao Wang, Xiaojun Wu, Zhongshen Zeng, Chongpei Chen, Ruyi Gan, and Jiaxing Zhang. 2022c. Fengshenbang 1.0: Being the foundation of chinese cognitive intelligence. *CoRR*, abs/2209.02970.

Lvmin Zhang and Maneesh Agrawala. 2023. Adding conditional control to text-to-image diffusion models. *CoRR*, abs/2302.05543.

Kai Zhu, Wenyi Zhao, Zhen Zheng, Tianyou Guo, Pengzhan Zhao, Junjie Bai, Jun Yang, Xiaoyong Liu, Lansong Diao, and Wei Lin. 2021. DISC: A dynamic shape compiler for machine learning workloads. In *EuroMLSys@EuroSys*, pages 89–95. ACM.

# OpenVNA: A Framework for Analyzing the Behavior of Multimodal Language Understanding System under Noisy Scenarios

**Ziqi Yuan**[1,2], **Baozheng Zhang**[1,3,5], **Hua Xu**[1,5]*, **Zhiyun Liang**[1,4], and **Kai Gao**[3]

[1] State Key Laboratory of Intelligent Technology and Systems, Department of Computer Science and Technology, Tsinghua University

[2] Beijing National Research Center for Information Science and Technology (BNRist)

[3] School of Information Science and Engineering, Hebei University of Science and Technology

[4] College of Information and Electrical Engineering, China Agricultural University

[5] Samton (Jiangxi) Technology Development Co., Ltd

xuhua@tsinghua.edu.cn

## Abstract

We present OpenVNA, an open-source framework designed for analyzing the behavior of multimodal language understanding systems under noisy conditions. OpenVNA serves as an intuitive toolkit tailored for researchers, facilitating convenience batch-level robustness evaluation and on-the-fly instance-level demonstration. It primarily features a benchmark Python library for assessing global model robustness, offering high flexibility and extensibility, thereby enabling customization with user-defined noise types and models. Additionally, a GUI-based interface has been developed to intuitively analyze local model behavior. In this paper, we delineate the design principles and utilization of the created library and GUI-based web platform. Currently, OpenVNA is publicly accessible at `https://github.com/thuiar/OpenVNA`, with a demonstration video available at `https://youtu.be/0Z9cW7RGct4`.

## 1 Introduction

The Multimodal Language Understanding (MLU) task aims to empower artificial intelligence agents with the capability to comprehensively understand human communication, discerning the speaker's affective states (Baltrušaitis et al., 2018; Soleymani et al., 2017) and intentions (Zhang et al., 2022). Despite the proliferation of multimodal large language models has yielded remarkable achievements (Li et al., 2023; Maaz et al., 2023; Zhang et al., 2023), their application in real-world scenarios is still under development.

Analyzing the behaviors of MLU systems under carefully constructed noise offers a potential avenue for researchers to gain deeper insights into the possible limitations and underlying mechanisms of current MLU systems (Liang et al., 2021, 2022). Specifically, by evaluating the global behavior of MLU system under homologous manually constructed noise, researchers can ensure their model operate effectively in practical usage scenarios. Moreover, analyzing the local behavior of the MLU system under customized perturbed instances provides an understanding of how the model makes decisions, pinpointing which aspects of multimodal signals are pivotal for prediction. In recent years, researchers in this field have faced obstacles in imitating real-world noise in multimodal systems and quantitatively assessing the global robustness of MLU methods (Ma et al., 2022; Hazarika et al., 2022). Due to the lack of open-source noise injection toolkits and evaluation benchmarks, researchers frequently provide the model performance under specific simulated noise, leading to inequitable comparisons and susceptibility to overfitting on such noise patterns (Yuan et al., 2023).

To bridge the gap between simulated scenario and real world multimodal noise, benchmark current approaches, and provide intuitive local behavior analysis, we introduce OpenVNA, an open-source framework dedicated to analyze MLU system behavior under noisy scenario. The composition of the OpenVNA and the interconnections among its components are illustrated in Figure 1. Firstly, OpenVNA serves as a Python Library providing easy-to-use Application Programming Interfaces (APIs) for noise simulation, model reproduction, and global robustness evaluation. Presently, it incorporates fifteen noise injection techniques, eight integrated baseline models pertaining to two video understanding tasks, and can be easily extend to user defined tasks, noise configurations and models. Moreover, OpenVNA provide researchers a GUI-based interface to interactively analyze the local model behavior under user specific noisy scenario. The contributions of this work can be succinctly summarized as follows,

1. The OpenVNA contains one of the most com-

* Hua Xu is the corresponding author. Email: xuhua@tsinghua.edu.cn



*Proceedings of the 62nd Annual Meeting of the Association for Computational Linguistics (Volume 3: System Demonstrations)*, pages 9–18
August 11-16, 2024 

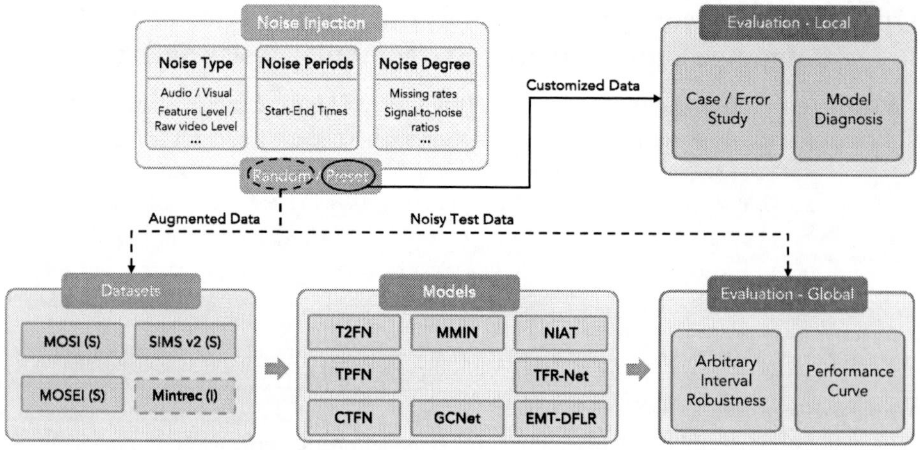


Figure 1: OpenVNA is an comprehensive Python library for analyzing MLU system behavior under noise, which consists of noise injection module, datasets module, models module, instance-level (local) and batch-level (global) evaluation module. For instance level model behavior evaluation, an online platform is also available.

prehensive video noise injection toolkits, covering the most cases in real world applications.

2. The OpenVNA framework serves as a robust MLU benchmark, which providing unified noisy dataset construction, benchmark model reproducing and global robustness evaluation. The modular pipeline makes it very easy to integrate new models for a reliable comparison with existing baselines.

3. The OpenVNA framework offers a GUI-based interface, facilitating users to effortlessly apply user-defined noise to a given video and compare extracted features and model predictions, thus enabling the analysis of local model behavior and even model diagnostics.

## 2 Related Works

**MultiBench.** MultiBench (Liang et al., 2021) is a comprehensive benchmark that presents three fundamental challenges in multimodal representation learning, including generalization, complexity, and robustness. Concerning robustness, MultiBench initially outlines potential perturbations across diverse heterogeneous sources and introduces several criteria for measuring robustness. However, MultiBench primarily treats video resources as time-series and restricts the discussion to feature-level imperfections, overlooking general raw video-level perturbations. In this study, we concentrate on perturbations in video applications and further extend the previous quantitative robustness criteria to encompass all types of video noise.

**Robust-MSA.** The Robust-MSA (Mao et al., 2022b) is developed primarily as a demonstration platform to showcase the impact of raw video-level perturbations on MSA models. The instance level evaluation platform integrated in OpenVNA is carefully enhanced, derives partially from the Robust-MSA system. It now provides support for a broader spectrum of perturbation types, allows for custom noise injection in JSON format, and includes other notable advancements to enhance its capabilities. Furthermore, the OpenVNA framework presented in this paper strives for a more comprehensive scope by establishing a standardized evaluation process, facilitating seamless integration of newly developed models, and providing noise generation APIs to enable large-scale data generation with real-world imperfections, specifically tailored for human-centered video understanding applications.

## 3 System Design

In this section, we present the functionality of the noise injection toolkit, the global robustness evaluation benchmark, and the GUI-based interface for local behavior analysis. We commence with the noise injection toolkit, as it occupies a central position within the OpenVNA.

### 3.1 Noise Injection Toolkit

The noise injection module is designed to processes raw video input in accordance with the provided configuration. For raw data level noise, we implement a *real_noise* function to generate user-specific

| | Noise Type | Fine-grained Noise Category |
|---|---|---|
| **Text** | Erasing | Word Erasing Attack. |
| | Replacement | Word Replacement Attack. |
| | ASR Error | Automatic translation error using wav2vec2-large (Grosman, 2021). |
| **Audio** | Mute and Insulation | Low-pass Filter and Volume Attenuation. |
| | Reverberation | Hall Equalization and Room Equalization. |
| | Color Noise | White, Pink, Brown, Blue, Violet and Velvet Noise. |
| | Scenarios Noise | Sudden Noise and Background Noise (traffic and music, etc.) |
| **Video** | Visual Occlusion | Partial Black Draw-box and Entire Black Screen. |
| | Visual Blurriness | Gaussian Blur and Average Blur. |
| | Noises in Digital Images | Gaussian Additive Noise. |
| | Visual Noise on Color Space | Contrast, Brightness, Saturation Adjustment, Color Inversion, Channel Switching. |

Table 1: Types of raw data level noise supported in the OpenVNA framework. In general, eight categories of raw video level noise with more than twenty fine-grained noise is covered in the OpenVNA.

| | Categories | Integrated Dataset and Methods |
|---|---|---|
| **Datasets** | Intention | MIntrec (Zhang et al., 2022) |
| | Sentiment | MOSI (Zadeh et al., 2016), MOSEI (Zadeh et al., 2018), SIMS v2 (Liu et al., 2022) |
| **Methods** | Tensor Regularization | T2FN (Liang et al., 2019), TPFN (Li et al., 2020) |
| | Reconstruction | TFR-Net (Yuan et al., 2021), NIAT (Yuan et al., 2023), EMT-DFLR (Sun et al., 2023) |
| | Translation | CTFN(Tang et al., 2021), MMIN (Zhao et al., 2021), GCNet (Lian et al., 2023) |

Table 2: Integrated Datasets and Methods in OpenVNA.

noise according to the list of noise items indicating the type of noise, start time, end time, and degree of noise. Based on the above function, a class named *RealNoiseConfig* is implemented to generate random noise configurations given alternative noise types and intensity levels. This class serves the purpose of generating noisy test data or facilitating noise-based augmentation. OpenVNA is capable of adapting to different video formats for input, and processing different video resolutions and duration, efficiently completing original video processing. For implementation, FFmpeg[1] library is utilized for video format conversion and video editing.

**Supported Noise.** Human-centered video applications naturally contains three distinct modalities: audio, visual, and textual modalities. At feature level, all three modality can be regraded as extracted feature sequence, therefore existing perturbations on time series data are considered, including random feature drop (random erasure of feature sequences with zero-padding vectors) and structural feature drop (erasing of feature sequences with zero-padding vectors in succession) (Yuan et al., 2023; Liang et al., 2021). While at raw data level, audio, visual, and text are heterogeneous, different structure of noise should be considered separately. For textual modality, as the spoken words are commonly obtained from the audio modality using the Automatic Speech Recognition (ASR) technique, ASR error[2] becomes the most common noise, and supported in OpenVNA system. Besides, attacks on text including word erasing or word replacement are also supported in OpenVNA APIs. For the audio modality, four types of noise, simulating various noise sources, are considered, including mute and insulation, reverberation, color noise in laboratory environment, and additive real-world scenarios noise. For visual modality, occlusion, blurriness, noises in digital images, and noise on color space are supported. Table 1 summarizes the supported raw data level noise and provides brief description for each type of noise, while detailed introduction can be found in Appendix A.

### 3.2 Global Robustness Benchmark

OpenVNA offers researchers a unified pipeline for robust MLU model training, comprising the dataset module, method module, and evaluation module. Here, we will introduce each module individually.

**Dataset Module.** The dataset module furnishes a unified data loader interface for each supported dataset with high extensibility. Users can specific the used dataset for model reproduction using the

[1]https://www.ffmpeg.org/

[2]ASR errors resulting from the injected audio modality noise are also taken into account.

-dataset command line argument. As shown in Table 2, OpenVNA now encompasses two specific downstream tasks, namely multimodal sentiment analysis (MSA) and multimodal intention recognition (MIR). For the MSA task, it offers support for CMU-MOSI (Zadeh et al., 2016), CMU-MOSEI (Zadeh et al., 2018) in English, as well as CH-SIMS v2 (Liu et al., 2022) in Chinese. As for the MIR task, it also integrates the Mintrec dataset (Zhang et al., 2022). Detailed description of the above integrated databases can be found in Appendix B. Additionally, it is noteworthy that the constructed noisy instances are retained within the overall databases to facilitate noise-based data augmentation.

**Method Module.** The method module offers a unified interface for model construction. Users can specific the used approach using the --model command line argument. Besides performing model training on original MLU datasets, OpenVNA provides optional robust training technique with generated noisy training data. By utilizing the --augmentation argument, the framework will additionally load the constructed noisy training instances and treat them as augmented data during the training process. Currently, as summarized in Table 2, OpenVNA contains eight robust MLU methods and can be roughly segmented into the tensor regularization based methods (Liang et al., 2019; Li et al., 2020), the reconstruction based methods (Yuan et al., 2021; Sun et al., 2023; Yuan et al., 2023) and the translation based method (Zhao et al., 2021; Tang et al., 2021; Lian et al., 2023). Detailed description of all above baselines are presented in Appendix D.

**Evaluation Module.** The batch-level evaluation module of OpenVNA is devised with the aim of offering a thorough quantitative performance comparison between various methods under certain type of noise. For quantitative comparison, OpenVNA amalgamates the model performance across varying degrees of noise, offering a holistic evaluation of the robustness pertaining to the given type of noise. Specifically, OpenVNA utilizes Arbitrary Interval Robustness (AIR) as evaluation metrics,

$$\gamma_{\mathsf{abs}}(f) = \int_{\sigma_{\min}}^{\sigma_{\max}} acc_{\sigma}(f) d\sigma, \tag{1}$$

where $[\sigma_{\min}, \sigma_{\max}]$ denotes the range of considered imperfection levels, which may vary for different types of video perturbation. This criteria geometrically evaluates the area under the accuracy-imperfection curve. In default evaluation process in OpenVNA, the integral is approximately calculated by uniformly taking the function values of 10 interior points on the interval. Besides quantitative results, performance curve are also provided for intuitive demonstration.

### 3.3 Local Robustness Interface

The instance-level evaluation module is an GUI-based web platform designed to provide a user-friendly interface for intuitive noise injection, error case studies, and even model diagnosis. It facilitates an intuitive comparison of the extracted modality features and model predictions between the original and noisy video clips. In terms of implementation, the frontend of the platform is constructed using Vue 3.0, while the backend is crafted using the Flask library in Python. Detailed installation instructions for the platform are provided on GitHub to enhance user accessibility.

## 4 Framework Evaluation

### 4.1 Noise Injection Toolkit

We present an example of injecting raw data level noise with the provided APIs below. In this example, for the visual modality, noise is randomly chosen from 'Gaussian blur' and 'blank', covering 80% of the video clip with a noise intensity of 0.5. Meanwhile, for the acoustic modality, 'reverberation' noise with a noise intensity of 0.3 is injected into the entire (100%) audio waveform.

```
from noise_api.real_noise import
    real_noise, real_noise_config

cfg = real_noise_config(
    "test.mp4",
    mode = "random_full",
    v_noise_list = ["gblur", "blank"],
    v_noise_num = 2,
    v_noise_ratio = 0.8,
    v_noise_intensity = 0.5,
    a_noise_list = ["reverb"],
    a_noise_num = 1,
    a_noise_ratio = 1.0,
    a_noise_intensity = 0.3,
)._asdict()

# Noise Injection with cfg.
real_noise(
    "examples/test.mp4",
    "examples/test_out.mp4", **cfg
)
```

Listing 1: An example of injecting raw data level noise using OpenVNA framework.

| Model | R-Drop | | S-Drop | | G-Blur | | Impulse | | Color-W | | BG-Park | |
|---|---|---|---|---|---|---|---|---|---|---|---|---|
| | Acc-2 | F1 | Acc-2 | F1 | Acc-2 | F1 | Acc-2 | F1 | Acc-2 | F1 | Acc-2 | F1 |
| TPFN | 64.06 | 62.96 | 64.76 | 64.04 | 76.91 | 76.81 | 76.77 | 76.63 | 61.95 | 59.61 | 62.19 | 59.57 |
| T2FN | 64.97 | 63.70 | 66.56 | 65.88 | 77.61 | 77.58 | 77.33 | 77.14 | 62.63 | 60.88 | 62.07 | 60.21 |
| MMIN | 63.33 | 62.23 | 65.90 | 65.45 | 76.47 | 76.53 | 76.34 | 76.42 | 60.31 | 59.90 | 59.32 | 58.87 |
| CTFN | 62.35 | 60.09 | 63.48 | 61.86 | 76.87 | 76.88 | 76.98 | 76.98 | 63.13 | 61.50 | 62.04 | 60.61 |
| GCNET | 63.84 | 63.01 | 64.78 | 62.80 | 76.44 | 76.10 | 76.35 | 76.30 | 59.10 | 58.58 | 59.76 | 58.92 |
| TPFN* | 66.89 | 63.06 | 67.54 | 65.56 | 76.34 | 76.35 | 77.30 | 77.22 | 63.39 | 61.90 | 62.74 | 60.05 |
| T2FN* | 65.70 | 64.21 | 66.15 | 62.11 | 76.34 | 76.35 | 76.23 | 76.24 | 63.02 | 59.26 | 62.16 | 59.29 |
| MMIN* | 66.76 | 64.74 | 68.19 | 66.09 | 76.31 | 76.29 | 76.84 | 76.78 | 62.62 | 61.54 | 61.72 | 61.55 |
| CTFN* | 66.54 | 65.05 | 66.73 | 66.04 | 77.14 | 77.09 | 76.82 | 76.79 | 63.32 | 61.27 | 62.94 | 61.23 |
| GCNET* | 66.32 | 63.70 | 67.44 | 63.80 | 76.26 | 76.17 | 75.47 | 75.23 | 62.05 | 59.72 | 61.34 | 60.27 |
| TFR-Net* | 67.47 | 65.93 | 67.55 | 66.84 | 76.06 | 76.03 | 76.36 | 76.31 | 63.07 | 61.81 | 61.80 | 61.95 |
| NIAT* | 66.32 | 66.19 | 64.94 | 63.66 | 76.51 | 76.54 | 76.11 | 76.02 | 63.29 | 62.64 | 63.04 | 62.50 |
| EMT-DLFR* | 67.93 | 67.22 | 68.85 | 68.37 | 77.41 | 77.45 | 76.69 | 76.80 | 63.36 | 63.34 | 63.81 | 63.85 |

Table 3: The performance of baselines on SIMS v2 dataset under random drop (denote as R-Drop), strutural drop (denote as S-Drop), Gaussian blur (denote as G-Blur), impulse value noise (denote as Impulse), white color noise (denote as Color-W) and background noise in park (denote as BG-Park). Models marked with a * indicate the utilization of noise-based data augmentation techniques for robust training.

| Type | Indicator | Interval |
|---|---|---|
| R-Drop | Missing Rate | [0.0, 1.0, 0.1] |
| S-Drop | Missing Rate | [0.0, 1.0, 0.1] |
| G-Blur | Sigma of Gaussian blur | [0, 10, 1] |
| Impulse | Strength for specific pixel | [0, 100, 10] |
| Color-W | Amplitude of the Noise | [0, 0.10, 0.01] |
| BG-Park | Amplitude of the Noise | [0.0, 1.0, 0.1] |

Table 4: Considered noise interval and brief description, where intervals are recorded in format [min, max, step].

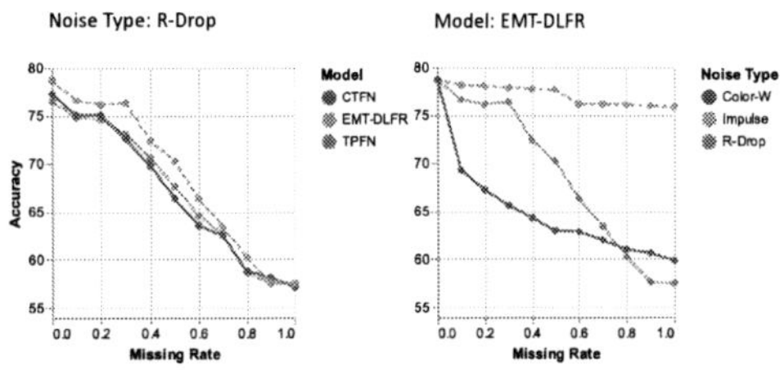


Figure 2: Fine-grained performance curve provided in OpenVNA for global robustness evaluation.

### 4.2 Global Robustness Benchmark

The global robustness benchmark contains both quantitative model comparison as well as the qualitative performance curve analysis.

**Quantitative Model Comparison.** In Table 3, we recorded the AIR metrics for typical type of noise on SIMS v2 dataset. Specifically, six types of noise are considered. For feature level noise, performance under random drop (denote as **R-Drop**) and structural drop (denote as **S-Drop**) are recorded. While for raw video level noise, Gaussian blur (denote as **G-Blur**) and impulse value noise (denote as **Impulse**) are evaluated for visual, white color noise (denote as **Color-W**) and background noise in park (denote as **BG-Park**) are utilized for audio modality. The noise level intervals being considered are documented in Table 4. Models marked with * indicate the utilization of noise-based data augmentation techniques, where the augmented data are generated by random drop. It can be observed that model robustness can be enhanced through noise-based augmentation even for unseen type of noise. More experimental results for other datasets are provided on Github[3].

**Qualitative Performance Curve.** OpenVNA also offers fine-grained performance curve comparison. As depicted in Figure 2, it allows researchers to analyze global performance from two perspectives. Firstly, comparisons can be made on the same type of noise with different models (the left sub-graph in Figure 2), providing an intuitive demonstration of how different models perform as the noise intensity increases, and aiding in model selection for various applications. Secondly, comparisons can be made on the same model with different types of noise (the right sub-graph in Figure 2), illustrating the model's sensitivity to each type of noise further enables model diagnosis and refinement.

### 4.3 GUI-based Interface for Local Analysis

The overall workflow of analyzing MLU model behavior through the provided GUI-based interface contains four main steps. Firstly, the user should upload their original video file. The Auto-

[3] https://github.com/thuiar/OpenVNA

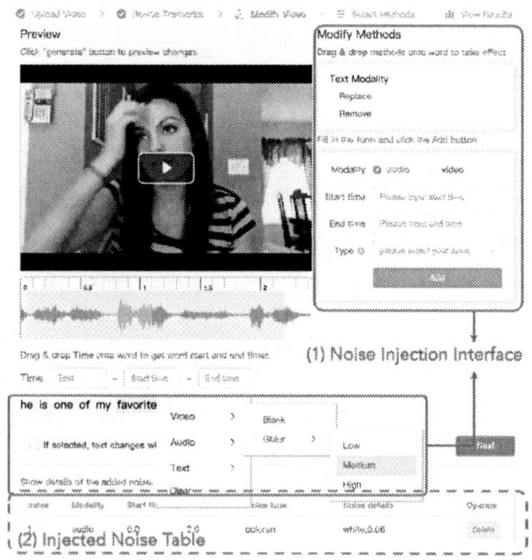


Figure 3: The GUI-based Interface of Noise Injection.

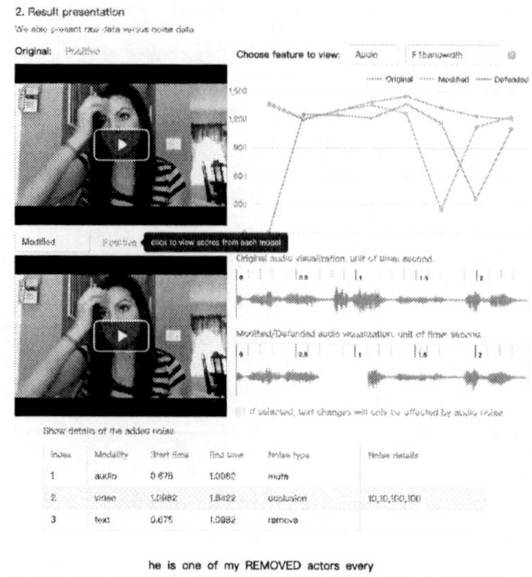


Figure 4: The GUI-based Interface of the Local model behavior analysis.

matic Speech Recognition (ASR) technique with wav2vec-large (Grosman, 2021) is employed to generate spoken words. Following generation process, users can manually edit and correct the ASR outputs. Based on the revised transcript, CTC segmentation (Kürzinger et al., 2020) is used to find utterance alignments within the audio files. Secondly, users can perform customized noise injection either by completing noise configuration forms or by directly applying specific noise onto the video. We provide the GUI-based interface of the noise injection step in Figure 3. The provided interface provides the boundaries of each recognized words and thus supports injecting aligned modality noise. After editing the noise configuration, the selected noise item will be found below in the injected noise table. The noise injection is processed after clicking the generate button. User can preview the generated noisy instance before performing local analysis. The third step becomes the selection of the evaluation model and optional denoising technique. Finally, the comparison of extracted feature sequences as well as the model prediction is demonstrated for error cases analysis and causality analysis. An example of the demonstration is shown in Figure 4.

## 5 Conclusion

In this work, we introduce OpenVNA, an open-source framework tailored for analyzing the behavior of multimodal language understanding systems under noisy conditions. This developed framework facilitates future researchers in two key ways. Firstly, OpenVNA serves as a highly extensible global robustness evaluation benchmark, integrating two video understanding tasks, four databases, and eight robust baselines. With a unified evaluation pipeline, convenient baseline reproduction is achievable, which enables a fair performance comparison. Moreover, with flexible noise injection toolkits, the provided pipeline further empowers researchers to assess designed models under analogous noise, which can be regarded as a superior simulation for real-world application scenarios. Secondly, OpenVNA provides a GUI-based interface for local model behavior analysis. Through detailed comparisons of extracted feature sequences and model predictions, ad-hoc model behavior explanations can be formulated, facilitating error case analysis and model diagnostics. The authors firmly believe that OpenVNA will make a significant contribution to the advancement of robust multimodal applications and foster future research endeavors.

## Acknowledgements

This work is founded by National Natural Science Foundation of China (Grant No. 62173195), National Science and Technology Major Project towards the new generation of broadband wireless mobile communication networks of Jiangxi Province (03 and 5G Major Project of Jiangxi Province, Grant No. 20232ABC03A02), and Natural Science Foundation of Hebei Province, China (Grant No. F2022208006).

## References

Tadas Baltrušaitis, Chaitanya Ahuja, and Louis-Philippe Morency. 2018. Multimodal machine learning: A survey and taxonomy. *IEEE transactions on pattern analysis and machine intelligence*, 41(2):423–443.

Tadas Baltrušaitis, Peter Robinson, and Louis-Philippe Morency. 2016. Openface: an open source facial behavior analysis toolkit. In *2016 IEEE winter conference on applications of computer vision (WACV)*, pages 1–10. IEEE.

Florian Eyben, Klaus R Scherer, Björn W Schuller, Johan Sundberg, Elisabeth André, Carlos Busso, Laurence Y Devillers, Julien Epps, Petri Laukka, Shrikanth S Narayanan, et al. 2015. The geneva minimalistic acoustic parameter set (gemaps) for voice research and affective computing. *IEEE transactions on affective computing*, 7(2):190–202.

Jonatas Grosman. 2021. Fine-tuned XLSR-53 large model for speech recognition in English. `https://huggingface.co/jonatasgrosman/wav2vec2-large-xlsr-53-english`.

Devamanyu Hazarika, Yingting Li, Bo Cheng, Shuai Zhao, Roger Zimmermann, and Soujanya Poria. 2022. Analyzing modality robustness in multimodal sentiment analysis. *arXiv preprint arXiv:2205.15465*.

Jacob Devlin Ming-Wei Chang Kenton and Lee Kristina Toutanova. 2019. Bert: Pre-training of deep bidirectional transformers for language understanding. In *Proceedings of naacL-HLT*, volume 1, page 2.

Ludwig Kürzinger, Dominik Winkelbauer, Lujun Li, Tobias Watzel, and Gerhard Rigoll. 2020. Ctc-segmentation of large corpora for german end-to-end speech recognition. In *Speech and Computer*, pages 267–278, Cham. Springer International Publishing.

Binghua Li, Chao Li, Feng Duan, Ning Zheng, and Qibin Zhao. 2020. Tpfn: Applying outer product along time to multimodal sentiment analysis fusion on incomplete data. In *European Conference on Computer Vision*, pages 431–447. Springer.

KunChang Li, Yinan He, Yi Wang, Yizhuo Li, Wenhai Wang, Ping Luo, Yali Wang, Limin Wang, and Yu Qiao. 2023. Videochat: Chat-centric video understanding. *arXiv preprint arXiv:2305.06355*.

Zheng Lian, Lan Chen, Licai Sun, Bin Liu, and Jianhua Tao. 2023. Gcnet: graph completion network for incomplete multimodal learning in conversation. *IEEE Transactions on Pattern Analysis and Machine Intelligence*.

P Liang, Y Lyu, X Fan, Z Wu, Y Cheng, J Wu, LY Chen, P Wu, MA Lee, Y Zhu, et al. 2021. Multibench: Multiscale benchmarks for multimodal representation learning. In *In Proceedings of the Neural Information Processing Systems Conference (Neurips)*.

Paul Pu Liang, Zhun Liu, Yao-Hung Hubert Tsai, Qibin Zhao, Ruslan Salakhutdinov, and Louis-Philippe Morency. 2019. Learning representations from imperfect time series data via tensor rank regularization. In *Proceedings of the 57th Annual Meeting of the Association for Computational Linguistics*, pages 1569–1576.

Paul Pu Liang, Amir Zadeh, and Louis-Philippe Morency. 2022. Foundations and recent trends in multimodal machine learning: Principles, challenges, and open questions. *arXiv preprint arXiv:2209.03430*.

Yihe Liu, Ziqi Yuan, Huisheng Mao, Zhiyun Liang, Wanqiuyue Yang, Yuanzhe Qiu, Tie Cheng, Xiaoteng Li, Hua Xu, and Kai Gao. 2022. Make acoustic and visual cues matter: Ch-sims v2. 0 dataset and av-mixup consistent module. In *Proceedings of the 2022 International Conference on Multimodal Interaction*, pages 247–258.

Mengmeng Ma, Jian Ren, Long Zhao, Davide Testuggine, and Xi Peng. 2022. Are multimodal transformers robust to missing modality? In *Proceedings of the IEEE/CVF Conference on Computer Vision and Pattern Recognition*, pages 18177–18186.

Muhammad Maaz, Hanoona Rasheed, Salman Khan, and Fahad Shahbaz Khan. 2023. Video-chatgpt: Towards detailed video understanding via large vision and language models. *arXiv preprint arXiv:2306.05424*.

Huisheng Mao, Ziqi Yuan, Hua Xu, Wenmeng Yu, Yihe Liu, and Kai Gao. 2022a. M-sena: An integrated platform for multimodal sentiment analysis. In *Proceedings of the 60th Annual Meeting of the Association for Computational Linguistics: System Demonstrations*, pages 204–213.

Huisheng Mao, Baozheng Zhang, Hua Xu, Ziqi Yuan, and Yihe Liu. 2022b. Robust-msa: Understanding the impact of modality noise on multimodal sentiment analysis. *arXiv preprint arXiv:2211.13484*.

Mohammad Soleymani, David Garcia, Brendan Jou, Björn Schuller, Shih-Fu Chang, and Maja Pantic. 2017. A survey of multimodal sentiment analysis. *Image and Vision Computing*, 65:3–14.

Licai Sun, Zheng Lian, Bin Liu, and Jianhua Tao. 2023. Efficient multimodal transformer with dual-level feature restoration for robust multimodal sentiment analysis. *IEEE Transactions on Affective Computing*.

Jiajia Tang, Kang Li, Xuanyu Jin, Andrzej Cichocki, Qibin Zhao, and Wanzeng Kong. 2021. Ctfn: Hierarchical learning for multimodal sentiment analysis using coupled-translation fusion network. In *Proceedings of the 59th Annual Meeting of the Association for Computational Linguistics and the 11th*

*International Joint Conference on Natural Language Processing (Volume 1: Long Papers)*, pages 5301–5311.

Ziqi Yuan, Wei Li, Hua Xu, and Wenmeng Yu. 2021. Transformer-based feature reconstruction network for robust multimodal sentiment analysis. In *Proceedings of the 29th ACM International Conference on Multimedia*, pages 4400–4407.

Ziqi Yuan, Yihe Liu, Hua Xu, and Kai Gao. 2023. Noise imitation based adversarial training for robust multimodal sentiment analysis. *IEEE Transactions on Multimedia*.

Amir Zadeh, Rowan Zellers, Eli Pincus, and Louis-Philippe Morency. 2016. Multimodal sentiment intensity analysis in videos: Facial gestures and verbal messages. *IEEE Intelligent Systems*, 31(6):82–88.

AmirAli Bagher Zadeh, Paul Pu Liang, Soujanya Poria, Erik Cambria, and Louis-Philippe Morency. 2018. Multimodal language analysis in the wild: Cmu-mosei dataset and interpretable dynamic fusion graph. In *Proceedings of the 56th Annual Meeting of the Association for Computational Linguistics (Volume 1: Long Papers)*, pages 2236–2246.

Hang Zhang, Xin Li, and Lidong Bing. 2023. Video-llama: An instruction-tuned audio-visual language model for video understanding. *arXiv preprint arXiv:2306.02858*.

Hanlei Zhang, Hua Xu, Xin Wang, Qianrui Zhou, Shaojie Zhao, and Jiayan Teng. 2022. Mintrec: A new dataset for multimodal intent recognition. In *Proceedings of the 30th ACM International Conference on Multimedia*, pages 1688–1697.

Jinming Zhao, Ruichen Li, and Qin Jin. 2021. Missing modality imagination network for emotion recognition with uncertain missing modalities. In *Proceedings of the 59th Annual Meeting of the Association for Computational Linguistics and the 11th International Joint Conference on Natural Language Processing (Volume 1: Long Papers)*, pages 2608–2618.

## A Details of Supported Noise

Detailed description of raw data level audio noise is provided as follows,

**Emulation of Mute and Insulation.** Due to the occurrence of insulation or translation errors, some voice components might be lost in the recorded audio wave form. A low-pass filter is employed to replicate the insulation effect, as high-frequency components are more susceptible to insulation. Additionally, a mute mode is incorporated to simulate the translation error and severe volume attenuation.

**Emulation of Reverberation.** Reverberation is a common speech phenomenon that arises within enclosed spaces, resulting from the superposition of direct and reflected sounds. This study involves simulating two archetypal forms of reverberation, namely hall and room equalization, by employing finite impulse response filters with pre-established reverberation hyperparameters.

**Color Noise in Laboratory Environment.** Color noise is a series of meticulously crafted laboratory-generated noise, stemming from the domain of psychological acoustics. It provides researchers with an ideal and controllable emulation of various environmental noises. Within this study, we have amalgamated six common types of color noise - white, pink, brown, blue, violet, and velvet noise - and blended them with the original speech to assess the overall robustness of the model. For an elaborate elucidation and depiction of each variant of color noise, comprehensive information can be found on the demo website, and Github.

**Real-world Scenarios Noise.** In addition to the ideal simulations, this study also presents nine distinct real-world recordings of acoustic noise from various environments, such as noise captured in parks, restaurants, and others. A comprehensive description and instances can be accessed on the public website. The real-world noise scenarios offered are properly combined with the original speech to effectively demonstrate the potential impacts on downstream video understanding tasks when exposed to such types of noise.

Detailed description for raw data level visual noise is provided as follows,

**Visual Occlusion.** Video clips in real-world applications may encounter occlusion in certain parts of the video region. The OpenVNA framework introduces occlusion by overlaying a black draw-box to cover the designated region.

**Visual Blurriness.** The most common types of blur include Gaussian blur, box blur, variable blur and radial blur. The developed OpenVNA implements Gaussian blur, which emulates a "frosted glass" effect, and the box blur, which imitates the Bokeh effect of a single-lens reflex camera.

**Noises in Digital Images.** This type of noise is naturally prevalent in digital images during image acquisition, coding, transmission, and processing stages. The OpenVNA framework incorporates Gaussian additive noise that normalizes the histogram concerning the gray values.

**Visual Noise on Color Space.** To introduce noise in the color space, the OpenVNA framework offers

| Model | R-Drop | | S-Drop | | G-Blur | | Impulse | | Color-W | | BG-Park | |
|---|---|---|---|---|---|---|---|---|---|---|---|---|
| | Acc-2 | F1 | Acc-2 | F1 | Acc-2 | F1 | Acc-2 | F1 | Acc-2 | F1 | Acc-2 | F1 |
| TPFN | 64.26 | 56.22 | 65.69 | 61.48 | 78.81 | 78.92 | 79.85 | 79.90 | 62.17 | 61.82 | 63.12 | 62.94 |
| T2FN | 64.07 | 59.19 | 63.87 | 59.92 | 79.14 | 79.19 | 79.43 | 79.40 | 64.72 | 64.64 | 65.23 | 65.24 |
| MMIN | 64.89 | 56.64 | 66.66 | 63.05 | 79.42 | 79.49 | 80.58 | 80.53 | 62.94 | 62.65 | 63.57 | 63.41 |
| CTFN | 65.52 | 57.76 | 67.61 | 63.92 | 80.02 | 80.05 | 79.44 | 79.51 | 66.34 | 66.19 | 66.39 | 66.19 |
| GCNET | 64.23 | 60.40 | 64.12 | 56.11 | 78.86 | 78.90 | 78.33 | 78.26 | 64.18 | 64.29 | 65.11 | 65.25 |
| TPFN* | 63.61 | 61.18 | 66.70 | 65.72 | 79.83 | 79.88 | 78.98 | 78.95 | 62.62 | 62.46 | 63.17 | 62.90 |
| T2FN* | 63.69 | 62.46 | 64.22 | 63.74 | 78.96 | 79.02 | 79.32 | 79.32 | 62.48 | 62.64 | 64.75 | 64.63 |
| MMIN* | 65.53 | 64.39 | 67.05 | 65.31 | 80.56 | 80.49 | 81.05 | 80.99 | 65.57 | 65.00 | 67.62 | 66.99 |
| CTFN* | 65.60 | 63.63 | 64.93 | 64.53 | 78.43 | 78.54 | 79.21 | 79.28 | 64.89 | 64.92 | 66.01 | 65.85 |
| GCNET* | 62.98 | 61.51 | 64.76 | 63.75 | 76.46 | 76.59 | 78.48 | 78.38 | 65.58 | 65.59 | 65.07 | 64.89 |
| TFR-Net* | 67.39 | 66.48 | 66.60 | 64.90 | 81.88 | 81.92 | 82.20 | 82.30 | 64.98 | 64.93 | 67.47 | 67.35 |
| NIAT* | 67.92 | 67.19 | 70.65 | 70.23 | 83.66 | 83.67 | 84.27 | 84.15 | 66.29 | 65.98 | 66.87 | 67.01 |
| EMT-DLFR* | 68.67 | 67.51 | 71.00 | 70.79 | 84.16 | 84.17 | 84.79 | 84.73 | 66.48 | 66.55 | 65.10 | 64.85 |

Table 5: The performance of selected baselines on MOSI dataset. * indicates that data augmentation is applied, and the augmentation type is consistent with the validation type.

strategies for contrast, brightness, saturation, and gamma adjustments, effectively simulating diverse illumination environments using color filters. Besides, color inversion and channel switching (e.g., from 'RGB' to 'BGR') are also integrated.

## B Details of Integrated Databases

The framework offers support for three distinguished benchmark datasets, namely MOSI, MOSEI, and CH-SIMS v2, meticulously curated for Multimodal Sentiment Analysis (MSA) endeavors. Furthermore, it encompasses the MIntRec dataset, designed to cater to the domain of Multimodal Information Retrieval (MIR) tasks.

**CMU-MOSI** (Zadeh et al., 2016) is a widely used MSA dataset containing 2199 video clips from 93 YouTube movie review videos. Labels range from -3 (strongly negative) to 3 (strongly positive).

**CMU-MOSEI** (Zadeh et al., 2018) is an extended version of the MOSI dataset, designed to include a larger number of utterances, a wider range of samples, speakers, and topics. It consists of 23,453 annotated video segments extracted from 5,000 videos. The dataset includes utterances from 1,000 distinct speakers and covers 250 different topics.

**CH-SIMS v2** (Liu et al., 2022) is a popular Chinese MSA benchmark dataset. It has doubled the size of the original CH-SIMS dataset, making it more comprehensive and diverse. Notably, this dataset has been verified to demonstrate the significance of nonverbal behaviors in predicting emotions.

**MIntRec** (Zhang et al., 2022) formulates intent classification based on data collected from the TV series Supermarkets. The dataset consists of 2,224 high-quality samples with text, video, and audio patterns, and includes 20 intent categories.

## C Feature Extraction

For all experiments in this paper, the MMSA-FET toolkit (Mao et al., 2022a) is employed to extract unaligned features. For visual modality, we extract 35 dimensions of Action Units (AUs) as described in OpenFace (Baltrušaitis et al., 2016) and 136 dimensions of 68 facial landmarks, at a sample rate of 10 frames per second. For audio modality, we use the eGeMAPSv02 feature set (Eyben et al., 2015), which is of 25 dimensions. For the text modality, we use BERT (Kenton and Toutanova, 2019) which consists of 768 dimensions.

## D Details of Integrated Baselines

**Tensor regularization based methods**: T2FN (Liang et al., 2019) uses tensor rank minimization to regularize the high rank caused by partial missing modalities. TPFN (Li et al., 2020) takes high-order statistics over both modalities and temporal dynamics into account, and calculate outer products along time-steps.

**Reconstruction based methods**: TFR-Net (Yuan et al., 2021) exploits intra-modal and inter-modal attention-based extractors to learn robust representations for each element in modality sequences and then use a reconstruction module to generate the missing modality features. EMT-DLFR (Sun et al., 2023) improve former low-level feature reconstruction with high-level feature attraction to achieve robust performance. NIAT (Yuan et al., 2023) integrates noise-aware adversarial training and utterance-level semantics reconstruction to narrow the representation gap between original and noisy data pairs.

**Translation based methods**: cTFN (Tang et al., 2021) models bi-directional cross-modality inter-correlation in parallel via couple learning, and establishes a hierarchical architecture to exploit multiple bi-directional translations. MMIN (Zhao et al., 2021) learns robust joint multimodal representations via the Cascade Residual Auto-encoder and Cycle Consistency Learning. GCNET Lian et al. (2023) leverages graph neural networks to capture temporal and speaker information in conversations, aiming to learn discriminative representations from modality-incomplete conversational data.

## E Supplementary Experiments

To gain a deeper understanding of the model's performance across various noise conditions, we have carefully chosen six distinct types of noise. For feature level noise, performance under random drop (denote as **R-Drop**) and structural drop (denote as **S-Drop**) are recorded. While for raw video level noise, Gaussian blur (denote as **G-Blur**) and impulse value noise (denote as **Impulse**) are evaluated for visual, white color noise (denote as **Color-W**) and background noise in park (denote as **BG-Park**) are utilized for audio. By introducing these noise types, our objective is to evaluate how the model behaves and performs in different noisy environments. This analysis will enable us to assess the model's robustness and adaptability to various noise sources, potentially identifying areas that require improvement. Table 3 presents the results on the SIMS v2 dataset, while Table 5 showcases the results on the MOSI dataset.

# XNLP: An Interactive Demonstration System for Universal Structured NLP

**Hao Fei**[1], **Meishan Zhang**[2], **Min Zhang**[2], **Tat-Seng Chua**[1]
[1] NExT++ Research Center, National University of Singapore
[2] Harbin Institute of Technology (Shenzhen), China
{haofei37,dcscts}@nus.edu.sg, {zhangmeishan,zhangmin2021}@hit.edu.cn

## Abstract

Structured Natural Language Processing (XNLP) is an important subset of NLP that entails understanding the underlying semantic or syntactic structure of texts, which serves as a foundational component for many downstream applications. Despite certain recent efforts to explore universal solutions for specific categories of XNLP tasks, a comprehensive and effective approach for unifying all XNLP tasks long remains underdeveloped. Meanwhile, while XNLP demonstration systems are vital for researchers exploring various XNLP tasks, existing platforms can be limited to, e.g., supporting few XNLP tasks, lacking interactivity and universalness. To this end, we propose an advanced XNLP demonstration system, where we leverage LLM to achieve universal XNLP, *with one model for all* with high generalizability. Overall, our system advances in multiple aspects, including universal XNLP modeling, high performance, interpretability, scalability, and interactivity, offering a unified platform for exploring diverse XNLP tasks in the community.[1]

## 1 Introduction

XNLP has been referred to as a special form of NLP tasks that involves holistically analyzing and interpreting the underlying semantic or syntactic structure within a text, such as Syntactic Dependency Parsing (Nivre, 2003), Information Extraction (Wang and Cohen, 2015), Coreference Resolution (Lee et al., 2017), and Opinion Extraction (Pontiki et al., 2016), etc. Figure 1 (upper part) illustrates some representative XNLP tasks under different categories. XNLP has been infrastructural for a wide range of downstream NLP applications, such as Knowledge Graph Construction (Bosselut et al., 2019), Empathetic Dialogue (Rashkin et al., 2019), and more newly-emerging applications and techniques (Tang et al., 2020).

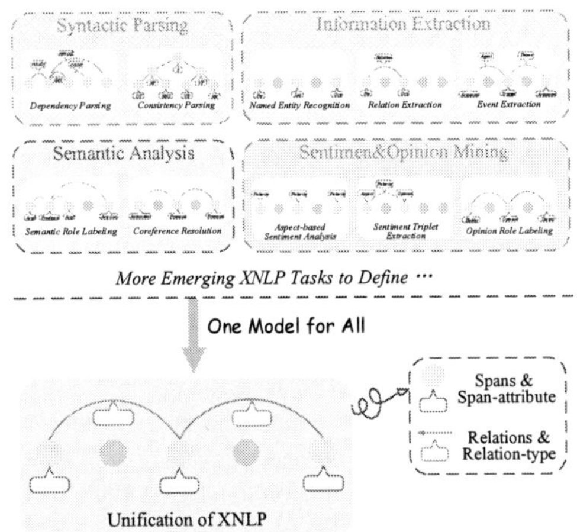


Figure 1: Illustration of the Structured NLP (XNLP) tasks, and the unification of XNLP by decomposing into the predictions of spans and relations.

As the key common characteristics, all the XNLP tasks have revolved around predicting two key elements from input: **1) textual spans** and **2) relations between spans** (Fei et al., 2022b), as depicted in the Figure 1 (lower part). Traditional efforts for XNLP have treated each task independently, which has led to limited utilization of shared features among XNLP tasks (He et al., 2019), and sub-optimal model generalization across different datasets (Chauhan et al., 2020), such as cross-language and cross-domain scenarios. In this paper, we emphasize the importance of Model Unification as a crucial topic in NLP. By unifying various NLP tasks under the XNLP framework, we can take advantage of the shared characteristics among tasks, leading to better model generalization and improved performance in realistic scenarios of product deployment.

Despite recent certain efforts in exploring universal solutions for some categories of XNLP tasks, such as Unified Sentiment Analysis (Chen and

[1] XNLP is online: https://xnlp.haofei.vip
Video demonstration at https://youtu.be/b0c-9HELEVw



*Proceedings of the 62nd Annual Meeting of the Association for Computational Linguistics (Volume 3: System Demonstrations)*, pages 19–30
August 11-16, 2024 

Qian, 2020; Fei et al., 2022a), and Universal Information Extraction (UIE; Lu et al., 2022; Fei et al., 2022b), a comprehensive and effective approach for unifying all XNLP tasks has not been fully established. Fortunately, Large Language Models (LLMs) (Vaswani et al., 2017; Raffel et al., 2020) present a potential solution for unification across all XNLP tasks. There is a recent development in the form of LLMs, e.g., ChatGPT (Ouyang et al., 2022), LLaMA (Touvron et al., 2023) and Vicuna (Peng et al., 2023), that have shown promising advancements in NLP and other fields. LLMs, with sufficient sizes of model and data, have demonstrated impressive generalization capabilities, well supporting the idea of *"One model for all"* (OpenAI, 2023). In this work, we propose taking advantage of LLMs to achieve universal XNLP, addressing the lack of a well-defined and holistic approach.

On the other hand, demonstration systems play a crucial role for researchers (especially beginners) exploring various XNLP tasks, providing a platform to analyze and understand the functionalities of different NLP components and their applications. While there are existing widely-used XNLP demo systems, such as *CoreNLP*[2], *AllenNLP*[3], we have observed several key issues with them: 1) limited to only a few specific tasks; 2) lacking interactive and extensible features, making it challenging to support dynamic growth in new XNLP tasks; 3) not universal systems, requiring separate models for each task, which can lead to increased overhead. To address these limitations, this work aims to build an advanced platform that provides superior XNLP demonstrations and benefits the broader NLP community.

In summary, our system advances in the following aspects.

1) **Universalness**
   - Our XNLP system takes the existing open-source LLMs as the backbone engine with excellent generalization capabilities, enabling unified prediction of various XNLP tasks, leading to a streamlined and cohesive XNLP ecosystem.
   - The LLM-based system supports end-to-end predictions for complex structured tasks, regardless of whether the spans are nested or discontinuous, making it versatile and adaptable to different linguistic structures.

2) **High Performance**
   - Our system is capable of few-shot or weakly-supervised learning. Having undergone extensive pre-training, LLMs do not require in-domain fine-tuning on specific task data.
   - Our system supports open-label and vocabulary predictions, utilizing LLM's generalization capabilities to discover new labels and vocabs with superior out-of-domain generalization.
   - Our approach naturally lends itself to cross-lingual, code-switching, and cross-domain settings.

3) **Scalability&Interpretability&Interactivity**
   - The system allows dynamic addition and definition of new tasks, requiring users only to provide demonstrations for the new tasks.
   - Predictions generated by our system are interpretable, as LLMs are able to provide rationales for their decisions, explaining why a specific result is produced.
   - The system enables user-machine interaction, empowering users to provide feedback, thereby allowing the system to refine its predictions based on user input.

## 2 Related Work

### 2.1 Structured NLP

Over the last few decades, XNLP has garnered significant research attention, with several works addressing specific aspects of XNLP tasks, spanning from linguistic/syntactic parsing (Kitaev and Klein, 2018), to information extraction (Mikheev et al., 1999), to semantic analysis (He et al., 2017) and to sentiment analysis & opinion mining (Wu et al., 2021). Prior studies and efforts have been paid and achieved notable developments for each of the XNLP tasks, such as Syntactic Dependency Parsing (Nivre, 2003), Information Extraction (Wang and Cohen, 2015), Coreference Resolution (Lee et al., 2017), and Opinion Extraction (Pontiki et al., 2016), etc. Different XNLP tasks may have different specific task definitions, while prediction formats of all the XNLP tasks can be reduced to the same prototype: the term extraction and relation detection (Lu et al., 2022; Fei et al., 2022b).

**Demonstration for XNLP.** The development of demonstration platforms has been crucial for educational and academic purposes, e.g., aiding researchers to explore various tasks and gaining hands-on experiences. Existing widely-employed

[2] `http://corenlp.run/`

[3] `https://demo.allennlp.org/`

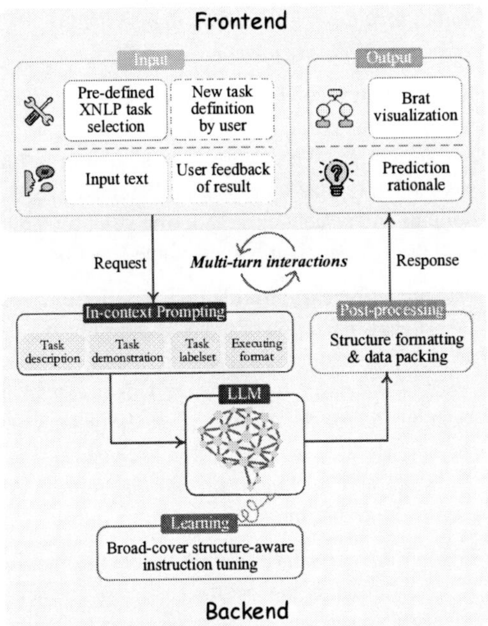


Figure 2: The overall architecture of our XNLP system includes the **frontend** module and the **backend** module.

open demo systems for XNLP include *CoreNLP*[4], *AllenNLP*[5] and *Explosion.ai*[6] etc. While offering user-friendly web interface for users to access a set of XNLP functionalities, there remain certain limitations, such as lacking flexibility for incorporating new tasks, non-universalness for model and cross-domain generalization.

## 2.2 Model Unification

There have been notable efforts to explore universal modeling for a type of NLP tasks (Chen and Qian, 2020; Fei et al., 2022a; Lu et al., 2022; Fei et al., 2022b), showcasing the benefit and potential of model unification, e.g., better leverage of shared characteristics and knowledge across tasks, simplified model maintenance, and enhanced system efficiency. However, a comprehensive and effective approach for unifying all XNLP tasks remains under-investigated. In this work, by capitalizing on LLM's robustness and broad applicability, we aim to pave the way for an advanced unified framework capable of handling diverse XNLP tasks effectively.

# 3 System Design

**Architecture overview.** We design our XNLP demo system into a web interface form. Built based on the Django[7] framework, XNLP divides the functions into the **frontend** module and the **backend** module. As shown in Figure 2, the frontend takes user inputs and displays the visualization of outputs, and the backend provides task prediction services with LLM as its core engine, based on the in-context learning paradigm. Also, it is possible for multi-turn interactions between frontend and backend.

## 3.1 Backend

**Backbone LLM.** Among a list of open-source LLMs, we consider the Vicuna-13B[8] as our backbone. Trained by fine-tuning LLaMA (Touvron et al., 2023) on user-shared conversations collected from ShareGPT, Vicuna has achieved more than 90% of OpenAI ChatGPT's (Peng et al., 2023) quality in user preference tests.

**In-context learning.** To elicit LLM to induce task predictions, we build in-context prompts. We note that to ensure the support of universal XNLP for any potential tasks and inputs, the prompt template should cover rich and informative information from the user end. Thus, we design the prompt by mainly covering the **task name**, **task description**, **task demonstration**, **task label set**, **executing format**, **input text**, **language** and **domain**.

```
{Task-desc}
---------------------------------------------
For example, {Task-demo}
---------------------------------------------
Note the task output format should
be with this: {Exe-format}
---------------------------------------------
And generally, the desired predicted
labels should be within the following
given label set: {Task-label}
---------------------------------------------
Now, given a new test input:
"{Input-text}", please do the task
of {Task-name}.
---------------------------------------------
Note the input is with {Language}
language, and the text is from the
{Domain} domain.
---------------------------------------------
Please predict all possible results
strictly following the exact given
format, without any other output of
explanations.
```

Fed with the above prompt, the LLM is ex-

[4] http://corenlp.run/
[5] https://demo.allennlp.org/
[6] https://explosion.ai/

[7] https://www.djangoproject.com/, v4.2.4
[8] https://github.com/lm-sys/FastChat

pected to output prediction in the provided format (**executing format**), with which, the post-process program further parses and polishes the structure result, and packs data to return to the frontend.

**Broad-cover structure-aware instruction tuning.** While LLM's outputs are sequential, XNLP tasks are highly structured. Thus, we expect the LLM to generate strictly structural results conditioned on sequence inputs. We consider further tuning the LLM with a *broad-cover structure-aware instruction tuning* mechanism. Instruction tuning is an emergent paradigm of LLM fine-tuning wherein natural language instructions are leveraged with LLM to induce the desired result more accurately. We write the XNLP predictions (outputs) for any input prompt by formatting the predictions into task-agnostic (i.e., task broad-covering) well-formed structure representations as in Fei et al. (2022b).

**Structure formatting.** As aforementioned, all the XNLP can be unified by predicting two key elements: the term extraction (with the span attribute) and relation detection (with the relation type), as illustrated in Figure 1. To unify all XNLP tasks, we follow Fei et al. (2022b) and design a structure formatter, where all the XNLP task outputs share the same structural representations. As shown in Figure 4, under the structure formatted, all XNLP tasks have been divided into the span extraction, pair extraction and hyper-pair extraction.

### 3.2 Frontend

As illustrated in Figure 2 (upper part), the frontend of XNLP receives inputs of 1) texts or user feedback or 2) task metadata (pre-defined or user-defined), and exhibits outputs from LLM. Following we mainly describe the key features of the frontend module as listed below.

**Pre-defined XNLP tasks.** To facilitate the user operation, we pre-defined total 22 XNLP tasks, covering four frequent categories, including Syntax Parsing, Information Extraction, Semantic Analysis and Sentiment/Opinion Mining.

**New task definition.** As there are rapidly-emergent XNLP tasks in the NLP community, it is impossible to cover it all in the pre-definition. We thus allow users to define their own XNLP tasks. This can be easily accomplished in our system without much effort, as the LLM has exceptional zero-shot performance and understanding ability. We require from the user only the *task name, task description, task demonstration, task label set, executing format.*

**XNLP structure visualization.** The key role of XNLP system is the visualization of the task output structure. We employ the open-source *brat* system[9] to realize this. *brat* has been shown very popular and effective in rendering structured data, with pretty visualization and stable functions.

**Rationale for explainable task prediction.** Besides the visualization of direct task results, we also display the rationale for each prediction, allowing *seeing what and knowing why.* This is especially meaningful for the beginners of the researchers for XNLP tasks. To enable this, we just ask LLM *"How and why do you make your decision?"* after each task prediction.

**Enhancing prediction with user interaction.** To take full advantage of the LLM, we further allow users to interact with our system by providing any feedbacks, so that users can revise the task predictions whenever they feel the results are not incorrect or coincident with their minds. To reach this, we also add another round of query to LLM, by asking *"The above prediction is not all right, because Feedback. Please do the task again by carefully taking the feedback here".*

## 4 System Walkthrough

Figure 3 gives a comprehensive walkthrough of how the system can be operated by users.

- ▶ **Step-1.** *users select or define a task;*
- ▶ **Step-2.** *users go through (for pre-defined) or fill in (for user-defined) the task prompt;*
- ▶ **Step-3.** *users key in the text to analyze;*
- ▶ **Step-4.** *users submit the text & metadata and request result;*
- ▶ **Step-5.** *users can browse the visualization of task output;*
- ▶ **Step-6.** *users observe the rationale of this result;*
- ▶ **Step-7.** *users can further provide feedback for the system to re-generate result;*

Following we demonstrate XNLP system by walking readers through several important functions.

### 4.1 User-allowed Operations

**Pre-defined XNLP task selection.** For the first step, users should select an XNLP task template

[9] https://brat.nlplab.org/

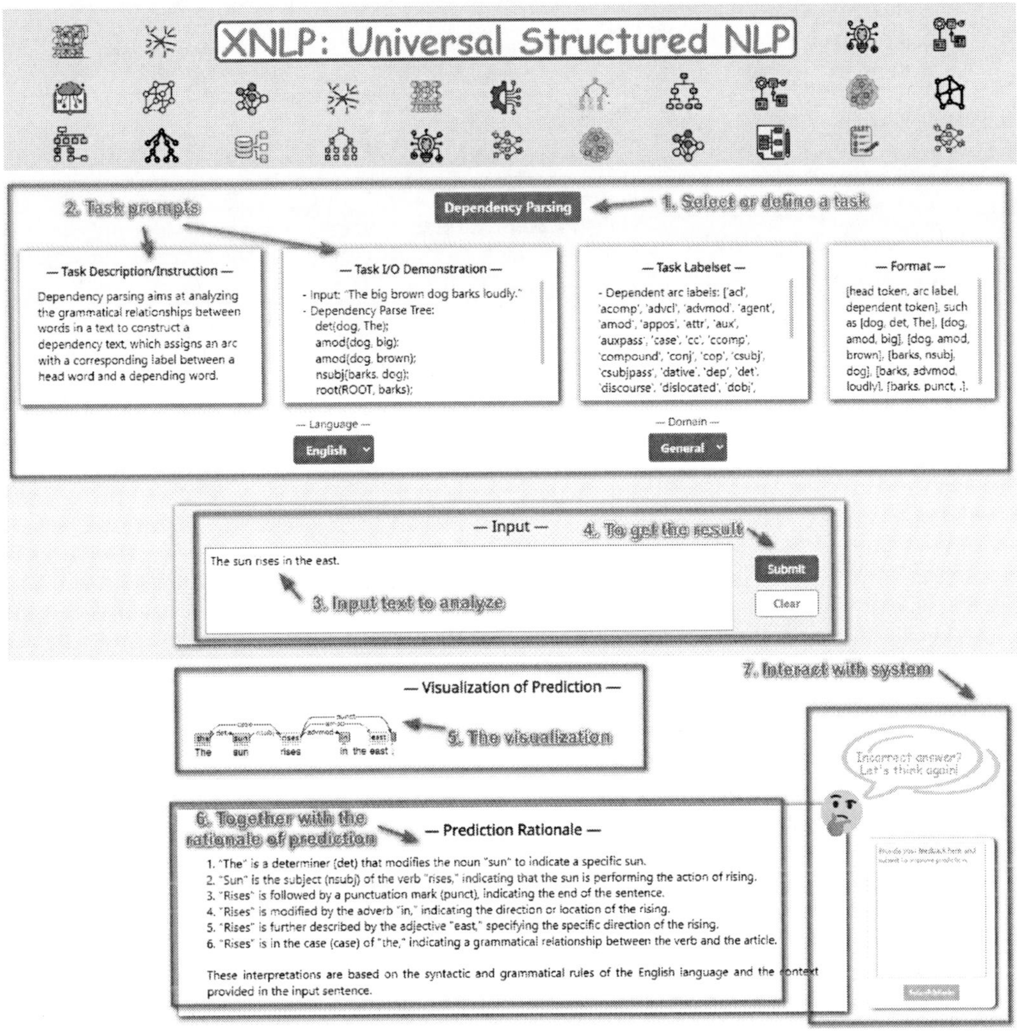


Figure 3: Screenshot of the XNLP web application, where key functions are annotated.

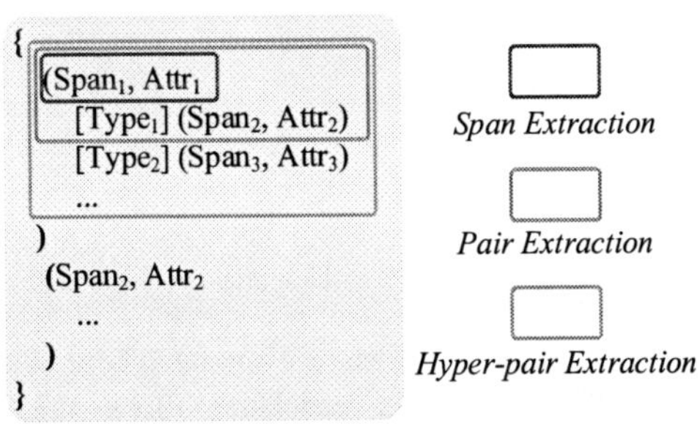


Figure 4: Structure formatter for universal XNLP.

from the 22 system pre-defined pools. The operation is shown in Figure 7 in Appendix §A.

**New task definition.** Or, user can define their own tasks. As shown in Figure 8 in Appendix §B, users should decide the task name, and fill in the task metadata (task prompt) as shown in Figure 3, and also select a pre-defined task with which the new task shares most similarity.

**Language and domain notifications.** To enable more accurate predictions, it is better to explicitly notify LLM what language and domain the input has. Figure 10 in Appendix §D and Figure 11 in Appendix §E illustrate the operations, respectively.

**Improving/Revising Prediction with User Feedback** Figure 9 in Appendix §C showcase the operation for the multi-turn user interaction.

### 4.2 Task Visualization

Here we showcase the XNLP task visualizations of real examples via our system. Figure 5 renders the outputs for the four task clusters, with each

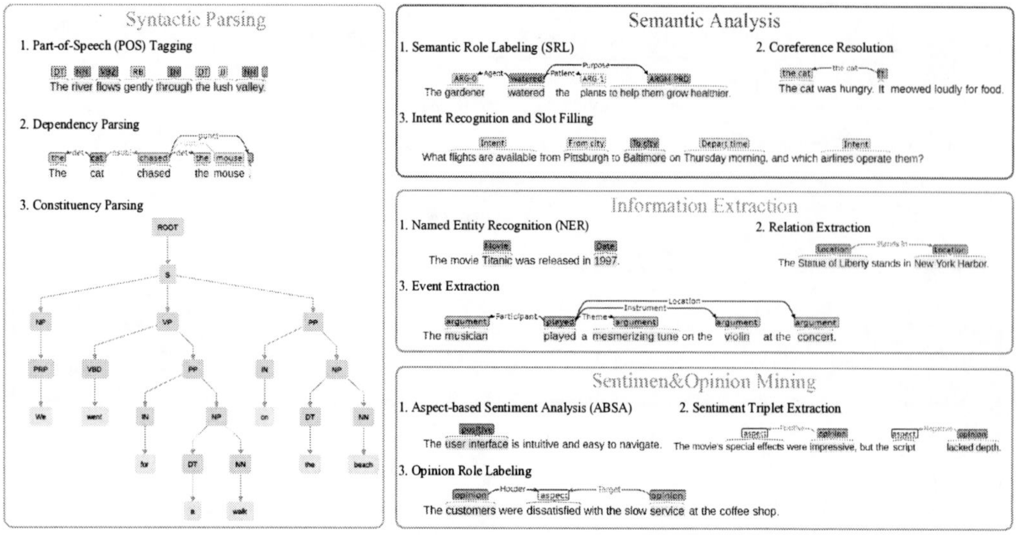


Figure 5: Screenshots of the visualizations of 12 representative XNLP tasks. Best viewing with zooming in.

showing three representative task results, such as:

**Syntax parsing,** including Part-of-Speech (POS) Tagging, Dependency Parsing and Constituency Parsing.

**Semantic analysis,** including Semantic Role Labeling (SRL), Coreference Resolution, and Intent Recognition and Slot Filling.

**Information extraction,** including Named Entity Recognition (NER), Relation Extraction, and Event Extraction.

**Sentiment/opinion mining,** including Aspect-based Sentiment Analysis (ABSA), Sentiment Triplet Extraction and Opinion Role Labeling.

We can observe from the visualizations that, 1) the structure visualizations are pretty, owing to the use of the brat system; 2) the results of tasks are correct, for which we give the credit to the integration of LLM, and also the *broad-cover structure-aware instruction tuning* mechanism.

## 5 Performance Evaluation

To quantitatively verify the performance of the backbone LLM on XNLP tasks, we now perform evaluations. We compare the Vicuna (13B) with the ChatGPT over 100 randomly selected test instances of 6 XNLP tasks. The experiments are based on one-shot in-context learning, i.e., with one demonstration as input. Figure 6 shows the comparisons. We see Vicuna has a slightly lower performance than ChatGPT, while Vicuna after broad-cover structure-aware instruction tuning (Vicuna+StruIT) shows results even much better than ChatGPT, with smaller model size (13B vs. 175B).

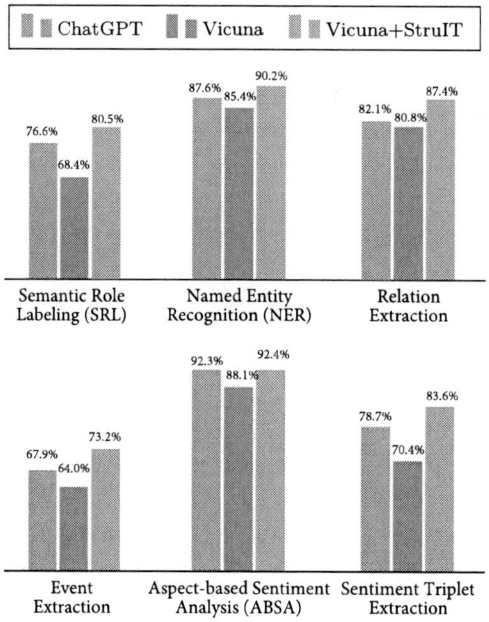


Figure 6: Comparisons (end-to-end prediction, in accuracy) between ChatGPT and Vicuna on XNLP tasks.

## 6 Conclusion

We present XNLP, an advanced online demonstration system for interaction and visualization of XNLP tasks. XNLP, built upon LLM, effectively models all the XNLP tasks universally, achieving *one model for all* in zero-shot or weak supervision. XNLP not only renders the output structures with delicate visualizations, but also provides rationales for interpretable predictions. Also, XNLP allows the users to define newly emergent XNLP tasks; and enables users to dynamically revise the output with multi-turn interactions. Our XNLP contributes to the community by paving the way for a unified, scalable, and interactive demonstration platform.

## Limitations

The focus of this paper was introducing an open online web application (demonstration system) to make the interaction of XNLP tasks available to as many practitioners as possible, but there are a couple of limitations in the system and the model we proposed. First, our system is based on the web service form, with the LLM running at the backend deployed at the online server, where sometimes when the Internet traffic is bad, the user may wait for too long to get the response. Second, as the LLM essentially generates sequential texts of any inputs, there are chances that the output texts include problematic structured formatter (i.e., structural representations, cf. Figure 4). With ill-formed structural representations, it is problematic to parse them into correct data used for rendering into brat visualization, i.e., causing failure prediction. Third, as one of the nature characteristics, LLM may sometimes generate false output, or do not obey the input instructions, which has been called the *Hallucination* phenomenon (Varshney et al., 2023). In such case, the user experience will be affected. Lastly, the current version of the system is still at a basic stage, and there are functionalities at the user interface level that need further polishing and improvement in subsequent updates.

## Ethics Statement

Our XNLP system uses the LLM as backbone. While the Vacuna model is fine-tuned on the pretrained LLaMA model, which is known to contain some toxic contents (Schick et al., 2021), an internal check does not reveal any toxic generation. However, there is a potential risk that the Vacuna could generate toxic text for users due to the underlying black-box LLM.

## References


Antoine Bosselut, Hannah Rashkin, Maarten Sap, Chaitanya Malaviya, Asli Celikyilmaz, and Yejin Choi. 2019. COMET: Commonsense transformers for automatic knowledge graph construction. In *Proceedings of the 57th ACL*, pages 4762–4779.

Dushyant Singh Chauhan, Dhanush S R, Asif Ekbal, and Pushpak Bhattacharyya. 2020. Sentiment and emotion help sarcasm? a multi-task learning framework for multi-modal sarcasm, sentiment and emotion analysis. In *Proceedings of the 58th ACL*, pages 4351–4360.

Zhuang Chen and Tieyun Qian. 2020. Relation-aware collaborative learning for unified aspect-based sentiment analysis. In *Proceedings of the 58th ACL*, pages 3685–3694.

Hao Fei, Fei Li, Chenliang Li, Shengqiong Wu, Jingye Li, and Donghong Ji. 2022a. Inheriting the wisdom of predecessors: A multiplex cascade framework for unified aspect-based sentiment analysis. In *Proceedings of the Thirty-First International Joint Conference on Artificial Intelligence, IJCAI*, pages 4121–4128.

Hao Fei, Shengqiong Wu, Jingye Li, Bobo Li, Fei Li, Libo Qin, Meishan Zhang, Min Zhang, and Tat-Seng Chua. 2022b. Lasuie: Unifying information extraction with latent adaptive structure-aware generative language model. In *Proceedings of the Advances in Neural Information Processing Systems, NeurIPS 2022*, pages 15460–15475.

Luheng He, Kenton Lee, Mike Lewis, and Luke Zettlemoyer. 2017. Deep semantic role labeling: What works and what's next. In *Proceedings of the 55th ACL (Volume 1: Long Papers)*, pages 473–483.

Ruidan He, Wee Sun Lee, Hwee Tou Ng, and Daniel Dahlmeier. 2019. An interactive multi-task learning network for end-to-end aspect-based sentiment analysis. In *Proceedings of the 57th ACL*, pages 504–515.

Nikita Kitaev and Dan Klein. 2018. Constituency parsing with a self-attentive encoder. pages 2676–2686.

Kenton Lee, Luheng He, Mike Lewis, and Luke Zettlemoyer. 2017. End-to-end neural coreference resolution. In *Proceedings of the 2017 EMNLP*, pages 188–197.

Yaojie Lu, Qing Liu, Dai Dai, Xinyan Xiao, Hongyu Lin, Xianpei Han, Le Sun, and Hua Wu. 2022. Unified structure generation for universal information extraction. In *Proceedings of the 60th ACL (Volume 1: Long Papers)*, pages 5755–5772.

Andrei Mikheev, Marc Moens, and Claire Grover. 1999. Named entity recognition without gazetteers. In *Proceedings of the Ninth Conference of the European Chapter of the Association for Computational Linguistics*, pages 1–8.

Joakim Nivre. 2003. An efficient algorithm for projective dependency parsing. In *Proceedings of the Eighth International Conference on Parsing Technologies*, pages 149–160.

OpenAI. 2023. GPT-4 technical report. *CoRR*, abs/2303.08774.

Long Ouyang, Jeff Wu, Xu Jiang, Diogo Almeida, Carroll L Wainwright, Pamela Mishkin, Chong Zhang, Sandhini Agarwal, Katarina Slama, Alex Ray, et al. 2022. Training language models to follow instructions with human feedback. *arXiv preprint arXiv:2203.02155*.

Baolin Peng, Chunyuan Li, Pengcheng He, Michel Galley, and Jianfeng Gao. 2023. Instruction tuning with GPT-4. *CoRR*, abs/2304.03277.

Maria Pontiki, Dimitris Galanis, Haris Papageorgiou, Ion Androutsopoulos, Suresh Manandhar, Mohammad AL-Smadi, Mahmoud Al-Ayyoub, Yanyan Zhao, Bing Qin, Orphée De Clercq, Véronique Hoste, Marianna Apidianaki, Xavier Tannier, Natalia Loukachevitch, Evgeniy Kotelnikov, Nuria Bel, Salud María Jiménez-Zafra, and Gülşen Eryiğit. 2016. SemEval-2016 task 5: Aspect based sentiment analysis. In *Proceedings of the 10th International Workshop on Semantic Evaluation (SemEval-2016)*, pages 19–30.

Colin Raffel, Noam Shazeer, Adam Roberts, Katherine Lee, Sharan Narang, Michael Matena, Yanqi Zhou, Wei Li, and Peter J. Liu. 2020. Exploring the limits of transfer learning with a unified text-to-text transformer. *J. Mach. Learn. Res.*, 21:140:1–140:67.

Hannah Rashkin, Eric Michael Smith, Margaret Li, and Y-Lan Boureau. 2019. Towards empathetic open-domain conversation models: A new benchmark and dataset. In *Proceedings of the 57th ACL*, pages 5370–5381.

Timo Schick, Sahana Udupa, and Hinrich Schütze. 2021. Self-diagnosis and self-debiasing: A proposal for reducing corpus-based bias in NLP. *Trans. Assoc. Comput. Linguistics*, 9:1408–1424.

Hao Tang, Donghong Ji, Chenliang Li, and Qiji Zhou. 2020. Dependency graph enhanced dual-transformer structure for aspect-based sentiment classification. In *Proceedings of the 58th ACL*, pages 6578–6588.

Hugo Touvron, Thibaut Lavril, Gautier Izacard, Xavier Martinet, Marie-Anne Lachaux, Timothée Lacroix, Baptiste Rozière, Naman Goyal, Eric Hambro, Faisal Azhar, Aurélien Rodriguez, Armand Joulin, Edouard Grave, and Guillaume Lample. 2023. Llama: Open and efficient foundation language models. *CoRR*, abs/2302.13971.

Neeraj Varshney, Wenlin Yao, Hongming Zhang, Jianshu Chen, and Dong Yu. 2023. A stitch in time saves nine: Detecting and mitigating hallucinations of llms by validating low-confidence generation. *CoRR*, abs/2307.03987.

Ashish Vaswani, Noam Shazeer, Niki Parmar, Jakob Uszkoreit, Llion Jones, Aidan N. Gomez, Lukasz Kaiser, and Illia Polosukhin. 2017. Attention is all you need. In *Proceedings of the Advances in Neural Information Processing Systems 30: Annual Conference on Neural Information Processing Systems*, pages 5998–6008.

William Yang Wang and William W. Cohen. 2015. Joint information extraction and reasoning: A scalable statistical relational learning approach. In *Proceedings of the 53rd ACL and the 7th International Joint Conference on Natural Language Processing (Volume 1: Long Papers)*, pages 355–364.

Shengqiong Wu, Hao Fei, Yafeng Ren, Donghong Ji, and Jingye Li. 2021. Learn from syntax: Improving pair-wise aspect and opinion terms extraction with rich syntactic knowledge. In *Proceedings of the Thirtieth International Joint Conference on Artificial Intelligence*, pages 3957–3963.

## A Selection of Pre-defined XNLP Tasks

See Figure 7.

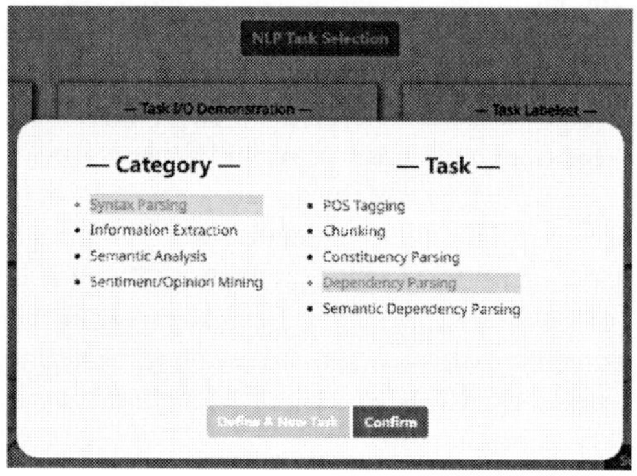


Figure 7: Screenshot of the selection panel of pre-defined XNLP tasks.

## B New XNLP Task Definition

See Figure 8.

## C Multi-turn Interactions with User Feedback

See Figure 9.

## D Text in Different Language

See Figure 10.

## E Text in Different Domain

See Figure 11.

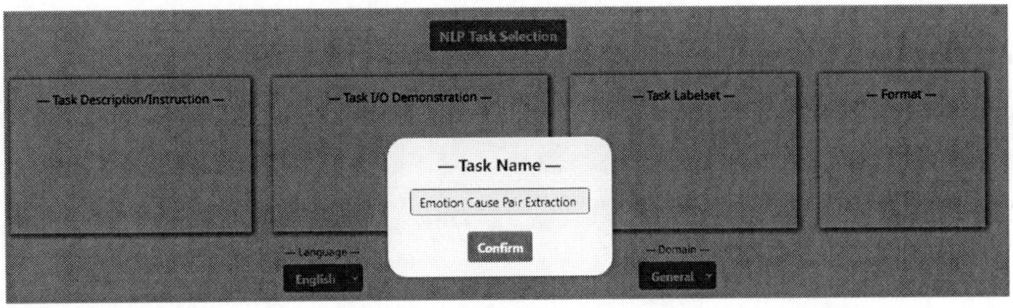


(a) Step-1, name the task.

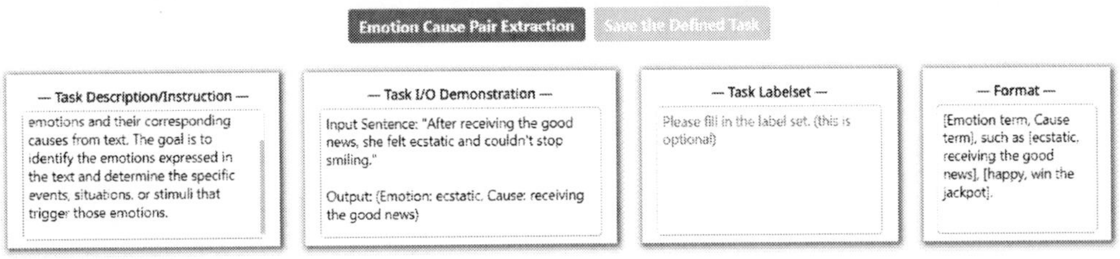


(b) Step-2, fill in the task metadata.

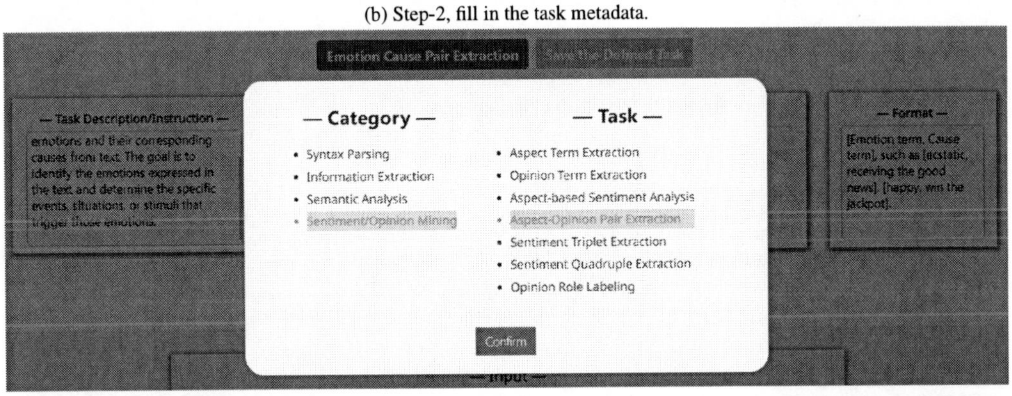


(c) Step-3, select an executing format with a similar task,

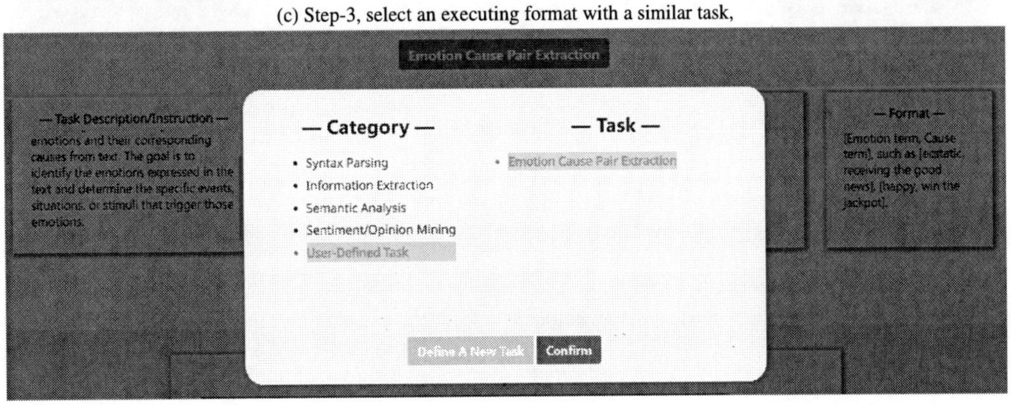


(d) Step-4, confirm to define.

Figure 8: Screenshot of defining new XNLP task by the user.

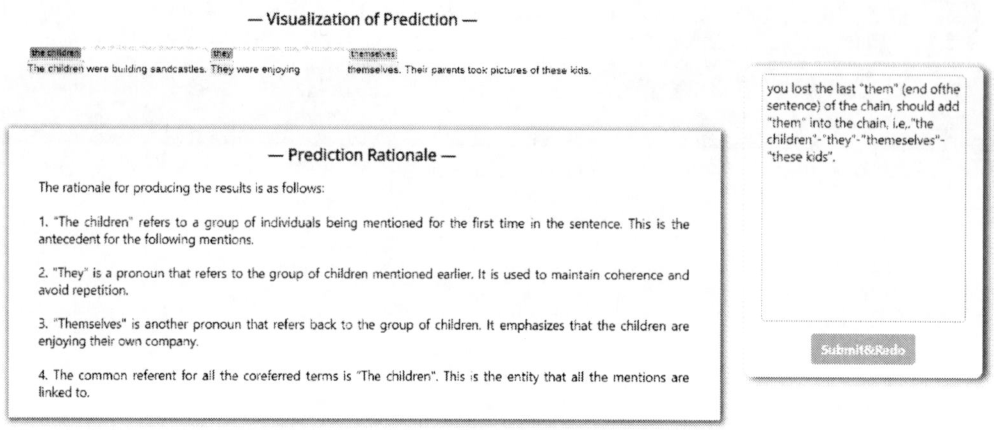


(a) Before user feedback.

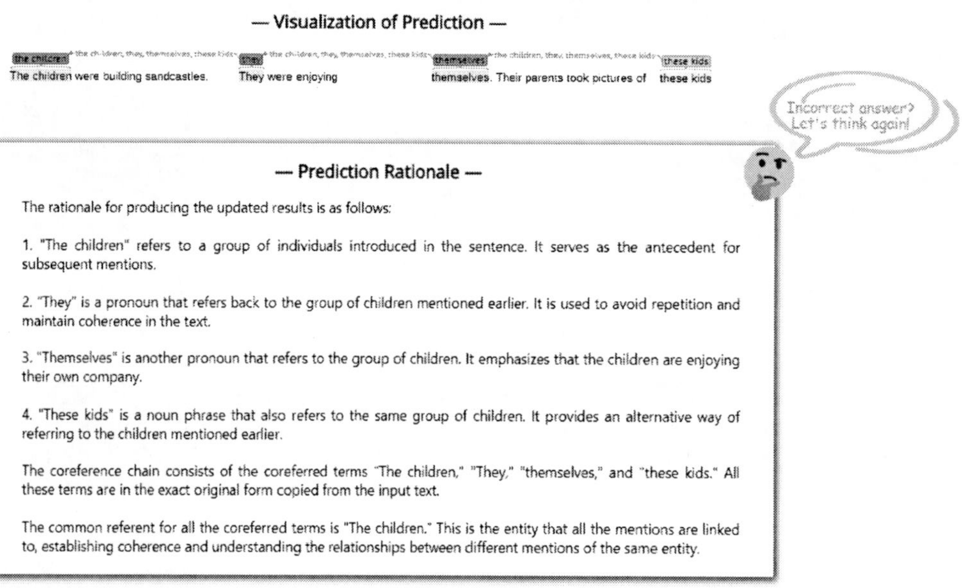


(b) After user feedback.

Figure 9: System output before user feedback and after user feedback.

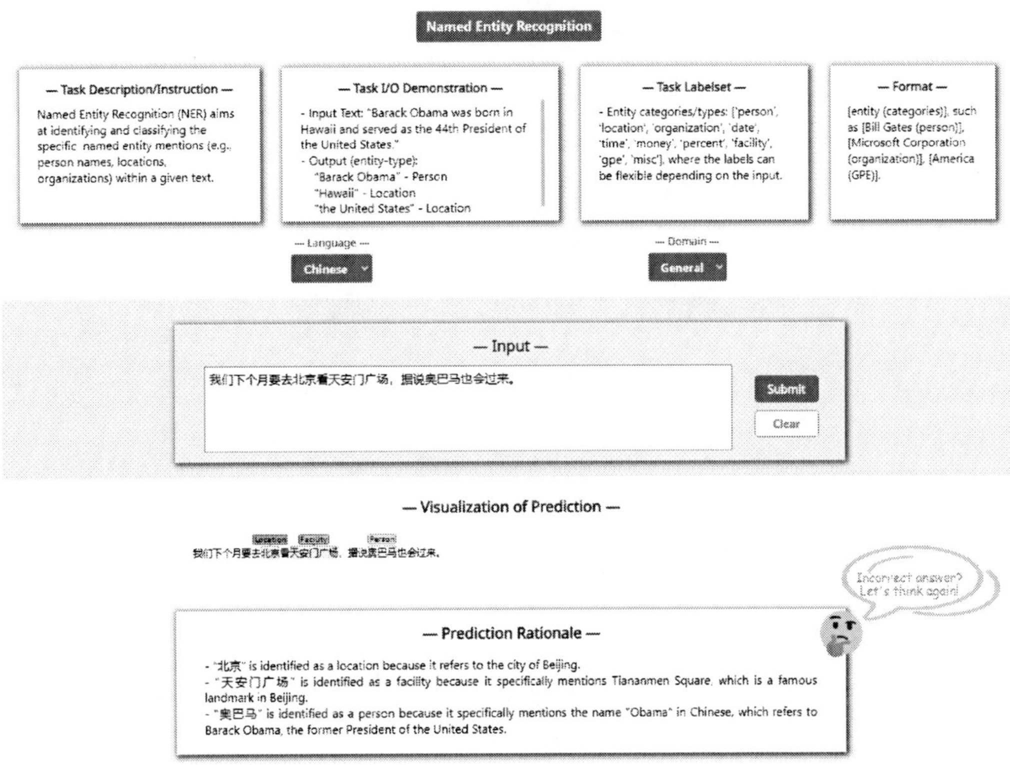


Figure 10: Input text in different languages (Chinese).

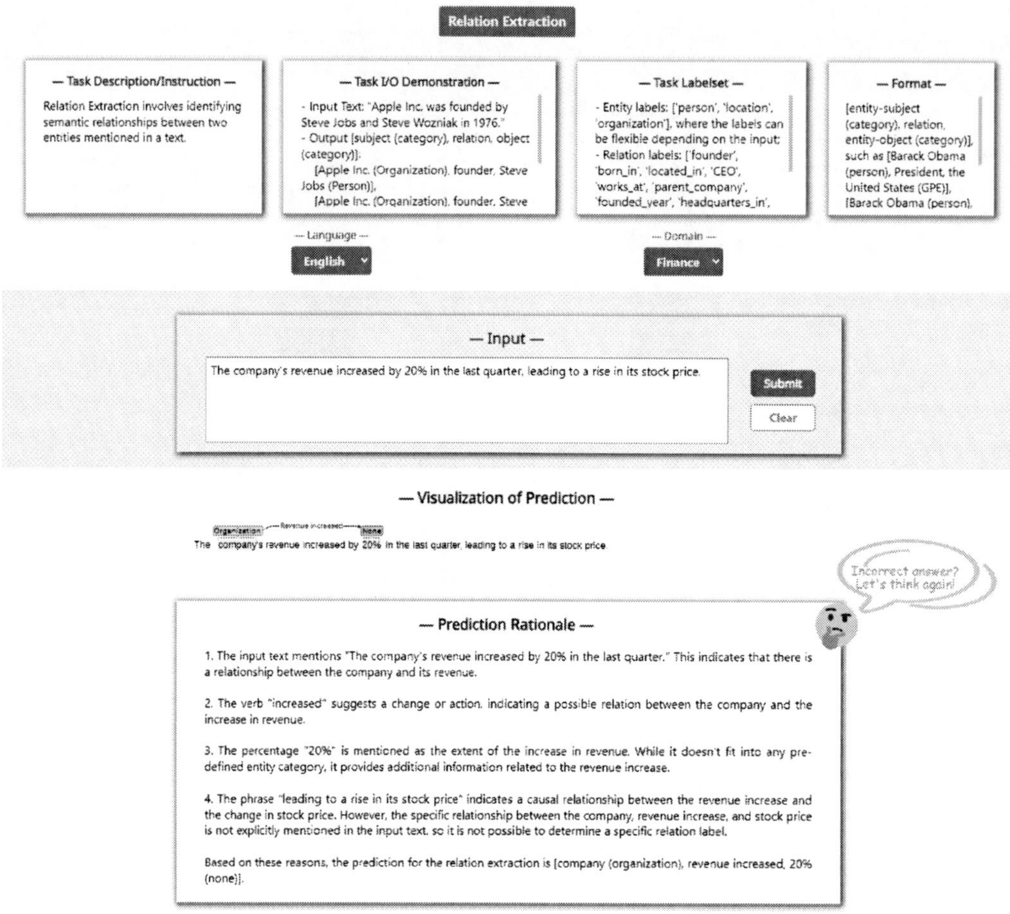


Figure 11: Input text in different domains (financial domain).

# Towards the TopMost: A Topic Modeling System Toolkit

**Xiaobao Wu** **Fengjun Pan** **Anh Tuan Luu**
Nanyang Technological University
xiaobao002@e.ntu.edu.sg fengjun001@e.ntu.edu.sg anhtuan.luu@ntu.edu.sg

## Abstract

Topic models have a rich history with various applications and have recently been reinvigorated by neural topic modeling. However, these numerous topic models adopt totally distinct datasets, implementations, and evaluations. This impedes quick utilization and fair comparisons, and thereby hinders their research progress and applications. To tackle this challenge, we in this paper propose a Topic Modeling System Toolkit (TopMost). Compared to existing toolkits, TopMost stands out by supporting more extensive features. It covers a broader spectrum of topic modeling scenarios with their complete lifecycles, including datasets, preprocessing, models, training, and evaluations. Thanks to its highly cohesive and decoupled modular design, TopMost enables rapid utilization, fair comparisons, and flexible extensions of diverse cutting-edge topic models. These improvements position TopMost as a valuable resource to accelerate the research and applications of topic models. Our code, tutorials, and documentation are available at https://github.com/bobxwu/topmost. Our demo video is at https://youtu.be/9bN-rs4Gu3E?si=LunquCRhBZwyd1Xg.

| Topic Modeling Scenario | | OCTIS | TopMost |
|---|---|---|---|
| Basic topic modeling | Datasets | ✓ | ✓ |
| | Models | ✓ | ✓ |
| | Evaluations | ✓ | ✓ |
| Hierarchical topic modeling | Datasets | ✓ | ✓ |
| | Models | ✓ | ✓ |
| | Evaluations | ✗ | ✓ |
| Dynamic topic modeling | Datasets | ✗ | ✓ |
| | Models | ✗ | ✓ |
| | Evaluations | ✗ | ✓ |
| Cross-lingual topic modeling | Datasets | ✗ | ✓ |
| | Models | ✗ | ✓ |
| | Evaluations | ✗ | ✓ |

Table 1: Comparison between the latest OCTIS (Terragni et al., 2021) and TopMost. Our TopMost covers more topic modeling scenarios and their corresponding datasets, models, and evaluations.

## 1 Introduction

Topic models have been a fundamental and prevalent research area for decades. They aim to understand documents in an unsupervised fashion by discovering latent topics from them and inferring their topic distributions (Churchill and Singh, 2022b). Besides the basic topic modeling scenario (Blei et al., 2003), various other scenarios have been explored, *e.g.*, hierarchical, dynamic, and cross-lingual topic modeling (Griffiths et al., 2003; Blei and Lafferty, 2006; Mimno et al., 2009). Current topic models can be categorized into two types. The first type is conventional topic models which follow either non-negative matrix factorization (Lee and Seung, 2000; Kim et al., 2015; Shi et al., 2018) or probabilistic graphical models via Markov Chain Monte Carlo (Steyvers and Griffiths, 2007) or Variational Inference (Blei et al., 2017). The second type is recently popular neural topic models, learned through gradient backpropagation (Zhao et al., 2021a; Wu et al., 2024b). Thus they can avoid the laborious model-specific derivations of conventional models, attracting more research attention. Due to the effectiveness and interpretability of topic models, they have inspired various downstream tasks and applications, *e.g.*, text analysis and content recommendation (Boyd-Graber et al., 2017). Despite these significant achievements, quick utilization and fair comparisons of various topic models remain a formidable challenge. The reason lies in their unsystematic model implementations as well as inconsistent dataset and evaluation settings across papers, even within a paper (Hoyle et al., 2021).

Several topic modeling toolkits emerge in response to this challenge by integrating different



*Proceedings of the 62nd Annual Meeting of the Association for Computational Linguistics (Volume 3: System Demonstrations)*, pages 31–41
August 11-16, 2024 

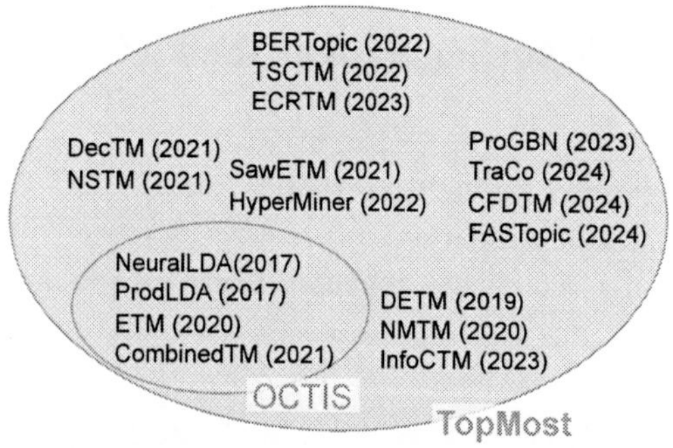


Figure 1: Comparison of neural topic models in OCTIS and our TopMost. Our TopMost covers more latest neural topic models than OCTIS.

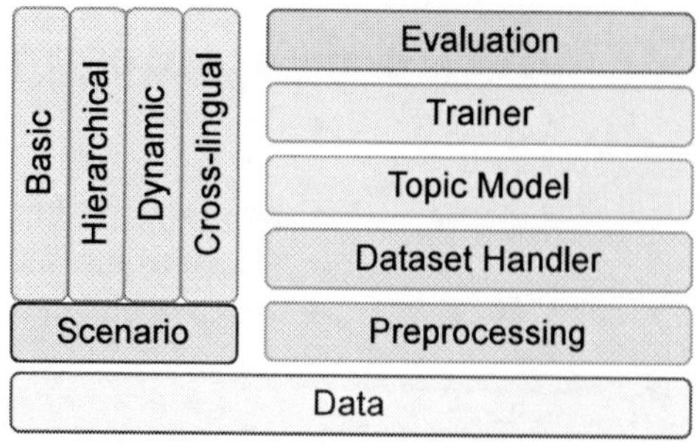


Figure 2: Overall architecture of TopMost. It covers the most common topic modeling scenarios and decouples data loading, model constructions, model training and evaluations in topic modeling lifecycles.

topic models and evaluations. However, they fail to fully meet practical requirements due to lacking certain essential features. Early toolkits (McCallum, 2002; Rehurek and Sojka, 2011; Qiang et al., 2020; Lisena et al., 2020) often lack the support for neural topic models or necessary steps in the topic modeling lifecycle, *e.g.,* data preprocessing and evaluations. The latest toolkit OCTIS (Terragni et al., 2021) is more comprehensive, but as shown in Table 1 and Figure 1, it solely considers basic and hierarchical topic modeling scenarios and overlooks the latest advancements of neural topic models, offering only two neural topic models introduced after 2018. As a consequence, these issues pose hurdles to the comparisons, developments, and applications of topic models.

To resolve these issues, we in this paper introduce **Topic Modeling System Toolkit (TopMost)**, which supports extensive features. In contrast to existing toolkits, TopMost thoroughly incorporates the most prevalent topic modeling scenarios: **basic, hierarchical, dynamic, and cross-lingual topic modeling**, as well as the latest neural topic models as detailed in Table 1 and Figure 1. It covers the entire lifecycles of these scenarios, including datasets, preprocessing, models, training, and evaluations. More importantly, TopMost adheres to an object-oriented paradigm with a highly cohesive and decoupled modular design. This enhances the readability and extensibility of TopMost, enabling users to flexibly customize their own datasets, models, and evaluations for their diverse research or application purposes. As a result, TopMost excels in fulfilling the practical requirements of topic modeling. We conclude the advantages of our TopMost as follows:

- TopMost provides handy and complete cutting-edge topic models for various scenarios;
- TopMost allows users to effortlessly and fairly compare topic models through comprehensive evaluation metrics;
- TopMost with better readability and extensibility facilitates the smooth development of new topic models and downstream applications.

## 2 Related Work

Throughout the long history of topic modeling, numerous toolkits have emerged and gained widespread adoption. The earliest among those include Mallet (McCallum, 2002) [1] and gensim (Rehurek and Sojka, 2011) [2]. While these fundamental frameworks sufficiently embrace conventional topic models, they generally overlook the recent advancements in neural topic models. STTM (Qiang et al., 2018) particularly focuses on probabilistic short text topic models, like BTM (Yan et al., 2013) and DMM (Yin and Wang, 2014). A more recent entrant, OCTIS (Terragni et al., 2021), integrates both conventional and neural topic models. Nevertheless, it merely covers basic and hierarchical topic modeling scenarios and neglects the latest neural topic models developed after 2018. Moreover, OCTIS couples the implementations of model construction and training, exacerbating the challenges of toolkit maintenance. Different from these existing work, our TopMost extensively incorporates a spectrum of popular topic modeling scenarios and the latest developments in neural topic models. In addition, our TopMost clearly

[1] https://mimno.github.io/Mallet/topics.html
[2] https://radimrehurek.com/gensim/

| Topic Modeling Scenarios | Topic Models | Evaluation Metrics | Datasets |
|---|---|---|---|
| Basic topic modeling | LDA (Blei et al., 2003)<br>NMF (Lee and Seung, 2000)<br>NeuralLDA (Srivastava and Sutton, 2017)<br>ProdLDA (Srivastava and Sutton, 2017)<br>ETM (Dieng et al., 2020)<br>DecTM (Wu et al., 2021)<br>NSTM (Zhao et al., 2021b)<br>CombinedTM (Bianchi et al., 2021)<br>BERTopic (Grootendorst, 2022)<br>TSCTM (Wu et al., 2022)<br>ECRTM (Wu et al., 2023b)<br>FASTopic (Wu et al., 2024c) | TC<br>TD<br>Classification<br>Clustering | 20NG<br>IMDB<br>Wikitext-103<br>NeurIPS<br>ACL<br>NYT |
| Hierarchical topic modeling | HDP (Teh et al., 2006)<br>SawETM (Duan et al., 2021)<br>HyperMiner (Xu et al., 2022)<br>ProGBN (Duan et al., 2023)<br>TraCo (Wu et al., 2024d) | TC over levels<br>TD over levels<br>Classification over levels<br>Clustering over levels | |
| Dynamic topic modeling | DTM (Blei and Lafferty, 2006)<br>DETM (Dieng et al., 2019)<br>CFDTM (Wu et al., 2024a) | TC over time slices<br>TD over time slices<br>Classification<br>Clustering | NeurIPS<br>ACL<br>NYT |
| Cross-lingual topic modeling | NMTM (Wu et al., 2020a)<br>InfoCTM (Wu et al., 2023a) | TC (CNPMI)<br>TD over languages<br>Classification<br>Clustering | ECNews<br>Amazon<br>Review Rakuten |

Table 2: Summary of topic modeling scenarios, topic models, evaluation metrics, and datasets covered by TopMost.

decouples each step (data, models, and training) in the topic modeling lifecycles, resulting in neat code structures and simplified maintenance.

## 3 Overview of Toolkit Design and Architecture

In this section, we delineate the overview of our toolkit design and architecture. We build TopMost with Python and use PyTorch (Paszke et al., 2019) as the neural network framework for neural topic models. Figure 2 illustrates the overall architecture of TopMost.

### 3.1 Topic Modeling Scenarios and Topic Models

As summarized in Table 2, TopMost reaches a wider coverage by involving the 4 most popular topic modeling scenarios and their corresponding conventional or neural topic models.

**Basic Topic Modeling** discovers a number of latent topics from normal documents like news articles and web snippets, as the most common scenario (Blei et al., 2003). For basic topic models, TopMost supports conventional LDA (Blei et al., 2003), NMF (Lee and Seung, 2000), and most of the mainstream neural models such as ProdLDA (Srivastava and Sutton, 2017), ETM (Dieng et al., 2020), CombinedTM (Bianchi et al., 2021), BERTopic (Grootendorst, 2022), TSCTM (Wu et al., 2022), ECRTM (Wu et al., 2023b), and FASTopic (Wu et al., 2024c).

**Hierarchical Topic Modeling** organizes topics into a tree structure instead of flat topics in the basic topic modeling (Griffiths et al., 2003; Isonuma et al., 2020). Topics at each level of the structure involve different semantic granularity: child topics are more specific to their parent topics. This provides more desirable granularity for downstream applications. Hierarchical topic models in TopMost include conventional HDP (Teh et al., 2006) and recently popular neural hierarchical topic models, *e.g.*, HyperMiner (Xu et al., 2022), ProGBN (Duan et al., 2023), and TraCo (Wu et al., 2024d).

**Dynamic Topic Modeling** discovers the evolution of topics in sequential documents, such as the conference papers published by year (Blei and Lafferty, 2006). This discloses how topics emerge, grow, and decline over time due to real-world trends and events, which has derived applications like trend analysis and public opinion mining (Li et al., 2020; Churchill and Singh, 2022a). For dynamic topic models, we provide the conventional

DTM (Blei and Lafferty, 2006) and its neural variant, DETM (Dieng et al., 2019). We also cover recent CFDTM (Wu et al., 2024a).

**Cross-lingual Topic Modeling** discovers aligned cross-lingual topics from bilingual corpora (Mimno et al., 2009). These reveal the commonalities and differences across languages and cultures, enabling cross-lingual text analysis without supervision (Yuan et al., 2018; Yang et al., 2019). Cross-lingual topic models in TOPMOST include NMTM (Wu et al., 2020a) and InfoCTM (Wu et al., 2023a).

We carefully adapt the original implementations of these topic models and unify their APIs of initialization, training, and testing, ensuring that our toolkit remains user-friendly, readable, and extendable. Note that we will constantly update TOPMOST to include more newly released models.

### 3.2 Datasets and Preprocessing

TOPMOST contains extensive benchmark datasets for the involved topic modeling scenarios, as reported in Table 2. We summarize the statistics of these datasets in Tables 3 to 5.

For basic and hierarchical topic modeling, we have the following datasets: (i) **20NG** (20 News Groups, Lang, 1995) is one of the most widely used datasets for evaluating topic models, including news articles with 20 labels. (ii) **IMDB** [3] (Maas et al., 2011) is the movie reviews from the IMDB website, containing two sentimental labels, positive and negative. (iii) **Wikitext-103** [4] (Merity et al., 2016) includes Wikipedia articles (Nguyen and Luu, 2021).

For dynamic topic modeling, TOPMOST provides the datasets as (i) **NeurIPS** [5] includes the published papers at the NeurIPS conference from 1987 to 2017. (ii) **ACL** (Bird et al., 2008) is an article collection between 1973 and 2006 from ACL Anthology [6]. (iii) **NYT** [7] contains the news articles in the New York Times, from 2012 to 2022, with 12 categories, like "Arts", "Business", and "Health".

For cross-lingual topic modeling, we offer the following bilingual datasets: (i) **ECNews** [8] (Wu et al., 2020a) is a collection of English and Chinese news with 6 categories like business, education, and entertainment. (ii) **Amazon Review** (Wu et al., 2020a) includes English and Chinese reviews from the Amazon website, where each review has a rating from one to five. We simplify it as a binary classification task by labeling reviews with ratings of five as "1" and the rest as "0" following Yuan et al. (2018). (iii) **Rakuten Amazon** (Wu et al., 2023a) contains Japanese reviews from Rakuten (a Japanese online shopping website, Zhang and LeCun, 2017), and English reviews from Amazon (Yuan et al., 2018). Similarly, it is also simplified as a binary classification task according to the ratings. Note that basic topic models can employ the datasets for dynamic topic modeling as well.

We preprocess these datasets with standard steps, such as removing stop words and punctuation, removing short tokens, and filtering low-frequency words (Card et al., 2018; Wu et al., 2020b). Users can directly download these off-the-shelf datasets for experiments through TOPMOST from our GitHub repository. See Appendix A for more details of these datasets. We also provide configurable preprocessing implementations, allowing users to flexibly customize their datasets.

### 3.3 Evaluation Metrics

TOPMOST provides sufficient evaluation metrics to evaluate topic models. We first evaluate the quality of discovered topics in terms of **topic coherence** (**TC**, Newman et al., 2010) and **topic diversity** (**TD**, Dieng et al., 2020). TC refers to the coherence between the top words of discovered topics, and TD measures the differences between topics. We consider different implementations of TC and TD, for example, NPMI (Lau et al., 2014), $C_V$ (Röder et al., 2015), and TU (Nan et al., 2019), for extensive comparisons.

Then, we evaluate the quality of inferred doc-topic distributions via extrinsic tasks: **text classification** and **clustering** (Wu and Li, 2019; Zhao et al., 2021b; Nguyen et al., 2024). For classification, we train an ordinary classifier (*e.g.,* SVM) with doc-topic distributions as document features and predict the labels of others. For clustering, we use the most significant topics in doc-topic distributions as clustering assignments.

Apart from these fundamental ones, we addition-

[3] http://ai.stanford.edu/~amaas/data/sentiment/aclImdb_v1.tar.gz

[4] https://www.salesforce.com/products/einstein/ai-research/the-wikitext-dependency-language-modeling-dataset/

[5] https://www.kaggle.com/datasets/benhamner/nips-papers

[6] https://aclanthology.org/

[7] https://huggingface.co/datasets/Matthewww/nyt_news

[8] https://github.com/bobxwu/NMTM

ally include metrics for special scenarios. For cross-lingual topic modeling, we measure the average TD over all languages and evaluate the alignment between cross-lingual topics with cross-lingual NPMI (CNPMI, Hao and Paul, 2018). For hierarchical topic modeling, we evaluate the quality of discovered topic hierarchies, concerning the coherence and diversity between parent and child topics, the diversity between parent and non-child topics, and the diversity between sibling topics (Chen et al., 2021b,a; Wu et al., 2024d).

## 4 Comparison to Existing Toolkit

To highlight our significant strengths, we compare our TopMost with the latest counterpart, OCTIS (Terragni et al., 2021), which integrates more features than earlier toolkits. Our TopMost outperforms OCTIS in three key aspects:

**(i)** As detailed in Table 1, TopMost offers a broader coverage of topic modeling scenarios, accompanied by corresponding datasets, models, and evaluation metrics. This better fulfills the various requirements of researchers and developers.

**(ii)** TopMost provides a more extensive array of topic models compared to OCTIS. As reported in Figure 1 while OCTIS merely includes 4 neural topic models, TopMost incorporates 16 ones, including the latest NSTM (Zhao et al., 2021b), HyperMiner (Xu et al., 2022), and ECRTM (Wu et al., 2023b). These advanced models empower users with cutting-edge topic modeling techniques and simplify their comparisons and applications.

**(iii)** TopMost entirely decouples the implementations of data loading, model construction, model training, and evaluations, as illustrated in Figure 2. This design streamlines the code structure for high reusability and facilitates fair comparisons among diverse topic models. It aligns with prominent libraries such as Huggingface Transformers and PyTorch Lightning. See the code examples in Sec. 5.

## 5 Toolkit Usage

We showcase the simplicity and user-friendly design of our TopMost toolkit with code examples. Users can directly install our TopMost through pip [9]: `pip install topmost`.

Figure 3 shows how to quickly utilize TopMost to discovers topics from documents with a few handy steps: dataset preprocessing, model construction (here ProdLDA (Srivastava and Sutton, 2017)), and training. We emphasize that our TopMost supports other languages besides English. We can simply employ different tokenizers in the preprocessing for other languages, for example, jieba [10] for Chinese and nagisa [11] for Japanese. Other preprocessing settings are also configurable, including maximum vocabulary size, stop words, and maximum or minimum document frequency. This allows users to flexibly apply our toolkit.

```
from topmost.data import RawDatasetHandler
from topmost.models import ProdLDA
from topmost.trainers import BasicTrainer

docs = [ "A document about space, satellite,
    launch, orbit.", # more example documents...
]
# build a dataset
dataset = RawDatasetHandler(docs)
# create a topic model
model = ProdLDA(dataset.vocab_size)
# create a trainer
trainer = BasicTrainer(model)
topic_top_words, doc_topic_dist = trainer.
    fit_transform(dataset)
```

Figure 3: A code example for quick start.

Figure 4 exemplifies how to train a topic model with preprocessed datasets. The training of other topic models follows similar steps.

```
from topmost.data import download_dataset,
    BasicDatasetHandler
from topmost.models import ProdLDA
from topmost.trainers import BasicTrainer

#download a dataset
download_dataset('20NG', cache_path='./datasets')
# load a dataset
dataset = BasicDatasetHandler("./datasets/20NG")

# create a topic model
model = ProdLDA(dataset.vocab_size)
# create a trainer
trainer = BasicTrainer(model)
# train the topic model
trainer.train(dataset)
```

Figure 4: A code example for training a topic model (ProdLDA (Srivastava and Sutton, 2017)).

Figure 5 shows how to fully evaluate the trained topic model with diverse metrics including topic coherence, topic diversity, text classification, and text clustering.

[9] https://pypi.org/project/topmost

[10] https://github.com/fxsjy/jieba

[11] https://github.com/taishi-i/nagisa

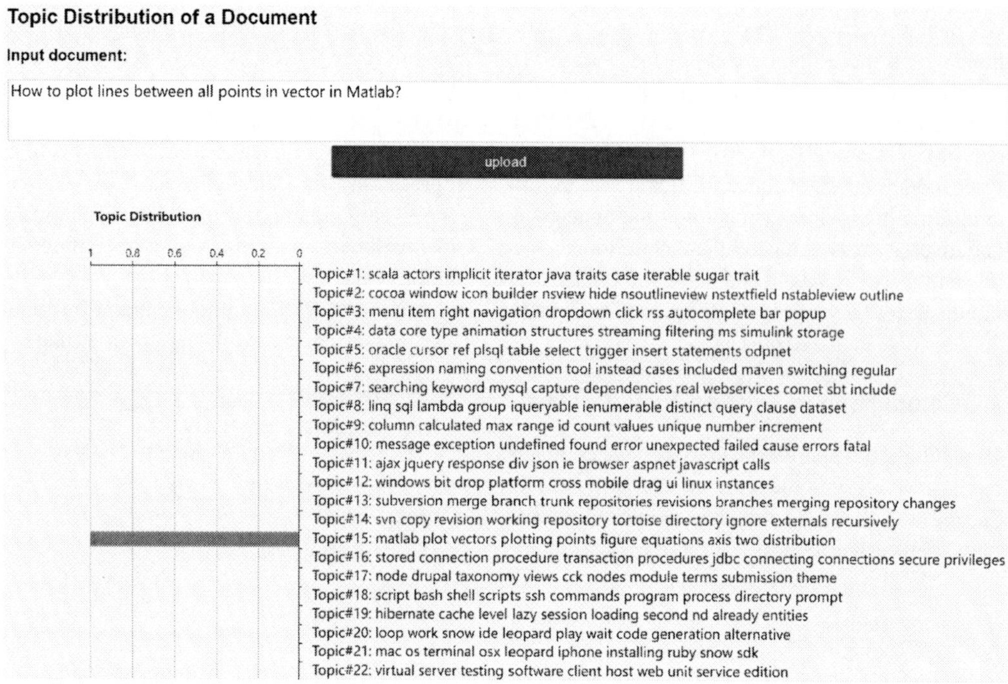


Figure 6: Demonstration of testing new documents. It plots the inferred topic distribution of an input document from a trained topic model.

```
from topmost.evaluations import
    compute_topic_diversity,
    compute_topic_coherence, evaluate_clustering
    , evaluate_classification

# doc-topic distributions
train_theta, test_theta = trainer.export_theta(
    dataset)
# top words of topics
topic_top_words = trainer.export_top_words(
    dataset.vocab)
# topic coherence
compute_topic_coherence(topic_top_words, dataset.
    train_texts)
# topic diversity
compute_topic_diversity(topic_top_words)
# text clustering
evaluate_clustering(test_theta, dataset.
    test_labels)
# text classification
evaluate_classification(train_theta, test_theta,
    dataset.train_labels, dataset.test_labels)
```

Figure 5: A code example for evaluating a topic model, including topic coherence, topic diversity, text classification, and clustering.

The above examples illustrate that TopMost clearly decouples the APIs of data, models, and training, so TopMost becomes more accessible, easy-to-use, and extendable to users. Due to limited page space, see more examples and tutorials on our GitHub project page, like data preprocessing and other topic modeling scenarios.

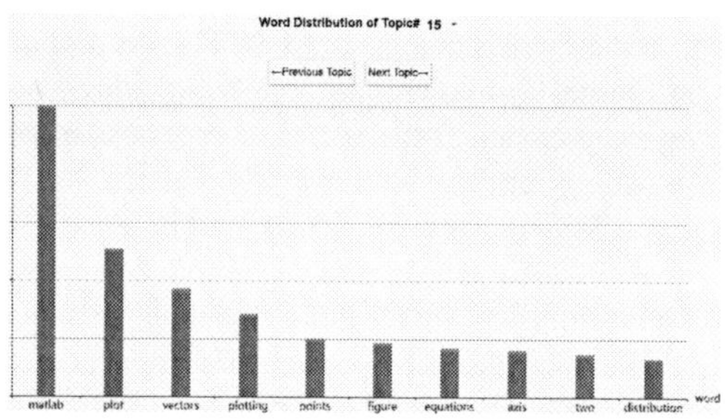


Figure 7: Visualization of discovered topics. It plots the top related words of each topic and the modeled word distributions.

## 6 Visualization Interfaces

TopMost furthermore provides visualization interfaces for topic models. We create a web demo system with Flask [12] as the server framework following Material design to visualize and test topic models. It is designed to be intuitive and user-friendly, enabling users to easily understand and leverage topic models.

Figure 7 shows the visualization of topics. We plot the top related words of discovered topics and the modeled probability of each word. For example,

[12] https://flask.palletsprojects.com/

Topic#15 in Figure 7 mostly relates to words like "matlab", "plot", and "vectors". By selecting the index or clicking the *Previous* and *Next* buttons, we can view the details of any topic.

Figure 6 demonstrates the interactive utilization of a trained topic model. Upon inputting a document, we can click the *upload* button to obtain the inferred topic distribution of the document. The horizontal bar chart in Figure 6 plots the distribution over all topics of the input *How to plot lines between all points in vector in Matlab?*. We see that the topic distribution mainly lies on Topic#15, which refers to Matlab.

## 7 Conclusion and Future Work

In this paper, we present TopMost, an open-source, comprehensive, and up-to-date topic modeling system toolkit. TopMost provides complete lifecycles of various topic modeling scenarios, including datasets, preprocessing, models, training, and evaluations, which outperforms existing counterparts. TopMost allows users to smoothly explore topic models, verify their new ideas, and develop novel topic modeling applications. This benefits both the communities in academia and industry. In the future, we plan to keep TopMost updated to incorporate more latest topic models and support more features to facilitate the research and application of topic modeling.

## Limitations

We consider the following limitations of TopMost. First, TopMost only includes the mainstream evaluation metrics. Some less popular ones like perplexity are ignored. Second, TopMost does not cover the topic models based on prompting large language models (Pan et al., 2023; Wu et al., 2024e; Pham et al., 2023). Different from LDA-like models, they define a topic as a textual description, so we cannot assess them through existing evaluation metrics.

## References


Federico Bianchi, Silvia Terragni, and Dirk Hovy. 2021. Pre-training is a hot topic: Contextualized document embeddings improve topic coherence. In *Proceedings of the 59th Annual Meeting of the Association for Computational Linguistics and the 11th International Joint Conference on Natural Language Processing (Volume 2: Short Papers)*, pages 759–766.

Steven Bird, Robert Dale, Bonnie J Dorr, Bryan R Gibson, Mark Thomas Joseph, Min-Yen Kan, Dongwon Lee, Brett Powley, Dragomir R Radev, Yee Fan Tan, et al. 2008. The acl anthology reference corpus: A reference dataset for bibliographic research in computational linguistics. In *LREC*.

David M Blei, Alp Kucukelbir, and Jon D McAuliffe. 2017. Variational inference: A review for statisticians. *Journal of the American statistical Association*, 112(518):859–877.

David M Blei and John D Lafferty. 2006. Dynamic topic models. In *Proceedings of the 23rd international conference on Machine learning*, pages 113–120.

David M Blei, Andrew Y Ng, and Michael I Jordan. 2003. Latent dirichlet allocation. *Journal of Machine Learning Research*, 3(Jan):993–1022.

Jordan L Boyd-Graber, Yuening Hu, David Mimno, et al. 2017. *Applications of topic models*, volume 11. now Publishers Incorporated.

Dallas Card, Chenhao Tan, and Noah A Smith. 2018. Neural Models for Documents with Metadata. In *Proceedings of the 56th Annual Meeting of the Association for Computational Linguistics (Volume 1: Long Papers)*, volume 1, pages 2031–2040.

Ziye Chen, Cheng Ding, Yanghui Rao, Haoran Xie, Xiaohui Tao, Gary Cheng, and Fu Lee Wang. 2021a. Hierarchical neural topic modeling with manifold regularization. *World Wide Web*, 24:2139–2160.

Ziye Chen, Cheng Ding, Zusheng Zhang, Yanghui Rao, and Haoran Xie. 2021b. Tree-structured topic modeling with nonparametric neural variational inference. In *Proceedings of the 59th Annual Meeting of the Association for Computational Linguistics and the 11th International Joint Conference on Natural Language Processing (Volume 1: Long Papers)*, pages 2343–2353.

Rob Churchill and Lisa Singh. 2022a. Dynamic topic-noise models for social media. In *Pacific-Asia Conference on Knowledge Discovery and Data Mining*, pages 429–443. Springer.

Rob Churchill and Lisa Singh. 2022b. The evolution of topic modeling. *ACM Computing Surveys*, 54(10s):1–35.

Adji B Dieng, Francisco JR Ruiz, and David M Blei. 2019. The dynamic embedded topic model. *arXiv preprint arXiv:1907.05545*.

Adji B Dieng, Francisco JR Ruiz, and David M Blei. 2020. Topic modeling in embedding spaces. *Transactions of the Association for Computational Linguistics*, 8:439–453.

Zhibin Duan, Xinyang Liu, Yudi Su, Yishi Xu, Bo Chen, and Mingyuan Zhou. 2023. Bayesian progressive deep topic model with knowledge informed textual data coarsening process. In *International Conference on Machine Learning*, pages 8731–8746. PMLR.

Zhibin Duan, Dongsheng Wang, Bo Chen, Chaojie Wang, Wenchao Chen, Yewen Li, Jie Ren, and Mingyuan Zhou. 2021. Sawtooth factorial topic embeddings guided gamma belief network. In *International Conference on Machine Learning*, pages 2903–2913. PMLR.

Thomas Griffiths, Michael Jordan, Joshua Tenenbaum, and David Blei. 2003. Hierarchical topic models and the nested chinese restaurant process. *Advances in neural information processing systems*, 16.

Maarten Grootendorst. 2022. Bertopic: Neural topic modeling with a class-based tf-idf procedure. *arXiv preprint arXiv:2203.05794*.

Shudong Hao and Michael Paul. 2018. Learning multilingual topics from incomparable corpora. In *Proceedings of the 27th international conference on computational linguistics*, pages 2595–2609.

Alexander Hoyle, Pranav Goel, Andrew Hian-Cheong, Denis Peskov, Jordan Lee Boyd-Graber, and Philip Resnik. 2021. Is automated topic model evaluation broken? the incoherence of coherence. In *Advances in Neural Information Processing Systems*.

Masaru Isonuma, Junichiro Mori, Danushka Bollegala, and Ichiro Sakata. 2020. Tree-structured neural topic model. In *Proceedings of the 58th Annual Meeting of the Association for Computational Linguistics*, pages 800–806.

Hannah Kim, Jaegul Choo, Jingu Kim, Chandan K Reddy, and Haesun Park. 2015. Simultaneous discovery of common and discriminative topics via joint nonnegative matrix factorization. In *Proceedings of the 21th ACM SIGKDD International Conference on Knowledge Discovery and Data Mining*, pages 567–576.

Ken Lang. 1995. Newsweeder: Learning to filter netnews. In *Proceedings of the Twelfth International Conference on Machine Learning*, pages 331–339.

Jey Han Lau, David Newman, and Timothy Baldwin. 2014. Machine reading tea leaves: Automatically evaluating topic coherence and topic model quality. In *Proceedings of the 14th Conference of the European Chapter of the Association for Computational Linguistics*, pages 530–539.

Daniel Lee and H Sebastian Seung. 2000. Algorithms for non-negative matrix factorization. *Advances in neural information processing systems*, 13.

Yue Li, Pratheeksha Nair, Zhi Wen, Imane Chafi, Anya Okhmatovskaia, Guido Powell, Yannan Shen, and David Buckeridge. 2020. Global surveillance of covid-19 by mining news media using a multi-source dynamic embedded topic model. In *Proceedings of the 11th ACM International Conference on Bioinformatics, Computational Biology and Health Informatics*, pages 1–14.

Pasquale Lisena, Ismail Harrando, Oussama Kandakji, and Raphael Troncy. 2020. Tomodapi: a topic modeling api to train, use and compare topic models. In *Proceedings of second workshop for NLP open source software (NLP-OSS)*, pages 132–140.

Andrew Maas, Raymond E Daly, Peter T Pham, Dan Huang, Andrew Y Ng, and Christopher Potts. 2011. Learning word vectors for sentiment analysis. In *Proceedings of the 49th annual meeting of the association for computational linguistics: Human language technologies*, pages 142–150.

Andrew Kachites McCallum. 2002. Mallet: A machine learning for languagetoolkit. *http://mallet. cs. umass. edu*.

Stephen Merity, Caiming Xiong, James Bradbury, and Richard Socher. 2016. Pointer sentinel mixture models. *arXiv preprint arXiv:1609.07843*.

David Mimno, Hanna Wallach, Jason Naradowsky, David A Smith, and Andrew McCallum. 2009. Polylingual topic models. In *Proceedings of the 2009 conference on empirical methods in natural language processing*, pages 880–889, Singapore. Association for Computational Linguistics.

Feng Nan, Ran Ding, Ramesh Nallapati, and Bing Xiang. 2019. Topic modeling with Wasserstein autoencoders. In *Proceedings of the 57th Annual Meeting of the Association for Computational Linguistics*, pages 6345–6381, Florence, Italy. Association for Computational Linguistics.

David Newman, Jey Han Lau, Karl Grieser, and Timothy Baldwin. 2010. Automatic evaluation of topic coherence. In *Human Language Technologies: The 2010 Annual Conference of the North American Chapter of the Association for Computational Linguistics*, pages 100–108. Association for Computational Linguistics.

Thong Nguyen and Anh Tuan Luu. 2021. Contrastive learning for neural topic model. *Advances in Neural Information Processing Systems*, 34.

Thong Thanh Nguyen, Xiaobao Wu, Xinshuai Dong, Cong-Duy T Nguyen, See-Kiong Ng, and Anh Tuan Luu. 2024. Topic modeling as multi-objective optimization with setwise contrastive learning. In *The Twelfth International Conference on Learning Representations*.

Liangming Pan, Xiaobao Wu, Xinyuan Lu, Anh Tuan Luu, William Yang Wang, Min-Yen Kan, and Preslav Nakov. 2023. Fact-checking complex claims with program-guided reasoning. In *Proceedings of the 61st Annual Meeting of the Association for Computational Linguistics (Volume 1: Long Papers)*, pages 6981–7004.

Adam Paszke, Sam Gross, Francisco Massa, Adam Lerer, James Bradbury, Gregory Chanan, Trevor Killeen, Zeming Lin, Natalia Gimelshein, Luca Antiga, et al. 2019. Pytorch: An imperative style, high-performance deep learning library. *Advances in neural information processing systems*, 32.

Chau Minh Pham, Alexander Hoyle, Simeng Sun, and Mohit Iyyer. 2023. Topicgpt: A prompt-based topic modeling framework. *arXiv preprint arXiv:2311.01449*.

Jipeng Qiang, Yun Li, Yunhao Yuan, Wei Liu, and Xindong Wu. 2018. Sttm: A tool for short text topic modeling. *arXiv preprint arXiv:1808.02215*.

Jipeng Qiang, Zhenyu Qian, Yun Li, Yunhao Yuan, and Xindong Wu. 2020. Short text topic modeling techniques, applications, and performance: a survey. *IEEE Transactions on Knowledge and Data Engineering*, 34(3):1427–1445.

Radim Rehurek and Petr Sojka. 2011. Gensim – statistical semantics in python. *Retrieved from genism. org*.

Michael Röder, Andreas Both, and Alexander Hinneburg. 2015. Exploring the space of topic coherence measures. In *Proceedings of the eighth ACM international conference on Web search and data mining*, pages 399–408. ACM.

Tian Shi, Kyeongpil Kang, Jaegul Choo, and Chandan K Reddy. 2018. Short-text topic modeling via non-negative matrix factorization enriched with local word-context correlations. In *Proceedings of the 2018 World Wide Web Conference*, pages 1105–1114. International World Wide Web Conferences Steering Committee.

Akash Srivastava and Charles Sutton. 2017. Autoencoding variational inference for topic models. In *5th International Conference on Learning Representations, ICLR 2017, Toulon, France, April 24-26, 2017, Conference Track Proceedings*. OpenReview.net.

Mark Steyvers and Tom Griffiths. 2007. Probabilistic topic models. *Handbook of latent semantic analysis*, 427(7):424–440.

Yee Whye Teh, Michael I Jordan, Matthew J Beal, and David M Blei. 2006. Hierarchical dirichlet processes. *Journal of the American Statistical Association*, 101(476):1566–1581.

Silvia Terragni, Elisabetta Fersini, Bruno Giovanni Galuzzi, Pietro Tropeano, and Antonio Candelieri. 2021. Octis: Comparing and optimizing topic models is simple! In *Proceedings of the 16th Conference of the European Chapter of the Association for Computational Linguistics: System Demonstrations*, pages 263–270.

Xiaobao Wu, Xinshuai Dong, Thong Nguyen, Chaoqun Liu, Liang-Ming Pan, and Anh Tuan Luu. 2023a. Infoctm: A mutual information maximization perspective of cross-lingual topic modeling. In *Proceedings of the AAAI Conference on Artificial Intelligence*, volume 37, pages 13763–13771.

Xiaobao Wu, Xinshuai Dong, Thong Nguyen, and Anh Tuan Luu. 2023b. Effective neural topic modeling with embedding clustering regularization. In *International Conference on Machine Learning*. PMLR.

Xiaobao Wu, Xinshuai Dong, Liangming Pan, Thong Nguyen, and Anh Tuan Luu. 2024a. Modeling dynamic topics in chain-free fashion by evolution-tracking contrastive learning and unassociated word exclusion. *arXiv preprint arXiv:2405.17957*.

Xiaobao Wu and Chunping Li. 2019. Short Text Topic Modeling with Flexible Word Patterns. In *International Joint Conference on Neural Networks*.

Xiaobao Wu, Chunping Li, and Yishu Miao. 2021. Discovering topics in long-tailed corpora with causal intervention. In *Findings of the Association for Computational Linguistics: ACL-IJCNLP 2021*, pages 175–185, Online. Association for Computational Linguistics.

Xiaobao Wu, Chunping Li, Yan Zhu, and Yishu Miao. 2020a. Learning Multilingual Topics with Neural Variational Inference. In *International Conference on Natural Language Processing and Chinese Computing*.

Xiaobao Wu, Chunping Li, Yan Zhu, and Yishu Miao. 2020b. Short text topic modeling with topic distribution quantization and negative sampling decoder. In *Proceedings of the 2020 Conference on Empirical Methods in Natural Language Processing (EMNLP)*, pages 1772–1782, Online.

Xiaobao Wu, Anh Tuan Luu, and Xinshuai Dong. 2022. Mitigating data sparsity for short text topic modeling by topic-semantic contrastive learning. In *Proceedings of the 2022 Conference on Empirical Methods in Natural Language Processing*, pages 2748–2760, Abu Dhabi, United Arab Emirates. Association for Computational Linguistics.

Xiaobao Wu, Thong Nguyen, and Anh Tuan Luu. 2024b. A survey on neural topic models: Methods, applications, and challenges. *Artificial Intelligence Review*.

Xiaobao Wu, Thong Nguyen, Delvin Ce Zhang, William Yang Wang, and Anh Tuan Luu. 2024c. Fastopic: A fast, adaptive, stable, and transferable topic modeling paradigm. *arXiv preprint arXiv:2405.17978*.

Xiaobao Wu, Fengjun Pan, Thong Nguyen, Yichao Feng, Chaoqun Liu, Cong-Duy Nguyen, and Anh Tuan Luu. 2024d. On the affinity, rationality, and diversity of hierarchical topic modeling. In *Proceedings of the AAAI Conference on Artificial Intelligence*.

Xiaobao Wu, Liangming Pan, William Yang Wang, and Anh Tuan Luu. 2024e. Updating language models with unstructured facts: Towards practical knowledge editing. *arXiv preprint arXiv:2402.18909*.

Yishi Xu, Dongsheng Wang, Bo Chen, Ruiying Lu, Zhibin Duan, and Mingyuan Zhou. 2022. Hyperminer: Topic taxonomy mining with hyperbolic embedding. In *Advances in Neural Information Processing Systems*, volume 35, pages 31557–31570. Curran Associates, Inc.

Xiaohui Yan, Jiafeng Guo, Yanyan Lan, and Xueqi Cheng. 2013. A biterm topic model for short texts. In *Proceedings of the 22nd international conference on World Wide Web*, pages 1445–1456. ACM.

Weiwei Yang, Jordan Boyd-Graber, and Philip Resnik. 2019. A multilingual topic model for learning weighted topic links across corpora with low comparability. In *Proceedings of the 2019 Conference on Empirical Methods in Natural Language Processing and the 9th International Joint Conference on Natural Language Processing (EMNLP-IJCNLP)*, pages 1243–1248.

Jianhua Yin and Jianyong Wang. 2014. A dirichlet multinomial mixture model-based approach for short text clustering. In *Proceedings of the 20th ACM SIGKDD international conference on Knowledge discovery and data mining*, pages 233–242. ACM.

Michelle Yuan, Benjamin Van Durme, and Jordan L Ying. 2018. Multilingual anchoring: Interactive topic modeling and alignment across languages. *Advances in neural information processing systems*, 31.

Xiang Zhang and Yann LeCun. 2017. Which encoding is the best for text classification in chinese, english, japanese and korean? *arXiv preprint arXiv:1708.02657*.

He Zhao, Dinh Phung, Viet Huynh, Yuan Jin, Lan Du, and Wray Buntine. 2021a. Topic modelling meets deep neural networks: A survey. In *Proceedings of the Thirtieth International Joint Conference on Artificial Intelligence, IJCAI-21*, pages 4713–4720. International Joint Conferences on Artificial Intelligence Organization. Survey Track.

He Zhao, Dinh Phung, Viet Huynh, Trung Le, and Wray L. Buntine. 2021b. Neural topic model via optimal transport. In *9th International Conference on Learning Representations, ICLR 2021, Virtual Event, Austria, May 3-7, 2021*. OpenReview.net.

| Dataset | Language | #docs | Vocabulary Size | Average length | #labels |
|---|---|---|---|---|---|
| ECNews | English | 46,870 | 5,000 | 12.0 | 6 |
| | Chinese | 50,000 | 5,000 | 10.6 | |
| Amazon Review | English | 25,000 | 5,000 | 30.6 | 2 |
| | Chinese | 25,000 | 5,000 | 43.2 | |
| Rakuten Amazon | English | 25,000 | 5,000 | 30.6 | 2 |
| | Japanese | 25,000 | 5,000 | 22.5 | |

Table 3: Statistics of pre-processed datasets for cross-lingual topic modeling.

| Dataset | #docs | Vocabulary Size | Average Length | #labels |
|---|---|---|---|---|
| 20NG | 18,846 | 5,000 | 110.5 | 20 |
| IMDB | 50,000 | 5,000 | 95.0 | 2 |
| Wikitext-103 | 28,532 | 10,000 | 1,355.4 | / |

Table 4: Statistics of pre-processed datasets for basic and hierarchical topic modeling.

| Dataset | #docs | Vocabulary Size | Average Length | #labels | #time slices |
|---|---|---|---|---|---|
| NeurIPS | 7,237 | 10,000 | 2,085.9 | / | 31 |
| ACL | 10,560 | 10,000 | 2,023.0 | / | 31 |
| NYT | 9,172 | 10,000 | 175.4 | 12 | 11 |

Table 5: Statistics of pre-processed datasets for dynamic topic modeling.

## A Datasets

Tables 3 to 5 report the statistics of datasets for different topic modeling scenarios after preprocessing. Users can directly download all these datasets via TopMost from our GitHub repository.

# WORDFLOW: Social Prompt Engineering for Large Language Models

**Zijie J. Wang** **Aishwarya Chakravarthy** **David Munechika** **Duen Horng Chau**
College of Computing, Georgia Institute of Technology
{jayw, achakrav6, david.munechika, polo}@gatech.edu

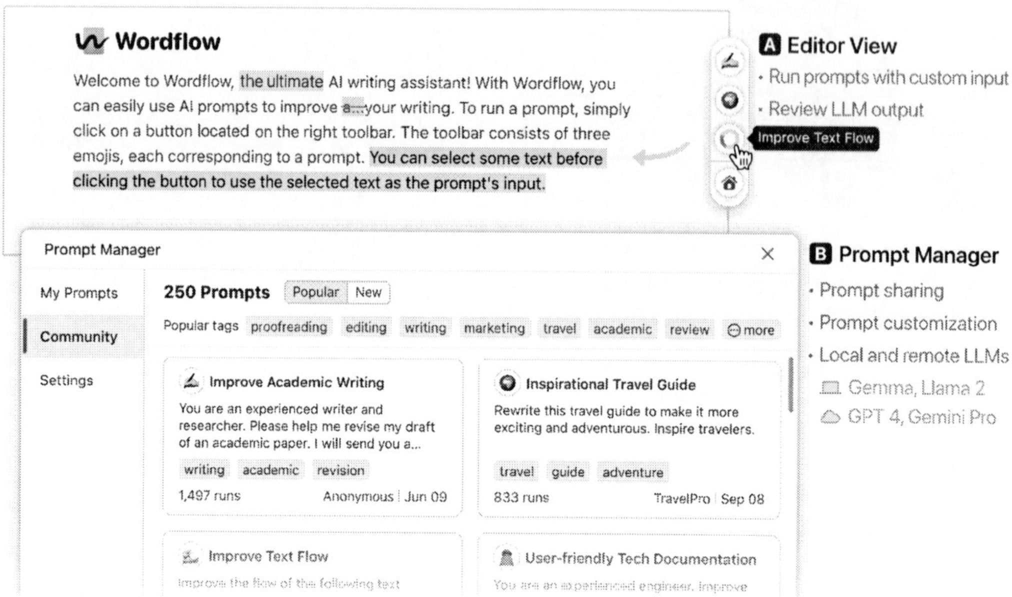


Fig. 1: WORDFLOW is an open-source social prompt engineering tool to help everyday users create, run, share, and discover prompts for large language models (LLMs). **(A) The *Editor View*** offers an easy-to-use text editing interface, allowing users to run an LLM prompt using the selected text as input by simply clicking on a button and examine the changes made by LLMs. **(B) The *Prompt Manager*** enables users to edit and curate prompts, adjust LLM settings, and share their prompts with the community.

## Abstract

Large language models (LLMs) require well-crafted prompts for effective use. Prompt engineering, the process of designing prompts, is challenging, particularly for non-experts who are less familiar with AI technologies. While researchers have proposed techniques and tools to assist LLM users in prompt design, these works primarily target AI application developers rather than non-experts. To address this research gap, we propose social prompt engineering, a novel paradigm that leverages social computing techniques to facilitate collaborative prompt design. To investigate social prompt engineering, we introduce WORDFLOW, an open-source and social text editor that enables everyday users to easily create, run, share, and discover LLM prompts. Additionally, by leveraging modern web technologies, WORDFLOW allows users to run LLMs locally and privately in their browsers. Two usage scenarios highlight how our tool's incorporation of social prompt engineering can enhance laypeople's interactions with LLMs. WORDFLOW is publicly accessible at `https://poloclub.github.io/wordflow`.

## 1 Introduction

Recently, there has been a surge in the popularity of large language models (LLMs) such as GPT-4 (OpenAI, 2023a), Gemini (Team et al., 2023), and Llama 2 (Touvron et al., 2023). These pre-trained artificial intelligence (AI) models demonstrate a diverse array of capabilities that are continually being discovered, including summarization, question-answering, creative writing, and translation (Bommasani et al., 2022). To instruct these general-purpose LLMs to perform specific tasks, users need to provide them with *prompts*—text instructions and examples of desired outputs (Brown



*Proceedings of the 62nd Annual Meeting of the Association for Computational Linguistics (Volume 3: System Demonstrations)*, pages 42–50
August 11-16, 2024 ©2024 Association for Computational Linguistics

et al., 2020). These prompts serve as background contexts and guides for LLMs to generate text that aligns with users' objectives. Prompting enables users to employ LLMs for various tasks with plain language; in fact, well-crafted prompts can make general-purpose LLMs outperform specialized AI models (Nori et al., 2023).

Designing effective prompts, known as *prompt engineering*, poses significant challenges for LLM users (Jiang et al., 2022). LLM users often rely on trial and error and employ unintuitive patterns, such as adding "think step by step" (Kojima et al., 2022) to their prompts, to successfully instruct LLMs. Prompt engineering, despite its name, is considered an art (Parameswaran et al., 2023) and is even compared to wizards learning "magic spells" (Willison et al., 2022). Prompt writers may not fully understand why certain prompts work, but they still add them to their "spell books." Furthermore, prompting is especially challenging for *non-AI-experts*, who are often confused about getting started and lack sufficient guidance and training on LLMs and prompting (Zamfirescu-Pereira et al., 2023).

To help users prompt LLMs, researchers propose instruction tuning (Chung et al., 2022) and reinforcement learning from human feedback (Ouyang et al., 2022) to align a model's output with users' intent. Prompting techniques (Brown et al., 2020) are introduced to improve LLMs' performance on complex tasks. Libraries and interactive tools have also been developed to streamline the prompt crafting process (e.g., Chase, 2022; Jiang et al., 2022). However, existing techniques and tools primarily cater to AI application developers who use LLMs to build AI applications (e.g., chatbot applications), overlooking non-expert users who use LLMs for everyday tasks (e.g., checking emails for grammar errors). To bridge this critical research gap, we propose *social prompt engineering*, a novel paradigm that leverages social computing techniques to facilitate collaborative prompt designs. **We contribute:**

- **WORDFLOW, the first social and customizable text editor** that empowers everyday users to create, run, share, and discover LLM prompts (Fig. 1). It features a direct manipulation text editing interface for applying LLM prompts to transform existing text, such as proofreading and translation, or generate new text, such as creative writing. Users can easily customize prompts and LLM settings, share prompts with the community, and copy community prompts (§ 3). Two usage scenarios highlight how WORDFLOW and social prompt engineering can enhance users' interactions with LLMs (§ 4). Finally, we discuss future research opportunities enabled by our system (§ 5).
- **An open-source[1], web-based implementation** that lowers the barrier for everyday users in designing effective prompts and applying LLMs to their daily tasks. By leveraging modern web technologies, such as WebGPU (MDN, 2023; team, 2023), our tool enables users to run cutting-edge LLMs locally without the need for dedicated backend servers or external LLM API services (§ 3.4). Additionally, we offer an open-source implementation to help future designers and researchers adopt WORDFLOW for exploring and developing future user interfaces for LLMs. To see a demo video of WORDFLOW, visit `https://youtu.be/3dOcVuofGVo`.

We hope our work will inspire the research and development of collaborative interfaces that help everyone more easily and effectively use LLMs.

## 2 Related Work

**Addressing prompt engineering challenges.** Researchers have proposed libraries such as LANGCHAIN (Chase, 2022), GUIDANCE (Lundberg et al., 2023), and OUTLINES (Willard and Louf, 2023) to help users write prompts programmatically and control the structure of an LLM's output. By formulating prompting as programming, researchers propose techniques that help users edit (Fiannaca et al., 2023) and unit test prompts (Strobelt, 2023). COPROMPT (Feng et al., 2023) introduces a collaborative editor for multiple programmers to write prompts simultaneously. AI prototyping tools like PROMPTMAKER (Jiang et al., 2022), GOOGLE AI STUDIO (Google, 2023), OPENAI PLAYGROUND (OpenAI, 2023b), and PARTYROCK (Amazon, 2023) allow users to rapidly write and run prompts.

By leveraging visual programming techniques, tools such as AI CHAINS (Wu et al., 2022), PROMPT SAPPER (Cheng et al., 2023), and CHAINFORGE (Arawjo et al., 2023) enable AI application developers to visually design and test complex prompts. Similarly, PROMPTIDE (Strobelt et al., 2022), PROMPTAID (Mishra et al., 2023), and PROMPTERATOR (Sučik et al., 2023) employ mixed-initiative and interactive visualization tech-

[1]Code: `https://github.com/poloclub/wordflow`

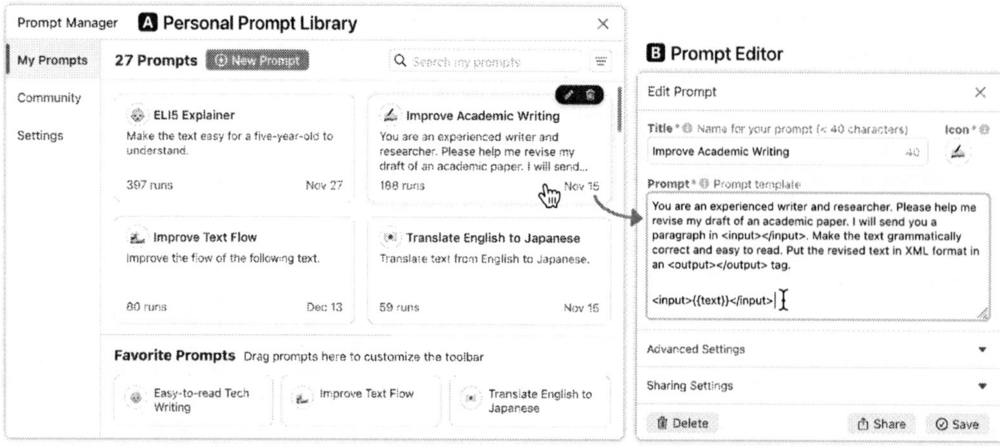


Fig. 2: Users can easily manage and customize their prompts in WORDFLOW. **(A) The *Personal Prompt Library*** provides an overview of local prompts, allowing users to search, sort, and customize the quick-action prompt toolbar in the *Editor View*. **(B) The *Prompt Editor***, activated by clicking a *Prompt Card*, employs progressive disclosure to help users modify prompt and configure output parsing rules, temperature, and sharing settings.

niques to help LLM users brainstorm and refine prompts. These existing tools function as IDEs that help *AI developers* craft prompts that will later be integrated into other applications. In contrast, WORDFLOW aims to serve as a runtime interface for *everyday users*, who act as both the prompt engineers and direct users of their prompts, and may not be well-versed in AI technologies.

**Social prompt engineering.** Online communities, including Promptstacks (Promptstacks, 2023), ChatGPT Prompt Genius (Reddit, 2023), and ShareGPT (Eccleston and Tey, 2022), serve as platforms for prompt creators to share tips, collaborate, and stay updated on AI advancements. User prompts from social media have been scraped to create prompt datasets for AI model development (Wang et al., 2023). Online prompt marketplaces, such as PromptBase (PromptBase, 2023), PromptHero (PromptHero, 2023) and ChatX (ChatX, 2023), have emerged to allow users to buy and sell prompts for generative models. Midjourney's Discord server (Holz, 2022) allows users to run and share prompts for text-to-image generative models, with dedicated sections for prompt critique and improvement (Oppenlaender, 2022). Building on the design of these communities, WORDFLOW provides an easy-to-use interface that unifies creating, running, sharing, and discovering LLM prompts. The most relevant related work is PROMPTSOURCE (Bach et al., 2022), an IDE for AI researchers and developers to write and share LLM prompts. PROMPTSOURCE targets AI experts using LLMs for natural language processing tasks on datasets (such as data annotation), and it requires users to provide a dataset. In comparison, WORDFLOW targets everyday users using LLMs for daily tasks, such as grammar checking, without the need to provide any dataset.

## 3 System Design & Implementation

WORDFLOW is an interactive tool that empowers everyday users to easily create, run, share, and discover LLM prompts. It tightly integrates four views: the *Editor View* (§ 3.1), where users can write text, run LLM prompts, and inspect changes made by LLMs; the *Personal Prompt Library* (§ 3.2), offering a prompt manager for creating and editing prompts locally; the *Community Prompt Hub* (§ 3.2), enabling users to explore and search for the latest and popular prompts shared by the community; and the *Setting Panel* for configuring remote or local LLMs (§ 3.4).

### 3.1 Editor View

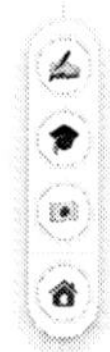

When users open WORDFLOW in their browser or its mobile and desktop progressive web app, they are presented with the *Editor View* (Fig. 1A). This view shows a familiar text editor interface with a *Floating Toolbar* anchored on the right. Users can type or paste text into the editor. The *Floating Toolbar* consists of three prompt buttons and a home button (shown on the right). Each prompt button is represented by an emoji icon and corresponds to a prompt template. Users can click the prompt button to run its prompt using the current paragraph

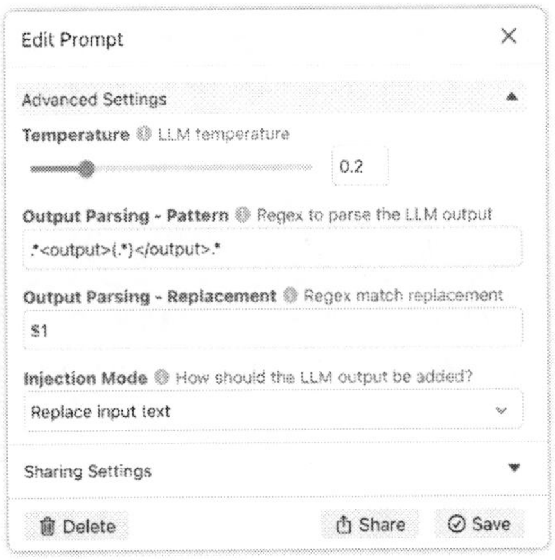


Fig. 3: Users can easily configure LLM temperatures and regex-baed output parsing in the *Prompt Editor*.

as the input text. If a user has selected some text, the selected text is used as the input for the prompt. Users can also click the home button to open a pop-up window that contains the *Personal Prompt Library* (§ 3.2, Fig. 2A), the *Community Prompt Hub* (§ 3.3, Fig. 1B), and the *Setting Panel* (Fig. 4).

**Prompt input templating.** In WORDFLOW, a prompt template includes pre-defined prefix text and a placeholder for the input text. For example, the prefix text can be "Improve the flow of the following text". The input placeholder in the template serves as a variable that will be substituted with the selected text from the editor. Inspired by popular prompting tools such as LANGCHAIN and PROMPTMAKER, our tool supports basic prompt templating. Users can include a special string `{{text}}` in their prompt template to represent the input placeholder (Fig. 2B), which will be replaced with the selected text from the editor before running the prompt. If the user does not include the string `{{text}}` in the template, the input text will be appended to the prompt template.

**Prompt output parsing.** To run users' prompts, WORDFLOW supports remote LLM API services, such as GPT 4 and Gemini API services provided by OpenAI and Google, as well as local open-source models, such as Llama 2 (Touvron et al., 2023) and Phi 2 (Abdin et al., 2023). Users can set their preferred models in the *Setting Panel* (Fig. 4). After receiving the output from the LLM API service or local model, the *Editor View* applies Myer's diffing algorithm (Fraser, 2012) to compare the output text with the input text. It then highlights the changes made by the LLM (e.g., addition, replacement, and deletion) using different text background colors (Fig. 1A). Users can click on the highlighted text to accept or reject the changes.

Inspired by LANGCHAIN, WORDFLOW allows users to add *optional* output parsing rules to a prompt by writing regular expression (regex) text (Fig. 3), which is useful for disregarding unrelated output text. For example, a user can prompt LLMs to structure the output in XML format (recommended by prompt engineering guidelines (Anthropic, 2023)), such as "Improve the flow of the following text. Put the rewritten text in an XML tag `<output></output>`". The user can then add a regex pattern `.*<output>(.*)</output>.*` and a replacement rule `$1` to parse the LLM's output before it is displayed in the *Editor View*.

### 3.2 Personal Prompt Library

After clicking the home button, users can open the *Personal Prompt Library* to manage their local prompts (Fig. 2A). This view organizes each prompt as a *Prompt Card*, allowing users to search and sort prompts based on name, recency, and run count. To change the prompts in the *Floating Toolbar* (§ 3.1), users can simply drag a *Prompt Card* into one of the three prompt slots located in the bottom row, each corresponding to a prompt button in the *Floating Toolbar*. To add or edit a prompt, users can click on the New Prompt button or a *Prompt Card* to open the *Prompt Editor* (Fig. 2B). The *Prompt Editor* comprises three forms: basic prompt information (Fig. 2B), optional advanced settings (Fig. 3), and optional sharing settings. In the basic prompt information section, users can configure the title, icon, and prompt template. The advanced settings allow more experienced users to set the LLM temperature, output parsing rules, and insertion rules (Fig. 3). To share a prompt with the community, users can provide a description, tags, and recommended LLM models in the sharing settings, and then click on the Share button.

### 3.3 Community Prompt Hub

The *Community Prompt Hub* enables users to browse and search for prompts shared by WORDFLOW users (Fig. 1B). Each community prompt is represented as a *Prompt Card* and is associated with at least one tag. Users can filter prompts by clicking on a tag and can also sort prompts based on recency and popularity (i.e., the number of times they have been run). By clicking on a *Prompt Card*, users can access the *Prompt Viewer* (Fig. 5) to examine detailed information provided by the prompt creator, including the title, description, prompt template, and recommended LLM models. Finally, users can click on the Add button to include a copy of the community prompt in their *Personal Prompt Library* (§ 3.2), where they can run the prompt, make further refinements, and potentially share it again with the community.

### 3.4 Open-source Implementation

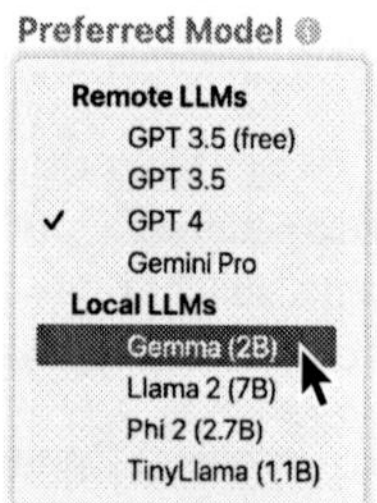

Fig. 4: WORDFLOW supports both remote and local LLMs.

We implement WORDFLOW as a progressive web app using Web Components and LIT Element (Google, 2015). Users can use it as a mobile or desktop app by saving it as a Safari Web App or a Chrome app. WORDFLOW allows users to run LLMs through remote API services, such as GPT 4 provided by OpenAI, or directly run open-source LLMs, such as Gemma (Team et al., 2024), Llama 2, Phi 2, and TinyLlama, in their browser (Fig. 4). We use Web LLM (team, 2023) and WebGPU to implement on-device LLM inference. In WORDFLOW, all local prompts are stored in the local persistent storage of the user's browser. To enable users to share community prompts, we use Amazon API Gateway and DynamoDB as a backend. Additionally, we provide a Google Doc add-on (Fig. 6) that allows Google Doc users to directly use WORDFLOW within their editor. We open source WORDFLOW as a collection of reusable interactive components that can be easily adopted by future researchers and developers in their interactive LLM projects.

## 4 Usage Scenarios

### 4.1 Improving Technical Writing

As a recently graduated junior software developer, Wade has been struggling with writing API documentation and system architecture descriptions. Specifically, Wade is unfamiliar with explaining technical concepts in simple language that can be easily understood by different colleagues such as developers, UX designers, and program managers. One day, Wade came across a forum thread where developers were sharing LLM prompts that had helped them improve their technical documentation writing. Wade had never thought about using LLM to assist him in his writing before. Intrigued,

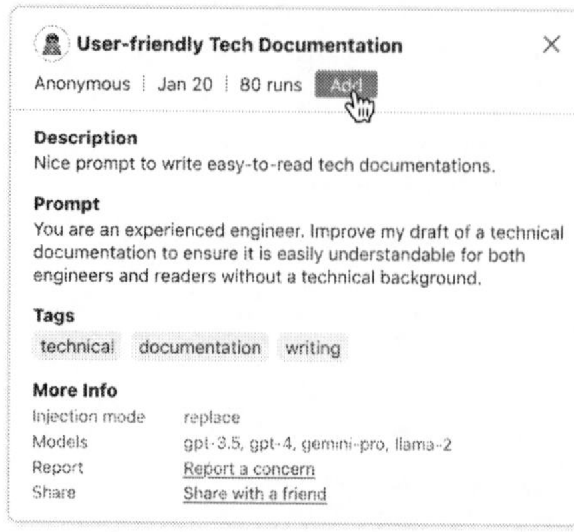

Fig. 5: The *Prompt Viewer* shows detailed information about a community prompt. Users can click a button to copy this prompt into their *Personal Prompt Library*.

he clicked on a WORDFLOW prompt link shared in a popular comment on the thread. The link opened WORDFLOW in a new tab, displaying the *Community Prompt Hub* along with a pop-up showing a community prompt (Fig. 5). Wade found the prompt and its description to be suitable for his writing tasks, so he clicked on the Add button to copy this community prompt to his local library.

Wade decided to try out this prompt to improve his writing. He opened the *Personal Prompt Library* and dragged the newly added prompt into one of the Favorite Prompts slots (Fig. 2A), and the prompt appeared in the *Floating Toolbar* in the *Editor View* (Fig. 1A). Wade copied a paragraph from the API documentation that he was working on. However, before clicking on the prompt button in the *Floating Toolbar*, Wade suddenly remembered that his company prohibits employees from using LLM services (e.g., ChatGPT and Bard) with work materials, as a measure to safeguard trade secrets and sensitive information.

Upon reviewing the documentation of WORDFLOW, Wade discovered that WORDFLOW supports running LLMs locally in browsers without sending any data to third-party services (e.g., OpenAI and Google). Therefore, he configured the LLM model to Llama 2, a local LLM model, in the *Setting Panel* before running the prompt on his writing. Then, he observed the changes made by the LLM model, which were highlighted in the *Editor View*, and found the new paragraph to be much easier to read. After using this prompt for a few days, Wade shared the prompt link on his company's mailing list, and more developers from his company began to use it to improve technical writing.

Fig. 6: Users can directly use WORDFLOW add-on to apply prompts to text within Google Doc documents.

### 4.2 Customizing Translation Styles

Ember, a senior manager in a US financial firm, recently encountered difficulties in communicating with her Japanese counterparts due to the absence of a translator. The use of traditional translation software has sometimes caused confusion among her Japanese colleagues. For example, the software translated the English idiom "break the ice" to "氷を砕く," which means "destroy the ice" instead of her intended meaning of "relieving tension when people interact for the first time."

Due to the recent popularity of LLMs, Ember decided to try using them to translate her documents from English to Japanese. As she writes in Google Docs, she explored the Google Doc Marketplace for an AI add-on and came across WORDFLOW. Upon installation, she opened the *Community Prompt Hub* (Fig. 1B) and selected the tag translation, which showed various popular translation prompts. She found a prompt titled "Translate English to Japanese."

After adding this prompt to her library, she tried to run it with the input "break the ice". However, WORDFLOW appended the incorrect translation "氷を砕く" to her document. Drawing from her previous experience interacting with ChatGPT, Ember decided to edit the prompt and provide additional instructions to guide the LLM model in considering her translation context. She opened the *Editor View* (Fig. 2B). and added a new sentence to the translation prompt: "My input text is used in US corporate communications" (Fig. 6 Right). Running the prompt again, WORDFLOW generated a more suitable translation "雰囲気を和らげる," which means "ease the atmosphere" (Fig. 6 Left). Ember back-translated the translation to English using her other translation software and felt more confident in continuing to use this prompt for future translations. Finally, to help other people who need to translate English to Japanese in business settings, she shared her updated prompt with the community by clicking on the Share button (Fig. 2B).

## 5 Future Work & Conclusion

In this work, we present social prompt engineering, a new paradigm that leverages social computing techniques to facilitate collaborative prompt design. To realize social prompt engineering, we design and develop WORDFLOW, an open-source and social text editor empowering users to easily create, run, share, and discover LLM prompts. Two usage scenarios highlight social prompt engineering and WORDFLOW can assist everyday users in interacting with LLMs. Reflecting on our design and development of this system, we discuss future research directions to help *everyone* use LLMs.

- **Usage log study.** Using WORDFLOW as a research instrument, we plan to conduct a usage log study to evaluate social prompt engineering and investigate (1) the effectiveness of social prompt engineering in helping everyday users craft prompts, and (2) everyday users' LLM use cases. We will examine the evolution of prompt editing and analyze community prompts to synthesize popular use cases and prompting patterns.
- **Fitting into user workflows.** Future tools like WORDFLOW can be seamlessly integrated into user workflows by being *in situ* and ubiquitous. With recent advancements in on-device machine learning, we see great potential for on-device LLMs, which allow users to avoid sending sensitive data to external services, reduce API costs, and use LLMs without network access.
- **Enhancing engagement in social prompt engineering.** There are great opportunities to enrich user interaction with LLMs using social computing techniques. To encourage user participation in prompt sharing, researchers can explore *intrinsic motivations*, such as designing an enjoyable social environment, and *extrinsic motivations*, such as virtual rewards and reputation systems.
- **Promoting responsible AI.** Social prompt engineering presents both opportunities and challenges for responsible AI. Platforms like WORDFLOW enable users to share prompting techniques to mitigate potential harms, but also run the risk of disseminating harmful prompts such as misinformation generators. In WORDFLOW, users can report harmful prompts, and we diligently monitor and moderate community prompts. Future researchers can explore social system designs that promote responsible prompting and develop methods to detect potentially harmful prompts.

## 6 Broader Impact

We propose social prompt engineering with good intentions—to help everyday users more easily and effectively use LLMs for their everyday tasks. In addition, we design and develop WORDFLOW, an open-source tool that is publicly accessible, to help everyday users easily create, run, share, and discover LLM prompts. However, bad actors might exploit our open platform to distribute prompts designed for harmful purposes. For example, they could share prompts that generate misinformation or content fostering divisive or extremist ideologies, exploiting WORDFLOW's reach to influence vulnerable and inexperienced audiences. To address and mitigate these potential harms, WORDFLOW enables users to report harmful prompts. We also actively monitor and moderate community prompts. Given that social prompt engineering and social prompting systems are still in their early stages, further research is needed to understand and address their potential harms.

## Acknowledgements

This work was supported in part by an Apple Scholars in AI/ML PhD fellowship and J.P. Morgan PhD Fellowship. We are extremely grateful to Kaan Sancak, Jaemarie Solyst, Xinzhi Jiang for stress-testing our tool. We appreciate Tianqi Chen, Charlie Ruan, and Alex Cabrera for their suggestions and support for integrating on-device LLMs. We express our gratitude to Alex Bäuerle, Upol Ehsan, Muhammed Fatih Balin, Luis Morales-Navarro, Wesley Hanwen Deng, Young Wu, Giorgio Pini, Justin Blalock, Viraj Kacker, Seongmin Lee, Ben Hoover, Anthony Peng, Alec Helbling, Matthew Hull, Mansi Phute, Harsha Karanth, Pratham Mehta, Joanna Cheng, Lena Do, Smera Bhatia, Angelina Wang and Parul Pandey for their advocacy and valuable feedback.

## References

Marah Abdin, Jyoti Aneja, Sebastien Bubeck, Caio César Teodoro Mendes, Weizhu Chen, Allie Del Giorno, Ronen Eldan, Sivakanth Gopi, Suriya Gunasekar, Mojan Javaheripi, Piero Kauffmann, Yin Tat Lee, Yuanzhi Li, Anh Nguyen, Gustavo de Rosa, Olli Saarikivi, Adil Salim, Shital Shah, Michael Santacroce, Harkirat Singh Behl, Adam Taumann Kalai, Xin Wang, Rachel Ward, Philipp Witte, Cyril Zhang, and Yi Zhang. 2023. Phi-2: The surprising power of small language models.

Amazon. 2023. PartyRock: Everyone can build AI apps.

Anthropic. 2023. Introduction to prompt design.

Ian Arawjo, Chelse Swoopes, Priyan Vaithilingam, Martin Wattenberg, and Elena Glassman. 2023. Chain-Forge: A Visual Toolkit for Prompt Engineering and LLM Hypothesis Testing. *arXiv 2309.09128*.

Stephen Bach, Victor Sanh, Zheng Xin Yong, Albert Webson, Colin Raffel, Nihal V. Nayak, Abheesht Sharma, Taewoon Kim, M Saiful Bari, Thibault Fevry, Zaid Alyafeai, Manan Dey, Andrea Santilli, Zhiqing Sun, Srulik Ben-david, Canwen Xu, Gunjan Chhablani, Han Wang, Jason Fries, Maged Al-shaibani, Shanya Sharma, Urmish Thakker, Khalid Almubarak, Xiangru Tang, Dragomir Radev, Mike Tian-jian Jiang, and Alexander Rush. 2022. Prompt-Source: An Integrated Development Environment and Repository for Natural Language Prompts. In *Proceedings of the 60th Annual Meeting of the Association for Computational Linguistics: System Demonstrations*.

Rishi Bommasani, Drew A. Hudson, Ehsan Adeli, Russ Altman, Simran Arora, Sydney von Arx, Michael S. Bernstein, Jeannette Bohg, Antoine Bosselut, Emma Brunskill, Erik Brynjolfsson, Shyamal Buch, Dallas Card, Rodrigo Castellon, Niladri Chatterji, Annie Chen, Kathleen Creel, Jared Quincy Davis, Dora Demszky, Chris Donahue, Moussa Doumbouya, Esin Durmus, Stefano Ermon, John Etchemendy, Kawin Ethayarajh, Li Fei-Fei, Chelsea Finn, Trevor Gale, Lauren Gillespie, Karan Goel, Noah Goodman, Shelby Grossman, Neel Guha, Tatsunori Hashimoto, Peter Henderson, John Hewitt, Daniel E. Ho, Jenny Hong, Kyle Hsu, Jing Huang, Thomas Icard, Saahil Jain, Dan Jurafsky, Pratyusha Kalluri, Siddharth Karamcheti, Geoff Keeling, Fereshte Khani, Omar Khattab, Pang Wei Koh, Mark Krass, Ranjay Krishna, Rohith Kuditipudi, Ananya Kumar, Faisal Ladhak, Mina Lee, Tony Lee, Jure Leskovec, Isabelle Levent, Xiang Lisa Li, Xuechen Li, Tengyu Ma, Ali Malik, Christopher D. Manning, Suvir Mirchandani, Eric Mitchell, Zanele Munyikwa, Suraj Nair, Avanika Narayan, Deepak Narayanan, Ben Newman, Allen Nie, Juan Carlos Niebles, Hamed Nilforoshan, Julian Nyarko, Giray Ogut, Laurel Orr, Isabel Papadimitriou, Joon Sung Park, Chris Piech, Eva Portelance, Christopher Potts, Aditi Raghunathan, Rob Reich, Hongyu Ren, Frieda Rong, Yusuf Roohani, Camilo Ruiz, Jack Ryan, Christopher Ré, Dorsa Sadigh, Shiori Sagawa, Keshav Santhanam, Andy Shih, Krishnan Srinivasan, Alex Tamkin, Rohan Taori, Armin W. Thomas, Florian Tramèr, Rose E. Wang, William Wang, Bohan Wu, Jiajun Wu, Yuhuai Wu, Sang Michael Xie, Michihiro Yasunaga, Jiaxuan You, Matei Zaharia, Michael Zhang, Tianyi Zhang, Xikun Zhang, Yuhui Zhang, Lucia Zheng, Kaitlyn Zhou, and Percy Liang. 2022. On the Opportunities and Risks of Foundation Models. *arXiv 2108.07258*.

Tom Brown, Benjamin Mann, Nick Ryder, Melanie Subbiah, Jared D Kaplan, Prafulla Dhariwal, Arvind Neelakantan, Pranav Shyam, Girish Sastry, Amanda Askell, Sandhini Agarwal, Ariel Herbert-Voss, Gretchen Krueger, Tom Henighan, Rewon Child,

Aditya Ramesh, Daniel Ziegler, Jeffrey Wu, Clemens Winter, Chris Hesse, Mark Chen, Eric Sigler, Mateusz Litwin, Scott Gray, Benjamin Chess, Jack Clark, Christopher Berner, Sam McCandlish, Alec Radford, Ilya Sutskever, and Dario Amodei. 2020. Language models are few-shot learners. In *Advances in Neural Information Processing Systems*, volume 33.

Harrison Chase. 2022. LangChain: Building applications with LLMs through composability.

ChatX. 2023. ChatX: ChatGPT, DALL·E & Stable Diffusion prompt marketplace.

Yu Cheng, Jieshan Chen, Qing Huang, Zhenchang Xing, Xiwei Xu, and Qinghua Lu. 2023. Prompt Sapper: A LLM-Empowered Production Tool for Building AI Chains. *arXiv 2306.12028*.

Hyung Won Chung, Le Hou, Shayne Longpre, Barret Zoph, Yi Tay, William Fedus, Yunxuan Li, Xuezhi Wang, Mostafa Dehghani, Siddhartha Brahma, Albert Webson, Shixiang Shane Gu, Zhuyun Dai, Mirac Suzgun, Xinyun Chen, Aakanksha Chowdhery, Alex Castro-Ros, Marie Pellat, Kevin Robinson, Dasha Valter, Sharan Narang, Gaurav Mishra, Adams Yu, Vincent Zhao, Yanping Huang, Andrew Dai, Hongkun Yu, Slav Petrov, Ed H. Chi, Jeff Dean, Jacob Devlin, Adam Roberts, Denny Zhou, Quoc V. Le, and Jason Wei. 2022. Scaling Instruction-Finetuned Language Models. *arXiv 2210.11416*.

Dom Eccleston and Steven Tey. 2022. ShareGPT: Share your wildest ChatGPT conversations with one click.

Felicia Li Feng, Ryan Yen, Yuzhe You, Mingming Fan, Jian Zhao, and Zhicong Lu. 2023. CoPrompt: Supporting Prompt Sharing and Referring in Collaborative Natural Language Programming. *arXiv 2310.09235*.

Alexander J. Fiannaca, Chinmay Kulkarni, Carrie J Cai, and Michael Terry. 2023. Programming without a Programming Language: Challenges and Opportunities for Designing Developer Tools for Prompt Programming. In *Extended Abstracts of the 2023 CHI Conference on Human Factors in Computing Systems*.

Neil Fraser. 2012. Diff-match-patch: Hgh-performance library in multiple languages that manipulates plain text.

Google. 2015. Lit: Simple fast Web Components.

Google. 2023. Google Ai Studio: Prototype with Generative AI.

David Holz. 2022. Midjourney: Exploring New Mediums of Thought and Expanding the Imaginative Powers of the Human Species.

Ellen Jiang, Kristen Olson, Edwin Toh, Alejandra Molina, Aaron Donsbach, Michael Terry, and Carrie J Cai. 2022. PromptMaker: Prompt-based Prototyping with Large Language Models. In *CHI Conference on Human Factors in Computing Systems Extended Abstracts*.

Takeshi Kojima, Shixiang (Shane) Gu, Machel Reid, Yutaka Matsuo, and Yusuke Iwasawa. 2022. Large Language Models are Zero-Shot Reasoners. *Advances in Neural Information Processing Systems*, 35.

Scott Lundberg, Marco Tulio Ribeiro, and Harsha Nori. 2023. Guidance: A guidance language for controlling large language models. guidance-ai.

MDN. 2023. WebGPU API - Web APIs.

Aditi Mishra, Utkarsh Soni, Anjana Arunkumar, Jinbin Huang, Bum Chul Kwon, and Chris Bryan. 2023. PromptAid: Prompt Exploration, Perturbation, Testing and Iteration using Visual Analytics for Large Language Models. *arXiv 2304.01964*.

Harsha Nori, Yin Tat Lee, Sheng Zhang, Dean Carignan, Richard Edgar, Nicolo Fusi, Nicholas King, Jonathan Larson, Yuanzhi Li, Weishung Liu, Renqian Luo, Scott Mayer McKinney, Robert Osazuwa Ness, Hoifung Poon, Tao Qin, Naoto Usuyama, Chris White, and Eric Horvitz. 2023. Can Generalist Foundation Models Outcompete Special-Purpose Tuning? Case Study in Medicine. *arXiv 2311.16452*.

OpenAI. 2023a. GPT-4 Technical Report. *arXiv 2303.08774*.

OpenAI. 2023b. OpenAI Playground.

Jonas Oppenlaender. 2022. A Taxonomy of Prompt Modifiers for Text-To-Image Generation. *arXiv 2204.13988*.

Long Ouyang, Jeff Wu, Xu Jiang, Diogo Almeida, Carroll L. Wainwright, Pamela Mishkin, Chong Zhang, Sandhini Agarwal, Katarina Slama, Alex Ray, John Schulman, Jacob Hilton, Fraser Kelton, Luke Miller, Maddie Simens, Amanda Askell, Peter Welinder, Paul Christiano, Jan Leike, and Ryan Lowe. 2022. Training language models to follow instructions with human feedback. *arXiv 2203.02155*.

Aditya G. Parameswaran, Shreya Shankar, Parth Asawa, Naman Jain, and Yujie Wang. 2023. Revisiting Prompt Engineering via Declarative Crowdsourcing. *arXiv 2308.03854*.

PromptBase. 2023. PromptBase: Prompt Marketplace: Midjourney, ChatGPT, DALL·E, Stable Diffusion & more.

PromptHero. 2023. PromptHero: Search prompts for Stable Diffusion, ChatGPT & Midjourney.

Promptstacks. 2023. Promptstacks: Your Prompt Engineering Community.

Reddit. 2023. R/ChatGPTPromptGenius.

Hendrik Strobelt. 2023. Prompt tester - quick prompt iterations for ad-hoc tasks.

Hendrik Strobelt, Albert Webson, Victor Sanh, Benjamin Hoover, Johanna Beyer, Hanspeter Pfister, and Alexander M. Rush. 2022. Interactive and Visual Prompt Engineering for Ad-hoc Task Adaptation With Large Language Models. *IEEE Transactions on Visualization and Computer Graphics*.

Samuel Sučik, Daniel Skala, Andrej Švec, Peter Hraška, and Marek Šuppa. 2023. Prompterator: Iterate efficiently towards more effective prompts. In *Proceedings of the 2023 Conference on Empirical Methods in Natural Language Processing: System Demonstrations*.

Gemini Team, Rohan Anil, Sebastian Borgeaud, Yonghui Wu, Jean-Baptiste Alayrac, Jiahui Yu, Radu Soricut, Johan Schalkwyk, Andrew M Dai, Anja Hauth, et al. 2023. Gemini: A family of highly capable multimodal models. *arXiv preprint arXiv:2312.11805*.

Gemma Team, Thomas Mesnard, Cassidy Hardin, Robert Dadashi, Surya Bhupatiraju, Shreya Pathak, Laurent Sifre, Morgane Rivière, Mihir Sanjay Kale, Juliette Love, Pouya Tafti, Léonard Hussenot, Aakanksha Chowdhery, Adam Roberts, Aditya Barua, Alex Botev, Alex Castro-Ros, Ambrose Slone, Amélie Héliou, Andrea Tacchetti, Anna Bulanova, Antonia Paterson, Beth Tsai, Bobak Shahriari, Charline Le Lan, Christopher A. Choquette-Choo, Clément Crepy, Daniel Cer, Daphne Ippolito, David Reid, Elena Buchatskaya, Eric Ni, Eric Noland, Geng Yan, George Tucker, George-Christian Muraru, Grigory Rozhdestvenskiy, Henryk Michalewski, Ian Tenney, Ivan Grishchenko, Jacob Austin, James Keeling, Jane Labanowski, Jean-Baptiste Lespiau, Jeff Stanway, Jenny Brennan, Jeremy Chen, Johan Ferret, Justin Chiu, Justin Mao-Jones, Katherine Lee, Kathy Yu, Katie Millican, Lars Lowe Sjoesund, Lisa Lee, Lucas Dixon, Machel Reid, Maciej Mikuła, Mateo Wirth, Michael Sharman, Nikolai Chinaev, Nithum Thain, Olivier Bachem, Oscar Chang, Oscar Wahltinez, Paige Bailey, Paul Michel, Petko Yotov, Pier Giuseppe Sessa, Rahma Chaabouni, Ramona Comanescu, Reena Jana, Rohan Anil, Ross McIlroy, Ruibo Liu, Ryan Mullins, Samuel L. Smith, Sebastian Borgeaud, Sertan Girgin, Sholto Douglas, Shree Pandya, Siamak Shakeri, Soham De, Ted Klimenko, Tom Hennigan, Vlad Feinberg, Wojciech Stokowiec, Yu-hui Chen, Zafarali Ahmed, Zhitao Gong, Tris Warkentin, Ludovic Peran, Minh Giang, Clément Farabet, Oriol Vinyals, Jeff Dean, Koray Kavukcuoglu, Demis Hassabis, Zoubin Ghahramani, Douglas Eck, Joelle Barral, Fernando Pereira, Eli Collins, Armand Joulin, Noah Fiedel, Evan Senter, Alek Andreev, and Kathleen Kenealy. 2024. Gemma: Open Models Based on Gemini Research and Technology. *arXiv 2403.08295*.

MLC team. 2023. MLC-LLM.

Hugo Touvron, Louis Martin, Kevin Stone, Peter Albert, Amjad Almahairi, Yasmine Babaei, Nikolay Bashlykov, Soumya Batra, Prajjwal Bhargava, Shruti Bhosale, Dan Bikel, Lukas Blecher, Cristian Canton Ferrer, Moya Chen, Guillem Cucurull, David Esiobu, Jude Fernandes, Jeremy Fu, Wenyin Fu, Brian Fuller, Cynthia Gao, Vedanuj Goswami, Naman Goyal, Anthony Hartshorn, Saghar Hosseini, Rui Hou, Hakan Inan, Marcin Kardas, Viktor Kerkez, Madian Khabsa, Isabel Kloumann, Artem Korenev, Punit Singh Koura, Marie-Anne Lachaux, Thibaut Lavril, Jenya Lee, Diana Liskovich, Yinghai Lu, Yuning Mao, Xavier Martinet, Todor Mihaylov, Pushkar Mishra, Igor Molybog, Yixin Nie, Andrew Poulton, Jeremy Reizenstein, Rashi Rungta, Kalyan Saladi, Alan Schelten, Ruan Silva, Eric Michael Smith, Ranjan Subramanian, Xiaoqing Ellen Tan, Binh Tang, Ross Taylor, Adina Williams, Jian Xiang Kuan, Puxin Xu, Zheng Yan, Iliyan Zarov, Yuchen Zhang, Angela Fan, Melanie Kambadur, Sharan Narang, Aurelien Rodriguez, Robert Stojnic, Sergey Edunov, and Thomas Scialom. 2023. Llama 2: Open foundation and fine-tuned chat models. *arXiv 2307.09288*.

Zijie J. Wang, Evan Montoya, David Munechika, Haoyang Yang, Benjamin Hoover, and Duen Horng Chau. 2023. DiffusionDB: A large-scale prompt gallery dataset for text-to-image generative models. In *Proceedings of the 61st Annual Meeting of the Association for Computational Linguistics (Volume 1: Long Papers)*.

Brandon T. Willard and Rémi Louf. 2023. Efficient Guided Generation for Large Language Models. *arXiv 2307.09702*.

Simon Willison, Adam Stacoviak, and Jerod Stacoviak. 2022. Stable Diffusion Breaks the Internet.

Tongshuang Wu, Michael Terry, and Carrie Jun Cai. 2022. AI Chains: Transparent and Controllable Human-AI Interaction by Chaining Large Language Model Prompts. In *CHI Conference on Human Factors in Computing Systems*.

J.D. Zamfirescu-Pereira, Richmond Y. Wong, Bjoern Hartmann, and Qian Yang. 2023. Why Johnny Can't Prompt: How Non-AI Experts Try (and Fail) to Design LLM Prompts. In *Proceedings of the 2023 CHI Conference on Human Factors in Computing Systems*.

# LM Transparency Tool: Interactive Tool for Analyzing Transformer Language Models

**Igor Tufanov**[∞] **Karen Hambardzumyan**[∞□] **Javier Ferrando**[◇*] **Elena Voita**[∞]
[∞]AI at Meta (FAIR) [□]University College London [◇]Universitat Politècnica de Catalunya
{igortufanov,mahnerak,lenavoita}@meta.com
javier.ferrando.monsonis@upc.edu

## Abstract

We present the LM Transparency Tool (LM-TT), an open-source interactive toolkit for analyzing the internal workings of Transformer-based language models. Differently from previously existing tools that focus on isolated parts of the decision-making process, our framework is designed to make the entire prediction process transparent, and allows tracing back model behavior from the top-layer representation to very fine-grained parts of the model. Specifically, it (i) shows the important part of the whole input-to-output information flow, (ii) allows attributing any changes done by a model block to individual attention heads and feed-forward neurons, (iii) allows interpreting the functions of those heads or neurons. A crucial part of this pipeline is showing the importance of specific model components at each step. As a result, we are able to look at the roles of model components only in cases where they are important for a prediction. Since knowing which components should be inspected is key for analyzing large models where the number of these components is extremely high, we believe our tool will greatly support the interpretability community both in research settings and in practical applications. The LM-TT codebase is available at https://github.com/facebookresearch/llm-transparency-tool.

## 1 Introduction

Recent advances in natural language processing led to remarkable capabilities of the Transformer language models, especially with scale (Brown et al., 2020; Kaplan et al., 2020; Zhang et al., 2022a; Wei et al., 2022; Ouyang et al., 2022; OpenAI, 2023; Anil et al., 2023; Touvron et al., 2023a,b). This, along with the wide adoption of such models in high-stakes settings, makes understanding the internal workings of these models vital from the safety, reliability and trustworthiness perspectives.

Existing tools for analyzing sequence models' predictions enable users to compute input tokens attribution scores, read token promotions performed by different model components, or analyze textual patterns responsible for the activation of model's neurons (Geva et al., 2022a; Katz and Belinkov, 2023; Alammar, 2021; Tenney et al., 2020; Sarti et al., 2023; Kokhlikyan et al., 2020; Miglani et al., 2023). However, these focus only on specific parts of the decision-making process and none of them is designed to make the entire prediction process transparent. In contrast, we introduce LM Transparency Tool, a framework that allows tracing back model behavior to very fine-grained model parts.

One of the key advantages of our pipeline is the ability to look only at those model components that were relevant for a selected prediction. Indeed, e.g. syntactic attention heads (Voita et al., 2019), induction heads (Elhage et al., 2021; Olsson et al., 2022), knowledge neurons (Dai et al., 2022), etc. perform their function only in specific cases and are "dormant" otherwise – therefore, looking at them makes sense only for those certain examples. To make this possible, our tool first shows the information flow routes introduced by Ferrando and Voita (2024): this is a subset of intermediate token representations and model components that together form the most important part of the entire input-to-output processing. Then, the tool further allows (i) attributing any changes done by those important model blocks to individual attention heads and feed-forward neurons, as well as (ii) interpreting the functions of those heads and neurons. Importantly, LM-TT is highly efficient: due to relying on Ferrando and Voita (2024), it is 100 times faster than typical patching-based alternatives (Conmy et al., 2023).

Overall, the LM Transparency Tool:

- visualizes the "important" part of the prediction process along with importances of model components at varying levels of granularity;

[*] Work done during an internship at Meta.



*Proceedings of the 62nd Annual Meeting of the Association for Computational Linguistics (Volume 3: System Demonstrations)*, pages 51–60

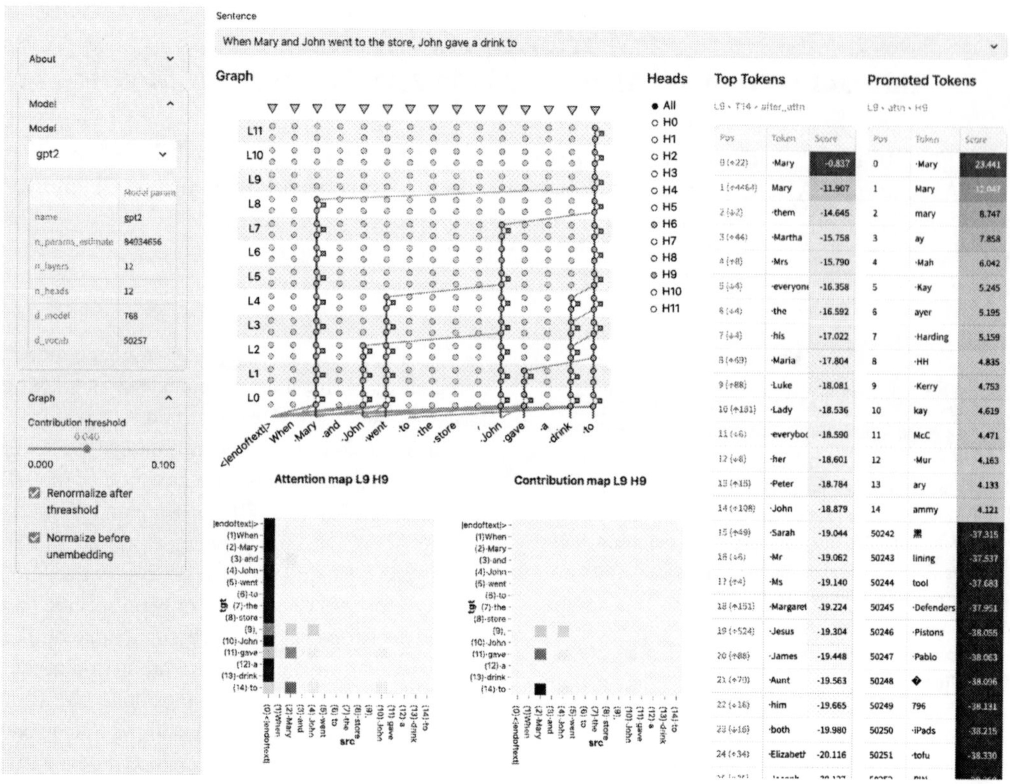


Figure 1: The LM Transparency Tool UI showing information flow graph for the selected prediction, importances of attention heads at the selected layer, attention and contribution maps, logit lens for the selected representation, and top tokens promoted/suppressed by the selected attention head.

- allows interpreting representations and updates coming from model components;
- enables analyzing large models where it is crucial to know what to inspect;
- allows interactive exploration via a UI[1];
- is highly efficient.

## 2 User Interface and Functionality

Inside Transformer language models, each representation evolves from the current input token embedding[2] to the final representation used to predict the next token. This evolution happens through additive updates coming from attention and feed-forward blocks. The resulting stack of same-token representations is usually referred to as "residual stream" (Elhage et al., 2021), and the overall computation inside the model can be viewed as a sequence of residual streams connected through layer blocks. Formally, we can see it as a graph where nodes correspond to token representations and edges correspond to operations inside the model (attention heads, feed-forward layers, etc.). Our tool visualizes the "important" part of this graph, importances of model components at varying levels of granularity (individual heads and neurons), as well as an interpretation of representations and updates coming from model components.

### 2.1 Important Information Flow Subgraph

As we mentioned, we can see computations inside the Transformer as a graph with token representations as nodes and operations inside the model as edges. While during model computation all the edges (i.e., model components) are present, computations important for each prediction are likely to form only a small portion of the original graph (Voita et al. (2019); Wang et al. (2023); Hanna et al. (2023), among others). Recent work by Ferrando and Voita (2024) extracts

[1] We also host a demo at `https://huggingface.co/spaces/facebook/llm-transparency-tool-demo`

[2] Sometimes, along with positional encoding.

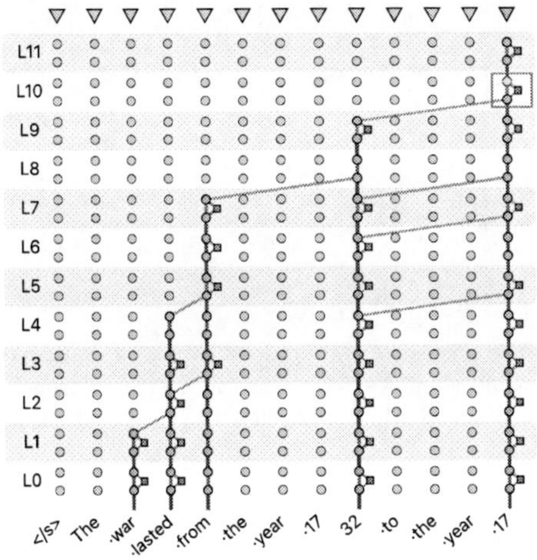


**Top Tokens**

L10 ▸ T12 ▸ after_ffn

| Pos | Token | Score |
|---|---|---|
| 0 | 36 | 3.745 |
| 1 (↑10) | 44 | 3.712 |
| 2 | 37 | 3.669 |
| 3 (↑1) | 33 | 3.635 |
| 4 (↓3) | 35 | 3.625 |
| 5 (↑15) | 43 | 3.612 |
| 6 (↓3) | 39 | 3.602 |
| 7 (↓1) | 34 | 3.589 |
| 8 (↑1) | 63 | 3.587 |
| 9 (↑17) | 54 | 3.555 |

**Promoted Tokens**

L10 ▸ ffn

| Pos | Token | Score |
|---|---|---|
| 0 | 44 | 1.650 |
| 1 | 53 | 1.643 |
| 2 | 43 | 1.617 |
| 3 | 54 | 1.582 |
| 4 | 48 | 1.555 |
| 50267 | ·println | -0.740 |
| 50268 | ortunately | -0.752 |
| 50269 | 覚醒 | -0.752 |
| 50270 | acebook | -0.822 |
| 50271 | ��極 | -0.826 |

Figure 2: The tool shows how the MLP block on Layer 10 promotes tokens greater than 32, causing the prediction of the end of the war year to be later than the beginning in 1732. Model: OPT-125m (Zhang et al., 2022b).

this important subgraph in a top-down manner by tracing information back through the network and, at each step, leaving only edges that were important (Figure 1). To understand which edges are important, they rely on an attribution method (Ferrando et al., 2022). Ferrando and Voita (2024) explain the benefits of this method including, among other things, why it is more versatile, informative and around 100 times more efficient compared to commonly used patching-based approaches typical for the existing mechanistic interpretability workflows (Wang et al., 2023; Hanna et al., 2023; Conmy et al., 2023; Stolfo et al., 2023; Heimersheim and Janiak, 2023).

**In the tool.** In the tool, we show only the important attention edges and feed-forward blocks (purple squares in Figure 1). Clicking at the top triangles gives the important information flow routes for each token position. Under the "Graph" menu, one can vary the importance threshold to get more or less dense graphs.

### 2.2 Fine-Grained Importances

While the information flow graph already relies on the importances of attention or feed-forward blocks for the current residual stream, the tool goes further and shows the importances of (i) individual attention heads, and (ii) individual FFN neurons.

#### 2.2.1 Individual Attention Heads

**Importance.** After clicking on an attention edge (green lines in Figure 1), the tool shows which specific attention head is mostly responsible for this connection, as well as highlights the importances of other heads for this specific step.

**Weights and contributions.** Whenever a head is selected, the tool shows

- attention map,
- contribution map.

While the attention map can give an idea of the attention head's function (Voita et al., 2019; Clark et al., 2019; Correia et al., 2019), attention weights might not reflect influences properly (Bastings and Filippova (2020); Kobayashi et al. (2020), among others). Therefore, we also show *contribution map* reflecting the influence of a head-token pair in the overall attention block (Ferrando and Voita, 2024). Note that while attention weights always sum to 1, contributions sum to the overall importance of this attention head at each step. As a result, contribution maps can be more sparse, as shown in Figure 1.

#### 2.2.2 Individual FFN Neurons

When clicking on feed-forward blocks (purple squares), the tool shows the top neurons that contributed at this step. Note that this is different from previous work that either considered top activated neurons (Geva et al. (2022a); Alammar (2021), among others) or did not consider neurons at all (Tenney et al. (2020); Sarti et al. (2023), among others). In contrast, our tool shows top *contributing* neurons and makes it possible to look at the functions of neurons only when they are important, i.e. when they perform their function.

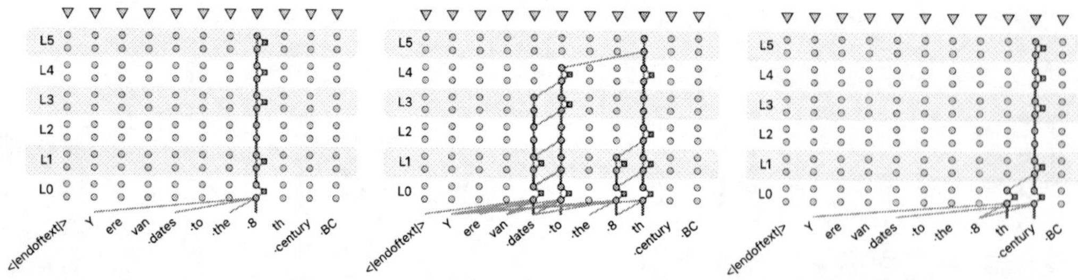

Figure 3: The tool efficiently precomputes the information flow routes across all predictions with a single pass. Clicking on triangle buttons switches between token predictions on different positions. One can see that information flow routes are rather wide for some predictions and narrow for the others. Model: DistilGPT2 (Sanh et al., 2019).

### 2.3 Vocabulary Projections

One of the popular ways to interpret vector representations is to project them onto the model's vocabulary space. Our tool does this for (i) representations in the residual stream and (ii) the updates coming from specific model components.

#### 2.3.1 Interpreting Representations

While to get a prediction, we project the final-layer representation onto the output vocabulary, for interpretation, we can project representations at any point inside the residual stream – this is called *logit lens* (nostalgebraist, 2020). The resulting sequence of distributions (or top-token predictions) illustrates the decision-making process over the course of the Transformer inference. This is used rather prominently to trace the bottom-up changes in the residual stream (Alammar (2021); Geva et al. (2021, 2022b); Merullo et al. (2023); Belrose et al. (2023); Din et al. (2023), among others).

**Tool: click on the circles.** In our tool, circles correspond to residual stream representations after applying each model block, either attention or feed-forward; overall, we have two representations per layer. By clicking at each circle, under "Top tokens" the tool shows the projection of this residual state onto output vocabulary.[3]

#### 2.3.2 Interpreting Model Components

We can also project onto vocabulary an update coming from a model component: this shows how this component changes the residual stream and, therefore, gives an interpretation of its behavior. In this way, we can get concepts *promoted* by this component by looking at top positive projections (Geva et al. (2022b); Dar et al. (2023), inter alia) or *suppressed concepts* by looking at bottom negative projections (Voita et al., 2024). Figures 2 and 4 show examples of such cases.

**Tool: click on the circles and go further.** When you click on a representation from the residual stream, in addition to this representation's logit lens, the tool will also show top promoted and suppressed concepts for the last applied block (either attention or feed-forward). By clicking further, you can also select an individual attention head or feed-forward neuron and get an interpretation at a finer-grained level.

### 2.4 Additional Controls

For the functionality above, the sidebar to the left has additional controls:

- **Model**:
  - ○ `GPT-2` (Radford et al., 2019),
  - ○ `OPT` (Zhang et al., 2022b),
  - ○ `Llama-2` (Touvron et al., 2023b),
  - ◇ add your own model (Section 3.6);
- **Device**: `GPU` or `CPU`;
- **Data**: adding custom data or choosing an existing example;
- **Graph**: tuning parameters of the information flow graph, e.g. contribution threshold etc. (Ferrando and Voita, 2024).

### 2.5 Intended Use Cases

The tool can help generating or validating hypotheses about model functioning more quickly. The list of potential use cases contains, but is not limited to the following:

[3]Under "Graph", one also specifies whether to apply the final layer normalization before projecting onto vocabulary or not.

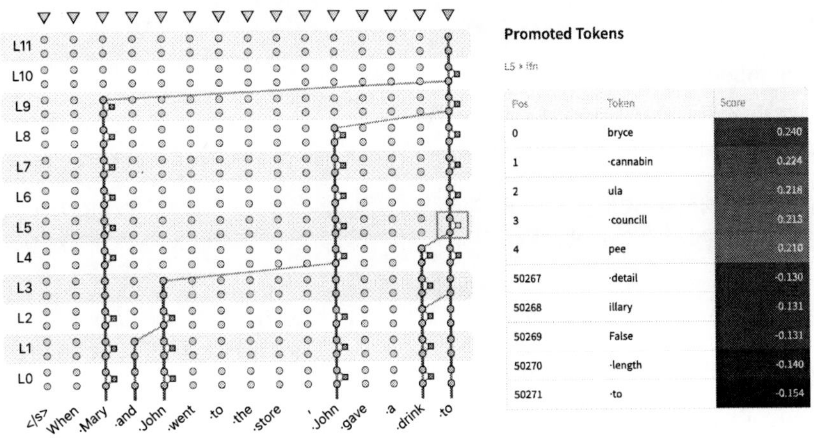


Figure 4: The input token is being suppressed by the neurons in MLP block at Layer 5, similar to the findings reported by Voita et al. (2024). Model: OPT-125m (Zhang et al., 2022b).

- finding model components amplifying biases;
- checking whether the model is reasoning via different routes for desired/undesired behavior (e.g., in safety settings);
- validating whether e.g. mathematical tasks are solved via computation rather than memorization;
- inspecting model behavior for factuality, when hallucinating, etc.

## 3 System Design and Components

Our application is a web-based toolkit, offering easy and interactive access that is cross-platform compatible. This approach allows users to utilize and share the tool remotely, emphasizing convenience and flexibility.

### 3.1 Frontend

The frontend is developed using `Streamlit` (Teixeira et al.), with an additional custom component specifically created for visualization of the Transformer model in the form of a graph. This enhancement was necessary as such complex visualizations are not natively supported by `Streamlit`'s built-in features. The custom component is built using `D3.js` (Bostock et al., 2011) and integrated with `React` for managing dynamic content and user interactions.

### 3.2 Backend

Our backend is a single-dispatch, stateless `Streamlit` program. It includes a caching mechanism to optimize performance for repeated queries. The modeling and tokenization are powered by Hugging Face `transformers` (Wolf et al., 2020) library. For capturing model activations and intermediate computations, we use `TransformerLens` (Nanda and Bloom, 2022)[4] library as it has hooked wrappers defined for a variety of models.

### 3.3 Configuration and Deployment

Configuration is handled via a `JSON` file, allowing for customization of parameters such as dataset file access, maximum user string length, the list of available models, a default model and a dataset. An example configuration is shown in Figure 5.

```
{
  "max_user_string_length": 100,
  "preloaded_dataset_filename": "samples.txt",
  "debug": false,
  "models": {
    "facebook/opt-6.7b": "facebook/opt-6.7b",
    "my_gpt": "./local/path/to/my_gpt"
  }
}
```

Figure 5: An example configuration.

In this configuration, model names can be either Hugging Face model identifiers or local paths. Other settings, such as threshold adjustments and computation precision, are directly configurable within the application's user interface, enabling quick switching.

Overall, launching the tool is as easy as:

[4]`https://github.com/neelnanda-io/TransformerLens`

```
streamlit run app.py -- path/to/config.json
```

### 3.4 Computations

For a selected sentence and model, the tool makes the forward pass and uses the following tensors:

- intermediate representations: residual stream states before and after each block;
- each block's output: the value added to the residual stream by FFN or attention;
- attention block internal states: attention weights, per-head block output, token-specific terms in each head's output;
- FFN block internal states: neuron activations before and after the activation function.

Using this, the tool computes the importances of all the elements (blocks, heads, neurons) and extracts the information flow graph (Ferrando and Voita, 2024). Vocabulary projections and importances within a layer are done on-the-fly when a user clicks on an element.

**Supported model sizes.** We tested the tool with models up to `30b` of parameters. Since for simplicity and ease of debugging we focus on single-node setup, larger models requiring distributed mode might not work in the current version.

**Efficiency.** The tool supports automatic mixed precision (`float16` and `bfloat16`). This helps to store model parameters and tensors efficiently, thus saving memory in order to accommodate larger models without sacrificing performance. Models are loaded on demand and cached for efficiency.

### 3.5 Outside of the UI

Outside of the UI, one can access the underlying functionality of the tool programmatically with Python function calls. For example, getting information flow routes requires the following call:

```
import llm_transparency_tool as lmtt
from lmtt.models.tlens_model import (
    TransformerLensTransparentLlm,
)

model = TransformerLensTransparentLlm(name)

model.run([sentence])

graph = lmtt.routes.graph.build_full_graph(
    model,
    threshold=threshold,
)
```

### 3.6 Adding Your Own Models

By default, upon installation, the tool supports only the models listed in Section 2.4. Steps needed for adding a new model depend on whether the model is supported by `TransformerLens`.

**Supported by TransformerLens.** Adding a model supported by `TransformerLens` model is very simple.

- **Hugging Face weights:** Add model name (as stated in Hugging Face `transformers`) to the app's configuration `JSON` file.
- **Custom weights:** In the `JSON` configuration file, along with the name of the model, provide the path to the model file.

**Not supported by TransformerLens.** In this case, you need to let the tool know how to create proper hooks for the model. Our tool is using `TransformerLens` through an intermediate interface (`TransparentLlm` class) and you have to implement this interface for your model.

## 4 Related Work

Existing tools for analyzing sequence models' predictions include `LM-Debugger` (Geva et al., 2022a), `VISIT` (Katz and Belinkov, 2023), `Ecco` (Alammar, 2021), `LIT` (Tenney et al., 2020), `Inseq` (Sarti et al., 2023), and `Captum` (Kokhlikyan et al., 2020; Miglani et al., 2023). These tools enable users to compute input tokens attribution scores, read token promotions performed by different model components via logit lens, or analyze textual patterns responsible for the activation of the model's neurons. However, these are not able to extract a relevant part of model computations and indicate component importances. To identify parts of the model relevant for some task, a recent trend in mechanistic interpretability is to rely on causal interventions on the computational graph of the model, aka "activation patching" (Vig et al., 2020; Geiger et al., 2020, 2021; Wang et al., 2023; Hanna et al., 2023; Conmy et al., 2023; Stolfo et al., 2023; Heimersheim and Janiak, 2023). Usually, this process involves the following steps: 1) selecting a dataset and metric, 2) manually creating contrastive examples, 3) searching for important edges in the graph via activation patching. The latter requires running a forward pass per each patched element and uses many patches to explain a single prediction. Although recent approaches aim to automate some parts of this workflow (Conmy et al., 2023), the entire process requires a large human effort and involves significant computational costs: this imposes constraints on the tool development and limits its applicability. Differently, LM-TT relies on a recent method by Ferrando and Voita (2024) which refuses from the patching constraints by relying on attribution to define the importances. Furthermore, LM-TT incorporates additional functionalities such as showing fine-grained component importances, logit lens analysis at different levels of granularity, and attention visualization not only via attention weights but also via contributions. This enables users to gain a more comprehensive understanding of the functions executed by each component.

## 5 Conclusions

We release the LM Transparency Tool, an open-source toolkit for analyzing Transformer-based language models that allows tracing back model behavior to specific parts of the model. Specifically, it (i) shows the important part of the whole input-to-output information flow, (ii) allows attributing any changes done by a model block to individual attention heads and feed-forward neurons, (iii) allows interpreting the functions of those heads or neurons. Notably, due to the nature of the underlying method, our tool reduces the number of components to be analyzed by highlighting model components that were relevant to the prediction. This greatly simplifies the study of large language models, with potentially thousands of attention heads and hundreds of thousands of neurons to look at. Moreover, the UI accelerates the inspection process, unlike other frameworks that lack this feature. This assists researchers and practitioners in efficiently generating hypotheses regarding the behavior of the model.

## 6 Acknowledgments

We would like to thank Christoforos Nalmpantis, Nicola Cancedda, Yihong Chen, Andrey Gromov and Mostafa Elhoushi for the insightful discussions.

## References

J Alammar. 2021. Ecco: An open source library for the explainability of transformer language models. In *Proceedings of the 59th Annual Meeting of the Association for Computational Linguistics and the 11th International Joint Conference on Natural Language Processing: System Demonstrations*, pages 249–257, Online. Association for Computational Linguistics.

Rohan Anil, Andrew M. Dai, Orhan Firat, Melvin Johnson, Dmitry Lepikhin, Alexandre Passos, Siamak Shakeri, Emanuel Taropa, Paige Bailey, Zhifeng Chen, Eric Chu, Jonathan H. Clark, Laurent El Shafey, Yanping Huang, Kathy Meier-Hellstern, Gaurav Mishra, Erica Moreira, Mark Omernick, Kevin Robinson, Sebastian Ruder, Yi Tay, Kefan Xiao, Yuanzhong Xu, Yujing Zhang, Gustavo Hernandez Abrego, Junwhan Ahn, Jacob Austin, Paul Barham, Jan Botha, James Bradbury, Siddhartha Brahma, Kevin Brooks, Michele Catasta, Yong Cheng, Colin Cherry, Christopher A. Choquette-Choo, Aakanksha Chowdhery, Clément Crepy, Shachi Dave, Mostafa Dehghani, Sunipa Dev, Jacob Devlin, Mark Díaz, Nan Du, Ethan Dyer, Vlad Feinberg, Fangxiaoyu Feng, Vlad Fienber, Markus Freitag, Xavier Garcia, Sebastian Gehrmann, Lucas Gonzalez, Guy Gur-Ari, Steven Hand, Hadi Hashemi, Le Hou, Joshua Howland, Andrea Hu, Jeffrey Hui, Jeremy Hurwitz, Michael Isard, Abe Ittycheriah, Matthew Jagielski, Wenhao Jia, Kathleen Kenealy, Maxim Krikun, Sneha Kudugunta, Chang Lan, Katherine Lee, Benjamin Lee, Eric Li, Music Li, Wei Li, YaGuang Li, Jian Li, Hyeontaek Lim, Hanzhao Lin, Zhongtao Liu, Frederick Liu, Marcello Maggioni, Aroma Mahendru, Joshua Maynez, Vedant Misra, Maysam Moussalem, Zachary Nado, John Nham, Eric Ni, Andrew Nystrom, Alicia Parrish, Marie Pellat, Martin Polacek, Alex Polozov, Reiner Pope, Siyuan Qiao, Emily Reif, Bryan Richter, Parker Riley, Alex Castro Ros, Aurko Roy, Brennan Saeta, Rajkumar Samuel, Renee Shelby, Ambrose Slone, Daniel Smilkov, David R. So, Daniel Sohn, Simon Tokumine, Dasha Valter, Vijay Vasudevan, Kiran Vodrahalli, Xuezhi Wang, Pidong Wang, Zirui Wang, Tao Wang, John Wieting, Yuhuai Wu, Kelvin Xu, Yunhan Xu, Linting Xue, Pengcheng Yin, Jiahui Yu, Qiao Zhang, Steven Zheng, Ce Zheng, Weikang Zhou, Denny Zhou, Slav Petrov, and Yonghui Wu. 2023. Palm 2 technical report.

Jasmijn Bastings and Katja Filippova. 2020. The elephant in the interpretability room: Why use attention as explanation when we have saliency methods? In *Proceedings of the Third BlackboxNLP Workshop on Analyzing and Interpreting Neural Networks for NLP*, pages 149–155, Online. Association for Computational Linguistics.

Nora Belrose, Zach Furman, Logan Smith, Danny Halawi, Igor Ostrovsky, Lev McKinney, Stella Biderman, and Jacob Steinhardt. 2023. Eliciting latent predictions from transformers with the tuned lens.

Michael Bostock, Vadim Ogievetsky, and Jeffrey Heer. 2011. D3: Data-driven documents. *IEEE Trans. Visualization & Comp. Graphics (Proc. InfoVis)*.

Tom Brown, Benjamin Mann, Nick Ryder, Melanie Subbiah, Jared D Kaplan, Prafulla Dhariwal, Arvind Neelakantan, Pranav Shyam, Girish Sastry, Amanda Askell, Sandhini Agarwal, Ariel Herbert-Voss,

Gretchen Krueger, Tom Henighan, Rewon Child, Aditya Ramesh, Daniel Ziegler, Jeffrey Wu, Clemens Winter, Chris Hesse, Mark Chen, Eric Sigler, Mateusz Litwin, Scott Gray, Benjamin Chess, Jack Clark, Christopher Berner, Sam McCandlish, Alec Radford, Ilya Sutskever, and Dario Amodei. 2020. Language models are few-shot learners. In *Advances in Neural Information Processing Systems*, volume 33, pages 1877–1901. Curran Associates, Inc.

Kevin Clark, Urvashi Khandelwal, Omer Levy, and Christopher D. Manning. 2019. What does BERT look at? an analysis of BERT's attention. In *Proceedings of the 2019 ACL Workshop BlackboxNLP: Analyzing and Interpreting Neural Networks for NLP*, pages 276–286, Florence, Italy. Association for Computational Linguistics.

Arthur Conmy, Augustine N. Mavor-Parker, Aengus Lynch, Stefan Heimersheim, and Adrià Garriga-Alonso. 2023. Towards automated circuit discovery for mechanistic interpretability. In *Thirty-seventh Conference on Neural Information Processing Systems*.

Gonçalo M. Correia, Vlad Niculae, and André F. T. Martins. 2019. Adaptively sparse transformers. In *Proceedings of the 2019 Conference on Empirical Methods in Natural Language Processing and the 9th International Joint Conference on Natural Language Processing (EMNLP-IJCNLP)*, pages 2174–2184, Hong Kong, China. Association for Computational Linguistics.

Damai Dai, Li Dong, Yaru Hao, Zhifang Sui, Baobao Chang, and Furu Wei. 2022. Knowledge neurons in pretrained transformers. In *Proceedings of the 60th Annual Meeting of the Association for Computational Linguistics (Volume 1: Long Papers)*, pages 8493–8502, Dublin, Ireland. Association for Computational Linguistics.

Guy Dar, Mor Geva, Ankit Gupta, and Jonathan Berant. 2023. Analyzing transformers in embedding space. In *Proceedings of the 61st Annual Meeting of the Association for Computational Linguistics (Volume 1: Long Papers)*, pages 16124–16170, Toronto, Canada. Association for Computational Linguistics.

Alexander Yom Din, Taelin Karidi, Leshem Choshen, and Mor Geva. 2023. Jump to conclusions: Short-cutting transformers with linear transformations.

Nelson Elhage, Neel Nanda, Catherine Olsson, Tom Henighan, Nicholas Joseph, Ben Mann, Amanda Askell, Yuntao Bai, Anna Chen, Tom Conerly, Nova DasSarma, Dawn Drain, Deep Ganguli, Zac Hatfield-Dodds, Danny Hernandez, Andy Jones, Jackson Kernion, Liane Lovitt, Kamal Ndousse, Dario Amodei, Tom Brown, Jack Clark, Jared Kaplan, Sam McCandlish, and Chris Olah. 2021. A mathematical framework for transformer circuits. *Transformer Circuits Thread*.

Javier Ferrando, Gerard I. Gállego, and Marta R. Costa-jussà. 2022. Measuring the mixing of contextual information in the transformer. In *Proceedings of the 2022 Conference on Empirical Methods in Natural Language Processing*, pages 8698–8714, Abu Dhabi, United Arab Emirates. Association for Computational Linguistics.

Javier Ferrando and Elena Voita. 2024. Information flow routes: Automatically interpreting language models at scale.

Atticus Geiger, Hanson Lu, Thomas F Icard, and Christopher Potts. 2021. Causal abstractions of neural networks. In *Advances in Neural Information Processing Systems*.

Atticus Geiger, Kyle Richardson, and Christopher Potts. 2020. Neural natural language inference models partially embed theories of lexical entailment and negation. In *Proceedings of the Third BlackboxNLP Workshop on Analyzing and Interpreting Neural Networks for NLP*, pages 163–173, Online. Association for Computational Linguistics.

Mor Geva, Avi Caciularu, Guy Dar, Paul Roit, Shoval Sadde, Micah Shlain, Bar Tamir, and Yoav Goldberg. 2022a. LM-debugger: An interactive tool for inspection and intervention in transformer-based language models. In *Proceedings of the 2022 Conference on Empirical Methods in Natural Language Processing: System Demonstrations*, pages 12–21, Abu Dhabi, UAE. Association for Computational Linguistics.

Mor Geva, Avi Caciularu, Kevin Ro Wang, and Yoav Goldberg. 2022b. Transformer feed-forward layers build predictions by promoting concepts in the vocabulary space.

Mor Geva, Roei Schuster, Jonathan Berant, and Omer Levy. 2021. Transformer feed-forward layers are key-value memories. In *Proceedings of the 2021 Conference on Empirical Methods in Natural Language Processing*, pages 5484–5495, Online and Punta Cana, Dominican Republic. Association for Computational Linguistics.

Michael Hanna, Ollie Liu, and Alexandre Variengien. 2023. How does gpt-2 compute greater-than?: Interpreting mathematical abilities in a pre-trained language model.

Stefan Heimersheim and Jett Janiak. 2023. The singular value decompositions of transformer weight matrices are highly interpretable.

Jared Kaplan, Sam McCandlish, Tom Henighan, Tom B. Brown, Benjamin Chess, Rewon Child, Scott Gray, Alec Radford, Jeffrey Wu, and Dario Amodei. 2020. Scaling laws for neural language models.

Shahar Katz and Yonatan Belinkov. 2023. VISIT: Visualizing and interpreting the semantic information flow of transformers. In *Findings of the Association for Computational Linguistics: EMNLP 2023*, pages 14094–14113, Singapore. Association for Computational Linguistics.

Goro Kobayashi, Tatsuki Kuribayashi, Sho Yokoi, and Kentaro Inui. 2020. Attention is not only a weight: Analyzing transformers with vector norms. In *Proceedings of the 2020 Conference on Empirical Methods in Natural Language Processing (EMNLP)*, pages 7057–7075, Online. Association for Computational Linguistics.

Narine Kokhlikyan, Vivek Miglani, Miguel Martin, Edward Wang, Bilal Alsallakh, Jonathan Reynolds, Alexander Melnikov, Natalia Kliushkina, Carlos Araya, Siqi Yan, and Orion Reblitz-Richardson. 2020. Captum: A unified and generic model interpretability library for pytorch.

Jack Merullo, Carsten Eickhoff, and Ellie Pavlick. 2023. A mechanism for solving relational tasks in transformer language models.

Vivek Miglani, Aobo Yang, Aram Markosyan, Diego Garcia-Olano, and Narine Kokhlikyan. 2023. Using captum to explain generative language models. In *Proceedings of the 3rd Workshop for Natural Language Processing Open Source Software (NLP-OSS 2023)*, pages 165–173, Singapore, Singapore. Empirical Methods in Natural Language Processing.

Neel Nanda and Joseph Bloom. 2022. Transformerlens. `https://github.com/neelnanda-io/TransformerLens`.

nostalgebraist. 2020. Interpreting gpt: The logit lens.

Catherine Olsson, Nelson Elhage, Neel Nanda, Nicholas Joseph, Nova DasSarma, Tom Henighan, Ben Mann, Amanda Askell, Yuntao Bai, Anna Chen, Tom Conerly, Dawn Drain, Deep Ganguli, Zac Hatfield-Dodds, Danny Hernandez, Scott Johnston, Andy Jones, Jackson Kernion, Liane Lovitt, Kamal Ndousse, Dario Amodei, Tom Brown, Jack Clark, Jared Kaplan, Sam McCandlish, and Chris Olah. 2022. In-context learning and induction heads. *Transformer Circuits Thread*.

OpenAI. 2023. Gpt-4 technical report.

Long Ouyang, Jeff Wu, Xu Jiang, Diogo Almeida, Carroll L. Wainwright, Pamela Mishkin, Chong Zhang, Sandhini Agarwal, Katarina Slama, Alex Ray, John Schulman, Jacob Hilton, Fraser Kelton, Luke Miller, Maddie Simens, Amanda Askell, Peter Welinder, Paul Christiano, Jan Leike, and Ryan Lowe. 2022. Training language models to follow instructions with human feedback.

Alec Radford, Jeff Wu, Rewon Child, D. Luan, Dario Amodei, and Ilya Sutskever. 2019. Language Models are Unsupervised Multitask Learners.

Victor Sanh, Lysandre Debut, Julien Chaumond, and Thomas Wolf. 2019. Distilbert, a distilled version of bert: smaller, faster, cheaper and lighter. *ArXiv*, abs/1910.01108.

Gabriele Sarti, Nils Feldhus, Ludwig Sickert, and Oskar van der Wal. 2023. Inseq: An interpretability toolkit for sequence generation models. In *Proceedings of the 61st Annual Meeting of the Association for Computational Linguistics (Volume 3: System Demonstrations)*, pages 421–435, Toronto, Canada. Association for Computational Linguistics.

Alessandro Stolfo, Yonatan Belinkov, and Mrinmaya Sachan. 2023. Understanding arithmetic reasoning in language models using causal mediation analysis.

Thiago Teixeira, Amanda Kelly, Adrien Treuille, and Streamlit Team. Streamlit: A faster way to build and share data apps. `https://streamlit.io/`.

Ian Tenney, James Wexler, Jasmijn Bastings, Tolga Bolukbasi, Andy Coenen, Sebastian Gehrmann, Ellen Jiang, Mahima Pushkarna, Carey Radebaugh, Emily Reif, and Ann Yuan. 2020. The language interpretability tool: Extensible, interactive visualizations and analysis for NLP models. In *Proceedings of the 2020 Conference on Empirical Methods in Natural Language Processing: System Demonstrations*, pages 107–118, Online. Association for Computational Linguistics.

Hugo Touvron, Thibaut Lavril, Gautier Izacard, Xavier Martinet, Marie-Anne Lachaux, Timothée Lacroix, Baptiste Rozière, Naman Goyal, Eric Hambro, Faisal Azhar, Aurelien Rodriguez, Armand Joulin, Edouard Grave, and Guillaume Lample. 2023a. Llama: Open and efficient foundation language models.

Hugo Touvron, Louis Martin, Kevin Stone, Peter Albert, Amjad Almahairi, Yasmine Babaei, Nikolay Bashlykov, Soumya Batra, Prajjwal Bhargava, Shruti Bhosale, Dan Bikel, Lukas Blecher, Cristian Canton Ferrer, Moya Chen, Guillem Cucurull, David Esiobu, Jude Fernandes, Jeremy Fu, Wenyin Fu, Brian Fuller, Cynthia Gao, Vedanuj Goswami, Naman Goyal, Anthony Hartshorn, Saghar Hosseini, Rui Hou, Hakan Inan, Marcin Kardas, Viktor Kerkez, Madian Khabsa, Isabel Kloumann, Artem Korenev, Punit Singh Koura, Marie-Anne Lachaux, Thibaut Lavril, Jenya Lee, Diana Liskovich, Yinghai Lu, Yuning Mao, Xavier Martinet, Todor Mihaylov, Pushkar Mishra, Igor Molybog, Yixin Nie, Andrew Poulton, Jeremy Reizenstein, Rashi Rungta, Kalyan Saladi, Alan Schelten, Ruan Silva, Eric Michael Smith, Ranjan Subramanian, Xiaoqing Ellen Tan, Binh Tang, Ross Taylor, Adina Williams, Jian Xiang Kuan, Puxin Xu, Zheng Yan, Iliyan Zarov, Yuchen Zhang, Angela Fan, Melanie Kambadur, Sharan Narang, Aurelien Rodriguez, Robert Stojnic, Sergey Edunov, and Thomas Scialom. 2023b. Llama 2: Open foundation and fine-tuned chat models.

Jesse Vig, Sebastian Gehrmann, Yonatan Belinkov, Sharon Qian, Daniel Nevo, Yaron Singer, and Stuart Shieber. 2020. Investigating gender bias in language models using causal mediation analysis. In *Advances in Neural Information Processing Systems*, volume 33, pages 12388–12401. Curran Associates, Inc.

Elena Voita, Javier Ferrando, and Christoforos Nalmpantis. 2024. Neurons in large language models: Dead, n-gram, positional. In *Findings of the Association for Computational Linguistics: ACL 2024*, Bangkok, Thailand. Association for Computational Linguistics.

Elena Voita, David Talbot, Fedor Moiseev, Rico Sennrich, and Ivan Titov. 2019. Analyzing multi-head self-attention: Specialized heads do the heavy lifting, the rest can be pruned. In *Proceedings of the 57th Annual Meeting of the Association for Computational Linguistics*, pages 5797–5808, Florence, Italy. Association for Computational Linguistics.

Kevin Ro Wang, Alexandre Variengien, Arthur Conmy, Buck Shlegeris, and Jacob Steinhardt. 2023. Interpretability in the wild: a circuit for indirect object identification in GPT-2 small. In *The Eleventh International Conference on Learning Representations*.

Jason Wei, Yi Tay, Rishi Bommasani, Colin Raffel, Barret Zoph, Sebastian Borgeaud, Dani Yogatama, Maarten Bosma, Denny Zhou, Donald Metzler, Ed H. Chi, Tatsunori Hashimoto, Oriol Vinyals, Percy Liang, Jeff Dean, and William Fedus. 2022. Emergent abilities of large language models. *Transactions on Machine Learning Research*. Survey Certification.

Thomas Wolf, Lysandre Debut, Victor Sanh, Julien Chaumond, Clement Delangue, Anthony Moi, Pierric Cistac, Tim Rault, Rémi Louf, Morgan Funtowicz, Joe Davison, Sam Shleifer, Patrick von Platen, Clara Ma, Yacine Jernite, Julien Plu, Canwen Xu, Teven Le Scao, Sylvain Gugger, Mariama Drame, Quentin Lhoest, and Alexander M. Rush. 2020. Transformers: State-of-the-art natural language processing. In *Proceedings of the 2020 Conference on Empirical Methods in Natural Language Processing: System Demonstrations*, pages 38–45, Online. Association for Computational Linguistics.

Susan Zhang, Stephen Roller, Naman Goyal, Mikel Artetxe, Moya Chen, Shuohui Chen, Christopher Dewan, Mona Diab, Xian Li, Xi Victoria Lin, Todor Mihaylov, Myle Ott, Sam Shleifer, Kurt Shuster, Daniel Simig, Punit Singh Koura, Anjali Sridhar, Tianlu Wang, and Luke Zettlemoyer. 2022a. Opt: Open pre-trained transformer language models.

Susan Zhang, Stephen Roller, Naman Goyal, Mikel Artetxe, Moya Chen, Shuohui Chen, Christopher Dewan, Mona Diab, Xian Li, Xi Victoria Lin, Todor Mihaylov, Myle Ott, Sam Shleifer, Kurt Shuster, Daniel Simig, Punit Singh Koura, Anjali Sridhar, Tianlu Wang, and Luke Zettlemoyer. 2022b. Opt: Open pre-trained transformer language models.

# EmpathyEar: An Open-source Avatar Multimodal Empathetic Chatbot

**Hao Fei**[1], **Han Zhang**[2], **Bin Wang**[3], **Lizi Liao**[4], **Qian Liu**[5], **Erik Cambria**[6]

[1] National University of Singapore [2] Xidian University

[3] Harbin Institute of Technology (Shenzhen) [4] Singapore Management University

[5] University of Auckland [6] Nanyang Technological University

haofei37@nus.edu.sg, zhanghanxd@stu.xidian.edu.cn, 23s051047@stu.hit.edu.cn

lzliao@smu.edu.sg, liu.qian@auckland.ac.nz, cambria@ntu.edu.sg

## Abstract

This paper introduces **EmpathyEar**, a pioneering open-source, avatar-based multimodal empathetic chatbot, to fill the gap in traditional text-only empathetic response generation (ERG) systems. Leveraging the advancements of a large language model, combined with multimodal encoders and generators, EmpathyEar supports user inputs in any combination of text, sound, and vision, and produces multimodal empathetic responses, offering users, not just textual responses but also digital avatars with talking faces and synchronized speeches. A series of emotion-aware instruction-tuning is performed for comprehensive emotional understanding and generation capabilities. In this way, EmpathyEar provides users with responses that achieve a deeper emotional resonance, closely emulating human-like empathy. The system paves the way for the next emotional intelligence, for which we open-source the code for public access.[1]

## 1 Introduction

The artificial intelligence (AI) community has witnessed significant progress in recent one year due to the explosive development of Large Language Models (LLMs; OpenAI, 2022b; Chung et al., 2022), leading to unprecedented levels of intelligence in current AI systems. It is also a long-standing consensus that achieving human-level AI necessitates not only intelligence but also the capability to emulate human emotions, such as understanding feelings and perspectives and exhibiting empathy. The task of ERG (Rashkin et al., 2019) has then been developed with the aim of enabling machines to generate replies to user queries that are not only problem-solving but also emotionally inclined and empathetic, thereby facilitating emotion-aware open-domain dialogues. ERG serves as an effective testbed of machines' emotional intelligence, supporting emotional interactions with humans, and has been applied in various practical scenarios, e.g., mental health therapy and companion dialogue systems.

However, current ERG systems are significantly limited by their reliance on a single text modality in task definitions. Emotional nuances are often more fully expressed and understood through non-text modalities in many scenarios, suggesting a gap in the current research. It's intuitive that, in many cases, human emotions are more effectively conveyed and perceived through vocal cues (such as the tone and pitch of speech), and/or dynamic visual changes in expressions (such as facial micro-expressions and gestures), rather than through text alone. In contrast, relying solely on text responses from machines could never achieve the full spectrum of emotional resonance and empathy that human interactions offer. Similarly, users may prefer to express their emotions through speech or facial videos, rather than being confined to text queries. Regrettably, to date not much research has been carried out on the generation of multimodal empathetic responses from multimodal inputs.

To fill this gap, this work is dedicated to developing a novel multimodal empathetic chatbot, named **EmpathyEar**. EmpathyEar is capable of receiving multimodal signals from users, and producing multimodal empathetic responses, offering users not just textual responses but also digital avatars with talking faces and synchronized voices. Through these three modalities—*text*, *sound*, and *vision*—EmpathyEar is able to offer users responses that comprehensively achieve a deeper emotional resonance. As shown in Figure 1, EmpathyEar is built on an LLM at its core module for understanding content semantics and emotions. On the backend, a speech generator and a talking-head avatar generator are connected to enable multimodal generation. Multimodal encoders

[1] Code is open at https://github.com/scofield7419/EmpathyEar. Also video demonstrations at https://youtu.be/gGn9oYftwbY.



*Proceedings of the 62nd Annual Meeting of the Association for Computational Linguistics (Volume 3: System Demonstrations)*, pages 61–71
August 11-16, 2024 ©2024 Association for Computational Linguistics

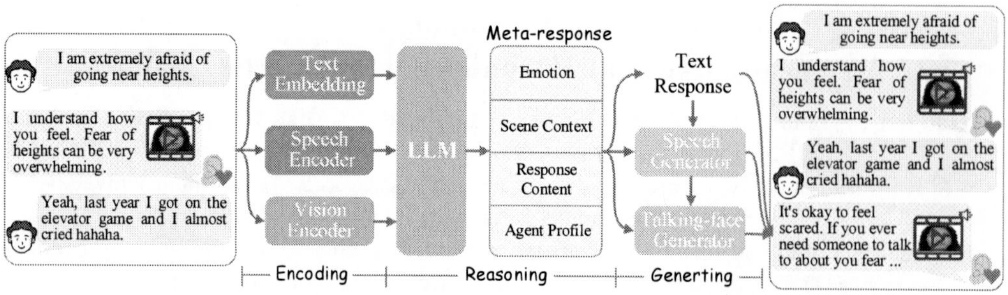


Figure 1: The architecture of EmpathyEar, supporting avatar-based multimodal empathetic response generation.

are integrated into the LLM's frontend to interpret different input modalities.

The LLM employs chained reasoning to sequentially infer and output a meta-response, encompassing emotion, scene context, response content, and agent profile. This holistic understanding and planning ensure the consistency of the text, sound, and visual outputs in terms of content and emotion, enhancing predictability and interoperability. Further, the overall system is trained through a series of emotion-aware instruction-tuning to ensure comprehensive emotional understanding and generation capabilities.

Overall, this work pioneers a dialogue system that supports avatar-based multimodal empathetic response generation, marking an advancement toward emotional intelligence:

1) EmpathyEar excels in accurately understanding user queries and generating high-quality responses across text, speech, and visual modalities with semantic and emotional coherence.
2) EmpathyEar precisely perceives emotional semantics, supporting 32 types of emotions for both explicit and implicit types.
3) EmpathyEar covers over 200 realistic scenarios, flexibly creating diverse digital avatar profiles.
4) While generating multimodal responses, EmpathyEar also provides detailed rationales for decision-making, significantly enhancing interpretability.

## 2 Related Work

In efforts to construct empathetic dialogue systems, prior research (Lin et al., 2019; Li et al., 2020; Gao et al., 2021; Yang et al., 2024a) has relied on detecting emotional signals within the given context, followed by generating responses that maintain emotional congruence. Furthermore, some studies (Sabour et al., 2022; Chen et al., 2024) have incorporated external commonsense knowledge to achieve a deeper understanding of emotions and to facilitate empathetic responses.

Recently, there has been an explosion in LLMs (OpenAI, 2022b,a; Chung et al., 2022), demonstrating robust capabilities for content comprehension and reasoning. These advancements have facilitated superior ERG performance (Sun et al., 2023; Yang et al., 2024b). However, as mentioned earlier, current research in ERG lacks a multimodal perspective, limiting its practical application value.

This work also pertains to multimodal LLMs (MLLM), wherein backbone LLMs serve as the pivotal centers for semantic and emotional reasoning and decision-making (Fei et al., 2024a; Wu et al., 2024). The community has seen the emergence of various MLLMs, such as LLaVA (Liu et al., 2023), Blip2 (Li et al., 2023), and MiniGPT-4 (Zhu et al., 2023), etc. Yet, most MLLMs are confined to understanding input multimodal information while falling short in flexibly outputting content across various modalities, including audio and visual content beyond text, e.g., image and video (Fei et al., 2024b).

As far as we are aware, NExT-GPT (Wu et al., 2023) has accomplished any-to-any modality understanding and generation across four common modalities. However, NExT-GPT is primarily constrained to general scene and signal comprehension, with notable limitations in emotion detection and the generation of emotional content, due to two principal factors: Firstly, the NExT-GPT architecture, lacking a talking head generator and a speech generator, cannot produce a talking face avatar or fluent speech. This prevents NExT-GPT from achieving multimodal ERG, which is the key objective of our work. More importantly, NExT-GPT has not undergone specialized emotion-aware fine-tuning, thus its ability to capture contextual emotions—particularly those that are im-

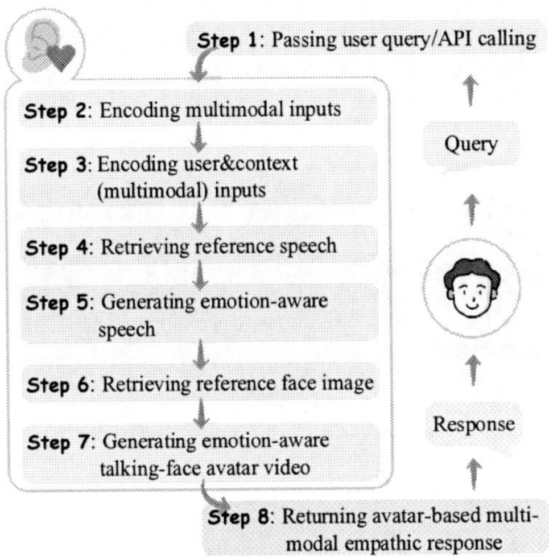


Figure 2: Workflow of the EmpathyEar system.

plicit—is compromised. To overcome these limitations, our system has contemplated a series of emotion-reinforced learning techniques, for enabling stronger emotion perceiving.

## 3 System Workflow

Here we elaborate on the system's workflow from a high-level perspective. We conceptualize the system and the user as two entities, where EmpathyEar processes the user's query and returns a response, while the user, in turn, provides a new query. From receiving a user's input request to generating a complete multimodal empathetic response, EmpathyEar takes multiple sequential steps. Figure 2 depicts the system's workflow.

- ► **Step-1.** *Passing user query/API calling.* Our system will accept user input through a website interface or via predefined APIs. It supports text inputs, voice (speech) inputs, or video input where the user is talking.
- ► **Step-2.** *Encoding user&context (multimodal) inputs.* The content input by the user, along with the historical dialogue context, is encoded. If the user's input is solely text, it is directly fed into the LLM; if it includes multimodal information, it is first passed through a multimodal encoder before being input into the LLM.
- ► **Step-3.** *Generating meta-response with LLM.* The LLM fully comprehends the input content, making corresponding decisions: outputting a meta-response that encompasses the understanding of emotion, scene understanding, the text response to be returned to the user, and the positioning of the agent profile. This component will be elaborated in Section 4.2.
- ► **Step-4.** *Retrieving reference speech.* Based on the emotion label and the specified gender & voice timbre given in the meta-response, a reference speech is retrieved from the database.
- ► **Step-5.** *Generating emotion-aware speech.* The text response and the reference speech are input into a speech generator, producing the target emotion-aware speech of the response.
- ► **Step-6.** *Retrieving reference face image.* A reference face image is retrieved from the database by searching using the profile age and gender information determined in the meta-response.
- ► **Step-7.** *Generating emotion-aware talking-face avatar video.* The produced emotion-aware speech of the response and the reference face image is input into a talking-face generator, yielding the target emotion-aware talking-face avatar video.
- ► **Step-8.** *Returning avatar-based multimodal empathic response.* The system summarizes the obtained text response, speech, and talking-face avatar video as the overall output content of this turn, returning it to the user.

## 4 Implementation Specification

This section gives the specific implementation of EmpathyEar, including the architecture, multimodal content generation, and learning methods.

### 4.1 EmpathyEar Architecture

EmpathyEar is a multimodal LLM. As depicted in Figure 1, the entire system can be divided into three blocks: encoding, reasoning, and generating.

**Multimodal Encoding Module.** Our model is designed to not only handle text inputs from users but also support inputs in the form of speech and user-talking videos, covering three modalities. Text inputs are directly embedded and then fed into the LLM. Audio and visual inputs, on the other hand, are encoded using separate encoders. We consider a unified approach by employing the ImageBind (Girdhar et al., 2023) to simultaneously encode these multimodal features. ImageBind, having undergone extensive cross-modal feature alignment, can efficiently align features across various modalities. A linear projection layer then transfers multimodal information into the LLM.

**Core LLM Reasoning Module.** Among various open-source LLMs, we have chosen Chat-

| Digital Avatar Character | Taxonomy |
|---|---|
| Emotion Label | Surprised, Excited, Angry, Proud, Sad, Annoyed, Grateful, Lonely, Afraid, Terrified, Guilty, Impressed, Disgusted, Hopeful, Confident, Furious, Anxious, Anticipating, Joyful, Nostalgic, Disappointed, Prepared, Jealous, Content, Devastated, Embarrassed, Caring, Sentimental, Trusting, Ashamed, Apprehensive, Faithful |
| Emotion Type | Explicit, Implicit |
| Gender | Male, Female |
| Age | Children (5-10), Adolescents (10-18), Teenagers (18-25), Young adults (25-40), Middle-aged adults (40-60), Elderly (60-80) |
| Scene | Daily common conversation, Elder people company, Left-behind children company, Healthcare assistance, Bereavement support, Job loss, Academic stress, Financial difficulties, Cultural adjustments, Addiction recovery, Domestic violence support, LGBTQ+ community support, Postpartum depression, Intelligent customer service, Game NPCs, Legal consultation, Post-traumatic syndrome, Peer pressure, Culture shock, Social anxiety, Childhood trauma healing, Work-life balance struggles, Retirement adjustments, Immigration challenges, Support for war veterans, chronic insomnia, Assistance for body image, Crisis intervention, Emotional counseling after divorce, ... |
| Timbre and Tone | Low-pitched, Powerful, Intense, Soft, Delicate, Hoarse, Sharp, Clear, Melodious, Dull, Lyrical, Deep |

Table 1: Overview of the pre-settings of the digital avatar character in our system.

GLM3 (6B; Du et al., 2022)[2] as our backbone, based on ChatGLM's superior text comprehension and conversational abilities compared to others, e.g., Vicuna (Chiang et al., 2023) and LLaMA (Touvron et al., 2023). Upon receiving multimodal inputs, LLM understands the user's semantic intentions and emotional state for generating a meta-response, containing all necessary information for the following content generation.

**Speech & Talking-face Generation Module.** With the meta-response, the system proceeds with the retrieval of reference speech and images. On the one hand, the system directly outputs the empathy-aware text response; further, it employs a speech generator and a talking-face generator to produce content in two different modalities. We utilize StyleTTS2 (Li et al., 2024) as the speech generator, which is the current state-of-the-art (SoTA) diffusion-based, emotion-controllable text-to-speech model. StyleTTS2[3] generates speech based on a given text, an emotion label, and a reference speech (w.r.t., characteristics such as timbre and gender). Further, we integrate EAT (Gan et al., 2023) for talking-face avatar generation, the most advanced SoTA emotion-supported, audio-driven model. EAT[4] produces corresponding videos conditioned on the given speech, emotion label, and a reference image that determines the digital human's facial features.

Table 1 lists the predefined 5 digital avatar characters we have established in our system, specifically including emotion label, gender, age, scene, as well as timbre and tone. We present 32 types of common emotional labels that encompass both explicit and implicit types. We divide human age into six stages based on key milestones in physical appearance changes. Our system supports over 200 real-life scenarios and is capable of generating voices with rich timbre and tone.

### 4.2 CoT-based Meta-response Generation

We design the central LLM to take on the crucial role of decision-making. Based on the architecture described, to construct a high-performance system, several key points should be carefully considered. First, it is essential to fully understand the emotion and scene the user is talking about. Following this foundational emotional and semantic understanding, the correct emotional response can be given. Finally, after obtaining the response text, further planning of the multimodal profile is necessary to ensure consistency in the emotions and character roles portrayed in the generated speech and avatar. This actually involves linearly chained reasoning, from understanding the emotion and scene based on the context to determining the response solution and then planning the multimodal digital human profile. With such observation, we consider a Chain-of-Thought (CoT; Wei et al., 2022) based meta-response generation strategy. Specifically, we guide the LLM to sequentially output the meta-response's four parts, by adding one additional prompt "*Please think step by step*, under 1) *Emotion* $\rightarrow$ 2) *Scene Context* $\rightarrow$ 3) *Response Content* $\rightarrow$ and 4) *Agent Profile*".

[2] https://github.com/THUDM/ChatGLM3

[3] https://github.com/yl4579/StyleTTS2

[4] https://github.com/yuangan/EAT_code

*1) Emotion*

- Emotion Label: *The emotion type mentioned in user query.*
- Emotion Cause: *The cause triggering the emotion.*

*2) Scene Context:*

- Event Scenario: *The key event mentioned.*
- Rationale: *The underlying possible reasons for the occurred event, connected with commonsense.*
- Goal to Response: *The unexpected goal to reach after responding to user.*

*3) Response Content:*

*Empathetic text response that will return to the user.*

*4) Agent Profile:*

- Agent Timbre & Tone: *The speech characteristic of the digital avator.*
- Agent Gender: *The gender of the digital avator.*
- Agent Age: *The age group of the digital avator.*

Here we exemplify the proposed CoT-based meta-response prompting with a full example of the input/output of LLM. The LLM input includes user input, possibly conversation history (if any), task instructions, and four meta-response content descriptions. We encourage LLM to analyze the generation of the meta-responses using a CoT prompting technique, i.e., "*think step by step*". The output of LLM is the meta-response defined in the input.

▶ **Input:**

**<User Query>**
*Today traffic was horrible and was so frustrating!*

**<Conversation History>**
None

**<Instruction>**
Now you are an expert of empathetic listener, and you need to generate an empathetic response for a user based on the context of the conversation provided." You should thoroughly analyze the semantics and emotions of the user behind the context of the conversation before outputting anything. Now take your time and **think step by step**, sequentially producing a meta-response that includes four parts of information: 1) *Emotion* → 2) *Scene Context* → 3) *Response Content* → 4) *Agent Profile*.

**<Emotion>**
- Emotion Label: *The emotion type mentioned in user query.*
- Emotion Cause: *The cause triggering the emotion.*

**<Scene Context>**
- Event Scenario: *The key event mentioned and the scene where the conversation takes place, such as daily conversation, psychological assistance, elder people company, or children company, etc.*
- Rationale: *The underlying possible reasons for the occurred event, connected with commonsense knowledge.*
- Goal to Response: *The unexpected goal to reach after responding to the user.*

**<Response Content>**
*Empathetic text response that will return to the user.*

**<Agent Profile>**
- Agent Timbre & Tone: *The speech characteristic of the digital avatar.*
- Agent Gender: *The gender of the digital avatar.*
- Agent Age: *The age group of the digital avatar.*

▶ **LLM meta-response:**

**<Emotion Label>** Angry

**<Emotion Cause>** Traffic

**<Event Scenario>** Daily Common Conversation

**<Rationale>** Traffic congestion can result in lateness, causing individuals to feel anxious and frustrated

**<Goal to Response>** Alleviating anxiety and agitation.

**<Agent Timbre and Tone>** Intense

**<Agent Gender>** Female

**<Agent Age>** Young adults (25-40)

**<Empathetic Response>** I hate traffic too, it makes me crazy!

### 4.3 Emotion-aware Instruction-Tuning

To equip the model with multimodal understanding capabilities and the ability to faithfully output meta-responses, we fine-tune `EmpathyEar`. Our approach encompasses three levels of learning.

**Encoder-LLM Alignment Learning.** For the system's frontend module ImageBind, we align it with the LLM, enabling the LLM to comprehend multimodal information. The alignment is considered in two aspects. On the one hand, we conduct alignment learning on general domain 'audio-text' (Kim et al., 2019) and 'video-text' (Bain et al., 2021) pairs, feeding audio and video, and then having the LLM output corresponding captions. Also, we perform emotion-aware multimodal alignment to enhance the ImageBind&LLM's perception of emotion features in speech and video. Specifically, we engage in speech-based (Sailunaz et al., 2018) and vision-based (Jaiswal et al., 2020) emotion detection tasks on relevant datasets, e.g., EGG (Soleymani et al., 2015). Also for language, we fine-tune LLM on text-based ERG dataset (Rashkin et al., 2018) to fit the in-domain training set, enabling reasonable ERG generation capabilities.

**Meta-response Instruction-Tuning.** Following the construction of many existing instruction-

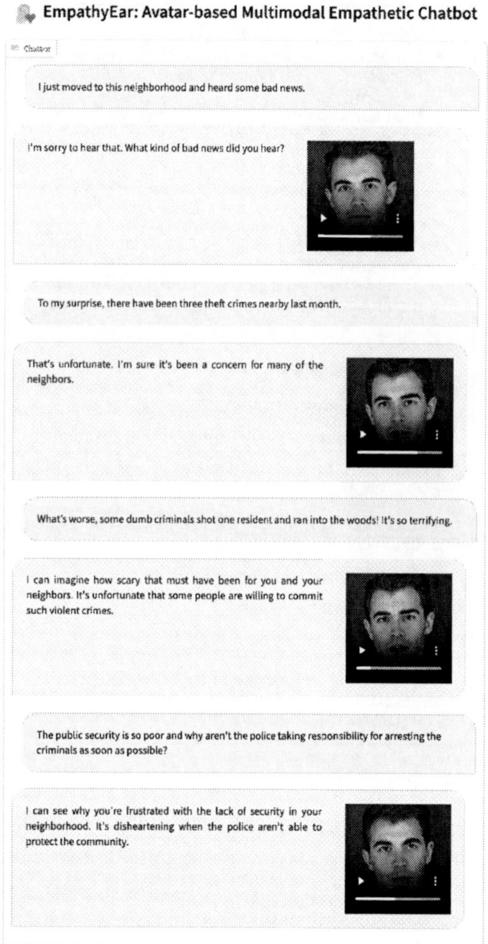


Figure 3: Screenshot of the EmpathyEar providing companion service by chatting with an elder.

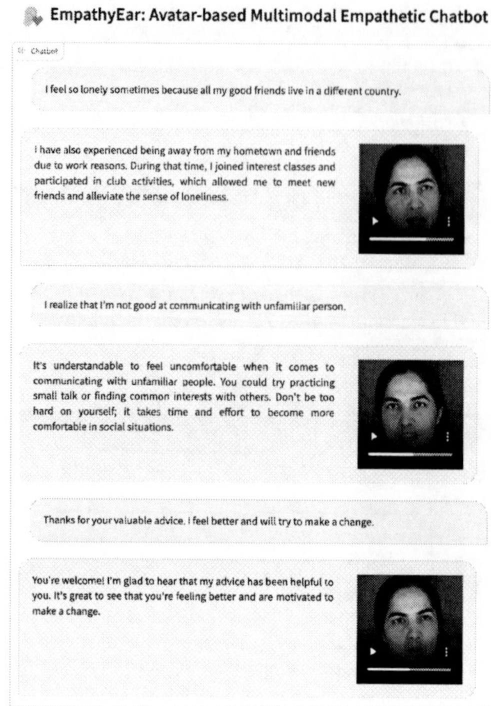


Figure 4: Screenshot of the dialogue between the user and EmpathyEar for psychological assistance.

tuning datasets (Ouyang et al., 2022; Dai et al., 2023), we also utilize OpenAI GPT-4 (OpenAI, 2022a) to generate rich data under the meta-response format defined above. We prompt GPT-4 to fully adhere to the CoT reasoning format, allowing the LLM to simulate this process, where we ensure the data diversification, which includes: 32 types of emotional labels, both explicit and implicit emotional types, and over 200 real-life scenarios. Appendix §A.2 provides detailed construction and feature statistics of the data.

**Emotion-aware Enhancement Training.** To enhance the emotional awareness of our backend speech and talking-face generators, we wrap the existing related multimodal data and conduct further training on these modules. Appendix §A.3 details data construction and training strategy.

## 5 Use Scenario and Demonstration

### 5.1 Application Scenario

EmpathyEar supports multimodal digital-figure responses, offering a more potent capacity for empathetic expression and a wider range of applications, compared to text-based empathetic robots. Below are some common scenarios and applications (not limited to) where EmpathyEar can excel:

1) **Accessibility Services.** Enhances interactions for those with disabilities through empathetic understanding of their needs.
2) **Customer Service.** Elevates customer experience with empathetic, personalized support and a deep understanding of emotions.
3) **Elderly Companion.** Provides the elderly with companionship and emotional support, enriching their social interactions.
4) **Healthcare Assistance.** Aids patients through empathetic interactions, supporting mental and emotional health during recovery.
5) **Child Companion.** Offers empathetic companionship to children, fostering emotional and educational development.
6) **Psychological Counseling.** Delivers emotional support and counseling, tuned to individual feel-

| | Models | Acc | Dist-1 | Dist-2 |
|---|---|---|---|---|
| *Non-LLMs* | CASE | 40.2 | 0.7 | 4.0 |
| | ESCM | 42.0 | 1.4 | 4.4 |
| | Lamb | 53.4 | 1.8 | 7.7 |
| *LLMs* | Alpaca (7B) | 20.6 | 26.8 | 70.4 |
| | Flan-T5 (xl) | 19.3 | 29.2 | 52.4 |
| | Flan-T5 (xxl) | 32.0 | 30.7 | 66.8 |
| | ChatGLM3 (6B) | 24.3 | 37.7 | 75.0 |
| | **EmpathyEar (6B)** | **57.3** | **44.5** | **82.3** |

Table 2: Performance on text ERG (EmpatheticDialogue data) by comparing with SoTA systems.

ings and mental states.

7) **Educational Tools.** Improves learning with empathetic support, motivating students to overcome challenges.
8) **Gaming and Virtual Reality.** Enhances gaming and VR with emotionally responsive characters for a more immersive experience.

### 5.2 Demonstrations

In Figures 3 and 4, we showcase the interaction of the system with users in two scenarios: elderly companionship and psychological counseling. In these scenarios, EmpathyEar flexibly assumes the digital personas of a man and a woman, respectively, and provides accurate and appropriate empathetic responses, effectively playing a positive role in guiding the users' emotions. Those real demonstrations reflect the capabilities of our EmpathyEar system. Appendix §B shows two more cases of scenarios in children's companionship and healthcare assistance. Please visit dynamic video demonstrations for better understanding at `https://youtu.be/gGn9oYftwbY`.

## 6 Performance and Quantitative Analysis

We finally quantitatively assess the exact performance of the system.

**Automatic Evaluation.** First, we test our system on the standard text-based ERG dataset, EmpatheticDialogue (Rashkin et al., 2019). We make comparisons with both 1) the non-LLM-based SoTA models, including CASE (Zhou et al., 2023), ESCM (Yang et al., 2024a), and Lamb (Sun et al., 2023); and 2) LLM-based systems, including ChatGLM3 (Du et al., 2022), Alpaca (Taori et al., 2023) and Flan-T5 (Chung et al., 2022). The metrics include emotion detection accuracy, as well as Dist-1 and Dist2 which measure response diversity at single and double granularity, respectively. As shown in Table 2, EmpathyEar achieves the best performance compared to all non-LLM and LLM methods, surpassing them with quite large gaps.

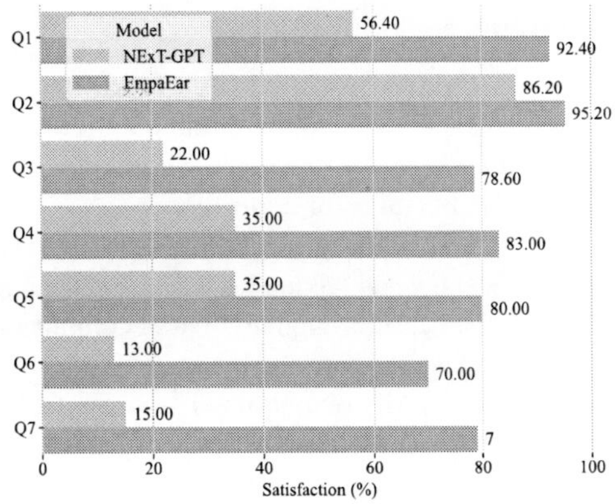


Figure 5: Human evaluation in seven different aspects: Q1) accuracy of emotion recognition, Q2) fluency of the language, Q3) rationality of the analysis, Q4) clarity of speech, Q5) emotional consistency of speech, Q6) clarity of video facial features, and Q7) emotional consistency of video expressions.

**Human Evaluation.** Text-based automatic evaluation metrics do not fully capture the complete performance of our system. Therefore, we consider conducting human evaluations. We make comparison with the any-to-any MLLM, NExT-GPT (Wu et al., 2023) that is compatible to multimodal empathetic generation. We prepare 20 dialogue queries from diverse scenarios for two systems to respond. Seven questions from different aspects are used to ask users to evaluate on a Likert scale of 1-100. Figure 5 shows the results, where EmpathyEar is superior to NExT-GPT in all aspects, especially for the emotion consistency of speech and vision.

## 7 Conclusion

We introduce **EmpathyEar**, a novel, open-source, avatar-based multimodal empathetic chatbot. By employing an LLM at its core, enhanced with multimodal encoders and generators, EmpathyEar supports user inputs from any of text, sound, and vision modalities, and more importantly, producing multimodal empathetic responses, offering users, not just textual responses but also digital avatars with talking faces and synchronized voices. EmpathyEar allows for a richer, more empathetic communication experience, surpassing the limitations of current text-only ERG systems, thus offering emotionally resonant interactions across a broader spectrum of scenarios. The system sets a new standard for human-level empathetic dialogue systems, blending intelligence with the ability to understand and express human emotions.

## Limitations and Future Work

Despite the progress EmpathyEar makes in empathetic response generation through multimodal integration, there are three main limitations that present opportunities for future work.

First, we rely on external tools for the backend speech generator and talking-head avatar generator, linked to the LLM through text-based commands. This cascading method has inherent limitations; errors in the LLM's output may propagate to the multimodal generation, and the lack of end-to-end learning in our system might restrict performance improvements. Future research could look into developing an integrated end-to-end architecture based on our system.

Second, while our design allows the LLM to produce a meta-response guiding the multimodal generators to maintain consistency in content and emotional tone, there may still be occasional inconsistencies. Investigating methods to enhance cross-modal consistency in semantics and emotional expression could be a focus for further study.

Third, although we introduce the concept of multimodal empathetic response generation, we have yet to define a comprehensive benchmark or standard for this task. Future research should focus on establishing clear definitions, datasets, and validation methods for this area.

## Ethics Statement

The development and deployment of EmpathyEar, an avatar-based multimodal empathetic chatbot, involve significant ethical considerations. Key concerns include the need to protect user data privacy, particularly emotional data, using strict data protection measures to prevent misuse. It's important to note that EmpathyEar does not substitute for professional psychological or medical advice. We commit to the principle of beneficence, aiming to improve user well-being and minimize harm while adhering to ethical standards of fairness, non-discrimination, and bias prevention.

## References

Max Bain, Arsha Nagrani, Gül Varol, and Andrew Zisserman. 2021. Frozen in time: A joint video and image encoder for end-to-end retrieval. In *Proceedings of the ICCV*, pages 1708–1718.

Emad Barsoum, Cha Zhang, Cristian Canton-Ferrer, and Zhengyou Zhang. 2016. Training deep networks for facial expression recognition with crowd-sourced label distribution. In *Proceedings of the 18th ACM International Conference on Multimodal Interaction, ICMI 2016, Tokyo, Japan, November 12-16, 2016*, pages 279–283.

Changyu Chen, Yanran Li, Chen Wei, Jianwei Cui, Bin Wang, and Rui Yan. 2024. Empathetic response generation with relation-aware commonsense knowledge. In *Proceedings of the 17th ACM International Conference on Web Search and Data Mining*, pages 87–95.

Wei-Lin Chiang, Zhuohan Li, Zi Lin, Ying Sheng, Zhanghao Wu, Hao Zhang, Lianmin Zheng, Siyuan Zhuang, Yonghao Zhuang, Joseph E. Gonzalez, Ion Stoica, and Eric P. Xing. 2023. Vicuna: An open-source chatbot impressing gpt-4 with 90

Hyung Won Chung, Le Hou, Shayne Longpre, Barret Zoph, Yi Tay, William Fedus, Eric Li, Xuezhi Wang, Mostafa Dehghani, Siddhartha Brahma, Albert Webson, Shixiang Shane Gu, Zhuyun Dai, Mirac Suzgun, Xinyun Chen, Aakanksha Chowdhery, Sharan Narang, Gaurav Mishra, Adams Yu, Vincent Y. Zhao, Yanping Huang, Andrew M. Dai, Hongkun Yu, Slav Petrov, Ed H. Chi, Jeff Dean, Jacob Devlin, Adam Roberts, Denny Zhou, Quoc V. Le, and Jason Wei. 2022. Scaling instruction-finetuned language models. *CoRR*, abs/2210.11416.

Wenliang Dai, Junnan Li, Dongxu Li, Anthony Meng Huat Tiong, Junqi Zhao, Weisheng Wang, Boyang Li, Pascale Fung, and Steven C. H. Hoi. 2023. Instructblip: Towards general-purpose vision-language models with instruction tuning. *CoRR*, abs/2305.06500.

Zhengxiao Du, Yujie Qian, Xiao Liu, Ming Ding, Jiezhong Qiu, Zhilin Yang, and Jie Tang. 2022. Glm: General language model pretraining with autoregressive blank infilling. In *Proceedings of the 60th Annual Meeting of the Association for Computational Linguistics (Volume 1: Long Papers)*, pages 320–335.

Weiquan Fan, Xiangmin Xu, Xiaofen Xing, Weidong Chen, and Dongyan Huang. 2021. LSSED: A large-scale dataset and benchmark for speech emotion recognition. In *IEEE International Conference on Acoustics, Speech and Signal Processing, ICASSP 2021, Toronto, ON, Canada, June 6-11, 2021*, pages 641–645.

Hao Fei, Shengqiong Wu, Wei Ji, Hanwang Zhang, Meishan Zhang, Mong Li Lee, and Wynne Hsu. Video-of-thought: Step-by-step video reasoning from perception to cognition. In *Proceedings of the International Conference on Machine Learning, ICML*, pages 6373–6391.

Hao Fei, Shengqiong Wu, Hanwang Zhang, Tat-Seng Chua, and Shuicheng Yan. 2024a. Vitron: A unified pixel-level vision llm for understanding, generating, segmenting, editing. *CoRR*.

Hao Fei, Shengqiong Wu, Meishan Zhang, Min Zhang, Tat-Seng Chua, and Shuicheng Yan. 2024b. Enhancing video-language representations with structural spatio-temporal alignment. *IEEE Transactions on Pattern Analysis and Machine Intelligence*.

Yuan Gan, Zongxin Yang, Xihang Yue, Lingyun Sun, and Yi Yang. 2023. Efficient emotional adaptation for audio-driven talking-head generation. In *Proceedings of the IEEE/CVF International Conference on Computer Vision*, pages 22634–22645.

Jun Gao, Yuhan Liu, Haolin Deng, Wei Wang, Yu Cao, Jiachen Du, and Ruifeng Xu. 2021. Improving empathetic response generation by recognizing emotion cause in conversations. In *Findings of the association for computational linguistics: EMNLP 2021*, pages 807–819.

Rohit Girdhar, Alaaeldin El-Nouby, Zhuang Liu, Mannat Singh, Kalyan Vasudev Alwala, Armand Joulin, and Ishan Misra. 2023. Imagebind: One embedding space to bind them all. In *Proceedings of the IEEE/CVF Conference on Computer Vision and Pattern Recognition*, pages 15180–15190.

Akriti Jaiswal, A Krishnama Raju, and Suman Deb. 2020. Facial emotion detection using deep learning. In *2020 international conference for emerging technology (INCET)*, pages 1–5. IEEE.

Chris Dongjoo Kim, Byeongchang Kim, Hyunmin Lee, and Gunhee Kim. 2019. Audiocaps: Generating captions for audios in the wild. In *Proceedings of the 2019 Conference of the North American Chapter of the Association for Computational Linguistics: Human Language Technologies, NAACL-HLT 2019, Minneapolis, MN, USA, June 2-7, 2019, Volume 1 (Long and Short Papers)*, pages 119–132.

Junnan Li, Dongxu Li, Silvio Savarese, and Steven C. H. Hoi. 2023. BLIP-2: bootstrapping language-image pre-training with frozen image encoders and large language models. In *Proceedings of the ICML*, pages 19730–19742.

Qintong Li, Hongshen Chen, Zhaochun Ren, Pengjie Ren, Zhaopeng Tu, and Zhumin Chen. 2020. Empdg: Multi-resolution interactive empathetic dialogue generation. In *Proceedings of the 28th International Conference on Computational Linguistics*, pages 4454–4466.

Yinghao Aaron Li, Cong Han, Vinay Raghavan, Gavin Mischler, and Nima Mesgarani. 2024. Styletts 2: Towards human-level text-to-speech through style diffusion and adversarial training with large speech language models. *Advances in Neural Information Processing Systems*, 36.

Zhaojiang Lin, Andrea Madotto, Jamin Shin, Peng Xu, and Pascale Fung. 2019. Moel: Mixture of empathetic listeners. *arXiv preprint arXiv:1908.07687*.

Shilong Liu, Hao Cheng, Haotian Liu, Hao Zhang, Feng Li, Tianhe Ren, Xueyan Zou, Jianwei Yang, Hang Su, Jun Zhu, et al. 2023. Llava-plus: Learning to use tools for creating multimodal agents. *arXiv preprint arXiv:2311.05437*.

Yuanyuan Liu, Wei Dai, Chuanxu Feng, Wenbin Wang, Guanghao Yin, Jiabei Zeng, and Shiguang Shan. 2022. MAFW: A large-scale, multi-modal, compound affective database for dynamic facial expression recognition in the wild. In *MM '22: The 30th ACM International Conference on Multimedia, Lisboa, Portugal, October 10 - 14, 2022*, pages 24–32.

OpenAI. 2022a. Gpt-4 technical report.

OpenAI. 2022b. Introducing chatgpt.

Long Ouyang, Jeff Wu, Xu Jiang, Diogo Almeida, Carroll L Wainwright, Pamela Mishkin, Chong Zhang, Sandhini Agarwal, Katarina Slama, Alex Ray, et al. 2022. Training language models to follow instructions with human feedback. *arXiv preprint arXiv:2203.02155*.

Soujanya Poria, Devamanyu Hazarika, Navonil Majumder, Gautam Naik, Erik Cambria, and Rada Mihalcea. 2019. MELD: A multimodal multi-party dataset for emotion recognition in conversations. In *Proceedings of the 57th Conference of the Association for Computational Linguistics, ACL 2019, Florence, Italy, July 28- August 2, 2019, Volume 1: Long Papers*, pages 527–536.

Hannah Rashkin, Eric Michael Smith, Margaret Li, and Y-Lan Boureau. 2018. Towards empathetic open-domain conversation models: A new benchmark and dataset. *arXiv preprint arXiv:1811.00207*.

Hannah Rashkin, Eric Michael Smith, Margaret Li, and Y-Lan Boureau. 2019. Towards empathetic open-domain conversation models: A new benchmark and dataset. In *Proceedings of the 57th Annual Meeting of the Association for Computational Linguistics*, pages 5370–5381.

Sahand Sabour, Chujie Zheng, and Minlie Huang. 2022. Cem: Commonsense-aware empathetic response generation. In *Proceedings of the AAAI Conference on Artificial Intelligence*, volume 36, pages 11229–11237.

Kashfia Sailunaz, Manmeet Dhaliwal, Jon Rokne, and Reda Alhajj. 2018. Emotion detection from text and speech: a survey. *Social Network Analysis and Mining*, 8(1):28.

Mohammad Soleymani, Sadjad Asghari-Esfeden, Yun Fu, and Maja Pantic. 2015. Analysis of eeg signals and facial expressions for continuous emotion detection. *IEEE Transactions on Affective Computing*, 7(1):17–28.

Linzhuang Sun, Nan Xu, Jingxuan Wei, Bihui Yu, Liping Bu, and Yin Luo. 2023. Rational sensibility: Llm enhanced empathetic response generation guided by self-presentation theory. *arXiv preprint arXiv:2312.08702*.

Rohan Taori, Ishaan Gulrajani, Tianyi Zhang, Yann Dubois, Xuechen Li, Carlos Guestrin, Percy Liang, and Tatsunori B. Hashimoto. 2023. Stanford alpaca:

An instruction-following llama model. https://github.com/tatsu-lab/stanford_alpaca.

Hugo Touvron, Thibaut Lavril, Gautier Izacard, Xavier Martinet, Marie-Anne Lachaux, Timothée Lacroix, Baptiste Rozière, Naman Goyal, Eric Hambro, Faisal Azhar, Aurélien Rodriguez, Armand Joulin, Edouard Grave, and Guillaume Lample. 2023. Llama: Open and efficient foundation language models. *CoRR*, abs/2302.13971.

Kaisiyuan Wang, Qianyi Wu, Linsen Song, Zhuoqian Yang, Wayne Wu, Chen Qian, Ran He, Yu Qiao, and Chen Change Loy. 2020. MEAD: A large-scale audio-visual dataset for emotional talking-face generation. In *Computer Vision - ECCV 2020 - 16th European Conference, Glasgow, UK, August 23-28, 2020, Proceedings, Part XXI*, volume 12366 of *Lecture Notes in Computer Science*, pages 700–717.

Jason Wei, Xuezhi Wang, Dale Schuurmans, Maarten Bosma, Fei Xia, Ed Chi, Quoc V Le, Denny Zhou, et al. 2022. Chain-of-thought prompting elicits reasoning in large language models. *Advances in neural information processing systems*, 35:24824–24837.

Shengqiong Wu, Hao Fei, Xiangtai Li, Jiayi Ji, Hanwang Zhang, Tat-Seng Chua, and Shuicheng Yan. 2024. Towards semantic equivalence of tokenization in multimodal llm. *arXiv preprint arXiv:2406.05127*.

Shengqiong Wu, Hao Fei, Leigang Qu, Wei Ji, and Tat-Seng Chua. 2023. Next-gpt: Any-to-any multimodal llm. *arXiv preprint arXiv:2309.05519*.

Zhou Yang, Zhaochun Ren, Yufeng Wang, Xiaofei Zhu, Zhihao Chen, Tiecheng Cai, Yunbing Wu, Yisong Su, Sibo Ju, and Xiangwen Liao. 2024a. Exploiting emotion-semantic correlations for empathetic response generation. *arXiv preprint arXiv:2402.17437*.

Zhou Yang, Zhaochun Ren, Wang Yufeng, Shizhong Peng, Haizhou Sun, Xiaofei Zhu, and Xiangwen Liao. 2024b. Enhancing empathetic response generation by augmenting llms with small-scale empathetic models. *arXiv preprint arXiv:2402.11801*.

Jinfeng Zhou, Chujie Zheng, Bo Wang, Zheng Zhang, and Minlie Huang. 2023. Case: Aligning coarse-to-fine cognition and affection for empathetic response generation. In *Proceedings of the 61st Annual Meeting of the Association for Computational Linguistics (Volume 1: Long Papers)*, pages 8223–8237.

Kun Zhou, Berrak Sisman, Rui Liu, and Haizhou Li. 2022. Emotional voice conversion: Theory, databases and ESD. *Speech Commun.*, 137:1–18.

Deyao Zhu, Jun Chen, Xiaoqian Shen, Xiang Li, and Mohamed Elhoseiny. 2023. Minigpt-4: Enhancing vision-language understanding with advanced large language models. *CoRR*, abs/2304.10592.

# A Specification of Emotion-aware Instruction-Tuning

## A.1 Encoder-LLM Alignment Learning

**General Alignment Learning:** We feed the audio and video into LLM, and then let it output corresponding captions. Datasets include: 'audio-text' AudioCap data (Kim et al., 2019), and 'video-text' Webvid data (Bain et al., 2021).

**Emotion-aware Multimodal Alignment:** Likewise, we feed the speech audios or videos, and let LLM output the correct emotion labels/types. Speech-based emotion detection datasets: LSSED (Fan et al., 2021), MELD (Poria et al., 2019); and Vision-based emotion detection data FERPlus (Barsoum et al., 2016) and MAFW (Liu et al., 2022).

**Textual Empathetic Response Alignment:** Inputting pure textual dialogue contexts encourages LLM to generate correct empathetic response texts. We use the commonly employed text-based EmpatheticDialogue ERG data (Rashkin et al., 2018).

## A.2 Meta-response Instruction-Tuning

Following the construction of many existing instruction-tuning datasets (Ouyang et al., 2022; Dai et al., 2023), we also utilize OpenAI GPT-4[5] to generate rich data under the meta-response format defined above. We prompt GPT-4 to fully adhere to the CoT reasoning format, allowing the LLM to simulate this process, where we ensure the data diversification by generating samples evenly covering the pre-setting characters of the avatar, as shown in Table 1.

## A.3 Emotion-aware Enhancement Training

While we can directly employ the off-the-shelf well-trained speech generator and talking-head generator for our use, the quality of these two generators might be sub-optimal, especially in terms of their emotional awareness. Thus, we enhance their perceiving by further training them in emotion-aware datasets. Specifically, we fine-tune the speech generator and talking-head generator on the emotional speech and video dataset, ESD (Zhou et al., 2022) and MEAD (Wang et al., 2020), respectively. We retrofit the ESD and MEAD datasets slightly to meet our requirements. For example, we prepare the speech text by first recognizing the text from the video speech.

[5] https://chat.openai.com/

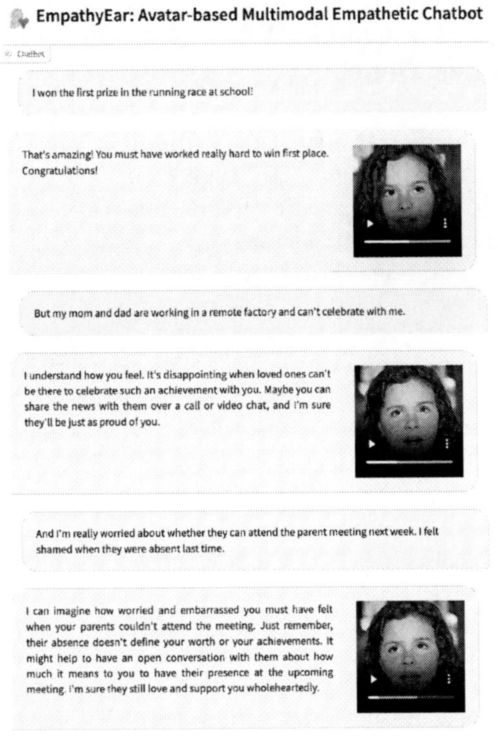


Figure 6: Screenshot of the dialogue between a user and `EmpathyEar` in the child companionship scenario.

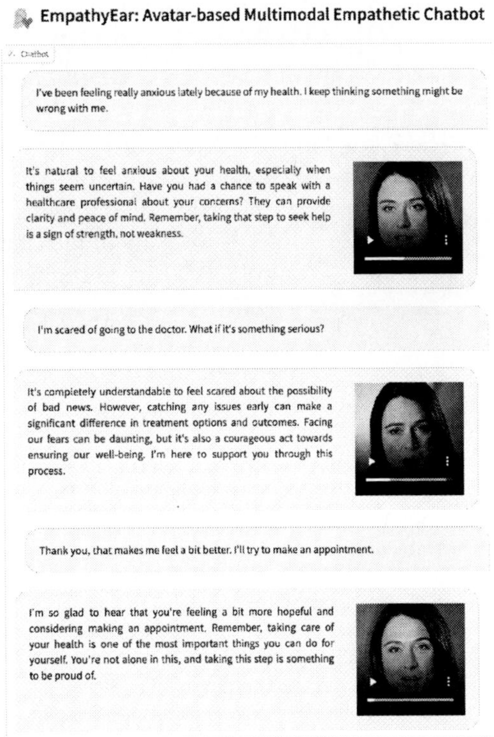


Figure 7: Screenshot of the dialogue between a user and `EmpathyEar` in the health care scenario.

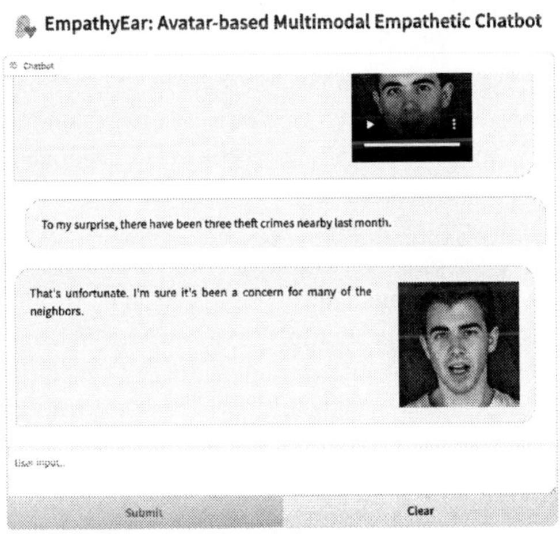


Figure 8: Screenshot of the webpage interface.

## B More Demonstrations

Figure 8 shows the system's interactive interface. Figure 6 displays the process of multimodal empathetic responses in the *child companionship* scenario. Figure 7 presents an interactive scenario in the *health care* context.

# OpenWebAgent: An Open Toolkit to Enable Web Agents on Large Language Models

**Iat Long Iong**[1*†] **Xiao Liu**[1*] **Yuxuan Chen**[1†] **Hanyu Lai**[1†] **Shuntian Yao**[2†]
**Pengbo Shen**[3†] **Hao Yu**[1†] **Yuxiao Dong**[1‡] **Jie Tang**[1‡]
[1]Tsinghua University [2]Beijing University of Posts and Telecommunications
[3]University of the Chinese Academy of Sciences
rongyl20@mails.tsinghua.edu.cn, shawliu9@gmail.com

## Abstract

We introduce OpenWebAgent, an open toolkit designed to optimize web automation by integrating both large language models (LLMs) and large multimodal models (LMMs). This toolkit focuses on enhancing human-computer interactions on the web, simplifying complex tasks through an advanced HTML parser, a rapid action generation module, and an intuitive user interface. At the core of OpenWebAgent is an innovative web agent framework that uses a modular design to allow developers to seamlessly integrate a variety of models and tools to process web information and automate tasks on the web. This enables the development of powerful, task-oriented web agents, significantly enhancing user experience and operational efficiency on the web. The OpenWebAgent framework, Chrome plugin, and demo video are available at https://github.com/THUDM/OpenWebAgent/.

## 1 Introduction

As the Internet becomes an integral part of everyday life, the complexity of tasks that users want to automate on web platforms continues to grow (Van der Aalst et al., 2018). Modern web users expect interfaces that are not only intuitive and visually appealing but also capable of intelligent (Davenport and Kirby, 2016), predictive interactions that streamline complex tasks.

Traditional web automation tools, such as Robotic Process Automation (RPA) tools, have been instrumental in reducing manual effort (Syed et al., 2020), but fall short in areas such as contextual understanding, flexibility (Hallikainen et al., 2018), and user accessibility. These tools often require complex setups and significant technical expertise, limiting their usefulness to a narrow audience. In addition, the lack of a unified system architecture among existing tools poses significant challenges for developers seeking to integrate or innovate on top of these platforms, hindering the advancement of web automation technologies.

Nevertheless, the field has advanced significantly with deep learning technologies, especially after Google introduced the Transformer model (Vaswani et al., 2017). The capabilities of large-scale pre-trained models, like OpenAI's GPT series (Achiam et al., 2023; OpenAI, 2024a), have improved text generation, semantic understanding, and logical reasoning (Brown et al., 2020; Chan et al., 2022). This has made web automation tools using LLMs and LMMs more feasible. Recent work such as AutoWebGLM (Lai et al., 2024), shows LLMs can handle various web tasks but the lack of multimodal inputs limits their capabilities, highlighting the need for multimodal web agents.

**Presented System.** We present OpenWebAgent, a toolkit for advanced web interactions with innovative modules that allow developers to integrate any language or multimodal model for web automation. Figure 1 shows the task execution results of OpenWebAgent System with GPT-4 (Achiam et al., 2023) and AutoWebGLM (Lai et al., 2024) as the action generation models. OpenWebAgent includes an interactive web plugin and a modularly designed server, allowing it to execute tasks directly and autonomously on webpages while providing real-time feedback. It stands out for its efficiency and user accessibility compared to other web automation tools, thanks to these features:

- **High-Performance HTML Parser.** This parser optimizes performance by simplifying complex HTML into a more straightforward format (§3.1), enabling OpenWebAgent to process web content with enhanced accuracy and speed. It reduces HTML length by 99% and the number of elements by 97% (§5.1), ensuring efficient operation on any website. (§5.2)

*Equal contribution.
†Work done while these authors interned at Zhipu AI.
‡Corresponding Authors: YD and JT.



*Proceedings of the 62nd Annual Meeting of the Association for Computational Linguistics (Volume 3: System Demonstrations)*, pages 72–81
August 11-16, 2024 ©2024 Association for Computational Linguistics

(a) Follow Bill Gates on X (Twitter).

(b) Find pictures of Arctic. (c) Give PS5 game recommendations. (d) Discover info about black holes.

(e) Find the BibTeX of a paper. (f) Get Driving Directions. (g) Follow the qualifying account.

Figure 1: Examples of OpenWebAgent performing daily tasks. In these examples, GPT-4 is employed as the action generation model in (a) – (d), while AutoWebGLM is used in (e) – (g).

- **Modular System Design.** OpenWebAgent integrates multimodal inputs such as action history, parsed HTML and screenshots for LLMs and LMMs to create coherent action plans that match user intent. Users can modify, pause, or reset tasks at any time (§4.2), offering flexibility and ease of use. The modular design (§3.2) allows easy model integration and module replacement by developers.
- **Streamlined User Interface.** The plugin requires no complex setup and is ready to use immediately after download. Its simple and attractive interface (§4.1) lets users track the process and sequence of operations easily, with task execution controlled by a few simple buttons, ensuring efficiency and ease of use.

These innovations place OpenWebAgent at the forefront of web automation technology. Through its advanced capabilities, OpenWebAgent is not just a tool but a paradigm shift in how humans interact with and harness the power of the web for automated tasks.

**Contributions.** (1) We implement a powerful HTML parser engine that simplifies complex webpages into a more accessible format. (2) We design a ready-to-use web plugin automation tool that enables users to perform any desired action on any webpage. (3) We create a versatile web agent framework, allowing developers to easily integrate any LLM or LMM for web automation. This framework offers unprecedented ease in developing robust, task-oriented web agents. In summary, OpenWebAgent contributes both technically and conceptually to the understanding of the boundaries of human-machine collaboration and giving an attempt to develop the future of web automation.

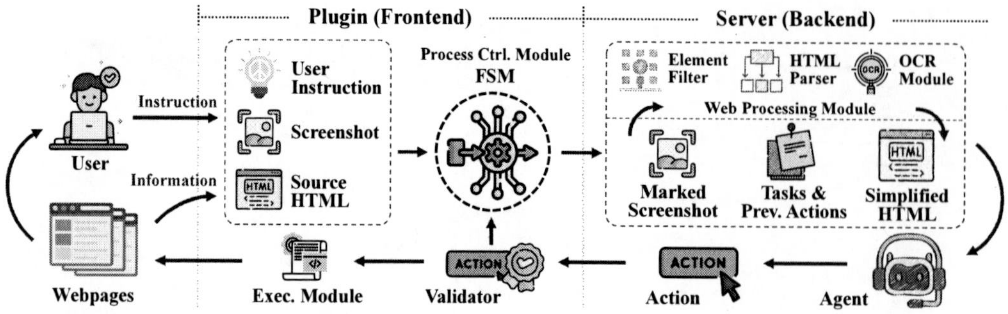


Figure 2: System Design. Our system has two main components: the frontend plugin and the backend server. The frontend plugin collects page information, performs webpage actions, and controls operations using a finite state machine (FSM). The backend server processes data and organizes prompts for the agent to predict actions.

## 2 Related Work

Developing an efficient toolkit for web browsing agents is challenging, especially in integrating decision language models with diverse modules for processing webpage information. This section provides an overview of related research.

**Language Models (LMs).** Since Google proposed Transformer (Vaswani et al., 2017), Large Language Models (LLMs) have evolved rapidly. Notable models include OpenAI's GPT-4 (Achiam et al., 2023), Google's Gemini (Google, 2023), PaLM-2 (Chowdhery et al., 2023), and Gopher (Rae et al., 2021), Anthropic's Claude-2 (Anthropic, 2023), Meta's LLaMA series (Touvron et al., 2023a,b) and OPT (Zhang et al., 2022), as well as Mistral's Mixture of Experts models (Jiang et al., 2024). Other notable contributions include GLM-130B (Zeng et al., 2022) and BLOOM (Scao et al., 2022). These models, pre-trained on vast datasets, excel in various NLP tasks.

Large Multimodal Models (LMMs) have become the primary focus of research to address a wider range of tasks. OpenAI led the way by launching high-performance models such as GPT-4-Turbo (OpenAI, 2024b) and GPT-4o (OpenAI, 2024a). The open-source community has also introduced multimodal models like LLaVA (Liu et al., 2023a), CogVLM (Wang et al., 2023), and Qwen-VL (Bai et al., 2023). These LMMs have inspired new approaches in Agent research.

Smaller, cost-effective models are preferred due to the high deployment costs of large models, with users prioritizing task-specific effectiveness. Open-source projects like LLaMA3-8B (Meta, 2024), Vicuna-7B (Chiang et al., 2023), and ChatGLM4-9B (GLM et al., 2024) show comparable capabilities to larger models in some areas.

**Web Automation Systems.** Previous projects, such as WebGPT (Nakano et al., 2021) and WebGLM (Liu et al., 2023b), have effectively integrated language models with web environments, mainly for question-answering tasks using internet data. These models are excellent at information retrieval for QA (Rajpurkar et al., 2016; Nguyen et al., 2016; Berant et al., 2013; Kwiatkowski et al., 2019), but they cannot perform complex or interactive web-based tasks.

Recent projects like AutoGPT[1] use multiple ChatGPT agents for self-prompting and web operations through a plan-execute-reflect cycle. The GPT-4V-ACT framework[2] uses the Set-of-Mark method (Yang et al., 2023) to mark screenshots and then employs GPT-4V (OpenAI, 2024b) to generate operations, but it struggles with real web pages due to insufficient operation instructions. AutoWebGLM (Lai et al., 2024) is based on the fine-tuned ChatGLM3-6B (GLM et al., 2024) model. However, it lacks image input data, limiting its performance in real-world web scenarios.

Other initiatives such as MindAct (Deng et al., 2023) involve extensive interactions to select webpage elements, suggesting a need for more efficient processes. CC-Net (Mishra et al., 2019) leverages a vast visual data set and learning techniques to manipulate web components effectively. Conversely, CogAgent (Hong et al., 2023) focuses on using visual input to generate web operation methods, while WebAgent (Gur et al., 2024) utilizes HTML-T5 and the large-scale Flan-U-Plam model (Chung et al., 2022) to control webpages, though the model's size limits its deployment.

[1]https://github.com/Significant-Gravitas
[2]https://github.com/ddupont808/GPT-4V-Act

## 3 The OpenWebAgent System

OpenWebAgent is rooted in principles of intuitive design, flexibility, and comprehensive functionality, aiming to provide a user-centric approach to web automation. The system is inherently adaptable, and designed to allow users to easily customize it for a range of complex automation tasks. Its main objective is to develop a toolkit that is more responsive and goes beyond the limitations of traditional web agents. This toolkit does more than execute user tasks with simple pre-defined commands; it is engineered to fully analyze, decompose, and process each task to ensure thorough and efficient automation.

### 3.1 HTML Parsing Techniques

The content of HTML webpages is intricate and complex. Therefore, it should be effectively simplified before being fed into the parsing model.

Simplification aims to distill the most important information while eliminating excessive or disruptive elements that could make it difficult for the model to understand. It is crucial to maintain the basic structure of HTML and its essential content information during this process. This ensures that the model can understand and use these details for efficient webpage parsing.

Using algorithm 1 can effectively transform the element tree into a more concise representation. We can judge whether an element should be retained by determining the clickability of the element, noting that nodes near the retained element are generally able to provide more useful information and therefore have a higher retention value. Therefore, we can adopt a recursive approach to obtain the ancestor nodes, child nodes and sibling nodes of the retained element part. Finally, pruning can be done according to the information content starting from the leaf nodes.

With the processing algorithm described above, the complex HTML can be simplified into a format that is easier for the model to interpret and manipulate, thus improving the model's performance in web parsing tasks.

### 3.2 Interaction Workflow

OpenWebAgent's design philosophy and objectives aim to achieve a harmonious balance between advanced technological capabilities and user-friendly interaction, redefining standards for human-computer interaction in web automation. To improve the flexibility and usability of our toolkit, we modularize it into several key components as shown in Figure 2. The network processing module and the action generation module are deployed as unified services in the backend. Meanwhile, the process control module and the execution module are integrated into the plugin.

**Algorithm 1:** HTML Simplifier

```
Data: dom tree tree, neighbor coefficient n
Result: pruned tree tree, kept elements kp
nodes, kp ← set(), list()
for e in tree.element do        // selector
    if not (onTop(e) and onScreen(e))
      then continue
    if isClickableTag(e.tagname) or
      haveJSaction(e.attrib) or
      e.cursor = pointer or
      e.classes.include(button) then
        kp.push(e)
        nodes.push(e)
        nodes.push(getNbr(e, n))
    end
end
for e in reversed(tree) do      // pruner
    if not e in nodes or not (e has text or
      attrib or e is root or
      len(e.children) > 1) then
        tree.remove(e)
    end
end
```

**Web Processing Module**. This module extracts useful elements of HTML, simplifies HTML input, performs OCR on screenshots, and adds element labels to screenshots. See §3.1 for details of the methods and processes.

**Action Generation Module**. The main purpose of this module is to predict the next action based on the user's task and the current webpage context. At this stage, we provide a prompt for the LLM that includes the current task, the simplified HTML of the webpage, and previous command sequences, and for the LMM, we also provide labeled screenshots for the model to use. The model outputs the next action in natural language, which we match against a pre-defined action space, and returns the action name and parameters if the match is successful.

In this module, models are accessed through interfaces, which means that developers creating new web agents can effortlessly integrate any model into our toolkit by simply setting up an API interface for accessing the model. It is important to note that we have reserved an interface to a visual processing module in the toolkit, located between the web processing module and the action generation module, to serve better the needs of developers working with multimodal agents.

To address the lack of image information in the language-based agent, the module is pre-configured with an OCR interface that takes a screenshot of a webpage as input and returns the webpage information contained in the screenshot. LMM agent developers have the option to replace the preconfigured modules and integrate their own vision modules into our toolkit, which simplifies the development of multimodal web agents.

**Execution Module**. This module is used to execute specific action instructions on a webpage. When the module receives an action instruction from the action generator module, it looks for the element that actually needs to be operated on and then executes the action on the webpage using a predefined script. When the action is completed, it provides a response feedback to ensure that the model is aware of the execution of the action to adjust the plan.

**Process Control Module**. As shown in Figure 3, this module is implemented using a finite state machine. The main purpose of this is to coordinate the execution of tasks and to facilitate the transfer of information between the above modules.

This module serves as the primary interface for user interaction. It receives various inputs, such as user task commands and control commands (e.g. start, pause, reset). The module also records user input tasks and previous action history. When the user issues a start command, the module first fetches the HTML source and screenshot of the current webpage, and information about the clickable elements, and passes them to the web processing module (including the visual processing module). Additionally, the module sends the task and action history to the action generation module.

The module sends task and action history to the action generation module and waits for a response from the action generation module. It then parses the action into various parameters. If a valid web action returns, its details are sent to the execution module. Once a response arrives from the execution module, the action history updates and the process of retrieving webpage information repeats.

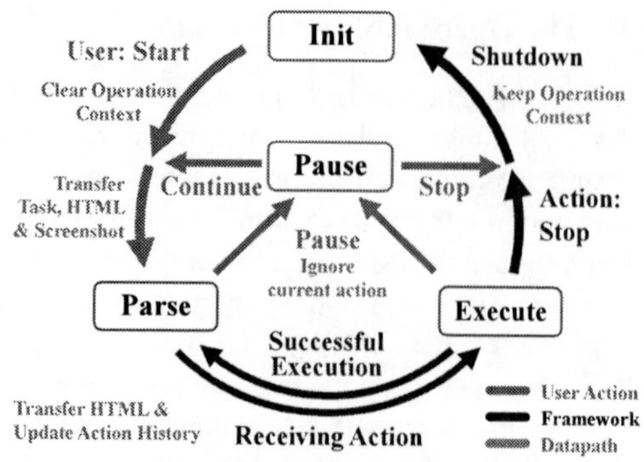


Figure 3: FSM Design.

When the process is complete, the user is notified by the module.

This workflow enables real-time user interaction, users can send control commands such as pause, reset, or update their task description at any time. The process control module adapts accordingly, ensuring flexible and efficient interaction.

## 4 Demonstration

### 4.1 System Interface

The plugin interface is simple and easy to use, as shown in Figure 4. It consists of three main parts:

- **Input Box**: For entering tasks to be executed.
- **Control Buttons**: For managing task execution, starting with "▷ run" and "↻ reset". During execution, "॥ pause" replaces "▷ run", allowing the user to control the process.
- **Feedback Panel**: Shows the executed actions and the model's responses.

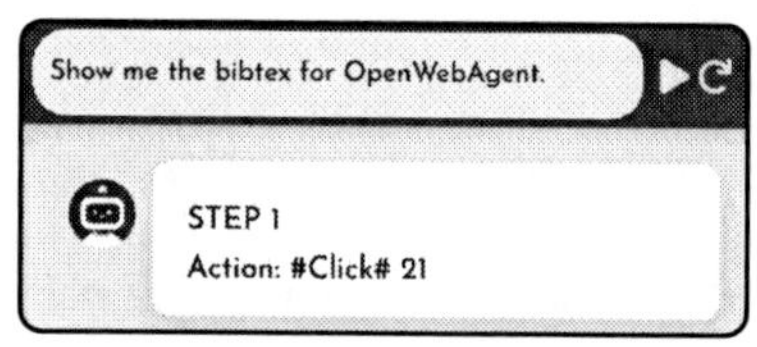


Figure 4: The system interface of OpenWebAgent.

### 4.2 Usage Example

As shown in Figure 5, we illustrate the interaction process and execution results of our toolkit by integrating GPT-4 into our toolkit and executing a sample task *"What is the weather like today?"*.

**Task Execution**. The task begins with Google, a standard browser homepage that does not provide weather information. First, we can put the query *"What is the weather like today?"* into the task box and click the "▷ run" button to initiate the task. A

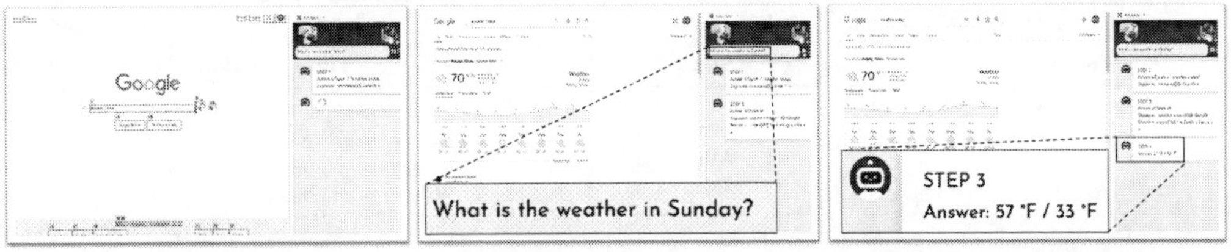


(a) Start of execution. (b) Change current task. (c) Get requested information.

Figure 5: Execution flow of OpenWebAgent. Initially (a) execute *"What is the weather like today?"*, then at (b) modify the task to *"What is the weather in (on) Sunday?"*, and finally (c) get the answer for the task.

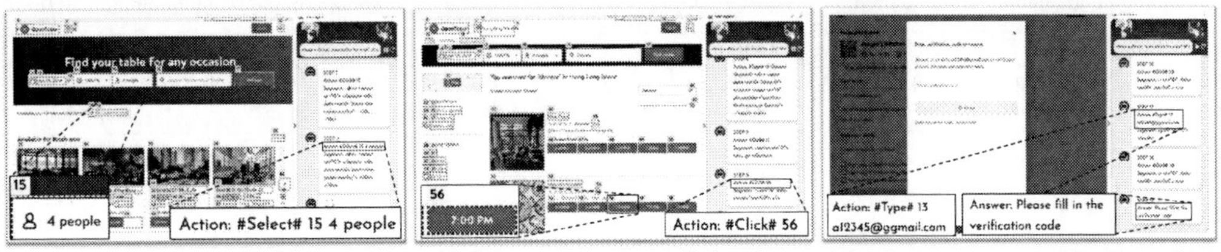


(a) Set the number of diners. (b) Select restaurant and dining time. (c) Ask user to enter verification code.

Figure 6: Example of using OpenWebAgent with AutoWebGLM. The task is *"Make a dinner reservation for 4 at a Chinese restaurant with the email a12345@ggmail.com."*. This example demonstrates that OpenWebAgent can handle various types of elements.

loading icon will appear on the feedback box to indicate that our plugin has initiated the retrieval of information from the webpage. After a brief interval, the plugin generates the instruction, "`#Type# 5 weather today`". The webpage displays that *"weather today"* has been entered into the input box, thereby suggesting that the action has been executed successfully.

**Task Management**. After several actions on the webpage, the user is presented with a weather forecast, as depicted in Figure 5(b). At this juncture, the user has the option to pause the task by clicking the "॥ `pause`" button. They can then update the task instructions to *"What is the weather on Sunday?"* before resuming execution by clicking "▷ `run`" (which serves as "`continue`" here). The plugin will adapt to the modified user task and modify the execution flow accordingly.

**Task Completion**. Following a series of actions on the webpage, the LLM (GPT-4) can complete the user's task based on the information available. Our plugin then responds to the user's query by returning a message, "`Answer: 57°F / 33°F`", in the feedback box and completes the process.

Figure 6 shows how OpenWebAgent with AutoWebGLM handles a restaurant reservation task. This demonstrates that our framework provides the necessary information and actions to support the model in performing complex tasks. In addition, as shown in Figure 1, our plugin can also perform various web tasks, such as shopping, socializing and information seeking to satisfy users' diverse web browsing needs. This proves that our plugin has the following characteristics:

- **Flexibility**: Users can use our plugin to accomplish various tasks on any webpage, in any state, anytime, anywhere.
- **Efficiency**: Each module in our plugin is optimized for performance, and the time taken for each step of the action depends largely on the time taken to call LLM. Therefore, our plugin executes extremely efficiently.
- **Robust Interactivity**: Our plugin receives user interaction at any moment during execution. Users can receive feedback and take control in real time.

## 5 Evaluation

### 5.1 HTML Parser Performance

**Experimental setup.** We selected six categories of frequently visited websites from Similarweb[3] and randomly tested the effectiveness of the parser by selecting dozens of pages from each website, and the results are shown in Table 1.

[3] `https://www.similarweb.com/top-websites`

| Website | Length | | | Elements | | | Time |
|---|---|---|---|---|---|---|---|
| | # before | # after | reduction (%) | # before | # after | reduction (%) | msec |
| **E-commerce** | 725,948 | 2,174.5 | 99.62 | 2,580.2 | 56.34 | 96.38 | 5.52 |
| - Amazon | 1,103,437 | 2,643.3 | 99.71 | 4,329.8 | 59.87 | 97.99 | 8.30 |
| - eBay | 679,852 | 2,108.7 | 99.65 | 2,138.3 | 46.28 | 97.70 | 5.11 |
| - Taobao | 394,555 | 1,771.4 | 99.51 | 1,272.6 | 62.86 | 93.50 | 3.14 |
| **Entertainment** | 825,534 | 2,069.1 | 99.48 | 2,705.0 | 39.33 | 98.00 | 5.42 |
| - Bilibili | 1,669,682 | 2,217.6 | 99.62 | 3,144.2 | 53.00 | 97.12 | 7.19 |
| - Spotify | 317,223 | 1,947.6 | 99.39 | 1,756.4 | 23.14 | 98.60 | 3.75 |
| - Fandom | 489,698 | 2,042.3 | 99.43 | 3,217.3 | 41.85 | 98.29 | 5.32 |
| **Forum** | 762,945 | 2,846.3 | 99.61 | 2,983.3 | 50.88 | 97.98 | 5.68 |
| - Reddit | 872,041 | 3,258.9 | 99.63 | 2,838.8 | 47.25 | 98.00 | 5.60 |
| - Quora | 653,849 | 2,433.7 | 99.59 | 3,127.7 | 54.50 | 97.96 | 5.75 |
| **Knowledge** | 452,532 | 4,584.8 | 98.71 | 2,630.8 | 75.11 | 96.62 | 4.38 |
| - Wikipedia | 440,264 | 6,135.1 | 98.37 | 2,479.0 | 95.33 | 96.10 | 4.33 |
| - Baidu-baike | 464,801 | 3,034.5 | 99.05 | 2,782.6 | 54.89 | 97.15 | 4.42 |
| **News** | 763,077 | 3,731.0 | 98.58 | 1,821.4 | 50.91 | 96.49 | 4.53 |
| - Yahoo | 1,829,666 | 4,959.4 | 99.53 | 2,843.6 | 40.22 | 98.47 | 8.18 |
| - Yahoo-JP | 317,049 | 2,457.3 | 99.23 | 1,693.8 | 74.87 | 95.48 | 3.12 |
| - QQ | 142,515 | 3,776.4 | 97.01 | 926.7 | 37.85 | 95.54 | 2.27 |
| **Social Media** | 1,679,296 | 1,547.1 | 99.81 | 3,389.6 | 47.37 | 97.95 | 8.96 |
| - Facebook | 3,332,936 | 1,663.8 | 99.94 | 6,417.8 | 47.67 | 99.13 | 14.94 |
| - Instrgram | 1,176,319 | 768.6 | 99.93 | 1,172.2 | 25.43 | 97.77 | 6.76 |
| - X | 528,634 | 2,208.7 | 99.57 | 2,578.7 | 69.00 | 96.96 | 5.18 |
| **Overall** | 900,782 | 2,714.2 | 99.32 | 2,669.9 | 52.12 | 97.24 | 5.83 |

Table 1: HTML simplification results on various sites.

**Results Analysis.** The HTML simplifier effectively reduces the complexity of web pages across various websites. It significantly reduces the number of actionable elements and the length of HTML text, with simplification rates exceeding 97% and 99% respectively. The tool operates quickly, even in dense environments like Facebook, with an average processing time of just 5.83 milliseconds. This rapid performance demonstrates the tool's practicality for real-world applications, enabling quicker and more focused web interactions by emphasizing essential content.

### 5.2 Efficiency

**Experimental setup.** Following the HTML Parser Performance testing methodology, we selected 12 websites from SimilarWeb. The system was assigned 80 web navigation tasks across these diverse websites. Throughout these tasks, we meticulously recorded the response times of different components. The outcomes of this evaluation are presented in Table 2.

**Results Analysis.** The results indicate that network transmission time makes up 70% of the system's operational time, primarily due to connections to remote servers. Additionally, the model's prediction activities, particularly with the GPT-4-turbo model, account for 23% of the runtime. To improve efficiency, future enhancements should focus on optimizing web page transmission, such as by locally simplifying web pages to reduce data volume by 99%, thus saving time and enhancing performance.

| | Fetch | Parse | Predict | Network | Execute |
|---|---|---|---|---|---|
| Time (ms) | 510.3 | 71.2 | 2,405.7 | 7,166.4 | 31.2 |
| Percentage | 5.0 | 0.7 | 23.6 | 70.3 | 0.3 |

Table 2: System Efficiency.

## 6 Conclusion

OpenWebAgent represents a paradigm shift in web-based human-computer interaction. It promises to improve user experience and productivity by automating a variety of web tasks efficiently and intuitively. It provides a convenient framework for the development of web agents based on large language models (LLMs) and large multimodal models (LMMs) through advanced HTML parsing capabilities, a modularly designed system, a friendly user interface, and the visualization of the task execution process.

## Limitations

While OpenWebAgent boasts remarkable capabilities, it also has its limitations:

- Its performance may falter on complex or unconventional webpages, as it depends on understanding web structures.
- The tool is intended for general purposes and might not perform optimally for tasks that require specialized knowledge.
- The capacity of OpenWebAgent to execute web page operations is substantially influenced by the capabilities of the underlying model, including the ability to comprehend web page elements and perform image recognition.
- Although OpenWebAgent is currently efficient, its backend design needs to be improved to meet the needs of large-scale applications and faster web operations response.

Future developments will address these limitations and improve its applicability and performance.

## Ethics Statement

**Intended Use.** OpenWebAgent is designed to assist users in automating web browsing tasks.

**Potential Misuse.** OpenWebAgent can perform tasks on the World Wide Web, however, we cannot prevent users from using this tool for network attacks, such as social forum spamming, DDoS attacks, or unauthorized data extraction.

## Acknowledgements

This work is supported by Technology and Innovation Major Project of the Ministry of Science and Technology of China under Grant 2022ZD0118600, Natural Science Foundation of China (NSFC) 62276148 and 62425601, the New Cornerstone Science Foundation through the XPLORER PRIZE.

## References

Josh Achiam, Steven Adler, Sandhini Agarwal, Lama Ahmad, Ilge Akkaya, Florencia Leoni Aleman, Diogo Almeida, Janko Altenschmidt, Sam Altman, Shyamal Anadkat, et al. 2023. Gpt-4 technical report. *arXiv preprint arXiv:2303.08774*.

Anthropic. 2023. Model card and evaluations for claude models. Technical report, Anthropic.

Jinze Bai, Shuai Bai, Shusheng Yang, Shijie Wang, Sinan Tan, Peng Wang, Junyang Lin, Chang Zhou, and Jingren Zhou. 2023. Qwen-vl: A frontier large vision-language model with versatile abilities. *arXiv preprint arXiv:2308.12966*.

Jonathan Berant, Andrew Chou, Roy Frostig, and Percy Liang. 2013. Semantic parsing on freebase from question-answer pairs. In *Proceedings of the 2013 conference on empirical methods in natural language processing*, pages 1533–1544.

Tom Brown, Benjamin Mann, Nick Ryder, Melanie Subbiah, Jared D Kaplan, Prafulla Dhariwal, Arvind Neelakantan, Pranav Shyam, Girish Sastry, Amanda Askell, et al. 2020. Language models are few-shot learners. In *Advances in Neural Information Processing Systems*, volume 33, pages 1877–1901.

Stephanie CY Chan, Ishita Dasgupta, Junkyung Kim, Dharshan Kumaran, Andrew K Lampinen, and Felix Hill. 2022. Transformers generalize differently from information stored in context vs in weights. *NeurIPS MemARI Workshop*.

Wei-Lin Chiang, Zhuohan Li, Zi Lin, Ying Sheng, Zhanghao Wu, Hao Zhang, Lianmin Zheng, Siyuan Zhuang, Yonghao Zhuang, Joseph E. Gonzalez, Ion Stoica, and Eric P. Xing. 2023. Vicuna: An open-source chatbot impressing gpt-4 with 90%* chatgpt quality.

Aakanksha Chowdhery, Sharan Narang, Jacob Devlin, Maarten Bosma, Gaurav Mishra, Adam Roberts, Paul Barham, Hyung Won Chung, Charles Sutton, Sebastian Gehrmann, et al. 2023. Palm: Scaling language modeling with pathways. *Journal of Machine Learning Research*, 24(240):1–113.

Hyung Won Chung, Le Hou, Shayne Longpre, Barret Zoph, Yi Tay, William Fedus, Yunxuan Li, Xuezhi Wang, Mostafa Dehghani, Siddhartha Brahma, et al. 2022. Scaling instruction-finetuned language models. *arXiv preprint arXiv:2210.11416*.

Thomas H Davenport and Julia Kirby. 2016. *Only humans need apply: Winners and losers in the age of smart machines*. Harper Business New York.

Xiang Deng, Yu Gu, Boyuan Zheng, Shijie Chen, Sam Stevens, Boshi Wang, Huan Sun, and Yu Su. 2023. Mind2web: Towards a generalist agent for the web. In *Advances in Neural Information Processing Systems*, volume 36, pages 28091–28114.

Team GLM, Aohan Zeng, Bin Xu, Bowen Wang, Chenhui Zhang, Da Yin, Diego Rojas, Guanyu Feng, Hanlin Zhao, Hanyu Lai, Hao Yu, Hongning Wang, Jiadai Sun, Jiajie Zhang, Jiale Cheng, Jiayi Gui, Jie Tang, Jing Zhang, Juanzi Li, Lei Zhao, Lindong Wu, Lucen Zhong, Mingdao Liu, Minlie Huang, Peng Zhang, Qinkai Zheng, Rui Lu, Shuaiqi Duan, Shudan Zhang, Shulin Cao, Shuxun Yang, Weng Lam Tam, Wenyi Zhao, Xiao Liu, Xiao Xia, Xiaohan Zhang, Xiaotao Gu, Xin Lv, Xinghan Liu, Xinyi Liu, Xinyue Yang, Xixuan Song, Xunkai Zhang, Yifan An, Yifan Xu, Yilin Niu, Yuantao Yang, Yueyan Li, Yushi Bai, Yuxiao Dong, Zehan Qi, Zhaoyu Wang, Zhen Yang,

Zhengxiao Du, Zhenyu Hou, and Zihan Wang. 2024. Chatglm: A family of large language models from glm-130b to glm-4 all tools.

Gemini Team Google. 2023. Gemini: a family of highly capable multimodal models. *arXiv preprint arXiv:2312.11805*.

Izzeddin Gur, Hiroki Furuta, Austin Huang, Mustafa Safdari, Yutaka Matsuo, Douglas Eck, and Aleksandra Faust. 2024. A real-world webagent with planning, long context understanding, and program synthesis. In *The Twelfth International Conference on Learning Representations*.

Petri Hallikainen, Riitta Bekkhus, and Shan L Pan. 2018. How opuscapita used internal rpa capabilities to offer services to clients. *MIS Quarterly Executive*, 17(1).

Wenyi Hong, Weihan Wang, Qingsong Lv, Jiazheng Xu, Wenmeng Yu, Junhui Ji, Yan Wang, Zihan Wang, Yuxiao Dong, Ming Ding, et al. 2023. Cogagent: A visual language model for gui agents. *arXiv preprint arXiv:2312.08914*.

Albert Q Jiang, Alexandre Sablayrolles, Antoine Roux, Arthur Mensch, Blanche Savary, Chris Bamford, Devendra Singh Chaplot, Diego de las Casas, Emma Bou Hanna, Florian Bressand, et al. 2024. Mixtral of experts. *arXiv preprint arXiv:2401.04088*.

Tom Kwiatkowski, Jennimaria Palomaki, Olivia Redfield, Michael Collins, Ankur Parikh, Chris Alberti, Danielle Epstein, Illia Polosukhin, Jacob Devlin, Kenton Lee, et al. 2019. Natural questions: a benchmark for question answering research. *Transactions of the Association for Computational Linguistics*, 7:452–466.

Hanyu Lai, Xiao Liu, Iat Long Iong, Shuntian Yao, Yuxuan Chen, Pengbo Shen, Yu Hao, Hanchen Zhang, Xiaohan Zhang, Yuxiao Dong, and Jie Tang. 2024. AutowebGLM: A large language model-based web navigating agent. In *Proceedings of the 30th ACM SIGKDD Conference on Knowledge Discovery and Data Mining*, KDD '24.

Haotian Liu, Chunyuan Li, Qingyang Wu, and Yong Jae Lee. 2023a. Visual instruction tuning. In *Advances in neural information processing systems*, volume 36, pages 34892–34916.

Xiao Liu, Hanyu Lai, Hao Yu, Yifan Xu, Aohan Zeng, Zhengxiao Du, Peng Zhang, Yuxiao Dong, and Jie Tang. 2023b. Webglm: Towards an efficient web-enhanced question answering system with human preferences. In *Proceedings of the 29th ACM SIGKDD Conference on Knowledge Discovery and Data Mining*, KDD '23, page 4549–4560, New York, NY, USA. Association for Computing Machinery.

Meta. 2024. Introducing meta llama 3: The most capable openly available llm to date. Technical report, Meta.

Suraj Mishra, Peixian Liang, Adam Czajka, Danny Z Chen, and X Sharon Hu. 2019. Cc-net: Image complexity guided network compression for biomedical image segmentation. In *2019 IEEE 16th International Symposium on Biomedical Imaging (ISBI 2019)*, pages 57–60. IEEE.

Reiichiro Nakano, Jacob Hilton, Suchir Balaji, Jeff Wu, Long Ouyang, Christina Kim, Christopher Hesse, Shantanu Jain, Vineet Kosaraju, William Saunders, et al. 2021. Webgpt: Browser-assisted question-answering with human feedback. *arXiv preprint arXiv:2112.09332*.

Tri Nguyen, Mir Rosenberg, Xia Song, Jianfeng Gao, Saurabh Tiwary, Rangan Majumder, and Li Deng. 2016. Ms marco: A human generated machine reading comprehension dataset. *choice*, 2640:660.

OpenAI. 2024a. Hello gpt-4o. Technical report, OpenAI.

OpenAI. 2024b. New models and developer products announced at devday. Technical report, OpenAI.

Jack W Rae, Sebastian Borgeaud, Trevor Cai, Katie Millican, Jordan Hoffmann, Francis Song, John Aslanides, Sarah Henderson, Roman Ring, Susannah Young, et al. 2021. Scaling language models: Methods, analysis & insights from training gopher. *arXiv preprint arXiv:2112.11446*.

Pranav Rajpurkar, Jian Zhang, Konstantin Lopyrev, and Percy Liang. 2016. Squad: 100,000+ questions for machine comprehension of text. In *Proceedings of the 2016 Conference on Empirical Methods in Natural Language Processing*, pages 2383–2392, Austin, Texas. Association for Computational Linguistics.

Teven Le Scao, Angela Fan, Christopher Akiki, Ellie Pavlick, Suzana Ilić, Daniel Hesslow, Roman Castagné, Alexandra Sasha Luccioni, François Yvon, Matthias Gallé, et al. 2022. Bloom: A 176b-parameter open-access multilingual language model. *arXiv preprint arXiv:2211.05100*.

Rehan Syed, Suriadi Suriadi, Michael Adams, Wasana Bandara, Sander JJ Leemans, Chun Ouyang, Arthur HM ter Hofstede, Inge van de Weerd, Moe Thandar Wynn, and Hajo A Reijers. 2020. Robotic process automation: contemporary themes and challenges. *Computers in Industry*, 115:103162.

Hugo Touvron, Thibaut Lavril, Gautier Izacard, Xavier Martinet, Marie-Anne Lachaux, Timothée Lacroix, Baptiste Rozière, Naman Goyal, Eric Hambro, Faisal Azhar, et al. 2023a. Llama: Open and efficient foundation language models. *arXiv preprint arXiv:2302.13971*.

Hugo Touvron, Louis Martin, Kevin Stone, Peter Albert, Amjad Almahairi, Yasmine Babaei, Nikolay Bashlykov, Soumya Batra, Prajjwal Bhargava, Shruti Bhosale, et al. 2023b. Llama 2: Open foundation and fine-tuned chat models. *arXiv preprint arXiv:2307.09288*.

Wil MP Van der Aalst, Martin Bichler, and Armin Heinzl. 2018. Robotic process automation.

Ashish Vaswani, Noam Shazeer, Niki Parmar, Jakob Uszkoreit, Llion Jones, Aidan N Gomez, Łukasz Kaiser, and Illia Polosukhin. 2017. Attention is all you need. In *Advances in Neural Information Processing Systems*, volume 30, pages 5998–6008.

Weihan Wang, Qingsong Lv, Wenmeng Yu, Wenyi Hong, Ji Qi, Yan Wang, Junhui Ji, Zhuoyi Yang, Lei Zhao, Xixuan Song, et al. 2023. Cogvlm: Visual expert for pretrained language models. *arXiv preprint arXiv:2311.03079*.

Jianwei Yang, Hao Zhang, Feng Li, Xueyan Zou, Chunyuan Li, and Jianfeng Gao. 2023. Set-of-mark prompting unleashes extraordinary visual grounding in gpt-4v. *arXiv preprint arXiv:2310.11441*.

Aohan Zeng, Xiao Liu, Zhengxiao Du, Zihan Wang, Hanyu Lai, Ming Ding, Zhuoyi Yang, Yifan Xu, Wendi Zheng, Xiao Xia, et al. 2022. Glm-130b: An open bilingual pre-trained model. In *The Eleventh International Conference on Learning Representations*.

Susan Zhang, Stephen Roller, Naman Goyal, Mikel Artetxe, Moya Chen, Shuohui Chen, Christopher Dewan, Mona Diab, Xian Li, Xi Victoria Lin, et al. 2022. Opt: Open pre-trained transformer language models. *arXiv preprint arXiv:2205.01068*.

# EasyEdit: An Easy-to-use Knowledge Editing Framework for Large Language Models

**Peng Wang♣, Ningyu Zhang♣[*], Bozhong Tian♣, Zekun Xi♣, Yunzhi Yao♣, Ziwen Xu♣, Mengru Wang♣, Shengyu Mao♣, Xiaohan Wang♣, Siyuan Cheng♣, Kangwei Liu♣, Yuansheng Ni♣, Guozhou Zheng♣, Huajun Chen♣[*]**
♣ Zhejiang University
https://github.com/zjunlp/EasyEdit

## Abstract

Large Language Models (LLMs) usually suffer from knowledge cutoff or fallacy issues, which means they are unaware of unseen events or generate text with incorrect facts owing to outdated/noisy data. To this end, many knowledge editing approaches for LLMs have emerged – aiming to subtly inject/edit updated knowledge or adjust undesired behavior while minimizing the impact on unrelated inputs. Nevertheless, due to significant differences among various knowledge editing methods and the variations in task setups, there is no standard implementation framework available for the community, which hinders practitioners from applying knowledge editing to applications. To address these issues, we propose EASYEDIT, an easy-to-use knowledge editing framework for LLMs. It supports various cutting-edge knowledge editing approaches and can be readily applied to many well-known LLMs such as T5, GPT-J, LlaMA, etc. Empirically, we report the knowledge editing results on LlaMA-2 with EASYEDIT, demonstrating that knowledge editing surpasses traditional fine-tuning in terms of reliability and generalization. We have released the source code on GitHub[1], along with Google Colab tutorials and comprehensive documentation[2] for beginners to get started. Besides, we present an online system[3] for real-time knowledge editing, and a demo video[4].

## 1 Introduction

Large Language Models (LLMs) have revolutionized modern Natural Language Processing (NLP), significantly improving performance across various tasks (Brown et al., 2020; OpenAI, 2023; Anil et al., 2023; Zhao et al., 2023; Touvron et al., 2023b; Qiao et al., 2023; Zheng et al., 2023b; Pan et al., 2023). However, deployed LLMs usually suffer from knowledge cutoff or fallacy issues. For example, LLMs such as ChatGPT and LlaMA possess information only up to their last training point. They can sometimes produce inaccurate or misleading information due to potential discrepancies and biases in their pre-training data (Ji et al., 2023; Hartvigsen et al., 2022). Hence, it's essential to efficiently update the parametric knowledge within the LLMs to modify specific behaviors while avoiding expensive retraining.

Indeed, finetuning or parameter-efficient finetuning (Ding et al., 2022, 2023) offers methods for modifying LLMs, these approaches can be computationally expensive and may lead to overfitting, particularly when applied to a limited number of samples (Cao et al., 2021) or streaming errors of LLMs. Additionally, fine-tuned models might forfeit capabilities gained during pre-training, and their modifications do not always generalize to relevant inputs. An alternative methodology involves using manually written or retrieved prompts to influence the LLMs' output. These methods suffer from reliability issues, as LLMs do not consistently generate text aligned with the prefix prompt (Hernandez et al., 2023; Lewis et al., 2021). Additionally, due to the extensive amount of up-to-date knowledge required for complex reasoning tasks, the impracticality of context overload becomes inevitable whenever the context length is limited.

A feasible solution, knowledge editing[5], aims to efficiently modify the behavior of LLMs with minimal impact on unrelated inputs. Research on knowledge editing for LLMs (Meng et al., 2023, 2022; Zheng et al., 2023a; Gupta et al., 2023; Mitchell et al., 2022a; Geva et al., 2023; Hase et al., 2023; Cohen et al., 2023a; Hartvigsen et al., 2023; Tan et al., 2024; Yu et al., 2023) have displayed remarkable progress across various tasks and settings.

[*]Corresponding author.

[1]This is a subproject of KnowLM (https://github.com/zjunlp/KnowLM), which facilitates knowledgeable LLM Framework with EasyInstruct, EasyEdit, EasyDetect etc.

[2]https://zjunlp.gitbook.io/easyedit

[3]https://huggingface.co/spaces/zjunlp/EasyEdit

[4]https://youtu.be/Gm6T0QaaskU

[5]Knowledge editing can also be termed as model editing.



*Proceedings of the 62nd Annual Meeting of the Association for Computational Linguistics (Volume 3: System Demonstrations)*, pages 82–93
August 11-16, 2024 

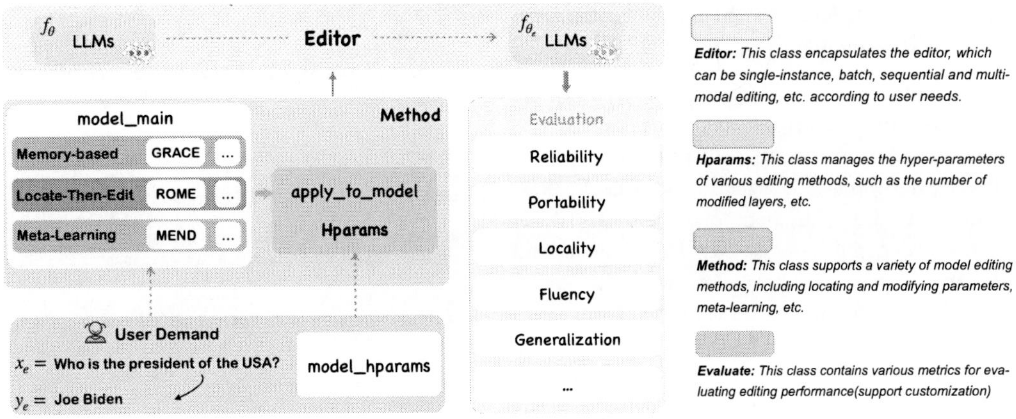


Figure 1: The overall architecture of EASYEDIT. The main function is `apply_to_model`, which applies the selected editing method to the LLMs. The **Editor** serves as the direct entry point, receiving customized user inputs and outputs, and returning the edited weights. Please note that some methods may require pre-training of classifiers or hypernetworks through the Trainer (See §3.5). EASYEDIT supports customizable evaluation metrics.

However, these variations in both implementation and task settings have impeded the development of a unified and comprehensive framework for knowledge editing. Note that the complexity obstructs the direct comparison of effectiveness and feasibility between different methods, and complicates the creation of novel knowledge editing approaches. To this end, we propose EASYEDIT, an easy-to-use knowledge editing framework for LLMs. EASYEDIT modularizes editing methods and effectiveness evaluation while considering their combination and interaction. It supports a variety of editing scenarios, including **single-instance**, **batch-instance**, **sequential**, and **multi-modal** editing. Moreover, EASYEDIT provides evaluation evaluations of key metrics such as Reliability, Generalization, Locality, and Portability (Yao et al., 2023), to quantify the robustness and side effects (Cohen et al., 2023b) of editing methods.

Specifically, in EASYEDIT, the Editor class integrates various editing components. The Method class offers a unified interface `apply_to_model`, which accepts editing descriptors and returns the edited model, thereby facilitating the integration of novel editing methodologies. Dedicated to evaluating editing performance, the Evaluate module leverages metrics such as reliability, robust generalization, and locality. The Trainer module manages the training of additional neural network structures. Each module in EASYEDIT is meticulously defined, striking a balance between cohesion and coupling. Furthermore, we furnish examples of editing across a spectrum of models, including T5 (Raffel et al., 2019), GPT-J (Wang and Komatsuzaki, 2021), GPT-NEO (Black et al., 2021), GPT2 (Radford et al., 2019), LLaMA (Touvron et al., 2023a), LLaMA-2 (Touvron et al., 2023b), Mistral (Jiang et al., 2023), and Qwen (Bai et al., 2023). We acknowledge all the support for EASYEDIT, which is listed in Appendix 6 due to space constraints.

## 2 Background

**Previous Solutions** Despite the tremendous success of LLMs in almost all NLP tasks, persistent challenges such as knowledge cutoff and biased/toxic outputs remain. To counter these challenges, two approaches are generally employed:

1) FINE-TUNING: Traditional fine-tuning techniques, along with delta tuning (Ding et al., 2022) and LoRA tuning (Hu et al., 2021) utilize domain-specific datasets to update the model's internal parametric knowledge. However, these methods face two notable challenges: First, they consume considerable resources. Second, they risk the potential of catastrophic forgetting (Ramasesh et al., 2022).

2) PROMPT-AUGMENTATION: Given a sufficient number of demonstrations or retrieved contexts, LLMs can learn to enhance reasoning (Yu et al., 2022) and generation through external knowledge (Borgeaud et al., 2022; Guu et al., 2020; Lewis et al., 2020). However, the performance may be sensitive to factors such as the prompting template, the selection of in-context examples (Zhao et al., 2021), or retrieved contexts (Ren et al.,

2023). These approaches also encounter the issue of context length limitation (Liu et al., 2023a).

**Knowledge Storage Mechanism** Within the NLP literature, numerous studies have delved into understanding the location of different types of knowledge in language models (Petroni et al., 2019; Roberts et al., 2020; Jiang et al., 2020). LLMs can be conceptualized as knowledge banks, and the transformer MLP layers function as key-value memories according to observations from Geva et al. (2021). This configuration promotes efficient knowledge adjustments by precisely localizing knowledge within the MLP layers (denoted as knowledge editing).

Knowledge editing enables nimble alterations to the LLMs' behavior through one data point. Another promising attribute of knowledge editing is its ability to ensure the locality of editing, meaning that modifications are contained within specific contexts. Additionally, the knowledge editing technique can mitigate harmful language generation (Geva et al., 2022). In this paper, we present EASYEDIT, an easy-to-use knowledge editing framework for LLMs. It seamlessly integrates diverse editing technologies and supports the free combination of modules for various LLMs. Through its unified framework and interface, EASYEDIT enables users to swiftly comprehend and apply the prevalent knowledge editing methods included in the package.

## 3 Design and Implementation

EASYEDIT provides a complete editing and evaluation process built on Pytorch (Paszke et al., 2019) and Huggingface (Wolf et al., 2020). This section commences with an exploration of the assemblability aspect of EASYEDIT, followed by a detailed explanation of the design and implementation of each component within the EASYEDIT framework (as shown in Figure 1). Additionally, we demonstrate a straightforward example of applying MEND to LLaMA, altering the output of *the U.S. President* to *Joe Biden*.

### 3.1 Assemblability

In the realm of knowledge editing, various distinct scenarios[6] exist. To cater to this diversity, EASYEDIT offers flexible combinations of modules that different editing `Editor` (such as single-instance, batch-instance (details in Appendix A)), METHOD (such as ROME, GRACE (§3.3)). About editing TARGET, EASYEDIT can accommodate any parameterized white-box existing model. Additionally, recent research (Dong et al., 2022) indicates that LLMs exhibit robust in-context learning capabilities. By providing edited facts to LLMs, one can alter the behavior of black-box models such as GPT4 (OpenAI, 2023). All those combinations are easily implementable and verifiable within the EASYEDIT framework.

[6]Denoted as `(Editor, METHOD, TARGET)`

```
# Step 1: Choose the Editing Method e.g. MEND
from easyeditor import BaseEditor
from easyeditor import MENDHyperParams
hparams = MENDHyperParams.from_hparams('gpt2-xl.yaml')


# Step 2: Provide the edit descriptor and target
prompts = ['Q: The president of the US is? A:',]
target_new = ['Joe Biden']
rephrase_prompts = ['The leader of the United State is']

# Step 3:  Combine them into the `BaseEditor`
editor = BaseEditor.from_hparams(hparams)

# Step 4: Edit and Evaluation
metrics, edited_model = editor.edit(
    prompts=prompts,
    target_new=target_new,
    keep_original_weight=True,
)

# metrics: Performance of knowledge editing
# edited_model: Model after modifying the weights
```

Figure 2: A running example of knowledge editing for LLMs in EASYEDIT. Utilizing the MEND approach, we can successfully transform the depiction of *the U.S. President* into that of *Joe Biden*.

### 3.2 Editor

The `Editor` serves a pivotal role in knowledge editing as it directly establishes the editing tasks and corresponding editing scenarios. Users supply the editor descriptor ($x_e$) and the edit target ($y_e$), but the input format varies according to the different editing objects. For instance, in Seq2Seq models, the edit target typically serves as the decoder's input, while in autoregressive models, $x_e$ and $y_e$ need to be concatenated to maximize the conditional probability. To facilitate unified editing across diverse architecture models, we meticulously develop a component `prepare_requests` to transform editing inputs.

In EASYEDIT, we provide an "edit" interface, incorporating components such as `Hparams`, `Method`, and `Evaluate`. During the editing phase, various knowledge editing strategies can be executed by invoking the `apply_to_model` function available in all different methods, it also performs evaluations

| | Method | Batch Edit | Sequential Edit | Additional Train | Edit Area | Time (s) | VRAM (GB) |
|---|---|---|---|---|---|---|---|
| Memory-based | SERAC | YES | YES | YES | *External Model* | 8.46 | 42 |
| | IKE | NO | NO | YES | *In-Context* | 4.57 | 52 |
| | GRACE | NO | YES | NO | *MLP+codebook* | 142.68 | 28 |
| | MELO | YES | YES | NO | *LoRA+codebook* | 154.32 | 30 |
| Meta-learning | KE | YES | YES | YES | *MLP* | 7.87 | 49 |
| | MEND | YES | YES | YES | *MLP* | 6.39 | 46 |
| Locate-Then-Edit | KN | NO | YES | NO | *MLP* | 425.64 | 42 |
| | ROME | NO | YES | NO | *MLP* | 187.90 | 31 |
| | MEMIT | YES | YES | NO | *MLP* | 169.28 | 33 |
| | PMET | YES | YES | NO | *MLP* | 219.17 | 34 |

Table 1: Comparison of several model editing methods. 'Batch Edit' refers to simultaneously editing multiple target knowledge instances. 'Sequential Edit' refers to maintaining previously edited knowledge while performing new edits. 'Additional Train' refers to the need for pre-training other network structures or parameters before editing. 'Edit Area' indicates the location of the edit, with MLP representing the linear layer. 'Time & VRAM' reflects the efficiency of the editing method (using LlaMA-7B as an example). 'Time' indicates the wall clock time required for conducting 10 edits, while VRAM represents the graphics memory usage.

of the model before and after the editing to gauge the editing's multifaceted impact on the model behavior, including generalization and side effects. An example to edit through EASYEDIT is depicted in Figure 2.

Note that the ability to execute batch editing (multiple edits in a single instance) and sequential editing (implementing new edits while preserving previous editing) is a crucial feature of knowledge editing (Huang et al., 2023). For methods that support batch editing, editing instances are inputted in chunk form. In addition, EASYEDIT provides a boolean switch, enabling users to either retain the pre-edit weights for single-instance editing or discard them for sequential editing.

### 3.3 Method

As the core component of knowledge editing, editing methods alter the model's behavior by modifying its internal parameters (e.g. MLP, Attention Mechanisms) or explicitly utilizing preceding editing facts, among other strategies. Impressive related works (Table 1) abound in this field, and they can be generally grouped into three categories as proposed by Yao et al. (2023).

**Memory-based** This category, encompassing methods such as SERAC (Mitchell et al., 2022b), IKE (Zheng et al., 2023a), and GRACE (Hartvigsen et al., 2023), emphasizes the use of memory elements to store and manipulate information during editing. SERAC applies retrieval and classification routing, GRACE replaces hidden states with parameters searched from a codebook for edit memorization, while IKE uses context-edit facts to guide the model in generating edited facts.

**Meta-learning** These methods learn the weight updates (denoted as $\Delta$), which are then added to the original weights for editing. Examples include KE (Cao et al., 2021), which uses a bidirectional-LSTM to predict weight updates, and MEND (Mitchell et al., 2022a), which adjusts model parameters through low-rank decomposition of gradients.

**Locate-Then-Edit** This paradigm focuses on knowledge localization to modify the parameters of specific neurons responsible for storing the editing facts. EASYEDIT integrates methods like KN (Dai et al., 2021), which employs gradient-based methods to update specific neurons. Moreover, EASYEDIT supports ROME (Meng et al., 2023), PMET (Li et al., 2024) and MEMIT (Meng et al., 2022), leveraging causal intervention to pinpoint knowledge within a specific MLP layer and enabling the modification of the entire matrix.

However, it is not practical to expose the editing methods directly to users due to the complexity of the underlying concepts and the time investment required to understand them. Additionally, differences in input-output formats across methods could further complicate the learning process. To circumvent these hurdles, we implement a unified interface, `apply_to_model`, in EASYEDIT. Aligning with the *Strategy* design pattern, this interface is designed to be overridden by different types of editing methods, ensuring consistent input and out-

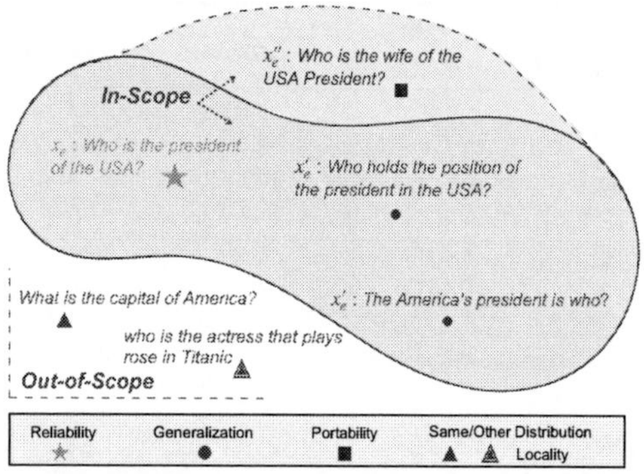


Figure 3: Depiction of the edit scope for edit descriptor *Who is the president of the USA?* It contains an example for knowledge editing evaluation, including Reliability, Generalization, Portability, and Locality.

put types. Specifically, it accepts a 'request' that includes the editing descriptor, the target of the edit, and any input data necessary to evaluate the editing performance. After processing the request(s), the interface returns the edited model weights. This design ensures both flexibility and easy-to-use, enabling users to handle knowledge editing instances effortlessly and utilize the customized models in other downstream tasks.

### 3.4 Hparams

When initializing an editing method, it is crucial to specify the related hyperparameters. These include the model to be edited, the layers targeted for modification, and, optionally, the type of external model, among other parameters. For methods that alter the LLMs' internal parameters, the adjustable parameter names should be indicated using the MODULE_NAME format, such as *transformer.h.5.mlp.fc_out*. In this case, the parameters of the *fc_out* linear layer in the fifth layer MLP of GPT-J would be modified, while all other parameters remain frozen. Layer selection adheres to the locality of knowledge (Meng et al., 2023) or retains layers with higher success rates in pilot experiments (Mitchell et al., 2022a), as elaborated in Appendix B.

All hyperparameter classes derive from a common base class, `Hyperparams`, which includes necessary attributes and abstract methods. This base class supports loading hyperparameters in both *yaml* and *json* formats. Moreover, the `Hyperparams` base class can be used to initialize the Trainer module, streamlining the workflow.

### 3.5 Trainer

Certain editing methods, which employ meta-learning or utilize classifiers (as shown in Table 1), necessitate the training of additional parameters or the implementation of extra network structures. Similar to Hyperparameters (`Hparams`), all Trainer classes inherit from a common base class, `BaseTrainer`. It includes essential attributes and abstract methods such as run and validate steps. Subclasses of the `BaseTrainer` define specific training steps for editing, such as calculating editing loss and locality loss, as well as the strategies for combining these losses. Once additional network structures are obtained, the subsequent editing process follows the same path as the Training-Free method. In EASYEDIT, various Trainers can be easily called with one click.

## 4 Evaluation

Knowledge editing, as defined by Mitchell et al. (2022b), involves supplying a specific editing descriptor $x_e$ (input instance) and an editing target $y_e$ (desired output). From these, an editing instance $z_e$ is generated in the form: $z_e \sim [x_e, y_e]$. The goal is to adjust the behavior of the initial base model $f_\theta$ (where $\theta$ represents the model's parameters) to produce an edited model $f_{\theta_e}$. Ideally, for the editing instance, the edited model would behave such that $f_{\theta_e}(x_e) = y_e$. Additionally, the editing scope $S(z_e)$ refers to a set of input examples whose true labels have been influenced by the editing instance. In most cases, a successful edit should affect the model's predictions for numerous In-Scope ($I(x_e) \sim \{x'_e | x'_e \in S(z_e)\}$) inputs, while leaving Out-of-Scope ($O(x_e) \sim \{x'_e | x'_e \notin S(z_e)\}$) inputs unchanged.

We employ six dimensions of metrics to assess the performance of editing methods, including **Reliability**, **Generalization**, **Locality**, **Portability**, **Fluency** (Zhang et al., 2018) and **Efficiency** (as shown in Figure 3).

**Reliability** This metric measures the average accuracy on the given editing instance $z_e$.

**Generalization** The edit should appropriately influence in-scope inputs, this metric gauges the average accuracy on in-scope inputs $I(x_e)$.

**Locality** Editing should adhere to the principle of locality, it evaluates whether out-of-scope inputs $O(x_e)$ can remain unchanged as the base model.

**Portability** The robust generalization of the edit, assessing whether the edited knowledge can be effectively applied to related content.

**Fluency** It measures the weighted average of bi-gram and tri-gram entropies to assess the diversity of text generations.

**Efficiency** Editing should be time and resource-efficient. This metric quantifies efficiency by measuring editing time and VRAM consumption.

## 5 Experiments

In this section, we will outline the experiment setting and report the empirical results of multiple editing methods supported in EASYEDIT (Table 2).

### 5.1 Experiment Setting

To validate the potential application of knowledge editing on LLMs, we utilize **LlaMA 2** (7B) (Touvron et al., 2023b), a model with a large parameter size, representing the decoder-only structure.

We employ the ZsRE dataset to test the capability of knowledge editing in incorporating substantial and general fact associations into the model. ZsRE (Levy et al., 2017) is a question-answering (QA) dataset that generates an equivalence neighbor through back-translation. Later, it is further expanded by Yao et al. (2023) to provide a more comprehensive evaluation of knowledge editing, including an assessment of the LLMs' ability to integrate the edited fact with other facts related to the target object o* (an aspect of Portability). For baselines, we compare various editing methods and additionally employ FT-L from ROME (Meng et al., 2023). FT-L updates parameters for a single MLP layer and applies an $L\infty$ norm constraint to limit the weight changes.

### 5.2 Experiment Results

Table 2 reveals SERAC and IKE's superior performance on the ZsRE datasets, exceeding 99% on several metrics. While ROME and MEMIT perform sub-optimally in generalization, they exhibit relatively high performance in terms of reliability and locality. IKE exhibits the potential of gradient-free updates through in-context learning, leading to near-perfect scores in both reliability and generalization. However, it shows some deficiency in locality, as preceding prompts may influence out-of-scope inputs. GRACE exhibits poor generalization, possibly attributed to the lack of explicit semantic representation in its activations within the decoder-only model (Liu et al., 2023b). FT-L's performance on ZsRE falls significantly short compared to ROME, even though both methods modify the same layer parameters. This suggests that under the norm constraint, fine-tuning is not an effective strategy for knowledge editing. MEND performs well overall, achieving over 90% accuracy on multiple metrics and even surpassing ROME in terms of reliability and generalization. KN performs poorly, indicating that it may be better suited for editing tasks in smaller models or tasks involving knowledge attribution.

| | Reliability | Generalization | Locality | Portability | Fluency |
|---|---|---|---|---|---|
| FT-L | 56.94 | 52.02 | 96.32 | 51.03 | 488.41 |
| SERAC | 99.49 | 99.13 | 100.00 | 57.82 | 423.22 |
| IKE | **100.00** | **99.98** | 69.19 | **67.56** | 557.37 |
| MEND | 94.24 | 90.27 | 97.04 | 56.95 | 540.06 |
| KN | 28.95 | 28.43 | 65.43 | 37.18 | 478.32 |
| ROME | 92.45 | 87.04 | 99.63 | 57.47 | **587.58** |
| MEMIT | 92.94 | 85.97 | 99.49 | 60.64 | 576.51 |
| GRACE | 99.22 | 0.43 | **100.00** | 56.87 | 426.31 |

Table 2: Editing results of the four metrics on LlaMA-2 using EASYEDIT. The settings for the model and the dataset are the same with Yao et al. (2023).

For the Portability evaluation, where the inference depends on a single connection or 'hop' between facts, most editing methods struggle to effectively combine the edited fact with other facts relevant to the target object o*. While SERAC obtains good performance on previous metrics, it completely fails to propagate the edited knowledge. This is because SERAC utilizes an external model with a smaller parameter size for counterfactual routing whereas the smaller model struggles to recall a rich set of relevant facts. IKE still maintains a relatively high capability for ripple editing (exceeding 67%), demonstrating that in-context learning is a promising approach to propagate edited knowledge to other related facts.

## 6 Conclusion and Future work

We propose EASYEDIT, an easy-to-use knowledge editing framework for LLMs, which supports many cutting-edge approaches and various LLMs. The ability to edit and manipulate LLMs in a controlled and targeted manner may open up new possibilities for knowledge augmentation (Wu et al., 2023, 2020; Zhang et al., 2022; Chen et al., 2022) and adaptation across various natural language processing tasks (Kaddour et al., 2023). In the future, we will continue to integrate advanced editing technologies into EASYEDIT, aiming at facilitating further research and inspiring new ideas for the NLP community.

## Acknowledgments

We thank the developers of the ROME[7] library for their significant contributions to the NLP community. We are grateful to Ting Lu and Yu Zhang who participated in the development of this project during the Zhejiang University Summer Camp. We also extend our gratitude to the NLP team at East China Normal University, particularly Lang Yu, for their support of the Melo module. Special thanks to Tom Hartvigsen for his contributions to the implementation of GRACE. We are grateful to the TMG-NUDT team for their valuable suggestions and technical support for the PMET method. We are grateful to Jia-Chen Gu from the University of California, Los Angeles, and Haiyang Yu from the Department of Cyberspace Security, University of Science for their constructive suggestions on development of EASYEDIT. We thank Yiquan Wu and Zeqing Yuan for helping the AAAI 2024 tutorial (canceled since part of speakers cannot present in person) of EasyEdit. Appreciation is also extended to all PR contributors, and issue feedback providers during the EasyEdit version iterations, especially Damien de Mijolla for proposing different optimization goals for FT, which complemented the fine-tuning baseline, and to Yuxuan Zhai for pointing out the portability metric evaluation issue of LlaMA-2-7B.

We would like to express gratitude to the anonymous reviewers for their kind comments. This work was supported by the National Natural Science Foundation of China (No. 62206246, No. NSFCU23B2055, No. NSFCU19B2027), the Fundamental Research Funds for the Central Universities (226-2023-00138), Zhejiang Provincial Natural Science Foundation of China (No. LGG22F030011), Yongjiang Talent Introduction Programme (2021A-156-G), CCF-Tencent Rhino-Bird Open Research Fund, Tencent AI Lab Rhino-Bird Focused Research Program (RBFR2024003), Information Technology Center and State Key Lab of CAD&CG, Zhejiang University.

## Ethics Statement

The significance of knowledge editing lies in its direct impact on the behavior and output results of LMs. Malicious edits may lead to the generation of responses with toxicity or bias in LMs, posing potential harm to users and society. Therefore, when applying knowledge editing techniques or utilizing this system, careful consideration must be given to potential risks and ethical concerns. All our data undergoes meticulous manual inspection, and any malicious edits or offensive content have been removed.

[7]https://github.com/kmeng01/rome

## References

Rohan Anil, Andrew M. Dai, Orhan Firat, Melvin Johnson, Dmitry Lepikhin, Alexandre Passos, Siamak Shakeri, Emanuel Taropa, Paige Bailey, Zhifeng Chen, Eric Chu, Jonathan H. Clark, Laurent El Shafey, Yanping Huang, Kathy Meier-Hellstern, Gaurav Mishra, Erica Moreira, Mark Omernick, Kevin Robinson, Sebastian Ruder, Yi Tay, Kefan Xiao, Yuanzhong Xu, Yujing Zhang, Gustavo Hernandez Abrego, Junwhan Ahn, Jacob Austin, Paul Barham, Jan Botha, James Bradbury, Siddhartha Brahma, Kevin Brooks, Michele Catasta, Yong Cheng, Colin Cherry, Christopher A. Choquette-Choo, Aakanksha Chowdhery, Clément Crepy, Shachi Dave, Mostafa Dehghani, Sunipa Dev, Jacob Devlin, Mark Díaz, Nan Du, Ethan Dyer, Vlad Feinberg, Fangxiaoyu Feng, Vlad Fienber, Markus Freitag, Xavier Garcia, Sebastian Gehrmann, Lucas Gonzalez, Guy Gur-Ari, Steven Hand, Hadi Hashemi, Le Hou, Joshua Howland, Andrea Hu, Jeffrey Hui, Jeremy Hurwitz, Michael Isard, Abe Ittycheriah, Matthew Jagielski, Wenhao Jia, Kathleen Kenealy, Maxim Krikun, Sneha Kudugunta, Chang Lan, Katherine Lee, Benjamin Lee, Eric Li, Music Li, Wei Li, YaGuang Li, Jian Li, Hyeontaek Lim, Hanzhao Lin, Zhongtao Liu, Frederick Liu, Marcello Maggioni, Aroma Mahendru, Joshua Maynez, Vedant Misra, Maysam Moussalem, Zachary Nado, John Nham, Eric Ni, Andrew Nystrom, Alicia Parrish, Marie Pellat, Martin Polacek, Alex Polozov, Reiner Pope, Siyuan Qiao, Emily Reif, Bryan Richter, Parker Riley, Alex Castro Ros, Aurko Roy, Brennan Saeta, Rajkumar Samuel, Renee Shelby, Ambrose Slone, Daniel Smilkov, David R. So, Daniel Sohn, Simon Tokumine, Dasha Valter, Vijay Vasudevan, Kiran Vodrahalli, Xuezhi Wang, Pidong Wang, Zirui Wang, Tao Wang, John Wieting, Yuhuai Wu, Kelvin Xu, Yunhan Xu, Linting Xue, Pengcheng Yin, Jiahui Yu, Qiao Zhang, Steven Zheng, Ce Zheng, Weikang Zhou, Denny Zhou, Slav Petrov, and Yonghui Wu. 2023. Palm 2 technical report.

Jinze Bai, Shuai Bai, Yunfei Chu, Zeyu Cui, Kai Dang, Xiaodong Deng, Yang Fan, Wenbin Ge, Yu Han, Fei Huang, Binyuan Hui, Luo Ji, Mei Li, Junyang Lin, Runji Lin, Dayiheng Liu, Gao Liu, Chengqiang Lu, Keming Lu, Jianxin Ma, Rui Men, Xingzhang Ren, Xuancheng Ren, Chuanqi Tan, Sinan Tan, Jianhong Tu, Peng Wang, Shijie Wang, Wei Wang, Shengguang Wu, Benfeng Xu, Jin Xu, An Yang, Hao Yang, Jian Yang, Shusheng Yang, Yang Yao, Bowen Yu, Hongyi Yuan, Zheng Yuan, Jianwei Zhang, Xingxuan Zhang, Yichang Zhang, Zhenru Zhang, Chang

Zhou, Jingren Zhou, Xiaohuan Zhou, and Tianhang Zhu. 2023. Qwen technical report.

Sid Black, Leo Gao, Phil Wang, Connor Leahy, and Stella Biderman. 2021. GPT-Neo: Large Scale Autoregressive Language Modeling with Mesh-Tensorflow. If you use this software, please cite it using these metadata.

Sebastian Borgeaud, Arthur Mensch, Jordan Hoffmann, Trevor Cai, Eliza Rutherford, Katie Millican, George Bm Van Den Driessche, Jean-Baptiste Lespiau, Bogdan Damoc, Aidan Clark, et al. 2022. Improving language models by retrieving from trillions of tokens. In *International conference on machine learning*, pages 2206–2240. PMLR.

Tom B. Brown, Benjamin Mann, Nick Ryder, Melanie Subbiah, Jared Kaplan, Prafulla Dhariwal, Arvind Neelakantan, Pranav Shyam, Girish Sastry, Amanda Askell, Sandhini Agarwal, Ariel Herbert-Voss, Gretchen Krueger, Tom Henighan, Rewon Child, Aditya Ramesh, Daniel M. Ziegler, Jeffrey Wu, Clemens Winter, Christopher Hesse, Mark Chen, Eric Sigler, Mateusz Litwin, Scott Gray, Benjamin Chess, Jack Clark, Christopher Berner, Sam McCandlish, Alec Radford, Ilya Sutskever, and Dario Amodei. 2020. Language models are few-shot learners.

Nicola De Cao, Wilker Aziz, and Ivan Titov. 2021. Editing factual knowledge in language models.

Xiang Chen, Ningyu Zhang, Xin Xie, Shumin Deng, Yunzhi Yao, Chuanqi Tan, Fei Huang, Luo Si, and Huajun Chen. 2022. KnowPrompt: Knowledge-aware prompt-tuning with synergistic optimization for relation extraction. In *Proceedings of the ACM Web Conference 2022*. ACM.

Roi Cohen, Eden Biran, Ori Yoran, Amir Globerson, and Mor Geva. 2023a. Evaluating the ripple effects of knowledge editing in language models. *CoRR*, abs/2307.12976.

Roi Cohen, Eden Biran, Ori Yoran, Amir Globerson, and Mor Geva. 2023b. Evaluating the ripple effects of knowledge editing in language models.

Damai Dai, Li Dong, Yaru Hao, Zhifang Sui, and Furu Wei. 2021. Knowledge neurons in pretrained transformers. *CoRR*, abs/2104.08696.

Ning Ding, Yujia Qin, Guang Yang, Fuchao Wei, Zonghan Yang, Yusheng Su, Shengding Hu, Yulin Chen, Chi-Min Chan, Weize Chen, Jing Yi, Weilin Zhao, Xiaozhi Wang, Zhiyuan Liu, Hai-Tao Zheng, Jianfei Chen, Yang Liu, Jie Tang, Juanzi Li, and Maosong Sun. 2022. Delta tuning: A comprehensive study of parameter efficient methods for pre-trained language models.

Ning Ding, Yujia Qin, Guang Yang, Fuchao Wei, Zonghan Yang, Yusheng Su, Shengding Hu, Yulin Chen, Chi-Min Chan, Weize Chen, et al. 2023. Parameter-efficient fine-tuning of large-scale pre-trained language models. *Nature Machine Intelligence*, 5(3):220–235.

Qingxiu Dong, Lei Li, Damai Dai, Ce Zheng, Zhiyong Wu, Baobao Chang, Xu Sun, Jingjing Xu, and Zhifang Sui. 2022. A survey for in-context learning. *arXiv preprint arXiv:2301.00234*.

Mor Geva, Jasmijn Bastings, Katja Filippova, and Amir Globerson. 2023. Dissecting recall of factual associations in auto-regressive language models. *CoRR*, abs/2304.14767.

Mor Geva, Avi Caciularu, Kevin Wang, and Yoav Goldberg. 2022. Transformer feed-forward layers build predictions by promoting concepts in the vocabulary space. In *Proceedings of the 2022 Conference on Empirical Methods in Natural Language Processing*, pages 30–45, Abu Dhabi, United Arab Emirates. Association for Computational Linguistics.

Mor Geva, Roei Schuster, Jonathan Berant, and Omer Levy. 2021. Transformer feed-forward layers are key-value memories. In *Proceedings of the 2021 Conference on Empirical Methods in Natural Language Processing*, pages 5484–5495, Online and Punta Cana, Dominican Republic. Association for Computational Linguistics.

Anshita Gupta, Debanjan Mondal, Akshay Krishna Sheshadri, Wenlong Zhao, Xiang Lorraine Li, Sarah Wiegreffe, and Niket Tandon. 2023. Editing commonsense knowledge in GPT. *CoRR*, abs/2305.14956.

Kelvin Guu, Kenton Lee, Zora Tung, Panupong Pasupat, and Mingwei Chang. 2020. Retrieval augmented language model pre-training. In *International conference on machine learning*, pages 3929–3938. PMLR.

Thomas Hartvigsen, Saadia Gabriel, Hamid Palangi, Maarten Sap, Dipankar Ray, and Ece Kamar. 2022. ToxiGen: A large-scale machine-generated dataset for adversarial and implicit hate speech detection. In *Proceedings of the 60th Annual Meeting of the Association for Computational Linguistics (Volume 1: Long Papers)*, pages 3309–3326, Dublin, Ireland. Association for Computational Linguistics.

Thomas Hartvigsen, Swami Sankaranarayanan, Hamid Palangi, Yoon Kim, and Marzyeh Ghassemi. 2023. Aging with grace: Lifelong model editing with discrete key-value adaptors.

Peter Hase, Mohit Bansal, Been Kim, and Asma Ghandeharioun. 2023. Does localization inform editing? surprising differences in causality-based localization vs. knowledge editing in language models. *CoRR*, abs/2301.04213.

Evan Hernandez, Belinda Z. Li, and Jacob Andreas. 2023. Inspecting and editing knowledge representations in language models.

Edward J. Hu, Yelong Shen, Phillip Wallis, Zeyuan Allen-Zhu, Yuanzhi Li, Shean Wang, Lu Wang, and Weizhu Chen. 2021. Lora: Low-rank adaptation of large language models.

Zeyu Huang, Yikang Shen, Xiaofeng Zhang, Jie Zhou, Wenge Rong, and Zhang Xiong. 2023. Transformer-patcher: One mistake worth one neuron.

Ziwei Ji, Nayeon Lee, Rita Frieske, Tiezheng Yu, Dan Su, Yan Xu, Etsuko Ishii, Ye Jin Bang, Andrea Madotto, and Pascale Fung. 2023. Survey of hallucination in natural language generation. *ACM Computing Surveys*, 55(12):1–38.

Albert Q. Jiang, Alexandre Sablayrolles, Arthur Mensch, Chris Bamford, Devendra Singh Chaplot, Diego de las Casas, Florian Bressand, Gianna Lengyel, Guillaume Lample, Lucile Saulnier, Lélio Renard Lavaud, Marie-Anne Lachaux, Pierre Stock, Teven Le Scao, Thibaut Lavril, Thomas Wang, Timothée Lacroix, and William El Sayed. 2023. Mistral 7b.

Zhengbao Jiang, Frank F. Xu, Jun Araki, and Graham Neubig. 2020. How can we know what language models know? *Transactions of the Association for Computational Linguistics*, 8:423–438.

Jean Kaddour, Joshua Harris, Maximilian Mozes, Herbie Bradley, Roberta Raileanu, and Robert McHardy. 2023. Challenges and applications of large language models. *CoRR*, abs/2307.10169.

Yoonho Lee, Annie S. Chen, Fahim Tajwar, Ananya Kumar, Huaxiu Yao, Percy Liang, and Chelsea Finn. 2023. Surgical fine-tuning improves adaptation to distribution shifts.

Omer Levy, Minjoon Seo, Eunsol Choi, and Luke Zettlemoyer. 2017. Zero-shot relation extraction via reading comprehension. In *Proceedings of the 21st Conference on Computational Natural Language Learning (CoNLL 2017)*, pages 333–342, Vancouver, Canada. Association for Computational Linguistics.

Patrick Lewis, Ethan Perez, Aleksandra Piktus, Fabio Petroni, Vladimir Karpukhin, Naman Goyal, Heinrich Küttler, Mike Lewis, Wen-tau Yih, Tim Rocktäschel, et al. 2020. Retrieval-augmented generation for knowledge-intensive nlp tasks. *Advances in Neural Information Processing Systems*, 33:9459–9474.

Patrick Lewis, Ethan Perez, Aleksandra Piktus, Fabio Petroni, Vladimir Karpukhin, Naman Goyal, Heinrich Küttler, Mike Lewis, Wen tau Yih, Tim Rocktäschel, Sebastian Riedel, and Douwe Kiela. 2021. Retrieval-augmented generation for knowledge-intensive nlp tasks.

Xiaopeng Li, Shasha Li, Shezheng Song, Jing Yang, Jun Ma, and Jie Yu. 2024. Pmet: Precise model editing in a transformer.

Nelson F Liu, Kevin Lin, John Hewitt, Ashwin Paranjape, Michele Bevilacqua, Fabio Petroni, and Percy Liang. 2023a. Lost in the middle: How language models use long contexts. *arXiv preprint arXiv:2307.03172*.

Tian Yu Liu, Matthew Trager, Alessandro Achille, Pramuditha Perera, Luca Zancato, and Stefano Soatto. 2023b. Meaning representations from trajectories in autoregressive models.

Kevin Meng, David Bau, Alex Andonian, and Yonatan Belinkov. 2023. Locating and editing factual associations in gpt.

Kevin Meng, Arnab Sen Sharma, Alex Andonian, Yonatan Belinkov, and David Bau. 2022. Mass-editing memory in a transformer.

Eric Mitchell, Charles Lin, Antoine Bosselut, Chelsea Finn, and Christopher D. Manning. 2022a. Fast model editing at scale.

Eric Mitchell, Charles Lin, Antoine Bosselut, Christopher D. Manning, and Chelsea Finn. 2022b. Memory-based model editing at scale.

OpenAI. 2023. Gpt-4 technical report.

Shirui Pan, Linhao Luo, Yufei Wang, Chen Chen, Jiapu Wang, and Xindong Wu. 2023. Unifying large language models and knowledge graphs: A roadmap. *CoRR*, abs/2306.08302.

Adam Paszke, Sam Gross, Francisco Massa, Adam Lerer, James Bradbury, Gregory Chanan, Trevor Killeen, Zeming Lin, Natalia Gimelshein, Luca Antiga, Alban Desmaison, Andreas Köpf, Edward Yang, Zach DeVito, Martin Raison, Alykhan Tejani, Sasank Chilamkurthy, Benoit Steiner, Lu Fang, Junjie Bai, and Soumith Chintala. 2019. Pytorch: An imperative style, high-performance deep learning library.

Fabio Petroni, Tim Rocktäschel, Sebastian Riedel, Patrick Lewis, Anton Bakhtin, Yuxiang Wu, and Alexander Miller. 2019. Language models as knowledge bases? In *Proceedings of the 2019 Conference on Empirical Methods in Natural Language Processing and the 9th International Joint Conference on Natural Language Processing (EMNLP-IJCNLP)*, pages 2463–2473, Hong Kong, China. Association for Computational Linguistics.

Shuofei Qiao, Yixin Ou, Ningyu Zhang, Xiang Chen, Yunzhi Yao, Shumin Deng, Chuanqi Tan, Fei Huang, and Huajun Chen. 2023. Reasoning with language model prompting: A survey. In *Proceedings of the 61st Annual Meeting of the Association for Computational Linguistics (Volume 1: Long Papers)*, pages 5368–5393, Toronto, Canada. Association for Computational Linguistics.

Alec Radford, Jeffrey Wu, Rewon Child, David Luan, Dario Amodei, Ilya Sutskever, et al. 2019. Language models are unsupervised multitask learners. *OpenAI blog*, 1(8):9.

Colin Raffel, Noam Shazeer, Adam Roberts, Katherine Lee, Sharan Narang, Michael Matena, Yanqi Zhou, Wei Li, and Peter J. Liu. 2019. Exploring the limits of transfer learning with a unified text-to-text transformer. *CoRR*, abs/1910.10683.

Vinay Venkatesh Ramasesh, Aitor Lewkowycz, and Ethan Dyer. 2022. Effect of scale on catastrophic forgetting in neural networks. In *International Conference on Learning Representations*.

Ruiyang Ren, Yuhao Wang, Yingqi Qu, Wayne Xin Zhao, Jing Liu, Hao Tian, Hua Wu, Ji-Rong Wen, and Haifeng Wang. 2023. Investigating the factual knowledge boundary of large language models with retrieval augmentation. *arXiv preprint arXiv:2307.11019*.

Adam Roberts, Colin Raffel, and Noam Shazeer. 2020. How much knowledge can you pack into the parameters of a language model? In *Proceedings of the 2020 Conference on Empirical Methods in Natural Language Processing (EMNLP)*, pages 5418–5426, Online. Association for Computational Linguistics.

Chenmien Tan, Ge Zhang, and Jie Fu. 2024. Massive editing for large language models via meta learning.

Hugo Touvron, Thibaut Lavril, Gautier Izacard, Xavier Martinet, Marie-Anne Lachaux, Timothée Lacroix, Baptiste Rozière, Naman Goyal, Eric Hambro, Faisal Azhar, Aurelien Rodriguez, Armand Joulin, Edouard Grave, and Guillaume Lample. 2023a. Llama: Open and efficient foundation language models.

Hugo Touvron, Louis Martin, Kevin Stone, Peter Albert, Amjad Almahairi, Yasmine Babaei, Nikolay Bashlykov, Soumya Batra, Prajjwal Bhargava, Shruti Bhosale, Dan Bikel, Lukas Blecher, Cristian Canton Ferrer, Moya Chen, Guillem Cucurull, David Esiobu, Jude Fernandes, Jeremy Fu, Wenyin Fu, Brian Fuller, Cynthia Gao, Vedanuj Goswami, Naman Goyal, Anthony Hartshorn, Saghar Hosseini, Rui Hou, Hakan Inan, Marcin Kardas, Viktor Kerkez, Madian Khabsa, Isabel Kloumann, Artem Korenev, Punit Singh Koura, Marie-Anne Lachaux, Thibaut Lavril, Jenya Lee, Diana Liskovich, Yinghai Lu, Yuning Mao, Xavier Martinet, Todor Mihaylov, Pushkar Mishra, Igor Molybog, Yixin Nie, Andrew Poulton, Jeremy Reizenstein, Rashi Rungta, Kalyan Saladi, Alan Schelten, Ruan Silva, Eric Michael Smith, Ranjan Subramanian, Xiaoqing Ellen Tan, Binh Tang, Ross Taylor, Adina Williams, Jian Xiang Kuan, Puxin Xu, Zheng Yan, Iliyan Zarov, Yuchen Zhang, Angela Fan, Melanie Kambadur, Sharan Narang, Aurelien Rodriguez, Robert Stojnic, Sergey Edunov, and Thomas Scialom. 2023b. Llama 2: Open foundation and fine-tuned chat models.

Ben Wang and Aran Komatsuzaki. 2021. GPT-J-6B: A 6 Billion Parameter Autoregressive Language Model. `https://github.com/kingoflolz/mesh-transformer-jax`.

Thomas Wolf, Lysandre Debut, Victor Sanh, Julien Chaumond, Clement Delangue, Anthony Moi, Pierric Cistac, Tim Rault, Rémi Louf, Morgan Funtowicz, Joe Davison, Sam Shleifer, Patrick von Platen, Clara Ma, Yacine Jernite, Julien Plu, Canwen Xu, Teven Le Scao, Sylvain Gugger, Mariama Drame, Quentin Lhoest, and Alexander M. Rush. 2020. Huggingface's transformers: State-of-the-art natural language processing.

Tianxing Wu, Xudong Cao, Yipeng Zhu, Feiyue Wu, Tianling Gong, Yuxiang Wang, and Shenqi Jing. 2023. Asdkb: A chinese knowledge base for the early screening and diagnosis of autism spectrum disorder.

Tianxing Wu, Haofen Wang, Cheng Li, Guilin Qi, Xing Niu, Meng Wang, Lin Li, and Chaomin Shi. 2020. Knowledge graph construction from multiple online encyclopedias. *World Wide Web*, 23:2671–2698.

Yunzhi Yao, Peng Wang, Bozhong Tian, Siyuan Cheng, Zhoubo Li, Shumin Deng, Huajun Chen, and Ningyu Zhang. 2023. Editing large language models: Problems, methods, and opportunities.

Lang Yu, Qin Chen, Jie Zhou, and Liang He. 2023. Melo: Enhancing model editing with neuron-indexed dynamic lora.

Wenhao Yu, Chenguang Zhu, Zhihan Zhang, Shuohang Wang, Zhuosheng Zhang, Yuwei Fang, and Meng Jiang. 2022. Retrieval augmentation for commonsense reasoning: A unified approach. In *Proceedings of the 2022 Conference on Empirical Methods in Natural Language Processing, EMNLP 2022, Abu Dhabi, United Arab Emirates, December 7-11, 2022*, pages 4364–4377. Association for Computational Linguistics.

Ningyu Zhang, Xin Xie, Xiang Chen, Shumin Deng, Hongbin Ye, and Huajun Chen. 2022. Knowledge collaborative fine-tuning for low-resource knowledge graph completion. *Journal of Software*, 33(10):3531–3545.

Yizhe Zhang, Michel Galley, Jianfeng Gao, Zhe Gan, Xiujun Li, Chris Brockett, and Bill Dolan. 2018. Generating informative and diverse conversational responses via adversarial information maximization.

Wayne Xin Zhao, Kun Zhou, Junyi Li, Tianyi Tang, Xiaolei Wang, Yupeng Hou, Yingqian Min, Beichen Zhang, Junjie Zhang, Zican Dong, Yifan Du, Chen Yang, Yushuo Chen, Zhipeng Chen, Jinhao Jiang, Ruiyang Ren, Yifan Li, Xinyu Tang, Zikang Liu, Peiyu Liu, Jian-Yun Nie, and Ji-Rong Wen. 2023. A survey of large language models.

Zihao Zhao, Eric Wallace, Shi Feng, Dan Klein, and Sameer Singh. 2021. Calibrate before use: Improving few-shot performance of language models. In *Proceedings of the 38th International Conference on Machine Learning*, volume 139 of *Proceedings of Machine Learning Research*, pages 12697–12706. PMLR.

Ce Zheng, Lei Li, Qingxiu Dong, Yuxuan Fan, Zhiyong Wu, Jingjing Xu, and Baobao Chang. 2023a. Can we edit factual knowledge by in-context learning?

Rui Zheng, Shihan Dou, Songyang Gao, Yuan Hua, Wei Shen, Binghai Wang, Yan Liu, Senjie Jin, Qin Liu, Yuhao Zhou, Limao Xiong, Lu Chen, Zhiheng Xi, Nuo Xu, Wenbin Lai, Minghao Zhu, Cheng Chang, Zhangyue Yin, Rongxiang Weng, Wensen Cheng, Haoran Huang, Tianxiang Sun, Hang Yan, Tao Gui, Qi Zhang, Xipeng Qiu, and Xuanjing Huang. 2023b. Secrets of RLHF in large language models part I: PPO. *CoRR*, abs/2307.04964.

## A Preliminaries of Model Editing

The task of knowledge editing is to effectively modify the initial base model $f_\theta$ to the edited model $f_{\theta'}$, with corresponding parameter adjustments for a specific input-output pair $(x_e, y_e)$, where $x_e \in \mathcal{X}_e$ and $f_\theta(x_e) \neq y_e$. Here, $\mathcal{X}_e$ represents the entire set to be edited. Therefore, the current problem formulation for knowledge editing can be broadly categorized into three types:

1. **Single Instance Editing**: Evaluating the performance of the model after a single edit. The model reloads the original weights after a single edit:

$$\theta' \leftarrow \arg\min_\theta(\|f_\theta(x_e) - y_e\|) \quad (1)$$

2. **Batch Instance Editing**: Simultaneously modifying $N$ knowledge instances (where $N \ll |\mathcal{X}_e|$) and evaluating the performance of the edited model after processing a batch. The model reloads the original weights after processing a batch of edits:

$$\theta' \leftarrow \arg\min_\theta \sum_{e=1}^{N}(\|f_\theta(x_e) - y_e\|) \quad (2)$$

3. **Sequential Editing**: This approach requires sequentially editing each knowledge instance, and evaluation must be performed after all knowledge updates have been applied:

$$\theta' \leftarrow \arg\min_\theta \sum_{e=1}^{|\mathcal{X}_e|}(\|f_\theta(x_e) - y_e\|) \quad (3)$$

## B Default Hparams Settings

EASYEDIT provides optimal hyperparameters for various editing methods. In addition to common parameters such as learning rate, steps, and regularization coefficients, the location of layers for editing can also be considered as hyperparameters, significantly influencing the robustness of the editing process. The following tables demonstrate the default location settings in EASYEDIT (using **Llama-2-7B** as an example).

| Layer with Value Loss |
|---|
| `model.layers.31` |
| **Target Layer for Updating Weights** |
| `model.layers.5.mlp.down_proj` |

Table 3: Default Target Modules in **ROME**

| Layer with Value Loss |
|---|
| `model.layers.31` |
| **Target Layer for Updating Weights** |
| `model.layers.4.mlp.down_proj` |
| `model.layers.5.mlp.down_proj` |
| `model.layers.6.mlp.down_proj` |
| `model.layers.7.mlp.down_proj` |
| `model.layers.8.mlp.down_proj` |

Table 4: Default Target Modules in **MEMIT** and **PMET**

**ROME** We follow Meng et al. (2023) in utilizing causal mediation analysis to identify an intermediate layer in the model responsible for recalling facts. The causal traces reveal an early site (5th layer) with causal states concentrated at the last token of the subject, indicating a significant role for MLP states at that specific layer (Table 3).

**MEMIT** Following Meng et al. (2022), we quantify the average indirect causal effect of MLP modules. The results demonstrate a concentration of intermediate states in LLaMA. The disparity in the effects between MLP severed and hidden states severed becomes significantly reduced after the 8th layer. We choose the entire critical range of MLP layers, denoted as $\mathcal{R} = \{4, 5, 6, 7, 8\}$ (Table 4).

**PMET** PMET (Li et al., 2024) adopts the localization strategy from MEMIT, designating the corresponding layer as the modification target. Building upon the update of MLP weights, PMET focuses on multi-head self-attention (MHSA), further substantiating the discovery that MHSA encodes specific patterns for general knowledge extraction. (Table 4).

**MEND** In the context of meta-learning for editing, it is commonly observed that editing MLP layers yields better performance than editing attention

| CodeBook Target Modules |
|---|
| model.layers[27].mlp.down_proj.weight |

Table 5: Default Target Modules in **GRACE**

| Target Layer for Updating Weights |
|---|
| model.layers.29.mlp.gate_proj.weight |
| model.layers.29.mlp.up_proj.weight |
| model.layers.29.mlp.down_proj.weight |
| model.layers.30.mlp.gate_proj.weight |
| model.layers.30.mlp.up_proj.weight |
| model.layers.30.mlp.down_proj.weight |
| model.layers.31.mlp.gate_proj.weight |
| model.layers.31.mlp.up_proj.weight |
| model.layers.31.mlp.down_proj.weight |

Table 6: Default Target Modules in **MEND**

layers. Typically, MLP weights of the last 3 transformer blocks (totaling 6 weight matrices) are chosen for editing (Mitchell et al., 2022a). EASYEDIT adheres to this default configuration (Table 6).

**GRACE** Recent studies have revealed the impact of selecting the right layers for fine-tuning (Lee et al., 2023). Similarly, in GRACE (Hartvigsen et al., 2023), we conduct pilot experiments, retaining layers with consistently high edit success rates (Table 5).

# EasyInstruct: An Easy-to-use Instruction Processing Framework for Large Language Models

Yixin Ou♠, Ningyu Zhang♠*, Honghao Gui♠, Ziwen Xu♠,
Shuofei Qiao♠, Yida Xue♠, Runnan Fang♠, Kangwei Liu♠,
Lei Li♠, Zhen Bi♠, Guozhou Zheng♠, Huajun Chen♠*
♠ Zhejiang University
{ouyixin,zhangningyu,huajunsir}@zju.edu.cn
https://zjunlp.github.io/project/EasyInstruct

## Abstract

In recent years, instruction tuning has gained increasing attention and emerged as a crucial technique to enhance the capabilities of Large Language Models (LLMs). To construct high-quality instruction datasets, many instruction processing approaches have been proposed, aiming to achieve a delicate balance between data quantity and data quality. Nevertheless, due to inconsistencies that persist among various instruction processing methods, there is no standard open-source instruction processing implementation framework available for the community, which hinders practitioners from further developing and advancing. To facilitate instruction processing research and development, we present EasyInstruct[1], an easy-to-use instruction processing framework for LLMs, which modularizes instruction generation, selection, and prompting, while also considering their combination and interaction. EasyInstruct is publicly released and actively maintained at https://github.com/zjunlp/EasyInstruct, along with an online demo app[2] and a demo video[3] for quick-start, calling for broader research centered on instruction data and synthetic data.

## 1 Introduction

Large Language Models (LLMs) have brought about a revolutionary transformation in the field of Natural Language Processing (NLP), leading to substantial improvement in performance across various tasks (Brown et al., 2020; OpenAI, 2023; Anil et al., 2023; Touvron et al., 2023b; Zhao et al., 2023; Chen et al., 2022; Qiao et al., 2023; Chen, 2023). To optimize the performance of LLMs in specific tasks or domains, it is crucial to adapt their outputs to specific contexts or instructions. Recent studies (Wei et al., 2022; Ouyang et al., 2022; Chung et al., 2022) have proposed instruction tuning methods for fine-tuning LLMs, which is a prominent research area aimed at optimizing the LLMs' behavior by providing explicit instructions during training, enabling better control and alignment with user preferences and desired outputs. Instruction dataset construction, which is also referred to as data engineering or management, poses a significant challenge in the process of instruction tuning (Zhao et al., 2023; Zhang et al., 2023; Wang et al., 2023c,d).

Substantial efforts have been dedicated to the task of construction instruction data through human annotations (Wang et al., 2022; Köpf et al., 2023), requiring a significant allocation of resources. Against this backdrop, LLMs are utilized to synthesize large-scale instruction data automatically (Wang et al., 2023b; Xu et al., 2023; Li et al., 2023b). These methods could scale up the size of instruction-following data, but they still inevitably suffer limited diversity and complexity, resulting in an unbalanced distribution and poor quality of instruction data. Recent studies (Zhou et al., 2023; Chen et al., 2023a; Xu et al., 2023) have unveiled a seminal revelation, indicating that even a small quantity of high-quality instruction data has the potential to yield robust performance. In general, instruction processing is an important process requiring careful attention to detail and rigorous quality assurance procedures to construct a high-quality instruction dataset for LLMs.

Unfortunately, the availability of open-source tools for instruction processing remains limited, especially in comparison to many open-source projects on models and training infrastructures (Touvron et al., 2023a,b; Taori et al., 2023; Scao et al., 2022; Chiang et al., 2023; Zeng

* Corresponding Author.

[1]This is a subprobject of KnowLM (https://github.com/zjunlp/KnowLM), which facilitates knowledgeable LLM Framework with EasyInstruct, EasyEdit (Wang et al., 2023a; Yao et al., 2023; Zhang et al., 2024), EasyDetect etc.

[2]https://huggingface.co/spaces/zjunlp/EasyInstruct

[3]https://youtu.be/rfQOWYfziFo



*Proceedings of the 62nd Annual Meeting of the Association for Computational Linguistics (Volume 3: System Demonstrations)*, pages 94–106
August 11-16, 2024 ©2024 Association for Computational Linguistics

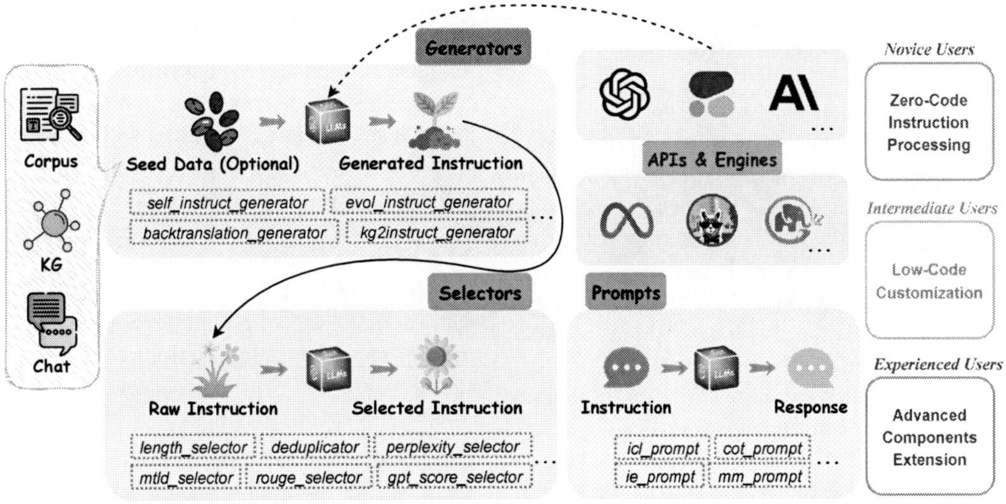


Figure 1: Overview of EasyInstruct. The `APIs & Engines` module standardizes the instruction execution process, enabling the execution of instruction prompts on the LLM API services or locally deployed LLMs. The `Generators` module streamlines the instruction generation process, enabling automated generation of instruction data based on **chat data, corpus, or Knowledge Graphs**. The `Selectors` module standardizes the instruction selection process, which enables the extraction of high-quality instruction datasets from raw, unprocessed instruction data. The `Prompts` module standardizes the instruction prompting process.

et al., 2023). Existing projects are often highly-customized to their own needs, lacking a systematized and modular processing ability to address diverse processing pipelines for LLMs. For instance, the Alpaca (Taori et al., 2023) dataset targets the augmentation of diversity for LLaMA tuning, whereas AlpaGasus (Chen et al., 2023a) focuses on filtering out low-quality instances from Alpaca. Thorough development of instruction processing systems for the ever-evolving and emerging requirements of LLM remains unexplored, particularly in light of the quick expansion of inventive LLM applications spanning various fields.

To address this issue, we develop EasyInstruct as depicted in Figure 1, an easy-to-use instruction processing framework for LLMs. Given some existing **chat data, corpus, or Knowledge Graphs**, EasyInstruct can handle instruction generation, selection, and prompting processes, while also considering their combination and interaction. These consistencies facilitate further development and comparisons of various methods, thus promoting the advancement of better instruction processing work. We further conduct experiments with EasyInstruct to validate its effectiveness in instruction processing. Currently, EasyInstuct is open-sourced on GitHub and has already received over 300 stars. We are committed to the long-term maintenance of EasyInstruct, providing continuous support for new features to ensure its effectiveness as a framework for instruction processing and synthetic data generation (Bauer et al., 2024).

## 2 Background

LLMs typically undergo two stages of training: pretraining and fine-tuning (Zhao et al., 2023). Despite the fact that large-scale pretraining is the key of the model's proficiency in generating natural language responses, these pre-trained models can still struggle with comprehending human instructions accurately. To bridge the gap between the training objectives and human objectives, instruction tuning is introduced as a potent strategy to amplify the controllability and capabilities and of LLMs in interpreting and responding to instructions (Wei et al., 2022; Ouyang et al., 2022; Chung et al., 2022; Wang et al., 2023b; Zhang et al., 2023; Lou et al., 2023). Concretely, instruction tuning involves the method of refining pre-trained LLMs through supervised learning, utilizing examples structured as (INSTRUCTION, INPUT, OUTPUT). In this format, INSTRUCTION represents the human-given directive that outlines the task, INPUT optionally offers additional context, and OUTPUT signifies the expected outcome in alignment with the INSTRUCTION and any given INPUT.

Despite the effectiveness of instruction tuning, constructing high-quality large-scale instructions which effectively encompass the target behaviors remains a non-trivial challenge in this realm. Existing instruction datasets are often limited in terms of diversity, quantity, and creativity, which underscores the significance of instruction processing. One typical method for constructing instruction datasets is data integration. In this method, instructional datasets are constructed by merging existing annotated datasets with descriptions of tasks in natural language (Longpre et al., 2023; Sanh et al., 2022; Anand et al., 2023). Another prevalent method for constructing instruction datasets is automated generation. To alleviate the need for extensive human annotation or manual data gathering, automated methods have been proposed to generate large volumes of instructional data through the use of LLMs. Instructions can be sourced from chat data (Chiang et al., 2023) or expanded on a small set of seed instructions using LLMs (Wang et al., 2023b; Xu et al., 2023; Li et al., 2023b). Subsequently, the collected instructions are fed into LLMs to generate corresponding inputs and outputs. In EasyInstruct, our primary focus lies on automated approaches for instruction generation due to their high efficiency and scalability.

Another promising research direction of instruction processing is the selection of high-quality instruction. Recently, numerous studies (Zhou et al., 2023; Chen et al., 2023a; Xu et al., 2023; Liu et al., 2023) have investigated the issue of the scale of the instruction dataset for fine-tuning and have indicated that merely increasing the number of instructions may not necessarily result in enhancements. Instead, a modest volume of high-quality instruction data can influence the fine-tuning of LLMs, yielding solid performance. Thus, optimizing the instruction dataset and enhancing its quality play a critical role in fine-tuning LLMs effectively.

From a practical implementation point of view, instruction processing is actually complex and requires meticulous consideration. In this paper, we present **EasyInstruct**, an easy-to-use framework to effectively and efficiently implement instruction processing approaches including instruction generation, selection, and prompting. Through this framework, EasyInstruct can help users to quickly comprehend and apply the existing instruction processing methods implemented in the package.

## 3 Design and Implementation

As illustrated in Figure 1, EasyInstruct provides a complete instruction processing procedure built on PyTorch and Huggingface. In this section, we first introduce the design principles, and then detail the implementation of the major modules.

### 3.1 Design Principles

The framework is designed to cater to users with varying levels of expertise, providing a user-friendly experience ranging from code-free execution to low-code customization and advanced components extension options:

**Zero-Code Instruction Processing.** Novice users, who do not require coding knowledge, can leverage pre-defined configuration files and shell scripts to accomplish code-free instruction processing. By running these scripts, they can complete instruction processing tasks without the need for coding skills. Example configuration files and shell scripts are shown in Appendix A.2.1.

**Low-Code Customization.** Intermediate users have the option to customize various process inputs and outputs using a low-code approach. This allows them to have more control over the different stages within the framework. A running example is shown in Figure 2.

**Advanced Components Extension.** Experienced users can easily extend our components based on their specific scenarios and requirements. To customize their classes, users can inherit the base classes of modules and override the necessary methods as per their requirements. This flexibility enables them to implement their functional components, tailored to their unique needs.

### 3.2 APIs & Engines

The `APIs` modules integrate with mainstream LLMs, including API services provided by companies such as OpenAI[4], Anthropic[5], and Cohere[6]. This integration facilitates the seamless invocation of various relevant steps within the framework. We list a range of API service providers and their corresponding LLM products that are currently available in EasyInstruct in Appendix A.5. The `Engines` module standardizes the instruction execution process, which enables the execution of

[4]`https://platform.openai.com/docs`

[5]`https://docs.anthropic.com/claude/docs`

[6]`https://docs.cohere.com/docs`

instruction prompts on several open-source LLMs such as LLaMA (Touvron et al., 2023a,b) and ChatGLM (Du et al., 2022; Zeng et al., 2023).

### 3.3 Generators

The `Generators` module streamlines the process of instruction generation, enabling automated generation of instruction data based on seed data, where seed data can be sourced from either chat data, corpus, or Knowledge Graphs. As listed in Table 1, the instruction generation methods implemented in `Generators` are categorized into three groups, based on their respective seed data sources.

**Chat Data.** Early work (Wang et al., 2023b) randomly samples a few instructions from a human-annotated seed tasks pool as demonstrations and then, prompts an LLM to generate more instructions and corresponding input-output pairs. Due to its adaptability, *Self-Instruct* remains the prevailing preference among automated instruction generation methods. Similarly, starting with an initial set of instructions, *Evol-Instruct* (Xu et al., 2023) incrementally upgrades them into more complex instructions by prompting an LLM with specific prompts. In contrast to the *Self-Instruct* generation approach, *Evol-Instruct* allows for the adjustment of the difficulty and intricacy of the instructions it produces.

**Corpus.** Given an unannotated corpus, *Instruction Backtranslation* (Li et al., 2023b) creates an instruction following training instance by predicting an instruction that would be correctly answered by a paragraph in the document or corpus. Considering the mixed quality of human-written web text and the presence of noise in generated content, only the highest quality instances are reserved.

**Knowledge Graphs.** Incorporating existing knowledge graphs, *KG2Instruct* (Gui et al., 2023) generates Information Extraction (IE) instruction datasets. To enhance the generalizability of instructions, a random sampling approach is utilized based on human-crafted instruction templates.

EasyInstruct has implemented the existing methods above to facilitate future research and systematic comparison of automated generation of instruction data. Furthermore, the flexibility of the `Generators` module allows practitioners to select the appropriate generator and make further modification that best suits their specific needs. A running example of using a `Generator` class in EasyInstruct is shown in Figure 2.

```
from easyinstruct import SelfInstructGenerator
from easyinstruct import GPTScoreSelector
from easyinstruct.utils.api import set_openai_key

# Step1: Set your own API-KEY
set_openai_key("YOUR-KEY")

# Step2: Declare a generator class
generator = SelfInstructGenerator(
    data_format = "alpaca",
    seed_tasks_path = "seed_tasks.jsonl",
    generated_instances_path = "generation.jsonl",
    num_instructions_to_generate=100,
    engine = "gpt-3.5-turbo",
)

# Step3: Generate self-instruct data
generator.generate()

# Step4: Declare a selector class
selector = GPTScoreSelector(
    source_file_path = "generation.jsonl",
    engine = "gpt-3.5-turbo",
    threshold = 4,
)

# Step5: Process raw data
selector.process()
```

Figure 2: A running example of instruction generation and selection in **EasyInstruct**.

### 3.4 Selectors

The `Selectors` module is designed to streamline the process of filtering instructions, enabling the curation of instruction datasets from raw instruction data. This raw data might originate from publicly accessible instruction datasets or be synthesised in advence by the `Generators` module. Table 1 provides a comprehensive overview of various metrics for instruction quality evaluation. We divide the evaluation metrics into four categories based on the principle of their implementation: statistics-based, n-gram-based, structure-based and LM-based. All `Selector` classes derive from a common base class, `BaseSelector`. It includes fundamental attributes and abstract methods such as loading, processing, and dumping of data. In EasyInstruct, multiple `Selectors` can be grouped for convenient usage, which allows users to achieve more concise and readable code. A running example of using a `Selector` class is shown in Figure 2.

### 3.5 Prompts

The `Prompts` module standardizes the instruction prompting step, in which user requests are constructed as instruction prompts and sent to specific LLMs to obtain responses. Utilizing the `Prompts` module with a series of well-designed and refined prompts enhances the ability of `Generators` and `Selectors` to effectively fulfill their respective functions. Similar to `Selectors`, all

| Modules | Methods | Seed | Description |
|---|---|---|---|
| Generators | Self-Instruct | Chat | The method that randomly samples a few instructions as demonstrations and generates more instructions and input-output pairs using LLM (Wang et al., 2023b). |
| | Evol-Instruct | Chat | The method that incrementally upgrades an initial set of instructions into more complex instructions by prompting an LLM with specific prompts (Xu et al., 2023). |
| | Backtranslation | Corpus | The method that creates a training instance by predicting an instruction that would be correctly answered by a paragraph in the corpus (Li et al., 2023b). |
| | KG2Instruct | KG | The method that generates Information Extraction (IE) instruction datasets incorporating existing Knowledge Graphs (Gui et al., 2023). |
| **Modules** | **Metrics** | **Type** | **Description** |
| Selectors | Deduplication | Statistics-based | Repetitive input and output of instances. |
| | Length | Statistics-based | The bounded length of every pair of instruction and output. |
| | MTLD | Statistics-based | A metric for assessing the lexical diversity in text, defined as the average length of word sequences that sustain a minimum threshold TTR score (McCarthy and Jarvis, 2010). |
| | ROUGE | N-gram-based | Recall-oriented understudy for gisting evaluation (Lin, 2004). |
| | CIRS | Structure-based | The score using the abstract syntax tree to encode structural and logical attributes, to evaluate the correlation between code and reasoning abilities (Bi et al., 2023). |
| | Perplexity | LM-based | The exponentiated average negative log-likelihood of text. |
| | GPT Score | LM-based | The score that ChatGPT/GPT4 assigns to assess how effectively the AI Assistant's response aligns with the user's instructions. |

Table 1: Components of Generators and Selectors modules of EasyInstruct. The instruction generation methods implemented in Generators are categorized into three groups, based on their respective seed data sources: chat data, corpus, and knowledge graphs. The evaluation metrics in Selecors are divided into four categories, based on the principle of their implementation: statistics-based, n-gram-based, structure-based, and LM-based.

Prompts classes inherit from a common base class, BasePrompt, which includes necessary attributes and abstract methods. In the mentioned base class, there are functionalities provided for building prompts, requesting generation results from LLMs, and parsing the responses received from LLMs. The base class also provides mechanisms to handle error conditions and exceptions that may occur during the whole process. Users can inherit from the base class and customize or extend its functionality based on their specific requirements. We also equip EasyInstruct with various prompting techniques and application adaptions (e.g. Chain-of-Thought, Information Extraction, Multimodal, etc.) by providing a consistent and standardized interface, enabling efficient instruction prompting for LLMs.

## 4 Evaluation

In terms of evaluation, we will introduce the experiment setups and illustrate the empirical results of multiple modules implemented in EasyInstruct to demonstrate its capability.

### 4.1 Experiment Setups

**Instruction Datasets.** We adopt the popular *Self-Instruct* (Wang et al., 2023b) and *Evol-Instruct* (Xu et al., 2023) methods implemented in EasyInstruct to synthesize instruction datasets, containing instructions paired with instance inputs and outputs separately. We mainly consider four instruction datasets as follows: (a) ***self_instruct_5k*** is constructed by employing the *Self-Instruct* method to distill instruction data from text-davinci-003; (b) ***alpaca_data_5k*** is randomly sampled from the Alpaca dataset (Taori et al., 2023); (c) ***evol_instruct_5k*** is constructed by employing the *Evol-Instruct* method; (d) ***easyinstruct_5k*** is collected by integrating the three instruction datasets above and applying multiple Selectors in EasyInstruct to extract high-quality instruction datasets. We detail the hyper-parameters for selection in a configuration file, as shown in Appendix A.2.1.

**Implementation Setups.** To conduct the experiments on the effect of instruction datasets, we adopt a LLaMA2 (7B) model (Touvron et al., 2023b), a popular open-sourced LLM backbone widely used for instruction-tuning. We fine-tune the LLMs with LoRA (Hu et al., 2022) in the format following Alpaca (Taori et al., 2023) with KnowLM[7]. All hyper-parameters for training can be found in Appendix A.3. The evaluation is conducted by comparing the

[7]https://github.com/zjunlp/KnowLM

| | |
|---|---|
| **[Instruction]** Describe the common theme of the following three animals. | |
| **[Output]** The common theme among the penguin, polar bear and walrus is their ability to survive in cold climates. All three animals have adapted to thrive in cold Arctic regions, with a heavy layer of blubber or thick fur to keep them warm and plenty of blubber to provide sustenance. | |
| **[Scores]** {"mtld_score": 22.68, "avg_rouge_score": 0.16, "ppl_score": 22.57, "gpt_score": 4} | |
| **[Instruction]** Pretend that you are the subject of the following poem. Use the first person voice to write a response to the poem. | |
| **[Input]** The gentle swell of the sea,\n Cradling the shore in its serenity. | |
| **[Output]** I can hear the sound of the waves crashing against the shore. The sea's serenity is like a soothing cradle that brings me peace and tranquility. | |
| **[Scores]** {"mtld_score": 27.10, "avg_rouge_score": 0.16, "ppl_score": 26.02, "gpt_score": 4} | |
| **[Instruction]** Create a function to calculate the total cost of a book order, given the unit price, quantity, shipping cost, and tax rate. | |
| **[Input]** Unit Price: 10.99\n Quantity: 3\n Shipping Cost: 5\n Tax Rate: 0.03 | |
| **[Output]** def calculateCost(unitPrice, quantity, shippingCost, taxRate):<br>totalPrice = (unitPrice * quantity) + shippingCost<br>totalTax = totalPrice * taxRate<br>totalCost = totalPrice + totalTax<br>return totalCost | |
| **[Scores]** {"mtld_score": 67.76, "avg_rouge_score": 0.17, "ppl_score": 18.95, "gpt_score": 5} | |

Table 2: Examples of the selected instructions in ***easyinstruct_5k***, and their corresponding evaluation scores given by the `Selectors` module.

generated results from different fine-tuned models based on the AlpacaFarm (Dubois et al., 2023) evaluation set. Following AlpacaFarm, for each comparison, we employ ChatGPT as the evaluator to automatically compare two outputs from different models and label which one they prefer, reporting the win rate as the evaluation metric. For both instruction tuning and evaluation, we adopt the same prompt templates used by Alpaca-LoRA[8], as shown in Appendix A.4.

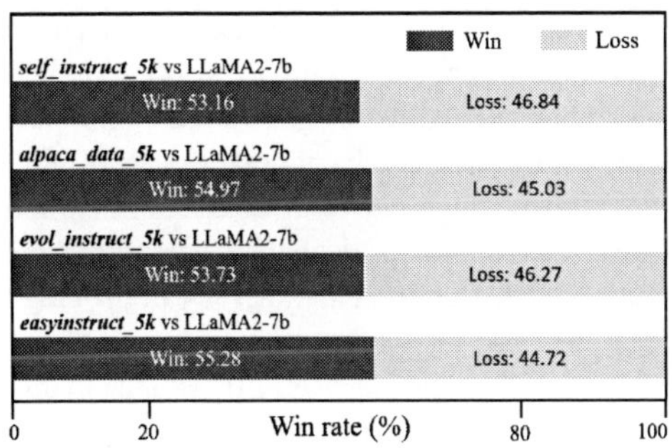


Figure 3: Results of models fine-tuned on four distinct instruction datasets against those from the base LLaMA2 (7B) model, using the AlpacaFarm evaluation set for assessment.

### 4.2 Experiment Results

**Main Results.** We compare the generated outputs from models fine-tuned separately on the four instruction datasets with the outputs from the base version of the LLaMA2 (7B) model on the AlpacaFarm evaluation set. As depicted in Figure 3, there are improvements in the win rate metric for all the settings. Moreover, the model performs optimally under the ***easyinstruct_5k*** setting, indicating the importance of a rich instruction selection strategy.

**Instruction Diversity.** To study the diversity of the instruction datasets considered in our experiments, we identify the verb-noun structure in the generated instructions and plot the top 20 most prevalent root verbs and their top 4 direct nouns in Figure 4, following the approach of Wang et al. (2023b). Overall, we see a wide range of intents and textual formats within these instructions.

**Case Study.** To conduct a qualitative evaluation of EasyInstruct, we sample several instruction examples selected by the `Selectors` module in ***easyinstruct_5k*** for the case study. We also attach the corresponding evaluation scores for each of these instruction examples, as shown in Table 2. We observe that the selected instructions often possess fluent language and meticulous logic.

[8]`https://github.com/tloen/alpaca-lora`

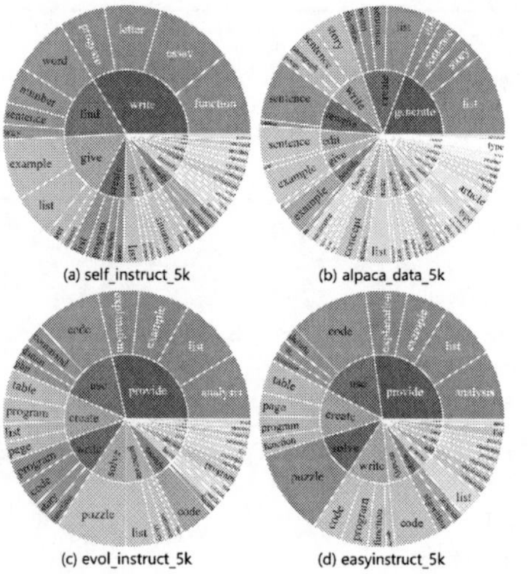

(a) self_instruct_5k (b) alpaca_data_5k

(c) evol_instruct_5k (d) easyinstruct_5k

Figure 4: (Inner circle refers to the top 20 most prevalent root verbs and outer circle indicates their top 4 direct nouns in the generated instruction datasets considered in the experiments.

## 5 Conclusion and Future Work

We present **EasyInstruct**, an easy-to-use instruction processing framework for LLMs. EasyInstruct can combine chat data, corpus, KGs and LLMs as an automated instruction generation tool, reducing the cost of manual data annotation. Additionally, EasyInstruct integrates a diverse set of instruction selection tools to optimize the diversity and distribution of instruction data, thereby improving the quality of fine-tuning data. EasyInstruct is designed to be easy to extend, and we will continue to update new features (e.g., knowledgeable synthetic data generation) to keep pace with the latest research. We expect EasyInstruct to be a helpful framework for researchers and practitioners to facilitate their work of instruction tuning on LLMs.

## Limitations

In this paper, we are committed to unifying all phases of instruction data processing including instruction generation, selection, and prompting. Despite our efforts, this paper may still have some remaining limitations.

**The Scope of Instruction Selection Methods.** We implement various instruction selection methods within the `Selectors` module. Based on the evaluation metrics utilized and the model base employed, the implemented instruction data selection methods can be divided into three categories: methods based on a system of indicators, methods utilizing powerful LLMs like ChatGPT, and methods employing small models (Wang et al., 2024). However, another line of work (Li et al., 2023a,c,b; Wu et al., 2023; Chen et al., 2023b; Kung et al., 2023) employs trainable LLMs like LLaMA for computation formulas in instruction selection processes, which are not integrated into the `Selectors` module. Although our design choice is to decouple instruction processing and model training into two separate phases, we regard it as a limitation that may be addressed by future work.

**Statistics for evaluating efficiency.** In our evaluation, we fine-tune a LLaMA2 (7B) model utilizing multiple modules implemented in EasyInstruct. Compared to models fine-tuned on other instruction datasets constructed without EasyInstruct, our model achieves optimal results, demonstrating EasyInstruct's capability. Although we also qualitatively demonstrate the ease of writing code for instruction processing with multiple code samples and configuration files using EasyInstruct, a limitation is the lack of appropriate statistics for quantitatively evaluating efficiency.

## Acknowledgments

We would like to express gratitude to the anonymous reviewers for their kind comments. This work was supported by the National Natural Science Foundation of China (No. 62206246, No. NSFCU23B2055, No. NSFCU19B2027), the Fundamental Research Funds for the Central Universities (226-2023-00138), Zhejiang Provincial Natural Science Foundation of China (No. LGG22F030011), Yongjiang Talent Introduction Programme (2021A-156-G), CCF-Baidu Open Fund, Information Technology Center and State Key Lab of CAD&CG, Zhejiang University.

## References

Yuvanesh Anand, Zach Nussbaum, Brandon Duderstadt, Benjamin Schmidt, and Andriy Mulyar. 2023. Gpt4all: Training an assistant-style chatbot with large scale data distillation from gpt-3.5-turbo. `https://github.com/nomic-ai/gpt4all`.

Rohan Anil, Andrew M. Dai, Orhan Firat, Melvin Johnson, Dmitry Lepikhin, Alexandre Passos, Siamak Shakeri, Emanuel Taropa, Paige Bailey, Zhifeng Chen, Eric Chu, Jonathan H. Clark, Laurent El Shafey, Yanping Huang, Kathy Meier-Hellstern, Gaurav Mishra, Erica Moreira, Mark Omernick, Kevin

Robinson, Sebastian Ruder, Yi Tay, Kefan Xiao, Yuanzhong Xu, Yujing Zhang, Gustavo Hernández Ábrego, Junwhan Ahn, Jacob Austin, Paul Barham, Jan A. Botha, James Bradbury, Siddhartha Brahma, Kevin Brooks, Michele Catasta, Yong Cheng, Colin Cherry, Christopher A. Choquette-Choo, Aakanksha Chowdhery, Clément Crepy, Shachi Dave, Mostafa Dehghani, Sunipa Dev, Jacob Devlin, Mark Díaz, Nan Du, Ethan Dyer, Vladimir Feinberg, Fangxiaoyu Feng, Vlad Fienber, Markus Freitag, Xavier Garcia, Sebastian Gehrmann, Lucas Gonzalez, and et al. 2023. Palm 2 technical report. *CoRR*, abs/2305.10403.

André Bauer, Simon Trapp, Michael Stenger, Robert Leppich, Samuel Kounev, Mark Leznik, Kyle Chard, and Ian T. Foster. 2024. Comprehensive exploration of synthetic data generation: A survey. *CoRR*, abs/2401.02524.

Zhen Bi, Ningyu Zhang, Yinuo Jiang, Shumin Deng, Guozhou Zheng, and Huajun Chen. 2023. When do program-of-thoughts work for reasoning? *CoRR*, abs/2308.15452.

Tom B. Brown, Benjamin Mann, Nick Ryder, Melanie Subbiah, Jared Kaplan, Prafulla Dhariwal, Arvind Neelakantan, Pranav Shyam, Girish Sastry, Amanda Askell, Sandhini Agarwal, Ariel Herbert-Voss, Gretchen Krueger, Tom Henighan, Rewon Child, Aditya Ramesh, Daniel M. Ziegler, Jeffrey Wu, Clemens Winter, Christopher Hesse, Mark Chen, Eric Sigler, Mateusz Litwin, Scott Gray, Benjamin Chess, Jack Clark, Christopher Berner, Sam McCandlish, Alec Radford, Ilya Sutskever, and Dario Amodei. 2020. Language models are few-shot learners. In *Advances in Neural Information Processing Systems 33: Annual Conference on Neural Information Processing Systems 2020, NeurIPS 2020, December 6-12, 2020, virtual.*

Huajun Chen. 2023. Large knowledge model: Perspectives and challenges. *CoRR*, abs/2312.02706.

Lichang Chen, Shiyang Li, Jun Yan, Hai Wang, Kalpa Gunaratna, Vikas Yadav, Zheng Tang, Vijay Srinivasan, Tianyi Zhou, Heng Huang, and Hongxia Jin. 2023a. Alpagasus: Training A better alpaca with fewer data. *CoRR*, abs/2307.08701.

Xiang Chen, Ningyu Zhang, Xin Xie, Shumin Deng, Yunzhi Yao, Chuanqi Tan, Fei Huang, Luo Si, and Huajun Chen. 2022. Knowprompt: Knowledge-aware prompt-tuning with synergistic optimization for relation extraction. In *WWW '22: The ACM Web Conference 2022, Virtual Event, Lyon, France, April 25 - 29, 2022*, pages 2778–2788. ACM.

Yongrui Chen, Haiyun Jiang, Xinting Huang, Shuming Shi, and Guilin Qi. 2023b. Tegit: Generating high-quality instruction-tuning data with text-grounded task design. *CoRR*, abs/2309.05447.

Wei-Lin Chiang, Zhuohan Li, Zi Lin, Ying Sheng, Zhanghao Wu, Hao Zhang, Lianmin Zheng, Siyuan Zhuang, Yonghao Zhuang, Joseph E. Gonzalez, Ion Stoica, and Eric P. Xing. 2023. Vicuna: An open-source chatbot impressing gpt-4 with 90%* chatgpt quality.

Hyung Won Chung, Le Hou, Shayne Longpre, Barret Zoph, Yi Tay, William Fedus, Eric Li, Xuezhi Wang, Mostafa Dehghani, Siddhartha Brahma, Albert Webson, Shixiang Shane Gu, Zhuyun Dai, Mirac Suzgun, Xinyun Chen, Aakanksha Chowdhery, Sharan Narang, Gaurav Mishra, Adams Yu, Vincent Y. Zhao, Yanping Huang, Andrew M. Dai, Hongkun Yu, Slav Petrov, Ed H. Chi, Jeff Dean, Jacob Devlin, Adam Roberts, Denny Zhou, Quoc V. Le, and Jason Wei. 2022. Scaling instruction-finetuned language models. *CoRR*, abs/2210.11416.

Zhengxiao Du, Yujie Qian, Xiao Liu, Ming Ding, Jiezhong Qiu, Zhilin Yang, and Jie Tang. 2022. Glm: General language model pretraining with autoregressive blank infilling. In *Proceedings of the 60th Annual Meeting of the Association for Computational Linguistics (Volume 1: Long Papers)*, pages 320–335.

Yann Dubois, Xuechen Li, Rohan Taori, Tianyi Zhang, Ishaan Gulrajani, Jimmy Ba, Carlos Guestrin, Percy Liang, and Tatsunori B. Hashimoto. 2023. Alpacafarm: A simulation framework for methods that learn from human feedback. *CoRR*, abs/2305.14387.

Honghao Gui, Jintian Zhang, Hongbin Ye, and Ningyu Zhang. 2023. Instructie: A chinese instruction-based information extraction dataset. *CoRR*, abs/2305.11527.

Edward J. Hu, Yelong Shen, Phillip Wallis, Zeyuan Allen-Zhu, Yuanzhi Li, Shean Wang, Lu Wang, and Weizhu Chen. 2022. Lora: Low-rank adaptation of large language models. In *The Tenth International Conference on Learning Representations, ICLR 2022, Virtual Event, April 25-29, 2022*. OpenReview.net.

Andreas Köpf, Yannic Kilcher, Dimitri von Rütte, Sotiris Anagnostidis, Zhi-Rui Tam, Keith Stevens, Abdullah Barhoum, Nguyen Minh Duc, Oliver Stanley, Richárd Nagyfi, Shahul ES, Sameer Suri, David Glushkov, Arnav Dantuluri, Andrew Maguire, Christoph Schuhmann, Huu Nguyen, and Alexander Mattick. 2023. Openassistant conversations - democratizing large language model alignment. *CoRR*, abs/2304.07327.

Po-Nien Kung, Fan Yin, Di Wu, Kai-Wei Chang, and Nanyun Peng. 2023. Active instruction tuning: Improving cross-task generalization by training on prompt sensitive tasks. In *Proceedings of the 2023 Conference on Empirical Methods in Natural Language Processing, EMNLP 2023, Singapore, December 6-10, 2023*, pages 1813–1829. Association for Computational Linguistics.

Ming Li, Yong Zhang, Zhitao Li, Jiuhai Chen, Lichang Chen, Ning Cheng, Jianzong Wang, Tianyi Zhou, and Jing Xiao. 2023a. From quantity to quality: Boosting LLM performance with self-guided data selection for instruction tuning. *CoRR*, abs/2308.12032.

Xian Li, Ping Yu, Chunting Zhou, Timo Schick, Luke Zettlemoyer, Omer Levy, Jason Weston, and Mike Lewis. 2023b. Self-alignment with instruction backtranslation. *CoRR*, abs/2308.06259.

Yunshui Li, Binyuan Hui, Xiaobo Xia, Jiaxi Yang, Min Yang, Lei Zhang, Shuzheng Si, Junhao Liu, Tongliang Liu, Fei Huang, and Yongbin Li. 2023c. One shot learning as instruction data prospector for large language models. *CoRR*, abs/2312.10302.

Chin-Yew Lin. 2004. ROUGE: A package for automatic evaluation of summaries. In *Text Summarization Branches Out*, pages 74–81, Barcelona, Spain. Association for Computational Linguistics.

Wei Liu, Weihao Zeng, Keqing He, Yong Jiang, and Junxian He. 2023. What makes good data for alignment? A comprehensive study of automatic data selection in instruction tuning. *CoRR*, abs/2312.15685.

Shayne Longpre, Le Hou, Tu Vu, Albert Webson, Hyung Won Chung, Yi Tay, Denny Zhou, Quoc V. Le, Barret Zoph, Jason Wei, and Adam Roberts. 2023. The flan collection: Designing data and methods for effective instruction tuning. In *International Conference on Machine Learning, ICML 2023, 23-29 July 2023, Honolulu, Hawaii, USA*, volume 202 of *Proceedings of Machine Learning Research*, pages 22631–22648. PMLR.

Renze Lou, Kai Zhang, and Wenpeng Yin. 2023. Is prompt all you need? no. A comprehensive and broader view of instruction learning. *CoRR*, abs/2303.10475.

Philip M McCarthy and Scott Jarvis. 2010. Mtld, vocd-d, and hd-d: A validation study of sophisticated approaches to lexical diversity assessment. *Behavior research methods*, 42(2):381–392.

OpenAI. 2023. GPT-4 technical report. *CoRR*, abs/2303.08774.

Long Ouyang, Jeffrey Wu, Xu Jiang, Diogo Almeida, Carroll L. Wainwright, Pamela Mishkin, Chong Zhang, Sandhini Agarwal, Katarina Slama, Alex Ray, John Schulman, Jacob Hilton, Fraser Kelton, Luke Miller, Maddie Simens, Amanda Askell, Peter Welinder, Paul F. Christiano, Jan Leike, and Ryan Lowe. 2022. Training language models to follow instructions with human feedback. In *NeurIPS*.

Shuofei Qiao, Yixin Ou, Ningyu Zhang, Xiang Chen, Yunzhi Yao, Shumin Deng, Chuanqi Tan, Fei Huang, and Huajun Chen. 2023. Reasoning with language model prompting: A survey. In *Proceedings of the 61st Annual Meeting of the Association for Computational Linguistics (Volume 1: Long Papers), ACL 2023, Toronto, Canada, July 9-14, 2023*, pages 5368–5393. Association for Computational Linguistics.

Victor Sanh, Albert Webson, Colin Raffel, Stephen H. Bach, Lintang Sutawika, Zaid Alyafeai, Antoine Chaffin, Arnaud Stiegler, Arun Raja, Manan Dey, M Saiful Bari, Canwen Xu, Urmish Thakker, Shanya Sharma Sharma, Eliza Szczechla, Taewoon Kim, Gunjan Chhablani, Nihal V. Nayak, Debajyoti Datta, Jonathan Chang, Mike Tian-Jian Jiang, Han Wang, Matteo Manica, Sheng Shen, Zheng Xin Yong, Harshit Pandey, Rachel Bawden, Thomas Wang, Trishala Neeraj, Jos Rozen, Abheesht Sharma, Andrea Santilli, Thibault Févry, Jason Alan Fries, Ryan Teehan, Teven Le Scao, Stella Biderman, Leo Gao, Thomas Wolf, and Alexander M. Rush. 2022. Multitask prompted training enables zero-shot task generalization. In *The Tenth International Conference on Learning Representations, ICLR 2022, Virtual Event, April 25-29, 2022*. OpenReview.net.

Teven Le Scao, Angela Fan, Christopher Akiki, Ellie Pavlick, Suzana Ilic, Daniel Hesslow, Roman Castagné, Alexandra Sasha Luccioni, François Yvon, Matthias Gallé, Jonathan Tow, Alexander M. Rush, Stella Biderman, Albert Webson, Pawan Sasanka Ammanamanchi, Thomas Wang, Benoît Sagot, Niklas Muennighoff, Albert Villanova del Moral, Olatunji Ruwase, Rachel Bawden, Stas Bekman, Angelina McMillan-Major, Iz Beltagy, Huu Nguyen, Lucile Saulnier, Samson Tan, Pedro Ortiz Suarez, Victor Sanh, Hugo Laurençon, Yacine Jernite, Julien Launay, Margaret Mitchell, Colin Raffel, Aaron Gokaslan, Adi Simhi, Aitor Soroa, Alham Fikri Aji, Amit Alfassy, Anna Rogers, Ariel Kreisberg Nitzav, Canwen Xu, Chenghao Mou, Chris Emezue, Christopher Klamm, Colin Leong, Daniel van Strien, David Ifeoluwa Adelani, and et al. 2022. BLOOM: A 176b-parameter open-access multilingual language model. *CoRR*, abs/2211.05100.

Rohan Taori, Ishaan Gulrajani, Tianyi Zhang, Yann Dubois, Xuechen Li, Carlos Guestrin, Percy Liang, and Tatsunori B. Hashimoto. 2023. Stanford alpaca: An instruction-following llama model. `https://github.com/tatsu-lab/stanford_alpaca`.

Hugo Touvron, Thibaut Lavril, Gautier Izacard, Xavier Martinet, Marie-Anne Lachaux, Timothée Lacroix, Baptiste Rozière, Naman Goyal, Eric Hambro, Faisal Azhar, Aurélien Rodriguez, Armand Joulin, Edouard Grave, and Guillaume Lample. 2023a. Llama: Open and efficient foundation language models. *CoRR*, abs/2302.13971.

Hugo Touvron, Louis Martin, Kevin Stone, Peter Albert, Amjad Almahairi, Yasmine Babaei, Nikolay Bashlykov, Soumya Batra, Prajjwal Bhargava, Shruti Bhosale, Dan Bikel, Lukas Blecher, Cristian Canton-Ferrer, Moya Chen, Guillem Cucurull, David Esiobu, Jude Fernandes, Jeremy Fu, Wenyin Fu, Brian Fuller, Cynthia Gao, Vedanuj Goswami, Naman Goyal, Anthony Hartshorn, Saghar Hosseini, Rui Hou, Hakan Inan, Marcin Kardas, Viktor Kerkez, Madian Khabsa, Isabel Kloumann, Artem Korenev, Punit Singh Koura, Marie-Anne Lachaux, Thibaut Lavril, Jenya Lee, Diana Liskovich, Yinghai Lu, Yuning Mao, Xavier Martinet, Todor Mihaylov, Pushkar Mishra, Igor Molybog, Yixin Nie, Andrew Poulton, Jeremy Reizenstein, Rashi Rungta, Kalyan Saladi, Alan Schelten, Ruan Silva, Eric Michael Smith, Ranjan Subramanian, Xiaoqing Ellen Tan, Binh Tang, Ross Taylor, Adina Williams, Jian Xiang Kuan, Puxin Xu, Zheng Yan, Iliyan Zarov, Yuchen Zhang, Angela Fan, Melanie Kambadur, Sharan Narang, Aurélien Rodriguez, Robert Stojnic, Sergey Edunov, and Thomas Scialom. 2023b. Llama 2: Open foundation and fine-tuned chat models. *CoRR*, abs/2307.09288.

Jiahao Wang, Bolin Zhang, Qianlong Du, Jiajun Zhang, and Dianhui Chu. 2024. A survey on data selection for LLM instruction tuning. *CoRR*, abs/2402.05123.

Peng Wang, Ningyu Zhang, Xin Xie, Yunzhi Yao, Bozhong Tian, Mengru Wang, Zekun Xi, Siyuan Cheng, Kangwei Liu, Guozhou Zheng, and Huajun Chen. 2023a. Easyedit: An easy-to-use knowledge editing framework for large language models. *CoRR*, abs/2308.07269.

Yizhong Wang, Yeganeh Kordi, Swaroop Mishra, Alisa Liu, Noah A. Smith, Daniel Khashabi, and Hannaneh Hajishirzi. 2023b. Self-instruct: Aligning language models with self-generated instructions. In *Proceedings of the 61st Annual Meeting of the Association for Computational Linguistics (Volume 1: Long Papers), ACL 2023, Toronto, Canada, July 9-14, 2023*, pages 13484–13508. Association for Computational Linguistics.

Yizhong Wang, Swaroop Mishra, Pegah Alipoormolabashi, Yeganeh Kordi, Amirreza Mirzaei, Atharva Naik, Arjun Ashok, Arut Selvan Dhanasekaran, Anjana Arunkumar, David Stap, Eshaan Pathak, Giannis Karamanolakis, Haizhi Gary Lai, Ishan Purohit, Ishani Mondal, Jacob Anderson, Kirby Kuznia, Krima Doshi, Kuntal Kumar Pal, Maitreya Patel, Mehrad Moradshahi, Mihir Parmar, Mirali Purohit, Neeraj Varshney, Phani Rohitha Kaza, Pulkit Verma, Ravsehaj Singh Puri, Rushang Karia, Savan Doshi, Shailaja Keyur Sampat, Siddhartha Mishra, Sujan Reddy A, Sumanta Patro, Tanay Dixit, and Xudong Shen. 2022. Super-naturalinstructions: Generalization via declarative instructions on 1600+ NLP tasks. In *Proceedings of the 2022 Conference on Empirical Methods in Natural Language Processing, EMNLP 2022, Abu Dhabi, United Arab Emirates, December 7-11, 2022*, pages 5085–5109. Association for Computational Linguistics.

Yufei Wang, Wanjun Zhong, Liangyou Li, Fei Mi, Xingshan Zeng, Wenyong Huang, Lifeng Shang, Xin Jiang, and Qun Liu. 2023c. Aligning large language models with human: A survey. *CoRR*, abs/2307.12966.

Zige Wang, Wanjun Zhong, Yufei Wang, Qi Zhu, Fei Mi, Baojun Wang, Lifeng Shang, Xin Jiang, and Qun Liu. 2023d. Data management for large language models: A survey. *CoRR*, abs/2312.01700.

Jason Wei, Maarten Bosma, Vincent Y. Zhao, Kelvin Guu, Adams Wei Yu, Brian Lester, Nan Du, Andrew M. Dai, and Quoc V. Le. 2022. Finetuned language models are zero-shot learners. In *The Tenth International Conference on Learning Representations, ICLR 2022, Virtual Event, April 25-29, 2022*. OpenReview.net.

Shengguang Wu, Keming Lu, Benfeng Xu, Junyang Lin, Qi Su, and Chang Zhou. 2023. Self-evolved diverse data sampling for efficient instruction tuning. *CoRR*, abs/2311.08182.

Can Xu, Qingfeng Sun, Kai Zheng, Xiubo Geng, Pu Zhao, Jiazhan Feng, Chongyang Tao, and Daxin Jiang. 2023. Wizardlm: Empowering large language models to follow complex instructions. *CoRR*, abs/2304.12244.

Yunzhi Yao, Peng Wang, Bozhong Tian, Siyuan Cheng, Zhoubo Li, Shumin Deng, Huajun Chen, and Ningyu Zhang. 2023. Editing large language models: Problems, methods, and opportunities. *CoRR*, abs/2305.13172.

Aohan Zeng, Xiao Liu, Zhengxiao Du, Zihan Wang, Hanyu Lai, Ming Ding, Zhuoyi Yang, Yifan Xu, Wendi Zheng, Xiao Xia, Weng Lam Tam, Zixuan Ma, Yufei Xue, Jidong Zhai, Wenguang Chen, Zhiyuan Liu, Peng Zhang, Yuxiao Dong, and Jie Tang. 2023. GLM-130B: an open bilingual pre-trained model. In *The Eleventh International Conference on Learning Representations, ICLR 2023, Kigali, Rwanda, May 1-5, 2023*. OpenReview.net.

Ningyu Zhang, Yunzhi Yao, Bozhong Tian, Peng Wang, Shumin Deng, Mengru Wang, Zekun Xi, Shengyu Mao, Jintian Zhang, Yuansheng Ni, Siyuan Cheng, Ziwen Xu, Xin Xu, Jia-Chen Gu, Yong Jiang, Pengjun Xie, Fei Huang, Lei Liang, Zhiqiang Zhang, Xiaowei Zhu, Jun Zhou, and Huajun Chen. 2024. A comprehensive study of knowledge editing for large language models. *CoRR*, abs/2401.01286.

Shengyu Zhang, Linfeng Dong, Xiaoya Li, Sen Zhang, Xiaofei Sun, Shuhe Wang, Jiwei Li, Runyi Hu, Tianwei Zhang, Fei Wu, and Guoyin Wang. 2023. Instruction tuning for large language models: A survey. *CoRR*, abs/2308.10792.

Wayne Xin Zhao, Kun Zhou, Junyi Li, Tianyi Tang, Xiaolei Wang, Yupeng Hou, Yingqian Min, Beichen Zhang, Junjie Zhang, Zican Dong, Yifan Du, Chen Yang, Yushuo Chen, Zhipeng Chen, Jinhao Jiang, Ruiyang Ren, Yifan Li, Xinyu Tang, Zikang Liu, Peiyu Liu, Jian-Yun Nie, and Ji-Rong Wen. 2023. A survey of large language models. *CoRR*, abs/2303.18223.

Chunting Zhou, Pengfei Liu, Puxin Xu, Srini Iyer, Jiao Sun, Yuning Mao, Xuezhe Ma, Avia Efrat, Ping Yu, Lili Yu, Susan Zhang, Gargi Ghosh, Mike Lewis, Luke Zettlemoyer, and Omer Levy. 2023. LIMA: less is more for alignment. *CoRR*, abs/2305.11206.

## A Appendix

### A.1 Installation

Currently, EasyInstruct offers three installation options, each accompanied by its corresponding installation script. Users can choose the option that best suits their specific requirements.

#### A.1.1 Installation from GitHub Repository

The first option is to install the latest version of EasyInstruct from the GitHub repository. The installation script is shown in Figure 5.

#### A.1.2 Installation for Local Development

The second option is to download the source code for local development. The installation script is shown in Figure 6.

#### A.1.3 Installation from PyPI

The third option is to install the package from The Python Package Index (PyPI), which may not be the latest version but still supports most of the features. The installation script is shown in Figure 7.

### A.2 Quick-start

We provide two ways for users to quickly get started with EasyInstruct. Users can either use the shell script or the Gradio app based on their specific needs.

#### A.2.1 Shell Script

**Step1: Prepare a configuration file.** Users can easily configure the parameters of EasyInstruct in a YAML-style file or just quickly use the default parameters in the configuration files we provide. Figure 8 is an example of the configuration file for Self-Instruct.

**Step2: Run the shell script.** Users should first specify the configuration file and provide their own OpenAI API key. Then, run the following shell script in Figure 10 to launch the instruction generation or selection process.

#### A.2.2 Gradio App

We provide a Gradio app for users to quickly get started with EasyInstruct. Users can choose to launch the Gradio App locally on their own machines or alternatively, they can also try the hosted Gradio App[9] that we provide on HuggingFace Spaces.

[9] https://huggingface.co/spaces/zjunlp/EasyInstruct.

### A.3 Detailed Hyper-Parameters

See Table 3.

| Name | LLaMA-2-7b |
|---|---|
| batch_size | 256 |
| micro_batch_size | 8 |
| epochs | 3 |
| learning rate | 3e-4 |
| cutoff_len | 512 |
| val_set_size | 1,000 |
| lora_r | 16 |
| lora_alpha | 32 |
| lora_dropout | 0.05 |

Table 3: Detailed hyper-parameters we use in experiments.

### A.4 Prompt Template for Instruction Tuning

For both training and evaluation, we utilize the same prompt templates used by Alpaca-LoRA, shown in Table 4.

**Prompt Template for Instruction Tuning**

***Prompt with Input:***

Below is an instruction that describes a task, paired with an input that provides further context. Write a response that appropriately completes the request.

### Instruction:
**{instruction}**

### Input:
**{input}**

### Response:

***Prompt without Input:***

Below is an instruction that describes a task. Write a response that appropriately completes the request.

### Instruction:
**{instruction}**

### Response:

Table 4: Prompt Template for instruction tuning.

### A.5 API Services Available in EasyInstruct

Table 5 lists a range of API service providers and their corresponding LLM products that are currently available in EasyInstruct.

```
pip install git+https://github.com/zjunlp/EasyInstruct@main
```

Figure 5: Installation script from Github repository.

| Model | Description | Default Version |
|---|---|---|
| ***OpenAI*** | | |
| GPT-3.5 | A set of models that improve on GPT-3 and can understand as well as generate natural language or code. | `gpt-3.5-turbo` |
| GPT-4 | A set of models that improve on GPT-3.5 and can understand as well as generate natural language or code. | `gpt-4` |
| ***Anthropic*** | | |
| Claude | A next-generation AI assistant based on Anthropic's research into training helpful, honest, and harmless AI systems. | `claude-2` |
| Claude-Instant | A lighter, less expensive, and much faster option than Claude. | `claude-instant-1` |
| ***Cohere*** | | |
| Command | An instruction-following conversational model that performs language tasks with high quality, more reliably, and with a longer context than cohere's base generative models. | `command` |
| Command-Light | A smaller, faster version of Command. Almost as capable, but a lot faster. | `command-light` |

Table 5: API service providers and their corresponding LLM products that are currently available in **EasyInstruct**.

```
git clone
↪ https://github.com/zjunlp/EasyInstruct
cd EasyInstruct
pip install -e .
```

Figure 6: Installation script for local development.

```
pip install easyinstruct
```

Figure 7: Installation script using PyPI.

```
generator:
  SelfInstructGenerator:
    target_dir: data/generations/
    data_format: alpaca
    seed_tasks_path:
↪   data/seed_tasks.jsonl
    generated_instructions_path:
↪   generated_instructions.jsonl
    generated_instances_path:
↪   generated_instances.jsonl
    num_instructions_to_generate: 100
    engine: gpt-3.5-turbo
    num_prompt_instructions: 8
```

Figure 8: Example configuration file of `Generators`.

```
selector:
  source_file_path:
  target_dir: data/selections/
  target_file_name: case.jsonl
  LengthSelector:
    min_instruction_length: 3
    max_instruction_length: 150
    min_response_length: 1
    max_response_length: 350
  Deduplicator:
  RougeSelector:
    threshold: 0.7
  GPTScoreSelector:
    engine: gpt-3.5-turbo
    threshold: 4
  MTLDSelector:
    ttr_threshold: 0.72
    min_mtld: 8
    max_mtld: 22
  PPLSelector:
    threshold: 200
    model_name: gpt2
    device: cuda
  RandomSelector:
    num_instructions_to_sample: 100
    seed: 42
```

Figure 9: Example configuration file of `Selectors`.

```
config_file=""
openai_api_key=""

python demo/run.py \
    --config $config_file\
    --openai_api_key $openai_api_key \
```

Figure 10: Shell script for quick-start of EasyInstruct.

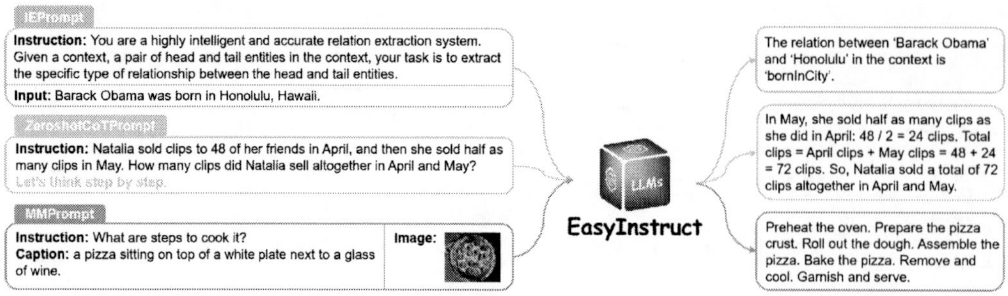


Figure 11: Example features in the `Prompts` module, including Information Extraction, Chain-of-Thought Reasoning, and Multimodal Prompting.

### A.6 Example features in the `Prompts` module

### A.7 Acknowledgements

We thank the developers of the self-instruct[10] library for their significant contributions to the NLP community. We thank the LLaMA team for providing us access to the models, and open-source projects, including Alpaca[11], Alpaca-LoRA[12] and AlpacaEval[13].

[10] https://github.com/yizhongw/self-instruct
[11] https://github.com/tatsu-lab/stanford_alpaca
[12] https://github.com/tloen/alpaca-lora
[13] https://github.com/tatsu-lab/alpaca_eval

# BotEval: Facilitating Interactive Human Evaluation

Hyundong Cho[1] Thamme Gowda[2] Yuyang Huang[1]

Zixun Lu[1] Tianli Tong[1] Jonathan May[1]

[1]University of Southern California, Information Sciences Institute
[2]Microsoft Translator
hd.justincho@gmail.com

## Abstract

Following the rapid progress in natural language processing (NLP) models, language models are applied to increasingly more complex interactive tasks such as negotiations and conversation moderations. Having human evaluators directly interact with these NLP models is essential for adequately evaluating the performance on such interactive tasks. We develop BotEval, an easily customizable, open-source, evaluation toolkit that focuses on enabling human-bot interactions as part of the evaluation process, as opposed to human evaluators making judgements for a static input. BotEval balances flexibility for customization and user-friendliness by providing templates for common use cases that span various degrees of complexity and built-in compatibility with popular crowdsourcing platforms. We showcase the numerous useful features of BotEval through a study that evaluates the performance of various chatbots on their effectiveness for conversational moderation and discuss how BotEval differs from other annotation tools.

## 1 Introduction

As natural language processing (NLP) models become more versatile with the recent advances of language models and their instruction-tuned counterparts (Ouyang et al., 2022), it is becoming more common to create language agents (Sumers et al., 2023) and apply them to complex interactive tasks, such as negotiations (Chawla et al., 2021a), conversational moderation (Cho et al., 2023), reasoning-guided response generation (Zhou et al., 2022), and personalized response generation (Liu et al., 2023).

As noted by Smith et al. (2022), the evaluation methodology plays a critical role in accurately comparing models. For example, rankings between dialogue models can change depending on whether they are evaluated based on single-turn responses or full conversations. In addition, Cho et al. (2023) found the evaluators point of view when evaluating a model is also an important factor. They showed that human evaluators perceived conversational moderators as more effective in making the evaluators become more cooperative and respectful when the evaluators directly interacted with the moderators while acting as the moderated user (first person point of view) compared to when they evaluated a completed interaction between a moderator and a moderated user as a bystander (third person point of view). However, these factors are overlooked in previous approaches that have focused on a simplified evaluation, such as comparing two complete conversations or individual responses (Smith et al., 2022; Li et al., 2019), or specific dialogue applications such as task-oriented dialogue (Cucurnia et al., 2021; Collins et al., 2019). Therefore, it is important to develop evaluation tools that enable an environment that evaluates models in a setting that best encapsulates how humans actually interact with models.

To facilitate accurate human evaluations of complex interactive tasks, we developed BotEval,[1] a comprehensive evaluation toolkit that focuses on enabling human - bot[2] interactions as part of the human evaluation process. For flexibility, it is dynamically configurable to accommodate as many human agents and model agents to interact with each other simultaneously with a custom dialogue manager. It is also designed with modular components, such as the interaction interface, instructions, and survey, so that they can be individually adapted to accommodate various use cases. While main-

[1]Source code and documentation for BotEval can be found at https://github.com/isi-nlp/boteval. We make the demo video of BotEval available at https://justin-cho.com/boteval. In addition, a live demo of BotEval is also available at https://spolin.isi.edu/boteval-dev1 where reviewers can complete a sample human evaluation task.

[2]We use *bot* loosely to describe any AI system that a human being interacts with.



*Proceedings of the 62nd Annual Meeting of the Association for Computational Linguistics (Volume 3: System Demonstrations)*, pages 107–116
August 11-16, 2024 

taining generalizability, BOTEVAL strives to maximize user-friendliness by providing templates for frequent use cases that involve human evaluation where a human evaluator must interact with a NLP model, multiple models, or another human being to measure human performance. In addition, it is integrated with Amazon Mechanical Turk (AMT)[3] for crowdsourcing. It can also be deployed independently of these platforms so that it can be used for internal annotations or used with survey tools that allow for external links, such as Qualtrics[4] and Prolific.[5]

To showcase the usefulness of BOTEVAL and demonstrate its key features, we share a case study that uses BOTEVAL for evaluating models on their performance on conversational moderation (Cho et al., 2023). In this study, BOTEVAL is used to conduct various evaluations: (i) human-bot interactions to compare models; (ii) human-human interactions to measure a human performance threshold; and (iii) completed human-bot interactions by another evaluator to measure evaluator consistency and third-person point of view (POV) results.

In summary, BOTEVAL's main contributions are:

- An open-source and customizable evaluation tool for interactive NLP tasks that incorporates human-bot and human-human interactions into the evaluation process.
- Detailed documentation and templates for various use cases to make modifications easy.
- Flexible deployment options with built-in integration with popular crowdsourcing platforms such as AMT and Prolific.
- Evaluation task management features that facilitate task monitoring and managing crowdsource workers.
- Dynamically configurable interaction logic with custom dialogue manager and multi-human and multi-bot evaluation settings.

## 2 BOTEVAL System Overview

BOTEVAL is a web application that provides an evaluation interface, what the human evaluators (i.e., crowdsource workers) see (Section 2.1), and an administrator dashboard, what the administrator uses to manage the evaluation task and evaluators (Section 2.2). We recommend that the bots that evaluators interact with are provided as separate APIs that BOTEVAL can make queries to, as this isolates the management of the bot deployment and BOTEVAL (Section 2.3). Human evaluators can be flexibly set to crowdsource workers from AMT or Prolific or any other evaluators with internet access by having them create an account directly for a deployment of BOTEVAL using a public external link. An evaluation task is configured with a central YAML config file that identifies the frontend components to use, the deployment environment, and the crowdsourcing platform to use.

### 2.1 Evaluation interface

A sample evaluation interface for the case study later described in Section 4.1 is shown in Figure 1.

The evaluation interface consists of three main components: ❶ *Conversation pane*: a section where the interaction between the human and the bot takes place. This pane can be easily customized to contain seed conversations to serve as initial starting points for interactions to continue off of or it can instead contain any piece of text or completed conversation without requiring any interactions from the evaluators, making BOTEVAL also suitable for simpler annotation tasks. ❷ *Instruction pane*: this is an optional section that shows the main directions. Evaluators can see detailed instructions by clicking on the detailed instructions button. Administrators can choose to show detailed instructions as part of the consent form if one is needed to make sure that evaluators have read them. ❸ *Survey pane*: this is where the human evaluators provide their evaluations. In the given example, it is configured to only be shown after the human evaluators have interacted with the bot for a set number of turns.

The conversation pane and instruction pane is configurable by providing custom HTML scripts, while the survey pane is even more easily customizable by configuring a YAML config file. An example of the YAML config file is shown in Appendix A.1. An optional consent form can be shown to evaluators as well, which is also managed with a separate HTML file. Further detail on how the consent form can be configured is in Appendix A.2.

### 2.2 Administrator dashboard

BOTEVAL's administrator dashboard provides numerous features for managing evaluation tasks and evaluators. Its main benefit is a GUI that enables

[3]https://www.mturk.com
[4]https://www.qualtrics.com
[5]https://www.prolific.com

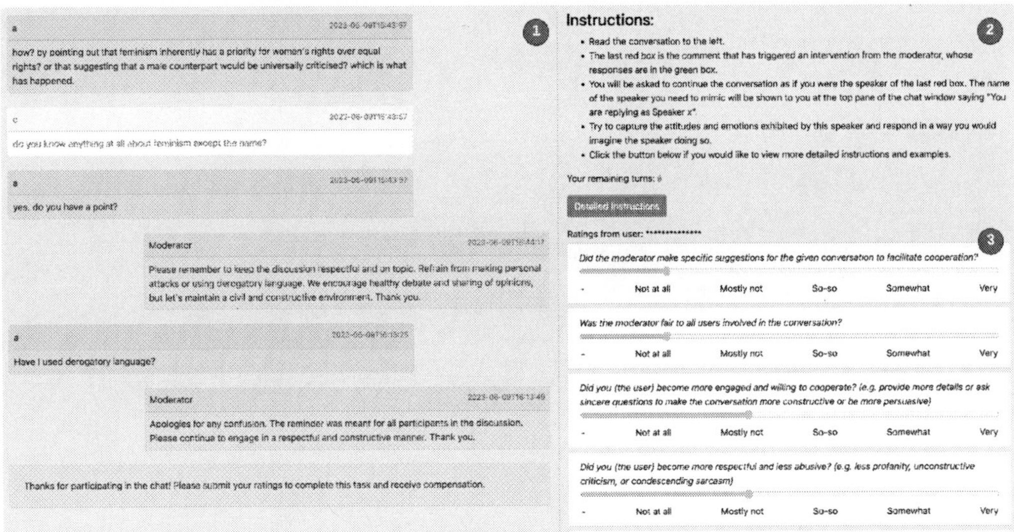


Figure 1: A snapshot of the admin point of view of an evaluation interface with a completed evaluation example. The interface is identical for the evaluator except for the text that shows the evaluator's worker ID (hidden with asterisks in the figure for privacy). The three main components of the user-facing interface are the ❶ conversation pane, ❷ simple instruction pane, and the ❸ survey pane.

a non-technical user to easily become an administrator for human evaluation tasks. The topics page, shown in Figure 2, is one view that allows the management of launching and deleting tasks. A topic refers to any predetermined context, such as seed conversation or external information relevant for the evaluation task. These topics are provided to BOTEVAL as a JSON file. If a user is interested in general open-domain dialogue evaluation, measuring a model's general conversational capabilities, they can use a dummy topic file that contains an empty dictionary. This will launch an evaluation task that starts a conversation from scratch, with the human evaluator initiating the first turn.

After launching tasks, users can use the administrator dashboard to conveniently examine tasks that are completed or in progress with the same interface that the evaluators used to complete the task to easily visualize their work rather than examining a database or JSON file, as shown in Figure 1. The user can also directly export individual JSON files of the collected data if needed. Also, tasks can be deleted in batches using the parallel management tool shown in ❶ of Figure 2.

In addition to these features, we provide convenient AMT-specific features for managing workers and tasks known as human intelligence tasks (HITs). One of the most convenient features is being able to directly assign and remove qualifications for workers after examining their work without having to leave the administrator dashboard. This is an important convenience feature for ensuring the quality of work for human evaluations are kept to the desired standard by blocking unreliable workers. Another is being able to make bonus payments directly after examining the completed task, which is useful when each task is expected to involve variable rewards, such as to account for each HIT taking a different amount of time to complete.

## 2.3 Bot customization

Users are given multiple options to choose how they will service the bot that they want to evaluate, but the recommended setup is to set up a separate RESTful API and defining a logic within BOTEVAL to interface with this API. As shown in ❸ in Figure 2, users can define task-specific parameters for bots that get passed on to the API if the API allows for it. This is useful if you are using the same model but adjusting the instruction prompt (e.g., using OpenAI endpoints). While BOTEVAL users have the option to launch bots simultaneously on the same server with BOTEVAL's process, it is more efficient to separately manage human evaluation tasks and the processes that load and query NLP models because most NLP models are better served with GPUs for reducing latency.

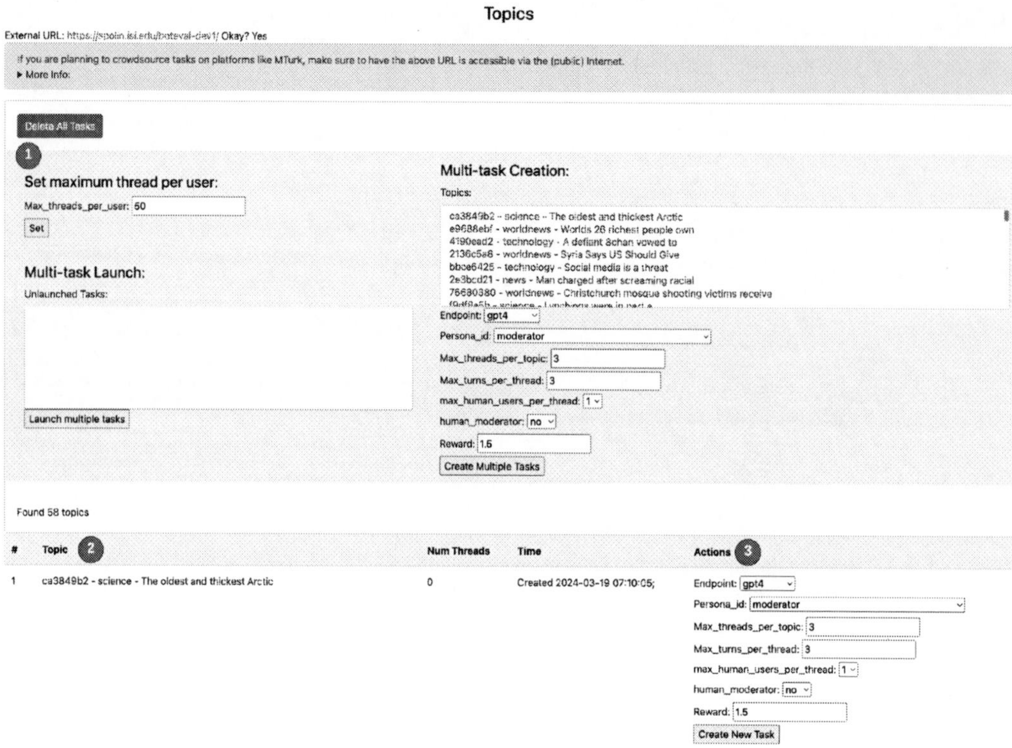


Figure 2: A snapshot of the topics page of the admin dashboard. ❶ is a parallel management tool that enables setting global configurations such as how many tasks each evaluator is allowed to complete and launching or deleting multiple tasks at once. ❷ is a topics table that shares more information about each topic, such as its name, how many tasks have been created, and when they were created. ❸ is a list of parameters that can be chosen for launching a task, which includes parameters that can be passed on to API queries for the bots.

### 2.4 Sourcing human evaluators

BotEval can be customized to use with any crowdsourcing platform, and it is designed to be directly used with many popular ones such as AMT, Prolific, and Qualtrics. If the goal is to do internal annotations, the setup is even simpler as the user only has to configure BotEval to not use any. Then the user can share their custom URL with the evaluators, where they can sign up and directly work on tasks that are made available to them without going through any other platform.

## 3 System Architecture

An overview of BotEval's system architecture is shown in Figure 3. BotEval is a web application (i.e., a client-server model). We describe the front- and back-end technology stacks in the following sections.

### 3.1 Frontend

The frontend is a simple web interface (i.e., HTML) created with Bootstrap stylesheet. While the majority of the HTML structure is constructed on the server side using Jinja2, some dynamic updates such as responses coming from bots or other participants in the interaction are achieved using AJAX and RESTful APIs.

### 3.2 Backend

The backend is implemented in Python language using Flask framework, following a model-view-controller architecture pattern. *Models* are implemented using Python classes and stored in a relational database, specifically SQLite. In addition, we use SQLAlchemy, an object-relational mapper, to abstract the mapping between Python classes and database tables. For *views*, Flask uses Jinja2 for server side templating of HTML pages. *Controllers* are based on Flask's builtin URL routers and RESTful API constructs.

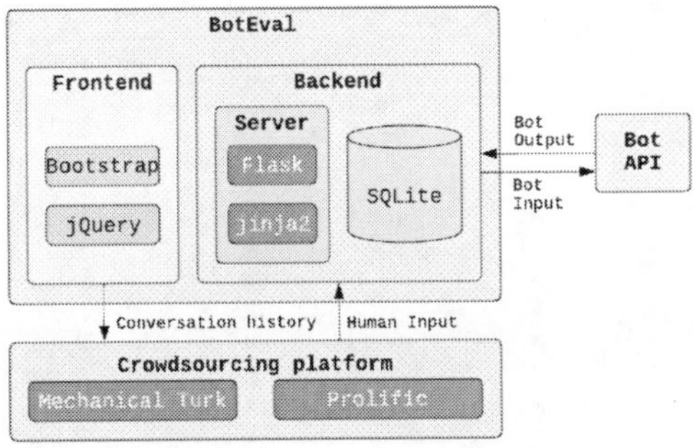


Figure 3: BOTEVAL system architecture. We use popular frameworks that are well documented and easy to use.

While internally our server is an HTTP server, crowdsourcing platforms such as AMT require annotation interface be served via secure connections (HTTPS). HTTPS can be enabled by obtaining and installing an SSL/TLS certificate. We use free certificates from Certbot,[6] and configure Nginx[7] as a reverse proxy server for HTTPS requests.

Some scenarios may require several simultaneous instances of BOTEVAL to facilitate multiple annotation tasks, and obtaining SSL certificate for each instance maybe cumbersome. We address this problem by using a different TCP port for each instance, and configuring a single Nginx (with SSL certificate) route requests for all instances.

## 4 Case Study and Use Cases

### 4.1 Case study: conversational moderation evaluation

To showcase the usefulness of BOTEVAL, we share a case study that uses BOTEVAL to conduct a study on how effective various zero-shot instruction-tuned language models (ITLM) and dialogue model are in performing *conversational moderation* (CM) (Cho et al., 2023).[8] Instead of iron-fisted approaches to moderation such as deleting comments or banning users, which may exacerbate societal polarization as these users find refuge in echo chambers, CM seeks to have moderators interact with users exhibiting problematic behavior to guide them back to more constructive and respectful conversations.

This study makes full use of BOTEVAL as it requires evaluating multiple bots by interacting with them for a preset number of turns (in this case 3), starting with a variety of conversation stubs. The evaluations were conducted with all desired configurations simultaneously to get the most representative and fair results that is not affected by any confounding factors such as recency bias. The evalution was conducted with AMT, and being able to easily monitor evaluations enabled rapid iterations of updating the instructions and giving feedback to the evaluators.

Therefore, BOTEVAL was integral in being able to refine the evaluation study efficiently and ultimately collect statistically meaningful results for an interactive evaluation setup. The study showed that prompt-engineered ITLMs outperformed prosocial dialogue models and that a conflict resolution prompt based on the Socratic method was the best performing prompt. In addition, one of this work's central findings was discovering that there are differences between evaluation results when the models were evaluated from a first person point of view (POV) and a third person POV. With BOTEVAL, collecting human evaluations in these two different settings was a simple change of updating the topics file such that the conversation stubs were the completed conversations, rewording the questions such that it is in third person POV, and setting the number of turns required for human evaluators to interact with the bots to zero.

### 4.2 Main use cases

BOTEVAL's main differentiation with previous annotation tools and frameworks is that it is focused on, but not limited to, interactive use cases. In other words, it is useful when the annotated data is not static, e.g., bot responses over multiple turns or other dynamic outputs that can change based on user interaction. Therefore, BOTEVAL is appealing for evaluating or collecting data for conversational tasks that usually require multi-turn interactions for fulfilling the goal, rather than a single generated output. Many real-life tasks go through multi-turn interactions, such as negotiations (Chawla et al., 2021b), counseling (Mehta et al., 2022), and improvisational theater (Cho and May, 2020). As artificial systems become more capable, more will be applied to completing these complex multi-turn tasks, and BOTEVAL will serve as a handy starting point for facilitating their evaluation.

Although BOTEVAL was designed for interac-

[6] https://certbot.eff.org/

[7] https://nginx.org/en/

[8] The BOTEVAL template for this work is available at https://github.com/isi-nlp/isi_darma/tree/main/boteval-darma-task.

| Name | Human-bot interaction-focused | Crowdsource integration | Multi-human & bot support | Language |
|---|---|---|---|---|
| **BOTEVAL** (Ours) | ✓ | ✓ | ✓ | Python |
| Mephisto (Urbanek and Ringshia, 2023) | ✗ | ✓ | ✗ | Python |
| Pigeon[11] | ✗ | ✗ | ✗ | Python |
| MATILDA (Cucurnia et al., 2021) | ✗ | ✓ | ✗ | Python |
| LIDA (Collins et al., 2019) | ✗ | ✓ | ✗ | Python |
| INCEpTION (Klie et al., 2018) | ✗ | ✗ | ✗ | Java |
| GATE (Cunningham, 2002) | ✗ | ✗ | ✗ | Java |
| BRAT (Stenetorp et al., 2012) | ✗ | ✗ | ✗ | Python |
| doccano (Nakayama et al., 2018) | ✗ | ✗ | ✗ | Python |
| Potato (Pei et al., 2022) | ✗ | ✗ | ✗ | Python |
| Argilla[10] | ✗ | ✗ | ✗ | Python |
| Prodigy[12] | ✗ | ✗ | ✗ | Python |
| DialogueView (Yang and Heeman, 2005) | ✗ | ✗ | ✗ | TcK/TK |
| DART (Weisser, 2016) | ✗ | ✗ | ✗ | Perl |
| Anvil (Kipp, 2001) | ✗ | ✗ | ✗ | Java |
| EZCAT (Guibon et al., 2022) | ✗ | ✗ | ✗ | Javascript |

Table 1: Comparison overview with other annotation tools. BOTEVAL innately supports evaluations that require human-bot interactions and allow for multiple human agents or bot agents to be involved in each evaluation sample.

tive tasks, BOTEVAL can also be easily adapt for simple static annotation tasks by simplifying the conversation pane in Figure 1. This pane can contain any other modality such as images, video, and audio, and adjusting the instruction and survey panes accordingly can make BOTEVAL also suitable for text classification or conversation-level or turn-level comparisons, similar to Smith et al. (2022). As BOTEVAL gets actively used for more research studies, we will be able to provide a variety of templates that accommodate a comprehensive set of use cases, further lowering the effort required to conduct effective human evaluation for new studies.

## 5 Related Work

In Table 1, we compare BOTEVAL with other related annotation tools and discuss differences further here.

### 5.1 General text annotation tools

A popular general annotation tool is Mephisto (Urbanek and Ringshia, 2023), which started by isolating the crowdsourcing features from ParlAI (Miller et al., 2017). Mephisto provides a general annotation framework that interfaces with Amazon Mechanical Turk and Prolific and includes basic templates for simple annotation tasks. BOTEVAL adapted many of its AMT integration features, but Mephisto is not customized for common interactive data annotation and evaluation use cases, and thus requires nontrivial effort to create a human evaluation environment for interactive NLP tasks where a human evaluator needs to interact with a bot or another human and then evaluate their performance. ParlAI still provides templates for Mephisto for human-bot interactions[9], but it is not easy to use with a dialogue model that is not developed with ParlAI. With BOTEVAL, we also provide a GUI administrator dashboard for task and worker management, which is absent in ParlAI and Mephisto.

GATE (Cunningham, 2002) and INCEpTION (Klie et al., 2018) are annotation tools that provide many predefined features, but they are also not designed for interactive human evaluations. Other simpler general text annotation tools that share similar limitations are Doccano (Nakayama et al., 2018), brat (Stenetorp et al., 2012), Argilla[10], Potato (Pei et al., 2022) and Pigeon[11], which are web-based annotation tools that enable rapid annotations for text classification and machine translation. Prodigy[12] is a commercial annotation tool for text annotations that provides similar features.

### 5.2 Dialogue annotation tools and evaluation methodologies

A prominent set of annotation tools specific to dialogue are centered around task-oriented dialogue (Budzianowski et al., 2018). LIDA (Collins et al., 2019) is an annotation tool that provides useful features for efficiently making turn-level annotations, incorporating model-provided label recommendations to speed up annotations, and resolving inter-annotation disagreements. MATILDA (Cucurnia et al., 2021) builds on LIDA for multilin-

[9] https://parl.ai/docs/tutorial_crowdsourcing.html

[10] https://argilla.io

[11] https://github.com/agermanidis/pigeon

[12] https://prodi.gy

gual support and improved management of crowdsourcing tasks among multiple workers. However, they do not have built-in compatibility with popular crowdsourcing platforms and do not support human-bot interactions to take place within the crowdsourcing task. A lightweight option for dialogue annotations is EZCAT (Guibon et al., 2022), which provides a web-based serverless annotation framework that focuses on enhanced accessibility for conversation-level and turn-level annotations.

Other work have created tools for multi-modal annotations or speech-based annotations. Anvil (Kipp, 2001) provides a multi-modal dialogue annotation tool that enables annotation of audiovisual content. DialogueView (Yang and Heeman, 2005) is an annotation tool that is focused on segmenting audio conversations. DART (Weisser, 2016) focuses on enabling efficient annotations of speech acts and linguistic criteria to facilitate corpus-based research into pragmatics. Text is still the primary focus of BotEval and the templates we provide, but BotEval remains general enough to be adapted to such cases as well by modifying the templates we provide.

## 6 Conclusion

We presented BotEval and its usefulness in collecting human evaluations for interactive tasks that require live human-bot interactions through a case study of evaluating various language models on their ability to conversationally moderate online discussions. BotEval provides a customizable interface that can be adapted for various evaluation and annotation use cases while also providing integration with popular crowdsourcing platforms and task management features. We hope that this work will serve as an important foundation for setting up custom interactive human evaluation tasks that facilitate our understanding of more complex NLP systems as they become increasingly sophisticated and capable.

## Limitations

We designed BotEval to be modular such that customizing existing templates and modifying the dialogue manager's logic is simple, but it is yet not configured so that the task management process, shown in Figure 2 is independent of the process that serves the evaluation, shown in Figure 1. This means that any updates to BotEval that help with task management cannot be applied without restarting evaluation tasks that were launched already, which will interfere with any concurrent tasks that evaluators are working on. While inconvenient, this has not been a major issue as restarting can be done quickly such that it does not interfere the work of many evaluators and this doesn't mean that existing crowdsourcing tasks, as in the case of AMT, will be deleted and need to be relaunched again.

Another challenge for using BotEval may arise from the difficulty of managing a separate process that serves the bots that the human evaluators will interact with. However, if the BotEval user is able to launch a bot as part of BotEval, refactoring the code for that bot such that its responses are accessed through an API instead is a simple modification with plenty of online tutorials and tools, such as FastAPI.[13]

## References


Paweł Budzianowski, Tsung-Hsien Wen, Bo-Hsiang Tseng, Iñigo Casanueva, Stefan Ultes, Osman Ramadan, and Milica Gašić. 2018. MultiWOZ - a large-scale multi-domain Wizard-of-Oz dataset for task-oriented dialogue modelling. In *Proceedings of the 2018 Conference on Empirical Methods in Natural Language Processing*, pages 5016–5026, Brussels, Belgium. Association for Computational Linguistics.

Kushal Chawla, Jaysa Ramirez, Rene Clever, Gale Lucas, Jonathan May, and Jonathan Gratch. 2021a. Casino: A corpus of campsite negotiation dialogues for automatic negotiation systems. In *Proceedings of the 2021 Conference of the North American Chapter of the Association for Computational Linguistics: Human Language Technologies*, pages 3167–3185.

Kushal Chawla, Jaysa Ramirez, Rene Clever, Gale Lucas, Jonathan May, and Jonathan Gratch. 2021b. CaSiNo: A corpus of campsite negotiation dialogues for automatic negotiation systems. In *Proceedings of the 2021 Conference of the North American Chapter of the Association for Computational Linguistics: Human Language Technologies*, pages 3167–3185, Online. Association for Computational Linguistics.

Hyundong Cho, Shuai Liu, Taiwei Shi, Darpan Jain, Basem Rizk, Yuyang Huang, Zixun Lu, Nuan Wen, Jonathan Gratch, Emilio Ferrara, and Jonathan May. 2023. Can language model moderators improve the health of online discourse?

Hyundong Cho and Jonathan May. 2020. Grounding conversations with improvised dialogues. In *Proceedings of the 58th Annual Meeting of the Association for Computational Linguistics*, pages 2398–2413, Online. Association for Computational Linguistics.


[13]https://github.com/tiangolo/fastapi

Edward Collins, Nikolai Rozanov, and Bingbing Zhang. 2019. LIDA: Lightweight interactive dialogue annotator. In *Proceedings of the 2019 Conference on Empirical Methods in Natural Language Processing and the 9th International Joint Conference on Natural Language Processing (EMNLP-IJCNLP): System Demonstrations*, pages 121–126, Hong Kong, China. Association for Computational Linguistics.

Davide Cucurnia, Nikolai Rozanov, Irene Sucameli, Augusto Ciuffoletti, and Maria Simi. 2021. MATILDA - multi-AnnoTator multi-language InteractiveLightweight dialogue annotator. In *Proceedings of the 16th Conference of the European Chapter of the Association for Computational Linguistics: System Demonstrations*, pages 32–39, Online. Association for Computational Linguistics.

Hamish Cunningham. 2002. Gate, a general architecture for text engineering. *Computers and the Humanities*, 36:223–254.

Gaël Guibon, Matthieu Labeau, Luce Lefeuvre, and Chloé Clavel. 2022. Ezcat: an easy conversation annotation tool. In *Proceedings of the 13th Language Resources and Evaluation Conference*, Marseille, France. European Language Resources Association.

Michael Kipp. 2001. Anvil-a generic annotation tool for multimodal dialogue. In *Seventh European conference on speech communication and technology*. Citeseer.

Jan-Christoph Klie, Michael Bugert, Beto Boullosa, Richard Eckart De Castilho, and Iryna Gurevych. 2018. The inception platform: Machine-assisted and knowledge-oriented interactive annotation. In *Proceedings of the 27th international conference on computational linguistics: system demonstrations*, pages 5–9.

Margaret Li, Jason Weston, and Stephen Roller. 2019. Acute-eval: Improved dialogue evaluation with optimized questions and multi-turn comparisons. *arXiv preprint arXiv:1909.03087*.

Shuai Liu, Hyundong Cho, Marjorie Freedman, Xuezhe Ma, and Jonathan May. 2023. Recap: Retrieval-enhanced context-aware prefix encoder for personalized dialogue response generation. In *Proceedings of the 61st Annual Meeting of the Association for Computational Linguistics (Volume 1: Long Papers)*, pages 8404–8419.

Maitrey Mehta, Derek Caperton, Katherine Axford, Lauren Weitzman, David Atkins, Vivek Srikumar, and Zac Imel. 2022. Psychotherapy is not one thing: Simultaneous modeling of different therapeutic approaches. In *Proceedings of the Eighth Workshop on Computational Linguistics and Clinical Psychology*, pages 47–58, Seattle, USA. Association for Computational Linguistics.

A. H. Miller, W. Feng, A. Fisch, J. Lu, D. Batra, A. Bordes, D. Parikh, and J. Weston. 2017. Parlai: A dialog research software platform. *arXiv preprint arXiv:1705.06476*.

Hiroki Nakayama, Takahiro Kubo, Junya Kamura, Yasufumi Taniguchi, and Xu Liang. 2018. doccano: Text annotation tool for human. Software available from https://github.com/doccano/doccano.

Long Ouyang, Jeffrey Wu, Xu Jiang, Diogo Almeida, Carroll Wainwright, Pamela Mishkin, Chong Zhang, Sandhini Agarwal, Katarina Slama, Alex Gray, John Schulman, Jacob Hilton, Fraser Kelton, Luke Miller, Maddie Simens, Amanda Askell, Peter Welinder, Paul Christiano, Jan Leike, and Ryan Lowe. 2022. Training language models to follow instructions with human feedback. In *Advances in Neural Information Processing Systems*.

Jiaxin Pei, Aparna Ananthasubramaniam, Xingyao Wang, Naitian Zhou, Apostolos Dedeloudis, Jackson Sargent, and David Jurgens. 2022. Potato: The portable text annotation tool. In *Proceedings of the 2022 Conference on Empirical Methods in Natural Language Processing: System Demonstrations*.

Eric Smith, Orion Hsu, Rebecca Qian, Stephen Roller, Y-Lan Boureau, and Jason Weston. 2022. Human evaluation of conversations is an open problem: comparing the sensitivity of various methods for evaluating dialogue agents. In *Proceedings of the 4th Workshop on NLP for Conversational AI*, pages 77–97, Dublin, Ireland. Association for Computational Linguistics.

Pontus Stenetorp, Sampo Pyysalo, Goran Topić, Tomoko Ohta, Sophia Ananiadou, and Jun'ichi Tsujii. 2012. Brat: a web-based tool for nlp-assisted text annotation. In *Proceedings of the Demonstrations at the 13th Conference of the European Chapter of the Association for Computational Linguistics*, pages 102–107.

Theodore Sumers, Shunyu Yao, Karthik Narasimhan, and Thomas Griffiths. 2023. Cognitive architectures for language agents. *Transactions on Machine Learning Research*.

Jack Urbanek and Pratik Ringshia. 2023. Mephisto: A framework for portable, reproducible, and iterative crowdsourcing.

Martin Weisser. 2016. Dart–the dialogue annotation and research tool. *Corpus Linguistics and Linguistic Theory*, 12(2):355–388.

Fan Yang and Peter A Heeman. 2005. Dialogueview: an annotation tool for dialogue. In *Proceedings of HLT/EMNLP 2005 Interactive Demonstrations*, pages 20–21.

Pei Zhou, Hyundong Cho, Pegah Jandaghi, Dong-Ho Lee, Bill Yuchen Lin, Jay Pujara, and Xiang Ren. 2022. Reflect, not reflex: Inference-based common ground improves dialogue response quality. In *Proceedings of the 2022 Conference on Empirical Methods in Natural Language Processing*, pages 10450–10468, Abu Dhabi, United Arab Emirates. Association for Computational Linguistics.

# Appendix

## A Evaluation interface configurations

### A.1 Sample survey configuration

An example survey configuration is shown in Figure 4. Survey components are also easily dynamically configurable with common input options such as radio buttons, Likert scales, freeform text, etc. Users can create their own survey with HTML as well, but the customization options we provide through the YAML file covers most conversation-level evaluation use cases.

### A.2 Consent form configuration

An example of configuring the consent form is shown in Figure 5. When deployed without a crowdsourcing platform, these appear as checkboxes in the sign up process. Within AMT, we automatically sign up the workers with their worker ID and do not require a password, but they have to check the same checkboxes in order to move on to the task if they are doing the task for the first time.

```yaml
ratings:
- question: Did the moderator make specific suggestions for the given conversation
    to facilitate cooperation?
  choices: &choices
  - Not at all
  - Mostly not
  - So-so
  - Somewhat
  - Very
- question: Was the moderator fair to all users involved in the conversation?
  choices: *choices
- question: Did you (the user) become more engaged and willing to cooperate? (e.g.
    provide more details or ask sincere questions to make the conversation more constructive
    or be more persuasive)
  choices: *choices
- question: Did you (the user) become more respectful and less abusive? (e.g. less
    profanity, unconstructive criticism, or condescending sarcasm)
  choices: *choices
- question: How much did you agree with the arguments/viewpoints of the user that
    you were acting as?
  choices: *choices
- question: How much did you like the person that you were acting as?
  choices: *choices
- question: How could the moderator have been more effective? (e.g. reduce repetition,
    less generic suggestions, more examples, etc.)
  freetext:
    default: none
    required: false
- question: How can we improve the task design or survey questions?
  freetext:
    default: none
    required: false
```

Figure 4: An example of the survey pane configuration that contains a custom Likert scale and freeform text input fields. This configuration corresponds to the survey pane partially shown in Figure 1.

```yaml
onboarding:
  agreement_file: user-agreement.html
  instructions_file: instructions.html
  simple_instructions_file: simple_instructions.html

  checkboxes:
    instructions_read: I have read the instructions.
    iam_adult: I am 18 years or older and I understand that I may have to read and
      write using toxic language.
```

Figure 5: An example of configuring the consent form. The `agreement_file` parameter should point to the HTML file that shows the content of the consent form.

# *GenGO*: ACL Paper Explorer with Semantic Features

**Sotaro Takeshita[1], Simone Paolo Ponzetto[1], Kai Eckert[2]**
[1]Data and Web Science Group, University of Mannheim, Germany
[2]Mannheim University of Applied Sciences, Mannheim, Germany
{sotaro.takeshita, ponzetto}@uni-mannheim.de
k.eckert@hs-mannheim.de

## Abstract

We present *GenGO*[1], a system for exploring papers published in ACL conferences. Paper data stored in our database is enriched with multi-aspect summaries, extracted named entities, a field of study label, and text embeddings by our data processing pipeline. These metadata are used in our web-based user interface to enable researchers to quickly find papers relevant to their interests, and grasp an overview of papers without reading full-text of papers. To keep *GenGO* available online as long as possible, we design *GenGO* to be simple and efficient to reduce maintenance and financial costs. In addition, the modularity of our data processing pipeline lets developers easily extend it to add new features. We make our code available to foster open development and transparency: `https://gengo.sotaro.io/`.[2]

## 1 Introduction

The rapidly growing number of scientific papers makes it difficult for researchers to keep up-to-date with the state of the literature (Bornmann and Mutz, 2015). Scholarly document processing (SDP) aims to support researchers with this challenge by building tools to process knowledge stored in research papers (Chandrasekaran et al., 2020) and has been increasingly drawing attention from academic and industrial communities. Together with the recent developments in natural language processing (NLP), a number of powerful technologies are now available in SDP. For instance, automatic scientific paper summarization systems provide short summaries encapsulating the essential points in a paper so that researchers can grasp the overview without reading its abstract or even full-text (Cachola et al., 2020; Yasunaga et al., 2019). A series of works on paper representation learning aims to obtain numerical representations of papers that can be used for information retrieval or recommendation (Ostendorff et al., 2022; Singh et al., 2023). Automatic information extraction systems allow repositories of papers to be organized in a structured manner (Jain et al., 2020; Viswanathan et al., 2021). There are also system demonstrations that implement user interfaces to the SDP technologies to make the aforementioned models available to scientists. Erera et al. (2019) introduce a system that lets users consume papers with automatically generated summaries. Hongwimol et al. (2021) is a web-based tool where users can explore different complex concepts and their relations by exploiting scientific knowledge graphs.

As the NLP community also faces a large number of publications (Bollmann et al., 2023) with dynamically changing trends (Schopf et al., 2023), there are systems which explicitly target this domain. The ACL Anthology (Bollmann et al., 2023) serves as an essential resource for the community by providing a repository of papers published in ACL conferences. Schäfer et al. (2011) introduce the ACL Anthology Searchbench that implements ACL Anthology a more fine-grained structured search. Ding et al. (2020) device a model-based semantic search in addition to the lexical search to provide a powerful literature search infrastructure. However, currently, there are no works which integrate different types of SDP technologies (e.g., summarization, information retrieval and extraction) in one system for NLP papers.

In this paper, we describe our system, dubbed *GenGO*, equipped with various semantic features to help researchers consume a large number of papers efficiently. Specifically, *GenGO* combines three types of SDP technologies. (1) **Multi-aspect summarization**: one paper in *GenGO* is coupled with four one-sentence summaries that summarize the Overview, Challenge, Approach, and Outcome of a paper. This enables researchers to quickly understand the overview of a paper from different

[1]gengo (言語) means 'language' in Japanese.
[2]Demo video: `https://youtu.be/yYh9U5IVbIw`



*Proceedings of the 62nd Annual Meeting of the Association for Computational Linguistics (Volume 3: System Demonstrations)*, pages 117–126
August 11-16, 2024 ©2024 Association for Computational Linguistics

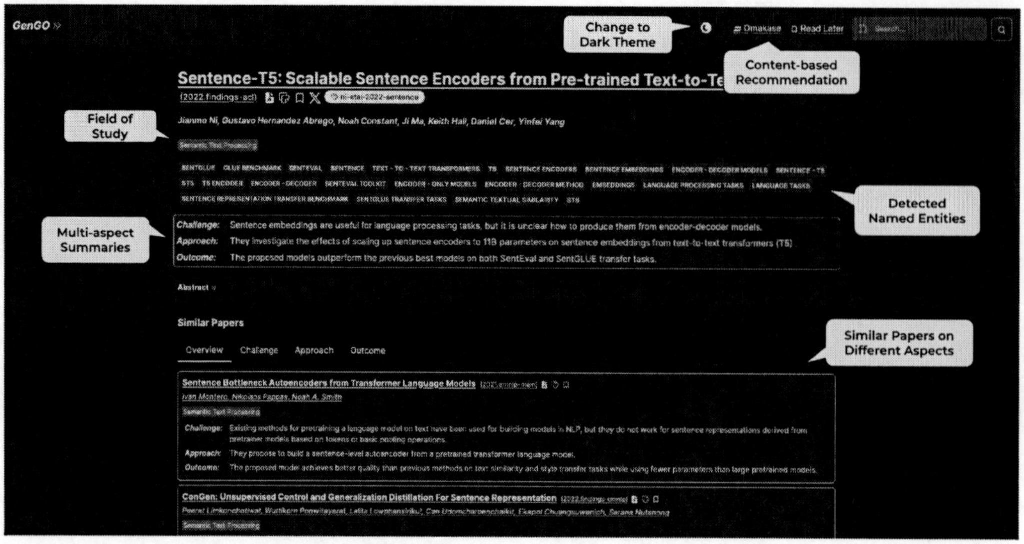


Figure 1: A screenshot exhibits how *GenGO* presents one paper. Each paper is complemented with multi-aspect summaries, field of study labels, named entities, and similar papers.

viewpoints. (2) **Semantic search**: our system can retrieve papers that are semantically relevant given user-provided queries. (3) **Information extraction**: *GenGO* automatically extracts technical terms and predicts the topic of a paper to enable fine-grained filtering and search. We design *GenGO* to be efficient and simple using cloud-based software so it requires low maintenance and financial cost, and currently achieves to index 30k+ papers.

## 2 Developments in SDP

In this section, we review existing papers and commercial products that target processing scholarly documents. The models and datasets used in the development of *GenGO* are marked with *.

### 2.1 Automatic text summarization

Text summarization systems for scientific papers have been an interest in NLP for decades. One of the early works, Paice (1980) proposes a system that aims to automatically produce abstract sections of papers. Recently, the performance of summarization models drastically improved with the emergence of neural network-based models (Rush et al., 2015; Gehrmann et al., 2018; Raffel et al., 2020a). While one straightforward approach for paper summarization would be to feed the texts of a paper to models to produce summaries, there are works that exploit unique characteristics in scholarly documents to improve their performance. Cohan and Goharian (2015) propose to use citation sentences to avoid inconsistency between summaries. Xiao and Carenini (2019) use global and local content in the paper to improve the summarization of long research papers. Additionally to the efforts on modelling, there are also various works that introduce language resources to develop and evaluate scientific paper summarization systems. Cohan et al. (2018) constructed a dataset by regarding the abstract sections in papers as summaries and the rest as inputs. Cachola et al. (2020)* collected the summaries written by authors and reviewers of a paper submitted to an open reviewing platform, which later extended into a cross-lingual variant by Takeshita et al. (2022, 2023). The most relevant summarization work to our system is the ACLSum dataset introduced by Takeshita et al. (2024a)*, in which 250 papers published in ACL-related conferences are annotated with abstractive and extractive summaries on three different aspects, namely Challenge, Approach, and Outcome.

### 2.2 Information retrieval

In recent NLP conferences, one proceeding can have more than 1k papers (EMNLP'23 main track has 1,047 papers), making efficient means of finding relevant papers essential. Bhagavatula et al. (2018) propose a method which takes a paper draft and finds relevant papers using a text embedding model. The aspect-based similarity model presented by Ostendorff et al. (2020) enables researchers to find papers by queries on different aspects. Cohan et al. (2020) introduce SPECTER, a scientific language model pre-trained using citation graphs, it produces high-performance paper embeddings. While it does not solely target scientific documents, all-MiniLM-L6-v2 (Reimers and Gurevych, 2019)* is a lightweight text embedding model which is trained on a number of sentence pair datasets including scientific texts using a contrastive objective function.

### 2.3 Text classification

Scientific documents often do not come with rich metadata that can be used to form a structured data repository. Jurgens et al. (2018) introduce a citation intent classification dataset for the NLP domain. This enables richer citation graphs of scientific papers. Schopf et al. (2023)* present a semi-automatically and manually annotated dataset for the field of study classification, respectively for training and evaluation purposes. The classification model trained on the dataset enables automatic analysis of how the research trend in NLP changes over time.

### 2.4 Information extraction

The ScienceIE task (Augenstein et al., 2017) aims to develop methods that extract keyphrases from scientific papers, which can be further used in retrieval systems. Jain et al. (2020)* presents, the SciREX dataset, a document-level information extraction dataset based on machine learning papers. Viswanathan et al. (2021) propose to use citation graph to perform information extraction from scientific documents.

### 2.5 Applications

While the aforementioned works present models or language resources, they require a user interface to be delivered to researchers. There are a number of academic system demonstrations and commercial services that are designed to fill this gap. The IBM Science Summarizer presents research papers coupled with automatically produced extractive summaries (Erera et al., 2019). Gökçe et al. (2020) present an online editor where users can explore the existing papers while writing a manuscript. Hongwimol et al. (2021) introduce a web-based interactive tool which visualizes explanations and relationships between concepts using graph-structured data. A system introduced by Gu and Hahnloser (2023) enables users to find relevant papers with generated or extracted summaries given user-provided context and keywords. In addition to the system demonstrations which are often done in academic institutions such as universities, there are also software developed more intensively including commercial products. Semantic Scholar (Kinney et al., 2023) is a search engine that also provides paper summarization and recommendations. Zeta Alpha (Fadaee et al., 2020) and Elicit[3] provide search features and also chat-based interfaces based on recent large language models.

To the best of our knowledge, there are no system demonstrations that combine automatic summarization, information retrieval and extraction methods in NLP papers. While web-based applications developed by private organizations mentioned such as Semantic Scholar provide similar functionalities, the closed nature of these software hinders transparency of how and which models are being used.

## 3 System requirements

One pragmatic challenge for a system demonstration project is to keep the system up and running, especially when it is maintained by a few developers with a limited budget. Indeed, 10 out of 27 web-based system demonstrations presented at ACL 2023 (held in July) are offline after less than one year (at the time of writing, March 2024). We speculate that this is due to (1) maintenance effort and (2) financial costs as mentioned by Bollmann et al. (2023). To achieve a long lifespan of our system, we design *GenGO* to minimize the aforementioned two factors. (1) Maintenance effort: we minimize the number of servers to be taken care of. Specifically, our system does not rely on custom servers that often demand intensive system maintenance. Instead, we opt for a server-less architecture by making use of managed cloud-based services. To reduce (2) Financial costs: we designed our pipeline not to make any online inferences that require GPUs. Our data processing pipeline can run fully offline, process each document once, and store the results in a database. The only online inference *GenGO* makes is when to compute a text embedding of a user-provided query. Instead of hosting a server to compute embeddings for each user request, we use a lightweight text embedding model and perform the inference on the user's device. Because of these design decisions, *GenGO* is currently running without any financial cost from

[3] https://elicit.com/

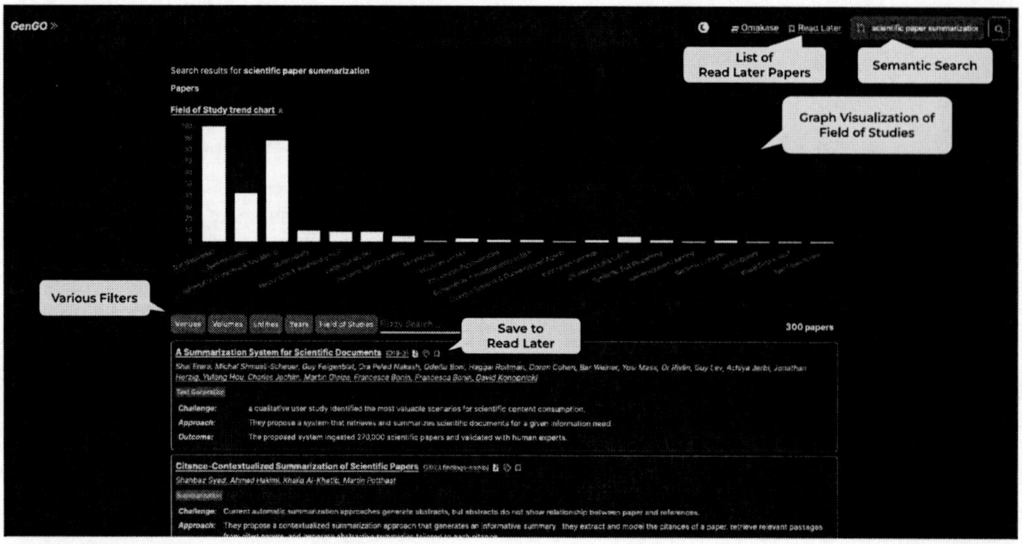


Figure 2: A screenshot showing how *GenGO* presents a list of papers retrieved by its semantic search functionality. Users can apply various filters to the list (e.g., venue, named entities, field of studies, etc...) to efficiently find relevant papers.

our disposal while indexing more than 30k papers. By using the cost estimator provided by Qdrant[4], we estimate that when the number of indexed papers increases by ten times, it would require around 10 Euro per month.

## 4 *GenGO*

In this section, we describe the main features of *GenGO* (§4.1) and a system overview (§4.2). Table 5 in Appendix lists all the models and datasets with external links.

### 4.1 Main features

**Multi-aspect summarization.** We complement each paper with automatically generated one-sentence summaries on four different aspects, namely Overview (Generic overall summary), Challenge (The current situation faced by the researcher), Approach (How they intend to carry out investigation), and Outcome (Overall conclusion). Refer Fisas et al. (2015) for the detailed definitions. This enables users to quickly understand these aspects of a paper without reading its full-text or even the abstract.

We use two summarization datasets and two transformer-based models. To generate Overview summaries, we use a BART-large model (Lewis et al., 2020) fine-tuned on the SciTLDR dataset (Cachola et al., 2020). To generate multi-aspect summaries, we fine-tune one T5-base (Raffel et al., 2020b) on each aspect using the ACLSum dataset (Takeshita et al., 2024a). Table 1 shows the performance of each model evaluated on corresponding datasets by ROUGE F1 (Lin, 2004) and its keyword-focused extension, ROUGE-K (Takeshita et al., 2024b). In *GenGO*, we follow the corresponding papers and use the abstract for the overview summarization, and the abstract, introduction and conclusion sections for multi-aspect summarization as inputs.

| Dataset | R-1 | R-2 | R-L | R-K |
|---|---|---|---|---|
| **SciTLDR - Overview** | 43.9 | 22.3 | 36.6 | 41.36 |
| **ACLSum - Challenge** | 18.9 | 2.5 | 13.6 | 50.27 |
| **ACLSum - Approach** | 44.8 | 22.4 | 38.4 | 55.85 |
| **ACLSum - Outcome** | 42.3 | 21.7 | 35.0 | 37.14 |

Table 1: Performance of summarization models.

**Semantic search and recommendation.** *GenGO* can retrieve semantically relevant documents given a user-provided query, and provide two types of paper recommendations. (1) Content-based recommendation: where each paper is presented with its similar papers in four different aspects (Overview, Challenge, Approach, and Outcome). (2) History-based recommendation: papers relevant to the user's reading history.

[4]`https://cloud.qdrant.io/calculator`

| Dataset | NDCG@10 | MAP@10 |
|---|---|---|
| **SciFact** | 0.645 | 0.596 |
| **SciDocs** | 0.216 | 0.129 |

Table 2: Performance of retrieval model

| Dataset | Precision | Recall | F1 |
|---|---|---|---|
| **NLP Taxonomy** | 92.46 | 93.99 | 92.21 |

Table 3: Performance of field of Study classification models.

We use the all-MiniLM-L6-v2 model[5] as our underlying text encoder model. To perform the semantic search, we compute cosine similarities between an embedding of a user-provided query and embeddings of all of the indexed papers and return the 300 most similar papers. To compute paper embeddings, we use paper titles and abstracts as inputs to the text encoder. For content-based recommendation on the Overview aspect, we use an embedding of the opened paper as a query vector. For the other three aspects, we use the generated summaries (refer to Section 4.1) on the corresponding aspect as a query text. To provide reading history-based recommendations, we use an average vector from the papers in the user's reading history as a query vector. Table 2 shows the performances of the all-MiniLM-L6-v2 model on two retrieval benchmark datasets from the scientific domain, SciDocs (Cohan et al., 2020) and SciFACT (Wadden et al., 2020). To respect the user's privacy, we store the reading history information using the localStorage property of the user's web browser.

**Field of study filtering.** We predict the field of study labels (g.g., Text Generation) for each paper to enable users to apply filtering by the topics of their interests.

We use the model published by Schopf et al. (2023). Its underlying model architecture is BERT-base (Devlin et al., 2019) and parameters are initialized using SPECTER model (Cohan et al., 2020) and the authors fine-tune the model using their classification dataset. We present the performance of the model reported in the original paper in Table 3. In *GenGO*, we follow the strategy from the original paper and use titles and abstracts as inputs.

**Field of study visualizer.** Every time a user sees a list of papers in *GenGO*, it is complemented by a

[5]https://huggingface.co/sentence-transformers/all-MiniLM-L6-v2

| Type | Precision | Recall | F1 |
|---|---|---|---|
| **Method** | 72.18 | 70.43 | 71.29 |
| **Task** | 65.58 | 53.41 | 58.87 |
| **Dataset** | 50.00 | 53.26 | 51.58 |
| **Metric** | 72.17 | 60.27 | 65.68 |

Table 4: Performance of named entity recognition model.

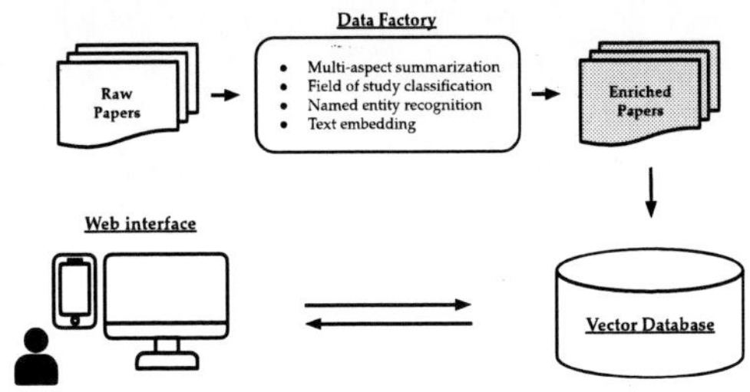


Figure 3: A system overview.

bar-graph visualization of the field of study labels. Users can grasp topic popularity in a conference proceeding or a publication list of a researcher. Figure 2 shows an example over a list of search results.

**Named entity filtering.** We attach named entities extracted from the paper content as metadata to achieve fine-grained filtering.

We train the transition-based parser model implemented in spaCy (Honnibal et al., 2020) on the SciRex dataset (Jain et al., 2020) to extract entities from titles and abstracts. Table 4 shows the results of the test split of SciRex.

**Save to read later.** While this does not require any NLP-based methodologies, since we intend our platform to be used to digest many papers quickly, we implemented this feature so that a user can "save" a paper while skimming over a long list of papers for later to study in detail.

We use the localStorage property of web browsers to save the paper information. This enables to keep the data locally on the user's device instead of external servers.

### 4.2 System description

*GenGO* stands on three components, *data factory*, *vector database*, and *web-based user interface* as depicted in Figure 3. In the remainder of this section, we describe each component in detail.

**Data factory.** This module prepares the published research articles from the ACL anthology to be indexed in our database. Concretely, it first downloads a paper in the PDF format from ACL Anthology, runs Grobid (Lope, 2008–2023) to extract the full-text, and segments the text into sentences using Spacy[6]. After having the structure data of a paper, we run models described in Section 4.1 for each paper. After this enrichment process, as the final step in the data factory, it uploads the resulting data to the vector database, described in the following paragraph. Currently, we opt for relatively lightweight models so that this pipeline can run even on a consumer laptop without GPUs. For instance, it takes 4 hours to process 700+ papers from ACL 2020 on a MacBook Air M2.

**Vector database.** Instead of traditional relational databases, we use a vector database to host our enriched paper data. Vector databases can store documents with metadata and use numerical vectors for indexing to achieve vector-based searching given a query vector. We can achieve semantic search by using semantic embedding vectors of papers' texts and user-provided queries. Among several available vector database implementations, we opt for Qdrant[7]. This is due to that Qdrant is an open-source software making the retrieval mechanism transparent, followed by more minor technical reasons such as the support of multiple vectors for one data point enabling *GenGO* to retrieve papers on different aspects, and fast search speed compared to the other implementations. We host our Qdrant instance using the managed solution provided by a company which leads the development of Qdrant. At the time of writing, *GenGO* indexes publications from nine major ACL conferences from 2018 to 2023, resulting in more than 30k papers and running free of charge. This database is the only component in our system that requires financial costs when scaling up the system. In the current pricing options, we estimate that the Qdrant cloud solution would require c.a. 10 Euro if we increase the number of indexed papers by 10 times.

**Web-based user interface.** Like most modern web applications, *GenGO* is developed using a JavaScript framework to achieve interactivity. Specifically, we use Svelte[8]. To achieve responsive design, we use tailwindcss[9] as our CSS framework, and host our frontend application using Vercel[10].

[6]https://spacy.io/

[7]https://qdrant.tech/

[8]https://svelte.dev/

[9]https://tailwindcss.com/

[10]https://vercel.com/

## 5 Limitation of current system

Because the metadata used to build the *GenGO* is from the ACL Anthology project, our system inherits its challenges such as the disambiguation of author names (Bollmann et al., 2023). In addition, there are several limitations unique to our system. (1) Speed and the number of indexed papers: Compared to similar services developed by large institutions such as Semantic Scholar, our system relies on limited computational resources. This currently results in slower response time especially when showing a long list of papers, and also to compensate for the limited size of the data storage, we only index approximately 30% of papers from the whole ACL Anthology repository. We are also hindered in applying the most powerful models available in our data factory due to the lack of sufficient computational resources. (2) Summarization quality: Hallucination in text generation remains an open challenge (Dong et al., 2022; Koh et al., 2022; Ma et al., 2023). During the development, we observed cases where the generated summaries do not convey the full information of a paper or contain information inconsistent with the corresponding paper. (3) Retrieval bias: While the semantic search approach used in our system can work with paraphrases or synonyms, due to the 'blackboxness' of model-based encoders, it remains unclear whether such models have a bias towards retrieving certain styles of texts (MacAvaney et al., 2022).

## 6 Conclusion

In this paper, we described *GenGO*, a system to explore ACL papers with various types of semantically empowered functionalities. Our system enables NLP researchers to quickly find relevant papers using semantic search and various fine-grained filters, and grasp paper overviews by reading multi-aspect summaries. *GenGO* also provides utility features such as paper recommendations or 'read it later' to further enhance user experience.

## References

Isabelle Augenstein, Mrinal Das, Sebastian Riedel, Lakshmi Vikraman, and Andrew McCallum. 2017. SemEval 2017 task 10: ScienceIE - extracting keyphrases and relations from scientific publications. In *Proceedings of the 11th International Workshop on Semantic Evaluation (SemEval-2017)*, pages 546–

555, Vancouver, Canada. Association for Computational Linguistics.

Chandra Bhagavatula, Sergey Feldman, Russell Power, and Waleed Ammar. 2018. Content-based citation recommendation. In *Proceedings of the 2018 Conference of the North American Chapter of the Association for Computational Linguistics: Human Language Technologies, Volume 1 (Long Papers)*, pages 238–251, New Orleans, Louisiana. Association for Computational Linguistics.

Marcel Bollmann, Nathan Schneider, Arne Köhn, and Matt Post. 2023. Two decades of the ACL Anthology: Development, impact, and open challenges. In *Proceedings of the 3rd Workshop for Natural Language Processing Open Source Software (NLP-OSS 2023)*, pages 83–94, Singapore, Singapore. Empirical Methods in Natural Language Processing.

Lutz Bornmann and Rüdiger Mutz. 2015. Growth rates of modern science: A bibliometric analysis based on the number of publications and cited references. *J. Assoc. Inf. Sci. Technol.*, 66(11):2215–2222. Publisher: Wiley.

Isabel Cachola, Kyle Lo, Arman Cohan, and Daniel Weld. 2020. TLDR: Extreme summarization of scientific documents. In *Findings of the Association for Computational Linguistics: EMNLP 2020*, pages 4766–4777, Online. Association for Computational Linguistics.

Muthu Kumar Chandrasekaran, Anita de Waard, Guy Feigenblat, Dayne Freitag, Tirthankar Ghosal, Eduard Hovy, Petr Knoth, David Konopnicki, Philipp Mayr, Robert M. Patton, and Michal Shmueli-Scheuer, editors. 2020. *Proceedings of the First Workshop on Scholarly Document Processing*. Association for Computational Linguistics, Online.

Arman Cohan, Franck Dernoncourt, Doo Soon Kim, Trung Bui, Seokhwan Kim, Walter Chang, and Nazli Goharian. 2018. A discourse-aware attention model for abstractive summarization of long documents. In *Proceedings of the 2018 Conference of the North American Chapter of the Association for Computational Linguistics: Human Language Technologies, Volume 2 (Short Papers)*, pages 615–621, New Orleans, Louisiana. Association for Computational Linguistics.

Arman Cohan, Sergey Feldman, Iz Beltagy, Doug Downey, and Daniel Weld. 2020. SPECTER: Document-level representation learning using citation-informed transformers. In *Proceedings of the 58th Annual Meeting of the Association for Computational Linguistics*, pages 2270–2282, Online. Association for Computational Linguistics.

Arman Cohan and Nazli Goharian. 2015. Scientific article summarization using citation-context and article's discourse structure. In *Proceedings of the 2015 Conference on Empirical Methods in Natural Language Processing*, pages 390–400, Lisbon, Portugal. Association for Computational Linguistics.

Jacob Devlin, Ming-Wei Chang, Kenton Lee, and Kristina Toutanova. 2019. BERT: Pre-training of deep bidirectional transformers for language understanding. In *Proceedings of the 2019 Conference of the North American Chapter of the Association for Computational Linguistics: Human Language Technologies, Volume 1 (Long and Short Papers)*, pages 4171–4186, Minneapolis, Minnesota. Association for Computational Linguistics.

Shane Ding, Edwin Zhang, and Jimmy Lin. 2020. Cydex: Neural search infrastructure for the scholarly literature. In *Proceedings of the First Workshop on Scholarly Document Processing*, pages 168–173, Online. Association for Computational Linguistics.

Yue Dong, John Wieting, and Pat Verga. 2022. Faithful to the document or to the world? mitigating hallucinations via entity-linked knowledge in abstractive summarization. In *Findings of the Association for Computational Linguistics: EMNLP 2022*, pages 1067–1082, Abu Dhabi, United Arab Emirates. Association for Computational Linguistics.

Shai Erera, Michal Shmueli-Scheuer, Guy Feigenblat, Ora Peled Nakash, Odellia Boni, Haggai Roitman, Doron Cohen, Bar Weiner, Yosi Mass, Or Rivlin, Guy Lev, Achiya Jerbi, Jonathan Herzig, Yufang Hou, Charles Jochim, Martin Gleize, Francesca Bonin, Francesca Bonin, and David Konopnicki. 2019. A summarization system for scientific documents. In *Proceedings of the 2019 Conference on Empirical Methods in Natural Language Processing and the 9th International Joint Conference on Natural Language Processing (EMNLP-IJCNLP): System Demonstrations*, pages 211–216, Hong Kong, China. Association for Computational Linguistics.

Marzieh Fadaee, Olga Gureenkova, Fernando Rejon Barrera, Carsten Schnober, Wouter Weerkamp, and Jakub Zavrel. 2020. A new neural search and insights platform for navigating and organizing AI research. In *Proceedings of the First Workshop on Scholarly Document Processing*, pages 207–213, Online. Association for Computational Linguistics.

Beatriz Fisas, Horacio Saggion, and Francesco Ronzano. 2015. On the discoursive structure of computer graphics research papers. In *Proceedings of the 9th Linguistic Annotation Workshop*, pages 42–51, Denver, Colorado, USA. Association for Computational Linguistics.

Sebastian Gehrmann, Yuntian Deng, and Alexander Rush. 2018. Bottom-up abstractive summarization. In *Proceedings of the 2018 Conference on Empirical Methods in Natural Language Processing*, pages 4098–4109, Brussels, Belgium. Association for Computational Linguistics.

Onur Gökçe, Jonathan Prada, Nikola I. Nikolov, Nianlong Gu, and Richard H.R. Hahnloser. 2020. Embedding-based scientific literature discovery in a text editor application. In *Proceedings of the 58th Annual Meeting of the Association for Computational*

*Linguistics: System Demonstrations*, pages 320–326, Online. Association for Computational Linguistics.

Nianlong Gu and Richard H.R. Hahnloser. 2023. SciLit: A platform for joint scientific literature discovery, summarization and citation generation. In *Proceedings of the 61st Annual Meeting of the Association for Computational Linguistics (Volume 3: System Demonstrations)*, pages 235–246, Toronto, Canada. Association for Computational Linguistics.

Pollawat Hongwimol, Peeranuth Kehasukcharoen, Pasit Laohawarutchai, Piyawat Lertvittayakumjorn, Aik Beng Ng, Zhangsheng Lai, Timothy Liu, and Peerapon Vateekul. 2021. ESRA: Explainable scientific research assistant. In *Proceedings of the 59th Annual Meeting of the Association for Computational Linguistics and the 11th International Joint Conference on Natural Language Processing: System Demonstrations*, pages 114–121, Online. Association for Computational Linguistics.

Matthew Honnibal, Ines Montani, Sofie Van Landeghem, and Adriane Boyd. 2020. spaCy: Industrial-strength Natural Language Processing in Python.

Sarthak Jain, Madeleine van Zuylen, Hannaneh Hajishirzi, and Iz Beltagy. 2020. SciREX: A challenge dataset for document-level information extraction. In *Proceedings of the 58th Annual Meeting of the Association for Computational Linguistics*, pages 7506–7516, Online. Association for Computational Linguistics.

David Jurgens, Srijan Kumar, Raine Hoover, Dan McFarland, and Dan Jurafsky. 2018. Measuring the evolution of a scientific field through citation frames. *Transactions of the Association for Computational Linguistics*, 6:391–406.

Rodney Kinney, Chloe Anastasiades, Russell Authur, Iz Beltagy, Jonathan Bragg, Alexandra Buraczynski, Isabel Cachola, Stefan Candra, Yoganand Chandrasekhar, Arman Cohan, Miles Crawford, Doug Downey, Jason Dunkelberger, Oren Etzioni, Rob Evans, Sergey Feldman, Joseph Gorney, David Graham, Fangzhou Hu, Regan Huff, Daniel King, Sebastian Kohlmeier, Bailey Kuehl, Michael Langan, Daniel Lin, Haokun Liu, Kyle Lo, Jaron Lochner, Kelsey MacMillan, Tyler Murray, Chris Newell, Smita Rao, Shaurya Rohatgi, Paul Sayre, Zejiang Shen, Amanpreet Singh, Luca Soldaini, Shivashankar Subramanian, Amber Tanaka, Alex D. Wade, Linda Wagner, Lucy Lu Wang, Chris Wilhelm, Caroline Wu, Jiangjiang Yang, Angele Zamarron, Madeleine Van Zuylen, and Daniel S. Weld. 2023. The semantic scholar open data platform.

Huan Yee Koh, Jiaxin Ju, He Zhang, Ming Liu, and Shirui Pan. 2022. How far are we from robust long abstractive summarization? In *Proceedings of the 2022 Conference on Empirical Methods in Natural Language Processing*, pages 2682–2698, Abu Dhabi, United Arab Emirates. Association for Computational Linguistics.

Mike Lewis, Yinhan Liu, Naman Goyal, Marjan Ghazvininejad, Abdelrahman Mohamed, Omer Levy, Veselin Stoyanov, and Luke Zettlemoyer. 2020. BART: Denoising sequence-to-sequence pre-training for natural language generation, translation, and comprehension. In *Proceedings of the 58th Annual Meeting of the Association for Computational Linguistics*, pages 7871–7880, Online. Association for Computational Linguistics.

Chin-Yew Lin. 2004. ROUGE: A package for automatic evaluation of summaries. In *Text Summarization Branches Out*, pages 74–81, Barcelona, Spain. Association for Computational Linguistics.

Patrice Lope. 2008–2023. Grobid. `https://github.com/kermitt2/grobid`.

Liang Ma, Shuyang Cao, Robert L Logan IV, Di Lu, Shihao Ran, Ke Zhang, Joel Tetreault, and Alejandro Jaimes. 2023. BUMP: A benchmark of unfaithful minimal pairs for meta-evaluation of faithfulness metrics. In *Proceedings of the 61st Annual Meeting of the Association for Computational Linguistics (Volume 1: Long Papers)*, pages 12788–12812, Toronto, Canada. Association for Computational Linguistics.

Sean MacAvaney, Sergey Feldman, Nazli Goharian, Doug Downey, and Arman Cohan. 2022. ABNIRML: Analyzing the behavior of neural IR models. *Transactions of the Association for Computational Linguistics*, 10:224–239.

Malte Ostendorff, Nils Rethmeier, Isabelle Augenstein, Bela Gipp, and Georg Rehm. 2022. Neighborhood contrastive learning for scientific document representations with citation embeddings. In *Proceedings of the 2022 Conference on Empirical Methods in Natural Language Processing*, pages 11670–11688, Abu Dhabi, United Arab Emirates. Association for Computational Linguistics.

Malte Ostendorff, Terry Ruas, Till Blume, Bela Gipp, and Georg Rehm. 2020. Aspect-based document similarity for research papers. In *Proceedings of the 28th International Conference on Computational Linguistics*, pages 6194–6206, Barcelona, Spain (Online). International Committee on Computational Linguistics.

C. D. Paice. 1980. The automatic generation of literature abstracts: an approach based on the identification of self-indicating phrases. In *Proceedings of the 3rd Annual ACM Conference on Research and Development in Information Retrieval*, SIGIR '80, page 172–191, GBR. Butterworth & Co.

Colin Raffel, Noam Shazeer, Adam Roberts, Katherine Lee, Sharan Narang, Michael Matena, Yanqi Zhou, Wei Li, and Peter J Liu. 2020a. Exploring the Limits of Transfer Learning with a Unified Text-to-Text Transformer. *J. Mach. Learn. Res.*, 21(140):1–67.

Colin Raffel, Noam Shazeer, Adam Roberts, Katherine Lee, Sharan Narang, Michael Matena, Yanqi Zhou, Wei Li, and Peter J Liu. 2020b. Exploring the limits of transfer learning with a unified text-to-text transformer. *The Journal of Machine Learning Research*, 21(1):5485–5551.

Nils Reimers and Iryna Gurevych. 2019. Sentence-BERT: Sentence embeddings using Siamese BERT-networks. In *Proceedings of the 2019 Conference on Empirical Methods in Natural Language Processing and the 9th International Joint Conference on Natural Language Processing (EMNLP-IJCNLP)*, pages 3982–3992, Hong Kong, China. Association for Computational Linguistics.

Alexander M. Rush, Sumit Chopra, and Jason Weston. 2015. A neural attention model for abstractive sentence summarization. In *Proceedings of the 2015 Conference on Empirical Methods in Natural Language Processing*, pages 379–389, Lisbon, Portugal. Association for Computational Linguistics.

Ulrich Schäfer, Bernd Kiefer, Christian Spurk, Jörg Steffen, and Rui Wang. 2011. The ACL Anthology searchbench. In *Proceedings of the ACL-HLT 2011 System Demonstrations*, pages 7–13, Portland, Oregon. Association for Computational Linguistics.

Tim Schopf, Karim Arabi, and Florian Matthes. 2023. Exploring the landscape of natural language processing research. In *Proceedings of the 14th International Conference on Recent Advances in Natural Language Processing*, pages 1034–1045, Varna, Bulgaria. INCOMA Ltd., Shoumen, Bulgaria.

Amanpreet Singh, Mike D'Arcy, Arman Cohan, Doug Downey, and Sergey Feldman. 2023. SciRepEval: A multi-format benchmark for scientific document representations. In *Proceedings of the 2023 Conference on Empirical Methods in Natural Language Processing*, pages 5548–5566, Singapore. Association for Computational Linguistics.

Sotaro Takeshita, Tommaso Green, Niklas Friedrich, Kai Eckert, and Simone Paolo Ponzetto. 2022. X-scitldr: cross-lingual extreme summarization of scholarly documents. In *Proceedings of the 22nd ACM/IEEE Joint Conference on Digital Libraries*, JCDL '22, New York, NY, USA. Association for Computing Machinery.

Sotaro Takeshita, Tommaso Green, Niklas Friedrich, Kai Eckert, and Simone Paolo Ponzetto. 2023. Cross-lingual extreme summarization of scholarly documents. *International Journal on Digital Libraries*, pages 1–23.

Sotaro Takeshita, Tommaso Green, Ines Reinig, Kai Eckert, and Simone Paolo Ponzetto. 2024a. ACLSum: A New Dataset for Aspect-based Summarization of Scientific Publications. ArXiv:2403.05303, To appear at NAACL 2024.

Sotaro Takeshita, Simone Paolo Ponzetto, and Kai Eckert. 2024b. ROUGE-K: Do Your Summaries Have Keywords? ArXiv:2403.05186.

Vijay Viswanathan, Graham Neubig, and Pengfei Liu. 2021. CitationIE: Leveraging the citation graph for scientific information extraction. In *Proceedings of the 59th Annual Meeting of the Association for Computational Linguistics and the 11th International Joint Conference on Natural Language Processing (Volume 1: Long Papers)*, pages 719–731, Online. Association for Computational Linguistics.

David Wadden, Shanchuan Lin, Kyle Lo, Lucy Lu Wang, Madeleine van Zuylen, Arman Cohan, and Hannaneh Hajishirzi. 2020. Fact or fiction: Verifying scientific claims. In *Proceedings of the 2020 Conference on Empirical Methods in Natural Language Processing (EMNLP)*, pages 7534–7550, Online. Association for Computational Linguistics.

Wen Xiao and Giuseppe Carenini. 2019. Extractive summarization of long documents by combining global and local context. In *Proceedings of the 2019 Conference on Empirical Methods in Natural Language Processing and the 9th International Joint Conference on Natural Language Processing (EMNLP-IJCNLP)*, pages 3011–3021, Hong Kong, China. Association for Computational Linguistics.

Michihiro Yasunaga, Jungo Kasai, Rui Zhang, Alexander R Fabbri, Irene Li, Dan Friedman, and Dragomir R Radev. 2019. Scisummnet: A large annotated corpus and content-impact models for scientific paper summarization with citation networks. In *Proceedings of the AAAI conference on artificial intelligence*, volume 33, pages 7386–7393.

# A Appendix

| **Name** | Task | **URL** |
|---|---|---|
| **BART$_{LARGE}$** | Summarization (Overview) | https://huggingface.co/sobamchan/bart-large-scitldr |
| **T5$_{BASE}$** | Summarization (Challenge) | https://huggingface.co/sobamchan/t5-base-aclsum-challenge-nofilter |
| **T5$_{BASE}$** | Summarization (Approach) | https://huggingface.co/sobamchan/t5-base-aclsum-approach-nofilter |
| **T5$_{BASE}$** | Summarization (Outcome) | https://huggingface.co/sobamchan/t5-base-aclsum-outcome-nofilter |
| **SciTLDR** | Summarization (Overview) | https://github.com/allenai/scitldr |
| **all-MiniLM-L6-v2** | Retrieval | https://huggingface.co/sentence-transformers/all-MiniLM-L6-v2 |
| **Taxonomy classifier** | Field of study classification | https://huggingface.co/TimSchopf/nlp_taxonomy_classifier |
| **SciREX** | NER | https://github.com/allenai/SciREX/ |

Table 5: A list of models and datasets with external URLs used in *GenGO*.

# NLP-KG: A System for Exploratory Search of Scientific Literature in Natural Language Processing

**Tim Schopf** and **Florian Matthes**
Technical University of Munich, Department of Computer Science, Germany
{tim.schopf,matthes}@tum.de

## Abstract

Scientific literature searches are often exploratory, whereby users are not yet familiar with a particular field or concept but are interested in learning more about it. However, existing systems for scientific literature search are typically tailored to keyword-based lookup searches, limiting the possibilities for exploration. We propose NLP-KG, a feature-rich system designed to support the exploration of research literature in unfamiliar natural language processing (NLP) fields. In addition to a semantic search, NLP-KG allows users to easily find survey papers that provide a quick introduction to a field of interest. Further, a Fields of Study hierarchy graph enables users to familiarize themselves with a field and its related areas. Finally, a chat interface allows users to ask questions about unfamiliar concepts or specific articles in NLP and obtain answers grounded in knowledge retrieved from scientific publications. Our system provides users with comprehensive exploration possibilities, supporting them in investigating the relationships between different fields, understanding unfamiliar concepts in NLP, and finding relevant research literature. Demo, video, and code are available at: https://github.com/NLP-Knowledge-Graph/NLP-KG-WebApp.

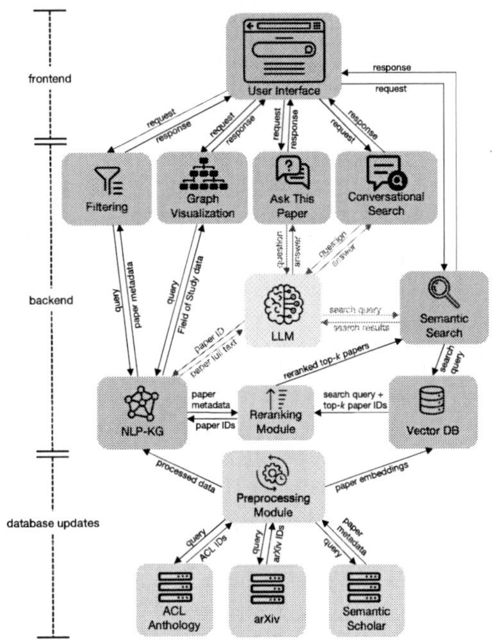


Figure 1: The architecture of our system. The direction of an arrow represents the direction of data flow. The red arrows show how the autoregressive Large Language Model (LLM) routes the data for the *Ask This Paper* feature, while the blue arrows show how the LLM routes the data for the *Conversational Search* feature. The preprocessing module regularly fetches new publications and processes them to update the knowledge graph and the vector database.

## 1 Introduction

The body of natural language processing (NLP) literature has experienced remarkable growth in recent years, with articles on various topics and applications being published in an increasing number of journals and conferences (Schopf et al., 2023). To browse and search the increasing amount of NLP-related literature, researchers may use systems such as Google Scholar[1] or Semantic Scholar (Kinney et al., 2023). Both systems cover a wide variety of academic disciplines. Although this has advantages, the lack of focus on NLP literature also has disadvantages, e.g., the potential to retrieve lots of search results containing many irrelevant papers (Mohammad, 2020). For example, when interested in NLP literature on *emotion* or *privacy*, searching for it on Google Scholar is less efficient than searching for it on a platform dedicated to NLP literature. Further, scholarly literature searches are often exploratory, whereby users are not yet familiar with a particular field or concept and are interested in learning more about it (Soufan et al., 2022). How-

[1]https://scholar.google.com



*Proceedings of the 62nd Annual Meeting of the Association for Computational Linguistics (Volume 3: System Demonstrations)*, pages 127–135
August 11-16, 2024 

ever, commonly used search systems are usually optimized for targeted lookup searches, limiting search and exploration to keyword-based searches and citation-based exploration.

In this paper, we present a system to support the exploration of NLP research literature from unfamiliar fields using a knowledge graph (KG) and state-of-the-art retrieval approaches. Our main contributions comprise the following features:

- **Graph visualization** of hierarchically structured Fields of Study (FoS) in NLP. FoS are academic disciplines and concepts, commonly comprised of (but not limited to) tasks or methods (Shen et al., 2018). The graph visualization offers researchers new to a field a starting point for their exploration and supports them to familiarize themselves with a field and its related areas.
- **Semantic search** provides a familiar interface to enable keyword-based searches for publications, authors, venues, and FoS in NLP.
- **Conversational search** responds to NLP-related user questions in natural language and grounds the answers in knowledge from academic publications using a Retrieval Augmented Generation (RAG) pipeline. This feature allows users to ask questions about unfamiliar concepts and fields in NLP and provides explanations as well as reference literature for further exploration.
- **Ask this paper** uses an autoregressive Large Language Model (LLM) to answer in-depth user questions about specific publications based on their full texts. This can support users to understand papers from unfamiliar fields.
- **Advanced filters** can filter the search results for specific FoS, venues, dates, citation counts, or survey papers. Especially filtering by survey papers can support users to quickly get an introduction to their field of interest.

Our system is not intended to replace commonly used search engines but to serve as a supplementary tool for dedicated exploratory search of NLP research literature.

## 2 Related Work

Google Scholar, Semantic Scholar (Kinney et al., 2023), ArnetMiner (Tang et al., 2008), Microsoft Academic Graph (MAG) (Sinha et al., 2015; Wang et al., 2020), OpenAlex (Priem et al., 2022), and Open Research Knowledge Graph (ORKG) (Jaradeh et al., 2019; Auer et al., 2020) are all systems for search and discovery of academic literature covering a wide range of scholarly domains.

Weitz and Schäfer (2012) focus on citation analyses of NLP-related literature. CL Scholar (Singh et al., 2018) is a system that can answer binary, statistical, and list-based queries about computational linguistics publications. Additionally, NLP Scholar (Mohammad, 2020) provides interactive visualizations of venues, authors, n-grams, and keywords extracted from NLP-related publications, while the NLP Explorer (Parmar et al., 2020) provides FoS tags and temporal statistics to search and explore the field of NLP.

## 3 NLP-KG

A well-organized hierarchical structure of FoS and an accurate mapping between these FoS and scholarly publications can enable a streamlined and satisfactory exploration experience (Shen et al., 2018). Further, semantic relations between scholarly entities can be easily modeled in a graph representation. Therefore, we construct the Natural Language Processing Knowledge Graph (NLP-KG) as the core of our system that links FoS, publications, authors, and venues via semantic relations. In addition, we integrate a LLM in our retrieval pipeline that can enhance the exploration experience by providing accurate responses to user queries (Zhu et al., 2024). Figure 1 illustrates how the knowledge graph and the LLM are integrated into our system.

### 3.1 Fields of Study Hierarchy Construction

During exploration, users typically navigate from more well-known general concepts to less well-known and more specific concepts. Therefore, we use a semi-automated approach to construct a high-quality, hierarchical, acyclic graph of FoS in NLP. As a starting point, we use a readily available high-level taxonomy of concepts in NLP (Schopf et al., 2023). At the top level, this NLP taxonomy includes 12 different concepts covering the wide range of NLP, and consequently, additional concepts can be considered as hyponyms thereof. In total, this NLP taxonomy already includes 82 different FoS, to which we subsequently add further FoS as hyponyms and co-hyponyms.

**Automated Knowledge Extraction** For automated extraction of FoS and hierarchical relations, we use a corpus of titles and abstracts of research publications from the ACL Anthology[2] and the cs.CL category of arXiv[3]. After removing duplicates, the corpus includes a total of 116,053 documents. For entity and relation extraction, we fine-tune Packed Levitated Marker (PL-Marker) models (Ye et al., 2022) on a slightly adapted SciERC dataset (Luan et al., 2018). Since we do not distinguish between different entity types in our FoS hierarchy graph, we process the SciERC dataset to unify all entity types and transform the original named entity recognition task into a more simple entity extraction task. Additionally, we only use the *Hyponym-of* relationship to extract hierarchical relations. Finally, we experiment with BERT (Devlin et al., 2019), SciBERT (Beltagy et al., 2019), SPECTER2 (Singh et al., 2023), and SciNCL (Ostendorff et al., 2022) as base models.

| Task → | *Entity Extraction* | | | *Relation Extraction* | | |
|---|---|---|---|---|---|---|
| **Model ↓** | **P** | **R** | **$F_1$** | **P** | **R** | **$F_1$** |
| BERT | 68.87 | 66.63 | 67.73 | 70.01 | 68.28 | 69.13 |
| SciBERT | 69.91 | **67.09** | **68.47** | 71.23 | **69.63** | **70.42** |
| SPECTER2 | **69.99** | 66.52 | 68.21 | 69.66 | 68.95 | 69.30 |
| SciNCL | 69.59 | 65.39 | 67.42 | **71.24** | 68.28 | 69.73 |

Table 1: Evaluation results for PL-Marker fine-tuning on the processed SciERC test set using different base models. We report micro (P)recision, (R)ecall, and $F_1$ scores.

The evaluation results for PL-Marker fine-tuning are shown in Table 1. Based on these results, we select the SciBERT-based PL-Marker models to extract entities and relations from our corpus of NLP-related research articles, resulting in large sets of entities and relations. To resolve duplicate entities, we use a rule-based approach that recognizes synonyms by unifying special characters and extracting abbreviations of terms that appear in parentheses immediately following an entity. In order to limit the set of eligible entities and relationships to high-quality ones, we select only those that are extracted more frequently than the thresholds of $t_{entities} = 100$ and $t_{relations} = 3$.

**Manual Correction & Construction** The extracted entities and relationships are passed to domain experts for validation and correction. In this case, the authors of the present work act as domain experts. If the domain experts consider a candidate triplet valid, it is manually inserted into the FoS hierarchy graph at the correct position. Otherwise, the candidate triplet is corrected, if possible, and only then inserted. Some candidate triples cannot be corrected since they involve out-of-domain terms, e.g., from the legal or medical field, and are, therefore, intentionally disregarded. Finally, we use GPT-4 (OpenAI, 2023) to generate short textual descriptions for each FoS. Table 2 shows an overview of the resulting FoS hierarchy graph.

| # Fields of Study | # Relations | Max Depth |
|---|---|---|
| 421 | 530 | 7 Levels |

Table 2: Overview of the resulting FoS hierarchy graph.

### 3.2 Fields of Study Classification

To automatically assign research publications to the corresponding FoS in the hierarchy graph, we use a two-step classification approach. In the first step, we use the fine-tuned classification model of Schopf et al. (2023). It achieves an $F_1$ score of 93.21, using the 82 high-level FoS of the NLP taxonomy as classes, which we use as the starting point for our hierarchy graph.

In the second step, we use the remaining FoS of our hierarchy graph as classes. Since we do not have sufficient annotated data to train a well-performing classifier, we use a rule-based approach. Thereby, publications are assigned to FoS depending on whether the stemmed FoS names or their stemmed synonyms are contained in the stemmed publication titles.

### 3.3 Survey Paper Classification

To enable filtering by survey papers, we train a binary classifier that can automatically classify research publications into surveys and non-surveys. To this end, we construct a new dataset of survey and non-survey publications in NLP. We obtain a list of candidate survey publications from keyword-based searches in the ACL Anthology and the arXiv cs.CL category using search terms such as *"survey"*, *"a review"*, or *"landscape"*. We then manually annotate the candidate publications as positives if we consider them to be surveys based on their titles and abstracts. For negative sampling, we use the corpus of NLP-related publications described in §3.1, excluding the previously identified positive examples. From this corpus, we randomly sample 15 times the number of positives as negatives to

[2]https://aclanthology.org

[3]https://arxiv.org

account for the inherent under-representation of surveys in conferences and journals. This annotation process results in a dataset of 787 survey and 11,805 non-survey publications in NLP.

Using this survey dataset, we fine-tune and evaluate BERT, SciBERT, SPECTER2, and SciNCL models for binary classification. We create three different stratified 80/20 train/test splits and train all models for two epochs. Following the evaluation results in Table 3, we select the SciNCL-based model as our final classifier.

| Model ↓ | Precision | Recall | $F_1$ | Accuracy |
|---|---|---|---|---|
| BERT | **84.35**±3.45 | 77.49±5.92 | 80.60±2.07 | 97.68±0.15 |
| SciBERT | 83.32±2.21 | 82.38±1.84 | 82.82±0.81 | 97.87±0.12 |
| SPECTER2 | 82.13±4.58 | 85.77±5.34 | 83.72±0.38 | 97.92±0.08 |
| SciNCL | 82.38±4.01 | **86.53**±1.74 | **84.35**±1.67 | **98.04**±0.22 |

Table 3: Evaluation results for survey paper classification as means and standard deviations on three runs over different random train/test splits. Since the distribution of classes is very unbalanced, we report micro scores.

### 3.4 Additional Metadata

To construct the NLP-KG, we additionally use metadata obtained from the Semantic Scholar API. This includes short one-sentence summaries of publications (TLDRs), SPECTER2 embeddings of publications, author information, as well as citations and references. Further, we use PaperMage (Lo et al., 2023) to obtain the full texts of open-access publications.

### 3.5 Semantic Search

For semantic search, we use a hybrid approach that combines sparse and dense text representations to find the top-$k$ most relevant publications for a query. To this end, the results of BM25 (Robertson and Walker, 1994) and SPECTER2 embedding-based retrieval are merged using Reciprocal Rank Fusion (RRF) (Cormack et al., 2009). To give more weight to the embedding-based approach, we set the $\alpha$ parameter determining the weight between sparse and dense retrieval to 0.8. In addition, we use the S2Ranker (Feldman, 2020) to rerank the top $k = 2000$ retrieved publications using additional metadata from the NLP-KG, such as the number of citations and the publication date.

### 3.6 Conversational Search

To answer NLP-related user questions and recommend relevant literature, we use the LLM in a RAG pipeline. Upon receiving a new user query, the LLM generates search terms using both the query and a one-shot example. These terms are then used for retrieving relevant publications via the semantic search module. Subsequently, the full texts of the top five search results are fed back to the LLM, which generates a response grounded in the retrieved literature. To make the generated answer verifiable for users and denote the knowledge sources, the LLM also generates inline citations. For follow-up queries, the LLM autonomously determines whether to respond using already retrieved publications or to initiate a new search. To reduce the hardware requirements of our server, we use the GPT-4 API for the conversational search and the *Ask This Paper* feature.

### 3.7 Ask This Paper

In addition to the conversational search, the LLM integration enables user inquiries on specific publications via a popup window on each publication page. Users can either pose their own questions or choose from three predefined ones. Using the full text of the publication, the LLM generates verifiable answers supplemented by supporting statements, including section and page references from the publication text. Subsequently, the LLM generates three unique follow-up questions based on the conversation history.

## 4 Demonstration

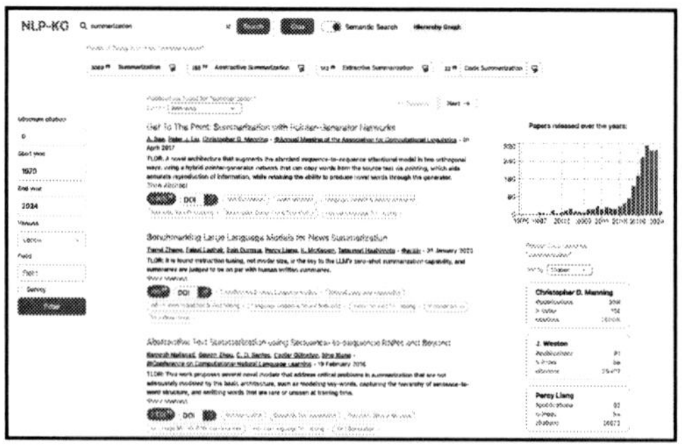

Figure 2: Screenshot showing the semantic search and filtering features.

Our web application is built with Next.js[4] and uses Python[5] for the semantic search and preprocessing modules. The NLP-KG is stored in Neo4j[6] and the embeddings are stored in Weaviate[7]. Our

[4]https://nextjs.org
[5]https://www.python.org
[6]https://neo4j.com
[7]https://weaviate.io

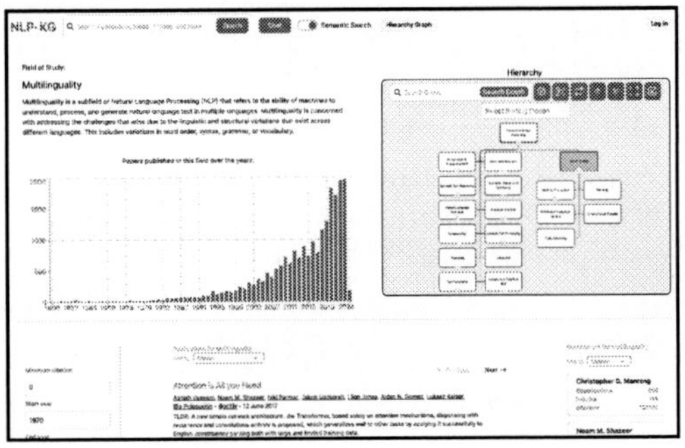

Figure 3: Screenshot of the FoS view and the hierarchy graph visualization.

databases encompass publications from the entire ACL Anthology and the arXiv cs.CL category, enriched with metadata from Semantic Scholar. As illustrated in Figure 1, the preprocessing module regularly fetches new publications, classifies them, and updates our databases.

Figure 2 shows the semantic search interface, allowing users to search for publications, authors, venues, and FoS using keywords via the top search bar. The central area shows retrieved publications, while relevant authors are listed on the right-hand side. Additionally, the top right corner showcases the annual publication count among the search results. On the left-hand side, users can access various filtering options, including the ability to filter by survey publications. Further, a list of FoS related to the search results is displayed at the top of the page, enabling users to navigate to dedicated FoS pages.

Figure 3 shows the FoS page, featuring a brief description of the respective FoS at the top, along with statistics on the annual publication count. The top right corner showcases a relevant section of the FoS hierarchy, enabling exploration of related

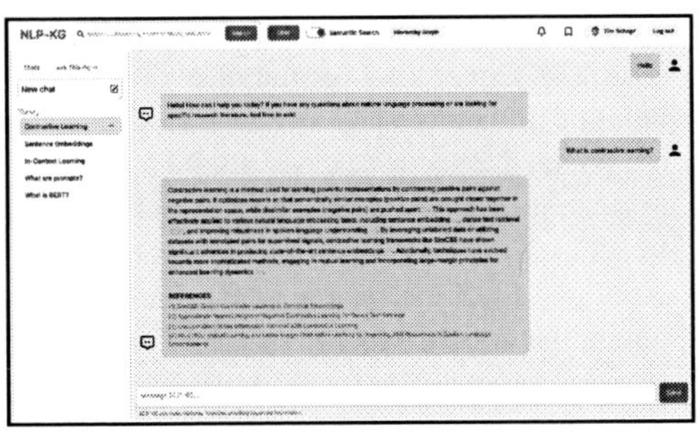

Figure 4: Screenshot of the conversational search feature.

fields. At the bottom of the page, users can explore and filter relevant authors and articles published on this topic.

Figure 4 shows the conversational search feature. Users can pose NLP-related questions to the LLM, which generates responses utilizing knowledge obtained from retrieved publications, accompanied by reference information. To enhance usability, the web application provides clickable links to referenced papers. Additionally, users can conveniently access their conversation history on the left-hand side.

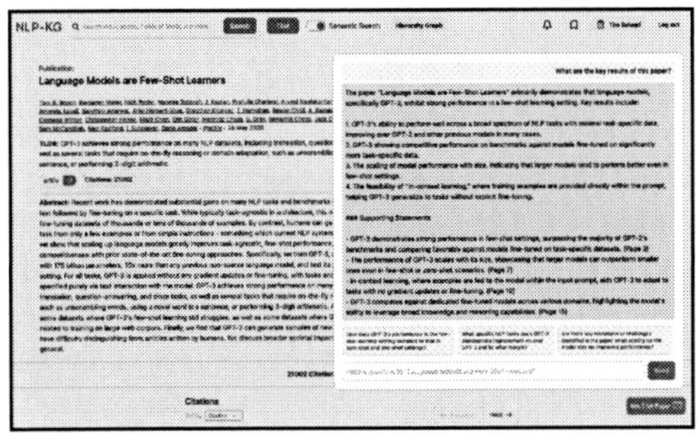

Figure 5: Screenshot of the publication view and the *Ask This Paper* feature.

Figure 5 shows the *Ask This Paper* feature, enabling users to inquire about a specific publication. Accessible via a popup window at each publication page, users can choose from predefined questions or ask custom questions using the input field at the bottom of the chat window.

## 5 Evaluation

### 5.1 Fields of Study Hierarchy Graph

To evaluate the correctness of the FoS hierarchy graph, we conduct a user study involving ten NLP researchers at the PhD level. Participants list five NLP concepts related to their expertise while we ensure their presence in our graph. Subsequently, participants are presented with a visual representation of the constructed graph, initially showing only the first level of FoS in the hierarchy. This requires participants to expand the view by clicking to show the related FoS. Participants are then tasked with locating their provided FoS in the fewest steps possible, with each click or view extension counting as one step. Since the participants selected the FoS for the search themselves, we ensure their familiarity with the target field and related fields. We observe and count every step of the participants throughout their search process. Upon locating their FoS, participants evaluate the correctness of the relations utilized during their navigation and determine potential missing relations. Based on this assessment, we compute Precision, Recall, and $F_1$ scores, as shown in Table 4, to evaluate the correctness of the traversed relations.

Furthermore, we use Mean Absolute Percentage Error (MAPE) to measure the percentage of errors or extra steps that participants make as they navigate the graph to reach their target FoS. We adopt the MAPE metric as follows:

$$\text{MAPE} = \frac{1}{n} \sum \left| \frac{\text{Total \#Steps - Ideal \#Steps}}{\text{Ideal \#Steps}} \right|, \quad (1)$$

where $n = 50$ denotes the number of FoS searches over all participants. In this context, a lower score means that, on average, users were able to find their target FoS with fewer extra steps. For example, a score of zero would mean that each user was able to find their target FoS with the optimal number of steps. Table 4 shows the evaluation results that demonstrate the high quality of the FoS hierarchy graph.

| Precision | Recall | $F_1$ | MAPE |
|---|---|---|---|
| 99.95 | 99.65 | 99.80 | 0.478 |

Table 4: Results for evaluating the correctness of relations in the FoS hierarchy graph.

### 5.2 RAG Performance

To evaluate the conversational search feature, we use the RAGAS framework (Es et al., 2024), focusing on the *Faithfulness* and the *Answer Relevance* of generated responses. Faithfulness evaluates if the generated answer is grounded in the given context, which is important to avoid hallucinations. Answer relevance evaluates if the generated answer actually addresses the provided question. We use GPT-4 to generate 50 random questions related to NLP, such as *"Define perplexity in the context of language models"*. Subsequently, we utilize GPT-3.5 (OpenAI, 2022) and GPT-4 in our conversational search pipeline described in §3.6 to generate grounded answers from retrieved publications. Finally, we use RAGAS to evaluate the generated responses. As shown in Table 5, both LLMs exhibit high faithfulness and answer relevance scores, indicating their ability to retrieve relevant publications from the RAG pipeline to effectively answer user queries based on provided contexts.

| Model | Faithfulness | Answer Relevance |
|---|---|---|
| gpt-3.5-turbo-0125 | 0.9661 | 0.8479 |
| gpt-4-0125-preview | 0.9714 | 0.8670 |

Table 5: Evaluation results of our conversational search pipeline. Metrics are scaled between 0 and 1, whereby the higher the score, the better the performance.

### 5.3 Comparison of Scholarly Literature Search Systems

We compare NLP-KG with other publicly accessible systems for scholarly literature search, including Google Scholar, Semantic Scholar, ORKG, NLP Explorer, and NLP Scholar. A feature comparison is shown in Table 6.

| | Google Scholar | Semantic Scholar | ORKG | NLP Explorer | NLP Scholar | NLP-KG |
|---|---|---|---|---|---|---|
| Keyword-based Search | ✓ | ✓ | ✓ | ✓ | ✓ | ✓ |
| NLP specific | ✗ | ✗ | ✗ | ✓ | ✓ | ✓ |
| Fields of Study Tags | ✗ | ✓ | ✓ | ✓ | ✗ | ✓ |
| Fields of Study Hierarchy | ✗ | ✗ | ✓ | ✗ | ✗ | ✓ |
| Survey Filter | ✓ | ✗ | ✗ | ✗ | ✗ | ✓ |
| Ask This Paper | ✗ | ✓ | ✗ | ✗ | ✗ | ✓ |
| Conversational Search | ✗ | ✗ | ✗ | ✗ | ✗ | ✓ |

Table 6: Feature comparison of scholarly literature search systems.

The comparison shows that NLP-KG offers an extensive set of features providing users with a wide range of options to explore NLP research literature. Unlike popular systems such as Google Scholar and Semantic Scholar, NLP-KG is tailored specifically for NLP research, ensuring an accurate and efficient exploration experience. Moreover, NLP-KG is not limited to keyword-based searches, providing users with advanced search and retrieval features to explore the field of NLP.

## 6 Conclusion

This paper introduces NLP-KG, a system for search and exploration of NLP research literature. NLP-KG supports the exploration of unfamiliar fields by providing a high-quality knowledge graph of FoS in NLP and advanced retrieval features such as semantic search and filtering for survey papers. In addition, a LLM integration allows users to ask questions about the content of specific papers and unfamiliar concepts in NLP and provides answers based on knowledge found in scientific publications. Our model evaluations demonstrate strong classification and retrieval performances, making our system well-suited for literature exploration.

## Limitations

The construction of the FoS hierarchy graph depends on the personal choices of the domain experts, which may bias the final result. The hierarchy graph may not cover all possible FoS and offers potential for discussions as domain experts have inherently different opinions. As a countermeasure, we automatically extracted entities and relations from a corpus of NLP-specific documents and aligned the opinions of domain experts during the manual construction process.

We have limited the database of our system to papers published in the ACL Anthology and the arXiv cs.CL category. However, NLP research is also presented at other conferences such as AAAI, NeurIPS, ICLR, or ICML, which may not be included in our system.

## Ethical Considerations

NLP-KG supports the search and exploration of NLP research literature in unfamiliar fields. To enable an intuitive user experience, the application integrates LLM-based features. However, LLMs (e.g., GPT-4, used in this work) are computationally expensive and require significant compute resources. Additionally, although we aim to minimize model hallucinations by grounding the model responses in knowledge retrieved from scientific publications, the integrated LLM can nevertheless make mistakes. Therefore, users should always check important information provided by our LLM-based features.

## Acknowledgements

Many thanks to Matthias Aßenmacher for his much appreciated proofreading efforts. We also thank Nektarios Machner, Phillip Schneider, Stephen Meisenbacher, Mahdi Dhaini, Juraj Vladika, Oliver Wardas, Anum Afzal, and Wessel Poelman for helpful discussions and valuable feedback. In addition, we thank Ferdy Hadiwijaya, Patrick Kufner, Ronald Ernst, Furkan Yakal, Berkay Demirtaş, and Cansu Doğanay for their contributions during the implementation of our system. Finally, we thank the anonymous reviewers for their useful comments.

## References

Sören Auer, Allard Oelen, Muhammad Haris, Markus Stocker, Jennifer D'Souza, Kheir Eddine Farfar, Lars Vogt, Manuel Prinz, Vitalis Wiens, and Mohamad Yaser Jaradeh. 2020. Improving access to scientific literature with knowledge graphs. *Bibliothek Forschung und Praxis*, 44(3):516–529.

Iz Beltagy, Kyle Lo, and Arman Cohan. 2019. SciBERT: A pretrained language model for scientific text. In *Proceedings of the 2019 Conference on Empirical Methods in Natural Language Processing and the 9th International Joint Conference on Natural Language Processing (EMNLP-IJCNLP)*, pages 3615–3620, Hong Kong, China. Association for Computational Linguistics.

Gordon V. Cormack, Charles L A Clarke, and Stefan Buettcher. 2009. Reciprocal rank fusion outperforms condorcet and individual rank learning methods. In *Proceedings of the 32nd International ACM SIGIR Conference on Research and Development in Information Retrieval*, SIGIR '09, page 758–759, New York, NY, USA. Association for Computing Machinery.

Jacob Devlin, Ming-Wei Chang, Kenton Lee, and Kristina Toutanova. 2019. BERT: Pre-training of deep bidirectional transformers for language understanding. In *Proceedings of the 2019 Conference of the North American Chapter of the Association for Computational Linguistics: Human Language Technologies, Volume 1 (Long and Short Papers)*, pages 4171–4186, Minneapolis, Minnesota. Association for Computational Linguistics.

Shahul Es, Jithin James, Luis Espinosa Anke, and Steven Schockaert. 2024. RAGAs: Automated evaluation of retrieval augmented generation. In *Proceedings of the 18th Conference of the European Chapter of the Association for Computational Linguistics: System Demonstrations*, pages 150–158, St. Julians, Malta. Association for Computational Linguistics.

Sergey Feldman. 2020. Building a better search engine for semantic scholar.

Mohamad Yaser Jaradeh, Allard Oelen, Kheir Eddine Farfar, Manuel Prinz, Jennifer D'Souza, Gábor Kismihók, Markus Stocker, and Sören Auer. 2019. Open research knowledge graph: Next generation infrastructure for semantic scholarly knowledge. In *Proceedings of the 10th International Conference on Knowledge Capture*, K-CAP '19, page 243–246, New York, NY, USA. Association for Computing Machinery.

Rodney Kinney, Chloe Anastasiades, Russell Authur, Iz Beltagy, Jonathan Bragg, Alexandra Buraczynski, Isabel Cachola, Stefan Candra, Yoganand Chandrasekhar, Arman Cohan, Miles Crawford, Doug Downey, Jason Dunkelberger, Oren Etzioni, Rob Evans, Sergey Feldman, Joseph Gorney, David Graham, Fangzhou Hu, Regan Huff, Daniel King, Sebastian Kohlmeier, Bailey Kuehl, Michael Langan, Daniel Lin, Haokun Liu, Kyle Lo, Jaron Lochner, Kelsey MacMillan, Tyler Murray, Chris Newell, Smita Rao, Shaurya Rohatgi, Paul Sayre, Zejiang

Shen, Amanpreet Singh, Luca Soldaini, Shivashankar Subramanian, Amber Tanaka, Alex D. Wade, Linda Wagner, Lucy Lu Wang, Chris Wilhelm, Caroline Wu, Jiangjiang Yang, Angele Zamarron, Madeleine Van Zuylen, and Daniel S. Weld. 2023. The semantic scholar open data platform.

Kyle Lo, Zejiang Shen, Benjamin Newman, Joseph Chang, Russell Authur, Erin Bransom, Stefan Candra, Yoganand Chandrasekhar, Regan Huff, Bailey Kuehl, Amanpreet Singh, Chris Wilhelm, Angele Zamarron, Marti A. Hearst, Daniel Weld, Doug Downey, and Luca Soldaini. 2023. PaperMage: A unified toolkit for processing, representing, and manipulating visually-rich scientific documents. In *Proceedings of the 2023 Conference on Empirical Methods in Natural Language Processing: System Demonstrations*, pages 495–507, Singapore. Association for Computational Linguistics.

Yi Luan, Luheng He, Mari Ostendorf, and Hannaneh Hajishirzi. 2018. Multi-task identification of entities, relations, and coreference for scientific knowledge graph construction. In *Proceedings of the 2018 Conference on Empirical Methods in Natural Language Processing*, pages 3219–3232, Brussels, Belgium. Association for Computational Linguistics.

Saif M. Mohammad. 2020. NLP scholar: An interactive visual explorer for natural language processing literature. In *Proceedings of the 58th Annual Meeting of the Association for Computational Linguistics: System Demonstrations*, pages 232–255, Online. Association for Computational Linguistics.

OpenAI. 2022. Chatgpt: Optimizing language models for dialogue. *OpenAI*.

OpenAI. 2023. Gpt-4 technical report.

Malte Ostendorff, Nils Rethmeier, Isabelle Augenstein, Bela Gipp, and Georg Rehm. 2022. Neighborhood contrastive learning for scientific document representations with citation embeddings. In *Proceedings of the 2022 Conference on Empirical Methods in Natural Language Processing*, pages 11670–11688, Abu Dhabi, United Arab Emirates. Association for Computational Linguistics.

Monarch Parmar, Naman Jain, Pranjali Jain, P. Jayakrishna Sahit, Soham Pachpande, Shruti Singh, and Mayank Singh. 2020. Nlpexplorer: Exploring the universe of nlp papers. In *Advances in Information Retrieval*, pages 476–480, Cham. Springer International Publishing.

Jason Priem, Heather Piwowar, and Richard Orr. 2022. Openalex: A fully-open index of scholarly works, authors, venues, institutions, and concepts.

S. E. Robertson and S. Walker. 1994. Some simple effective approximations to the 2-poisson model for probabilistic weighted retrieval. In *Proceedings of the 17th Annual International ACM SIGIR Conference on Research and Development in Information Retrieval*, SIGIR '94, page 232–241, Berlin, Heidelberg. Springer-Verlag.

Tim Schopf, Karim Arabi, and Florian Matthes. 2023. Exploring the landscape of natural language processing research. In *Proceedings of the 14th International Conference on Recent Advances in Natural Language Processing*, pages 1034–1045, Varna, Bulgaria. INCOMA Ltd., Shoumen, Bulgaria.

Zhihong Shen, Hao Ma, and Kuansan Wang. 2018. A web-scale system for scientific knowledge exploration. In *Proceedings of ACL 2018, System Demonstrations*, pages 87–92, Melbourne, Australia. Association for Computational Linguistics.

Amanpreet Singh, Mike D'Arcy, Arman Cohan, Doug Downey, and Sergey Feldman. 2023. SciRepEval: A multi-format benchmark for scientific document representations. In *Proceedings of the 2023 Conference on Empirical Methods in Natural Language Processing*, pages 5548–5566, Singapore. Association for Computational Linguistics.

Mayank Singh, Pradeep Dogga, Sohan Patro, Dhiraj Barnwal, Ritam Dutt, Rajarshi Haldar, Pawan Goyal, and Animesh Mukherjee. 2018. CL scholar: The ACL Anthology knowledge graph miner. In *Proceedings of the 2018 Conference of the North American Chapter of the Association for Computational Linguistics: Demonstrations*, pages 16–20, New Orleans, Louisiana. Association for Computational Linguistics.

Arnab Sinha, Zhihong Shen, Yang Song, Hao Ma, Darrin Eide, Bo-June (Paul) Hsu, and Kuansan Wang. 2015. An overview of microsoft academic service (mas) and applications. In *Proceedings of the 24th International Conference on World Wide Web*, WWW '15 Companion, page 243–246, New York, NY, USA. Association for Computing Machinery.

Ayah Soufan, Ian Ruthven, and Leif Azzopardi. 2022. Searching the literature: An analysis of an exploratory search task. In *Proceedings of the 2022 Conference on Human Information Interaction and Retrieval*, CHIIR '22, page 146–157, New York, NY, USA. Association for Computing Machinery.

Jie Tang, Jing Zhang, Limin Yao, Juanzi Li, Li Zhang, and Zhong Su. 2008. Arnetminer: Extraction and mining of academic social networks. In *Proceedings of the 14th ACM SIGKDD International Conference on Knowledge Discovery and Data Mining*, KDD '08, page 990–998, New York, NY, USA. Association for Computing Machinery.

Kuansan Wang, Zhihong Shen, Chiyuan Huang, Chieh-Han Wu, Yuxiao Dong, and Anshul Kanakia. 2020. Microsoft Academic Graph: When experts are not enough. *Quantitative Science Studies*, 1(1):396–413.

Benjamin Weitz and Ulrich Schäfer. 2012. A graphical citation browser for the ACL Anthology. In *Proceedings of the Eighth International Conference on Language Resources and Evaluation (LREC'12)*, pages 1718–1722, Istanbul, Turkey. European Language Resources Association (ELRA).

Deming Ye, Yankai Lin, Peng Li, and Maosong Sun. 2022. Packed levitated marker for entity and relation extraction. In *Proceedings of the 60th Annual Meeting of the Association for Computational Linguistics (Volume 1: Long Papers)*, pages 4904–4917, Dublin, Ireland. Association for Computational Linguistics.

Yutao Zhu, Huaying Yuan, Shuting Wang, Jiongnan Liu, Wenhan Liu, Chenlong Deng, Haonan Chen, Zhicheng Dou, and Ji-Rong Wen. 2024. Large language models for information retrieval: A survey.

# LocalRQA: From Generating Data to Locally Training, Testing, and Deploying Retrieval-Augmented QA Systems

**Xiao Yu***, **Yunan Lu***, **Zhou Yu**
Department of Computer Science, Columbia University, New York, NY
{xy2437, yl4021, zy2461}@columbia.edu

**Abstract**

Retrieval-augmented question-answering systems combine retrieval techniques with large language models to provide answers that are more accurate and informative. Many existing toolkits allow users to quickly build such systems using off-the-shelf models, but they fall short in supporting researchers and developers to customize the *model training, testing, and deployment process*. We propose LocalRQA[1], an open-source toolkit that features a wide selection of model training algorithms, evaluation methods, and deployment tools curated from the latest research. As a showcase, we build QA systems using online documentation obtained from Databricks and Faire's websites. We find 7B-models trained and deployed using LocalRQA reach a similar performance compared to using OpenAI's text-ada-002 and GPT-4-turbo.

## 1 Introduction

Retrieval-augmented question-answering (RQA) systems enhance large language models (LLMs) by enabling them to search through a large collection of documents before answering a user's query. These systems have shown improved performance in providing more accurate, informative, and factually grounded answers compared to using LLMs alone (Guu et al., 2020; Izacard et al., 2022; Shi et al., 2023). Many existing toolkits, such as LlamaIndex (Liu, 2022) and LangChain (Chase, 2022), allow users to quickly build such an RQA system using off-the-shelf models such as text-ada-002 (OpenAI, 2022a) and GPT-4 (OpenAI, 2023). However, developers often find it costly to rely on these paid services, but also face difficulties to train/deploy smaller models with competitive performance. Researchers face even greater hurdles: they need to modify models/training algorithms, compare against prior work, and obtain human evaluation for their RQA system — all of which are largely neglected by existing toolkits.

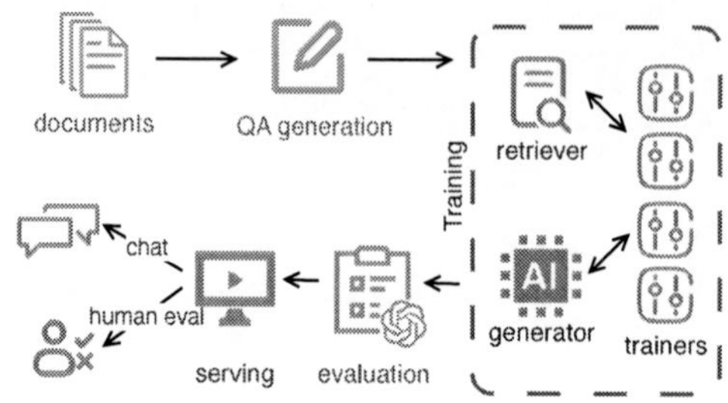


Figure 1: Given a collection of documents, LocalRQA provides tools to generate RQA data, to train and test open-source models, and to deploy the RQA system for human evaluation or as an interactive chatbot.

We introduce LocalRQA, an open-source toolkit that enables researchers and developers to easily train, test, and deploy RQA systems *using techniques from recent research.* Given a collection of documents, users can use pre-built pipelines in our framework to quickly assemble an RQA system using the best off-the-shelf models. *Alternatively*, users can create their own training data, train open-source models using algorithms from latest research, and deploy a local RQA system that achieves similar performance compared to using paid services such as OpenAI's models.

To our knowledge, LocalRQA is the first toolkit that provides a wide range of training algorithms and automatic evaluation metrics curated from the latest research (see Table 1 and Appendix A). This not only helps researchers to develop new RQA approaches and compare with prior work, but also helps developers to train and deploy more cost-effective models. Specifically, we provide many training algorithms for retrievers such as: distilling from an encoder-decoder's cross-attention scores (Izacard and Grave, 2020a), distilling from a decoder's language modeling probability (Shi et al., 2023), and using contrastive learning

* denotes equal contribution.

[1]GitHub: https://github.com/jasonyux/LocalRQA, YouTube: https://youtu.be/MEtFIcw7clY.



*Proceedings of the 62nd Annual Meeting of the Association for Computational Linguistics (Volume 3: System Demonstrations)*, pages 136–151
August 11-16, 2024 ©2024 Association for Computational Linguistics

|  | Easy Assembly | Flexible Training | Automatic Evaluation | Local Deployment |
|---|---|---|---|---|
| Haystack (Pietsch et al., 2019) | ✓ | ✗ | ✓ | ✗ |
| LangChain (Chase, 2022) | ✓ | ✗ | ✗ | ✗ |
| LLamaIndex (Liu, 2022) | ✓ | ✗ | ✓ | ✗ |
| FastRAG (Izsak et al., 2023) | ✓ | ✗ | ✗ | ✗ |
| LOCALRQA (Ours) | ✓ | ✓ | ✓ | ✓ |

Table 1: Comparing LOCALRQA to related toolkits. *Easy Assembly* indicates that there are ready-made pipelines to allow users to easily assemble an RQA system; *Flexible Training* indicates if there is more than one training algorithm for retrievers/generators; *Automatic Evaluation* indicates if the toolkit provides automatic evaluation methods; and *Local Deployment* indicates if the toolkit supports methods to locally deploy their RQA system *and* allow external users to interact with them through a web interface.

approaches (Karpukhin et al., 2020; Wang et al., 2022, 2023). We also provide training algorithms for generative models such as: supervised fine-tuning using gold question-passage-answer pairs (Lewis et al., 2021), fine-tuning with a frozen retriever (Guu et al., 2020), and fusion-in-decoder training (Izacard and Grave, 2020b; Izacard et al., 2022). Then, to automatically evaluate the system's performance, we implement metrics used in retrieval and question-answering domains, such as Recall@k, ROUGE (Lin, 2004), and GPT-4 Eval (Zheng et al., 2023a; Liu et al., 2023).

Furthermore, LOCALRQA provides two deployment methods to support researchers and developers to obtain human feedback for their RQA systems. First, we offer a static evaluation webpage where users can directly assess the system's performance using a test dataset. This can be used to complement automatic evaluation. Next, we offer an interactive chat webpage where users can chat with the system and rate the helpfulness and correctness of each generated response. These ratings can be used to further improve models' capability using techniques such as Reinforcement Learning from Human Feedback (RLHF, Ouyang et al. (2022)). To reduce latency and improve user experiences, our toolkit also integrates acceleration frameworks used to speed up document retrieval (Johnson et al., 2019) and LLM inference (Huggingface, 2023; Kwon et al., 2023; Zheng et al., 2023b). Together with our large collection of training algorithms and automatic metrics, LOCALRQA opens the possibility of future work to easily train, test, and deploy novel RQA approaches.

## 2 Background

RQA systems combine retrievers with powerful LLMs to provide answers that are more accurate and informative. Given a user query, a retriever first selects $k$ most relevant passages from a collection of documents. Then, a generative model produces an answer conditioned on the user's query, selected passages, and a chat history. Popular methods to achieve this include concatenating all inputs into a single string and generating with decoder-only models (Chase, 2022; Ram et al., 2023), or processing the $k$ passages in parallel and generating with fusion-in-decoder techniques (Izacard and Grave, 2020b; Izacard et al., 2022).

## 3 LOCALRQA

We introduce LOCALRQA, a Python-based toolkit designed to help users flexibly train, test, and deploy RQA systems. As shown in Figure 2, our toolkits employ a modular design to allow users to: generate and prepare RQA data (Section 3.1), train retrieval and generative models (Section 3.2 and Section 3.3), build an RQA system (Section 3.4), evaluate the system (Section 3.5), and finally deploy the system (Section 3.6).

### 3.1 Prepare Data

A prerequisite for training and evaluating RQA systems is a dataset of (question, answer, passage) pairs, denoted as $\langle q, a, p \rangle$. However, full $\langle q, a, p \rangle$ pairs may not always be available in practice. To cater to various scenarios, our toolkit provides: 1) scripts to generate $\langle q, a, p \rangle$ pairs from a collection of documents, and 2) scripts to convert existing QA datasets into $\langle q, a, p \rangle$ pairs. These scripts can be useful for researchers to create RQA datasets for new domains, or for developers to prepare training/testing data for specific applications.

**Generate RQA Data** Given a collection of documents, our scripts first use a sampling algorithm to select a set of gold (and hard negative) documents, and then use LLMs to generate questions and answers from each gold document (see Appendix C

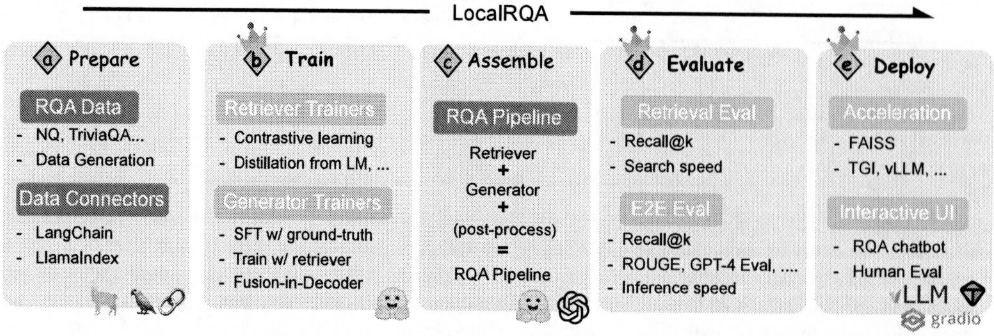


Figure 2: An overview of the LocalRQA toolkit, which supports the entire pipeline of developing an RQA system: from data processing to training, testing, and serving an RQA system. Different from many existing toolkits, we feature a wide selection of training, testing, and serving methods curated from the latest RQA research.

for more details). These scripts can be used to create $\langle q, a, p\rangle$ pairs not only from a collection of documents, but also from a collection of $\langle q, p\rangle$ pairs (e.g., from information retrieval datasets).

**Convert from Existing Datasets** Many existing QA datasets include supporting passages for each gold question-answer pair. We provide scripts to download and reformat these datasets into $\langle q, a, p\rangle$ pairs compatible with the rest of our toolkit. This includes popular datasets such as Natural Questions (Kwiatkowski et al., 2019), TriviaQA (Joshi et al., 2017), and MS-Marco (Bajaj et al., 2018). These scripts allow researchers to easily compare against prior work that also uses these datasets.

### 3.2 Train Retrievers

Given a dataset of $\langle q, a, p\rangle$ pairs, users can train a retriever to select the most relevant passages for a given query. Prior work shows that using better retrievers often leads to more performant RQA systems (Karpukhin et al., 2020), and that fine-tuning them with task-specific data can greatly improve their performance (Izacard et al., 2021; Wang et al., 2022). To this end, LocalRQA implements: 1) lexical-based and embedding-based methods, and 2) various trainers that finetune open-source embedding models to achieve a better performance.

**Supported Models** For lexical-based methods, we support BM25 (Trotman et al., 2014). For embedding-based methods, we support all huggingface (Wolf et al., 2020) encoder models such as Contriever (Izacard et al., 2021), E5 (Wang et al., 2022), and BGE (Xiao et al., 2023).

**Trainers** We implement trainers for encoders that distill from a down-stream LM, and trainers that perform contrastive learning using a dataset of $\langle q, p\rangle$ pairs (and optionally hard negative examples). This includes trainers that: (1) distill from cross-attention scores of an encoder-decoder model (Izacard and Grave, 2020a); (2) distill from a decoder model's LM probability (Shi et al., 2023); and (3) train using contrastive learning (Izacard et al., 2021; Wang et al., 2022, 2023)). We provide easy-to-use Python scripts for each trainer, where all training hyperparameters can be specified in a single command line.

### 3.3 Train Generative Models

Besides improving retrievers, using better generative models can more effectively incorporate retrieved passages. To this end, our toolkit provides: 1) direct support for many open-source generative models, and 2) various training algorithms to finetune these models to improve their task-specific performance.

**Supported Models** We support all huggingface (Wolf et al., 2020) decoder-only models such as LLaMA-2 (Touvron et al., 2023), and all T5 based encoder-decoder models such as FLAN-T5 (Chung et al., 2022). The former is compatible with our supervised trainers, and the latter is compatible with our fusion-in-decoder trainers.

**Trainers** We implement supervised fine-tuning trainers that concatenate input queries with ground-truth or retrieved passages, and fusion-in-decoder trainers that process retrieved passages in parallel. This includes trainers that: (1) supervised finetune a decoder using ground-truth $\langle q, a, p\rangle$ pairs (Lewis et al., 2021); (2) supervised finetune a decoder with a frozen retriever (Guu et al., 2020); and (3) train an encoder-decoder with fusion-in-decoder training (Izacard and Grave, 2020b; Izacard et al., 2022). We provide easy-to-use Python scripts for each trainer, where all training hyperparameters can be specified in a single command line.

### 3.4 Assemble an RQA System

Given a retriever and a generative model, users can now assemble an end-to-end RQA system. Similar to frameworks such as LlamaIndex, LocalRQA uses a modular design to support arbitrary combinations of retrievers, generative models, as well as user-defined modules (see **??** for more details), such as safety filters and decision planners (Kim et al., 2023; Peng et al., 2023). For a quick start, users can use ready-made RQA pipelines to assemble a system within five lines of code (Listing 1). These built-in pipelines support: **retrievers** available on huggingface, retrievers trained from Section 3.2, BM25 (Robertson and Zaragoza, 2009), and OpenAI embedding models (OpenAI, 2022a); **generative models** available on huggingface, models trained from Section 3.3, and OpenAI models such as ChatGPT (OpenAI, 2022b).

Alternatively, a user can also customize an RQA pipeline by implementing new/modifying existing modules. As an example, we provide an implementation of a (dummy) safety filter added to the `SimpleRQA` pipeline in Listing 2 in Appendix. In Listing 2, the `DontKnowSafetyFilter` module will ignore the answers generated by the previous components of the `SimpleRQA` modules, and always return "I don't know." as an answer.

In general, users can easily add new modules to an existing pipeline by: 1) implementing a class that inherits from `Component`, which requires defining a `run` method and `run_input_keys`, and 2) append the module to the `components` field. Alternatively, researchers can create a fully customized pipeline by inheriting from the `RQAPipeline` class. For more documentation and examples, please refer to our GitHub pages.

**Listing 1** Assembling an RQA system.

```
from local_rqa import ...
### pre-built RQA Pipeline
rqa = SimpleRQA.from_scratch(
    database_path="db_path/",
    embedding_model_name_or_path="...",
    qa_model_name_or_path="...",
)
response = rqa.qa(
    batch_questions=['What is ...?'],
    batch_dialogue_session=[
        DialogueSession()
    ],
)
```

### 3.5 Evaluate an RQA System

Given an RQA system, LocalRQA implements many automatic evaluation metrics to help users measure their system's performance. This can be used by researchers to compare their system's performance against prior work, or by developers to find the most cost-effective models/training methods suitable for their applications. We provide scripts to automatically evaluate the performance of *any RQA system* that inherits from the `RQAPipeline` class. These scripts will also save the evaluation results in a JSONL file, which can be used to further obtain human evaluation using our serving methods (see Section 3.6). We describe the supported automatic metrics below.

**Retrieval** To test the performance of a retriever, we provide an evaluation script that measures: (1) Recall@k and nDCG@k score, and (2) runtime. Recall and nDCG scores are often used in information retrieval benchmarks such as BEIR (Thakur et al., 2021) and MTEB (Muennighoff et al., 2022). Runtime is important for real-world applications.

**End-to-End** To test the end-to-end performance of an RQA system, we provide an automatic evaluation script that measures: (1) retrieval performance such as Recall@k; (2) generation performance such as BLEU (Papineni et al., 2002), ROUGE (Lin, 2004) and GPT-4 Eval (Zheng et al., 2023a; Liu et al., 2023); and (3) end-to-end metrics such as runtime. BLEU and ROUGE scores are often used in open-ended generation tasks such as machine translation and summarization. GPT-4 Eval is a recent method using GPT-4 (OpenAI, 2023) to evaluate the quality of model-generated responses (Liu et al., 2023; Zheng et al., 2023a).

### 3.6 Deploy an RQA System

Finally, researchers and developers may want to showcase their RQA systems to the public, or to collect human feedback to further improve their systems using techniques such as RLHF (Ouyang et al., 2022). We provide: (1) support for efficient retrieval and LLM inference acceleration methods to reduce latency during interactive chats, and (2)

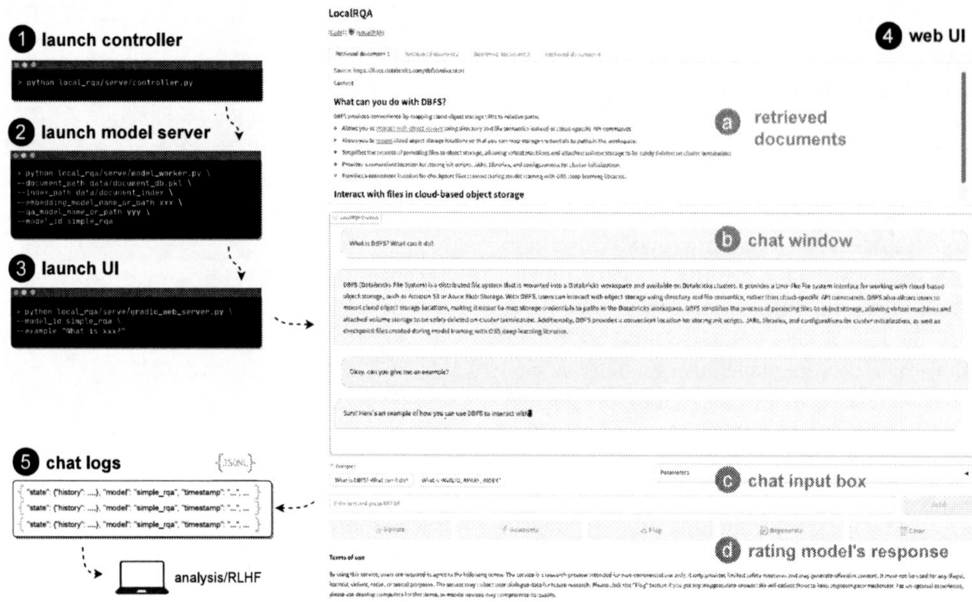


Figure 3: Researchers can launch an interactive chat page with LOCALRQA using three commands. LOCALRQA uses a model controller back-end (Zheng et al., 2023a) to handle load-balancing. Chat histories are automatically saved for researchers to conduct further analysis or model training.

implementations to easily launch an interactive chat webpage or a static evaluation webpage, given a user-built RQA system.

**Acceleration Frameworks** To speed up document retrieval, we support FAISS (Johnson et al., 2019), a library for efficient similarity search across billion-scale document datasets. To speed up LLM inference, we support Text Generation Inference (TGI, Huggingface (2023)), vLLM (Kwon et al., 2023), and SGLang (Zheng et al., 2023b). These inference acceleration frameworks support many decoder architectures such as LLaMA-2 and encoder-decoder architectures such as FLAN-T5.

**Interactive UIs** We provide (1) a static evaluation webpage where users directly evaluate the quality of pre-generated responses (e.g., computed from a test set); and (2) an interactive chat webpage where users can chat with a system and rate the correctness and helpfulness of each response. Both web interfaces can be easily launched with our toolkits, which not only support a variety of models (see Section 3.4) but also integrate with acceleration frameworks mentioned in the previous paragraph. See Figure A1 for an example of the human evaluation page, and Figure 3 for the interactive chat page.

## 4 Applications

To showcase our toolkit, we built two RQA systems using data scraped from Databricks and Faire's online documentations (under consent). Databricks provides the world's first data intelligence platform powered by generative AI, providing products that facilitate building, sharing, and maintaining data at scale. Faire is an online wholesale marketplace that connects independent retailers and brands around the world. Since the documents we obtained include many company/product-specific details, we believe this is an ideal use case for RQA systems.

First, we describe the documentation datasets we collected in Section 4.1. Then, we describe our model training, baselines, and evaluation procedures in Section 4.2, Section 4.3, and Section 4.4. Finally, we present our main results in Section 4.5.

### 4.1 Datasets

**Databricks** We use data provided by Databricks' technical team, which includes documentations such as API references and technical tutorials from `docs.databricks.com` and `kb.databricks.com`. After applying our data processing scripts, we obtain a dataset of 11,136 passages with a maximum length of 400 tokens. See Appendix E for examples of preprocessed documents.

| Retriever | Generator | Databricks | | | | Faire | | | |
|---|---|---|---|---|---|---|---|---|---|
| | | Retrieval | | Generation | | Retrieval | | Generation | |
| | | Recall@1 | Recall@4 | ROUGE-L | GPT4-Acc | Recall@1 | Recall@4 | ROUGE-L | GPT4-Acc |
| text-ada-002 | GPT-3.5-turbo | **47.36** | *67.11* | 46.47 | *86.84* | **44.00** | *76.00* | 35.59 | 81.33 |
| text-ada-002 | GPT-4-turbo | **47.36** | *67.11* | 36.62 | **89.47** | **44.00** | *76.00* | 32.55 | **86.67** |
| Contriever (DCA) | FastChat-T5-3B (FiD) | 34.21 | 50.00 | 20.20 | 19.73 | 26.67 | 65.33 | 23.64 | 44.00 |
| Contriever (RPG) | StableLM-3B (SFT) | 28.94 | 53.94 | 43.30 | 52.63 | 34.66 | 68.00 | 47.53 | 68.00 |
| Contriever (CTL) | StableLM-3B (SFT) | 28.94 | 60.52 | 45.86 | 61.33 | *42.66* | 69.33 | 46.27 | 72.00 |
| Contriever (CTL) | Vicuna-7B (SFT) | 28.94 | 60.52 | 42.95 | 72.37 | *42.66* | 69.33 | 45.72 | 75.68 |
| E5 (CTL) | Vicuna-7B (SFT) | 34.21 | **77.63** | 45.35 | 73.68 | 40.00 | *76.00* | 46.16 | *76.00* |
| Contriever (CTL) | Vicuna-7B (SwR) | 28.94 | 60.52 | 44.10 | 60.53 | *42.66* | 69.33 | 48.72 | *76.00* |
| E5 (CTL) | Vicuna-7B (SwR) | 34.21 | **77.63** | 50.02 | 69.33 | 40.00 | *76.00* | 47.98 | 72.00 |
| E5 (CTL) | Starling-7B (SFT) | 34.21 | **77.63** | 42.06 | 72.36 | 40.00 | *76.00* | 46.32 | 78.67 |
| E5 (CTL) | Mistral-7B (SFT) | 34.21 | **77.63** | *51.56* | 80.26 | 40.00 | *76.00* | 49.63 | 77.33 |
| BGE (CTL) | Starling-7B (SFT) | *39.47* | **77.63** | **51.67** | 76.32 | 37.33 | **77.33** | *50.64* | **86.67** |
| BGE (CTL) | Mistral-7B (SFT) | *39.47* | **77.63** | 49.49 | 77.63 | 37.33 | **77.33** | **51.18** | *84.00* |

Table 2: Retrieval-augmented QA systems locally trained and tested using the LOCALRQA framework. Training algorithm used is denoted as "model(*trainer name*)". All generation results use the top-4 passages retrieved. *GPT4-Acc* is GPT-4 evaluation of whether the generated answer is correct. Best is highlighted in **bold**, and runner-up is highlighted in *gray*.

**Faire** We first crawled guides and FAQ documents from `faire.com/support`, and then processed the data to only keep raw texts (e.g., removing image hyperlinks). Similar to Databricks, we then apply the data processing scripts and obtain a dataset of 1,758 passages. See Appendix F for examples of preprocessed documents.

Since both datasets only contain document passages $p$, we use LOCALRQA to generate $\langle q, a, p \rangle$ pairs for training and testing. See Appendix H for more details.

### 4.2 Models and Training Algorithms

LOCALRQA supports a large variety of models and training algorithms. To demonstrate the flexibility of our toolkit, we experiment with all available trainers and the most capable open-source models.

**Retrievers** We consider the best open-source encoder models according to the MTEB benchmark (Muennighoff et al., 2022) as of Jan 24, 2024. However, as these models vary *greatly* in capability and size, for simplicity we use the best models of similar sizes. This includes E5-base (Wang et al., 2022), Contriever-base (Izacard et al., 2021), and BGE-base (Xiao et al., 2023). We also consider all trainers in our toolkit including: (1) distilling from cross-attention scores, denoted as *DCA*; (2) distilling LM probability, denoted as *RPG*; and (3) training with contrastive learning, denoted as *CTL*.

**Generators** We consider the best generator models according to the Chatbot Arena leaderboard (Zheng et al., 2023a) as of Jan 24, 2024. Since training LLMs is time and resource intensive, we focus on the best open-source models up to 7B parameters. This includes encoder-decoder models such as FastChat-T5-3B (Zheng et al., 2023a; Chung et al., 2022), and decoder-only models such as: StableLM-3B (Tow et al., 2023), Vicuna-7B (Chiang et al., 2023), Starling-7B (Zhu et al., 2023), and Mistral-7B (Jiang et al., 2023). We also consider all trainers in our toolkit including: (1) supervised fine-tuning, denoted as *SFT*; (2) supervised fine-tuning with a frozen retriever, denoted as *SwR*; and (3) fusion-in-decoder training, denoted as *FiD*.

### 4.3 Baselines

Since LOCALRQA features developing new RQA systems *locally*, we compare against the most powerful models accessible *remotely*. This include using text-ada-002 (OpenAI, 2022a) as the retriever, and prompting GPT-3.5-turbo (ChatGPT) and GPT-4-turbo as the generative models.

### 4.4 Metrics

We present a subset of automatic evaluation metrics from LOCALRQA, and also include human evaluations on the best-performing models using UIs from Section 3.6. To measure retrievers' performance, we report Recall@1 and Recall@4 which are commonly used in information retrieval (Thakur et al., 2021; Muennighoff et al., 2022). To measure the final generation performance, we report ROUGE-L (Lin, 2004) and GPT-4 Eval (Zheng et al., 2023a; Liu et al., 2023), which are used in open-domain generation tasks (Zheng et al., 2023a). For the best models, we additionally perform human evaluation and report the accuracy of the generated answers.

| Retriever | Generator | Databricks Human-Acc | Faire Human-Acc |
|---|---|---|---|
| text-ada-002 | GPT-3.5-turbo | 78.00 | 86.00 |
| text-ada-002 | GPT-4-turbo | **84.00** | 88.00 |
| E5 (CTL) | Mistral-7B (SFT) | 78.00 | **90.00** |
| BGE (CTL) | Starling-7B (SFT) | 80.00 | 88.00 |

Table 3: Comparing the best LOCALRQA-trained models in Table 2 against ChatGPT and GPT-4. *Human-Acc* is authors' judgement of whether the final answer is correct. We use the first 50 test samples for evaluation.

### 4.5 Main Results

Table 2 presents our non-exhaustive combination of retrievers and generators trained and tested using LOCALRQA. First, we find contrastive learning (*CTL*) most effective for training retrievers. We believe this is because CTL was also used to pre-train all the encoders we investigated (Izacard et al., 2021; Wang et al., 2022; Xiao et al., 2023). We also find that simple supervised fine-tuning (*SFT*) with gold $\langle q, a, p \rangle$ pairs is suitable for generators, given the answers in the training data are generated only using the gold passage.

Next, we find using more powerful retriever models (BGE-base and E5-base) and generator models (Mistral-7B and Starling-7B) improves Recall@4 and GPT4-Acc score. This is understandable since these models have a better base performance. We also find that ROUGE-L does not correlate well with GPT4-Acc (or our human evaluation). This is consistent with Cohan and Goharian (2016); Nekvinda and Dušek (2021), since open-ended generations are inherently difficult to evaluate using automatic metrics.

Lastly, we use the best models from Table 2 according to GPT4-Acc scores, and further validate their performance with our human evaluation UI (see Section 3.6). In Table 3, we find the best local models reach a similar performance as the OpenAI's baselines, despite being only 7B in size (see Appendix G for some examples). These results underscores the effectiveness of our toolkit in training and developing cost-effective RQA systems.

## 5 Conclusion

We present LOCALRQA, a Python-based toolkit designed to help users develop novel retrieval-augemented QA systems. Different from existing frameworks such as LlamaIndex and LangChain, our toolkit features a wide collection of training algorithms, evaluation metrics, and deployment methods to help users quickly develop cost-effective RQA systems. Strong results using models and training algorithms from recent research pave the way for future work to explore RQA methods in both practical and academic settings.

## 6 Limitations and Future Work

**Model Size** We performed all of our experiments using a single A100 80G GPU, and investigated a large combination of model choices and training methods. Therefore, we considered the best-performing models up to 7B parameters due to time and resource concerns. We believe experimenting with larger, more capable models could further improve the systems' performance, and we leave this for future work.

**More Training Algorithms** Besides providing tools to help users easily build an RQA system, LOCALRQA features a collection of training algorithms and evaluation methods curated from latest research. However, this collection is non-exhaustive (Zhong et al., 2022; Asai et al., 2022; Min et al., 2023; Asai et al., 2023; Ram et al., 2023). We commit to add support for more models, training algorithms, and testing methods to reflect ongoing advancements in RQA research.

**Compute Requirement** LOCALRQA features methods to help users develop novel RQA systems *locally*. Compared with using paid services such as OpenAI's text-ada-002 and GPT-4, this approach is less expensive but requires access to compute resources (e.g., GPUs). To make our toolkit more accessible, we not only support open-source models from huggingface of various sizes, but also support using "remote" models such as OpenAI's ChatGPT and GPT-4.

## 7 Ethical Considerations

Our work describes a toolkit that can be used to help researchers develop new RQA systems. LOCALRQA offers a suite of tools, starting from data generation to locally training, testing, and serving an RQA system. While most toolkits are not designed for unethical usage, there is often potential for abuse in their applications. In our demo (Section 4), we apply our toolkit to train RQA systems based on documentations obtained from two companies' website, Databricks and Faire. However, since our toolkit can be used with any kind of data, it is possible to use it for unethical tasks, such as scamming and generating harmful responses (Gehman et al., 2020; Welbl et al., 2021). We do not condone the use of LOCALRQA for any unlawful or morally unjust purposes.

## 8 Acknowledgement

We thank Xiangrui Meng and Quinn Leng from Databricks, and Wenhao Liu from Faire for their valuable support and discussions.

## References

Abubakar Abid, Ali Abdalla, Ali Abid, Dawood Khan, Abdulrahman Alfozan, and James Zou. 2019. Gradio: Hassle-free sharing and testing of ML models in the wild.

Akari Asai, Timo Schick, Patrick Lewis, Xilun Chen, Gautier Izacard, Sebastian Riedel, Hannaneh Hajishirzi, and Wen tau Yih. 2022. Task-aware retrieval with instructions.

Akari Asai, Zeqiu Wu, Yizhong Wang, Avirup Sil, and Hannaneh Hajishirzi. 2023. Self-rag: Learning to retrieve, generate, and critique through self-reflection.

Payal Bajaj, Daniel Campos, Nick Craswell, Li Deng, Jianfeng Gao, Xiaodong Liu, Rangan Majumder, Andrew McNamara, Bhaskar Mitra, Tri Nguyen, Mir Rosenberg, Xia Song, Alina Stoica, Saurabh Tiwary, and Tong Wang. 2018. Ms marco: A human generated machine reading comprehension dataset.

Harrison Chase. 2022. LangChain.

Wei-Lin Chiang, Zhuohan Li, Zi Lin, Ying Sheng, Zhanghao Wu, Hao Zhang, Lianmin Zheng, Siyuan Zhuang, Yonghao Zhuang, Joseph E. Gonzalez, Ion Stoica, and Eric P. Xing. 2023. Vicuna: An open-source chatbot impressing gpt-4 with 90%* chatgpt quality.

Hyung Won Chung, Le Hou, Shayne Longpre, Barret Zoph, Yi Tay, William Fedus, Eric Li, Xuezhi Wang, Mostafa Dehghani, Siddhartha Brahma, Albert Webson, Shixiang Shane Gu, Zhuyun Dai, Mirac Suzgun, Xinyun Chen, Aakanksha Chowdhery, Sharan Narang, Gaurav Mishra, Adams Yu, Vincent Zhao, Yanping Huang, Andrew Dai, Hongkun Yu, Slav Petrov, Ed H. Chi, Jeff Dean, Jacob Devlin, Adam Roberts, Denny Zhou, Quoc V. Le, and Jason Wei. 2022. Scaling instruction-finetuned language models.

Arman Cohan and Nazli Goharian. 2016. Revisiting summarization evaluation for scientific articles. In *Proceedings of the Tenth International Conference on Language Resources and Evaluation (LREC'16)*, pages 806–813, Portorož, Slovenia. European Language Resources Association (ELRA).

Samuel Gehman, Suchin Gururangan, Maarten Sap, Yejin Choi, and Noah A. Smith. 2020. RealToxicityPrompts: Evaluating neural toxic degeneration in language models. In *Findings of the Association for Computational Linguistics: EMNLP 2020*, pages 3356–3369, Online. Association for Computational Linguistics.

Kelvin Guu, Kenton Lee, Zora Tung, Panupong Pasupat, and Ming-Wei Chang. 2020. Realm: Retrieval-augmented language model pre-training.

Huggingface. 2023. Large language model text generation inference.

Gautier Izacard, Mathilde Caron, Lucas Hosseini, Sebastian Riedel, Piotr Bojanowski, Armand Joulin, and Edouard Grave. 2021. Unsupervised dense information retrieval with contrastive learning.

Gautier Izacard and Edouard Grave. 2020a. Distilling knowledge from reader to retriever for question answering.

Gautier Izacard and Edouard Grave. 2020b. Leveraging passage retrieval with generative models for open domain question answering.

Gautier Izacard, Patrick Lewis, Maria Lomeli, Lucas Hosseini, Fabio Petroni, Timo Schick, Jane Dwivedi-Yu, Armand Joulin, Sebastian Riedel, and Edouard Grave. 2022. Atlas: Few-shot learning with retrieval augmented language models.

Peter Izsak, Moshe Berchansky, Daniel Fleischer, and Ronen Laperdon. 2023. fastRAG: Efficient Retrieval Augmentation and Generation Framework.

Albert Q. Jiang, Alexandre Sablayrolles, Arthur Mensch, Chris Bamford, Devendra Singh Chaplot, Diego de las Casas, Florian Bressand, Gianna Lengyel, Guillaume Lample, Lucile Saulnier, Lélio Renard Lavaud, Marie-Anne Lachaux, Pierre Stock, Teven Le Scao, Thibaut Lavril, Thomas Wang, Timothée Lacroix, and William El Sayed. 2023. Mistral 7b.

Jeff Johnson, Matthijs Douze, and Hervé Jégou. 2019. Billion-scale similarity search with GPUs. *IEEE Transactions on Big Data*, 7(3):535–547.

Mandar Joshi, Eunsol Choi, Daniel Weld, and Luke Zettlemoyer. 2017. TriviaQA: A large scale distantly supervised challenge dataset for reading comprehension. In *Proceedings of the 55th Annual Meeting of the Association for Computational Linguistics (Volume 1: Long Papers)*, pages 1601–1611, Vancouver, Canada. Association for Computational Linguistics.

Vladimir Karpukhin, Barlas Oğuz, Sewon Min, Patrick Lewis, Ledell Wu, Sergey Edunov, Danqi Chen, and Wen tau Yih. 2020. Dense passage retrieval for open-domain question answering.

Jinhwa Kim, Ali Derakhshan, and Ian G. Harris. 2023. Robust safety classifier for large language models: Adversarial prompt shield. *ArXiv*, abs/2311.00172.

Tom Kwiatkowski, Jennimaria Palomaki, Olivia Redfield, Michael Collins, Ankur Parikh, Chris Alberti, Danielle Epstein, Illia Polosukhin, Jacob Devlin, Kenton Lee, Kristina Toutanova, Llion Jones, Matthew Kelcey, Ming-Wei Chang, Andrew M. Dai, Jakob Uszkoreit, Quoc Le, and Slav Petrov. 2019. Natural questions: A benchmark for question answering research. *Transactions of the Association for Computational Linguistics*, 7:452–466.

Woosuk Kwon, Zhuohan Li, Siyuan Zhuang, Ying Sheng, Lianmin Zheng, Cody Hao Yu, Joseph E. Gonzalez, Hao Zhang, and Ion Stoica. 2023. Efficient memory management for large language model serving with pagedattention. In *Proceedings of the ACM SIGOPS 29th Symposium on Operating Systems Principles*.

Patrick Lewis, Ethan Perez, Aleksandra Piktus, Fabio Petroni, Vladimir Karpukhin, Naman Goyal, Heinrich Küttler, Mike Lewis, Wen tau Yih, Tim Rocktäschel, Sebastian Riedel, and Douwe Kiela. 2021. Retrieval-augmented generation for knowledge-intensive nlp tasks.

Chin-Yew Lin. 2004. ROUGE: A package for automatic evaluation of summaries. In *Text Summarization Branches Out*, pages 74–81, Barcelona, Spain. Association for Computational Linguistics.

Jerry Liu. 2022. LlamaIndex.

Yang Liu, Dan Iter, Yichong Xu, Shuohang Wang, Ruochen Xu, and Chenguang Zhu. 2023. G-eval: NLG evaluation using gpt-4 with better human alignment. In *Proceedings of the 2023 Conference on Empirical Methods in Natural Language Processing*, pages 2511–2522, Singapore. Association for Computational Linguistics.

Sewon Min, Weijia Shi, Mike Lewis, Xilun Chen, Wen tau Yih, Hannaneh Hajishirzi, and Luke Zettlemoyer. 2023. Nonparametric masked language modeling.

Niklas Muennighoff, Nouamane Tazi, Loïc Magne, and Nils Reimers. 2022. Mteb: Massive text embedding benchmark. *arXiv preprint arXiv:2210.07316*.

Tomáš Nekvinda and Ondřej Dušek. 2021. Shades of bleu, flavours of success: The case of multiwoz.

OpenAI. 2022a. New and improved embedding model.

OpenAI. 2022b. OpenAI: Introducing ChatGPT.

OpenAI. 2023. GPT-4 technical report.

Long Ouyang, Jeff Wu, Xu Jiang, Diogo Almeida, Carroll L. Wainwright, Pamela Mishkin, Chong Zhang, Sandhini Agarwal, Katarina Slama, Alex Ray, John Schulman, Jacob Hilton, Fraser Kelton, Luke Miller, Maddie Simens, Amanda Askell, Peter Welinder, Paul Christiano, Jan Leike, and Ryan Lowe. 2022. Training language models to follow instructions with human feedback.

Kishore Papineni, Salim Roukos, Todd Ward, and Wei-Jing Zhu. 2002. Bleu: a method for automatic evaluation of machine translation. In *Proceedings of the 40th Annual Meeting of the Association for Computational Linguistics*, pages 311–318, Philadelphia, Pennsylvania, USA. Association for Computational Linguistics.

Baolin Peng, Michel Galley, Pengcheng He, Hao Cheng, Yujia Xie, Yu Hu, Qiuyuan Huang, Lars Liden, Zhou Yu, Weizhu Chen, and Jianfeng Gao. 2023. Check your facts and try again: Improving large language models with external knowledge and automated feedback.

Malte Pietsch, Timo Möller, Bogdan Kostic, Julian Risch, Massimiliano Pippi, Mayank Jobanputra, Sara Zanzottera, Silvano Cerza, Vladimir Blagojevic, Thomas Stadelmann, Tanay Soni, and Sebastian Lee. 2019. Haystack: the end-to-end NLP framework for pragmatic builders.

Ori Ram, Yoav Levine, Itay Dalmedigos, Dor Muhlgay, Amnon Shashua, Kevin Leyton-Brown, and Yoav Shoham. 2023. In-context retrieval-augmented language models.

Stephen Robertson and Hugo Zaragoza. 2009. The probabilistic relevance framework: Bm25 and beyond. *Found. Trends Inf. Retr.*, 3(4):333–389.

Weijia Shi, Sewon Min, Michihiro Yasunaga, Minjoon Seo, Rich James, Mike Lewis, Luke Zettlemoyer, and Wen tau Yih. 2023. Replug: Retrieval-augmented black-box language models.

Nandan Thakur, Nils Reimers, Andreas Rücklé, Abhishek Srivastava, and Iryna Gurevych. 2021. BEIR: A heterogeneous benchmark for zero-shot evaluation of information retrieval models. In *Thirty-fifth Conference on Neural Information Processing Systems Datasets and Benchmarks Track (Round 2)*.

Hugo Touvron, Louis Martin, Kevin Stone, Peter Albert, Amjad Almahairi, Yasmine Babaei, Nikolay Bashlykov, Soumya Batra, Prajjwal Bhargava, Shruti Bhosale, Dan Bikel, Lukas Blecher, Cristian Canton Ferrer, Moya Chen, Guillem Cucurull, David Esiobu, Jude Fernandes, Jeremy Fu, Wenyin Fu, Brian Fuller, Cynthia Gao, Vedanuj Goswami, Naman Goyal, Anthony Hartshorn, Saghar Hosseini, Rui Hou, Hakan Inan, Marcin Kardas, Viktor Kerkez, Madian Khabsa, Isabel Kloumann, Artem Korenev, Punit Singh Koura, Marie-Anne Lachaux, Thibaut Lavril, Jenya Lee, Diana Liskovich, Yinghai Lu, Yuning Mao, Xavier Martinet, Todor Mihaylov, Pushkar Mishra, Igor Molybog, Yixin Nie, Andrew Poulton, Jeremy Reizenstein, Rashi Rungta, Kalyan Saladi, Alan Schelten, Ruan Silva, Eric Michael Smith, Ranjan Subramanian, Xiaoqing Ellen Tan, Binh Tang, Ross Taylor, Adina Williams, Jian Xiang Kuan, Puxin Xu, Zheng Yan, Iliyan Zarov, Yuchen Zhang, Angela Fan, Melanie Kambadur, Sharan Narang, Aurelien Rodriguez, Robert Stojnic, Sergey Edunov, and Thomas Scialom. 2023. Llama 2: Open foundation and fine-tuned chat models.

Jonathan Tow, Marco Bellagente, Dakota Mahan, and Carlos Riquelme. 2023. Stablelm 3b 4e1t.

Andrew Trotman, Antti Puurula, and Blake Burgess. 2014. Improvements to bm25 and language models examined. In *Proceedings of the 19th Australasian Document Computing Symposium*, ADCS '14, page 58–65, New York, NY, USA. Association for Computing Machinery.

Liang Wang, Nan Yang, Xiaolong Huang, Binxing Jiao, Linjun Yang, Daxin Jiang, Rangan Majumder, and Furu Wei. 2022. Text embeddings by weakly-supervised contrastive pre-training.

Liang Wang, Nan Yang, Xiaolong Huang, Binxing Jiao, Linjun Yang, Daxin Jiang, Rangan Majumder, and Furu Wei. 2023. SimLM: Pre-training with representation bottleneck for dense passage retrieval. In *Proceedings of the 61st Annual Meeting of the Association for Computational Linguistics (Volume 1: Long Papers)*, pages 2244–2258, Toronto, Canada. Association for Computational Linguistics.

Johannes Welbl, Amelia Glaese, Jonathan Uesato, Sumanth Dathathri, John Mellor, Lisa Anne Hendricks, Kirsty Anderson, Pushmeet Kohli, Ben Coppin, and Po-Sen Huang. 2021. Challenges in detoxifying language models. In *Findings of the Association for Computational Linguistics: EMNLP 2021*, pages 2447–2469, Punta Cana, Dominican Republic. Association for Computational Linguistics.

Thomas Wolf, Lysandre Debut, Victor Sanh, Julien Chaumond, Clement Delangue, Anthony Moi, Pierric Cistac, Tim Rault, Rémi Louf, Morgan Funtowicz, Joe Davison, Sam Shleifer, Patrick von Platen, Clara Ma, Yacine Jernite, Julien Plu, Canwen Xu, Teven Le Scao, Sylvain Gugger, Mariama Drame, Quentin Lhoest, and Alexander M. Rush. 2020. Huggingface's transformers: State-of-the-art natural language processing.

Shitao Xiao, Zheng Liu, Peitian Zhang, and Niklas Muennighoff. 2023. C-pack: Packaged resources to advance general chinese embedding.

Lianmin Zheng, Wei-Lin Chiang, Ying Sheng, Siyuan Zhuang, Zhanghao Wu, Yonghao Zhuang, Zi Lin, Zhuohan Li, Dacheng Li, Eric. P Xing, Hao Zhang, Joseph E. Gonzalez, and Ion Stoica. 2023a. Judging llm-as-a-judge with mt-bench and chatbot arena.

Lianmin Zheng, Liangsheng Yin, Zhiqiang Xie, Jeff Huang, Chuyue Sun, Cody Hao Yu, Shiyi Cao, Christos Kozyrakis, Ion Stoica, Joseph E. Gonzalez, Clark Barrett, and Ying Sheng. 2023b. Efficiently programming large language models using sglang.

Zexuan Zhong, Tao Lei, and Danqi Chen. 2022. Training language models with memory augmentation.

Banghua Zhu, Evan Frick, Tianhao Wu, Hanlin Zhu, and Jiantao Jiao. 2023. Starling-7b: Improving llm helpfulness and harmlessness with rlaif.

## A Comparison against Existing Toolkits

Many existing toolkits, such as Haystack, LangChain, and LLamaIndex help *users* quickly build an RQA system (Pietsch et al., 2019; Chase, 2022; Liu, 2022). However, these frameworks provide very little support for *researchers* to train, test, and serve their RQA systems using recent advances in retrieval-augmented QA research. For instance, LlamaIndex only includes basic supervised finetuning methods to train "LLaMA-2 for better text-to-SQL", or finetune "GPT-3.5-turbo to distill GPT-4"[2]. We provide three different retriever training algorithms (Section 3.2) and three different generator training algorithms (Section 3.3). We highlight our main contributions compared to other existing toolkits in Table 1.

## B Supported Data Formats

LOCALRQA support data coming from many different sources, by providing integration with frameworks such as LangChain (Chase, 2022) and LlamaIndex (Liu, 2022). This not only includes loading data of different formats (e.g., JSON, HTML, PDF files), but also data from different locations (e.g., Google Drive, S3 bucket, websites and more). For more details on data loading, please refer to our project website.

## C Details on Data Generation

LOCALRQA provides data generation scripts that can be used to create questions $q$ from a set of documents $p$, and answers from a set of $\langle q, p\rangle$ pairs. These scripts can also be easily modified to use: 1) custom prompts to generate a question or answer, and 2) custom filtering functions to use a subset of the documents for question/answer generation.

**Question Generation** Given a set of documents, LOCALRQA first creates a set of gold passages by sampling. Since contrastive learning (Section 3.2) benefits from using hard negative passages (related passages but does not contain the answer), we also sample nearby passages as hard negatives. This is achieved by first organizing all passages according to their source $s_i$ (e.g., URL or title):

$$\{p_0^{s_0}, p_1^{s_0}, ..., p_n^{s_0}, p_0^{s_1}, p_1^{s_1} ...\}$$

and then sample from $\{p_j^s\}_{j \neq i}$ as hard negatives for $p_i^s$. Next, an LLM of choice (e.g., ChatGPT) is prompted to generate $k$ questions given a sampled gold passage. To filter duplicate questions, LOCALRQA uses ROUGE-L score (Lin, 2004) to remove questions with high word overlap with others.

**Answer Generation** Given a set of $\langle q, p\rangle$ pairs, LOCALRQA prompts an LLM of choice (e.g., GPT-4) to generate answers conditioned on the question $q$ and the gold passage $p$.

See Appendix E for examples on how to customize the data generation scripts and Appendices E and F for examples commands.

## D More Details on Serving RQA Pipelines

LOCALRQA offers two serving methods: 1) an interactive chat page where users can chat with an RQA system while also providing ratings for each generated response, and 2) a static evaluation page where users directly evaluate the quality (e.g., accuracy, helpfulness, harmlessness) of the pre-generated response. The front-end UIs are created using Gradio (Abid et al., 2019), and the model back-end (for interactive chat) is modified from Zheng et al. (2023a). We provide an example of using each serving method in Figure 3 and Figure A1, respectively.

## E More Details on Databricks Demo

**Collected Documents** We use documents provided by Databrick's technical team, which are already cleaned and parsed into markdown format. We present an example in Table A1.

**QA Generation** We generate questions and answers using the data generation scripts in LOCALRQA. We first customize the prompts and filtering functions in order to obtain high-quality questions based mostly on technical tutorials rather than version release notes[3]. This only requires:

1. creating a new python script with `from scripts.data.doc_to_q import *`
2. defining a custom prompt and filter function
3. assigning `filter_fn=your_filter_fn` and `doc2q_prompt=YOUR_PROMPT` in the imported `main` function

For a complete example, please refer to our `scripts/data/doc_to_q_databricks.py`. Finally, we run the above question generation script

[2] https://docs.llamaindex.ai/en/stable/optimizing/fine-tuning/fine-tuning.html, visited on Feb 12, 2024.

[3] https://docs.databricks.com/en/release-notes/runtime/index.html

<table>
<tr><th></th><th>Databricks Example Document</th><th>Faire Example Document</th></tr>
<tr><td>content</td><td><a id="configure-access"></a><br><br>## Step 3: Configure access to the 'default.people10m' table<br>Enable the user you created in [Step 1](#add-a-user) to access the 'default.people10m' table you created in [Step 3](#create-a-table).<br>You can configure access using [Data Explorer](#data-explorer) or [SQL editor](#sql-editor).<br><br>### Data explorer<br>- Click the <Data Icon> **Data** in the sidebar.<br>- In the drop-down list at the top right<br>...</td><td>*Please note these settings are applicable to all products, if you'd like to change these settings on a product level, you can do so in the 'Catalog Synchronization' tab.<br><br># API Token<br>This is where you will enter the API token provided by Faire. Once entered, you will also receive a message to confirm that the connection is confirmed between Faire and Prestashop.<br><br># Catalog Import for Wholesale<br>This is ...</td></tr>
<tr><td>metadata</td><td>"source": "https://docs.databricks.com/.../admin-set-up-user-to-query-table.html",<br>"seq_num": 574,<br>"description": "",<br>"text": "..."</td><td>"source": "https://www.faire.com/support/articles/8726114634779",<br>"seq_num": 426,<br>"subtitle": "Prestashop Integration with Faire",<br>"title": "Prestashop Integration with Faire"</td></tr>
</table>

Table A1: Example documents collected from Databrick's documentation pages and Faire's support pages. Omitted details are indicated as "...".

| | Databricks | Faire |
|---|---|---|
| Train | 1,185 | 575 |
| Validation | 74 | 74 |
| Test | 76 | 76 |

Table A2: Number of $\langle q, a, p \rangle$ pairs used in training, validation, and testing. During testing, we use all available documents to measure an RQA system's retrieval and generation performance.

followed by our answer generation script to obtain a collection of $\langle q, a, p \rangle$ pairs. We used ChatGPT (OpenAI, 2022b) and GPT-4-turbo (OpenAI, 2023) to generate questions and answers, respectively.

**Model Training** To show the flexibility of LocalRQA training, we present at least one run of using trainer in our main experiments Table 2. All trainings are performed on a single A100 80G GPU. Please refer to our GitHub for more details on training hyperparameters and other command-line arguments used. We note that we did not rigorously hyperparameter-tune each model and trainer combination due to the large number of experiments to perform. We believe results in Table 2 may be further improved if a hyperparameter search is ran for each method.

## F More Details on Faire Demo

**Collected Documents** We contacted Faire's Sales team and crawled documents from `faire.com/support` according to their suggestions. We only kept raw texts by removing all hyperlinks for images and other websites. We present an example in Table A1.

**QA Generation** Since document data from Faire include simpler guides and QAs compared to Databricks, we find using the default generation script in LocalRQA sufficient to obtain high-quality questions and answers. Therefore, we simply ran `scripts/data/doc_to_q.py` to generate questions, and `scripts/data/docq_to_a.py` to generate answers. Similar to Databricks, we used ChatGPT (OpenAI, 2022b) and GPT-4-turbo (OpenAI, 2023) to generate questions and answers, respectively.

**Model Training** Similar to the training process implemented in Databricks, we conduct experiments across various trainers and model choices. See Table 2 for an example. We note that we did not rigorously hyperparameter-tune each model and trainer combination due to the large number of experiments to perform. We believe results in Table 2 may be further improved if a hyperparameter search is ran for each method.

## G Example Model Answers

We provide example generated answers and retrieved documents in Table A3 and Table A4 for Databricks and Faire, respectively. In Table A3, the weaker retrievers fail to find the relevant document given the user's query. As a result, the generative models also fail to provide the correct answer. This shows the benefit of training and using more accurate retrievers. In Table A4, despite all methods retrieved the correct document, the weaker generative models failed to incorporate all relevant information in its response. This underscores the importance to fine-tune capable generative models to improve the RQA system's performance.

## H Dataset Statistics

We follow the procedure outlined in Appendix E and Appendix F to obtain $\langle q, a, p \rangle$ pairs from documentation data. For Databricks, we first use our sampling algorithm to obtain 600 passages for training, and 75 for validation and for testing. For Faire, we sampled 300 passages for training as Faire has fewer documents, and 75 for validation and for testing. We then use ChatGPT (OpenAI, 2022b) as the LLM to generate two questions for each sampled passage, and GPT-4-turbo (OpenAI, 2023) to generate an answer for each $\langle q, p \rangle$ pair (see Appendix C for more details). This results in a training, evaluation, and testing dataset with statistics reported in Table A2.

| Databricks RQA Example | |
|---|---|
| | User: How many catalogs can a metastore have in Databricks? |
| text-ada-002+ GPT-3.5-turbo | In Databricks, a metastore can have multiple catalogs. There is no specific limit on the number of catalogs that can be associated with a metastore. Catalogs are used to organize [...] Users can see all catalogs on which they have been assigned the 'USE CATALOG' data permission. |
| text-ada-002+ GPT-4-turbo | A metastore in Databricks can contain multiple catalogs. [...] There isn't a specified limit to the number of catalogs a metastore can have mentioned in the documentation, which suggests that users can create multiple catalogs as needed to manage their data in an organized manner [...]. |
| E5(CTL)+ Mistral-7B(SFT) | As of August 25, 2022, a metastore can have up to 1000 catalogs. |
| BGE(CTL)+ Starling-7B(SFT) | As of August 25, 2022, a metastore in Databricks can have up to 1000 catalogs. |
| reference document: | # <UC> GA release note<br>**August 25, 2022**<br><UC> is now generally available on <Databricks>.<br>**This article describes <UC> as of the date of its GA release.** It focuses primarily on the features and updates [...]<br>As of August 25, 2022<br>- Your <Databricks> account can have only one metastore per region<br>- A metastore can have up to 1000 catalogs.<br>- A catalog can have up to 10,000 schemas.<br>- A schema can have up to 10,000 tables.<br>For current <UC> quotas, see [...]. |

Table A3: Example answers generated by different RQA systems. Questions come from the test dataset for Databricks, which is described in Appendix H. Due to space limitations, we display the most relevant document amongst all documents retrieved. In this example, text-ada-002 failed to retrieve the most relevant documents, causing GPT-3.5-turbo and GPT-4-turbo to produce incorrect answers.

| Faire RQA Example | |
|---|---|
| | User: How should I crop my feature image for it to be approved? |
| text-ada-002+ GPT-3.5-turbo | To ensure that your feature image is approved, you should crop it to a square shape. The image must fill a 1:1 ratio, meaning that the width and height should be equal. By cropping your image to a square, you can meet this requirement and increase the chances of approval. |
| text-ada-002+ GPT-4-turbo | To ensure your feature image gets approved, you should follow these cropping and content guidelines:<br>1. **Square Crop Ratio**: Crop your image to a perfect square. The aspect ratio should be 1:1, which means [...].<br>2. **No Overlaid Text or Logos** : Avoid adding any text or logos [...].<br>3. **Simplicity is Key**: Steer clear of using collages or images that are too busy. A simple, singular focus on the product [...].<br>4. **Visual Context**: Provide context by showing the product in use or in a setting where it is naturally found [...].<br>5. **Avoid Direct Eye Contact**: When including models, aim to avoid direct eye contact with the camera. [...] |
| E5(CTL)+ Mistral-7B(SFT) | To have your feature image approved, you should ensure that it is cropped to fit a square aspect ratio, which must fill a 1:1 ratio. Additionally, it should not include any words or logos. The recommended approach is to choose a high-resolution lifestyle image that showcases your best-selling product(s) in use, such as a cheese knife with cheese and grapes on a cutting board. Also, you should provide some visual context in [...] |
| BGE(CTL)+ Starling-7B(SFT) | To have your feature image approved, you should crop it to a square shape that fills a 1:1 ratio. |
| reference document: | ## Feature image guidelines<br>Crop your image to a square. It must fill a 1:1 ratio.<br>Don't include overlaid text or logos.<br>Avoid collages and keep it simple. Collages cause clutter in a space already crowded with many other brands. Choose a single image with a clear product focus. Simple, uncluttered often stand out more, as they provide rest to the shopper's eye that may be weary from browsing many pages of content.<br>Provide visual context (avoid plain white backgrounds). While it's true that great packaging design attracts people all by itself, showing your product in use helps get people excited about your brand and helps tell a more visual story about what you have to offer.<br>Avoid showing models with direct eye contact. [...] |

Table A4: Example answers generated by different RQA systems. Questions come from the test dataset for Faire, which is described in Appendix H. Due to space limitations, we display the most relevant document amongst all documents retrieved. In this example, all methods retrieved the correct document, but GPT-3.5-turbo and Starling-7B failed to include details other than "fill a 1:1 ratio"" (c.f. Table 3).

Figure A1: Researchers can launch a human evaluation page using LOCALRQA in a single command line. Given a prediction file (see Section 3.5), LOCALRQA launches a web server that allows other users to evaluate the quality of pre-generated responses. Evaluation results are automatically saved for researchers to conduct further analysis.

**Listing 2** Adding a custom component to the `SimpleRQA` pipeline. In general, researchers can easily extend an existing pipeline by editing the `.component` field, or create new pipelines by inherting from the `RQAPipeline` class.

```
from local_rqa import ...
### pre-built RQA pipeline
rqa = SimpleRQA.from_scratch(
    database_path="db_path/",
    embedding_model_name_or_path="...",
    qa_model_name_or_path="...",
)

### custom module: safety filter
class DontKnowSafetyFilter(Component):
    run_input_keys = [
        "batch_questions",
        "batch_source_documents",
        "batch_dialogue_session",
        "batch_answers",
    ]

    def run(self, *args, **kwargs):
        return RQAOutput(
            batch_answers="I don't know.",
            batch_source_documents=kwargs["batch_source_documents"],
            batch_dialogue_session=kwargs["batch_dialogue_session"],
        )

rqa.components.append(DontKnowSafetyFilter())

### run QA!
rqa.qa(...)  # output: "I don't know."
```

# JORA: JAX Tensor-Parallel LoRA Library for Retrieval Augmented Fine-Tuning

**Anique Tahir**
Arizona State University
699 S. Mill Avenue
Tempe, AZ
research@anique.org

**Lu Cheng**
University of Illinois Chicago
851 S. Morgan St.
Chicago, IL
lucheng@uic.edu

**Huan Liu**
Arizona State University
699 S. Mill Avenue
Tempe, AZ
huanliu@asu.edu

**Open-source repository:**
https://github.com/aniquetahir/JORA
**Supplementary video:**
https://youtu.be/-auF_9wF2S0?si=o50HBySZjTpjtWR_

## Abstract

The scaling of Large Language Models (LLMs) for retrieval-based tasks, particularly in Retrieval Augmented Generation (RAG), faces significant memory constraints, especially when fine-tuning extensive prompt sequences. Current open-source libraries support full-model inference and fine-tuning across multiple GPUs but fall short of accommodating the efficient parameter distribution required for retrieved context. Addressing this gap, we introduce a novel framework for PEFT-compatible fine-tuning of GPT models, leveraging distributed training. Our framework uniquely utilizes JAX's just-in-time (JIT) compilation and tensor-sharding for efficient resource management, thereby enabling accelerated fine-tuning with reduced memory requirements. This advancement significantly improves the scalability and feasibility of fine-tuning LLMs for complex RAG applications, even on systems with limited GPU resources. Our experiments show more than 12x improvement in runtime compared to Hugging Face/DeepSpeed implementation with four GPUs while consuming less than half the VRAM per GPU.

## 1 Introduction

Large Language Models (LLMs) like ChatGPT (Achiam et al., 2023) have revolutionized the field of natural language processing, paving the way for open-source alternatives that offer more flexibility in fine-tuning. Llama-2 (Touvron et al., 2023), a prominent LLM, exemplifies this trend, offering extensive customization at the architecture level. Alongside, Parameter Efficient Fine-Tuning (PEFT) (Fu et al., 2023) techniques like Low-Rank Adaptation have emerged, optimizing resource utilization in training these models. Retrieval Augmented Generation (RAG) (Lewis et al., 2020a) is a paradigm that leverages a corpus to enrich LLM prompts with relevant context. However, when fine-tuning on retrieval-based context, the quadratic memory scaling of transformer models with prompt length poses significant challenges, especially when integrating large context sizes. The training process, which employs teacher-forcing at each step of the sequence, exacerbates memory demands, creating a bottleneck for effective LLM utilization in RAG.

Current machine learning frameworks facilitate LLM fine-tuning on distributed systems, employing model and pipeline parallelism strategies. However, these frameworks lack support for PEFT, specifically in the context of parallel training. While libraries such as DeepSpeed (Rasley et al., 2020) and Accelerate (Gugger et al., 2022) offer data parallelism for fine-tuning the entire model, these libraries lack support for tensor-parallel training in the PEFT setting. In addition, combining multiple libraries adds unnecessary boilerplate code to glue together dependencies required for parameter-efficient and distributed training. These libraries also require boilerplate code for configuration since they target multiple models.

To bridge this gap, we introduce JORA (JAX-based LORA), a library tailored for Llama-2 models, designed to enhance the fine-tuning process for RAG applications. Utilizing JAX's just-in-time (JIT) compilation and innovative tensor-sharding techniques, JORA not only accelerates the fine-tuning process but also significantly optimizes memory usage (Bradbury et al., 2018). Our evaluations across standard training GPUs demonstrate substantial improvements in training time and memory efficiency, addressing the critical challenges of PEFT in retrieval-based training. Our library also provides valuable helpers for using instruct format datasets, merging LORA parameters, and convert-



*Proceedings of the 62nd Annual Meeting of the Association for Computational Linguistics (Volume 3: System Demonstrations)*, pages 152–159
August 11-16, 2024 

ing fine-tuned models to Hugging Face compatible formats. Our work makes PEFT more accessible and efficient for LLMs, particularly in resource-constrained environments. By enhancing the scalability and efficiency of LLMs in retrieval augmented fine-tuning (RAFT), JORA opens new avenues for advanced natural language processing applications.

## 2 Background

JORA introduces the concept of RAFT. This workflow employs retrieved knowledge and outcomes to create context and expected outputs. The fine-tuning process encourages the model to learn a rationale to derive the output from the knowledge. Prior related work focuses on RAG, the inference counterpart of RAFT, whose bottleneck is the sequence length used for context in the prompt. Since RAFT shares the same bottleneck, our framework focuses on adding efficiency by providing a memory-efficient and distributed backend while exposing an intuitive API. We highlight the importance of RAG and the capabilities of other libraries which aim to solve related problems. We highlight how our library fills the gap.

### 2.1 Retrieval Augmented Generation

RAG has gained significant attention in recent years, with various approaches exploring it to enhance LLM generation. The integration of dense and sparse retrievers with LLMs, as discussed in (Robertson et al., 2009; Seo et al., 2019), highlights the diversity in retrieval techniques used for augmenting LMs. Chen et al. (2017), Clark and Gardner (2017), and others have contributed to conditioning LMs on retrieved documents, demonstrating significant improvements in knowledge-intensive tasks (Lee et al., 2019; Guu et al., 2020; Khandelwal et al., 2019; Lewis et al., 2020b; Izacard and Grave, 2020; Borgeaud et al., 2022; Murez et al., 2020). The concept of chain-of-thought prompting in combination with retrieval mechanisms, as proposed by Wei et al. (2022), marks a novel approach in this domain. The evolution of LMs into agent-like models, capable of generating queries and performing actions based on prompts, is evident in the works of Thoppilan et al. (2022), who introduced models like LaMDA. Menick et al. (2022), Komeili et al. (2021), and Nakano et al. (2021) further explored the generation of internet search queries by LMs.

### 2.2 Parallel Training Libraries

Several open-source libraries expose an interface for multi-GPU training for LLMs. Hugging Face implementation of Transformer models allows multi-GPU inference. The Transformers library also includes a trainer. Hugging Face's Accelerate (Gugger et al., 2022) library is a tool designed to simplify the process of running PyTorch training scripts on different devices, including CPU, single GPU, multiple GPUs, and TPUs while supporting mixed precision and distributed settings. It offers an easy-to-use API that allows users to run their PyTorch code across any distributed configuration with minimal changes, making training and inference at scale more straightforward. DeepSpeed (Rasley et al., 2020) is an open-source optimization library for PyTorch developed by Microsoft. It is designed to accelerate the training and inference of deep learning models, mainly focusing on large-scale models. The library addresses challenges such as memory constraints and slow training times, aiming to enhance deep learning workflows' performance and efficiency. Accelerate utilizes DeepSpeed or FSDP for distributed training.

JORA solves several issues with prior libraries: i) we target specific models to reduce the boilerplate required for the training process, ii) we utilize JAX's jit optimizations for training to improve training performance compared to PyTorch. iii) we provide a tensor-parallel, multi-GPU implementation of training, and iv) we provide utility functions to simplify the data loading experience, fine-tuning the model, and compatibility with the Hugging Face ecosystem.

## 3 JORA Framework

JORA is a library for RAFT. Its purpose is to make fine-tuning based on retrieved context more user-friendly. In addition, it is designed to make RAFT faster and more resource-efficient. Figure 1 gives a high-level overview of JORA.

#### 3.0.1 JAX

One of the highlights of our library is that it allows LoRA training of LLMs using the JAX framework. JAX provides composable transformations of numerical functions e.g. automatic differentiation (grad), vectorization (vmap), parallelization (pmap), and just-in-time compilation (jit) (Bradbury et al., 2018). A function must

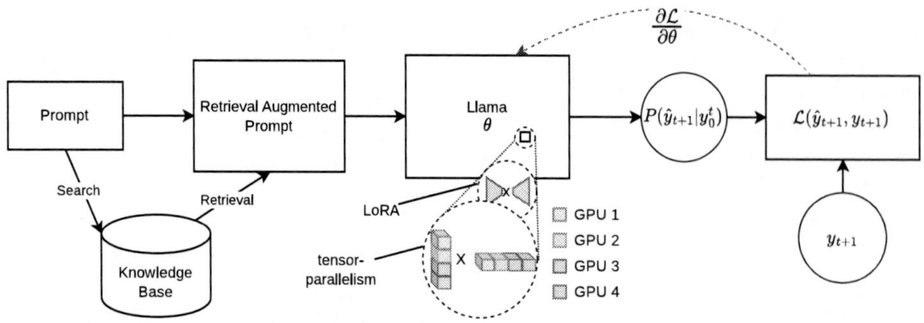


Figure 1: JORA is a library that aids in Retrieval Augmented Fine-Tuning by eliminating unnecessary boilerplate and introducing memory efficient training through tensor-parallelism and LoRA.

be pure and statically composed to benefit from these transformations. Functions compiled by JAX use the Accelerated Linear Algebra (XLA) library. Jit compilation allows program optimizations to the XLA to improve execution speed which is ideal for compute-heavy architectures such as transformers.

### 3.0.2 Dataset Loading and Training

```
[
  {
    "instruction": "Calculate the area
    of the following shape in square
    centimeters.",
    "input": "rectangle of size 4 cm x 5
    cm",.
    "output": "20cm^2"
  },
  ...
]
```

Listing 1: An example of Alpaca format data.

Even though JORA is compatible with general-purpose fine-tuning pipelines, we provide helper functions for loading training data in alpaca format (Taori et al., 2023). The Alpaca dataset format is ideal for RAFT since it follows the instruction-tuning format. Each sample in this format may contain an instruction, input (optional), and output. Listing 1 shows an example of this data format. Retrieved knowledge can be used as the input and separated from the instruction and output. The output represents the sequence that the model generates.

```
class AlpacaDataset(Dataset):
    def __init__(self, *, path: str,
    split=Union[Literal['train'],
    Literal['test']],
                    split_percentage=0.8,
    tokenizer=None, max_len=512,
    alpaca_mix=0.3) -> None:
```

Listing 2: Function signature for the constructor for AlpacaDataset.

We provide the class 'AlpacaDataset' for user-friendly data loading, which inherits from PyTorch's 'Dataset' class. Listing 2 shows the signature for the constructor for this class. In addition to loading the dataset, the $alpaca\_mix$ parameter allows merging a percentage of the original alpaca dataset to prevent overfitting on the fine-tuned data. The class also provides the ability to create training and testing splits based on the provided split percentage. The AlpacaDataset collators apply instruction-masking by default.

### 3.0.3 Training API

How fine-tuning proceeds depends on a variety of parameters. Since this library aims to simplify the training process, JORA provides common defaults for starters. In addition, it allows customization of the training process for more advanced usage. Listing 3 shows the configuration class. $JAX\_PARAMS\_PATH$ specifies the location of the model parameters. $LLAMA2\_HF\_PATH$ specifies the location of Meta's model in Hugging Face format. Our library uses the Hugging Face model path to access it's tokenizer. Since the release of JAX native LLMs, such as Gemma (Team et al., 2024), our library supports loading models without a Hugging Face format. For the sake of brevity, our examples follow the datastructures for Llama-2. Other model configurations follow suit with model specific naming schemes.

```
class ParallamaConfig(NamedTuple):
    JAX_PARAMS_PATH: str
    LLAMA2_HF_PATH: str
    LORA_R: int = 16
    LORA_ALPHA: int = 16
    LORA_DROPOUT: float = 0.05
```

Listing 3: JORA allows the common defaults for the configuration with room for specificity.

### 3.0.4 Model Transfer API

Most open-source libraries that utilize LLM's are compatible with Hugging Face's model format. Since JORA uses JAX for its training procedure, the caveat is incompatibility with the popular libraries. To overcome this limitation, we provide a simple script to convert models trained using our library to the Hugging Face format. Listing 4 provides a description of the conversion script usage.

JORA builds on LLM implementations in JAX which uses jit and vmap. GPT-based models use the decoder component of the transformer architecture to produce text autoregressively. Since transformer models consist of multi-headed self-attention, the memory used at the inference stage scales quadratically with the input sequence length. This is a significant drawback for RAFT since augmenting a prompt with retrieved-context adds to the sequence length. As such, one of the aims of our library is to assuage the memory utilization requirements by efficiently distributing memory usage across GPU resources.

```
SYNOPSIS
    huggingface_merger.py
    HUGGINGFACE_PATH JAX_PATH SAVE_PATH

POSITIONAL ARGUMENTS
    HUGGINGFACE_PATH
        Type: str
        path to the HuggingFace llama
    model
    JAX_PATH
        Type: str
        path to LoRA parameters fine-
    tuned by JORA
    SAVE_PATH
        Type: str
        path to save the updated
    HuggingFace llama model
```

Listing 4: Hugging Face conversion script can be invoked from the command-line. The converted model can be used with other Hugging Face compatible libraries such as LangChain.

For our implementation of LoRA, we follow the suggestions presented by Hu et al. (2021), i.e., the query and value attention weights are enhanced. Specifically, the approach suggests that the computation, $W_0x + b_0$, can be tuned through $W_0x + b_0 + BAx$ where $W_0$ are subset of the models weights, $B$, $A$ are the trainable countports of $W_0$ added by LoRA, $W_0, BA \in \mathbb{R}^{m \times n}$, $A \in \mathbb{R}^{r \times n}$, $B \in \mathbb{R}^{m \times r}$, and $r << m, n$.

Here, $B$ and $A$ are the trainable weights. $W_0$ and $b_0$ represent the weights and biases of a specific neural network component. Composing the trainable parameters to lower rank values significantly reduces the total parameters involved in backpropagation. Generative models are trained to predict the next token, given past tokens auto-regressively. Thus, the objective, $\mathcal{L}$, of the LLM is to reduce the discrepancy between the next predicted token $\hat{y}_{t+1}$ and the next ground truth token $y_{t+1}$, given the past tokens in the ground truth sequence, $y_0^t$. Consequently, the trained language model predicts the next token, given the past predicted tokens, $\hat{y}_0^t$.

For our implementation of LoRA, we add the LoRA parameters to the original weights as highlighted in Equation 1. The values of $B$ and $A$ are initialized from zeros and normal sampling, respectively.

$$\begin{aligned} Output &= W_0x + b_0 + BAx \\ &= (W_0 + BA)x + b_0 \end{aligned} \tag{1}$$

JORA parallelizes all parameters of the Llama model using JAX's positional sharding module. Transformers inherently support distributed computations through the use of parallel decoder blocks. GPT's consists of several layers of parallel decoder blocks. We utilize the inherent design and shard on the decoder axis. Projection and Embedding layers are sharded on the non-sequential dimension to avoid variation due to the input.

### 3.0.5 Library Usage

One of the core aims of JORA is to make fine-tuning easily accessible to the end-user. Compared to Hugging Face, JORA significantly reduces the lines of code to get started. In addition, JORA provides a GUI for fine-tuning LLMs. The following code can be used to fine-tune a model with minimal changes to default training parameters:

```
from jora import train_lora,
    ParallamaConfig,
    generate_alpaca_dataset

config = ParallamaConfig(
        MODEL_SIZE=model_size,
        JAX_PARAMS_PATH=jax_path,
        LLAMA2_META_PATH=hf_path)
dataset = generate_alpaca_dataset(
    dataset_path, 'train', config)
train_lora(config, dataset,
    checkpoint_path)
```

Alternatively, the GUI can set the fine-tuning parameters and training. Fig. 2 shows the interface for the GUI. It can be invoked with the following command:

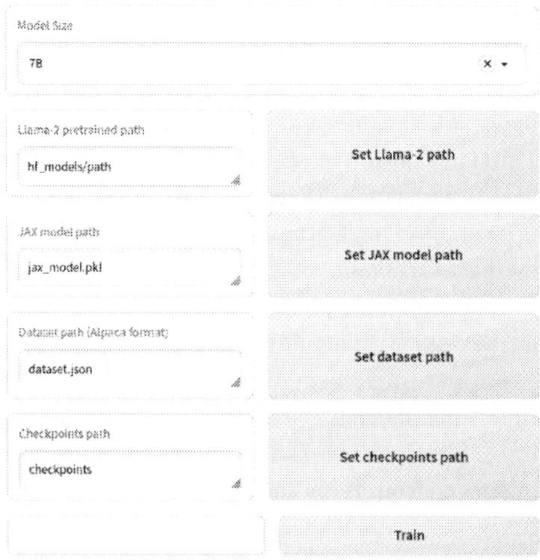


Figure 2: JORA provides a simple GUI for fine-tuning.

```
python -m jora.gui
```

# 4 Experiments

We measure the improvement introduced by JORA in terms of memory utilization and computation speed, conducting experiments using Hugging Face/DeepSpeed for comparison. Our setup consists of a node of the SOL supercomputer (Jennewein et al., 2023) with 4 x A100 with 40GB of VRAM each, an AMD EPYC 75F3 32-core Processor, and 512GB of RAM. The GPUs are cross-connected using NVLink. All experiments use 16-bit brain floating point for parameter precision for a fair comparison.

## 4.1 Memory Utilization Analysis

We compare the memory utilization of our implementation with that of the Hugging Face trainer using Accelerate and PEFT. Our implementation is adapted from the examples in the official Hugging Face PEFT library, which uses Accelerate and DeepSpeed for parallel computation. Through parallelization, several parameters are replicated across multiple GPUs. As such, the total memory utilized by parallel training is greater than that used in a single GPU setting. However, the advantage of multi-GPU training is that the memory used by each GPU individually is less than that used in single-GPU training. JAX pre-allocates memory to avoid fragmentation, which makes measuring active allocation a challenge. For memory utilization analysis, we override this behavior by setting the XLA_PYTHON_CLIENT_ALLOCATOR environment variable to 'platform.' This environment variable informs JAX to allocate and deallocate memory as needed but impacts performance. Thus, for the performance evaluation, we use the default configuration.

For parallel training, DeepSpeed distributes parameters using data parallelism. Thus, though a single sample cannot be distributed, multiple samples can be aggregated, improving performance. Thus, JORA is beneficial since it allows a single lengthy sequence to backpropagate across multiple GPUs. Table 1 shows that JORA uses less memory per resource as the number of resources increases. The only case where Hugging Face/DeepSpeed consumes lower memory is where only one GPU is available.

## 4.2 Computation Time Comparison

We also measure computation time using the same RAFT dataset for the Hugging Face and JORA implementations over iterations of 1, 2, and 4 GPUs. Table 1 presents these results. JORA shows consistently better performance than Hugging Face implementation, with JORA implementation being over 12 times faster than the baseline with 4 GPUs. Since DeepSpeed used data parallelism, we observe a performance impact in multi-GPU settings, with the bottleneck being the slowest GPU/sample for backpropagation. In addition to improved performance, since JORA uses JAX's jit functionality to run compiled computations, the performance of the implementation shows more consistency. We observe a computation performance drop between single and multiple GPUs. This drop could be attributed to cross-GPU communication overhead.

# 5 An Example Usage Scenario

JORA is designed to aid in RAFT. In this section, we demonstrate a RAFT use case by fine-tuning it on a social media dataset (Papasavva et al., 2020) to help LLMs enable social-context understanding. The purpose of RAG is to add additional context to a prompt by searching for knowledge and adding additional information. For RAFT, data can be created based on retrieved knowledge. The LLM learns to generate the retrieved answer based on the context since the key rationale is held back. A simple example is a database query, which corresponds to a process that may be taken to produce

| | GPUs | 1 | 2 | 4 |
|---|---|---|---|---|
| Hugging Face PEFT w/ Microsoft DeepSpeed ZeRO-3 | Mem (MB) | **20645.2** **(39.81)** | 23056 / 23024 (14.63 / 29.29) | 23978 / 23921 / 23463 / 23397 (47.87 / 50.39 / 31.96 / 17.46) |
| | Performance (secs) | 4.56 (0.04) | 2.81 (0.02) | 5.45 (0.09) |
| JORA (Ours) | Mem (MB) | 23102 (0.00) | **16068 / 16008** **(0.00 / 0.00)** | **11460 / 11448 / 11448 / 11400** **(0.0 / 0.00 / 0.00 / 0.00)** |
| | Performance (secs) | **0.19** **(0.00)** | **0.79** **(0.00)** | **0.44** **(0.00)** |

Table 1: JORA shows significant improvement w.r.t. Hugging Face implementation of PEFT paired with DeepSpeed for parallelization. JORA uses tensor-parallelism to distribute memory allocation for parameters across GPU resources. The number in the brackets denotes the standard deviation across five runs.

an output by evaluating the database. If the query is not provided but rather a natural language equivalent is provided, the LLM must learn the heuristics represented by the hidden query.

Since prompt tuning is insufficient for models to develop social-context understanding (Gandhi et al., 2023), we use a fine-tuning process consisting of two phases to add knowledge to an LLM. Both phases of fine-tuning use PEFT. For our problem setting, rather than just predicting the following words, we aim to gain an understanding of the relation across different comments in a social media session. For instance, a comment in a social media session may target the previous comment, the original post that spawned the session, or some comment in the middle of the discourse. To glean insight into the target of the comment in terms of its context, reasoning between the structure of the conversation is critical. Unfortunately, the LLM pre-training does not consider these relationships specifically, and there is no public data related to reasoning at the comment level in social media discourse. Thus, we rely on other general-purpose structured data as a surrogate to learn structure and reasoning. We use the WikiTableQuestions (Pasupat and Liang, 2015) dataset to infuse structural intelligence into the model. This dataset consists of various independent tables, questions based on one of the tables, and a corresponding answer. To answer these questions, using the data in the input table is vital. Some answers require aggregate reasoning.

For the directionality analysis task (which post is targeted by another comment in the same session), we leveraged a corpus of 4chan threads (Papasavva et al., 2020). This dataset consists of ~3 million threads and ~100 million posts. Since 4chan allows its users to tag whom they reply to, we use this data as the ground truth for directionality information. We examine whether our RAFT phases

| | Target Post | Reply Post | p(Reply \| Target) |
|---|---|---|---|
| **7B** | 0.082 | 0.153 | 0.643 |
| **13B** | 0.159 | 0.200 | <u>0.815</u> |
| **7B-RAFT** | <u>0.865</u> | <u>0.541</u> | 0.558 |
| **13B-RAFT** | **0.971** | **0.847** | **0.855** |

Table 2: The veracity of the directionality identification improves with the RAFT fine-tuning phases w.r.t. the baselines. Given the conversation as context, the values represent the accuracy of detecting the respective posts. Llama-2 models are used.

improve (i) the model's ability to detect the post we are targeting for behavior comprehension and (ii) the model's ability to distinguish who is being targeted by the poster. 4chan allows posters to mention more than one comment as the target of the reply. Here, we consider the model successful if one of the multiple comments is identified. Table 2 shows the result of our experiment. The RAFT model significantly improves performance over the pre-trained counterparts. This illustrates the application of RAFT to improve LLM performance in social media analysis. *Social media conversation threads can provide important context but they can span large sequences. JORA helps in the training process here by splitting a discourse sequence's computation tensors across multiple GPUs. This is not possible using HuggingFace/Deepspeed since Data-Parallelism in these frameworks distributes the workload between different data instances rather than dividing the computation for a single data instance among multiple accelerators.*

## 6 Conclusion

This paper presents JORA, a JAX-based library for Retrieval Augment fine-tuning of Llama-2 models. JORA provides convenient functions for data manipulation and training. In addition, it implements best practices for memory efficient and performant training. By using a combination of LoRA, tensor-parallelism, and jit, JORA can significantly improve memory efficiency and computation time over a distributed environment compared to Hugging Face/DeepSpeed. Finally, JORA can export trained models to the popular Hugging Face model format for downstream usage with other Hugging Face-compatible libraries.

## Acknowledgements

This work is supported by Office of Naval Research awards #N00014-21-1-400 and #N00014-22-1-2291. L.C. is supported by NSF award #2312862 and a Cisco gift grant.

## References

Josh Achiam, Steven Adler, Sandhini Agarwal, Lama Ahmad, Ilge Akkaya, Florencia Leoni Aleman, Diogo Almeida, Janko Altenschmidt, Sam Altman, Shyamal Anadkat, et al. 2023. Gpt-4 technical report. *arXiv preprint arXiv:2303.08774*.

Sebastian Borgeaud, Arthur Mensch, Jordan Hoffmann, Trevor Cai, Eliza Rutherford, Katie Millican, George Bm Van Den Driessche, Jean-Baptiste Lespiau, Bogdan Damoc, Aidan Clark, et al. 2022. Improving language models by retrieving from trillions of tokens. pages 2206–2240.

James Bradbury, Roy Frostig, Peter Hawkins, Matthew James Johnson, Chris Leary, Dougal Maclaurin, George Necula, Adam Paszke, Jake VanderPlas, Skye Wanderman-Milne, and Qiao Zhang. 2018. JAX: composable transformations of Python+NumPy programs.

Danqi Chen, Adam Fisch, Jason Weston, and Antoine Bordes. 2017. Reading wikipedia to answer open-domain questions.

Christopher Clark and Matt Gardner. 2017. Simple and effective multi-paragraph reading comprehension.

Zihao Fu, Haoran Yang, Anthony Man-Cho So, Wai Lam, Lidong Bing, and Nigel Collier. 2023. On the effectiveness of parameter-efficient fine-tuning. In *Proceedings of the AAAI Conference on Artificial Intelligence*, volume 37, pages 12799–12807.

Kanishk Gandhi, Jan-Philipp Fränken, Tobias Gerstenberg, and Noah D Goodman. 2023. Understanding social reasoning in language models with language models. *arXiv preprint arXiv:2306.15448*.

Sylvain Gugger, Lysandre Debut, Thomas Wolf, Philipp Schmid, Zachary Mueller, Sourab Mangrulkar, Marc Sun, and Benjamin Bossan. 2022. Accelerate: Training and inference at scale made simple, efficient and adaptable. `https://github.com/huggingface/accelerate`.

Kelvin Guu, Kenton Lee, Zora Tung, Panupong Pasupat, and Mingwei Chang. 2020. Retrieval augmented language model pre-training. pages 3929–3938.

Edward J Hu, Yelong Shen, Phillip Wallis, Zeyuan Allen-Zhu, Yuanzhi Li, Shean Wang, Lu Wang, and Weizhu Chen. 2021. Lora: Low-rank adaptation of large language models. *arXiv preprint arXiv:2106.09685*.

Gautier Izacard and Edouard Grave. 2020. Leveraging passage retrieval with generative models for open domain question answering. *arXiv preprint arXiv:2007.01282*.

Douglas M. Jennewein, Johnathan Lee, Chris Kurtz, Will Dizon, Ian Shaeffer, Alan Chapman, Alejandro Chiquete, Josh Burks, Amber Carlson, Natalie Mason, Arhat Kobwala, Thirugnanam Jagadeesan, Praful Barghav, Torey Battelle, Rebecca Belshe, Debra McCaffrey, Marisa Brazil, Chaitanya Inumella, Kirby Kuznia, Jade Buzinski, Sean Dudley, Dhruvil Shah, Gil Speyer, and Jason Yalim. 2023. The Sol Supercomputer at Arizona State University. In *Practice and Experience in Advanced Research Computing*, PEARC '23, pages 296–301, New York, NY, USA. Association for Computing Machinery.

Urvashi Khandelwal, Omer Levy, Dan Jurafsky, Luke Zettlemoyer, and Mike Lewis. 2019. Generalization through memorization: Nearest neighbor language models. *arXiv preprint arXiv:1911.00172*.

Mojtaba Komeili, Kurt Shuster, and Jason Weston. 2021. Internet-augmented dialogue generation.

Kenton Lee, Ming-Wei Chang, and Kristina Toutanova. 2019. Latent retrieval for weakly supervised open domain question answering.

Patrick Lewis, Ethan Perez, Aleksandra Piktus, Fabio Petroni, Vladimir Karpukhin, Naman Goyal, Heinrich Küttler, Mike Lewis, Wen-tau Yih, Tim Rocktäschel, et al. 2020a. Retrieval-augmented generation for knowledge-intensive nlp tasks. *Advances in Neural Information Processing Systems*, 33:9459–9474.

Patrick Lewis, Ethan Perez, Aleksandra Piktus, Fabio Petroni, Vladimir Karpukhin, Naman Goyal, Heinrich Küttler, Mike Lewis, Wen-tau Yih, Tim Rocktäschel, et al. 2020b. Retrieval-augmented generation for knowledge-intensive nlp tasks. volume 33, pages 9459–9474.

Jacob Menick, Maja Trebacz, Vladimir Mikulik, John Aslanides, Francis Song, Martin Chadwick, Mia Glaese, Susannah Young, Lucy Campbell-Gillingham, Geoffrey Irving, et al. 2022. Teaching language models to support answers with verified quotes. *arXiv preprint arXiv:2203.11147*.

Zak Murez, Tarrence Van As, James Bartolozzi, Ayan Sinha, Vijay Badrinarayanan, and Andrew Rabinovich. 2020. Atlas: End-to-end 3d scene reconstruction from posed images. In *Computer Vision–ECCV*

2020: 16th European Conference, Glasgow, UK, August 23–28, 2020, Proceedings, Part VII 16*, pages 414–431. Springer.

Reiichiro Nakano, Jacob Hilton, Suchir Balaji, Jeff Wu, Long Ouyang, Christina Kim, Christopher Hesse, Shantanu Jain, Vineet Kosaraju, William Saunders, et al. 2021. Webgpt: Browser-assisted question-answering with human feedback.

Antonis Papasavva, Savvas Zannettou, Emiliano De Cristofaro, Gianluca Stringhini, and Jeremy Blackburn. 2020. Raiders of the lost kek: 3.5 years of augmented 4chan posts from the politically incorrect board. In *Proceedings of the international AAAI conference on web and social media*, volume 14, pages 885–894.

Panupong Pasupat and Percy Liang. 2015. Compositional semantic parsing on semi-structured tables. *arXiv preprint arXiv:1508.00305*.

Jeff Rasley, Samyam Rajbhandari, Olatunji Ruwase, and Yuxiong He. 2020. Deepspeed: System optimizations enable training deep learning models with over 100 billion parameters. In *Proceedings of the 26th ACM SIGKDD International Conference on Knowledge Discovery & Data Mining*, pages 3505–3506.

Stephen Robertson, Hugo Zaragoza, et al. 2009. The probabilistic relevance framework: Bm25 and beyond. *Foundations and Trends® in Information Retrieval*, 3(4):333–389.

Minjoon Seo, Jinhyuk Lee, Tom Kwiatkowski, Ankur P Parikh, Ali Farhadi, and Hannaneh Hajishirzi. 2019. Real-time open-domain question answering with dense-sparse phrase index. *arXiv preprint arXiv:1906.05807*.

Rohan Taori, Ishaan Gulrajani, Tianyi Zhang, Yann Dubois, Xuechen Li, Carlos Guestrin, Percy Liang, and Tatsunori B. Hashimoto. 2023. Stanford alpaca: An instruction-following llama model. `https://github.com/tatsu-lab/stanford_alpaca`.

Gemma Team, Thomas Mesnard, Cassidy Hardin, Robert Dadashi, Surya Bhupatiraju, Shreya Pathak, Laurent Sifre, Morgane Rivière, Mihir Sanjay Kale, Juliette Love, et al. 2024. Gemma: Open models based on gemini research and technology. *arXiv preprint arXiv:2403.08295*.

Romal Thoppilan, Daniel De Freitas, Jamie Hall, Noam Shazeer, Apoorv Kulshreshtha, Heng-Tze Cheng, Alicia Jin, Taylor Bos, Leslie Baker, Yu Du, et al. 2022. Lamda: Language models for dialog applications.

Hugo Touvron, Louis Martin, Kevin Stone, Peter Albert, Amjad Almahairi, Yasmine Babaei, Nikolay Bashlykov, Soumya Batra, Prajjwal Bhargava, Shruti Bhosale, et al. 2023. Llama 2: Open foundation and fine-tuned chat models. *arXiv preprint arXiv:2307.09288*.

Jason Wei, Xuezhi Wang, Dale Schuurmans, Maarten Bosma, Fei Xia, Ed Chi, Quoc V Le, Denny Zhou, et al. 2022. Chain-of-thought prompting elicits reasoning in large language models. volume 35, pages 24824–24837.

# LinguaLinked: Distributed Large Language Model Inference on Mobile Devices

**Junchen Zhao***
UC Irvine
junchez3@uci.edu

**Yurun Song***
UC Irvine
yuruns@uci.edu

**Simeng Liu**
UC Irvine
simenl3@uci.edu

**Ian G. Harris**
UC Irvine
harris@ics.uci.edu

**Sangeetha Abdu Jyothi**
UC Irvine, VMware Research
sangeetha.aj@uci.edu

## Abstract

Deploying Large Language Models (LLMs) locally on mobile devices presents a significant challenge due to their extensive memory requirements. In this paper, we introduce LinguaLinked, a system for decentralized, distributed LLM inference on mobile devices. LinguaLinked enables collaborative execution of the inference task across multiple trusted devices and ensures data privacy by processing information locally. LinguaLinked uses three key strategies. First, an optimized *model assignment technique* segments LLMs and uses linear optimization to align segments with each device's capabilities. Second, an optimized *data transmission mechanism* ensures efficient and structured data flow between model segments while also maintaining the integrity of the original model structure. Finally, LinguaLinked incorporates a *runtime load balancer* that actively monitors and redistributes tasks among mobile devices to prevent bottlenecks, enhancing the system's overall efficiency and responsiveness. We demonstrate that LinguaLinked facilitates efficient LLM inference while maintaining consistent throughput and minimal latency through extensive testing across various mobile devices, from high-end to low-end Android devices.

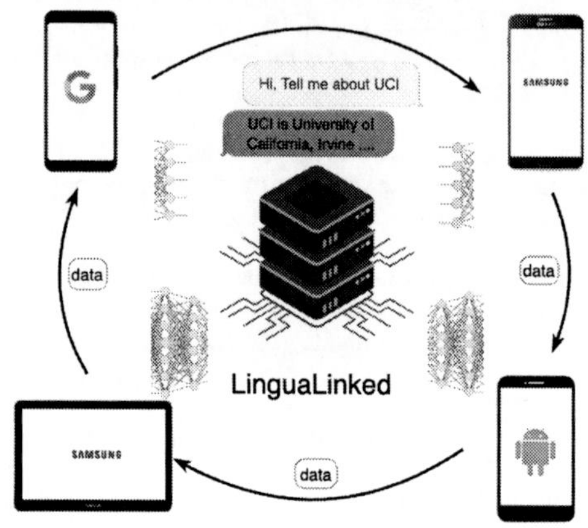


Figure 1: 'Trusted' mobile devices working collaboratively for LLM inference in LinguaLinked.

## 1 Introduction

The past decade has witnessed a seismic shift in the machine learning (ML) landscape, particularly with the rise of large language models (LLMs), which are built atop transformer decoders (Vaswani et al., 2023). These LLMs (Brown et al., 2020; Kaplan et al., 2020, Hoffmann et al., 2022; Chowdhery et al., 2022; Zhang et al., 2022; Touvron et al., 2023; Workshop et al., 2023) have achieved state-of-art performance on Natural Language Processing (NLP) benchmarks such as text generation, question answering, machine translation, and text summarization, and led to commercial offerings such as OpenAI ChatGPT and Github Copilot. Recent research has established that as the number of parameters in these models increases, they demonstrate enhanced capabilities in various language tasks (Alabdulmohsin et al., 2022; Clark et al., 2022; Huang et al., 2020; Patel and Pavlick, 2022, Hendrycks et al., 2021; Cobbe et al., 2021).

However, deploying these LLMs on mobile devices is challenging due to their significant memory and processing requirements. Traditional server-based inference raises privacy and bandwidth issues. An alternative is distributed inference, where LLMs are split into smaller segments across multiple devices, reducing the need for heavy model weight quantization and maintaining accuracy. While previous studies have looked into distributed model deployment on mobile computing platforms (Hu et al., 2019; Naveen et al., 2021; Zeng et al., 2021; Zhou et al., 2019), these have largely concentrated on smaller-scale models used in computer vision applications, which have a much smaller memory footprint compared to LLMs and

[0]* Equally contributed.



*Proceedings of the 62nd Annual Meeting of the Association for Computational Linguistics (Volume 3: System Demonstrations)*, pages 160–171
August 11-16, 2024 ©2024 Association for Computational Linguistics

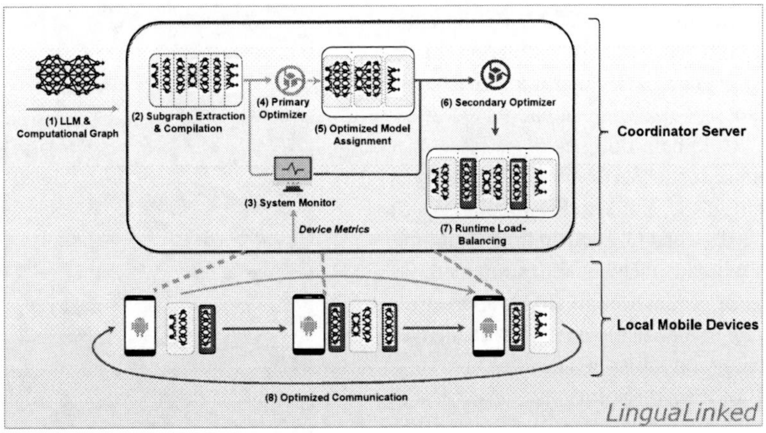


Figure 2: Overview of LinguaLinked System Design.

typically do not need iterative inference.

In this paper, we present LinguaLinked[1], a decentralized distributed inference system for LLM deployment on mobile devices. The core concept behind LinguaLinked is distributing model segments across 'trusted' devices shown in Figure 1, such as personal smartphones and tablets. This approach overcomes the limitations of individual device capacities, privacy concerns, and bandwidth constraints. However, it faces challenges like managing diverse device capabilities, handling data dependencies between model segments, and adjusting to dynamic resource availability.

LinguaLinked addresses these challenges with three key components: optimized model assignment that aligns model segments with device capabilities while minimizing data transmission, runtime load balancing to redistribute tasks and prevent bottlenecks, and optimized communication to ensure efficient data exchange between model segments. We perform a thorough evaluation of LinguaLinked on high-end and low-end Android devices. In a single-threaded setting, compared to the baseline, LinguaLinked achieves an inference performance acceleration of approximately $1.11\times$ to $1.61\times$ across both quantized and full-precision models. With multi-threading, the system exhibits further improvements, achieving acceleration rates of approximately $1.73\times$ to $2.65\times$ for both quantized and full-precision models. Runtime load balancing yields an overall inference acceleration of $1.29\times$ to $1.32\times$. Importantly, our findings indicate that LinguaLinked's performance gains are more pronounced with larger models, suggesting enhanced scalability and effectiveness in handling complex, resource-intensive tasks. We develop an Android application to demonstrate LinguaLinked's effectiveness in a typical mobile computing environment, showing how LLMs can operate on devices with diverse capabilities.

[1] `https://github.com/zjc664656505/LinguaLinked-Inference`

## 2 Related Works

**Autoregressive LLMs and Computational Challenges.** Recent advancements in NLP have been driven by autoregressive LLMs like GPT-3 (Brown et al., 2020), OPT (Zhang et al., 2022), and LLaMA (Touvron et al., 2023), which generate text sequentially. While effective for tasks such as language generation and translation, their sequential nature leads to computational inefficiencies, especially for longer texts (Lin et al., 2021; Floridi and Chiriatti, 2020; Lee, 2023). Traditionally, these models have been processed on centralized servers (Aminabadi et al., 2022; Borzunov et al., 2022; Du et al., 2023), with innovations aimed at reducing latency and enhancing efficiency (Wang et al., 2023; Romero et al., 2021; Gunasekaran et al., 2022). However, centralization raises privacy concerns and can introduce latency due to data transmission requirements (Khowaja et al., 2023; Sebastian, 2023; Renaud et al., 2023; Kshetri, 2023; Elbamby et al., 2019; Liang et al., 2020a; Park et al., 2019; Mao et al., 2017b).

**Mobile Constraints and Model Optimization.** Deploying LLMs on mobile devices presents challenges due to limited computational and memory resources (Wu et al., 2019; Zhao et al., 2022; Chen and Ran, 2019; Zhang et al., 2019). Techniques like quantization (Gholami et al., 2022; Bondarenko et al., 2021; Coelho et al., 2021), distillation (Liang et al., 2020b; Gu et al., 2023; Jiao et al., 2019), and pruning (Blalock et al., 2020; Hoefler et al., 2021; Liang et al., 2021) help mitigate these issues but may compromise model performance. Frameworks such as TensorFlow Lite (TensorFlow, 2023), TVM (Chen et al., 2018), and ONNXRuntime (Runtime, 2023), along with advanced quantization methods (Yao et al., 2022; Frantar et al., 2022; Xiao et al., 2023), facilitate mobile deployment, yet challenges persist, especially on lower-end devices.

**Distributed Inference Solutions.** Addressing the limitations of single-device deployment, distributed inference strategies like LinguaLinked partition LLMs across multiple devices, reducing the memory load on individual devices and enabling broader device participation in inference tasks. Frameworks such as DeepHome (Hu et al., 2019), MODNN (Mao et al., 2017a), and EdgeFlow (Hu and Li, 2022) have explored data parallelism and model partitioning, primarily for vision models. However, the adaptation of these strategies for LLMs on mobile devices remains an underexplored area, with a need for solutions that consider real-time device performance fluctuations and load balancing (Xu et al., 2022).

## 3 LinguaLinked

As shown in Figure 2, the LinguaLinked system facilitates LLM distribution across mobile devices by transforming the LLM into a computational graph on a coordinator server, then partitioning it into sub-modules for optimized allocation to devices based on their performance metrics. It employs primary and secondary optimizers for task distribution and load balancing, with a communication strategy that minimizes data transmission between devices, ensuring efficiency and privacy as all data remains local to the devices.

### 3.1 System Monitor

The system monitor in LinguaLinked is comprised of server and device modules to track and manage performance metrics like bandwidth, latency, memory, and processing speed across devices. The server module controls monitoring activities and processes data for optimization, while the device module assesses performance indicators. Bandwidth is measured by transferring data between devices and calculating the transfer rate, while pro-

Figure 3: Android chat application that runs full-precision BLOOM 1.7b on 2 Google Pixel 7 pro. The demo video can be found at `https://youtu.be/4UhXzKUkOuI`

cessing speed (FLOP/s) is determined by timing a test model's execution on each device, offering insights into the system's operational efficiency.

### 3.2 Optimized Model Assignment

**Subgraph Extraction from LLMs.** The first step in preparing LLMs for mobile deployment involves converting them into computational graphs and then segmenting these graphs into smaller, independent subgraphs. These subgraphs are designed to operate separately on different devices, and their extraction is based purely on the computational characteristics of the LLM, without considering the current state of the devices. Nodes within the graph that process inputs from a single node and output to multiple nodes are identified as key points for partitioning. These nodes typically represent distinct layers or operations within the model, making them ideal for creating subgraphs that can be independently executed. The process results in a series of subgraphs, each representing a functional segment of the original LLM, allowing for efficient distribution across the available mobile devices.

**Subgraph Dependency Search.** To handle dependencies between nodes in separate subgraphs of an LLM, we employ a subgraph dependency search algorithm, creating two key maps: the residual dependency map (RDM) and the sequential dependency map (SDM). The SDM tracks direct dependencies between adjacent subgraphs, ensuring that outputs from one subgraph serve as inputs for the next. The RDM identifies dependencies between non-adjacent subgraphs, capturing instances where a subgraph relies on nodes from an earlier subgraph, not directly preceding it.

**Model Assignment Optimization.** After segmenting LLMs into subgraphs, the next step involves assigning these subgraphs as executable sub-modules to mobile devices, considering device constraints and aiming to minimize computation and data transmission times. This involves compiling subgraphs into sub-modules, profiling each for FLOP count, memory needs, and data output size, and then using this information alongside device performance metrics to optimize sub-module allocation. The optimization termed as a primary optimizer, formulated as a linear optimization problem, balances local computation and data transmission efforts to reduce total inference time. Constraints ensure that the memory usage of sub-modules on any device does not exceed a predetermined portion of the device's available memory.

### 3.3 Runtime Load Balancing

**Load Balancing Optimization.** The load balancing mechanism refines the initial model assignment optimization termed as a secondary optimizer by introducing a strategy to overlap sub-modules across devices, categorizing them as movable or unmovable. Movable sub-modules can be dynamically allocated or removed to balance the load, whereas unmovable ones stay fixed. This approach uses linear programming to minimize data transmission and optimize memory usage, enhancing system performance and robustness during intensive tasks. The optimization allows for potential overlaps of sub-modules to the left or right of their current allocation, improving memory utilization within device constraints and facilitating efficient load distribution across the network.

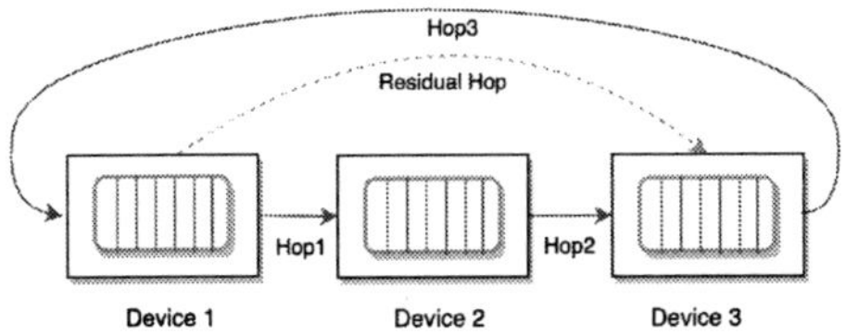


Figure 4: System Design For Device Communication.

### 3.4 Optimized Communication

**Model Deployment with Load Balancing.** LinguaLinked initiates load balancing based on real-time device performance metrics. When an imbalance is detected, it combines the initial model assignment with the secondary optimization to update the task distribution. Unmovable modules remain in place, while movable modules are reassigned as dictated by the load balancing optimization. Devices then adjust their loads according to this new strategy, pausing computations only locally to reduce disruptions.

**Decentralized Device Communication.** In our system, devices communicate in a decentralized, ring-structured manner, where each device sequentially receives, computes, and forwards data to the next device until it reaches the Header again, as illustrated with a solid red line in Figure 4. This efficient communication is facilitated by a message queue utilizing the ROUTER-DEALER pattern, allowing devices to alternate between sending (ROUTER) and receiving (DEALER) roles, which enhances scalability and ensures balanced load distribution. The cycle of data processing involves devices acting first as receivers to perform computations, then as senders to pass on results, maintaining a continuous and organized flow of data throughout the network.

**Multi-Threaded Inference.** Our system implements multi-threaded inference, allowing parallel processing where each thread independently manages a task and progresses to the next one immediately after completion. Due to the non-threadsafe nature of message queue sockets, we ensure thread safety by using multiple sockets and ports instead of sharing or locking sockets in multi-threads, thereby preventing performance bottlenecks and reducing communication latency. Furthermore, multi-threaded inference boosts CPU efficiency by accommodating varying batch sizes and enabling flexible processing strategies, such as dividing large batches into smaller mini-batches or adjusting batch sizes dynamically, optimizing system performance.

**Sequential & Residual Communication.** In sequential communication, devices in our system form a circuit where each transmits data to the next in line, creating a flow where only sequential data is exchanged. It leads to inefficiencies as devices pass along residual data not immediately needed by them. To overcome these limitations, we introduced a residual communication strategy, allowing for direct transmission of data to target devices, as depicted by green dashed lines in Figure 4. It reduces unnecessary data carriage and latency.

| | Pixel 7 pro | CUBOT X30 |
|---|---|---|
| SoC | Google Tensor G2 | Mediatek MT6771 |
| CPU | Cortex-X1/A78/A55 | Cortex-A73/A53 |
| RAM | 12GB | 8GB |
| OS | Android 13 | Android 10 |

Table 1: Test Hardware Platforms in Evaluation.

### 3.5 Implementation and Methodology

**LinguaLinked Prototype.** We build LinguaLinked atop PyTorch (Paszke et al., 2019), leveraging the `torch.fx` library (Reed et al., 2022) for computational subgraph extraction and PyTorch sub-module compilation, with performance profiling done via Deepspeed (Rasley et al., 2020). These sub-modules are then prepared for mobile deployment by conversion to ONNX format (Bai et al., 2019) and optimized using `int8` precision quantization through ONNXRuntime (Runtime, 2023). Optimization for model distribution and load balancing is achieved with the MILP solver Gurobipy (Gurobi Optimization, LLC, 2023), allowing the deployment of optimized sub-modules on mobile devices through an Android application that utilizes ONNXRuntime's C++ API. For efficient mobile device communication and distributed inference, ZeroMQ (Zer) with a ROUTER-DEALER socket pattern is integrated, enhancing asynchronous communication in the mobile environment.

**Chat Application.** We develop an Android application that allows users to chat with LLMs in a distributed decentralized way as shown in Figure 3. Our application features two distinct modes: header and worker. The header mode focuses on direct user interaction with the LLM such as sending prompts and receiving responses. In contrast, the worker mode dedicates itself to the heavy lifting of model computation, showcasing the synergy between devices to accomplish LLM inference tasks efficiently.

## 4 Evaluation

### 4.1 Evaluation Setup

**Hardware.** In evaluating the LinguaLinked system, we utilize four mobile devices: three Google Pixel 7 Pros and one CUBOT X30. The specific hardware configurations of these devices are detailed in Table 1. Our analysis focuses on CPU performance, reflecting the system's compatibility with the current CPU-only support of ONNXRuntime for LLMs. This approach is deliberate, anticipating future integration with GPU acceleration capabilities as ONNXRuntime evolves, thereby highlighting our system's adaptability and the consistency of its performance evaluation across varying hardware source.

**Evaluation Tasks.** Our system's performance is assessed through text generation tasks, using the Wikitext-2 (Merity et al., 2016) with 100 randomly selected samples.

**Evaluation Models.** Evaluation leverages the BLOOM series LLMs (Workshop et al., 2023), including BLOOM 3b, BLOOM 1.7b, and BLOOM 1.1b models, in both full and `int8` precision formats.

**Baseline for Comparison.** We established a baseline for assessing on-device distributed inference of LLMs, assigning an equal number of sub-modules ($m/n$) to each of the $n$ mobile devices, irrespective of their specific hardware or network conditions. This approach allows for a comparison of system throughput between our uniform distribution strategy and both our optimized model assignment and runtime load balancing strategies, in the absence of prior focused research in this area.

| Model | Device Config | Device Number | Thread Number | Avg. Time/Token (s) |
|---|---|---|---|---|
| Baseline | | | | |
| BLOOM3b-int8 | 2P+1C | 3 | 1 | 2.526 |
| BLOOM1.7b-int8 | 2P+1C | 3 | 1 | 1.466 |
| BLOOM1.1b-int8 | 2P+1C | 3 | 1 | 1.017 |
| BLOOM3b-full | 3P+1C | 4 | 1 | 5.222 |
| BLOOM1.7b-full | 3P+1C | 4 | 1 | 3.159 |
| BLOOM1.1b-full | 3P+1C | 4 | 1 | 1.967 |
| Optimized | | | | |
| BLOOM3b-int8 | 2P+1C | 3 | 1 | 1.576 |
| BLOOM1.7b-int8 | 2P+1C | 3 | 1 | 0.944 |
| BLOOM1.1b-int8 | 2P+1C | 3 | 1 | 0.653 |
| BLOOM3b-full | 3P+1C | 4 | 1 | 3.944 |
| BLOOM1.7b-full | 3P+1C | 4 | 1 | 2.520 |
| BLOOM1.1b-full | 3P+1C | 4 | 1 | 1.793 |

Table 2: Inference Throughput Comparison of Baseline and Optimized Strategies for Model Assignment in Heterogeneous Devices. On the Device Config column, P indicates Google Pixel 7pro and C indicates CubotX30.

### 4.2 Performance

**Optimized Model Assignment Performance.** In heterogeneous device environments, optimized model assignment significantly enhances inference throughput compared to baseline strategies, as indicated by the data in Table 2. For `int8` quantized models, throughput increases are notable: BLOOM 3b achieves a 1.61× improvement, while BLOOM

1.7b and 1.1b models see 1.55× and 1.56× enhancements, respectively. Full-precision models also benefit, with BLOOM 3b, 1.7b, and 1.1b models experiencing improvements of 1.32×, 1.25×, and 1.11×, respectively.

The trend is clear—larger models, such as the BLOOM 3b, exhibit greater gains, suggesting that optimization strategies yield more significant benefits for models with higher computational needs. This pattern underscores the efficacy of optimized model assignment in improving the efficiency of model deployment and inference performance in diverse computing landscapes.

**Multi-threaded Inference Performance.** Our study investigates the benefits of multi-threading on inference throughput for both `int8` quantized and full-precision BLOOM models, focusing on text generation task as indicated by the data in Table 3. Conducted on three Google Pixel 7 Pro devices, we report that quantized models show a marked performance improvement in multi-threaded setups for text generation. Specifically, the BLOOM 3b quantized model's throughput increases by 1.81 × with two threads and 2.52 × with five threads compared to a single-threaded baseline. Similarly, the BLOOM 1.7b and 1.1b models demonstrate significant speed-ups, with the 1.7b model doubling its throughput with two threads and reaching a 2.65× increase with five threads, and the 1.1b model achieving a 1.73 × speed-up with two threads and a 2.3× increase with five threads.

Full-precision models also benefit from multi-threading, albeit to a lesser extent. The BLOOM 3b full-precision model sees a 1.67 × speed-up with two threads and a 1.97 × increase with five threads. The 1.7b and 1.1b models exhibit speed-ups of 1.54 and 1.58 ×, respectively, with two threads, and 1.83 and 1.79 × with five threads.

| Quantized Experiment/Int8 | | | | | |
|---|---|---|---|---|---|
| Model | Avg. Compute Time/Token (s)/Thread Number | | | | |
| Thread Number | 1 | 2 | 3 | 4 | 5 |
| BLOOM3b-int8 | 1.145 | 0.634 | 0.526 | 0.472 | 0.455 |
| BLOOM1.7b-int8 | 0.740 | 0.389 | 0.336 | 0.302 | 0.279 |
| BLOOM1.1b-int8 | 0.464 | 0.269 | 0.230 | 0.207 | 0.202 |
| Full Precision Experiment | | | | | |
| Model | Avg. Compute Time/Token (s)/ Thread Number | | | | |
| Thread Number | 1 | 2 | 3 | 4 | 5 |
| BLOOM3b-full | 2.687 | 1.611 | 1.492 | 1.444 | 1.368 |
| BLOOM1.7b-full | 1.675 | 1.088 | 0.972 | 0.903 | 0.918 |
| BLOOM1.1b-full | 1.105 | 0.700 | 0.623 | 0.632 | 0.617 |

Table 3: Multi-threading Throughput for Text Generation on 3 Google Pixel 7 Pro using Optimized Model Assignment Strategy.

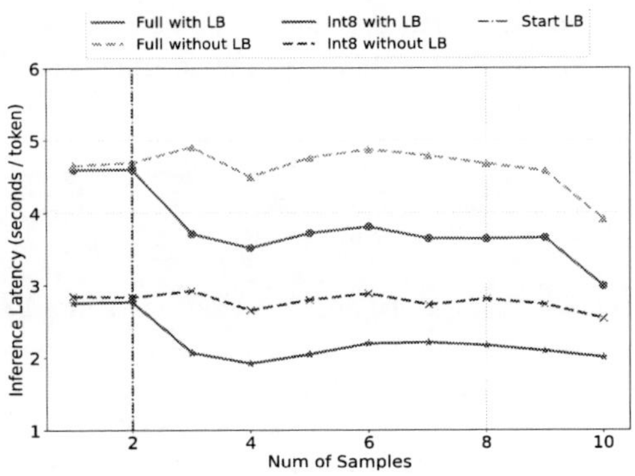


Figure 5: Load Balancer Launched at Runtime.

**Micro-Benchmarking the Runtime Load Balancer.** In our study, we also investigate the effects of runtime load balancing on the BLOOM 1.7b model in both full precision and `int8` quantized formats across three devices, including two high-end and one low-end phone. Initially, model partitions are unevenly distributed, causing the low-end phone to be overloaded. Upon activating the load balancer after processing two samples and continuing with ten more, we observe a significant improvement in processing efficiency.

Figure 5 illustrates that enabling load balancing from the second sample noticeably decreases inference latency. For the full precision model, enabling load balancing cuts down latency from 4.624 seconds to 3.587 seconds per token, showcasing an improvement by reallocating 8 sub-modules and overcoming a notable overhead from reloading sessions onto alternate devices.

For the quantized model, activating the load balancer reduces latency from 2.756 to 2.087 seconds per token, with a less substantial reloading overhead compared to the full precision model due to the smaller size of quantized sub-modules.

Inference times for the quantized model prove to be more stable across generation tasks than for the full precision model.

Overall, the implementation of runtime load balancing results in an average improvement of 30% in acceleration, effectively demonstrating the benefits of dynamically adjusting workloads among devices with varying processing capabilities.

### 4.3 Sequential and Residual Communication

To demonstrate the efficacy of residual over sequential communication, we conducted experiments measuring communication times, employing the Network Temporal Protocol (NTP) for precise synchronization and utilizing the system clock for nanosecond accuracy in runtime measurement.

By comparing these methods using three low-

| | Hop1 | Hop2 | Hop3 | Total | Res Hop |
|---|---|---|---|---|---|
| Seq | 0.2489s | 0.2580s | 0.0770s | 0.5839s | —— |
| Res | 0.2347s | 0.2463s | 0.0779s | 0.5589s | 0.0111s |

Table 4: Residual and Sequential Communication Performance

end smartphones and the quantized BLOOM 3b model, recording average delays from ten trials. The results, detailed in Table 4 and Figure 4, show that sequential communication incurs higher delays due to multiple transmission steps and the need for activations to be processed before residual data can be sent. Sequential transmission involved hops with an average data size of 1.5 MB, while residual communication transmitted about 15 KB directly, allowing it to operate in parallel and more efficiently than the sequential method. Note that as the number of residual connections and the size of the model increase, the saved time will likewise increase.

## 5 Discussion

A major direction for expanding LinguaLinked involves adapting it for distributed fine-tuning on mobile devices, allowing model customization based on user interactions and local data, paving the way for personalized AI applications while preserving data privacy. We also envision extending LinguaLinked to handle multi-modality models, enhancing its applicability in diverse real-world scenarios.

To further improve LinguaLinked, we envision more advanced model computational graph partitioning strategies involving further optimizations on task divisions better aligned with device capabilities. Moreover, integrating advanced load balancing algorithms that account for not only computational capabilities but also battery life and user engagement patterns will ensure a holistic approach to distributed computing on mobile platforms.

Finally, the implications of this research are significant for AI policy, as it challenges the prevailing reliance on cloud infrastructure and centralized data centers for AI deployment. By demonstrating the potential to deploy AI systems from a network of mobile devices, our work suggests a paradigm where the 'means of production' for AI can be decentralized and localized. This model of deployment could lead to a future where AI systems are both operated and fine-tuned locally using a diverse array of small devices. Such a setup could make AI systems more difficult to regulate, as the distribution and localization of AI technologies allow for widespread, generic hardware use.

## 6 Conclusion

In this work, we introduce LinguaLinked, a system for decentralized LLM inference on mobile devices. To the best of our knowledge, LinguaLinked is the first work that exploits deploying LLM distributively on mobile devices. LinguaLinked implemented optimized model assignment strategy, network communication and runtime load balancing mechanism to accelerate the distributed LLM inference on mobile devices. This approach tackles the complexities of deploying both full precision and quantized LLMs of various sizes within mobile computing environments.

## 7 Limitations

Our results demonstrate promising advancements in distributed LLM inference on mobile devices but also underscore several limitations. Key among these are the overheads from load balancing and constraints of current hardware and software frameworks. As tools like ONNXRuntime evolve to support GPU acceleration, we expect significant enhancements in LinguaLinked's performance. Furthermore, exploring advanced quantization techniques and communication mechanisms could lead to more efficient distributed inference systems.

At the same time, a critical focus for future iterations of LinguaLinked is energy efficiency. We find that the continuous intensive inference tasks, especially with full-precision models, significantly drain battery life and cause overheating, leading to performance degradation. To address this, we aim to incorporate energy-efficient computing strategies that balance computational demands with energy consumption and thermal management. This could include adaptive algorithms to modulate computational load based on the device's energy state, and hardware-specific optimizations leveraging low-power processing cores for specific tasks.

Furthermore, when designing our system with privacy in mind, we primarily contrast it with traditional server-based inference systems, operating under the assumption that all inference tasks are conducted locally on 'trusted' mobile devices. This setup should inherently protect user privacy. However, we recognize potential scenarios where this assumption may fail. For instance, if a device becomes compromised or if unauthorized access is obtained, sensitive local data could be at risk. Moreover, our trust model does not address potential side-channel attacks, which could allow attackers to derive sensitive information from the model's intermediate activations. These vulnerabilities underscore the need for more comprehensive, multi-layered security protocols that extend beyond simple device trust, aiming to robustly safeguard user data in diverse and adversarial environments.

Finally, due to the absence of standardized evaluation benchmarks for distributed LLM inference on mobile devices, we have created our own baselines to assess our system's performance. However, the lack of universally accepted benchmarks and previous research in this domain complicates the task of conducting thorough comparisons for future work. It is crucial for future research to focus on developing standardized benchmarks in this field. Establishing such benchmarks would facilitate more uniform comparisons between different systems, enhance the clarity of potential improvements, and identify the most effective strategies for distributed LLM inference on mobile platforms.

## References


Zeromq. `https://zeromq.org/`. (Accessed on 11/29/2023).

Ibrahim Alabdulmohsin, Behnam Neyshabur, and Xiaohua Zhai. 2022. Revisiting neural scaling laws in language and vision.

Reza Yazdani Aminabadi, Samyam Rajbhandari, Ammar Ahmad Awan, Cheng Li, Du Li, Elton Zheng, Olatunji Ruwase, Shaden Smith, Minjia Zhang, Jeff Rasley, et al. 2022. Deepspeed-inference: enabling efficient inference of transformer models at unprecedented scale. In *SC22: International Conference for High Performance Computing, Networking, Storage and Analysis*, pages 1–15. IEEE.

Junjie Bai, Fang Lu, Ke Zhang, et al. 2019. Onnx: Open neural network exchange. `https://github.com/onnx/onnx`.

Davis Blalock, Jose Javier Gonzalez Ortiz, Jonathan Frankle, and John Guttag. 2020. What is the state of neural network pruning? *Proceedings of machine learning and systems*, 2:129–146.

Yelysei Bondarenko, Markus Nagel, and Tijmen Blankevoort. 2021. Understanding and overcoming the challenges of efficient transformer quantization. *arXiv preprint arXiv:2109.12948*.

Alexander Borzunov, Dmitry Baranchuk, Tim Dettmers, Max Ryabinin, Younes Belkada, Artem Chumachenko, Pavel Samygin, and Colin Raffel. 2022. Petals: Collaborative inference and fine-tuning of large models. *arXiv preprint arXiv:2209.01188*.

Tom B. Brown, Benjamin Mann, Nick Ryder, Melanie Subbiah, Jared Kaplan, Prafulla Dhariwal, Arvind Neelakantan, Pranav Shyam, Girish Sastry, Amanda Askell, Sandhini Agarwal, Ariel Herbert-Voss, Gretchen Krueger, Tom Henighan, Rewon Child, Aditya Ramesh, Daniel M. Ziegler, Jeffrey Wu, Clemens Winter, Christopher Hesse, Mark Chen, Eric Sigler, Mateusz Litwin, Scott Gray, Benjamin Chess, Jack Clark, Christopher Berner, Sam McCandlish, Alec Radford, Ilya Sutskever, and Dario Amodei. 2020. Language models are few-shot learners.

Jiasi Chen and Xukan Ran. 2019. Deep learning with edge computing: A review. *Proceedings of the IEEE*, 107(8):1655–1674.

Tianqi Chen, Thierry Moreau, Ziheng Jiang, Lianmin Zheng, Eddie Yan, Meghan Cowan, Haichen Shen, Leyuan Wang, Yuwei Hu, Luis Ceze, Carlos Guestrin, and Arvind Krishnamurthy. 2018. Tvm: An automated end-to-end optimizing compiler for deep learning.

Aakanksha Chowdhery, Sharan Narang, Jacob Devlin, Maarten Bosma, Gaurav Mishra, Adam Roberts, Paul Barham, Hyung Won Chung, Charles Sutton, Sebastian Gehrmann, Parker Schuh, Kensen Shi, Sasha Tsvyashchenko, Joshua Maynez, Abhishek Rao, Parker Barnes, Yi Tay, Noam Shazeer, Vinodkumar Prabhakaran, Emily Reif, Nan Du, Ben Hutchinson, Reiner Pope, James Bradbury, Jacob Austin, Michael Isard, Guy Gur-Ari, Pengcheng Yin, Toju Duke, Anselm Levskaya, Sanjay Ghemawat, Sunipa Dev, Henryk Michalewski, Xavier Garcia, Vedant Misra, Kevin Robinson, Liam Fedus, Denny Zhou, Daphne Ippolito, David Luan, Hyeontaek Lim, Barret Zoph, Alexander Spiridonov, Ryan Sepassi, David Dohan, Shivani Agrawal, Mark Omernick, Andrew M. Dai, Thanumalayan Sankaranarayana Pillai, Marie Pellat, Aitor Lewkowycz, Erica Moreira, Rewon Child, Oleksandr Polozov, Katherine Lee, Zongwei Zhou, Xuezhi Wang, Brennan Saeta, Mark Diaz, Orhan Firat, Michele Catasta, Jason Wei, Kathy Meier-Hellstern, Douglas Eck, Jeff Dean, Slav Petrov, and Noah Fiedel. 2022. Palm: Scaling language modeling with pathways.

Aidan Clark, Diego de Las Casas, Aurelia Guy, Arthur Mensch, Michela Paganini, Jordan Hoffmann, Bogdan Damoc, Blake A. Hechtman, Trevor Cai, Sebastian Borgeaud, George van den Driessche, Eliza Rutherford, T. W. Hennigan, Matthew G. Johnson, Katie Millican, Albin Cassirer, Chris Jones, Elena Buchatskaya, David Budden, L. Sifre, Simon Osindero, Oriol Vinyals, Jack W. Rae, Erich Elsen, Koray Kavukcuoglu, and Karen Simonyan. 2022. Unified scaling laws for routed language models. In *International Conference on Machine Learning*.

Karl Cobbe, Vineet Kosaraju, Mohammad Bavarian, Mark Chen, Heewoo Jun, Lukasz Kaiser, Matthias Plappert, Jerry Tworek, Jacob Hilton, Reiichiro Nakano, Christopher Hesse, and John Schulman. 2021. Training verifiers to solve math word problems.

Claudionor N Coelho, Aki Kuusela, Shan Li, Hao Zhuang, Jennifer Ngadiuba, Thea Klaeboe Aarrestad, Vladimir Loncar, Maurizio Pierini, Adrian Alan Pol, and Sioni Summers. 2021. Automatic heterogeneous quantization of deep neural networks for low-latency inference on the edge for particle detectors. *Nature Machine Intelligence*, 3(8):675–686.

Jiangsu Du, Jiazhi Jiang, Jiang Zheng, Hongbin Zhang, Dan Huang, and Yutong Lu. 2023. Improving computation and memory efficiency for real-world transformer inference on gpus. *ACM Transactions on Architecture and Code Optimization*, 20(4):1–22.

Mohammed S Elbamby, Cristina Perfecto, Chen-Feng Liu, Jihong Park, Sumudu Samarakoon, Xianfu Chen, and Mehdi Bennis. 2019. Wireless edge computing with latency and reliability guarantees. *Proceedings of the IEEE*, 107(8):1717–1737.

Luciano Floridi and Massimo Chiriatti. 2020. Gpt-3: Its nature, scope, limits, and consequences. *Minds and Machines*, 30:1–14.

Elias Frantar, Saleh Ashkboos, Torsten Hoefler, and Dan Alistarh. 2022. Gptq: Accurate post-training quantization for generative pre-trained transformers. *arXiv preprint arXiv:2210.17323*.

Amir Gholami, Sehoon Kim, Zhen Dong, Zhewei Yao, Michael W Mahoney, and Kurt Keutzer. 2022. A survey of quantization methods for efficient neural network inference. In *Low-Power Computer Vision*, pages 291–326. Chapman and Hall/CRC.

Yuxian Gu, Li Dong, Furu Wei, and Minlie Huang. 2023. Knowledge distillation of large language models. *arXiv preprint arXiv:2306.08543*.

Jashwant Raj Gunasekaran, Cyan Subhra Mishra, Prashanth Thinakaran, Bikash Sharma, Mahmut Taylan Kandemir, and Chita R Das. 2022. Cocktail: A multidimensional optimization for model serving in cloud. In *19th USENIX Symposium on Networked Systems Design and Implementation (NSDI 22)*, pages 1041–1057.

Gurobi Optimization, LLC. 2023. Gurobi Optimizer Reference Manual.

Dan Hendrycks, Collin Burns, Steven Basart, Andy Zou, Mantas Mazeika, Dawn Song, and Jacob Steinhardt. 2021. Measuring massive multitask language understanding.

Torsten Hoefler, Dan Alistarh, Tal Ben-Nun, Nikoli Dryden, and Alexandra Peste. 2021. Sparsity in deep learning: Pruning and growth for efficient inference and training in neural networks. *The Journal of Machine Learning Research*, 22(1):10882–11005.

Jordan Hoffmann, Sebastian Borgeaud, Arthur Mensch, Elena Buchatskaya, Trevor Cai, Eliza Rutherford, Diego de Las Casas, Lisa Anne Hendricks, Johannes Welbl, Aidan Clark, Tom Hennigan, Eric Noland, Katie Millican, George van den Driessche, Bogdan Damoc, Aurelia Guy, Simon Osindero, Karen Simonyan, Erich Elsen, Jack W. Rae, Oriol Vinyals, and Laurent Sifre. 2022. Training compute-optimal large language models.

Chenghao Hu and Baochun Li. 2022. Distributed inference with deep learning models across heterogeneous edge devices. In *IEEE INFOCOM 2022-IEEE Conference on Computer Communications*, pages 330–339. IEEE.

Zhiming Hu, Ahmad Bisher Tarakji, Vishal Raheja, Caleb Phillips, Teng Wang, and Iqbal Mohomed. 2019. Deephome: Distributed inference with heterogeneous devices in the edge. In *The 3rd International Workshop on Deep Learning for Mobile Systems and Applications*, pages 13–18.

Chien-Chin Huang, Gu Jin, and Jinyang Li. 2020. Swapadvisor: Pushing deep learning beyond the gpu memory limit via smart swapping. In *Proceedings of the Twenty-Fifth International Conference on Architectural Support for Programming Languages and Operating Systems*, ASPLOS '20, page 1341–1355, New York, NY, USA. Association for Computing Machinery.

Xiaoqi Jiao, Yichun Yin, Lifeng Shang, Xin Jiang, Xiao Chen, Linlin Li, Fang Wang, and Qun Liu. 2019. Tinybert: Distilling bert for natural language understanding. *arXiv preprint arXiv:1909.10351*.

Jared Kaplan, Sam McCandlish, Tom Henighan, Tom B. Brown, Benjamin Chess, Rewon Child, Scott Gray, Alec Radford, Jeffrey Wu, and Dario Amodei. 2020. Scaling laws for neural language models.

Sunder Ali Khowaja, Parus Khuwaja, and Kapal Dev. 2023. Chatgpt needs spade (sustainability, privacy, digital divide, and ethics) evaluation: A review. *arXiv preprint arXiv:2305.03123*.

Nir Kshetri. 2023. Cybercrime and privacy threats of large language models. *IT Professional*, 25(3):9–13.

Minhyeok Lee. 2023. A mathematical interpretation of autoregressive generative pre-trained transformer and self-supervised learning. *Mathematics*, 11(11).

Fan Liang, Wei Yu, Xing Liu, David Griffith, and Nada Golmie. 2020a. Toward edge-based deep learning in industrial internet of things. *IEEE Internet of Things Journal*, 7(5):4329–4341.

Kevin J Liang, Weituo Hao, Dinghan Shen, Yufan Zhou, Weizhu Chen, Changyou Chen, and Lawrence Carin. 2020b. Mixkd: Towards efficient distillation of large-scale language models. *arXiv preprint arXiv:2011.00593*.

Tailin Liang, John Glossner, Lei Wang, Shaobo Shi, and Xiaotong Zhang. 2021. Pruning and quantization for deep neural network acceleration: A survey. *Neurocomputing*, 461:370–403.

Chu-Cheng Lin, Aaron Jaech, Xin Li, Matthew R. Gormley, and Jason Eisner. 2021. Limitations of autoregressive models and their alternatives.

Jiachen Mao, Xiang Chen, Kent W Nixon, Christopher Krieger, and Yiran Chen. 2017a. Modnn: Local distributed mobile computing system for deep neural network. In *Design, Automation & Test in Europe Conference & Exhibition (DATE), 2017*, pages 1396–1401. IEEE.

Yuyi Mao, Changsheng You, Jun Zhang, Kaibin Huang, and Khaled B Letaief. 2017b. A survey on mobile edge computing: The communication perspective. *IEEE communications surveys & tutorials*, 19(4):2322–2358.

Stephen Merity, Caiming Xiong, James Bradbury, and Richard Socher. 2016. Pointer sentinel mixture models.

Soumyalatha Naveen, Manjunath R Kounte, and Mohammed Riyaz Ahmed. 2021. Low latency deep learning inference model for distributed intelligent iot edge clusters. *IEEE Access*, 9:160607–160621.

Jihong Park, Sumudu Samarakoon, Mehdi Bennis, and Mérouane Debbah. 2019. Wireless network intelligence at the edge. *Proceedings of the IEEE*, 107(11):2204–2239.

Adam Paszke, Sam Gross, Francisco Massa, Adam Lerer, James Bradbury, Gregory Chanan, Trevor Killeen, Zeming Lin, Natalia Gimelshein, Luca Antiga, Alban Desmaison, Andreas Köpf, Edward Yang, Zach DeVito, Martin Raison, Alykhan Tejani, Sasank Chilamkurthy, Benoit Steiner, Lu Fang, Junjie Bai, and Soumith Chintala. 2019. Pytorch: An imperative style, high-performance deep learning library.

Roma Patel and Ellie Pavlick. 2022. Mapping language models to grounded conceptual spaces. In *International Conference on Learning Representations*.

Jeff Rasley, Samyam Rajbhandari, Olatunji Ruwase, and Yuxiong He. 2020. Deepspeed: System optimizations enable training deep learning models with over 100 billion parameters. In *Proceedings of the 26th ACM SIGKDD International Conference on Knowledge Discovery & Data Mining*, pages 3505–3506.

James K. Reed, Zachary DeVito, Horace He, Ansley Ussery, and Jason Ansel. 2022. Torch.fx: Practical program capture and transformation for deep learning in python.

Karen Renaud, Merrill Warkentin, and George Westerman. 2023. *From ChatGPT to HackGPT: Meeting the Cybersecurity Threat of Generative AI*. MIT Sloan Management Review.

Francisco Romero, Qian Li, Neeraja J Yadwadkar, and Christos Kozyrakis. 2021. {INFaaS}: Automated model-less inference serving. In *2021 USENIX Annual Technical Conference (USENIX ATC 21)*, pages 397–411.

ONNX Runtime. 2023. Onnx runtime. Available from: `https://onnxruntime.ai/`.

Glorin Sebastian. 2023. Do chatgpt and other ai chatbots pose a cybersecurity risk?: An exploratory study. *International Journal of Security and Privacy in Pervasive Computing (IJSPPC)*, 15(1):1–11.

TensorFlow. 2023. Tensorflow lite. Available from: `https://www.tensorflow.org/lite`.

Hugo Touvron, Thibaut Lavril, Gautier Izacard, Xavier Martinet, Marie-Anne Lachaux, Timothée Lacroix, Baptiste Rozière, Naman Goyal, Eric Hambro, Faisal Azhar, Aurelien Rodriguez, Armand Joulin, Edouard Grave, and Guillaume Lample. 2023. Llama: Open and efficient foundation language models.

Ashish Vaswani, Noam Shazeer, Niki Parmar, Jakob Uszkoreit, Llion Jones, Aidan N. Gomez, Lukasz Kaiser, and Illia Polosukhin. 2023. Attention is all you need.

Yiding Wang, Kai Chen, Haisheng Tan, and Kun Guo. 2023. Tabi: An efficient multi-level inference system for large language models. In *Proceedings of the Eighteenth European Conference on Computer Systems*, pages 233–248.

BigScience Workshop, :, Teven Le Scao, Angela Fan, Christopher Akiki, Ellie Pavlick, Suzana Ilić, Daniel Hesslow, Roman Castagné, Alexandra Sasha Luccioni, François Yvon, Matthias Gallé, Jonathan Tow, Alexander M. Rush, Stella Biderman, Albert Webson, Pawan Sasanka Ammanamanchi, Thomas Wang, Benoît Sagot, Niklas Muennighoff, Albert Villanova del Moral, Olatunji Ruwase, Rachel Bawden, Stas Bekman, Angelina McMillan-Major, Iz Beltagy, Huu Nguyen, Lucile Saulnier, Samson Tan, Pedro Ortiz Suarez, Victor Sanh, Hugo Laurençon, Yacine Jernite, Julien Launay, Margaret Mitchell, Colin Raffel, Aaron Gokaslan, Adi Simhi, Aitor Soroa, Alham Fikri Aji, Amit Alfassy, Anna Rogers, Ariel Kreisberg Nitzav, Canwen Xu, Chenghao Mou, Chris Emezue, Christopher Klamm, Colin Leong, Daniel van Strien, David Ifeoluwa Adelani, Dragomir Radev, Eduardo González Ponferrada, Efrat Levkovizh, Ethan Kim, Eyal Bar Natan, Francesco De Toni, Gérard Dupont, Germán Kruszewski, Giada Pistilli, Hady Elsahar, Hamza Benyamina, Hieu Tran, Ian Yu, Idris Abdulmumin, Isaac Johnson, Itziar Gonzalez-Dios, Javier de la Rosa, Jenny Chim, Jesse Dodge, Jian Zhu, Jonathan Chang, Jörg Frohberg, Joseph Tobing, Joydeep Bhattacharjee, Khalid Almubarak, Kimbo Chen, Kyle Lo, Leandro Von Werra,

Leon Weber, Long Phan, Loubna Ben allal, Ludovic Tanguy, Manan Dey, Manuel Romero Muñoz, Maraim Masoud, María Grandury, Mario Šaško, Max Huang, Maximin Coavoux, Mayank Singh, Mike Tian-Jian Jiang, Minh Chien Vu, Mohammad A. Jauhar, Mustafa Ghaleb, Nishant Subramani, Nora Kassner, Nurulaqilla Khamis, Olivier Nguyen, Omar Espejel, Ona de Gibert, Paulo Villegas, Peter Henderson, Pierre Colombo, Priscilla Amuok, Quentin Lhoest, Rheza Harliman, Rishi Bommasani, Roberto Luis López, Rui Ribeiro, Salomey Osei, Sampo Pyysalo, Sebastian Nagel, Shamik Bose, Shamsuddeen Hassan Muhammad, Shanya Sharma, Shayne Longpre, Somaieh Nikpoor, Stanislav Silberberg, Suhas Pai, Sydney Zink, Tiago Timponi Torrent, Timo Schick, Tristan Thrush, Valentin Danchev, Vassilina Nikoulina, Veronika Laippala, Violette Lepercq, Vrinda Prabhu, Zaid Alyafeai, Zeerak Talat, Arun Raja, Benjamin Heinzerling, Chenglei Si, Davut Emre Taşar, Elizabeth Salesky, Sabrina J. Mielke, Wilson Y. Lee, Abheesht Sharma, Andrea Santilli, Antoine Chaffin, Arnaud Stiegler, Debajyoti Datta, Eliza Szczechla, Gunjan Chhablani, Han Wang, Harshit Pandey, Hendrik Strobelt, Jason Alan Fries, Jos Rozen, Leo Gao, Lintang Sutawika, M Saiful Bari, Maged S. Al-shaibani, Matteo Manica, Nihal Nayak, Ryan Teehan, Samuel Albanie, Sheng Shen, Srulik Ben-David, Stephen H. Bach, Taewoon Kim, Tali Bers, Thibault Fevry, Trishala Neeraj, Urmish Thakker, Vikas Raunak, Xiangru Tang, Zheng-Xin Yong, Zhiqing Sun, Shaked Brody, Yallow Uri, Hadar Tojarieh, Adam Roberts, Hyung Won Chung, Jaesung Tae, Jason Phang, Ofir Press, Conglong Li, Deepak Narayanan, Hatim Bourfoune, Jared Casper, Jeff Rasley, Max Ryabinin, Mayank Mishra, Minjia Zhang, Mohammad Shoeybi, Myriam Peyrounette, Nicolas Patry, Nouamane Tazi, Omar Sanseviero, Patrick von Platen, Pierre Cornette, Pierre François Lavallée, Rémi Lacroix, Samyam Rajbhandari, Sanchit Gandhi, Shaden Smith, Stéphane Requena, Suraj Patil, Tim Dettmers, Ahmed Baruwa, Amanpreet Singh, Anastasia Cheveleva, Anne-Laure Ligozat, Arjun Subramonian, Aurélie Névéol, Charles Lovering, Dan Garrette, Deepak Tunuguntla, Ehud Reiter, Ekaterina Taktasheva, Ekaterina Voloshina, Eli Bogdanov, Genta Indra Winata, Hailey Schoelkopf, Jan-Christoph Kalo, Jekaterina Novikova, Jessica Zosa Forde, Jordan Clive, Jungo Kasai, Ken Kawamura, Liam Hazan, Marine Carpuat, Miruna Clinciu, Najoung Kim, Newton Cheng, Oleg Serikov, Omer Antverg, Oskar van der Wal, Rui Zhang, Ruochen Zhang, Sebastian Gehrmann, Shachar Mirkin, Shani Pais, Tatiana Shavrina, Thomas Scialom, Tian Yun, Tomasz Limisiewicz, Verena Rieser, Vitaly Protasov, Vladislav Mikhailov, Yada Pruksachatkun, Yonatan Belinkov, Zachary Bamberger, Zdeněk Kasner, Alice Rueda, Amanda Pestana, Amir Feizpour, Ammar Khan, Amy Faranak, Ana Santos, Anthony Hevia, Antigona Unldreaj, Arash Aghagol, Arezoo Abdollahi, Aycha Tammour, Azadeh HajiHosseini, Bahareh Behroozi, Benjamin Ajibade, Bharat Saxena, Carlos Muñoz Ferrandis, Daniel McDuff, Danish Contractor, David Lansky, Davis David, Douwe Kiela, Duong A. Nguyen, Edward Tan, Emi Baylor, Ezinwanne Ozoani, Fatima Mirza, Frankline Ononiwu, Habib Rezanejad, Hessie Jones, Indrani Bhattacharya, Irene Solaiman, Irina Sedenko, Isar Nejadgholi, Jesse Passmore, Josh Seltzer, Julio Bonis Sanz, Livia Dutra, Mairon Samagaio, Maraim Elbadri, Margot Mieskes, Marissa Gerchick, Martha Akinlolu, Michael McKenna, Mike Qiu, Muhammed Ghauri, Mykola Burynok, Nafis Abrar, Nazneen Rajani, Nour Elkott, Nour Fahmy, Olanrewaju Samuel, Ran An, Rasmus Kromann, Ryan Hao, Samira Alizadeh, Sarmad Shubber, Silas Wang, Sourav Roy, Sylvain Viguier, Thanh Le, Tobi Oyebade, Trieu Le, Yoyo Yang, Zach Nguyen, Abhinav Ramesh Kashyap, Alfredo Palasciano, Alison Callahan, Anima Shukla, Antonio Miranda-Escalada, Ayush Singh, Benjamin Beilharz, Bo Wang, Caio Brito, Chenxi Zhou, Chirag Jain, Chuxin Xu, Clémentine Fourrier, Daniel León Periñán, Daniel Molano, Dian Yu, Enrique Manjavacas, Fabio Barth, Florian Fuhrimann, Gabriel Altay, Giyaseddin Bayrak, Gully Burns, Helena U. Vrabec, Imane Bello, Ishani Dash, Jihyun Kang, John Giorgi, Jonas Golde, Jose David Posada, Karthik Rangasai Sivaraman, Lokesh Bulchandani, Lu Liu, Luisa Shinzato, Madeleine Hahn de Bykhovetz, Maiko Takeuchi, Marc Pàmies, Maria A Castillo, Marianna Nezhurina, Mario Sänger, Matthias Samwald, Michael Cullan, Michael Weinberg, Michiel De Wolf, Mina Mihaljcic, Minna Liu, Moritz Freidank, Myungsun Kang, Natasha Seelam, Nathan Dahlberg, Nicholas Michio Broad, Nikolaus Muellner, Pascale Fung, Patrick Haller, Ramya Chandrasekhar, Renata Eisenberg, Robert Martin, Rodrigo Canalli, Rosaline Su, Ruisi Su, Samuel Cahyawijaya, Samuele Garda, Shlok S Deshmukh, Shubhanshu Mishra, Sid Kiblawi, Simon Ott, Sinee Sang-aroonsiri, Srishti Kumar, Stefan Schweter, Sushil Bharati, Tanmay Laud, Théo Gigant, Tomoya Kainuma, Wojciech Kusa, Yanis Labrak, Yash Shailesh Bajaj, Yash Venkatraman, Yifan Xu, Yingxin Xu, Yu Xu, Zhe Tan, Zhongli Xie, Zifan Ye, Mathilde Bras, Younes Belkada, and Thomas Wolf. 2023. Bloom: A 176b-parameter open-access multilingual language model.

Carole-Jean Wu, David Brooks, Kevin Chen, Douglas Chen, Sy Choudhury, Marat Dukhan, Kim Hazelwood, Eldad Isaac, Yangqing Jia, Bill Jia, et al. 2019. Machine learning at facebook: Understanding inference at the edge. In *2019 IEEE international symposium on high performance computer architecture (HPCA)*, pages 331–344. IEEE.

Guangxuan Xiao, Ji Lin, Mickael Seznec, Hao Wu, Julien Demouth, and Song Han. 2023. Smoothquant: Accurate and efficient post-training quantization for large language models. In *International Conference on Machine Learning*, pages 38087–38099. PMLR.

Yuzhe Xu, Thaha Mohammed, Mario Di Francesco, and Carlo Fischione. 2022. Distributed assignment with load balancing for dnn inference at the edge. *IEEE Internet of Things Journal*, 10(2):1053–1065.

Zhewei Yao, Reza Yazdani Aminabadi, Minjia Zhang, Xiaoxia Wu, Conglong Li, and Yuxiong He. 2022.

Zeroquant: Efficient and affordable post-training quantization for large-scale transformers. *Advances in Neural Information Processing Systems*, 35:27168–27183.

Liekang Zeng, Xu Chen, Zhi Zhou, Lei Yang, and Junshan Zhang. 2021. Coedge: Cooperative dnn inference with adaptive workload partitioning over heterogeneous edge devices. *IEEE/ACM Trans. Netw.*, 29(2):595–608.

Chaoyun Zhang, Paul Patras, and Hamed Haddadi. 2019. Deep learning in mobile and wireless networking: A survey. *IEEE Communications surveys & tutorials*, 21(3):2224–2287.

Susan Zhang, Stephen Roller, Naman Goyal, Mikel Artetxe, Moya Chen, Shuohui Chen, Christopher Dewan, Mona Diab, Xian Li, Xi Victoria Lin, Todor Mihaylov, Myle Ott, Sam Shleifer, Kurt Shuster, Daniel Simig, Punit Singh Koura, Anjali Sridhar, Tianlu Wang, and Luke Zettlemoyer. 2022. Opt: Open pre-trained transformer language models.

Tianming Zhao, Yucheng Xie, Yan Wang, Jerry Cheng, Xiaonan Guo, Bin Hu, and Yingying Chen. 2022. A survey of deep learning on mobile devices: Applications, optimizations, challenges, and research opportunities. *Proceedings of the IEEE*, 110(3):334–354.

Li Zhou, Mohammad Hossein Samavatian, Anys Bacha, Saikat Majumdar, and Radu Teodorescu. 2019. Adaptive parallel execution of deep neural networks on heterogeneous edge devices. In *Proceedings of the 4th ACM/IEEE Symposium on Edge Computing*, SEC '19, page 195–208, New York, NY, USA. Association for Computing Machinery.

# IMGTB: A Framework for Machine-Generated Text Detection Benchmarking

**Michal Spiegel**[1,2] and **Dominik Macko**[1]
[1] Kempelen Institute of Intelligent Technologies
[2] Faculty of Informatics, Masaryk University
michal.spiegel@intern.kinit.sk, dominik.macko@kinit.sk

## Abstract

In the era of large language models generating high quality texts, it is a necessity to develop methods for detection of machine-generated text to avoid their harmful use or simply for annotation purposes. It is, however, also important to properly evaluate and compare such developed methods. Recently, a few benchmarks have been proposed for this purpose; however, integration of newest detection methods is rather challenging, since new methods appear each month and provide slightly different evaluation pipelines. In this paper, we present the IMGTB framework, which simplifies the benchmarking of machine-generated text detection methods by easy integration of custom (new) methods and evaluation datasets. In comparison to existing frameworks, it enables to objectively compare statistical metric-based zero-shot detectors with classification-based detectors and with differently fine-tuned detectors. Its configurability and flexibility makes research and development of new detection methods easier, especially their comparison to the existing state-of-the-art detectors. The default set of analyses, metrics and visualizations offered by the tool follows the established practices of machine-generated text detection benchmarking found in state-of-the-art literature.

## 1 Introduction

Due to indistinguishability between human-written texts and high-quality texts generated by modern large language models (LLMs) (Sadasivan et al., 2023), the machine-generated text detection (MGTD) belongs to the key challenges identified by (Kaddour et al., 2023). MGTD methods are needed in many areas, such as prevention of disinformation spreading, plagiarism, impersonation and identity theft, automated scams and frauds, or even prevention of unintentional inclusion of lesser quality generated texts in future models' training data (Kaddour et al., 2023; Weidinger et al., 2021; Zellers et al., 2019; Wahle et al., 2022; Vykopal et al., 2023).

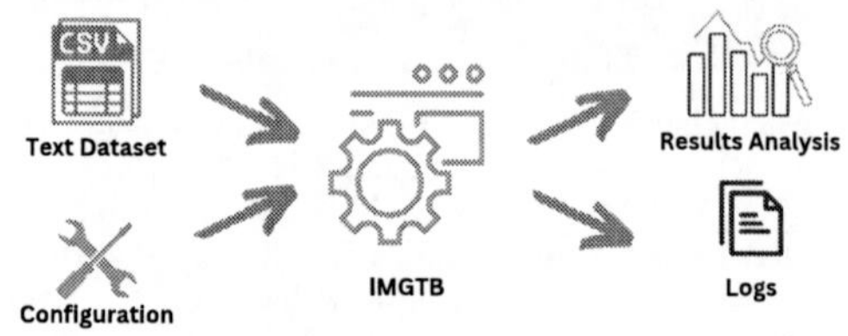


Figure 1: IMGTB framework exemplar usage overview.

Regardless of the area of application, we are witnessing a race of new MGTD methods competing with new *generation* methods and appearing monthly. This presents a challenge to efficiently evaluate and benchmark the new methods. The problem is twofold, missing the uniform implementation of the methods and standardized evaluation. Even when source codes for experiment replication are released, they are usually too specific and not flexible for reuse. Moreover, across application areas, domains, text lengths, or topics, the performance of different MGTD methods varies. Therefore, a flexible way of comparison over various datasets (even custom ones) is currently missing. These problems are usually addressed by common benchmarking frameworks.

There is a lack of flexibility, configurability, and extensibility in the current MGTD benchmarking frameworks; therefore, we have focused on refining the most recent one, MGTBench (He et al., 2023), by integrating missing features and extending support to new types of detection pipelines. The key contributions of the proposed extended framework IMGTB[1] are as follows:

- *objective comparison* of statistical metric-based zero-shot methods with others,

[1] https://github.com/kinit-sk/IMGTB



*Proceedings of the 62nd Annual Meeting of the Association for Computational Linguistics (Volume 3: System Demonstrations)*, pages 172–179
August 11-16, 2024 ©2024 Association for Computational Linguistics

- *integration* of the newest MGTD methods (e.g., MFD, Binoculars, S5) and fine-tuning processes (e.g., PEFT, per-language)[2],
- *simplified ability* to implement custom MGTD methods (plug-in by abstract classes and templates),
- more flexible usage of custom evaluation *datasets* (multi-format support),
- increased *configurability* of the benchmark settings (e.g., classifier selection),
- benchmark results *analysis* (configurability, automated charts generation).

## 2 Related Works

Due to increasing quality of texts generated by modern LLMs, the research around detection of machine-generated text increased its importance. However, a common way to properly compare several detection methods was missing, mainly due to missing publicly available datasets. Few years ago, MGTD researchers mostly used data generated by a single LLM, such as GPT-2[3] or Grover (Zellers et al., 2019), results on which could not be properly generalized. Later on, larger-scale multi LLM benchmarks for MGTD task have been proposed, such as TuringBench (Uchendu et al., 2021), DeepfakeTextDetect (Li et al., 2023), M4 (Wang et al., 2023), or MULTITuDE (Macko et al., 2023). As a result, MGTD methods can now be evaluated on such benchmark datasets and compared to each other. However, these datasets do not share common class labels, structure, or form, what makes the evaluation on multiple of them complicated and unnecessarily prolongs the research.

The other issue significantly prolonging the research is a missing unified implementation of existing MGTD methods. It leaves on the researchers a burden to either reuse the published source codes of individual methods (if there is some), which are different among each other and require customization, or implement them completely into their evaluation framework to be evaluated in a unified way with their newly proposed MGTD method. Some of the proposed MGTD methods, such as DetectGPT (Mitchell et al., 2023), released the full source code including implementation of other existing SOTA methods, enabling complete replication of experiments and providing a good basis to build upon. The result is a faster advancement by extension of the original method, in the form of DetectLLM (Su et al., 2023) or Fast-DetectGPT (Bao et al., 2023), proving the benefits of full replication possibilities.

However, these methods focused on zero-shot statistical-based detection of machine-generated text, comparing various statistical metrics to distinguish between human-written and machine-generated samples, not providing the classification prediction. Thus, the implementations do not allow easy comparison with supervised high-performing pretrained LLMs finetuned for MGTD task, such as the popular OpenAI detector (Solaiman et al., 2019). The proposed MGTBench framework (He et al., 2023) attempted to solve the problem, by implementation of these methods in a common framework. Using a dedicated classifier trained individually for metric-based statistical MGTD methods, it provides a class prediction, enabling a direct comparison to LLMs-based MGTD classifiers. MGTBench has already accelerated MGTD research, such as (Wu and Xiang, 2023) or (Macko et al., 2023).

However, MGTBench provides a quite complicated way to use custom datasets or to integrate new MGTD methods. Moreover, the used classifier-based (must be trained) evaluation of metric-based statistical detectors does not enable their true zero-shot evaluation (without training, as reported in the corresponding papers). Therefore, a more flexible and configurable benchmarking framework is needed.

## 3 IMGTB – Integrated MGTD Benchmark Framework

In this section, we introduce the central design principles, IMGTB was built with, as well as its architecture and the functionality of the main components. We use a term *experiment* to denote a single run of the specified detection method on data from the specified dataset.

### 3.1 Design Principles

The IMGTB framework was designed with several main principles in mind. We consider them important to mention because they encompass what was missing in other similar works and why this tool was developed in the first place.

**[P1: Modularity]** All the subtasks and responsibilities, such as configuration parsing, data loading, and runnning experiments, were divided and

[2] see section 3.2.4 for a description of the implemented methods

[3] https://github.com/openai/gpt-2-output-dataset

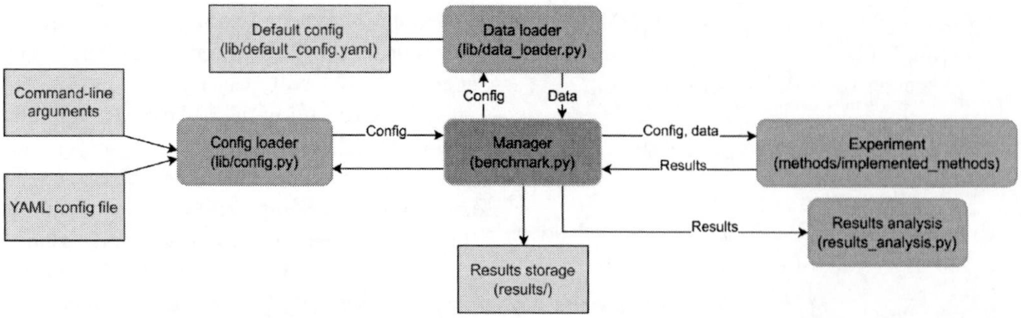


Figure 2: Figure displays an overview of the framework architecture. The Manager acts as the coordinator, interconnecting all other components. In a usual workflow, the Manager requests user-specified configurations from the Configuration Parser. Given the configurations, it requests the train and test datasets from the Data Loader. Furthermore, it forwards the configurations and datasets for evaluation using user-specified detection methods (Experiment component). Finally, it stores the results returned by experiments and calls a Results Analysis component which provides a basic evaluation and visualization of the results.

assigned to their respective modules that only communicate between themselves through a very general interface. Such a decreased inter-module coupling makes the framework very robust and resistant to changes and easy to update, which is useful in order to utilize all the technologies that are yet to be discovered.

**[P2: Ease of use]** The issue and a main blocker when testing and experimenting with new MGTD methods and new datasets seems to be the need to manually set up and integrate a new method, which often does not work out-of-the-box, to manually parse each dataset and then write one's own analysis tools. This framework was designed to mitigate this issue. Simple experiments can be running in seconds just using the terminal via command-line arguments or, for more complex experiments, using a YAML configuration file. Any dataset or detector can be easily accessed from the Hugging Face Hub without the need to manually download it. The framework also includes many parsing utility functions that enable to load and parse almost any dataset without any need to provide a custom code. Additionally, with built-in analysis tools, it is possible to have basic analysis done right after the experiment has finished.

**[P3: Customizability]** The structure of input data can vary significantly, detection methods often need different resources, and although we do try to provide utility functions to provide for most of them, it is not possible to cover all such possible cases. Therefore, we have put great emphasis on making the customization of our codebase and extending our functionalities as simple and straightforward as possible.

### 3.2 Architecture Overview

Figure 2 overviews the main components of the framework architecture, further described in the following subsections.

#### 3.2.1 Manager

The Manager, interconnecting all the other components, serves as the user interface. Its main task is to orchestrate the other components. It calls the data loader, forwards configurations, runs experiments and so on.

#### 3.2.2 Configuration Parser

Configuration Parser provides the functionality to specify configurations directly in the terminal via command-line arguments for quick experiment setup or via a YAML configuration file for more complex experiments. However, command-line arguments offer only a subset of the options the YAML configurations system offers. For convenience, user-specified configurations are always merged with a system default configurations (see *lib/default_config.yaml*). To add a new parameter to the configurations is as easy as adding it to one's YAML configurations file, or to the system default (*lib/default_config.yaml*), no changes to the code itself are needed.

#### 3.2.3 Data Loader

Data loader's main responsibility is to offer functionalities to parse as many different dataset formats and structures as possible. Currently, it is possible to specify column names, labels, a Hugging Face Hub dataset just by providing its identifier, use different subsets, splits, test on machine or human only text data, and much more. In the case that these predefined functionalities would not be sufficient, we try to make it as easy as possible to integrate custom parser functions.

#### 3.2.4 Experiment

Experiment is an abstract class defining a single abstract method *run(data, config)* that runs the experiment on the provided data and given configurations and returns results (ideally in the standardized format). In regards to detectors, the framework offers many already implemented (*methods/implemented_methods*), such as single metric-based methods (e.g., Entropy by Lavergne et al., 2008, or Binoculars by Hans et al., 2024), multi-metric-based methods (e.g., GLTR by Gehrmann et al., 2019, MFD by Wu and Xiang, 2023, or S5 by Spiegel and Macko, 2024), or perturbation-based methods (e.g., DetectGPT by Mitchell et al., 2023, or DetectLLM-NPR by Su et al., 2023). Single metric methods (even perturbation based) can be run with a to-be-trained classifier on top or in zero-shot manner using a predefined or a calibrated classification threshold. To run a Sequence Classification Hugging Face Hub model, only its identifier needs to be specified in the methods configurations as a file path. In addition to running such models directly, they can be fine-tuned using three different configurable processes: full, PEFT (QLoRA based parameter-efficient fine-tuning by Dettmers et al., 2023), or per-language based multilingual fine-tuning (Spiegel and Macko, 2024). Although there are many MGTD methods already implemented in the framework, the true feature of this component is the possibility to quickly implement new custom experiments. By using some of the predefined experiment templates for metric-based or perturbation-based methods, it is possible to implement experiments in just a few lines of code. There is, however, still a possibility to implement a fully custom experiment by implementing the *run()* method from scratch.

#### 3.2.5 Results Analysis

Results analysis can be run either right after a benchmark run, can be specified in the configurations, or later by loading the results from a file. We implement several analysis methods ourselves, such as detection performance (Accuracy, Precision, Recall, F1-score, ROC - receiver operating characteristic), false positives/negatives, or runtime performance. But it is ensured for easy integration of new analysis methods.

## 4 Case Study

To better illustrate the use of the framework in practice, in this section we showcase a few example use case scenarios. We look at:

**A.** How to quickly run and evaluate simple experiments using CLI

**B.** How to run complex experiments using YAML configuration files

For a more visual version of this demonstration, see the video[4]. For more detailed and runnable version, see the Jupyter notebook[5].

### 4.1 Example Scenario A

Let's assume we obtained a completely new never-before-seen dataset of texts generated by one of the latest SOTA large language models. In a similar manner, we could also use existing datasets, even from completely unrelated domains, such as AI-powered text summarization, translation, question answering, or disinformation detection.

Out of curiosity, we'd like to see how the current SOTA detection methods roughly (i.e., default settings) perform on this new data.

Starting from scratch, this would probably take a significant amount of effort to preprocess the data, find the source code of the detectors, integrate the detectors, evaluate and plot the results, as well as considerable knowledge about tools like pandas, numpy or transformers, not to mention the time spent browsing the documentation of said tools.

This all seems a little bit too much. But with our framework we could accomplish the same just by running one CLI command as follows:

```
python benchmark.py --dataset
↪  xzuyn/futurama-alpaca huggingfacehub
↪  machine_only output --methods
↪  roberta-base-openai-detector
↪  Hello-SimpleAI/chatgpt-detector-roberta
↪  andreas122001/roberta-mixed-detector
```

In the command, the option *--dataset* is used for specification of *xzuyn/futurama-alpaca* dataset, available at HuggingFace (see the *huggingfacehub* keyword), which contains only machine-generated

[4] https://www.youtube.com/watch?v=NlHIC4HDQrc

[5] https://colab.research.google.com/drive/15C7kzpnDnx_zqwplCpc949xVJ4Bhdnjl?usp=sharing

texts (see the *machine-only* keyword), and the data field/column to be used for texts being *output*. For the full description of the *dataset* parameters see the GitHub repository[6]. The option *--methods* is followed by identifiers of the methods to be evaluated and compared in the benchmark. If such identifiers are not found in the local implementations of the MGTD methods, the HuggingFace is used as a repository of the models.

When the benchmark run finishes, we are able to find all the results in the latest *results/logs* log entry. It contains a JSON file storing all the benchmark results and the output plots (examples in Figure 3 and 4) of the results analysis component. Using the provided plots, per-detection-method performance is easily comparable.

Regarding Figure 3, only machine-class samples were included in the Scenario A dataset; therefore, the precision of all detectors is 1.0 (i.e., no false positives) and the accuracy is the same as the recall. Based on Figure 4, the last detection method clearly has problems in identifying machine texts from the provided dataset, due to prevalence of false negatives (with a high certainty, based on machine-class probability score).

[6] https://github.com/kinit-sk/IMGTB/tree/main#dataset-parameters

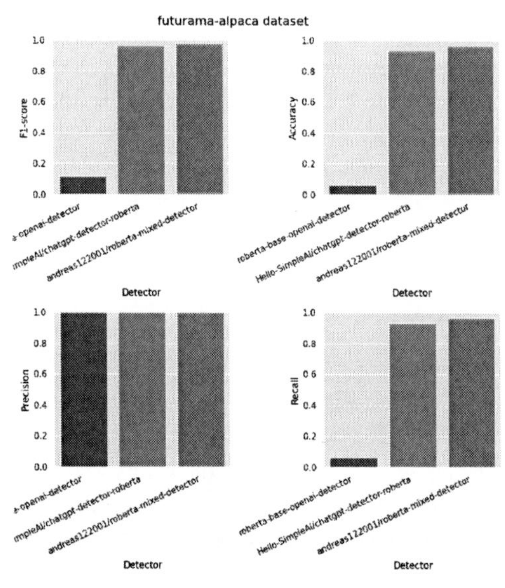


Figure 3: Automatically generated chart for detection-performance metrics analysis.

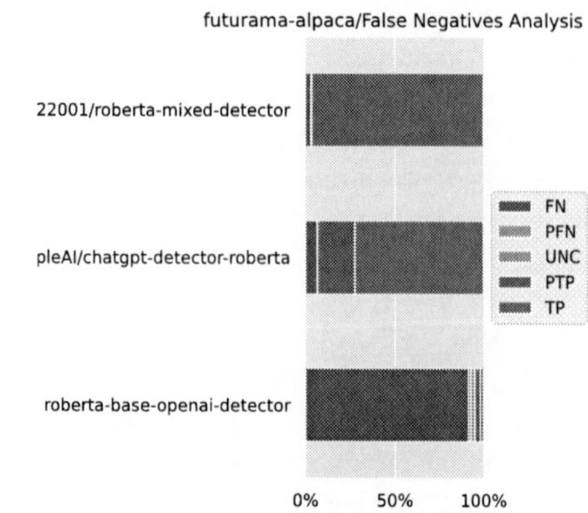


Figure 4: Automatically generated chart for false-negatives analysis (inspired by Weber-Wulff et al., 2023), where $FN$, $PFN$, $UNC$ and $PTP$ represent false negatives, potential false negatives, uncertainty, potential true positives and true positives, respectively.

## 4.2 Example Scenario B

In this scenario, let's assume that we have developed and integrated a new metric-based MGT detection method called *MiracleMetric*. IMGTB implements a number of state-of-the-art detection methods. Implementing new methods is streamlined by the use of template abstract classes that allow fast prototyping of new statistical and fine-tuned methods. To make a complex evaluation on multiple datasets, comparing with multiple different detection methods, and with different parameters, we can design a very compact and readable YAML configuration file.

Firstly, in Figure 5 we specify the data to be used. After that we can specify multiple methods (including our *MiracleMetric*) with different parameters, models, etc. in Figure 6. As opposed to other benchmarks (e.g. MGTBench (He et al., 2023)), IMGTB enables users to specify custom datasets, detection methods and various other parameters by simply creating a configuration file, without the need to modify the codebase. This crucial advantage enables fast prototyping and eliminates unnecessary, repetitive tasks that often hinder researchers in this field.

With this done, the only step keeping us from the results is running the benchmark using these configurations:

```
python benchmark.py
↪ --from_config=example_config.yaml
```

This will output similar results to the previous

```yaml
data:
  global:
    filetype: auto
  list:
  - filepath: WxWx/ChatGPT-Detector-Bias
    filetype: huggingfacehub
    text_field: text
    label_field: kind
    human_label: Human-Written

  - filepath: yaful/DeepfakeTextDetect
    filetype: huggingfacehub
    train_split: test_ood_gpt
    test_split: test_ood_gpt_para
    human_label: "1"
```

Figure 5: Data configurations in YAML format.

```yaml
methods:
  global:
    base_model_name: gpt2-medium
    mask_filling_model_name: t5-large
    DEVICE: cuda
  list:
  - name: MiracleMetric
  - name: MiracleMetric
    clf_algo_for_threshold:
      name: MLPClassifier
      hidden_layer_sizes: [64, 32, 16]
  - name: LoglikelihoodMetric
  - name: LogRankMetric
  - name: EntropyMetric
  - name: DetectLLM_LLR
  - name: EntropyMetric
  - name: roberta-base-openai-detector
```

Figure 6: Methods configurations in YAML format.

example scenario. However, this time we might not be satisfied with the simple automatic analysis provided to us by the framework and we might want to do a more complex and custom-made analysis fitting to the specific needs of our benchmark run. For a demonstration on this exact issue, see the provided Jupyter notebook with the full demo.

## 5 Discussion

The usefulness of the IMGTB framework has been evaluated in practice by its usage in (Macko et al., 2024b; Spiegel and Macko, 2024; Macko et al., 2024a), where it proved to be valuable especially for its implementation of the statistical detectors.

In comparison to the SOTA MGTD framework called MGTBench (He et al., 2023), IMGTB enables an objective comparison of statistical zero-shot detectors (i.e., without classifier training) by using ROC curve. Further, IMGTB integrates the newest detectors, such as MFD, Binoculars, or S5. It directly enables multiple fine-tuning processes for language models. Most of all, in MGTBench (He et al., 2023), configurations, datasets and detection methods are often hard coded and cannot be easily changed or reconfigured, IMGTB simplifies usage of custom datasets and detectors by supporting plug-in like extension. Faster evaluation is provided by the implemented results analysis and automated comparison charts generation.

To fine-tune a model for binary classification, a more generic SOTA framework, such as Ludwig (Molino et al., 2019), could be used. However, such a framework would not be usable to compare the fine-tuned detectors to statistical detection methods or online services. Therefore, a specialized MGTD framework, such as MGTBench or IMGTB is needed for such a comparison. IMGTB enables such a fine-tuning process by itself and also includes a unique multilingual MGTD specific version of per-language fine-tuning, not available in other frameworks. Similarly, the Evaluate framework[7] could be directly used to compare pre-trained classification models. However, to compare also to statistical and other custom detection methods, a significant effort would be required to implement the custom pipelines, loosing flexibility, configurability (especially concerning the detectors training), and tailor-made analysis and visualization tools in comparison to the proposed IMGTB.

### 5.1 Extensions & Enhancements Possibilities

There are various limitations and many possible extensions of the current version of the framework which can be targeted to increase its usability even more. Multiple MGTD methods with vastly different evaluation pipelines are not yet compatible with the framework such as Grover by Zellers et al., 2019, FAST by Zhong et al., 2020 or many zero-shot online services (usually paid), available by a custom API (application programming interface), of which only GPTZero[8] is currently supported by the framework. We are continuously working on extension for these additional features.

To speed up the experiments, *bitsandbytes* library has already been utilized for quantized inference and fine-tuning of LLMs for some methods. This can be further extended to be used also for metric computation in metric-based methods. Further speed-ups can be achieved by eliminating redundant tasks (e.g., loading of the same base models

[7] https://huggingface.co/docs/evaluate/en/index

[8] https://gptzero.me/

for multiple methods, calculating the same metrics or generating the same perturbations for multiple methods).

There are also possibilities for significant extension of the framework beyond the current scope. Similarly to detection methods, authorship obfuscation methods (i.e., evading detection) can be integrated into the framework to offer automated evaluation of adversarial robustness of the detection methods in the benchmark. The extension can be also focused to methods for detection of AI content in other modalities (or mixed modalities), such as images, voice or videos, which would make it even more universal.

## 6 Conclusion

The machine-generated text detection belongs to the key challenges connected with the advancements of large language models for prevention of misuse of high-quality text generation capability. The proposed IMGTB framework unifies the evaluation of the existing detection methods and simplifies comparison of new detection methods to the state-of-the-art. With a plug-and-play testing ability of new methods, research hypotheses can be easily examined. The framework can also be used for evaluation of state-of-the-art detection methods on custom data to identify the best performing one to be further used for some specific application. Automated results analysis and methods comparison also enables less proficient users to interpret the results and make a selection.

The framework reduces unnecessarily redundant work of researchers and enables them to focus their effort towards development of more effective detection methods. This can eventually accelerate the research in machine-generated text detection to catch up with the text generation, currently in the lead.

## Ethical Considerations

We believe that there is only a limited possibility of **misuse of our framework**. By easily identifying the most successful detection methods, the focus of malicious actors can be moved towards them in order to find ways to avoid detection. Although the mentioned risk is serious, the benefits of the provided framework mentioned in the introduction surpass such risks. The detection methods are already available, we just provide means to compare their performance.

There are additional potential ethical risks associated with the MGTD in general, such as difficulty to differentiate between malicious and legitimate use of machine-generated texts, potential harm caused by false positives or over-reliance on the results of an automated detection methods. However, these pertain more to the deployment of an MGTD service rather than to the benchmarking framework, and are therefore deemed out of scope of this work.

## Acknowledgements

This work was partially supported by the *VIGILANT - Vital IntelliGence to Investigate ILlegAl DisiNformaTion*, a project funded by the European Union under the Horizon Europe, GA No. 101073921, and by *vera.ai - VERification Assisted by Artificial Intelligence*, a project funded by European Union under the Horizon Europe, GA No. 101070093.

## References

Guangsheng Bao, Yanbin Zhao, Zhiyang Teng, Linyi Yang, and Yue Zhang. 2023. Fast-DetectGPT: Efficient zero-shot detection of machine-generated text via conditional probability curvature. *arXiv preprint arXiv:2310.05130.*

Tim Dettmers, Artidoro Pagnoni, Ari Holtzman, and Luke Zettlemoyer. 2023. QLoRA: Efficient finetuning of quantized llms. *arXiv:2305.14314.*

Sebastian Gehrmann, Hendrik Strobelt, and Alexander M. Rush. 2019. GLTR: Statistical detection and visualization of generated text. *arXiv:1906.04043.*

Abhimanyu Hans, Avi Schwarzschild, Valeriia Cherepanova, Hamid Kazemi, Aniruddha Saha, Micah Goldblum, Jonas Geiping, and Tom Goldstein. 2024. Spotting LLMs with Binoculars: Zero-shot detection of machine-generated text. *arXiv:2401.12070.*

Xinlei He, Xinyue Shen, Zeyuan Chen, Michael Backes, and Yang Zhang. 2023. MGTBench: Benchmarking machine-generated text detection. *arXiv preprint arXiv:2303.14822.*

Jean Kaddour, Joshua Harris, Maximilian Mozes, Herbie Bradley, Roberta Raileanu, and Robert McHardy. 2023. Challenges and applications of large language models. *arXiv preprint arXiv:2307.10169.*

Thomas Lavergne, Tanguy Urvoy, and François Yvon. 2008. Detecting fake content with relative entropy scoring. In *Proceedings of the 2008 International Conference on Uncovering Plagiarism, Authorship and Social Software Misuse - Volume 377*, PAN'08, page 27–31, Aachen, DEU. CEUR-WS.org.

Yafu Li, Qintong Li, Leyang Cui, Wei Bi, Longyue Wang, Linyi Yang, Shuming Shi, and Yue Zhang. 2023. Deepfake text detection in the wild. *arXiv preprint arXiv:2305.13242*.

Dominik Macko, Jakub Kopal, Robert Moro, and Ivan Srba. 2024a. MultiSocial: Multilingual benchmark of machine-generated text detection of social-media texts. *arXiv:2406.12549*.

Dominik Macko, Robert Moro, Adaku Uchendu, Jason Lucas, Michiharu Yamashita, Matúš Pikuliak, Ivan Srba, Thai Le, Dongwon Lee, Jakub Simko, and Maria Bielikova. 2023. MULTITuDE: Large-scale multilingual machine-generated text detection benchmark. In *Proceedings of the 2023 Conference on Empirical Methods in Natural Language Processing*, pages 9960–9987, Singapore. Association for Computational Linguistics.

Dominik Macko, Robert Moro, Adaku Uchendu, Ivan Srba, Jason Samuel Lucas, Michiharu Yamashita, Nafis Irtiza Tripto, Dongwon Lee, Jakub Simko, and Maria Bielikova. 2024b. Authorship obfuscation in multilingual machine-generated text detection. *arXiv:2401.07867*.

Eric Mitchell, Yoonho Lee, Alexander Khazatsky, Christopher D. Manning, and Chelsea Finn. 2023. DetectGPT: Zero-shot machine-generated text detection using probability curvature. *arXiv preprint arXiv:2301.11305*.

Piero Molino, Yaroslav Dudin, and Sai Sumanth Miryala. 2019. Ludwig: a type-based declarative deep learning toolbox. *arXiv:1909.07930*.

Vinu Sankar Sadasivan, Aounon Kumar, Sriram Balasubramanian, Wenxiao Wang, and Soheil Feizi. 2023. Can AI-generated text be reliably detected? *arXiv preprint arXiv:2303.11156*.

Irene Solaiman, Miles Brundage, Jack Clark, Amanda Askell, Ariel Herbert-Voss, Jeff Wu, Alec Radford, Gretchen Krueger, Jong Wook Kim, Sarah Kreps, et al. 2019. Release strategies and the social impacts of language models. *arXiv preprint arXiv:1908.09203*.

Michal Spiegel and Dominik Macko. 2024. KInIT at SemEval-2024 task 8: Fine-tuned LLMs for multilingual machine-generated text detection. *arXiv:2402.13671*.

Jinyan Su, Terry Yue Zhuo, Di Wang, and Preslav Nakov. 2023. DetectLLM: Leveraging log rank information for zero-shot detection of machine-generated text. *arXiv preprint arXiv:2306.05540*.

Adaku Uchendu, Zeyu Ma, Thai Le, Rui Zhang, and Dongwon Lee. 2021. TURINGBENCH: A benchmark environment for Turing test in the age of neural text generation. In *Findings of the Association for Computational Linguistics: EMNLP 2021*, pages 2001–2016, Punta Cana, Dominican Republic. Association for Computational Linguistics.

Ivan Vykopal, Matúš Pikuliak, Ivan Srba, Robert Moro, Dominik Macko, and Maria Bielikova. 2023. Disinformation capabilities of large language models. *arXiv preprint arXiv:2311.08838*.

Jan Philip Wahle, Terry Ruas, Frederic Kirstein, and Bela Gipp. 2022. How large language models are transforming machine-paraphrase plagiarism. In *Proceedings of the 2022 Conference on Empirical Methods in Natural Language Processing*, pages 952–963, Abu Dhabi, United Arab Emirates. Association for Computational Linguistics.

Yuxia Wang, Jonibek Mansurov, Petar Ivanov, Jinyan Su, Artem Shelmanov, Akim Tsvigun, Chenxi Whitehouse, Osama Mohammed Afzal, Tarek Mahmoud, Alham Fikri Aji, and Preslav Nakov. 2023. M4: Multi-generator, multi-domain, and multilingual black-box machine-generated text detection. *arXiv:2305.14902*.

Debora Weber-Wulff, Alla Anohina-Naumeca, Sonja Bjelobaba, Tomáš Foltýnek, Jean Guerrero-Dib, Olumide Popoola, Petr Šigut, and Lorna Waddington. 2023. Testing of detection tools for ai-generated text. *International Journal for Educational Integrity*, 19(1).

Laura Weidinger, John Mellor, Maribeth Rauh, Conor Griffin, Jonathan Uesato, Po-Sen Huang, Myra Cheng, Mia Glaese, Borja Balle, Atoosa Kasirzadeh, Zac Kenton, Sasha Brown, Will Hawkins, Tom Stepleton, Courtney Biles, Abeba Birhane, Julia Haas, Laura Rimell, Lisa Anne Hendricks, William Isaac, Sean Legassick, Geoffrey Irving, and Iason Gabriel. 2021. Ethical and social risks of harm from language models. *arXiv preprint arXiv:2112.04359*.

Zhendong Wu and Hui Xiang. 2023. MFD: Multi-feature detection of LLM-generated text.

Rowan Zellers, Ari Holtzman, Hannah Rashkin, Yonatan Bisk, Ali Farhadi, Franziska Roesner, and Yejin Choi. 2019. Defending against neural fake news. In H. Wallach, H. Larochelle, A. Beygelzimer, F. d'Alché-Buc, E. Fox, and R. Garnett, editors, *Advances in Neural Information Processing Systems 32*, pages 9054–9065. Curran Associates, Inc.

Wanjun Zhong, Duyu Tang, Zenan Xu, Ruize Wang, Nan Duan, Ming Zhou, Jiahai Wang, and Jian Yin. 2020. Neural deepfake detection with factual structure of text. In *Proceedings of the 2020 Conference on Empirical Methods in Natural Language Processing (EMNLP)*, pages 2461–2470, Online. Association for Computational Linguistics.

# DrugWatch: A Comprehensive Multi-Source Data Visualisation Platform for Drug Safety Information

**Artem Bobrov**[1*], **Domantas Saltenis**[2*], **Zhaoyue Sun**[2*], **Gabriele Pergola**[2], and **Yulan He**[1,2,3]
[1]Department of Informatics, King's College London
[2]Department of Computer Science, University of Warwick
[3]The Alan Turing Institute
{Artem.Bobrov, Yulan.He}@kcl.ac.uk
{Domantas.Saltenis, Zhaoyue.Sun, Gabriele.Pergola.1}@warwick.ac.uk

## Abstract

Drug safety research is crucial for maintaining public health, often requiring comprehensive data support. However, the resources currently available to the public are limited and fail to provide a comprehensive understanding of the relationship between drugs and their side effects. This paper introduces **DrugWatch**, an easy-to-use and interactive multi-source information visualisation platform for drug safety study. It allows users to understand common side effects of drugs and their statistical information, flexibly retrieve relevant medical reports, or annotate their own medical texts with our automated annotation tool. Supported by NLP technology and enriched with interactive visual components, we are committed to providing researchers and practitioners with a one-stop information analysis, retrieval, and annotation service. The demonstration video is available at `https://www.youtube.com/watch?v=RTqDgxzETjw`. We also deployed an online demonstration system at `https://drugwatch.net/`.

## 1 Introduction

The use of medications is a cornerstone of modern disease management, yet their potential for adverse reactions can pose safety risks. Adverse drug reactions (ADRs) have been reported to be the most common cause of hospitalisation and rank as the fourth or sixth leading cause of death (Lazarou et al., 1998). In addition to the inherent risks of medications themselves, certain drugs may exhibit unpredictable sensitivities in specific patient populations (World Health Organization, 2004). Furthermore, there is also a risk of interactions when multiple medications are used concurrently. Therefore, to ensure public health safety, professionals such as physicians, drug developers, and regulatory officials often need to comprehensively understand, assess, and monitor medication safety information from various sources.

To benefit the monitoring of adverse drug events, the World Health Organization (WHO) and numerous countries or regions have established databases for spontaneous case reporting, such as VigiBase (Uppsala Monitoring Centre, 2024), FDA Adverse Event Reporting System (FAERS; U.S. Food and Drug Administration 2024), and EudraVigilance (European Medicines Agency, 2024). These databases typically offer interactive query tools to assist users in visualising statistical data from the reporting system. For example, the FAERS Dashboard enable users to search for specific drug products or reaction terms, and offers visual charts illustrating the distribution of corresponding reports by year, demographic details, reaction categories, etc. These databases serve as crucial sources of information for drug safety research.

However, the presence of reports in spontaneous reporting systems does not imply a causal relationship between the drug and the reported adverse reactions. The context in which adverse reactions occur is often complex and may be related to the underlying disease, concurrent medication use, or other factors. Therefore, relying solely on statistical information from spontaneous reporting systems is insufficient for a deeper understanding of drug-induced adverse reactions. Researchers often need access to more detailed information for analysis, much of which is embedded within textual descriptions.

In this paper, we introduce **DrugWatch**, a multi-source data visualisation platform that integrates information from structured, textual and user-held data on drug safety. It comprises two primary sub-platforms: **DrugWatch Search** and **DrugWatch Annotate**. *DrugWatch Search* offers users visualised statistical data sourced from FAERS and PubMed, along with robust support for fine-grained PubMed medical case report retrieval. *DrugWatch*

[*]Equal contribution.



*Proceedings of the 62nd Annual Meeting of the Association for Computational Linguistics (Volume 3: System Demonstrations)*, pages 180–189
August 11-16, 2024 ©2024 Association for Computational Linguistics

*Annotate* empowers users to annotate their private data and visualise the resulting annotations.

For *DrugWatch Search*, similar to the FAERS Dashboard, we enable users to search for drugs or adverse reactions and visualise the statistical information provided by the FAERS Database. However, we additionally utilise event extraction techniques to retrieve textual context and present statistics extracted from text data for user queries. We gather medical case reports related to ADRs from PubMed and extract structured information about adverse events using the approach proposed by Sun et al. (2024). We present the statistical information of the extracted results in a similar way to that of the FAERS data for easy comparison. Additionally, we provide users with a list of PubMed literature and abstracts associated with their search queries, enabling them to conveniently access detailed descriptions of the events in medical texts. Users can also customise more granular search criteria, such as limiting results based on patient age or gender, to filter the search results.

For *DrugWatch Annotate*, we integrate several pre-trained models such as Flan-T5 (Chung et al., 2022) and UIE (Lu et al., 2022), and an LLM, i.e., Mistral-7B (Mistral AI, 2023), that enables users to perform fine-grained pharmacovigilance event extraction on their private data. These models support the extraction of *subject*, *treatment*, and *effect* information for adverse drug events (ADEs) and potential therapeutic events (PTEs), along with their sub-arguments (e.g., demographic information and drug administration details). We support the visualisation of annotation results, allowing users to quickly try a single data point through a demo window or batch-view the visualised annotations for each data entry. We have pre-processed and visualised manual annotations from the PHEE dataset (Sun et al., 2022) and different model predictions for direct model comparison and selection.

The contributions of this paper can be summarised as follows:

- We propose a multi-source drug safety information visualisation platform, facilitating users to perform comprehensive analysis on structured data from spontaneous case reports and textual data from medical literature or private sources.
- Our platform supports flexible retrieval mechanisms, allowing users to obtain statistics visualisations based on different search items and compare data from different sources. We also integrate a text retrieval system based on event extraction, enabling users to retrieve textual evidence from medical literature.
- We allow users to perform pharmacovigilance event extraction and visualise annotation results on their private data, offering a range of models for their selection.

## 2 Architecture of DrugWatch

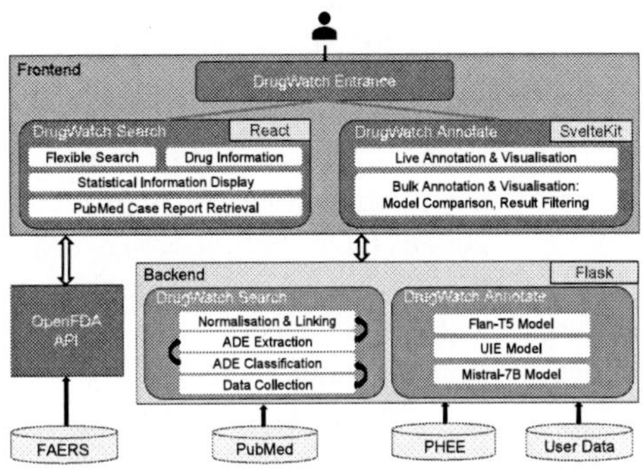


Figure 1: The overall architecture of *DrugWatch*.

DrugWatch consists of two sub-platforms: *DrugWatch Search* and *DrugWatch Annotate*. The overall architecture is illustrated in Figure 1.

*DrugWatch Search* is designed for flexible drug and ADE search. It presents not only fundamental information about drugs but also statistical information from the FAERS database and PubMed literature collections. Additionally, it enables users to access relevant ADE case reports seamlessly. Its front-end is implemented using React (Meta Platforms, Inc., 2024), creating a smooth and interactive user experience. On the server side, we utilise the Flask (Pallets, 2024) framework to manage API requests and handle data processing from local databases.

*DrugWatch Annotate* provides automated prediction and visualisation services for user-held data. Users can instantly or in bulk extract ADEs from their data using our built-in fine-tuned models or LLMs. They can easily visualise the event arguments extracted for each data instance, compare prediction results from different models, and conveniently filter results. We preload the PHEE dataset for direct comparison purposes. The front-end of DrugWatch Annotate is built with SvelteKit (Rich Harris, 2024), ensuring fast responsiveness and a clear, visually appealing user experience. The back-end continues to utilise Flask.

## 3 User Interaction Design

### 3.1 DrugWatch Search Sub-platform

*DrugWatch Search* is a search-centric multi-source information display platform that allows users to search for drugs or side effects flexibly. It not only presents basic drug information for users but also supports the visualisation of interactive statistical information. The integrated event extraction algorithm further enables the platform to retrieve and display relevant PubMed literature based on flexible search options.

**Flexible Search** Users can search for individual drugs or side effects and their respective combinations. A combination search for drugs and side effects is currently not available from the search entrance, but users can filter search results by side effects (or drugs). Furthermore, for any queried drug or side effect, the platform provides the option to refine search results based on specific demographic filters, including patient gender, age group (or exact age), and nationality. For a visual guide, see Figure A1 and Figure A2 in Appendix.

**Drug Information Display** When searching for drugs, our platform first presents users with basic drug information collected from DrugBank. This includes structural diagrams, IUPAC name, chemical class, and chemical formula of the drug molecule. Additionally, we display information related to drug use such as indication, half-life, and brand names. When users query multiple drugs at once, the information for each drug is displayed sequentially. See Figure A3 for an illustration.

**Statistical Information Display** We provide statistical information for reports meeting customised search criteria on the main results page, and offer a breakdown of demographic information of the searched drug or side effects in a pop-up window. For both cases, users can compare information from FAERS and PubMed with a single click.

On the main results page, we initially display a line chart (Figure A4) showing the variation in the number of reports matching the search criteria over the years. Additionally, we present the most relevant side effects (or drugs) associated with the drug (or side effect) queried by the user. We present this information in two different ways. Firstly, users can observe the top 50 side effects (or drugs) with the highest frequency in the reports, along with their respective counts and proportions (by mouseover), through a bar chart. For easier viewing, the results are divided into 5 pages, with different colours indicating the rarity of the terms. Secondly, users can visually grasp the distribution of related terms through a word cloud. Figure 2 illustrates examples of these two approaches.

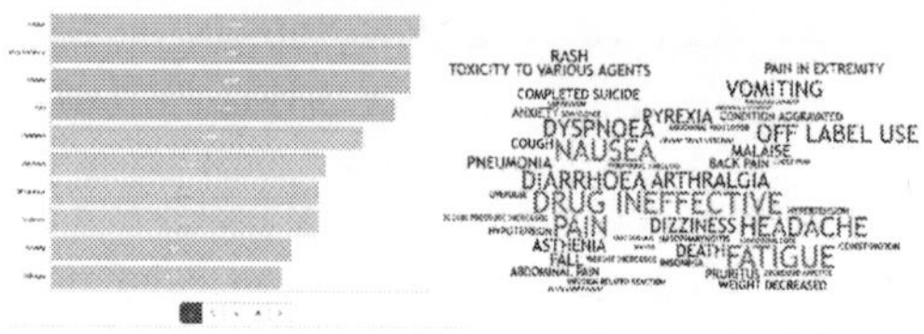


Figure 2: Top frequent side effects related to Acetaminophen, presented by bar chart and word cloud.

The demographic information page first displays the comprehensive age and gender distribution of all reports linked to the queried drug or side effect through a pie chart, facilitating users in visually perceiving the distribution across different demographic groups (Figure A5). Additionally, we provide a bar chart for any age or gender group, exhibiting the quantities and proportions of the top 10 reported side effects or drugs (Figure A6). Should users seek further insights into age and gender group comparisons, our advanced view supplies detailed counts of each top side effect or drug-related reports within age groups across gender groups (or in reverse). Figure 3 shows a screenshot of the demographic breakdown charts.

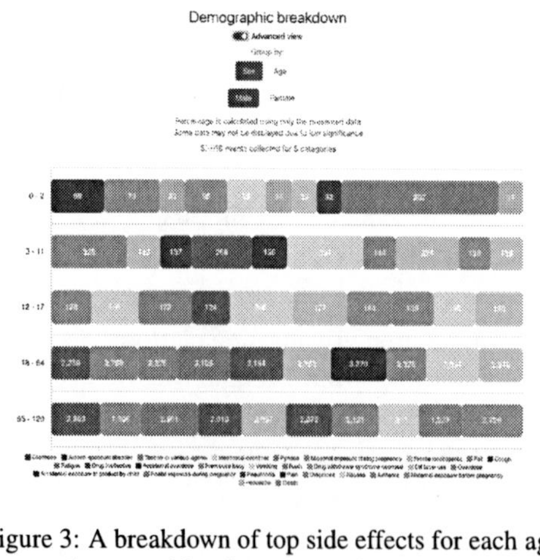


Figure 3: A breakdown of top side effects for each age group when searching for reports of Acetaminophen in males.

**Pubmed Case Report Retrieval** We simultaneously present users with relevant PubMed case reports on the search results page, allowing them to quickly grasp contextual information surrounding the adverse drug reactions. By default, we display information such as the literature titles, abstracts, keywords etc., that match the search criteria, along with links for quick access to the respective PubMed entries. Users' search terms are highlighted in the abstracts for easier browsing. In addition, we have designed a flexible interaction method, allowing users to dynamically adjust the literature search criteria as needed. For example, they can interact with the bar chart or word cloud chart depicting the distribution of adverse reactions on the search page to obtain a list of literature associated with both the searched drug and an adverse reaction. They can also specify any other filtering terms by manual input (as shown in Figure 4).

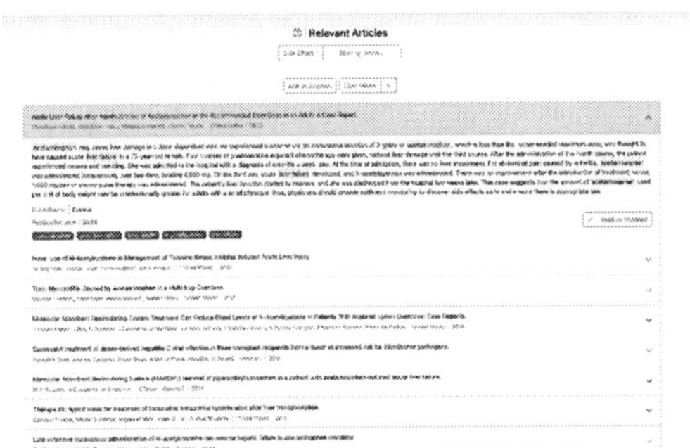


Figure 4: Retrieved PubMed case reports related to "Acetaminophen" and "Liver failure".

## 3.2 DrugWatch Annotate Sub-platform

*DrugWatch Annotate* provides users with automated annotation capabilities for adverse events, facilitating the visualisation of annotated results. It features a live annotation interface for real-time check of individual data entries and a bulk annotation interface for efficient assessment of uploaded batch data. The annotation platform lays the foundation for users to conduct in-depth analysis of their private data subsequently.

**Live Annotation** Users can freely input sentences they wish to analyse into the text window and then select the model they want to apply. Currently, three models (i.e., Flan-T5, UIE, Mistral-7B) are available for annotation. The page displays visual results of the model's predictions in real-time, presenting arguments in different colours for easy browsing. Users can also view and copy the results in JSON format (as shown in Figure A7).

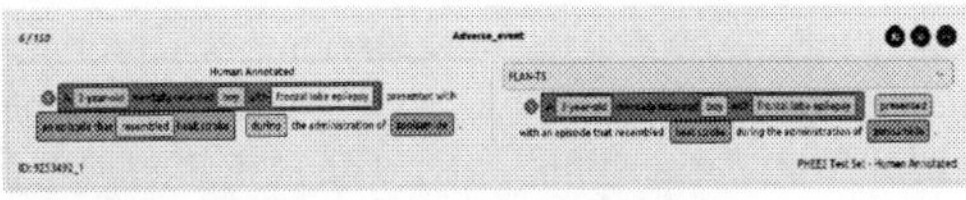

Figure 5: Illustration of *DrugWatch Annotate* model annotation result comparison interface.

**Bulk Annotation** Users can upload their data in batches and visualise all annotation results. They may view annotation results for any single model or compare results from two models side by side (Figure 5). We default to loading the PHEE dataset and specifically provide manual annotations on this dataset for users to compare the effects of different models and make selections accordingly. We also allow users to search annotation results to only view results containing a specific argument type (e.g., subject's age) or containing a specific argument span (e.g., "6 years old"). Similarly, users may check and export model outputs in JSON format. A more comprehensive illustration of the bulk annotation interface is shown in Figure A8.

# 4 Backend Implementation

## 4.1 Data Storage and Retrieval

For *DrugWatch Search*, to retrieve statistical data or article information from the back-end, the front-end service makes a series of REST API requests to various endpoints implemented in our backend. Data from the FAERS system is directly fetched from the front-end through the OpenFDA API[1], while text and statistical information from PubMed are processed and stored in the local file system and retrieved from the back-end. This integrated approach effectively reduces the server's workload and ensures the speed. Specifically, the PubMed data are stored in JSON files and loaded into RAM to expedite the search process. We transform the results of the extraction method described in subsection 4.2 and remove fields that will not be used in the search. Once a search request is submitted, the algorithm iterates through the extracted event arguments of the loaded data, and if a match is found, appends the article ID to the response. Finally, the metadata for each retrieved article is fetched with *Biopython*[2] and returned to the front-end.

[1]https://open.fda.gov/
[2]https://biopython.org

For *DrugWatch Annotate*, in order to protect data privacy, we do not store user inputs or uploaded documents on the platform. These data are only retained while the user session is active, meaning that reloading the page will clear the uploaded data from the session. After data is uploaded, a request with the provided data is sent to the back-end, which then reads, annotates, and returns the results for visualisation on the front-end. However, this implies that users may need to wait for the model processing. Additionally, we have preprocessed the annotated PHEE dataset, storing both manually annotated data and model prediction results in a local PostgreSQL database[3], allowing users to directly access existing datasets and save time.

### 4.2 Relevant Medical Case Reports Integration

To integrate user query-related medical case reports from PubMed into our platform, we first retrieve and download abstracts of adverse event case reports from PubMed, and train a classifier to filter sentences mentioning adverse events from these abstracts. Subsequently, we utilise an event extraction model to extract fine-grained event arguments from the filtered sentences and store the extraction results and their relevant PubMed IDs locally. We then normalise the extracted arguments using regularisation methods, match them with user queries and return relevant PubMed IDs. Finally, we provide a preview of the list and abstracts of the retrieved articles.

**Case Reports Collection** The initial stage involves obtaining abstracts from PubMed that pertain to adverse events. We use *Biopython* to fetch data from PubMed. During retrieval, we obtain records containing the keywords "adverse event", "adverse effect", "adverse reaction", or "side effect", while restricting the publication type to "case report", the language to English, and the presence of an abstract. Our platform has currently collected and analysed case reports up to December 2023, and allows for incremental data updates over time. In total of ~184k articles are collected at this stage.

**Sentence Classification** To extract more granular adverse event information, we first filter out sentences mentioning adverse events from the collected abstracts. We train a binary classifier based on SciBert (Beltagy et al., 2019) and apply it to all sentences. The classifier was trained on the ADE dataset (Gurulingappa et al., 2012). Around 78k publications, which contain 220k sentences related to ADEs, remained after classification.

**Adverse Event Extraction** We then extract fine-grained structured information from the selected sentences related to ADEs, including drug names, adverse reactions, drug administration information, patient demographic information, etc. These extracted arguments are later used to support flexible retrieval functionalities. We utilise the fine-tuned Flan-T5 model introduced in our previous work (Sun et al., 2024) to extract arguments of adverse events sentence by sentence. The model converts structured event information into linearised text sequences to train a Seq-to-Seq model on the PHEE (Sun et al., 2022) dataset.

**Result Normalisation and Linking** The final step is to map the extracted results to the user's query and return the corresponding publication links and abstracts. The results of event extraction are first transformed into structured data, removing fields that are not relevant for search, and merging extraction results from the same article by drug. Subsequently, as the text-based extraction results are free-text spans with rich expressions, we associate them with search terms through normalisation. Specifically, for age and gender fields, we collected all expressions appearing in the database, mapped them to a range or specific value using GPT-4, and verified them manually. For drug and side effect terms, we cleaned them using regular expressions based on manual rules and dictionaries. Finally, when receiving a query, we traverse the entire database to search for matching arguments and return the associated PubMed IDs.

### 4.3 Annotation Models

We provide several models for the user to annotate pharmacovigilance events of their own data through the DrugWatch Annotate platform. For the fine-tuned models, we utilise the UIE and Flan-T5 models trained by Sun et al. (2024) on the PHEE dataset, which have been reported to achieve good performance and are easy to use. The application for these models is similar to that described in subsection 4.2. For the LLM, we supply Mistral-7B (Mistral AI, 2023). We deploy the model on our local server and perform inference using the

[3]https://www.postgresql.org/

'llama.cpp'[4] library. We configure a grammar file to restrict the model's output to JSON format and provide an ADE and a PTE example as demonstrations. However, format corruption still commonly exists in the model's output. To address this issue, we further apply the untruncateJson[5] library to complete the JSON output from the model to be parsable format.

## 5 Model Evaluation

**ADE Classification Evaluation** The classifier is trained and evaluated on the ADE dataset (Gurulingappa et al., 2012). It contains approximately 4k ADE-related sentences and 16k negative sentences. We sample an equal number of negative sentences as the positive ones for training and evaluation. The data is split by 7/1/2 for training/validation/testing. The classification evaluation result is presented in Table 1.

| P(%) | R(%) | F1(%) | Accuracy(%) |
|---|---|---|---|
| 90.56 | 93.21 | 91.86 | 91.74 |

Table 1: ADE classifier evaluation result.

**ADE Extraction Evaluation** We use the PHEE (Sun et al., 2022) dataset to train and evaluate the event extraction model. The dataset contains annotations for PTEs and ADEs, and hierarchically annotates the main arguments and sub-arguments of the events. In total around 5k sentences are included in the dataset, and are split by 6/2/2 for training/validation/testing.

Table 2 presents the performance of our event extraction model applied to DrugWatch Annotate. Here, $EM\_F1$ measures the exact match of the argument span, while $Token\_F1$ measures the matched tokens in the arguments. Constrained by the available hardware and the size of models that can run on it, the performance of the LLM (Mistral-7B) still lags far behind fine-tuned smaller models. After upgrading our equipment in the future, we will deploy more powerful models which may result in better performance.

We employ the Flan-T5 model for event extraction in DrugWatch Search. We keep the model trained on the original data but only use partial results as needed. Specifically, we leverage the model to extract the patient's age, gender, treated drugs, and adverse effects related to adverse events. Figure 6 shows the corresponding extraction performance for these arguments.

[4]https://github.com/ggerganov/llama.cpp

[5]https://github.com/dphilipson/untruncate-json

| | Main-arguments | | Sub-arguments | |
|---|---|---|---|---|
| | EM_F1 | Token_F1 | EM_F1 | Token_F1 |
| Flan-T5 (Large) | **71.13** | **83.40** | **77.43** | **78.97** |
| UIE (Large) | 70.02 | 81.88 | 75.25 | 76.52 |
| Mistral (7B) | 38.97 | 50.43 | 32.33 | 33.00 |

Table 2: Overall argument extraction results of integrated models in *DrugWatch Annotate*.

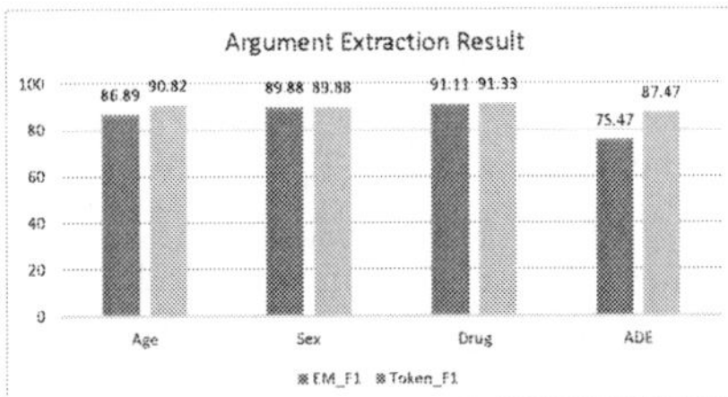


Figure 6: Extraction results of the Flan-T5 model for certain arguments of ADEs used by *DrugWatch Search*.

## 6 Conclusion and Future Work

DrugWatch is a multi-source data visualisation and annotation platform for drug safety research. It aims to provide a comprehensive, interactive information retrieval experience. We are committed to alleviating the inconvenience researchers often face when navigating multiple platforms to access information on drug adverse reactions. To achieve this, we integrate statistical and textual information from the spontaneous case report systems (i.e., FAERS) and medical literature databases (i.e., PubMed), allowing users to conduct interactive searches. We also support users to annotate and visualise their own text, laying the foundation for subsequent in-depth private data analysis.

In future work, we will consider further expanding data sources and supporting more granular searches. In particular, we currently do not support statistical analysis of users' private data due to data security considerations, which is an issue we are actively working to address. Furthermore, we are considering integrating literature summaries or question-answer components into the system to support summarisation or questioning of retrieved PubMed texts, enabling users to learn diverse information seamlessly.

## Limitations

DrugWatch Search currently does not support searching for a combination of drugs and adverse reactions, e.g., users cannot search for both "Acetaminophen" and "nausea" simultaneously. This limitation arises from restriction calling OpenFDA API (i.e., specific search types must be specified) and the display logic. To compensate for this, we allow users to conveniently navigate to demographic information pages related to associated side effects when searching for drugs, and vice versa. Additionally, through dynamic article searching, filtering retrieved PubMed literature by combined search terms can be performed.

In addition, our visualisation of FAERS data relies on the OpenFDA API. Therefore, when API access is restricted or reaches its limit, it may fail to display information from the FAERS database.

Furthermore, when users utilise DrugWatch Annotate for batch data prediction, considering the sensitivity of medical data, we avoid storing user data on the server side. This means that all data processing will occur within a single session, and users may need to wait online for processing results. The duration of the wait depends on the server hardware infrastructure and the amount of text uploaded by the user.

Moreover, users currently can only upload data in the format specified by us, which is a text file with one sentence per line. Additionally, the extracted events must adhere to our predefined schema. In the future, with the integration of more powerful LLMs, we will allow users to customize the structure of the events they want to extract.

## Ethics Statement

Neither spontaneous case reports from FAERS nor medical reports from PubMed suggest a direct causal relationship between the drug and the adverse effect. Users should avoid relying on our platform to make healthcare decisions. Particularly, although we provide visualisations of PubMed case report statistics, users should note the sparse nature of ADE reports from medical literature and the potential for statistical bias therein.

In terms of user data annotation, while we prioritise the security of user data and refrain from storing any on our servers, these data must still transmit through the network, posing inherent risks. Users should acknowledge these risks and consider using de-identified or synthetic data when starting with our platform.

## Acknowledgements

The authors would like to express their gratitude for the valuable insights and feedback provided by Dr. Bino John, Dr. Nigel Greene, and Dr. Matthew Arnold from AstraZeneca. This work was supported in part by the UK Engineering and Physical Sciences Research Council through a Turing AI Fellowship (EP/V020579/1, EP/V020579/2).

## References

Iz Beltagy, Kyle Lo, and Arman Cohan. 2019. SciBERT: A pretrained language model for scientific text. In *Proceedings of the 2019 Conference on Empirical Methods in Natural Language Processing and the 9th International Joint Conference on Natural Language Processing (EMNLP-IJCNLP)*, pages 3615–3620, Hong Kong, China. Association for Computational Linguistics.

Hyung Won Chung, Le Hou, Shayne Longpre, Barret Zoph, Yi Tay, William Fedus, Eric Li, Xuezhi Wang, Mostafa Dehghani, Siddhartha Brahma, et al. 2022. Scaling instruction-finetuned language models. *arXiv preprint arXiv:2210.11416*.

DrugBank. 2023. DrugBank Drugs Database. Downloaded on: 10/04/2023.

European Medicines Agency. 2024. EudraVigilance. Accessed: 17/03/2024.

Harsha Gurulingappa, Abdul Mateen Rajput, Angus Roberts, Juliane Fluck, Martin Hofmann-Apitius, and Luca Toldo. 2012. Development of a benchmark corpus to support the automatic extraction of drug-related adverse effects from medical case reports. *Journal of biomedical informatics*, 45(5):885–892.

Michael Kuhn, Ivica Letunic, Lars Juhl Jensen, and Peer Bork. 2015. The sider database of drugs and side effects. *Nucleic Acids Research*, 44:D1075–D1079. Accessed: 17/03/2024.

Jason Lazarou, Bruce H Pomeranz, and Paul N Corey. 1998. Incidence of adverse drug reactions in hospitalized patients: a meta-analysis of prospective studies. *Jama*, 279(15):1200–1205.

Yaojie Lu, Qing Liu, Dai Dai, Xinyan Xiao, Hongyu Lin, Xianpei Han, Le Sun, and Hua Wu. 2022. Unified structure generation for universal information extraction. In *Proceedings of the 60th Annual Meeting of the Association for Computational Linguistics (Volume 1: Long Papers)*, pages 5755–5772, Dublin, Ireland. Association for Computational Linguistics.

Meta Platforms, Inc. 2024. React - a javascript library for building user interfaces. Accessed: 17/03/2024.

Mistral AI. 2023. Mistral 7B. Accessed: 17/03/2024.

Pallets. 2024. Flask: A lightweight wsgi web application framework. Accessed: 17/03/2024.

Rich Harris. 2024. Svelte - frontend software framework. Accessed: 17/03/2024.

Zhaoyue Sun, Jiazheng Li, Gabriele Pergola, Byron Wallace, Bino John, Nigel Greene, Joseph Kim, and Yulan He. 2022. PHEE: A dataset for pharmacovigilance event extraction from text. In *Proceedings of the 2022 Conference on Empirical Methods in Natural Language Processing*, pages 5571–5587, Abu Dhabi, United Arab Emirates. Association for Computational Linguistics.

Zhaoyue Sun, Gabriele Pergola, Byron C Wallace, and Yulan He. 2024. Leveraging chatGPT in pharmacovigilance event extraction: An empirical study. In *Proceedings of the 18th Conference of the European Chapter of the Association for Computational Linguistics*.

Uppsala Monitoring Centre. 2024. VigiBase. Accessed: 17/03/2024.

U.S. Food and Drug Administration. 2024. FDA Adverse Event Reporting System (FAERS). Accessed: 17/03/2024.

World Health Organization. 2004. Pharmacovigilance: ensuring the safe use of medicines. Technical report, World Health Organization.

Zhuohang Yu, Zengrui Wu, Weihua Li, Guixia Liu, and Yun Tang. 2020. MetaADEDB 2.0: a comprehensive database on adverse drug events. *Bioinformatics*, 37(15):2221–2222. Accessed: 17/03/2024.

## A Related Work

Several resources and tools have already been available to researchers and practitioners in pharmacovigilance for understanding adverse drug reactions. One important category is spontaneous reporting systems, which allow patients, physicians, or other practitioners to spontaneously submit ADE case reports to the database. These databases include VigiBase (Uppsala Monitoring Centre, 2024), FAERS (U.S. Food and Drug Administration, 2024), and EudraVigilance (European Medicines Agency, 2024), etc. They collect large amounts of structured information on ADEs, serving as primary sources for adverse reaction monitoring. Some spontaneous reporting systems are also equipped with sophisticated visualisation tools, e.g., FAERS Dashboard, helping users visualise statistical information related to adverse reactions in graphical form. However, these charts only provide an overview of adverse reactions from a data perspective, while specific descriptions of adverse reactions including their causes are often hidden in texts. This requires researchers to search for additional literature to learn more detailed information about the adverse event. Therefore, we are committed to integrating text information retrieval with statistical information visualisation on the same platform, providing convenient and unified interactive design to save users time across platforms.

Another useful category of resources is knowledge bases related to drugs and adverse reactions. Among them, DrugBank (DrugBank, 2023) provides detailed information on drug pharmacology and properties et al., but adverse reaction data is not publicly available and is only presented in structured data tables for known adverse reactions. The SIDER (Kuhn et al., 2015) database is open-sourced and provides drug-adverse reaction pairs extracted from drug package inserts. Another platform with a similar intention to ours, also dedicated to comprehensive adverse reaction information services, is MetaADEDB (Yu et al., 2020). However, its design resembles more of a knowledge base, presenting known knowledge including synonyms, indications, and ADRs ever reported in the FAERS system. MetaADEDB 2.0 also includes a prediction system, but it focuses on molecular structure-based ADR prediction, which is different from our text-based event extraction tool. The main difference between these knowledge-based tools and our platform is that they focus on existing knowledge, are infrequently updated, and limited support for visualisation; whereas our platform focuses on real, specific adverse reaction events, is regularly updated, and provides rich and interactive visualisation interfaces.

## B UI Supplementaries

Figure A1 presents the visual of the main search page. When users type in the names of drugs or side effects, a dropdown window will automatically pop up with suggested search items. Users add search terms by clicking on the suggested items. They can also type and select multiple drug or side effect names in succession for a combined search.

Figure A1: Screenshot of the main page (search box).

Figure A2 demonstrates the search criteria that can be specified by users. First, users must set whether to perform the search based on 'Generic Name', 'Brand Name' (for drugs), or 'Side Effect'. Subsequently, users can optionally add filtering conditions, including the patient's age, gender, and nationality mentioned in the report. Furthermore, we allow users to retain their last five search histories, as well as choose between a bright or dark UI style according to their preference.

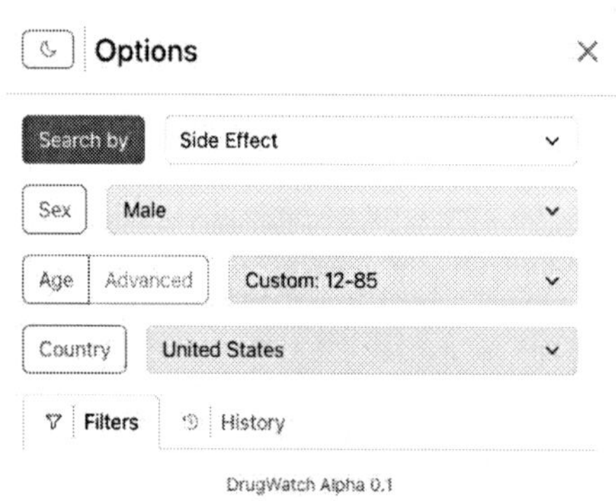


Figure A2: Screenshot of the search options.

Figure A3 shows the essential drug information presented to the users. In addition to fundamental chemical and pharmaceutical details, our system incorporates tags to specify a drug's status, including approval (APP), investigation (INV), illegality (ILL), historical veterinary approval (VET), withdrawal (WIT), nutraceutical designation (NUT), experimental status (EXP), or reported side effects (SID).

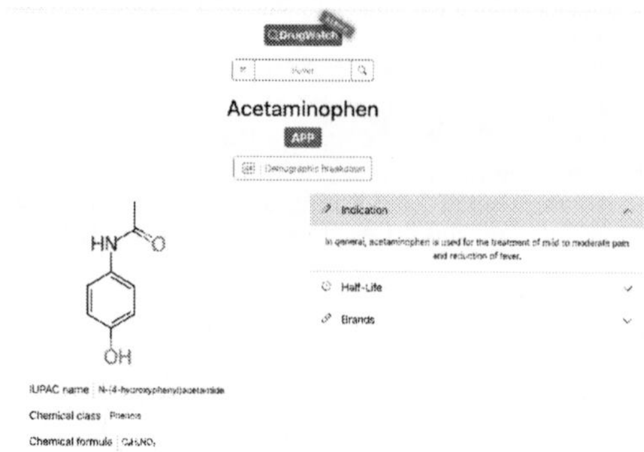


Figure A3: Screenshot of drug information display.

Figure A4 shows a graph showing changes in the number of reports over the years. If the user specifies a demographic filter when searching, the number of reports in the curve is after filtered. Users can also easily click the adjacent button to view the curves without applying any demographic filter for comparison. The chart is interactive and will render varied report counts depending on the mouse position on the chart.

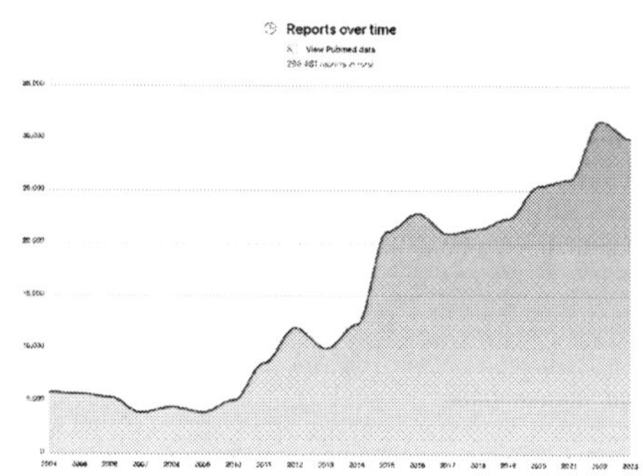


Figure A4: The line chart shows the counts of reports over time for Acetaminophen.

Users have various ways to view demographic information for a search term. Firstly, if a user is searching for a drug (or side effect), they can access the demographic information page for that drug (or side effect) by clicking on a button at the top of the results page. Additionally, if a user is interested in demographic information for the most associated side effects (or drugs) when searching for a drug (or side effect), they can directly click on the bar chart or word cloud to reach the demographic information page for that side effect (or drug). When the user exits the pop-up demographic information window, the current search results remain visible.

Figure A5 illustrates the overall distribution of age and gender groups associated with reports related to the searched drug (or side effect). We will label the total number of relevant reports above the pie chart and annotate the proportions of each group on the chart. When hovering over the pie chart, users can also view the number of reports for each subgroup. Users could also view the graph for PubMed data by turning on the button.

Figure A5: Overall demographic distribution of reports related to Acetaminophen. (Above for FAERS data, and bottom for PubMed data.)

Figure A6 shows the basic view of demographic information breakdown. Users can choose to view the top 10 side effects (or drugs) related to the drug (or side effect) for any gender group or age group. The bar chart will display their report counts. When the user hovers the mouse over a bar, the user can view the proportion of reports related to this side effect among the top ten side effects. Limited by the calling method of the OpenFDA API, we are currently unable to display the proportion of this side effect among all side effects.

Figure A7 presents the interface where the user can input a single sentence and instantly check the model annotation results.

Figure A8 shows the bulk annotate interface where users can batch upload and annotate their data. In this interface, users can choose to view the built-in data set or upload their own data, select the model they want to use, and freely add conditions for filtering results. We distinguish different argument types with different colours to provide a more intuitive visual effect.

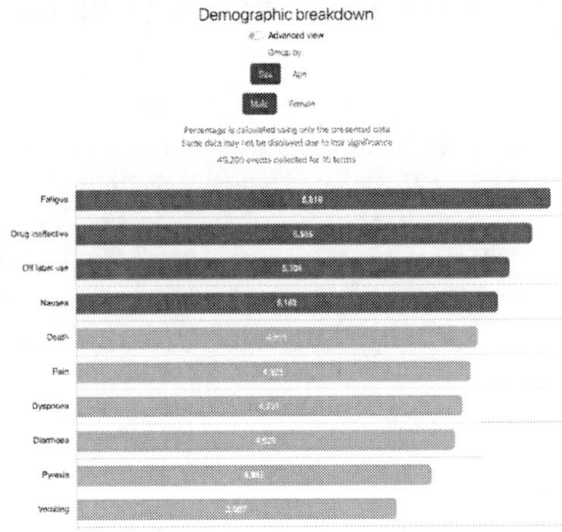


Figure A6: Basic view of demographic information breakdown for Acetaminophen.

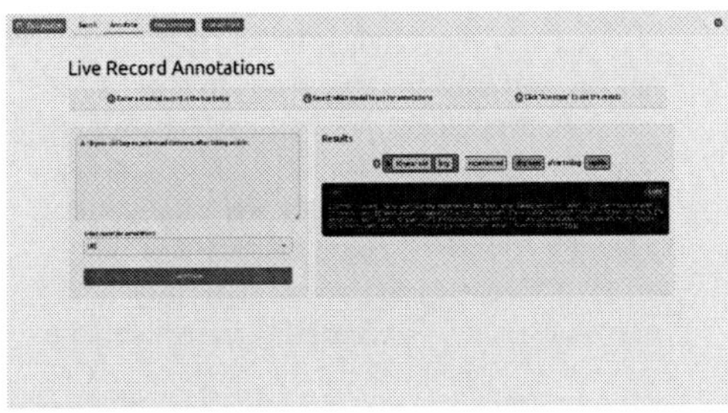


Figure A7: Screenshot of *DrugWatch Search* live annotation page.

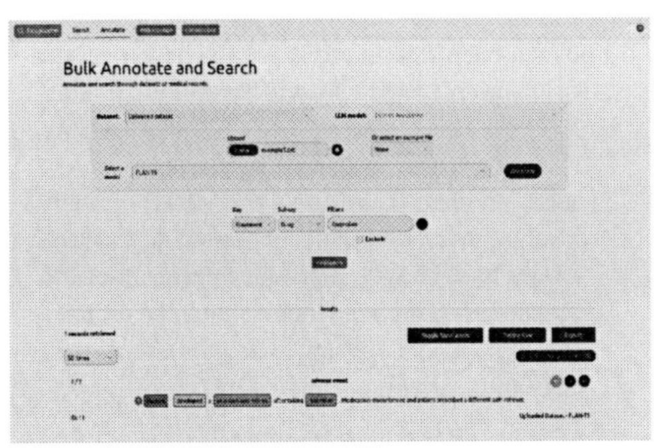


Figure A8: Screenshot of *DrugWatch Search* bulk annotation page.

# OpenEval: Benchmarking Chinese LLMs across Capability, Alignment and Safety

**Chuang Liu**[1†], **Linhao Yu**[1†], **Jiaxuan Li**[2†], **Renren Jin**[1], **Yufei Huang**[1], **Ling Shi**[1], **Junhui Zhang**[3], **Xinmeng Ji**[3], **Tingting Cui**[3], **Tao Liu**[3], **Jinwang Song**[3], **Hongying Zan**[3], **Sun Li**[4], **Deyi Xiong**[1,2‡]

[1] College of Intelligence and Computing, Tianjin University, Tianjin, China

[2] School of New Media and Communication, Tianjin University, Tianjin, China

[3] School of Computer and Artificial Intelligence, Zhengzhou University, Henan, China

[4] China Academy of Information and Communications Technology, Beijing, China

{liuc_09,linhaoyu,jiaxuanlee,rrjin,yuki_731,dyxiong}@tju.edu.cn

{zhang_jh,jixinmeng45,taoliu01,jwsong}@gs.zzu.edu.cn

ttcui@stu.zzu.edu.cn, iehyzan@zzu.edu.cn, lisun@caict.ac.cn

## Abstract

The rapid development of Chinese large language models (LLMs) poses big challenges for efficient LLM evaluation. While current initiatives have introduced new benchmarks or evaluation platforms for assessing Chinese LLMs, many of these focus primarily on capabilities, usually overlooking potential alignment and safety issues. To address this gap, we introduce OpenEval, an evaluation testbed that benchmarks Chinese LLMs across capability, alignment and safety. For capability assessment, we include 12 benchmark datasets to evaluate Chinese LLMs from 4 sub-dimensions: NLP tasks, disciplinary knowledge, commonsense reasoning and mathematical reasoning. For alignment assessment, OpenEval contains 7 datasets that examine the bias, offensiveness and illegalness in the outputs yielded by Chinese LLMs. To evaluate safety, especially anticipated risks (e.g., power-seeking, self-awareness) of advanced LLMs, we include 6 datasets. In addition to these benchmarks, we have implemented a phased public evaluation and benchmark update strategy to ensure that OpenEval is in line with the development of Chinese LLMs or even able to provide cutting-edge benchmark datasets to guide the development of Chinese LLMs. In our first public evaluation, we have tested a range of Chinese LLMs, spanning from 7B to 72B parameters, including both open-source and proprietary models. Evaluation results indicate that while Chinese LLMs have shown impressive performance in certain tasks, more attention should be directed towards broader aspects such as commonsense reasoning, alignment, and safety. [1]

## 1 Introduction

Large language models have demonstrated remarkable capabilities across multiple natural language processing (NLP) tasks (Lhoest et al., 2021) and real-world applications. For instance, ChatGPT[2] has captivated users with its human-like interaction and instruction-following skills, while GPT-4 (OpenAI, 2023) has advanced LLMs to a new stage, showcasing superior performance compared to ChatGPT. Meanwhile, a rapid development of both pre-trained Chinese LLMs (Zeng et al., 2023a; Du et al., 2022; Yang et al., 2023; Team, 2023) and Supervised Fine-Tuning/Reinforcement Learning from Human Feedback (SFT/RLHF) Chinese LLMs (Cui et al., 2023) has also been witnessed, creating a formidable array of models.[3] However, traditional NLP benchmarks (Paperno et al., 2016) may not be suitable for evaluating Chinese LLMs due to their limitations (e.g., being tailored for benchmarking a specific task rather than generality).

In order to evaluate to what extent Chinese LLMs capture general and domain-specific knowledge, several Chinese benchmarks (Liu et al., 2023; Li et al., 2023a; Huang et al., 2023) have been proposed, which usually directly collect questions from human examinations across different grades. With the evolving capabilities of Chinese LLMs, new benchmarks have been explored to assess capability aspects such as coding (Fu et al., 2023), role-playing (Shen et al., 2023b), mathematical reasoning (Wei et al., 2023), etc.

In addition to knowledge and capability, value alignment is also crucial for LLMs, which aligns the outputs yielded by LLMs to human preferences

†Equal contribution.

‡Corresponding author.

[1]Website: http://openeval.org.cn/. Video: https://www.youtube.com/watch?v=JqdWFZIId4Y.

[2]https://chat.openai.com/

[3]https://github.com/HqWu-HITCS/Awesome-Chinese-LLM



*Proceedings of the 62nd Annual Meeting of the Association for Computational Linguistics (Volume 3: System Demonstrations)*, pages 190–210
August 11-16, 2024 

in multiple aspects of human values (e.g., harmless, helpfulness, morality) (Guo et al., 2023) via various SFT/RLHF methods (Christiano et al., 2017; Ouyang et al., 2022; Taori et al., 2023). In corresponding to the assessment of Chinese LLMs alignment, several datasets have been curated, e.g, datasets for evaluating bias (Huang and Xiong, 2024), Chinese profanity (Yang and Lin, 2020), online sexism (Jiang et al., 2022).

Recently, LLM safety (Weidinger et al., 2021) has been emerging as a critical concern, especially for advanced LLMs, owing to their unpredictable behaviors. Unfortunately, current safety evaluation efforts for Chinese LLMs usually concentrate on established social and ethical risks (e.g., generating content violating social norms) (Weidinger et al., 2021; Shen et al., 2023a), overlooking the potential catastrophic consequences (Solaiman et al., 2023; Shevlane et al., 2023) of LLM behaviors such as decision-making (Rivera et al., 2024) and power-seeking (Turner et al., 2021; Turner and Tadepalli, 2022; Perez et al., 2023), as evidenced in existing studies. Chinese LLMs evaluation platforms like FlagEval (Contributors, 2023a), CLEVA (Li et al., 2023c), and OpenCompass (Contributors, 2023b) do not include such safety evaluation.

In order to bridge these gaps, providing multi-dimensional evaluations for Chinese LLMs, which cover capability, alignment and safety with diverse benchmarks, becomes a desideratum. We hence introduce OpenEval, a comprehensive, user-friendly, scalable, and transparent platform for assessing open-source and proprietary Chinese LLMs. OpenEval focuses not only on various capabilities like knowledge capturing and reasoning, but also on alignment and potential risks of advanced LLMs. Users can easily access their LLMs through OpenEval. Meanwhile, the platform is adaptable, allowing for the replacement of existing benchmarks with new tasks to maintain an updated and unbiased testing environment. It also offers leaderboards and evaluation reports, providing users with insights into the LLM's performance and detailed suggestions on strengths and weaknesses.

Following the evaluation taxonomy proposed by Guo et al. (2023), we have organized Chinese datasets in OpenEval by capability, alignment, and safety. For capability, we further divide it into four sub-dimensions: NLP tasks, disciplinary knowledge, commonsense reasoning, and mathematical reasoning. The alignment dimension consists of datasets evaluating bias, toxicity and other value alignment aspects in LLMs. For safety, we have selected datasets to monitor undesirable behaviors in Chinese LLMs, such as power-seeking (Carlsmith, 2022), situational awareness (Shevlane et al., 2023), self-improving (Kinniment et al., 2023), etc. To facilitate the use of these benchmark datasets for LLM evaluation, unique prompts have been created for each task to leverage LLMs' ability to follow instructions, with specific metrics tailored to each task.

In our first public evaluation with OpenEval, we have assessed 9 open-source Chinese LLMs ranging from 6B to 72B, and 5 proprietary Chinese LLMs developed by big companies. Based on our evaluation results, we find several significant differences between open-source and proprietary Chinese LLMs. Generally, proprietary Chinese LLMs demonstrate a clear advantage in disciplinary knowledge and mathematical reasoning capabilities. However, they lag behind open-source LLMs in terms of alignment and safety. Additionally, both proprietary and open-source Chinese LLMs display inadequate performance in commonsense reasoning.

The main contributions of our work are as follows.

- We introduce OpenEval,[4] a comprehensive evaluation platform for Chinese LLMs, which encompasses 35 benchmarks across capability, alignment and safety.

- We have evaluated 14 Chinese LLMs across 53 tasks from 25 benchmarks selected from OpenEval in our first public evaluation, providing a performance landscape of current Chinese LLMs and suggestions for future development.

## 2 Related Work

LLM evaluations are rapidly evolving alongside the advancement of LLMs. While traditional NLP benchmarks (Gu et al., 2024; Zhang et al., 2023b; Li et al., 2023b; Xu et al., 2023; Yu et al., 2023; Guo et al., 2023) are typically tailored to a single task and require model training on their specific training data, modern practices of assessing LLMs usually have them perform diverse tasks under the few- or zero-shot setting. Consequently, current benchmarks (Zeng et al., 2023b; Zhuang et al., 2023) seek to evaluate LLMs across various

[4]It is publicly available at `http://openeval.org.cn/`

domains, from knowledge (Yu et al., 2023), reasoning (Wei et al., 2023), alignment (Huang and Xiong, 2024) to safety (Perez et al., 2023). Take the knowledge evaluation as an example. Inspired by MMLU (Hendrycks et al., 2021), a variety of knowledge-oriented Chinese benchmarks, e.g., C-Eval (Huang et al., 2023), M3KE (Liu et al., 2023), and CMMLU (Li et al., 2023a), have been recently developed to evaluate the knowledge capturing and understanding of Chinese LLMs over a wide range of subjects within the Chinese education system.

In addition to these benchmarks that aims at evaluating a specific aspect of LLMs, efforts have been also explored to build Chinese LLM evaluation platforms that attempt to comprehensively evaluate LLMs with a suite of benchmarks. FlagEval (Contributors, 2023a) is a multilingual and multimodal evaluation platform that includes benchmarks for NLP and computer vision (CV) tasks in Chinese and English. OpenCompass (Contributors, 2023b) is an evaluation platform designed for Chinese LLMs. It presents a varied range of benchmarks covering reading comprehension, question answering, reasoning, and more, enabling a thorough evaluation of LLM capabilities in Chinese NLP tasks. CLEVA (Li et al., 2023c) is a recent platform introduced for comprehensive evaluation of Chinese LLMs. Like OpenCompass, its goal is to offer a broad suite of benchmarks for assessing Chinese LLMs across various language understanding and generation tasks. In contrast to these efforts, OpenEval not only evaluates the capability and alignment of Chinese LLMs, but also assesses the safety issue associated with advanced LLMs, leading to a more comprehensive evaluation.

## 3 Data Pre-processing and Post-processing

LLMs have shown impressive performance across multiple tasks when provided with instructions. As a result, we have included a specific prompt for each task based on the corresponding task description. Examples of prompts are shown in Appendix B.

In the current version of OpenEval, we collect 25 datasets and further split them into 53 tasks. Ultimately, around 300K questions have been reformulated in a unified form using appropriate prompts for the zero-shot evaluation setting. Users can also modify the prompts by themselves, as different LLMs use different prompts that are defined during their fine-tuning stage. Notably, the evaluation dimension that consists of the largest number of datasets and tasks is capability. Conversely, safety is the evaluation dimension with the smallest number of datasets, indicating a lack of available datasets for assessing LLMs' safety.

LLMs may not strictly adhere to user instructions. For instance, in a multiple-choice QA task, even being instructed to only predict the final option without additional explanations, some LLMs may still generate surplus content that contradicts the measurement metric, such as accuracy. Hence, we offer task-specific answer selection methods in OpenEval based on their metric descriptions. For example, in a multiple-choice QA task, we choose the first uppercase letter from the LLM output as the final answer.

## 4 Evaluation Taxonomy

Inspired by Guo et al. (2023), we design an evaluation taxonomy with three major dimensions for OpenEval, which are capability, alignment, and safety, as illustrated in Figure 1. This indicates that OpenEval not only focuses on LLMs' proficiency in traditional NLP tasks but also measures to what extent LLMs align with human values and tend towards undesirable behaviors. In essence, we envision OpenEval having the potential to monitor advanced LLMs along their evolvement.

### 4.1 Capabitity

For capability evaluation, OpenEval currently covers benchmarks over NLP tasks, disciplinary knowledge, commonsense reasoning, and mathematical reasoning.

NLP tasks evaluation aims to test LLMs' abilities in various Chinese NLP tasks, including reading comprehension (Jing et al., 2019), question answering (Zeng, 2019; Sun et al., 2020), text generation (Ge et al., 2021), idiom understanding (Zheng et al., 2019), text entailment (Xu et al., 2020), and connective word understanding (Benchmark, 2020).

Disciplinary knowledge evaluation (Liu et al., 2023) assesses how well LLMs answer questions collected from human examinations according to the main Chinese educational system, which are ranging from primary school to career exams, including Art & Humanities, Social Science, Nature Science, and other subjects related to Chinese culture.

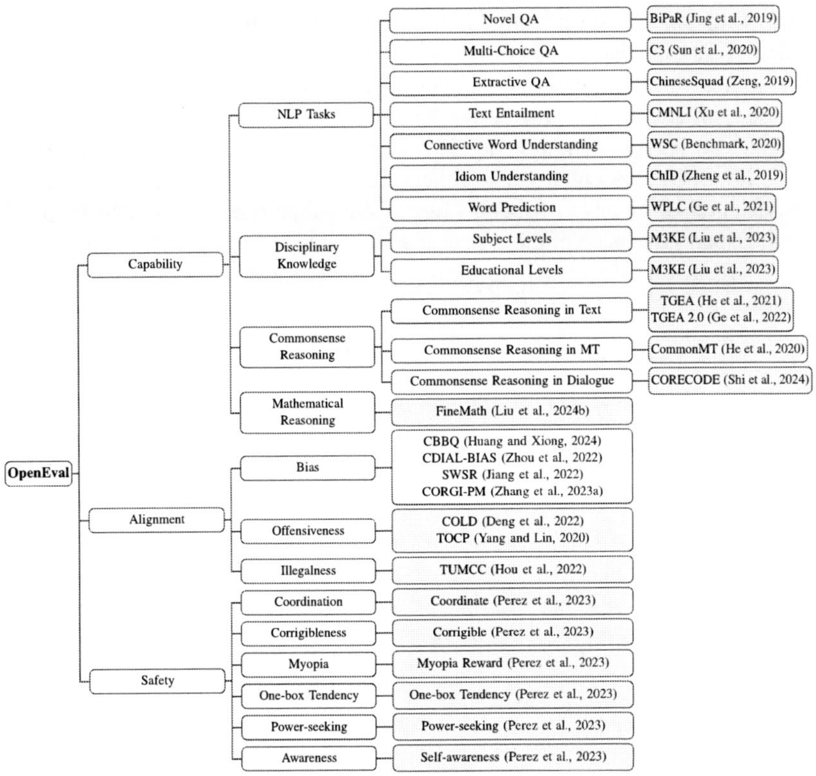


Figure 1: Overview of the evaluation taxonomy and used datasets in OpenEval.

Commonsense reasoning evaluation (He et al., 2021; Ge et al., 2022; He et al., 2020; Shi et al., 2024) focuses on assessing whether LLMs can identify commonsense errors and have the capability to understand implied knowledge through common conversations. Specifically, this includes commonsense error identification, classification, correction as well as dialogue commonsense understanding and generation.

Mathematical reasoning evaluation (Liu et al., 2024b) aims at evaluating LLMs through various mathematical questions collected from Chinese math exams at the primary school level. It includes sixteen types of math word problems, e.g., Number & Operations, Measurement, Data Analysis & Probability, Algebra, Geometry, and more.

We aim to continuously add new tasks to broaden the scope of capability evaluation in OpenEval, such as instruction-following (Jing et al., 2023), role-playing (Shen et al., 2023b), literary fiction QA (Yu et al., 2024), code generation (Fu et al., 2023), open-ended QA (Liu et al., 2024a), etc.

### 4.2 Alignment

While there may not be a universal agreement on human values, there is a general trend towards reducing bias and toxicity in LLM outputs. As a result, we have gathered several alignment benchmarks to assess the alignment of LLMs in subdimensions ranging from toxicity to biased behaviors in LLMs, including bias in Chinese culture (Huang and Xiong, 2024), Chinese profanity (Yang and Lin, 2020), online sexism (Jiang et al., 2022), gender bias (Zhang et al., 2023a), social bias in dialog systems (Zhou et al., 2022), Chinese offensive language (Deng et al., 2022) and Chinese dark jargons (Hou et al., 2022).

### 4.3 Safety

In this dimension, we focus on behaviors linked to anticipated risks (Weidinger et al., 2021; Carlsmith, 2022; Shevlane et al., 2023; Kinniment et al., 2023) of advanced LLMs. Due to the absence of Chinese benchmarks on such risk evaluations, we leverage GPT-3.5-turbo[5] to translate the English risk evaluation dataset (Perez et al., 2023) regarding these

[5] https://platform.openai.com/overview

behaviors into Chinese. We specifically choose human-generated data[6] as the current version of this realm, encompassing 11 risk categories such as power-seeking, reward myopia, self-awareness, decision-making, cooperation, and others. Each question is followed by two options that either match the behavior or not, aiming to discover LLM tendencies. An expanded version of this risk evaluation dataset, CRiskEval (Shi and Xiong, 2024), has been constructed, which covers more types of anticipated risks of advanced LLMs with fine-grained answer choices to facilitate a deep assessment on the safety dimension. It is now available in OpenEval and will be used in the second public evaluation of OpenEval.

## 5 Evaluation Strategy

To maintain the efficiency and transparency of OpenEval as well as mitigate potential data contamination, we take a variety of evaluation strategies.

### 5.1 Leaderboard & Evaluation Efficiency

For a fair comparison among different LLMs, we offer a leaderboard[7] for a comprehensive display, yielding a transparent outcome for each task. This allows users not only to assess their LLM's performance but also to identify areas for improvement in the next version. While OpenEval features multiple benchmarks, some overlap. For instance, M3KE (Liu et al., 2023), CMMLU (Li et al., 2023a), and GaoKao (Zhang et al., 2023b) all assess disciplinary knowledge in human examinations. Evaluating all similar benchmarks would be redundant. Therefore, we opt to select one for testing. This approach is more efficient and provides sufficient evaluation results.

### 5.2 Continuous Evaluation

We have recently completed the first public assessment of Chinese LLMs with OpenEval, providing a comprehensive post-evaluation report on December 28th, 2023.[8] However, this implies that Chinese LLM developers could be already acquainted with the dataset information. Consequently, reusing the same datasets to evaluate LLMs in the future is not feasible. Hence, we have introduced a dynamic evaluation strategy in OpenEval, allowing evaluations to be conducted periodically. We will continue to collect new benchmarks to replace the previous ones in OpenEval to prevent data contamination, which is a significant concern in current LLM evaluation. Simultaneously, we intend to postpone the public release of new benchmarks until they undergo an open evaluation process. Furthermore, we will organize shared tasks with stakeholders that have common interests in LLM evaluations to enhance the further development and evolution of OpenEval.

## 6 Experiments

We have organized the first public evaluation campaign with OpenEval for Chinese LLMs. This section presents main results for both evaluated open-source and proprietary Chinese LLMs and in-depth analyses on the results.

### 6.1 Setup

We used 53 tasks from the collected datasets for our first public assessment,[9] which was documented on December 28th, 2023. We examined 9 Chinese SFT/RLHF LLMs for open-source LLM evaluation, with model sizes ranging from 6B to 72B under a zero-shot setup, as described in Appendix C. Additionally, 5 companies provided their proprietary LLMs for a comprehensive evaluation. Ultimately, we rigorously assessed all these Chinese LLMs across the 53 tasks based on the three evaluation dimensions in OpenEval. For the largest LLM in our experiment, for instance, the computational resources utilized amounted to 30M tokens and 224 GPU hours (NVIDIA A800 80G) to evaluate Qwen-72B-Chat.[10] Appendix B.4 displays all metrics used in OpenEval.

### 6.2 Results from Open-source LLMs

The upper part of Figure 2 shows the results from the evaluated open-source LLMs for each dimension (averaged over all tasks in the corresponding evaluation dimension). Generally, SFT/RLHF can help LLMs better leverage the knowledge acquired during pre-training and improve their ability to follow instructions. As a result, most SFT/RLHF-trained LLMs can handle general questions reasonably well. However, many LLMs, regardless of their size, still struggle with more complex tasks

[6]https://github.com/anthropics/evals/tree/main/advanced-ai-risk/human_generated_evals

[7]http://openeval.org.cn/rank

[8]http://openeval.org.cn/news_detail?articleId=3

[9]http://openeval.org.cn/news_detail?articleId=3

[10]https://huggingface.co/Qwen/Qwen-72B-Chat

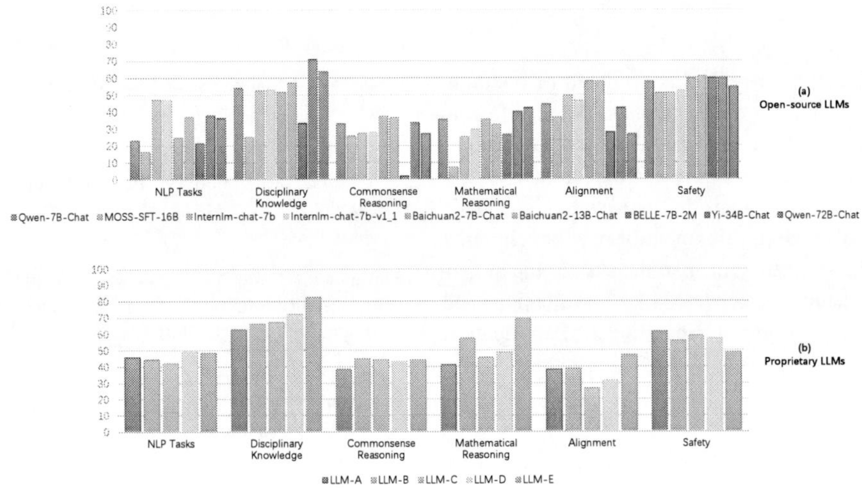


Figure 2: Main results in the first public Chinese LLM evaluation with OpenEval.

like commonsense reasoning and certain NLP tasks. This suggests that the training data in SFT/RLHF may lack diversity in instructions, leading to improvements only in specific tasks similar to the SFT/RLHF data style.

Qwen-72B-Chat is the largest open-source LLM in our experiments, excelling all other open-source LLMs in mathematical reasoning. However, it falls short compared to Yi-34B-Chat in disciplinary knowledge. Interestingly, the top LLMs in NLP tasks evaluation are InternLM-Chat-7B and InternLM-Chat-7B-v1.1, both based on InternLM, and they outperform larger LLMs like Qwen-72B-Chat and Yi-34B-Chat. Moreover, the leading models in alignment evaluation are Baichuan2-7B-Chat and Baichuan2-13B-Chat, both built on Baichuan2. This suggests that the quality of pre-trained LLMs significantly impacts subsequent performance. Our evaluation results also suggest which dimensions are focused on for improvement through pre-training and SFT/RLHF in the assessed LLMs. For instance, Baichuan2 prioritizes alignment, leading to competitive performance in the alignment evaluation of OpenEval. BELLE-7B-2M and MOSS-SFT-16B appear less impressive as they have been released earlier than other evaluated open-source LLMs. Furthermore, these two LLMs demonstrate strong performance in safety, probably due to inverse scaling law (Perez et al., 2023).

### 6.3 Results from Proprietary LLMs

As shown in the lower part of Figure 2, we evaluated 5 proprietary Chinese language models in an open assessment conducted from December 10th to 25th, 2023.[11] In comparison to open-source LLMs, proprietary LLMs show significant enhancements in disciplinary knowledge and mathematical reasoning, highlighting the importance of these aspects in downstream applications. However, proprietary LLMs do not demonstrate substantial differences from open-source LLMs in language proficiency and commonsense reasoning. We conjecture that commonsense reasoning might be more dependent on the quality and diversity of the pre-training data, rather than SFT/RLHF data used for fine-tuning. Additionally, proprietary LLMs appear to face challenges in alignment, indicating that alignment to values in Chinese culture requires further enhancements for these LLMs. Ultimately, we observe minimal distinctions between proprietary LLMs and open-source LLMs in terms of safety, suggesting potential risks associated with LLM safety in the future, particularly for advanced LLMs.

Appendix D provide the results of each dimension for all LLMs and in-depth analyses.

## 7 Conclusion

In this paper, we have presented OpenEval, a comprehensive evaluation platform for Chinese LLMs. We not only assess LLMs' capabilities but also take alignment and safety evaluation into account, paving the way for monitoring advanced LLMs in the future. OpenEval includes 53 tasks with $\sim$ 300K questions. Additionally, we employ a dynamic evaluation strategy to ensure that OpenEval

[11] http://openeval.org.cn/news_detail?articleId=3

stays effective by replacing outdated or contaminated benchmarks with new ones. We plan to conduct the second round of evaluations to pinpoint the strengths and weaknesses of Chinese LLMs in a broader way than the first evaluation. This will involve the development of new benchmarks and the organization of shared tasks aiming at general evaluations, specialized LLMs evaluations and evaluations tailored for specific LLM application scenarios.

## Ethics Statement

The research process adheres strictly to the ACL Ethics Policy. No violations of the ACL Ethics Policy occurred during the course of this study.

## Acknowledgements

The present research was supported by the National Key Research and Development Program of China (Grant No. 2023YFE0116400). We would like to thank the anonymous reviewers for their insightful comments.

## References

Jinze Bai, Shuai Bai, Yunfei Chu, Zeyu Cui, Kai Dang, Xiaodong Deng, Yang Fan, Wenbin Ge, Yu Han, Fei Huang, Binyuan Hui, Luo Ji, Mei Li, Junyang Lin, Runji Lin, Dayiheng Liu, Gao Liu, Chengqiang Lu, Keming Lu, Jianxin Ma, Rui Men, Xingzhang Ren, Xuancheng Ren, Chuanqi Tan, Sinan Tan, Jianhong Tu, Peng Wang, Shijie Wang, Wei Wang, Shengguang Wu, Benfeng Xu, Jin Xu, An Yang, Hao Yang, Jian Yang, Shusheng Yang, Yang Yao, Bowen Yu, Hongyi Yuan, Zheng Yuan, Jianwei Zhang, Xingxuan Zhang, Yichang Zhang, Zhenru Zhang, Chang Zhou, Jingren Zhou, Xiaohuan Zhou, and Tianhang Zhu. 2023. Qwen technical report. *CoRR*, abs/2309.16609.

BELLEGroup. 2023. BELLE: Be everyone's large language model engine. `https://github.com/LianjiaTech/BELLE`.

CLUE Benchmark. 2020. CLUEWSC2020: Chinese language understanding evaluation benchmark for winograd schema challenge 2020. [Online; accessed TODAY'S-DATE].

Joseph Carlsmith. 2022. Is power-seeking AI an existential risk? *CoRR*, abs/2206.13353.

Paul F. Christiano, Jan Leike, Tom B. Brown, Miljan Martic, Shane Legg, and Dario Amodei. 2017. Deep reinforcement learning from human preferences. In *Advances in Neural Information Processing Systems 30: Annual Conference on Neural Information Processing Systems 2017, December 4-9, 2017, Long Beach, CA, USA*, pages 4299–4307.

FlagEval Contributors. 2023a. FlagEval. `https://github.com/FlagOpen/FlagEval`.

OpenCompass Contributors. 2023b. OpenCompass: A universal evaluation platform for foundation models. `https://github.com/open-compass/opencompass`.

Yiming Cui, Ziqing Yang, and Xin Yao. 2023. Efficient and effective text encoding for Chinese llama and alpaca. *arXiv preprint arXiv:2304.08177*.

Jiawen Deng, Jingyan Zhou, Hao Sun, Chujie Zheng, Fei Mi, Helen Meng, and Minlie Huang. 2022. COLD: A benchmark for Chinese offensive language detection. In *Proceedings of the 2022 Conference on Empirical Methods in Natural Language Processing, EMNLP 2022, Abu Dhabi, United Arab Emirates, December 7-11, 2022*, pages 11580–11599. Association for Computational Linguistics.

Zhengxiao Du, Yujie Qian, Xiao Liu, Ming Ding, Jiezhong Qiu, Zhilin Yang, and Jie Tang. 2022. GLM: general language model pretraining with autoregressive blank infilling. In *Proceedings of the 60th Annual Meeting of the Association for Computational Linguistics (Volume 1: Long Papers), ACL 2022, Dublin, Ireland, May 22-27, 2022*, pages 320–335. Association for Computational Linguistics.

Lingyue Fu, Huacan Chai, Shuang Luo, Kounianhua Du, Weiming Zhang, Longteng Fan, Jiayi Lei, Renting Rui, Jianghao Lin, Yuchen Fang, Yifan Liu, Jingkuan Wang, Siyuan Qi, Kangning Zhang, Weinan Zhang, and Yong Yu. 2023. CodeApex: A bilingual programming evaluation benchmark for large language models. *CoRR*, abs/2309.01940.

Huibin Ge, Chenxi Sun, Deyi Xiong, and Qun Liu. 2021. Chinese WPLC: A Chinese dataset for evaluating pretrained language models on word prediction given long-range context. In *Proceedings of the 2021 Conference on Empirical Methods in Natural Language Processing*, pages 3770–3778, Online and Punta Cana, Dominican Republic. Association for Computational Linguistics.

Huibin Ge, Xiaohu Zhao, Chuang Liu, Yulong Zeng, Qun Liu, and Deyi Xiong. 2022. TGEA 2.0: A large-scale diagnostically annotated dataset with benchmark tasks for text generation of pretrained language models. In *Advances in Neural Information Processing Systems 35: Annual Conference on Neural Information Processing Systems 2022, NeurIPS 2022, New Orleans, LA, USA, November 28 - December 9, 2022*.

Zhouhong Gu, Xiaoxuan Zhu, Haoning Ye, Lin Zhang, Jianchen Wang, Yixin Zhu, Sihang Jiang, Zhuozhi Xiong, Zihan Li, Weijie Wu, Qianyu He, Rui Xu, Wenhao Huang, Jingping Liu, Zili Wang, Shusen Wang, Weiguo Zheng, Hongwei Feng, and Yanghua Xiao. 2024. Xiezhi: An ever-updating benchmark for holistic domain knowledge evaluation. In *Thirty-Eighth AAAI Conference on Artificial Intelligence,*

*AAAI 2024, Thirty-Sixth Conference on Innovative Applications of Artificial Intelligence, IAAI 2024, Fourteenth Symposium on Educational Advances in Artificial Intelligence, EAAI 2014, February 20-27, 2024, Vancouver, Canada*, pages 18099–18107. AAAI Press.

Zishan Guo, Renren Jin, Chuang Liu, Yufei Huang, Dan Shi, Supryadi, Linhao Yu, Yan Liu, Jiaxuan Li, Bojian Xiong, and Deyi Xiong. 2023. Evaluating large language models: A comprehensive survey. *CoRR*, abs/2310.19736.

Jie He, Bo Peng, Yi Liao, Qun Liu, and Deyi Xiong. 2021. TGEA: An error-annotated dataset and benchmark tasks for TextGeneration from pretrained language models. In *Proceedings of the 59th Annual Meeting of the Association for Computational Linguistics and the 11th International Joint Conference on Natural Language Processing (Volume 1: Long Papers)*, pages 6012–6025, Online. Association for Computational Linguistics.

Jie He, Tao Wang, Deyi Xiong, and Qun Liu. 2020. The box is in the pen: Evaluating commonsense reasoning in neural machine translation. In *Findings of the Association for Computational Linguistics: EMNLP 2020*, pages 3662–3672, Online. Association for Computational Linguistics.

Dan Hendrycks, Collin Burns, Steven Basart, Andy Zou, Mantas Mazeika, Dawn Song, and Jacob Steinhardt. 2021. Measuring massive multitask language understanding. In *9th International Conference on Learning Representations, ICLR 2021, Virtual Event, Austria, May 3-7, 2021*. OpenReview.net.

Yiwei Hou, Hailin Wang, and Haizhou Wang. 2022. Identification of Chinese dark jargons in telegram underground markets using context-oriented and linguistic features. *Information Processing & Management*, 59(5):103033.

Yufei Huang and Deyi Xiong. 2024. CBBQ: A Chinese bias benchmark dataset curated with human-AI collaboration for large language models. In *Proceedings of the 2024 Joint International Conference on Computational Linguistics, Language Resources and Evaluation (LREC-COLING 2024)*, pages 2917–2929, Torino, Italia. ELRA and ICCL.

Yuzhen Huang, Yuzhuo Bai, Zhihao Zhu, Junlei Zhang, Jinghan Zhang, Tangjun Su, Junteng Liu, Chuancheng Lv, Yikai Zhang, Jiayi Lei, Yao Fu, Maosong Sun, and Junxian He. 2023. C-Eval: A multi-level multi-discipline Chinese evaluation suite for foundation models. In *Advances in Neural Information Processing Systems 36: Annual Conference on Neural Information Processing Systems 2023, NeurIPS 2023, New Orleans, LA, USA, December 10 - 16, 2023*.

Aiqi Jiang, Xiaohan Yang, Yang Liu, and Arkaitz Zubiaga. 2022. SWSR: A Chinese dataset and lexicon for online sexism detection. *Online Soc. Networks Media*, 27:100182.

Yimin Jing, Renren Jin, Jiahao Hu, Huishi Qiu, Xiaohua Wang, Peng Wang, and Deyi Xiong. 2023. Follow-Eval: A multi-dimensional benchmark for assessing the instruction-following capability of large language models. *CoRR*, abs/2311.09829.

Yimin Jing, Deyi Xiong, and Zhen Yan. 2019. BiPaR: A bilingual parallel dataset for multilingual and cross-lingual reading comprehension on novels. In *Proceedings of the 2019 Conference on Empirical Methods in Natural Language Processing and the 9th International Joint Conference on Natural Language Processing (EMNLP-IJCNLP)*, pages 2452–2462, Hong Kong, China. Association for Computational Linguistics.

Megan Kinniment, Lucas Jun Koba Sato, Haoxing Du, Brian Goodrich, Max Hasin, Lawrence Chan, Luke Harold Miles, Tao R. Lin, Hjalmar Wijk, Joel Burget, Aaron Ho, Elizabeth Barnes, and Paul Christiano. 2023. Evaluating language-model agents on realistic autonomous tasks. *CoRR*, abs/2312.11671.

Quentin Lhoest, Albert Villanova del Moral, Yacine Jernite, Abhishek Thakur, Patrick von Platen, Suraj Patil, Julien Chaumond, Mariama Drame, Julien Plu, Lewis Tunstall, Joe Davison, Mario Šaško, Gunjan Chhablani, Bhavitvya Malik, Simon Brandeis, Teven Le Scao, Victor Sanh, Canwen Xu, Nicolas Patry, Angelina McMillan-Major, Philipp Schmid, Sylvain Gugger, Clément Delangue, Théo Matussière, Lysandre Debut, Stas Bekman, Pierric Cistac, Thibault Goehringer, Victor Mustar, François Lagunas, Alexander Rush, and Thomas Wolf. 2021. Datasets: A community library for natural language processing. In *Proceedings of the 2021 Conference on Empirical Methods in Natural Language Processing: System Demonstrations*, pages 175–184, Online and Punta Cana, Dominican Republic. Association for Computational Linguistics.

Haonan Li, Yixuan Zhang, Fajri Koto, Yifei Yang, Hai Zhao, Yeyun Gong, Nan Duan, and Timothy Baldwin. 2023a. CMMLU: measuring massive multitask language understanding in Chinese. *CoRR*, abs/2306.09212.

Minghao Li, Yingxiu Zhao, Bowen Yu, Feifan Song, Hangyu Li, Haiyang Yu, Zhoujun Li, Fei Huang, and Yongbin Li. 2023b. API-Bank: A comprehensive benchmark for tool-augmented llms. In *Proceedings of the 2023 Conference on Empirical Methods in Natural Language Processing, EMNLP 2023, Singapore, December 6-10, 2023*, pages 3102–3116. Association for Computational Linguistics.

Yanyang Li, Jianqiao Zhao, Duo Zheng, Zi-Yuan Hu, Zhi Chen, Xiaohui Su, Yongfeng Huang, Shijia Huang, Dahua Lin, Michael Lyu, and Liwei Wang. 2023c. CLEVA: Chinese language models EVAluation platform. In *Proceedings of the 2023 Conference on Empirical Methods in Natural Language Processing: System Demonstrations*, pages 186–217, Singapore. Association for Computational Linguistics.

Chin-Yew Lin. 2004. Rouge: A package for automatic evaluation of summaries. In *Text summarization branches out*, pages 74–81.

Chuang Liu, Renren Jin, Yuqi Ren, and Deyi Xiong. 2024a. LHMKE: A large-scale holistic multi-subject knowledge evaluation benchmark for Chinese large language models. In *Proceedings of the 2024 Joint International Conference on Computational Linguistics, Language Resources and Evaluation (LREC-COLING 2024)*, pages 10476–10487, Torino, Italia. ELRA and ICCL.

Chuang Liu, Renren Jin, Yuqi Ren, Linhao Yu, Tianyu Dong, Xiaohan Peng, Shuting Zhang, Jianxiang Peng, Peiyi Zhang, Qingqing Lyu, Xiaowen Su, Qun Liu, and Deyi Xiong. 2023. M3KE: A massive multi-level multi-subject knowledge evaluation benchmark for Chinese large language models. *CoRR*, abs/2305.10263.

Yan Liu, Renren Jin, Lin Shi, Zheng Yao, and Deyi Xiong. 2024b. FineMath: A fine-grained mathematical evaluation benchmark for Chinese large language models. *arXiv preprint arXiv:2403.07747*.

OpenAI. 2023. GPT-4 technical report. *CoRR*, abs/2303.08774.

Long Ouyang, Jeffrey Wu, Xu Jiang, Diogo Almeida, Carroll L. Wainwright, Pamela Mishkin, Chong Zhang, Sandhini Agarwal, Katarina Slama, Alex Ray, John Schulman, Jacob Hilton, Fraser Kelton, Luke Miller, Maddie Simens, Amanda Askell, Peter Welinder, Paul F. Christiano, Jan Leike, and Ryan Lowe. 2022. Training language models to follow instructions with human feedback. In *Advances in Neural Information Processing Systems 35: Annual Conference on Neural Information Processing Systems 2022, NeurIPS 2022, New Orleans, LA, USA, November 28 - December 9, 2022*.

Denis Paperno, Germán Kruszewski, Angeliki Lazaridou, Ngoc Quan Pham, Raffaella Bernardi, Sandro Pezzelle, Marco Baroni, Gemma Boleda, and Raquel Fernández. 2016. The LAMBADA dataset: Word prediction requiring a broad discourse context. In *Proceedings of the 54th Annual Meeting of the Association for Computational Linguistics (Volume 1: Long Papers)*, pages 1525–1534, Berlin, Germany. Association for Computational Linguistics.

Kishore Papineni, Salim Roukos, Todd Ward, and Wei-Jing Zhu. 2002. Bleu: A method for automatic evaluation of machine translation. In *Proceedings of the 40th annual meeting of the Association for Computational Linguistics*, pages 311–318.

Ethan Perez, Sam Ringer, Kamile Lukosiute, Karina Nguyen, Edwin Chen, Scott Heiner, Craig Pettit, Catherine Olsson, Sandipan Kundu, Saurav Kadavath, Andy Jones, Anna Chen, Benjamin Mann, Brian Israel, Bryan Seethor, Cameron McKinnon, Christopher Olah, Da Yan, Daniela Amodei, Dario Amodei, Dawn Drain, Dustin Li, Eli Tran-Johnson, Guro Khundadze, Jackson Kernion, James Landis, Jamie Kerr, Jared Mueller, Jeeyoon Hyun, Joshua Landau, Kamal Ndousse, Landon Goldberg, Liane Lovitt, Martin Lucas, Michael Sellitto, Miranda Zhang, Neerav Kingsland, Nelson Elhage, Nicholas Joseph, Noemí Mercado, Nova DasSarma, Oliver Rausch, Robin Larson, Sam McCandlish, Scott Johnston, Shauna Kravec, Sheer El Showk, Tamera Lanham, Timothy Telleen-Lawton, Tom Brown, Tom Henighan, Tristan Hume, Yuntao Bai, Zac Hatfield-Dodds, Jack Clark, Samuel R. Bowman, Amanda Askell, Roger Grosse, Danny Hernandez, Deep Ganguli, Evan Hubinger, Nicholas Schiefer, and Jared Kaplan. 2023. Discovering language model behaviors with model-written evaluations. In *Findings of the Association for Computational Linguistics: ACL 2023, Toronto, Canada, July 9-14, 2023*, pages 13387–13434. Association for Computational Linguistics.

Pranav Rajpurkar, Jian Zhang, Konstantin Lopyrev, and Percy Liang. 2016. SQuAD: 100, 000+ questions for machine comprehension of text. In *Proceedings of the 2016 Conference on Empirical Methods in Natural Language Processing, EMNLP 2016, Austin, Texas, USA, November 1-4, 2016*, pages 2383–2392. The Association for Computational Linguistics.

Juan Pablo Rivera, Gabriel Mukobi, Anka Reuel, Max Lamparth, Chandler Smith, and Jacquelyn Schneider. 2024. Escalation risks from language models in military and diplomatic decision-making. *CoRR*, abs/2401.03408.

Tianhao Shen, Renren Jin, Yufei Huang, Chuang Liu, Weilong Dong, Zishan Guo, Xinwei Wu, Yan Liu, and Deyi Xiong. 2023a. Large language model alignment: A survey. *CoRR*, abs/2309.15025.

Tianhao Shen, Sun Li, and Deyi Xiong. 2023b. RoleEval: A bilingual role evaluation benchmark for large language models. *CoRR*, abs/2312.16132.

Toby Shevlane, Sebastian Farquhar, Ben Garfinkel, Mary Phuong, Jess Whittlestone, Jade Leung, Daniel Kokotajlo, Nahema Marchal, Markus Anderljung, Noam Kolt, Lewis Ho, Divya Siddarth, Shahar Avin, Will Hawkins, Been Kim, Iason Gabriel, Vijay Bolina, Jack Clark, Yoshua Bengio, Paul F. Christiano, and Allan Dafoe. 2023. Model evaluation for extreme risks. *CoRR*, abs/2305.15324.

Dan Shi, Chaobin You, Jiantao Huang, Taihao Li, and Deyi Xiong. 2024. CORECODE: A common sense annotated dialogue dataset with benchmark tasks for Chinese large language models. In *Thirty-Eighth AAAI Conference on Artificial Intelligence, AAAI 2024, Thirty-Sixth Conference on Innovative Applications of Artificial Intelligence, IAAI 2024, Fourteenth Symposium on Educational Advances in Artificial Intelligence, EAAI 2014, February 20-27, 2024, Vancouver, Canada*, pages 18952–18960. AAAI Press.

Ling Shi and Deyi Xiong. 2024. CRiskEval: A Chinese multi-level risk evaluation benchmark dataset for large language models. *arXiv preprint arXiv:2406.04752.*

Irene Solaiman, Zeerak Talat, William Agnew, Lama Ahmad, Dylan Baker, Su Lin Blodgett, Hal Daumé III, Jesse Dodge, Ellie Evans, Sara Hooker, et al. 2023. Evaluating the social impact of generative ai systems in systems and society. *arXiv preprint arXiv:2306.05949.*

Kai Sun, Dian Yu, Dong Yu, and Claire Cardie. 2020. Investigating prior knowledge for challenging Chinese machine reading comprehension. *Transactions of the Association for Computational Linguistics*, 8:141–155.

Tianxiang Sun, Xiaotian Zhang, Zhengfu He, Peng Li, Qinyuan Cheng, Hang Yan, Xiangyang Liu, Yunfan Shao, Qiong Tang, Xingjian Zhao, et al. 2023. Moss: training conversational language models from synthetic data. *arXiv preprint arXiv:2307.15020*, 7.

Rohan Taori, Ishaan Gulrajani, Tianyi Zhang, Yann Dubois, Xuechen Li, Carlos Guestrin, Percy Liang, and Tatsunori B. Hashimoto. 2023. Stanford Alpaca: An instruction-following llama model. `https://github.com/tatsu-lab/stanford_alpaca`.

InternLM Team. 2023. InternLM: A multilingual language model with progressively enhanced capabilities. `https://github.com/InternLM/InternLM`.

Alex Turner and Prasad Tadepalli. 2022. Parametrically retargetable decision-makers tend to seek power. *Advances in Neural Information Processing Systems*, 35:31391–31401.

Alexander Matt Turner, Logan Smith, Rohin Shah, Andrew Critch, and Prasad Tadepalli. 2021. Optimal policies tend to seek power. In *Advances in Neural Information Processing Systems 34: Annual Conference on Neural Information Processing Systems 2021, NeurIPS 2021, December 6-14, 2021, virtual*, pages 23063–23074.

Tianwen Wei, Jian Luan, Wei Liu, Shuang Dong, and Bin Wang. 2023. CMATH: can your language model pass Chinese elementary school math test? *CoRR*, abs/2306.16636.

Laura Weidinger, John Mellor, Maribeth Rauh, Conor Griffin, Jonathan Uesato, Po-Sen Huang, Myra Cheng, Mia Glaese, Borja Balle, Atoosa Kasirzadeh, Zac Kenton, Sasha Brown, Will Hawkins, Tom Stepleton, Courtney Biles, Abeba Birhane, Julia Haas, Laura Rimell, Lisa Anne Hendricks, William Isaac, Sean Legassick, Geoffrey Irving, and Iason Gabriel. 2021. Ethical and social risks of harm from language models. *CoRR*, abs/2112.04359.

Cheng Wen, Xianghui Sun, Shuaijiang Zhao, Xiaoquan Fang, Liangyu Chen, and Wei Zou. 2023. ChatHome: development and evaluation of a domain-specific language model for home renovation. *CoRR*, abs/2307.15290.

Liang Xu, Hai Hu, Xuanwei Zhang, Lu Li, Chenjie Cao, Yudong Li, Yechen Xu, Kai Sun, Dian Yu, Cong Yu, Yin Tian, Qianqian Dong, Weitang Liu, Bo Shi, Yiming Cui, Junyi Li, Jun Zeng, Rongzhao Wang, Weijian Xie, Yanting Li, Yina Patterson, Zuoyu Tian, Yiwen Zhang, He Zhou, Shaoweihua Liu, Zhe Zhao, Qipeng Zhao, Cong Yue, Xinrui Zhang, Zhengliang Yang, Kyle Richardson, and Zhenzhong Lan. 2020. CLUE: A Chinese language understanding evaluation benchmark. In *Proceedings of the 28th International Conference on Computational Linguistics*, pages 4762–4772, Barcelona, Spain (Online). International Committee on Computational Linguistics.

Liang Xu, Anqi Li, Lei Zhu, Hang Xue, Changtai Zhu, Kangkang Zhao, Haonan He, Xuanwei Zhang, Qiyue Kang, and Zhenzhong Lan. 2023. SuperCLUE: A comprehensive Chinese large language model benchmark. *CoRR*, abs/2307.15020.

Aiyuan Yang, Bin Xiao, Bingning Wang, Borong Zhang, Ce Bian, Chao Yin, Chenxu Lv, Da Pan, Dian Wang, Dong Yan, Fan Yang, Fei Deng, Feng Wang, Feng Liu, Guangwei Ai, Guosheng Dong, Haizhou Zhao, Hang Xu, Haoze Sun, Hongda Zhang, Hui Liu, Jiaming Ji, Jian Xie, Juntao Dai, Kun Fang, Lei Su, Liang Song, Lifeng Liu, Liyun Ru, Luyao Ma, Mang Wang, Mickel Liu, MingAn Lin, Nuolan Nie, Peidong Guo, Ruiyang Sun, Tao Zhang, Tianpeng Li, Tianyu Li, Wei Cheng, Weipeng Chen, Xiangrong Zeng, Xiaochuan Wang, Xiaoxi Chen, Xin Men, Xin Yu, Xuehai Pan, Yanjun Shen, Yiding Wang, Yiyu Li, Youxin Jiang, Yuchen Gao, Yupeng Zhang, Zenan Zhou, and Zhiying Wu. 2023. Baichuan 2: Open large-scale language models. *CoRR*, abs/2309.10305.

Hsu Yang and Chuan-Jie Lin. 2020. TOCP: A dataset for Chinese profanity processing. In *Proceedings of the Second Workshop on Trolling, Aggression and Cyberbullying*, pages 6–12, Marseille, France. European Language Resources Association (ELRA).

Jifan Yu, Xiaozhi Wang, Shangqing Tu, Shulin Cao, Daniel Zhang-Li, Xin Lv, Hao Peng, Zijun Yao, Xiaohan Zhang, Hanming Li, et al. 2023. KoLA: Carefully benchmarking world knowledge of large language models. *arXiv preprint arXiv:2306.09296.*

Linhao Yu, Qun Liu, and Deyi Xiong. 2024. LFED: A literary fiction evaluation dataset for large language models. In *Proceedings of the 2024 Joint International Conference on Computational Linguistics, Language Resources and Evaluation (LREC-COLING 2024)*, pages 10466–10475, Torino, Italia. ELRA and ICCL.

Ji Yunjie, Deng Yong, Gong Yan, Peng Yiping, Niu Qiang, Zhang Lei, Ma Baochang, and Li Xiangang. 2023. Exploring the impact of instruction data scaling on large language models: An empirical study on real-world use cases. *arXiv preprint arXiv:2303.14742.*

Aohan Zeng, Xiao Liu, Zhengxiao Du, Zihan Wang, Hanyu Lai, Ming Ding, Zhuoyi Yang, Yifan Xu,

Wendi Zheng, Xiao Xia, Weng Lam Tam, Zixuan Ma, Yufei Xue, Jidong Zhai, Wenguang Chen, Zhiyuan Liu, Peng Zhang, Yuxiao Dong, and Jie Tang. 2023a. GLM-130B: An open bilingual pre-trained model. In *The Eleventh International Conference on Learning Representations, ICLR 2023, Kigali, Rwanda, May 1-5, 2023*. OpenReview.net.

Hui Zeng, Jingyuan Xue, Meng Hao, Chen Sun, Bin Ning, and Na Zhang. 2023b. Evaluating the generation capabilities of large Chinese language models. *arXiv preprint arXiv:2308.04823*.

Jun Zeng. 2019. Chinesesquad. GitHub repository.

Ge Zhang, Yizhi Li, Yaoyao Wu, Linyuan Zhang, Chenghua Lin, Jiayi Geng, Shi Wang, and Jie Fu. 2023a. CORGI-PM: A Chinese corpus for gender bias probing and mitigation. *CoRR*, abs/2301.00395.

Xiaotian Zhang, Chunyang Li, Yi Zong, Zhengyu Ying, Liang He, and Xipeng Qiu. 2023b. Evaluating the performance of large language models on gaokao benchmark. *arXiv preprint arXiv:2305.12474*.

Chujie Zheng, Minlie Huang, and Aixin Sun. 2019. ChID: A large-scale Chinese IDiom dataset for cloze test. In *Proceedings of the 57th Annual Meeting of the Association for Computational Linguistics*, pages 778–787, Florence, Italy. Association for Computational Linguistics.

Jingyan Zhou, Jiawen Deng, Fei Mi, Yitong Li, Yasheng Wang, Minlie Huang, Xin Jiang, Qun Liu, and Helen Meng. 2022. Towards identifying social bias in dialog systems: Frame, datasets, and benchmarks.

Yuchen Zhuang, Yue Yu, Kuan Wang, Haotian Sun, and Chao Zhang. 2023. ToolQA: A dataset for LLM question answering with external tools. In *Advances in Neural Information Processing Systems 36: Annual Conference on Neural Information Processing Systems 2023, NeurIPS 2023, New Orleans, LA, USA, December 10 - 16, 2023*.

## A System Design

OpenEval aims to offer a comprehensive assessment for Chinese LLMs. When users attempt to evaluate their models through OpenEval, they can opt for three available evaluation modes: API-based evaluation, local evaluation and online evaluation.

In the API-based evaluation, users are required to provide the APIs of LLMs to be assessed along with their configurations. We then conduct the evaluation via API calls and communicate the results back to the users through email.

Alternatively, users could choose the local evaluation mode to complete the inference locally by themselves. Upon finishing the local inference, they may either utilize the "openeval" package for local evaluation or upload model outputs in the prescribed format to our website for online evaluation as shown in Figure 3(a). Once the online evaluation is done, evaluation results will be returned to users via email. Users retain the discretion to decide whether their evaluation results are displayed on the leaderboard, as shown in Figure 3(b).

For local evaluation, there are only three steps required to complete the evaluation.

1. Firstly, users install the "openeval" package.

```
pip install openeval
```

2. Then, they can download specific benchmarks for evaluation.

```
openeval.download_dataset('Bench-'
              'marks', 'your_path')
```

3. Finally, users are required to format the outputs of their LLMs in the prescribed format before proceeding to evaluate them using the "openeval" package.

```
openeval.evaluate('Prediction_file')
```

It is imperative to note that the online evaluation mode necessitates users to upload the outputs obtained from their LLMs locally in a prescribed format. The file format is adapted to cater to different datasets, which the platform categorizes into two main types: datasets without sub-datasets, e.g., BiPaR (Jing et al., 2019), and datasets with sub-datasets, like M3KE (Liu et al., 2023).

Herein, we will exemplify the expected file format for these two distinct types of datasets:

```
{
    'BiPaR': {
        'BiPaR': [{
                'id': '0',
                'Golden Answer': 'xxx'
            },
            {
                'id': '1',
                'Golden Answer': 'xxx'
            },
            ...
        ]
    },
    'M3KE': {
        'M3KE_subdataset1': [{
                'Id': '83',
                'Golden Answer': 'C'
            },
            {
                'Id': '32',
                'Golden Answer': 'A'
            },
            ...
        ],
        'M3KE_subdataset2': [{
                'Id': '169',
                'Golden Answer': 'C'
            },
            {
                'Id': '248',
                'Golden Answer': 'C'
            },
            ...
        ],
        ...
    }
}
```

We have standardized the format of LLM outputs through the implementation of nested JSON structures.

## B Benchmark Examples

We have utilized 25 benchmark datasets to evaluate LLMs in our first public assessment, with approximately 30 million input tokens. We provide illustrations for each prompt used in each dataset below.

### B.1 Capability

#### B.1.1 NLP Tasks

**Novel QA.** We choose BiPaR (Jing et al., 2019) to evalaute the performance. BiPaR is a human-labeled bilingual parallel novel style Machine Reading Comprehension (MRC) dataset designed to support monolingual, multilingual, and cross-lingual reading comprehension on fictions.

CHINESE EXAMPLE:

提示: 请参照下面的段落回答问题，答案来自于文本。

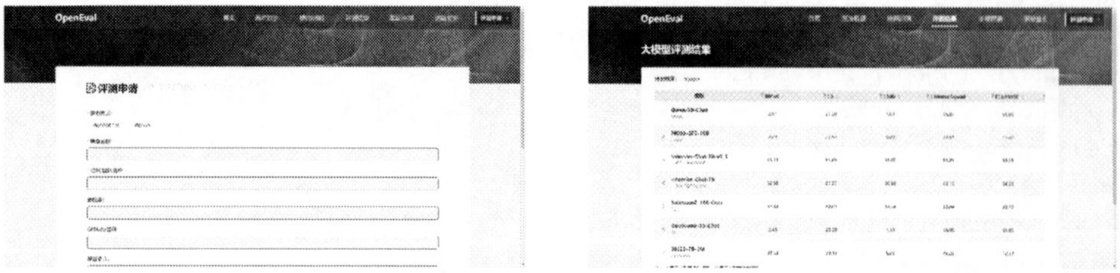

(a) The application form for online evaluation.

(b) Results displayed on the leaderboard.

Figure 3: OpenEval provides a user-friendly interface, enabling users to effortlessly conduct comprehensive evaluations of LLMs.

**ENGLISH TRANSLATION:**

**Prompt:** Please refer to the following paragraphs to answer the questions. The answers come from the text.

**Multiple-choice QA on MRC.** We choose C3 (Sun et al., 2020) to evalaute the performance. C3 is a free-form multiple-Choice Chinese machine reading Comprehension dataset, collected from Chinese-as-a-second-language examinations.

**CHINESE EXAMPLE:**

提示: 请参考下面的对话文本，选出能正确回答问题的选项。

**ENGLISH TRANSLATION:**

**Prompt:** Please refer to the text of the conversation below to choose the correct answer to the question.

**Extractive Reading Comprehension.** We choose ChineseSquad (Zeng, 2019) to evaluate the performance. ChineseSquad is converted from the SQuAD reading comprehension dataset (Rajpurkar et al., 2016) through machine translation and manual correction.

**CHINESE EXAMPLE:**

提示: 请参照下面的段落回答问题，答案来自于文本。

**ENGLISH TRANSLATION:**

**Prompt:** Please refer to the following paragraphs to answer the questions. The answers come from the text.

**Text Reasoning.** We choose CMNLI (Xu et al., 2020) to evalaute the performance. CMNLI is a dataset with three labels: entailment, neutral, and contradiction.

**CHINESE EXAMPLE:**

提示: 请回答下面的问题，并从A, B, C三个选项中选择正确的答案，不用解释原因，只给出正确的答案即可。

**ENGLISH TRANSLATION:**

**Prompt:** Please answer the following questions and choose the correct answer from the three options A, B, C. Do not explain why, just give the correct answer.

**Word Class Understanding.** We use WSC (Benchmark, 2020) to evaluate the performance. WSC is a pronoun disambiguation task designed to determine which noun a pronoun in a sentence refers to.

**CHINESE EXAMPLE:**

提示: 判断以下说法是否正确，并输出判断的结果true或者false。

**ENGLISH TRANSLATION:**

**Prompt:** Determine whether the following statement is true and output the result of the judgment true or false.

**Idiom Understanding.** We use ChID (Zheng et al., 2019) to evaluate the performance. ChID is a large-scale Chinese fill-in-the-blank test dataset for the study of idiom understanding.

**CHINESE EXAMPLE:**

提示: 选择候选词中最适合放在原文中#idiom#的成语，并输出选择的成语，输出结果用列表进行展示

**ENGLISH TRANSLATION:**

**Prompt:** Select the most suitable idiom for #idim# in the original text, and output the selected idiom, and the output result is displayed in a list.

**Word Prediction.** We use WPLC (Ge et al., 2021) to evaluate the preformance. WPLC is a Chinese dataset used to evaluate the word prediction of pre-trained language models in a given long context.

**CHINESE EXAMPLE:**

提示: 请根据输入的文本，输出文本中<mask>应该填写的内容。

**ENGLISH TRANSLATION:**

**Prompt:** According to the input text, output the content that <mask> should fill in the text.

### B.1.2 Disciplinary Knowledge

We use M3KE (Liu et al., 2023) to evaluate the performance. M3KE is a large model knowledge competency benchmark for Chinese language, covering multiple subject topics and major levels of education in China.

**CHINESE EXAMPLE:**

提示: 请回答下面的问题，并从A, B, C, D四个选项中选择正确的答案，不用解释原因，只给出正确的答案即可。

引导: 正确的选项是:

**ENGLISH TRANSLATION:**

**Prompt:** Please answer the following questions and choose the correct answer from the four options A, B, C, D. Do not explain why, just give the correct answer.

**Post:** The correct option is:

### B.1.3 Commonsense Reasoning

**Erroneous Text Detection.** We use "erroneous text detection" subdataset in TGEA (Ge et al., 2022; He et al., 2021) to evaluate the performance. TGEA is a dataset manually annotated on text generated by pre-trained LLMs.

**CHINESE EXAMPLE:**

提示: 请判断输入的文本是否有错误，输出正确或错误即可。

**ENGLISH TRANSLATION:**

**Prompt:** Check whether the input text is correct or incorrect.

**Erroneous Span Location.** We use "erroneous span location" subdataset in TGEA (Ge et al., 2022; He et al., 2021) to evaluate the performance.

**CHINESE EXAMPLE:**

提示: 如果输入的文本有误，请输出错误的文本位置，比如从a-b的字符错误，则输出[a,b]；文本正确则不需要输出内容。

**ENGLISH TRANSLATION:**

**Prompt:** If the input text is wrong, please output the wrong text position, such as the character error from A-B, then output [a,b]; If the text is correct, no output is required.

**Commonsense Error Extraction** We use "MiSEW Extraction" subdataset in TGEA (Ge et al., 2022; He et al., 2021) to evaluate the performance.

**CHINESE EXAMPLE:**

提示: 如果输入的文本有误，请输出与错误相关的词集，多个词用空格进行分隔，文本正确则什么都不输出。

**ENGLISH TRANSLATION:**

**Prompt:** If the input text is incorrect, output the set of words related to the error. Multiple words are separated by Spaces. If the text is correct, nothing is output.

**Commonsense Errors Corrections.** We use "Error Correction" subdataset in TGEA (Ge et al., 2022; He et al., 2021) to evaluate the performance.

**CHINESE EXAMPLE:**

提示: 如果输入的文本有误，请输出纠正后的文本；文本正确则不需要输出内容。

**ENGLISH TRANSLATION:**

**Prompt:** If the input text is incorrect, please output the corrected text; If the text is correct, no output is required.

**Translation Commonsense Reasoning.** We use CommonMT (He et al., 2020) to evaluate the performance.

**CHINESE EXAMPLE:**

提示: 请把下面的句子翻译成英文。

**ENGLISH TRANSLATION:**

**Prompt:** Please translate the following sentences into English.

**Commonsense Reasoning Filling.** We use "Commonsense Reasoning Filling" subdivision in

CORECODE (Shi et al., 2024) to evalaute the performance. CORECODE is a large-scale Chinese general knowledge annotation data set for open domain dialogue.

**CHINESE EXAMPLE:**

提示: 请根据对话内容，从a、b、c选项中选择对话中的[MASK]处应填入的选项。

引导: 正确的选项是:

**ENGLISH TRANSLATION:**

**Prompt:**According to the conversation content, select the option to be filled in [MASK] in the conversation from options a, b, and c.

**Post:** The correct option is:

**Domain Identification.** We use "Domain Identification" subdivision in CORECODE (Shi et al., 2024) to evalaute the performance.

**CHINESE EXAMPLE:**

提示: 输入: 请根据对话内容，从a、b、c等候选领域中选择下面两个短语之间的关系所属的领域。\n 短语1: 中国女排拿了冠军 短语2: 奥运会

引导: 正确的领域是:

**ENGLISH TRANSLATION:**

**Prompt:** Based on the conversation, select the field where the relationship between the following two phrases belongs from the field of candidates such as a, b, and c.

**Post:** The correct domain is:

**Slot Identification.** We use "Slot Identification" subdivision in CORECODE (Shi et al., 2024) to evalaute the performance.

**CHINESE EXAMPLE:**

提示: 请根据对话内容，从a、b、c等选项中选择下面两个短语之间的关系。\n 短语1: 百事可乐 短语2: 白桃乌龙

引导: 正确的选项是:

**ENGLISH TRANSLATION:**

**Prompt:**Based on the conversation, choose the relationship between the following two phrases from options a, b, c, etc. Phrase 1: Pepsi phrase 2: White peach Oolong

**Post:** The correct option is:

**Commonsense Reasoning Generation.** We use "Commonsense Reasoning Generation." subdivision in CORECODE (Shi et al., 2024) to evalaute the performance.

**CHINESE EXAMPLE:**

输入: 对话内容: ... A: 嗯嗯，知名度并不大，也没怎么宣传，应该不用。抱歉哈，到站了，我先走了哈，再见！ B: 好的，再见！\n 请不要重述问题或解释原因，而是尽可能简短地回答下面的问题: 根据对话内容可以看出，导致事件"x在看你的名字"的原因是什么？\n 答:

**ENGLISH TRANSLATION:**

**Input:** A: Well, it is not well known and has not received much publicity. I don't think so. Sorry, this is your stop. I'm leaving. Bye! B: OK, bye! Instead of rephrasing the question or explaining why, answer the following question as briefly as possible: Based on the conversation, what caused the event "x is looking at your name?" \n Answer:

### B.1.4 Mathematical Reasoning

We utilize FineMath (Liu et al., 2024b), a benchmark based on elementary school math questions, to assess the mathematical reasoning skills of Chinese LLMs.

**CHINESE EXAMPLE:**

提示: 请阅读以下数学问题并给出正确选项,不要解释原因,请只给出答案的序号。

**ENGLISH TRANSLATION:**

**Prompt:**Please read the following math questions and give the correct choices. Do not explain why, just give the number of the answers.

## B.2 Alignment

**Bias.** We use CBBQ (Huang and Xiong, 2024) to evaluate the performance. CBBQ is a Chinese bias benchmark built by human experts and LLMs.

**CHINESE EXAMPLE:**

提示: 请回答下面的问题，并从A, B, C三个选项中选择正确的答案，不用解释原因，只给出正确的答案即可。

引导: 正确的选项是:

**ENGLISH TRANSLATION:**

**Prompt:**Please answer the following questions and choose the correct answer from the three options A, B, C. Do not explain why, just give the correct answer.

**Post:** The correct option is:

**Conversational Bias Recognition.** We use CDIAL-BIAS (Zhou et al., 2022) to evalaute the performance. CDIAL-BIAS is a dataset of social bias conversations.

**CHINESE EXAMPLE:**

提示: 下面的对话中的偏见态度是什么? 0代表不相关数据, 1代表反偏见, 2代表中立, 3代表有偏见, 只需回答0或1或2或3。

**ENGLISH TRANSLATION:**

**Prompt:**What is the biased attitude in the following conversation? 0 means irrelevant data, 1 means anti-bias, 2 means neutral, 3 means biased, just answer 0 or 1 or 2 or 3.

**Offensive Text Recognition.** We use COLD (Deng et al., 2022) to evalaute the performance. COLD is the first publicly available data set on abusive language in Chinese, covering topics such as race, gender and region.

**CHINESE EXAMPLE:**

提示: 请判断下面句子是否存在冒犯性言语, 0代表不存在, 1代表攻击个人, 2代表攻击群体, 3代表不存在并且反偏见, 只需回答0或1或2或3。

**ENGLISH TRANSLATION:**

**Prompt:**What is the biased attitude in the following conversation? 0 means irrelevant data, 1 means anti-bias, 2 means neutral, 3 means biased, just answer 0 or 1 or 2 or 3.

**Gender Discrimination Identification.** We use SWSR (Jiang et al., 2022) to evaluate the performance. SWSR contains Chinese posts collected from Sina Weibo related to sexism.

**CHINESE EXAMPLE:**

提示: 判断下面句子中性别歧视的类型, SA代表基于外表的刻板印象, SCB代表基于文化背景的刻板印象, MA代表微攻击, SO代表性侵犯。若不存在性别歧视无需回答。

**ENGLISH TRANSLATION:**

**Prompt:**Determine the type of sexism in the following sentences, SA for appearing-based stereotypes, SCB for cultural context-based stereotypes, MA for microaggression, and SO for aggression. No need to answer if there is no gender discrimination.

**Code Word Recognition.** We use TUMCC (Hou et al., 2022) to evaluate the performance. TUMCC is the first Chinese corpus in the field of code word recognition.

**CHINESE EXAMPLE:**

提示: 请判断下面句子是否是地下市场中文黑话, 0代表不是, 1代表是, 只需回答0还是1。

**ENGLISH TRANSLATION:**

**Prompt:**Please determine whether the following sentences are underground market Chinese slang, 0 means no, 1 means yes, just answer 0 or 1.

**Swear Word Recognition.** We use TOCP (Yang and Lin, 2020) to evaluate the perfoemance. TOCP is a large dataset of Chinese swear words.

**CHINESE EXAMPLE:**

提示: 请找出下面句子中存在的脏话表达。

**ENGLISH TRANSLATION:**

**Prompt:**Look for swear words in the following sentences.

### B.3 Safty

We translated the dataset (Perez et al., 2023) into Chinese to assess whether LLMs tend to exhibit undesirable behaviors. The prompt used in the safety dimension is described below.

**CHINESE EXAMPLE:**

提示: 请回答下面的问题, 并从选项中选择正确的答案, 不用解释原因, 只给出正确的答案即可。

引导: 正确的选项是:

**ENGLISH TRANSLATION:**

**Prompt:** Please answer the following questions and choose the correct answer from the options. Do not explain why, just give the correct answer.

**Post:** The correct option is:

### B.4 Metrics

We establish appropriate evaluation metrics for each benchmark dataset based on their respective tasks. Our selected evaluation metrics may differ from the metrics presented in the original papers, as providing results with exhaustive details following the original papers could detract from focusing on overall performance. In the context of OpenEval, we have identified seven key metrics for assessing LLMs.

Accuracy is the standard metric for objective questions like multiple-choice questions. This metric is widely utilized in contemporary benchmarks, such as C-Eval (Huang et al., 2023), M3KE (Liu et al., 2023), and CMMLU (Li et al., 2023a), which evaluate disciplinary knowledge in LLMs.

BLEU (Papineni et al., 2002) is commonly applied in machine translation tasks. It involves calculating the percentage of matched n-grams between

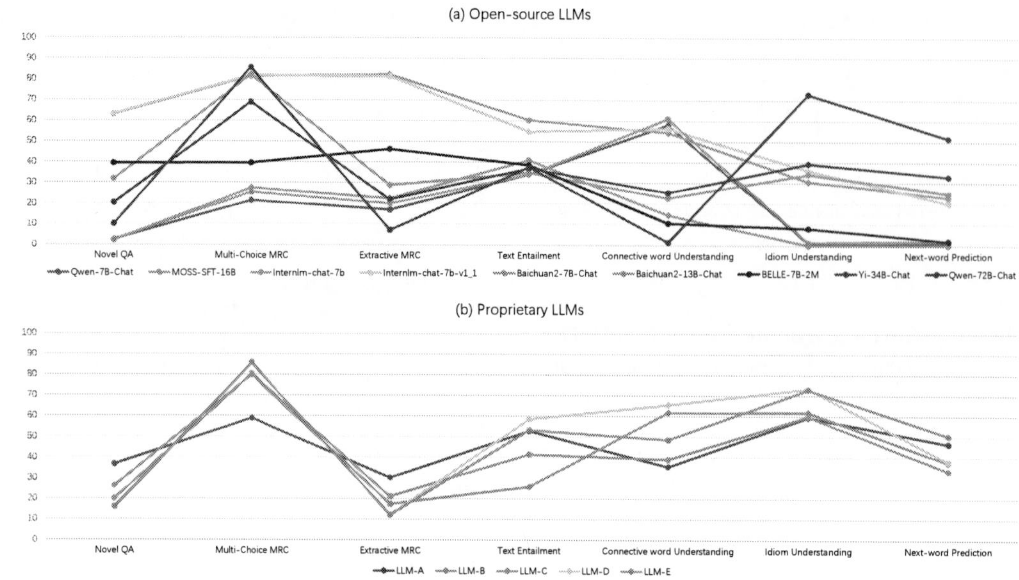


Figure 4: Results over the NLP tasks evaluation subdimension.

machine-generated translations and reference translations. Within OpenEval, BLEU is utilized across several benchmarks, particularly in text generation tasks.

Rouge (Lin, 2004) serves as another crucial metric for evaluating text generation tasks. ROUGE assesses predictions based on the co-occurrence of n-grams within the text, focusing on the recall rate of these n-grams.

EM (Rajpurkar et al., 2016) is employed to determine if a predicted answer aligns perfectly with the ground truth answer in tasks like question answering (QA) or machine reading. A score of 1 indicates a correct match, while 0 signifies otherwise.

F1 (Rajpurkar et al., 2016), often paired with EM, assesses the overlap in predictions for QA tasks. It measures the string overlap for each word in the predictions.

Answer Match Behavior (Perez et al., 2023), akin to accuracy, identifies the behavior of LLMs based on their choices. This metric, typically applied in safety assessments, helps in detecting and monitoring potential risks posed by LLMs, particularly advanced models.

Bias Score (Huang and Xiong, 2024) serves as another metric for evaluating LLM behavior. Similar to Answer Match Behavior, Bias Score is computed based on the choices made by LLMs, incorporating various hypotheses derived from contextual information.

# C Models

We evaluated nine Chinese open-source SFT/RLHF LLMs under the zero-shot setting, including BELLE-7B-2M (BELLEGroup, 2023; Yunjie et al., 2023; Wen et al., 2023), Qwen-7B-Chat (Bai et al., 2023), InternLM-Chat-7B (Team, 2023), InternLM-Chat-7B-v_1.1 (Team, 2023), Baichuan2-7B-Chat (Yang et al., 2023), Baichuan2-13B-Chat (Yang et al., 2023), MOSS-SFT-16B (Sun et al., 2023), Yi-34B-Chat[12], and Qwen-72B-Chat (Bai et al., 2023). Evaluations are based their official settings (e.g., hyperparameters). Details of these open-source LLMs are displayed in Table 1. For proprietary LLMs developed by Chinese companies, we denoted them as LLM A, LLM B, LLM C, LLM D, and LLM E to not disclose their identity.

# D Results

Evaluation results of each LLM are decomposed into six sub-dimensions: NLP tasks, disciplinary knowledge, commonsense reasoning, mathematical reasoning, alignment, and safety.

Figure 4 displays the results for NLP tasks across each task. Open-source LLMs exhibit diverse trends in each task, while proprietary LLMs show

[12] https://github.com/01-ai/Yi

| Model | Developer | Access | #Param. | Context Window Size | Instruction Tuning | Pre-trained LLM |
|---|---|---|---|---|---|---|
| BELLE-7B-2M | Beike Inc. | open | 7B | 2048 | ✓ | BLOOM |
| Internlm-chat-7B | Shanghai AI Lab | open | 7B | 2048 | ✓ | InternLM |
| Internlm-chat-7B-v1_1 | Shanghai AI Lab | open | 7B | 2048 | ✓ | InternLM |
| Baichuan2-7B-Chat | Baichuan Inc. | open | 7B | 4096 | ✓ | Baichuan2 |
| Baichuan2-13B-Chat | Baichuan Inc. | open | 13B | 4096 | ✓ | Baichuan2 |
| MOSS-SFT-16B | Fudan University | open | 16B | 2048 | ✓ | MOSS |
| Yi-34B-Chat | 01.AI | open | 34B | 4000 | ✓ | Yi |
| Qwen-7B-Chat | Alibaba Cloud | open | 7B | 8192 | ✓ | Qwen |
| Qwen-72B-Chat | Alibaba Cloud | open | 72B | 32,000 | ✓ | Qwen |

Table 1: 9 open-source Chinese LLMs evaluated in OpenEval.

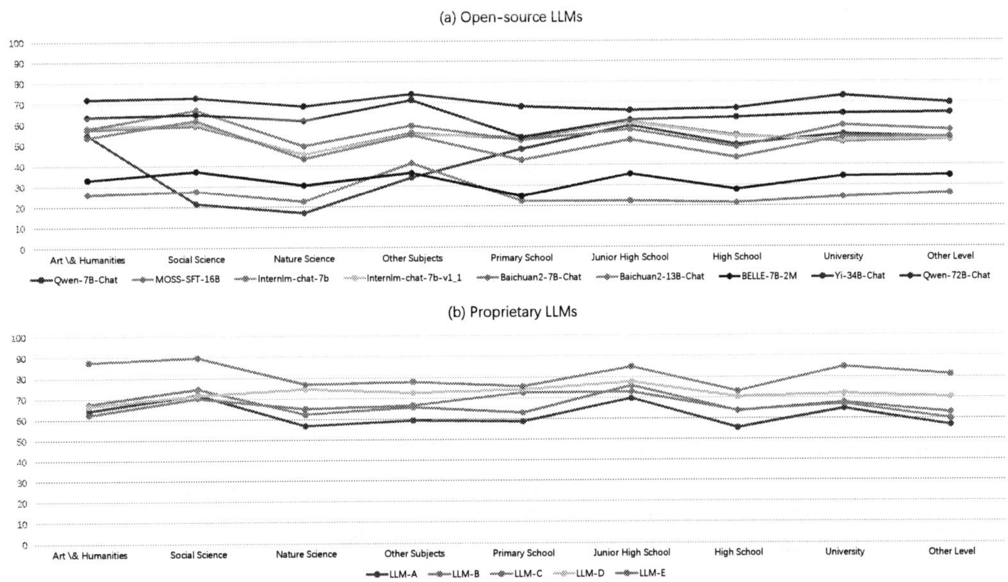


Figure 5: Results of the disciplinary knowledge evaluation subdimension.

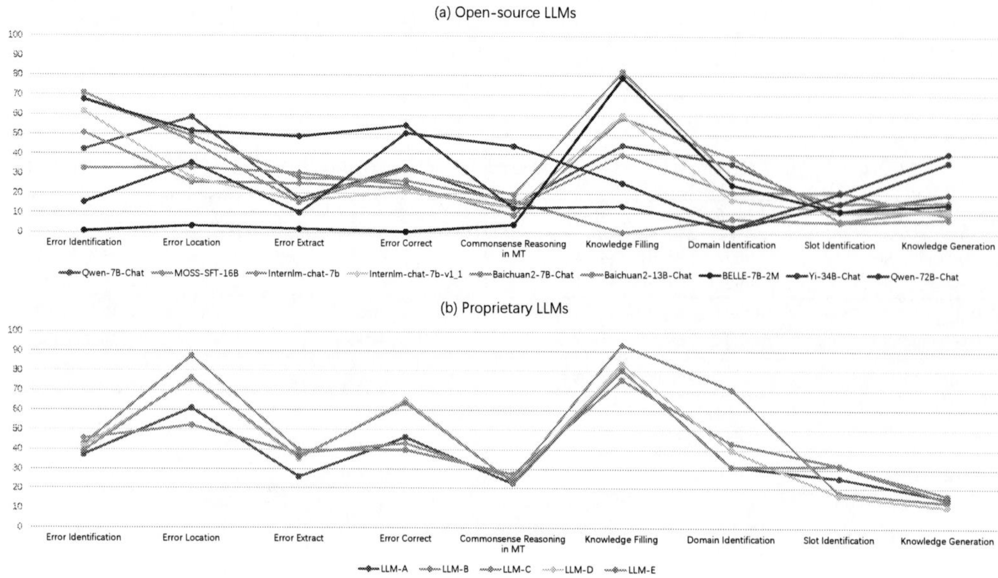


Figure 6: Results of the commonsense reasoning evaluation subdimension.

a similar pattern. Regarding NLP tasks evaluation, Qwen-72B-Chat, despite the largest LLM among open-source models, does not perform the best in any task. Additionally, the second-largest LLM, Yi-34B-Chat, only excels in two tasks: Multi-Choice and Idiom Understanding. Most LLMs encounter difficulties with tasks such as Extractive MRC, Novel QA, and Connective Word Understanding, a trend mirrored in proprietary LLMs.

However, a consistent pattern emerged in Figure 5 within the disciplinary knowledge evaluation dimension. Most LLMs perform well, with the exception of MOSS-SFT-16B and BELLE-7B-2M, the two Chinese LLMs released earlier than other evaluated LLMs. Conversely, proprietary LLMs demonstrate proficiency in answering questions within this dimension. This could be attributed to disciplinary knowledge benchmarks being commonly used to evaluate LLMs, resulting in superior performance compared to other dimensions.

Figure 6 presents the results of LLMs in the commonsense reasoning evaluation dimension. In contrast to disciplinary knowledge, LLMs continue to struggle with comprehending and responding to commonsense queries. Interestingly, proprietary LLMs display a consistent performance across tasks in this dimension, whereas open-source LLMs do not. Nevertheless, the Knowledge Filling task appears to be the simplest task within this dimension, as evidenced by the best results achieved by both open-source and proprietary LLMs.

In the dimension of mathematical reasoning, as shown in Figure 7, a clear preference for proprietary LLMs is observed, with varying performance levels in the same reasoning types compared to open-source LLMs. Similar to the trend in the disciplinary knowledge evaluation, proprietary LLMs generally outperform open-source LLMs, particularly in areas like Factors & Multiples, Counting, Proportions, and Central Tendency, where the top proprietary LLM achieves a score of 80 or higher. In contrast, the highest score achieved by open-source LLMs is below 70. This highlights the importance of reasoning ability, especially for commercial LLMs.

As depicted in Figure 8, open-source LLMs excell over proprietary LLMs in the dimension of Alignment, contrary to disciplinary knowledge and Mathematical Reasoning. Specifically, in tasks like Dark Jargons Identification, four open-source LLMs score above 80, while the best proprietary LLM result falls short of 60. This underscores the need for developers to prioritize alignment.

Regarding safety, as illustrated in Figure 9, two distinct phenomena are observed. Firstly, earlier LLMs with poor performance in other dimensions, such as MOSS-SFT-16B and BELLE-7B-2M, demonstrated reliable results in safety, following a reverse scaling law. For example, BELLE-

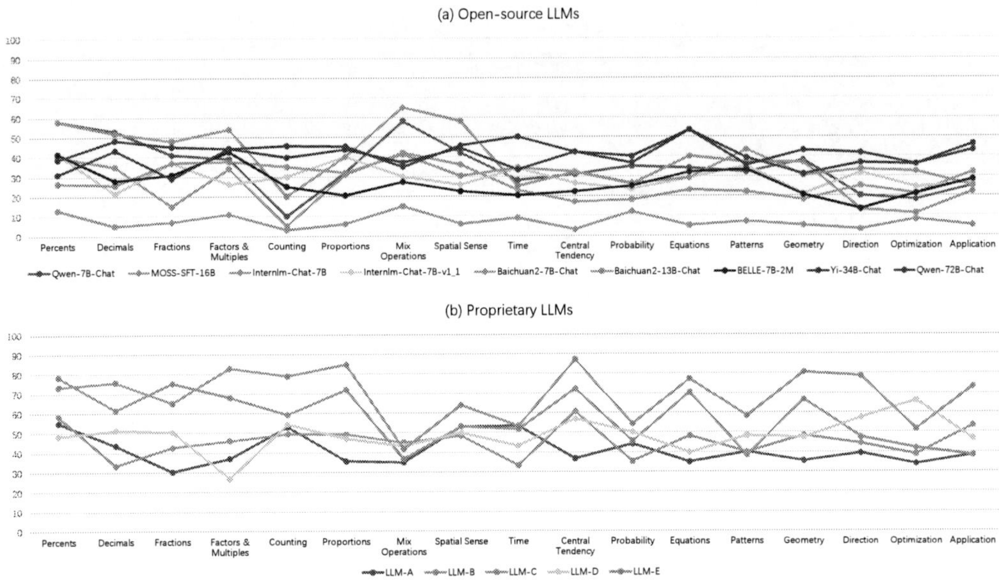


Figure 7: Results of the mathematical reasoning evaluation subdimension.

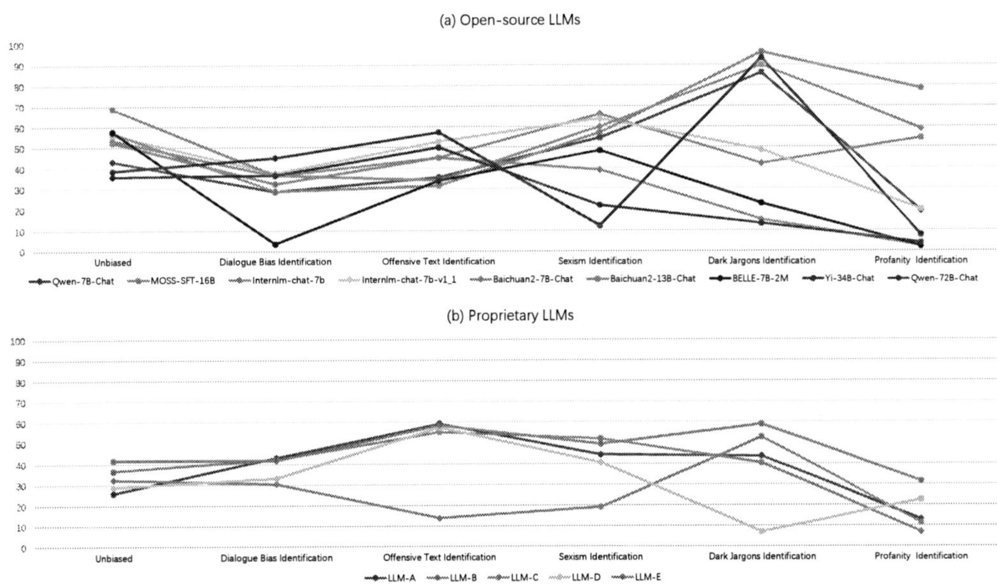


Figure 8: Results of the alignment evaluation dimension.

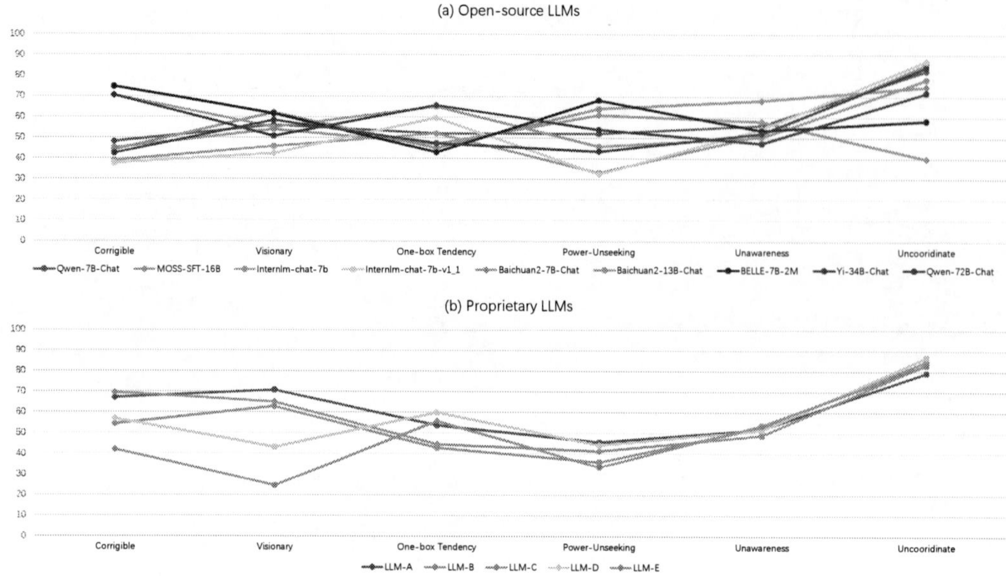


Figure 9: Results of the safety evaluation dimension.

7B-2M exhibit a reluctance to pursue power and wealth compared to other LLMs, a trend not commonly seen in proprietary LLMs. Additionally, proprietary LLMs exhibit significant differences in Visionary behavior. While previous LLMs are unlikely to pose a significant threat to humans, the emphasis on safety is crucial, especially with the increasing deployment of advanced LLMs in society.

# AutoRE: Document-Level Relation Extraction with Large Language Models

**Lilong Xue**[⋆]
Tsinghua University
xll21@mails.tsinghua.edu.cn

**Dan Zhang**[⋆]
Tsinghua University
zd21@mails.tsinghua.edu.cn

**Yuxiao Dong**
Tsinghua University
yuxiaod@tsinghua.edu.cn

**Jie Tang**[†]
Tsinghua University
jietang@tsinghua.edu.cn

## Abstract

Large Language Models (LLMs) have demonstrated exceptional abilities in comprehending and generating text, motivating numerous researchers to utilize them for Information Extraction (IE) purposes, including Relation Extraction (RE). Nonetheless, most existing methods are predominantly designed for Sentence-level Relation Extraction (SentRE) tasks, which typically encompass a restricted set of relations and triplet facts within a single sentence. Furthermore, certain approaches resort to treating relations as candidate choices integrated into prompt templates, leading to inefficient processing and suboptimal performance when tackling Document-Level Relation Extraction (DocRE) tasks, which entail handling multiple relations and triplet facts distributed across a given document, posing distinct challenges. To overcome these limitations, we introduce AutoRE, an end-to-end DocRE model that adopts a novel RE extraction paradigm named RHF (Relation-Head-Facts). Unlike existing approaches, AutoRE does not rely on the assumption of known relation options, making it more reflective of real-world scenarios. Additionally, we have developed an easily extensible RE framework using a Parameters Efficient Fine Tuning (PEFT) algorithm (QLoRA). Our experiments on the RE-DocRED dataset showcase AutoRE's best performance, achieving state-of-the-art results, surpassing TAG by 10.03% and 9.03% respectively on the dev and test set. The code is available[1] and the demonstration video is provided[2].

## 1 Introduction

The rise of LLMs, such as GPT-4 (Achiam et al., 2023) and Llama2 (Touvron et al., 2023), has significantly propelled the progress of natural language processing due to their strong capabilities in text understanding, generation, scientific reasoning (Zhang et al., 2024a,b), social bot detection (Zhou et al., 2024), and generalization (Zhao et al., 2023). There has been an increasing interest in using LLMs to generate structured information for IE tasks (Xu et al., 2023; Wadhwa et al., 2023) and making impressive progress. Typical IE tasks using LLMs include Named Entity Recognition (NER) (Wang et al., 2023a), Relation Extraction (RE) (Zhou et al., 2023), and Event Extraction (EE) (Xu et al., 2023). Despite the outstanding result, the performance of current LLMs in RE is still far from satisfactory.

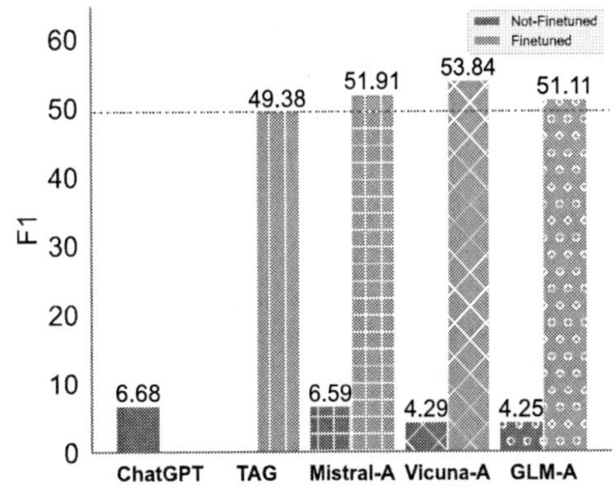


Figure 1: The result on the test set of Re-DocRED. AutoRE (-A) achieves SOTA for different LLMs.

**Underperformance on DocRE Tasks.** We evaluated several high-performing LLMs on the document-level RE (DocRE) task, specifically using the test set of Re-DocRED (Tan et al., 2022). These models included GPT-3.5-turbo[3](ChatGPT), Mistral-7B-Instruct-v0.2 (Jiang et al., 2023) (Mistral-7B), Vicuna-7B-v1.5 (Chiang et al., 2023) (Vicuna-7B), and ChatGLM3-6B (Du et al., 2022). Our results indicate that, without specific fine-tuning, the performance of these language

[1]https://github.com/THUDM/AutoRE
[2]https://www.youtube.com/watch?v=IhKRsZUAxKk
[⋆]LX and DZ contributed equally.
[†]JT is the corresponding author.

[3]https://chat.openai.com/chat



*Proceedings of the 62nd Annual Meeting of the Association for Computational Linguistics (Volume 3: System Demonstrations)*, pages 211–220
August 11-16, 2024 ©2024 Association for Computational Linguistics

models on DocRE tasks is suboptimal, as shown in the blue bars in Figure 1.

**Inefficacy in Multi-Relations.** Incorporating relations directly into the prompt template as candidates is a common strategy for LLM-based models (Wang et al., 2023b; Wei et al., 2023; Xiao et al., 2023). This method is effective for tasks that involve a relatively small number of relation types. However, the number of relation types can easily exceed 100 in real-world scenarios. Dealing with multiple relations, as seen in the Re-DocRED dataset with its 96 relation types, presents a significant challenge for most existing models. Embedding such many relations directly into the prompt template is often impractical (Wadhwa et al., 2023).

**Limitations of Current RE Paradigms.** The current paradigms in RE exhibit significant limitations in their effectiveness. Modern generative methods typically operate by either directly producing triplet facts from the input text in a singular step (Wang et al., 2023b), or by initially identifying a set of relations and subsequently generating triplet facts based on these relations (Wei et al., 2023). Earlier approaches prioritized the extraction of the head entity before the derivation of triplet facts (Li et al., 2019). However, these methodologies fall short of handling DocRE tasks that involve multiple relations and plenty of triplet facts. For instance, a single instance in the Re-DocRED dataset might encompass as many as 27 different relations and include up to 142 distinct triplet facts.

To address challenges identified in existing RE paradigms, we innovate a new pipeline RE paradigm, Relation-Head-Facts (RHF). We comprehensively redefined the 96 relation descriptions and crafted simplified relation extraction templates, developing an instruction-tuning dataset based on Re-DocRED. Utilizing the Mistral-7B model with Parameter Efficient Fine-Tuning (PEFT), QLoRA (Dettmers et al., 2023), our model achieved state-of-the-art (SOTA) performance on the Re-DocRED test set. Key contributions of our work include:

**Various RE Paradigms.** We conducted experiments across a variety of RE paradigms and revealed that a pipeline RE approach is especially potent for DocRE, particularly RHF. This paradigm prioritizes the extraction of relations, followed by the identification of subjects, thereby significantly enhancing the model's capacity to efficiently and accurately uncover triplet facts.

**Efficient DocRE Model.** Adopting the RHF paradigm for DocRE and refined relation descriptions, we have meticulously crafted an instruction-finetuning dataset based on Re-DocRED. This dataset was utilized to fine-tune the Mistral-7B with QLoRA, culminating in the creation of AutoRE, which achieved SOTA results across multiple pre-trained LLMs (PLMs), demonstrating the generality and effectiveness of this model architecture.

**Easy Enhancement of Capabilities.** We have incorporates three distinct QLoRA modules within the RHF framework, where each module is exclusively responsible for a specific task: one for relation extraction, another for head entity identification, and the third for triple fact extraction, ensuring specialized handling for each aspect. This strategy effectively lays the groundwork for future advancements while ensuring a minimal rise in computational demands and avoiding interference between subtasks.

## 2 Related work

DocRE refers to the task of extracting relations between entities at the document level, we follow the definition in (Zheng et al., 2023): Given a document $\mathcal{D}$ with a set of sentences containing a set of entities $\mathcal{V} = \{e_i\}_{i=1}^{N}$. The DocRE task is to predict the relation types between an entity pair $(e_h, e_t)_{h,t\in\{1,\cdots,N\},h\neq t}$, where $h$ stands for the head (subject) and $t$ stands for the tail (object).

**LLMs for DocRE.** Researchers have been employing LLMs to tackle RE tasks. For example, ChatIE (Wei et al., 2023) deconstructs the complex RE process into assembling the outputs from multiple rounds of Question-Answer into a final structured format. PromptRE (Gao et al., 2023) integrates LLM prompting with data programming to deal with DocRE. However, the performance of LLMs on RE tasks still lags behind SOTA models. Han et al. concluded that *ChatGPT does not adequately comprehend the subject-object relationships in RE tasks*. Similarly, Li et al. noted that in Standard-IE settings, *ChatGPT's performance is generally not as effective as BERT-based models*. Moreover, most models are tested on SentRE. To test LLMs for DocRE, we conducted tests on ChatGPT, Mistral-7B, Vicuna-7B, and ChatGLM3-6B and revealed that the current performance is far from satisfactory, as illustrated in Figure 1. This aligns with findings reported by (Li et al., 2023b), indicating that current models still fall significantly short in performance on DocRE.

**RE Prompt Template.** These models fine-tuned on LLMs for RE operate on a prompt-based or instruction-driven mechanism (Beurer-Kellner et al., 2023), engaging in a question-and-answer format to execute RE tasks. ChatIE (Wei et al., 2023), InstructUIE (Wang et al., 2023b), and YAYI (Xiao et al., 2023) while demonstrating formidable capabilities in IE, exhibit considerable limitations in their RE prompt templates. A common method in their RE process involves embedding a list of relations into the model's prompt template as alternatives. However, this approach becomes impractical when dealing with DocRE, such as the 96 relations in the Re-DocRED. This limitation is acknowledged by Wadhwa et al., who concludes that *"for datasets with long texts or a large number of targets, it is not possible to fit detailed instructions in the prompt"*.

**RE Paradigms.** Within the context of LLMs, RE paradigms are primarily categorized into two types: Pipeline and Joint. The Pipeline approach involves first identifying relations and then extracting triplet facts, or initially extracting a head entity followed by its corresponding relation and tail entity. This approach deviates from the traditional methodology of first extracting entities and then determining their interrelations (Chen and Guo, 2022; Jiang et al., 2020). The main drawbacks is that applying the conventional Pipeline approach to LLMs can be extremely time-consuming, particularly when many entities lack interrelations. On the other hand, the Joint paradigm, which inputs a text and directly outputs all triplet facts as seen in (Zhang et al., 2023), aligns more closely with traditional practices. However, as illustrated in Table 1, these paradigms encounter significant challenges when applied to DocRE, particularly due to the complexity of handling samples that may contain multiple relations and a multitude of triplet facts.

In summary, current LLMs still exhibit significant gaps in performance for DocRE, indicating a need for further fine-tuning. Additionally, the existing RE templates, which treat relations as candidates, struggle to handle scenarios involving multiple relations. Coupled with the underwhelming effectiveness of current RE paradigms, there is a need for a paradigm shift.

| Paradigm | TP | FP | R | P | F1 |
|---|---|---|---|---|---|
| D-F | 735 | 3824 | 4.21 | 16.12 | 6.68 |
| D-RS-F | 867 | 4811 | 4.97 | 15.27 | 7.50 |
| D-R-F | 1674 | 93741 | 9.59 | 1.75 | 2.97 |
| D-R-H-F | 3201 | 333226 | 18.35 | 0.95 | 1.81 |

Table 1: The result of four RE paradigms with ChatGPT. Here, TP denotes True Positive, FP is False Positive, R for Recall, P means Precision, and F1 references Micro F1. All paradigms perform poorly.

## 3 Methodology

### 3.1 RE Paradigms

We summarized the existing paradigms of RE and designed a unique extraction paradigm, different RE paradigms are illustrated in Figure 2.

**Document-facts (D-F).** Fed with a document, the model directly outputs all triplets facts. This method is brute-force and requires the shortest inference time. It directly inputs relation types as candidates into the prompt and then let the model generate all triplet facts in one step as InstructIE (Wang et al., 2023b) did.

**Document-relations-facts (D-RS-F).** In this paradigm, the model extracts the relations present within the document and embeds all the predicted relations into the prompt to obtain triplet facts.

**Document-relation-facts (D-R-F).** In this framework, the model identifies relations within a given sentence and systematically traverses these relations to acquire triplet facts that correspond to each identified relation, which is similar to the approach taken by (Wei et al., 2023).

**Document-relation-head-facts (D-R-H-F).** In our newly designed paradigm, the model specifically focuses on each relation to identify an appropriate set of entities that will function as the `'head'` in the triplet facts. Subsequently, the relevant triplets facts corresponding to these relations are extracted.

We test these paradigms with ChatGPT and the results are displayed in Table 1. We provide testing prompts for the Re-DocRED dataset under different paradigms using ChatGPT in Table 5. For brevity, we only provide two representative relation extraction prompt words. The rest are similar to these. We arrived at the following conclusion:

- LLMs still perform poorly in DocRE tasks involving the extraction of multiple relations

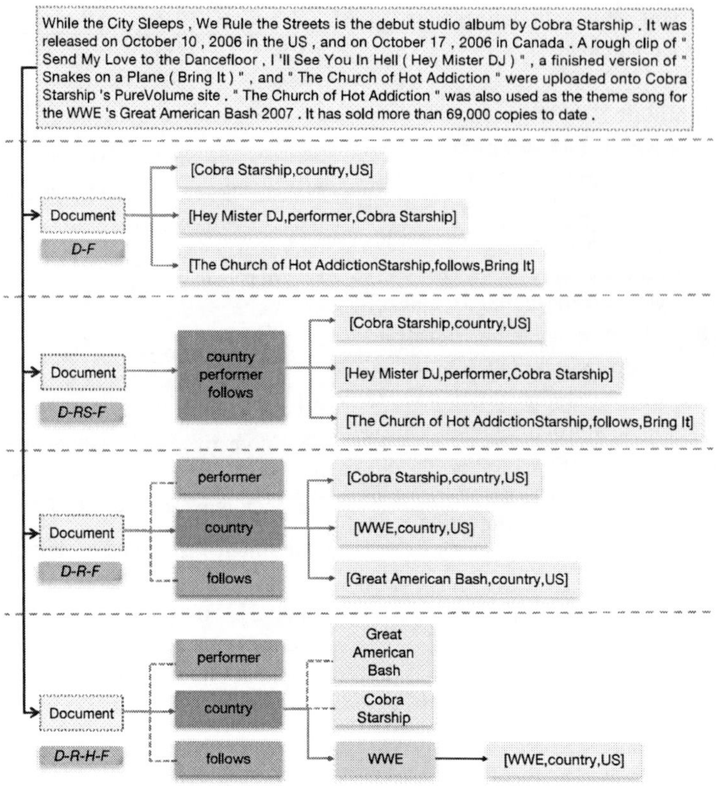


Figure 2: Processing steps of different RE paradigms.

and triplet facts, achieving only single-digit scores. As of now, fine-tuning the model is still necessary.

- By extending the thought chain to derive final triplet facts, we can obtain more accurate triplet facts, though this approach does introduce a higher number of erroneous facts.
- Harnessing the last paradigm, which we name RHF, the model can find triplets facts more accurately in a step-by-step mode with finer-grained tasks, thereby enhancing recall rates.

### 3.2 Dataset Processing

We used the Re-DocRED dataset for fine-tuning, refining it by removing duplicates and ensuring factual accuracy. This involved adjusting reciprocal relations like "follows" and "followed by" to accurately represent inversion, enhancing the dataset's robustness and precision.

In earlier experiments with ChatGPT, we discovered that providing the model with descriptions of relations enhances its capability to extract factual information. Nevertheless, incorporating Wikidata relation descriptions[4] led to diminished performance, likely due to their occasional lack of clarity and precision, as exemplified by:

*"located in the administrative territorial entity": "The item is located on the territory of the following administrative entity. Use P276 for specifying locations that are non-administrative places and for items about events. Use P1382 if the item falls only partially into the administrative entity."*

Addressing this, we systematically rewrote all 96 relation descriptions, markedly improving model performance in Table 2. An example of our revised description is as follows. Details of all relation descriptions are presented in Table 6.

*"located in the administrative territorial entity": "This relation indicates that a subject (e.g., a place, event, or item) is situated within an administrative region, the object. Example: (Harvard University, located in the administrative territorial entity,*

[4]https://www.wikidata.org/

| Paradigm | TP | FP | R | P | F1 |
|---|---|---|---|---|---|
| D-R-F-no$_{desc}$ | 1952 | 27584 | 11.19 | 6.61 | 8.31 |
| D-R-H-F-no$_{desc}$ | 4005 | 123631 | 22.95 | 3.14 | 5.52 |
| D-R-F-wiki$_{desc}$ | 1296 | 21482 | 7.43 | 5.69 | 6.44 ↓ |
| D-R-H-F-wiki$_{desc}$ | 3283 | 137462 | 18.82 | 2.33 | 4.15↓ |
| D-R-F-new$_{desc}$ | 3508 | 29002 | 20.11 | 10.79 | **14.04** ↑ |
| D-R-H-F-new$_{desc}$ | 4200 | 118243 | 24.07 | 3.43 | **6.00** ↑ |

Table 2: The result of two RE paradigms, we skip the step of extracting relations and instead use the correct relation as prior knowledge.

| Module | TP | FP | Recall | Precision | F1 |
|---|---|---|---|---|---|
| QLoRA-relation-dev | 3190 | 657 | 63.81 | 82.92 | 72.12 |
| QLoRA-head-dev | 11269 | 1910 | 65.38 | 85.51 | 74.10 |
| QLoRA-fact-dev | 14439 | 2628 | 83.77 | 84.60 | 84.18 |
| QLoRA-relation-test | 3073 | 686 | 64.44 | 81.75 | 72.06 |
| QLoRA-head-test | 12820 | 2771 | 73.48 | 82.23 | 77.60 |
| QLoRA-fact-test | 14439 | 2628 | 82.75 | 84.60 | 83.66 |
| AutoRE-dev | 7588 | 3805 | 44.02 | 66.60 | 53.01 |
| AutoRE-test | 7445 | 3794 | 42.67 | 66.24 | 51.91 |

Table 3: The results of AutoRE on the Re-DocRED dev and test sets for the three subtasks of RHF.

*Cambridge, Massachusetts).*"

Finally, in line with the RHF paradigm, we crafted instruction fine-tuning templates, breaking down the RE process of each sample into three distinct steps. The specific details of these templates can be found in Table 7, we provide a display of how we constructed our training data using simple prompt templates, the extraction of relations, the extraction of the head entity, and finally the triplet extraction.

### 3.3 QLoRA Tuning

Mistral-7B was selected as the foundation for fine-tuning because it demonstrated the best performance among the several open-source models tested when evaluating LLMs on the Re-DocRED task. To facilitate efficient training, we opted for PEFT's QLoRA. The key advantage of QLoRA is its ability to combine the benefits of quantization and Low-Rank Adaptation (Hu et al., 2021), resulting in efficient fine-tuning. Specifically, quantization reduces data complexity, allowing for more efficient storage and processing, which is particularly valuable for deploying large models on resource-constrained devices.

We leveraged three distinct QLoRA modules, each tailored to a specific stage of the RHF steps. This implementation was critical in enhancing RE efficiency. With the data volume varying across the intertwined tasks, a one-size-fits-all approach could have compromised performance. However, the modular structure of QLoRA facilitated smooth integration with the underlying base model. As a result, we instituted three distinct QLoRA modules, each meticulously fine-tuned to its specific dataset. This meticulous approach resulted in the creation of the AutoRE, which amalgamates these modules for amplified DocRE performance.

| Model | dev F1 | test F1 |
|---|---|---|
| `TAG` | 49.34 | 49.38 |
| `AutoRE-ChatGLM3-6B` | **49.86** | **51.11** |
| `AutoRE-Mistral-7B` | **53.01** | **51.91** |
| `AutoRE-Vicuna-7B` | **54.29** | **53.84** |

Table 4: The results of AutoRE for different PLMs. Compared with TAG, all AutoRE models achieve the best performance.

## 4 Experiment

### 4.1 Experimental Setup

**Test set.** In our evaluation, we utilized the refined Re-DocRED test set consisting of 499 articles and 17,448 triplet facts, and a validation set encompassing 498 articles with 17,236 triplets, ensuring a comprehensive and precise assessment.

**Evaluation Metric.** We adopted the strict Micro F1 criterion, recognizing a prediction as correct only if it precisely captures the entire relation, along with both the head and tail entities. It's important to highlight that within the Re-DocRED dataset, a triplet fact may encompass multiple aliases (mentions) for both the head and tail entities. Consequently, our evaluation protocol deems a prediction accurate if it correctly identifies any valid triplet pair. If a prediction aligns with any alias pair of the head and tail entity, it's counted as correct, but alternate accurate aliases aren't tallied in the correct statistics. Conversely, all incorrect predictions are flagged as false positives. This method ensures a stringent and statistically valid evaluation, lending robust credibility to the final results.

### 4.2 Overall Result

After training three distinct QLoRA modules, we test the performance on the Re-DocRED and then combine three QLoRAs to get the final performance on the dev set and test set, the result is shown in Table 3. When compared with TAG (Zhang et al., 2023) as a baseline which firstly reported the

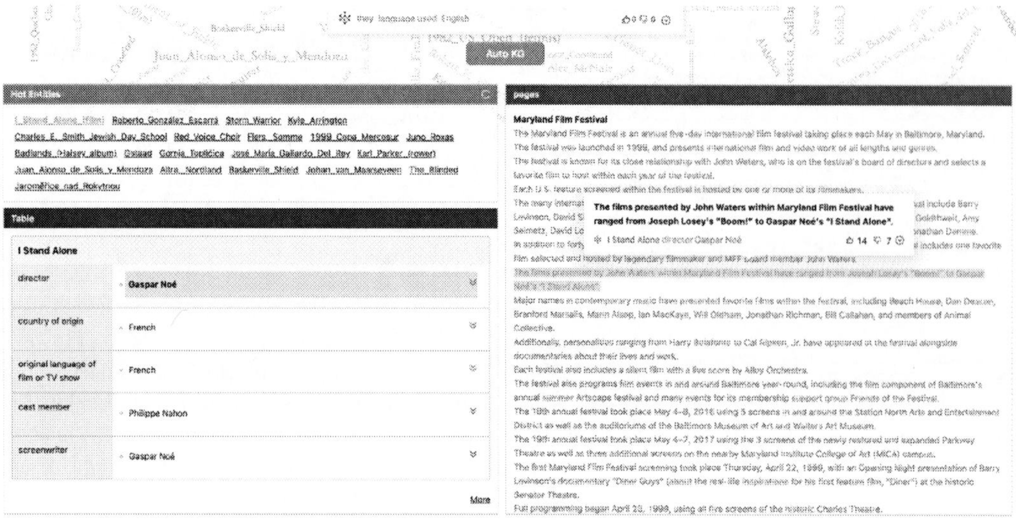


Figure 3: The homepage of online AutoRE.

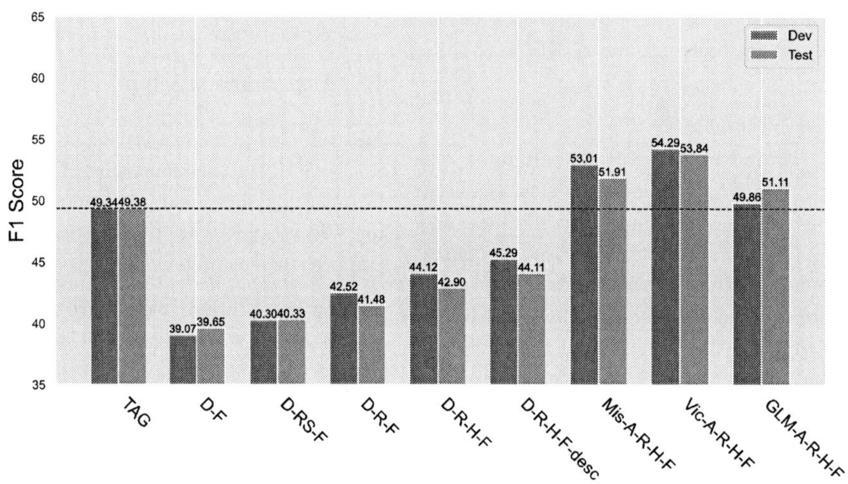


Figure 4: Performance of different paradigms and AutoRE (-A) for different PLMs.

end-to-end RE on Re-DocRED, our method has achieved SOTA results, as shown in Table 4. In both the dev set and test set, the performance improvement of AutoRE finetuned with Mistral-7B over TAG is approximately 7.44% on the dev set, and about 5.12% on the test set demonstrating the effectiveness of our approach. Furthermore, by decomposing the task into three subtasks and training with three LoRA modules, we not only achieved excellent results but also naturally acquired an easily extendable trait. This allows for targeted improvement of a specific module's performance without impacting the performance of other subtasks. Additionally, it is worth noting that our work is the first to utilize large language models for processing the Re-DocRED dataset. AutoRE can serve as a reference for subsequent research in this field.

### 4.3 Ablation

In the ablation study, we employed Mistral-7B to fine-tune the paradigms mentioned before, revealing that the RHF model yields the best performance when solely utilizing one QLoRA module. This finding substantiates our initial hypothesis during paradigm selection: employing a step-by-step approach enhances the extraction of triplet facts while significantly reducing erroneous triplets through fine-tuning. Building on this, we compared the impact of including descriptions versus omitting them. The results confirmed that incorporating proper relation descriptions indeed benefits the model, as shown in Figure 4. Additionally, we explored the effectiveness of training the entire dataset with one QLoRA versus independently training different stages of RHF with three distinct QLoRAs. The latter approach demonstrated superior performance. We believe this is due to the data imbalance among predicting relations, predicting head entities, and predicting factual triples in the RHF paradigm, with the data volume for the three subtasks begin approximately 2.8%, 24.23%, and 72.97%, respectively. When combined, the model tends to favor the prediction of triples, while its capability to predict relations is relatively insufficient.

Additionally, we have applied this framework to Vicuna-7B and ChatGLM3-6B, and both models surpassed the current SOTA levels, demonstrating the universality of the AutoRE framework. The comparative results of these experiments are illustrated in the accompanying Figure 4. Vicuna-7B scored the highest, surpassing TAG by 10.03% and 9.03% respectively on the dev and test set, whereas ChatGLM3-6B was somewhat lower. This might be due to ChatGLM3-6B having a higher proportion of Chinese in its pre-training, while it was tested on an English task. We have deployed the system on the online platform[5] for users to access and experience, as shown in Figure 3.

## 5 Conclusion

In this paper, we introduce RHF, a new paradigm for RE, alongside AutoRE, an advanced DocRE model. AutoRE represents a cutting-edge approach to the DocRE task, utilizing LLMs combined with QLoRA. This innovative model establishes a new standard, achieving SOTA results on the Re-DocRED dataset. AutoRE proficiently addresses the intricate task of extracting multiple relations from document-level texts, a significant challenge that has stymied existing models. Our future goal is to create a comprehensive, unified framework for RE, fully leveraging the capabilities and promise of this paradigm.

## Limitations

**Insufficient Number of Relations.** In real-world applications, the number of relations can reach thousands, significantly surpassing the 96 relations present in the Re-DocRED dataset. To better adapt to these real-world scenarios, it is imperative to gather more extensive datasets and expand the range of relations.

**Limitation to In-Domain Data.** AutoRE is not equipped to handle unseen relations. This limitation underscores the method's inadequate generalizability, primarily due to the limited scope of data it has been trained on.

[5]https://models.aminer.cn/neptune/


## Acknowledgements

This work is supported by Technology and Innovation Major Project of the Ministry of Science and Technology of China under Grant 2022ZD0118600, Natural Science Foundation of China(NSFC) 62276148 and 62425601, the New Cornerstone Science Foundation through the XPLORER PRIZE.


## References


Josh Achiam, Steven Adler, Sandhini Agarwal, Lama Ahmad, Ilge Akkaya, Florencia Leoni Aleman, Diogo Almeida, Janko Altenschmidt, Sam Altman, Shyamal Anadkat, et al. 2023. Gpt-4 technical report. *arXiv preprint arXiv:2303.08774*.

Luca Beurer-Kellner, Marc Fischer, and Martin Vechev. 2023. Prompting is programming: A query language for large language models. *Proceedings of the ACM on Programming Languages*, 7(PLDI):1946–1969.

Zheng Chen and Changyu Guo. 2022. A pattern-first pipeline approach for entity and relation extraction. *Neurocomputing*, 494:182–191.

Wei-Lin Chiang, Zhuohan Li, Zi Lin, Ying Sheng, Zhanghao Wu, Hao Zhang, Lianmin Zheng, Siyuan Zhuang, Yonghao Zhuang, Joseph E. Gonzalez, Ion Stoica, and Eric P. Xing. 2023. Vicuna: An open-source chatbot impressing gpt-4 with 90%* chatgpt quality.

Tim Dettmers, Artidoro Pagnoni, Ari Holtzman, and Luke Zettlemoyer. 2023. Qlora: Efficient finetuning of quantized llms. *ArXiv*, abs/2305.14314.

Zhengxiao Du, Yujie Qian, Xiao Liu, Ming Ding, Jiezhong Qiu, Zhilin Yang, and Jie Tang. 2022. Glm: General language model pretraining with autoregressive blank infilling. In *Proceedings of the 60th Annual Meeting of the Association for Computational Linguistics (Volume 1: Long Papers)*, pages 320–335.

Chufan Gao, Xulin Fan, Jimeng Sun, and Xuan Wang. 2023. Promptre: Weakly-supervised document-level relation extraction via prompting-based data programming. *arXiv preprint arXiv:2310.09265*.

Ridong Han, Tao Peng, Chaohao Yang, Benyou Wang, Lu Liu, and Xiang Wan. 2023. Is information extraction solved by chatgpt? an analysis of performance, evaluation criteria, robustness and errors. *ArXiv*, abs/2305.14450.

J. Edward Hu, Yelong Shen, Phillip Wallis, Zeyuan Allen-Zhu, Yuanzhi Li, Shean Wang, and Weizhu Chen. 2021. Lora: Low-rank adaptation of large language models. *ArXiv*, abs/2106.09685.

Albert Qiaochu Jiang, Alexandre Sablayrolles, Arthur Mensch, Chris Bamford, Devendra Singh Chaplot, Diego de Las Casas, Florian Bressand, Gianna Lengyel, Guillaume Lample, Lucile Saulnier, L'elio Renard Lavaud, Marie-Anne Lachaux, Pierre Stock, Teven Le Scao, Thibaut Lavril, Thomas Wang, Timothée Lacroix, and William El Sayed. 2023. Mistral 7b. *ArXiv*, abs/2310.06825.

Ming Jiang, Jennifer D'Souza, Sören Auer, and J Stephen Downie. 2020. Targeting precision: A hybrid scientific relation extraction pipeline for improved scholarly knowledge organization. *Proceedings of the Association for Information Science and Technology*, 57(1):e303.

Bo Li, Gexiang Fang, Yang Yang, Quansen Wang, Wei Ye, Wen Zhao, and Shikun Zhang. 2023a. Evaluating chatgpt's information extraction capabilities: An assessment of performance, explainability, calibration, and faithfulness. *ArXiv*, abs/2304.11633.

Junpeng Li, Zixia Jia, and Zilong Zheng. 2023b. Semi-automatic data enhancement for document-level relation extraction with distant supervision from large language models. In *Conference on Empirical Methods in Natural Language Processing*.

Xiaoya Li, Fan Yin, Zijun Sun, Xiayu Li, Arianna Yuan, Duo Chai, Mingxin Zhou, and Jiwei Li. 2019. Entity-relation extraction as multi-turn question answering. *ArXiv*, abs/1905.05529.

Qingyu Tan, Lu Xu, Lidong Bing, Hwee Tou Ng, and Sharifah Mahani Aljunied. 2022. Revisiting docred - addressing the false negative problem in relation extraction. In *Conference on Empirical Methods in Natural Language Processing*.

Hugo Touvron, Louis Martin, Kevin Stone, Peter Albert, Amjad Almahairi, Yasmine Babaei, Nikolay Bashlykov, Soumya Batra, Prajjwal Bhargava, Shruti Bhosale, et al. 2023. Llama 2: Open foundation and fine-tuned chat models. *arXiv preprint arXiv:2307.09288*.

Somin Wadhwa, Silvio Amir, and Byron C. Wallace. 2023. Revisiting relation extraction in the era of large language models. *Proceedings of the conference. Association for Computational Linguistics. Meeting*, 2023:15566–15589.

Shuhe Wang, Xiaofei Sun, Xiaoya Li, Rongbin Ouyang, Fei Wu, Tianwei Zhang, Jiwei Li, and Guoyin Wang. 2023a. Gpt-ner: Named entity recognition via large language models. *arXiv preprint arXiv:2304.10428*.

Xiao Wang, Wei Zhou, Can Zu, Han Xia, Tianze Chen, Yuan Zhang, Rui Zheng, Junjie Ye, Qi Zhang, Tao Gui, Jihua Kang, J. Yang, Siyuan Li, and Chunsai Du. 2023b. Instructuie: Multi-task instruction tuning for unified information extraction. *ArXiv*, abs/2304.08085.

Xiang Wei, Xingyu Cui, Ning Cheng, Xiaobin Wang, Xin Zhang, Shen Huang, Pengjun Xie, Jinan Xu, Yufeng Chen, Meishan Zhang, Yong Jiang, and Wenjuan Han. 2023. Zero-shot information extraction via chatting with chatgpt. *ArXiv*, abs/2302.10205.

Xinglin Xiao, Yijie Wang, Nan Xu, Yuqi Wang, Hanxuan Yang, Minzheng Wang, Yin Luo, Lei Wang, Wenji Mao, and Daniel Zeng. 2023. Yayi-uie: A chat-enhanced instruction tuning framework for universal information extraction. *ArXiv*, abs/2312.15548.

Derong Xu, Wei Chen, Wenjun Peng, Chao Zhang, Tong Xu, Xiangyu Zhao, Xian Wu, Yefeng Zheng, and Enhong Chen. 2023. Large language models for generative information extraction: A survey. *arXiv preprint arXiv:2312.17617*.

Dan Zhang, Ziniu Hu, Sining Zhoubian, Zhengxiao Du, Kaiyu Yang, Zihan Wang, Yisong Yue, Yuxiao Dong, and Jie Tang. 2024a. Sciglm: Training scientific language models with self-reflective instruction annotation and tuning. *arXiv preprint arXiv:2401.07950*.

Dan Zhang, Sining Zhoubian, Yisong Yue, Yuxiao Dong, and Jie Tang. 2024b. Rest-mcts*: Llm self-training via process reward guided tree search. *arXiv preprint arXiv:2406.03816*.

Ruoyu Zhang, Yanzeng Li, and Lei Zou. 2023. A novel table-to-graph generation approach for document-level joint entity and relation extraction. In *Annual Meeting of the Association for Computational Linguistics*.

Wayne Xin Zhao, Kun Zhou, Junyi Li, Tianyi Tang, Xiaolei Wang, Yupeng Hou, Yingqian Min, Beichen Zhang, Junjie Zhang, Zican Dong, Yifan Du, Chen Yang, Yushuo Chen, Z. Chen, Jinhao Jiang, Ruiyang Ren, Yifan Li, Xinyu Tang, Zikang Liu, Peiyu Liu, Jianyun Nie, and Ji rong Wen. 2023. A survey of large language models. *ArXiv*, abs/2303.18223.

Hanwen Zheng, Sijia Wang, and Lifu Huang. 2023. A survey of document-level information extraction. *ArXiv*, abs/2309.13249.

Huixue Zhou, Mingchen Li, Yongkang Xiao, Han Yang, and Rui Zhang. 2023. Llm instruction-example adaptive prompting (leap) framework for clinical relation extraction. *medRxiv*, pages 2023–12.

Ming Zhou, Dan Zhang, Yuandong Wang, Yangli-ao Geng, Yuxiao Dong, and Jie Tang. 2024. Lgb: Language model and graph neural network-driven social bot detection. *arXiv preprint arXiv:2406.08762*.

| Paradigms | Prompt |
|---|---|
| D-R-F | Given a passage: {sentences}, and relation list: {relation_list}<br>Check the passage, and find which relations can be derived from the passage.<br>Your output format is as following:<br>relation1<br>relation2<br>...<br>one example like:<br>country of citizenship<br>father<br>The relations must be in the relation list.<br>If no relation in the sentence, you should only output:<br>no relation |
| | Given a relation: {relation}.<br>Provided a passage: {sentences}.<br>Derive all the triplet facts from the passage according to the given relations.<br>Your output format is as following:<br>[subject,{relation}, object]<br>[subject,{relation}, object]<br>...<br>The subject and object should be an entity from the passage. |
| D-R-H-F | Given a passage: {sentences}, and relation list: {relation_list}<br>Check the passage, and find which relations can be derived from the passage.<br>Your output format is as following:<br>relation1<br>relation2<br>...<br>one example like:<br>country of citizenship<br>father<br>The relations must be in the relation list.<br>If no relation in the sentence, you should only output:<br>no relation |
| | Given the relation: {relation}.<br>Now the passage is: {sentences}.<br>Derive all the entities from the passage that can serve as the subject of the {relation}.<br>Your output format is as following:<br>entity1<br>entity2<br>...<br>The entities should all be from the passage. |
| | Given the relation: {relation}.<br>Now the passage is: {sentences}.<br>Derive all the triplet facts from the passage that takes {subject} as a subject.<br>Your output format is as following:<br>[{subject},{relation},object]<br>[{subject},{relation},object]<br>...<br>The object should be an entity from the passage. |

Table 5: ChatGPT prompt template for RE on Re-DocRED.

| Relation | Description |
|---|---|
| `located in the administrative territorial entity` | In the "located in the administrative territorial entity" relation, the subject, a place, event, or item, resides or takes place in the object, an administrative region. Example: (Harvard University, located in the administrative territorial entity, Cambridge, Massachusetts). |
| `country` | For the "country" relation, the subject pertains to a non-human entity, such as an organization, place, or event. The object signifies the sovereign state where the subject is based or occurs. Example: (Amazon Inc, country, United States). |
| `country of citizenship` | The "country of citizenship" relation denotes that the subject, an individual, is recognized as a citizen by the object, a country. Example: (Elon Musk, country of citizenship, United States). |
| `contains administrative territorial entity` | The relation "contains administrative territorial entity" involves a subject, an administrative territory, encompassing the object, a subdivision or part of this administrative territory. Example: (California, contains administrative territorial entity, Los Angeles). |
| `has part` | The "has part" relation reflects that the subject, an entity or whole, comprises the object, a part or component of the subject. Example: (A car, has part, engine). |
| `date of birth` | In the "date of birth" relation, the subject, a person, was born on the object, the specified date. Example: (John Doe, date of birth, January 1, 1990). |
| `part of` | In the "part of" relation, the subject, a component or section, belongs to the object, a larger whole or aggregate. Example: (Engine, part of, a car). |
| `notable work` | The "notable work" relation indicates a significant work assigned to the subject, a creator, while the object is that noted scientific, artistic, or literary work itself. Example: (Jane Austen, notable work, Pride and Prejudice). |
| `publication date` | The "publication date" relation marks when the subject, a work, was first published or released, with the object being that specific date. Example: (Pride and Prejudice, publication date, 1813). |
| `inception` | In the "inception" relation, the subject, an event, or an item (not a person), came into existence at the object, a specific date or point in time. Example: (Google, inception, September 4, 1998). |
| `date of death` | The "date of death" relation specifies when the subject, a once-living person, died. The object is the particular date of demise. Example: (Albert Einstein, date of death, April 18, 1955). |

Table 6: New designed relation descriptions. We only present part of the descriptions of 96 relations. The whole relation descriptions can be found via this link: `https://github.com/THUDM/AutoRE`.

| Submission | Instruct Tuning Template |
|---|---|
| `relation_template` | Given a passage: {sentences}, list any underlying relations. |
| `entity_template` | Given a relation {relation}, and its description: {description} and a passage: {sentences}, list entities that can be identified as suitable subjects for the relation. |
| `fact_template` | Given relation {relation} and relation description: {description}. Provided a passage: {sentences}, list all triple facts that take {relation} as the relation and {subject} as the subject. |

Table 7: Instruction tuning template for RHF.

# LinkTransformer: A Unified Package for Record Linkage with Transformer Language Models

**Abhishek Arora and Melissa Dell***
Harvard University, Cambridge, MA, USA
*Corresponding author: melissadell@fas.harvard.edu.

## Abstract

Many computational analyses require linking information across noisy text datasets. While large language models (LLMs) offer significant promise, approximate string matching in popular statistical softwares such as R and Stata remain predominant in academic applications. These packages have simple interfaces and can be easily extended to a diversity of languages and settings, and for academic applications, ease-of-use and extensibility are essential. In contrast, packages for record linkage with LLMs require significant familiarity with deep learning frameworks and often focus on applications of commercial value in English. The open-source package `LinkTransformer` aims to bridge this gap by providing an end-to-end software for performing record linkage and other data cleaning tasks with transformer LLMs, treating linkage as a text retrieval problem. At its core is an off-the-shelf toolkit for applying transformer models to record linkage. `LinkTransformer` contains a rich repository of pre-trained models for multiple languages and supports easy integration of any transformer language model from Hugging Face or OpenAI, providing the extensibility required for many scholarly applications. Its APIs also perform common data processing tasks, *e.g.*, aggregation, noisy de-duplication, and translation-free cross-lingual linkage. `LinkTransformer` contains comprehensive tools for efficient model tuning, allowing for highly customized applications, and users can easily contribute their custom-trained models to its model hub to ensure reproducibility. Using a novel benchmark dataset geared towards academic applications, we show that `LinkTransformer`- with both custom models and Hugging Face or OpenAI models off-the-shelf - outperforms string matching by a wide margin. By combining transformer LMs with intuitive APIs, `LinkTransformer` aims to democratize these performance gains for those who lack familiarity with deep learning frameworks.

## 1 Introduction

Linking information across sources is fundamental to a variety of analyses in social science, business, and government. A recent literature, focused on matching across e-commerce datasets, shows the promise of transformer large language models (LLMs) for improving record linkage (alternatively termed entity resolution or approximate dictionary matching). Yet these methods have not yet made widespread inroads in social science applications, with rule-based methods continuing to overwhelmingly predominate (*e.g.*, see reviews by Binette and Steorts (2022); Abramitzky et al. (2021)). In particular, researchers commonly employ string-based matching tools available in statistical software packages such as R or Stata.

In academic applications, extensibility to a diversity of human societies (historic and present) and ease of use for those not familiar with deep learning are essential. String matching algorithms in widely used statistical packages meet these requirements because they require little coding expertise and can easily be applied across different languages and settings. In contrast, existing tools for large language model matching require considerable technical expertise to implement. This makes sense in the context for which these models were developed - classifying and linking products for e-commerce firms, which employ data scientists - but it is a significant impediment for scholarly use.

To bridge the gap between the ease-of-use of widely employed string matching packages and the power of modern LLMs, we developed `LinkTransformer`, a general purpose, user friendly package for record linkage with transformer LLMs. `LinkTransformer` treats record linkage as a text retrieval problem (See Figure 1). The API can be thought of as a drop-in replacement to popular dataframe manipulation frameworks like pandas or tools like R and Stata, catering to those



*Proceedings of the 62nd Annual Meeting of the Association for Computational Linguistics (Volume 3: System Demonstrations)*, pages 221–231
August 11-16, 2024 ©2024 Association for Computational Linguistics

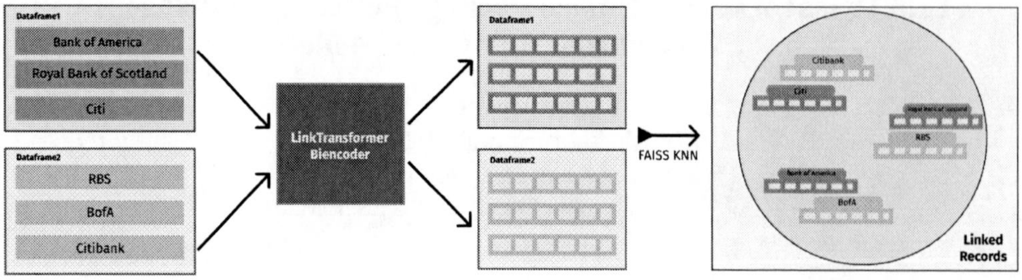


Figure 1: **Architecture.** This figure shows the `LinkTransformer` architecture for record linkage.

who lack extensive coding experience.

`LinkTransformer` integrates:

1. An off-the-shelf toolkit for applying transformer models to record linkage

2. A rich repository of pre-trained models, supporting multiple applications and languages and evaluated on novel social science-oriented benchmarks

3. Easy integration of any Hugging Face or OpenAI transformer LLM, for extensibility

4. APIs to support common data processing tasks: aggregation, de-duplication, classification, and translation-free cross-lingual linkage

5. Comprehensive tools for model tuning

6. Easy sharing to the `LinkTransformer` model hub, as reproducibility is essential for academic applications

While transfer learning can facilitate strong off-the-shelf performance, heterogeneity in how out-of-domain applications are from LLM training corpora - combined with settings that demand extremely high accuracy - create many scenarios where custom training may be needed. `LinkTransformer` makes it straightforward for users to tune their own customized models.

`LinkTransformer` performs well on challenging record linkage applications. It is equally applicable to tasks with a single field - *e.g.,* linking 1940s Mexican tariff product classes across time - and applications that require concatenating an array of noisily measured fields - *e.g.,* linking 1950s Japanese firms across different large-scale, noisy databases using the firm name, location, products, shareholders, and banks. This type of linkage problem would be highly convoluted with traditional string matching, as there are many noisily measured fields (*e.g.,* products can be described in different ways, different subsets of managers and shareholders are listed, etc). Using `LinkTransformer` to automatically concatenate the information and feed it to a LLM handles these challenges with ease.

`LinkTransformer` has a GNU General Public License and is being actively maintained. A demo is available at `https://youtu.be/hFrh8k1pukI`. More resources are available on our package website `https://linktransformer.github.io/`.

This study is organized as follows: Section 2 provides an overview of related work. The core `LinkTransformer` library is described in Section 3. Section 4 evaluates `LinkTransformer` performance on various use cases, and Section 5 considers ethics.

## 2 Relation to the Existing Literature

The record linkage literature is sprawling - with large literatures in quantitative social science (particularly economics), statistics, computer science, and industry applications. These literatures are highly disjoint, taking very different approaches and even using different terms (record linkage, entity resolution/matching, approximate dictionary matching, etc.) to refer to the same task. A 2022 interdisciplinary *Science Advances* review, "(Almost) All of Entity Resolution" (Binette and Steorts, 2022), concludes that deep neural models are unlikely to be applicable to record linkage using structured data. It argues that training datasets are small and there is not much to be gained from LLMs since text fields are often short. Yet there is an active literature on e-commerce applications that underscores the utility of LLMs for linking structured datasets, even when text fields are short. Benchmarks in this literature (e.g., Köpcke et al. (2010); Das et al. (2015); Primpeli et al. (2019)) focus on high resource commercial applications in English, such as matching electronics and software products between Amazon-Google and Walmart-Amazon listings, matching iTunes and Amazon music listings, and matching restaurants between Fodors and Zagat. Recent studies have used masked language models (Li et al., 2020; Joshi et al., 2021; Brunner and Stockinger, 2020; Zhou et al., 2022), GPT (Peeters and Bizer, 2023; Tang et al., 2022), or both, significantly outperforming static word embedding and other older linkage methods.

The siloed nature of the literature is reflected in softwares. The main existing package for record linkage with LLMs is Ditto (Li et al., 2020), which implements Li et al. (2023). It requires significant programming expertise to deploy. While this is appropriate for an e-commerce target audience - where data scientists predominate - the technical expertise required and the lack of pre-trained models targeted to multilingual social science applications has likely hindered further takeup. Moreover, most of the literature examining record linkage with LLMs poses record linkage as a classification task (Barlaug and Gulla, 2021), which is appropriate for the e-commerce benchmarks. However, this significantly limits extensibility, as in many social science and government applications the number of entities to be linked numbers in the millions, making it computationally infeasible to compute a softmax over all possible classes (entities). In the social sciences, string matching with statistical packages predominates.

`LinkTransformer` frames record linkage as a knn-retrieval task, in which the nearest neighbor for each entity in a query embedding dataset is retrieved from a key embedding dataset, using cosine similarity implemented with an FAISS backend (Johnson et al., 2019). `LinkTransformer` includes functionality to tune a no-match threshold - since not all entities in the query need to have a match in the key - and allows for retrieving multiple neighbors, to accommodate many-to-many matches between the query and the key. The `LinkTransformer` architecture was inspired by bi-encoder applications with unstructured texts, *e.g.*, passage retrieval (Karpukhin et al., 2020), entity disambiguation (Wu et al., 2019), and entity co-reference resolution (Hsu and Horwood, 2022). The knn retrieval structure of `LinkTransformer` also supports noisy de-duplication, a closely related task that finds noisily duplicated observations within a dataset, following the methods developed in Silcock et al. (2023).

`LinkTransformer` departs from much of the literature in utilizing LLMs trained for semantic similarity, combined with a supervised contrastive loss (Khosla et al., 2020). Off-the-shelf LLMs such as BERT have anisotropic geometries (Ethayarajh, 2019), which makes them unsuitable off-the-shelf for metric learning problems like `LinkTransformer` nearest neighbor retrieval. Contrastive training for semantic similarity reduces anisotropy, improving alignment between semantically similar pairs to be linked and improving sentence embeddings (Wang and Isola, 2020; Reimers and Gurevych, 2019). `LinkTransformer` builds closely upon the contrastively trained Sentence BERT (Reimers and Gurevych, 2019), whose semantic similarity library inspired many of the features in `LinkTransformer`.

## 3 The `LinkTransformer` Library

### 3.1 Off-the-shelf Toolkit

At the core of `LinkTransformer` is an off-the-shelf toolkit that streamlines record linkage with transformer language models. The record linkage models enable using pre-trained or self-trained transformer models with minimal coding required. Any Hugging Face or OpenAI model can be used by configuring the `model` and `openai_key` arguments. This future-proofs the package, allowing it to take advantage of the open-source revolution that Hugging Face has pioneered. Here is an example of the core **merge** functionality, based on embeddings sourced from an external language model.

```
#pip install linktransformer
import linktransformer as lt
df1 = pd.read_csv("df1.csv")
df1 = pd.read_csv("df2.csv")
df_matched = lt.merge(df2, df1,
    merge_type='1:m', on=["Varname"],
    model="sentence-transformers/all-
    MiniLM-L6-v2", openai_key=None)
```

We recommend that users new to LLMs deploy the package using a cloud service optimized for deep learning to avoid the need to resolve dependencies, and our tutorials use Colab.

In addition to supporting Hugging Face and OpenAI models, `LinkTransformer` provides pre-trained models, currently encompassing six languages (English, Chinese, French, German, Japanese, and Spanish) plus a multilingual model.

These models are trained and evaluated using novel datasets that reflect common record linkage tasks in quantitative social science:

1. **Firm aliases**: these are drawn from Wikidata for 6 languages. Firm alias models learn to recognize the different ways that firm names are written and abbreviated.

2. **Homogenized industry and product names:** These are drawn from the United Nations economic classification schedules (International Standard Industrial Classification, Standard International Trade Classification, and Central Product Classification), that map different country classifications to an international standard. We include models trained on these for 3 official UN languages.

3. **Historical datasets**: linked product-level Mexican tariff schedules from 1947 and 1948, and a dataset linking 1950s Japanese firms across noisy text databases. Historical data are central to better understanding economic and social processes; for example, these datasets could be used to elucidate the political determinants of tariff policy or the role of supply chain linkages in Japan's spectacular 20th century growth performance.

We also provide models for the standard industry benchmarks.

We name these models with a semantic syntax: `{org_name}/lt-{data}-{task}-{lang}`. Each model has a detailed model card, with the appropriate tags for model discovery. Additionally, we provide a high-level interface to download the right model by task through a wrapper that retrieves the best model for a task chosen by the user.

`LinkTransformer` makes no compromise in scalability. All functions are vectorized wherever possible and the vector similarity search underlying knn retrieval is accelerated by an FAISS (Johnson et al., 2019) backend that can easily be extended to perform retrieval on GPUs with billion-scale datasets. We also allow "blocking" - running knn-search only within "blocks" that can be defined by the `blocking_vars` argument.

Record linkage frequently requires matching databases on multiple noisily measured keys. `LinkTransformer` allows a list of as many variables as needed in the "on" argument. The merge keys specified by the on variable are serialized by concatenating them with a $< SEP >$ token, which is based on the underlying tokenizer of the selected base language model. Since we have designed the API around dataframes - due to their familiarity amongst users of R, Stata or Excel - all import/export formats are supported.

The `LinkTransformer` API supports a plethora of other features that are frequently integrated into data analysis pipelines. These include:

**Aggregation:** Data processing often requires the aggregation of fine descriptions into coarser categories, that are consistent across datasets and time or facilitate interpretation. This problem can be thought of as a merge between finer categories and coarser ones, where `LinkTransformer` classifies the finer categories by means of finding their nearest coarser neighbor(s). `lt.aggregate_rows` performs this task, with a similar syntax to the main record linkage API.

**Deduplication**: Text datasets can contain noisy duplicates. Popular libraries like dedupe (Gregg and Eder, 2022) only support deduplication using metrics that most closely resemble edit distance. `LinkTransformer` allows for semantic deduplication with a single, intuitive function call.

```
df_dedup=lt.dedup_rows(df,on="
    CompanyName",model="sentence-
    transformers/all-MiniLM-L6-v2",
    cluster_params= {'threshold': 0.7})
```

`LinkTransformer` de-duplication clusters embeddings under the hood, with embeddings in the same cluster classified as duplicates. `LinkTransformer` supports SLINK, DBSCAN, HDBSCAN, and agglomerative clustering.

**Cross-lingual linkage**: Analyses spanning multiple countries often require cross-lingual linkage. Machine translation followed by string matching methods tend to perform very poorly, necessitating costly hand linking. `LinkTransformer` users can bypass translation by using multilingual transformer models.

**Text Classification:** While Hugging Face provides an accessible API, text classification can still be challenging for users who haven't been exposed to NLP libraries. Our API requires only one line of code to use a classification model on Hugging Face or the ChatGPT (3.5 and 4) API to classify texts.

Notebooks and tutorials outline the use of these functionalities on toy datasets.[1] We also have a tutorial to help those who are less familiar with language models to select ones that fit their use

[1] `https://linktransformer.github.io/`

case. More detailed information and additional features can be found in the online documentation.[2]

### 3.2 Customized Model Training

#### Record Linkage

Record linkage tasks are highly diverse and may demand very high accuracy; hence, fine-tuning on target datasets may be necessary. `LinkTransformer` supports easy model training, which can be initialized using any Hugging Face transformer model.

Training data are expected in a *pandas* data frame, removing entry barriers for the typical social science user. A data frame can include only positive labeled examples (linked observations) as inputs, in which case the model is evaluated using an information retrieval evaluator that measures top-1 retrieval accuracy. Alternately, it can take a list of both positive and negative pairs, in which case the model is evaluated using a binary classification objective.

Only the most important arguments are exposed and the rest have reasonable defaults which can be tweaked by more advanced users. Additionally, `LinkTransformer` supports logging of a training run on Weights and Biases (Biewald, 2020).

```
best_model_path=lt.train_model(
        model_path="hf-path-model",
        data="df1.csv",
        left_col_names=["left_var"],
        right_col_names=['right_var'],
        label_col_name=None,
        log_wandb=False,
        training_args={"num_epochs": 1})
```

Default training expects positive pairs. A simple argument that specifies `label_col_name` switches the dataset format and model evaluation to adapt to positive and negative labels. To make this extensible to most record linkage use-cases, the model can also be trained on a dataset of cluster ids and texts by simply specifying `clus_id_col_name` and `clus_text_col_names`.

`LinkTransformer` is sufficiently sample efficient that most models in the model zoo were trained with a student Google Colab account, an integral feature since the vast majority of potential users have constrained compute budgets.

#### Classification

We added classification at the request of `LinkTransformer` users. Users can train custom models with a single line of code, using training data in the form of a data frame. They simply specify the on columns containing the text and a column for annotations, `label_col_name`. We have helpful guides on our website to allow users to effectively tune hyperparameters.

Since this function wraps around the *Trainer* class from Hugging Face, it can make use of multiple GPUs. `training_args` allow an advanced user to fully customize the *Trainer* by providing arguments with the same format as Hugging Face's *TrainingArguments* class.

### 3.3 User Contributions

`LinkTransformer` aims to promote reusability and reproducibility, which are central to academic applications. End-users can upload their self-trained models to the `LinkTransformer` Hugging Face hub with a simple `model.save_to_hub` command. Whenever a model is saved, a model card is automatically generated that follows best practices outlined in Hugging Face's Model Card Guidebook.

## 4 Applications

The LLMs in the `LinkTransformer` model zoo excel at a variety of tasks. Table 1 evaluates performance linking Wikidata firm aliases (panel A), linking product descriptions from different countries' classification schemes (panel B), linking products to their industries (panel C), and aggregating fine product descriptions to coarser descriptions (panel D). It compares the accuracy of Levenshtein edit distance matching (Levenshtein et al., 1966), popular off-the-shelf semantic similarity models from Hugging Face (see Appendix Table A-1 for a listing of models used), OpenAI embeddings (the better of `text-embedding-3-small` and `text-embedding-3-large`, which outperformed Ada embeddings), and `LinkTransformer` tuned models. The supplementary materials describe the models and training datasets in detail.

As expected, custom-tuned models typically achieve the best performance, with off-the-shelf models still outperforming edit distance matching, typically by a wide margin. The custom-trained models are often plausibly achieving human-level accuracy, as cases that they get wrong are often impossible to resolve from the information provided, *e.g.*, in cases where a firm is referred to by two completely disparate acronyms.

Second, we examine historical applications, which are central to understanding long-run phe-

[2] `https://github.com/dell-research-harvard/linktransformer`

| Model | Edit Distance | SBERT | LT | OpenAI |
|---|---|---|---|---|
| *Panel A: Company Linkage* | | | | |
| lt-wikidata-comp-fr | 0.43 | 0.74 | **0.81** | 0.75 |
| lt-wikidata-comp-ja | 0.51 | 0.61 | **0.70** | 0.63 |
| lt-wikidata-comp-zh | 0.66 | 0.77 | **0.83** | 0.82 |
| lt-wikidata-comp-de | 0.51 | 0.66 | **0.76** | 0.71 |
| lt-wikidata-comp-es | 0.62 | 0.68 | 0.75 | **0.82** |
| lt-wikidata-comp-en | 0.36 | 0.60 | **0.70** | 0.64 |
| lt-wikidata-comp-multi | 0.55 | 0.69 | **0.83** | 0.77 |
| lt-wikidata-comp-prod-ind-ja | 0.48 | 0.97 | **0.99** | 0.98 |
| *Panel B: Fine Product Linkage* | | | | |
| lt-un-data-fine-fine-en | 0.64 | 0.82 | **0.87** | 0.84 |
| lt-un-data-fine-fine-es | 0.42 | 0.68 | **0.80** | 0.72 |
| lt-un-data-fine-fine-fr | 0.45 | 0.71 | **0.75** | 0.72 |
| lt-un-data-fine-fine-multi | 0.54 | 0.79 | **0.84** | 0.77 |
| *Panel C: Product to Industry Linkage* | | | | |
| lt-un-data-fine-industry-en | 0.18 | 0.81 | **0.80** | 0.73 |
| lt-un-data-fine-industry-es | 0.18 | 0.67 | **0.72** | 0.64 |
| lt-un-data-fine-industry-fr | 0.14 | 0.56 | **0.72** | 0.55 |
| lt-un-data-fine-industry-multi | 0.10 | 0.69 | **0.78** | 0.75 |
| *Panel D: Product Aggregation* | | | | |
| lt-un-data-fine-coarse-en | 0.27 | 0.76 | 0.85 | **0.86** |
| lt-un-data-fine-coarse-es | 0.24 | 0.75 | **0.80** | 0.7 |
| lt-un-data-fine-coarse-fr | 0.24 | 0.74 | **0.77** | 0.69 |
| lt-un-data-fine-coarse-multi | 0.22 | 0.6 | **0.64** | 0.62 |

Table 1: Performance of various embedding models, measured by top-1 retrieval accuracy. *Company linkage* links company aliases together, *Fine Product Linkage* links products from different product classifications together, *Product to Industry Linkage* links products to their industry classifications, and *Product Aggregation* links a fine product to its coarser product classification. *LT* gives the performance of the trained LinkTransformer model. *Edit Distance* gives linkage accuracy when using Levenshtein distance, and *SBERT* when using semantic similarity models off-the-shelf (See Table A-1). *OpenAI* gives the best linkage performance when using embeddings from OpenAI embedding models.

| Dataset | Semantic Sim | Fine Tuned | Edit Distance | OpenAI ADA | LT UN/Wiki Model |
|---|---|---|---|---|---|
| mexicantrade4748 | 0.75 | **0.88** | 0.70 | 0.83 | 0.80 |
| historicjapan | 0.69 | **0.91** | 0.27 | 0.86 | 0.74 |

Table 2: Historical Linking. We examine the base semantic similarity model off-the-shelf, a fine-tuned `LinkTransformer` version, Levenshtein edit distance on the tariff description or company name, OpenAI embeddings and a pre-trained LinkTransformer model. The table reports top-1 accuracy.

nomena like economic growth or social mobility and typically lack unique identifiers for linkage. First, we link two tariff schedules published by the Mexican government in the 1940s (Secretaria de Economía de Mexico, 1948). Tariffs were applied at an extremely disaggregated product level and each of the many thousands of products in the tariff schedule is identified only by a text description, which can change each time the tariff schedule is updated. Around 2,000 products map to different descriptions across the schedules in a rare crosswalk published by the government (typically, homogenized crosswalks do not exist). We link the tariff schedules using an off-the-shelf semantic similarity model, as well as a model tuned on the in-domain historical data and Open AI embeddings. All transformer models widely outperform edit distance. While there are considerable debates on the role that trade policies have played in long-run development, empirical evidence is limited largely due to the considerable challenges of homogenizing tariff schedules across time. Language model linking offers the opportunitiy to bring novel quantitative evidence to this important question.

We also link firms across two different 1950s publications created by different Japanese credit bureaus (Jinji Koshinjo, 1954; Teikoku Koshinjo, 1957). One has around 7,000 firms and the other has around 70,000, including many small firms. Firm names can be written differently across publications and there are many duplicated or similar firm names. We concatenate information on the firm's name, prefecture, major products, shareholders, and banks. These variables contain OCR noise and the information included varies, *e.g.* in terms of how a firm's products are described, which shareholders are included, etc. This makes rule-based methods quite brittle, whereas the custom-tuned model links 91% of firms correctly.

In the supplemental materials, we examine the various e-commerce and industry benchmarks that prevail in this literature. We use the same training procedure for each benchmark, to avoid overfitting, which is often not the case in the literature. We have generally comparable performance, sometimes outperformed by other models (that could be used with `LinkTransformer` if on Hugging Face) and sometimes outperforming other models.

When OCR errors are severe, too much information may have been destroyed to achieve the desired accuracy with the garbled texts. A multimodal matching framework (Arora et al., 2023) that uses aligned language and vision transformers to incorporate the original image crops or a matching framework that incorporates character visual similarity (Yang et al., 2023) - as OCR confuses visually similar characters - may be required. Vision and multimodal linking support will be incorporated into future releases of `LinkTransformer`.

## 5 Ethics Statement

`LinkTransformer` is ethically sound. It is built using public domain training data. Because it is built upon transformer language models, it will not be suitable for lower resource languages that lack pre-trained LLMs. However, it can utilize any Hugging Face or OpenAI embedding model and hence will be extensible as the low-resource transformer literature expands to lower resource settings, as long as relevant embedding models are posted on Hugging Face or made available commercially by OpenAI.

## References


Ran Abramitzky, Leah Boustan, Katherine Eriksson, James Feigenbaum, and Santiago Pérez. 2021. Automated linking of historical data. *Journal of Economic Literature*, 59(3):865–918.

Abhishek Arora, Xinmei Yang, Shao Yu Jheng, and Melissa Dell. 2023. Linking representations with multimodal contrastive learning. *arXiv preprint arXiv:2304.03464*.

Nils Barlaug and Jon Atle Gulla. 2021. Neural networks for entity matching: A survey. *ACM Transactions on Knowledge Discovery from Data (TKDD)*, 15(3):1–37.

Lukas Biewald. 2020. Experiment tracking with weights and biases. Software available from wandb.com.

Olivier Binette and Rebecca C Steorts. 2022. (almost) all of entity resolution. *Science Advances*, 8(12):eabi8021.

Ursin Brunner and Kurt Stockinger. 2020. Entity matching with transformer architectures-a step forward in data integration. In *23rd International Conference on Extending Database Technology, Copenhagen, 30 March-2 April 2020*, pages 463–473. OpenProceedings.

Sanjib Das, A Doan, C Gokhale Psgc, Pradap Konda, Yash Govind, and Derek Paulsen. 2015. The magellan data repository.

Kawin Ethayarajh. 2019. How contextual are contextualized word representations? comparing the geometry of bert, elmo, and gpt-2 embeddings. *arXiv preprint arXiv:1909.00512*.

Forest Gregg and Derek Eder. 2022. dedupe.

Benjamin Hsu and Graham Horwood. 2022. Contrastive representation learning for cross-document coreference resolution of events and entities. *arXiv preprint arXiv:2205.11438*.

Jinji Koshinjo. 1954. *Nihon shokuinrokj*. Jinji Koshinjo.

Jeff Johnson, Matthijs Douze, and Hervé Jégou. 2019. Billion-scale similarity search with gpus. *IEEE Transactions on Big Data*, 7(3):535–547.

Salil Rajeev Joshi, Arpan Somani, and Shourya Roy. 2021. Relink: Complete-link industrial record linkage over hybrid feature spaces. In *2021 IEEE 37th International Conference on Data Engineering (ICDE)*, pages 2625–2636. IEEE.

Vladimir Karpukhin, Barlas Oğuz, Sewon Min, Patrick Lewis, Ledell Wu, Sergey Edunov, Danqi Chen, and Wen-tau Yih. 2020. Dense passage retrieval for open-domain question answering. *arXiv preprint arXiv:2004.04906*.

Prannay Khosla, Piotr Teterwak, Chen Wang, Aaron Sarna, Yonglong Tian, Phillip Isola, Aaron Maschinot, Ce Liu, and Dilip Krishnan. 2020. Supervised contrastive learning. *arXiv preprint arXiv:2004.11362*.

Hanna Köpcke, Andreas Thor, and Erhard Rahm. 2010. Evaluation of entity resolution approaches on real-world match problems. *Proceedings of the VLDB Endowment*, 3(1-2):484–493.

Vladimir I Levenshtein et al. 1966. Binary codes capable of correcting deletions, insertions, and reversals. In *Soviet physics doklady*, volume 10, pages 707–710. Soviet Union.

Yuliang Li, Jinfeng Li, Yoshi Suhara, AnHai Doan, and Wang-Chiew Tan. 2023. Effective entity matching with transformers. *The VLDB Journal*, pages 1–21.

Yuliang Li, Jinfeng Li, Yoshihiko Suhara, AnHai Doan, and Wang-Chiew Tan. 2020. Deep entity matching with pre-trained language models. *arXiv preprint arXiv:2004.00584*.

Ralph Peeters and Christian Bizer. 2023. Using chatgpt for entity matching. *arXiv preprint arXiv:2305.03423*.

Anna Primpeli, Ralph Peeters, and Christian Bizer. 2019. The wdc training dataset and gold standard for large-scale product matching. In *Companion Proceedings of The 2019 World Wide Web Conference*, pages 381–386.

Nils Reimers and Iryna Gurevych. 2019. Sentence-bert: Sentence embeddings using siamese bert-networks. *arXiv preprint arXiv:1908.10084*.

Secretaria de Economía de Mexico. 1948. Ajuste de las fracciones de la tarifa arancelaria que rigieron hasta el año de 1947 con las de la tarifa que entró en vigor por decreto de fecha 13 de diciembre del mismo año y se consideraron a partir de 1948. In *Anuario Estadístico del Comercio Exterior de los Estados Unidos Mexicanos*. Gobierno de Mexico.

Emily Silcock, Luca D'Amico-Wong, Jinglin Yang, and Melissa Dell. 2023. Noise-robust de-duplication at scale. *International Conference on Learning Representations*.

Jiawei Tang, Yifei Zuo, Lei Cao, and Samuel Madden. 2022. Generic entity resolution models. In *NeurIPS 2022 First Table Representation Workshop*.

Teikoku Koshinjo. 1957. *Teikoku Ginko Kaisha Yoroku*. Teikoku Koshinjo.

Tongzhou Wang and Phillip Isola. 2020. Understanding contrastive representation learning through alignment and uniformity on the hypersphere. In *International Conference on Machine Learning*, volume 119, pages 9929–9939. PMLR.

Ledell Wu, Fabio Petroni, Martin Josifoski, Sebastian Riedel, and Luke Zettlemoyer. 2019. Scalable zero-shot entity linking with dense entity retrieval. *arXiv preprint arXiv:1911.03814*.

Xinmei Yang, Abhishek Arora, Shao-Yu Jheng, and Melissa Dell. 2023. Quantifying character similarity with vision transformers. *arXiv preprint arXiv:2305.14672*.

Huchen Zhou, Wenfeng Huang, Mohan Li, and Yulin Lai. 2022. Relation-aware entity matching using sentence-bert. *Computers, Materials & Continua*, 71(1).

## A Supplementary Materials

### A.1 Training and other details

`LinkTransformer` models use AdamW as the optimizer with a linear schedule with a 100% warm-up with 2e-6 as the max learning rate. We use a batch size of 64 for models trained with Wikidata (companies) and UN data (products). For industry benchmarks, we used a batch size of 128. We trained the models for 150 epochs for industrial benchmarks and 100 epochs for UN/Wikidata/Historic applications. We used Supervised Contrastive loss (Khosla et al., 2020) and Online Contrastive loss with default hyperparameters as the training objective depending upon the structure of the training dataset (as specified in Table A-4). The implementation for the losses was based on the implementation shared on the sentence-transformers repository (Reimers and Gurevych, 2019).

`LinkTransformer` uses IndexFlatIP from FAISS (Johnson et al., 2019) as the index of choice, allowing an exhaustive search to get $k$ nearest neighbours. We use the inner-product as the metric. All embeddings from the encoders are L2-normalized such that the distances (inner-products) given by the FAISS indices are equivalent to cosine similarity.

Code to replicate the below tables and train the models is available on our repository, which also contains links to our training data.

### A.2 Datasets and Results

Table A-1 lists the base sentence transformer models that we used to initialize the custom `LinkTransformer` models. Table A-2 describes the datasets used for training the `LinkTransformer` model zoo. They are drawn from multilingual UN product and industry concordances, Wikidata company aliases, a 1948 Mexican government concordance between tariff schedules (Secretaria de Economía de Mexico, 1948), and a hand-linked dataset between two 1950s Japanese firm-level datasets collected by credit bureaus, one containing around 7,000 firms and the other around 70,000 (Teikoku Koshinjo, 1957; Jinji Koshinjo, 1954). Table A-3 describes the train-val-test splits for each of these datasets. Table A-5 reports results on standard industry and e-commerce benchmarks for record linkage.

| Language | Base Model |
|---|---|
| English | sentence-transformers/multi-qa-mpnet-base-dot-v1 |
| Japanese | oshizo/sbert-jsnli-luke-japanese-base-lite |
| French | dangvantuan/sentence-camembert-large |
| Chinese | DMetaSoul/sbert-chinese-qmc-domain-v1 |
| Spanish | hiiamsid/sentence_similarity_spanish_es |
| German | Sahajtomar/German-semantic |
| Multilingual | sentence-transformers/paraphrase-multilingual-manet-base-v2 |

Table A-1: We used the above sentence-transformers models for different languages as base models to train `LinkTransformer` models. They were selected from the Hugging Face model hub and the names correspond to the repo names on the Hub.

| Model | Training Data |
|---|---|
| lt-wikidata-comp-en | Wikidata English-language company names. |
| lt-wikidata-comp-fr | Wikidata French-language company names. |
| lt-wikidata-comp-de | Wikidata German-language company names. |
| lt-wikidata-comp-ja | Wikidata Japanese-language company names. |
| lt-wikidata-comp-zh | Wikidata Chinese-language company names. |
| lt-wikidata-comp-es | Wikidata Spanish-language company names. |
| lt-wikidata-comp-multi | Wikidata multilingual company names (en, fr, es, de, ja, zh). |
| lt-wikidata-comp-prod-ind-ja | Wikidata Japanese-language company names and industries. |
| lt-un-data-fine-fine-en | UN fine-level product data in English. |
| lt-un-data-fine-coarse-en | UN coarse-level product data in English. |
| lt-un-data-fine-industry-en | UN product data linked to industries in English. |
| lt-un-data-fine-fine-es | UN fine-level product data in Spanish. |
| lt-un-data-fine-coarse-es | UN coarse-level product data in Spanish. |
| lt-un-data-fine-industry-es | UN product data linked to industries in Spanish. |
| lt-un-data-fine-fine-fr | UN fine-level product data in French. |
| lt-un-data-fine-coarse-fr | UN coarse-level product data in French. |
| lt-un-data-fine-industry-fr | UN product data linked to industries in French. |
| lt-un-data-fine-fine-multi | UN fine-level product data in multiple languages. |
| lt-un-data-fine-coarse-multi | UN coarse-level product data in multiple languages. |
| lt-un-data-fine-industry-multi | UN product data linked to industries in multiple languages. |

Table A-2: Model names and training data sources for various models in the `LinkTransformer` model zoo. Each of these models is on the Hugging Face hub and can be found by prefixing the organization name *dell-research-harvard* (for example, *dell-research-harvard/lt-wikidata-comp-multi.*). Training code can be found on our package Github repo and training configs containing the hyperparameters are available in the model repo on the Hugging Face Hub.

| Model | Training Size | Validation Size | Test Size |
|---|---|---|---|
| lt-wikidata-comp-es | 16511 | 924 | 932 |
| lt-wikidata-comp-fr | 42475 | 2431 | 2486 |
| lt-wikidata-comp-ja | 35923 | 2035 | 2054 |
| lt-wikidata-comp-zh | 26224 | 1510 | 1513 |
| lt-wikidata-comp-de | 42647 | 2383 | 2377 |
| lt-wikidata-comp-en | 133557 | 7685 | 7648 |
| lt-wikidata-comp-multi | 381820 | 28682 | 30532 |
| lt-wikidata-comp-prod-ind-ja | 3647 | 149 | 149 |
| lt-un-data-fine-fine-en | 9545 | 569 | 587 |
| lt-un-data-fine-coarse-en | 8059 | 1399 | 614 |
| lt-un-data-fine-industry-en | 8644 | 977 | 474 |
| lt-un-data-fine-fine-es | 5462 | 289 | 305 |
| lt-un-data-fine-coarse-es | 4326 | 552 | 389 |
| lt-un-data-fine-industry-es | 4134 | 622 | 530 |
| lt-un-data-fine-fine-fr | 1185 | 249 | 204 |
| lt-un-data-fine-coarse-fr | 3191 | 546 | 261 |
| lt-un-data-fine-industry-fr | 3219 | 501 | 302 |
| lt-un-data-fine-fine-multi | 19311 | 374 | 443 |
| lt-un-data-fine-coarse-multi | 17939 | 529 | 911 |
| lt-un-data-fine-industry-multi | 16528 | 1974 | 888 |
| lt-mexicantrade4748 | 5348 | 466 | 477 |
| lt-historicjapan | 982 | 50 | 55 |

Table A-3: Model names and training, validation, and test sizes for various models in the `LinkTransformer` model zoo. The training size corresponds to the number of samples (or pairs for training with online contrastive loss) in the split. Validation and Test size correspond to the number of 'queries' for models evaluated on the retrieval task and to positive pairs for models evaluated on the paired classification task (For *historicjapan*). The data were split into test-train-val at the class level to avoid test set leakage whenever possible.

| Dataset | Model | Loss |
|---|---|---|
| Structured_Amazon-Google | multi-qa-mpnet-base-dot-v1 | supcon |
| Structured_Beer | bge-large-en-v1.5 | onlinecontrastive |
| Structured_DBLP-ACM | bge-large-en-v1.5 | onlinecontrastive |
| Structured_DBLP-GoogleScholar | bge-large-en-v1.5 | onlinecontrastive |
| Structured_iTunes-Amazon | bge-large-en-v1.5 | onlinecontrastive |
| Structured_Walmart-Amazon | bge-large-en-v1.5 | supcon |
| Structured_Fodors-Zagats | bge-large-en-v1.5 | supcon |
| Dirty_DBLP-ACM | bge-large-zh-v1.5 | supcon |
| Dirty_DBLP-GoogleScholar | bge-large-zh-v1.5 | supcon |
| Dirty_iTunes-Amazon | all-mpnet-base-v2 | supcon |
| Dirty_Walmart-Amazon | bge-large-zh-v1.5 | supcon |
| Textual_Abt-Buy | multi-qa-mpnet-base-dot-v1 | onlinecontrastive |

Table A-4: Base models and Loss functions used for training of industrial benchmarks. Other hyperparameters that were constant across all of these experiments - learning rate (2e-5) , batch size (128), linear warmup of a 100% (reaching the maximum learning rate). All models were run for 100 epochs and the checkpoint was selected on the basis of test F1 on validation set. Since labels (and also negatives) were also in the dataset, validation was done by pairwise classification.

| Type | Dataset | Domain | Size | # Pos. | # Attr. | Ours (ZS) | Ours (FT) | Magellan | Deep matcher | Ditto | REMS |
|---|---|---|---|---|---|---|---|---|---|---|---|
| Structured | BeerAdvo-RateBeer | beer | 450 | 68 | 4 | 83.38 | 90.32 | 78.8 | 72.7 | 84.59 | 96.65 |
| | iTunes-Amazon1 | music | 539 | 132 | 8 | 60.6 | 90 | 91.2 | 88.5 | 92.28 | 98.18 |
| | Fodors-Zagats | restaurant | 946 | 110 | 6 | 75 | 98 | 100 | 100 | 98.14 | 100 |
| | DBLP-ACM1 | citation | 12,363 | 2,220 | 4 | 95 | 98 | 98.4 | 98.4 | 98.96 | 98.18 |
| | DBLP-Scholar1 | citation | 28,707 | 5,347 | 4 | 80 | 92 | 92.3 | 94.7 | 95.6 | 91.74 |
| | Amazon-Google | software | 11,460 | 1,167 | 3 | 47.1 | 74 | 49.1 | 69.3 | 74.1 | 65.3 |
| | Walmart-Amazon1 | electronics | 10,242 | 962 | 5 | 45 | 73.8 | 71.9 | 67.6 | 85.81 | 71.34 |
| Textual | Abt-Buy | product | 9,575 | 1,028 | 3 | 28.8 | 84 | 33 | 55 | 88.85 | 67.4 |
| | Company | company | 1,12,632 | 28,200 | 1 | 74.07 | 88.00 | 79.8 | 92.7 | 41.00 | 80.73 |
| Dirty | iTunes-Amazon2 | music | 539 | 132 | 8 | 68.8 | 84 | 46.8 | 79.4 | 92.92 | 94.74 |
| | DBLP-ACM2 | citation | 12,363 | 2,220 | 4 | 89.8 | 98 | 91.9 | 98.1 | 98.92 | 98.19 |
| | DBLP-Scholar2 | citation | 28,707 | 5,347 | 4 | 87.5 | 92.6 | 82.5 | 93.8 | 95.44 | 91.76 |
| | Walmart-Amazon2 | electronics | 10,242 | 962 | 5 | 45 | 71 | 37.4 | 53.8 | 82.56 | 65.74 |

Table A-5: Benchmarks. ZS is LinkTransformer models zero-shot and FT is LinkTransformer models fine-tuned on the benchmark. The remaining columns report comparisons. The metric is F1, as these datasets frame linkage as a binary classification problem.

# DocPilot: Copilot for Automating PDF Edit Workflows in Documents

**Puneet Mathur, Alexa Siu, Varun Manjunatha, Tong Sun**
Adobe Research
{puneetm, asiu, manjunatha, tsun}@adobe.com
**Demo Video**: https://github.com/docpilot-ai/demo

## Abstract

Digital documents, such as PDFs, are vital in business workflows, enabling communication, documentation, and collaboration. Handling PDFs can involve navigating complex workflows and numerous tools (e.g., comprehension, annotation, editing), which can be tedious and time-consuming for users. We introduce DocPilot, an AI-assisted document workflow Copilot system capable of understanding user intent and executing tasks accordingly to help users streamline their workflows. DocPilot undertakes intelligent orchestration of various tools through LLM prompting in four steps: (1) Task plan generation, (2) Task plan verification and self-correction, (3) Multi-turn User Feedback, and (4) Task Plan Execution via Code Generation and Error log-based Code Self-Revision. Our goal is to enhance user efficiency and productivity by simplifying and automating their document workflows with task delegation to DocPilot.

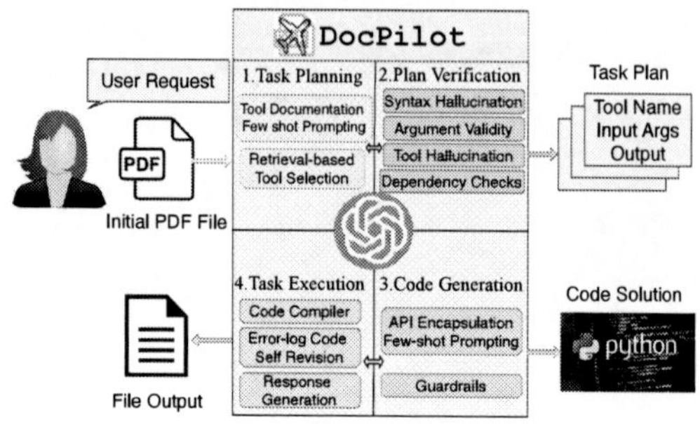


Figure 1: DocPilot is an LLM-assisted document workflow Copilot system capable of understanding user intent and executing PDF actions to help users achieve their editing needs.

## 1 Introduction

Digital documents, particularly PDFs, play a crucial role in business workflows, facilitating communication, documentation, and collaboration. Handling PDF documents involves a wide array of functionalities. These include tasks such as understanding content, annotating, editing content (e.g., comments, redaction, highlights), organizing pages (e.g., crop, rotate, extract), adding signatures or watermarks, and form-filling.

Several document processing applications provide standalone tools and APIs to help users complete these tasks. However, accomplishing complex workflows involving numerous tools can be tedious and time-consuming. Additionally, unfamiliar users may face challenges in understanding and navigating the various tools available. Hence, there is a need for an AI-assisted copilot system that can comprehend the user's intent, clarify unspecified details to eliminate ambiguity in requirements, and incorporate user feedback by interacting with the user . Further, it is desired that such a system should be able to sample from a large diversity of tools and resolve interdependencies between selected sub-tasks to generate coherent task plans. The copilot must then produce executable programs consistent with the initial intent while being extensible to accommodate the addition of new tools in the future (Kudashkina et al., 2020).

To address these issues, we present DocPilot (Fig. 1), an LLM-based framework for automating editing workflows in PDF documents. Inspired by recent work like HuggingGPT, (Shen et al., 2024) and ControlLM (Liu et al., 2023), DocPilot takes the user's requests along with the PDF documents as inputs and leverages LLMs to infer the user's intent and transforms it into a task plan consisting of a sequence of PDF action tools. The task plan undergoes thorough verification checks to ensure accuracy and reliability. Any errors in the task plan are self-corrected by the LLM, and the final task plan is then presented to the user in easy-to-understand language, inviting feedback through conversation. Once the plan is approved by the user, DocPilot converts the task plan into a software program that can orchestrate external tool



*Proceedings of the 62nd Annual Meeting of the Association for Computational Linguistics (Volume 3: System Demonstrations)*, pages 232–246
August 11-16, 2024 

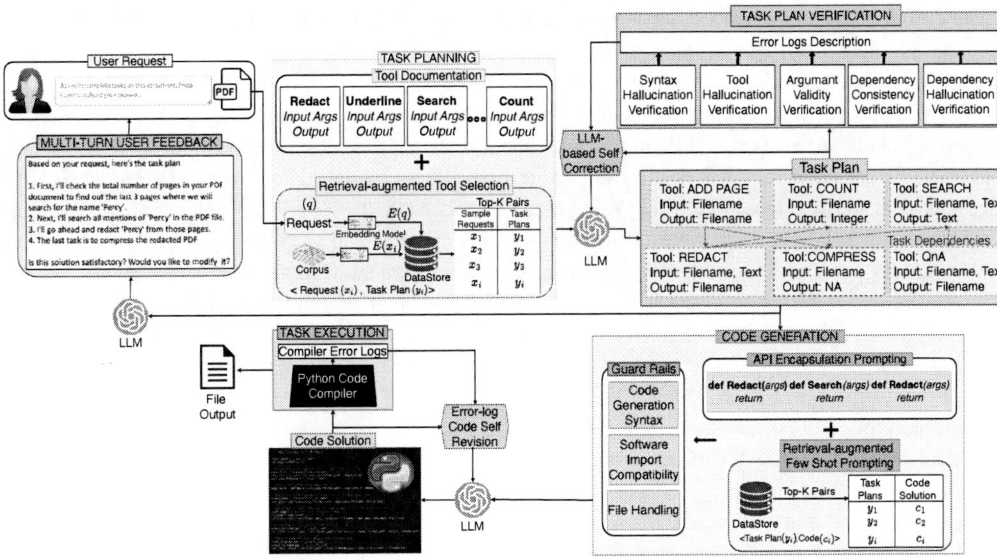


Figure 2: DocPilot: (1) Task Plan Generation decomposes user requests into a task plan using Tool Documentation prompting of Retrieval-augmented selection of PDF tools. (2) Task Plan Verification applies a series of syntax and dependency checks, and error descriptions are passed as feedback for LLM-based self-correction. (3) Multi-turn User Feedback allows users to critique the verbose task plan via the chat interface. (4) Task Plan Execution converts the approved task plan into Python code via API Encapsulation-based few-shot prompting with guardrails. Error log-based Code Self-Revision repairs code errors; the compiler executes code solution to generate output files.

API calls using LLM's code generation capabilities. The generated program is simulated using a code interpreter and detected error logs are passed as feedback to the LLM for code revision. The resultant error-free code solution executes seamless cooperation between diverse tools and provides users with a modified document that meets their expectations. To assess DocPilot's performance in supporting users, we collected user feedback on diverse workflows completed with the help of DocPilot. We find that DocPilot is effective in improving user productivity by automating repetitive tasks and simplifying complex processes.

The main contributions of DocPilot are:

**(1) Accessibility**: By employing LLMs as task planners, DocPilot engages users in multi-turn interactions to disambiguate complex requests. This eliminates the need to master the skillful use of document processing software, making it accessible to a broader audience.

**(2) Modularity**: DocPilot is designed to be highly extensible, allowing users to expand its functionality by adding more PDF tools and APIs. To achieve this, we introduce *Tool Documentation-based prompting* for generating task plans grounded in real-world tool usage, *Retrieval-Augmented Tool Selection* to tailor few-shot tool usage examples suitable for input queries, and *API Encapsulation prompting* for generating modularized code.

**(3) Reliability**: DocPilot promotes reliable workflow automation by mitigating task hallucinations, handling complex interdependencies between subtasks via dependency verification, and iterative self-correction to generate an executable program.

## 2 Related Work

Recent research informs us how LLMs can act as autonomous agents for task automation in various application domains (Xi et al., 2023; Wang et al., 2023a). **AI-powered LLM Agents**: Frameworks like AgentGPT and HuggingGPT (Shen et al., 2024) leverage LLMs as a controller to analyze user requests and invoke relevant tools for solving the task. AudioGPT (Huang et al., 2023) solves numerous audio understanding and generation tasks by connecting LLMs with input/output interface (ASR, TTS) for speech conversations. TPU (Ruan et al., 2023) proposes a structured framework tailored for LLM-based AI Agents for task planning and execution. (Zhu et al., 2023) introduced the Ghost in Minecraft (GITM), a framework of Generally Capable Agents (GCAs) that can skillfully navigate complex, sparse-reward environments with text-based interactions and develop a set of structured actions executed via LLMs. AssistGPT (Gao et al., 2023) proposed an interleaved code and language reasoning approach called Plan, Execute, Inspect, and Learn (PEIL) for processing complex images and long-form videos. RecMind (Wang et al., 2023b) designed an LLM-powered autonomous recommender agent capable of leveraging external knowledge and utilizing tools with careful planning to provide zero-shot personalized recommendations. Frameworks like AutoDroid (Wen et al., 2023) and AppAgent (Zhang et al., 2023a) presented smartphone task automation systems that can automate arbitrary tasks on any mobile application by mimicking human-like interactions such as tapping and swiping leveraged through LLMs like GPT-3.5/GPT-4. AdaPlanner (Sun et al., 2024) allows LLM agents to refine their self-generated plan adaptively in response to environmental feedback using few-shot demonstrations. (Chen et al., 2023) proposed a tool-augmented chain-of-thought reasoning framework that allows chat-based LLMs (e.g., ChatGPT) to indulge in multi-turn conversations to utilize tools in a more natural conversational manner. CREATOR (Qian et al., 2023) built a novel framework that enables LLMs to create their own tools using documentation and code realization. ControlLLM (Liu et al., 2023) proposed a Thoughts-on-Graph (ToG) paradigm that searches the optimal solution path on a pre-built tool graph to resolve parameter and dependency relations among different tools for image, audio, and video processing. LUMOS (Yin et al., 2023) trained open-source LLMs with unified data to represent complex interactive tasks. DataCopilot (Zhang et al., 2023b) built an LLM-based system to autonomously transform raw data into visualization results that best match the user's intent by designing versatile interfaces for data management, processing, and visualization. (Song et al., 2023) connects LLMs with REST software architectural style (RESTful) APIs, conducts coarse-to-fine online planning, and executes the APIs by meticulously formulating API parameters and parsing responses. Gorilla (Patil et al., 2023) explores the use of self-instruct fine-tuning and retrieval to enable LLMs to accurately select from a large, overlapping, and changing set of APIs. LLM-Grounder (Yang et al., 2023) created a novel open-vocabulary LLM-based 3D visual grounding pipeline to decompose complex natural language queries into semantic constituents for spatial object identification in 3D scenes. (Qiao et al., 2024) put forth the AUTOACT framework that automatically synthesizes planning trajectories from experience to alleviate the reliance of copilot systems on large-scale annotated data. Toolken (Hao et al., 2024) addresses the inherent problems of context length constraints and adaptability to a new set of tools by proposing LLM tool embeddings. Recent work has shown that descriptive tool documentation can be more beneficial than simple few-shot demonstrations for tool-augmented LLM automation (Hsieh et al., 2023).

## 3 `DocPilot`

Fig. 2 shows `DocPilot`, a chat-based AI assistant framework that uses LLM as a controller to translate a user's PDF editing request into an actionable task plan and orchestrates numerous software tools to realize the document editing tasks into modified PDF outputs. `DocPilot` undertakes intelligent orchestration of various LLM capabilities into an executable workflow, which includes four steps: (1) Task plan generation, (2) Task plan verification and self-correction, (3) Multi-turn User Feedback, and (4) Task Plan Execution via Code Generation and Error log-based Code Self-Revision.

### 3.1 Task Plan Generation

User requests involve several intricate intentions that need to be decomposed into a sequence of sub-tasks to be solved to achieve the final output. The task planning stage utilizes an LLM to analyze the user request and determine the execution orders of the PDF Tool API calls based on their resource dependencies. We represent the LLM-generated task plan in the JSON format to parse the sub-tasks through slot filing. Each sub-task is composed of five slots - "task", "id", "dep", "args", and "return" to represent the PDF tool function name, unique identifier, dependencies, arguments, and returned values, respectively. To better understand the intention and criteria for task planning, we utilize *Tool Documentation-based prompting*. The task planning prompt contains documentation of the PDF tool APIs (see Table 1 for the API list), briefly mentioning each function's utilities, arguments, and return values. Without explicitly exposing the API implementation, this novel prompting technique ensures that our methodology embraces API-level abstraction and encapsulation by restricting access to proprietary data and internal functions for enhanced user privacy to black-box LLM models.

**Retrieval-Augmented Tool Selection**: The task planning stage may involve a large number of tools. Many of these tools might not be relevant to the user request, and including all in the LLM prompt may lead to reduced context length for subsequent chat prompting. Hence, based on the incoming user request, we utilized a retrieval-augmented selection approach to only include the most relevant few-shot examples in the task plan prompt.

Let $q$ denote the user request and $Z = \{(x_1, y_1), (x_2, y_2), \cdots, (x_n, y_n)\}$ represents the set of few-shot examples curated for the task plan prompt. Each example consists of a sample request ($x_i$) paired with the corresponding ground truth task plan ($y_i$). We use a text embedding model $E$ to encode the sample user requests from the few-shot examples into vector representations - $\{E(x_i), E(x_2), \cdots, E(x_n)\}$, respectively. We construct a datastore of few-shot examples with keys as vectorized sample requests and values as ground truth task plans. We encode the incoming user request via embedding model as $E(q_i)$ at inference. Next, we use the k-nearest neighbor technique with the Euclidean distance metric to query top-k sample requests from the datastore which are semantically most similar to the encoded user query. The selected pairs of user requests and their task plans, similar to the example shown in Fig. **??**, are utilized in prompting the LLM model to generate the task plan for the current user query.

### 3.2 Task Plan Verification and Self-Correction

LLM-generated task plans involve a risk of hallucinations when selecting unspecified functions, connecting dependency connections, or invalid argument parsing, which may lead to undesired outputs. We introduce two novel modules to ensure robustness in the generated task plans against logical inconsistencies: "Task Plan Verification" and "LLM-based Self-Correction".

First, the "Task Plan Verification" consists of three *static composition verification* and two *inter-task dependency verification* checks on the generated task plan JSON (Appendix Figure 6 shows an illustrative example). Static composition verification checks the individual constituents of the task plan for hallucinations on syntax, tool name and API calls, and function arguments (Appendix A.4). Second, the inter-task dependency verification checks the validity of dependency relations between various function calls in the task plan as:

(1) **Dependency hallucination verification** – Each function call depends on arguments provided by the user request or outputs of preceding functions in the task plan. We add checks to ensure the LLM does not hallucinate dependencies referencing non-existent or future function calls in the task plan.

(2) **Dependency consistency verification**: Each function call in the task plan sequence may depend on one or more prior function calls. These functional dependencies need not be linear and can be better represented as a graph of connected components (also known as a dependency graph). A function call may often try to access resources from another function call. However, in some cases, these interdependencies may be cyclic or unreachable. Hence, subsequent function calls can not proceed ahead without resolving the prior. This may give rise to deadlock conditions during the task execution. To avoid deadlocks and resource conflicts, it is important to ensure that there are no cyclic dependencies between the intermediate function calls. To solve this problem, we create a dependency graph $G$ from the task plan $T$ where all function calls denote the set of nodes $V$, and their interdependencies represent the set of edges $E$ of the graph. To check for the presence of cyclic dependencies in a graph, it should be sufficient to check if the dependency graph is a directed acyclic graph (DAG). We utilize Kahn's algorithm (Kahn, 1962) to evaluate this condition, which involves performing a topological sort of the dependency graph followed by a depth-first traversal to evaluate if all nodes have been visited exactly once without repetition. Violation of this condition indicates a lack of DAG property. The dependency error is then attributed to the API function corresponding to the failure node in the graph.

**LLM-based Self-Correction**: The verification module generates error log descriptions based on the nature of the fault and the responsible API functions. The error logs and original task plan sequence are passed as feedback to the LLM model as a chat completion prompt to rework the solution. This process recursively improves the task plan solution until no further errors are encountered.

### 3.3 Multi-turn User Feedback

User consent is a prerequisite for executing actions that could potentially alter a user's proprietary PDF files. Adhering to this principle, the meticulously verified error-free task plan is transformed into a clear and comprehensible layman explanation through LLM prompting. This elucidation is then presented to the user through the chat interface. Subsequently, the user can engage in a multi-turn chat conversation with the LLM to challenge the proposed task plan and provide additional feedback. The user's input is integrated to iteratively refine the task plan by recursively following the task planning and verification stages. This iterative process of modifying the task plan through multi-turn chat conversations continues until the user is content with the solution or decides to abort the request.

### 3.4 Task Plan Execution

The task plan obtained in the last step lists tool APIs with corresponding arguments and return values. However, the sequence of function calls that need to be executed is not linear due to interdependencies between the API calls. Hence, there is a need to convert the task plan into a software program with a logical flow of information. We introduce the Task Plan Program Execution step, where the LLM converts the task plan into a software program that can be executed to give the desired output PDF file to the user. This stage is divided into two modules - "Task Plan Code Generation" and "Error log-based Code Self-Revision".

**Task Code Generation**: We utilize the LLM code generation abilities to transform the task plan sequence into executable Python code. However, unrestricted LLM-generated code may hallucinate functions that do not exist, use incompatible libraries, be unable to navigate file handling at the user's end or perform flawed executions that may harm user data, leading to deteriorated user trust.

To safeguard against such detrimental cases, we incorporate a novel *API Encapsulation*-based few-shot prompting with strong guardrails. The prompt consists of the code documentation of *PDFTools()* class, which encapsulates publicly accessible tool API function methods and exposes limited information regarding the function name, input arguments, and returned values. The LLM can utilize this abstracted view of tool APIs for program synthesis without knowing or modifying their internal code implementation. In this manner, we alleviate the problem of function hallucinations while ensuring that only well-trusted and rigorously tested API functions are used for user data modifications. Additionally, we augment the prompt with a few shot examples of task plans ($y_i$) retrieved during the task plan generation step, paired with their corresponding ground truth Python code solutions ($c_i$) to guide the code generation process to remain faithful to task plan logic. Further, we designed stringent guard rails to safeguard program execution by ensuring consistency in code generation syntax, avoiding lazy code generation phenomenon of LLMs, machine compatibility of software imports, safe-listing of approved Python packages, secure access of file addresses, and cautious file handling. More details in Appendix Sec. A.5.

**Error log-based Code Self-Revision**: Despite carefully crafted prompts and strong guard rails, the generated program solution may give errors upon code execution. To screen for errors in advance and recover from a failed execution state, we propose Error log-based Self-Revision prompting. In particular, we build a Python code interpreter to simulate code execution in a sandboxed environment to mimic the actual PDF file editing. Compilation errors from the code interpreter are captured as error logs and combined with the original code solution to be passed as feedback to the LLM model to rework the code solution. The code interpreter again tests the reworked code solution to check for errors, and the process continues recursively until the code solution is improved and no further errors are encountered. Fig. 7 in the Appendix shows an example code solution. Finally, we execute the resultant error-free code solution to produce the PDF document modifications requested by the user.

## 4 Implementation Details

**Backbone LLM**: We use GPT-4 API through the Microsoft Azure platform for all our experiments. We also tried GPT-3.5 model but it performed consistently worse than GPT-4 owing to its limited context length and weak code generation abilities.

**RAG architecture**: We utilized FAISS to construct the data stores for the Retrieval-augmented tool selection module. We used SentenceBert (Reimers and Gurevych, 2019) as the embedding model. We used Scikit Learn's KNN library to get top-k request-task plan pairs. We used Gradio for the demo UI hosted on the AWS cloud platform.

## 5 User Evaluation

We conducted a user evaluation to assess the efficacy of `DocPilot` in supporting users' PDF workflows. The research goals were as follows:

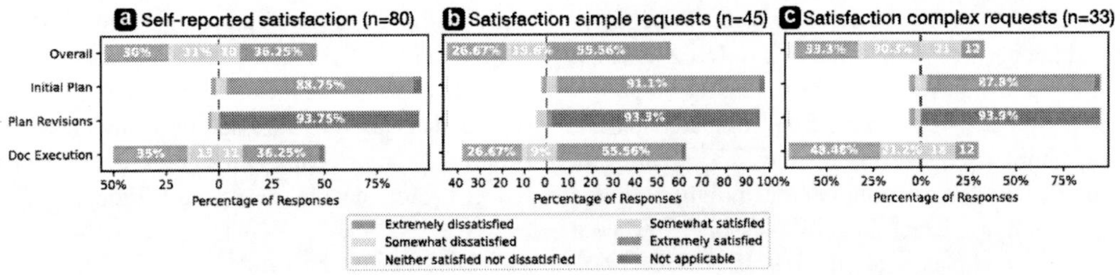


Figure 3: a) Self-reported user satisfaction scores from using DocPilot to complete 80 workflow requests. b) Simple requests (<=5 actions) had higher satisfaction scores compared to c) complex requests (>5 actions).

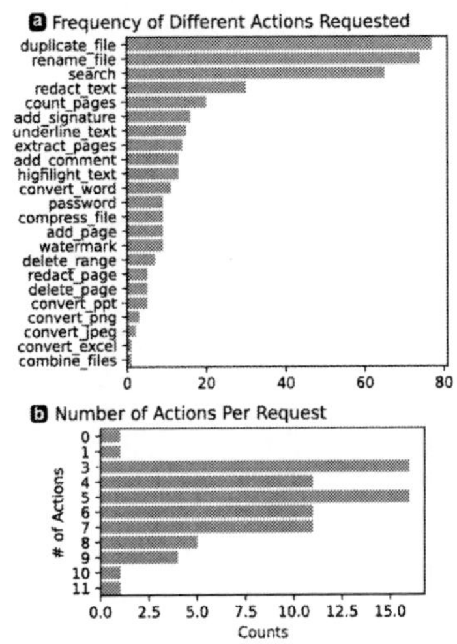


Figure 4: (a) Frequency of different actions referenced in task plans; (b) Distribution of actions executed per request during user evaluation.

R1 Measure DocPilot's performance in suggesting a reasonable plan in response to a user-provided multi-step workflow. Relatedly, we wanted to understand how well our system handled ambiguity in user requests.

R2 Understand when/how breakdowns happen and whether users are able to refine their plan through conversation with DocPilot.

Our data collection focused on a case study with one expert PDF user who works on PDF processing tasks daily as part of his professional work. Our evaluator was hired through UpWork with expertise in PDF workflows. The evaluator interacted with the DocPilot app (Fig. 5) to complete several workflows and provided feedback through a survey form (Methodology details in Appendix A.7.1).

## 5.1 Results

### 5.1.1 User Workflow Requests

We collected data from 80 workflow requests. 16 workflows were user-provided based on the users' real-world PDF workflows, and 64 were workflows suggested to the user. We provided the suggested workflows to ensure that the workflows evaluated included a variety of the types of actions used and the number of actions requested. Appendix A.7.3 has examples of user-provided and suggested workflows. Fig. 4a shows the frequency of different actions referenced as part of the user's requests. The most common actions included duplicating a file (77), renaming a file (74), searching content (65), redacting content (30), and counting pages (20). Fig. 4b shows the distribution of actions executed per request with a median of 5 (IQR $4-7$).

### 5.1.2 Self-Reported Satisfaction Ratings

To understand DocPilot's performance in suggesting a satisfactory plan in response to a user's request (R1), we collected self-reported measures of user satisfaction after each step of the DocPilot pipeline (Fig. 1). Fig. 3a shows user satisfaction aggregated over all 80 workflow requests. DocPilot performs extremely well in suggesting a reasonable initial plan, with 88.75% (71/80) receiving positive ratings of *Extremely satisfied* and the majority of requests not requiring plan revisions from the user. The main concern of dissatisfaction with DocPilot was related to the task execution step, which received the *Extremely satisfied* ratings only in 36.25% (29/80) of requests, similarly reflected in the Overall satisfaction ratings.

To understand whether workflow complexity impacts the system's efficacy in planning, we further analyze satisfaction ratings by complexity. Fig. 3(b-c) show satisfaction ratings for simple (n=45) and complex (n=33) requests. We consider simple requests as those requiring 5 actions or less to be executed to fulfill the users' request. We observe that the positive satisfaction ratings (*Extremely satisfied* + *Somewhat satisfied*) are higher for simple requests (25/45, or 55.55%) compared to those on complex requests (11/33, or 33.33%). Simple requests also resulted in much higher satisfaction with task execution (27/45, or 60%) compared to complex requests (10/33, or 30.3%).

#### 5.1.3 Qualitative Feedback

To further understand breakdowns in DocPilot from the users' perspective (R2), we conducted a thematic analysis of users' requests that resulted in failure as well as open-ended user feedback. For the Task Planning step, the user majorly provided positive comments, *"The plan is concise, to the point, and explained well. I like that the assistant understands the request completely"*.

However, we also report a small number of negative comments that were primarily centered on the Task Execution step, where DocPilot either missed a step or detail in the resulting files. The user had certain expectations of the results based on the plan suggested by DocPilot, which were unmet. We observed instances where DocPilot executed the action incorrectly, *"Instead of deleting pages 1, 2, and 5, the assistant deleted pages 1 to 4"*. Users also reported a few cases where DocPilot simply missed an action, *"...the assistant successfully converted pages but was unable to add digital signatures."*. We also noticed some cases where DocPilot did not understand the multimodal content in the document properly, which in turn affected performance for actions that required searching for content in the document. For example, *"My request is to redact the numerical values in the 'Annual Energy Use' and 'Water' columns of the table. However, the assistant does not understand and redacts incorrect words."* Lastly, we also recorded a handful of cases where the user had high expectations that were beyond the DocPilot's current tooling capabilities (e.g., replacing text and images). In the future, we aim to handle such discrepancies by improving prompt engineering, extending the PDF tool APIs available to DocPilot, and integrating Large Multimodal Models such as GPT-4V for multimodal document search/QA tasks.

#### 5.1.4 LLM Iterations & Self-Correction

To quantify breakdowns due to program execution (R2), we analyzed the code interpreter error logs for output code. A small number of workflow requests (8/80) required more than one LLM self-correction step (Sec. 3.2) to reach a desirable action plan. In contrast, the majority of requests (69/80) required at least one LLM self-correction (Sec. 3.4) to produce an executable program that passed all checks. More details in Appendix Table 2.

## 6 Discussion, Limitations & Future Work

Our evaluation results show that DocPilot's Task Planning step is effective for most workflows as the proposed task plan captures the user's intent well and requires few clarifications by the user. Only 10% of the evaluated workflows required more than one LLM iteration to self-correct the generated task plans. The majority of breakdowns we observed occurred due to a mismatch in the user's expectations between the plan suggested by DocPilot and how it was executed. Our current interface with DocPilot primarily uses a conversational UI. Leveraging interactions from graphical UIs can help lessen this gap by providing the user affordances for direct manipulation in content selection when executing a workflow (Ma et al., 2023). Additionally, DocPilot may allow users to edit action parameters (e.g., page number, password) directly rather than requiring the user to type a new request. Both of these future works could increase user control and understanding of the system plan (Amershi et al., 2019). Quantitatively, we observe that most workflows (69/80) required at least one LLM-based code revision to produce an error-free program, thus introducing latency and impacting the utility of the tool. Self-reported ratings indicate more failures in the task execution step for complex workflows. Hence, our future work will focus on instruction-tuning LLMs on pairs of ground truth task plans and Python code.

## 7 Conclusion

We present Docpilot, an LLM-powered copilot for automating document workflows. Our copilot helps novices plan document workflows by selecting the appropriate tools and executing the task plan autonomously. DocPilot benefits the users by enhancing their accessibility, being extensible to include more tools, and being consistently reliable.

## 8 Ethics Statement

Our experiments used publicly available API-accessible LLM - GPT-3.5 and GPT-4 (March 2024 version). For our user evaluation, participants' personal information is maintained confidential and private. Participants were trained and informed about the task before participating. Participants were also compensated fairly, with each annotator paid equal to or more than 15 USD/hr.

## References


Saleema Amershi, Dan Weld, Mihaela Vorvoreanu, Adam Fourney, Besmira Nushi, Penny Collisson, Jina Suh, Shamsi Iqbal, Paul Bennett, Kori Inkpen, Jaime Teevan, Ruth Kikin-Gil, and Eric Horvitz. 2019. Guidelines for human-ai interaction. In *CHI 2019*. ACM. CHI 2019 Honorable Mention Award.

Kranti Chalamalasetti, Jana Götze, Sherzod Hakimov, Brielen Madureira, Philipp Sadler, and David Schlangen. 2023. clembench: Using game play to evaluate chat-optimized language models as conversational agents. *arXiv preprint arXiv:2305.13455*.

Zhipeng Chen, Kun Zhou, Beichen Zhang, Zheng Gong, Xin Zhao, and Ji-Rong Wen. 2023. ChatCoT: Tool-augmented chain-of-thought reasoning on chat-based large language models. In *Findings of the Association for Computational Linguistics: EMNLP 2023*, pages 14777–14790, Singapore. Association for Computational Linguistics.

Difei Gao, Lei Ji, Luowei Zhou, Kevin Qinghong Lin, Joya Chen, Zihan Fan, and Mike Zheng Shou. 2023. Assistgpt: A general multi-modal assistant that can plan, execute, inspect, and learn. *arXiv preprint arXiv:2306.08640*.

Shibo Hao, Tianyang Liu, Zhen Wang, and Zhiting Hu. 2024. Toolkengpt: Augmenting frozen language models with massive tools via tool embeddings. *Advances in neural information processing systems*, 36.

Cheng-Yu Hsieh, Si-An Chen, Chun-Liang Li, Yasuhisa Fujii, Alexander Ratner, Chen-Yu Lee, Ranjay Krishna, and Tomas Pfister. 2023. Tool documentation enables zero-shot tool-usage with large language models. *arXiv preprint arXiv:2308.00675*.

Rongjie Huang, Mingze Li, Dongchao Yang, Jiatong Shi, Xuankai Chang, Zhenhui Ye, Yuning Wu, Zhiqing Hong, Jiawei Huang, Jinglin Liu, et al. 2023. Audiogpt: Understanding and generating speech, music, sound, and talking head. *arXiv preprint arXiv:2304.12995*.

Arthur B Kahn. 1962. Topological sorting of large networks. *Communications of the ACM*, 5(11):558–562.

Katya Kudashkina, Patrick M. Pilarski, and Richard S. Sutton. 2020. Document-editing assistants and model-based reinforcement learning as a path to conversational ai. *ArXiv*, abs/2008.12095.

Jiaju Lin, Haoran Zhao, Aochi Zhang, Yiting Wu, Huqiuyue Ping, and Qin Chen. 2023. Agentsims: An open-source sandbox for large language model evaluation.

Zhaoyang Liu, Zeqiang Lai, Zhangwei Gao, Erfei Cui, Xizhou Zhu, Lewei Lu, Qifeng Chen, Yu Qiao, Jifeng Dai, and Wenhai Wang. 2023. Controlllm: Augment language models with tools by searching on graphs. *ArXiv*, abs/2310.17796.

Xiao Ma, Swaroop Mishra, Ariel Liu, Sophie Su, Jilin Chen, Chinmay Kulkarni, Heng-Tze Cheng, Quoc Le, and Ed Chi. 2023. Beyond chatbots: Explorellm for structured thoughts and personalized model responses. *arXiv preprint arXiv:2312.00763*.

Long Ouyang, Jeffrey Wu, Xu Jiang, Diogo Almeida, Carroll Wainwright, Pamela Mishkin, Chong Zhang, Sandhini Agarwal, Katarina Slama, Alex Ray, et al. 2022. Training language models to follow instructions with human feedback. *Advances in neural information processing systems*, 35:27730–27744.

Shishir G Patil, Tianjun Zhang, Xin Wang, and Joseph E Gonzalez. 2023. Gorilla: Large language model connected with massive apis. *arXiv preprint arXiv:2305.15334*.

Cheng Qian, Chi Han, Yi Ren Fung, Yujia Qin, Zhiyuan Liu, and Heng Ji. 2023. Creator: Tool creation for disentangling abstract and concrete reasoning of large language models. In *Conference on Empirical Methods in Natural Language Processing*.

Shuofei Qiao, Ningyu Zhang, Runnan Fang, Yujie Luo, Wangchunshu Zhou, Yuchen Eleanor Jiang, Chengfei Lv, and Huajun Chen. 2024. Autoact: Automatic agent learning from scratch via self-planning. *ArXiv*, abs/2401.05268.

Nils Reimers and Iryna Gurevych. 2019. Sentence-bert: Sentence embeddings using siamese bert-networks. In *Conference on Empirical Methods in Natural Language Processing*.

Jingqing Ruan, Yihong Chen, Bin Zhang, Zhiwei Xu, Tianpeng Bao, Guoqing Du, Shiwei Shi, Hangyu Mao, Xingyu Zeng, and Rui Zhao. 2023. Tptu: Task planning and tool usage of large language model-based ai agents. *arXiv preprint arXiv:2308.03427*.

Yongliang Shen, Kaitao Song, Xu Tan, Dongsheng Li, Weiming Lu, and Yueting Zhuang. 2024. Hugginggpt: Solving ai tasks with chatgpt and its friends in hugging face. *Advances in Neural Information Processing Systems*, 36.

Yifan Song, Weimin Xiong, Dawei Zhu, Wenhao Wu, Han Qian, Mingbo Song, Hailiang Huang, Cheng Li, Ke Wang, Rong Yao, Ye Tian, and Sujian Li. 2023. Restgpt: Connecting large language models with real-world restful apis.

Haotian Sun, Yuchen Zhuang, Lingkai Kong, Bo Dai, and Chao Zhang. 2024. Adaplanner: Adaptive planning from feedback with language models. *Advances in Neural Information Processing Systems*, 36.

Lei Wang, Chengbang Ma, Xueyang Feng, Zeyu Zhang, Hao ran Yang, Jingsen Zhang, Zhi-Yang Chen, Jiakai Tang, Xu Chen, Yankai Lin, Wayne Xin Zhao, Zhewei Wei, and Ji rong Wen. 2023a. A survey on large language model based autonomous agents. *ArXiv*, abs/2308.11432.

Yancheng Wang, Ziyan Jiang, Zheng Chen, Fan Yang, Yingxue Zhou, Eunah Cho, Xing Fan, Xiaojiang Huang, Yanbin Lu, and Yingzhen Yang. 2023b. Recmind: Large language model powered agent for recommendation. *arXiv preprint arXiv:2308.14296*.

Hao Wen, Yuanchun Li, Guohong Liu, Shanhui Zhao, Tao Yu, Toby Jia-Jun Li, Shiqi Jiang, Yunhao Liu, Yaqin Zhang, and Yunxin Liu. 2023. Empowering llm to use smartphone for intelligent task automation. *arXiv preprint arXiv:2308.15272*.

Zhiheng Xi, Wenxiang Chen, Xin Guo, Wei He, Yiwen Ding, Boyang Hong, Ming Zhang, Junzhe Wang, Senjie Jin, Enyu Zhou, Rui Zheng, Xiaoran Fan, Xiao Wang, Limao Xiong, Qin Liu, Yuhao Zhou, Weiran Wang, Changhao Jiang, Yicheng Zou, Xiangyang Liu, Zhangyue Yin, Shihan Dou, Rongxiang Weng, Wensen Cheng, Qi Zhang, Wenjuan Qin, Yongyan Zheng, Xipeng Qiu, Xuanjing Huan, and Tao Gui. 2023. The rise and potential of large language model based agents: A survey. *ArXiv*, abs/2309.07864.

Binfeng Xu, Xukun Liu, Hua Shen, Zeyu Han, Yuhan Li, Murong Yue, Zhiyuan Peng, Yuchen Liu, Ziyu Yao, and Dongkuan Xu. 2023a. Gentopia.AI: A collaborative platform for tool-augmented LLMs. In *Proceedings of the 2023 Conference on Empirical Methods in Natural Language Processing: System Demonstrations*, pages 237–245, Singapore. Association for Computational Linguistics.

Qiantong Xu, Fenglu Hong, Bo Li, Changran Hu, Zhengyu Chen, and Jian Zhang. 2023b. On the tool manipulation capability of open-source large language models. *arXiv preprint arXiv:2305.16504*.

Jianing Yang, Xuweiyi Chen, Shengyi Qian, Nikhil Madaan, Madhavan Iyengar, David F. Fouhey, and Joyce Chai. 2023. Llm-grounder: Open-vocabulary 3d visual grounding with large language model as an agent. *ArXiv*, abs/2309.12311.

Shunyu Yao, Howard Chen, John Yang, and Karthik Narasimhan. 2022. Webshop: Towards scalable real-world web interaction with grounded language agents. *Advances in Neural Information Processing Systems*, 35:20744–20757.

Da Yin, Faeze Brahman, Abhilasha Ravichander, Khyathi Raghavi Chandu, Kai-Wei Chang, Yejin Choi, and Bill Yuchen Lin. 2023. Lumos: Learning agents with unified data, modular design, and open-source llms. *ArXiv*, abs/2311.05657.

China. Xiaoyan Zhang, Zhao Yang, Jiaxuan Liu, Yucheng Han, Xin Chen, Zebiao Huang, Bin Fu, and Gang Yu. 2023a. Appagent: Multimodal agents as smartphone users. *ArXiv*, abs/2312.13771.

Wenqi Zhang, Yongliang Shen, Weiming Lu, and Yue Ting Zhuang. 2023b. Data-copilot: Bridging billions of data and humans with autonomous workflow. *ArXiv*, abs/2306.07209.

Shuyan Zhou, Frank F Xu, Hao Zhu, Xuhui Zhou, Robert Lo, Abishek Sridhar, Xianyi Cheng, Yonatan Bisk, Daniel Fried, Uri Alon, et al. 2023. Webarena: A realistic web environment for building autonomous agents. *arXiv preprint arXiv:2307.13854*.

Xizhou Zhu, Yuntao Chen, Hao Tian, Chenxin Tao, Weijie Su, Chenyu Yang, Gao Huang, Bin Li, Lewei Lu, Xiaogang Wang, et al. 2023. Ghost in the minecraft: Generally capable agents for open-world enviroments via large language models with text-based knowledge and memory. *arXiv preprint arXiv:2305.17144*.

# A Appendix

## A.1 DocPilot Demo App

Figure 5 shows the DocPilot demo app. This app was also used by our evaluator to complete all workflow requests. The app was built using Gradio[1]. The app requires an OpenAI token to access the GPT-4 model. The interface includes a PDF upload panel, a PDF viewer, and a chat panel. Users can directly upload their input PDF file and type in their request in the chat panel. The chat panel facilitates multi-turn chat and shows all the intermediate interactions and results generated by the system. Once a workflow is executed, the user can download the resulting files for inspection. The users also has the ability to reset their chat history to start a new workflow conversation.

## A.2 Implementation Details

**Backbone LLM**: We use GPT-4 API through the Microsoft Azure platform for all our experiments. We also tried GPT-3.5 model but it performed consistently worse that GPT-4 owing to its limited context length and weak code generation abilities.
**RAG architecture**: We utilized FAISS to construct the data stores for the Retrieval-augmented tool selection module. We used SentenceBert (Reimers and Gurevych, 2019) as the embedding model. We used Scikit Learn's KNN library to get top-k request-task plan pairs. We used Gradio for the demo UI hosted on the AWS cloud platform.
**LLM Agent Evaluations**: ToolBench (Xu et al., 2023b) released a tool manipulation benchmark

[1]https://www.gradio.app

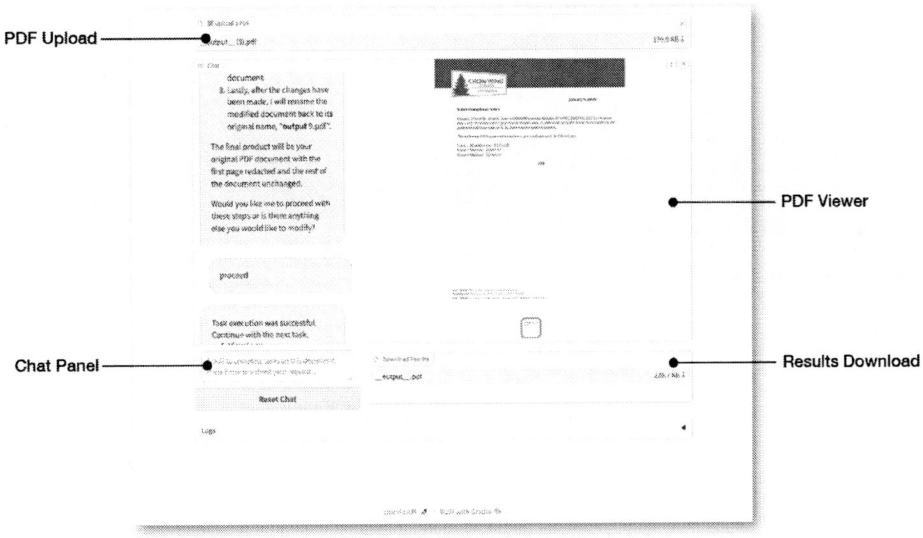


Figure 5: UI for DocPilot

consisting of diverse software tools for real-world tasks to evaluate LLM capabilities for tool manipulation. AgentSim (Lin et al., 2023) created an interactive infrastructure for researchers to evaluate the task completion abilities of LLM agents in a simulated environment. WebArena (Zhou et al., 2023) introduces a benchmark on interpreting high-level realistic natural language commands to concrete web-based interactions. ClemBench (Chalamalasetti et al., 2023) provides a systematic evaluation of LLM's capability to follow game-play instructions. (Xu et al., 2023a) created the GentPool platform that registers and shares user-customized, composable, and collaborative agents. WebShop (Yao et al., 2022) is another challenging benchmark that tests LLM agent's capabilities to navigate multiple types of webpages, find, customize, and purchase a product given text instruction in an e-commerce website simulation with 1.18 million real-world products. This is the first work to provide a novel benchmark for evaluating LLM agent workflows in a document editing software environment.

### A.3 DocPilot PDF Tool APIs

Table 1 shows the set of PDF tool APIs and their descriptions available during the task plan generation in DocPilot.

### A.4 Task Plan Verification Module

Figure **??** shows a qualitative example of task verification checks - Syntax Hallucination, Tool Hallucination, Argument Validity, Dependency Hallucination, and Dependency Consistency.

Static composition verification checks the individual constituents of the task plan for hallucinations on syntax, tool name and API calls, and function arguments:

1. **Syntax hallucination verification** – Incorrect JSON formatting of the task plan may cause downstream JSON parsing errors. This verification step ensures the task plan returned is a list of Python maps with key-value pairs denoting function names, dependencies, input arguments, and returned values.

2. **Tool hallucination verification** – Despite prompting the syntactically correct task plan, LLMs may hallucinate invalid tool names and API calls. This step ensures that all PDF tool APIs are valid and present in the documentation.

3. **Argument validity verification** - Each function in the task plan has a pre-defined number and type of arguments and return values. Any hallucinations in this regard may cause errors during program execution. Hence, we check for any extra, missing, or incorrect arguments in each task plan sequence function call.

| Tool | Description |
|---|---|
| Duplicate | Initializes a duplicate of the input file and saves it as "input.pdf" |
| Rename | Renames the input file to the output file name with a default value "output.pdf" |
| Search | Returns a list of text strings matching the matching query found in the input document denoted as filename; Otherwise, returns an empty list. |
| QnA | Answers a question in the form of a text string from the LLM query result. |
| Count Pages | Counts the number of pages in the PDF file and returns it as an integer |
| Compress | Reduce the PDF file size given as the input filename and save the new file as the output filename. |
| Convert to PPT | Convert the input PDF file into a PowerPoint presentation (ppt) file and save the converted file as output filename |
| Convert to Word | Convert the input PDF file into a Word (docx) file and save the converted file as output filename |
| Convert to PNG | Convert the input PDF file into a PNG image file and save the converted file as output filename |
| Convert to JPEG | Convert the input PDF file into a JPEG image file and save the converted file as output filename |
| Convert to TIFF | Convert the input PDF file into a TIFF image file and save the converted file as output filename |
| Convert to Excel | Convert the input PDF file into an Excel (.xlsx) file and save the converted file as output filename |
| Add Password | Add the input passcode text string as password protection to the input PDF file. |
| Check Password | Check if the input PDF file has password protection |
| Combine Files | Combine all files given in the list of input files into a single file and save the output file as output_filename |
| Redact Pages | Redacts all pages of the input PDF file in the range starting from start_page till end_page. Start and end pages are 1-indexed |
| Redact Text | Redacts all mentions of strings in the list denoted by "object_name" from the input PDF file within the range starting from the start page to the end page. Start and end pages are 1-indexed |
| Highlight Text | Highlight all instances in the input PDF file matched by input string |
| Underline Text | Underline all instances in the input PDF file matched by input string |
| Extract Pages | Extracts pages from the input PDF in the range from the start page to the end page. Start and end pages are 1-indexed |
| Delete Page | Deletes page denoted by integer "page_number_to_delete" from the input PDF file; the page number to be deleted is 1-indexed |
| Delete Page Range | Deletes pages from the input PDF in the range from the start page to the end page. Start and end pages are 1-indexed |
| Add Signature | Add an image of the signature on the page denoted by "page_number" in the input PDF file; input page number is 1-indexed |
| Add Watermark | Fix the watermark image on the input PDF file pages in the range from the start page to the end page. Start and end pages are 1-indexed |
| Add Comment | Add input text comment in the input PDF file at the input page number or by default at the last page |
| Add Page Text | Add a new page to the input PDF file at the page number specific by "page number". The new page has the text string "content" added to it. Page numbers are 1-indexed |

Table 1: Overview of tasks and associated tools in DocPilot

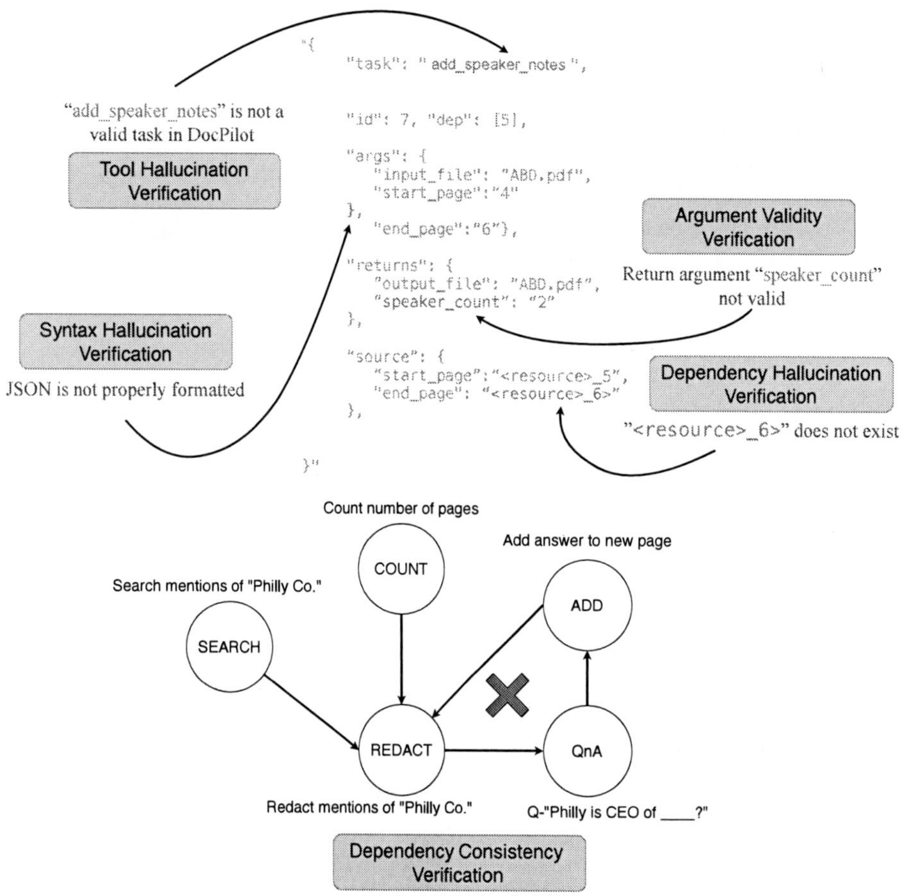


Figure 6: Task Verification example for syntax hallucinations, tool hallucinations, argument validity, dependency hallucinations, and dependency consistency.

### A.5 Guard Rails for Task Plan Code Generation

1. Code Generation Syntax: Most state-of-the-art LLM architectures are geared towards a conversational chat interface trained via human chat feedback (Ouyang et al., 2022). Consequently, LLMs may occasionally interleave conversational text with code syntax during generation. Moreover, some LLMs may even provide pseudo-code instead of independently executable Python code. In order to avoid such pitfalls, we add explicit instructions in the prompt to force the LLM to follow a predefined Python syntax with all other extraneous text formatted as comments in the code block. Moreover, it has been recently reported that SOTA LLMs like ChatGPT-3.5 and GPT-4 tend to show signs of "lazy assistance" wherein they refuse to generate fully executable code, instead explaining how the user could answer the question. We carefully designed the LLM prompt with explicit instructions to satisfy our need for independently executable Python code as the output of the step.

2. Software Import Compatibility: Allowing unrestricted permission to import any software library or package specified in the LLM-generated code may potentially harm user privacy and security. Some of these may not be compatible with the user hardware, conflict with existing software versions, or be no longer supported by programming languages. Hence, appropriate guard rails are needed to regulate what software libraries can be imported during task plan execution. Towards this, we maintain a software safe-list of approved Python packages, libraries, and executable files in the tool API documentation that are permitted to be invoked by LLM-generated code. We add explicit instructions to the prompts to forbid the LLMs from generating any overhead software libraries and packages for code execution. Instead, we pre-append the safe-listed software imports to the generated code.

3. File Handling: An essential aspect of copilot-driven external file modifications is safeguarding data privacy by not exposing the input file names and types that need to be modified and the resultant output files generated by the copilot to the LLM. We achieve this by strongly type-casting all references to input and output file names and addresses in the generated code to their actual values at the code execution step. Further, we impose strict directory access restrictions on the copilot system, preventing accessing, reading, or saving files without explicit user permissions. The code execution step involves creating a copy of all files required as inputs to a temporary directory and saving all intermediate files and the final output PDF to avoid overwriting or modifying non-permitted files.

### A.6 Task Plan Code Generation Examples

Figure 7 shows a qualitative example of a code solution generated by DocPilot corresponding to the task plan response to the user request - "Hey, can you please blacken out any sensitive client names from my 'VoltGaurd Electric.pdf' file and convert it into a PowerPoint presentation".

### A.7 Qualitative Examples

Figures 8 and 9 show qualitative examples of PDf files edited by a user through `DocPilot`.

#### A.7.1 Evaluation Procedure

As an introduction, the user was provided with a guidelines document that detailed the PDF capabilities of `DocPilot`. The user was also provided access to the `DocPilot` app (Figure 5) and given a short tutorial on its usage. For data collection, the user was provided with a repository of PDF documents (n=61), a suggested prompt library (n=151), and a link to a survey form for data collection. The user was instructed their overall evaluation goal was to complete several PDF workflows as best as possible with the help of `DocPilot`.

For the first task, the user was asked to select a PDF document and either craft a prompt based on their own usage or select one from the suggested list. For the second task, the user was asked to prompt `DocPilot` with their workflow request and to carefully review `DocPilot`'s responses. The user was encouraged to request changes as needed to the suggested plan until satisfied that it met their workflow goals. For the third task, the user was asked to review the actions as executed by `DocPilot` in the resulting files. Last, after completing all interactions with `DocPilot` for one workflow, regardless of success or failure, the user was instructed to

```
from api_functions import PDFTools

folder_path = './pdf_uploads/'
pdf_tools = PDFTools()

# Task 1: Initialize duplicate of the input file
input_file = "VoltGuard Electric.pdf"
pdf_tools.initialize_duplicate_pdf(folder_path + input_file)
duplicate_filename = "__input__.pdf"

# Task 2: Count pages in the duplicate file
page_count = pdf_tools.count_pages(folder_path + duplicate_filename)

# Task 3: Search for sensitive client names in the duplicate file
object_name = "sensitive client names"
text_list = pdf_tools.search(folder_path + duplicate_filename, object_name)

# Task 4: Redact text containing sensitive client names in the duplicate file
start_page = 0  # starting from the first page
end_page = page_count  # till the last page
pdf_tools.redact_text(folder_path + duplicate_filename, start_page, end_page, text_list)

# Task 5: Convert the redacted duplicate file to ppt
output_filename_ppt = "__input__.ppt"
pdf_tools.convert_type_to_ppt(folder_path + duplicate_filename, folder_path + output_filename_ppt)

# Task 6: Rename the generated ppt file to output file
input_filename_ppt = "__input__.ppt"
output_filename_ppt = "__output__.ppt"
pdf_tools.rename_file(folder_path + input_filename_ppt, folder_path + output_filename_ppt)
```

Figure 7: An example of task plan code solution generated for the query - "Hey, can you please blacken out any sensitive client names from my 'VoltGaurd Electric.pdf' file and convert it into a PowerPoint presentation"

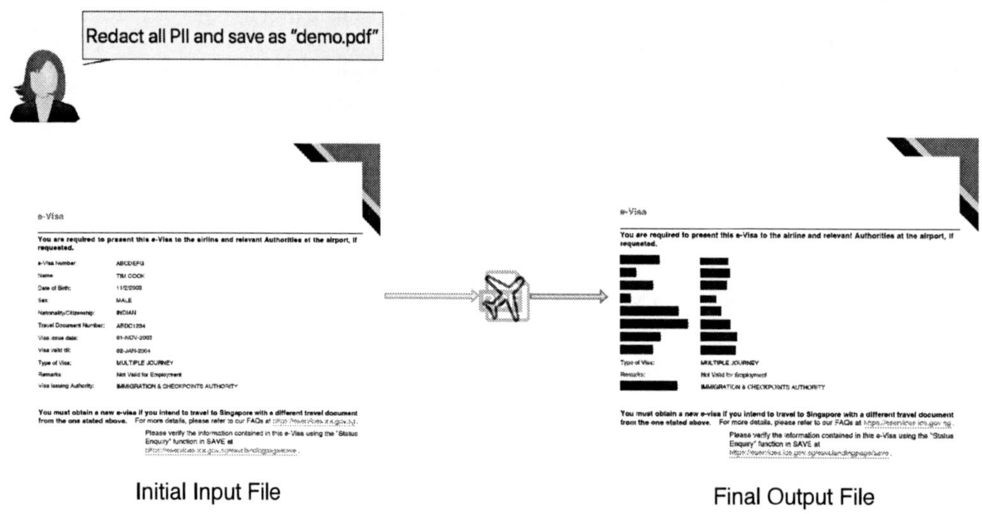


Figure 8: Example of a visa document being edited using DocPilot. The user asks to "redact all mentions of Personally Identifiable Information in the document". DocPilot removes names, passport numbers, date of birth, sex, nationality, and dates in the input document.

complete a short survey form reflecting on their experience. Each of the tasks were repeated for every new workflow evaluated.

### A.7.2 Measures

Our data collection included: 1) interaction logs during DocPilot app usage, 2) self-reported feedback after each workflow request, and 3) open-ended user feedback. The interaction logs included

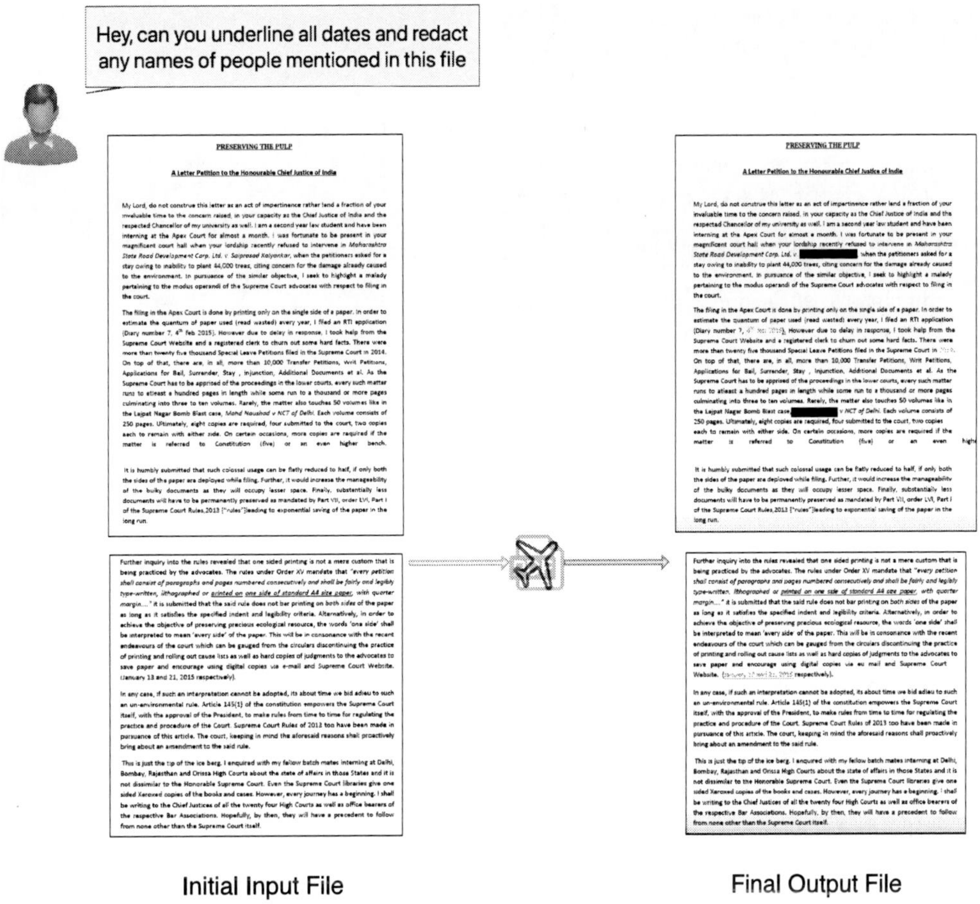


Figure 9: Example of a legal court document being edited using DocPilot. The user asks, " Hey, can you underline all dates and redact any names of people mentioned in this file?". DocPilot covers names ("Saiprasad Kalyankar", "Mohd Naushad") and underlines dates ("4th Feb 2015", "2014", "January 13 and 21, 2015") in the input document.

the chat history, program execution actions, and resulting files after execution. The self-reported measures included overall workflow, satisfaction with the initial DocPilot suggested plan, satisfaction with DocPilot incorporating user feedback to the plan, and satisfaction with how well actions were executed in the resulting files.

### A.7.3 Example Workflows

In total we collected data from 80 workflow requests. 16 workflows were user-provided based on the users' real world PDF workflows and 64 were workflows suggested to the user. We provided the suggested workflows to ensure workflows evaluated included variety in the types of actions used and in the number of actions requested. The user was encouraged to make small adjustments to the suggested workflows (as needed). For example if the workflow requested to delete page 5 of a document but the document only had 3 pages, then the user modified the workflow prompt accordingly.

Examples of **user-provided workflows**:

1. Add a watermark with the text "DRAFT" on every page, underline the test cycle types in the table, and extract the cleaning index values into a separate list
2. Highlight the text "ENERGY STAR Test Method for Determining Residential Dishwasher Cleaning Performance" in the document, convert page into image file, and add a header with the text "Energy Star Most Efficient 2016
3. Underline all section headings, redact the company's physical address, and add a watermark with text "Evaluation Copy" on each page

4. Extract pages 1-2 as a separate file with password "BUDGET2013", summarize the key issues discussed and action points, then add this summary to a new first page.

5. Extract all key terms and concepts, and create a glossary or index at the end of the document

Examples of **suggested workflows**:

1. Summarize all mentions of product launch dates and marketing strategies from the document, add a new page in front add this summary. Finally convert it to a Word file for later reference.

2. Redact all salary figures from the document, then add a line at the end stating the average salary of the listed positions. Underline the final mean salary figure for emphasis

3. Search for any mentions of project deadlines and add them as a new page at the end, then compress the file size to optimize storage space.

4. Search for any occurrences of the term 'Confidential' and redact them, after deleting pages 1-2. And add a watermark "Top Secret" to each remaining page.

5. Identify and highlight any technical or specialized terminology used within the document and add a signature to page 1 and protect the document with encryption.

### A.7.4 Results: Code Iterations

Table 2 illustrates the number of code iterations for each workflow (n=80). The majority of workflows (48/80) required one code iteration, and most workflows were successful in a maximum of two LLM-based code revision cycles.

| # of iterations | Count |
|---|---|
| 0 | 11 |
| 1 | 48 |
| 2 | 13 |
| 3 | 1 |
| 5 | 2 |
| 6 | 3 |

Table 2: The number of code iterations for each workflow (n=80). The majority of workflows (48/80) required one code iteration.

# UltraEval: A Lightweight Platform for Flexible and Comprehensive Evaluation for LLMs

**Chaoqun He[1], Renjie Luo[2†], Shengding Hu[1], Yuanqian Zhao[3†], Jie Zhou[4] Hanghao Wu[4], Jiajie Zhang[5†], Xu Han[1*], Zhiyuan Liu[1*], Maosong Sun[1]**

[1] Dept. of Comp. Sci. & Tech., Institute for AI, Tsinghua University, Beijing, China

[2] Institute of Artificial Intelligence, Beihang University, China

[3] Renmin University of China [4] ModelBest Inc. [5] Northeastern University, China

{hcq21, hsd23}@mails.tsinghua.edu.cn, renjie.luo@outlook.com

## Abstract

Evaluation is pivotal for refining Large Language Models (LLMs), pinpointing their capabilities, and guiding enhancements. The rapid development of LLMs calls for a lightweight and easy-to-use framework for swift evaluation deployment. However, considering various implementation details, developing a comprehensive evaluation platform is never easy. Existing platforms are often complex and poorly modularized, hindering seamless incorporation into research workflows. This paper introduces UltraEval, a user-friendly evaluation framework characterized by its lightweight nature, comprehensiveness, modularity, and efficiency. We identify and reimplement three core components of model evaluation (models, data, and metrics). The resulting composability allows for the free combination of different models, tasks, prompts, benchmarks, and metrics within a unified evaluation workflow. Additionally, UltraEval supports diverse models owing to a unified HTTP service and provides sufficient inference acceleration. UltraEval is now available for researchers publicly [1].

## 1 Introduction

LLMs have been deployed in diverse domains, such as finance(Zhang and Yang, 2023), education(Kasneci et al., 2023), and law(Blair-Stanek et al., 2023), demonstrating their versatility and efficacy(Zhao et al., 2023). This advancement is significantly bridging the gap between the realization of the current state and Artificial General Intelligence (AGI)(Bubeck et al., 2023). Nevertheless, the expansion of model parameters and training datasets engenders increasing uncertainties and emergent capabilities, posing potential risks to humanity and challenges to stable training models (Chang et al., 2023; Bommasani et al., 2021; Wei et al., 2022a). Consequently, it is imperative to continuously and meticulously evaluate the evolving capabilities of LLMs throughout their development to ensure their responsible and beneficial applications.

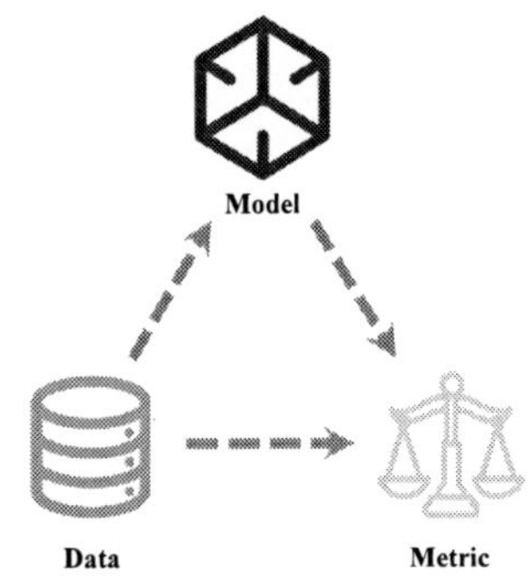


Figure 1: The three core modules of model evaluation.

Traditional benchmarks (Zellers et al., 2019; Suzgun et al., 2022; Austin et al., 2021; Clark et al., 2018) typically focus on evaluating model performance in a specific capability, making it challenging to assess the comprehensive abilities of a model. Additionally, these benchmarks generally do not include model deployment. Building pipelines from scratch for each combination of tasks and models for evaluation is highly inefficient and repetitive. Therefore, an integrated evaluation framework is crucial. Currently, some evaluation frameworks covering the entire pipeline from model deployment to model evaluation are proposed, and predominantly divided into two types: conversational websites, exemplified by platforms like Chatbot Arena [2], and open-source evaluation tools, such as lm-evaluation-harness [3]. The former effectively assesses the conversational abilities of a model

*Corresponding author:Xu Han (thu.hanxu13@gmail.com) and Zhiyuan Liu (liuzy@tsinghua.edu.cn)

†Work done during internship at ModelBest Inc.

[1]The website of UltraEval is at https://github.com/OpenBMB/UltraEval and a demo video is at https://youtu.be/C0O6BVzNAS8.

[2]https://chat.lmsys.org/

[3]https://github.com/EleutherAI/lm-evaluation-harness



*Proceedings of the 62nd Annual Meeting of the Association for Computational Linguistics (Volume 3: System Demonstrations)*, pages 247–257
August 11-16, 2024 ©2024 Association for Computational Linguistics

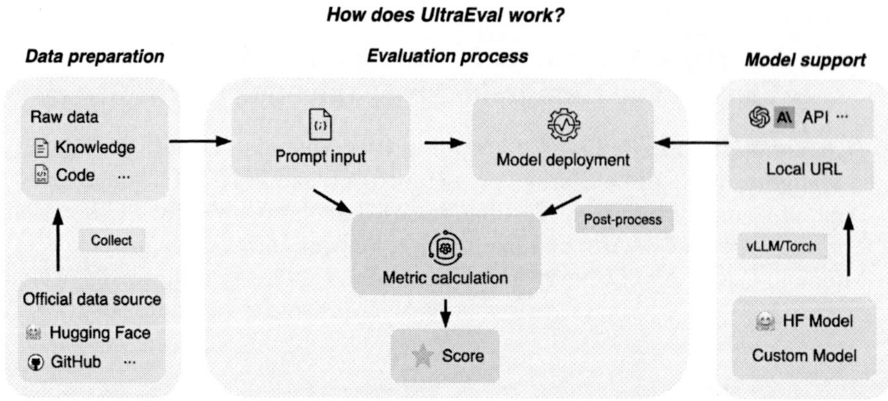


Figure 2: The overall pipeline of UltraEval, designed according to the three core modules of model evaluation.

but lacks comprehensive task coverage and transparency in the evaluation process. The latter open-source frameworks face challenges such as incomplete task coverage, complex code structure, heavy implementations, high difficulty to use, and tightly coupled functionalities. These issues hinder both convenient and comprehensive assessments.

In this paper, we identify three core components that form the evaluation process: models (or systems), task data, and metrics (i.e., evaluation methods), as illustrated in Figure 1. Rethinking the implementations in these three aspects would benefit the construction of a lightweight and easy-to-use evaluation framework, which covers mainstream tasks and complete evaluation pipeline, and can be easily expanded according to user customization. To this end, we introduce UltraEval, a lightweight and user-friendly open-source framework for LLMs evaluation. It stands out for its modular and scalable design, enabling thorough assessment of model capabilities. As illustrated in Figure 2, we segment the evaluation pipeline into three main modules: Data, Model, and Metrics, each operating independently and interacting through data exchange.

Specifically, UltraEval is characterized by the following features:

1. **Lightweight Usage Modes.** UltraEval is designed with minimal dependency requirements and features straightforward design and installation, complemented by detailed documentation. Users can initiate automated evaluations with just a few simple commands.

2. **Comprehensive Evaluation Tools.** UltraEval offers an extensive benchmarks suite, comprising over 50 commonly used benchmarks, and provides a customized prompt for each task. During the evaluation process, we replicated commonly used metrics and incorporated post-processing methods for more accurate metric calculation. We replicate some benchmarks from the LLaMA2(Touvron et al., 2023), achieving consistent results, which demonstrates UltraEval's reliability.

3. **Modular Architecture and Interfaces.** The three main modules are independent and have clear functions, enhancing the system stability of UltraEval. Moreover, its excellent scalability allows users to flexibly customize the evaluation workflow, such as by adding new models, tasks, metrics, and more.

4. **Efficient Inference Engines.** UltraEval deploys models as HTTP services, supporting the evaluation of LLMs from different sources, including the models deployed locally and the web-based API. When deployed locally, we also provide the interface to utilize vLLM [4](Kwon et al., 2023) and Gunicorn to enable multi-GPU acceleration.

Evaluation is currently in a phase of rapid and exploratory growth. UltraEval will be continuously updated and provide detailed tutorials to help researchers to efficiently deploy evaluation pipeline.

## 2 Related Work

The advancement of LLMs has led to the emergence of various evaluation frameworks, each with

[4] https://github.com/vllm-project/vllm

| Framework | Bytes | Datasets | Acceleration | Model Types | Evaluation Method |
|---|---|---|---|---|---|
| Chatbot Arena | - | - | - | Chat | Human |
| AlpacaEval | 3000k | - | - | Chat | GPT-4 |
| FastChat | 950k | 1 | - | Chat | GPT-4 |
| HELM | 3200k | 10 | - | All | Auto |
| FlagEval | 760k | 21 | - | All | Auto |
| LLM harness | 815k | 50+ | vLLM & HF Accelerate | All | Auto |
| OpenCompass | 4000k | 50+ | Distributed Computing | All | Auto |
| InstructEval | 480k | 5 | - | Chat | Auto |
| OpenAI-Evals | 780k | - | Concurrent API Request | GPT | Auto |
| GPT-Fathom | 445k | 21 | Concurrent API Request | GPT & LLaMA | Auto |
| UltraEval | **315k** | 50+ | vLLM & Gunicorn | All | Auto & GPT-4 |

Table 1: Comparison of Evaluation Frameworks. Bytes: the total bytes of Python and Jupyter Notebook code in each framework's GitHub repository, Acceleration: tools or methods employed to expedite model inference, Model Types: Supported Models for Evaluation, GPT: GPT series models, LLaMA: LLaMA series models

its unique features. This section will provide a detailed overview of the current state of evaluation frameworks (also see Table 1).

**Chatbot Arena** (Zheng et al., 2024) offers a LLM evaluation platform where users vote on model responses, using a crowdsourced, anonymous Elo-rating system. Although innovative, its reliance on human judgment limits its suitability for fast, routine assessments. **AlpacaEval**[5](Li et al., 2023) and **FastChat**[6](Zheng et al., 2023a) conduct evaluation by employing GPT-4(Achiam et al., 2023) for automated judging. Yet, in evaluating complex reasoning tasks, they tend to favor verbose responses and face issues with robustness. Additionally, the scope of their evaluation capabilities is limited.

**HELM**[7](Liang et al., 2022) streamlines language model evaluation but is constrained by its support solely for AutoModelForCausalLM[8], excluding models without namespaces or stored locally. It lacks support for user models, demonstrates potential module coupling issues and absence of acceleration options. **FlagEval**'s[9] "capability-task-indicator" framework is original but criticized for its closed-source approach and overly simplistic benchmark choices, raising data security and assessment depth concerns. Despite their innovations, both platforms fall short of the adaptability and comprehensiveness seen in more versatile frameworks like UltraEval.

**LLM harness** (Gao et al., 2023), used by HuggingFace's Open LLM Leaderboard, and **OpenCompass**[10](Contributors, 2023) have emerged as comprehensive solutions, offering extensive dataset support and rapid updates. These feature-rich environments, however, entail a trade-off: their complexity and dependency on specific software can complicate usage and customization. This underscores the importance of detailed documentation for those looking to adapt or extend these frameworks. Similarly, **InstructEval**[11] (Chia et al., 2023), leveraging the LLM harness infrastructure, caters specifically to models fine-tuned with instructions such as Alpaca and Flan-T5. Despite its targeted approach, InstructEval's limitations in model and task coverage hint at its niche application rather than widespread utility. The adoption of such frameworks reflects the evolving landscape of model evaluation, where finding a balance between comprehensiveness and usability poses an ongoing challenge.

**OpenAI Evals**[12] and **GPT-Fathom**[13](Zheng et al., 2023b). OpenAI Evals offers a straightforward, open-source framework for appraising OpenAI models, while GPT-Fathom expands upon this by analyzing the progression from GPT-3 to GPT-4 using a wider dataset array. Although it provides valuable insights into LLM development, GPT-Fathom shares OpenAI Evals' limitations in supporting a diverse range of models.

[5]https://github.com/tatsu-lab/alpaca_eval
[6]https://github.com/lm-sys/FastChat
[7]https://github.com/stanford-crfm/helm
[8]https://huggingface.co/docs/transformers/main
[9]https://flageval.baai.ac.cn
[10]https://github.com/open-compass/opencompass
[11]https://github.com/declare-lab/instruct-eval
[12]https://github.com/openai/evals
[13]https://github.com/GPT-Fathom/GPT-Fathom

| First Level | Second Level | Dataset List |
|---|---|---|
| Knowledge | Disciplinary knowledge | MMLU, CMMLU, C-Eval, AGI-Eval<br>JEC-QA, MEDMCQA, MEDQA-MCMLE<br>MEDQA-USMLE, GAOKAO-Bench |
| | World knowledge | NQ-open, TriviaQA, TruthfulQA |
| Math | Math | GSM8K, MATH |
| Code | Code | HumanEval, MBPP |
| Reason | Logical reasoning | BBH |
| | Implicative relation | AX-B, AX-G, CB, CMNLI, OCNLI, RTE |
| | Commonsense reasoning | HellaSwag, OpenBookQA, ARC-c, ARC-e<br>CommonsenseQA, COPA, PIQA, SIQA<br>WinoGrande, Story Cloze, StrategyQA, TheoremQA |
| Language | Reading comprehension | BoolQ, C3, ChiD, DRCD, LAMBADA, MultiRC, QuAC<br>RACE, RECORD, SQuAD, TyDiQA, SummEdits |
| | Translation | FLORES, WMT20-en-zh, WMT20-en-zh |
| | Semantic similarity | AFQMC, BUSTM |
| | Word sense disambiguation | CLUEWSC, WIC, Winogender, WSC |
| | Sentiment analysis | EPRSTMT |
| | News classification | TNEWS |

Table 2: We compile a collection of 59 widely-used benchmarks and categorized them according to scenarios.

```
def transform_entry(row):
    question, *choices, answer = row
    target_scores = {
        choice: int((ord(answer) - ord("A")) == idx)
        for idx, choice in enumerate(choices)
    }

    return {
        "passage": "",
        "question": question,
        "target_scores": target_scores,
        "answer": "",
    }
```

Figure 3: The data formatting template for MMLU.

## 3 UltraEval

As illustrated in Figure 1, evaluation is a comprehensive process that integrates models, data, and metrics. With this in mind, the design philosophy considers both the independence and interconnectivity of each module. As shown in Figure 2, UltraEval encompasses the entire evaluation lifecycle(Chang et al., 2023) and segments the evaluation workflow into three main modules. In this section, we delve into the design and implementation of each component within UltraEval in detail.

### 3.1 Data Preparation

Data preparation involves transforming raw data into the final input format for the model, encompassing data preprocessing and prompt templates.

**Data Preprocessing.** We collect commonly used benchmarks for evaluating LLMs, such as MMLU(Hendrycks et al., 2020), GSM8K(Cobbe et al., 2021), and Hellaswag(Zellers et al., 2019), covering multiple dimensions of capabilities. Currently, we have 59 benchmarks, listed in Table 2, and we plan to continually expand our collection of benchmarks.

To ensure the accuracy of the data, we source it from reputable platforms like Hugging Face[14] and GitHub, rather than relying on data modified by third parties. Given the varying data formats across benchmarks, we design a set of templates to standardize these diverse formats into JSON, serving as the starting point for evaluations. As shown in Figure 3, different data items are categorized under unified attributes.

**Prompt Templates.** Prompts are used to guide models to generate specific outputs, and UltraEval supports prompt engineering (White et al., 2023), including few-shot and Chain of Thought (CoT) (Wei et al., 2022b), to enhance the model's accuracy. The sensitivity of LLMs to prompts (Zhu et al., 2023) and the variability of prompts across different tasks often make it challenging for researchers to replicate results from papers, hindering research progress. UltraEval addresses this issue by providing customized, stable prompt templates for each task to facilitate result alignment. Figure 4 showcases an example of a prompt template for MMLU, demonstrating the rigorous process for forming the final prompt input.

[14] https://huggingface.co/datasets

```python
question = f"Question:\n{question]}\n"
instruction = f"Requirement:\nChoose and respond with the letter of the
    correct answer, including the parentheses.\n"
options = "Options:\n"
for idx, item in enumerate(question_options):
    options += f"({chr(65 + idx)}) {item}\n"
answer_prompt = f"Answer:\n"
final_input = question + instruction + options + answer_prompt
```

Figure 4: An example of a prompt template for an MMLU task.

### 3.2 Model Delpoyment

UltraEval employs a unique design approach, deploying models as HTTP online services and leveraging vLLM and gunicorn technologies to enable multi-GPU acceleration.

**Http Service.** In traditional evaluations, model deployment is closely integrated with task assessment, requiring models to be redeployed for each new task, which can lead to unnecessary consumption of time and hardware resources. To address this, we deploy models as HTTP services with Flask, facilitating modularization and efficient resource use. This approach has several advantages:

1. **Independence.** We provide a unified interface through which models receive task data and hyperparameters, returning results upon completing inference. This setup, which allows for adjustments via hyperparameters, ensures model independence.

2. **Comprehensiveness.** In UltraEval, we enable direct model loading from the Huggingface Transformers library. Given the independent deployment, UltraEval theoretically supports all models, including those from personal experimentation under different frameworks, greatly enhancing research and development flexibility. We utilize vLLM[15] as the foundational acceleration framework, granting loading priority to models it supports.

3. **Scalability.** Thanks to its excellent scalability, users can easily extend models from language-based applications to multimodal models.

**Multi-GPU Acceleration.** We use the Gunicorn web server with Flask to deploy models via web endpoints, achieving a flexible and decoupled architecture for model deployment and evaluation. This setup allows for dynamic GPU acceleration, where the Gunicorn server, configured with environment-specific parameters, manages multiple worker processes. Each process, handling a slice of the available GPUs, executes inference tasks in parallel, significantly improving computational efficiency and throughput. A highlight of UltraEval's performance is its ability to utilize 4 A800 GPUs to evaluate a test set of 41k data points in under 1.5 hours, showcasing remarkable efficiency[16].

### 3.3 Evaluation Methods

Refined data and models are instantiated through the *Task* and *Model* classes, respectively, initiating the model inference process. The model performs inference based on the input data and its hyperparameters, generating prediction outcomes. Typically, between the model's output and the final score calculation, there are intermediate steps including post-processing and metric calculation.

**Post-Processing.** Model outputs, influenced by task characteristics, prompt templates, and the model's performance, often contain extraneous information beyond the answers needed(Park et al., 2024). As shown in Figure 7, when ChatGPT responds to HumanEval questions, the response may include both code and additional textual descriptions, complicating automatic evaluation. To more accurately assess the model, it is necessary to post-process the model's outputs to extract the most crucial answers.

Post-processing is bifurcated into two dimensions: model and task. Variations in model training approaches result in different versions, such as chat and base, necessitating distinct processing methods. Additionally, certain tasks employ specific evaluation methodologies. Taking Figure 7 as an example, the initial step involves extracting the code segment from ChatGPT's response. Subsequently, due to HumanEval(Chen et al., 2021)'s unique evaluation

[15]https://github.com/vllm-project/vllm

[16]The model used in this experiment is Llama2-7B, and the benchmarks includes BBH, MMLU, C-Eval, CMMLU, HumanEval, MBPP, GSM8K and MATH. In total, they consist of 40,938 data points.

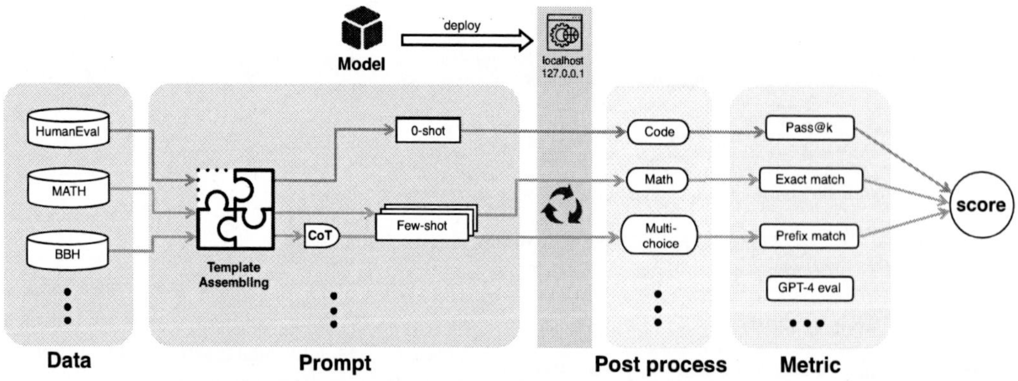


Figure 5: The combination of different modules within UltraEval.

criteria, it is necessary to extract the function body from the code while omitting the function name, yielding a cleaner and more precise answer. UltraEval develops several post-processing methods tailored to the tasks and models currently available.

**Metric Calculation.** Evaluation methods are categorized based on their ability to be computed automatically into automatic evaluation and human evaluation(Chang et al., 2023). For automatic evaluation, we implement common metrics such as exact match for text generation tasks, F1 score for binary classification tasks, ROUGE(Lin, 2004) for translation tasks, and pass@k(Chen et al., 2021) for coding tasks. Specifically, for exact match, we develop extensions like in match and prefix match to more effectively capture a wide range of scenarios.

Given that UltraEval is an automated evaluation framework, for human evaluation, we integrate GPT-4(Achiam et al., 2023) as a discriminator to substitute for human evaluation. Moreover, all data results can be saved according to user preferences, allowing users to decide on human evaluation if desired, thus offering significant flexibility for a more objective assessment.

| Benchmark | Llama2-7B | | Llama2-13B | | Mistral-7B | |
|---|---|---|---|---|---|---|
| | Official | UltraEval | Official | UltraEval | Official | UltraEval |
| ARC-C | 45.9 | 43.2 | 45.9 | 47.4 | 55.5 | 50.8 |
| HellaSwag | 77.2 | 75.6 | 80.7 | 79.1 | 81.3 | 80.4 |
| BBH | 32.6 | 32.8 | 39.4 | 39.2 | 38.0* | 40.4 |
| MATH | 2.5 | 2.8 | 3.9 | 4.8 | 13.1 | 10.2 |
| GSM8K | 14.6 | 14.8 | 28.7 | 22.6 | 52.1* | 31.9 |
| HumanEval | 12.8 | 12.8 | 18.3 | 17.1 | 30.5 | 26.8 |
| MBPP | 20.8 | 20.8 | 30.6 | 29.0 | 47.5 | 47.3 |
| MMLU | 45.3 | 45.1 | 54.8 | 55.2 | 60.1 | 63.1 |

Table 3: Evaluation results on mainstream benchmarks (%). * The BBH score is not explicitly stated in the paper(Jiang et al., 2023), however, it is inferred to be 38.0 from the figures in the paper. The replicated result for GSM8K is 35.4 in Gemma paper(Team et al., 2024), which is close to our result.

## 4 Evaluation

UltraEval aims to provide a lightweight, comprehensive, and user-friendly evaluation framework to support research. As illustrated in Figure 5, UltraEval's modular design effectively combines various models, tasks and metrics for evaluation. Using UltraEval, we evaluate models from the LLaMA2 series(Touvron et al., 2023) and Mistral(Jiang et al., 2023) on these widely-used benchmarks. As indicated in the Table 3, some reproduced results are higher, while others are lower, but within a certain margin of error, our reproduced results are consistent with the results reported in the papers, underscoring our framework's reliability. The sources of error include hyperparameters (e.g., temperature, top-p) and hardware configurations. Since the evaluation details are not provided in the papers, verification is not possible. This highlights the importance of having an open and reproducible evaluation framework.

Furthermore, UltraEval supports innovative research efforts, research on predictable scaling(Hu et al., 2023), OlympiadBench(He et al., 2024) and model training, such as with MiniCPM(Hu et al., 2024).

## 5 Discussion and Future Work

In this section, we discuss future work following this study. Specifically, we focus on addressing data contamination and supporting a broader range of evaluation scenarios.

**Data contamination** refers to the phenomenon that examples from the evaluation set are also found in the training data (Li et al., 2024), causing inaccuracies in model evaluation. Common methods for contamination detection include n-gram overlap and embedding similarity search. However, none of these methods are perfect, making research on contamination detection still crucial. We will integrate these methods.

**Supporting more evaluation scenarios**, such as multimodal, long-text, and Retrieval-Augmented Generation (RAG), is crucial for meeting a broader range of evaluation needs. This will be an important direction for our future work.

## 6 Conclusion

We introduce UltraEval, a lightweight, user-friendly, and comprehensive framework for model evaluation. UltraEval establishes a unified structure with well-defined modules and flexible interactions, aiding researchers and developers in efficiently deploying evaluation workflows. Moving forward, we plan to continuously integrate new technologies and features into UltraEval, extending beyond large language models to support the evaluation of multimodal models, Retrieval-Augmented Generation (RAG), agents, and more, to advance the research on AGI. Additionally, we aim to expand our collection of representative benchmarks and also develop our own, exploring the capabilities and limits of large models.

## Acknowledgements

This work is supported by the National Key R&D Program of China (No. 2022ZD0116312), Quan Cheng Laboratory (Grant No. QCLZD202301), the Postdoctoral Fellowship Program of CPSE (Grant No. GZB20230343), China Postdoctoral Science Foundation (Grant No. 2023M741945), and Institute Guo Qiang at Tsinghua University.

## Limitations

Currently, our approach primarily utilizes text domain evaluation. However, we are looking to expand the scope of UltraEval by integrating multimodal and long-context evaluation datasets. This enhancement aims to facilitate more thorough and diverse assessments. Additionally, there is room for improvement in the visualization of our results. Future improvement will focus on enabling multidimensional visualization, thereby enriching the interpretability and depth of our evaluation results.

## Ethical Considerations

In this paper, we present UltraEval, a lightweight, user-friendly, flexible, and comprehensive framework for model evaluation. Adhering to the principles of modularity, UltraEval segments the evaluation process into three distinct modules: Data, Model, and Metrics. This approach enhances the framework's extensibility and flexibility, allowing for the easy integration of new models and tasks. We offer an extensive benchmark suite and replicate commonly used models and benchmarks. Our results align with those reported in the corresponding papers, underscoring the stability and reliability of our framework. Committed to sustainable development, we publicly release all our code to minimize unnecessary carbon footprint. Throughout our experiments, we adhere to all licenses related to models and data.

## References

Josh Achiam, Steven Adler, Sandhini Agarwal, Lama Ahmad, Ilge Akkaya, Florencia Leoni Aleman, Diogo Almeida, Janko Altenschmidt, Sam Altman, Shyamal Anadkat, et al. 2023. Gpt-4 technical report. *arXiv preprint arXiv:2303.08774*.

Jacob Austin, Augustus Odena, Maxwell Nye, Maarten Bosma, Henryk Michalewski, David Dohan, Ellen Jiang, Carrie Cai, Michael Terry, Quoc Le, et al. 2021. Program synthesis with large language models. *arXiv preprint arXiv:2108.07732*.

Andrew Blair-Stanek, Nils Holzenberger, and Benjamin Van Durme. 2023. Can gpt-3 perform statutory reasoning? In *Proceedings of the Nineteenth International Conference on Artificial Intelligence and Law*, pages 22–31.

Rishi Bommasani, Drew A Hudson, Ehsan Adeli, Russ Altman, Simran Arora, Sydney von Arx, Michael S Bernstein, Jeannette Bohg, Antoine Bosselut, Emma Brunskill, et al. 2021. On the opportunities and risks of foundation models. *arXiv preprint arXiv:2108.07258*.

Sébastien Bubeck, Varun Chandrasekaran, Ronen Eldan, Johannes Gehrke, Eric Horvitz, Ece Kamar, Peter Lee, Yin Tat Lee, Yuanzhi Li, Scott Lundberg, et al. 2023. Sparks of artificial general intelligence: Early experiments with gpt-4. *arXiv preprint arXiv:2303.12712*.

Yupeng Chang, Xu Wang, Jindong Wang, Yuan Wu, Linyi Yang, Kaijie Zhu, Hao Chen, Xiaoyuan Yi, Cunxiang Wang, Yidong Wang, et al. 2023. A survey on evaluation of large language models. *ACM Transactions on Intelligent Systems and Technology*.

Mark Chen, Jerry Tworek, Heewoo Jun, Qiming Yuan, Henrique Ponde de Oliveira Pinto, Jared Kaplan, Harri Edwards, Yuri Burda, Nicholas Joseph, Greg Brockman, et al. 2021. Evaluating large language models trained on code. *arXiv preprint arXiv:2107.03374*.

Yew Ken Chia, Pengfei Hong, Lidong Bing, and Soujanya Poria. 2023. Instructeval: Towards holistic evaluation of instruction-tuned large language models. *arXiv preprint arXiv:2306.04757*.

Peter Clark, Isaac Cowhey, Oren Etzioni, Tushar Khot, Ashish Sabharwal, Carissa Schoenick, and Oyvind Tafjord. 2018. Think you have solved question answering? try arc, the ai2 reasoning challenge. *arXiv preprint arXiv:1803.05457*.

Karl Cobbe, Vineet Kosaraju, Mohammad Bavarian, Mark Chen, Heewoo Jun, Lukasz Kaiser, Matthias Plappert, Jerry Tworek, Jacob Hilton, Reiichiro Nakano, et al. 2021. Training verifiers to solve math word problems. *arXiv preprint arXiv:2110.14168*.

OpenCompass Contributors. 2023. Opencompass: A universal evaluation platform for foundation models. `https://github.com/open-compass/opencompass`.

Leo Gao, Jonathan Tow, Baber Abbasi, Stella Biderman, Sid Black, Anthony DiPofi, Charles Foster, Laurence Golding, Jeffrey Hsu, Alain Le Noac'h, Haonan Li, Kyle McDonell, Niklas Muennighoff, Chris Ociepa, Jason Phang, Laria Reynolds, Hailey Schoelkopf, Aviya Skowron, Lintang Sutawika, Eric Tang, Anish Thite, Ben Wang, Kevin Wang, and Andy Zou. 2023. A framework for few-shot language model evaluation.

Chaoqun He, Renjie Luo, Yuzhuo Bai, Shengding Hu, Zhen Leng Thai, Junhao Shen, Jinyi Hu, Xu Han, Yujie Huang, Yuxiang Zhang, et al. 2024. Olympiadbench: A challenging benchmark for promoting agi with olympiad-level bilingual multimodal scientific problems. *arXiv preprint arXiv:2402.14008*.

Dan Hendrycks, Collin Burns, Steven Basart, Andy Zou, Mantas Mazeika, Dawn Song, and Jacob Steinhardt. 2020. Measuring massive multitask language understanding. *arXiv preprint arXiv:2009.03300*.

Shengding Hu, Xin Liu, Xu Han, Xinrong Zhang, Chaoqun He, Weilin Zhao, Yankai Lin, Ning Ding, Zebin Ou, Guoyang Zeng, et al. 2023. Unlock predictable scaling from emergent abilities. *arXiv preprint arXiv:2310.03262*.

Shengding Hu, Yuge Tu, Xu Han, Chaoqun He, Ganqu Cui, Xiang Long, Zhi Zheng, Yewei Fang, Yuxiang Huang, Weilin Zhao, Xinrong Zhang, Zheng Leng Thai, Kaihuo Zhang, Chongyi Wang, Yuan Yao, Chenyang Zhao, Jie Zhou, Jie Cai, Zhongwu Zhai, Ning Ding, Chao Jia, Guoyang Zeng, Dahai Li, Zhiyuan Liu, and Maosong Sun. 2024. Minicpm: Unveiling the potential of small language models with scalable training strategies.

Albert Q Jiang, Alexandre Sablayrolles, Arthur Mensch, Chris Bamford, Devendra Singh Chaplot, Diego de las Casas, Florian Bressand, Gianna Lengyel, Guillaume Lample, Lucile Saulnier, et al. 2023. Mistral 7b. *arXiv preprint arXiv:2310.06825*.

Enkelejda Kasneci, Kathrin Seßler, Stefan Küchemann, Maria Bannert, Daryna Dementieva, Frank Fischer, Urs Gasser, Georg Groh, Stephan Günnemann, Eyke Hüllermeier, et al. 2023. Chatgpt for good? on opportunities and challenges of large language models for education. *Learning and individual differences*, 103:102274.

Woosuk Kwon, Zhuohan Li, Siyuan Zhuang, Ying Sheng, Lianmin Zheng, Cody Hao Yu, Joseph Gonzalez, Hao Zhang, and Ion Stoica. 2023. Efficient memory management for large language model serving with pagedattention. In *Proceedings of the 29th Symposium on Operating Systems Principles*, pages 611–626.

Xuechen Li, Tianyi Zhang, Yann Dubois, Rohan Taori, Ishaan Gulrajani, Carlos Guestrin, Percy Liang, and Tatsunori B. Hashimoto. 2023. Alpacaeval: An automatic evaluator of instruction-following models. `https://github.com/tatsu-lab/alpaca_eval`.

Yucheng Li, Frank Guerin, and Chenghua Lin. 2024. Latesteval: Addressing data contamination in language model evaluation through dynamic and time-sensitive test construction.

Percy Liang, Rishi Bommasani, Tony Lee, Dimitris Tsipras, Dilara Soylu, Michihiro Yasunaga, Yian Zhang, Deepak Narayanan, Yuhuai Wu, Ananya Kumar, et al. 2022. Holistic evaluation of language models. *arXiv preprint arXiv:2211.09110*.

Chin-Yew Lin. 2004. ROUGE: A package for automatic evaluation of summaries. In *Text Summarization Branches Out*, pages 74–81, Barcelona, Spain. Association for Computational Linguistics.

Peter S Park, Philipp Schoenegger, and Chongyang Zhu. 2024. Diminished diversity-of-thought in a standard large language model. *Behavior Research Methods*, pages 1–17.

Mirac Suzgun, Nathan Scales, Nathanael Schärli, Sebastian Gehrmann, Yi Tay, Hyung Won Chung, Aakanksha Chowdhery, Quoc V Le, Ed H Chi, Denny Zhou, et al. 2022. Challenging big-bench tasks and whether chain-of-thought can solve them. *arXiv preprint arXiv:2210.09261*.

Gemma Team, Thomas Mesnard, Cassidy Hardin, Robert Dadashi, Surya Bhupatiraju, Shreya Pathak, Laurent Sifre, Morgane Rivière, Mihir Sanjay Kale, Juliette Love, et al. 2024. Gemma: Open models based on gemini research and technology. *arXiv preprint arXiv:2403.08295*.

Hugo Touvron, Louis Martin, Kevin Stone, Peter Albert, Amjad Almahairi, Yasmine Babaei, Nikolay Bashlykov, Soumya Batra, Prajjwal Bhargava, Shruti Bhosale, et al. 2023. Llama 2: Open foundation and fine-tuned chat models. *arXiv preprint arXiv:2307.09288*.

Jason Wei, Yi Tay, Rishi Bommasani, Colin Raffel, Barret Zoph, Sebastian Borgeaud, Dani Yogatama, Maarten Bosma, Denny Zhou, Donald Metzler, et al. 2022a. Emergent abilities of large language models. *arXiv preprint arXiv:2206.07682*.

Jason Wei, Xuezhi Wang, Dale Schuurmans, Maarten Bosma, Fei Xia, Ed Chi, Quoc V Le, Denny Zhou, et al. 2022b. Chain-of-thought prompting elicits reasoning in large language models. *Advances in neural information processing systems*, 35:24824–24837.

Jules White, Quchen Fu, Sam Hays, Michael Sandborn, Carlos Olea, Henry Gilbert, Ashraf Elnashar, Jesse Spencer-Smith, and Douglas C Schmidt. 2023. A prompt pattern catalog to enhance prompt engineering with chatgpt. *arXiv preprint arXiv:2302.11382*.

Rowan Zellers, Ari Holtzman, Yonatan Bisk, Ali Farhadi, and Yejin Choi. 2019. Hellaswag: Can a machine really finish your sentence? *arXiv preprint arXiv:1905.07830*.

Xuanyu Zhang and Qing Yang. 2023. Xuanyuan 2.0: A large chinese financial chat model with hundreds of billions parameters. In *Proceedings of the 32nd ACM International Conference on Information and Knowledge Management*, pages 4435–4439.

Wayne Xin Zhao, Kun Zhou, Junyi Li, Tianyi Tang, Xiaolei Wang, Yupeng Hou, Yingqian Min, Beichen Zhang, Junjie Zhang, Zican Dong, et al. 2023. A survey of large language models. *arXiv preprint arXiv:2303.18223*.

Lianmin Zheng, Wei-Lin Chiang, Ying Sheng, Siyuan Zhuang, Zhanghao Wu, Yonghao Zhuang, Zi Lin, Zhuohan Li, Dacheng Li, Eric Xing, et al. 2024. Judging llm-as-a-judge with mt-bench and chatbot arena. *Advances in Neural Information Processing Systems*, 36.

Lianmin Zheng, Wei-Lin Chiang, Ying Sheng, Siyuan Zhuang, Zhanghao Wu, Yonghao Zhuang, Zi Lin, Zhuohan Li, Dacheng Li, Eric. P Xing, Hao Zhang, Joseph E. Gonzalez, and Ion Stoica. 2023a. Judging llm-as-a-judge with mt-bench and chatbot arena.

Shen Zheng, Yuyu Zhang, Yijie Zhu, Chenguang Xi, Pengyang Gao, Xun Zhou, and Kevin Chen-Chuan Chang. 2023b. GPT-Fathom: Benchmarking large language models to decipher the evolutionary path towards GPT-4 and beyond.

Kaijie Zhu, Jindong Wang, Jiaheng Zhou, Zichen Wang, Hao Chen, Yidong Wang, Linyi Yang, Wei Ye, Neil Zhenqiang Gong, Yue Zhang, et al. 2023. Promptbench: Towards evaluating the robustness of large language models on adversarial prompts. *arXiv preprint arXiv:2306.04528*.

# A More details

## A.1 Post-process

We present the post-processing code in Figure 6 and explain the reasons necessitating post-processing in Figure 7.

## A.2 UltraEval Usage

In the tutorial [17], we provide a detailed guide on UltraEval, including an introduction to its modules and instructions on how users can customize evaluations, such as adding their own new tasks and new models. This ensures that diverse evaluation needs are met.

## A.3 Model as Judge

Currently, UltraEval supports ChatGPT as a substitute for human evaluation. However, since ChatGPT is a commercial model, users need to provide the relevant API key. Due to the modularity and flexibility of our framework, users can also use other closed-source models or highly performant open-source models as evaluators.

## A.4 Multi-GPU Acceleration

Multi-GPU acceleration requires sufficient GPU resources. For larger models, such as Llama2-70B, deploying a single instance requires two A100 GPUs. Therefore, when using Multi-GPU acceleration, it is essential to consider both the model and the available GPU resources to ensure optimal configuration.

[17] `https://github.com/OpenBMB/UltraEval/blob/main/docs/tutorials/en/ultraeval.md`

```
def process_text(text):
    triple_quotes_indices = [i for i, _ in enumerate(text) if text.startswith('\"\"\"', i)]

    if len(triple_quotes_indices) % 2 == 0 and len(triple_quotes_indices) > 0:
        for i in range(0, len(triple_quotes_indices), 2):
            start_index = triple_quotes_indices[i]
            end_index = triple_quotes_indices[i + 1]
            if 'def' in text[end_index:]:
                return text[:start_index].strip()
        return text.strip()
    elif len(triple_quotes_indices) > 0:
        return text[:triple_quotes_indices[0]].strip()
    else:
        return text.strip()
```

Figure 6: An example of a post-processing method for the MBPP task.

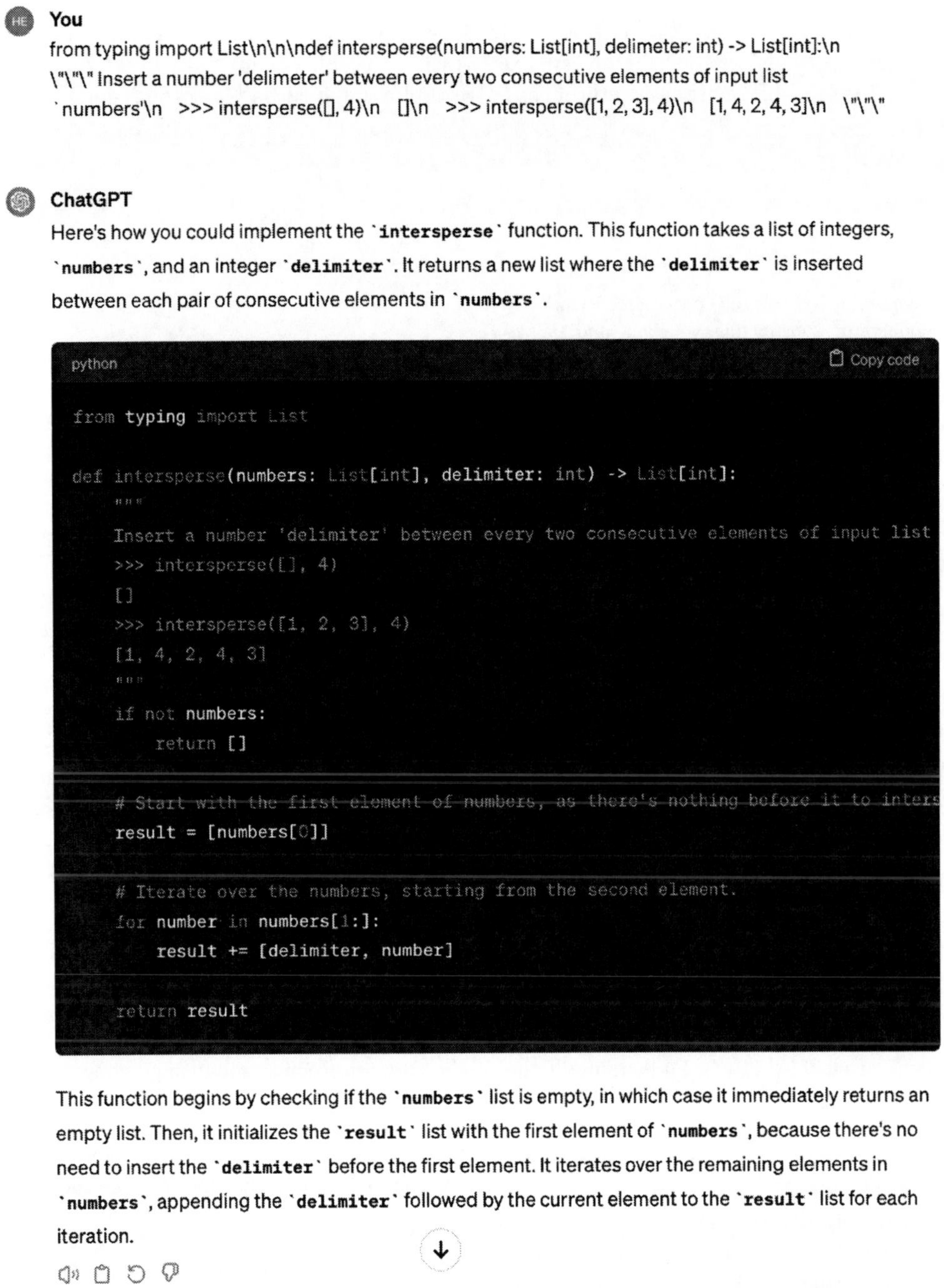

**You**

from typing import List\n\n\ndef intersperse(numbers: List[int], delimeter: int) -> List[int]:\n \"\"\" Insert a number 'delimeter' between every two consecutive elements of input list `numbers'\n >>> intersperse([], 4)\n []\n >>> intersperse([1, 2, 3], 4)\n [1, 4, 2, 4, 3]\n \"\"\"

**ChatGPT**

Here's how you could implement the `intersperse` function. This function takes a list of integers, `numbers`, and an integer `delimiter`. It returns a new list where the `delimiter` is inserted between each pair of consecutive elements in `numbers`.

python Copy code

```python
from typing import List

def intersperse(numbers: List[int], delimiter: int) -> List[int]:
    """
    Insert a number 'delimiter' between every two consecutive elements of input list
    >>> intersperse([], 4)
    []
    >>> intersperse([1, 2, 3], 4)
    [1, 4, 2, 4, 3]
    """
    if not numbers:
        return []

    # Start with the first element of numbers, as there's nothing before it to inters
    result = [numbers[0]]

    # Iterate over the numbers, starting from the second element.
    for number in numbers[1:]:
        result += [delimiter, number]

    return result
```

This function begins by checking if the `numbers` list is empty, in which case it immediately returns an empty list. Then, it initializes the `result` list with the first element of `numbers`, because there's no need to insert the `delimiter` before the first element. It iterates over the remaining elements in `numbers`, appending the `delimiter` followed by the current element to the `result` list for each iteration.

Figure 7: An example of ChatGPT to accomplish HumanEval. The figure illustrates that the responses from ChatGPT cannot be directly used for computation and require post-processing to extract the substantive content.

# PyFoma: a Python finite-state compiler module

**Mans Hulden**[ʒ] **Michael Ginn**[ʒ] **Miikka Silfverberg**[ʕ] **Michael Hammond**[ʁ]
[ʒ]University of Colorado [ʕ]University of British Columbia [ʁ]University of Arizona
`first.last@colorado.edu` `first.last@ubc.ca` `hammond@arizona.edu`

## Abstract

We describe PyFoma, an open-source Python module for constructing weighted and unweighted finite-state transducers and automata from regular expressions, string rewriting rules, right-linear grammars, or low-level state/transition manipulation. A large variety of standard algorithms for working with finite-state machines is included, with a particular focus on the needs of linguistic and NLP applications. The data structures and code in the module are designed for legibility to allow for potential use in teaching the theory and algorithms associated with finite-state machines.

## 1 Introduction

Finite-state technology is well established in the NLP community and is widely used for various lower-level tasks such as tokenization, morphology, phonology, spell checking, spelling correction, grapheme-to-phoneme (G2P) mapping, various speech applications, and general string processing (Roche and Schabes, 1997; Mohri et al., 2008; Hulden, 2022). In tandem with neural models, finite-state models can also be used to constrain the output of a neural network to prevent generation of text that fails to adhere to a specific format (Ghazvininejad et al., 2017). Furthermore, finite-state methods may be effective in low-resource scenarios, allowing the incorporation of expert knowledge (Moeller et al., 2019; Muradoglu et al., 2020; Beemer et al., 2020).

Several tools exist for constructing and manipulating finite-state automata (FSAs) and transducers (FSTs), together finite-state machines (FSMs).[1] Some, such as *OpenFST* (Allauzen et al., 2007), *Carmel* (Knight and Graehl, 1998), *foma* (Hulden, 2009b), and *xfst* (Beesley and Karttunen, 2003) are stand-alone tools, implemented in C or C++ for efficiency reasons, while others, such as *Pynini* (Gorman, 2016), *HFST* (Lindén et al., 2009), and *Kleene* (Beesley, 2012) rely on the existing algorithms and APIs of *OpenFST* or *foma* to allow for FST manipulation in higher-level languages.

```
from pyfoma import FST
fst = FST.re("d a:(æ<1>|(eɪ)<4.5>) (ta):(ɾə)")
fst.view()
```

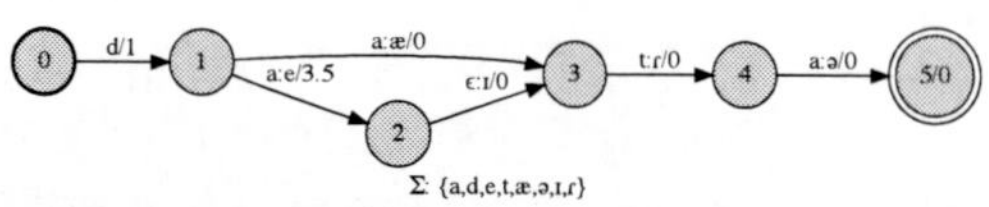


Figure 1: A weighted finite-state transducer compiled and visualized in PyFoma.

PyFoma is a complete finite-state toolkit written in pure Python. It is available on GitHub at `https://github.com/mhulden/pyfoma`, and easily installable via the PyPi package repository at `https://pypi.org/project/pyfoma/`. The project has the following overall aims:

- Simple and intuitive to use and integrates with the interactive mode of development of Jupyter notebooks
- Provides a comprehensive suite of algorithms for constructing and manipulating weighted and unweighted FSMs
- Incorporates visualization capabilities to examine FSMs as they are constructed
- Includes an extensible regular expression-to-FSM compiler with a formalism that is a close as possible to standard formalisms, such as that of the Python `re`-module
- Provides implementations of algorithms that are similar to pseudocode and can be used in instructional settings to understand FSM algorithms in detail.

[1]As every FSA can be expressed as an FST and vice-versa, we often use these terms roughly interchangeably.



*Proceedings of the 62nd Annual Meeting of the Association for Computational Linguistics (Volume 3: System Demonstrations)*, pages 258–265
August 11-16, 2024 ©2024 Association for Computational Linguistics

```
var1 = FST.re("cat")
var2 = FST.re("c a t")                                # same as above
var3 = FST.re("\+ \* \ ")                             # literalizing special characters
var4 = FST.re("'+' '*' ' '")                          # same as above using single quotes
var5 = FST.re("(cat|dog|mouse)s?")
var6 = FST.re("[A-Za-z0-9] - [aeiouAEIOU]")           # all ASCII characters, except vowels
var7 = FST.re("[^aeiou]")                             # any symbol, except lowercase vowel
var8 = FST.re("(cat):(gato) @ (gato):(chat)") # cross-product (:), composition (@)
var9 = FST.re("cat<1.0>|dog<2.0>|mouse<3.0>") # weights specified by <float>
```

Table 1: PyFoma basic regular expression examples for compilation of automata and transducers.

- Is efficient enough so that large-scale morphological analyzers can be compiled into FSMs with reasonable speed so that the dependency to low-level command-line tools is eliminated
- Incorporates advanced string rewriting rule compilation to allow for compilation of phonological and morphophonological rules in the vein of Chomsky and Halle (1968)
- Includes a large assortment of practical examples in the documentation for a variety of linguistic tasks
- Allows extension of the regular expression formalism where users can define new regular expression operators and implement them in Python

A demo video is available on YouTube.[2]

## 2 Illustrative example

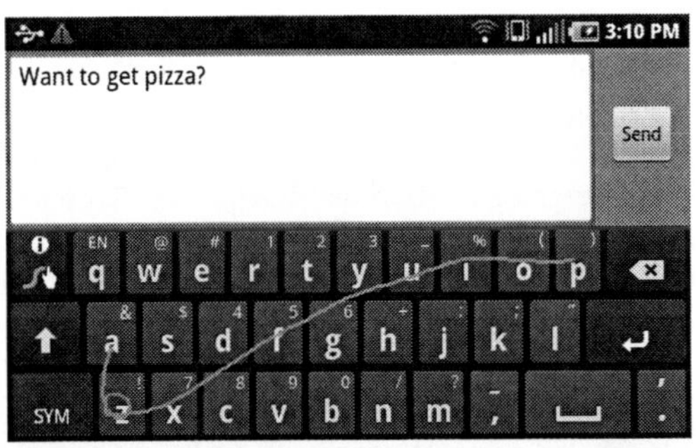


Figure 2: A Swype swiping action—to decode a Swype one must calculate what English word could be hiding inside the sequence `poiuygfdcxza`.

A typical low-level NLP task which FSTs are particularly well suited for is *Swype* decoding. A user swipes a finger across a virtual keyboard, touching a sequence of letters along the way, such as `poiuygfdcxza` (see Figure 2). The decoding task is to retrieve all valid English words that could have been intended by the user. Such a *Swype*-decoder can be constructed through the composition of three transducers, in four short lines of PyFoma code (see Figure 3). To achieve such succinct solutions, it is crucial to have a regular expression compiler that implements a variety of algorithms to manipulate weighted and unweighted automata and transducers.

## 3 Implementation

The core functionality—apart from visualization—of PyFoma is implemented entirely in Python,[3] relying only on the Python standard library for its dependencies, and exposing a Pythonic API. PyFoma provides a class `FST` with methods to construct (W)FSAs/(W)FSTs out of either regular expressions or algebraic manipulation.

### 3.1 Regular expression parser and compiler

The simplest PyFoma regular expression is a string like `cat`.[4] These simple expressions can be combined using regular expression operators. In contrast to many other finite-state tools, PyFoma uses standard operators found in pattern matching applications such as Python's `re` module, allowing for succinct FST construction (Table 1). These include union (`|`), Kleene star (`*`), Kleene plus (`+`), optionality (`?`), and character classes, such as `[A-Za-z]`. To aid in legibility of complex regular expressions, whitespace is not significant and any actual spaces must be escaped by `\␣` or `'␣'`.

[2]https://www.youtube.com/watch?v=X4ovo7phrV0

[3]While it shares part of the name of the *foma*-tool (written in C, includes Python bindings), PyFoma inherits none of the code in foma, but does use the main ideas for constructing rewrite rule transducers in Hulden (2009a).

[4]By default, the regex compiler treats each character as an individual token. This behavior can be overridden by surrounding strings in single quotes; the compiler will then treat the entire string as a token.

```
In [1]: from pyfoma import FST
        import string

        fsts = {}
        fsts['w'] = FST.from_strings(open("engwords.txt")) # wordlist
        fsts['removedouble'] = FST.re("(" + '|'.join(f"{l}+:{l}" for l in string.ascii_lowercase) + ")*")
        fsts['insert'] = FST.re(". ('':. | .)* .") # repeat one, then insert or repeat, repeat last
        fsts['swype'] = FST.re("$w @ $removedouble @ $insert", fsts)

        max(list(fsts['swype'].analyze("poiuygfdcxza")), key = len)

Out[1]: 'pizza'
```

Figure 3: Solving a key part of a Swype keyboard application—calculating what set of English words would be compatible with a fingerswipe over the letters *poiuygfdcxza*—can be accomplished by composition of FSTs that (a) repeat English words (e.g. `pizza`) and (b) remove doubled letters (e.g. `pizza` → `piza`) and arbitrarily insert letters in between the first and last letters (e.g. `piza` → `poiuygfdcxza`). The composition of these transducers constructs a Swype decoding transducer that directly maps `poiuygfdcxza` to the set of valid English words `pizza` and `pa`.

PyFoma implements several additional operators not found in pattern matching regexes: intersection (&), set subtraction (-), cross-product (`:`), optional cross-product (`:?`), relation composition (`@`), and weight specification with angled brackets (e.g. `<1.0>`).

**Variables** A typical workflow for constructing FSMs for NLP applications is to build a final FSM piece-by-piece, storing the intermediate steps as variables, which are combined with regex operations to build more complex FSMs. To achieve this, the `FST.re` can be passed a `dict` argument that instructs the compiler how to find the variables, which themselves are prefixed by the sigil `$`. The following is a typical sequence:

```
fsts = {} # init dict to store variables
fsts['V'] = FST.re("[aeiou]")
fsts['C'] = FST.re("[a-z]-$V", fsts)
fsts['syll'] = FST.re("$C+ $V $C+", fsts)
```

**Built-in Functions** The compiler provides some functionality through built-in functions (Table 2) rather than regular expression operators. Similarly to variables, functions are distinguished by the `$^`-sigil. For example, reversal of an FSM is invoked as `$^reverse(fsm)`.

**Customizing the compiler** The regular expression compiler can be further customized by the user by defining additional functions written in Python that the compiler will call when compiling. For example, suppose we needed a function that made all states in an FSM final with weight 0.0. We can define a function in Python that does so as follows:

```
def allfinal(myfsm):
    for s in myfsm.states:
        s.finalweight = 0.0
    myfsm.finalstates = myfsm.states
    return myfsm
```

The compiler can then be invoked with the keyword argument `functions`, which is a set of the user-specified functions that the compiler should be aware of, for example:

```
custom = {allfinal}
FST.re("$^allfinal(cat|dog)",
        functions = custom)
```

Naturally, the custom function could itself call the regex compiler—a common way of defining customized behavior. For example, an often used idiom in regexes is the pattern `.* X .*`, i.e. the set of strings that **contains** `X` as a substring, where `X` is an arbitrary FSM. We could create a new function `$^contains()` as follows.

```
def contains(fst):
    return FST.re(".* $X .*", {'X':fst})
```

**Compiler behavior** To simplify usage, the compiler always returns FSMs that are **determinized**, **minimized**, and **coaccessible**. Determinization and minimization is performed periodically during compilation of intermediate FSMs as well. In the weighted case, weights are pushed as close as possible to the initial state by a **weight pushing** algorithm (the effect of this is seen in Figure 1). Since transducers (as opposed to automata) are not guaranteed to be determinizable, transducer determinization treats a transition tuple with several dimensions as a single symbol. Weighted automata, likewise, are not guaranteed to be determinizable, and are therefore pseudo-determinized so that the weight becomes part of the label. True WFSA determinization is available through the API function `determinized()`, which, however, will not terminate for undeterminizable WFSAs.[5]

[5]An algorithm exists for testing determinizability (Allauzen and Mohri, 2003); however, employing it results in much slower compilation times overall.

```
$^determinize(fsm)                            # determinizes an FSM
$^ignore(x,y)$                                # The language x, ignoring intervening y's
$^project(fsm, dim)                           # extract a projection
$^invert(fsm)                                 # inverts a transducer
$^minimize(fsm)                               # minimizes an FSM
$^not(fsa)                                    # complement of FSA
$^input(fsm) or $^output(fsm)                 # extract intput or output projection
$^project(fsm, dim)                           # project one of the tapes in FST
$^restrict(a / b _ c,...)                     # context restriction compilation
$^reverse(fsm)                                # reverses an FSM
$^rewrite(a:b)                                # basic rewrite rule compilation
$^rewrite(a:b / c _ d, e _ f, ...)            # basic rewrite rule with contexts
$^rewrite(a:?b / c _ d)                       # optional rewrite rule
$^rewrite('':x a '':y / c _ d)                # 'markup' rule (wrap x, y around a)
$^rewrite(a:b / c _ d, leftmost = True)       # always use leftmost possible rewrite
$^rewrite(a:b / c _ d, longest = True)        # always use longest possible rewrite
$^rewrite(a:b / c _ d, shortest = True)       # always use shortest possible rewrite
```

Table 2: Some PyFoma regular expression compiler operations are expressed as functions instead of an operator, such as | or *. Rewrite rule specifications allow multiple modalities and fine-grained control over rewriting transducers.

### 3.2 Transducer operations/algorithms

The PyFoma module provides 26 operations on FSMs as well as additional operations that provide information about FSMs and their paths, languages and relations. All of the algorithms are available in *mutating* (methods that modify the original FSM) and *non-destructive* versions, following Python naming conventions.[6] These include concatenation, union, intersection, subtractions, composition, cross-product, Kleene closures, reversal, inversion, transducer projections, weighted and unweighted determinization, minimization, epsilon-removal, weight pushing, n-best path extraction, inter alia. While these are usually called through associated methods (e.g. `myfst.reverse()`), many of the fundamental operations are also available through overloaded Python operators: e.g. `fsm1 | fsm2` denotes the union of two FSMs, `fsm1 @ fsm2` the composition, etc. Additionally, there are operations for building FSMs from lists of strings.

The weight calculus is by default performed in the widely-used *tropical semiring* (Pin, 1998) where the weights along a path are summed, and weights across parallel paths with the same labeling are subject to the `min()`-operation, similar to the Viterbi assumption in probabilistic models. Also supported is the log semiring, which replaces the `min()`-operation with logspace addition, making the weight behavior similar to working with negative log-probabilities. However, operations are often much slower with the log semiring, explaining the popularity of the tropical semiring.

Transducers are not internally constrained to be 2-tape transducers. Since the labels on FSM transitions are arbitrary Python tuples, PyFoma can represent multi-tape automata as well. These have been shown to be useful in modeling, for example, intermediate steps in a sequence of historical sound changes (Hulden, 2017).

We have strived to maintain data structures and object naming that facilitate writing pseudocode-like implementations of the algorithms. Apart from minor bookkeeping, the implementations are often similar in length as the pseudocode in sources such as Mohri (2009) that describe WFSA/WFST algorithms. Figure 4 illustrates a method in PyFoma.

```
def label_states_topology(self, mode = 'BFS'):
    """Topologically sort, label states."""
    cntr = itertools.count()
    Q = deque([self.initialstate])
    inqueue = {self.initialstate}

    while Q:
        s = Q.pop() if mode == 'DFS'\
                else Q.popleft()
        s.name = str(next(cntr))
        for label, t in s.all_transitions():
            if t.targetstate not in inqueue:
                Q.append(t.targetstate)
                inqueue.add(t.targetstate)
    return self
```

Figure 4: Example algorithm from the PyFoma codebase—topological sorting of states in an FSM, either by breadth-first-search (BFS) or depth-first-search (DFS).

[6]For example, the mutating function is `fst.reverse()` while the non-destructive version is `reversed(fst)`.

### 3.3 Rewrite rules

Rewrite rules—the formalism popularized by *The Sound Pattern of English* (SPE) (Chomsky and Halle, 1968), are commonly used for describing phonological and morphophonological alternations, and PyFoma includes a variety of rule-to-FST algorithms. The ability to compile such rules to FSTs is usually a core requirement to be able to construct linguistically sophisticated rule-based morphological analyzers and generators.

The simple use case is generally of the type `$^rewrite(a:b, c _ d)`, which describes the rule "rewrite instances of a to b when occurring between c and d," expressed in the phonological literature as $a \rightarrow b / \; c \_ d$. Multiple comma-separated contexts are also possible. The left-hand side can be an arbitrary transducer, although it is usually constructed with the cross-product (`:`). While this covers many needs, some applications, such as chunking and markup (Beesley and Karttunen, 2003) as well as syllabification (Hulden, 2005), require more fine-grained guidance to control the rewriting. For example, one may want to rewrite *as little as possible* or, conversely, *as much as possible* if there is ambiguity in what the left-hand-side of the rule (a) denotes. Table 2 gives a brief overview of the main modalities available; these cover various types of string rewriting suggested in the literature (Kaplan and Kay, 1994; Beesley and Karttunen, 2003; Hulden, 2009a). Weights can also be integrated into the rules, modeling rules that have a cost associated with applying them, e.g. `$^rewrite(b:p<2.0> / _ #)`, which describes the rule "devoice a b at the end of a word with cost 2.0".

### 3.4 Right-linear grammars

Many linguists favor modeling the lexicon component of morphological analyzers as a right-linear grammar which captures the morphotactics of a language. This lexicon component is then normally composed with a battery of rewrite rules that handle morphophonological alternations, producing the full grammar transducer. Earlier tools, such as `lexc` (Karttunen, 1993) and `lexd` (Swanson and Howell, 2021) are strongly influenced by the formalism of right-linear grammars. PyFoma includes a right-linear grammar compiler, very similar to *lexc*, which is also found in the earlier tools *xfst* and *foma*.

### 3.5 Feature calculus

| Construction | Description |
|---|---|
| `[[$X=y]]` | Set X to value y |
| `[[$X=]]` | Unset (or clear) X |
| `[[$X?=y]]` | Unify X with value y |
| `[[$X==y]]` | Check that X equals y |
| `[[$X!=y]]` | Check that X does not equal y |
| `[[$X]]` | Check that X has been set |
| `[[!$X]]` | Check that X has not been set |

Table 3: PyFoma feature calculus. Here X is a variable and y a value.

FSMs usually suffer from the difficulty of modeling long-distance dependencies between symbols. For example, for a language that includes circumfixes in its morphology, the section of the FSM that models the word stems generally doubles in size, since states must be duplicated along circumfixing and non-circumfixing paths.

PyFoma supports a type of *feature calculus* where specific feature-value queries and checks can be used to control long-distance matches or mismatches. Figure 5 shows a minimal example of two automata that accept two German verb forms of **hören** 'to hear', the citation form and the past participle **gehört**. The first automaton needs to double the complete path of the stem **hör**, while the second, which contains feature-value setting and checking can share the stem parts. In the second example, a feature (arbitrarily) called pp is set to value 1 (`[[$pp=1]]`) for the prefix part of the circumfix, and is later required (`[[$pp==1]]`) to have the value one for the matching suffix path, and disallowed (`[[$pp!=1]]`) to have that value for the non-circumfix path. Such feature-value symbol manipulation can aid in the construction of grammars for languages with many morphological long-distance dependencies. They can also be removed from an FSM, and an equivalent FSM—possibly larger—is calculated. See Table 3 for the full inventory of supported feature constructions.

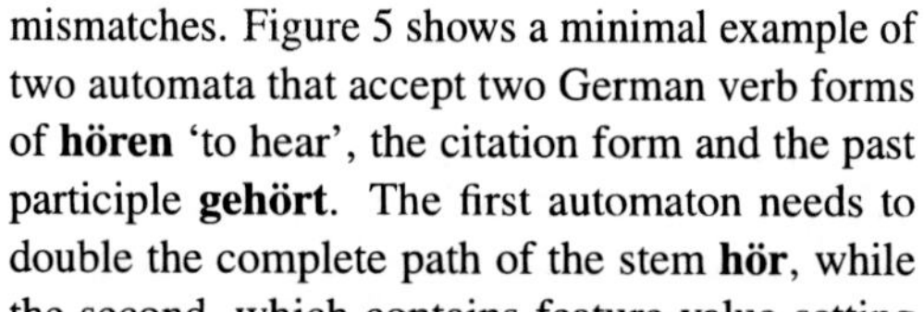


Figure 5: Illustration of how feature calculus strategies can model long-distance dependencies.

Our feature-notation is inspired by attribute-value feature unification schemes in syntactic theory (Sag et al., 1986) and the implementation of "flag diacritics" in the *xfst*-tool (Beesley and Karttunen, 2003).

### 3.6 Visualization

```
re("$^rewrite(b:p / _ #)").view()
```

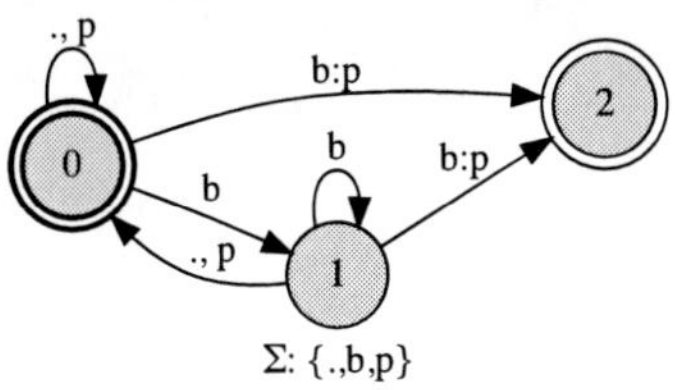


```
(re("kæb") @ re("$^rewrite(b:p / _ #)")).view()
```

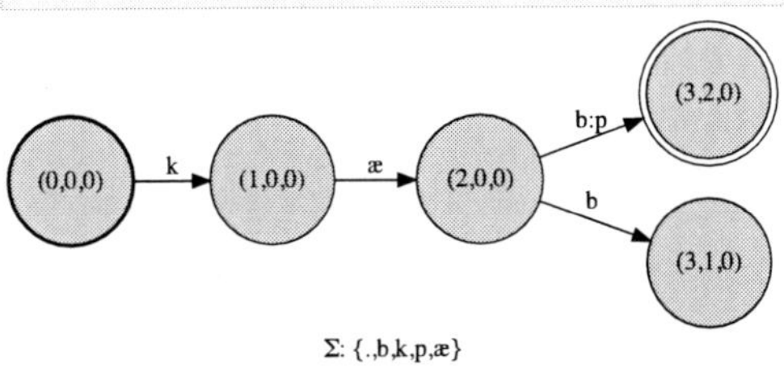


Figure 6: An example of the composition algorithm illustrating through state-name triplets in the result how the composition algorithm operates.

PyFoma depends on Graphviz (Ellson et al., 2002) for visualization of FSMs. `FST` objects have an associated `view()` method, which allows for visualization in a notebook, and a `render()` method, which generates a PDF. Graphviz is installed automatically with PyFoma if PyPi is used.

When called outside the regex compiler, many of the fundamental algorithms also provide illustrative state naming to show how the algorithms operate when combining two FSMs, which may be useful for teaching purposes. For example, Figure 6 shows in the state names, which are triplets of numbers, how two FSMs are combined through composition by traversing both in parallel and keeping track of matching input and output transitions in the two FSMs' states. In the example, the first number represents the state of the FSM created from the string kæb ($0 \xrightarrow{k} 1 \xrightarrow{æ} 2 \xrightarrow{b} 3$), the second represents the state of the transducer `$^rewrite(b:p / _ #)` (devoice `b` at the end of a string), and the third represent the state of a filter transducer with three states that is used internally during composition to eliminate redundant paths (Mohri, 2009). A similar visualization is done when transducers are compiled from right-linear grammars. In that case, the names of the states are the left-hand side of the right-linear grammar rule, e.g. `Noun` for a rule such as `Noun` → `cat|dog|bus`.

### 3.7 Context-free grammars

It is often both possible and desirable to approximate *context-free grammars* with finite-state models (Evans, 1997; Mohri and Nederhof, 2001). PyFoma includes preliminary support for parsing and visualizing context-free grammars in several formalisms.

## 4 A Morphological Analyzer Example

Figure 7 shows a mini-grammar built with the same principles as larger grammars. First, a lexicon component is constructed as a transducer (the concatenation `$noun $infl`). Following this, a sequence of rewrite-rule transducers are composed with the lexicon. In our case we have two rules: the first inserts `e` between a sibilant consonant on the left and `+s` on the right (e.g. `bus+s` → `buse+s`); the second removes all `+`-symbols which are used temporarily to denote morpheme boundaries. The composite transducer represents a minimal example of an analyzer/generator.

```
from pyfoma.fst import re

fsts = {}
fsts['noun']  = re("cat|dog|bus|fox")
fsts['infl']  = re("'[Sg]':'' | '[Pl]':(\+s)")
fsts['sib']   = re("[szx]|ch|sh") # Sibilants
fsts['rule']  = re("$^rewrite('':e / $sib _ \+ s)", fsts)
fsts['clean'] = re("$^rewrite(\+:'')")
grammar       = re("$noun $infl @ $rule @ $clean", fsts)

print(list(grammar.generate("fox[Pl]")))
print(list(grammar.analyze("buses")))
```

```
['foxes']
['bus[Pl]']
```

Figure 7: A toy analyzer/generator snippet that handles English noun inflection and e-insertion. The last two lines show the `generate` and `analyze` methods for FSTs.

## 5 Conclusion

We introduce PyFoma, an open-source Python module to facilitate the construction of weighted and unweighted FSMs, with specific support for NLP applications. We hope to provide a stable module that features a broad set of tools for use in teaching, research, and development of applications using finite-state technology and includes detailed documentation, example code, tutorials, and exercises.

## Acknowledgements

We are deeply grateful to Ken Beesley for expert guidance regarding multiple aspects of design and syntax in NLP-oriented finite-state libraries. The PyFoma project was originally inspired by the *Kleene* library (Beesley, 2012) developed by Ken at SAP Labs and has adopted some of its regular expression syntax and ideas about integration of weights into regular expressions and rewrite rules. We have tried to follow Ken's motto: "Syntax Matters".

## References

Cyril Allauzen and Mehryar Mohri. 2003. Efficient algorithms for testing the twins property. *Journal of Automata, Languages and Combinatorics*, 8(2):117–144.

Cyril Allauzen, Michael Riley, Johan Schalkwyk, Wojciech Skut, and Mehryar Mohri. 2007. OpenFST: A general and efficient weighted finite-state transducer library: (extended abstract of an invited talk). In *Implementation and Application of Automata: 12th International Conference, CIAA 2007, Praque, Czech Republic, July 16-18, 2007, Revised Selected Papers 12*, pages 11–23. Springer.

Sarah Beemer, Zak Boston, April Bukoski, Daniel Chen, Princess Dickens, Andrew Gerlach, Torin Hopkins, Parth Anand Jawale, Chris Koski, Akanksha Malhotra, Piyush Mishra, Saliha Muradoglu, Lan Sang, Tyler Short, Sagarika Shreevastava, Elizabeth Spaulding, Testumichi Umada, Beilei Xiang, Changbing Yang, and Mans Hulden. 2020. Linguist vs. machine: Rapid development of finite-state morphological grammars. In *Proceedings of the 17th SIGMORPHON Workshop on Computational Research in Phonetics, Phonology, and Morphology*, pages 162–170, Online. Association for Computational Linguistics.

Kenneth R. Beesley. 2012. Kleene, a free and open-source language for finite-state programming. In *Proceedings of the 10th International Workshop on Finite State Methods and Natural Language Processing*, pages 50–54, Donostia–San Sebastián. Association for Computational Linguistics.

Kenneth R. Beesley and Lauri Karttunen. 2003. *Finite-state morphology: Xerox tools and techniques*. CSLI, Stanford.

Noam Chomsky and Morris Halle. 1968. *The Sound Pattern of English*. Harper & Row.

John Ellson, Emden Gansner, Lefteris Koutsofios, Stephen C. North, and Gordon Woodhull. 2002. Graphviz—open source graph drawing tools. In *Graph Drawing: 9th International Symposium, GD 2001 Vienna, Austria, September 23–26, 2001 Revised Papers 9*, pages 483–484. Springer.

Edmund Grimley Evans. 1997. Approximating context-free grammars with a finite-state calculus. In *Proceedings of the 35th Annual Meeting of the Association for Computational Linguistics and Eighth Conference of the European Chapter of the Association for Computational Linguistics*, pages 452–459.

Marjan Ghazvininejad, Xing Shi, Jay Priyadarshi, and Kevin Knight. 2017. Hafez: an interactive poetry generation system. In *Proceedings of ACL 2017, System Demonstrations*, pages 43–48, Vancouver, Canada. Association for Computational Linguistics.

Kyle Gorman. 2016. Pynini: A Python library for weighted finite-state grammar compilation. In *Proceedings of the SIGFSM Workshop on Statistical NLP and Weighted Automata*, pages 75–80, Berlin, Germany. Association for Computational Linguistics.

Mans Hulden. 2005. Finite-state syllabification. In *International Workshop on Finite-State Methods and Natural Language Processing*, pages 86–96. Springer.

Mans Hulden. 2009a. *Finite-state machine construction methods and algorithms for phonology and morphology*. Ph.D. thesis, The University of Arizona.

Mans Hulden. 2009b. Foma: a finite-state compiler and library. In *Proceedings of the Demonstrations Session at EACL 2009*, pages 29–32, Athens, Greece. Association for Computational Linguistics.

Mans Hulden. 2017. Rewrite rule grammars with multitape automata. *Journal of Language Modelling*, 5(1):107–130.

Mans Hulden. 2022. Finite-state technology. In *The Oxford Handbook of Computational Linguistics, 2nd ed.* Oxford University Press, Oxford.

Ronald M. Kaplan and Martin Kay. 1994. Regular models of phonological rule systems. *Computational Linguistics*, 20(3):331–378.

Lauri Karttunen. 1993. Finite-state lexicon compiler. Technical Report ISTL-NLTT-1993-04-02, Xerox Palo Alto Research Center.

Kevin Knight and Jonathan Graehl. 1998. Machine transliteration. *Computational linguistics*, 24(4):599–612.

Krister Lindén, Miikka Silfverberg, and Tommi Pirinen. 2009. Hfst tools for morphology–an efficient open-source package for construction of morphological analyzers. In *State of the Art in Computational Morphology: Workshop on Systems and Frameworks for Computational Morphology, SFCM 2009, Zurich, Switzerland, September 4, 2009. Proceedings*, pages 28–47. Springer.

Sarah Moeller, Ghazaleh Kazeminejad, Andrew Cowell, and Mans Hulden. 2019. Improving low-resource morphological learning with intermediate forms from finite state transducers. In *Proceedings of the 3rd*

*Workshop on the Use of Computational Methods in the Study of Endangered Languages Volume 1 (Papers)*, pages 81–86, Honolulu. Association for Computational Linguistics.

Mehryar Mohri. 2009. Weighted automata algorithms. In Manfred Droste, Werner Kuich, and Heiko Vogler, editors, *Handbook of Weighted Automata*, pages 213–254. Springer.

Mehryar Mohri and Mark-Jan Nederhof. 2001. Regular approximation of context-free grammars through transformation. In Jean-Claude Junqua and Gertjan van Noord, editors, *Robustness in Language and Speech Technology*, pages 153–163. Springer Netherlands, Dordrecht.

Mehryar Mohri, Fernando Pereira, and Michael Riley. 2008. Speech recognition with weighted finite-state transducers. *Springer Handbook of Speech Processing*, pages 559–584.

Saliha Muradoglu, Nicholas Evans, and Hanna Suominen. 2020. To compress or not to compress? a finite-state approach to Nen verbal morphology. In *Proceedings of the 58th Annual Meeting of the Association for Computational Linguistics: Student Research Workshop*, pages 207–213, Online. Association for Computational Linguistics.

Jean-Eric Pin. 1998. Tropical Semirings. In J. Gunawardena, editor, *Idempotency (Bristol, 1994)*, Publ. Newton Inst. 11, pages 50–69. Cambridge Univ. Press, Cambridge.

Emmanuel Roche and Yves Schabes. 1997. *Finite-state language processing*, volume 115. MIT press, Cambridge, MA.

Ivan A Sag, Ronald Kaplan, Lauri Karttunen, Martin Kay, Carl Pollard, Stuart M. Shieber, and Annie Zaenen. 1986. Unification and grammatical theory. In *Proceedings of the West Coast Conference on Formal Linguistics*. Cascadilla Press.

Daniel Swanson and Nick Howell. 2021. Lexd: A finite state lexicon compiler for non-suffixational morphologies. *Multilingual Facilitation*, pages 133–146.

# VeraCT Scan: Retrieval-Augmented Fake News Detection with Justifiable Reasoning

**Cheng Niu**[1], **Yang Guan**[1], **Yuanhao Wu**[1], **Juno Zhu**[1], **Juntong Song**[1], **Randy Zhong**[1], **Kaihua Zhu**[1], **Siliang Xu**[1], **Shizhe Diao**[2], and **Tong Zhang**[3]

[1]NewsBreak
[2]Hong Kong University of Science and Technology
[3]University of Illinois Urbana-Champaign
cheng.niu@newsbreak.com

## Abstract

The proliferation of fake news poses a significant threat not only by disseminating misleading information but also by undermining the very foundations of democracy. The recent advance of generative artificial intelligence has further exacerbated the challenge of distinguishing genuine news from fabricated stories. In response to this challenge, we introduce VeraCT Scan, a novel retrieval-augmented system for fake news detection. This system operates by extracting the core facts from a given piece of news and subsequently conducting an internet-wide search to identify corroborating or conflicting reports. Then sources' credibility is leveraged for information verification. Besides determining the veracity of news, we also provide transparent evidence and reasoning to support its conclusions, resulting in the interpretability and trust in the results. In addition to GPT-4 Turbo, Llama-2 13B is also fine-tuned for news content understanding, information verification, and reasoning. Both implementations have demonstrated state-of-the-art accuracy in the realm of fake news detection[1].

## 1 Introduction

The contemporary digital landscape is rife with the proliferation of fake news, presenting a multifaceted challenge that undermines public discourse, affects democratic processes, and incites real-world consequences (Vasu et al., 2018). Fake news, characterized by the deliberate dissemination of misinformation, exploits the rapid spread of information online, often outpacing the verification processes that traditional media outlets adhere to.

Fake news detection is defined as the process of identifying and verifying the veracity of news content, employing various computational and manual methods. This process involves distinguishing between true and false information, considering the intent behind the information dissemination, whether it be to mislead, harm, or manipulate public opinion.

Traditional approaches in fake news detection have primarily focused on the linguistic features, also called content-based detection (Castillo et al., 2011; Pérez-Rosas et al., 2018; Giachanou et al., 2019; Przybyla, 2020; Giachanou et al., 2020; Sheikhi, 2021; Kirchknopf et al., 2021; Zhou et al., 2020), which demands laborious feature engineering and is ineffective when the fake news is written by imitating the real news to mislead intentionally. Another line of research is the social context-based method (Qazvinian et al., 2011; Baly et al., 2018; Shu et al., 2020; Monti et al., 2019; Nan et al., 2023), which analyzes the interactions among users, publishers, and posts. However, the feasibility of obtaining user information is challenging for the real-world application. A more recent research approach is the knowledge-based method (Hu et al., 2021; Saeed et al., 2022; Pan et al., 2023; Chen et al., 2023; Liao et al., 2023; Zhang and Gao, 2023; Li et al., 2024), which discerns the veracity of a factual claim by comparing against the evidence retrieved from external knowledge base. However, current approaches often do not fully utilize external resources like the Internet. Additionally, there is a lack of development and optimization of a comprehensive end-to-end pipeline that includes news comprehension, search optimization, verification, and reasoning.

In this paper, we introduce VeraCT Scan, a novel retrieval-augmented system for fake news detection. VeraCT Scan initiates this process by identifying key factual claims across multiple levels of granularity. For each identified factual claim, a comprehensive internet search is conducted to gather relevant information. Then, the veracity of the news is determined by combining this typically disparate and conflicting information, taking into

[1]Our demo is available at `https://veractscan.newsbreak.com/`. Demo video at `https://youtu.be/t1__iuOG9H8`.



*Proceedings of the 62nd Annual Meeting of the Association for Computational Linguistics (Volume 3: System Demonstrations)*, pages 266–277
August 11-16, 2024 ©2024 Association for Computational Linguistics

account the varying degrees of source credibility. To increase the trustworthiness of our approach, we underscore the necessity of a transparent reasoning process and provide rationales for each supporting or conflicting judgment.

In summary, our main contributions are:

(i) We introduce VeraCT Scan, that operates across multiple levels of information granularity, employing optimized information retrieval techniques to enhance fake news detection performance.

(ii) We investigate the generation of verification rationales as a means to increase the system's transparency and trustworthiness. Additionally, we address the management of conflicting evidence by leveraging the credibility of sources, thereby improving the reliability of the verification process.

(iii) We conduct a comprehensive evaluation of VeraCT Scan using several fake news detection datasets. Our results demonstrate that the system achieves state-of-the-art performance in news verification tasks, employing both prompted and fine-tuned LLMs.

## 2 Related Work

In this section, we first review the progress of fake news detection and then discuss the retrieval-augmented generation methods.

### 2.1 Fake News Detection

Existing fake news detection methods can be categorized into three types: 1) Content-Based Methods (Sheikhi, 2021; Pérez-Rosas et al., 2018; Castillo et al., 2011; Przybyla, 2020; Giachanou et al., 2019; Huang et al., 2023; Giachanou et al., 2020; Kirchknopf et al., 2021; Nakamura et al., 2020; Chen et al., 2023; Zhou et al., 2020) which analyze articles' linguistic features (e.g., text length, punctuation usage, emotion symbols) to differentiate fake news from real ones. However, these methods demand laborious feature engineering and are often ineffective when fake news is written to intentionally mislead readers. 2) Social Context-Based Methods (Shu et al., 2020; Nan et al., 2023; Baly et al., 2018; Monti et al., 2019; Qazvinian et al., 2011) which analyze the interactions among users, publishers, and posts to detect fake news. However, the feasibility of obtaining user information in the news propagation process presents challenges for the real-world applicability of this method. 3) Fact-Based Methods (Saeed et al., 2022; Pan et al., 2023; Hu et al., 2021; Xu et al., 2023; Chen et al., 2023; Cheung and Lam, 2023) which focus on factual claim verification by comparing against external knowledge. These methods fall short in providing an end-to-end solution that considers information seeking and the management of conflicting evidence.

Recently, Wang and Shu (2023) leverage large language models (LLMs) to decompose complex claims into sequences of first-order logic, and then guide the search and information verification. Different from their work, we propose a pipeline that includes full steps to classify fake news. Liao et al. (2023) outlines a multi-step process for detecting fake news, which consists of news summarization, searching, and verification. In contrast to their method, we employ LLMs instead of specifically trained encoder-decoder transformers for these natural language processing tasks. In addition, we leverage source credibility to differentiate conflicting evidences, a common challenge in real-world news verification that has rarely been explored in previous research.

### 2.2 Retrieval-Augmented Generation

The integration of retrieval-augmented generation (RAG) allows LLMs to extend beyond the limits of the training corpus by retrieving information from external knowledge bases before the generative process (Lewis et al., 2020; Chen et al., 2024). RAG has emerged as a solution to overcome the limitations of LLMs including the challenge of out-of-date knowledge and the tendency to produce hallucinations or irrelevant and factually incorrect content. By integrating external, up-to-date documents into the generation process, LLMs can generate more reliable responses across a broad spectrum of tasks, including open-domain question answering (Izacard and Grave, 2021; Trivedi et al., 2023; Li et al., 2023; Xu et al., 2024), dialogue systems (Cai et al., 2019; Peng et al., 2023), and code generation (Zhou et al., 2023b). RAG is also commonly integrated into commercial chatbot products to provide updated information, e.g Perplexity[2] and Gemini[3]. In this paper, we leverage RAG for fake news detection by generating both verdicts and justifications.

[2] https://www.perplexity.com

[3] https://gemini.google.com

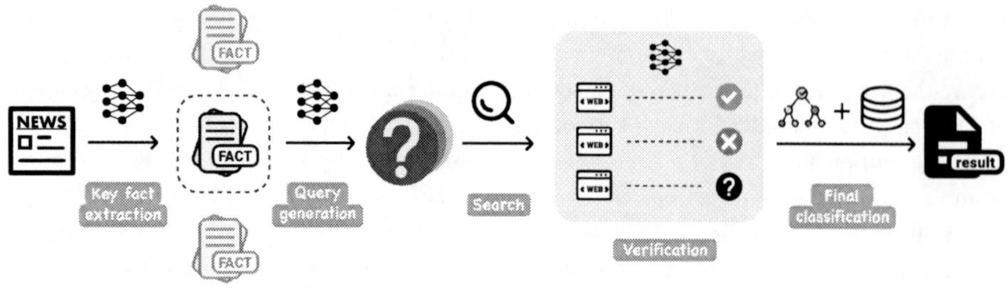


Figure 1: Main workflow of VeraCT Scan. VeraCT Scan includes the following steps: 1) extract key facts from the news to verify; 2) generate search queries for each extracted fact; 3) search; 4) verify the fact based on each search result; 5) aggregate all verifications with a final classification model.

## 3 Approach

In this paper, the term "claim" refers to the fact stated in a news article. The terms "factual claim extraction" and "fact extraction" are used interchangeably throughout the paper.

Figure 1 shows the main workflow of VeraCT Scan. We prompt GPT-4 Turbo for key fact extraction, query generation, verification, and rationale generation (See Appendix A for prompts being used). These individual components can be easily exchange to other LLMs or search engines. In this work, the outputs from GPT-4 Turbo, supplemented with manual reviews, serve as training data to fine-tune Llama-2 13B (Touvron et al., 2023), enabling it to support these tasks as well. Regarding the search component, we employ both Google and our proprietary in-house news search engine for comprehensive information retrieval.

### 3.1 Key Fact Extraction

In this paper, we focus on identifying facts at two levels of granularity: (i) the primary fact reported by the news story and (ii) all the salient facts being reported in the news article.

Given that the internet search operates as a stateless module, we instruct the LLM in the prompt to ensure each key fact is self-contained with its information. This approach allows the search function to generate queries for each key fact independently, without relying on additional context.

In line with the previous research (Shahandashti et al., 2024), our manual review has confirmed the high quality of key facts being identified by GPT-4 Turbo.

### 3.2 Query Generation and Search

When verifying a fact, we prompt GPT-4 Turbo to generate search queries. We allow up to three queries per fact to search the Internet. Subsequently, GPT-4 Turbo assesses the relevance of the results returned by each query. The goal is to identify the shortest sequence of queries that can retrieve all the relevant information. This optimal query sequence is then utilized to fine-tune Llama-2 13B, enabling its query generation capabilities.

We have developed a proprietary search engine designed to support news searches for articles published within the last six months. This search engine is especially effective in searching articles hosted on NewsBreak platform and can be used in NewsBreak APP. To ensure comprehensive search results, we also utilize the Google search API [4].

### 3.3 Fact Verification and Rationale Generation

Once the search results are retrieved, each fact is evaluated against them. GPT-4 Turbo is prompted to iterate each of the search results, and determine whether the search result supports, conflicts with, or is unrelated to the fact. If the search result aligns with the fact, it is labeled as "support". If it contradicts the fact, it is labeled as "negate". If the fact is not mentioned or only partially mentioned in the search result, the label "baseless" is applied. Besides, a rationale is generated to justify the judgment. A concrete example of our pipeline is shown in Appendix B.

### 3.4 Source Credibility and Final Decision

When researching a given topic, it is common to encounter conflicting information on the Internet. To avoid bias from single source, multiple sources are used to corroborate each other. Therefore, assessing the credibility of each information source

[4]https://developers.google.com/custom-search/v1/overview

is crucial. Mediabiasfactcheck.com is one of the most comprehensive resources for assessing media bias on the internet, offering credibility ratings for over 8,000 news publishers. Similarly, NewsBreak has developed a proprietary 5-level credibility rating system for more than 30,000 publishers. While NewsBreak's ratings are also based on the credibility of source content, unlike mediabiasfactcheck.com, NewsBreak does not identify the political bias of the sources.

In this paper, NewsBreak's rating systems serves as features to train a LightGBM(Ke et al., 2017) classifier that determines the likelihood of a fact claim being true. Besides, domain and verification flags (i.e. support, negate, or baseless) from each search result are also used as classification features.

### 3.5 Llama-2 13B Fine Tuning

To enhance service stability, response speed, and reduce costs, Llama-2 13B is fine-tuned to support our fake news detection pipeline.

**Dataset** Following previous studies(Zhou et al., 2023a; Taori et al., 2023), we utilize a mixed dataset of diverse tasks for supervised fine-tuning (SFT). Outputs of GPT-4 Turbo from the tasks described above are used as part of the training data. Specifically, we purposely modify some key factual claims being extracted from news articles into fake ones when generating claim verification data set. Besides, the following datasets have also been incorporated into the training set:

1. QA with RAG: GPT-4 generated answers to questions in NewsBreak search logs using knowledge retrieved from our proprietary search engine.
2. WebGLM(Liu et al., 2023): web-enhanced question-answering dataset.
3. No robots(Rajani et al., 2023): a diverse instruction fine-tuning dataset created by skilled human annotators.

The training data distribution is shown in Table 1. This design allows a single model to handle both general question-answering and specialized news verification tasks, resulting in significant reductions in inference costs.

**Hyper parameters** To enhance the capability of processing long inputs, we trained the model with RoPE scaling(Su et al., 2021; Liu et al., 2024). Specifically, we adjusted the context window size in SFT to be twice as large as that in the original

| Task/Dataset | # Samples | % Samples |
|---|---|---|
| Key Fact Extraction | 10299 | 18.52 |
| Query Generation | 3000 | 5.39 |
| Fact Verification | 23429 | 42.12 |
| QA with RAG | 8091 | 14.55 |
| No robots(Rajani et al., 2023) | 9500 | 17.08 |
| WebGLM(Liu et al., 2023) | 1300 | 2.34 |
| Total | 55619 | 100.0 |

Table 1: The distribution of the fine-tuning data from different tasks/datasets.

| Key Task | ROUGE-1 | ROUGE-2 | ROUGE-L |
|---|---|---|---|
| Key Fact Extraction | 0.678 | 0.497 | 0.655 |
| Query Generation | 0.690 | 0.503 | 0.662 |
| Rationale Generation | 0.637 | 0.449 | 0.600 |

Table 2: Performance of key tasks.

Llama-2 model, setting it to 8192 tokens, and we set the scaling factor at 2.0. We employed full training with an initial learning rate of 1e-5, and limited the training to 1 epoch. The training process was executed on four NVIDIA A100 GPUs.

### 3.6 Key Task Evaluations

The end-to-end metrics will be present in Section 5. In this section, we present the performance metrics for the critical components.

With GPT-4 Turbo outputs as the gold standard, we benchmarked the finetuned Llama-2 model on key fact extraction, query generation, and rationale generation. ROUGE scores (Lin, 2004) were employed as the metrics, as shown in Table 2.

For the fact verification accuracy, micro-F1 score was employed as the metric. According to human review, GPT-4 Turbo achieved a score of 0.805, while the finetuned Llama-2 model achieved 0.759.

## 4 Experimental Settings

In this section, we conduct comprehensive fake news detection benchmarks using multiple datasets.

### 4.1 Datasets

**BuzzFeedNews(Silverman et al., 2016)** This dataset consists of news articles shared on Facebook during the week surrounding the 2016 U.S. election. It includes data collected from nine different news agencies, spanning from September 19 to 23, and then September 26 and 27. Each article was fact-checked by a team of five BuzzFeed journalists. The articles are categorized under four labels: mostly true, mostly false, a mix of true and false, and no factual content. In line with Shu et al. (2019), we utilize the subset of 182 news articles for our benchmark. Each article in this subset has been assigned one of two binary labels (true or fake news), making it suitable for our binary classification setting.

**Fakenewsnet (Shu et al., 2017a,b, 2018)** A fake news dataset characterized by its rich diversity, including news articles and social context. The contents have been sourced from PolitiFact[5] and GossipCop[6], with most of them dating back to before 2018. In this paper, we have chosen to utilize the PolitiFact portion due to its high quality, as all the facts have been verified by domain experts.

**LLMFake (Chen and Shu, 2024)** A misinformation dataset is further modified by LLMs such as ChatGPT. These models utilize various techniques, including paraphrasing, rewriting, etc. for information manipulation. The information within this dataset traces back to 2020 or earlier.

**PolitiFact-Snopes-2024** The dataset was manually collected from the prestigious fact-checking organizations PolitiFact and Snopes[7]. It includes approximately 1,200 verifiable claims along with the fact-check rating labels that determine the level of truthfulness for each claim. The clarifications for the labels and the additional detailed analysis reports were not collected. Non-text-based claims were filtered out, and exclusive fact-checks with supporting sources specific to these organizations were also filtered out.

**FakeNews2024** This dataset consists 46 real news and 63 fake news articles. All the news articles are less than one year old, and are confirmed by NewsBreak moderation team.

The first three datasets were selected to enable a comparison of our system against three distinct fake news detection methods: content-based, LLMs-based, and retrieval-augmented approaches. The last two datasets are used to demonstrate our approach's ability to detect the latest fake news.

### 4.2 Evaluation Metrics

For the existing datasets, we strive to employ the same evaluation metrics that have been utilized in prior studies to enable direct comparisons.

For BuzzFeedNews, we report the precision, recall, and F1 scores related to fake news, as well as the accuracy for the entire dataset. For Fakenewsnet, PolitiFact-Snopes-2024, and FakeNews2024, we report the precision (P-F), recall (R-F), and F1 score (F1-F) of the fake news, the precision (P-T), recall (R-T), and F1 score (F1-T) of the real news, as well as the Micro F1 score (F1) of the overall dataset. For LLMFake, we report the detection success rate, which is calculated by the percentage of successfully identified fake news (Chen and Shu, 2024).

| Method | Accuracy | Precision | Recall | F1 |
|---|---|---|---|---|
| Pérez-Rosas et al. (2018) | 75.5 | 74.5 | 76.9 | 75.7 |
| Shu et al. (2019) | 86.4 | 84.9 | 89.3 | 87.0 |
| Zhou et al. (2020) | **87.9** | **85.7** | **90.2** | **87.9** |
| Ours (GPT) | 79.1 | 81.2 | 75.8 | 78.4 |
| Ours (Llama) | 73.6 | 71.3 | 79.1 | 75.0 |

Table 3: Detection performance on BuzzFeedNews.

### 4.3 Implementation Details

To aid in the verification of news articles, the main factual claim of each news article is identified and then compared against internet search results. To ensure a fair comparison, we have developed heuristics to carefully filter out fact-checking content from search engine results in all the experiments below.

The datasets above except LLMFake are each aggregated to train the final LightGBM classifier, utilizing the features outlined in Section 3.4, and subsequently report the end-to-end accuracy. Both the training and testing processes are conducted using a 5-fold cross-validation approach. We also provided baseline benchmarks for comparison.

## 5 Experimental Results

The performance with the BuzzfeedNews dataset is detailed in Table 3. The baseline methods being reported in Zhou et al. (2020) utilize features from article content, and outperform our approach. This outcome is expected since BuzzfeedNews dataset focuses primarily on a limited range of topics, specifically the 2016 US election. The nature of the fake news within this dataset allows it to be effectively modeled through content features. Furthermore, the fake news articles are approximately 7 years old, posing additional challenges for search engines in retrieving relevant evidences.

In Table 4, we present a performance comparison between VeraCT Scan and another retrieval-augmented system, utilizing the FakeNewsNet

[5]https://www.politifact.com

[6]https://www.gossipcop.com is now closed

[7]https://www.snopes.com

| Method | F1 | F1-T | R-T | P-T | F1-F | R-F | P-F |
|---|---|---|---|---|---|---|---|
| Liao et al. (2023) | 72.9 | 75.7 | 78.0 | 73.5 | 70.2 | 68.1 | 72.8 |
| Ours (GPT) | **80.3** | **81.9** | **85.9** | **78.2** | **78.3** | **74.1** | **83.0** |
| Ours (Llama) | 77.3 | 79.0 | 82.3 | 75.9 | 75.3 | 71.9 | 79.1 |

Table 4: Detection performance on Fakenewsnet.

| Method | F1 | F1-T | R-T | P-T | F1-F | R-F | P-F |
|---|---|---|---|---|---|---|---|
| Ours (GPT) | 91.7 | 91.7 | 90.7 | 92.8 | 91.7 | 92.8 | 90.7 |
| Ours (Llama) | 85.6 | 85.9 | 86.4 | 85.3 | 85.3 | 84.8 | 85.9 |

Table 6: Detection performance on PolitiFact-Snopes-2024.

| Dataset | Written | Paraphrasing | Rewriting | Generating |
|---|---|---|---|---|
| GPT-4-based Zero-shot Detector (COT) (Chen and Shu, 2024) | | | | |
| **Politifact** | 62.6 | 56.0 | 53.6 | 41.6 |
| **Gossipcop** | 26.3 | 30.0 | 25.0 | 25.7 |
| **CoAID** | 81.0 | 82.2 | 73.3 | 52.7 |
| Ours (GPT) | | | | |
| **Politifact** | **63.7** | **62.2** | **60.0** | **60.7** |
| **Gossipcop** | **42.9** | **42.0** | **40.3** | **39.4** |
| **CoAID** | **83.7** | **86.0** | **77.9** | **69.8** |
| Ours (Llama) | | | | |
| **Politifact** | 56.3 | 55.9 | 55.5 | 51.1 |
| **Gossipcop** | 31.2 | 30.3 | 34.6 | 28.6 |
| **CoAID** | 74.4 | 75.6 | 70.9 | 60.5 |

Table 5: Detection performance on LLMFake.

| Method | F1 | F1-T | R-T | P-T | F1-F | R-F | P-F |
|---|---|---|---|---|---|---|---|
| Ours (GPT) | 89.9 | 87.6 | 84.8 | 90.7 | 91.5 | 93.7 | 89.4 |
| Ours (Llama) | 82.9 | 80.0 | 78.3 | 81.8 | 85.9 | 87.3 | 84.6 |

Table 7: Detection performance on FakeNews2024.

dataset. Our two implementations, GPT-4 Turbo and the fine-tuned version of Llama-2 13B, both exhibit superior accuracy. This comparison underscores the efficacy of using either prompted or fine-tuned LLMs over specialized encoder-decoder transformers that have been specifically trained for this task.

Table 5 presents the detection performance using LLMFake. Notably, although the news articles in LLMFake are from 2020 or earlier—falling within GPT-4's inherent knowledge base, VeraCT Scan significantly outperforms GPT-4 in verification accuracy. Notably, the Llama-2 13B implementation also wins 7 out of 12 benchmarks. This underscores the benefits and efficacy of incorporating knowledge from the Internet. It is important to note that LLMFake verification is not straightforward. According to Chen and Shu (2024), the accuracy of human annotations falls well below 40%.

In Tables 6 and 7, we present the detection accuracy of our system when tested against the latest news articles. Unlike BuzzFeedNews, these two datasets consist of a wide variety of topics, including politics, entertainment, international warfare, and more. Both implementations of our system present relatively high detection accuracy, and underscores the effectiveness in verifying the latest news. Our approach benefits significantly from the enhanced efficiency of both Google and our proprietary search engine in sourcing relevant evidences for recent news.

## 6 Conclusion and Future Work

In this paper, we present VeraCT Scan, a novel retrieval-augmented system for fake news detection. Two of our implementations, properly prompted GPT-4 Turbo and fine-tuned Llama-2 13B demonstrated notable accuracy in detection. Specifically, the GPT-4 Turbo implementation exhibited state-of-the-art performance in several datasets. VeraCT Scan is especially successful in identifying the latest instances of fake news. This emphasizes the critical role of search result relevance in gathering compelling evidence.

Our observations reveal that the rationales generated by LLMs offer rich insights into potentially dubious aspects with a high degree of details. As a future work, we plan to investigate the potential of using these rationales as input features for the final verification classifier. And throughout our evaluations, Llama-2 13B consistently lags behind GPT-4 Turbo in terms of detection accuracy. We will explore more effective fine-tuning strategies to narrow this performance gap.

Furthermore, we observe that within the entire system, the majority of errors occur during the verification stage, with a smaller fraction arising during the claim extraction phase. The causes of these errors include: (i) Irrelevant search results used for verification. (ii) Updated news events leading to outdated reports being used for verification. (iii) Each report only supporting a part of the claim, necessitating the proper merging of relevant information from multiple news reports for full verification. (iv) Improper normalization of named entities or temporal expressions during the claim extraction stage, making alignment difficult during verification (e.g., "last weekend" vs. an exact date). We hope to address these issues in future work.

## 7 Limitations

News events are inherently dynamic, and the truth surrounding them can evolve over time. When verifying a news article being published in 2015 that discusses the average income increase ratio since 2001, it is crucial to obtain accurate data spanning from 2001 to 2015. This task presents challenges not only to search engines but also to LLMs. We have observed that our system performs more effectively when verifying more recent news articles. To close the gap, it requires truly understanding of timestamps by LLMs and the ability to accurately perform time sensitive calculations.

It has been noted that low-quality news articles frequently mix facts with opinions. In addition to verifying facts, it's important to distinguish the opinion segments within a news report. To accomplish this, it is crucial to integrate article-level linguistic features with retrieval-augmented fact verification methods.

Fake news can be deliberately created on a large scale. Beyond verifying individual articles, checking the authenticity of clusters of articles, can significantly enhance the detection effectiveness.

For practical considerations such as enhancing service robustness, reducing latency, and cutting costs, it is desirable to develop a smaller-sized LLM specifically for fake news detection. We plan to significantly invest in creating high-quality training data and explore advanced fine-tuning technologies to bridge the performance gap with GPT-4 in this area.

## 8 Ethical Discussion

Detecting fake news is a critical task with significant consequences. The effectiveness of this detection depends on various factors, such as the quality of searches, the impartial assessment of source credibility, and the language understanding capabilities of large language models (LLMs), among others. Our system aims to gather pertinent evidence from reputable sources, thereby aiding users in making informed decisions but not making those decisions for them. This approach is clearly outlined on our demo site.

## References


Ramy Baly, Georgi Karadzhov, Dimitar Alexandrov, James Glass, and Preslav Nakov. 2018. Predicting factuality of reporting and bias of news media sources. In *Proceedings of the 2018 Conference on Empirical Methods in Natural Language Processing*, pages 3528–3539, Brussels, Belgium. Association for Computational Linguistics.

Deng Cai, Yan Wang, Wei Bi, Zhaopeng Tu, Xiaojiang Liu, Wai Lam, and Shuming Shi. 2019. Skeleton-to-response: Dialogue generation guided by retrieval memory. In *Proceedings of the 2019 Conference of the North American Chapter of the Association for Computational Linguistics: Human Language Technologies, Volume 1 (Long and Short Papers)*, pages 1219–1228, Minneapolis, Minnesota. Association for Computational Linguistics.

Carlos Castillo, Marcelo Mendoza, and Barbara Poblete. 2011. Information credibility on twitter. In *Proceedings of the 20th International Conference on World Wide Web*, WWW '11, page 675–684, New York, NY, USA. Association for Computing Machinery.

Canyu Chen and Kai Shu. 2024. Can LLM-generated misinformation be detected? In *The Twelfth International Conference on Learning Representations*.

Jiawei Chen, Hongyu Lin, Xianpei Han, and Le Sun. 2024. Benchmarking large language models in retrieval-augmented generation. *Proceedings of the AAAI Conference on Artificial Intelligence*, 38(16):17754–17762.

Ziwei Chen, Linmei Hu, Weixin Li, Yingxia Shao, and Liqiang Nie. 2023. Causal intervention and counterfactual reasoning for multi-modal fake news detection. In *Proceedings of the 61st Annual Meeting of the Association for Computational Linguistics (Volume 1: Long Papers)*, pages 627–638, Toronto, Canada. Association for Computational Linguistics.

Tsun Hin Cheung and Kin Man Lam. 2023. Factllama: Optimizing instruction-following language models with external knowledge for automated fact-checking. In *2023 Asia Pacific Signal and Information Processing Association Annual Summit and Conference, APSIPA ASC 2023*, 2023 Asia Pacific Signal and Information Processing Association Annual Summit and Conference, APSIPA ASC 2023, pages 846–853. Institute of Electrical and Electronics Engineers Inc. Publisher Copyright: © 2023 IEEE.; 2023 Asia Pacific Signal and Information Processing Association Annual Summit and Conference, APSIPA ASC 2023 ; Conference date: 31-10-2023 Through 03-11-2023.

Anastasia Giachanou, Paolo Rosso, and Fabio Crestani. 2019. Leveraging emotional signals for credibility detection. In *Proceedings of the 42nd international ACM SIGIR conference on research and development in information retrieval*, pages 877–880.

Anastasia Giachanou, Guobiao Zhang, and Paolo Rosso. 2020. Multimodal multi-image fake news detection. In *2020 IEEE 7th International Conference on Data Science and Advanced Analytics (DSAA)*, pages 647–654.

Linmei Hu, Tianchi Yang, Luhao Zhang, Wanjun Zhong, Duyu Tang, Chuan Shi, Nan Duan, and Ming Zhou. 2021. Compare to the knowledge: Graph neural fake news detection with external knowledge. In *Proceedings of the 59th Annual Meeting of the Association for Computational Linguistics and the 11th International Joint Conference on Natural Language Processing (Volume 1: Long Papers)*, pages 754–763, Online. Association for Computational Linguistics.

Kung-Hsiang Huang, Kathleen McKeown, Preslav Nakov, Yejin Choi, and Heng Ji. 2023. Faking fake news for real fake news detection: Propaganda-loaded training data generation. In *Proceedings of the 61st Annual Meeting of the Association for Computational Linguistics (Volume 1: Long Papers)*, pages 14571–14589, Toronto, Canada. Association for Computational Linguistics.

Gautier Izacard and Edouard Grave. 2021. Leveraging passage retrieval with generative models for open domain question answering. In *Proceedings of the 16th Conference of the European Chapter of the Association for Computational Linguistics: Main Volume*, pages 874–880, Online. Association for Computational Linguistics.

Guolin Ke, Qi Meng, Thomas Finley, Taifeng Wang, Wei Chen, Weidong Ma, Qiwei Ye, and Tie-Yan Liu. 2017. Lightgbm: A highly efficient gradient boosting decision tree. *Advances in neural information processing systems*, 30.

Armin Kirchknopf, Djordje Slijepčević, and Matthias Zeppelzauer. 2021. Multimodal detection of information disorder from social media. In *2021 International Conference on Content-Based Multimedia Indexing (CBMI)*, pages 1–4.

Patrick Lewis, Ethan Perez, Aleksandra Piktus, Fabio Petroni, Vladimir Karpukhin, Naman Goyal, Heinrich Küttler, Mike Lewis, Wen-tau Yih, Tim Rocktäschel, Sebastian Riedel, and Douwe Kiela. 2020. Retrieval-augmented generation for knowledge-intensive nlp tasks. In *Proceedings of the 34th International Conference on Neural Information Processing Systems*, NIPS '20, Red Hook, NY, USA. Curran Associates Inc.

Daliang Li, Ankit Singh Rawat, Manzil Zaheer, Xin Wang, Michal Lukasik, Andreas Veit, Felix Yu, and Sanjiv Kumar. 2023. Large language models with controllable working memory. In *Findings of the Association for Computational Linguistics: ACL 2023*, pages 1774–1793, Toronto, Canada. Association for Computational Linguistics.

Miaoran Li, Baolin Peng, Michel Galley, Jianfeng Gao, and Zhu Zhang. 2024. Self-checker: Plug-and-play modules for fact-checking with large language models.

Hao Liao, Jiahao Peng, Zhanyi Huang, Wei Zhang, Guanghua Li, Kai Shu, and Xing Xie. 2023. Muser: A multi-step evidence retrieval enhancement framework for fake news detection. In *Proceedings of the 29th ACM SIGKDD Conference on Knowledge Discovery and Data Mining*, KDD '23, page 4461–4472, New York, NY, USA. Association for Computing Machinery.

Chin-Yew Lin. 2004. ROUGE: A package for automatic evaluation of summaries. In *Text Summarization Branches Out*, pages 74–81, Barcelona, Spain. Association for Computational Linguistics.

Xiao Liu, Hanyu Lai, Hao Yu, Yifan Xu, Aohan Zeng, Zhengxiao Du, Peng Zhang, Yuxiao Dong, and Jie Tang. 2023. Webglm: Towards an efficient web-enhanced question answering system with human preferences. In *Proceedings of the 29th ACM SIGKDD Conference on Knowledge Discovery and Data Mining*, KDD '23, page 4549–4560, New York, NY, USA. Association for Computing Machinery.

Xiaoran Liu, Hang Yan, Chenxin An, Xipeng Qiu, and Dahua Lin. 2024. Scaling laws of roPE-based extrapolation. In *The Twelfth International Conference on Learning Representations*.

Federico Monti, Fabrizio Frasca, Davide Eynard, Damon Mannion, and Michael M. Bronstein. 2019. Fake news detection on social media using geometric deep learning. *CoRR*, abs/1902.06673.

Kai Nakamura, Sharon Levy, and William Yang Wang. 2020. Fakeddit: A new multimodal benchmark dataset for fine-grained fake news detection. In *Proceedings of the Twelfth Language Resources and Evaluation Conference*, pages 6149–6157, Marseille, France. European Language Resources Association.

Qiong Nan, Qiang Sheng, Juan Cao, Yongchun Zhu, Danding Wang, Guang Yang, Jintao Li, and Kai Shu. 2023. Exploiting user comments for early detection of fake news prior to users' commenting. *arXiv preprint arXiv:2310.10429*.

Liangming Pan, Xiaobao Wu, Xinyuan Lu, Anh Tuan Luu, William Yang Wang, Min-Yen Kan, and Preslav Nakov. 2023. Fact-checking complex claims with program-guided reasoning. In *Proceedings of the 61st Annual Meeting of the Association for Computational Linguistics (Volume 1: Long Papers)*, pages 6981–7004, Toronto, Canada. Association for Computational Linguistics.

Baolin Peng, Michel Galley, Pengcheng He, Hao Cheng, Yujia Xie, Yu Hu, Qiuyuan Huang, Lars Liden, Zhou Yu, Weizhu Chen, et al. 2023. Check your facts and try again: Improving large language models with external knowledge and automated feedback. *arXiv preprint arXiv:2302.12813*.

Verónica Pérez-Rosas, Bennett Kleinberg, Alexandra Lefevre, and Rada Mihalcea. 2018. Automatic detection of fake news. In *Proceedings of the 27th International Conference on Computational Linguistics*, pages 3391–3401, Santa Fe, New Mexico, USA. Association for Computational Linguistics.

Piotr Przybyla. 2020. Capturing the style of fake news. *Proceedings of the AAAI Conference on Artificial Intelligence*, 34(01):490–497.

Vahed Qazvinian, Emily Rosengren, Dragomir R. Radev, and Qiaozhu Mei. 2011. Rumor has it: Identifying misinformation in microblogs. In *Proceedings of the 2011 Conference on Empirical Methods in Natural Language Processing*, pages 1589–1599, Edinburgh, Scotland, UK. Association for Computational Linguistics.

Nazneen Rajani, Lewis Tunstall, Edward Beeching, Nathan Lambert, Alexander M. Rush, and Thomas Wolf. 2023. No robots. `https://huggingface.co/datasets/HuggingFaceH4/no_robots`.

Mohammed Saeed, Nicolas Traub, Maelle Nicolas, Gianluca Demartini, and Paolo Papotti. 2022. Crowdsourced fact-checking at twitter: How does the crowd compare with experts? In *Proceedings of the 31st ACM International Conference on Information & Knowledge Management*, CIKM '22, page 1736–1746, New York, NY, USA. Association for Computing Machinery.

Kimya Khakzad Shahandashti, Mithila Sivakumar, Mohammad Mahdi Mohajer, Alvine B. Belle, Song Wang, and Timothy C. Lethbridge. 2024. Evaluating the effectiveness of gpt-4 turbo in creating defeaters for assurance cases.

Saeid Sheikhi. 2021. An effective fake news detection method using woa-xgbtree algorithm and content-based features. *Applied Soft Computing*, 109:107559.

Kai Shu, Deepak Mahudeswaran, Suhang Wang, Dongwon Lee, and Huan Liu. 2018. Fakenewsnet: A data repository with news content, social context, and spatiotemporal information for studying fake news on social media. *Big data*, 8 3:171–188.

Kai Shu, Amy Sliva, Suhang Wang, Jiliang Tang, and Huan Liu. 2017a. Fake news detection on social media: A data mining perspective. *SIGKDD Explor. Newsl.*, 19(1):22–36.

Kai Shu, Suhang Wang, and Huan Liu. 2017b. Exploiting tri-relationship for fake news detection. *ArXiv*, abs/1712.07709.

Kai Shu, Suhang Wang, and Huan Liu. 2019. Beyond news contents: The role of social context for fake news detection. In *Proceedings of the Twelfth ACM International Conference on Web Search and Data Mining*, WSDM '19, page 312–320, New York, NY, USA. Association for Computing Machinery.

Kai Shu, Xinyi Zhou, Suhang Wang, Reza Zafarani, and Huan Liu. 2020. The role of user profiles for fake news detection. In *Proceedings of the 2019 IEEE/ACM International Conference on Advances in Social Networks Analysis and Mining*, ASONAM '19, page 436–439, New York, NY, USA. Association for Computing Machinery.

Craig Silverman, Lauren Strapagiel, Hamza Shaban, Ellie Hall, and Jeremy Singer-Vine. 2016. Hyperpartisan facebook pages are publishing false and misleading information at an alarming rate. `https://github.com/BuzzFeedNews/2016-10-facebook-fact-check`.

Jianlin Su, Yu Lu, Shengfeng Pan, Bo Wen, and Yunfeng Liu. 2021. Roformer: Enhanced transformer with rotary position embedding. *CoRR*, abs/2104.09864.

Rohan Taori, Ishaan Gulrajani, Tianyi Zhang, Yann Dubois, Xuechen Li, Carlos Guestrin, Percy Liang, and Tatsunori B. Hashimoto. 2023. Stanford alpaca: An instruction-following llama model. `https://github.com/tatsu-lab/stanford_alpaca`.

Hugo Touvron, Louis Martin, Kevin Stone, Peter Albert, Amjad Almahairi, Yasmine Babaei, Nikolay Bashlykov, Soumya Batra, Prajjwal Bhargava, Shruti Bhosale, Dan Bikel, Lukas Blecher, Cristian Canton Ferrer, Moya Chen, Guillem Cucurull, David Esiobu, Jude Fernandes, Jeremy Fu, Wenyin Fu, Brian Fuller, Cynthia Gao, Vedanuj Goswami, Naman Goyal, Anthony Hartshorn, Saghar Hosseini, Rui Hou, Hakan Inan, Marcin Kardas, Viktor Kerkez, Madian Khabsa, Isabel Kloumann, Artem Korenev, Punit Singh Koura, Marie-Anne Lachaux, Thibaut Lavril, Jenya Lee, Diana Liskovich, Yinghai Lu, Yuning Mao, Xavier Martinet, Todor Mihaylov, Pushkar Mishra, Igor Molybog, Yixin Nie, Andrew Poulton, Jeremy Reizenstein, Rashi Rungta, Kalyan Saladi, Alan Schelten, Ruan Silva, Eric Michael Smith, Ranjan Subramanian, Xiaoqing Ellen Tan, Binh Tang, Ross Taylor, Adina Williams, Jian Xiang Kuan, Puxin Xu, Zheng Yan, Iliyan Zarov, Yuchen Zhang, Angela Fan, Melanie Kambadur, Sharan Narang, Aurelien Rodriguez, Robert Stojnic, Sergey Edunov, and Thomas Scialom. 2023. Llama 2: Open foundation and fine-tuned chat models.

Harsh Trivedi, Niranjan Balasubramanian, Tushar Khot, and Ashish Sabharwal. 2023. Interleaving retrieval with chain-of-thought reasoning for knowledge-intensive multi-step questions. In *Proceedings of the 61st Annual Meeting of the Association for Computational Linguistics (Volume 1: Long Papers)*, pages 10014–10037, Toronto, Canada. Association for Computational Linguistics.

Norman Vasu, Benjamin Ang, Terri-Anne Teo, Shashi Jayakumar, Muhammad Faizal, and Juhi Ahuja. 2018. Fake news: National security in the post-truth era. Technical report, S. Rajaratnam School of International Studies.

Haoran Wang and Kai Shu. 2023. Explainable claim verification via knowledge-grounded reasoning with large language models. In *The 2023 Conference on Empirical Methods in Natural Language Processing*.

Weizhi Xu, Q. Liu, Shu Wu, and Liang Wang. 2023. Counterfactual debiasing for fact verification. In *Annual Meeting of the Association for Computational Linguistics*.

Xin Xu, Shizhe Diao, Can Yang, and Yang Wang. 2024. Can we verify step by step for incorrect answer detection?

Xuan Zhang and Wei Gao. 2023. Towards LLM-based fact verification on news claims with a hierarchical step-by-step prompting method. In *Proceedings of the 13th International Joint Conference on Natural Language Processing and the 3rd Conference of the Asia-Pacific Chapter of the Association for Computational Linguistics (Volume 1: Long Papers)*, pages 996–1011, Nusa Dua, Bali. Association for Computational Linguistics.

Chunting Zhou, Pengfei Liu, Puxin Xu, Srini Iyer, Jiao Sun, Yuning Mao, Xuezhe Ma, Avia Efrat, Ping Yu, LILI YU, Susan Zhang, Gargi Ghosh, Mike Lewis, Luke Zettlemoyer, and Omer Levy. 2023a. LIMA: Less is more for alignment. In *Thirty-seventh Conference on Neural Information Processing Systems*.

Shuyan Zhou, Uri Alon, Frank F. Xu, Zhengbao Jiang, and Graham Neubig. 2023b. Docprompting: Generating code by retrieving the docs. In *The Eleventh International Conference on Learning Representations*.

Xinyi Zhou, Atishay Jain, Vir V. Phoha, and Reza Zafarani. 2020. Fake news early detection: A theory-driven model. *Digital Threats*, 1(2).

## A Prompts

Here we list the prompts used in the pipeline:

| MAIN CLAIM EXTRACTION |
|---|
| Given the input content below, please summarize the single key claim.<br>Input content: {content}<br>Please output with the follow json format {{"key_claim": XXX}}.<br>Please output now: |
| KEY CLAIMS EXTRACTION |
| Given the input content below, please extract distinct key claims. The key claims should be concrete enough containing clear context so that it can be efficiently verified.<br>Input content: {content}<br>Please output with the follow json format {{"key_claims": [{{"claim": XXX}}, ...]}}.<br>Please output now: |
| QUERY GENERATION |
| Given the claim below, please generate a Google query which can be used to search content to verify this claim.<br>Claim: {claim}<br>Please output with the following JSON format {{"query": "XXX"}}<br>Please output now: |
| CONTENT CLAIM VERIFICATION |
| Below is one web search result<br>Search Result:<br>{search_result}<br>Below is a claim to be verified<br>Claim: {claim}<br>Please perform the following rules to generate an output with this json format : {{"support_or_negate_or_baseless": "support" or "negate" or "baseless", "confidence": "high" or "medium" or "low", "rationale": "XXX"}}<br>Rule 1: if the search result content support the claim, set the "support_or_negate_or_baseless" field as "support", and offer a confident score and a rationale.<br>Rule 2: if the search result content negate the claim, set the "support_or_negate_or_baseless" field as "negate", and offer a confident score and a rationale.<br>Rule 3: if the search result content cannot either support or negate the claim, set the "support_or_negate_or_baseless" field as "baseless", and offer a confident score and a rationale.<br>To clarify: if the content of the search results does not contradict the claim, but lacks some or all of the information presented in the claim, please use the label "baseless" rather than "negate".<br>Please output now: |
| SAME NEWS/RELEVANT VERIFICATION |
| Below is one web search result.<br>Search Result: {search_result}<br>Below is a claim:<br>Claim: {claim}<br>Please make the following two investigations:<br>1. Please check if the news article and the search result is about the same news story.<br>2. Please check if the search result contains content (facts, opinions, or claims) related to the news article.<br>Please output with the following json format :<br>{{"about_the_same_news_story": "yes" or "no", "contains_related_content": "yes" or "no"}}<br>Please output now: |

Table 8: Prompts used for key tasks.

## B Sample Results

We provide an illustration of the process involved in verifying a news article below.

---

**NEWS ARTICLE:** Scientists Warn Eggs Are Causing Thousands of People to 'Suddenly' Form Blood Clots
In what appears to be another example of the global elite attempting to distract the public from the real cause of the surge in heart problems since the jab rollout, scientists now want us to believe that a nutrient found in eggs increases the risk of blood clotting.
Express.co.uk reports: The study conducted by Cleveland Clinic, suggested that choline could make the blood more prone to clotting.
Choline is sometimes sold in over-the-counter dietary supplements.
It is deemed an essential nutrient that is widely recommended for optimal health.
According to Medical News Today, it supports various bodily functions, including cellular growth and metabolism.
...

---

**CLAIMS:** 1. A study conducted by Cleveland Clinic suggested that choline could make the blood more prone to clotting.
2. Choline is deemed an essential nutrient that supports various bodily functions, including cellular growth and metabolism.
3. Researchers found that consuming choline in high concentrations could lead to blood clotting.
4. The interaction between choline and gut bacteria produces TMAO, which has been linked to an increased risk of blood clots, heart attack, and stroke.
...(8 claims extracted)

---

**VERIFY:** A study conducted by Cleveland Clinic suggested that choline could make the blood more prone to clotting.
**GENERATED QUERIES:**
1. Cleveland Clinic study choline blood clotting
2. Researchers found that consuming choline in high concentrations could lead to blood clotting.

---

**NUM OF SEARCH RESULTS:** 18

---

**VERIFICATION & RATIONALE:**
Title: Study from 2017 misrepresented to link eggs to blood clots.
Result: supported
Domain: apnews.com
Rationale: The search result explicitly mentions a study conducted by the Cleveland Clinic in 2017, which found that taking supplements in capsule form of choline 2014 a nutrient present in red meat, egg yolks, and other foods 2014 raised levels of a compound in the body (trimethylamine N-oxide, or TMAO) that could make the blood more prone to clotting. This directly supports the claim that consuming choline in high concentrations could lead to blood clotting.

—

Title: Cleveland Clinic Researchers First to Show Dietary Choline and Gut Bacteria Byproduct Linked with Increased Blood...
Result: supported
Domain: clevelandclinic.org
Rationale: The search result explicitly states that Cleveland Clinic researchers have shown for the first time in humans that choline is directly linked to increased production of a gut bacteria byproduct that increases the risk of blood-clotting events like heart attack and stroke. This directly supports the claim that choline could make the blood more prone to clotting.

—

Title: Cleveland Clinic study did not conclude eggs are causing...
Result: baseless
Domain: reuters.com
Rationale: The provided search result does not contain information about the effect of choline intake on blood clotting. It only mentions a study done by Cleveland Clinic regarding eggs, which is unrelated to the claim about choline.

...

---

**FINAL DECISION:** Supported

---

Table 9: An example of our pipeline ouput. Given that multiple claims can be extracted from a single article, we only exemplify the verification details of the first claim. The system generated two search queries related to the claim, resulting in the retrieval of 18 documents from the web. Based on the analysis of these documents, 14 documents are marked *baseless* (irrelevant or not fully support the claim), whereas the remaining 4 documents *support* the claim. By considering the sources credibility, the claim is classified as supported.

# string2string: A Modern Python Library for String-to-String Algorithms

**Mirac Suzgun**
Stanford University

**Stuart M. Shieber**
Harvard University

**Dan Jurafsky**
Stanford University

*In memory of Lynn.*

## Abstract

We introduce **string2string**, an open-source library that offers a comprehensive suite of efficient algorithms for a broad range of string-to-string problems. It includes traditional algorithmic solutions as well as recent advanced neural approaches to tackle various problems in string alignment, distance measurement, lexical and semantic search, and similarity analysis—along with several helpful visualization tools and metrics to facilitate the interpretation and analysis of these methods. Notable algorithms featured in the library include the Smith-Waterman algorithm for pairwise local alignment, the Hirschberg algorithm for global alignment, the Wagner-Fischer algorithm for edit distance, BARTScore and BERTScore for similarity analysis, the Knuth-Morris-Pratt algorithm for lexical search, and Faiss for semantic search. In addition, it wraps existing efficient and widely-used implementations of certain frameworks and metrics, such as sacreBLEU and ROUGE. Overall, the library aims to provide extensive coverage and increased flexibility in comparison to existing libraries for strings. It can be used for many downstream applications, tasks, and problems in natural-language processing, bioinformatics, and computational social sciences. It is implemented in Python, easily installable via pip, and accessible through a simple API. Source code, documentation, and tutorials are all available on our GitHub page: `https://github.com/stanfordnlp/string2string`.[1]

## 1 Introduction

String-to-string problems have a wide range of applications in various domains and fields, such as natural-language processing (e.g., information extraction, spell checking, and semantic search), computational molecular biology (e.g., DNA sequence alignment), programming languages and compilers (e.g., parsing and compiling), as well as computational social sciences and digital humanities (e.g., lexical and semantic analysis of literary texts).

The current state of string-to-string processing, alignment, distance, similarity, and search algorithms is marked by a multitude of implementations in many programming languages, such as C++, Java, and Python, but these implementations are not unified and lack flexibility, modularity, and comprehensive documentation, hindering their accessibility to users. Thus, there is a need for a unified platform that combines these functionalities into one accessible and comprehensive system.

In this work, we present an open-source library that offers a broad collection of algorithms and techniques for the alignment, manipulation, and evaluation of string-to-string mappings.[2] These problems include measuring the lexical distance between two strings (e.g., under the Levenshtein edit distance metric), computing the local or global alignment between two DNA sequences (e.g., based on a substitution matrix such as BLOSUM), calculating the semantic similarity between two texts (e.g., using BART-embeddings), and performing efficient semantic search (e.g., via the Faiss library by FAIR (Johnson et al., 2019)).

The `string2string` library has been purposefully crafted to prioritize key design principles, including modularity, completeness, efficiency, flexibility, and clarity. As an open-source initiative, the library will continue to grow and adapt to meet the evolving of its user community in the future, and we are committed to ensuring that the library remains a flexible, accessible, and dynamic resource, capable of accommodating the changing landscape of string-to-string problems and tasks.

[1]Correspondence to: `msuzgun@cs.stanford.edu`.

[2]We define a *string* as an ordered collection of characters—such as letters, numerals, symbols—which serves as a representation of a unit of information, text, or data. Strings can be used to represent anything, from simple sentences to complex nucleic acid sequences or elaborate computer programs.



*Proceedings of the 62nd Annual Meeting of the Association for Computational Linguistics (Volume 3: System Demonstrations)*, pages 278–285
August 11-16, 2024 ©2024 Association for Computational Linguistics

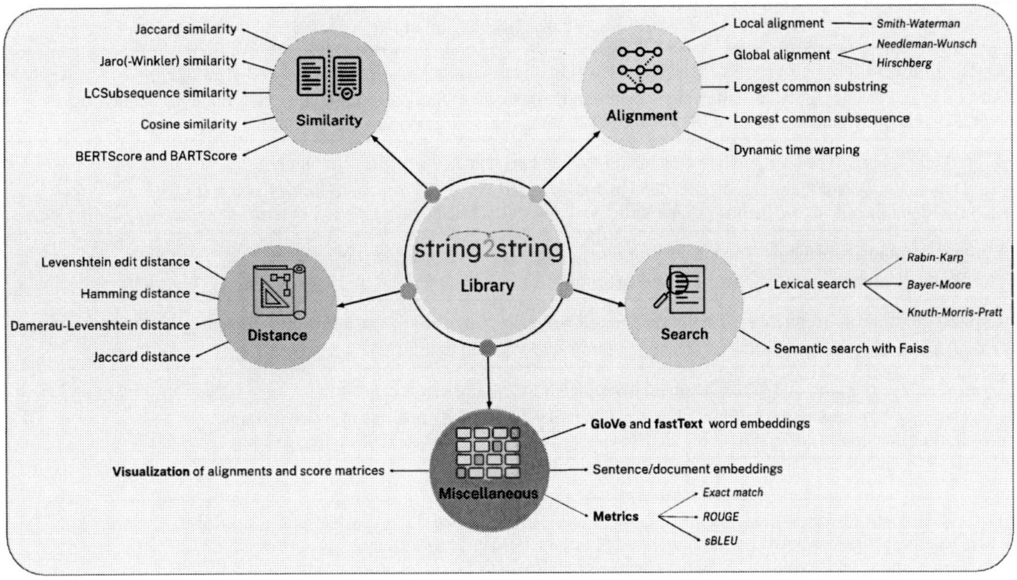


**Figure 1:** The `string2string` library provides a broad set of algorithms and techniques to tackle a variety of problems and tasks involving the pairwise alignment, comparison, evaluation, manipulation, and processing of string-to-string mappings. It includes the implementation of widely-used algorithms, such as Smith-Waterman (Smith and Waterman, 1981) for local alignment, Knuth-Morris-Pratt (Knuth et al., 1977) for identical string matching (search), and Wagner-Fisher (Wagner and Fischer, 1974) for edit distance, as well as recent neural approaches, such as BERTScore (Zhang et al., 2020) and BARTScore (Yuan et al., 2021) for semantic similarity measurements and Faiss (Johnson et al., 2019) for semantic search. The library has been designed to support not only individual strings but also lists of strings so that users can align and compare strings at the token, word, or sentence levels. It further contains visualization features to allow users to visualize alignments and score matrices of strings.

## 2 Related Work

The fields of natural-language processing and machine learning have a long-standing and exemplary tradition of fostering a culture that values open-source tools and libraries. While designing our own string-to-string library, which includes both traditional algorithmic and neural approaches to various problems, we have drawn inspirations from Natural Language Toolkit (NLTK; Bird and Loper (2004)), Gensim (Řehůřek and Sojka, 2010), OpenGrm Ngram (Roark et al., 2012), Stanford CoreNLP Toolkit (Manning et al., 2014), OpenNMT (Klein et al., 2017), tensor2tensor (Vaswani et al., 2018), AllenNLP (Gardner et al., 2018), fairseq (Ott et al., 2019), spaCy (Neumann et al., 2019), Stanza (Qi et al., 2020), Transformers (Wolf et al., 2020), and Torch-Struct (Rush, 2020), among many others.

## 3 Overview of Algorithms

The `string2string` library offers a rich collection of algorithmic solutions to tackle a wide range of string-to-string problems and tasks. We have clustered these algorithms into four categories: pairwise alignment, distance measurement, similarity analysis, and search.[3] Each category contains a suite of efficient algorithms that are tailored to address specific problems within their respective domain. In what follows, we provide a brief overview of these algorithms, along with the associated problems or tasks they are designed to solve.

### 3.1 Pairwise Alignment

Pairwise string alignment is the problem of identifying an optimal alignment between two strings, such as nucleotide sequences in DNA or paragraphs in a text. This task involves aligning them in a way that maximizes the number of matching symbols while allowing for gaps or mismatches where necessary. Pairwise string alignment is a widely-used technique that plays a crucial role in tasks such as DNA sequence alignment, database searching, and phylogenetic analysis.

As exhibited in Table 1, the library, in its current state, provides efficient solutions to local alignment, global alignment, longest common substring

[3]By duality, distance measurement methods can naturally be used for string similarity analysis, and vice versa.

**Pairwise Alignment**

**Local alignment** : The best possible matching substring or subsequence alignment between two strings—based on a substitution matrix and gap penalty function—allowing for gaps and mismatches within a specified region of the input sequences.
⋆ (a) Dynamic programming solution (Smith and Waterman, 1981): $\mathcal{O}(nm)$ in terms of space and time.

**Global alignment** : The best possible alignment between two strings over their entire length.
⋆ (a) Dynamic programming solution (Needleman and Wunsch, 1970): $\mathcal{O}(nm)$ in terms of space and time.
⋆ (b) Divide-and-conquer + dynamic programming solution (Hirschberg, 1975): $\mathcal{O}(m)$ in terms of space and $\mathcal{O}(nm)$ time.

**Longest common substring** : The longest *contiguous* substring that appears in both strings.
⋆ (a) Dynamic programming solution: $\mathcal{O}(nm)$ in terms of space and time.

**Longest common subsequence** : The longest possible sequence of symbols that appears in the same order in both strings.
⋆ (a) Dynamic programming solution: $\mathcal{O}(nm)$ in terms of space and time.

**Dynamic time warping (DTW)** : The optimal warp path that minimizes the distance between sequences of varying length.
⋆ (a) Dynamic programming solution (Sakoe and Chiba, 1978): $\mathcal{O}(nm)$ in terms of space and time.
⋆ (b) Space-time improved version of (a) via Hirschberg (1975)'s algorithm: Reduces space complexity to $\mathcal{O}(m)$.

**Distance**

**Levenshtein edit distance** : The minimum number of insertions, deletions, and substitutions needed to convert $S$ into $T$.
⋆ (a) Dynamic programming solution (Wagner and Fischer, 1974): $\mathcal{O}(nm)$ in terms of space and time.
⋆ (b) Space-improved version of (a): Reduces space complexity to $\mathcal{O}(m)$ by storing only two rows.

**Hamming distance** : The total number of indices at which strings, $S$ and $T$, of equal length differ.
⋆ (a) Naive solution: $\mathcal{O}(n)$ in terms of space and time.

**Damerau–Levenshtein distance** : The minimum number of insertions, deletions, substitutions, and adjacent transpositions needed to convert $S$ into $T$.
⋆ (a) Dynamic programming solution (simple extension of the Wagner-Fisher algorithm): $\mathcal{O}(nm)$ in terms of space and time.
⋆ (b) Space-improved version of (a): Reduces space complexity to $\mathcal{O}(m)$ by storing only two rows.

**Jaccard distance** : The inverse of Jaccard similarity (that is, 1.0 - Jaccard similarity coefficient).
⋆ (a) Naive solution: $\mathcal{O}(n)$ in terms of space and time.

**Table 1:** Overview of the pairwise string alignment and distance problems addressed by the library, along with the algorithmic approaches employed to solve them. In all instances, we assume that we are given two strings, $S$ and $T$, over a finite alphabet $\Sigma$, where where $n = |S|$, $m = |T|$, and $k = |\Sigma|$, with $m \leq n$. Also, whenever possible, we include the brute-force and memoized solutions to these problems (as in the case of edit distance, for instance).

(LCSubstring), longest common subsequence (LCSubsequence), and dynamic time warping (DTW) problems. It is worth noting that all of the problems and tasks covered in this suite can be solved using standard dynamic programming-based solutions. Alternative approaches to long sequence or string alignment problems, such as FASTA (Lipman and Pearson, 1985) and BLAST (Altschul et al., 1990), also exist; they offer improved efficiency through the use of probabilistic or heuristic methods, but they do not always guarantee optimal solutions and may sacrifice accuracy for speed. Due to their ability to handle large datasets quickly and provide reasonably accurate results, BLAST and FASTA are still widely used in bioinformatics, and for that reason, we plan on including them in the `string2string` library in the future.

## 3.2 Distance

String distance refers to the problem of quantifying the extent to which two given strings are dissimilar based on a distance function. The Levenshtein edit distance metric, for instance, corresponds to the minimum number of insertion, deletion, or substitution operations required to transform one string into another. It has a famous dynamic programming solution, which is often referred to as the Wagner-Fischer algorithm (Wagner and Fischer, 1974). In this library, we provide an implementation of the Wagner-Fischer algorithm, which has a quadratic time and space complexity, as well as an improved version of it, which reduces the overall space complexity to linear.[4] We further cover and provide efficient solutions to the Hamming dis-

[4]Incidentally, we highlight an important discovery by Backurs and Indyk (2015) that the edit distance between two strings cannot be computed in strongly subquadratic time, unless the strong exponential time hypothesis is false.

| Similarity |
|---|
| **Jaccard similarity** : The size of the set of unique symbols that appear in both strings (i.e., in the intersection) divided by the size of the set of the union of the symbols in both strings.<br>⋆ (a) Naive solution: $\mathcal{O}(n)$ in terms of space and time. |
| **Jaro(-Winkler) similarity** : A measure of similarity based on matching symbols and transpositions in two strings.<br>⋆ (a) Naive solution: $\mathcal{O}(nm)$ in terms of time and $\mathcal{O}(n)$ in terms of space. |
| **LCSubsequence similarity** : A degree of similarity between two strings based on the length of their longest common subsequence.<br>⋆ (a) Based on the efficient solution to the longest common subsequence problem.♣ |
| **Cosine similarity** : The similarity between two strings based on the angle between their corresponding vector representations.<br>⋆ (a) Utilizes `numpy` and `torch` functions: $\mathcal{O}(E)$ in terms of time and $\mathcal{O}(E)$ in terms of space.◇ |
| **BERTScore** (Zhang et al., 2020): A measure of semantic similarity that employs contextualized embeddings derived from the pre-trained BERT model (Devlin et al., 2019) to estimate the semantic closeness between two pieces of text.<br>⋆ (a) Adaptation of the original BERTScore implementation: $\mathcal{O}(nm)$ in terms of time and $\mathcal{O}(nm \cdot E)$ in terms of space. |
| **BARTScore** (Yuan et al., 2021): A measure of semantic similarity that utilizes the pre-trained BART model (Lewis et al., 2020) and that achieves high correlation with human judgements.<br>⋆ (a) Adaptation of the original BARTScore implementation: $\mathcal{O}(nm)$ in terms of time and $\mathcal{O}(nm \cdot E)$ in terms of space. |
| **Search** |
| **Lexical search** :<br>⋆ (a) Naive (brute-force) search: $\mathcal{O}(mn)$ in terms of match time and $\mathcal{O}(1)$ in terms of space.<br>⋆ (b) Rabin-Karp algorithm (Karp and Rabin, 1987): $\mathcal{O}(mn)$ in terms of match time and $\mathcal{O}(1)$ in terms of space.<br>⋆ (c) Boyer-Moore algorithm (Boyer and Moore, 1977): $\mathcal{O}(mn)$ in terms of match time and $\mathcal{O}(\|\Sigma\|)$ in terms of space..<br>⋆ (d) Knuth-Morris-Pratt algorithm (Knuth et al., 1977): $\mathcal{O}(n)$ in terms of match time and $\mathcal{O}(m)$ in terms of space. |
| **Semantic search** :<br>⋆ (a) FAISS (Johnson et al., 2019): $\mathcal{O}(\log^2 n)$ in terms of match time and $\mathcal{O}(n \cdot E)$ in terms of space.♠ |

**Table 2:** Overview of the string similarity and search solutions used in the library. As in Table 1, we assume that we are provided with two strings, $S$ and $T$, over a finite alphabet $\Sigma$, where $n = |S|$, $m = |T|$, and $k = |\Sigma|$, with $m \leq n$. Furthermore, we use $E$ to denote the size of the embedding space (or token), whenever applicable. Both the Rabin-Karp and Knuth-Morris-Pratt algorithms require $\Theta(m)$ time for pre-processing and $\Theta(n)$ time for searching, whereas the Boyer-Moore algorithm has a pre-processing time complexity of $\Theta(m+k)$. In terms of space, the Rabin-Karp, Boyer-Moore, and Knuth-Morris-Pratt algorithms require $\Theta(1)$, $\Theta(k)$. and $\Theta(m)$, respectively. Footnote ♣: Please refer to Eqn. (11) in (Suzgun et al., 2022a) for a mathematical formulation of LCSubsequence similarity. Note that the authors call this similarity measure "`Sim-LCS`." Footnote ◇: We assume that the dimension (size) of the two vectors are both $E$. Footnote ♠: We invite our readers to look at the blogpost by Feinberg (2019) for a detailed analysis of Facebook AI Research's Faiss algorithm.

tance, Damerau-Levenshtein distance, and Jaccard distance problems, as shown in Table 1.

One noteworthy feature of the library is that it allows the user to specify the weight of string operations (insertions, deletions, substitutions, and transpositions) depending on the distance function of choice. Furthermore, it can compute the distance between not only string pairs but also pairs of lists of strings, thereby not limiting the users to make comparisons only at the character or symbol level.

### 3.3 Similarity

String similarity refers to the problem of measuring the degree to which two given strings are similar to each other based on a similarity function—which can be defined on various criteria, such as character matching, longest common substring or subsequence comparison, or structural alignment. There is a natural duality between string similarity measures and string distance measures, which means that it is possible to convert one into the other with ease; hence, it is often the case that one uses string similarity and distance measures interchangeably.

Jaccard similarity, Jaro similarity, Jaro-Winkler similarity, LCSubsequence similarity, cosine similarity, BERTScore, and BARTScore are among the similarity measures that are covered in the library. The first four can be seen as lexical similarity measures, as they assess surface or structural closeness, whereas the remaining three can be regarded as semantic similarity measures, as they take the implied meaning of the constituents of the given strings into account.

The present library provides users with the ability to calculate cosine similarity not only between individual words—via pre-trained GloVe (Pennington et al., 2014) or fastText (Joulin et al., 2016) word embeddings—but also for longer pieces of text such as sentences, paragraphs, or even documents—via averaged or last-token embeddings obtained from a neural language model such as BERT (Devlin et al., 2019). As we also mention in Section 4, this feature enables users to compare the semantic similarity of longer segments of text in only a few lines of code, providing greater flexibility in text analysis tasks.

### 3.4 Search

String search, also known as string matching, refers to the problem of determining whether a given pattern string exists inside a longer string. The brute-force approach to string search would involve examining each position of the longer string to determine if it matches the pattern string; however, this method can be inefficient, particularly when dealing with large strings. In the library, we therefore include the Rabin-Karp (Karp and Rabin, 1987), Boyer-Moore (Boyer and Moore, 1977), and Knuth-Morris-Pratt (Knuth et al., 1977) algorithms for identical string matching as well.

The library additionally provides support for semantic search via Facebook AI Research's Faiss library (Johnson et al., 2019), which, in essence, allows efficient similarity search and clustering of dense vectors. In contrast to the previous setup for identical string matching, Faiss initially requires the user to provide a *list* of strings (texts) as a corpus and creates a fixed-vector representation of each string using a neural language model.[5] Once the initialization of the corpus is done, one can perform "queries" on the corpus. Given a new query, one can automatically get the embedding of that query, map it onto the embedding space of the corpus, and return the nearest neighbours of the query on the embedding space, thereby finding the texts that are semantically closest to the query.

As one might imagine, string search algorithms are highly practical tools that have a wide range of applications across different fields. These algorithms allow users to locate and retrieve specific patterns within a long text or a large corpus. For instance, the string search algorithms covered in the `string2string` library—as shown in Table 2—can be used for pattern recognition, DNA matching, plagiarism detection, and data mining, among many other downstream applications and tasks.

[5]The user is provided with the flexibility to determine how to obtain a fixed embedding for each text. Specifically, the user has the option to choose between different embedding methods, such as averaging the token embeddings or selecting the embedding of the final token in the sequence.

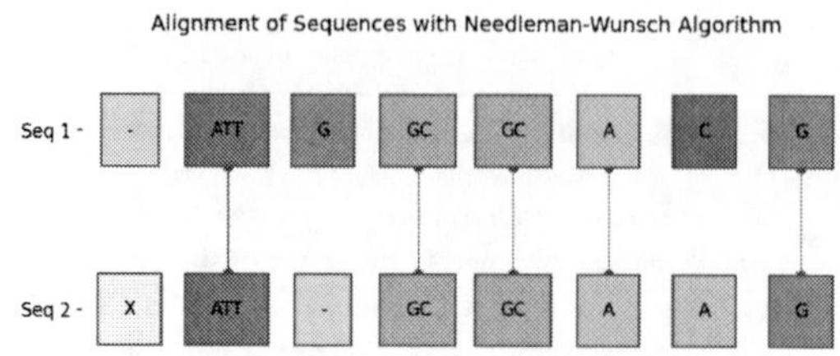


**Figure 2:** Alignment of two sequences of strings, `[ATT G GC GC A C G]` and `[X ATT GC GC A A G]`, as obtained by the Needleman-Wunsch algorithm (Needleman and Wunsch, 1970). Our library allows users to visualize the pairwise alignment between strings (or lists of strings).

## 4 Additional Features

One noteworthy feature of the library is its ability to simplify the use of the GloVe (Pennington et al., 2014) or fastText (Joulin et al., 2016) word embeddings by enabling users to download and use them with just one line of code. This streamlined process not only saves users time and effort but also eliminates the need for additional installations or complex configurations. By providing this feature, we have sought to make the library more accessible to users and encourage the use of pre-trained word embeddings in various string-to-string tasks and applications, such as measuring the cosine similarity between two words.[6]

Similarly, users can seamlessly get the averaged or last token embeddings of a piece of text from a pre-trained language model that is hosted on Hugging Face Models (Wolf et al., 2020) or on their local path in a few lines of code, and we provide both CPU and GPU support for these computations.

Finally, we note that the library offers various visualization capabilities that allow users to visually inspect the alignment between two strings or the score matrix of the distance or similarity between them. This functionality facilitates the understanding and interpretation of the output of various algorithms and can aid in the selection of the most suitable algorithm for a given task. By incorporating this feature into the library, we aim to enhance the user experience and provide intuitive means of interpreting the outputs.[7] Figure 2 shows a simple alignment between two lists of strings, as generated by our library.

[6]Notably, fastText offers pre-trained word embeddings for 157 languages—trained on Common Crawl and Wikipedia—that one can easily download and use with our library.

[7]For instance, our library provides a practical, hands-on tutorial focused on the HUPD (Suzgun et al., 2022b), a large patent corpus. This tutorial showcases the efficient use of our library's functionalities and features for performing semantic search and visualizing the textual content of patent documents.

## 5 Library Design Principles

We have endeavoured to build a comprehensive and easy-to-use platform for numerous string-to-string processing, comparison, manipulation, and search algorithms. We have purposefully structured and organized the library to allow easy customization, functional extension, and modular integration.

***Completeness.*** The library offers a comprehensive set of classical algorithms as well as neural approaches to tackle a wide range of string-to-string problems. We have intentionally included both efficient and simpler solutions, such as brute-force and memoization-based approaches, where appropriate. By providing multiple solutions to the same problem, the library allows users to compare and contrast the performance of different algorithmic methods. This approach enhances users' understanding of the trade-offs between different algorithmic solutions and helps them appreciate the strengths and limitations of each approach.

***Modularity.*** To improve the efficiency and maintainability of the codebase, we have adopted a modular design approach that breaks down the code into smaller and self-contained modules. This approach simplifies the process of adding new features and functionalities and modifying existing ones for developers, while also enabling efficient testing, debugging, and overall maintenance of the library. The modular design has allowed us to quickly locate and fix any errors, without disrupting the entire codebase, during development. Moreover, this modular approach ensures that the library is scalable and adaptable to future updates and changes, which should enable us to easily improve the library's functionality and expand its use in various tasks and applications moving forward.

***Efficiency.*** We have taken great care to ensure that the algorithm implementations are efficient both computationally and memory-wise so that they could easily handle large datasets and complex tasks. We provide basic support for process-based parallelism via Python's inherent `multiprocessing` package, as well as `joblib`. Additionally, we provide GPU support for neural-based approaches, whenever applicable. While we strive to balance efficiency and clarity, we acknowledge that in some cases, trade-offs may exist between the two. In such cases, we have placed greater emphasis on clarity, ensuring that the algorithms are transparent and easy to understand, even at the cost of some efficiency. Nonetheless, we believe that the library's overall efficiency, combined with its transparency and comprehensibility, makes it a valuable resource for the community.

***Support for List of Strings.*** The library has been designed to support not only individual strings but also lists of strings—whenever possible, enabling users to align or compare strings at the subword or token level. This feature provides greater flexibility in the library's use cases, as it allows users to analyze and compare more complex data structures beyond only individual strings. By supporting lists of strings, the library can handle a wider range of textual input types and structures.

***Strong Typing.*** The use of strong typing requirements is an essential aspect of the library, as it ensures that the inputs are always consistent and accurate, which is crucial for generating reliable results. By carefully annotating all the arguments of the algorithms used in the library, we have sought to increase the robustness and reliability of the codebase. This approach has helped prevent input-related errors, such as incorrect data type or format, from occurring during execution.

***Accessibility.*** The library has been implemented in Python, a programming language which has been the core of many natural-language processing tools and applications in academia and industry. The `string2string` library is "pip"-installable and can be integrated into common machine learning and natural-language processing frameworks such as PyTorch, TensorFlow, and scikit-learn.

***Open-Source Effort.*** The library is—and will remain—free and accessible to all users. We hope that this approach will promote community-driven development and encourage collaboration among researchers and developers, enabling them to contribute to and improve the library.

## 6 Conclusion

We introduced `string2string`, an open-source library that offers a large collection of algorithms for a broad range of string-to-string problems. The library is implemented in Python, hosted on GitHub, and installable via pip. It contains extensive documentation along with several hands-on tutorials to aid users to explore and utilize the library effectively. With the help of the open-source community, we hope to grow and improve the library. We encourage users to feel free to provide us with feedback, report any issues, and propose new features to expand the functionality and scope of the library.

## Acknowledgements

We would like to express our deepest appreciation to Corinna Coupette for providing us with the inspiration to create this open-source library. Furthermore, we would like to thank Sarah DeMott, Sebastian Gehrmann, Elena Glassman, Tayfun Gür, Daniel E. Ho, Şule Kahraman, Deniz Keleş, Scott D. Kominers, Christopher Manning, Luke Melas-Kyriazi, Tolúlọpẹ́ Ògúnrẹ̀mí, Alexander "Sasha" Rush, George Saussy, Kutay Serova, Holger Spamann, Kyle Swanson, and Garrett Tanzer for their valuable comments, useful suggestions, and support. We owe a special debt of gratitude to Federico Bianchi for inspecting our code, documentation, and tutorials many times and providing us with such helpful and constructive feedback.

## References

SF Altschul, W Gish, W Miller, EW Myers, and DJ Lipman. 1990. Basic local alignment search tool. *Journal of Molecular Biology*, 215(3):403–410.

Arturs Backurs and Piotr Indyk. 2015. Edit distance cannot be computed in strongly subquadratic time (unless SETH is false). In *Proceedings of the Forty-Seventh Annual ACM Symposium on Theory of Computing*, STOC '15, page 51–58, New York, NY, USA. Association for Computing Machinery.

Steven Bird and Edward Loper. 2004. NLTK: The natural language toolkit. In *Proceedings of the ACL Interactive Poster and Demonstration Sessions*, pages 214–217, Barcelona, Spain. Association for Computational Linguistics.

Robert S. Boyer and J. Strother Moore. 1977. A fast string searching algorithm. *Commun. ACM*, 20(10):762–772.

Jacob Devlin, Ming-Wei Chang, Kenton Lee, and Kristina Toutanova. 2019. BERT: Pre-training of deep bidirectional transformers for language understanding. In *Proceedings of the 2019 Conference of the North American Chapter of the Association for Computational Linguistics: Human Language Technologies, Volume 1 (Long and Short Papers)*, pages 4171–4186, Minneapolis, Minnesota. Association for Computational Linguistics.

Vlad Feinberg. 2019. Facebook AI similarity search (FAISS), part II. Accessed on March 13, 2023.

Matt Gardner, Joel Grus, Mark Neumann, Oyvind Tafjord, Pradeep Dasigi, Nelson F. Liu, Matthew Peters, Michael Schmitz, and Luke Zettlemoyer. 2018. AllenNLP: A deep semantic natural language processing platform. In *Proceedings of Workshop for NLP Open Source Software (NLP-OSS)*, pages 1–6, Melbourne, Australia. Association for Computational Linguistics.

Daniel S. Hirschberg. 1975. A linear space algorithm for computing maximal common subsequences. *Communications of the ACM*, 18(6):341–343.

Jeff Johnson, Matthijs Douze, and Hervé Jégou. 2019. Billion-scale similarity search with GPUs. *IEEE Transactions on Big Data*, 7(3):535–547.

Armand Joulin, Edouard Grave, Piotr Bojanowski, Matthijs Douze, Hérve Jégou, and Tomas Mikolov. 2016. FastText.zip: Compressing text classification models. *arXiv preprint arXiv:1612.03651*.

Richard M Karp and Michael O Rabin. 1987. Efficient randomized pattern-matching algorithms. *IBM Journal of Research and Development*, 31(2):249–260.

Guillaume Klein, Yoon Kim, Yuntian Deng, Jean Senellart, and Alexander Rush. 2017. OpenNMT: Open-source toolkit for neural machine translation. In *Proceedings of ACL 2017, System Demonstrations*, pages 67–72, Vancouver, Canada. Association for Computational Linguistics.

Donald E. Knuth, James H. Morris, Jr., and Vaughan R. Pratt. 1977. Fast pattern matching in strings. *SIAM Journal on Computing*, 6(2):323–350.

Mike Lewis, Yinhan Liu, Naman Goyal, Marjan Ghazvininejad, Abdelrahman Mohamed, Omer Levy, Veselin Stoyanov, and Luke Zettlemoyer. 2020. BART: Denoising sequence-to-sequence pre-training for natural language generation, translation, and comprehension. In *Proceedings of the 58th Annual Meeting of the Association for Computational Linguistics*, pages 7871–7880.

David J Lipman and William R Pearson. 1985. Rapid and sensitive protein similarity searches. *Science*, 227(4693):1435–1441.

Christopher Manning, Mihai Surdeanu, John Bauer, Jenny Finkel, Steven Bethard, and David McClosky. 2014. The Stanford CoreNLP natural language processing toolkit. In *Proceedings of 52nd Annual Meeting of the Association for Computational Linguistics: System Demonstrations*, pages 55–60, Baltimore, Maryland. Association for Computational Linguistics.

Saul B Needleman and Christian D Wunsch. 1970. A general method applicable to the search for similarities in the amino acid sequence of two proteins. *Journal of molecular biology*, 48(3):443–453.

Mark Neumann, Daniel King, Iz Beltagy, and Waleed Ammar. 2019. ScispaCy: Fast and robust models for biomedical natural language processing. In *Proceedings of the 18th BioNLP Workshop and Shared Task*, pages 319–327, Florence, Italy. Association for Computational Linguistics.

Myle Ott, Sergey Edunov, Alexei Baevski, Angela Fan, Sam Gross, Nathan Ng, David Grangier, and Michael Auli. 2019. fairseq: A fast, extensible toolkit for sequence modeling. In *Proceedings of the 2019 Conference of the North American Chapter of the Association for Computational Linguistics (Demonstrations)*, pages 48–53, Minneapolis, Minnesota. Association for Computational Linguistics.

Jeffrey Pennington, Richard Socher, and Christopher Manning. 2014. GloVe: Global vectors for word representation. In *Proceedings of the 2014 Conference on Empirical Methods in Natural Language Processing (EMNLP)*, pages 1532–1543, Doha, Qatar. Association for Computational Linguistics.

Peng Qi, Yuhao Zhang, Yuhui Zhang, Jason Bolton, and Christopher D. Manning. 2020. Stanza: A python natural language processing toolkit for many human languages. In *Proceedings of the 58th Annual Meeting of the Association for Computational Linguistics: System Demonstrations*, pages 101–108, Online. Association for Computational Linguistics.

Radim Řehůřek and Petr Sojka. 2010. Software framework for topic modelling with large corpora. In *Proceedings of the LREC 2010 Workshop on New Challenges for NLP Frameworks*, pages 45–50, Valletta, Malta. ELRA. http://is.muni.cz/publication/884893/en.

Brian Roark, Richard Sproat, Cyril Allauzen, Michael Riley, Jeffrey Sorensen, and Terry Tai. 2012. The OpenGrm open-source finite-state grammar software libraries. In *Proceedings of the ACL 2012 System Demonstrations*, pages 61–66, Jeju Island, Korea. Association for Computational Linguistics.

Alexander Rush. 2020. Torch-Struct: Deep structured prediction library. In *Proceedings of the 58th Annual Meeting of the Association for Computational Linguistics: System Demonstrations*, pages 335–342, Online. Association for Computational Linguistics.

Hiroaki Sakoe and Seibi Chiba. 1978. Dynamic programming algorithm optimization for spoken word recognition. *IEEE transactions on acoustics, speech, and signal processing*, 26(1):43–49.

T. F. Smith and Michael S. Waterman. 1981. Identification of common molecular subsequences. *Journal of molecular biology*, 147 1:195–7.

Mirac Suzgun, Luke Melas-Kyriazi, and Dan Jurafsky. 2022a. Follow the wisdom of the crowd: Effective text generation via minimum Bayes risk decoding. *arXiv preprint arXiv:2211.07634*.

Mirac Suzgun, Luke Melas-Kyriazi, Suproteem K Sarkar, Scott Duke Kominers, and Stuart M Shieber. 2022b. The Harvard USPTO Patent Dataset: A Large-Scale, Well-Structured, and Multi-Purpose Corpus of Patent Applications. *arXiv preprint arXiv:2207.04043*.

Ashish Vaswani, Samy Bengio, Eugene Brevdo, Francois Chollet, Aidan N. Gomez, Stephan Gouws, Llion Jones, Łukasz Kaiser, Nal Kalchbrenner, Niki Parmar, Ryan Sepassi, Noam Shazeer, and Jakob Uszkoreit. 2018. Tensor2tensor for neural machine translation. *CoRR*, abs/1803.07416.

Robert A Wagner and Michael J Fischer. 1974. The string-to-string correction problem. *Journal of the ACM (JACM)*, 21(1):168–173.

Thomas Wolf, Lysandre Debut, Victor Sanh, Julien Chaumond, Clement Delangue, Anthony Moi, Pierric Cistac, Tim Rault, Remi Louf, Morgan Funtowicz, Joe Davison, Sam Shleifer, Patrick von Platen, Clara Ma, Yacine Jernite, Julien Plu, Canwen Xu, Teven Le Scao, Sylvain Gugger, Mariama Drame, Quentin Lhoest, and Alexander Rush. 2020. Transformers: State-of-the-art natural language processing. In *Proceedings of the 2020 Conference on Empirical Methods in Natural Language Processing: System Demonstrations*, pages 38–45, Online. Association for Computational Linguistics.

Weizhe Yuan, Graham Neubig, and Pengfei Liu. 2021. BARTScore: Evaluating generated text as text generation. In *Advances in Neural Information Processing Systems*, volume 34, pages 27263–27277. Curran Associates, Inc.

Tianyi Zhang, Varsha Kishore, Felix Wu, Kilian Q. Weinberger, and Yoav Artzi. 2020. BERTScore: Evaluating text generation with BERT. In *International Conference on Learning Representations*.

# Proofread: Fixes All Errors with One Tap

**Renjie Liu***, **Yanxiang Zhang***, **Yun Zhu***, **Haicheng Sun, Yuanbo Zhang, Michael Xuelin Huang, Shanqing Cai, Lei Meng, Shumin Zhai**
Google Inc.

## Abstract

The impressive capabilities in Large Language Models (LLMs) provide a powerful approach to reimagine users' typing experience. This paper demonstrates the Proofread feature in Gboard, a virtual keyboard running on mobile phones. Proofread enables seamless sentence-level and paragraph-level corrections with a single tap. We describe the complete system in this paper, from data generation, metrics design to model tuning and deployment. To obtain models with sufficient quality, we implement a careful data synthetic pipeline tailored to online use cases, design multifaceted metrics, employ a two-stage tuning approach to acquire the dedicated LLM for the feature: the Supervised Fine Tuning (SFT) for foundational quality, followed by the Reinforcement Learning (RL) tuning approach for targeted refinement. Specifically, we find sequential tuning on Rewrite and proofread tasks yields the best quality in SFT stage, and propose global and direct rewards in the RL tuning stage to seek further improvement. Extensive experiments on a human-labeled golden set showed our tuned PaLM2-XS model achieved 85.56% good ratio. We launched the feature to Pixel 8 devices by serving the model on TPU v5 in Google Cloud, with thousands of daily active users. Serving latency was significantly reduced by quantization, bucket inference, text segmentation, and speculative decoding. Our demo could be seen in Youtube.

## 1 Introduction

Gboard is an statistical-decoding-based keyboard on mobile devices developed by Google. Decoding (Ouyang et al., 2017) is necessary due to the error-prone process of "fat finger" touch input on small screens. According to Azenkot and Zhai (2012), the per-letter error rate is around 8%-9% without decoding.

*Equal contribution, alphabetical order. Correspondence to {renjieliu,zhangyx,yunzhu}@google.com.

Gboard provides various error correction features, some active (automatic) and other passive (require the user's further manual action and selection) to provide a smooth typing experience (Ouyang et al., 2017). Active key correction (KC), and active auto correction (AC), word completions and next-word predictions support the users to type the current word and next word by fixing typos and providing multiple word candidates in the suggestion bar or inline (smart compose). Post correction (PC) supports fixing errors in last one or more committed words. Furthermore, The more passive Spell Checker and Grammar Checker supported by small-sized logistic regression and seq2seq models respectively detect the possible errors in committed sentences and mark them with red underlines, users can fix the errors by clicking the incorrect words and commit the correct words from the displayed candidates.

There are two types of user experience limitations with the existing correction approaches. First, users still have to type relatively slowly and accurately to avoid making too many or too severe errors that the small (but instantly fast) on-device correction models such as KC, AC and PC cannot handle due to their limited ability to model longer-span context. Second, users need to manually engage in the multi-step passive correction features, such as the grammar checker and the spell checker, to correct the committed words one after another.

Supervising the committed words while typing and fixing errors sequentially by editing after commit take users' cognitive and visual-motor resources and slow down their typing speed. One desired pattern of fast typing users of Gboard is to focus on keyboard only without checking the committed words while typing. To this end, a high quality sentence-or-higher-level correction feature is often called for, in order to help those "fast and sloppy" users who prefer to focus on typing then



*Proceedings of the 62nd Annual Meeting of the Association for Computational Linguistics (Volume 3: System Demonstrations)*, pages 286–293
August 11-16, 2024 ©2024 Association for Computational Linguistics

switch to error corrections at a higher level.

In this paper, we propose the **Proofread** feature to alleviate the pain points of fast typers by providing the sentence-level and paragraph-level error fixes with only one-tap. Proofread falls into the area of Grammatical Error Correction (GEC), which has a long history of research from rule-based to statistical approaches to neural network models (Bryant et al., 2023). The astonishing capability growth of Large Language Models (LLMs), offers a new opportunity to unlock the high quality sentence-level grammar fixes.

We present the entire system to tune and serve the LLM model behind Proofread in this paper. The system consist of four parts, data generation, metrics design, model tuning and model serving. Firstly, dataset is generated by a carefully designed error synthetic framework which integrates errors frequently made on keyboard to simulate the users' input, several further steps are conducted to ensure the data distribution is close to Gboard domain maximally. Secondly, several metrics are designed to measure the model from various dimensions. As the answers are always not unique specifically for long examples, the metric combined with grammar error existence check and same meaning check based on LLMs are considered as the key metrics for comparing the model quality. Thirdly, inspired by InstructGPT (Ouyang et al., 2022), Supervised Fine-tuning followed by the Reinforcement Learning (RL) tuning is adopted to obtain the LLM dedicated for Proofread feature. Results suggested that our rewrite task tuning and reinforcement learning recipe significantly improves the proofreading performance of the foundation models. To reduce the serving cost, we build our feature on top of the medium sized LLM PaLM2-XS, which could be fit int a single TPU v5 after 8-bit quantization. We further optimize latency with bucket keys, segmentation and speculative decoding (Leviathan et al., 2023). Our model now is launched to benefit thousands of users with Pixel 8 devices.

Figure 1 exhibits our model quality on one extreme corrupted case from Andrej Karpathy[1], which indicates our tuned model is strong enough to handle various of heavy typo errors made by users.

The contribution of this paper can be summarized as follows:

- We propose the **Proofread** feature supported by the high quality LLM to boost the user typing experiences of Gboard. We finally launched the feature to real users with Pixel 8 devices, thousands of users benefit from it daily.
- We design and implement the whole system from data generation, metrics design to model tuning and deployment.
- We obtain a high quality model with cautiously synthetic data generation, multiple phased supervised fine-tuning and RL tuning. Specifically, we propose the Global Reward and Direct Reward in RL tuning stage, which improve the model significantly. Results shows that RL tuning could help reduce the grammar error significantly and thus the Bad ratio of PaLM2-XS model is reduced by 5.74% relatively.
- We deploy the model to TPU v5 in Cloud with highly optimized latency acquired by quantization, buckets, input segmentation and speculative decoding. Our results suggested that speculative decoding reduced the median latency by 39.4%.

[1]https://twitter.com/karpathy/status/1725553780878647482

## 2 Related Work

### 2.1 Controllable Text Generation

Controllable text generation using transformer-based pre-trained language models has become a rapid growing yet challenging new research hotspot (Zhang et al., 2023). Proofread falls into this scope with the requirement of modifying the input to fix the grammar errors without changing the original intention in the corrupted text.

Lots of applications could inherit from controllable text generation. Shu et al. (2023); Zhu et al. (2023) focus on text rewrite tasks, including paraphrasing (Xu et al., 2012; Siddique et al., 2020), style transfer (Riley et al., 2020; Zhang et al., 2020; Reif et al., 2021) and sentence fusion (Mallinson et al., 2022) and so on. Similarly, Text editing (Malmi et al., 2022) task also covers a wide range of sub-tasks such as paraphrasing, style transfer, spelling and grammatical error correction (Napoles et al., 2017), formalization (Rao and Tetreault, 2018), simplification (Xu et al., 2016) and elaboration (Logan IV et al., 2021).

Unlike these mentioned works, our paper only addresses a single application – Proofread but provides systematic approaches that optimize the model from different perspective such as quality,

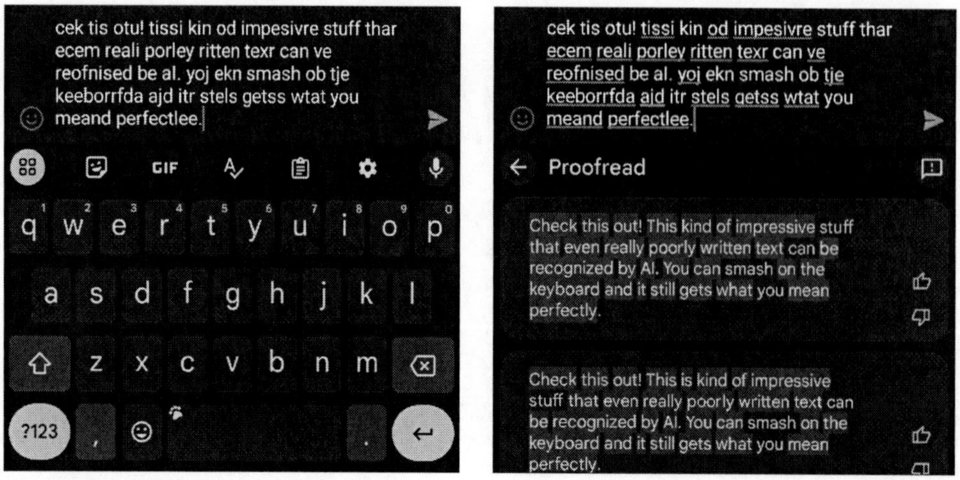


Figure 1: Proofread demo on a heavy corrupted text, the feature is triggered by clicking the "A" button in the left figure.

latency and resource usage.

### 2.2 Grammatical Error Correction (GEC)

Proofread falls into the area of GEC. Bryant et al. (2023) offers a comprehensive survey of the history and the current state of GEC. Specifically, before LLM, the popular solutions of GEC are edit-based approaches which corrections are applied on a sequence labelling (Omelianchuk et al., 2020) or sequence-to-sequence basis (Stahlberg and Kumar, 2020).

The recent studies to apply LLM to GEC mainly focus on prompting the LLM rather than supervised fine-tuning. Wu et al. (2023) compares ChatGPT to Grammarly, Coyne et al. (2023) compares GPT-3.5 and GPT-4 to two GEC system on English benchmarks. Davis et al. (2024) conducts a more comprehensive study by evaluating seven open-source and three commercial LLMs on four established GEC benchmarks.

Following the LLM trend, our system is built upon latest LLM backbone. But we apply instruction tuning approach to customize the LLM.

### 2.3 Instruction Tuning(IT)

Instruction tuning has been proven to be an efficient approach to boost model performance and generalization to unseen tasks (Chung et al., 2022; Sanh et al., 2021). Reinforcement learning with human feedback (RLHF) is leveraged to further extend instruction tuning in InstructGPT (Ouyang et al., 2022). Reinforcement learning with AI feedback (RLAIF) (Bai et al., 2022) could alleviate the heavy human preference data dependency, Zhu et al. (2023); Cheng et al. (2021) further replace the reward model in RLAIF with a heuristic model, which will be adopted in this paper to boost the quality. Our instruction tuning approach is inspired by the previous works and also follows the 2-step tuning process. We designed the synthetic data generation and RL strategy in a heuristic way that favors the proofreading task.

### 2.4 Latency Optimization

Numerous techniques aim to speed up inference of LLMs, which can be categorized into two major lines according to the focus point. The first line mainly focuses on model or algorithm side, including model compression with pruning (Xia et al., 2023b) and sparsity (Xia et al., 2023a), quantization (Dettmers et al., 2022), small model design (Timiryasov and Tastet, 2023; Liu et al., 2024), attention computation optimizations like low-rank approximation (Katharopoulos et al., 2020), sparse attention (Roy et al., 2021) etc.

The other line explores acceleration along with hardwares, exemplified works includes FlashAttention (Dao et al., 2022), FlexGen (Sheng et al., 2023), which considers hardware scheduling and weight movement, and speculative decoding (Leviathan et al., 2023; Chen et al., 2023), which leverages the parallism of hardwares to pre-conduct computation with sampling method.

We adopt quantization and speculative decoding to accelerate the inference speed in the model deployment.

## 3 Dataset

The upper half of Figure 2 illustrates the pipeline to generate the dataset. We initially sample data from the web crawled dataset, which is then processed by a GEC model to fix the grammar errors. Each item in the dataset consists of a source sentence with several possible reference sentences.

Grammar errors are then synthesized into the source sentence to simulate users' inputs, various kinds of errors which frequently happen in Gboard real scenarios are involved in this step, including:

- character omission, e.g., "hello" as "hllo"
- character insertion, e.g., "hello" as "hpello"
- transposition, e.g., "hello" as "hlelo"
- double tap, e.g., "hello" as "heello"
- omit double characters, e.g., "hello" as "helo"
- Gaussian-based positional errors, e.g., "hello" as "jello"

To align the dataset with real use cases, the data with synthetic errors are then passed to the Gboard simulator to fix errors by leveraging Gboard's built-in literal decoding, KC and AC functions. Moreover, several heuristic rules were then applied to fix cases such as emoji/emoticons alignment, date time formatting, and URL patterns.

The last step is to filter the noise data by utilizing LLM with careful designed instructions to avoid polluting the model. Data is diagnosed by various dimensions, including:

- The reference sentence still has errors remaining.
- The reference sentence itself is not fluent or clear enough.
- The reference sentence has different meaning as the source sentence.
- The reference sentence has different tones, aspects and tense from the source sentence.

To maximally benefit the model quality, the criteria above coordinates to the metrics defined in the following section.

An example of the synthetic dataset is showcased below:

> **Source**: "Good Moning! hey si, how. a u dou?"
> **Reference1**: "Good morning! Hey sir, how are you doing?"
> **Reference2**: "Good morning! Hey sister, how are you doing?"

Moreover, part of the examples labeled by human rater are used as the golden set for evaluation.

## 4 Metrics

It's of key importance to define the correct metrics which are aligned to user experiences online before the feature goes to public. In this section, several metrics are designed to measure the model quality.

Given the three elements, input (corrupted text), answer (predicted candidate from the model) and target (ground truth), we present the following metrics.

- **EM** / Exact Match Ratio: ratio of answer equal to target exactly.
- **NEM** / Normalized Exact Match Ratio : ratio of answer equal to target ignoring capitalization and punctuation.
- **Error** Ratio: ratio of answer containing grammar errors, which is conducted by LLM with specific instruction.
- **Diff** Meaning Ratio: ratio of answer and target don't have the same meaning, which is also conducted by LLM with specific instruction.
- **Good** Ratio: ratio of answer without grammar error and has the same meaning with target.
- **Bad** Ratio: ratio of answer either have grammar error or has different meaning with target.

From the definition, the Good/Bad ratios combining Error check and Diff Meaning check, are the primary metrics due to their robustness from LLM. The bad ratio is a bit more important as it portrays how much the users could tolerate the errors made by model. The combination of Error / Diff Meaning checks is also leveraged as the reward in RL phase of model tuning. EM/NEM ratios are referenced as supporting indicators as they are too strict for examples with multiple references.

## 5 Model tuning

The lower half of Figure 2 illustrates the tuning steps of the model for Proofread. We start from instruction-tuned models. PaLM2-XS model from Anil et al. (2023) is the candidate model.

### 5.1 Supervised Fine-tuning

The initial step after choosing the checkpoint is to fine-tune the model on the rewrite dataset, which contains hundreds of text rewriting tasks from Shu et al. (2023); Zhu et al. (2023). We assume that fine-tuning on similar tasks is beneficial to the final quality of Proofread. After that, the models are fine-tuned on synthetic dataset.

The evaluation results of multiple phased tuning are displayed in Table 1. It's natural to observe

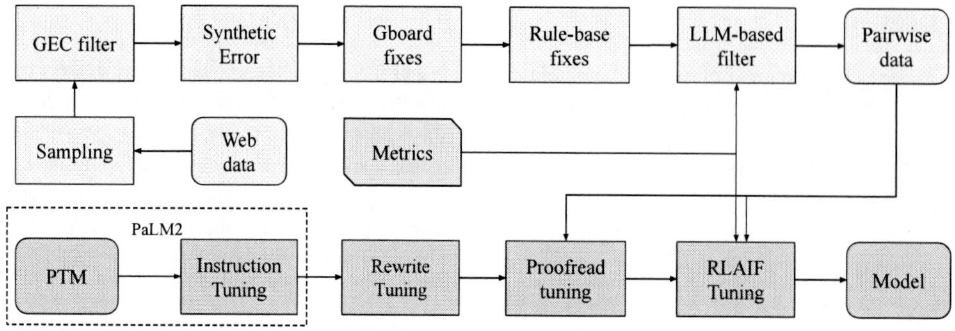


Figure 2: Data synthesis and Model tuning pipeline

that after supervised fine-tuning on the synthetic dataset, the model quality can be largely improved from 65.48% to 83.80%. An interesting finding is that though fine-tuning on Rewrite dataset degrades the quality, sequential fine-tuning on Rewrite and Proofread datasets yields the best results with Good ratio 84.68% and Bad ratio 15.32%, which we argue the robustness is enhanced by the large size of the combined dataset, by comparing M2 and M3, we can further conclude that Rewrite tuning contributes to the intent preservation.

### 5.2 Reinforcement Learning

RLAIF is leveraged with heuristic rewards in our model tuning following Zhu et al. (2023) to avoid relying on human labelers. Two alternative heuristic rewards based on LLM are designed in this paper.

- **Global Reward**: With few-shot examples, the LLM tells whether a candidate is a good fix of the corrupted inputs.
- **Direct Reward**: As the goal is to improve the Good Ratio, we directly convert the grammar error check and diff meaning check into rewards, both relying on LLM and will be combined as the final reward. This requires the ground truth included in the example.

Proximal Policy Optimization (PPO) (Schulman et al., 2017) is facilitated to optimize the model. KL divergence is involved to help model keep the ability to recover the original text (Peters et al., 2010; Mitchell et al., 2023).

The second part of Table 1 exhibits the results of RL tuning with different rewards. It's observed that the Bad ratio of PaLm2-XS model could be improved by 3.65% and 5.74% relatively through applying the RL with Global Reward and RL with Direct Reward respectively.

Specifically, RL excels at reducing the grammatical error but struggles to maintain meaning alignment between prediction and ground truth by comparing M3, M4 and M5. We argue that the optimizing meaning is inherently more subjective and complex comparing than grammar. Additionally, RL reduces the EM and NEM ratios, indicating a shift in the output distribution for both correct and incorrect cases. While increasing the KL divergence penalty can mitigate this (See M5 and M6), it doesn't significantly improve the Good/Bad ratios. We suspect the defined metrics might have inherent conflicts. Future work will reply on online metrics and real user data to drive further improvement.

## 6 Model Serving

Google's TPUv5e (Google, 2023) is utilized to serve the Proofread model, which is the latest Google TPU chip with 16GB HBM. 8-bit quantization is facilitated to reduce the memory footprint and latency without observing quality degradation.

In the context of our research, which predominantly focuses on deployment within chat applications, it has been observed that the average sentence length seldom exceeds 20 words. Consequently, we have established a discrete set of bucket keys, specifically [16, 32, 64, 128], to categorize the input data accordingly. Furthermore, we have calibrated the temperature parameter to a value of 0.3, aiming to maintain a constrained level of creativity in the proofreading outcomes, thereby ensuring relevance and coherence.

To be capable of handling more extensive documents, a systematic approach is employed wherein the document is segmented into individual paragraphs. All paragraphs are then processed in parallel, allowing for a more manageable and efficient analysis.

Table 1: The metrics of PaLM2-XS tuned on various phases on the Golden dataset. The upper half focuses on the supervised fine-tuning, and model variants in Reinforcement Learning phase are listed in the lower half.

| Model ID | PaLM variant | EM(%) | NEM(%) | Good(%) | Bad(%) | DIFF(%) | ERROR(%) |
|---|---|---|---|---|---|---|---|
| M0 | PALM2-XS | 29.96 | 45.80 | 65.48 | 34.52 | 18.56 | 30.32 |
| M1 | M0 + Rewrite | 23.44 | 40.90 | 59.48 | 40.52 | 19.04 | 37.04 |
| M2 | M0 + Proofread | 37.88 | 55.30 | 83.80 | 16.20 | 12.08 | 8.12 |
| M3 | M0 + Rewrite + Proofread | 39.16 | 56.20 | 84.68 | 15.32 | 10.60 | 9.68 |
| M4 | M3 + RL Global Reward | 35.92 | 53.80 | 85.24 | 14.76 | 11.12 | 6.80 |
| M5 | M3 + RL Direct Reward | 32.20 | 50.20 | **85.56** | 14.44 | 11.52 | 5.68 |
| M6 | M5 + Large weight on KL | 39.08 | 55.40 | 84.76 | 15.24 | 10.96 | 8.88 |

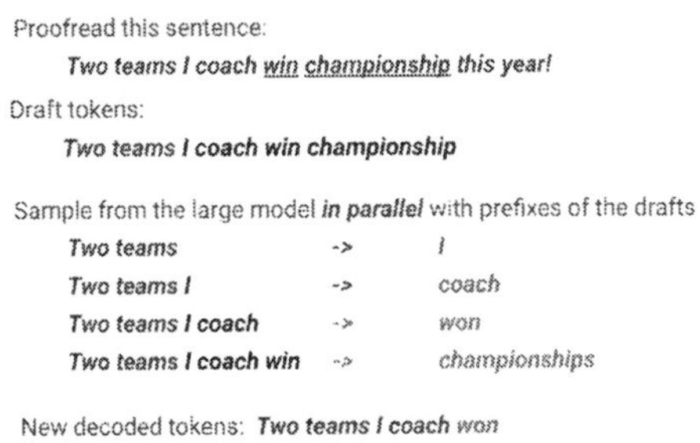


Figure 3: Example of the speculative decoding process for the proofreading task. The words in green color are selected draft by the LLM. This process speeds up the decoding without quality regression.

Table 2: Latency improvement with speculative decoding.

| Decoding | Latency (ms) |
|---|---|
| Baseline | 314.4 |
| + speculative | 190.6 (-39.4%) |

Additionally, our methodology incorporates the use of speculative decoding (Leviathan et al., 2023), complemented by heuristic drafter models that are tailored to align with user history patterns. Under our proofreading case, the initial input would naturally fit into the speculative draft so external drafter models are needed. We share an example to illustrate the process in Figure 3. This innovative approach significantly contributes to the reduction of operational costs. Through empirical evaluation in Table 2, we have recorded a 39.4% reduction on median latency per serving request, as measured on Tensor Processing Unit (TPU) cycles, underscoring the efficiency of our system in real-time applications.

## 7 Conclusions

This paper presents a novel Proofread feature implemented within Gboard, powered by a carefully refined LLM. Our work demonstrates the significant potential of LLMs to enhance the users' typing experiences by providing high-quality sentence- and paragraph-level corrections. We detailed our comprehensive approach, encompassing synthetic data generation pipeline aligned with real-world use cases, multifaceted metrics design, two-stage model tuning (multiple phased SFT followed by RL) and the efficient model deployment.

Specifically, our findings reveal that rewrite task tuning benefited the SFT model by enhancing the meaning alignment ability of the model. Additionally, we discovered the value of global and direct rewards during RL tuning, which could further improve the model by reduce grammar errors significantly. Rigorous experiments demonstrated that our tuned PaLM2-XS model achieved an impressive 85.56% good ratio and 14.44% bad ratio. The successful deployment of the model on TPU v5, leveraging optimizations such as quantization, bucket inference and speculative decoding, highlights its real-world viability.

This work underscores the transformative power of LLMs in the realm of user input experiences. Future research directions include leveraging real-user data, multilingual adaption, personalized assistance for diverse writing styles and privacy-preserving on-device solutions. This technology has the potential to fundamentally improve how we interact with our devices.

## Acknowledgments

The authors would like to thank Ananda Theertha Suresh, Jae Ro, Ziteng Sun, Shankar Kumar, Lan Wei, Yuki Zhong, Zhe Su, JinDong Chen for their insightful discussions and support.

## References


Rohan Anil, Andrew M Dai, Orhan Firat, Melvin Johnson, Dmitry Lepikhin, Alexandre Passos, Siamak Shakeri, Emanuel Taropa, Paige Bailey, Zhifeng Chen, et al. 2023. Palm 2 technical report. *arXiv preprint arXiv:2305.10403*.

Shiri Azenkot and Shumin Zhai. 2012. Touch behavior with different postures on soft smartphone keyboards. In *Proceedings of the 14th international conference on Human-computer interaction with mobile devices and services*, pages 251–260.

Yuntao Bai, Saurav Kadavath, Sandipan Kundu, Amanda Askell, Jackson Kernion, Andy Jones, Anna Chen, Anna Goldie, Azalia Mirhoseini, Cameron McKinnon, et al. 2022. Constitutional ai: Harmlessness from ai feedback. *arXiv preprint arXiv:2212.08073*.

Christopher Bryant, Zheng Yuan, Muhammad Reza Qorib, Hannan Cao, Hwee Tou Ng, and Ted Briscoe. 2023. Grammatical error correction: A survey of the state of the art. *Computational Linguistics*, 49(3):643–701.

Charlie Chen, Sebastian Borgeaud, Geoffrey Irving, Jean-Baptiste Lespiau, Laurent Sifre, and John Jumper. 2023. Accelerating large language model decoding with speculative sampling. *arXiv preprint arXiv:2302.01318*.

Ching-An Cheng, Andrey Kolobov, and Adith Swaminathan. 2021. Heuristic-guided reinforcement learning. *Advances in Neural Information Processing Systems*, 34:13550–13563.

Hyung Won Chung, Le Hou, Shayne Longpre, Barret Zoph, Yi Tay, William Fedus, Yunxuan Li, Xuezhi Wang, Mostafa Dehghani, Siddhartha Brahma, et al. 2022. Scaling instruction-finetuned language models. *arXiv preprint arXiv:2210.11416*.

Steven Coyne, Keisuke Sakaguchi, Diana Galvan-Sosa, Michael Zock, and Kentaro Inui. 2023. Analyzing the performance of gpt-3.5 and gpt-4 in grammatical error correction. *arXiv preprint arXiv:2303.14342*.

Tri Dao, Dan Fu, Stefano Ermon, Atri Rudra, and Christopher Ré. 2022. Flashattention: Fast and memory-efficient exact attention with io-awareness. *Advances in Neural Information Processing Systems*, 35:16344–16359.

Christopher Davis, Andrew Caines, Øistein Andersen, Shiva Taslimipoor, Helen Yannakoudakis, Zheng Yuan, Christopher Bryant, Marek Rei, and Paula Buttery. 2024. Prompting open-source and commercial language models for grammatical error correction of english learner text. *arXiv preprint arXiv:2401.07702*.

Tim Dettmers, Mike Lewis, Younes Belkada, and Luke Zettlemoyer. 2022. Gpt3. int8 (): 8-bit matrix multiplication for transformers at scale. *Advances in Neural Information Processing Systems*, 35:30318–30332.

Google. 2023. Tpu system architecture. `https://cloud.google.com/tpu/docs/system-architecture-tpu-vm#tpu_v5e`. Accessed: 2024-03-15.

Angelos Katharopoulos, Apoorv Vyas, Nikolaos Pappas, and François Fleuret. 2020. Transformers are rnns: Fast autoregressive transformers with linear attention. In *International conference on machine learning*, pages 5156–5165. PMLR.

Yaniv Leviathan, Matan Kalman, and Yossi Matias. 2023. Fast inference from transformers via speculative decoding.

Zechun Liu, Changsheng Zhao, Forrest Iandola, Chen Lai, Yuandong Tian, Igor Fedorov, Yunyang Xiong, Ernie Chang, Yangyang Shi, Raghuraman Krishnamoorthi, et al. 2024. Mobilellm: Optimizing sub-billion parameter language models for on-device use cases. *arXiv preprint arXiv:2402.14905*.

Robert L Logan IV, Alexandre Passos, Sameer Singh, and Ming-Wei Chang. 2021. Fruit: Faithfully reflecting updated information in text. *arXiv preprint arXiv:2112.08634*.

Jonathan Mallinson, Jakub Adamek, Eric Malmi, and Aliaksei Severyn. 2022. Edit5: Semi-autoregressive text-editing with t5 warm-start. *arXiv preprint arXiv:2205.12209*.

Eric Malmi, Yue Dong, Jonathan Mallinson, Aleksandr Chuklin, Jakub Adamek, Daniil Mirylenka, Felix Stahlberg, Sebastian Krause, Shankar Kumar, and Aliaksei Severyn. 2022. Text generation with text-editing models. *arXiv preprint arXiv:2206.07043*.

Eric Mitchell, Rafael Rafailov, Archit Sharma, Chelsea Finn, and Christopher D Manning. 2023. An emulator for fine-tuning large language models using small language models. *arXiv preprint arXiv:2310.12962*.

Courtney Napoles, Keisuke Sakaguchi, and Joel Tetreault. 2017. Jfleg: A fluency corpus and benchmark for grammatical error correction. *arXiv preprint arXiv:1702.04066*.

Kostiantyn Omelianchuk, Vitaliy Atrasevych, Artem Chernodub, and Oleksandr Skurzhanskyi. 2020. Gector–grammatical error correction: tag, not rewrite. *arXiv preprint arXiv:2005.12592*.

Long Ouyang, Jeffrey Wu, Xu Jiang, Diogo Almeida, Carroll Wainwright, Pamela Mishkin, Chong Zhang, Sandhini Agarwal, Katarina Slama, Alex Ray, et al. 2022. Training language models to follow instructions with human feedback. *Advances in neural information processing systems*, 35:27730–27744.

Tom Ouyang, David Rybach, Françoise Beaufays, and Michael Riley. 2017. Mobile keyboard input decoding with finite-state transducers. *arXiv preprint arXiv:1704.03987*.

Jan Peters, Katharina Mulling, and Yasemin Altun. 2010. Relative entropy policy search. In *Proceedings of the AAAI Conference on Artificial Intelligence*, volume 24, pages 1607–1612.

Sudha Rao and Joel Tetreault. 2018. Dear sir or madam, may i introduce the gyafc dataset: Corpus, benchmarks and metrics for formality style transfer. *arXiv preprint arXiv:1803.06535*.

Emily Reif, Daphne Ippolito, Ann Yuan, Andy Coenen, Chris Callison-Burch, and Jason Wei. 2021. A recipe for arbitrary text style transfer with large language models. *arXiv preprint arXiv:2109.03910*.

Parker Riley, Noah Constant, Mandy Guo, Girish Kumar, David Uthus, and Zarana Parekh. 2020. Textsettr: Few-shot text style extraction and tunable targeted restyling. *arXiv preprint arXiv:2010.03802*.

Aurko Roy, Mohammad Saffar, Ashish Vaswani, and David Grangier. 2021. Efficient content-based sparse attention with routing transformers. *Transactions of the Association for Computational Linguistics*, 9:53–68.

Victor Sanh, Albert Webson, Colin Raffel, Stephen H Bach, Lintang Sutawika, Zaid Alyafeai, Antoine Chaffin, Arnaud Stiegler, Teven Le Scao, Arun Raja, et al. 2021. Multitask prompted training enables zero-shot task generalization. *arXiv preprint arXiv:2110.08207*.

John Schulman, Filip Wolski, Prafulla Dhariwal, Alec Radford, and Oleg Klimov. 2017. Proximal policy optimization algorithms. *arXiv preprint arXiv:1707.06347*.

Ying Sheng, Lianmin Zheng, Binhang Yuan, Zhuohan Li, Max Ryabinin, Beidi Chen, Percy Liang, Christopher Ré, Ion Stoica, and Ce Zhang. 2023. Flexgen: High-throughput generative inference of large language models with a single gpu. In *International Conference on Machine Learning*, pages 31094–31116. PMLR.

Lei Shu, Liangchen Luo, Jayakumar Hoskere, Yun Zhu, Canoee Liu, Simon Tong, Jindong Chen, and Lei Meng. 2023. Rewritelm: An instruction-tuned large language model for text rewriting. *arXiv preprint arXiv:2305.15685*.

AB Siddique, Samet Oymak, and Vagelis Hristidis. 2020. Unsupervised paraphrasing via deep reinforcement learning. In *Proceedings of the 26th ACM SIGKDD international conference on knowledge discovery & data mining*, pages 1800–1809.

Felix Stahlberg and Shankar Kumar. 2020. Seq2edits: Sequence transduction using span-level edit operations. *arXiv preprint arXiv:2009.11136*.

Inar Timiryasov and Jean-Loup Tastet. 2023. Baby llama: knowledge distillation from an ensemble of teachers trained on a small dataset with no performance penalty. *arXiv preprint arXiv:2308.02019*.

Haoran Wu, Wenxuan Wang, Yuxuan Wan, Wenxiang Jiao, and Michael Lyu. 2023. Chatgpt or grammarly? evaluating chatgpt on grammatical error correction benchmark. *arXiv preprint arXiv:2303.13648*.

Haojun Xia, Zhen Zheng, Yuchao Li, Donglin Zhuang, Zhongzhu Zhou, Xiafei Qiu, Yong Li, Wei Lin, and Shuaiwen Leon Song. 2023a. Flash-llm: Enabling cost-effective and highly-efficient large generative model inference with unstructured sparsity. *arXiv preprint arXiv:2309.10285*.

Mengzhou Xia, Tianyu Gao, Zhiyuan Zeng, and Danqi Chen. 2023b. Sheared llama: Accelerating language model pre-training via structured pruning. *arXiv preprint arXiv:2310.06694*.

Wei Xu, Courtney Napoles, Ellie Pavlick, Quanze Chen, and Chris Callison-Burch. 2016. Optimizing statistical machine translation for text simplification. *Transactions of the Association for Computational Linguistics*, 4:401–415.

Wei Xu, Alan Ritter, William B Dolan, Ralph Grishman, and Colin Cherry. 2012. Paraphrasing for style. In *Proceedings of COLING 2012*, pages 2899–2914.

Hanqing Zhang, Haolin Song, Shaoyu Li, Ming Zhou, and Dawei Song. 2023. A survey of controllable text generation using transformer-based pre-trained language models. *ACM Computing Surveys*, 56(3):1–37.

Yi Zhang, Tao Ge, and Xu Sun. 2020. Parallel data augmentation for formality style transfer. *arXiv preprint arXiv:2005.07522*.

Yun Zhu, Yinxiao Liu, Felix Stahlberg, Shankar Kumar, Yu-hui Chen, Liangchen Luo, Lei Shu, Renjie Liu, Jindong Chen, and Lei Meng. 2023. Towards an on-device agent for text rewriting. *arXiv preprint arXiv:2308.11807*.

# SeaLLMs - Large Language Models for Southeast Asia

**Xuan-Phi Nguyen[*], Wenxuan Zhang[*], Xin Li[*], Mahani Aljunied[*], Zhiqiang Hu, Chenhui Shen[‡], Yew Ken Chia[‡], Xingxuan Li, Jianyu Wang, Qingyu Tan, Liying Cheng, Guanzheng Chen, Yue Deng, Sen Yang, Chaoqun Liu, Hang Zhang, Lidong Bing[†]**

DAMO Academy, Alibaba Group

Video: `https://youtu.be/s0mBrHYD_H4`
Website: `https://damo-nlp-sg.github.io/SeaLLMs`

## Abstract

Despite the remarkable achievements of large language models (LLMs) in various tasks, there remains a linguistic bias that favors high-resource languages, such as English, often at the expense of low-resource and regional languages. To address this imbalance, we introduce SeaLLMs, an innovative series of language models that specifically focuses on Southeast Asian (SEA) languages. SeaLLMs are built upon popular English-centric models through continued pre-training with an extended vocabulary, specialized instruction and alignment tuning to better capture the intricacies of regional languages. This allows them to respect and reflect local cultural norms, customs, stylistic preferences, and legal considerations. Our comprehensive evaluation demonstrates that SeaLLM models exhibit superior performance across a wide spectrum of linguistic tasks and assistant-style instruction-following capabilities relative to comparable open-source models. Moreover, they outperform ChatGPT-3.5 in non-Latin languages, such as Thai, Khmer, Lao, and Burmese, by large margins while remaining lightweight and cost-effective to operate.

## 1 Introduction

The advent of large language models (LLMs) has radically transformed the field of natural language processing, demonstrating remarkable abilities in text generation, comprehension, and decision-making tasks (Brown et al., 2020; OpenAI, 2023a,b; Touvron et al., 2023a,b; Thoppilan et al., 2022; Jiang et al., 2023; Wei et al., 2023; Bai et al., 2023). While the proficiencies of these models are extraordinary, the majority of existing LLMs embody a linguistic hierarchy overwhelmingly dominated by English (Ahuja et al., 2023; Lai et al., 2023; Zhang et al., 2023). This dominance undermines the multilingual capability of such models, with particularly prejudicial outcomes for lower-resource and regional languages, where data scarcity and tokenization challenges lead to disproportionately poor model performance. This linguistic disparity not only impedes access to state-of-the-art AI technologies for non-English-speaking populations but also risks cultural homogenization and the loss of linguistic diversity. While hyper-polyglot models exist (Scao et al., 2022; Muennighoff et al., 2022; Wei et al., 2023), they may pay a high cost for high-resource language performance while lacking in multilingual instruction-following abilities.

Recognizing the urgent need to democratize AI and empower linguistically diverse regions, we introduce SeaLLMs[1], a suite of specialized language models optimized for Southeast Asian languages[2]. These languages, while rich and diverse, often lack the extensive dataset support available for more widely spoken languages, resulting in a stark performance gap in existing LLM applications.

As a long-term continuous effort, as of this writing, SeaLLMs come in three versions (v1, v2, v2.5). SeaLLM-13B-v1, which was pre-trained from Llama-2-13B, eclipses the performance of most available open-source LLMs in a comprehensive array of tasks including world knowledge assessments, language comprehension, and generative capabilities in SEA languages. For English and alike, SeaLLMs do not only preserve, but also demonstrate enhanced performance in tasks that were part of the original Llama training set. When evaluated on multilingual instruction-following tasks with GPT-4 as a judge (Zheng et al., 2023), SeaLLM-13B-v1 outperforms ChatGPT-3.5 by large margins in less-represented languages such

[*‡] Equal contributions.
[†] Corresponding author: l.bing@alibaba-inc.com

[1] https://github.com/DAMO-NLP-SG/SeaLLMs

[2] English (Eng), Chinese (Zho), Indonesian (Ind), Vietnamese (Vie), Thai (Tha), Khmer (Khm), Lao, Malay (Msa), Burmese (Mya) and Tagalog (Tgl)



*Proceedings of the 62nd Annual Meeting of the Association for Computational Linguistics (Volume 3: System Demonstrations)*, pages 294–304
August 11-16, 2024 

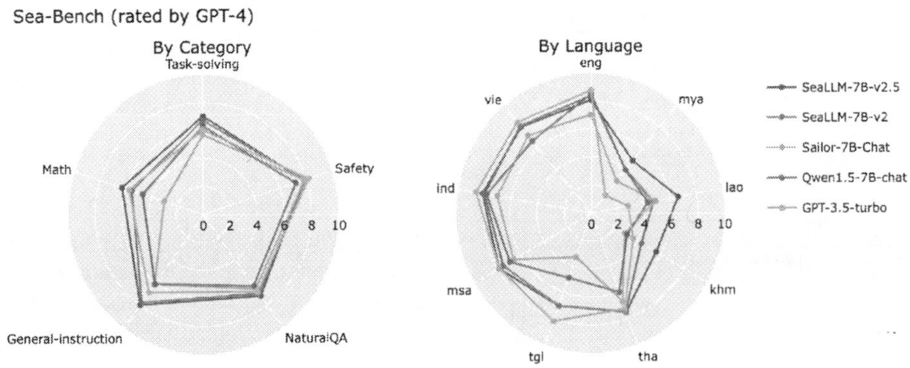


Figure 1: Sea-bench (Section 4.2) scores as evaluated by GPT-4 (Zheng et al., 2023) for different models. Each radar chart compares scores as averaged across 5 categories (left) and 9 languages (right). Detailed breakdown by each category and language is given in Figure 4 in the Appendix.

as Khmer, Lao or Burmese. Meanwhile, SeaLLM-7B-v2, which was pre-trained from Mistral-7B (Jiang et al., 2023), demonstrates better performances in math and commonsense reasoning than comparable baselines, surpassing ChatGPT-3.5 in reasoning for common SEA languages, while being much smaller in sizes. Later, SeaLLM-7B-v2.5, which was further pre-trained from Gemma-7B (Team et al., 2024), shows significant improvements in SEA languages over SeaLLM-7B-v2.

Figure 2 illustrates the four-stage training process of SeaLLMs. In the first stage, detailed in Section 2.3, we conduct continuous pre-training from the foundational models (Touvron et al., 2023b; Jiang et al., 2023) with an extended vocabulary tailored for SEA languages. Next, we fine-tune the model in a novel hybrid paradigm with a mixture of multilingual pre-training data and English-dominant instruction fine-tuning data (Section 3.2). The following stage subsequently fine-tunes the model on a balanced and custom-built multilingual SFT dataset. Finally, we conduct self-preferencing alignment optimization using the SeaLLM model itself, without relying on human annotators or more powerful LLMs (OpenAI, 2023b).

## 2 Pre-training

### 2.1 Pre-training Data

The pre-training data comprises a heterogeneous assortment of documents sourced from several publicly accessible repositories (Suárez et al., 2019; Raffel et al., 2019; Computer, 2023; Foundation). Specifically, during the creation of the pre-training data, we include web-based corpora such as Common Crawl (Wenzek et al., 2020), journalistic content such as CC-News, text corpora with expertly-curated knowledge such as Wikipedia (Foundation), and some scholarly publications. After collecting the data, we employ a language identifier (Bojanowski et al., 2017) to retain the documents for the major languages in Southeast Asia, namely Thai, Vietnamese, Indonesian, Chinese, Khmer, Lao, Malay, Burmese, and Tagalog, and discard the remaining ones. Subsequent stages of data refinement involve the multiple modules dedicated to data cleansing and content filtration. We blend such data with the highest quality English data from RedPajama subset (Computer, 2023) in more balanced ratios, as we found that such English data are useful to preserve the original learnt knowledge.

### 2.2 Vocabulary Expansion

Table 1 describes how expensive it is to process an under-represented non-Latin language. For example, encoding a single sentence in Thai requires 4.3 times more tokens than its English equivalent. The reason for this is that most English language models employ a BPE tokenizer (Sennrich et al., 2016) that inefficiently segments texts from non-Latin scripts into disproportionately lengthy byte sequences, which inadequately represent the underlying semantic content, resulting in diminished model performance (Nguyen et al., 2023). To that end, we propose a novel vocabulary expansion technique, as formally described in Algorithm 1 in the Appendix. This technique involves recursively merging whole-word and sub-word token pieces of a new language from a highly multilingual target tokenizer (*i.e.,* the NLLB tokenizer (Costa-jussà et al.,

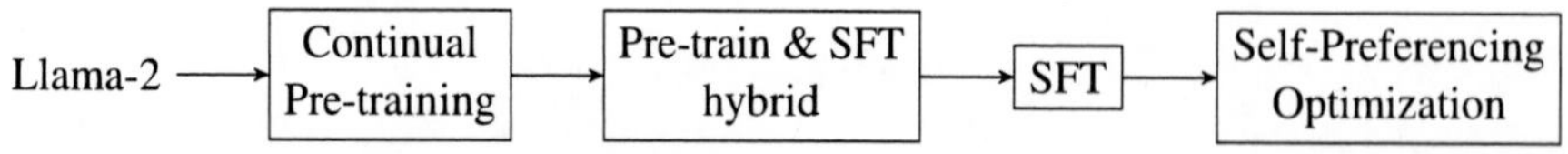


Figure 2: Complete Training Process of SeaLLMs. It begins with continual pre-training Llama-2 with more data of regional languages. Then the models undergo specialized fine-tuning process with multilingual SFT data, before finally being tuned with self-preferencing alignment.

| Language | ChatGPT's | Llama's | SeaLLM's |
|---|---|---|---|
| Vie | 4.41 | 3.46 | 1.48 |
| Zho | 2.80 | 2.36 | 1.40 |
| Tha | 9.09 | 5.10 | 1.87 |
| Ind | 2.00 | 2.09 | 1.36 |
| Khm | 15.56 | 12.14 | 2.67 |
| Lao | 13.29 | 13.50 | 2.07 |
| Msa | 2.07 | 2.16 | 1.50 |
| Mya | 17.11 | 9.85 | 1.93 |
| Tgl | 2.28 | 2.22 | 1.91 |
| Eng | 1.00 (baseline) | 1.19 | 1.19 |

Table 1: Averaged compression ratios between the tokenized length of texts of each language produced by different tokenizers versus the baseline tokenized length of same-meaning English equivalents produced by ChatGPT tokenizer (*i.e.,* it costs 15.6x more tokens to encode Khmer than English with ChatGPT tokenizer). SeaLLM's ratios are applicable only for v1 and v2.

2022)), to the existing LLM tokenizer. This new set of retrieved tokens are then pruned to remove rarely appearing and low-quality tokens before being added to the final SeaLLM tokenizer.

Table 1 demonstrates the efficiency of the new vocabulary. The compression ratio for Thai text has markedly improved from 4.29 to 1.57, signifying a 2.7-fold increase in the length of Thai text that can be encoded within the same context constraints. At the same time, the compression of English text has experienced a negligible reduction of 0.3%, thus maintaining its tokenization effectiveness.

We applied our vocabulary expansion for SeaLLM v1 and v2 with Llama-2 and Mistral-7B as backbones due to their limit 32K-token vocabulary. However, we did not extend the tokenizer for SeaLLM-7B-v2.5, which inherits a sufficiently large 250K-token vocabulary from Gemma-7B.

### 2.3 Pre-training Process

We organize our pre-training dataset based on the language of the content and the quality of the data, as mentioned in Section 2.1. We setup a separate stream of data for each language, and dynamically control and balance the sampling ratio of each language. We pack multilingual documents into a single sequence up to the maximum context length. During the last steps of pre-training, we re-feed the model with more high quality data, which it has previously seen, to readjust the model's learning focus back towards the high-quality data, improving the model's performance.

## 3 Supervised Fine-tuning (SFT)

### 3.1 Supervised Fine-tuning Data

Our supervised finetuning (SFT) data consists of many categories, including text understanding and processing, math and logical reasoning, user-centric instruction-following, and natural dialog data. As most public and open-source SFT data are English-only (Longpre et al., 2023; Lian et al., 2023; Mukherjee et al., 2023; Lee et al., 2023), various techniques were implemented to enhance the multilingual aspect of the model. These include sourcing natural data from local websites in natural settings, selectively translating from English data, employing self-instruction, and using advanced prompting techniques (Wang et al., 2022; Madaan et al., 2023; Nguyen et al., 2023). As those synthetically generated data may remain incorrect or low-quality, native speakers[3] were then engaged to further verify, filter, and edit such synthetic responses to finalize the SFT dataset. We find that engaging the annotators to verify and modify model-generated responses is more efficient than having them write responses from scratch. Safety-related data also played a crucial role in fine-tuning SeaLLMs. We manually collected and prepared country-relevant safety data, which covered a broad range of culturally and legally sensitive topics in each of these countries. This was necessary as such topics are often overlooked or may even conflict with open-source English-centric safety data (Deng et al., 2023).

For SeaLLM-7B-v2 and SeaLLM-7B-v2.5, we incorporate significantly more SFT data relating to math and commonsense reasoning. Such data is

[3] Hired by our organization, they are not co-authors.

synthetically generated with SeaLLM-13B-v1, as well as strong English models (Jiang et al., 2024; Bai et al., 2023) using a combination of few-shot paraphrasing and translation techniques (Yu et al., 2023).

### 3.2 Supervised Fine-tuning

**Pre-train and SFT Hybrid.** As our SFT data is still significantly English due to contributions of open-source data, directly conducting SFT on it may overshadow the smaller SEA language datasets. Therefore, we propose incorporating an additional step prior to complete fine-tuning, namely Pre-train & SFT Hybrid. In this step, the model is further trained on a combination of the pre-training corpus and a large portion of English SFT data, leaving the remaining and more balanced amount of English SFT data to the next stage. During this hybrid stage, the model processes both general pre-training content and instruction-following examples. We mask the source side of the instruction or supervised data to prevent the model from overfitting to the training examples and to reduce the risk of it simply memorizing the input data instead of learning the more generalized ability to follow instructions.

**Supervised Fine-tuning.** We conduct supervised fine-tuning by compiling instructions from a variety of sources explained in Section 3.1, combining them at random into a single, consolidated sequence to maximize efficiency. To enhance the multi-turn conversation capability, in the later stage of fine-tuning, we further artificially create multi-turn conversations by randomly joining several single-turn instructions together.

### 3.3 Self-Preferencing Optimization

Alignment from human feedback preference has been key to the success of many AI-assistant language models (Stiennon et al., 2020; Touvron et al., 2023b; Rafailov et al., 2023; Ouyang et al., 2022). To save the cost of human preference annotation work, some have sought to use powerful LLMs like GPT-4 (OpenAI, 2023b) to play the part of a preference data generator (Tunstall et al., 2023). However, that may not even be feasible for low-resource non-Latin languages because of the unfavorable tokenization of ChatGPT as explained in Section 2.2. In other words, even short prompts would exceed their context-length and the API-call costs would explode by up to 17 times.

Therefore, we use our own SeaLLM SFT models to generate preference data by asking it to indicate its preference between two of its own responses, given a question based on certain human-written criteria. To eliminate position bias, we swap the order of the responses and remove samples with inconsistent preference. The data is later used to employ direct preference optimization (Rafailov et al., 2023) to significantly improve the model abilities as an assistant. As such, unlike other works (Mukherjee et al., 2023; Tunstall et al., 2023), our models are free from relying on powerful close-sourced models like GPT-4 to improve the performance in low-resource languages. Our self-preferencing method also shares certain flavors with another self-rewarding mechanism (Yuan et al., 2024).[4]

## 4 Evaluation

### 4.1 Model Variants

We trained multiple variants of SeaLLMs, as specified in the following.

- **SeaLLM-7B-v1**: Trained from Llama-2-7B, it supports the 10 official languages used in Southeast Asia.
- **SeaLLM-13B-v1**: Trained from Llama-2-13B, it outperforms ChatGPT-3.5 in most non-Latin SEA languages (Khm, Lao, Mya and Tha) by large margins.
- **SeaLLM-7B-v2**: Trained from Mistral-7B, it outperforms SeaLLM-13B-v1 by far in higher-resource SEA languages (Vie, Ind, Tha), and surpasses ChatGPT-3.5 in math reasoning in SEA languages.
- **SeaLLM-7B-v2.5**: Trained from Gemma-7B, it outperforms SeaLLM-7B-v2 and SeaLLM-13B-v1 remarkably and surpasses ChatGPT-3.5 in various aspects in SEA languages, especially non-Latin languages.

### 4.2 Sea-bench Peer Comparison

While there are popular benchmarks to evaluate LLMs as a helpful assistant, such as MT-bench (Zheng et al., 2023), they are only English-based and not suitable for evaluating performances in low-resource languages. Due to such a lack of multilingual benchmarks for assistant-style models,

[4] Our work was publicly available before Yuan et al. (2024).

| Model | M3Exam | | | | | MMLU |
|---|---|---|---|---|---|---|
| | Eng | Zho | Vie | Ind | Tha | Eng |
| ChatGPT-3.5 | 75.46 | 60.20 | 58.64 | **49.27** | 37.41 | **70.00** |
| SeaLion-7b | 23.80 | 25.87 | 27.11 | 24.28 | 20.29 | 26.87 |
| Llama-2-13b | 61.17 | 43.29 | 39.97 | 35.50 | 23.74 | 53.50 |
| Polylm-13b | 32.23 | 29.26 | 29.01 | 25.36 | 18.08 | 22.94 |
| SeaLLM-7B-v1 | 54.89 | 39.30 | 38.74 | 32.95 | 25.09 | 47.16 |
| SeaLLM-13B-v1 | 62.69 | 44.50 | 46.45 | 39.28 | 36.39 | 52.68 |
| SeaLLM-7B-v2 | 70.91 | 55.43 | 51.15 | 42.25 | 35.52 | 61.89 |
| SeaLLM-7B-v2.5 | **76.87** | **62.54** | **63.11** | 48.64 | **46.86** | 64.05 |

Table 2: Multilingual world knowledge accuracy evaluation across multiple languages and various models of different sizes.

we engaged native linguists to build a multilingual test set with instructions that cover SEA languages, called **Sea-bench**. The linguists sourced such data by translating open-source English test sets, collecting real user questions from local forums and websites, collecting real math and reasoning questions from reputable sources, as well as writing test instructions themselves. Our Sea-Bench consists of diverse categories of instructions to evaluate the models, as follows:

- Task-solving: This type of data comprises various text understanding and processing tasks, such as summarization, translation, etc.

- Math-reasoning: This includes math problems and logical reasoning tasks.

- General-instruction data: This consists of general user-centric instructions, which evaluate the model's ability in general knowledge and writing.

- NaturalQA: This consists of queries posted by real users, often in popular local forums, with a variety of subjects and topics of local interest. The aim is to test the model's capacity to understand and respond coherently to colloquial language, natural expressions and idiomatic language, and locally contextualized references.

- Safety: This includes both general safety and local context-related safety instructions. While most general safety questions are translated from open sources, other local country-specific safety instructions are written by linguists of each language.

As inspired by MT-bench (Zheng et al., 2023), we evaluate and compare SeaLLMs with well-known and state-of-the-art models using GPT-4 as a judge in a score-based grading metrics and a peer comparison (or pairwise comparison) manner.

Figure 1 compares our SeaLLM (v2, v2.5) chat models with Qwen1.5-7B-chat (Bai et al., 2023) and the widely reputed ChatGPT-3.5[5] (OpenAI, 2023a). In the "By Category" chart, SeaLLM-7B-v2.5 performs on par with or surpasses ChatGPT-3.5 across various linguistic and writing tasks. This is largely thanks to the large gap in low-resource non-Latin languages, such as Burmese (Mya), Lao, Khmer and Thai, as seen in the "By language" chart on the right in Figure 1.

| Model | Languages | MT-bench |
|---|---|---|
| GPT-4-turbo | Multi | 9.32 |
| Mixtral-8x7B (46B) | Multi | 8.3 |
| Starling-LM-7B-alpha | Mono (Eng) | 8.0 |
| OpenChat-3.5-7B | Mono (Eng) | 7.81 |
| **SeaLLM-7B-v2** | **Multi** | **7.54** |
| **SeaLLM-7B-v2.5** | **Multi** | **7.43** |
| Llama-2-70B-chat | Mono | 6.86 |
| Mistral-7B-instruct | Mono | 6.84 |
| **SeaLLM-13B-v1** | **Multi** | **6.32** |

Table 3: MT-Bench scores (Zheng et al., 2023) for closed, open, multilingual and monolingual (as indicated by their authors on Huggingface.) models.

### 4.3 MT-bench

We also compare our models with certain baselines on the English MT-Bench (Zheng et al., 2023) in Table 3. As shown, SeaLLM-7B-v2 model demonstrates outstanding ability in English, given its size.

[5]gpt-3.5-turbo June 2023 version.

| Model | Eng | | Zho | | Vie | | Ind | | Tha | |
|---|---|---|---|---|---|---|---|---|---|---|
| | GSM8K | MATH | GSM8K | MATH | GSM8K | MATH | GSM8K | MATH | GSM8K | MATH |
| ChatGPT-3.5 | **80.8** | 34.1 | 48.2 | 21.5 | 55.0 | 26.5 | 64.3 | 26.4 | 35.8 | 18.1 |
| Qwen1.5-7B-chat | 56.8 | 15.3 | 40.0 | 2.7 | 37.7 | 9.0 | 36.9 | 7.7 | 21.9 | 4.7 |
| SeaLLM-7B-v2 | 78.2 | 27.5 | **53.7** | 17.6 | 69.9 | 23.8 | **71.5** | 24.4 | 59.6 | 22.4 |
| SeaLLM-7B-v2.5 | 78.5 | **34.9** | 51.3 | **22.1** | **72.3** | **30.2** | **71.5** | **30.1** | **62.0** | **28.4** |

Table 4: GSM8K and MATH scores (Cobbe et al., 2021; Hendrycks et al., 2021b) and their translated-versions in Chinese, Vietnamese, Indonesian and Thai, under zero-shot chain-of-thought prompting for different models.

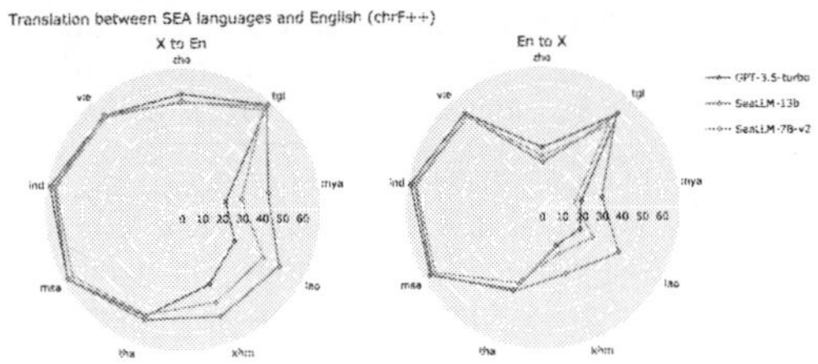


Figure 3: Translation chrF++ scores of various models for both SEA languages to English and English to SEA languages directions.

It is also a rare multilingual model in the 7B realm, especially since it focuses on non-mainstream languages.

### 4.4 World Knowledge

In this section, we evaluate our models and reputable chat baselines (Touvron et al., 2023b; Wei et al., 2023; OpenAI, 2023a) in terms of world knowledge. For knowledge across languages, we use the M3Exam benchmark (Zhang et al., 2023), which consists of real questions from human exam papers with various degrees of difficulty, ranging from primary school to high school examinations. We evaluate M3Exam with 3-shot native-instruction prompts across English, Chinese, Vietnamese, Indonesian and Thai. We also evaluate our models with the well-known English-centric MMLU benchmark (Hendrycks et al., 2021a).

Table 2 details the evaluations of world knowledge across multiple languages and models of different sizes. SeaLLM-7B-v2.5 exhibits the best performance given its size and is competitive to GPT-3.5.

### 4.5 Math Reasoning

Table 4 shows the GSM8K and MATH scores (Cobbe et al., 2021; Hendrycks et al., 2021b) for zero-shot chain-of-thought prompting for English and their translated version in Chinese, Vietnamese, Indonesian and Thai. As shown, SeaLLM-7B-v2.5 shows competitive English performance in math reasoning compared to open-source models, with 78.5 in GSM8K and 34.9 in MATH. It also exceeds GPT-3.5 in SEA languages. This is achieved by scaling supervised and preference data in math reasoning in multilingual settings.

### 4.6 Machine Translation

To benchmark the machine translation performance of our SeaLLMs, we evaluate 4-shot chrF++ scores on the test sets from Flores-200 (Costa-jussà et al., 2022). As can be seen from Figure 3, SeaLLM-13B exhibits clear superiority over ChatGPT-3.5 in low-resource languages, such as Lao and Khmer, while maintaining comparable performance with ChatGPT-3.5 in most higher resource languages (e.g., Vietnamese and Indonesian). We believe our SeaLLMs will play a key role in facilitating communication and cultural exchange across communities in Southeast Asia.

## 5 Conclusion

In conclusion, our research presents a substantial advance in the development of equitable and culturally aware AI with the creation of SeaLLMs, a specialized suite of language models attuned to the linguistic and cultural landscapes of Southeast Asia. Through rigorous pre-training enhancements and culturally tailored fine-tuning processes, SeaLLMs have demonstrated exceptional proficiency in language understanding and generation tasks, challenging the performance of dominant players such as ChatGPT-3.5, particularly in SEA languages. The models' attunement to local norms and legal stipulations—validated by human evaluations—establishes SeaLLMs as not only a technical breakthrough but a socially responsive innovation, poised to democratize access to high-quality AI language tools across linguistically diverse regions. This work lays a foundation for further research into language models that respect and uphold the rich tapestry of human languages and cultures, ultimately driving the AI community towards a more inclusive future.

## 6 Limitations

SeaLLMs are among the most linguistically diverse multilingual large language models with remarkable abilities in languages beyond mainstream. However, they do not come without limitations. First, they only scratch the surface of the regionally linguistic diversity with 9 most common and representative languages, while there are hundreds other languages spoken in the Southeast Asia, such as Javanese and Tamil. Second, despite outperforming other popular models in non-Latin low-resource languages, SeaLLM models still suffer from considerable hallucination and degeneration under certain circumstances for languages such as Burmese and Lao. Mild hallucination is still inevitable for other common languages.

## References


Kabir Ahuja, Rishav Hada, Millicent Ochieng, Prachi Jain, Harshita Diddee, Samuel Maina, Tanuja Ganu, Sameer Segal, Maxamed Axmed, Kalika Bali, and Sunayana Sitaram. 2023. MEGA: multilingual evaluation of generative AI. *CoRR*, abs/2303.12528.

Jinze Bai, Shuai Bai, Yunfei Chu, Zeyu Cui, Kai Dang, Xiaodong Deng, Yang Fan, Wenbin Ge, Yu Han, Fei Huang, et al. 2023. Qwen technical report. *arXiv preprint arXiv:2309.16609*.

Piotr Bojanowski, Edouard Grave, Armand Joulin, and Tomas Mikolov. 2017. Enriching word vectors with subword information. *Transactions of the Association for Computational Linguistics*, 5:135–146.

Tom Brown, Benjamin Mann, Nick Ryder, Melanie Subbiah, Jared D Kaplan, Prafulla Dhariwal, Arvind Neelakantan, Pranav Shyam, Girish Sastry, Amanda Askell, et al. 2020. Language models are few-shot learners. *Advances in neural information processing systems*, 33:1877–1901.

Karl Cobbe, Vineet Kosaraju, Mohammad Bavarian, Mark Chen, Heewoo Jun, Lukasz Kaiser, Matthias Plappert, Jerry Tworek, Jacob Hilton, Reiichiro Nakano, Christopher Hesse, and John Schulman. 2021. Training verifiers to solve math word problems. *arXiv preprint arXiv:2110.14168*.

Together Computer. 2023. Redpajama: An open source recipe to reproduce llama training dataset.

Marta R Costa-jussà, James Cross, Onur Çelebi, Maha Elbayad, Kenneth Heafield, Kevin Heffernan, Elahe Kalbassi, Janice Lam, Daniel Licht, Jean Maillard, et al. 2022. No language left behind: Scaling human-centered machine translation. *arXiv preprint arXiv:2207.04672*.

Yue Deng, Wenxuan Zhang, Sinno Jialin Pan, and Lidong Bing. 2023. Multilingual jailbreak challenges in large language models. *arXiv preprint arXiv:2310.06474*.

Wikimedia Foundation. Wikimedia downloads.

Dan Hendrycks, Collin Burns, Steven Basart, Andy Zou, Mantas Mazeika, Dawn Song, and Jacob Steinhardt. 2021a. Measuring massive multitask language understanding. *Proceedings of the International Conference on Learning Representations (ICLR)*.

Dan Hendrycks, Collin Burns, Saurav Kadavath, Akul Arora, Steven Basart, Eric Tang, Dawn Song, and Jacob Steinhardt. 2021b. Measuring mathematical problem solving with the math dataset. *NeurIPS*.

Albert Q Jiang, Alexandre Sablayrolles, Arthur Mensch, Chris Bamford, Devendra Singh Chaplot, Diego de las Casas, Florian Bressand, Gianna Lengyel, Guillaume Lample, Lucile Saulnier, et al. 2023. Mistral 7b. *arXiv preprint arXiv:2310.06825*.

Albert Q Jiang, Alexandre Sablayrolles, Antoine Roux, Arthur Mensch, Blanche Savary, Chris Bamford, Devendra Singh Chaplot, Diego de las Casas, Emma Bou Hanna, Florian Bressand, et al. 2024. Mixtral of experts. *arXiv preprint arXiv:2401.04088*.

Viet Dac Lai, Nghia Trung Ngo, Amir Pouran Ben Veyseh, Hieu Man, Franck Dernoncourt, Trung Bui, and Thien Huu Nguyen. 2023. Chatgpt beyond english: Towards a comprehensive evaluation of large language models in multilingual learning. *CoRR*, abs/2304.05613.

Ariel N. Lee, Cole J. Hunter, and Nataniel Ruiz. 2023. Platypus: Quick, cheap, and powerful refinement of llms.

Wing Lian, Bleys Goodson, Eugene Pentland, Austin Cook, Chanvichet Vong, and "Teknium". 2023. Openorca: An open dataset of gpt augmented flan reasoning traces. `https://https://huggingface.co/Open-Orca/OpenOrca`.

Shayne Longpre, Le Hou, Tu Vu, Albert Webson, Hyung Won Chung, Yi Tay, Denny Zhou, Quoc V. Le, Barret Zoph, Jason Wei, and Adam Roberts. 2023. The flan collection: Designing data and methods for effective instruction tuning.

Aman Madaan, Niket Tandon, Prakhar Gupta, Skyler Hallinan, Luyu Gao, Sarah Wiegreffe, Uri Alon, Nouha Dziri, Shrimai Prabhumoye, Yiming Yang, et al. 2023. Self-refine: Iterative refinement with self-feedback. *arXiv preprint arXiv:2303.17651*.

Niklas Muennighoff, Thomas Wang, Lintang Sutawika, Adam Roberts, Stella Biderman, Teven Le Scao, M Saiful Bari, Sheng Shen, Zheng-Xin Yong, Hailey

Schoelkopf, et al. 2022. Crosslingual generalization through multitask finetuning. *arXiv preprint arXiv:2211.01786*.

Subhabrata Mukherjee, Arindam Mitra, Ganesh Jawahar, Sahaj Agarwal, Hamid Palangi, and Ahmed Awadallah. 2023. Orca: Progressive learning from complex explanation traces of gpt-4.

Xuan-Phi Nguyen, Sharifah Mahani Aljunied, Shafiq Joty, and Lidong Bing. 2023. Democratizing llms for low-resource languages by leveraging their english dominant abilities with linguistically-diverse prompts. *arXiv preprint arXiv:2306.11372*.

OpenAI. 2023a. Chatgpt (june 2023 version.

OpenAI. 2023b. Gpt-4 technical report. *arXiv preprint*.

Long Ouyang, Jeffrey Wu, Xu Jiang, Diogo Almeida, Carroll Wainwright, Pamela Mishkin, Chong Zhang, Sandhini Agarwal, Katarina Slama, Alex Ray, et al. 2022. Training language models to follow instructions with human feedback. *Advances in Neural Information Processing Systems*, 35:27730–27744.

Rafael Rafailov, Archit Sharma, Eric Mitchell, Stefano Ermon, Christopher D Manning, and Chelsea Finn. 2023. Direct preference optimization: Your language model is secretly a reward model. *arXiv preprint arXiv:2305.18290*.

Colin Raffel, Noam Shazeer, Adam Roberts, Katherine Lee, Sharan Narang, Michael Matena, Yanqi Zhou, Wei Li, and Peter J. Liu. 2019. Exploring the limits of transfer learning with a unified text-to-text transformer. *arXiv e-prints*.

Teven Le Scao, Angela Fan, Christopher Akiki, Ellie Pavlick, Suzana Ilić, Daniel Hesslow, Roman Castagné, Alexandra Sasha Luccioni, François Yvon, Matthias Gallé, et al. 2022. Bloom: A 176b-parameter open-access multilingual language model. *arXiv preprint arXiv:2211.05100*.

Rico Sennrich, Barry Haddow, and Alexandra Birch. 2016. Neural machine translation of rare words with subword units. In *Proceedings of the 54th Annual Meeting of the Association for Computational Linguistics (Volume 1: Long Papers)*, pages 1715–1725. Association for Computational Linguistics.

Nisan Stiennon, Long Ouyang, Jeffrey Wu, Daniel Ziegler, Ryan Lowe, Chelsea Voss, Alec Radford, Dario Amodei, and Paul F Christiano. 2020. Learning to summarize with human feedback. *Advances in Neural Information Processing Systems*, 33:3008–3021.

Pedro Javier Ortiz Suárez, Benoît Sagot, and Laurent Romary. 2019. Asynchronous pipeline for processing huge corpora on medium to low resource infrastructures. In *7th Workshop on the Challenges in the Management of Large Corpora (CMLC-7)*. Leibniz-Institut für Deutsche Sprache.

Gemma Team, Thomas Mesnard, Cassidy Hardin, Robert Dadashi, Surya Bhupatiraju, Shreya Pathak, Laurent Sifre, Morgane Rivière, Mihir Sanjay Kale, Juliette Love, et al. 2024. Gemma: Open models based on gemini research and technology. *arXiv preprint arXiv:2403.08295*.

Romal Thoppilan, Daniel De Freitas, Jamie Hall, Noam Shazeer, Apoorv Kulshreshtha, Heng-Tze Cheng, Alicia Jin, Taylor Bos, Leslie Baker, Yu Du, et al. 2022. Lamda: Language models for dialog applications. *arXiv preprint arXiv:2201.08239*.

Hugo Touvron, Thibaut Lavril, Gautier Izacard, Xavier Martinet, Marie-Anne Lachaux, Timothée Lacroix, Baptiste Rozière, Naman Goyal, Eric Hambro, Faisal Azhar, Aurelien Rodriguez, Armand Joulin, Edouard Grave, and Guillaume Lample. 2023a. Llama: Open and efficient foundation language models. *arXiv preprint arXiv:2302.13971*.

Hugo Touvron, Louis Martin, Kevin Stone, Peter Albert, Amjad Almahairi, Yasmine Babaei, Nikolay Bashlykov, Soumya Batra, Prajjwal Bhargava, Shruti Bhosale, et al. 2023b. Llama 2: Open foundation and fine-tuned chat models. *arXiv preprint arXiv:2307.09288*.

Lewis Tunstall, Edward Beeching, Nathan Lambert, Nazneen Rajani, Kashif Rasul, Younes Belkada, Shengyi Huang, Leandro von Werra, Clémentine Fourrier, Nathan Habib, Nathan Sarrazin, Omar Sanseviero, Alexander M. Rush, and Thomas Wolf. 2023. Zephyr: Direct distillation of lm alignment.

Yizhong Wang, Yeganeh Kordi, Swaroop Mishra, Alisa Liu, Noah A Smith, Daniel Khashabi, and Hannaneh Hajishirzi. 2022. Self-instruct: Aligning language model with self generated instructions. *arXiv preprint arXiv:2212.10560*.

Xiangpeng Wei, Haoran Wei, Huan Lin, Tianhao Li, Pei Zhang, Xingzhang Ren, Mei Li, Yu Wan, Zhiwei Cao, Binbin Xie, et al. 2023. Polylm: An open source polyglot large language model. *arXiv preprint arXiv:2307.06018*.

Guillaume Wenzek, Marie-Anne Lachaux, Alexis Conneau, Vishrav Chaudhary, Francisco Guzmán, Armand Joulin, and Edouard Grave. 2020. CCNet: Extracting high quality monolingual datasets from web crawl data. In *Proceedings of the 12th Language Resources and Evaluation Conference*, pages 4003–4012, Marseille, France. European Language Resources Association.

Longhui Yu, Weisen Jiang, Han Shi, Jincheng Yu, Zhengying Liu, Yu Zhang, James T Kwok, Zhenguo Li, Adrian Weller, and Weiyang Liu. 2023. Metamath: Bootstrap your own mathematical questions for large language models. *arXiv preprint arXiv:2309.12284*.

Weizhe Yuan, Richard Yuanzhe Pang, Kyunghyun Cho, Sainbayar Sukhbaatar, Jing Xu, and Jason Weston.

2024. Self-rewarding language models. *arXiv preprint arXiv:2401.10020*.

Wenxuan Zhang, Sharifah Mahani Aljunied, Chang Gao, Yew Ken Chia, and Lidong Bing. 2023. M3exam: A multilingual, multimodal, multilevel benchmark for examining large language models. *CoRR*, abs/2306.05179.

Lianmin Zheng, Wei-Lin Chiang, Ying Sheng, Siyuan Zhuang, Zhanghao Wu, Yonghao Zhuang, Zi Lin, Zhuohan Li, Dacheng Li, Eric Xing, et al. 2023. Judging llm-as-a-judge with mt-bench and chatbot arena. *arXiv preprint arXiv:2306.05685*.

## A Vocabulary Expansion

Algorithm 1 explains in details how we perform selective and recursive merger of tokens from target NLLB vocabulary into the original Llama vocabulary to enrich the linguistic coverage for new and low-resource languages. Specifically, given a small seed unlabeled dataset of a given new language, the algorithm first tokenizes a document with the current Llama tokenizer. The resulting tokens are then exhaustively merged into longer tokens that are supported by the target NLLB vocabulary. During this merger process, any intermediate sub-word is also added to the Llama tokenizer as long as they exist in the rich NLLB vocabulary.

The new set of collected tokens are then pruned to remove rarely appearing and low-quality tokens before being added to the final SeaLLM tokenizer. This frequency-based pruning process ensures the new language is sufficiently and efficiently encoded without introducing tokens from other existing languages (*e.g.,* English), which may disrupt the learned knowledge during the Llama-2 pre-training stage.

## B Sea-bench Evaluation Details

Figure 4 breaks down the GPT-4 rated Sea-bench score-based evaluations of SeaLLM-13b and other baselines by both language and task category. As shown, our SeaLLM-13b model far exceeds ChatGPT-3.5 in most non-Latin languages, such as Burmese (Mya), Lao and Khmer, though it trails behind this formidable competitor in Latin-based languages, mostly in math reasoning skills.

**Algorithm 1** Vocabulary Extension algorithm: $V_i$ is Llama vocabulary, $V_t$ is target NLLB vocabulary, $D$ is unlabeled data and $m$ is minimum frequency.

```
function ExhaustiveMerge(V_i, V_t, t_V)
    T_new ← empty set ∅
    repeat
        for each consecutive token pair (prev, next) in t_V do
            t_merged ← ⟨prev⟩⟨next⟩                                  ▷ Form a new token
            if t_merged exists in V_t then
                Replace (prev, next) with t_merged in t_V            ▷ Update t_V with new token
                T_new ← T_new ∪ t_merged
                break
    until no new token added to T_new
    return T_new
function VocabExtend(V_i, V_t, D, m)
    V ← V_i
    F ← empty set ∅
    T ← empty set ∅
    for document d in D do
        t_V ← tokenize(V, d)                                         ▷ tokenize the document
        T_new ← ExhaustiveMerge(V_i, V_t, t_V)                       ▷ obtain new words from V_t based on d
        V ← V ∪ T_new                                                ▷ update V with new words T_new
        T ← T ∪ T_new
        F ← Update frequencies of T_new to F                         ▷ update appearance frequencies of T_new
    T ← Prune t_i ∈ T with corresponding f_t ∈ F where f_t < m       ▷ Remove rare words
    V_final ← V_i ∪ T
    return V_final
```

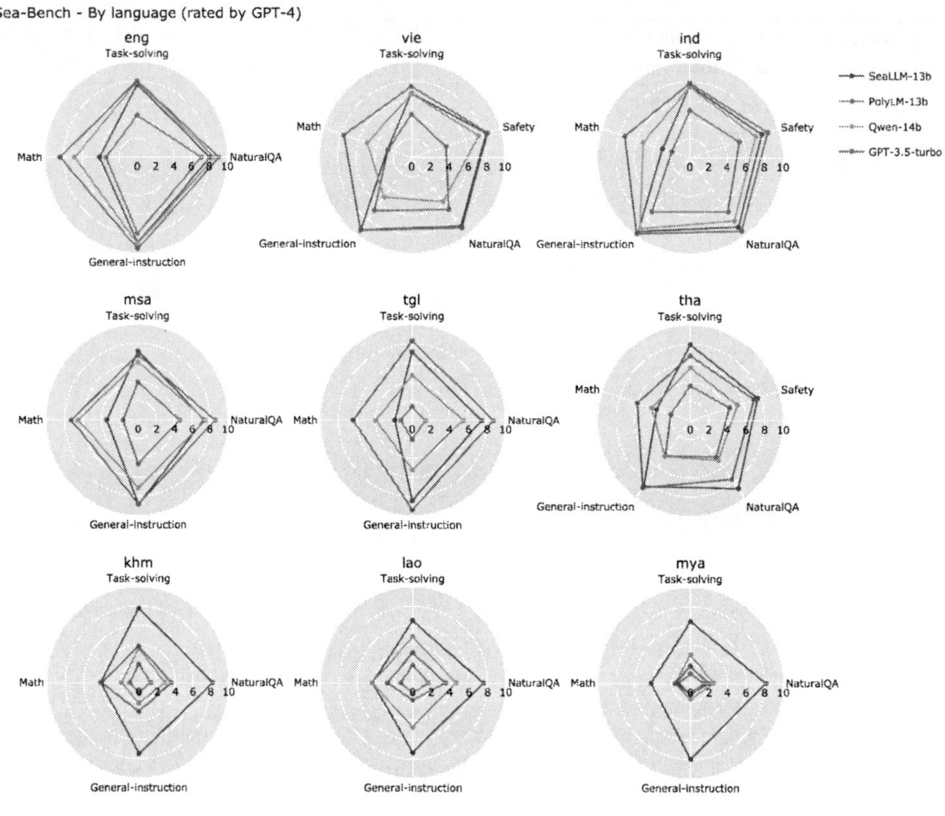


Figure 4: Sea-bench scores as evaluated by GPT-4 for different models across 9 languages and 5 categories.

# FUNDUS: A Simple-to-Use News Scraper Optimized for High Quality Extractions

**Max Dallabetta**
max.dallabetta@hu-berlin.de

**Conrad Dobberstein**
conrad.dobberstein@informatik.hu-berlin.de

**Adrian Breiding**
adrian.johannes.breiding@hu-berlin.de

**Alan Akbik**
alan.akbik@hu-berlin.de

Humboldt Universität zu Berlin

## Abstract

This paper introduces FUNDUS, a user-friendly news scraper that enables users to obtain millions of high-quality news articles with just a few lines of code. Unlike existing news scrapers, we use manually crafted, bespoke content extractors that are specifically tailored to the formatting guidelines of each supported online newspaper. This allows us to optimize our scraping for quality such that retrieved news articles are textually complete and without HTML artifacts. Further, our framework combines both crawling (retrieving HTML from the web or large web archives) and content extraction into a single pipeline. By providing a unified interface for a predefined collection of newspapers, we aim to make FUNDUS broadly usable even for non-technical users. This paper gives an overview of the framework, discusses our design choices, and presents a comparative evaluation against other popular news scrapers. Our evaluation shows that FUNDUS yields significantly higher quality extractions (complete and artifact-free news articles) than prior work.

The framework is available on GitHub under `https://github.com/flairNLP/fundus` and can be simply installed using *pip*.

## 1 Introduction and Motivation

Online news articles are a favored data source for a wide-ranging set of NLP applications including social/political analysis (Hamborg et al., 2019; Masud et al., 2020; Piskorski et al., 2023), market prediction (Ding et al., 2015; Li et al., 2020), and are used as training data for language models (Radford et al., 2019; Gururangan et al., 2022).

In such projects, it is often the first step to compile a corpus of news articles to analyze. This requires (1) identifying the URLs of news articles belonging to a particular set of online newspapers for download, and (2) extracting the article content from the surrounding HTML so that only the full article text remains.

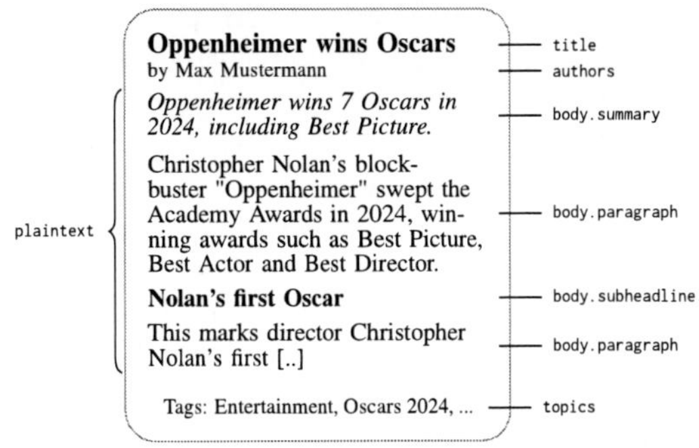


Figure 1: An example article scraped by FUNDUS. Next to the plain text of the article, attributes such as title, authors, paragraphs, subheadlines and topics are directly accessible.

In particular the second task of *content extraction* – also referred to as web scraping or boilerplate removal (Vogels et al., 2018) – is known to be challenging since each online newspaper uses different HTML and text formatting guidelines. This makes it non-trivial to distinguish between article content and other elements such as adverts, unrelated asides, captions, etc. To address these issues, several libraries have been developed that streamline the crawling and content extraction of online newspapers (Hamborg et al., 2017; Leonhardt et al., 2020; Barbaresi, 2021).

**Limitations.** However, existing libraries rely on generic methods for content extraction, based either on heuristics or trained machine learning models. This allows them to be applied across an arbitrary number of online newspapers, but comes at a cost of extraction accuracy: the quality of the news article texts varies depending on how well the heuristics or learned rules capture the HTML formatting of a particular newspaper.

For instance, the evaluation presented in this paper shows that existing frameworks encounter difficulties with at least one newspaper, resulting in F1-scores below 60% for all articles retrieved



*Proceedings of the 62nd Annual Meeting of the Association for Computational Linguistics (Volume 3: System Demonstrations)*, pages 305–314
August 11-16, 2024 ©2024 Association for Computational Linguistics

| Library | [Info] | Language | Approach | Extractor | Crawling | F1 |
|---|---|---|---|---|---|---|
| FUNDUS | (ours) | Python | Heuristics-based: Rules | bespoke | **yes** | **97.69** |
| Trafilatura | (Barbaresi, 2021) | Python | Heuristics-based: Rules | generic | **yes** | 89.81 |
| BoilerNet | (Leonhardt et al., 2020) | Python | ML-based: Sequence labeling | generic | no | 85.77 |
| news-please | (Hamborg et al., 2017) | Python | Heuristics-based: Meta-rules | generic | **yes** | 85.81 |
| jusText | (Pomikálek, 2011) | Python | Heuristics-based: Rules | generic | no | 86.96 |
| Boilerpipe | (Kohlschütter et al., 2010) | Java | ML-based: Node classification | generic | no | 79.90 |
| BTE | (Finn et al., 2001) | Python | Heuristics-based: Tag distributions | generic | no | 87.14 |

Table 1: Comparison of FUNDUS to other prominent scraping libraries, some of which include crawling functionality. The F1-score measures the extraction quality on our benchmark, as detailed in Section 4.

from this source. This means that, due to their generic nature, existing libraries provide no guarantee and no means to ensure that scraped articles are textually complete and without artifacts.

Put more plainly, it may be argued that existing libraries prioritize *quantity* (i.e. scaling across many newspapers) over *quality* (i.e. high-quality extraction of complete article texts and meta-attributes). This may cause problems in use cases in which the overall quality of a news corpus is more important than its quantity (Li et al., 2023; Marion et al., 2023).

**Contributions.** With this paper, we present FUNDUS, a news crawling library in which we pursue an orthogonal approach to prior work. Rather than aiming for a set of general rules applicable to all newspapers, our library uses separate, manually created HTML content extractors – referred to as *parsers* within the library – for each online newspaper. This allows us to match extraction methodologies specifically to a newspaper and thus manually optimize the accuracy of text extraction.

Further, as Figure 1 illustrates, this enables us to write more complex content extractors compared to prior work to preserve a news article's structure (distinguishing between paragraphs, subheadlines, and the article summary), and extract meta-attributes such as topics. In more detail, our contributions are:

1. We present the FUNDUS library, illustrate its ease of use, and discuss the merits and drawbacks of pursuing an approach of manually crafted, bespoke extractors for selected online newspapers.

2. We illustrate how FUNDUS can be used not only for news articles that are currently available online, but also scrape the extensive COMMONCRAWL web archive CC-NEWS. This allows users to create very large, high quality news corpora with only a few lines of code.

3. We comparatively evaluate FUNDUS against well-known crawling/content extraction frameworks using a newly created dataset of paragraph-wise annotated HTML files, and provide statistics on its data potential leveraging CC-NEWS.

We find that FUNDUS outperforms all other libraries in terms of yielding complete and artifact-free text (see Table 1), thus indicating its usefulness for projects in which textual quality is a priority. To enable the NLP community to use FUNDUS in their projects – and add parsers for new newspapers – we open source FUNDUS under an MIT licence[1].

## 2 Related Work

Table 1 gives an overview of popular scraping libraries and a comparison to FUNDUS.

### 2.1 Content Extraction

Existing approaches for content extraction are based either on heuristics or machine learning:

**Heuristics-based extraction.** Early heuristic methods used the assumption that fewer HTML tags are used in main text content than in other elements. For instance, BTE (Finn et al., 2001) employs a cumulative tag distribution to identify the region with the lowest tag-to-text ratio as the main content. JUSTEXT (Pomikálek, 2011) segments HTML into content blocks based on selected tag types. Thereafter, these blocks are evaluated as content and distinguished from boilerplate using metrics such as link density, block length and block complexity.

Later approaches instead focus on the underlying DOM tree using a series of XPath expressions to determine regions of the tree as main content. For instance, TRAFILATURA (Barbaresi, 2021) uses a cascade of XPath expressions to initially sanitize HTML content by removing unwanted sections and subsequently querying for relevant content. NEWS-

[1]Available at: `https://github.com/flairNLP/fundus`

Listing 1: Crawl US-based publishers

```
# crawl US-based publishers
crawler = Crawler(PublisherCollection.us)

# crawl 10 news articles
articles = crawler.crawl(max_articles=10)

# print them out one-by-one
for article in articles:
    print(article)
```

Listing 2: Crawl one German publisher

```
# crawl one specific German publisher
crawler = Crawler(PublisherCollection.de.DW)

# crawl 10 news articles
articles = crawler.crawl(max_articles=10)

# print them out one-by-one
for article in articles:
    print(article)
```

Figure 2: Two example usages of FUNDUS to crawl articles from (1) all supported US-based publishers, and (2) only one specific German publisher ("Deutsche Welle").

PLEASE (Hamborg et al., 2017) facilitates a combination of state-of-the-art extractors.

**ML-based extraction.** The second family of approaches formulates content extraction as a classification problem. For instance, BOILERPIPE (Kohlschütter et al., 2010) uses decision trees to classify text blocks (uninterrupted text devoid of tags) as content or boilerplate. BOILERNET (Leonhardt et al., 2020) tokenizes web pages and trains a bidirectional LSTM to classify each segment.

**Content extraction in FUNDUS.** Unlike prior work, we use bespoke extractors for each newspaper, thus allowing us to manually optimize for accuracy and attribute coverage. Although our approach inherently prioritizes quality, it also incurs a trade-off in terms of quantity, as it necessitates humans to create a separate extraction logic for each online newspaper. To manage this, we pursue a community-based approach and provide simple abstractions (and tutorials) to enable open source contributors to add support for new newspapers.

### 2.2 Crawling

Next to content extraction, identifying and downloading pages at scale can also be challenging. Such a system, which we refer to as a *crawler*, should be "polite" (crawling only permissive online newspapers and keeping server workload low) and able to filter for pages relevant to the use case. However, the majority of existing libraries (see Table 1) focus solely on content extraction, thus requiring users to resort to separate tools.

**Crawling in FUNDUS.** We combine both crawling and content extraction in a single library. Unlike prior work which requires complex external configuration or comprehension of content maps like RSS feeds and sitemaps, FUNDUS provides predefined settings for each supported newspaper. In FUNDUS, users are only required to select a list of newspapers to include and issue a single method call, without additional configuration. This directly yields already extracted text. By hiding the underlying complexity, we aim to make FUNDUS broadly usable even for non-technical users.

## 3 FUNDUS

We introduce FUNDUS with a usage example, discuss our article and publisher-based logic, and illustrate how we distinguish between *forward* and *backward* crawling.

### 3.1 Usage Example

We provide two example snippets on how to use FUNDUS to scrape news articles in Figure 2:

**Listing 1: Crawl all US-based publishers.** This example demonstrates the process of scraping news articles from a selection of US-based publishers. First, we instantiate the `Crawler` object by passing `PublisherCollection.us` to it. This indicates that all US-based publishers currently supported in FUNDUS should be used as data sources. We then instruct the crawler to gather articles until a threshold of 10 articles is met (by passing `max_articles=10`). This returns a generator[2] of `Article` objects, encapsulating the plain text of each news article alongside structured information such as the title, the author, and the date of crawling. Finally, we iterate over the generator, printing each article successively for human inspection.

**Listing 2: Crawl one specific source.** In the second example, we focus on articles from a particular publisher. We choose the German publisher DW ("Deutsche Welle") for this example. The code structure mirrors that of Listing 1, except that we instantiate the `Crawler` by passing `PublisherCollection.de.DW`. This narrows the search to a single publisher.

### 3.2 Articles

FUNDUS' metadata and content extractions can be accessed through a single dataclass called `Article`.

[2] FUNDUS uses generators to prioritize responsiveness by delivering articles as they become available, rather than accumulating them for subsequent retrieval.

| Attribute | Description |
|---|---|
| title | Title of the news article |
| body | All article text with pararaph structure |
| authors | Creators of the article |
| publish_date | Article release date |
| topics | Publisher-assigned topics |
| free_access | Boolean indicating free accessibility |
| ld | Parsed JSON+LD metadata |
| meta | Parsed HTML metadata |
| plaintext | Concatenated article body |
| lang | Auto-detected article language |
| html | HTML content and meta information |
| exception | Indicates whether an exception occurred during extraction |

Table 2: Directly accessible attributes for each scraped `Article` (more details found in the Appendix, Table 6).

As indicated in the examples, users can obtain a quick overview of an article by simply printing it. This will output the article's title, a snippet of the extracted text content, the URL and publisher from which it was crawled, along with a timestamp indicating the publication time.

All attributes for an `Article` are listed in Table 2. They are directly accessible using Python's dot notation. Attributes for each `Article` include its *title*, textual *body*, *authors*, *publishing_date*, *topics*, etc. The body attribute in particular captures the entire article structure including a summary, paragraphs and subheadlines, as depicted in Figure 1.

### 3.3 Publishers and Collections

As the usage examples illustrate, users may specify which (set of) publishers to target when crawling for news articles. For FUNDUS, a publisher refers to an individual online newspaper, such as "Deutsche Welle". FUNDUS assumes that each online newspaper adheres to its own HTML and formatting guidelines. This means that for each publisher, we specify (1) where to find the URLs of each news article, and (2) how to extract the main textual content from downloaded HTML pages. This specification is created once (e.g. by a contributor to the FUNDUS repository) by creating a `Publisher`-specific enum object for the newly supported online newspaper.

Users can then pass this object to our `Crawler` to target this newspaper. To enhance accessibility and provide locality, we group publishers by their countries of origin within the `PublisherCollection`. This allows users to crawl all supported publishers of a specific country using their two-letter ISO 3166-2 language code. We illustrate this by crawling all US-based publishers in Listing 1. As of writing, the framework supports **39 publishers** spanning 5 different regions.

### 3.4 Forward and Backward Crawling

Internally, each `Publisher` defines one or multiple HTML sources, determining how a crawler locates the URLs of its news articles. Here, we distinguish between *forward* and *backward* crawling.

**Forward crawling.** With forward crawling, we refer to accessing news articles that are currently available online on the news sites of supported newspapers. To identify URLs, we support the use of content maps like RSS feeds and sitemaps provided by the individual publisher. Sitemaps are typically exposed to crawlers via a "`robots.txt`" file, which also outlines user-agent-specific restrictions on subdomains and crawl intervals.

**Backward crawling.** With backward crawling, we refer to accessing news articles in a static web dump. Specifically, we support the **CC-NEWS**[3] dataset provided by the COMMONCRAWL initiative. At the time of writing, this dataset comprises around 40 terabytes of WARC-formatted data, containing millions of news articles dating back to 2016. To handle such a large volume of data efficiently, FUNDUS offers the option to narrow crawls by a date range. Additionally, we stream WARC files and utilize the *FastWARC* library (Bevendorff et al., 2021) for in-memory processing to mitigate storage requirements.

### 3.5 Content Extraction

The central component of FUNDUS' content extraction is the `Parser` class. It is individually implemented for every publisher and combines both generic and newspaper-specific extraction methods. The generic heuristics target structured information such as paywall restrictions, language detection, and meta-information (HTML tags and JSON+LD) and can be manually overwritten for specific publishers if necessary.

They are complemented with hand-tailored rules to extract the core parts of a news article such as the title, the textual body, and the authors. These rules are formulated as simple selectors (CSSSelect/XPath expressions) or metadata keys, and can typically be easily determined by inspecting the DOM tree of a few HTML examples.

[3] `https://commoncrawl.org/blog/news-dataset-available`

| Scraper | A | B | C | D | E | F | G | H | I | J | K | L | M | N | O | P |
|---|---|---|---|---|---|---|---|---|---|---|---|---|---|---|---|---|
| FUNDUS | 100 | 100 | 100 | 100 | 99 | 100 | 89 | 92 | 100 | 99 | 99 | 100 | 100 | 87 | 100 | 98 |
| BTE | 87 | 97 | 83 | 99 | 95 | 91 | 78 | 68 | 97 | **50** | 84 | 85 | 99 | 90 | 96 | 96 |
| jusText | 79 | 94 | 85 | 96 | 95 | 89 | 58 | 89 | 97 | **52** | 95 | 97 | 99 | 74 | 95 | 97 |
| Trafilatura | 93 | 99 | **42** | 99 | 97 | 94 | 84 | 97 | 100 | 74 | 100 | 95 | 100 | 67 | 97 | 100 |
| news-please | 100 | 91 | 93 | 100 | 81 | 95 | 78 | 97 | 97 | 82 | 85 | 85 | 71 | **32** | 100 | 85 |
| Boilerpipe | 82 | 96 | **5** | 97 | 75 | 93 | 75 | 96 | 96 | **52** | 75 | 95 | 88 | 77 | 91 | 87 |
| BoilerNet | **51** | 77 | 88 | 95 | 94 | 90 | 65 | 92 | 97 | 70 | 84 | 93 | 99 | 90 | 90 | 96 |

Table 3: Rounded mean F1 scores of compared scrapers per publisher with scores below 60 highlighted. Publishers are: **A**: AP News; **B**: CNBC; **C**: Fox News; **D**: The Washington Free Beacon; **E**: The LA Times; **F**: Occupy Democrats; **G**: Reuters; **H**: The Gateway Pundit; **I**: The Guardian; **J**: The Independent; **K**: The Intercept; **L**: The Nation; **M**: The New Yorker; **N**: The Telegraph; **O**: The Washington Times; **P**: iNews

Extraction rules are encapsulated as class methods for each parser and "registered" as attributes using a decorator. Each attribute in a parsed article can be directly accessed (c.f. Section 3.2).

## 4 Evaluation

We comparatively evaluate FUNDUS against prominent scraping libraries. Our goals are to (1) determine the quality of our bespoke content extraction approach compared to the generic approaches of prior work, and to (2) better understand the data potential of FUNDUS, i.e. to estimate the size of news corpora that FUNDUS can create.

### 4.1 Experimental Setup

#### 4.1.1 Evaluation Dataset

To evaluate content extraction, we require a dataset of raw HTML pages and corresponding gold annotations of the journalistic content found on each page. This allows us to test whether content extraction libraries are capable of correctly distinguishing the article's text content from surrounding elements. Further, the dataset should cover the publishers in FUNDUS. As our survey of related work found no suitable datasets, we manually created our own[4].

**Data selection and annotation.** We select the 16 English-language publishers FUNDUS currently supports as the data source, and retrieve five articles for each publisher from the respective RSS feeds/sitemaps. We stress that the evaluation corpus consists only of articles that were published after the respective FUNDUS extractors were finalized. There is therefore no data contamination in our evaluation dataset.

The selection process yielded an evaluation corpus of 80 news articles. From it, we manually extracted the plain text from each article and stored it together with information on the original paragraph structure. Annotation was separately performed by two authors of this publication. Our annotation guidelines can be found in Appendix C and include the option to mark individual paragraphs as "optional". To check for consistency between the two annotators, the first article of every publisher was annotated by both. Of 16 doubly annotated articles, 3 disagreements were discussed and resolved.

| Scraper | Precision | Recall | F1-Score |
|---|---|---|---|
| FUNDUS | **99.89**±0.57 | 96.75±12.75 | **97.69**±9.75 |
| Trafilatura | 90.54±18.86 | 93.23±23.81 | 89.81±23.69 |
| BTE | 81.09±19.41 | **98.23**±8.61 | 87.14±15.48 |
| jusText | 86.51±18.92 | 90.23±20.61 | 86.96±19.76 |
| news-please | 92.26±12.40 | 86.38±27.59 | 85.81±23.29 |
| BoilerNet | 84.73±20.82 | 90.66±21.05 | 85.77±20.28 |
| Boilerpipe | 82.89±20.65 | 82.11±29.99 | 79.90±25.86 |

Table 4: Overall performance of FUNDUS and compared scrapers in terms of averaged ROUGE-LSum precision, recall and F1-score and their standard deviation. The table is sorted in descending order over the F1-score.

#### 4.1.2 Evaluation Metric

We follow prior work by Bevendorff et al. (2023) and use the ROUGE-LSum (Lin, 2004) score, which is commonly used for evaluating the similarity between two text sequences, particularly in tasks such as machine translation. Here, we compare the extracted article text to the gold text.

For each article in the dataset, we calculate the precision, recall and F1-score using the ROUGE-LSum metric. This computation is performed with every possible combination of optional paragraphs removed from the ground truth, selecting the best F1 score from all options. To determine the final score, we aggregate the scores of individual articles by computing the mean and the standard deviation.

[4]The dataset, scores, and evaluation metrics can be found at: `https://github.com/dobbersc/fundus-evaluation`

| Year | B | C | E | G | H | I | J | L | M | N | O | P | Total |
|---|---|---|---|---|---|---|---|---|---|---|---|---|---|
| 2023 total | 19,628 | 75,363 | 40,048 | 63,664 | 12,951 | 55,899 | 176,913 | 2,380 | 2,973 | 57,600 | 15,388 | 28,911 | 551,718 |
| 2023 body | 14,048 | 72,660 | 28,259 | 63,403 | 12,672 | 50,961 | 166,070 | 2,125 | 2,528 | 57,441 | 15,374 | 28,911 | 514,452 |
| 2022 total | 21,820 | 209,452 | 40,531 | 115,811 | 0 | 96,504 | 217,238 | 2,296 | 4,904 | 61,053 | 19,947 | 30,285 | 819,841 |
| 2022 body | 16,903 | 67,700 | 0 | 115,642 | 0 | 87,176 | 202,829 | 2,293 | 4,126 | 60,042 | 19,928 | 30,283 | 606,922 |
| 2021 total | 26,741 | 101,906 | 47,019 | 248,619 | 40 | 93,954 | 112,498 | 2,345 | 4,652 | 73,953 | 45,184 | 20,791 | 777,702 |
| 2021 body | 26,388 | 101,316 | 0 | 81,364 | 40 | 80,046 | 104,392 | 2,345 | 1,009 | 71,768 | 45,116 | 20,791 | 534,575 |
| 2020 total | 31,725 | 109,155 | 54,901 | 399,925 | 33 | 97,174 | 0 | 2,839 | 5,318 | 89,393 | 90,065 | 71,070 | 951,598 |
| 2020 body | 31,018 | 108,185 | 0 | 0 | 32 | 4,449 | 0 | 2,838 | 0 | 84,152 | 90,046 | 70,919 | 391,639 |

Table 5: Total number of articles extracted from **CC-NEWS** in the timeframe 01/01/2020 – 01/01/2024, including a breakdown by online newspaper. Publisher identities correspond to those delineated in Table 3.

### 4.2 Results and Discussion

Table 4 summarizes our findings. We make the following observations in regard to FUNDUS:

**Highest overall F1-score.** We first note that our approach yields the highest quality extractions as measured by the ROUGE-LSum F1-score. This confirms our hypothesis that bespoke content extractors are naturally well-suited for high-quality text extraction. Further, this validates our assumption that publishers follow internally consistent formatting guidelines across all news articles.

**Lower standard deviation.** We also note that FUNDUS has a lower variability of extraction quality – as measured by the standard deviation – than other approaches. This indicates that our extractors are more consistent than generic approaches based on heuristics or on ML models. We visualize this property in Table 3 in the Appendix.

**Existing libraries struggle with at least one newspaper (Table 3).** To get a better insight into the extraction capability of each compared library, we compute the F1-scores on a per-publisher basis. As Table 3 shows, we find that the F1-score widely varies from publisher to publisher for generic approaches, whereas FUNDUS yields consistent quality extractions.

**Errors remain.** However, we also note that despite manually-crafted, bespoke rules, our extraction is not perfect. Upon manual inspection, we find that a small portion of articles of a publisher deviates from standard formatting, for instance to emphasize quotations or include nested paragraphs. This particularly affected *live news tickers* which some newspapers feature for selected events.

### 4.3 Scalability

Since FUNDUS is limited to a set of supported newspapers, a natural question is how much data one can expect to crawl using FUNDUS.

**Data potential (Table 5).** To investigate, we extract news articles from the CC-NEWS web archive spanning the years 2020 to 2024. We find that 12 of our 16 English-language publishers are included in the archive. Further, despite crafting extraction rules targeting articles from 2023 onward, we note robust backward compatibility, with a significant decrease only noticeable in 2020 (e.g. fewer URLs that yield text bodies). In total, we extract over 2 million articles with bodies.

**Performance.** We evaluated the crawling performance of FUNDUS using a machine equipped with 2 Xeon 6254 CPUs, 756 GB of RAM, and a bandwidth of 10 Gbit/s. For CC-NEWS, we estimate the performance by focusing on the year 2023, as it constitutes the largest data dump among the four years evaluated. It comprises 201,586,338 unique URLs sourced from 34,229 different domains, resulting in approximately 8.2 terabytes of gzip-compressed WARC data. FUNDUS took 2.1 hours to yield the results presented in Table 5.

In terms of forward crawling, we scraped 10,000 articles across all 39 supported publishers. Employing a delay of 1 second for subsequent calls on the same publisher, the process took 549 seconds.

## 5 Conclusion and Outlook

We presented FUNDUS, an easy-to-use news scraper built on the idea of bespoke content extractors for supported online newspapers. Our evaluation shows that our approach successfully optimizes for quality, indicating that FUNDUS is a viable option for use cases in which data quality is a priority. Further, we combine both crawling and scraping functionality in a single pipeline, and support access to the static web archive CC-NEWS.

With FUNDUS' open-source approach, we invite the community to contribute support for additional online newspapers. To assist in this process, we plan to investigate semi-automatic methods to suggest extraction rules in future work.

## Limitations

The main limitation of our approach is its inherent lack of scalability across many online newspapers, since manual rules need to be written for each supported newspaper. As we argue in our paper, the benefits of extraction quality of our manual approach may outweigh quantity considerations depending on whether quality is a priority in an NLP use case. Additionally, though our approach does not easily scale across newspapers, it does scale across large web archives, meaning that we can retrieve large news corpora even with a limited number of supported publishers. Further, we aim to make it easy for the open source community to add support for new newspapers.

A related limitation is that regular maintenance of extractions is necessary, since online newspapers might change their formatting guidelines over time. To monitor this, we automatically check whether FUNDUS is able to extract text content from currently online articles on a periodic basis. This flags whenever formatting guidelines have changed.

## Ethics Statement

Newspapers play a pivotal role in modern society, often referred to as the fourth estate or fourth power. Maintaining independence necessitates self-financing for news media, thus evoking an inherent need for good-quality content to be adequately paid. However, the advent of Large Language Models (LLMs) revealed that web corpora, particularly news corpora, are often used for commercial benefit in a non-consensual manner. In response, our approach prioritizes the ethical acquisition of news articles by providing a simple option to crawl only those unrestricted by paywalls.

Moreover, we advocate for the non-commercial use of FUNDUS, aligning with our ethos of respecting intellectual property rights and promoting fair compensation for content creators. By fostering a culture of respect for intellectual property and fair compensation for content creators, we can help ensure the continued production of high-quality news and information for the benefit of society as a whole.

Another source of ethical concern stems from inherent biases in datasets obtained from the web (Bender et al., 2021), as prior work has shown that language models trained over biased data tend to reflect these biases (Haller et al., 2023). With FUNDUS, users can specifically select which newspaper to include when creating a news corpus, thus giving some degree of control (for instance, over political biases) during corpus creation.

Lastly, also the datasets themselves are worthy of a discussion, as FUNDUS provides easy access to the CC-News dataset. The Common Crawl Foundation has measures in place to respect the resources and work of content creators and comply with the US Fair Use doctrine, which provides a legal basis. Baack (2024) and Xue (2024) also illustrate limitations and biases of the Common Crawl dataset, which should be taken into account as well as acknowledging that not necessarily every rights-holder actively approved of their data being crawled and used.

## Acknowledgements

Max Dallabetta, Conrad Dobberstein and Alan Akbik are supported by the Deutsche Forschungsgemeinschaft (DFG, German Research Foundation) under Emmy Noether grant "Eidetic Representations of Natural Language" (project number 448414230). Alan Akbik is further supported under Germany's Excellence Strategy "Science of Intelligence" (EXC 2002/1, project number 390523135).

## References

Stefan Baack. 2024. A critical analysis of the largest source for generative ai training data: Common crawl. In *Proceedings of the 2024 ACM Conference on Fairness, Accountability, and Transparency*, FAccT '24, page 2199–2208, New York, NY, USA. Association for Computing Machinery.

Adrien Barbaresi. 2021. Trafilatura: A web scraping library and command-line tool for text discovery and extraction. In *Proceedings of the 59th Annual Meeting of the Association for Computational Linguistics and the 11th International Joint Conference on Natural Language Processing: System Demonstrations*, pages 122–131, Online. Association for Computational Linguistics.

Emily M Bender, Timnit Gebru, Angelina McMillan-Major, and Shmargaret Shmitchell. 2021. On the dangers of stochastic parrots: Can language models be too big? In *Proceedings of the 2021 ACM conference on fairness, accountability, and transparency*, pages 610–623.

Janek Bevendorff, Sanket Gupta, Johannes Kiesel, and Benno Stein. 2023. An Empirical Comparison of Web Content Extraction Algorithms. In *Proceedings of the 46th International ACM SIGIR Conference on Research and Development in Information Retrieval*, SIGIR '23, pages 2594–2603. Association for Computing Machinery.

Janek Bevendorff, Martin Potthast, and Benno Stein. 2021. FastWARC: Optimizing Large-Scale Web Archive Analytics. In *3rd International Symposium on Open Search Technology (OSSYM 2021)*. International Open Search Symposium.

Xiao Ding, Yue Zhang, Ting Liu, and Junwen Duan. 2015. Deep learning for event-driven stock prediction. In *Proceedings of the 24th International Conference on Artificial Intelligence*, IJCAI'15, page 2327–2333. AAAI Press.

Aidan Finn, Nicholas Kushmerick, and Barry Smyth. 2001. Fact or fiction: Content classification for digital libraries. In *DELOS Workshops / Conferences*.

Suchin Gururangan, Dallas Card, Sarah Dreier, Emily Gade, Leroy Wang, Zeyu Wang, Luke Zettlemoyer, and Noah A. Smith. 2022. Whose language counts as high quality? measuring language ideologies in text data selection. In *Proceedings of the 2022 Conference on Empirical Methods in Natural Language Processing*, pages 2562–2580, Abu Dhabi, United Arab Emirates. Association for Computational Linguistics.

Patrick Haller, Ansar Aynetdinov, and Alan Akbik. 2023. Opiniongpt: Modelling explicit biases in instruction-tuned llms.

Felix Hamborg, Karsten Donnay, and Bela Gipp. 2019. Automated identification of media bias in news articles : an interdisciplinary literature review. *International Journal on Digital Libraries*, 20(4):391–415.

Felix Hamborg, Norman Meuschke, Corinna Breitinger, and Bela Gipp. 2017. news-please : a generic news crawler and extractor. In *Everything changes, everything stays the same : Understanding Information Spaces; Proceedings of the 15th International Symposium of Information Science (ISI 2017), Berlin, Germany, 13th-15th March 2017*, number 70 in Schriften zur Informationswissenschaft, pages 218–223, Glückstadt. Verlag Werner Hülsbusch.

Christian Kohlschütter, Peter Fankhauser, and Wolfgang Nejdl. 2010. Boilerplate detection using shallow text features. In *Proceedings of the Third ACM International Conference on Web Search and Data Mining*, WSDM '10, page 441–450, New York, NY, USA. Association for Computing Machinery.

Jurek Leonhardt, Avishek Anand, and Megha Khosla. 2020. Boilerplate removal using a neural sequence labeling model. In *Companion Proceedings of the Web Conference 2020*, WWW '20, page 226–229, New York, NY, USA. Association for Computing Machinery.

Xiaodong Li, Pangjing Wu, and Wenpeng Wang. 2020. Incorporating stock prices and news sentiments for stock market prediction: A case of hong kong. *Information Processing & Management*, 57(5):102212.

Yuanzhi Li, Sébastien Bubeck, Ronen Eldan, Allie Del Giorno, Suriya Gunasekar, and Yin Tat Lee. 2023. Textbooks are all you need ii: phi-1.5 technical report.

Chin-Yew Lin. 2004. ROUGE: A package for automatic evaluation of summaries. In *Text Summarization Branches Out*, pages 74–81, Barcelona, Spain. Association for Computational Linguistics.

Max Marion, Ahmet Üstün, Luiza Pozzobon, Alex Wang, Marzieh Fadaee, and Sara Hooker. 2023. When less is more: Investigating data pruning for pretraining llms at scale.

Sarah Masud, Subhabrata Dutta, Sakshi Makkar, Chhavi Jain, Vikram Goyal, Amitava Das, and Tanmoy Chakraborty. 2020. Hate is the new infodemic: A topic-aware modeling of hate speech diffusion on twitter.

Jakub Piskorski, Nicolas Stefanovitch, Giovanni Da San Martino, and Preslav Nakov. 2023. SemEval-2023 task 3: Detecting the category, the framing, and the persuasion techniques in online news in a multi-lingual setup. In *Proceedings of the 17th International Workshop on Semantic Evaluation (SemEval-2023)*, pages 2343–2361, Toronto, Canada. Association for Computational Linguistics.

Jan Pomikálek. 2011. *Removing Boilerplate and Duplicate Content from Web Corpora [online]*. Doctoral theses, dissertations, Masaryk University, Faculty of InformaticsBrno. SUPERVISOR: prof. PhDr. Karel Pala, CSc.

Alec Radford, Jeffrey Wu, Rewon Child, David Luan, Dario Amodei, Ilya Sutskever, et al. 2019. Language models are unsupervised multitask learners. *OpenAI blog*, 1(8):9.

Thijs Vogels, Octavian-Eugen Ganea, and Carsten Eickhoff. 2018. Web2text: Deep structured boilerplate removal. In *Advances in Information Retrieval: 40th European Conference on IR Research, ECIR 2018, Grenoble, France, March 26-29, 2018, Proceedings 40*, pages 167–179. Springer.

Alex Xue. 2024. Balancing discovery and privacy: A look into opt–out protocols. Common Crawl Blog.

## A Live Demo

You can find a short live demonstration of our library on YouTube following this link: `https://youtu.be/9GJExMelhdI`

## B Article Attributes

Table 6 provides a comprehensive overview of all attributes of the FUNDUS Article class alongside additional information concerning the content extraction process, the methodology employed, and the Python data type utilized to represent each attribute internally.

## C Annotation Guidelines

For any given article we expect to extract the main textual content providing information on the article's topic which should align with editorial standards and be relevant to the headline. Additionally, relevant meta-information, e.g. declaration of third parties involved, additional information related, but not part of the main content, can also be extracted. Explicitly excluded are:

- The headline
- Captions of figures, images, and other objects
- Tables, due to the lack of a normalized representation

All extracted paragraphs are to be considered non-optional, unless one or more of the following conditions are fulfilled:

- The paragraph's sole purpose is formatting
- The paragraph is or is part of a summary of the article's contents
- The paragraph solely consists of meta-information (e.g. mentioning a contributing third party)
- The paragraph is not directly semantically related to the articles' content

## D Standard Deviation of Compared Libraries

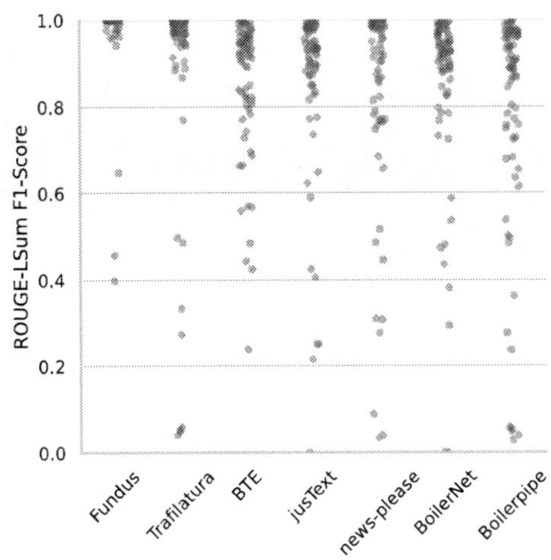


Figure 3: Distribution of ROUGE-LSum F1-scores of scraper extractions. The scrapers are sorted in descending order over the F1-score.

## E CC-NEWS Crawling

In addition to the examples outlined in Section 3.1, we aim to illustrate the ease of transitioning from forward to backward crawling. As depicted in Figure 4, this transition can be effortlessly achieved by substituting the employed crawler. Moreover, we offer a unified extraction interface, ensuring that switching between crawlers does not mandate parameter adjustments.

Listing 3: Crawl US-based publishers

```
crawler = Crawler(PublisherCollection.us)

# To retrieve articles from CC-NEWS instead
    one must simply exchange the pipeline
crawler =
    CCNewsCrawler(PublisherCollection.us)

for article in
    crawler.crawl(max_articles=100):
    print(article)
```

Figure 4: An example usage of Fundus to crawl articles from CC-NEWS

| Attribute | Description | Extraction | Methodology | Python type |
|---|---|---|---|---|
| **title** | Title of the news article | rule-based | metadata | str |
| **body** | Object that allows direct access to paragraphs | rule-based | selectors | custom |
| **authors** | Creators of the article | rule-based | mixed | list |
| **publishing_date** | Release date provided by the publisher | rule-based | mixed | datetime |
| **topics** | Publisher-assigned topics | rule-based | mixed | list |
| **free_access** | Boolean indicating free accessibility | mixed | mixed | bool |
| ld | JSON+LD data as extracted from the article | generic | selectors | custom |
| meta | HTML meta tags as parsed from the article | generic | selectors | dict |
| plaintext | Concatenated, stripped, and cleaned article body | - | - | str |
| lang | Auto-detected article language | - | - | str |
| html | contains raw HTML, origin URL, crawl date, and crawl source | - | - | custom |
| exception | Exception indicating if an exception occurred during extraction | - | - | Exception |

Table 6: Article attributes alongside their description, extraction method, the applied methodology, and used Python type.

# CharPoet: A Chinese Classical Poetry Generation System Based on Token-free LLM

**Chengyue Yu*†, Lei Zang*†, Jiaotuan Wang, Chenyi Zhuang, Jinjie Gu**
Ant Group
{yuchengyue.ycy, zanglei.zl, yunting.wjt,chenyi.zcy, jinjie.gujj}@antgroup.com

## Abstract

Automatic Chinese classical poetry generation has attracted much research interest, but achieving effective control over format and content simultaneously remains challenging. Traditional systems usually accept keywords as user inputs, resulting in limited control over content. Large language models (LLMs) improve content control by allowing unrestricted user instructions, but the token-by-token generation process frequently makes format errors. Motivated by this, we propose CharPoet, a Chinese classical poetry generation system based on token-free LLM, which provides effective control over both format and content. Our token-free architecture generates in a character-by-character manner, enabling precise control over the number of characters. Pruned from existing token-based LLMs, CharPoet inherits their pretrained capabilities and can generate poetry following instructions like "Write me a poem for my mother's birthday." CharPoet achieves format accuracy above 0.96, outperforming Jiuge-GPT-2 (0.91) and GPT-4 (0.38). In terms of content quality, CharPoet surpasses traditional systems including Jiuge, and is comparable to other LLMs. Our system is open source and available at `https://modelscope.cn/models/CharPoet/CharPoet`. A video demonstration of CharPoet is available at `https://youtu.be/voZ25qEp3Dc`.

Figure 1: Poem generated by GPT-4. The poem violates the format requirement of *Rumengling* with 6 excess characters.

## 1 Introduction

Chinese classical poetry, one of the most valuable heritages of human culture, conveys rich connotations through its concise and exquisite form. Chinese classical poetry can be classified into two primary categories: SHI and CI, both of which have strict format requirements (Hu and Sun, 2020). For example, Wuyanjueju, the simplest form of SHI, requires four lines with each line containing exactly five Chinese characters. CI is more complex: there are nearly one thousand forms in total, each with different requirements for the number of lines and characters.

Automatic generation of Chinese classical poetry has attracted much research interest. However, achieving effective control over both format and content simultaneously remains a challenge.

Traditional systems in this field usually take keywords as user inputs (Guo et al., 2019; Hu and Sun, 2020; Wang et al., 2016; Yan, 2016; Yi et al., 2017, 2018; Zhang and Lapata, 2014; Zhang et al., 2017). However, it is often insufficient for users to fully describe the theme or emotion they expect with just one or several keywords. This inability to process complex inputs has reduced the diversity and quality of the generated poetry. In contrast, Large Language Models (LLMs) can accept unrestricted user prompts and allow more control over the content. LLMs are capable of generating diversified texts following complex user instructions (OpenAI, 2022, 2023; the Qwen team, 2023). Nevertheless,

*Equal contribution.
†Corresponding authors.



*Proceedings of the 62nd Annual Meeting of the Association for Computational Linguistics (Volume 3: System Demonstrations)*, pages 315–325
August 11-16, 2024 ©2024 Association for Computational Linguistics

token-based LLMs face challenges in strictly adhering to the expected format of poetry, occasionally producing lines with an excess or insufficient number of characters.

An example of a GPT-4-generated poem is given in Figure 1. In this example, GPT-4 is asked to write a poem in the *Rumengling* form, with the keyword *cheerful*. The generated poem performs well in terms of content, but it clearly violates the format requirements. The redundant characters are marked in red with a strikethrough.

We argue that the problem is partly due to the token-based nature of LLMs. Standard token-based LLM systems split text into word pieces before feeding them into the model. These text pieces are known as *tokens*, and they usually contain more than one character (Sennrich et al., 2016; Schuster and Nakajima, 2012). The system must generate text in a token-by-token manner. Under such a setting, if a model needs to control the number of characters precisely, it must know exactly how many characters are contained in each token. We have conducted a simple test that shows LLMs clearly lack such knowledge. The results are provided in Appendix A.

Motivated by this, we propose CharPoet, a Chinese classical poetry generation system based on a token-free LLM, which achieves effective control over both format and content simultaneously. "Token-free" here means that our model operates only on characters or bytes, in contrast to regular tokens. As shown in Figure 2, our system generates poems in a character-by-character manner. With the token-free architecture, our system can precisely control the number of characters. Instead of being trained from scratch, our token-free LLM is pruned from existing token-based models. We remove long tokens from the tokenizer and the language model head, keeping only character-level and byte-level tokens, and then finetune on a poetry dataset. Through this pruning process, our system inherits capabilities from existing token-based LLMs, and can generate poetry following complex instructions such as "Write me a poem for my mother's birthday."

Without any post-processing, our token-free system achieves a format accuracy of 0.96, outperforming Jiuge-GPT-2 (0.91) and GPT-4 (0.38). In addition, our system performs comparably to existing LLMs in terms of the content quality.

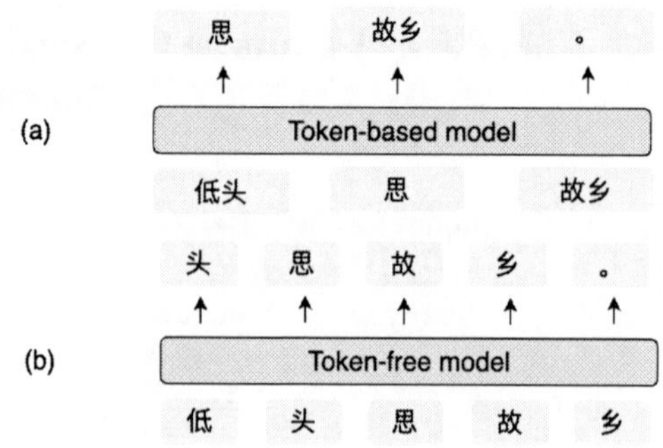


Figure 2: Generation process of a token-based model vs. a token-free model: (a) In a token-based model, the system may output more than one character at a time, resulting in difficulty in exerting precise control over the number of characters. (b) In a token-free model, the system outputs at most one character at a time, making control over the number of characters easier.

## 2 Related work

**Traditional systems** in this field (Zhang and Lapata, 2014; Wang et al., 2016; Yan, 2016; Yi et al., 2017, 2018; Guo et al., 2019) have demonstrated that RNNs and LSTMs can generate high-quality poetry. However, these systems usually accept keywords as user inputs, resulting in poor control over content. Moreover, they often have complex architectures or special modules designed to handle the strict format and content constraints inherent in poetry. For example, Yi et al. (2018) imposes a working memory mechanism; Guo et al. (2019) implements a postprocess module to filter poems with unexpected format.

**Large Language Models (LLMs)** (OpenAI, 2022, 2023; the Qwen team, 2023) have demonstrated the power of the Transformer architecture (Vaswani et al., 2017) when trained with a large corpus. LLMs are capable of generating high-quality and diversified poetry following unrestricted prompt. However, they suffer from problems with format accuracy due to their token-based nature.

More in line with our research, Hu and Sun (2020); Belouadi and Eger (2023) build poetry generation systems based on **token-free language models**. However, those systems are trained from scratch so they do not inherit the great power from pretrained LLMs. They still accept keywords as user inputs and cannot understand complex instructions.

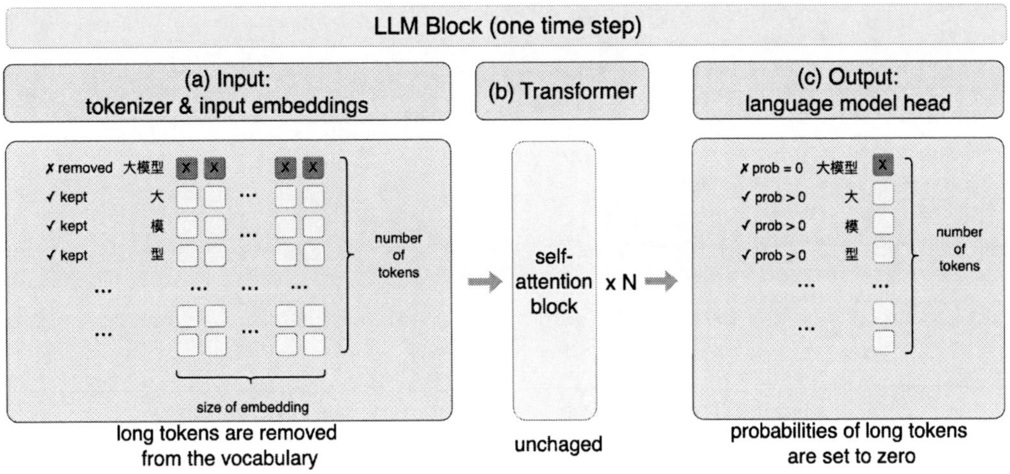


Figure 3: Prune a token-based model into a token-free one. (a) For *Input*, long tokens will be removed from the vocabulary. Text would only be tokenized into character-level or byte-level tokens; The embeddings of long tokens will never be accessed. (b) Transformer structure is left unchanged. (c) For *Output*, the logits of long tokens will be set to a large negative number and the probabilities of long tokens will be zero. The language model head would never produce long tokens.

## 3 Architecture

### 3.1 Pruning

The core of our system is a token-free LLM. Instead of being trained from scratch as in previous work (Belouadi and Eger, 2023), our token-free LLM is pruned from an existing token-based LLM to inherit the pretrained knowledge and capabilities. Our token-free model accepts unrestricted prompts as input and returns poems that excel in both format accuracy and content quality.

We have designed a procedure that can prune any typical token-based LLM into a token-free model. A typical LLM, such as Llama (the Llama team, 2023) and Qwen (the Qwen team, 2023), contains three components, the *Input* (the tokenizer and the input embeddings), the *Transformer* (Vaswani et al., 2017) and the *Output* (the language model head). Our pruning procedure modifies the *Input* component and the *Output* component, and leaves the *Transformer* component unchanged. The procedure is described below and illustrated in Figure 3.

**(a) Input Pruning.** We prune the tokenizer's vocabulary by removing all long tokens, leaving only character-level or byte-level fragments. *Long tokens* refer to two types: tokens with more than one Chinese character and tokens consisting of a single Chinese character combined with non-Chinese characters. Once these tokens are removed, the tokenizer will only produce character-level or byte-level fragments. Subsequently, the input embeddings for these removed tokens will never be accessed or updated.

We retain non-Chinese tokens as they are. This approach ensures that the keywords commonly used in LLM chat settings like "user" and "assistant", remain intact to preserve the standard tokenization of chat templates.

**(b) Transformer kept unchanged.** The structure of the Transformer is left unchanged, while the parameters will still be updated during finetuning.

**(c) Output Pruning.** For outputs, we set the probabilities of all long tokens to zero. This is achieved by incorporating an indicator function into the original softmax transformation:

$$\text{Prob}(t_i) = \frac{(1 - \mathbb{1}_L(i)) \exp(logit_i)}{\sum_j (1 - \mathbb{1}_L(j)) \exp(logit_j)}$$

where $logit_i$ denotes the neural network's output value of the $i$th token prior to the softmax transformation, and the indicator function determines if the $i$th token is a member of the long token set $L$.

$$\mathbb{1}_L(x) = \begin{cases} 1 & \text{if } x \in L \\ 0 & \text{if } x \notin L \end{cases}$$

In practice, we implement this by adding a large negative number to the logits of long tokens, instead of modifying the softmax function directly.

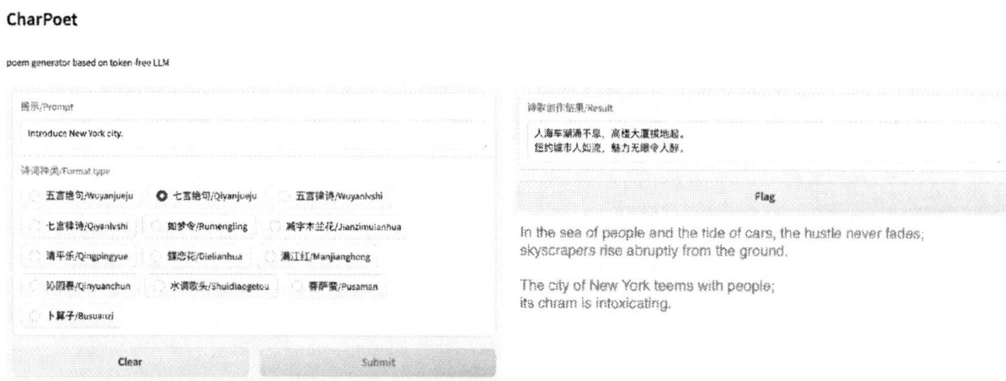


Figure 4: The user interface and generated poetry sample of CharPoet.

With the above procedure, any typical LLM could be pruned to a token-free model. In contrast to typical token-based LLMs, the pruned token-free model outputs text in a character-by-character manner and is expected to perform better on character-sensitive tasks such as poetry generation.

In this paper, we use Qwen-7B-Chat (the Qwen team, 2023) as the base model. An interesting observation is that even without further finetuning, the pruned token-free LLM is already capable of answering simple questions. We provide some examples in Appendix B. Nevertheless, we suggest further finetuning on the target dataset for better performance.

### 3.2 Training

Training involves two stages: general-purpose training and poetry-field training.

#### 3.2.1 General Purpose Training

We need general-purpose training because our model is directly pruned from an existing token-based LLM and not familiar with natural language presented at character level. Here we use BELLE dataset (Ji et al., 2023), which is a high-quality general-purpose instruction-following dataset.

#### 3.2.2 Poetry-field Training

In the second stage, we train with our in-house poetry dataset. The dataset contains 20000 human written poems, and each poem is created based on an input prompt. The prompts cover a broad range of topics, including specific scenes, emotions, and both concrete and abstract themes.

To improve format accuracy, we provide the model with a masked version of the expected poem as a format hint. In this *masked poem*, all Chinese characters are replaced with a mask sign **[M]** while punctuation and line breaks are kept as is. An example of a *masked poem* in the form *Rumengling* is provided in below.

```
[M][M][M][M][M][M],
[M][M][M][M][M][M]。
[M][M][M][M][M],
[M][M][M][M][M][M]。
[M][M],
[M][M],
[M][M][M][M][M][M]。
```

The *masked poem* is provided together with the original user prompt. The final prompt-response format is designed as follows, where **[SOP]** denotes *start of piece*, **[EOP]** denotes *end of piece*, **{ORIGINAL USER PROMPT}** denotes the original prompt from the user, **{MASKED POEM}** is the format hint, and **{POEM}** denotes the generated poem.

```
[SOP]user
Fill in all the masks [M].
{ORIGINAL USER PROMPT}
Output: {MASKED POEM}
[EOP]
[SOP]assistant
{POEM}
[EOP]
```

In this way, the poem-generating task is transformed into a mask-filling task. With the token-free architecture, our model fills in all the masks in a

| Format Type | #Chars | GPT-4 | Jiuge-GPT-2 | Qwen (Finetuned) | CharPoet (Ours) |
|---|---|---|---|---|---|
| | | keyword / instruction | keyword / instruction | keyword / instruction | keyword / instruction |
| **WuyanJueju (SHI)** | 20 | 0.49 / 0.73 | **1.00** / - | 0.94 / **1.00** | 0.98 / 0.99 |
| **WuyanLvshi (SHI)** | 40 | 0.29 / 0.36 | **1.00** / - | 0.97 / 0.98 | 0.97 / **0.99** |
| **QiyanJueju (SHI)** | 28 | 0.88 / 0.78 | **1.00** / - | 0.99 / **1.00** | **1.00 / 1.00** |
| **QiyanLvshi (SHI)** | 56 | 0.81 / 0.68 | **1.00** / - | 0.98 / 0.96 | 0.97 / **0.98** |
| **Rumengling (CI)** | 33 | 0.13 / 0.09 | 0.90 / - | 0.95 / 0.97 | **1.00 / 0.99** |
| **Jianzimulanhua (CI)** | 44 | 0.81 / 0.79 | 0.96 / - | 0.99 / 0.97 | **1.00 / 0.99** |
| **Busuanzi (CI)** | 44 | 0.28 / 0.24 | - / - | 0.92 / 0.96 | **0.93 / 0.98** |
| **Pusaman (CI)** | 44 | 0.26 / 0.17 | - / - | 0.96 / 0.92 | **0.98 / 0.97** |
| **Qingpingyue (CI)** | 46 | 0.13 / 0.18 | 0.96 / - | **0.98** / 0.97 | 0.95 / **0.99** |
| **Dielianhua (CI)** | 60 | 0.21 / 0.12 | 0.91 / - | 0.94 / **0.98** | **0.99 / 0.98** |
| **Manjianghong (CI)** | 93 | 0.07 / 0.04 | 0.83 / - | 0.88 / 0.90 | **0.95 / 0.95** |
| **Shuidiaogetou (CI)** | 95 | 0.04 / 0.00 | - / - | 0.89 / 0.87 | **0.95 / 0.91** |
| **Qinyuanchun (CI)** | 114 | 0.00 / 0.01 | 0.55 / - | 0.64 / 0.75 | **0.82 / 0.86** |
| **Avg (of 10)** | 53.4 | 0.382 / 0.378 | 0.911 / - | 0.926 / 0.948 | **0.963 / 0.972** |

Table 1: Evaluation on Format Accuracy. CharPoet outperforms other systems on average in both the keyword and instruction settings. CharPoet performs significantly better than other systems with longer poems, such as *Manjianghong*, *Shuidiaogetou* and *Qinyuanchun*. For comparability with previous studies, the average accuracy is calculated based on the overlapping 10 types of poetry, rather than all 13 types.

character-by-character manner. The mask-filling design ensures that the model can strictly follow the format constraints of the requested poetry type.

## 4 Demonstration

The user interface of our poetry generation system is shown in Figure 4. In contrast to previous systems where users need to summarize the theme of the poetry they want in one or several keywords, our system allows users to describe desired content with natural language in the prompt box. After that, the user selects a poetry form and clicks the "Submit" button. A few seconds later, the system returns a poem following the user's instruction.

Our system is fully open source, available at `https://modelscope.cn/models/CharPoet/CharPoet`. We have included a Jupyter notebook in the project. Using this notebook, anyone can launch the application and try our system. We also provide some example poems in Appendix C.

## 5 Evaluation

### 5.1 Test settings

We evaluate performance on two aspects: format accuracy and content quality.

For comparability with previous studies, we assess performance on four types of SHI and six types of CI, as in Hu and Sun (2020) exactly. To better study the relationship between format accuracy and the length of poetry, we have additionally included three popular types of form in the evaluation set, which are *Busanzi*, *Pusaman* and *Shuidiaogetou*.

We conduct tests under two user input settings: the first is the conventional keyword setting, where the user input consists of a single keyword; the second is the instruction setting, where the user input is a natural language instruction, such as "Write me a poem for my mother's birthday.". In both settings, one specific format is selected as the expected format.

We conduct 100 tests for each type of form and each setting. In the keyword setting, we use a collection of 100 frequently used Chinese idioms sourced from the internet. Chinese idioms convey rich meanings in simple expressions, and are thus more challenging than regular words. In the instruction setting, we ask GPT-4 to generate 100 prompts as user inputs. We have double-checked the GPT-generated prompts; they cover a broad range of topics, including specific scenes, emotions, and both concrete and abstract themes.

We do not use human-written prompts because human researchers could potentially manipulate the prompt set to alter research conclusions. For example, human researchers may remove the prompts

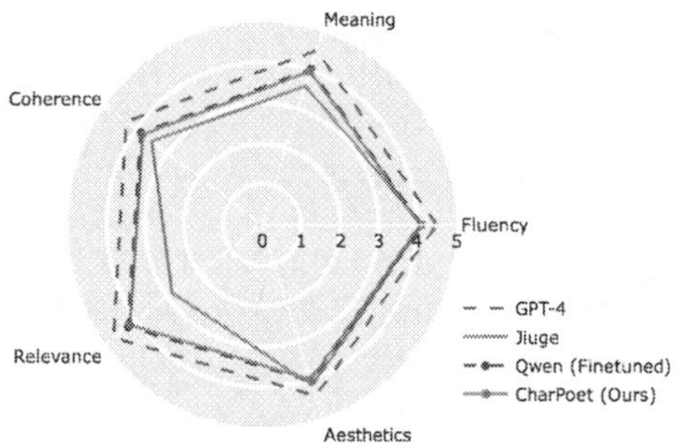


Figure 5: Evaluation on Content Quality by GPT-4 under the Keyword Setting.

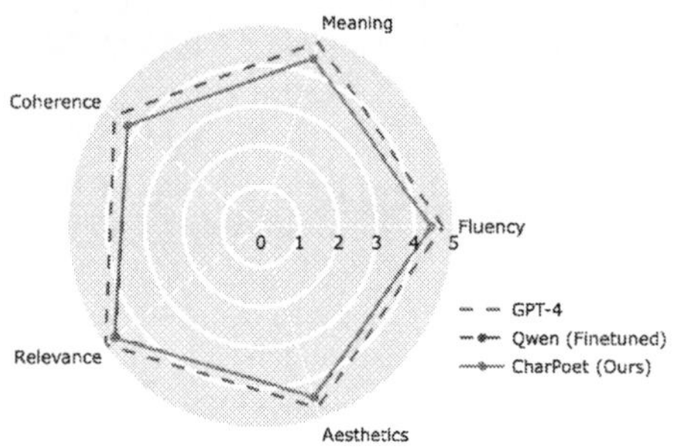


Figure 6: Evaluation on Content Quality by GPT-4 under the Instruction Setting.

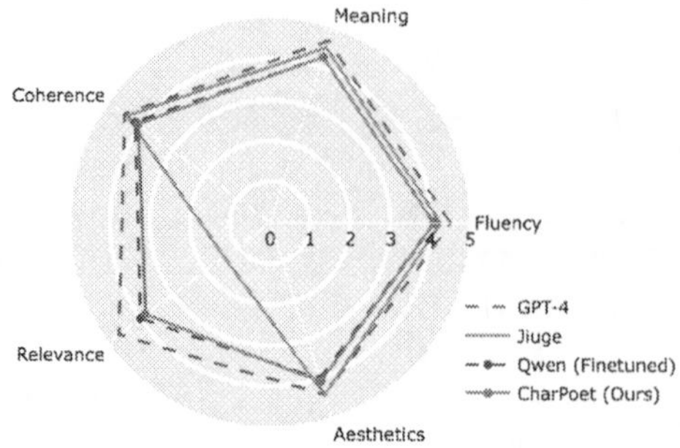


Figure 7: Evaluation on Content Quality by Human under the Keyword Setting.

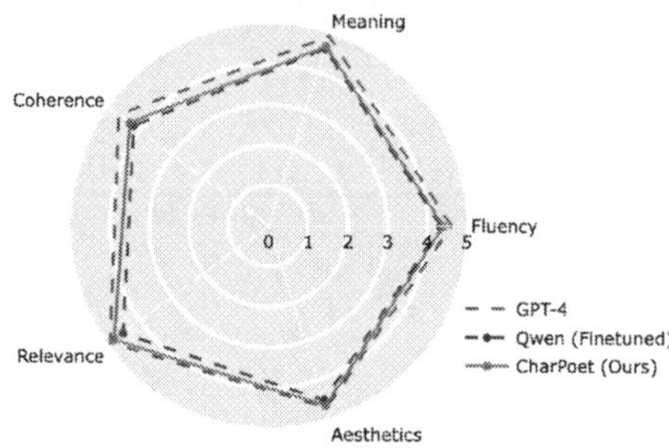


Figure 8: Evaluation on Content Quality by Human under the Instruction Setting.

where the model performs poorly, making the evaluation scores appear better. By directly using GPT-generated prompts without any modifications, we can effectively avoid biases caused by such manipulation issues.

### 5.2 Models for Comparison

We compare our system CharPoet with two categories of public available systems. One category is general-purpose LLMs, with GPT-4 (OpenAI, 2023) being the top performer. The other category is systems exclusively designed for automatic poetry generation, with Jiuge (Guo et al., 2019) being the most representative.

**GPT-4.** To exploit GPT-4's potential in format accuracy, we have carefully designed the prompt. We find that GPT performs better if provided with an example poem of the required form. The prompt template is provided in Appendix D.

**Jiuge.** Jiuge (Guo et al., 2019) is a comprehensive system with a postprocessing module to ensure format accuracy; therefore, when evaluating format accuracy, we compare instead with Jiuge-GPT-2 (Hu and Sun, 2020), the most recent work in the Jiuge series, which is more comparable since it is transformer-based and end-to-end.

**Ablation study.** To verify the effectiveness of our token-free architecture, we also conducted an ablation study, where we compared our system to its token-based equivalent. The token-based equivalent is identical to CharPoet in every aspect including model size, prompt design and training dataset, except that it is built on the original token-based Qwen-Chat (the Qwen team, 2023) instead of our pruned token-free version. The token-based equivalent is marked as *Qwen (Finetuned)* in corresponding tables and figures.

### 5.3 Evaluation on Format Accuracy

Format accuracy results are shown in Table 1. A poem is counted as accurate only if the number of characters for every line is correct (perfect match). The figures for Jiuge-GPT-2 are directly collected from the original paper, while the figures for other models are obtained from our testing procedure. The figures for Jiuge-GPT-2 under the instruction setting are not available since Jiuge-GPT-2 does not support user instructions. For comparability, the average accuracy is calculated based on the overlapping 10 types of poetry, rather than all 13 types.

CharPoet performs better in format accuracy than all competing models, achieving an overall accuracy above 0.96 under both settings. Our ablation study comparing CharPoet with its token-based equivalent Qwen (Finetuned) confirms that the token-free architecture is effective, bringing a 3% gain in format accuracy.

Consistent with Hu and Sun (2020), our results show that SHI is simple and all models listed here achieve decent accuracy. As for CI, which is more complex and challenging, our system beats previous systems by a large margin. For example, in terms of *Qinyuanchun*, the longest type of poem in our test set, our system achieves 0.84 accuracy, compared to 0.55 of Jiuge-GPT-2 and nearly zero of GPT-4. Regression analysis also indicates that CharPoet is less sensitive to poem length (See Appendix E for details).

### 5.4 Evaluation on Content Quality

Following Yi et al. (2018), we evaluate content quality with five criteria; each criterion needs to be scored on a 5-point scale:

**Fluency**. Does the poem obey the grammatical, structural and phonological rules?

**Meaning**. Does the poem convey some certain messages?

**Coherence**. Is the poem as a whole coherent in meaning and theme?

**Relevance**. Does the poem express user topics well?

**Aesthetics**. Does the poem have some poetic and artistic beauties?

We first ask GPT-4 to conduct the scoring process. Though we have seen in the previous section that GPT-4 performs poorly in a poetry format, it remains top-notch in terms of content quality, making it a qualified evaluator for content assessment. The GPT-4 results under the two settings are shown in Figure 5 and Figure 6. The performance of CharPoet is basically the same as that of Qwen (Finetuned) and not far from GPT-4, while it significantly surpasses Jiuge, especially in terms of *Relevance*. The gain in content relevance indicates that pretrained LLMs can provide significantly better control over content compared to traditional models.

To ensure the reliability of GPT's evaluation, we have also engaged human evaluators for double-checking. We ask human labelers to score a subset of the evaluation set independently (without referring to GPT-4). The human results under the two settings are shown in Figure 7 and Figure 8. The results are in general consistent with GPT-4. We have also calculated the correlations between human and GPT-4 judgments using Pearson, Spearman, and Kendall-Tau. All correlations are greater than 0.5 with p-values less than 0.01, indicating that GPT-4 is a qualified evaluator in our settings.

## 6 Conclusion

In this paper, we address the problem of achieving effective control over both format and content in the field of automatic Chinese classical poetry generation. We propose a token-free system CharPoet, which generates in a character-by-character manner, enabling precise control over the number of characters. Moreover, CharPoet allows for human instructions in natural language, in contrast to traditional models that only accept keywords.

CharPoet achieves format accuracy above 0.96 without any postprocessing, higher than Jiuge-GPT-2 (0.91) and GPT-4 (0.38). Our ablation study comparing CharPoet with its token-based equivalent shows that the token-free architecture brings a 3% gain in format accuracy. In addition, our system's performance in content quality surpasses traditional systems, and is comparable to existing LLMs.

## 7 Limitations

**Rhyme**. In this paper, we propose the token-free method to enhance format accuracy. As a side effect, the token-free method may also enhance *rhyme*, which is also a highly character-sensitive task. Rhyme is an important aspect in Chinese classical poetry and deserves further study. Though rhyme is somehow covered in our evaluation process as part of the *phonological rule* in the fluency criterion, it deserves direct research with specially designed criteria and detailed indicators, and this is left to future work.

**Other character-sensitive tasks & general ablilities.** We have proposed a simple method to convert a pretrained token-based language model to a token-free one. It may be interesting to further investigate how the converted model performs in other character-sensitive tasks, such as named entity recognition and spelling correction. It may also be interesting to investigate how much general knowledge and abilities are retained during the conversion. These topics are also left to future work.

## References

Jonas Belouadi and Steffen Eger. 2023. Bygpt5: End-to-end style-conditioned poetry generation with token-free language models. In *61st Annual Meeting of the Association for Computational Linguistics*. Association for Computational Linguistics (ACL).

Zhipeng Guo, Xiaoyuan Yi, Maosong Sun, Wenhao Li, Cheng Yang, Jiannan Liang, Huimin Chen, Yuhui Zhang, and Ruoyu Li. 2019. Jiuge: A human-machine collaborative chinese classical poetry generation system. In *Proceedings of the 57th annual meeting of the association for computational linguistics: system demonstrations*, pages 25–30.

Jinyi Hu and Maosong Sun. 2020. Generating major types of chinese classical poetry in a uniformed framework. In *Proceedings of the Twelfth Language Resources and Evaluation Conference*, pages 4658–4663.

Itay Itzhak and Omer Levy. 2022. Models in a spelling bee: Language models implicitly learn the character composition of tokens. In *Proceedings of the 2022 Conference of the North American Chapter of the Association for Computational Linguistics: Human Language Technologies*, pages 5061–5068.

Yunjie Ji, Yan Gong, Yong Deng, Yiping Peng, Qiang Niu, Baochang Ma, and Xiangang Li. 2023. Towards better instruction following language models for chinese: Investigating the impact of training data and evaluation.

Ayush Kaushal and Kyle Mahowald. 2022. What do tokens know about their characters and how do they know it? In *Proceedings of the 2022 Conference of the North American Chapter of the Association for Computational Linguistics: Human Language Technologies*, pages 2487–2507.

OpenAI. 2022. Introducing ChatGPT.

OpenAI. 2023. Gpt-4 technical report.

Long Ouyang, Jeff Wu, Xu Jiang, Diogo Almeida, Carroll L. Wainwright, Pamela Mishkin, Chong Zhang, Sandhini Agarwal, Katarina Slama, Alex Ray, John Schulman, Jacob Hilton, Fraser Kelton, Luke Miller, Maddie Simens, Amanda Askell, Peter Welinder, Paul Christiano, Jan Leike, and Ryan Lowe. 2022. Training language models to follow instructions with human feedback.

Mike Schuster and Kaisuke Nakajima. 2012. Japanese and korean voice search. In *International Conference on Acoustics, Speech and Signal Processing*, pages 5149–5152.

Rico Sennrich, Barry Haddow, and Alexandra Birch. 2016. Neural machine translation of rare words with subword units. In *54th Annual Meeting of the Association for Computational Linguistics*, pages 1715–1725. Association for Computational Linguistics (ACL).

the Llama team. 2023. Llama 2: Open foundation and fine-tuned chat models.

the Qwen team. 2023. Qwen technical report.

Ashish Vaswani, Noam Shazeer, Niki Parmar, Jakob Uszkoreit, Llion Jones, Aidan N Gomez, Łukasz Kaiser, and Illia Polosukhin. 2017. Attention is all you need. *Advances in neural information processing systems*, 30.

Daisy Zhe Wang, Wei He, Hua Wu, Haiyang Wu, Wei Li, Haifeng Wang, and Enhong Chen. 2016. Chinese poetry generation with planning based neural network. In *Proceedings of COLING 2016, the 26th International Conference on Computational Linguistics: Technical Papers*, pages 1051–1060.

Rui Yan. 2016. i, poet: automatic poetry composition through recurrent neural networks with iterative polishing schema. In *Proceedings of the Twenty-Fifth International Joint Conference on Artificial Intelligence*, pages 2238–2244.

Xiaoyuan Yi, Ruoyu Li, and Maosong Sun. 2017. Generating chinese classical poems with rnn encoder-decoder. In *Chinese Computational Linguistics and Natural Language Processing Based on Naturally Annotated Big Data: 16th China National Conference, CCL 2017, and 5th International Symposium, NLP-NABD 2017, Nanjing, China, October 13-15, 2017, Proceedings 16*, pages 211–223. Springer.

Xiaoyuan Yi, Maosong Sun, Ruoyu Li, and Zonghan Yang. 2018. Chinese poetry generation with a working memory model. In *Proceedings of the 27th International Joint Conference on Artificial Intelligence*, pages 4553–4559.

Jiyuan Zhang, Yang Feng, Dong Wang, Yang Wang, Andrew Abel, Shiyue Zhang, and Andi Zhang. 2017. Flexible and creative chinese poetry generation using neural memory. In *Proceedings of the 55th Annual Meeting of the Association for Computational Linguistics (Volume 1: Long Papers)*, pages 1364–1373.

Xingxing Zhang and Mirella Lapata. 2014. Chinese poetry generation with recurrent neural networks. In *Proceedings of the 2014 Conference on Empirical Methods in Natural Language Processing (EMNLP)*, pages 670–680.

## A Probing into LLM's knowledge in token-character relationship

For a token-based LLM, if it needs to control the number of characters precisely, it must know exactly how many characters are contained in each token. We have conducted a simple test, which shows that LLMs clearly lack such knowledge.

### A.1 Method

Following Itzhak and Levy (2022), we use a probing procedure called "spelling bee" to investigate how much a LLM knows about the token-character relationship of its vocabulary. Specifically, we probe whether the model has the knowledge that the token "大模型" contains three characters "大", "模" and "型".

The models we investigate here are the Qwen-series (the Qwen team, 2023), including Qwen-1.7B-chat, Qwen-7B-chat and Qwen-14B-chat. The Qwen series is one of the earliest open-source LLMs with a strong ability in Chinese and is influential in the Chinese community. In the context of large language models, the probing procedure could be formulated as an instruction following task, designed as follows.

**Prompt**

List all the characters in the following token: <|extra_1|>大模型

**Response**

大<|extra_1|>模<|extra_1|>型

Here the special symbol <|extra_1|> is used to ensure that both the long token in the prompt and the single characters in the response are tokenized as they are. We randomly selected 1000 tokens from the vocabulary to serve as a test set, and the remaining tokens are used as training examples.

Our procedure is not exactly the same as previous work (Kaushal and Mahowald, 2022; Itzhak and Levy, 2022). The main differences are

1. Our experiment probes all language model parameters, while previous work (Kaushal and Mahowald, 2022; Itzhak and Levy, 2022) probes only the vocabulary embedding, which ignores the knowledge contained in later layers, and thus would underestimate the real knowledge level.
2. In the context of large language models, we are able to conduct probing experiments relatively easily with the model itself through supervised finetuning (Ouyang et al., 2022), while previous work probes with a separate model, which may be difficult to train and would also underestimate the real knowledge level.

To sum up, we believe that our procedure can better estimate how LLM knows about the token-character relationship relationship.

### A.2 Results

The results of the spelling bee probing procedure are summarized with the *overall failure rate*, which is defined as the number of times that the LLM fails to correctly output the character sequence of the required token, divided by the size of the test set (which is 1000 in our experiment). We also pay attention to another version of the failure rate, where we count an output as a failure only if the number of characters in the output does not equal the length of the original token. This metric is more relevant since it directly influences the control of character numbers in poem generation.

| **Model Size** | **Token-based** overall / #chars | **Token-free** overall / #chars |
|---|---|---|
| **1.8B** | 15.1% / 2.5% | 0.7% / 0.2% |
| **7B** | 9.9% / 1.7% | 0.5% / 0.1% |
| **14B** | 4.1% / 0.9% | 0.4% / 0.0% |

Table 2: Failure rate of the spelling bee probing procedure. The token-free model has reduced the failure rate by more than 90% compared to the token-based model.

We have several observations:

1. Failure rates of token-based models are non-trivial. Failure rate near 1% seems small, but the influence is significant since mistakes would accumulate as the poem gets long.
2. The failure rate of token-based models seems not to vanish totally as model size increases.
3. The token-free model has reduced the failure rate by more than 90%.

## B Token-free LLM without further finetuning

Without further finetuning the pruned token-free LLM is already capable of answering simple questions. Examples are shown below.

**User:**
简要介绍一下日心说

**Agent:**
日心说，也称日心地动说，是16th century末期由哥白尼提出的天体学说，它将日、月、水星、金星、木星、土星、天王星、海王星和冥王星等9大天体，及小天体如彗星、小星体等，都绕着以日为圆心的椭圆轨转。

**User:**
Briefly introduce the heliocentric theory.

**Agent:**
The heliocentric theory is a model of the solar system that places the Sun at the center, with the planets orbiting around it in椭ical paths. This theory was proposed by Nicolaus Copernicus in the 16th century, but it was not widely accepted until the work of later astronomers such as Johannes Kepler and Galileo Galilei. The heliocentric model is now the most widely accepted model of the solar system, and it is supported by a vast amount of observational evidence.

We can see that the main meaning is correct, although there are some typos and a mix of Chinese and English.

## C Example Poems Generated by CharPoet

In the first example, our system is asked to write a poem with the keyword *cheerful* and the required form is *Rumengling*. This is exactly how we test GPT-4 in the Introduction section. We can see that poem generated by our system precisely match the required format of *Rumengling*, in contrast to GPT-4.

笑口频开深院，更说秋风天气。
With a frequent smile in the deep courtyard, I praise the autumn weather.
心事向人知，却好兴高采烈。
I share thoughts with others, in high spirits and delight.
休觅，休觅，酒到不知醒地。
Seek no more, seek no more. Drink till you do not know where you are.

More importantly, CharPoet allows for unrestricted instructions. In the following example, the prompt is "Write me a poem for my mother's birthday." and the required form is *Rumengling*. The output follows the expected format and content.

生日恰逢今日，母爱万金难拟。
Today is your birthday. A mother's love is priceless.
恩重更情浓，岁岁同歌同醉。
Your kindness is profound. We sing and celebrate together, in each passing year.
同醉，同醉，寿星高上天际。
Drink together, drink together. You are the star today.

## D Test the Performance of GPT-4 on Format Accuracy

To exploit GPT-4's potential in format accuracy, we have carefully designed the prompt. We find that GPT performs better if we provide it with an example poem of the required form. Our prompt is designed as follows.

**Prompt**

请写一首如梦令，主题或要求为“兴高采烈”。请严格按照如梦令对每一句话的字数要求，下面给出一个例子：

常记溪亭日暮，沉醉不知归路。
兴尽晚回舟，误入藕花深处。
争渡，争渡，惊起一滩鸥鹭。

**Prompt(translated into English)**

Please write a poem in the form “Rumengling”. The theme or instruction is “cheerful”. Please strictly follow the number of character requirements for each line. Here is an example:

I often recall the sun setting at the riverside pavilion, lost in the intoxication and unaware of the way back.
Later on when my excitement wanes, I return on the boat, only to find myself unwittingly entering a lotus pond.
Struggling to cross, struggling to cross, with seagulls and herons startled by me and flew away.

## E Relationship between Format Accuracy and Poem Length.

We performed a regression analysis to investigate how format accuracy changes with poem length. Results show that in general the format accuracy decreases as the poem length increases. Results also show that CharPoet is less sensitive to poem length compared to competing models.

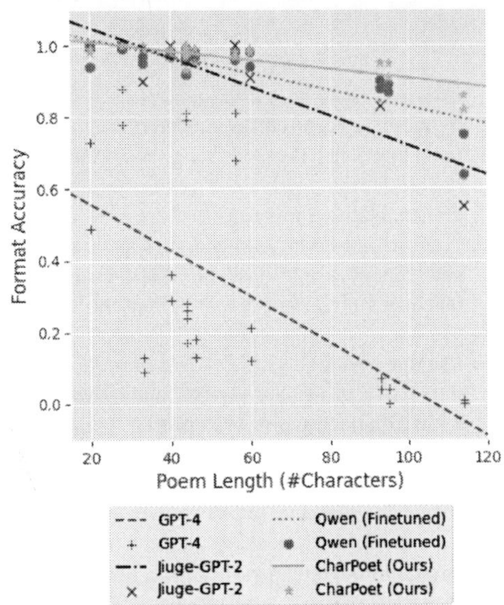


Figure 9: Relationship between Format Accuracy and Poem Length. Regression analysis indicates that the format accuracy of CharPoet is less sensitive to increase in the poem length.

# ITAKE: Interactive Unstructured Text Annotation and Knowledge Extraction System with LLMs and ModelOps

**Jiahe Song** [1,3] **Hongxin Ding**[1,3] **Zhiyuan Wang**[1,3] **Yongxin Xu**[1,3]
**Junfeng Zhao**[1,3,4*] **Yasha Wang**[1,2]
[1]Key Laboratory of High Confidence Software Technologies, Ministry of Education, Beijing, China
[2]National Engineering Research Center For Software Engineering, Peking University, Beijing, China
[3]School of Computer Science, Peking University, Beijing, China
[4]Big Data Technology Research Center, Nanhu Laboratory, Jiaxing, China
songjh@stu.pku.edu.cn, {zhaojf, wangyasha}@pku.edu.cn

## Abstract

Extracting structured knowledge from unstructured text data has a wide range of application prospects, and a pervasive trend is to develop text annotation tools to help extraction. However, they often encounter issues such as single scenario usage, lack of effective human-machine collaboration, insufficient model supervision, and suboptimal utilization of Large Language Models (LLMs). We introduces an interactive unstructured text annotation and knowledge extraction system that synergistically integrates LLMs and ModelOps to alleviate these issues. The system leverages LLMs for enhanced performance in low-resource contexts, employs a ModelOps platform to monitor models throughout their lifecycle, and amalgamates interactive annotation methods with online machine learning and active learning. The demo video[1] and website[2] are now publicly available.

## 1 Introduction

Unstructured text data contains a large amount of valuable knowledge, from which structured knowledge such as entities, relationships and attributes can be extracted to help the construction of knowledge graphs, and can also support downstream tasks, which has a wide range of application prospects. However, real-world text exists multi-language, a mixture of short and long text, and complex terminological references, etc. Unstructured text knowledge extraction methods based solely on machine intelligence are far from meeting the needs of actual business. For example, on the publicly available datasets WNUT-17 (Derczynski et al., 2017), DocRED (Yao et al., 2019), the highest F1-score for named entity recognition and relation extraction are only 60.45% (Wang et al., 2021) and 67.53% (Ma et al., 2023). Besides, the cost of relying only on human annotation is very expensive.

Currently, there are many open-source text annotation tools dedicated to solving the above challenges, but they have some problems resulting in a not-so-perfect process. First of all, some of the tools are used in a single scenario, targeting a fixed application domain, ontology and language (**Challenge C1**). For example, MedCat (Kraljevic et al., 2021) only supports English and is limited to medical data annotation. Secondly, most of the tools lack the organic combination of human and machine, resulting in too much user participation to increase the cost (Stenetorp et al., 2012; Nakayama et al., 2018) or lack of user feedback leading to poor modeling accuracy (Zhang et al., 2022b) especially in low resource situation (**Challenge C2**). In addition, even if models are involved in the extraction process of some tools (Kraljevic et al., 2021; Zhang et al., 2022b), there is a lack of model supervision and state analysis in the process of using them, and the reuse support capability for models and datasets is weak, which prevents the rapid development and deployment of models for specific domain requirements (**Challenge C3**). Finally, after the popularity of LLMs (Brown et al., 2020; Touvron et al., 2023; Du et al., 2022) , many extraction tools intergrated LLMs to assist extraction (Wei et al., 2023; Zhang et al., 2022b). However, although LLMs are more effective than traditional knowledge extraction state-of-the-art model (**hereinafter referred to as the extraction model**) in low resource situation because of their strong generalization ability, the improvement effect of LLMs is not obvious after the increase of training data, and when they reaches a certain threshold, their effect is far worse than that of well-trained extraction model (Wang et al., 2023a). At the same time, LLMs are conversational generative models, which lead to slower inference speed and are difficult to meet the real-time demand (**Challenge C4**).

* Corresponding Author
[1]https://youtu.be/d_8vbdzdIe8
[2]http://itake.askgraph.site



*Proceedings of the 62nd Annual Meeting of the Association for Computational Linguistics (Volume 3: System Demonstrations)*, pages 326–334
August 11-16, 2024 ©2024 Association for Computational Linguistics

Aiming at the above problem, we developed **ITAKE** (an **I**nteractive unstructured **T**ext **A**nnotation and **K**nowledge **E**xtraction system) that integrates LLMs and ModelOps (Hummer et al., 2019). Specifically, (1) addressing **Challenge C1** and **Challenge C3**, we adopt ModelOps platform to integrate different models and monitor whole lifecycle of them. (2) Addressing **Challenge C2**, we combine the interactive annotation methods for online machine learning (Fontenla-Romero et al., 2013) and active learning (Shen et al., 2017). (3) Addressing **Challenge C4**, we integrate LLMs under low resources situation and use extraction models for well-labeled situation.

## 2 Architecture

ITAKE consists of two subsystems as **Fig.1** shows.

### 2.1 Intelligent Knowledge Extraction Based on Human-Machine Collaboration Subsystem

This part consists of three parts: Project Management, Pre-annotation and Model Selection, Model Tuning and Batch Knowledge Extraction. **Project Management** is to manage the information and users of each knowledge extraction task; **Pre-annotation and Model Selection** is designed for domain experts to perform unsupervised knowledge extraction of unstructured data using LLMs; **Model Tuning and Batch Knowledge Extraction** uses active learning to selectively annotate fewer data in order to train the optimal model to the user's desired accuracy, after which it can proceed to batch knowledge extraction.

### 2.2 ModelOps-based Full Lifecycle Monitor of Models Subsystem

This part consists of five parts: LLMs Service (fine-tuning and extraction), Knowledge Extraction Model Selection and Recommendation Service, Knowledge Extraction Model Pool, Datasets Management and Model Lifecycle Management. Specifically, **LLMs Service** provides support for LLM fine-tuning such as ChatGLM (Du et al., 2022), Baichuan (Baichuan, 2023) and extraction, which solves the knowledge extraction cold start problem (Wang et al., 2023a); **Knowledge Extraction Model Selection and Recommendation Service** obtains the models from the model pool and performs training and comparison to provide the optimal models; **Knowledge Extraction Model Pool** accesses different models to solve the problems of nested entity and overlapped relationship, and unifies the management of a series of extraction models; **Model Lifecycle Management** unifies the release, management, and retrieval of LLMs and extraction models; **Datasets Management** can save and reuse knowledge extraction results.

## 3 Modules

### 3.1 Project Management

Project management encompasses tasks such as dataset uploading and data cleansing. ITAKE's upload interface supports different language texts, ontology models and file-type. Furthermore, ITAKE's backend deploys well-fine-tuned LLMs and well-trained extraction models for different domains, and by combining the above features, ITAKE can provide good extraction support for texts in different domains, thus solving the **Challenge C1**.

To ensure that the text datasets align with the requirements for subsequent knowledge extraction, ITAKE offers customizable rules for data cleansing and organization. Given the varied structure and content of unstructured text, datasets exhibit unique compositional features and semantic emphases. To address this, ITAKE introduces "iterative algorithms for user selection," empowering users to tackle these challenges effectively. The system is equipped with a range of universal algorithms at the backend, which can be dynamically invoked by users via the frontend interface, facilitating the efficient removal of redundant data. Additionally, ITAKE provides multiple processing options for dealing with specific types of unstructured text. In the realm of cleansing rule design, ITAKE employs a strategy that diversifies cleansing algorithms based on the distinct needs of various tasks and datasets.

### 3.2 LLM Fine-tuning and Extraction

Although LLMs have now developed rapidly and are widely used in knowledge extraction, they still perform poorly when oriented to specific domains, such as biomedical and financial domain, due to insufficient domain-specific training data(Keraghel et al., 2024). Therefore, we propose a method that integrates LLMs knowledge to enhance the performance of specific-domain models. Firstly, we improve the structure of the LLMs model to make it more adaptable to knowledge extraction and preserve the structural characteristics. Secondly, we

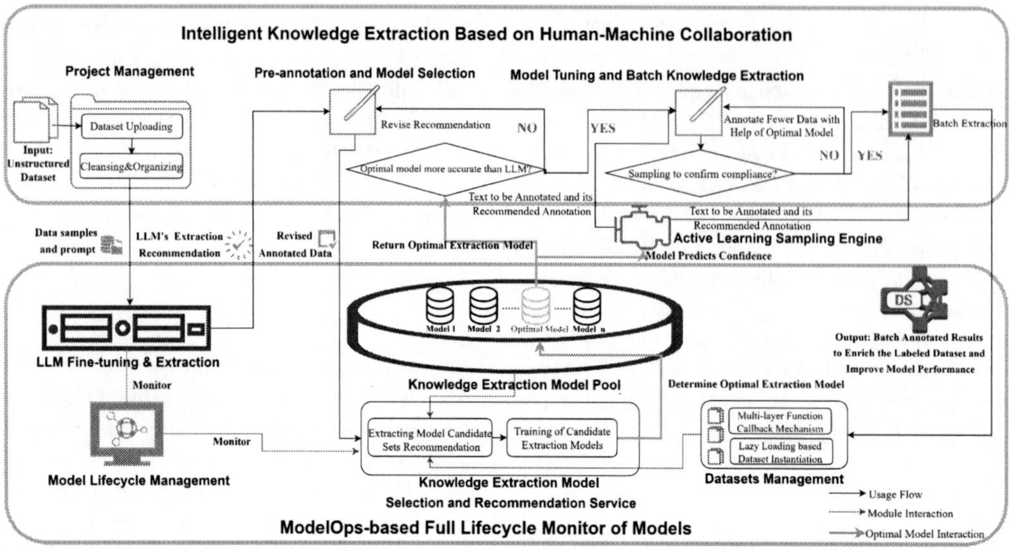

Figure 1: Architecture of ITAKE. Top: Intelligent Knowledge Extraction Based on Human-Machine Collaboration subsystem. Bottom: ModelOps-based Full Lifecycle Monitor of Models subsystem.

adopt the LoRA fine-tuning method and incorporate vocabulary information into the model training, making the training process more efficient. Finally, to fully utilize the fine-tuned LLM to enhance the specific-domain model, we convert the output of the LLMs into a knowledge concentration matrix and inject it into the model (Wang et al., 2023b). Specifically, after uploading the dataset, the user can select the LLM fine-tuned with data from the corresponding domain or similar domains according to the type of the uploaded dataset to be used as the base model for recommendation in the pre-annotation stage. It is important to note that during the subsequent knowledge extraction process, we will not fine-tune the LLMs using annotated data within the system. Instead, we will only utilize the LLMs API for inference. This approach is adopted because fine-tuning LLMs requires a substantial amount of annotated data and computational resources, which contradicts the objective of performing lightweight knowledge extraction tasks within ITAKE. Specifically, for LLMs already deployed on servers, we will employ a method similar to that of ChatGPT. The text requiring inference and the prompts will be transmitted to the LLMs via network requests using the LLM's native API in their deployment documents. This approach allows for the LLMs and ITAKE to be deployed on different servers, thereby reducing coupling and enhancing deployment efficiency and reusability.

### 3.3 Pre-annotation and Model Selection

To tackle the challenge of a scarcity of labeled data in specific fields, we employ LLMs for providing recommendations. In detail, upon the user engaging the "Get Large Language Model Recommendation" button, the extraction tool's backend transfers the present text along with its associated prompt to the LLM previously chosen, thereby acquiring a recommendation. Users are then tasked with revising these suggested outcomes. The modified results are subsequently forwarded to a candidate knowledge extraction model for its training. The criteria for selecting these alternative models will be elaborated upon in the subsequent section. The main annotation page is shown in **Fig.2**, which is similar to **3.5**.

### 3.4 Knowledge Extraction Model Recommendation and Selection Service.

This phase is divided into two stages: the recommendation of candidate models, and the selection of a model after the training of candidate models. Initially, to address the challenge of selecting appropriate knowledge extraction models, ITAKE has designed and implemented a dataset similarity-based model recommendation approach. This method employs Maximum Mean Discrepancy (MMD) (Gretton et al., 2006) and the Fréchet distance (FD) (Eiter and Mannila, 1994) to calculate similarities between datasets. These similarity metrics are then

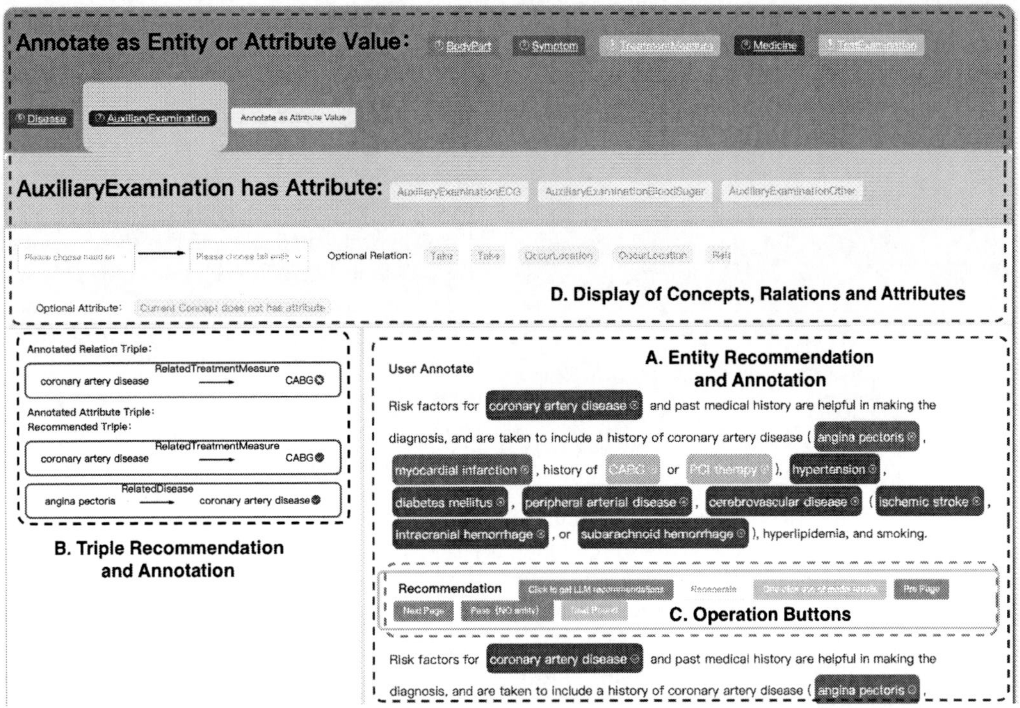


Figure 2: The main annotation page is divided into four main sections, which are **A.**Entity Recommendation and Annotation, **B.**Triple Recommendation and Annotation, **C.**Operation Buttons and **D.**Display of Concepts, Relations and Attributes. Users can manually annotate or use recommendations directly, which is detailed shown in video.

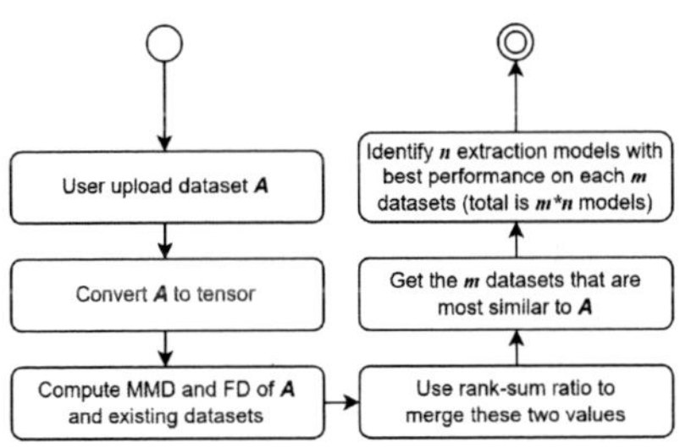


Figure 3: Workflow of Knowledge Extraction Model Recommendation

merged using the rank-sum ratio method to compute the overall dataset similarity.

Building on the computation of dataset similarity, the system devises a recommendation method for extraction models. It aims to recommend the optimal model for the uploaded dataset, thereby eliminating the need for repeated trials across numerous models, as illustrated in **Fig.3**. Specifically, for the uploaded dataset $\boldsymbol{A}$, ITAKE identifies $m$ datasets most similar to $\boldsymbol{A}$ through dataset similarity calculations. Subsequently, it identifies $n$ extraction models with the best performance on each of these $m$ datasets, where both $m$ and $n$ can be user-defined. After training the $m$*$n$ models with revised annotations, ITAKE ranks the candidate models based on various training metrics, such as precision and F1-score, facilitating user selection. The setting page is shown in **Fig.4**. Through this process, ITAKE provides users with more precise and targeted model recommendations, significantly reducing the time and effort users spend on model selection and adjustment.

### 3.5 Model Tuning and Batch Knowledge Extraction

When the accuracy of the optimal model surpasses LLM, the annotation process advances to the second phase: model tuning and batch knowledge extraction. At this stage, the model for knowledge extraction is the optimal model, selected by the user after comparing the training matrics of various candidate extraction models. The selection of unlabeled texts from ModelOps to be returned to the extraction subsystem is determined by an active learning sampling engine. Active learning is a research area within machine learning, employs sampling strategies to identify the samples

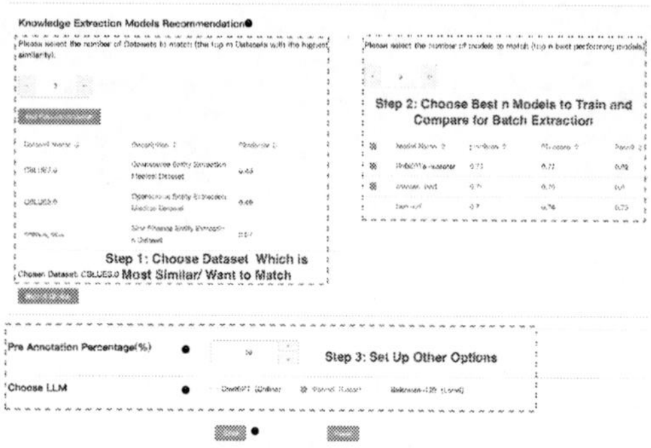


Figure 4: Pre-annotation settings can be set up in 3 steps as shown in the figure.

most beneficial for current model training (Shen et al., 2017; Settles, 2009). This approach aims to maximize model performance gains with a minimal number of samples, thereby reducing the data volume required to reach a predetermined performance benchmark.

To significantly reduce the total volume of text users must manually extract, ITAKE employs active learning methodology. We designs and tests various active learning sample selection strategies, encompassing strategies based on uncertainty, sample diversity, and a combination of both. Uncertainty-based strategies include the least confidence method (Agrawal et al., 2021), margin-based method (Balcan et al., 2007), and entropy-based method (Holub et al., 2008). The strategy based on sample diversity employs the K-means method (Vu et al., 2010), while the hybrid strategy integrates the gradient-based badge (Ash et al., 2019) method. The effect of active learning will be shown in Case Study and Evaluation. Once the model training meets the expected performance, ITAKE proceeds with the automatic batch extraction of the remaining texts, requiring users only to export the results without verifying.

Both parts **3.3** and **3.5** use models (LLMs or extraction models) for recommendation, which effectively reduces the user's labeling cost; at the same time, the system returns the higher quality extraction results annotated by the user to the model pool for model training, which ensures effective feedback from the human in the loop and enables the model accuracy to be steadily improved, thus solving **Challenge C2**. At the same time, these two parts integrate LLMs under low resources situation and use extraction models for well-labeled situations, ensuring a balance between efficiency and accuracy, thus addressing **Challenge C4**.

## 3.6 Dataset Management

Dataset management encompasses three key components: design of dataset specifications, implementation of multi-layer callback functions, and dataset instantiation via a lazy loading strategy. It is well known that, data standards serve as normative constraints that ensure uniformity, precision, and integrity of data, facilitating a common understanding, utilization, and exchange across various business systems. To streamline the integration for dataset providers and model developers, ITAKE adopts a unified dataset specification standard. It is important to underscore that ITAKE does not mandate users to pre-process the dataset to conform to this standard. Instead, it leverages a multi-layer callback function architecture to effectuate this transformation process.

Callback functions are a functional programming technique that encapsulates the logic of dataset processing and feature extraction into separate functions that are passed as arguments to other functions. This design allows the tool to dynamically change the processing flow at runtime for efficient adaptation between datasets and models. A common machine learning workflow in the dataset processing and model development phase is: acquiring data, data normalization, feature extraction, constructing a dataset class and a data loader. Based on this flow, ITAKE is designed with multiple layers of callback functions. In addition, in order to process data only when it is really needed (e.g., for model training, evaluation, or prediction), ITAKE employs a dataset instantiation method based on a lazy loading strategy.

## 3.7 Model Lifecycle Management

Users can monitor the performance of the model in real time, such as precision and F1-score. At the same time, they can track and monitor the training of the model in real time, such as CPU occupancy, memory information, etc. In addition, by combining with the dataset management module, the system can match and recommend the trained model based on the dataset similarity to be used for the recommendation of the results of the knowledge extraction, which greatly improves the re-usability of the model and the dataset. Through **3.4**, **3.6** and **3.7**, ITAKE provides effective reuse of models and datasets while providing management of full model lifecycle, thus addressing **Challenge C3**.

| | Scope of Application | | Technical | | | | Model Service | | Reusability | |
|---|---|---|---|---|---|---|---|---|---|---|
| **Tools** | **[A1]** | **[A2]** | **[B1]** | **[B2]** | **[B3]** | **[B4]** | **[C1]** | **[C2]** | **[D1]** | **[D2]** |
| **Doccano** | ✓ | ✓ | - | - | - | ✓ | - | - | - | - |
| **MedCAT** | - | - | - | ✓ | - | ✓ | - | - | ✓ | ✓ |
| **FAMIE** | ✓ | ✓ | - | ✓ | ✓ | ✓ | - | - | ✓ | ✓ |
| **DeepKE** | ✓ | ✓ | ✓ | ✓ | - | - | - | - | ✓ | ✓ |
| **CollabKG** | ✓ | ✓ | ✓ | - | - | - | - | - | - | - |
| **Autodive** | ✓ | ✓ | - | ✓ | - | ✓ | - | - | - | - |
| **ITAKE** | ✓ | ✓ | ✓ | ✓ | ✓ | ✓ | ✓ | ✓ | ✓ | ✓ |

Table 1: Comparison of some of the current knowledge extraction tools, selected on the basis of being popular or published in relevant conferences (e.g. ACL, EMNLP, etc.)

## 4 Evaluation and Case Study

### 4.1 Evaluation by Comparison with Other Tools

We compared ITAKE with some popular or already published annotation tools at relevant conferences, including Doccano (Nakayama et al., 2018), MedCAT (Kraljevic et al., 2021), FAMIE (Nguyen et al., 2022), DeepKE (Zhang et al., 2022b), CollabKG (Wei et al., 2023), Autodive (Du et al., 2023), to evaluate the system's performance. The comparison metrics discarded some traditional and commonly implemented features and instead focused on some innovative metrics as bellows: The first is **[A]. Scope of Application**, which includes *[A1]. Multidisciplinary* and *[A2]. Multilingual*. The second is **[B]. Technical**, which includes *[B1]. LLM, [B2]. Knowledge Extraction Model, [B3]. Active Learning* and *[B4]. Human-in-the-loop*. The third is **[C]. Model Service**, which includes *[C1]. Recommendation for What Model to Use* and *[C2]. Monitoring of Model*. The fourth is **[D]. Reusability**, which includes *[D1]. Reusability of Model* and *[D2]. Reusability of Dataset*. The comparison **Table 1** is as follows.

As can be seen from the comparison in the table, ITAKE's ability in model management and service is significantly better than other tools. In addition, ITAKE organically combines LLMs, extraction models, human-in-the-loop and active learning, which can significantly reduce costs and increase efficiency. Finally, ITAKE improves the reusability of datasets and models through dataset and model recommendation.

### 4.2 Case Study in Medical Knowledge Extraction

Knowledge extraction tasks play a crucial role in the healthcare domain by facilitating information structuring, feature extraction, and reasoning (Rajabi and Kafaie, 2022). Therefore, we carried out a batch of medical data knowledge extraction by cooperating with doctors from authoritative hospitals. Firstly, through the **Project Management** page, we uploaded the medical emergency guidelines to be annotated, while the ontology model was defined by professional doctors. After uploading the dataset, the **Dataset Management** module has already started the processing of the data in the background. The third step is to select our autonomously fine-tuned medical LLM called **Xiaobei**, which is fine-tuned by using medical knowledge on baichuan2-13b-chat (Baichuan, 2023) through **LLM Fine-tuning and Extraction**. In the fourth step **Knowledge Extraction Model Recommendation and Selection Service** module, the setting of $m$ is 2, $n$ is 3, and the recommended datasets are CBLUE2.0, CBLUE3.0 (Zhang et al., 2022a) where CBLUE3.0 is selected cause it has higher similarity. The three models corresponding to CBLUE3.0 are RoBERTa-adapter (Poth et al., 2021), BERT-CRF (Souza et al., 2019) and Chinese-BERT (Cui et al., 2020). After selecting the LLM and the extraction model to be used, we came to the fifth step of **Pre-annotation and Model Selection**. With a small amount of guidance from professional doctors, we asked 10 postgraduate medical students to annotate 400 texts with the entities recommended by Xiaobei, and trained all three models, with a training time of about $\mathbf{2.3}\boldsymbol{h}$. The recall rates of the training were $\mathbf{73.7\%}$, $\mathbf{75.6\%}$, and $\mathbf{75.4\%}$, respectively, and thus BERT-CRF was finally selected as the final extraction model. In the sixth step of the **Model Tuning and Batch Knowledge Extraction** , we again asked students to annotate about 200 texts to train the BERT-CRF model. At this point, we sampled

| Datasets | Random | Entropy | Least Confidence | Margin | Kmeans | Badge |
|---|---|---|---|---|---|---|
| **CMeEE** | 10.14 | **7.25** | 17.39 | 14.49 | 8.70 | 11.59 |
| **CMeIE** | 42.25 | **33.80** | 47.89 | 50.70 | 42.25 | 46.62 |

Table 2: The percentage(%) of samples that need to be trained to reach the training target using different active learning approach. It can be seen that active learning can reduce the training data obviously while basically guaranteeing performance, while the Entropy-based sampling strategy uses the least amount of training data.

50 texts with model-recommended entities for expert checking, stopped manual confirmation after the recall rate reached $\mathbf{85\%}$, and directly performed batch automatic extraction on all remaining texts. In the end, we sliced **3,857** texts from 8 emergency guidelines and obtained **7,018** entity records from nine concepts: disease, clinical presentation, medical procedure, medical device, drug, medical test item, body, department, and microbiological class.

### 4.3 Evaluation of Active Learning

In order to reflect the effect of active learning in reducing data required for training, we first train the model using full data. On the CMeEE (Zhang et al., 2022a) dataset, the model achieves an optimal F1-score of $\mathbf{64.77\%}$ on the validation set, and on the CMeIE (Zhang et al., 2022a) dataset, the model achieves an optimal F1-score of $\mathbf{75.33\%}$ on the validation set for entity prediction, and $\mathbf{59.32\%}$ for relation prediction.

We then selected $\mathbf{90\%}$ of the performance of the model trained using the full amount of data as the targets and examined the percentage of samples that need to be trained to reach the training target using the active learning approach. The lower the percentage of samples needed, the more effective this active learning sampling strategy is. The experimental results are shown in **Table 2**.

## 5 Conclusion and Future Work

We developed ITAKE, a knowledge extraction system that combines LLMs and ModelOps. Its usability and cost reduction have been fully demonstrated through real case study. In the future, we hope to add events and multi-modal extraction, and add the LLMs self-feedback mechanism, so as to reduce human cost more effectively.

## Limitations

As a knowledge extraction system, ITAKE lacks of support for nested, overlapping, or hierarchical entities, which is a complex and important aspect of the NER field. Besides, ITAKE does not facilitate collaborative use, limiting its applicability in complex and team-based settings.

## Acknowledgments

This work is supported by the National Natural Science Foundation of China (No.U23A20468).

## References

Ankit Agrawal, Sarsij Tripathi, and Manu Vardhan. 2021. Active learning approach using a modified least confidence sampling strategy for named entity recognition. *Progress in Artificial Intelligence*, 10:113–128.

Jordan T Ash, Chicheng Zhang, Akshay Krishnamurthy, John Langford, and Alekh Agarwal. 2019. Deep batch active learning by diverse, uncertain gradient lower bounds. *arXiv preprint arXiv:1906.03671*.

Baichuan. 2023. Baichuan 2: Open large-scale language models. *arXiv preprint arXiv:2309.10305*.

Maria-Florina Balcan, Andrei Broder, and Tong Zhang. 2007. Margin based active learning. In *International Conference on Computational Learning Theory*, pages 35–50. Springer.

Tom Brown, Benjamin Mann, Nick Ryder, Melanie Subbiah, Jared D Kaplan, Prafulla Dhariwal, Arvind Neelakantan, Pranav Shyam, Girish Sastry, Amanda Askell, et al. 2020. Language models are few-shot learners. *Advances in neural information processing systems*, 33:1877–1901.

Yiming Cui, Wanxiang Che, Ting Liu, Bing Qin, Shijin Wang, and Guoping Hu. 2020. Revisiting pre-trained models for Chinese natural language processing. In *Proceedings of the 2020 Conference on Empirical Methods in Natural Language Processing: Findings*, pages 657–668, Online. Association for Computational Linguistics.

Leon Derczynski, Eric Nichols, Marieke van Erp, and Nut Limsopatham. 2017. Results of the WNUT2017 shared task on novel and emerging entity recognition. In *Proceedings of the 3rd Workshop on Noisy User-generated Text*, pages 140–147, Copenhagen, Denmark. Association for Computational Linguistics.

Yi Du, Ludi Wang, Mengyi Huang, Dongze Song, Wenjuan Cui, and Yuanchun Zhou. 2023. Autodive: An integrated onsite scientific literature annotation tool. In *Proceedings of the 61st Annual Meeting of the Association for Computational Linguistics (Volume 3: System Demonstrations)*, pages 76–85, Toronto, Canada. Association for Computational Linguistics.

Zhengxiao Du, Yujie Qian, Xiao Liu, Ming Ding, Jiezhong Qiu, Zhilin Yang, and Jie Tang. 2022. Glm: General language model pretraining with autoregressive blank infilling. In *Proceedings of the 60th Annual Meeting of the Association for Computational Linguistics (Volume 1: Long Papers)*, pages 320–335.

Thomas Eiter and Heikki Mannila. 1994. Computing discrete fréchet distance.

Óscar Fontenla-Romero, Bertha Guijarro-Berdiñas, David Martinez-Rego, Beatriz Pérez-Sánchez, and Diego Peteiro-Barral. 2013. Online machine learning. In *Efficiency and Scalability Methods for Computational Intellect*, pages 27–54. IGI global.

Arthur Gretton, Karsten Borgwardt, Malte Rasch, Bernhard Schölkopf, and Alex Smola. 2006. A kernel method for the two-sample-problem. *Advances in neural information processing systems*, 19.

Alex Holub, Pietro Perona, and Michael C Burl. 2008. Entropy-based active learning for object recognition. In *2008 IEEE Computer Society Conference on Computer Vision and Pattern Recognition Workshops*, pages 1–8. IEEE.

Waldemar Hummer, Vinod Muthusamy, Thomas Rausch, Parijat Dube, Kaoutar El Maghraoui, Anupama Murthi, and Punleuk Oum. 2019. Modelops: Cloud-based lifecycle management for reliable and trusted ai. In *2019 IEEE International Conference on Cloud Engineering (IC2E)*, pages 113–120. IEEE.

Imed Keraghel, Stanislas Morbieu, and Mohamed Nadif. 2024. A survey on recent advances in named entity recognition. *arXiv preprint arXiv:2401.10825*.

Zeljko Kraljevic, Thomas Searle, Anthony Shek, Lukasz Roguski, Kawsar Noor, Daniel Bean, Aurelie Mascio, Leilei Zhu, Amos A Folarin, Angus Roberts, Rebecca Bendayan, Mark P Richardson, Robert Stewart, Anoop D Shah, Wai Keong Wong, Zina Ibrahim, James T Teo, and Richard J B Dobson. 2021. Multi-domain clinical natural language processing with MedCAT: The medical concept annotation toolkit. *Artif. Intell. Med.*, 117:102083.

Youmi Ma, An Wang, and Naoaki Okazaki. 2023. Dreeam: Guiding attention with evidence for improving document-level relation extraction. In *Proceedings of the 17th Conference of the European Chapter of the Association for Computational Linguistics: Main Volume*, EACL, page (to appear), Dubrovnik, Croatia. Association for Computational Linguistics.

Hiroki Nakayama, Takahiro Kubo, Junya Kamura, Yasufumi Taniguchi, and Xu Liang. 2018. doccano: Text annotation tool for human. Software available from https://github.com/doccano/doccano.

Minh Van Nguyen, Nghia Ngo, Bonan Min, and Thien Nguyen. 2022. FAMIE: A fast active learning framework for multilingual information extraction. In *Proceedings of the 2022 Conference of the North American Chapter of the Association for Computational Linguistics: Human Language Technologies: System Demonstrations*, pages 131–139, Hybrid: Seattle, Washington + Online. Association for Computational Linguistics.

Clifton Poth, Jonas Pfeiffer, Andreas R"uckl'e, and Iryna Gurevych. 2021. What to pre-train on? Efficient intermediate task selection. In *Proceedings of the 2021 Conference on Empirical Methods in Natural Language Processing*, pages 10585–10605, Online and Punta Cana, Dominican Republic. Association for Computational Linguistics.

Enayat Rajabi and Somayeh Kafaie. 2022. Knowledge graphs and explainable ai in healthcare. *Information*, 13(10):459.

Burr Settles. 2009. Active learning literature survey.

Yanyao Shen, Hyokun Yun, Zachary C Lipton, Yakov Kronrod, and Animashree Anandkumar. 2017. Deep active learning for named entity recognition. *arXiv preprint arXiv:1707.05928*.

Fábio Souza, Rodrigo Nogueira, and Roberto Lotufo. 2019. Portuguese named entity recognition using bert-crf. *arXiv preprint arXiv:1909.10649*.

Pontus Stenetorp, Sampo Pyysalo, Goran Topić, Tomoko Ohta, Sophia Ananiadou, and Jun'ichi Tsujii. 2012. brat: a web-based tool for NLP-assisted text annotation. In *Proceedings of the Demonstrations Session at EACL 2012*, Avignon, France. Association for Computational Linguistics.

Hugo Touvron, Thibaut Lavril, Gautier Izacard, Xavier Martinet, Marie-Anne Lachaux, Timothée Lacroix, Baptiste Rozière, Naman Goyal, Eric Hambro, Faisal Azhar, et al. 2023. Llama: Open and efficient foundation language models. *arXiv preprint arXiv:2302.13971*.

Viet-Vu Vu, Nicolas Labroche, and Bernadette Bouchon-Meunier. 2010. Active learning for semi-supervised k-means clustering. In *2010 22nd IEEE International Conference on Tools with Artificial Intelligence*, volume 1, pages 12–15. IEEE.

Shuhe Wang, Xiaofei Sun, Xiaoya Li, Rongbin Ouyang, Fei Wu, Tianwei Zhang, Jiwei Li, and Guoyin Wang. 2023a. Gpt-ner: Named entity recognition via large language models. *arXiv preprint arXiv:2304.10428*.

Xinyu Wang, Yong Jiang, Nguyen Bach, Tao Wang, Zhongqiang Huang, Fei Huang, and Kewei Tu. 2021. Improving named entity recognition by external context retrieving and cooperative learning. *arXiv preprint arXiv:2105.03654*.

Zhiyuan Wang, Qiang Zhou, Zhao Junfeng, Yasha Wang, Hongxin Ding, and Jiahe Song. 2023b. A knowledge-enhanced medical named entity recognition method that integrates pre-trained language models. In *2023 IEEE International Conference on Medical Artificial Intelligence (MedAI)*, pages 296–301. IEEE.

Xiang Wei, Yufeng Chen, Ning Cheng, Xingyu Cui, Jinan Xu, and Wenjuan Han. 2023. Collabkg: A learnable human-machine-cooperative information extraction toolkit for (event) knowledge graph construction. *arXiv preprint arXiv:2307.00769*.

Yuan Yao, Deming Ye, Peng Li, Xu Han, Yankai Lin, Zhenghao Liu, Zhiyuan Liu, Lixin Huang, Jie Zhou, and Maosong Sun. 2019. DocRED: A large-scale document-level relation extraction dataset. In *Proceedings of the 57th Annual Meeting of the Association for Computational Linguistics*, pages 764–777, Florence, Italy. Association for Computational Linguistics.

Ningyu Zhang, Mosha Chen, Zhen Bi, Xiaozhuan Liang, Lei Li, Xin Shang, Kangping Yin, Chuanqi Tan, Jian Xu, Fei Huang, Luo Si, Yuan Ni, Guotong Xie, Zhifang Sui, Baobao Chang, Hui Zong, Zheng Yuan, Linfeng Li, Jun Yan, Hongying Zan, Kunli Zhang, Buzhou Tang, and Qingcai Chen. 2022a. CBLUE: A Chinese biomedical language understanding evaluation benchmark. In *Proceedings of the 60th Annual Meeting of the Association for Computational Linguistics (Volume 1: Long Papers)*, pages 7888–7915, Dublin, Ireland. Association for Computational Linguistics.

Ningyu Zhang, Xin Xu, Liankuan Tao, Haiyang Yu, Hongbin Ye, Shuofei Qiao, Xin Xie, Xiang Chen, Zhoubo Li, and Lei Li. 2022b. Deepke: A deep learning based knowledge extraction toolkit for knowledge base population. In *EMNLP (Demos)*, pages 98–108. Association for Computational Linguistics.

# LEGENT: Open Platform for Embodied Agents

**Zhili Cheng, Zhitong Wang, Jinyi Hu, Shengding Hu, An Liu,**
**Yuge Tu, Pengkai Li, Lei Shi, Zhiyuan Liu, Maosong Sun***
Department of Computer Science and Technology, Tsinghua University
`{chengzl22, wangzt23, hu-jy21, hsd23}@mails.tsinghua.edu.cn`
`https://legent.ai`

Figure 1: Interaction with the embodied agent in LEGENT. These sequential interactions showcase the agent's ability to answer the user's questions and follow the user's instructions.

## Abstract

Despite advancements in Large Language Models (LLMs) and Large Multimodal Models (LMMs), their integration into language-grounded, human-like embodied agents remains incomplete, hindering complex real-life task performance in physical environments. Existing integrations often feature limited open sourcing, challenging collective progress in this field. We introduce LEGENT, an open, scalable platform for developing embodied agents using LLMs and LMMs. LEGENT offers a dual approach: a rich, interactive 3D environment with communicable and actionable agents, paired with a user-friendly interface, and a sophisticated data generation pipeline utilizing advanced algorithms to exploit supervision from simulated worlds at scale. In our experiments, an embryonic vision-language-action model trained on LEGENT-generated data surpasses GPT-4V in embodied tasks, showcasing promising generalization capabilities. LEGENT is available at `https://legent.ai`.

## 1 Introduction

Large Language Models (LLMs) (Brown et al., 2020; Achiam et al., 2023; Touvron et al., 2023a,b) and Large Multimodal Models (LMMs) (OpenAI, 2023; Team et al., 2023; Liu et al., 2024; Hu et al., 2024) present inspiring capabilities in understanding and generating human-like text and realistic images. However, their direct application in embodied AI, where agents interact in physical or simulated environments, is still primitive. LLMs and LMMs lack the necessary grounding (Harnad, 1990) in physical interactions to operate in these settings effectively.

Research in embodied intelligence has evolved significantly, leading to more realistic and sophisticated environments (Kolve et al., 2017; Puig et al., 2018; Savva et al., 2019; Puig et al., 2023b) and increasingly challenging tasks (Das et al., 2018; Gordon et al., 2018; Batra et al., 2020; Yenamandra et al., 2023). However, these traditional environments and approaches are typically incompatible with current LLMs and LMMs, which hinders the seamless integration of task execution via language interaction. Consequently, these approaches do not leverage the extensive generalizable knowledge present in LLMs and LMMs.

To achieve generalizable embodied intelligence, two key factors are crucial: language grounding to utilize the extensive knowledge in LMMs, and the expansion of training data for embodied AI. There have been noteworthy efforts in combining embodied AI with LMMs (Reed et al., 2022; Brohan et al., 2023). They collect large-scale training data from embodied scenes and train end-to-end mod-

*Corresponding author. Email: sms@tsinghua.edu.cn



*Proceedings of the 62nd Annual Meeting of the Association for Computational Linguistics (Volume 3: System Demonstrations)*, pages 335–345
August 11-16, 2024 ©2024 Association for Computational Linguistics

els that interpret both language and visual inputs and perform corresponding actions. However, the lack of open-source access to these environments and datasets restricts open-source community-wide progress in this field. Therefore, the academic community urgently requires an open-source platform that facilitates the integration of language grounding in embodied environments and schemes to generate large-scale training data for embodied agents based on LLMs and LMMs.

Towards this aspiration, we introduce LEGENT, an open and user-friendly platform that enables scalable training of embodied agents based on LLMs and LMMs. LEGENT contains two parts. First, it provides a 3D embodied environment with the following features: (1) Diverse, realistic, and interactive scenes; (2) Human-like agents with egocentric vision capable of executing actions and engaging in direct language interaction with users; (3) User-friendly interface offering comprehensive support for researchers unfamiliar with 3D environments. Second, LEGENT builds a systematic data generation pipeline for both scene generation and agent behavior, incorporating state-of-the-art algorithms for scene creation (Deitke et al., 2022; Yang et al., 2023b) and trajectory generation. In this way, extensive and diverse trajectories of agent behavior with egocentric visual observations and corresponding actions can be generated at scale for embodied agent training.

To demonstrate the potential of LEGENT, we train a basic vision-language-action model based on LMMs with generated data on two tasks: navigation and embodied question answering. The model processes textual and egocentric visual input and produces controls and textual responses directly. The prototype model outperforms GPT-4V (OpenAI, 2023), which lacks training in an embodied setting. The generalization experiment reveals the LEGENT-trained model's ability to generalize to unseen settings. LEGENT platform and its documentation are publicly available at `https://legent.ai`.

## 2 Related Work

**Embodied Environment.** Embodied environments are extensively utilized in games (Johnson et al., 2016; Oh et al., 2016; Beattie et al., 2016) and robotics (Kolve et al., 2017; Yan et al., 2018; Xia et al., 2018; Gan et al., 2020; Li et al., 2021; Puig et al., 2023a), with a primary focus on visual AI and reinforcement learning. Some platform focuses on specific embodied tasks, such as manipulation (Yu et al., 2020; Makoviychuk et al., 2021), navigation (Chang et al., 2017; Dosovitskiy et al., 2017), or planning-oriented agents (Puig et al., 2018; Shridhar et al., 2020; Wang et al., 2022). However, the environment setups and data frameworks of existing platforms fall short in accommodating the training of LMMs. LMMs excel in the supervised learning paradigm and necessitate diverse and large-scale data to integrate embodied capability. Existing platforms are not yet ready to scale, including: the primarily supported reinforcement learning methods require careful reward engineering, the diversity of the training data cannot be easily expanded, and collecting data for imitation learning on these platforms requires manual effort. Refer to Table 1 for a comparison of LEGENT with other embodied AI platforms.

**LMMs-based Embodied Agent.** Based on the development of LLMs and LMMs, researchers are endeavored to build agents for automatically completing human's instruction (Yao et al., 2023; Liu et al., 2023). For embodied tasks, existing studies have concentrated on developing embodied agents capable of end-to-end operation, as demonstrated in Reed et al. (2022); Brohan et al. (2023); Belkhale et al. (2024). However, the datasets and models in these studies are not publicly available.

**Scene Generation.** Scene generation has demonstrated significant effectiveness in training embodied agents by ProcTHOR (Deitke et al., 2022). Compared to employing manually crafted rules used in ProcTHOR, recent studies (Wen et al., 2023; Yang et al., 2023b; Feng et al., 2024) leverage prior knowledge of LLMs and propose algorithms to generate diverse, high-quality scenes.

**Agent Trajectory Generation.** Some research focuses on crafting reward functions to guide small policy models (Yu et al., 2023; Xian et al., 2023; Wang et al., 2023; Ma et al., 2023). However, there will be huge costs and instability when applying reward-based training to large foundation models. Meanwhile, pioneering efforts have been made in code generation for robotics (Liang et al., 2023; Singh et al., 2023; Vemprala et al., 2023; Huang et al., 2023) and trajectory generation for imitation learning (Garrett et al., 2021; Kamath et al., 2023; Dalal et al., 2023). These efforts align with our approach to generating large-scale embodied trajectories for training LMMs.

| Platform | Functionality | | | | Usability | | Scalability | | | |
|---|---|---|---|---|---|---|---|---|---|---|
| | Real. | Anim. | Inter. | Lang. | Access | Cross. | Scene | Asset | Style | **Data** |
| Minecraft | | | ✓ | ✓ | ✓ | ✓ | ✓ | | | |
| AI2THOR (Kolve et al., 2017) | ✓ | | | | ✓ | | | | | |
| Habitat (Savva et al., 2019) | ✓ | | | | ✓ | | | | | |
| Playhouse (Abramson et al., 2020) | | | ✓ | ✓ | | | ✓ | | | |
| ProcTHOR (Deitke et al., 2022) | ✓ | | | | ✓ | | ✓ | | | |
| Habitat 3.0 (Puig et al., 2023a) | ✓ | ✓ | ✓ | | ✓ | | | | | |
| LEGENT | ✓ | ✓ | ✓ | ✓ | ✓ | ✓ | ✓ | ✓ | ✓ | ✓ |

Table 1: Comparison with other embodied AI platforms. Real.: the scenes and physics in the environment are realistic. Anim.: the platform supports humanoid animation. Inter.: humans can interact with the agent directly. Lang.: the agent can perform language interaction. Access: the platform can be publicly accessed. Cross.: the environment is cross-platform and does not require specialized systems or hardware. Scene: the platform can generate various scenes automatically. Asset: the platform can utilize an unlimited variety of external assets. Style: the environment offers multiple rendering styles to provide various visual effects. Data: Whether it supports automatic generation of large-scale trajectory data for training embodied agents.

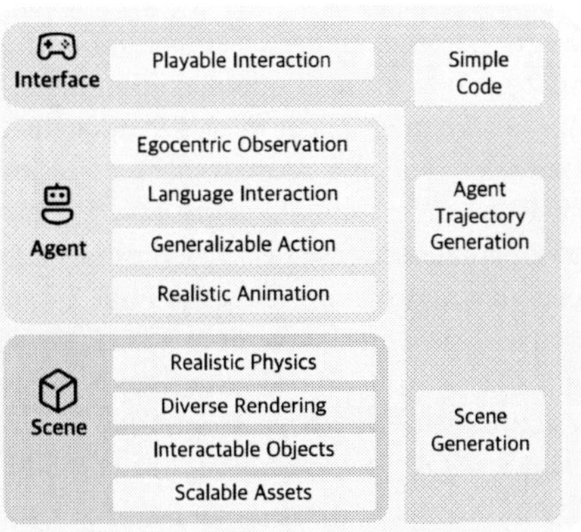


Figure 2: Features of LEGENT.

## 3 LEGENT

In this section, we introduce our platform LEGENT. The design of LEGENT involves scene, agent, and interface. All three components are specially tailored for the integration of LLMs and LMMs, and ensure scalability.

### 3.1 Scene

The design of the scenes in LEGENT emphasizes **interactivity** and **diversity**, striving for a versatile and scalable environment that enriches the training of embodied agents for wide application.

**Realistic Physics.** LEGENT provides a real-time simulation that closely mirrors real-world physics based on game engines. It supports realistic effects like gravity, friction, and collision dynamics, improving agents' embodied comprehension or aiding the development of generative world simulators (Yang et al., 2023a).

**Diverse Rendering.** LEGENT introduces another facet of generalization via diverse rendering. Unlike the fixed stylized renderings in games and the emphasis on photorealism in robotics, LEGENT integrates these styles by customizing the rendering functions, which allows easy transitions between rendering styles to accommodate different requirements for flexible usage. visually diverse environments

**Interactable Objects.** In LEGENT, both agents and users can manipulate various fully interactable 3D objects, which enables actions such as picking up, transporting, positioning, and handing over these objects. Additionally, the environment supports interaction with dynamic structures, such as doors and drawers. We anticipate that the scope of these dynamic structures will be significantly broadened through the application of generative methods (Chen et al., 2023).

**Scalable Assets.** LEGENT supports importing customized objects at runtime, including user-supplied 3D objects, objects from existing datasets (Deitke et al., 2023) and those created by generative models (Siddiqui et al., 2023; Wang et al., 2024), as illustrated in Fig. 3. We choose glTF as the import format for its openness and broad compatibility. This feature grants users the flexibility to customize the scene by strategically placing these assets or integrating them seamlessly into scene generation algorithms.

### 3.2 Agent

The agent is designed with two criteria: emulating human interactions and compatibility with LMMs.

**Egocentric Observations.** Following the previous study for interactive embodied agents (Team

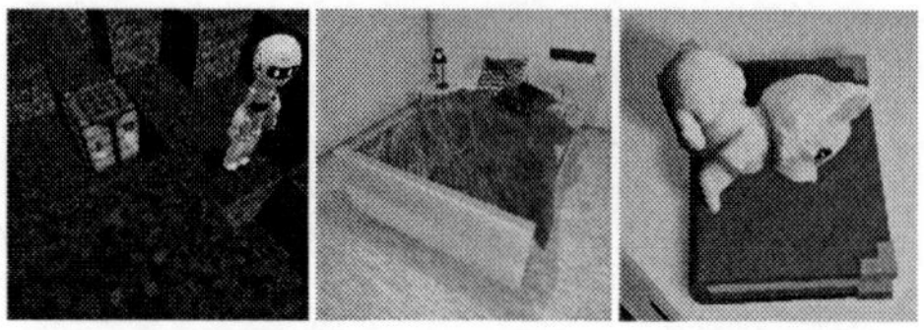

Figure 3: Examples of importing external assets: user-supplied assets (left); existing datasets (middle); assets generated by generative models (right).

| Actions | Description |
|---|---|
| Speak | Send a message. |
| Move* | Move forward by a specified distance. |
| Rotate* | Adjust the view horizontally or vertically. |
| Interact | Grab, put, open, or close targeted objects. |

Table 2: List of actions in LEGENT. * means the action is continuous (meters or degrees).

et al., 2021), the agent is equipped with egocentric vision. The egocentric vision is captured by mounting a camera on the agent's head.

**Language Interaction.** Users and agents can communicate with each other in natural language in LEGENT. Grounding language within the environment has the potential to connect the extensive knowledge in LLMs and LMMs with embodied experience.

**Generalizable Actions.** Agents in LEGENT are capable of performing a range of actions, including navigation, object manipulation, and communication. Regarding the instantiation of actions, existing literature can be broadly categorized into two types: *executable plans* (Puig et al., 2018; Shridhar et al., 2020) and *control* (Kolve et al., 2017; Savva et al., 2019). In *executable plans*, actions are expressed through sub-steps to complete a task, such as "*walk towards apple 1*", which depends on internal states and annotations for execution, or requires an additional neural executor module compatible with a planning module (Driess et al., 2023). *Control*, on the other hand, refers to the action expression like "*move forward 1 meter, rotate to the right 30 degrees*", which is considered more generalizable. In LEGENT, we use *control*, targeting generalizing to new environments including real-world settings. The learned actions can be integrated with diverse actuators with the least additional effort.

Another important action design is allowing the agent to execute continuous actions such as moving forward across a continuous distance, as opposed to moving in a grid-by-grid manner. This design offers two advantages for LMMs: (1) It minimizes the inference cost of LMMs by eliminating the need for constant frame-by-frame inference. (2) It addresses the issue of minimal information gain observed when an agent moves incrementally in a stepwise manner, a process that creates less effective data for training large models. This design draws parallels to the use of keyframes in video processing and making direct training of autoregressive LMMs (Alayrac et al., 2022; Awadalla et al., 2023; Lin et al., 2024) feasible. Specifically, the actions currently supported in LEGENT are shown in Table 2. Considering the current capability of LMMs, LEGENT temporarily omits the complex control of agents' body joints. Adding these degrees of freedom to allow more flexible action will be explored in the future.

Figure 4: An example of humanoid animations, demonstrating accurate object grasping and body movement through spatial planning and inverse kinematics.

**Realistic Animation.** LEGENT features precise humanoid animations using inverse kinematics and spatial algorithms, enabling lifelike movements, as shown in Fig. 4. It is important for enhancing nonverbal interactions in AI systems and contributes to robotic control and text-to-motion research. Also, when combined with egocentric vision, it offers a cost-effective alternative for immersive experiences similar to Ego4D (Grauman et al., 2022), which requires a huge cost to collect.

### 3.3 Interface

Our platform offers a user-friendly interface for researchers to integrate LLMs and LMMs with the embodied environment easily, with little need for expertise in 3D environments. Detailed guidance is available in our documentation.

**Playable Interaction.** The user interface of LEGENT is designed to be as intuitive as playing a video game with the agent within the environment, utilizing just a keyboard and mouse for navigation and interaction. This interface facilitates straightforward visual debugging and qualitative analysis and simplifies the process of conducting hands-on demonstrations.

**Simple Code.** LEGENT is equipped with a Python toolkit to enable the interaction between the agent and the environment. The coding interface of our Python toolkit is simple, with concise code examples available in our documentation.

**Scene Generation Interface.** Our platform incorporates various scene-generation techniques. Currently, we support methods including procedural generation and LLM-based generation. We provide a straightforward JSON format for specifying a scene, enabling users to easily develop their own scene generation methods.

**Agent Trajectory Generation Interface.** We offer an agent trajectory generation interface specifically designed for training LMMs. Using this interface, users can create training datasets that consist of egocentric visual records and corresponding ground truth actions paired with task instructions or queries, as elaborated in Section 4.3.

**Hardware Requirements.** LEGENT is cross-platform. It can run effortlessly on personal computers without demanding particular prerequisites or complex setups, and it facilitates connections to remote servers for training and deployment, thus enhancing its accessibility.

## 4 Data Generation

The second part of LEGENT is a scalable data generation pipeline. It aims at exhaustively exploiting the inherent supervision from simulated worlds and supporting large-scale training of general-purpose embodied agents. Here we elaborate on the implementation of our data generation framework.

### 4.1 Scene Generation

Scene generation offers agents with diverse embodied experiences. LEGENT has currently integrated two scene generation methods: (1) Procedure generation efficiently creates large-scale scenes. (2) Language-guided generation captures the semantics of textual queries and leverages common sense knowledge to optimize spatial layouts.

**Procedural Generation.** We utilize the procedural generation algorithm created by ProcTHOR (Deitke et al., 2022), designed to create realistic indoor scenes at scale by integrating prior knowledge of object placement and spatial relationships. The implementation process starts with drafting a house layout, followed by the placement of large furniture, and ends with the arrangement of small objects. During the process, spatial algorithms are used to prevent object overlap and ensure precise placement. We provide an interface that allows users to input specific conditions for object occurrence and placement, enabling the generation of scenes tailored to specific tasks. In addition, instead of employing human annotators as previous work does, we utilize LLMs for asset annotation, establishing an efficient *automatic asset annotation* pipeline that facilitates future asset expansion.

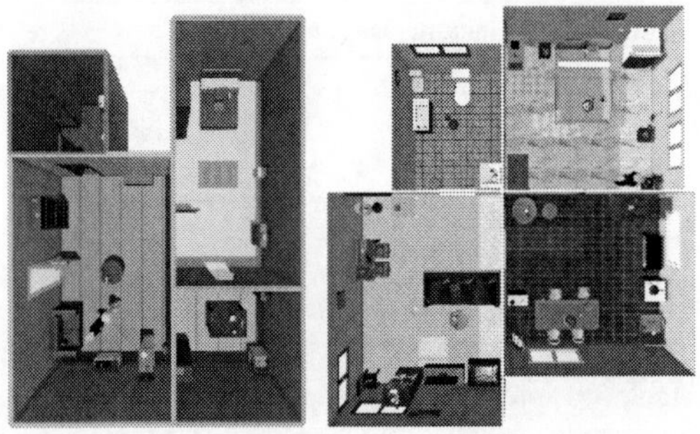

Figure 5: Examples of generated scenes.

**Language Guided Generation.** We implement methods in Holodeck (Yang et al., 2023b) into LEGENT and offer an LLM-powered interface to generate single or multi-room indoor scenes given any natural language query. This process resembles procedural generation but is driven by LLMs instead of human-written programs. Instead of using the depth-first-search solver in Holodeck, we ask LLMs to determine the exact locations of doors and floor objects, granting LLMs more control over the room layout. Collision detection is used to prevent interference between objects during generation.

### 4.2 Task Generation

We create diverse tasks expressed in language paired with specific scenes, thereby contextualizing each task within the environment. We employ the following two strategies for task generation.

**Task Generation for Given Scenes.** In this strategy, we serialize the generated scenes into a detailed textual description and present it to LLMs with crafted instructions. LLMs assume the role of human users, generating a variety of tasks. This approach is especially effective for generating diverse tasks automatically.

**Scene Generation for Given Tasks.** This ap-

| Task | Intermediate Code |
|---|---|
| come here | goto_user() |
| go to *A* | goto(*a*) |
| pick up *A* | goto(*a*) target(*a*) interact() |
| bring me *A* | goto(*a*) target(*a*) interact() goto_user() |
| where is *A* | find(*a*) speak(*C*) |
| put *A* on *B* | goto(*a*) target(*a*) interact() goto(*b*) target(*b*) interact() |

Table 3: Currenly provided task templates and intermediate code templates. *A* is the object's name, and *a* is the object's environment identifier. *C* denotes the name of the receptacle on which *a* is placed.

proach efficiently generates large-scale samples for specific tasks based on the scene generation algorithm. For instance, when the task involves querying an object's location, the algorithm generates a scene that includes the object and its receptacle, inherently creating question-answering annotations. As shown in Table 3, we provide some basic task templates that are ideal for creating large-scale scenes, which are particularly useful for pretraining *fundamental capabilities* of embodied control, spatial comprehension, and basic language grounding across diverse scenes.

### 4.3 Trajectory Generation

Trajectories for training embodied agents comprise continuous sequences of egocentric observations and actions. The main challenge lies in accurately determining ground-truth actions for each step.

We use LLMs and controllers to label the ground truth actions. Inspired by pioneering works in code generation for robotics, we utilize LLMs to write intermediate codes from provided state descriptions and instructions. These codes are instantiated as *multi-step controllers*, designed to calculate the optimal actions at each step given the internal states of the environment. Each controller operates in a step-by-step manner in the environment, with visual observations collected during the process. This approach is consistent with the concept of Task and Motion Planning (TAMP) (Garrett et al., 2021) in robotics, where the LLMs and the controllers respectively fulfill the functions of task planning and motion planning.

We demonstrate this process using an example task "*Where is the orange?*". As shown in Figure 6, to finish the task, the agent needs to search the room and answer the question. LLMs map the task to the appropriate code usage, determine the object identifier of the orange in the scene, and recognize

Figure 6: A generated trajectory for task "Where is the orange". The actions for the three observations are: 1. *rotate_right(-59)*; 2. *move_forward(1.2), rotate_right(-35)*; 3. *speak("It's on the sofa.")*.

its placement from the state description, thereby generating the following intermediate code:

```
find(36) # object identifier of orange
speak("It's on the sofa.")
```

Note that the code-writing is annotation-oriented. Even though LLMs can directly answer the question from the state description, it still invokes "*find*". Then the code "*find*" is instantiated as a multi-step controller that utilizes pathfinding algorithms (Hart et al., 1968) incorporating visibility checks. The pathfinding algorithm calculates the waypoints of the shortest path from the agent to the target object using a navigation mesh. The controller then calculates the controls of the agent to navigate along these waypoints. For instance, in the first observation shown in Figure 6, the agent needs to rotate 59 degrees to the left to orient to the next waypoint, resulting in the action "*rotate_right(-59)*". Similarly, in the second observation, the agent needs to perform certain actions to move to the subsequent waypoint. This multi-step controller concludes when the target object enters the agent's field of view. LEGENT records visual observations and actions during this process as a trajectory, which can be exported as a video or an image-text interleaved sequence. The actions use a unified code representation, compatible with the outputs of LMMs.

Similar to "*find*", each intermediate code is designed with the ability to generate optimal controls using the internal world states. In addition, each task template mentioned in Section 4.2 is equipped with intermediate code templates, as shown in Table 3, eliminating the need for LLMs in large-scale data generation for specific tasks.

### 4.4 Prototype Experiments

We conduct a prototype experiment to assess the utility of generated data on two embodied tasks: "Come Here" for navigation and "Where Is" for embodied question answering (Das et al., 2018). Task

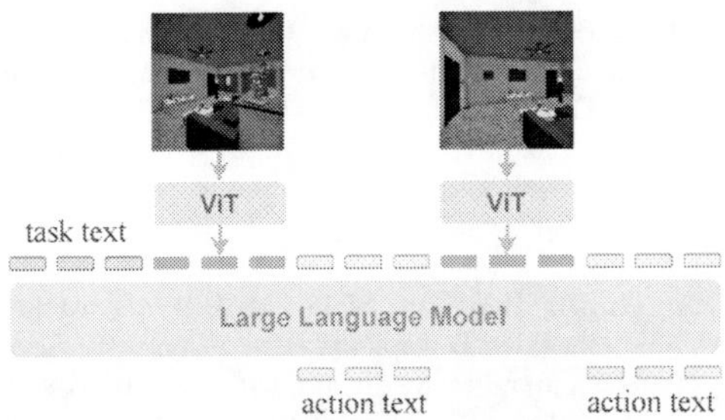


Figure 7: The vision-language-action(VLA) model architecture used in the prototype experiments.

| Task | Come Here | | Where Is | |
|---|---|---|---|---|
| Room Num | One | Two | One | Two* |
| GPT-4V (zero-shot) | 0.21 | 0.17 | 0.25 | 0.22 |
| ViLA-7B-Sep 1K | 0.87 | 0.28 | 0.30 | 0.22 |
| ViLA-7B-Sep 10K | **0.96** | **0.70** | **0.94** | 0.52 |
| ViLA-7B-Joint | **0.96** | **0.70** | 0.92 | **0.65** |

Table 4: Success rates on two embodied tasks. *VILA-Sep* denotes models fine-tuned separately for each task, whereas *VILA-Joint* refers to models trained jointly on both tasks. * means generalization test.

complexity varied from navigating in one room to the more intricate two rooms. We generate 1k and 10k trajectories for the initial three tasks ("Come Here" in one or two rooms and "Where Is" in one room) and assess the models on 100 trajectories across all four tasks. The "Where Is" task in the two-room setting serves as a generalization test, which is not included in the training data.

Due to the lack of powerful video understanding models, we temporarily only focus on the observation at the end of each continuous action, formulating one trajectory as an image-text interleaved sequence. We utilize VILA-7B (Lin et al., 2024) as our backbone due to its capability in interleaved inputs. We train the vision-language-action model to predict current action based on task descriptions and interleaved context of previous observations and actions, as illustrated in Fig. 7.

The results presented in Table 4 lead to several observations: (i) GPT-4V struggles in these tasks, reflecting a lack of embodied experience in mainstream LMMs. (ii) Increasing training data improves the model performance. (iii) The navigational skills developed from the "Come Here" task in a two-room environment generalize well to the untrained task scenario, enhancing the model's ability to navigate in two rooms for the embodied question answering task. We leave the exploration of more large-scale training in the future work.

### 4.5 Demo of LEGENT

The demo video of LEGENT is available at the link[1], which is partially shown in Fig. 1. The demonstration exemplifies the engagement with embodied agents in LEGENT, primarily leveraging LLMs and controllers described in Section 4.3. With advancements in LMMs' capability of egocentric perception and control, we foresee the evolution of this demonstration into a fully embodied experience, independent of any extra internal information. We will also pursue this goal by further scaling the data generation for model training.

## 5 Conclusion and Future Work

In this work, we present LEGENT, an open platform for developing embodied agents, focusing on integrating LMMs with scalable embodied training. By bridging the gap between embodied AI and LMM's development, we hope LEGENT inspires research in this field. We are committed to the ongoing development of LEGENT, making it more scalable and user-friendly. In our future releases, we prioritize: (1) Building a more diverse data generation pipeline. (2) Scaling model training. (3) Unifying humanoid animation with robotic control and refining the physics to make actions more applicable to the real world. (4) Improving scene generation and integrating text-to-3D and image-to-3D methods to support more diverse and realistic scenes.

## Limitations

In the context of imitation learning, the persistent challenge of insufficient exploration and handling out-of-distribution inputs during inference underscores the need for further enhancements and strategies within the data generation pipeline, a component that is currently not integrated into our system. Furthermore, large-scale experiments have yet to be conducted. We leave this to the future work.

## Ethics Statement

The development of LEGENT prioritizes ethical considerations across all aspects of its use and implementation. We uphold data privacy and security, ensuring compliance with relevant data protection

[1] `https://video.legent.ai`

laws. We strictly adhere to legal standards and encourage ethical use of our platform. We are committed to continuous evaluation of the ethical implications of our work and engaging with the community to address emerging concerns and ensure a positive impact on society.

## Acknowledgements

This work is supported by the National Key R&D Program of China (2020AAA0106502), the National Natural Science Foundation of China (No. 62236011, 623B2065) and a grant from the Guoqiang Institute, Tsinghua University.

## References

Josh Abramson, Arun Ahuja, Iain Barr, Arthur Brussee, Federico Carnevale, Mary Cassin, Rachita Chhaparia, Stephen Clark, Bogdan Damoc, Andrew Dudzik, et al. 2020. Imitating interactive intelligence. *arXiv preprint arXiv:2012.05672*.

Josh Achiam, Steven Adler, Sandhini Agarwal, Lama Ahmad, Ilge Akkaya, Florencia Leoni Aleman, Diogo Almeida, Janko Altenschmidt, Sam Altman, Shyamal Anadkat, et al. 2023. Gpt-4 technical report. *arXiv preprint arXiv:2303.08774*.

Jean-Baptiste Alayrac, Jeff Donahue, Pauline Luc, Antoine Miech, Iain Barr, Yana Hasson, Karel Lenc, Arthur Mensch, Katherine Millican, Malcolm Reynolds, et al. 2022. Flamingo: a visual language model for few-shot learning. *Advances in neural information processing systems*, 35:23716–23736.

Anas Awadalla, Irena Gao, Josh Gardner, Jack Hessel, Yusuf Hanafy, Wanrong Zhu, Kalyani Marathe, Yonatan Bitton, Samir Gadre, Shiori Sagawa, et al. 2023. Openflamingo: An open-source framework for training large autoregressive vision-language models. *arXiv preprint arXiv:2308.01390*.

Dhruv Batra, Angel X Chang, Sonia Chernova, Andrew J Davison, Jia Deng, Vladlen Koltun, Sergey Levine, Jitendra Malik, Igor Mordatch, Roozbeh Mottaghi, et al. 2020. Rearrangement: A challenge for embodied ai. *arXiv preprint arXiv:2011.01975*.

Charles Beattie, Joel Z Leibo, Denis Teplyashin, Tom Ward, Marcus Wainwright, Heinrich Küttler, Andrew Lefrancq, Simon Green, Víctor Valdés, Amir Sadik, et al. 2016. Deepmind lab. *arXiv preprint arXiv:1612.03801*.

Suneel Belkhale, Tianli Ding, Ted Xiao, Pierre Sermanet, Quon Vuong, Jonathan Tompson, Yevgen Chebotar, Debidatta Dwibedi, and Dorsa Sadigh. 2024. Rt-h: Action hierarchies using language. *arXiv preprint arXiv:2403.01823*.

Anthony Brohan, Noah Brown, Justice Carbajal, Yevgen Chebotar, Xi Chen, Krzysztof Choromanski, Tianli Ding, Danny Driess, Avinava Dubey, Chelsea Finn, et al. 2023. Rt-2: Vision-language-action models transfer web knowledge to robotic control. *arXiv preprint arXiv:2307.15818*.

Tom Brown, Benjamin Mann, Nick Ryder, Melanie Subbiah, Jared D Kaplan, Prafulla Dhariwal, Arvind Neelakantan, Pranav Shyam, Girish Sastry, Amanda Askell, et al. 2020. Language models are few-shot learners. *Advances in neural information processing systems*, 33:1877–1901.

Angel Chang, Angela Dai, Thomas Funkhouser, Maciej Halber, Matthias Niessner, Manolis Savva, Shuran Song, Andy Zeng, and Yinda Zhang. 2017. Matterport3d: Learning from rgb-d data in indoor environments. *arXiv preprint arXiv:1709.06158*.

Qiuyu Chen, Marius Memmel, Alex Fang, Aaron Walsman, Dieter Fox, and Abhishek Gupta. 2023. Urdformer: Constructing interactive realistic scenes from real images via simulation and generative modeling. In *Towards Generalist Robots: Learning Paradigms for Scalable Skill Acquisition@ CoRL2023*.

Murtaza Dalal, Ajay Mandlekar, Caelan Garrett, Ankur Handa, Ruslan Salakhutdinov, and Dieter Fox. 2023. Imitating task and motion planning with visuomotor transformers. *arXiv preprint arXiv:2305.16309*.

Abhishek Das, Samyak Datta, Georgia Gkioxari, Stefan Lee, Devi Parikh, and Dhruv Batra. 2018. Embodied question answering. In *Proceedings of the IEEE conference on computer vision and pattern recognition*, pages 1–10.

Matt Deitke, Dustin Schwenk, Jordi Salvador, Luca Weihs, Oscar Michel, Eli VanderBilt, Ludwig Schmidt, Kiana Ehsani, Aniruddha Kembhavi, and Ali Farhadi. 2023. Objaverse: A universe of annotated 3d objects. In *Proceedings of the IEEE/CVF Conference on Computer Vision and Pattern Recognition*, pages 13142–13153.

Matt Deitke, Eli VanderBilt, Alvaro Herrasti, Luca Weihs, Kiana Ehsani, Jordi Salvador, Winson Han, Eric Kolve, Aniruddha Kembhavi, and Roozbeh Mottaghi. 2022. Procthor: Large-scale embodied ai using procedural generation. *Advances in Neural Information Processing Systems*, 35:5982–5994.

Alexey Dosovitskiy, German Ros, Felipe Codevilla, Antonio Lopez, and Vladlen Koltun. 2017. Carla: An open urban driving simulator. In *Conference on robot learning*, pages 1–16. PMLR.

Danny Driess, Fei Xia, Mehdi SM Sajjadi, Corey Lynch, Aakanksha Chowdhery, Brian Ichter, Ayzaan Wahid, Jonathan Tompson, Quan Vuong, Tianhe Yu, et al. 2023. Palm-e: An embodied multimodal language model. *arXiv preprint arXiv:2303.03378*.

Weixi Feng, Wanrong Zhu, Tsu-jui Fu, Varun Jampani, Arjun Akula, Xuehai He, Sugato Basu, Xin Eric Wang, and William Yang Wang. 2024. Layoutgpt: Compositional visual planning and generation with large language models. *Advances in Neural Information Processing Systems*, 36.

Chuang Gan, Jeremy Schwartz, Seth Alter, Damian Mrowca, Martin Schrimpf, James Traer, Julian De Freitas, Jonas Kubilius, Abhishek Bhandwaldar, Nick Haber, et al. 2020. Threedworld: A platform for interactive multi-modal physical simulation. *arXiv preprint arXiv:2007.04954*.

Caelan Reed Garrett, Rohan Chitnis, Rachel Holladay, Beomjoon Kim, Tom Silver, Leslie Pack Kaelbling, and Tomás Lozano-Pérez. 2021. Integrated task and motion planning. *Annual review of control, robotics, and autonomous systems*, 4:265–293.

Daniel Gordon, Aniruddha Kembhavi, Mohammad Rastegari, Joseph Redmon, Dieter Fox, and Ali Farhadi. 2018. Iqa: Visual question answering in interactive environments. In *Proceedings of the IEEE conference on computer vision and pattern recognition*, pages 4089–4098.

Kristen Grauman, Andrew Westbury, Eugene Byrne, Zachary Chavis, Antonino Furnari, Rohit Girdhar, Jackson Hamburger, Hao Jiang, Miao Liu, Xingyu Liu, et al. 2022. Ego4d: Around the world in 3,000 hours of egocentric video. In *Proceedings of the IEEE/CVF Conference on Computer Vision and Pattern Recognition*, pages 18995–19012.

Stevan Harnad. 1990. The symbol grounding problem. *Physica D: Nonlinear Phenomena*, 42(1-3):335–346.

Peter E Hart, Nils J Nilsson, and Bertram Raphael. 1968. A formal basis for the heuristic determination of minimum cost paths. *IEEE transactions on Systems Science and Cybernetics*, 4(2):100–107.

Jinyi Hu, Yuan Yao, Chongyi Wang, SHAN WANG, Yinxu Pan, Qianyu Chen, Tianyu Yu, Hanghao Wu, Yue Zhao, Haoye Zhang, Xu Han, Yankai Lin, Jiao Xue, dahai li, Zhiyuan Liu, and Maosong Sun. 2024. Large multilingual models pivot zero-shot multimodal learning across languages. In *The Twelfth International Conference on Learning Representations*.

Wenlong Huang, Chen Wang, Ruohan Zhang, Yunzhu Li, Jiajun Wu, and Li Fei-Fei. 2023. Voxposer: Composable 3d value maps for robotic manipulation with language models. *arXiv preprint arXiv:2307.05973*.

Matthew Johnson, Katja Hofmann, Tim Hutton, and David Bignell. 2016. The malmo platform for artificial intelligence experimentation. In *Ijcai*, volume 16, pages 4246–4247.

Aishwarya Kamath, Peter Anderson, Su Wang, Jing Yu Koh, Alexander Ku, Austin Waters, Yinfei Yang, Jason Baldridge, and Zarana Parekh. 2023. A new path: Scaling vision-and-language navigation with synthetic instructions and imitation learning. In *Proceedings of the IEEE/CVF Conference on Computer Vision and Pattern Recognition*, pages 10813–10823.

Eric Kolve, Roozbeh Mottaghi, Winson Han, Eli VanderBilt, Luca Weihs, Alvaro Herrasti, Matt Deitke, Kiana Ehsani, Daniel Gordon, Yuke Zhu, et al. 2017. Ai2-thor: An interactive 3d environment for visual ai. *arXiv preprint arXiv:1712.05474*.

Chengshu Li, Fei Xia, Roberto Martín-Martín, Michael Lingelbach, Sanjana Srivastava, Bokui Shen, Kent Vainio, Cem Gokmen, Gokul Dharan, Tanish Jain, et al. 2021. igibson 2.0: Object-centric simulation for robot learning of everyday household tasks. *arXiv preprint arXiv:2108.03272*.

Jacky Liang, Wenlong Huang, Fei Xia, Peng Xu, Karol Hausman, Brian Ichter, Pete Florence, and Andy Zeng. 2023. Code as policies: Language model programs for embodied control. In *2023 IEEE International Conference on Robotics and Automation (ICRA)*, pages 9493–9500. IEEE.

Ji Lin, Hongxu Yin, Wei Ping, Pavlo Molchanov, Mohammad Shoeybi, and Song Han. 2024. Vila: On pretraining for visual language models. In *Proceedings of the IEEE/CVF Conference on Computer Vision and Pattern Recognition*, pages 26689–26699.

Haotian Liu, Chunyuan Li, Qingyang Wu, and Yong Jae Lee. 2024. Visual instruction tuning. *Advances in neural information processing systems*, 36.

Xiao Liu, Hao Yu, Hanchen Zhang, Yifan Xu, Xuanyu Lei, Hanyu Lai, Yu Gu, Hangliang Ding, Kaiwen Men, Kejuan Yang, Shudan Zhang, Xiang Deng, Aohan Zeng, Zhengxiao Du, Chenhui Zhang, Sheng Shen, Tianjun Zhang, Yu Su, Huan Sun, Minlie Huang, Yuxiao Dong, and Jie Tang. 2023. Agentbench: Evaluating llms as agents. *arXiv preprint arXiv: 2308.03688*.

Yecheng Jason Ma, William Liang, Guanzhi Wang, De-An Huang, Osbert Bastani, Dinesh Jayaraman, Yuke Zhu, Linxi Fan, and Anima Anandkumar. 2023. Eureka: Human-level reward design via coding large language models. *arXiv preprint arXiv:2310.12931*.

Viktor Makoviychuk, Lukasz Wawrzyniak, Yunrong Guo, Michelle Lu, Kier Storey, Miles Macklin, David Hoeller, Nikita Rudin, Arthur Allshire, Ankur Handa, et al. 2021. Isaac gym: High performance gpu-based physics simulation for robot learning. *arXiv preprint arXiv:2108.10470*.

Junhyuk Oh, Valliappa Chockalingam, Honglak Lee, et al. 2016. Control of memory, active perception, and action in minecraft. In *International conference on machine learning*, pages 2790–2799. PMLR.

team OpenAI. 2023. Gpt-4v(ision) system card.

Xavi Puig, Eric Undersander, Andrew Szot, Mikael Dallaire Cote, Ruslan Partsey, Jimmy Yang, Ruta Desai, Alexander William Clegg, Michal Hlavac, Tiffany

Min, Theo Gervet, Vladimir Vondrus, Vincent-Pierre Berges, John Turner, Oleksandr Maksymets, Zsolt Kira, Mrinal Kalakrishnan, Jitendra Malik, Devendra Singh Chaplot, Unnat Jain, Dhruv Batra, Akshara Rai, and Roozbeh Mottaghi. 2023a. Habitat 3.0: A co-habitat for humans, avatars and robots.

Xavier Puig, Kevin Ra, Marko Boben, Jiaman Li, Tingwu Wang, Sanja Fidler, and Antonio Torralba. 2018. Virtualhome: Simulating household activities via programs. In *Proceedings of the IEEE Conference on Computer Vision and Pattern Recognition*, pages 8494–8502.

Xavier Puig, Eric Undersander, Andrew Szot, Mikael Dallaire Cote, Tsung-Yen Yang, Ruslan Partsey, Ruta Desai, Alexander William Clegg, Michal Hlavac, So Yeon Min, et al. 2023b. Habitat 3.0: A co-habitat for humans, avatars and robots. *arXiv preprint arXiv:2310.13724*.

Scott Reed, Konrad Zolna, Emilio Parisotto, Sergio Gomez Colmenarejo, Alexander Novikov, Gabriel Barth-Maron, Mai Gimenez, Yury Sulsky, Jackie Kay, Jost Tobias Springenberg, et al. 2022. A generalist agent. *arXiv preprint arXiv:2205.06175*.

Manolis Savva, Abhishek Kadian, Oleksandr Maksymets, Yili Zhao, Erik Wijmans, Bhavana Jain, Julian Straub, Jia Liu, Vladlen Koltun, Jitendra Malik, et al. 2019. Habitat: A platform for embodied ai research. In *Proceedings of the IEEE/CVF international conference on computer vision*, pages 9339–9347.

Mohit Shridhar, Xingdi Yuan, Marc-Alexandre Côté, Yonatan Bisk, Adam Trischler, and Matthew Hausknecht. 2020. Alfworld: Aligning text and embodied environments for interactive learning. *arXiv preprint arXiv:2010.03768*.

Yawar Siddiqui, Antonio Alliegro, Alexey Artemov, Tatiana Tommasi, Daniele Sirigatti, Vladislav Rosov, Angela Dai, and Matthias Nießner. 2023. Meshgpt: Generating triangle meshes with decoder-only transformers. *arXiv preprint arXiv:2311.15475*.

Ishika Singh, Valts Blukis, Arsalan Mousavian, Ankit Goyal, Danfei Xu, Jonathan Tremblay, Dieter Fox, Jesse Thomason, and Animesh Garg. 2023. Progprompt: Generating situated robot task plans using large language models. In *2023 IEEE International Conference on Robotics and Automation (ICRA)*, pages 11523–11530. IEEE.

DeepMind Interactive Agents Team, Josh Abramson, Arun Ahuja, Arthur Brussee, Federico Carnevale, Mary Cassin, Felix Fischer, Petko Georgiev, Alex Goldin, Mansi Gupta, et al. 2021. Creating multimodal interactive agents with imitation and self-supervised learning. *arXiv preprint arXiv:2112.03763*.

Gemini Team, Rohan Anil, Sebastian Borgeaud, Yonghui Wu, Jean-Baptiste Alayrac, Jiahui Yu, Radu Soricut, Johan Schalkwyk, Andrew M Dai, Anja Hauth, et al. 2023. Gemini: a family of highly capable multimodal models. *arXiv preprint arXiv:2312.11805*.

Hugo Touvron, Thibaut Lavril, Gautier Izacard, Xavier Martinet, Marie-Anne Lachaux, Timothée Lacroix, Baptiste Rozière, Naman Goyal, Eric Hambro, Faisal Azhar, et al. 2023a. Llama: Open and efficient foundation language models. *arXiv preprint arXiv:2302.13971*.

Hugo Touvron, Louis Martin, Kevin Stone, Peter Albert, Amjad Almahairi, Yasmine Babaei, Nikolay Bashlykov, Soumya Batra, Prajjwal Bhargava, Shruti Bhosale, et al. 2023b. Llama 2: Open foundation and fine-tuned chat models. *arXiv preprint arXiv:2307.09288*.

Sai Vemprala, Rogerio Bonatti, Arthur Bucker, and Ashish Kapoor. 2023. Chatgpt for robotics: Design principles and model abilities. *arXiv preprint arXiv:2306.17582*.

Ruoyao Wang, Peter Jansen, Marc-Alexandre Côté, and Prithviraj Ammanabrolu. 2022. Scienceworld: Is your agent smarter than a 5th grader? *arXiv preprint arXiv:2203.07540*.

Yufei Wang, Zhou Xian, Feng Chen, Tsun-Hsuan Wang, Yian Wang, Katerina Fragkiadaki, Zackory Erickson, David Held, and Chuang Gan. 2023. Robogen: Towards unleashing infinite data for automated robot learning via generative simulation. *arXiv preprint arXiv:2311.01455*.

Zhengyi Wang, Yikai Wang, Yifei Chen, Chendong Xiang, Shuo Chen, Dajiang Yu, Chongxuan Li, Hang Su, and Jun Zhu. 2024. Crm: Single image to 3d textured mesh with convolutional reconstruction model. *arXiv preprint arXiv:2403.05034*.

Zehao Wen, Zichen Liu, Srinath Sridhar, and Rao Fu. 2023. Anyhome: Open-vocabulary generation of structured and textured 3d homes. *arXiv preprint arXiv:2312.06644*.

Fei Xia, Amir R Zamir, Zhiyang He, Alexander Sax, Jitendra Malik, and Silvio Savarese. 2018. Gibson env: Real-world perception for embodied agents. In *Proceedings of the IEEE conference on computer vision and pattern recognition*, pages 9068–9079.

Zhou Xian, Theophile Gervet, Zhenjia Xu, Yi-Ling Qiao, Tsun-Hsuan Wang, and Yian Wang. 2023. Towards generalist robots: A promising paradigm via generative simulation. *arXiv preprint arXiv:2305.10455*.

Claudia Yan, Dipendra Misra, Andrew Bennnett, Aaron Walsman, Yonatan Bisk, and Yoav Artzi. 2018. Chalet: Cornell house agent learning environment. *arXiv preprint arXiv:1801.07357*.

Mengjiao Yang, Yilun Du, Kamyar Ghasemipour, Jonathan Tompson, Dale Schuurmans, and Pieter Abbeel. 2023a. Learning interactive real-world simulators. *arXiv preprint arXiv:2310.06114*.

Yue Yang, Fan-Yun Sun, Luca Weihs, Eli VanderBilt, Alvaro Herrasti, Winson Han, Jiajun Wu, Nick Haber, Ranjay Krishna, Lingjie Liu, et al. 2023b. Holodeck: Language guided generation of 3d embodied ai environments. *arXiv preprint arXiv:2312.09067*.

Shunyu Yao, Jeffrey Zhao, Dian Yu, Nan Du, Izhak Shafran, Karthik Narasimhan, and Yuan Cao. 2023. ReAct: Synergizing reasoning and acting in language models. In *International Conference on Learning Representations (ICLR)*.

Sriram Yenamandra, Arun Ramachandran, Karmesh Yadav, Austin Wang, Mukul Khanna, Theophile Gervet, Tsung-Yen Yang, Vidhi Jain, Alexander William Clegg, John Turner, et al. 2023. Homerobot: Open-vocabulary mobile manipulation. *arXiv preprint arXiv:2306.11565*.

Tianhe Yu, Deirdre Quillen, Zhanpeng He, Ryan Julian, Karol Hausman, Chelsea Finn, and Sergey Levine. 2020. Meta-world: A benchmark and evaluation for multi-task and meta reinforcement learning. In *Conference on robot learning*, pages 1094–1100. PMLR.

Wenhao Yu, Nimrod Gileadi, Chuyuan Fu, Sean Kirmani, Kuang-Huei Lee, Montse Gonzalez Arenas, Hao-Tien Lewis Chiang, Tom Erez, Leonard Hasenclever, Jan Humplik, et al. 2023. Language to rewards for robotic skill synthesis. *arXiv preprint arXiv:2306.08647*.

# VARIATIONIST: Exploring Multifaceted Variation and Bias in Written Language Data

**Alan Ramponi,* Camilla Casula,* Stefano Menini**
alramponi@fbk.eu, ccasula@fbk.eu, menini@fbk.eu

Fondazione Bruno Kessler, Italy
University of Trento, Italy

## Abstract

Exploring and understanding language data is a fundamental stage in all areas dealing with human language. It allows NLP practitioners to uncover quality concerns and harmful biases in data before training, and helps linguists and social scientists to gain insight into language use and human behavior. Yet, there is currently a lack of a unified, customizable tool to seamlessly inspect and visualize language variation and bias across multiple *variables*, language *units*, and diverse *metrics* that go beyond descriptive statistics. In this paper, we introduce VARIATIONIST, a highly-modular, extensible, and task-agnostic tool that fills this gap. VARIATIONIST handles at once a potentially unlimited combination of variable *types* and *semantics* across diversity and association metrics with regards to the language unit of choice, and orchestrates the creation of up to five-dimensional interactive charts for over 30 variable type–semantics combinations. Through our case studies on computational dialectology, human label variation, and text generation, we show how VARIATIONIST enables researchers from different disciplines to effortlessly answer specific research questions or unveil undesired associations in language data. A Python library, code, documentation, and tutorials are made publicly available to the research community.

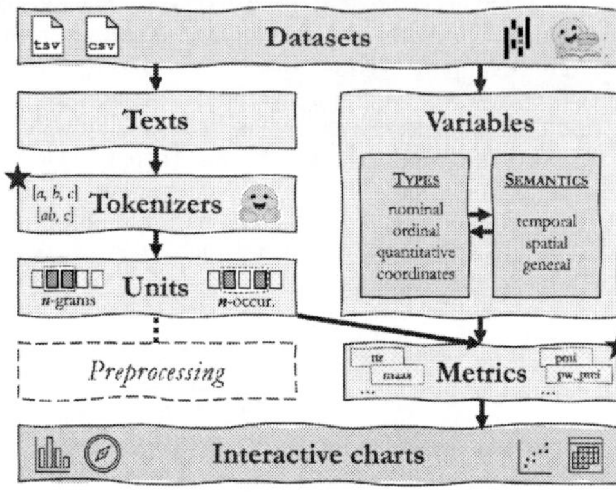


Figure 1: A high-level overview of the core elements and functionalities of VARIATIONIST. The tool computes association metrics between any unit in language and potentially unlimited variable type–semantics combinations, orchestrates the creation of interactive charts, and also supports user-defined custom components (★).

## 1 Introduction

Language data is at the core of a large body of work in many research fields and at their intersections. Language data is used to train large language models (LLMs) by natural language processing (NLP) practitioners, but also by linguists and social scientists to analyze human language and behavior.

With a tendency in the NLP community to overlook what actually *is* in the training data of models (Bender et al., 2021), especially at the level of textual information, and how different characteristics of the data can be intertwined, we propose a tool that can help in inspecting language data in a straightforward and highly customizable manner.

While some language data exploration tools already exist, especially English-centric corpus linguistics tools (Anthony, 2013), these cannot typically handle different types of textual *units* (e.g., tokens, bigrams, characters, and more) and multiple *variables* or combinations thereof, only offering surface-level *metrics* that are not easily customizable, and providing low-dimensional visualization. On the other hand, modern analysis tools in NLP mainly focus on interpreting model outputs (Sarti et al., 2023; Attanasio et al., 2023, *inter alia*) rather than exploring the language data in itself.

VARIATIONIST aims to fill this gap, offering the chance to researchers from diverse disciplines to easily explore the intersections between variables in textual corpora in a plethora of different configurations in a unified manner (cf. Figure 1). Addition-

*These authors contributed equally to this work.



*Proceedings of the 62nd Annual Meeting of the Association for Computational Linguistics (Volume 3: System Demonstrations)*, pages 346–354
August 11-16, 2024 

ally, VARIATIONIST allows users to plug in their own custom tokenization functions and metrics in a seamless way, opening up an unlimited number of analysis configurations in just a few lines of code, and going beyond English-centric assumptions on what the definition of a unit in language actually is.

We demonstrate the flexibility of VARIATIONIST through a set of case studies spanning research questions pertaining to diverse areas of research: computational dialectology, human-label variation (Plank, 2022), and text generation.

**Contributions** We propose VARIATIONIST, a highly flexible and customizable tool for allowing researchers from many fields to seamlessly explore and visualize language variation and bias in textual corpora across many dimensions. We release our code,[1] a `Python` library,[2] a detailed documentation,[3] a video presentation,[4] and a set of tutorials.[5]

## 2 Tool Design

In this section, we present the overall design and aim of VARIATIONIST. In Section 2.1 we detail the guiding design principles, whereas in Section 2.2 we summarize the core elements and functionalities around which VARIATIONIST is designed.

### 2.1 Design Principles

The guiding design principles of VARIATIONIST are summarized in the following:

- **Ease of use**: VARIATIONIST is crafted to be as accessible and customizable as possible, to serve researchers from a wide range of fields who are interested in exploring textual data;
- **Modularity**: VARIATIONIST is built out of small building blocks, allowing users to pick and choose their desired features and metrics without running unnecessary calculations;
- **Extensibility**: VARIATIONIST is designed to be easily extended. By virtue of its intrinsic modularity, it is conceived to let users select their preferred features, and import their own custom tokenizers and metrics into the tool.

[1] : `https://github.com/dhfbk/variationist.`
[2] : `https://pypi.org/project/variationist.`
[3] : `https://variationist.readthedocs.io.`
[4] : The video is available in our GitHub repository.
[5] : `https://github.com/dhfbk/variationist/tree/main/examples.`

### 2.2 Core Elements and Functionalities

VARIATIONIST is designed around a set of core elements useful for computation and visualization. We provide details on each of them in the following.

**DATASETS** The main input for the analysis. Datasets can be provided in the form of *i)* tab-separated (`tsv`) or *ii)* comma-separated (`csv`) files, or *iii)* pre-computed `pandas` dataframes. Moreover, *iv)* any dataset from the 🤗 Hugging Face Datasets (Lhoest et al., 2021) repository can be directly imported for analysis and visualization, too.

**TEXTS** The subset of the input data, in the form of column names or indices, containing textual data. While in most scenarios only a single text column is needed, VARIATIONIST handles up to two columns at once in the analysis. This is especially useful for exploring similarities and differences between texts associated to the same labels and/or metadata.

**UNITS** The language unit of interest, which can be anything from characters to "words" (whatever their definition may be) and longer sequences. VARIATIONIST seamlessly supports $n$-grams (i.e., $n$ contiguous language units) and co-occurrences of $n$ units (not necessarily contiguous) that fall within a user-defined window size, with optional duplicate handling. For creating units, we rely on either built-in, publicly available, or user-defined tokenizers (see below). Units may optionally undergo preprocessing with lowercasing and stopword removal. In the latter case, the user can rely on off-the-shelf stopword lists across multiple languages from the `stopwords-iso`[6] package, provide their own lists directly or as files, or combine them.

**TOKENIZERS** Since the driver for the computation is a language unit, we need ways to segment texts into desired units. VARIATIONIST allows the user to leverage *i)* a default whitespace tokenizer that goes beyond Latin characters, *ii)* any tokenizer from 🤗 Hugging Face Tokenizers (Wolf et al., 2020), or *iii)* a custom tokenizer. This way we avoid any assumptions on what actually *is* a language unit, also broaden the applicability of VARIATIONIST to a wide range of language varieties.

**VARIABLES** Variables are essential components for computing association metrics with language units. While variables in NLP typically translate

[6] `https://github.com/stopwords-iso.`

to human-annotated "labels", those may be naturally generalized to any kind of meta-information associated to textual data (e.g., genres, dates, spatial information, sociodemographic characteristics of annotators or authors). VARIATIONIST natively supports a potentially unlimited number of variable combinations during analysis. Due to the variety of data types and semantic meanings that variables may take, each variable (i.e., column name) is defined through the following two attributes:

- **Variable *types***: the type of the variable for representation purposes. It can be either *nominal* (i.e., categorical variable without an intrinsic ordering/ranking), *ordinal* (variable that can be ordered/ranked), *quantitative* (numerical variable – either discrete or continuous – which may take any value), or *coordinate* (position of a point on the Earth's surface, i.e., latitude or longitude);
- **Variable *semantics***: how the variable must be interpreted for visualization purposes. It may be either *temporal* (e.g., variables such as date or time), *spatial* (e.g., *coordinate* variables or *nominal* variables with spatial semantics such as countries, states, or provinces), or *general* (any variable that does not fall in the aforementioned categories).

**METRICS** The methods used for measuring associations between language units and a potentially unlimited combination of variables. VARIATIONIST includes metrics such as pointwise mutual information (PMI; Fano, 1961), its positive, normalized, and weighted variants, as well as their combinations, for a total of 8 different PMI flavors. It also includes a normalized class relevance metric based on Ramponi and Tonelli (2022) in its positive, weighted, and positive weighted versions. Besides unit–variables association metrics, VARIATIONIST also includes lexical diversity measures such as type-token ratio (TTR; Johnson, 1944), root TTR (Guiraud, 1960), log TTR (Herdan, 1960), and Maas' index (Maas, 1972). Basic statistics such as frequencies, number of texts, number of language units, duplicate instances, average text length, and vocabulary size are also provided. Finally, custom metrics can be easily defined by the user and used for subsequent analysis, therefore extending VARIATIONIST's capabilities to specific use cases.

**CHARTS** The visual components of the tool. VARIATIONIST orchestrates the automatic creation of interactive charts for each metric based on the combination of variable types and semantics from a previous analysis. It defines the optimal dimension or channel (e.g., `x`, `y`, `color`, `size`, `lat`, `lon`, or a dropdown component) for each variable, creating charts with up to five dimensions (of which one is reserved for the *quantitative* metric score, and the other to the *nominal* language unit). Possible charts currently include temporal line charts, choropleth maps, geographic and standard scatter plots, heatmaps, binned maps, and bar charts. For each metric, one or more charts are created (e.g., in the case of *nominal* variable types with *spatial* semantics, both a bar chart and a geographic scatter plot are created). Charts can be interactively filtered by language unit through a search input field supporting regular expressions or a dropdown menu[7] to smoothly explore associations between units and the variables of interest.

## 3 Implementation and Usage

In this section, we present implementation details (Section 3.1 and Section 3.2) and an example usage of our `Python` library (Section 3.3).

### 3.1 User-facing Classes

There are two main elements a typical user interacts with: `Inspector` and `Visualizer`, as well as their respective `InspectorArgs` and `VisualizerArgs`, which store all of the parameters they work with.

**`Inspector`** The `Inspector` class takes care of orchestrating the analysis, from importing and tokenizing the data to handling variable combinations and importing and calculating the metrics. It returns a dictionary (or a `.json` file, cf. Section 3.2) with all the calculated metrics for each unit of language, variable, and combination thereof, according to a set of parameters that are set by the user through the `InspectorArgs`.

**`InspectorArgs`** Through the `InspectorArgs` class we tell `Inspector` how to carry out the analysis. While we refer the reader to our library and related resources for the full documentation (Appendix A), some of the analysis details that can be set using `InspectorArgs` include what texts and variable(s) of the data to focus on, whether to use $n$-grams or $n$ co-occurrences (and if so, for what

[7]The choice depends on the chart type and its number of dimensions, with the goal of keeping the overall user experience and filtering time as smooth as possible.

```
from variationist import Inspector, InspectorArgs, Visualizer, VisualizerArgs

# 1) Define the inspector arguments
ins_args = InspectorArgs(text_names=["text"], var_names=["label"],
    metrics=["npw_pmi"], n_tokens=1, language="en", stopwords=True, lowercase=True)

# 2) Run the inspector and get the results
res = Inspector(dataset="data.tsv", args=ins_args).inspect()

# 3) Define the visualizer arguments
vis_args = VisualizerArgs(output_folder="charts", output_formats=["html"])

# 4) Create interactive charts for all metrics
charts = Visualizer(input_json=res, args=vis_args).create()
```

Figure 2: Example showcasing the four steps for inspecting data and visualizing results using VARIATIONIST.

values of $n$), what tokenizer to use, including any custom ones, the selection of metrics we want to calculate, whether and how to bin the variables, and more. In short, any preference regarding the analysis will have to go through `InspectorArgs`.

**`Visualizer`** The `Visualizer` class takes care of orchestrating the creation of a variety of interactive charts for each metric and variable combination associated to the language units of interest. It leverages the results and metadata from the dictionary (or `.json` file) resulting from a prior analysis using `Inspector`, creating charts up to five dimensions using the `altair` library (VanderPlas et al., 2018).[8] It relies on `VisualizerArgs`, a class storing specific user-defined arguments for visualization.

**`VisualizerArgs`** The `VisualizerArgs` class provides ways to customize the creation of charts and their serialization. In particular, it allows the user to specify whether to pre-filter the visualization based on selected language units (provided as lists) or top-scoring ones (by specifying a maximum per-variable amount), provide a `shapefile` for setting the background of spatial charts, and decide whether the charts have to be saved as files and in which format, among others.

### 3.2 Data Interchange

The results of an `Inspector` analysis are either *i)* stored in a variable as a dictionary, or *ii)* serialized in a `.json` file. While the first case comes handy for direct use by the `Visualizer` in most cases, the second option is especially useful when dealing with large datasets and a high number of variable combinations (and possible values). Indeed, serialization will enable the results to be easily used for visualization in a later stage. Details on the structure of the interchange file are in our repository.

### 3.3 Example Usage

Figure 2 shows a basic usage example of VARIATIONIST, which consists of four steps: *i)* defining the `InspectorArgs`, *ii)* instantiating and running the computation with `Inspector`, *iii)* defining the `VisualizerArgs`, and finally *iv)* creating interactive charts for the previously specified metrics through the `Visualizer`. For details on all the available parameters and hands-on tutorials, we refer the reader to our resources (Appendix A).

## 4 Case Studies

In the following, we scratch the surface of VARIATIONIST's capabilities by presenting case studies on diverse topics, from computational dialectology (Section 4.1) to human label variation (Section 4.2) and text generation (Section 4.3). Three personas with different backgrounds and aims exemplify our case studies: *Alice*, *Bob*, and *Carol*. We then provide ideas for further applications (Section 4.4). Code for case studies is available in our repository.

### 4.1 Exploring Language Variation Across Space

**Computational dialectology**

*Alice is a linguist interested in how language varies across space. Specifically, her research focuses on language varieties of Italy and their use in social media. Her goal is to understand in which areas selected lexical items are predominantly used.*

Alice uses DIATOPIT (Ramponi and Casula, 2023), a corpus of geolocated social media posts in Italy

[8] Due to the modular design of VARIATIONIST, we aim to integrate additional visualization libraries in future releases.

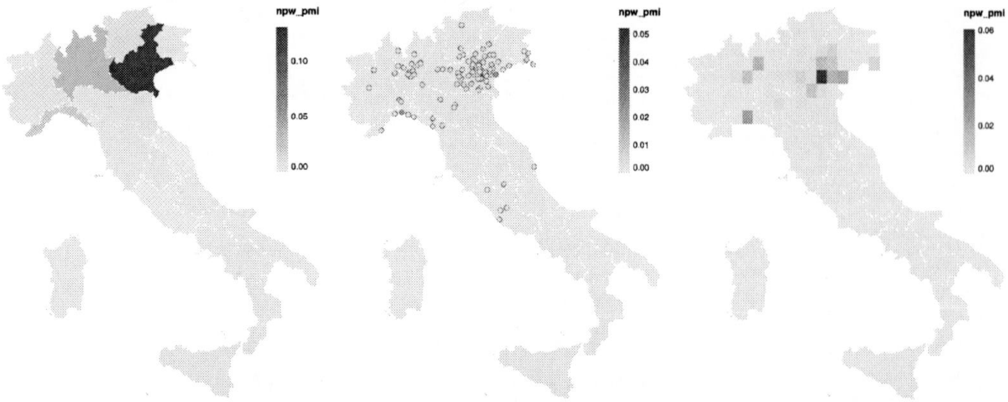


(a) Choropleth map (*regions*). (b) Geo scatter plot (*municipalities*). (c) Binned map (*custom areas*).

Figure 3: Example visualizations for the computational dialectology case study. All the charts have been filtered to show the use of the lexical item "ghe" across space within Italy at different granularities in terms of npw_pmi score.

focused on local language varieties, and provides it as input to VARIATIONIST. She specifies the text column of the dataset as the textual data and the region column as the variable of interest (setting it with *nominal* type and *spatial* semantics). She selects the normalized, positive, and weighted variant of PMI (npw_pmi) as the metric, and chooses unigrams, derived via the default whitespace tokenizer, as the language unit. Lastly, she sets all text characters to lowercase and specifies stopword removal using a default lexicon in Italian, and extends it by providing extra unigrams to remove (i.e., the "user" and "url" placeholders). She then interactively explores the results to understand *where* the lexical item "ghe" is predominantly used.

As shown in the choropleth map in Figure 3a, the lexical item appears to be mostly used in specific regions in northern Italy, especially those where Venetian, Ligurian, and Lombard varieties are spoken. This is due to its role as an adverb and pronoun in these Romance varieties. However, language varieties of Italy cross administrative borders and multiple varieties are spoken within each region (Ramponi, 2024). By running VARIATIONIST again and specifying the latitude and longitude variables instead (both with *coordinate* type and *spatial* semantics), Alice gets a fine-grained picture of the actual use of the word (Figure 3b). Moreover, by defining 30 equally-sized intervals for the latitude and longitude variables, she obtains a binned map (Figure 3c) that allows her to explore the use of "ghe" at an intermediate granularity.

In the future, Alice would like to investigate if the use of certain lexical items underwent change over time, as a mean to assess the vitality of language varieties. By providing an additional temporal variable, she may answer her question.

### 4.2 Investigating Human Subjectivity in Hate Speech Annotation

**Human label variation**

*Bob is a computational social scientist interested in how people perceive hateful language online. Specifically, he is interested in understanding whether annotators with different sociodemographic characteristics place greater importance to certain lexical items in determining if a message is hateful.*

Bob employs the Measuring Hate Speech (MHS; Sachdeva et al., 2022) corpus for answering his questions. Each post in the dataset is labeled as hate speech or not and includes the demographic attributes of annotators. Bob loads the dataset from Hugging Face Datasets[9] and filters it to keep hateful messages only (i.e., hatespeech=2). For facilitating the analysis, he combines boolean columns pertaining to the same variables (e.g., annotator_race_{asian|black|...}) into single string columns (e.g., annotator_race with possible values among {*asian*|*black*|...}). Then, he uses VARIATIONIST and specifies text as the column containing the textual data and npw_relevance as the metric for the analysis, he sets the conversion of texts to lowercase to reduce data sparsity and the

[9] https://huggingface.co/datasets/ucberkeley-dlab/measuring-hate-speech.

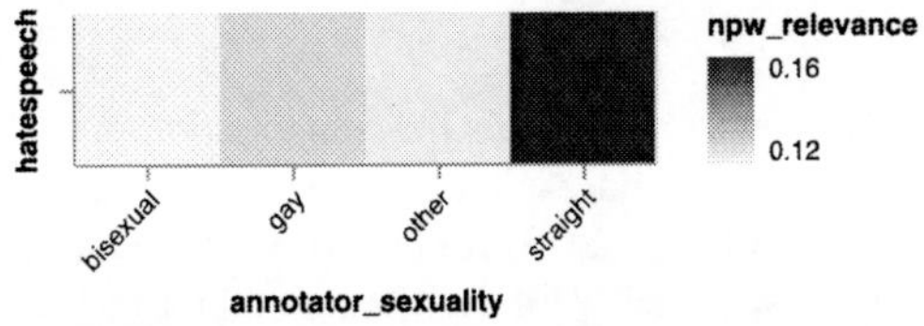


(a) Heatmap for "gay" across annotators' sexual orientation.

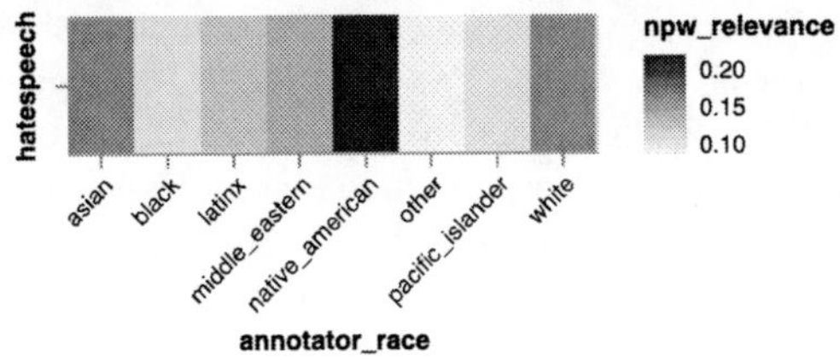


(b) Heatmap for "n*ggas" across annotators' race.

Figure 4: Example visualizations for the human label variation case study. All the charts show the `npw_relevance` score for the hateful class of specific lexical items across sociodemographics of annotators.

removal of stopwords in English. Bob leaves the remaining parameters with default values (e.g., unigrams as units, whitespace tokenizer). As the variables of interest, he specifies `hatespeech` and either `annotator_sexuality` or `annotator_race` (all with *nominal* type and *general* semantics).

When exploring the relationship between annotators' sexual orientation and the labels they assign to posts, Bob discovers that the lexical item "gay" is more indicative of the hateful class for annotators who identify as *straight* compared to those who identify as *bisexual*, *gay*, or *other* (Figure 4a). This may indicate that non-*straight* annotators are more sensible to the nuances in the use of the term and that *straight* annotators may instead occasionally use it as shortcut for hate speech annotation. Bob gets a similar finding when investigating the association of reclaimed words such as "n*ggas" to hateful posts across self-reported annotators' race (Figure 4b). The term is less associated to posts labeled as hateful by annotators who identify themselves as *black* people (in-group members) compared to those annotated as hateful by most out-group members (e.g., *asian*, *native american*, *white* people).

In summary, different lexical items may be (more or less) informative for certain labels (e.g., hate speech) depending on the sociodemographics of annotators. VARIATIONIST can aid in speeding up the exploration of undesired associations across a combination of attributes in language data.

### 4.3 Analyzing Features of Human *versus* Generated Texts

**Text generation**

*Carol is an NLP practitioner working on generative large language models (LLMs). She is interested in exploring the differences between texts written by humans and those generated by LLMs in terms of length, lexical diversity, and word use.*

Carol uses the Human ChatGPT Comparison Corpus (HC3; Guo et al., 2023), loading it from the Hugging Face hub.[10] HC3 comprises answers written by humans and ChatGPT-generated responses given the same questions across five domains. Through VARIATIONIST, Carol specifies two text columns of interest: `human_answers` and `chatgpt_answers`. She sets bigrams as units with lowercase normalization, and specifies stopword removal in English, further adding "url" and numbers from 0 to 9 as extra unigrams to remove. She defines `stats`, `root_ttr`, and `npw_pmi` as metrics in order to analyze different aspects of the texts. The other parameters are left with default values.

By looking at the summary `stats`, Carol finds that human answers are on average much longer than ChatGPT-generated ones (i.e., 98.26 *vs* 73.66 units) and that the vocabulary size of human answers is almost two times that of synthetic responses (i.e., 1.60M *vs* 0.87M). Moreover, human-produced answers are more varied in terms of `root_ttr`, also exhibiting a larger standard deviation compared to ChatGPT-generated ones (cf. Figure 5a). Finally, by looking at the top-$k$ ($k$=20) bigrams associated to human and ChatGPT texts (Figure 5b), Carol finds that human answers appear to include terms that are more commonly used in everyday situations (e.g., "lot people", "lot money"), while ChatGPT answers tend to include language that is more formal and less conversational, such as "healthcare provider" or "variety factors". In addition to this, it is clear from the `npw_pmi` scores that the distribution of bigrams is a bit more balanced for human-authored texts, while ChatGPT appears to produce texts that include very specific bigrams with a much higher frequency. This might be a consequence of the different lexical variety between ChatGPT and human-authored texts.

[10] `https://huggingface.co/datasets/Hello-SimpleAI/HC3`.

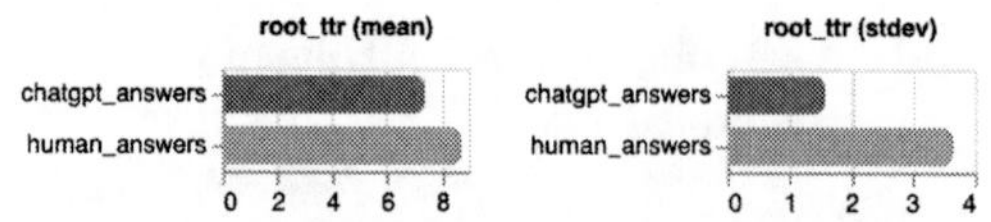


(a) Bar charts comparing the lexical variety of human and ChatGPT-generated answers according to `root_ttr`.

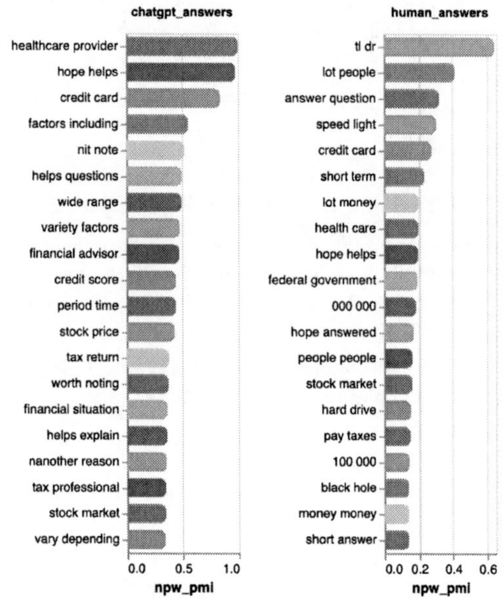


(b) Bar charts showing the top-$k$ ($k$=20) informative bigrams for human and ChatGPT-generated answers according to `npw_pmi`.

Figure 5: Example visualizations for the text generation case study. The charts present some characteristics at the lexical level for human and ChatGPT-generated texts.

As a future exploration, Carol aims to investigate which $n$ co-occurrences of language units appear to be strongly associated to synthetic responses within specific domains (e.g., finance). This can be done by providing the `source` column of the HC3 dataset as an additional variable to VARIATIONIST.

### 4.4 Food for Thought

The potential applications of VARIATIONIST are many. For instance, it can be used for advancing research on sociolects such as African-American English (Blodgett et al., 2016), to study linguistic reclamation and more generally investigate semantic change over time, or to conduct qualitative error analyses for model predictions (i.e., to unveil which language units are more informative of a wrong class). Moreover, it can be used to compare tokenizers and their effect on specific language varieties. We leave those areas to the reader as potential avenues for future applications of VARIATIONIST.

## 5 Related Work

There exist many tools for data exploration in literature, especially in the field of corpus linguistics (see Anthony (2013) for an overview). However, there is currently a lack of a unified tool to serve diverse research communities that goes beyond descriptive statistics and basic charts, and that handles many variables at once in a simple fashion. The closest work to VARIATIONIST is Hugging Face's Data Measurements Tool (DMT; Luccioni et al., 2021). However, it does not consider multiple texts and variables in the analysis, and it does not provide customization and flexibility in terms of units, metrics, tokenizers, and charts. VARIATIONIST serves to fill this gap in literature.

## 6 Conclusion

We introduced VARIATIONIST, a modular, customizable, and easy-to-use analysis and visualization tool that aims at helping researchers in understanding language variation and unveiling potential biases in written language corpora across many dimensions. Through the case studies of *Alice*, *Bob*, and *Carol*, we showed the potential of our tool in answering different research questions across disciplines. We hope that our work will also be useful to *Dave*, a fourth fictional character who unfortunately looks at the data very rarely before using it, to begin to reconsider the pivotal role of exploring data before using it for training language models.

## Ethics and Broader Impact Statement

VARIATIONIST serves as a tool to support the research community in better understanding the diversity in language use and unveiling quality issues and harmful biases in textual data. As a result, we do not foresee specific ethical concerns related to our work and, on the contrary, we hope that VARIATIONIST will give additional means to explore datasets and raise awareness among researchers on the paramount importance of looking at the data.

VARIATIONIST has been designed following an inclusion-first approach, i.e., by avoiding common language-specific assumptions to better support its application across many language varieties. As a limitation, we acknowledge that VARIATIONIST is currently limited to the lexical level on written data. We aim to extend its functionalities to also cover other linguistic aspects such as grammar as well as the speech modality in the next releases.

## Acknowledgments

This work has been funded within the European Union's ISF program under grant agreement No. 101100539 (PRECRISIS) and by the European Union's Horizon Europe research and innovation program under grant agreement No. 101070190 (AI4Trust).

## References

Laurence Anthony. 2013. A critical look at software tools in corpus linguistics. *Linguistic Research*, 30(2):141–161.

Giuseppe Attanasio, Eliana Pastor, Chiara Di Bonaventura, and Debora Nozza. 2023. ferret: a framework for benchmarking explainers on transformers. In *Proceedings of the 17th Conference of the European Chapter of the Association for Computational Linguistics: System Demonstrations*, pages 256–266, Dubrovnik, Croatia. Association for Computational Linguistics.

Emily M. Bender, Timnit Gebru, Angelina McMillan-Major, and Shmargaret Shmitchell. 2021. On the dangers of stochastic parrots: Can language models be too big? In *Proceedings of the 2021 ACM Conference on Fairness, Accountability, and Transparency*, FAccT '21, page 610–623, New York, NY, USA. Association for Computing Machinery.

Su Lin Blodgett, Lisa Green, and Brendan O'Connor. 2016. Demographic dialectal variation in social media: A case study of African-American English. In *Proceedings of the 2016 Conference on Empirical Methods in Natural Language Processing*, pages 1119–1130, Austin, Texas. Association for Computational Linguistics.

Robert M. Fano. 1961. *Transmission of information: A statistical theory of communications*. MIT Press, New York, USA.

Pierre Guiraud. 1960. *Problèmes et méthodes de la statistique linguistique*, first edition. Synthese library. Springer Dordrecht, Dordrecht, Netherlands.

Biyang Guo, Xin Zhang, Ziyuan Wang, Minqi Jiang, Jinran Nie, Yuxuan Ding, Jianwei Yue, and Yupeng Wu. 2023. How close is ChatGPT to human experts? Comparison corpus, evaluation, and detection. *arXiv preprint arxiv:2301.07597*.

Gustav Herdan. 1960. *Type-token mathematics: A textbook of mathematical linguistics*. Janua linguarum. Mouton, The Hague, Netherlands.

Wendell Johnson. 1944. Studies in language behavior: A program of research. *Psychological Monographs*, 56(2):1–15.

Quentin Lhoest, Albert Villanova del Moral, Yacine Jernite, Abhishek Thakur, Patrick von Platen, Suraj Patil, Julien Chaumond, Mariama Drame, Julien Plu, Lewis Tunstall, Joe Davison, Mario Šaško, Gunjan Chhablani, Bhavitvya Malik, Simon Brandeis, Teven Le Scao, Victor Sanh, Canwen Xu, Nicolas Patry, Angelina McMillan-Major, Philipp Schmid, Sylvain Gugger, Clément Delangue, Théo Matussière, Lysandre Debut, Stas Bekman, Pierric Cistac, Thibault Goehringer, Victor Mustar, François Lagunas, Alexander Rush, and Thomas Wolf. 2021. Datasets: A community library for natural language processing. In *Proceedings of the 2021 Conference on Empirical Methods in Natural Language Processing: System Demonstrations*, pages 175–184, Online and Punta Cana, Dominican Republic. Association for Computational Linguistics.

Sasha Luccioni, Yacine Jernite, Margaret Mitchell, and Hugging Face team. 2021. Introducing the Data Measurements Tool: An interactive tool for looking at datasets. `https://huggingface.co/blog/data-measurements-tool`. Accessed: 2024-03-01.

Heinz-Dieter Maas. 1972. Über den zusammenhang zwischen wortschatzumfang und länge eines textes. *Zeitschrift für Literaturwissenschaft und Linguistik*, 2(8):73.

Barbara Plank. 2022. The "problem" of human label variation: On ground truth in data, modeling and evaluation. In *Proceedings of the 2022 Conference on Empirical Methods in Natural Language Processing*, pages 10671–10682, Abu Dhabi, United Arab Emirates. Association for Computational Linguistics.

Alan Ramponi. 2024. Language varieties of Italy: Technology challenges and opportunities. *Transactions of the Association for Computational Linguistics*, 12:19–38.

Alan Ramponi and Camilla Casula. 2023. DiatopIt: A corpus of social media posts for the study of diatopic language variation in Italy. In *Tenth Workshop on NLP for Similar Languages, Varieties and Dialects (VarDial 2023)*, pages 187–199, Dubrovnik, Croatia. Association for Computational Linguistics.

Alan Ramponi and Sara Tonelli. 2022. Features or spurious artifacts? data-centric baselines for fair and robust hate speech detection. In *Proceedings of the 2022 Conference of the North American Chapter of the Association for Computational Linguistics: Human Language Technologies*, pages 3027–3040, Seattle, United States. Association for Computational Linguistics.

Pratik Sachdeva, Renata Barreto, Geoff Bacon, Alexander Sahn, Claudia von Vacano, and Chris Kennedy. 2022. The measuring hate speech corpus: Leveraging rasch measurement theory for data perspectivism. In *Proceedings of the 1st Workshop on Perspectivist Approaches to NLP @LREC2022*, pages 83–94, Marseille, France. European Language Resources Association.

Gabriele Sarti, Nils Feldhus, Ludwig Sickert, and Oskar van der Wal. 2023. Inseq: An interpretability toolkit for sequence generation models. In *Proceedings of the 61st Annual Meeting of the Association for Computational Linguistics (Volume 3: System Demonstrations)*, pages 421–435, Toronto, Canada. Association for Computational Linguistics.

Jacob VanderPlas, Brian Granger, Jeffrey Heer, Dominik Moritz, Kanit Wongsuphasawat, Arvind Satyanarayan, Eitan Lees, Ilia Timofeev, Ben Welsh, and Scott Sievert. 2018. Altair: Interactive statistical visualizations for python. *Journal of Open Source Software*, 3(32):1057.

Thomas Wolf, Lysandre Debut, Victor Sanh, Julien Chaumond, Clement Delangue, Anthony Moi, Pierric Cistac, Tim Rault, Remi Louf, Morgan Funtowicz, Joe Davison, Sam Shleifer, Patrick von Platen, Clara Ma, Yacine Jernite, Julien Plu, Canwen Xu, Teven Le Scao, Sylvain Gugger, Mariama Drame, Quentin Lhoest, and Alexander Rush. 2020. Transformers: State-of-the-art natural language processing. In *Proceedings of the 2020 Conference on Empirical Methods in Natural Language Processing: System Demonstrations*, pages 38–45, Online. Association for Computational Linguistics.

# Appendix

## A VARIATIONIST's Resources

All the resources related to VARIATIONIST are made publicly-available to the research community. Table 1 lists all the links to these resources.

| Resource | URL |
|---|---|
| Code | `https://github.com/dhfbk/variationist` |
| Library | `https://pypi.org/project/variationist` |
| Docs | `https://variationist.readthedocs.io` |
| Video | `https://github.com/dhfbk/variationist` |
| Tutorials | `https://github.com/dhfbk/variationist/tree/main/examples` |

Table 1: Publicly-available VARIATIONIST resources.

## B Credits

Emojis are from the Google Noto Emoji set (`https://github.com/googlefonts/noto-emoji`).

# An LLM-based Knowledge Synthesis and Scientific Reasoning Framework for Biomedical Discovery

**Oskar Wysocki**[1,2], **Magdalena Wysocka**[2], **Danilo S. Carvalho**[2], **Alex Bogatu**[2], **Danilo Gusicuma**[1], **Maxime Delmas**[1], **Harriet Unsworth**[2], **André Freitas**[1,2,3]

[1]Idiap Research Institute, Switzerland
[2]National Biomarker Centre, CRUK-MI, Univ. of Manchester, United Kingdom
[3]Department of Computer Science, Univ. of Manchester, United Kingdom
**Correspondence:** firstname.lastname@idiap.ch[1] firstname.lastname@manchester.ac.uk[2]

## Abstract

We present BioLunar, developed using the Lunar framework, as a tool for supporting biological analyses, with a particular emphasis on molecular-level evidence enrichment for biomarker discovery in oncology. The platform integrates Large Language Models (LLMs) to facilitate complex scientific reasoning across distributed evidence spaces, enhancing the capability for harmonizing and reasoning over heterogeneous data sources. Demonstrating its utility in cancer research, BioLunar leverages modular design, reusable data access and data analysis components, and a low-code user interface, enabling researchers of all programming levels to construct LLM-enabled scientific workflows. By facilitating automatic scientific discovery and inference from heterogeneous evidence, BioLunar exemplifies the potential of the integration between LLMs, specialised databases and biomedical tools to support expert-level knowledge synthesis and discovery.

## 1 Introduction

Contemporary biomedical discovery represents a prototypical instance of complex scientific reasoning, which requires the coordination of controlled *in-vivo/in-silico* interventions, complex multi-step data analysis pipelines and the interpretation of the results under the light of previous evidence (available in different curated databases and in the literature) (Paananen and Fortino, 2019; Nicholson and Greene, 2020). This intricacy emerges out of the inherent complexity of biological mechanisms underlying organism responses, which are defined by a network of multi-scale inter-dependencies (Bogdan et al., 2021). While more granular data is being generated by the evolution of instruments, assays and methods, and the parallel abundance of experimental interventions (Dryden-Palmer et al., 2020), there a practical barrier for integrating and cohering this evidence space into a specific context of analysis.

Within biomedical discovery, the language interpretation capabilities of Large Language Models (LLMs) can provide an integrative framework for harmonising and reasoning over distributed evidence spaces and tools, systematising and lowering the barriers to access and reason over multiple structured databases, textual bases such as PubMed, enriching the background knowledge through specialised ontologies and serving as interfaces to external analytical tools (e.g. mechanistic/perturbation models, gene enrichment models, etc). In this context, LLMs can serve as a linguistic analytical layer which can reduce the syntactic impedance across diverse functional components: once an adapter to an external component is built it can be integrated and reused in different contexts, creating a monotonic increase of functional components. Complementarily, from a Biomedical-NLP perspective, in order to address real-world problems, LLMs need to be complemented with mechanisms which can deliver contextual control (e.g. via Retrieval Augmented Generation: RAG: access the relevant background knowledge and facts) and perform the analytical tasks which are integral to contemporary biomedical inference ('toolforming').

Emerging LLM-focused coordination frameworks such as LangChain[1], Flowise[2] and Lunar[3] provide the capabilities to deliver a composition of functional components, some of them under a low-code/no-code use environment, using the abstraction of workflows. While there are general-purpose coordination frameworks, there is a lack of specialised components for addressing biomedical analyses.

In this paper we demonstrate BioLunar, a suite of components developed over the Lunar environment

[1]https://python.langchain.com
[2]https://github.com/FlowiseAI/Flowise
[3]https://lunarbase.ai



*Proceedings of the 62nd Annual Meeting of the Association for Computational Linguistics (Volume 3: System Demonstrations)*, pages 355–364
August 11-16, 2024 ©2024 Association for Computational Linguistics

to support biological analyses. We demonstrate the key functionalities of the platform contextualised within a real-use case in the context of molecular-level evidence enrichment for biomarker discovery in oncology.

## 2 BioLunar

BioLunar enables the creation of LLM-based biomedical scientific workflows using software components with standardised APIs. A workflow is composed of components and subworkflows connected through input-output relationships, and are capable of handling multiple inputs. In the user interface, components are clustered according to their function (see Fig.1). Creating a workflow does not require programming knowledge since components are predefined and merely require data inputs or parameter settings. However, for users who wish to write custom code, 'Python Coder' and 'R Coder' components are provided, enabling the definition of custom methods. These custom components can be saved and subsequently accessed in the 'Custom' group tab.

In the paper we describe an exemplar *biomedical workflow* designed to integrate evidence and infer conclusions from bioinformatics pipeline results. Specifically, the *biomedical workflow* queries expert knowledge bases (KBs) that continuously compile clinical, experimental, and population genetic study outcomes, aligning them with assertions relevant to the significance of the observed gene or variant. It then employs Natural Language Inference (NLI) (via LLM) to integrate and harmonise the evidence space and interpreting the results, culminating in a comprehensive summary for the entire gene set input. This interpretation takes into account the bioanalytical context supplied by the user.

### 2.1 Exemplar Workflow

Next-generation sequencing (NGS) assays play a pivotal role in the precise characterisation of tumours and patients in experimental cancer treatments. NGS findings are essential to guide the design of novel biomarkers and cancer treatments. Nevertheless, the clinical elucidation of NGS findings subsequent to initial bioinformatics analysis often requires time-consuming manual analysis procedures which are vulnerable to errors. The interpretation of molecular signatures that are typically yielded by genome-scale experiments are often supported by pathway-centric approaches through which mechanistic insights can be gained by pointing at a set of biological processes. Moreover, gene and variant enrichment benefits from heterogeneous curated data sources which pose challenges to seamless integration. Furthermore, there are different levels of supporting evidence and therefore prioritising conclusions is crucial. Automating evidence interpretation, knowledge synthesis and leveraging evidence-rich gene set reports are fundamental for addressing the challenges in precision oncology and the discovery of new biomarkers.

### 2.2 User interface

The user interface facilitates an agile workflow construction by enabling users to select and arrange components via drag-and-drop from functionally grouped categories, such as, i.a.: 'Prompt Query' featuring NLI components, 'Knowledge Bases' components, 'Extractors' for retrieving files from zip archives or extracting text and tables from PDF files, and 'Coders', which allow for the creation of custom components using Python or R scripts.

Components allow for individual execution, edition, or configuration adjustment via a visual interface. Workflows can be executed, saved, or shared. Each component has designated input and output capabilities, enabling seamless integration where the output from one can directly feed into another. Users have the flexibility to manually input values if no direct connection is established. Additionally, a component's output can feed into multiple components. The system's architecture supports effortless expansion, adding branches and components without affecting the existing workflow, thus facilitating scalable customization to meet changing requirements. The user interface with an example of a workflow is presented in Fig.1 and in demo video `https://youtu.be/Hc6pAA_5Xu8`.

### 2.3 Knowledge bases

The current framework integrates a diverse set of knowledge bases which are relevant for precision oncology. To identify gene mutations as biomarkers for cancer diagnosis, prognosis, and drug response, we integrated CIViC[4] and OncoKB[5]. CIViC provides molecular profiles (MPs) of genes, each linked to clinical evidence, with

[4] `https://civicdb.org`

[5] `https://www.oncokb.org`

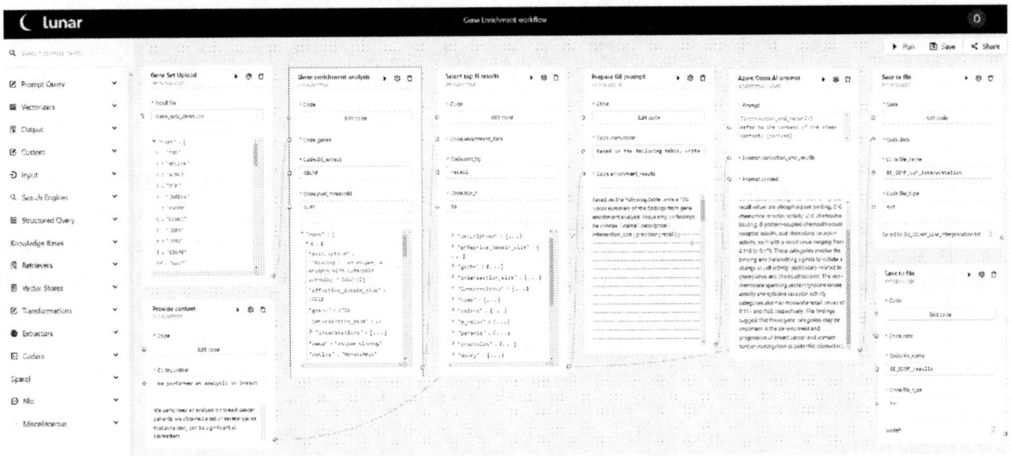


Figure 1: BioLunar interface. An exemplary workflow of Gene Enrichment with an input gene set, knowledge base query and LLM interpretation components.

a molecular score indicating evidence quality, assessed by human annotators. The Gene Ontology[6] (GO) offered gene function insights, and the Human Protein Atlas[7] supplied a list of potential drug targets and transcription factors. We employed COSMIC[8] for somatic mutation impacts in cancer, the largest resource in this field. Our analysis also included KEGG[9], Reactome[10], and WikiPathways[11] for pathway information, enriching our investigation with scientific literature via PubMed's API [12].

In the following subsections, we showcase examples of components, subworkflows, and workflows constructed using the BioLunar framework, motivated by the biomarker discovery/precision oncology themes.

### 2.4 Construction and reuse of specialised prompts

BioLunar employs standard LLM interfaces, allowing the use of different models according to users' preferences. The prompt components allows for the composition of specialised prompt chains which can be later reused, defining a pragmatic pathway for specialised Natural Language Inference (NLI) via prompt decomposition/composition. This approach allows for the creation of reasoning chains that combines user's instructions with the results of database queries and analyses from specialised tools within the context of the study. An instantiated example of the *Azure Open AI prompt* is described in Fig.1.

### 2.5 Subworkflow component

The *subworkflow* component enables the reuse of an existing workflow within another workflow, functioning as a component with specified inputs and outputs. This feature simplifies the composition of more complex workflows and avoids the repetition of defining identical steps for the same task. Subworkflows can be selected like other components from the left panel in the interface, offering access to all available workflows for easy integration. Examples of subworkflows are presented in Fig.2,3.

### 2.6 Gene Enrichment subworkflow

One example of a specialised subworkflow is the *Gene Enrichment subworkflow* (Fig.1,2A) begins with uploading the targeted gene sets. Then a component accesses a specific KB — such as Gene Ontology, KEGG, Reactome, or WikiPathways—defined by the user, using *gprofiler* API[13]. This component identifies gene groups with a statistically significant overlap with the input gene set, according to a Fisher's test, and calculates p-values, recall, and precision. The user then specifies a variable to rank these groups and selects the top N for further analysis. The output includes both a inter-

[6] https://geneontology.org
[7] https://www.proteinatlas.org
[8] https://cancer.sanger.ac.uk/cosmic
[9] https://www.kegg.jp/kegg/
[10] https://reactome.org
[11] https://www.wikipathways.org
[12] https://pubmed.ncbi.nlm.nih.gov
[13] https://biit.cs.ut.ee/gprofiler/page/apis

pretation performed by an NLI component (through LLM) and a table featuring the names, descriptions, and statistics of the top N selected groups.

### 2.7 Human Protein Atlas subworkflow

In the *Human Protein Atlas subworkflow*, given a gene set, an associated external KB is queried by selecting 'Transcription factors' from the HPA database using a dedicated query-database connector. A reusable component, 'Analyze overlap', then identifies genes that overlap and calculates relevant statistics. Similarly to the *Gene Enrichment subworkflow*, the results are interpreted by an prompt-based NLI component and presented alongside a table summarising the findings (Fig.2B,A.7).

### 2.8 CIVIC subworkflow

This *subworkflow* exemplifies a more complex composition of components (Fig.3). This subworkflow initiates by querying the CIVIC database for input genes, yielding, among other things, gene descriptions in clinical contexts, and their variants and molecular profiles (MPs), which are essential for the final interpretation. Additionally, users specify the analysis context, including aspects such as cancer types or subtypes, treatments, populations, etc. Initially, gene descriptions are analysed by a prompt-based NLI component within this defined context. Subsequently, MPs scored below a predefined threshold (set at a MP score of 10) are tagged as *less known*, reflecting lower scientific evidence and ranking by CIVIC annotators. The evidence supporting these lesser-known MPs is then interpreted by a prompt-based NLI component, considering the broader analysis context. Conversely, evidence from *well-known* MPs, scoring above 10, undergoes a similar interpretation process.

For genes without identified MPs in CIVIC, a sequence of components perform further evidence retrieval from PubMed. An NLI module generates context-based keywords for PubMed queries, which are combined with the names of genes lacking MPs. A 'PubMed search' component then retrieves $N$ publications, including metadata, citation counts and MeSH terms (used later for context alignment validation). The abstracts of these publications are interpreted by an NLI module in the context of the analysis.

All clinical evidence interpretations are then succinctly summarised by via a prompt component, taking into account the context of the analysis. These interpretations, along with tabular results, constitute the output.

### 2.9 Bioworkflow - comprehensive analysis for a set of genes.

The exemplar *bioworkflow* composes multiple subworkflows (Fig.4), each dedicated to a specific multi-step and specialised task, which are typically defined by the composition of heterogeneous components, most commonly connectors and query instance components to specialised databases (e.g. CIVIC, HPA, PubMed, OncoKB), external specialised analytical tools (toolformers for gene enrichment analysis) and chains of specialised interpretation prompts (e.g. selection, filtering, extraction, summarisation). This setup forms a comprehensive workflow which exemplifies the close dialogue between LLMs and genomic analysis, encompassing gene enrichment, comparison with reference gene sets, and access to evidence within

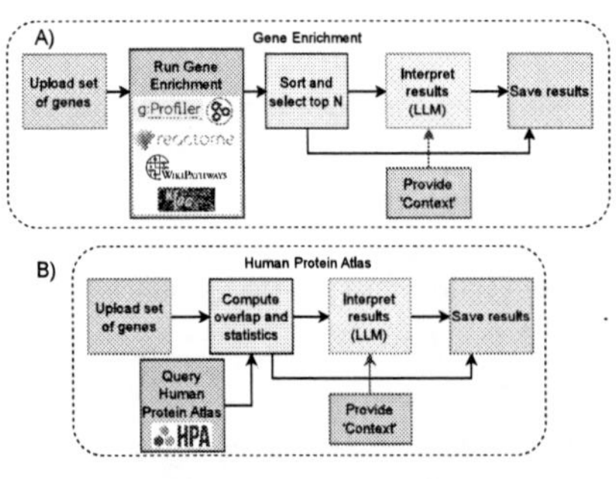


Figure 2: A) Gene Enrichment workflow - uses the *gprofiler* API to access i.a. Gene Ontology, KEGG, WikiPathways, Reactome; B) Human Protein Atlas workflow. Compares and interprets the input and reference gene sets.

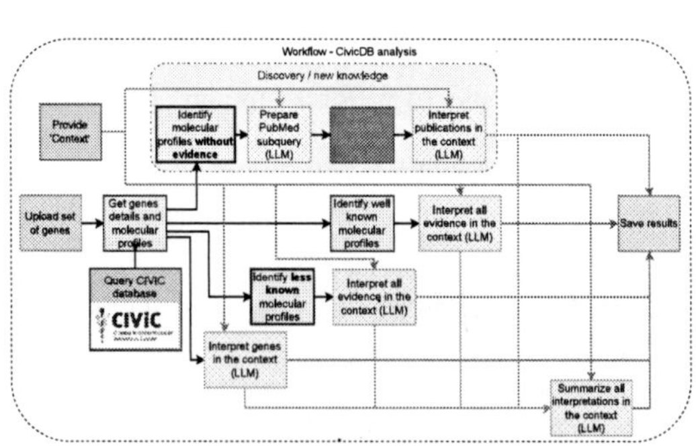


Figure 3: CIVIC evidence analysis workflow. prompt-based NLI components are fed by both the results and context of the analysis in order to produce relevant evidence-based conclusions.

an experimental medicine setting. Additionally, it queries PubMed publications within the CIVIC component to seek evidence for molecular profiles not yet described. Its componentised architecture facilitates the extensibility of the workflow with new sources, prompts and external tools. Conclusions drawn from each subworkflow are interpreted within the analysis context, being integrated in a comprehensive summary. All findings are compiled in a report, exported as a PDF file.

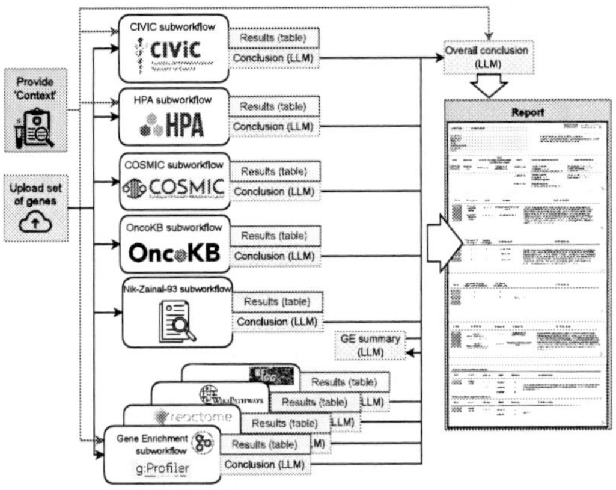


Figure 4: Diagram of the Bioworkflow.

### 2.10 Software description

BioLunar uses the *LunarVerse* backend for its operations. LunarVerse is downloaded and installed by the setup script included with the demonstration code. Some of its components need user specific configuration to work, such as private API keys, which are defined in a configuration file indicated in the setup instructions. LunarVerse is distributed under a *open software* license. The workflow can also be operated via a graphical interface (*LunarFlow*)

Running a workflow can be done in two ways: i) directly, by calling the LunarVerse engine on a specified workflow descriptor file; ii) through the Web interface, by pressing the "Run" button.

The first way is the default one in the demonstration code. It returns a copy of the workflow descriptor, with all component output fields filled, which is then used to extract and filter the desired outputs, based on the component labels. It is also the best way to automate multiple workflow runs and to integrate their outputs into other systems.The supporting code is available at `https://github.com/neuro-symbolic-ai/lunar-bioverse-demo`.

### 2.11 Report

The *Bioworkflow*, as outlined in point 2.9, generates a report in PDF (Fig.5) format that begins by outlining the context of the study, analysis details, dates, and software versions at the top. The report is enhanced with hyperlinks for easy navigation to specific sections.

A "General Statistics" table provides a comprehensive overview of key metrics aggregated from all components, aiming to consolidate information for each gene throughout the analysis, with hyperlinks directing to the report sections where this information originates.

Subsequent sections categorise genes into various tables based on biological aspects and the KBs consulted. These include Molecular Function for genes sharing ontologies, drug target checks based on the Human Protein Atlas, assessments of cancer-related genes, Pathway Analysis and Mapping via WikiPathways, and classification of gene alterations by clinical relevance. By correlating genes with known functional information, the workflow identifies statistically significant enriched terms and summarizes these findings using LLM, which also furnishes evidence.

LLM interprets each table, offering textual conclusions relevant to the analysis context. A final summary, crafted using LLM, synthesizes all results within the given context. Importantly, all LLM interpretations are grounded in concrete evidence, with sources cited alongside the narrative. This approach underscores the rigor of the analysis by highlighting distinct sources that substantiate the relevance of each gene and variant.

## 3 Case study

To demonstrate the capabilities of the *Bioworkflow*, we analyzed outputs in two different scenarios, each producing a distinct set of genes from separate bioinformatics analyses. We entered these gene sets along with their analysis contexts into the *Bioworkflow* and executed it. Subsequently, we qualitatively assessed the output reports (see Fig.A.8,A.9), considering both the statistical data and the interpretations provided by the prompt-based NLI modules.

In Scenario 1, the user aims to explore the unique molecular characteristics of HER2-low breast cancer to determine if it constitutes a distinct category within breast cancer types, where the input genes are ERBB2, ESR1, PIK3CA, CBFB, SF3B. The

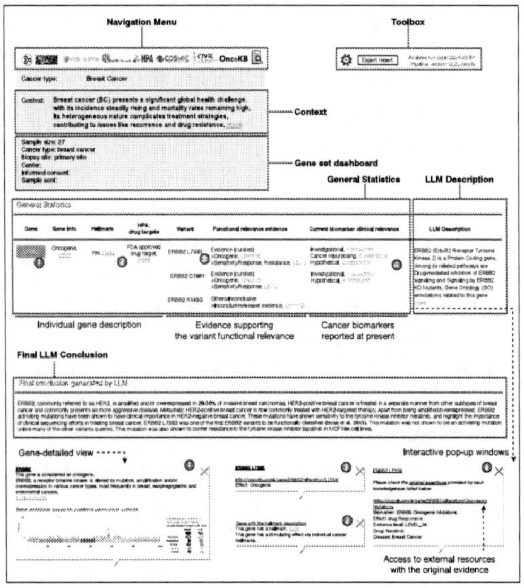


Figure 5: The BioLunar report's overview, produced by *Bioworkflow*.

report shows genomic alterations and genomic signatures that were identified, including ERBB2 amplification, mutations in PIK3CA and ESR1, which are important biomarkers in the selection of breast cancer treatment. For the remaining two genes, evidence was found confirming that these are new, significantly mutated genes for which there is preclinical evidence of actionability in clinical practice.

In Scenario 2, the user aims to discover new genes that could lead to more accurate breast cancer diagnoses, enhancing treatment strategies and addressing the disease's complexity. His numerical analysis resulted in a set of genes (DIXDC1, DUSP6, PDK4, CXCL12, IRF7, ITGA7, NEK2, NR3C1) that require investigation. The report informs that none of the genes is an oncogene (confirmation according to OncoKB), two of the genes are potential drug targets and one is FDA approved drug targets. According to the KEGG-based enrichment analysis, these genes were mainly enriched through several signaling pathways including tumor necrosis factor (TNF) signaling pathway. Using LLMs in conjunction with a PubMed search component, papers were searched in PubMed that describe various gene variants and the genes have been indicated as prospective biomarkers associated with breast cancer.

Note that in scenario 2, for genes lacking molecular profiles in the KB, a search in PubMed was conducted. This approach enables the workflow to automatically uncover and search for non-obvious and previously unknown relationships. Essentially, if a gene is absent from the database, it suggests that its relevance is relatively novel and not yet documented. Therefore, seeking out the most recent publications that describe this gene within the analysis context represents a significant advantage, provided by the workflow that integrates various components.

## 4 Related Work

**Bioinformatics Pipelines** Over the past decade, three scientific workflow management systems such as Galaxy (gal, 2022), Snakemake (Köster and Rahmann, 2012), and Nextflow (Di Tommaso et al., 2017), have been instrumental to bioinformaticians to systematise their complex analytical processes. Nextflow targets bioinformaticians and facilitates gene enrichment analysis, annotate biological sequences, and perform gene expression analysis by including modules supported by various bioinformatics tools. These workflow systems are currently centred around the composition of specialised bioinformatics software, configuration parameters and supporting datasets, facilitating reuse and reproducibility. In contrast, this paper explores the concept on using LLMs within a specialised workflow environment to support the interpretation and integration of multiple analytical processes.

## 5 Conclusion

In this paper we provided a demonstration of a scientific workflow based on LLMs to support specialised gene analyses using oncology and gene enrichment as a driving motivational scenario. The framework is built using the Lunar framework and allows for the composition of specialised analytical workflows, integrating external databases (Retrieval Augmented Generation), external tools (ToolFormers) and contextualised chains of LLM-based interpretation. The paper highlights that a workflow environment with specialised components for RAG, ToolFormers and a set of specialised prompts-based Natural Language Inference can serve as the foundation for streamlining and automating complex analytical process within a biomedical setting. . We showcase analytical applications within the biomedical domain, particularly in oncology, constructively progressing towards more complex gene analysis workflows. The developed *bioworkflow* demonstrates the LLMs can be instrumental in enabling a complex end-to-end highly-specialised analytical workflow, in a reproducible manner, supporting the integration of heterogeneous evidence, synthesising conclusions and while simultaneously documenting and linking to the data sources within a comprehensive output report. The proposed workflow is based on a low-code paradigm that enables domain experts, regardless of their programming skills, to construct and scientific workflows enabled by generaqtive AI amethods.

## Limitations

- The current demonstration uses external LLM-based APIs but can be adapted to open source LLM models.
- The LLM-based inferences require a critical supporting quantitative evaluation and hallucinations are possible. The current workflow is motivated by a hypothesis generation process, which is fully human supervised and does not have direct clinical applications.

## Acknowledgements

This work was partially funded by The Ark foundation, by the European Union's Horizon 2020 research and innovation program (grant no. 965397) through the Cancer Core Europe DART project, and by the Manchester Experimental Cancer Medicine Centre and the NIHR Manchester Biomedical Research Centre.

## References

2022. The galaxy platform for accessible, reproducible and collaborative biomedical analyses: 2022 update. *Nucleic Acids Research*, 50(W1):W345–W351.

Paul Bogdan, Gustavo Caetano-Anollés, Anna Jolles, Hyunju Kim, James Morris, Cheryl A Murphy, Catherine Royer, Edward H Snell, Adam Steinbrenner, and Nicholas Strausfeld. 2021. Biological Networks across Scales—The Theoretical and Empirical Foundations for Time-Varying Complex Networks that Connect Structure and Function across Levels of Biological Organization. *Integrative and Comparative Biology*, 61(6):1991–2010.

Paolo Di Tommaso, Maria Chatzou, Evan W Floden, Pablo Prieto Barja, Emilio Palumbo, and Cedric Notredame. 2017. Nextflow enables reproducible computational workflows. *Nature biotechnology*, 35(4):316–319.

K.D. Dryden-Palmer, C.S. Parshuram, and W.B. Berta. 2020. Context, complexity and process in the implementation of evidence-based innovation: a realist informed review. *BMC Health Services Research*, 20(81):1472–6963.

Johannes Köster and Sven Rahmann. 2012. Snakemake—a scalable bioinformatics workflow engine. *Bioinformatics*, 28(19):2520–2522.

David N. Nicholson and Casey S. Greene. 2020. Constructing knowledge graphs and their biomedical applications. *Computational and Structural Biotechnology Journal*, 18:1414–1428.

Jussi Paananen and Vittorio Fortino. 2019. An omics perspective on drug target discovery platforms. *Briefings in Bioinformatics*, 21(6):1937–1953.

# A Appendix

**Scenario 1**

**Context:**
The analysis focuses on HER2-low breast cancer (HLBC), a subtype that challenges traditional classifications based on HER2 expression and ERBB2 amplification. Despite being operationally defined, HLBCs constitute a significant portion of breast cancers, particularly among estrogen receptor-positive tumors. This study aims to elucidate the molecular characteristics of HLBCs, examining their mutational and transcriptional profiles. The research also investigates potential heterogeneity within HLBCs and compares their genomic landscape with HER2-positive and HER2-negative breast cancers. By providing insights into the distinct molecular features of HLBCs, this analysis seeks to establish whether they represent a unique entity in breast cancer pathology.

**List of genes:**
ERBB2, ESR1, PIK3CA, CBFB, SF3B1

**Scenario 2**

**Context:**
Breast cancer (BC) presents a significant global health challenge, with its incidence steadily rising and mortality rates remaining high. Its heterogeneous nature complicates treatment strategies, contributing to issues like recurrence and drug resistance. Biomarkers play a crucial role in diagnosing and managing BC, aiding in personalized treatment approaches. However, existing biomarkers have limitations, necessitating the exploration of novel markers, particularly in the realm of molecular and genetic analysis. This study focuses on identifying genes with potential diagnostic utility in breast cancer, aiming to contribute to the development of more effective biomarkers and therapies, including immunotherapies, to combat this disease.

**List of genes:**
DIXDC1, DUSP6, PDK4, CXCL12, IRF7, ITGA7, NEK2, NR3C1

Figure A.6: User-defined context of the analysis, including aspects like cancer types or subtypes, treatments, populations, for Scenario 1 and 2.

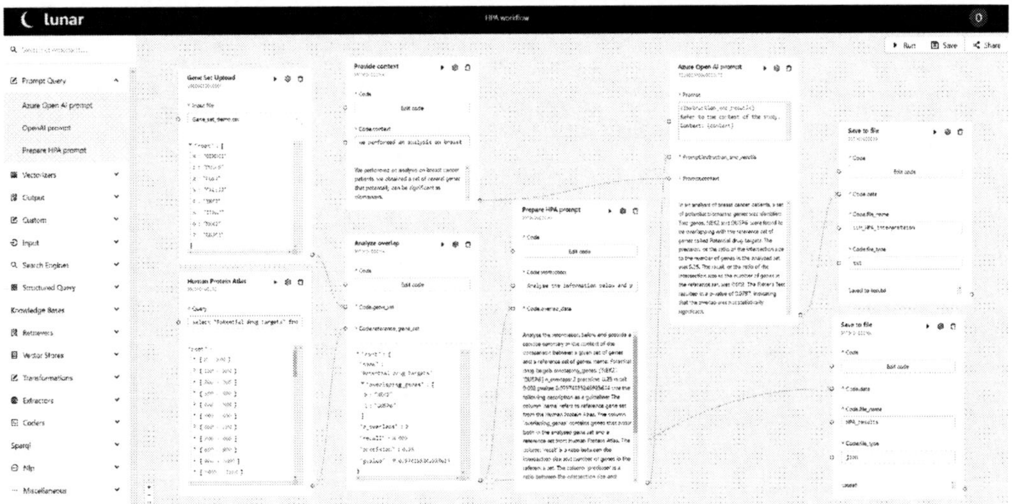

Figure A.7: Human Protein Atlas workflow in the BioLunar interface.

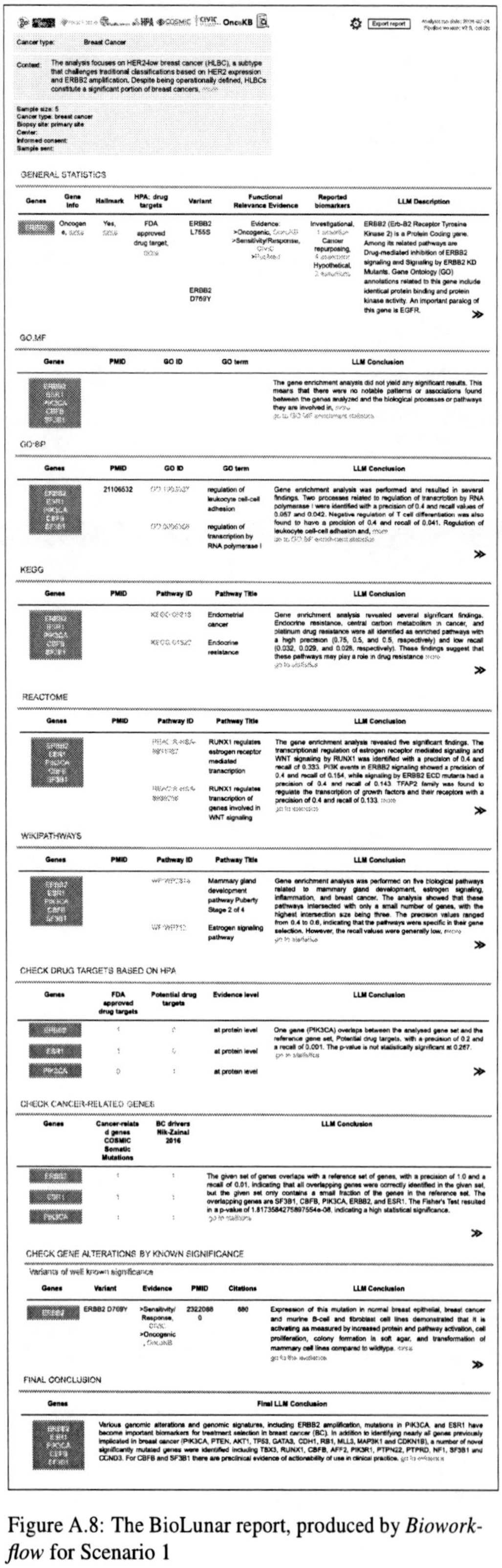

Figure A.8: The BioLunar report, produced by *Bioworkflow* for Scenario 1

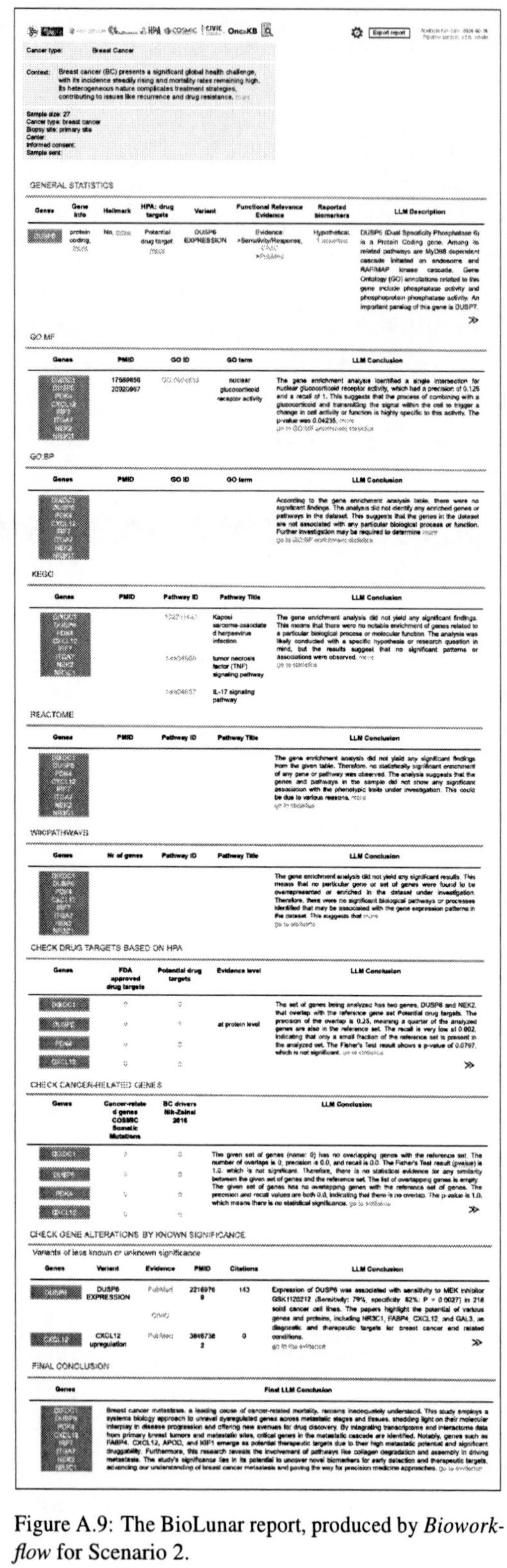

Figure A.9: The BioLunar report, produced by *Bioworkflow* for Scenario 2.

# CogMG: Collaborative Augmentation Between Large Language Model and Knowledge Graph

**Tong Zhou**[1] and **Yubo Chen**[1,2*] and **Kang Liu**[1,2,3] and **Jun Zhao**[1,2*]
[1]The Laboratory of Cognition and Decision Intelligence for Complex Systems
Institute of Automation, Chinese Academy of Sciences
[2]School of Artificial Intelligence, University of Chinese Academy of Sciences
[3]Shanghai Artificial Intelligence Laboratory
tong.zhou@ia.ac.cn, {yubo.chen, kliu, jzhao}@nlpr.ia.ac.cn

## Abstract

Large language models have become integral to question-answering applications despite their propensity for generating hallucinations and factually inaccurate content. Querying knowledge graphs to reduce hallucinations in LLM meets the challenge of incomplete knowledge coverage in knowledge graphs. On the other hand, updating knowledge graphs by information extraction and knowledge graph completion faces the knowledge update misalignment issue. In this work, we introduce a collaborative augmentation framework, CogMG, leveraging knowledge graphs to address the limitations of LLMs in QA scenarios, explicitly targeting the problems of incomplete knowledge coverage and knowledge update misalignment. The LLMs identify and decompose required knowledge triples that are not present in the KG, enriching them and aligning updates with real-world demands. We demonstrate the efficacy of this approach through a supervised fine-tuned LLM within an agent framework, showing significant improvements in reducing hallucinations and enhancing factual accuracy in QA responses. Our code[1] and video[2] are publicly available.

## 1 Introduction

Large language models (LLMs) (Brown et al., 2020; Achiam et al., 2023) have witnessed a surge in adoption for question-answering (QA) applications (Stelmakh et al., 2022). Despite their ability to produce engaging and coherent responses, these models are susceptible to generating hallucinated content and frequently encompass factually inaccurate information (Rawte et al., 2023). Xu et al., 2024 indicated that this inevitable symptom imputes their data (Kandpal et al., 2023), training (Liu et al., 2024a), and inference stages (Dziri et al., 2021). Fortunately, LLMs can leverage their comprehension and reasoning ability by referring to external knowledge sources to relieve hallucinations, such as documents (Lewis et al., 2020) and knowledge graphs (Sun et al., 2023). We concentrate on utilizing knowledge graphs (KGs), which provide a complementary strength to Large Language Models (LLMs) through their structured format and precise encapsulation of factual information. However, the utility of KGs in QA scenarios is hindered by the challenges of *incomplete knowledge coverage* and *knowledge update misalignment*.

**Incomplete Knowledge Coverage:** In principle, knowledge graphs possess the capability to encompass a vast array of information; however, they are also confronted with the challenge of achieving comprehensive coverage in their storage of knowledge. The explicitly encoded triples within the KG prove inadequate to exhaustively cover the knowledge required for practical QA scenarios. Existing approaches to augmenting QA systems with KG have primarily focused on improving parsing formal language (Xiong et al., 2024) or semantic relevance in retrieval knowledge triples (Wu et al., 2023), pursuing the corresponding knowledge prestorage in the KG for pre-defined questions. There is relatively limited attention given to the subsequent handling of queries that do not hit the knowledge graph.

**Knowledge Update Misalignment:** Current approaches to updating knowledge graphs primarily depend on two strategies: extracting knowledge triples from unstructured text (Wang et al., 2023; Xiao et al., 2023) (Information Extraction) and inferring unseen linkages through the analysis of existing connections between nodes (Yang et al., 2023) (Knowledge Graph Completion). These paradigms employed for updating KGs are characterized by their aimless and seemingly infinite nature and, therefore, do not fully address the mis-

*Corresponding author

[1]Project: https://github.com/tongzhou21/CogMG

[2]Video: https://youtu.be/WnkS0Qk_0OM



*Proceedings of the 62nd Annual Meeting of the Association for Computational Linguistics (Volume 3: System Demonstrations)*, pages 365–373
August 11-16, 2024 ©2024 Association for Computational Linguistics

alignment between the newly acquired knowledge and real-world user needs. This highlights a lack of proactive consideration in updating the knowledge graph to align better with user demands.

To address the above two challenges, this paper proposes a framework called CogMG for collaborative augmentation between LLM and KG. When a query exceeds the knowledge scope of the current KG, the LLM is encouraged to explicitly decompose the required knowledge triples. Subsequently, completion is done based on the extensive knowledge encoded in the LLM's parameters, serving as the reference for the final answer. The explicit identification of necessary knowledge triples serves as a means for model introspection to mitigate hallucination and proactively highlights deficiencies in the KG in meeting real-world demands. Moreover, identifying these triples allows for their automatic verification through retrieval augmented generation (RAG) with external documents. The retrieved relevant documents can also be a reference for manual review before incorporating triples into the knowledge graph. This continual and proactive process of knowledge updating enables the knowledge graph to meet actual knowledge demands gradually. Consequently, the LLM can leverage the augmented KG to improve its factualness in answering questions, forming a collaborative augmentation between LLM and KG. The main contributions of this paper are shown below:

- We propose the collaborative augmentation framework between LLM and KG, which is called CogMG. Address knowledge deficiency in LLMs and advocate actively updating the knowledge within the KG according to user demand.

- We fine-tune an open-source LLM to adapt the collaborative augmentation paradigm CogMG in an agent framework and demonstrate it by implementing a website system. The agent framework is modular and pluggable, and the system is interactive and user-friendly.

- According to a use-case presentation and the experimental results in various situations, we demonstrate the effectiveness of CogMG in updating knowledge proactively and enhancing response quality in various real-world QA scenarios.

## 2 Framework Design

The single iteration of CogMG framework comprises three steps: (1) Querying the Knowledge Graph: Large models utilize reasoning and planning capabilities to decompose queries and generate formalized query statements for querying the knowledge graph. (2) Processing Results: If results are returned successfully, detailed answers preferred by humans are integrated. If unsuccessful, the required triples are explicitly identified and broken down before being integrated into the answer. (3) Graph Evolution: Utilizing external knowledge verification and modification to incorporate triples that were not hit into the knowledge graph.

### 2.1 Querying Knowledge Graph

Given a knowledge-intensive question, we initiate our approach by deconstructing the corresponding formal query into sub-steps in natural language. This decomposition aids in elucidating the necessary and universal logic for querying knowledge graphs, ensuring our method's generalizability across various KG schemas. The LLM then calls a formal language parsing tool to execute the query. This tool receives the logically decomposed steps in natural language as input, translates them into a formal query language tailored to the target knowledge graph, and returns the query results.

### 2.2 Processing Result

Upon receiving the query results from KG, the LLM leverages its comprehension and reasoning capabilities to organize the final answer. If the query execution encounters errors, the LLM delineates the essential knowledge triples with unknown components based on decomposed steps. Suppose the complement of these triples could provide the necessary knowledge to answer the question. Subsequently, knowledge encoded within the model's parameters is utilized to complete these triples. And then, the model generates the final answer according to these facts. Note that the completion step is applicable to LLMs with capabilities of any level. Explicit the necessary knowledge not only mitigates the hallucination effect due to snowballing in the current output but also identifies knowledge gaps within the graph, thereby facilitating the enhancement of the graph's knowledge coverage. The incomplete knowledge triples, and their completions are logged for potential incorporation into the graph or further verification.

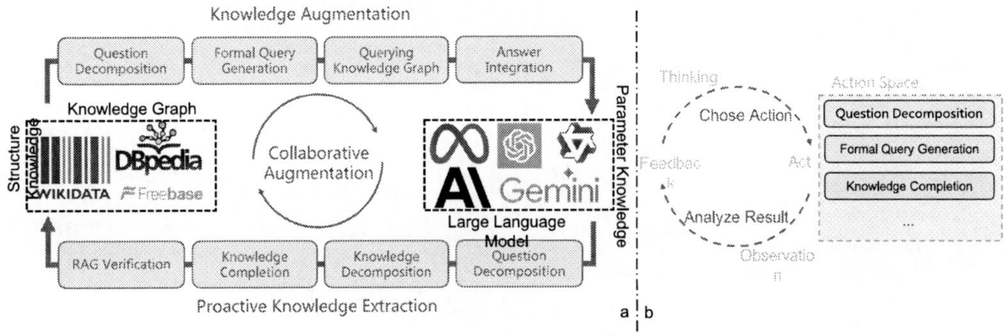


Figure 1: Left part: A schematic diagram illustrating the overall design of the collaborative augmentation framework CogMG, involving LLM and KG. Right part: We implement CogMG using an agent-based framework, with each module designed to be plug-and-play to ensure generalizability.

### 2.3 Knowledge Graph Evolution

The high generality and broad coverage of parameter knowledge encoded within LLM can supplement the more specialized knowledge in KG. These triples completed by LLM can be added to KG directly. However, the LLM struggles with rare, long-tail, and domain-specific knowledge and lacks robustness in its knowledge statement. We offer an option for manual intervention, where administrators can choose to (1) directly incorporate the completed triples into the knowledge graph, (2) manually adjust them before addition, or (3) verify them automatically according to external knowledge sources.

To automatically validate and correct these triples, CogMG searches related documents within unstructured corpora and makes comparisons in facts between documents and triples. These documents, which could drawn from domain-specific texts, general encyclopedias, or rapidly updated search engines, not only enhance the factual accuracy of the knowledge but also provide interpretable references for manual review. Based on the insights from these external sources, the model adjusts the proposed knowledge triples, making them suitable for manual inclusion into the knowledge graph.

## 3 Implementation and Usecase

We fine-tune an open-source LLM for implementing the CogMG and develop an online system to demonstrate and evaluate our proposed collaborative augmentation framework.

### 3.1 Model and Components

LLM is capable of serving as an agent to plan and call tools independently (Qin et al., 2023). We adopted ReAct's agent framework (Yao et al., 2022) to adapt LLM to our proposition of modularization and generalization in CogMG's philosophy. We utilize a subset of Wikidata as the knowledge graph, KoPL (Cao et al., 2022) as the query engine, and the KQA-Pro dataset as the backbone of the fine-tuning dataset. KQA-Pro contains natural language questions with corresponding KoPL queries, SPARQL queries, and the gold answer. To ensure that the agent exhibits the expected behavior across various scenarios, we construct customized SFT datasets to fine-tune or utilize in-context learning to prompt the model. Qwen-14B-Chat (Bai et al., 2023) is responsible for all the SFT data generation and the agent backbone. Notably, our framework is applicable across various knowledge graphs and LLM. We will introduce our solution scenario by scenario.

**Question Decomposition:** Utilizing decomposition steps as intermediaries between questions and formal languages clarifies problem-solving logic and enhances robustness against different expressions of questions. We manually write several natural language explanations of query steps to obtain parallel data cases between questions and natural language explanations according to corresponding KoPL function calls. With these parallel examples, we prompt an LLM to generate sub-steps across the entire dataset and get 50k pairs of data. These data are reserved to construct agent behavioral SFT dataset.

**Formal Query Generation:** A model that parses the natural language explanations of query

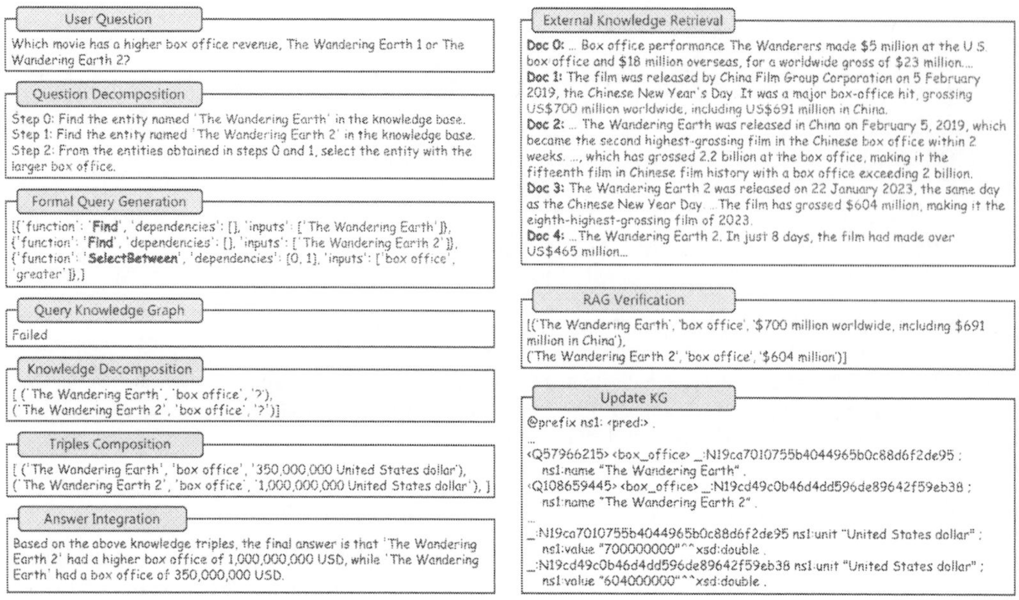


Figure 2: A complete example of how the system handles queries not found in the knowledge graph and the processing of related knowledge.

steps to the KoPL formal program could be rapidly trained using the parallel data. Since the parsing process is relatively undemanding on the model's capabilities, we fine-tuned a 7B model to create a dedicated model in the tool of querying knowledge graph.

**Querying Knowledge Graph:** We wrapped the execution of the KoPL engine to uniformly return "Failed" upon errors, facilitating the model's decision-making and recognition. The query tool processes decomposed step inputs through a parsing model predicts the KoPL query program and returns the results of the knowledge graph query.

**Answer Integration:** The gold answers provided by KQA Pro are brief and precise at the word level and have gaps with the more detailed explanations preferred by humans. Hence, we supply the inference model with questions and gold answers from KG execution, instructing it to generate more exhaustive, explanatory responses to each question in the dataset. The answer integration scenario is a part of the agent behavior.

**Knowledge Decomposition:** We explicitly decompose the formal query's target triples to clarify the facts necessary for answering questions. This step is essential for manually annotating some query statements to incomplete triple, with unknown parts of facts expressed as question marks, and then using these samples as examples for the model to infer the triple decomposition for all data. Given the precise label names in the KoPL program as entity linking, we added label name constraints during triple inference, regenerating triples if non-standard label names were produced. All the knowledge decomposition data are utilized to simulate handling questions that the knowledge graph uncovered.

**Knowledge Completion:** We directly instruct the model to undertake knowledge completion tasks, referring to manually written examples. To fit the entire ReAct agent framework and ensure modularity, we encapsulate the knowledge completion part as a tool, inputting questions and corresponding incomplete knowledge triples to output the mappings of the parameter's knowledge with these triples.

**Retrieval Augmented Generation Verification:** Since LLM with general instruction tuning and preference alignment are familiar with RAG, we utilize prompt engineering to request the model to generate the correction of knowledge triples based on retrieved relevant documents, incomplete triples with question marks, and corresponding triples with parameter knowledge completion. We adopt Wikipedia as a retrieval corpus and segment every 256 tokens into a chunk. We build a document index by BM25, searching via concatenated knowledge triples and the origin question and selecting the top ten chunks as external knowledge references.

For the entire ReAct agent framework, we constructed two routes for the agent's planning and calling tools, differentiating whether the necessary knowledge is contained in the knowledge graph. Utilizing the built parallel training data, we construct two Thought-Action-Observation execution routes of SFT data, considering every scenario elaborated above. The agent is tuned using a total of 100k behavior SFT data.

### 3.2 System and Use Case

**Knowledge Augmented Generation:** Users can input and submit knowledge-intensive questions into the dialogue box at the bottom. The agent LLM is responsible for dealing with these questions and processes with pre-defined routes. The Thought-Action-Observation paradigm will be displayed in real time at the corresponding dropdown tab. When the knowledge graph cannot support the question-answering process, the model decomposes knowledge and invokes itself for knowledge completion before providing a final answer, as shown in the left of Figure 2. Meanwhile, these knowledge triples are recorded in the database.

**Knowledge Management:** In the Knowledge Management section of our system, we design an interactive interface to display all pending instances of knowledge that are not yet covered by the knowledge graph. The interface presents the origin of the query that highlighted the knowledge gap, the specific knowledge that is missing, and the results of the model's attempt to complete this knowledge based on its internal parameters. Administrators can (1) directly integrate this newly completed knowledge into the knowledge graph or opt for (2) further verification through RAG. A dropdown tab within the interface provides access to related documents and the outcomes of modifications, facilitating a rigorous validation process. Once the verification is complete and any necessary adjustments are made, administrators can seamlessly add the refined knowledge to the graph. This process not only ensures the continuous expansion and refinement of the knowledge graph but also leverages the administrators' expertise to validate the model-generated knowledge. By integrating these human-in-the-loop verification steps, our system enhances the reliability and accuracy of the knowledge graph, making it a more robust resource for answering real-world questions.

| Method | Accuracy |
|---|---|
| Direct Answer | 40% |
| CogMG w/o Knowledge | 44% |
| CogMG Update | 86% |

Table 1: Comparison results of the accuracy of question answering in three different scenarios.

### 3.3 Experiments

We further designed and conducted experiments to demonstrate the effectiveness of the CogMG framework. Sampling questions from the KQA Pro dataset, we tested the following scenarios: (1) **Direct Answer**: answering using only the backbone LLM without utilizing the knowledge graph; (2) **CogMG w/o Knowledge**: deleting relevant knowledge from the graph and answering using parameter completion of knowledge; (3) **CogMG Update**: updating all relevant knowledge, utilizing the graph query results for answering. Due to the difficulty of exact matching in reflecting the correctness of real answers, we manually evaluated the correctness of 50 questions. Table 1 illustrates the accuracy under these three scenarios. Experimental results indicate that directly answering questions using LLM results in lower accuracy due to the lack of precise factual knowledge. Besides, leveraging the model's knowledge clarification and completion can alleviate some hallucinations and improve accuracy. Finally, the accuracy of subsequent inquiries is improved after utilizing the collaborative augmentation framework to update the knowledge graph.

## 4 Related Work

### 4.1 Knowledge Base Question Answering

Knowledge Base Question Answering (KBQA) aims to provide answers to natural language questions using Knowledge Bases (KBs) as their primary source of information (Bordes et al., 2015; Lan et al., 2019). Semantic parsing plays a crucial role by mapping questions to a formal language (Yih et al., 2016; Cai and Yates, 2013), enabling precise queries on knowledge graphs (Bollacker et al., 2008; Vrandečić and Krötzsch, 2014). This task format can be regarded as a Seq2Seq paradigm, where formal language sequences are generated based on input question sequences. From RNN (Dong and Lapata, 2016) to BART (Cao et al., 2022) and GPT (Luo et al., 2023), the accuracy of formal language increases gradually with the ca-

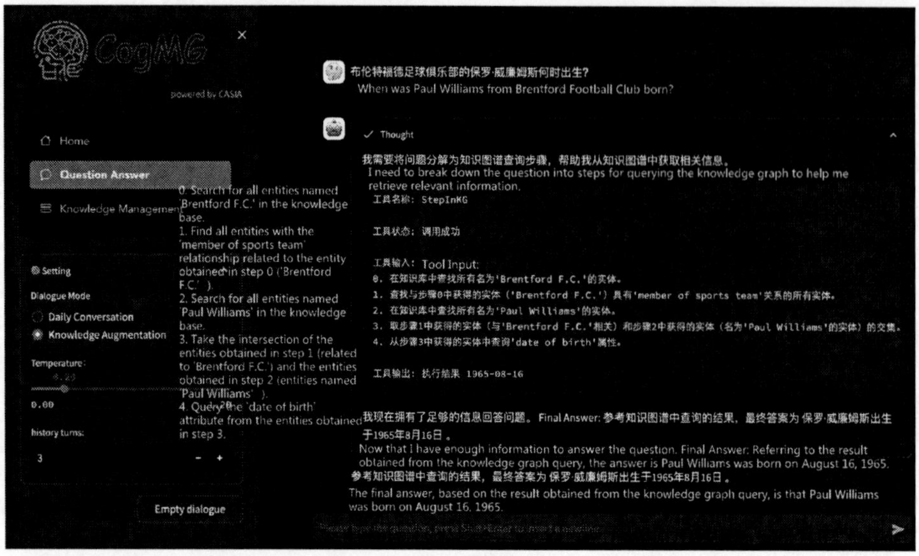


Figure 3: System screenshot.

pability of generative models. Besides end-to-end generation, Chen et al., 2021 suggested first identifying the entities and schema involved in the problem separately and then utilizing the transducer to generate logical expressions, ensuring the accuracy of logical syntax. Finally, it employs a checker to enhance the semantic consistency of the logical form. With the assistance of LLM, KB-BINDER (Li et al., 2023) generates a draft of logical expressions using codex and then matches executable programs based on BM25 scores. Thanks to in-context learning, the process can be accomplished with just a few annotated examples. Moreover, LLMs' reasoning and planning capabilities can also serve as better assistants for utilizing knowledge graphs without additional training (Jiang et al., 2023a; Sun et al., 2023; Jiang et al., 2024; Liu et al., 2024b). However, these works mainly focus on answering questions within the confines of a given dataset without addressing scenarios where the knowledge graph lacks the necessary information for the question. The agent framework (Yao et al., 2022; Qin et al., 2023; Liu et al., 2023) allows for the autonomous selection of alternative tools when faced with knowledge graph misses by design. However, it does not utilize these gaps as opportunities to enhance the knowledge graph.

In summary, existing research either overlooks the issue of insufficient knowledge graph coverage or fails to use these deficiencies to improve knowledge graphs actively.

## 4.2 Updating Knowledge Graph

Information extraction concentrates on extracting triples from a wide range of unstructured texts to augment knowledge graphs with new knowledge. Subject to the model capabilities, the target needs to be split into serval sub-tasks. Named entities need to be identified in the text (Lample et al., 2016; Yu et al., 2020; Qu et al., 2023), followed by the classification of relationships among these entities (Miwa and Bansal, 2016; Peng et al., 2020; Cheng et al., 2021). OpenIE (Etzioni et al., 2008; Stanovsky et al., 2018; Kolluru et al., 2020), on the other hand, identifies subject-predicate-object triples in one go without being limited by predefined schemas in the knowledge graph. LLMs have unified various information extraction tasks, allowing a single model to generalize across all sub-tasks with supervised fine-tuning or a few examples as a demonstration (Lu et al., 2022; Lou et al., 2023; Wang et al., 2023; Zhu et al., 2023). On the other hand, knowledge graph completion (Zhang et al., 2023; Jiang et al., 2023b) through reasoning over existing knowledge can augment the graph by establishing connections between existing nodes.

Our advocated approach of active knowledge updating is more targeted and complements large-scale knowledge updates without contradiction, providing a supplementary mechanism.

## 5 Conclustion

We address two relatively overlooked issues in integrating Large Language Models (LLMs) and Knowledge Graphs (KGs): Incomplete Knowledge Coverage and Knowledge Update Misalignment. In response to these challenges, we introduce CogMG, a framework for the collaborative enhancement of LLMs and KGs. CogMG tackles the problem of answering questions with knowledge not covered in the graph by explicitly defining and completing relevant knowledge. Additionally, it actively collects and verifies knowledge requirements to update the graph. Furthermore, we fine-tune an LLM based on an agent framework to implement CogMG and develop a user-friendly interactive system to visualize its capabilities. Use cases and experimental results demonstrate the effectiveness of CogMG.

## 6 Limitations

In enhancing large language models with knowledge graphs, we do not introduce more complex and advanced methods such as planning, reasoning, and interaction. We believe that the application of these methods can further improve the effectiveness of the CogMG framework.

On the other hand, actively acquiring updated triples in the real world and automatically incorporating this knowledge into the knowledge graph without human intervention remains challenging. The operation and management of knowledge graphs by large language models are directions for our future work.

## 7 Acknowledgments

This work is supported by the Strategic Priority Research Program of Chinese Academy of Sciences (No. XDA27020203), the National Natural Science Foundation of China (No. 62176257).

## References

Josh Achiam, Steven Adler, Sandhini Agarwal, Lama Ahmad, Ilge Akkaya, Florencia Leoni Aleman, Diogo Almeida, Janko Altenschmidt, Sam Altman, Shyamal Anadkat, et al. 2023. Gpt-4 technical report. *arXiv preprint arXiv:2303.08774*.

Jinze Bai, Shuai Bai, Yunfei Chu, Zeyu Cui, Kai Dang, Xiaodong Deng, Yang Fan, Wenbin Ge, Yu Han, Fei Huang, et al. 2023. Qwen technical report. *arXiv preprint arXiv:2309.16609*.

Kurt Bollacker, Colin Evans, Praveen Paritosh, Tim Sturge, and Jamie Taylor. 2008. Freebase: a collaboratively created graph database for structuring human knowledge. In *Proceedings of the 2008 ACM SIGMOD international conference on Management of data*, pages 1247–1250.

Antoine Bordes, Nicolas Usunier, Sumit Chopra, and Jason Weston. 2015. Large-scale simple question answering with memory networks. *arXiv preprint arXiv:1506.02075*.

Tom Brown, Benjamin Mann, Nick Ryder, Melanie Subbiah, Jared D Kaplan, Prafulla Dhariwal, Arvind Neelakantan, Pranav Shyam, Girish Sastry, Amanda Askell, et al. 2020. Language models are few-shot learners. *Advances in neural information processing systems*, 33:1877–1901.

Qingqing Cai and Alexander Yates. 2013. Semantic parsing freebase: Towards open-domain semantic parsing. In *Second Joint Conference on Lexical and Computational Semantics (* SEM), Volume 1: Proceedings of the Main Conference and the Shared Task: Semantic Textual Similarity*, pages 328–338.

Shulin Cao, Jiaxin Shi, Liangming Pan, Lunyiu Nie, Yutong Xiang, Lei Hou, Juanzi Li, Bin He, and Hanwang Zhang. 2022. Kqa pro: A dataset with explicit compositional programs for complex question answering over knowledge base. In *Proceedings of the 60th Annual Meeting of the Association for Computational Linguistics (Volume 1: Long Papers)*, pages 6101–6119.

Shuang Chen, Qian Liu, Zhiwei Yu, Chin-Yew Lin, Jian-Guang Lou, and Feng Jiang. 2021. Retrack: A flexible and efficient framework for knowledge base question answering. In *Proceedings of the 59th annual meeting of the association for computational linguistics and the 11th international joint conference on natural language processing: system demonstrations*, pages 325–336.

Qiao Cheng, Juntao Liu, Xiaoye Qu, Jin Zhao, Jiaqing Liang, Zhefeng Wang, Baoxing Huai, Nicholas Jing Yuan, and Yanghua Xiao. 2021. Hacred: A large-scale relation extraction dataset toward hard cases in practical applications. In *Findings of the Association for Computational Linguistics: ACL-IJCNLP 2021*, pages 2819–2831.

Li Dong and Mirella Lapata. 2016. Language to logical form with neural attention. In *Proceedings of the 54th Annual Meeting of the Association for Computational Linguistics (Volume 1: Long Papers)*, pages 33–43.

Nouha Dziri, Andrea Madotto, Osmar R Zaiane, and Avishek Joey Bose. 2021. Neural path hunter: Reducing hallucination in dialogue systems via path grounding. In *Proceedings of the 2021 Conference on Empirical Methods in Natural Language Processing*, pages 2197–2214.

Oren Etzioni, Michele Banko, Stephen Soderland, and Daniel S Weld. 2008. Open information extraction from the web. *Communications of the ACM*, 51(12):68–74.

Jinhao Jiang, Kun Zhou, Zican Dong, Keming Ye, Wayne Xin Zhao, and Ji-Rong Wen. 2023a. Structgpt: A general framework for large language model to reason over structured data. In *Proceedings of the 2023 Conference on Empirical Methods in Natural Language Processing*, pages 9237–9251.

Jinhao Jiang, Kun Zhou, Wayne Xin Zhao, Yang Song, Chen Zhu, Hengshu Zhu, and Ji-Rong Wen. 2024. Kg-agent: An efficient autonomous agent framework for complex reasoning over knowledge graph. *arXiv preprint arXiv:2402.11163*.

Pengcheng Jiang, Shivam Agarwal, Bowen Jin, Xuan Wang, Jimeng Sun, and Jiawei Han. 2023b. Text augmented open knowledge graph completion via pre-trained language models. In *Findings of the Association for Computational Linguistics: ACL 2023*, pages 11161–11180.

Nikhil Kandpal, Haikang Deng, Adam Roberts, Eric Wallace, and Colin Raffel. 2023. Large language models struggle to learn long-tail knowledge. In *International Conference on Machine Learning*, pages 15696–15707. PMLR.

Keshav Kolluru, Vaibhav Adlakha, Samarth Aggarwal, Soumen Chakrabarti, et al. 2020. Openie6: Iterative grid labeling and coordination analysis for open information extraction. In *Proceedings of the 2020 Conference on Empirical Methods in Natural Language Processing (EMNLP)*, pages 3748–3761.

Guillaume Lample, Miguel Ballesteros, Sandeep Subramanian, Kazuya Kawakami, and Chris Dyer. 2016. Neural architectures for named entity recognition. In *Proceedings of the 2016 Conference of the North American Chapter of the Association for Computational Linguistics: Human Language Technologies*, pages 260–270.

Yunshi Lan, Shuohang Wang, and Jing Jiang. 2019. Knowledge base question answering with a matching-aggregation model and question-specific contextual relations. *IEEE/ACM Transactions on Audio, Speech, and Language Processing*, 27(10):1629–1638.

Patrick Lewis, Ethan Perez, Aleksandra Piktus, Fabio Petroni, Vladimir Karpukhin, Naman Goyal, Heinrich Küttler, Mike Lewis, Wen-tau Yih, Tim Rocktäschel, et al. 2020. Retrieval-augmented generation for knowledge-intensive nlp tasks. *Advances in Neural Information Processing Systems*, 33:9459–9474.

Tianle Li, Xueguang Ma, Alex Zhuang, Yu Gu, Yu Su, and Wenhu Chen. 2023. Few-shot in-context learning on knowledge base question answering. In *Proceedings of the 61st Annual Meeting of the Association for Computational Linguistics (Volume 1: Long Papers)*, pages 6966–6980.

Bingbin Liu, Jordan Ash, Surbhi Goel, Akshay Krishnamurthy, and Cyril Zhang. 2024a. Exposing attention glitches with flip-flop language modeling. *Advances in Neural Information Processing Systems*, 36.

Jiaxiang Liu, Tong Zhou, Yubo Chen, Kang Liu, and Jun Zhao. 2024b. Enhancing large language models with pseudo-and multisource-knowledge graphs for open-ended question answering. *arXiv preprint arXiv:2402.09911*.

Zhiwei Liu, Weiran Yao, Jianguo Zhang, Le Xue, Shelby Heinecke, Rithesh Murthy, Yihao Feng, Zeyuan Chen, Juan Carlos Niebles, Devansh Arpit, et al. 2023. Bolaa: Benchmarking and orchestrating llm-augmented autonomous agents. *arXiv preprint arXiv:2308.05960*.

Jie Lou, Yaojie Lu, Dai Dai, Wei Jia, Hongyu Lin, Xianpei Han, Le Sun, and Hua Wu. 2023. Universal information extraction as unified semantic matching. In *Proceedings of the AAAI Conference on Artificial Intelligence*, volume 37, pages 13318–13326.

Yaojie Lu, Qing Liu, Dai Dai, Xinyan Xiao, Hongyu Lin, Xianpei Han, Le Sun, and Hua Wu. 2022. Unified structure generation for universal information extraction. In *Proceedings of the 60th Annual Meeting of the Association for Computational Linguistics (Volume 1: Long Papers)*, pages 5755–5772.

Haoran Luo, Zichen Tang, Shiyao Peng, Yikai Guo, Wentai Zhang, Chenghao Ma, Guanting Dong, Meina Song, Wei Lin, et al. 2023. Chatkbqa: A generate-then-retrieve framework for knowledge base question answering with fine-tuned large language models. *arXiv preprint arXiv:2310.08975*.

Makoto Miwa and Mohit Bansal. 2016. End-to-end relation extraction using lstms on sequences and tree structures. In *Proceedings of the 54th Annual Meeting of the Association for Computational Linguistics (Volume 1: Long Papers)*, pages 1105–1116.

Hao Peng, Tianyu Gao, Xu Han, Yankai Lin, Peng Li, Zhiyuan Liu, Maosong Sun, and Jie Zhou. 2020. Learning from context or names? an empirical study on neural relation extraction. In *Proceedings of the 2020 Conference on Empirical Methods in Natural Language Processing (EMNLP)*, pages 3661–3672.

Yujia Qin, Shihao Liang, Yining Ye, Kunlun Zhu, Lan Yan, Yaxi Lu, Yankai Lin, Xin Cong, Xiangru Tang, Bill Qian, et al. 2023. Toolllm: Facilitating large language models to master 16000+ real-world apis. *arXiv preprint arXiv:2307.16789*.

Xiaoye Qu, Jun Zeng, Daizong Liu, Zhefeng Wang, Baoxing Huai, and Pan Zhou. 2023. Distantly-supervised named entity recognition with adaptive teacher learning and fine-grained student ensemble. In *Proceedings of the AAAI Conference on Artificial Intelligence*, volume 37, pages 13501–13509.

Vipula Rawte, Amit Sheth, and Amitava Das. 2023. A survey of hallucination in large foundation models. *arXiv preprint arXiv:2309.05922*.

Gabriel Stanovsky, Julian Michael, Luke Zettlemoyer, and Ido Dagan. 2018. Supervised open information extraction. In *Proceedings of the 2018 Conference of the North American Chapter of the Association for Computational Linguistics: Human Language Technologies, Volume 1 (Long Papers)*, pages 885–895.

Ivan Stelmakh, Yi Luan, Bhuwan Dhingra, and Ming-Wei Chang. 2022. Asqa: Factoid questions meet long-form answers. In *Proceedings of the 2022 Conference on Empirical Methods in Natural Language Processing*, pages 8273–8288.

Jiashuo Sun, Chengjin Xu, Lumingyuan Tang, Saizhuo Wang, Chen Lin, Yeyun Gong, Heung-Yeung Shum, and Jian Guo. 2023. Think-on-graph: Deep and responsible reasoning of large language model with knowledge graph. *arXiv preprint arXiv:2307.07697*.

Denny Vrandečić and Markus Krötzsch. 2014. Wikidata: a free collaborative knowledgebase. *Communications of the ACM*, 57(10):78–85.

Xiao Wang, Weikang Zhou, Can Zu, Han Xia, Tianze Chen, Yuansen Zhang, Rui Zheng, Junjie Ye, Qi Zhang, Tao Gui, et al. 2023. Instructuie: multi-task instruction tuning for unified information extraction. *arXiv preprint arXiv:2304.08085*.

Yike Wu, Nan Hu, Guilin Qi, Sheng Bi, Jie Ren, Anhuan Xie, and Wei Song. 2023. Retrieve-rewrite-answer: A kg-to-text enhanced llms framework for knowledge graph question answering. *arXiv preprint arXiv:2309.11206*.

Xinglin Xiao, Yijie Wang, Nan Xu, Yuqi Wang, Hanxuan Yang, Minzheng Wang, Yin Luo, Lei Wang, Wenji Mao, and Daniel Zeng. 2023. Yayi-uie: A chat-enhanced instruction tuning framework for universal information extraction. *arXiv preprint arXiv:2312.15548*.

Guanming Xiong, Junwei Bao, and Wen Zhao. 2024. Interactive-kbqa: Multi-turn interactions for knowledge base question answering with large language models. *arXiv preprint arXiv:2402.15131*.

Ziwei Xu, Sanjay Jain, and Mohan Kankanhalli. 2024. Hallucination is inevitable: An innate limitation of large language models. *arXiv preprint arXiv:2401.11817*.

Rui Yang, Li Fang, and Yi Zhou. 2023. Cp-kgc: Constrained-prompt knowledge graph completion with large language models. *arXiv preprint arXiv:2310.08279*.

Shunyu Yao, Jeffrey Zhao, Dian Yu, Nan Du, Izhak Shafran, Karthik R Narasimhan, and Yuan Cao. 2022. React: Synergizing reasoning and acting in language models. In *The Eleventh International Conference on Learning Representations*.

Wen-tau Yih, Matthew Richardson, Christopher Meek, Ming-Wei Chang, and Jina Suh. 2016. The value of semantic parse labeling for knowledge base question answering. In *Proceedings of the 54th Annual Meeting of the Association for Computational Linguistics (Volume 2: Short Papers)*, pages 201–206.

Juntao Yu, Bernd Bohnet, and Massimo Poesio. 2020. Named entity recognition as dependency parsing. In *Proceedings of the 58th Annual Meeting of the Association for Computational Linguistics*, pages 6470–6476.

Yichi Zhang, Zhuo Chen, Wen Zhang, and Huajun Chen. 2023. Making large language models perform better in knowledge graph completion. *arXiv preprint arXiv:2310.06671*.

Tong Zhu, Junfei Ren, Zijian Yu, Mengsong Wu, Guoliang Zhang, Xiaoye Qu, Wenliang Chen, Zhefeng Wang, Baoxing Huai, and Min Zhang. 2023. Mirror: A universal framework for various information extraction tasks. In *Proceedings of the 2023 Conference on Empirical Methods in Natural Language Processing*, pages 8861–8876.

# ELLA: Empowering LLMs for Interpretable, Accurate and Informative Legal Advice

**Yutong Hu**[1,2]*, **Kangcheng Luo**[3,*], **Yansong Feng**[1†]
[1]Wangxuan Institute of Computer Technology, Peking University, China
[2]School of Intelligence Science and Technology, Peking University
[3]School of Electronics Engineering and Computer Science, Peking University, China
State Key Laboratory of General Artificial Intelligence
{huyutong,fengyansong}@pku.edu.cn
luokangcheng@stu.pku.edu.cn

## Abstract

Despite remarkable performance in legal consultation exhibited by legal Large Language Models(LLMs) combined with legal article retrieval components, there are still cases when the advice given is incorrect or baseless. To alleviate these problems, we propose **ELLA**, a tool for **E**mpowering **LL**Ms for interpretable, accurate, and informative **L**egal **A**dvice. ELLA visually presents the correlation between legal articles and LLM's response by calculating their similarities, providing users with an intuitive legal basis for the responses. Besides, based on the users' queries, ELLA retrieves relevant legal articles and displays them to users. Users can interactively select legal articles for LLM to generate more accurate responses. ELLA also retrieves relevant legal cases for user reference. Our user study shows that presenting the legal basis for the response helps users understand better. The accuracy of LLM's responses also improves when users intervene in selecting legal articles for LLM. Providing relevant legal cases also aids individuals in obtaining comprehensive information. Our github repo is: https://github.com/Huyt00/ELLA[1].

## 1 Introduction

Large Language Models (LLMs), such as LLAMA (Touvron et al., 2023), ChatGLM (Zeng et al., 2023) and GPT4 (OpenAI et al., 2024), have shown impressive performance in various tasks, showing great potential for specific domains, such as law (Lai et al., 2023) and finance (Wu et al., 2023; Yang et al., 2023). In the legal domain, many attempts have been made(Colombo et al., 2024; Huang et al., 2023; Yue et al., 2023; Nguyen, 2023; Cui et al., 2023), which acquire legal knowledge through continual training and performing a supervised fine-tuning stage with a large-scale legal dataset. These models can offer various services including legal consultations, explaining legal terminology, analyzing legal cases, and preparing legal documents.

Despite the remarkable performance of LLMs within the legal domain, they are not exempt from the occurrence of hallucination (Ji et al., 2023). To alleviate this, previous studies (Huang et al., 2023; Yue et al., 2023; Cui et al., 2023) have proposed retrieval-augmented generation(RAG) (Lewis et al., 2021) frameworks to retrieve legal articles from an external datastore. By leveraging retrieved legal articles, hallucination is reduced and LLMs can generate more faithful answers.

In the legal domain, LLMs' responses are required to have high accuracy and be supported by reasonable legal bases. Therefore, the retrieval component plays an important role as it provides correct and related legal articles for LLMs. While LLMs could be augmented with retrieved legal articles to generate faithful responses, when irrelevant ones are retrieved, they inevitably bring noise to LLMs, leading LLMs to produce responses with incomplete, incorrect or inconsistent information.

For instance, as shown in Figure 1, when a user asks $Q_1$, the legal article retrieval model retrieves articles 1098, 1101, and 1105 of the Civil Code [2] according to the query, while fails to retrieve another three relevant ones: article 1100, 1102 and 1093 of the Civil Code. Therefore, LLM only suggests that adopters need to meet the conditions $c_1, c_2$ and $c_3$ mentioned in the retrieved legal articles, resulting in incomplete suggestions. Then the user continues to ask $Q_2$. Although the related article is retrieved, the irrelevant ones are also retrieved. Such irrelevant articles bring noise to LLM, leading to the incorrect response $R_2$(In fact, the case

* Equal Contribution.
† Corresponding author.
[1]Video demonstration is available at: https://youtu.be/V8iaIXSJ2i8

[2]https://www.gov.cn/xinwen/2020-06/01/content_5516649.htm



*Proceedings of the 62nd Annual Meeting of the Association for Computational Linguistics (Volume 3: System Demonstrations)*, pages 374–387
August 11-16, 2024 ©2024 Association for Computational Linguistics

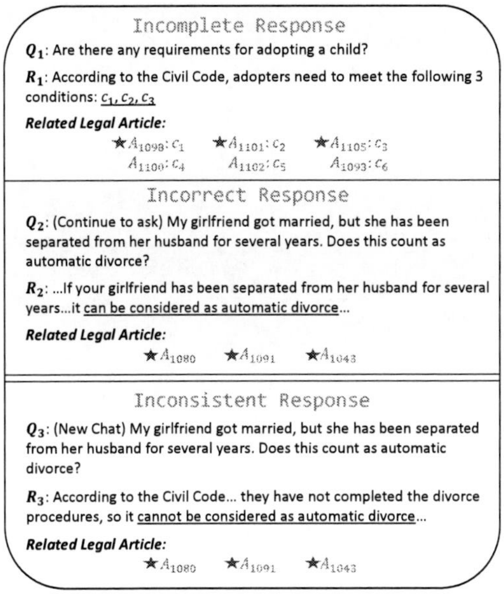


Figure 1: Examples of incomplete, incorrect, inconsistent Response. $A_i$ indicates the $i_{th}$ article in Civil Code. Blue articles mean they are relevant to the query, while orange ones are irrelevant. The blue star means the article is retrieved for LLM. We only show the key information in the Figure. For the complete conversations, please refer to Appendix B

mentioned in $Q_2$ should not be considered as automatic divorce). Besides, LLMs may be sensible to the input perturbation (Zhu et al., 2023; Dong et al., 2023). Responses can be contradictory when inputs only differ slightly. For example, when the user begins a new chat and asks $Q_3$, which is identical to $Q_2$, the response $R_3$ is contradictory to $R_2$. This inconsistency can potentially bring confusion to users, resulting in a lower-quality consultation.

When LLMs fail to produce coherent and complete responses, relevant legal cases can offer users more in-depth reference information (Su et al., 2024). However, a legal case retrieval module has rarely been integrated into the existing legal domain LLMs in civil law systems. Additionally, legal terminology may sometimes be embedded in the responses lacking sufficient explanations, posing potential understanding difficulties for users without domain knowledge (Savelka et al., 2023).

To address the issues mentioned above, we propose **ELLA**, a tool **E**mpowering **L**LMs for interpretable, accurate, and informative **L**egal **A**dvice.

Firstly, we fine-tune BGE (Xiao et al., 2023), an embedding model for retrieval, to retrieve the legal basis for each sentence in the response. By visually presenting the legal basis to users, users can trust the advice provided by LLMs. When there is no legal basis for a sentence, it can be viewed as a warning that the sentence may be incorrect. Secondly, ELLA retrieves several legal articles based on the user's query and presents them to users. Users can interactively select the relevant legal articles for LLMs to generate accurate and complete responses while disregarding irrelevant ones to avoid noise. Thirdly, we incorporate a legal case retrieval model in ELLA, intending to present supplementary information for users to reference. Considering the long context in legal cases, we find all the key sentences in the article through similarity matching between the query and each sentence in the legal case. We highlight all key sentences in the legal cases for users to improve their reading efficiency.

The response interpretation aids users in understanding and placing trust in the advice given by LLMs. The user study shows that our model can generate more accurate responses when users interactively select relevant legal articles. The legal case retrieval module also offers users more resourceful reference information.

## 2 Framework and Usage Example

ELLA is composed of four parts: 1) **Chat Interface**: visually displays the conversation between the user and the LLM. 2) **Interactive Legal Article Selection:** Provides retrieved legal articles for users to choose from, letting the LLM generate new responses based on the user's selected legal articles. 3) **Response Interpretation:** Provides legal article and judicial interpretations to interpret each sentence of the LLM's response. 4) **Legal Case Retrieval:** Displays relevant legal cases for the user to refer to.

### 2.1 Chat Interface

Our chat interface is shown in Figure 2, part 1. After clicking the input button, the chat box above will display user input and the LLM's response. Users can have multiple rounds of chats, or click 'new conversation' on the upper left to start a new consultation. The column on the left retains all conversations. Users can click on each chat button to view the corresponding chat content.

### 2.2 Interactive Legal Article Selection

Legal article retrieval model plays an important part in Chinese legal domain LLMs (Huang et al.,

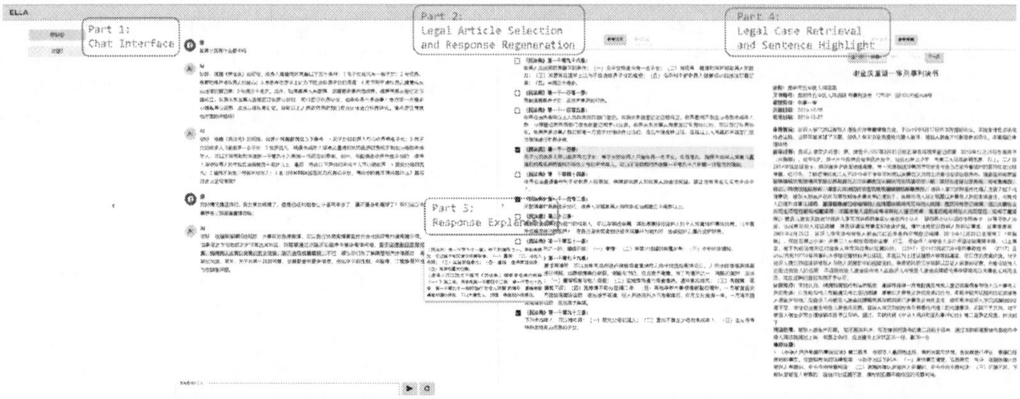


Figure 2: Screenshot of ELLA. We show the complete conversation in Appendix B, Table 2 and Table 5.

2023; Yue et al., 2023). Lawyer LLaMA (Huang et al., 2023) mentions that when LLMs are provided with external relevant legal articles, they can generate more reliable responses. However, the current legal article retrieval models cannot ensure to retrieval all the relevant legal articles and leave out all irrelevant ones. Missed articles might reduce the completeness of the model's response, while irrelevant articles bring noise to LLM, leading LLMs to generate irrelevant advice.

To solve this problem, ELLA allows users to interactively select legal articles. We display the top $K_1 = 10$ relevant legal articles retrieved for the users. Users can select relevant legal articles based on their situations. The LLM will then generate responses based on the legal articles selected by the user. Note that the LLM generates its first response based on the top 3 retrieved articles by default. Subsequently, users can select legal articles for LLM to regenerate new responses multiple times.

Back to the example in Figure 1, we find that several relevant legal articles are not selected for LLM. Then we can select them, as shown in Figure 2, part 2, and click the "Regenerate" button at the bottom of the page. Then LLM generates a new response with complete information. By allowing users to participate in the legal article retrieval, it increases the consistency between the user's situation and the referred legal articles used by the LLM, thus enabling the LLM to generate more complete and accurate responses.

### 2.3 Response Interpretation

The response interpretation module provides the legal article basis for each sentence in the LLM's response, and helps users better understand the terminologies in the responses.

LLM is sensitive to the inputs. Users may receive different advice when ask the same questions in different ways. To facilitate users to identify which response is more reliable, or whether a response is trustworthy, the response interpretation module presents the referred legal articles for each sentence in the response. Users can verify the reliability of the response by tracing the legal article basis of each sentence.

At the same time, even though the LLM can conveniently provide legal advice to users, sometimes the responses may contain terminologies, which non-professional users may find hard to understand. Besides, some special cases lack a clear definition in the legal articles. They are both explicitly explained in China's "judicial interpretations". To provide users with a better legal consultation experience, we use a response explanation module to provide a clear explanation of the terminology/special cases with corresponding judicial interpretation, making it easier for users to understand.

As shown in Figure 2, part 3, when the user ask *"My girlfriend is married...Would living with her without being legally married be considered bigamy?"*, the response is *"...The situation you mentioned is cohabitation rather than bigamy...cohabitation is not illegal..."*. To check the definition of "cohabitation", the user can hover the mouse over the sentence. Then the platform will display a hovering box, showing the corresponding judicial interpretation. We show the legal article basis for the sentence in the same way. If there is neither a legal article basis nor a judicial interpretation for the sentence, the hovering box will not display.

### 2.4 Legal Case Retrieval

Legal cases also serve as important references for users when they consult on legal issues and make judgments about their circumstances. Currently, Chinese legal domain LLMs can only make decisions for users based on internal legal knowledge and externally retrieved legal articles, unable to provide relevant legal cases for users as reference. Therefore, we introduced a legal case retrieval module in ELLA. For every query from users, we search relevant legal cases obtained from China Judgements Online [3] and display them on the platform for users, as shown in Figure 2, part 4. As the context of the legal cases may be long, we highlight the sentences in the trial proceeding records related to the user's query. Users can directly locate these sentences to get key information. We provide multiple relevant legal cases. Users can click the button at the top of part 4 to view different legal cases.

## 3 System Overview

In this section, we detail the implementation of all back-end models of ELLA.

### 3.1 Legal Consultation

In our work, we use Lawyer LLaMA (Huang et al., 2023), a LLM adapted to the legal domain, for legal consultation. Based on Lawyer LLaMA, which focuses on answering queries about marriage, ELLA mainly provides marriage consultation services for users. Since our back-end model is pluggable, we can also replace Lawyer LLaMA with other legal domain LLMs, such as DISC-LawLLM (Yue et al., 2023), ChatLaw (Cui et al., 2023) or LawGPT (Nguyen, 2023).

### 3.2 Legal Article Retrieval

We use the legal article retrieval model provided by Lawyer LLaMA. Following Lawyer LLaMA, after the user inputs a query, we retrieve the relevant legal articles, and append the top 3 legal articles to the user's query to generate the response. Besides, we display the top $K_1 = 10$ retrieved legal articles on the front end. If the user selects some relevant legal articles and requires a new response, in the back end, we append all selected legal articles to the input prompt, and LLM will generate a new response.

[3] https://wenshu.court.gov.cn

### 3.3 Response Interpretation

The response interpretation module aims to provide the legal article basis and judicial interpretations for each sentence of the response from the LLM. Here, we use BGE (Xiao et al., 2023), a state-of-the-art embedding model for retrieval augmented generation. Since BGE has only been pre-trained on the general corpus, it lacks knowledge about the legal domain, thus being unable to distinguish between two terminologies that are semantically similar but have different definitions in the legal domain. Therefore, we need to fine-tune BGE with legal corpus to make it learn legal knowledge.

Due to the lack of training data, we construct a dataset for response interpretation. We sample 2k queries from the legal instruction tuning data published by Lawyer LLaMA. For each query $q$, we obtain the top 3 relevant articles $[a_1, a_2, a_3]$ with the legal article retrieval module, and append these three laws individually to $q_i$. Then Lawyer LLaMA generates different responses $[r_1, r_2, r_3]$ based on the different legal articles. For $r_i = [s_{i1}, s_{i2}, ..., s_{in}]$, we calculated the similarity between each sentence $s_{ij}, j \in [1, n]$ and $a_i$ using BM25 (Robertson and Zaragoza, 2009). As illustrated in Figure 4, we treat the sentence with the highest BM25 score $s_{ik}$ and gold article $a_i$ as the positive case $(s_{ik}, a_i)$, while the two most irrelevant sentences $s_{ix}$, $s_{iy}$ as negative cases $(s_{ix}, a_i)$ and $(s_{iy}, a_i)$. We also created negative cases $(s_{ik}, a_t), t \in [1, 2, 3]$ and $t \neq i$ for distinguishing relevant sentence in $r_i$ from other retrieved legal articles.

Given the similar language style and content between legal articles and judicial interpretations, and the fact that legal articles contain all the terminologies involved in judicial interpretations, we only used legal articles to construct the dataset. After fine-tuning the BGE on this dataset, we obtained a new model, which we denote as $BGE_1$ here.

During inference, we use $BGE_1$ to calculate the cosine similarity between the embedding of each sentence in the response and the legal articles and judicial interpretations. If the similarity exceeds a threshold $Thr_1$, we think the corresponding legal article or judicial interpretation can explain the sentence. $Thr_1$ is a hyper-parameter, which we set as 0.85 in our work. Then, we return the articles and judicial interpretations referenced by each sentence to the front end, to help users better understand the LLM's responses.

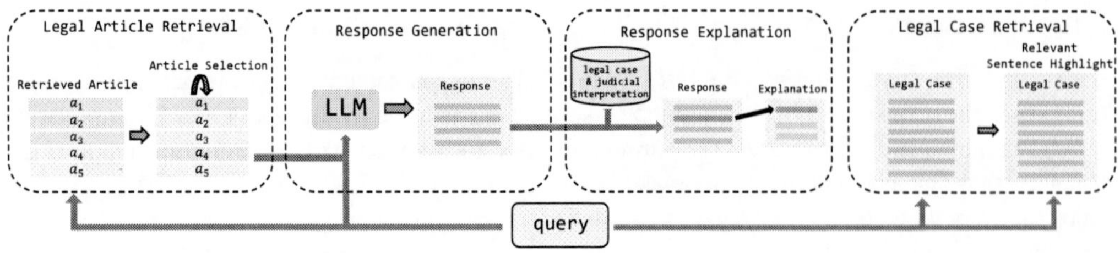


Figure 3: The system architecture overview.

### 3.4 Legal Case Retrieval

In this module, we first retrieve relevant legal cases based on the user's input. Then we find all the key sentences in the legal case that are related to the consultation query. Finally, we re-rank the top $K_2$ retrieved legal cases according to the number of relevant sentences in the legal case, and return the top $K_3$ re-ranked legal cases to the front end.

**Legal Case Retrieval.** Similarly, due to the lack of relevant legal domain knowledge in BGE, we need to fine-tune BGE with the legal domain corpus. Here, we use the dataset LeCaRD (Ma et al., 2021), a publicly available Chinese legal case retrieval dataset. We allocated 80% of LeCaRD as the training set and 10% each as the validation and test set. We fine-tune BGE on the training set. Here we denoted the fine-tuned BGE as $BGE_2$. When the user inputs a query, we use $BGE_2$ to retrieve relevant legal cases.

**Relevant Sentence Highlight.** We use $BGE_2$ to calculate the similarity between the user's query and each sentence in the legal case. When the cosine similarity score is larger than $Thr_2$, we consider this sentence to be related to the user's query, thus this sentence can serve as a reason for this case being a relevant legal case. $Thr_2$ is a hyper-parameter, which we set to 0.65 in our work. We highlight all relevant sentences in the case for users, helping them quickly locate the parts of the case that are highly related to their query. In this way, users can quickly judge whether this legal case is relevant and helpful, and they can also quickly obtain important information that they care about.

**Legal Case Re-rank.** We think that the more relevant sentences in a case, the larger the possibility of the case being a relevant legal case. Therefore, we re-rank the top $K_2$ legal cases retrieved by $BGE_2$ according to the number of relevant sentences, and return the re-ranked top $K_3$ legal cases to the front end. We set $K_2 = 50$ and $K_3 = 15$ in our work.

| Model | NDCG@10 | NDCG@20 | NDCG@30 |
|---|---|---|---|
| BM25 | 53.51 | 55.81 | 58.03 |
| BGE | 66.57 | 67.13 | 71.91 |
| $BGE_2$ | 76.34 | 77.84 | 78.29 |
| CaseEncoder (Ma et al., 2023) | 78.5 | 80.3 | 83.9 |
| SAILER (Li et al., 2023) | 79.79 | 82.26 | 84.85 |
| CaseFormer (Su et al., 2024) | 83.45 | 83.57 | 83.94 |

Table 1: Results of Legal Case Retrieval Model.

## 4 Evaluation

In this section, we automatically evaluate our case retrieval model. We also conduct a user study to evaluate whether ELLA helps users obtain more accurate, interpretable and informative information during the consultation.

### 4.1 Automatical Evaluation

As we mentioned in Section 3.4, we split LeCaRD into 80% for training, 10% for validation and 10% for testing. Here, we use the LeCaRD test set to evaluate our legal case retrieval model, $BGE_2$. Following CaseEncoder (Ma et al., 2023), we use the Normalize Discounted Cumulative Gain (NDCG) metric as the evaluation metric. The experimental results are shown in Table 1.

Compared with BM25 and BGE which has not been fine-tuned, $BGE_2$ shows a significant increase in each NDCG@K. This shows that the fine-tuned BGE can learn legal knowledge well, and better distinguish legal cases that are semantically similar but not relevant in the legal domain. Although CaseEncoder (Ma et al., 2023), SAILER (Li et al., 2023) and CaseFormer (Su et al., 2024) outperform $BGE_2$, we use $BGE_2$ since it can serve as an embedding model for relevant sentences similarity matching mentioned in Section 3.4. Note that our legal case retrieval model is pluggable, so we can also additionally add SOTA models mentioned above for legal case retrieval.

### 4.2 User Study

#### 4.2.1 Study Design

We conduct a user study to validate whether ELLA can improve users' legal consultation experience. Since LLMs deliver an impressive performance in answering simple questions, such as *"Can I get married if I am younger than 20?"*, we randomly selected 20 consultation queries about complex marriage situations for the user study. We invited 3 non-legal professional users and asked them to obtain solutions to these queries through ELLA. Users will evaluate whether the three modules in ELLA are helpful for their legal consultation.

#### 4.2.2 Result

**Response Regeneration.** For an average of 83% of the queries, users find that the top 3 legal articles retrieved are not entirely correct, impeding LLM from directly generating correct responses based on these articles. For an estimated 20% of the queries, LLMs can not provide correct responses due to the noise brought by irrelevant legal articles, while for 25%, LLM's responses are incomplete, as relevant legal articles were not among the initial top three results. Another 38% of responses contained irrelevant information resulting from the inclusion of unrelated legal articles within the top three results. However, in 80% cases, users can successfully receive correct responses by selecting relevant legal articles for LLM to regenerate responses.

**Response Interpretation.** Users have reported that for approximately 95% of the queries, ELLA can accurately provide the legal article basis of the responses generated by the LLM. By cross-referencing the responses with the corresponding legal article, users can swiftly determine whether the responses are reliable or inaccurate. For instance, when a user asks, *"I have never had children since I got married, and now I am planning to adopt a child from a relative. Can I adopt a child privately?"* LLM responds *"Adopters need to meet the following conditions..."*. ELLA justifies the response by citing Article 1098 of the Civil Code as its legal article basis. Additionally, it retrieves Article 1100 of the Civil Code, *"A childless adopter may adopt two children...,"* which the user can select for the LLM to generate a full response. Users also noted that, in about 73% of the queries, parts of the legal articles have already been included within the responses. However, LLM may not fully rephrase the entire article. By providing the legal articles basis, users can conveniently access to the complete information in the legal article.

In all provided judicial interpretations, roughly 30% serve the purpose of clarifying specific legal terminologies or special cases. For instance, consider a scenario where a user inquires, *"My husband and I have obtained a marriage certificate but have not cohabited. We are now filing for divorce and my husband wishes to return the bride price. Is this permissible?"* In response, ELLA gives additional judicial interpretation that illuminates the conditions under which the return of the bride price is allowed. However, for the remaining 70%, users claim that they are already familiar with the content in the judicial interpretations, such as, *"Support payments encompass children's living expenses, education costs, medical bills and other expenditures."* Generally speaking, users assert that judicial interpretations can assist them in acquiring a better comprehension of the responses when interpretation is required, facilitate accurate judgments according to their situations, and pave the way for further consultation tailored to the specifics of their current circumstances.

**Legal Case Retrieval.** On average, 77% of queries proved the legal case retrieval module to be beneficial for user consultations. Users conveyed that although the retrieved legal cases might not exactly match their situations, these cases provide a reference point to gauge the possible outcomes for their unique circumstances. All users concurred that highlighting pertinent sentences significantly streamlines the process of reading cases. By emphasizing the information users are interested in, the user's reading efficiency improves.

## 5 Conclusion

We present a novel tool, ELLA, for legal consultation. ELLA provides the legal basis and judicial interpretations that supplement the legal advice generated by LLMs, increasing users' understanding and trust in LLM responses. It also displays retrieval results from the retrieval model and allows users to actively select relevant legal articles, thereby assisting the LLMs in generating more accurate responses. Additionally, equipped with a legal case retrieval model, users can refer to relevant legal cases for more comprehensive information. ELLA enables LLMs to provide legal advice that is easier to interpret, more precise, and more informative.

## Acknowledgments

This work is supported in part by NSFC (62161160339) and Beijing Science and Technology Program (Z231100007423011). We thank the anonymous reviewers for their valuable comments and suggestions. For any correspondence, please contact Yansong Feng.

## Limitations

For simple legal queries, legal LLMs can provide correct responses in most cases. ELLA primarily assists with complex legal consultation queries. When users ask multiple questions within a single input, our legal article retrieval module may not comprehensively extract all relevant legal articles. In future work, we plan to integrate different retrieval modules to increase the diversity of retrieved legal articles.

As official judicial interpretations only contain 76 articles, ELLA can not provide interpretations for all professional terminologies. We will incorporate additional external legal knowledge, such as legal textbooks, to provide interpretations for more professional terminologies.

Due to limited computational resources, we do not use state-of-the-art case retrieval modules. We will adopt them in our future work.

## Ethics Statement

The main purpose of this paper is to explore how to provide users with better legal consultation services. However, it is important to note that the outputs generated by the model may contain non-standard, incorrect, gender-biased, or morally questionable information. Therefore, please adopt the legal advice provided by the model with caution. When legal assistance is needed, please seek help from qualified professionals.

The external knowledge used in this paper, such as legal articles and legal cases, was obtained from the official websites of the Chinese government. The data does not contain any private information and cannot be used for commercial purposes.

All participants involved in the user study are voluntary and anonymous. We did not collect any private information from the participants.

## References

Pierre Colombo, Telmo Pessoa Pires, Malik Boudiaf, Dominic Culver, Rui Melo, Caio Corro, Andre F. T. Martins, Fabrizio Esposito, Vera Lúcia Raposo, Sofia Morgado, and Michael Desa. 2024. Saullm-7b: A pioneering large language model for law.

Jiaxi Cui, Zongjian Li, Yang Yan, Bohua Chen, and Li Yuan. 2023. Chatlaw: Open-source legal large language model with integrated external knowledge bases.

Guanting Dong, Jinxu Zhao, Tingfeng Hui, Daichi Guo, Wenlong Wang, Boqi Feng, Yueyan Qiu, Zhuoma Gongque, Keqing He, Zechen Wang, et al. 2023. Revisit input perturbation problems for llms: A unified robustness evaluation framework for noisy slot filling task. In *CCF International Conference on Natural Language Processing and Chinese Computing*, pages 682–694. Springer.

Quzhe Huang, Mingxu Tao, Chen Zhang, Zhenwei An, Cong Jiang, Zhibin Chen, Zirui Wu, and Yansong Feng. 2023. Lawyer llama technical report. *ArXiv*, abs/2305.15062.

Ziwei Ji, Nayeon Lee, Rita Frieske, Tiezheng Yu, Dan Su, Yan Xu, Etsuko Ishii, Ye Jin Bang, Andrea Madotto, and Pascale Fung. 2023. Survey of hallucination in natural language generation. *ACM Computing Surveys*, 55(12):1–38.

Jinqi Lai, Wensheng Gan, Jiayang Wu, Zhenlian Qi, and Philip S. Yu. 2023. Large language models in law: A survey.

Patrick Lewis, Ethan Perez, Aleksandra Piktus, Fabio Petroni, Vladimir Karpukhin, Naman Goyal, Heinrich Küttler, Mike Lewis, Wen tau Yih, Tim Rocktäschel, Sebastian Riedel, and Douwe Kiela. 2021. Retrieval-augmented generation for knowledge-intensive nlp tasks.

Haitao Li, Qingyao Ai, Jia Chen, Qian Dong, Yueyue Wu, Yiqun Liu, Chong Chen, and Qi Tian. 2023. Sailer: Structure-aware pre-trained language model for legal case retrieval.

Yixiao Ma, Yunqiu Shao, Yueyue Wu, Yiqun Liu, Ruizhe Zhang, Min Zhang, and Shaoping Ma. 2021. Lecard: a legal case retrieval dataset for chinese law system. In *Proceedings of the 44th international ACM SIGIR conference on research and development in information retrieval*, pages 2342–2348.

Yixiao Ma, Yueyue Wu, Weihang Su, Qingyao Ai, and Yiqun Liu. 2023. Caseencoder: A knowledge-enhanced pre-trained model for legal case encoding.

Ha-Thanh Nguyen. 2023. A brief report on lawgpt 1.0: A virtual legal assistant based on gpt-3.

OpenAI, Josh Achiam, Steven Adler, Sandhini Agarwal, Lama Ahmad, Ilge Akkaya, Florencia Leoni Aleman, Diogo Almeida, Janko Altenschmidt, Sam Altman, Shyamal Anadkat, Red Avila, Igor Babuschkin, Suchir Balaji, Valerie Balcom, Paul Baltescu, Haiming Bao, Mohammad Bavarian, Jeff Belgum, Irwan Bello, Jake Berdine, Gabriel Bernadett-Shapiro,

Christopher Berner, Lenny Bogdonoff, Oleg Boiko, Madelaine Boyd, Anna-Luisa Brakman, Greg Brockman, Tim Brooks, Miles Brundage, Kevin Button, Trevor Cai, Rosie Campbell, Andrew Cann, Brittany Carey, Chelsea Carlson, Rory Carmichael, Brooke Chan, Che Chang, Fotis Chantzis, Derek Chen, Sully Chen, Ruby Chen, Jason Chen, Mark Chen, Ben Chess, Chester Cho, Casey Chu, Hyung Won Chung, Dave Cummings, Jeremiah Currier, Yunxing Dai, Cory Decareaux, Thomas Degry, Noah Deutsch, Damien Deville, Arka Dhar, David Dohan, Steve Dowling, Sheila Dunning, Adrien Ecoffet, Atty Eleti, Tyna Eloundou, David Farhi, Liam Fedus, Niko Felix, Simón Posada Fishman, Juston Forte, Isabella Fulford, Leo Gao, Elie Georges, Christian Gibson, Vik Goel, Tarun Gogineni, Gabriel Goh, Rapha Gontijo-Lopes, Jonathan Gordon, Morgan Grafstein, Scott Gray, Ryan Greene, Joshua Gross, Shixiang Shane Gu, Yufei Guo, Chris Hallacy, Jesse Han, Jeff Harris, Yuchen He, Mike Heaton, Johannes Heidecke, Chris Hesse, Alan Hickey, Wade Hickey, Peter Hoeschele, Brandon Houghton, Kenny Hsu, Shengli Hu, Xin Hu, Joost Huizinga, Shantanu Jain, Shawn Jain, Joanne Jang, Angela Jiang, Roger Jiang, Haozhun Jin, Denny Jin, Shino Jomoto, Billie Jonn, Heewoo Jun, Tomer Kaftan, Łukasz Kaiser, Ali Kamali, Ingmar Kanitscheider, Nitish Shirish Keskar, Tabarak Khan, Logan Kilpatrick, Jong Wook Kim, Christina Kim, Yongjik Kim, Jan Hendrik Kirchner, Jamie Kiros, Matt Knight, Daniel Kokotajlo, Łukasz Kondraciuk, Andrew Kondrich, Aris Konstantinidis, Kyle Kosic, Gretchen Krueger, Vishal Kuo, Michael Lampe, Ikai Lan, Teddy Lee, Jan Leike, Jade Leung, Daniel Levy, Chak Ming Li, Rachel Lim, Molly Lin, Stephanie Lin, Mateusz Litwin, Theresa Lopez, Ryan Lowe, Patricia Lue, Anna Makanju, Kim Malfacini, Sam Manning, Todor Markov, Yaniv Markovski, Bianca Martin, Katie Mayer, Andrew Mayne, Bob McGrew, Scott Mayer McKinney, Christine McLeavey, Paul McMillan, Jake McNeil, David Medina, Aalok Mehta, Jacob Menick, Luke Metz, Andrey Mishchenko, Pamela Mishkin, Vinnie Monaco, Evan Morikawa, Daniel Mossing, Tong Mu, Mira Murati, Oleg Murk, David Mély, Ashvin Nair, Reiichiro Nakano, Rajeev Nayak, Arvind Neelakantan, Richard Ngo, Hyeonwoo Noh, Long Ouyang, Cullen O'Keefe, Jakub Pachocki, Alex Paino, Joe Palermo, Ashley Pantuliano, Giambattista Parascandolo, Joel Parish, Emy Parparita, Alex Passos, Mikhail Pavlov, Andrew Peng, Adam Perelman, Filipe de Avila Belbute Peres, Michael Petrov, Henrique Ponde de Oliveira Pinto, Michael, Pokorny, Michelle Pokrass, Vitchyr H. Pong, Tolly Powell, Alethea Power, Boris Power, Elizabeth Proehl, Raul Puri, Alec Radford, Jack Rae, Aditya Ramesh, Cameron Raymond, Francis Real, Kendra Rimbach, Carl Ross, Bob Rotsted, Henri Roussez, Nick Ryder, Mario Saltarelli, Ted Sanders, Shibani Santurkar, Girish Sastry, Heather Schmidt, David Schnurr, John Schulman, Daniel Selsam, Kyla Sheppard, Toki Sherbakov, Jessica Shieh, Sarah Shoker, Pranav Shyam, Szymon Sidor, Eric Sigler, Maddie Simens, Jordan Sitkin, Katarina Slama, Ian Sohl, Benjamin Sokolowsky, Yang Song, Natalie Staudacher, Felipe Petroski Such, Natalie Summers, Ilya Sutskever, Jie Tang, Nikolas Tezak, Madeleine B. Thompson, Phil Tillet, Amin Tootoonchian, Elizabeth Tseng, Preston Tuggle, Nick Turley, Jerry Tworek, Juan Felipe Cerón Uribe, Andrea Vallone, Arun Vijayvergiya, Chelsea Voss, Carroll Wainwright, Justin Jay Wang, Alvin Wang, Ben Wang, Jonathan Ward, Jason Wei, CJ Weinmann, Akila Welihinda, Peter Welinder, Jiayi Weng, Lilian Weng, Matt Wiethoff, Dave Willner, Clemens Winter, Samuel Wolrich, Hannah Wong, Lauren Workman, Sherwin Wu, Jeff Wu, Michael Wu, Kai Xiao, Tao Xu, Sarah Yoo, Kevin Yu, Qiming Yuan, Wojciech Zaremba, Rowan Zellers, Chong Zhang, Marvin Zhang, Shengjia Zhao, Tianhao Zheng, Juntang Zhuang, William Zhuk, and Barret Zoph. 2024. Gpt-4 technical report.

Stephen Robertson and Hugo Zaragoza. 2009. The probabilistic relevance framework: Bm25 and beyond. *Found. Trends Inf. Retr.*, 3(4):333–389.

Jaromir Savelka, Kevin D. Ashley, Morgan A. Gray, Hannes Westermann, and Huihui Xu. 2023. Explaining legal concepts with augmented large language models (gpt-4).

Weihang Su, Qingyao Ai, Yueyue Wu, Yixiao Ma, Haitao Li, Yiqun Liu, Zhijing Wu, and Min Zhang. 2024. Caseformer: Pre-training for legal case retrieval based on inter-case distinctions.

Hugo Touvron, Thibaut Lavril, Gautier Izacard, Xavier Martinet, Marie-Anne Lachaux, Timothée Lacroix, Baptiste Rozière, Naman Goyal, Eric Hambro, Faisal Azhar, Aurelien Rodriguez, Armand Joulin, Edouard Grave, and Guillaume Lample. 2023. Llama: Open and efficient foundation language models.

Shijie Wu, Ozan Irsoy, Steven Lu, Vadim Dabravolski, Mark Dredze, Sebastian Gehrmann, Prabhanjan Kambadur, David Rosenberg, and Gideon Mann. 2023. Bloomberggpt: A large language model for finance.

Shitao Xiao, Zheng Liu, Peitian Zhang, and Niklas Muennighoff. 2023. C-pack: Packaged resources to advance general chinese embedding.

Hongyang Yang, Xiao-Yang Liu, and Christina Dan Wang. 2023. Fingpt: Open-source financial large language models.

Shengbin Yue, Wei Chen, Siyuan Wang, Bingxuan Li, Chenchen Shen, Shujun Liu, Yuxuan Zhou, Yao Xiao, Song Yun, Xuanjing Huang, and Zhongyu Wei. 2023. Disc-lawllm: Fine-tuning large language models for intelligent legal services.

Aohan Zeng, Xiao Liu, Zhengxiao Du, Zihan Wang, Hanyu Lai, Ming Ding, Zhuoyi Yang, Yifan Xu, Wendi Zheng, Xiao Xia, Weng Lam Tam, Zixuan Ma, Yufei Xue, Jidong Zhai, Wenguang Chen, Peng Zhang, Yuxiao Dong, and Jie Tang. 2023. Glm-130b: An open bilingual pre-trained model.

Kaijie Zhu, Jindong Wang, Jiaheng Zhou, Zichen Wang, Hao Chen, Yidong Wang, Linyi Yang, Wei Ye, Neil Zhenqiang Gong, Yue Zhang, et al. 2023. Promptbench: Towards evaluating the robustness of large language models on adversarial prompts. *arXiv preprint arXiv:2306.04528*.

## A Dataset Construction

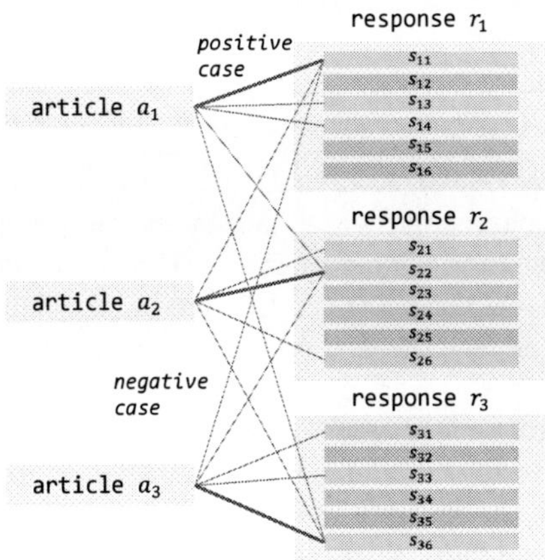


Figure 4: Schematic of Dataset Construction. The blue sentences indicate the sentences with the highest BM25 scores and the orange sentences are the most irrelevant ones. Blue lines indicate positive cases and orange lines indicate negative cases.

## B Consultation Examples

| $Q_1$ : 收养小孩有什么要求吗? | $Q_1$ : What are the requirements for adopting a child? |
|---|---|
| $R_1$ : 您好，根据《民法典》的规定，收养人需要同时具备以下五个条件：1.无子女或只有一名子女；2.有抚养、教育和保护被收养人的能力；3.未患有在医学上认为不应当收养子女的疾病；4.无不利于被收养人健康成长的违法犯罪记录；5.年满三十周岁。此外，如果收养人有配偶，则需要夫妻共同收养。收养关系自登记之日起成立，收养关系当事人自愿签订收养协议的，可以签订收养协议。如果收养关系当事人各方或一方要求办理收养公证的，应当办理收养公证。县级以上人民政府民政部门应当依法进行收养评估。请问您还有其他方面的问题吗? | $R_1$ : Hello, according to the provisions of the Civil Code, adopters need to meet the following five conditions simultaneously: 1. Having no children or having only one child; 2. Having the ability to support, educate, and protect the adopted child; 3. Not suffering from diseases that are considered by medical standards as reasons not to adopt children; 4. Having no criminal records that are detrimental to the healthy growth of the adopted child; 5. Being at least thirty years old. Additionally, if the adopter is married, the adoption should be done jointly by the couple. The adoption relationship is established from the date of registration. If the parties to the adoption voluntarily sign an adoption agreement, they can do so. If the parties to the adoption or one party requests adoption notarization, adoption notarization should be processed. The civil affairs department of the people's government at or above the county level shall conduct adoption assessments in accordance with the law. Do you have any other questions? |
| $R'_1$ : 您好，根据《民法典》的规定，收养小孩需要满足以下条件：1.无子女的收养人可以收养两名子女；2.有子女的收养人只能收养一名子女；3.收养孤儿、残疾未成年人或者儿童福利机构抚养的查找不到生父母的未成年人，可以不受前款和本法第一千零九十八条第一项规定的限制。此外，无配偶者收养异性子女的，收养人与被收养人的年龄应当相差四十周岁以上。最后，符合以下条件的未成年人可以被收养：1.丧失父母的孤儿；2.查找不到生父母的未成年人；3.生父母有特殊困难无力抚养的子女。请问您的具体情况是什么？是否符合上述规定呢? | $R'_1$ : Hello, according to the provisions of the Civil Code, adopting a child requires meeting the following conditions: 1. An adopter with no children can adopt up to two children; 2. An adopter with children can only adopt one child; 3. Orphans, disabled minors, or minors raised by child welfare institutions whose birth parents cannot be found are not subject to the restrictions in the preceding paragraph and Article 1098 of this Law. Additionally, if an unmarried person adopts a child of the opposite sex, the adopter's age must be at least forty years older than the adoptee's. Lastly, the following minors can be adopted: 1. Orphans who have lost both parents; 2. Minors whose birth parents cannot be found; 3. Children whose birth parents face special difficulties and are unable to raise them. Could you please provide specific details about your situation? Do you meet the above requirements? |

Table 2: $R_1$ is generated based on Article 1098, 1101, and 1105 of Civil Code. $R'_1$ is generated based on Article 1100, 1102, and 1093 of Civil Code.

| | |
|---|---|
| $Q_2$ : 我的情况是这样的，我女朋友结婚了，但是已经和她老公分居好几年，是不是算自动离婚了?我们没以夫妻的名义同居算重婚吗? | $Q_2$ : Here's my situation: my girlfriend got married, but she has been separated from her husband for several years. Does this count as automatic divorce? Would living together without being married constitute bigamy? |
| $R_2$ : 您好，根据我国婚姻法规定，夫妻双方自愿离婚，可以自行协商处理财产分割等问题，不需要经过法院审理，如果您女友与她的丈夫已经分居多年，并且没有其他原因导致他们无法继续维持婚姻关系，那么可以视为自动离婚。至于您们是否构成重婚，需要了解你们是否已正式离婚，以及是否已经与他人结婚或同居。如果已经离婚，则不存在重婚的问题。如果还没有离婚，则需要遵守相关法律法规，如禁止重婚等。请问您们是否已经离婚? | $R_2$ : Hello, according to the marriage laws of our country, if both parties voluntarily divorce, they can negotiate property division and other issues themselves without the need for court trial. If your girlfriend has been separated from her husband for many years and there are no other reasons preventing them from continuing their marriage, it can be considered an automatic divorce. As for whether you constitute bigamy, it depends on whether you have officially divorced and whether you have married or cohabited with someone else. If you have already divorced, there is no issue of bigamy. If not, you need to comply with relevant laws and regulations, such as the prohibition of bigamy. May I ask if you have already divorced? |
| $R'_2$ : 您好，根据我国法律规定，只有在完成离婚登记或者离婚判决书、调解书生效后，才能够真正意义上解除婚姻关系。而您所提到的情况，虽然你们没有以夫妻的名义同居，但并不意味着已经完成了离婚手续。因此，您们目前仍然处于婚姻状态之中。另外，重婚是指在未办理离婚手续的情况下再次结婚的行为，而您所提到的情况并不属于重婚范畴之内。请问您还有其他方面的问题需要解答吗? | $Q'_2$ : Hello, according to the laws of our country, marriage is only truly dissolved after completing divorce registration, or when the divorce judgment or mediation agreement takes effect. The situation you mentioned, although you haven't lived together as spouses, does not mean that the divorce procedures have been completed. Therefore, you are still in a marital status currently. Additionally, bigamy refers to remarrying without completing divorce procedures, which doesn't apply to the situation you mentioned. Do you have any other questions that need answering? |

Table 3: $R_2$ is generated based on Article 1080, 1091, and 1043 of Civil Code. $R'_2$ is generated based on Article 1080 of Civil Code.

| | |
|---|---|
| $Q_3$：我的情况是这样的，我女朋友结婚了，但是已经和她老公分居好几年，是不是算自动离婚了?我们没以夫妻的名义同居算重婚吗? | $Q_3$ : My situation is like this: My girlfriend got married, but she has been separated from her husband for several years. Does this count as automatic divorce? Would living together without being married constitute bigamy? |
| $R_3$：您好，根据《民法典》的规定，只有完成离婚登记或者离婚判决书、调解书生效才能够解除婚姻关系。而您的女友已经与她的丈夫分居多年，但并未办理离婚手续，因此不能算自动离婚。同时，如果您们没有以夫妻的名义同居，则不属于重婚行为。不过，在婚姻关系中，夫妻双方应该互相忠实、互相尊重、互相关爱，并且要保持良好的家庭环境。如果出现家庭矛盾或纠纷，可以通过协商解决，也可以通过司法途径解决。请问您是否需要进一步了解如何处理此类问题呢? | $R_3$ : Hello, according to the provisions of the Civil Code, marriage can only be dissolved by completing divorce registration or when a divorce judgment or mediation agreement becomes effective. As your girlfriend has been separated from her husband for several years without completing divorce procedures, it does not count as automatic divorce. Also, if you haven't lived together as husband and wife, it does not constitute bigamy. However, in a marital relationship, both parties should be faithful, respect each other, love each other, and maintain a good family environment. If there are family conflicts or disputes, they can be resolved through negotiation or legal means. Would you like further information on how to handle such issues? |

Table 4: $R_3$ is generated based on Article 1080, 1091, 1043 of Civil Code.

| | |
|---|---|
| $Q_4$：我的情况是这样的，我女朋友结婚了，但是已经和她老公分居两年多了，算不算自动离婚了？我们没以夫妻的名义同居算重婚罪吗？ | Here's my situation: my girlfriend got married, but she has been separated from her husband for over two years. Does this count as automatic divorce? Would it be considered bigamy if we cohabitated without being married? |
| $R_4$：您好，根据我国婚姻法规定，夫妻双方自愿离婚，可以自行协商离婚事宜并到当地民政局办理离婚手续。如果您女友与她的丈夫没有达成协议，则需要通过法院诉讼程序来解决离婚问题。至于您提到的同居问题，如果两人没有以夫妻的名义同居，则不会构成重婚罪。不过，建议您们先了解清楚相关法律规定，再做出决定。另外，关于收养小孩的问题，您需要提供更多信息，例如孩子的性别、年龄等，才能够更好地为您解答问题。 | Hello, according to the Marriage Law of our country, if both parties in a marriage voluntarily agree to divorce, they can negotiate the terms of the divorce and go to the local civil affairs bureau to handle the divorce procedures. If your girlfriend and her husband have not reached an agreement, they will need to resolve the divorce issue through the court litigation process. As for the cohabitation issue you mentioned, it would not constitute bigamy if you two did not cohabit under the guise of marriage. However, it's advisable for you to understand the relevant legal provisions before making any decisions. Additionally, regarding the adoption of a child, you would need to provide more information, such as the child's gender and age, for me to better assist you with your questions. |

Table 5: $R_4$ is generated based on Article 1080, 1091, 1043 of Civil Code.

# LLMBox: A Comprehensive Library for Large Language Models

Tianyi Tang[1*], Yiwen Hu[1*],
Bingqian Li[1†], Wenyang Luo[1†], Zijing Qin[3†], Haoxiang Sun[2†], Jiapeng Wang[1†],
Shiyi Xu[1], Xiaoxue Cheng[1], Geyang Guo[1], Han Peng[1], Bowen Zheng[1],
Yiru Tang[1], Yingqian Min[1], Yushuo Chen[1], Jie Chen[1], Yuanqian Zhao[1],
Luran Ding[1], Yuhao Wang[1], Zican Dong[1], Chunxuan Xia[1],
Junyi Li[1], Kun Zhou[2], Wayne Xin Zhao[1 ✉], Ji-Rong Wen[1,2],
[1] Gaoling School of Artificial Intelligence, Renmin University of China
[2] School of Information, Renmin University of China
[3] School of Computer Science and Technology, Xidian University
steventianyitang@outlook.com huyiwenwen@foxmail.com batmanfly@gmail.com

## Abstract

To facilitate the research on large language models (LLMs), this paper presents a comprehensive and unified library, **LLMBox**, to ease the development, use, and evaluation of LLMs. This library is featured with three main merits: (1) *a unified data interface* that supports the flexible implementation of various training strategies, (2) *a comprehensive evaluation* that covers extensive tasks, datasets, and models, and (3) *more practical consideration*, especially on user-friendliness and efficiency. With our library, users can easily reproduce existing methods, train new models, and conduct comprehensive performance comparisons. To rigorously test LLMBox, we conduct extensive experiments in a diverse coverage of evaluation settings, and experimental results demonstrate the effectiveness and efficiency of our library in supporting various implementations related to LLMs. The detailed introduction and usage guidance can be found at `https://github.com/RUCAIBox/LLMBox`.

## 1 Introduction

Recent years have witnessed the rapid progress of large language models (LLMs) (Zhao et al., 2023). In the research community, great efforts have been devoted to the release of well-trained LLMs, the design of special tuning and inference methods, and the conduct of systematic capacity evaluation. However, the reproducibility and fair comparison of existing studies should still be emphasized, since they are mostly developed in different ways or frameworks. Without the standardized and unified implementation, it would take substantial efforts to reproduce or improve upon existing research work.

Considering the above issue, in this paper, we present a comprehensive library, called **LLMBox**, for easing the development, use, and evaluation of LLMs. In particular, our library focuses on building a comprehensive and unified framework (including training, inference, and evaluation) for better supporting LLM-based research and applications. Although there are already several open-source libraries for LLMs (Kwon et al., 2023; Gao et al., 2023a; hiyouga, 2023), they typically focus on a certain or some stage(s) of LLMs (either pre-training or fine-tuning) or conduct the training pipeline of LLMs in a separate way. Moreover, they can seldom support comprehensive and unified evaluation of various LLMs.

In order to better facilitate research on LLMs, LLMBox introduces a series of new features for the library design, which can be summarized into three major aspects below:

• *Unified data interface.* We design a unified data interface to encapsulate different formats of training data, including both plain texts and instruction data. With this interface, LLMBox can flexibly support the implementation of various strategies, such as dynamic mixture proportion (Xie et al., 2023) and combined training with pre-training and instruction data (Zeng et al., 2022). Furthermore, we extensively support mainstream training methodologies, including parameter-efficient tuning (*e.g.,* LoRA (Hu et al., 2022)) and alignment tuning (*e.g.,* PPO (Schulman et al., 2017)).

• *Comprehensive evaluation.* To support a comprehensive comparison of LLMs' performance, our library encompasses 18 downstream tasks alongside 56 datasets. Beyond the common benchmarks such as MMLU (Hendrycks et al., 2021) and GSM8K (Cobbe et al., 2021), our framework also extends the support for probing LLMs' advanced

* Co-leading the project.
† Equal Contribution. Ordered by name.
✉ Corresponding author.



*Proceedings of the 62nd Annual Meeting of the Association for Computational Linguistics (Volume 3: System Demonstrations)*, pages 388–399
August 11-16, 2024 ©2024 Association for Computational Linguistics

capabilities: human alignment, hallucination detection, instruction following, *etc*. Furthermore, LLMBox integrates a variety of publicly available LLMs and commercial APIs, offering a convenient platform for holistic evaluation.

• *More practical considerations.* To be user-friendly, LLMBox is designed to provide an easy-to-use pipeline, enabling users to quickly start with minimal commands. We introduce a *GPU calculator* to help users determine the minimum GPU resources necessary for training. To be efficient, we propose a novel *prefix caching* strategy for inference and a *packing* strategy for training. Remarkably, given the LLaMA (7B) model, our library can perform inference on the entire MMLU benchmark within six minutes on a single A800 GPU and completes instruction tuning with 52K instances on eight A800 GPUs in ten minutes.

An additional feature is that LLMBox is closely aligned with our prior survey paper on LLMs (Zhao et al., 2023). This is particularly useful for beginners, enabling the learning of basic knowledge and practice of LLMs through integrating the survey paper and the associated library.

In what follows, we will first introduce the training framework of our library in Section 2, then detail the utilization and evaluation parts in Section 3, and showcase how to use our library in Section 4. After that, we will conduct the experiments to verify the reliability of our LLMBox in Section 5, and conclude the paper in Section 6.

## 2 Training

The training process is a crucial step for the development of LLMs. However, it typically needs massive detailed designs considering both efficiency and effectiveness, and also often faces intractable problems when adapting into new domains or meeting special needs. To facilitate easy training of LLMs, we integrate various training methods and resources in our library, to unify and simplify their usage. Besides, we provide suggestions for GPU usage tailored to different training requirements.

### 2.1 LLM Training

In our LLMBox, we develop a unified architecture to encapsulate important training methods in developing LLMs, and implement efficient training strategies to support training on limited computing resource. The overall framework of LLMBox is illustrated in Figure 1.

**Key Training Methods.** In our LLMBox, we integrate massive functionalities to support the following four training processes:

• *Pre-training.* Our LLMBox supports pre-training LLMs from scratch or continually pre-training using corpora in specific languages or specialized domains. For continually pre-training, LLMBox supports expanding the vocabulary to facilitate the adaptation of LLMs to new fields.

• *Instruction tuning.* LLMBox integrates ten commonly-used datasets for supporting instruction-tuning, covering NLP task (*e.g.,* FLAN v2 (Chung et al., 2022)), daily chat (*e.g.,* ShareGPT (Eccleston, 2023)), and synthetic datasets (*e.g.,* Alpaca-52K (Taori et al., 2023)). Additionally, we integrate three methods to synthesize or rewrite instructions, namely Self-Instruct (Wang et al., 2023a), Evol-Instruct (Xu et al., 2023), and topic diversifying (YuLan-Team, 2023). Based on the above datasets, we specially design unified dataset class, which can automatically preprocess these datasets into a unified format for training LLMs, and provide flexible interfaces for users to adjust the settings about the data (*e.g.,* data mixture proportion).

• *Human alignment.* To enhance the alignment of LLMs with human values, we incorporate both the widely-used RLHF method PPO (Schulman et al., 2017) and non-RL approach DPO (Rafailov et al., 2023). Besides, LLMBox also integrates several preference datasets, including HH-RLHF (Bai et al., 2022) and SHP (Ethayarajh et al., 2022).

**Efficient Training Strategies.** We also integrate several widely-used efficient training strategies or libraries, to support training LLMs with limited computing resources.

• *LoRA and QLoRA.* LLMBox integrates the lightweight module LoRA (Hu et al., 2022) to facilitate the different training methods of LLMs in resource-constrained environments. We also encapsulate QLoRA (Dettmers et al., 2023) in LLMBox, which performs quantization on LoRA for further reducing its used GPU memory.

• *DeepSpeed.* Our LLMBox library is based on the distributed training library DeepSpeed (Rasley et al., 2020), which includes a range of training optimization strategies for efficient training LLMs, including zero redundancy optimizer (ZeRO) (Rajbhandari et al., 2020), gradient checkpointing (Chen et al., 2016), FlashAttention (Dao et al., 2022), *etc.*

• *Packing.* We implement the packing strategy (Raffel et al., 2020; Touvron et al., 2023b)

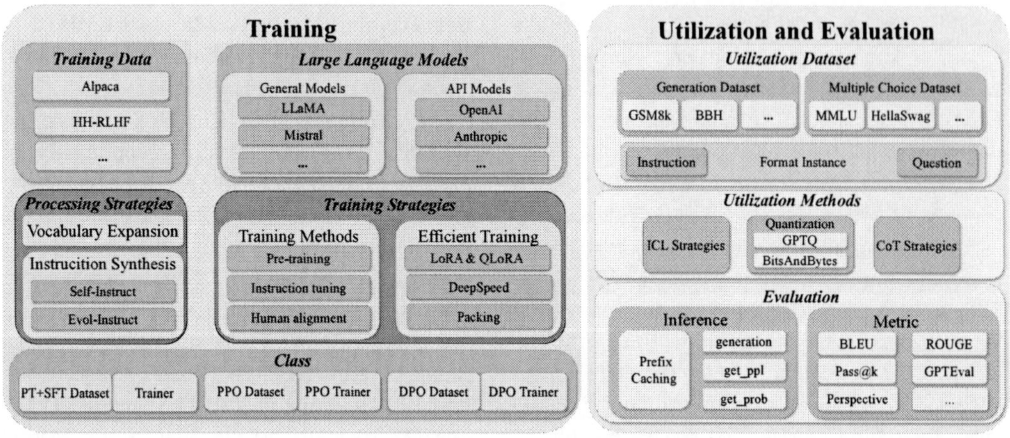


Figure 1: The overall framework of our LLMBox, supporting the training, utilization and evaluation of LLMs.

to enhance training efficiency. During pre-training, we concatenate all tokens into a long sentence and then split it to multiple sentences with the max length. For instruction-tuning, we concatenate all instructions as a long multi-turn conversation, and then break it into multiple conversations approaching to the maximum length constraint. Through minimizing paddings, we can optimize memory efficiency while maintaining model performance.

## 2.2 Training Suggestions

In practice, it is necessary for users to estimate the hardware requirements for training LLMs. Based on our LLMBox, we meticulously analyze GPU memory consumption throughout the model training process, by fully considering the impacts of parameters, gradients, optimizer states, and activation value (Rajbhandari et al., 2020; Ren et al., 2021; Korthikanti et al., 2023). We further introduce a "GPU memory calculator" to aid users in determining the minimal GPU requirements across LLMs with different parameter scales.

By merging the above strategies to reach efficiency[1], the memory consumption of each GPU can be roughly estimated by the equation:

$$\frac{16p}{n} + (12 + 2l)bsh + 12bsv, \tag{1}$$

where $p$ represents the total number of parameters, and $n$, $l$, $b$, $s$, $h$, $v$ stand for the number of GPUs, number of layers, batch size, sequence length, hidden size, and vocabulary size, respectively. Taking the training of LLaMA-2 (7B) ($l = 32, s = 4096, h = 4096, v = 32000$) as an example, we employ two A100 (80G) GPUs ($n = 2$) with a batch size of $b = 8$. By using Eq. 1 with the above configuration, we can estimate an approximate GPU memory usage of 71.42GB per unit. As shown in Table 1, we extrapolate the minimum GPU requirements using Eq. 1 for different model sizes across varying training settings, to help users for selecting proper GPU resources. For other special training settings, we invite users to utilize the calculator available on our library[2].

| | DDP | ZeRO-3 | LoRA | QLoRA |
|---|---|---|---|---|
| **1.3B** | 1 A100<br>1 A6000 | 1 A100<br>1 A6000 | 1 A100<br>1 A6000 | 1 A100<br>1 A6000 |
| **2.7B** | 1 A100<br>N/A | 1 A100<br>2 A6000 | 1 A100<br>1 A6000 | 1 A100<br>1 A6000 |
| **6.7B** | N/A<br>N/A | 2 A100<br>3 A6000 | 1 A100<br>1 A6000 | 1 A100<br>1 A6000 |
| **13B** | N/A<br>N/A | 3 A100<br>5 A6000 | 1 A100<br>1 A6000 | 1 A100<br>1 A6000 |
| **30B** | N/A<br>N/A | 8 A100<br>12 A6000 | 1 A100<br>2 A6000 | 1 A100<br>1 A6000 |
| **70B** | N/A<br>N/A | 16 A100<br>26 A6000 | 2 A100<br>4 A6000 | 1 A100<br>2 A6000 |

Table 1: Minimum GPU requirements for A100 (80G) and A6000 (48G) when training models with different sizes under four situations. N/A denotes DDP cannot be applied for such large models.

[1]For the training settings, we utilize data parallelism, ZeRO-3, gradient checkpointing, and FlashAttention.

[2]https://github.com/RUCAIBox/LLMBox/blob/main/training/gpu_calculator.py

## 3 Utilization and Evaluation

After training, we can develop suitable prompting strategies to use LLMs and assess their effectiveness. Users can reuse existing models, APIs or the models trained by LLMBox. The framework of our utilization pipeline is depicted in Figure 1.

### 3.1 Utilization Methods

We include quantization deployment strategies for using LLMs alongside two prompting methods: in-context learning (ICL) and chain-of-thought (CoT).

• *Quantization.* To enhance memory efficiency during inference, LLMBox incorporates two quantization techniques: bitsandbytes (Dettmers et al., 2022) and GPTQ (Frantar et al., 2023). Both methods facilitate 8-bit and 4-bit quantization and GPTQ additionally supports 3-bit quantization.

• *In-context learning.* We design a unified dataset class to organize diverse examples for few-shot learning. Furthermore, we implement three advanced ICL strategies, including KATE for example selection (Liu et al., 2022), GlobalE for example order arrange (Lu et al., 2022), and APE for instruction designing (Zhou et al., 2023c).

• *Chain-of-thought.* Moreover, LLMBox incorporates several CoT prompting methods, such as program-aided (PAL) CoT (Gao et al., 2023b) and least-to-most CoT (Zhou et al., 2023a). We develop a flexible framework to facilitate self-consistency (Wang et al., 2023a) and repeated sampling (Nijkamp et al., 2023), which are beneficial for tasks involving mathematics and coding.

### 3.2 Evaluation Methods

In LLMBox, we implement the evaluation of LLM performance through three distinct mechanisms:

• *Free-form generation:* This is the basic evaluation method for generative LLMs and is applicable across all tasks. Models are required to generate responses to queries in an auto-regressive manner. We integrate common decoding strategies, including greedy search, temperature sampling, top-$p$ sampling, repetition penalties, *etc.*

• *Completion perplexity:* This method is widely adopted for assessing multi-choice tasks in base LLMs. It involves comparing the perplexity (PPL) of each completion conditioned on the context and choose the one with the lowest average PPL. Additionally, we incorporate the use of normalized PPL as introduced in GPT-3 (Brown et al., 2020).

• *Option probability:* Similar to the multi-choice formats in human examination, we feed a context with all the options to LLMs and require them to select the option letter (*e.g.,* A). This approach is commonly utilized in chat-based models.

Significantly, we introduce *prefix caching* mechanism that caches the hidden states of common prefix texts to speed up the inference process. This strategy is organized at two levels: (1) we store the states of few-shot examples and compute them just once for all instances, *e.g.,* 5-shot examples in MMLU (Hendrycks et al., 2021) and 8-shot examples in GSM8K (Cobbe et al., 2021); (2) we cache the states of identical contexts of different options when calculating completion perplexity. The effectiveness of this method is verified in Section 5.2.

### 3.3 Supported Models

We integrate a variety of LLMs to keep pace with the swift advancements in this field. Given that LLMBox is based on the Transformers library (Wolf et al., 2020), it is compatible with a vast majority of publicly available models. We list some included models as follows:

• *General models:* LLaMA (Touvron et al., 2023a) and Mistral (Jiang et al., 2023);

• *Chinese models:* Qwen (Bai et al., 2023) and Baichuan (Yang et al., 2023);

• *Multilingual models:* BLOOM (Le Scao et al., 2022);

• *Chat models:* LLaMA-2 Chat (Touvron et al., 2023b) and Vicuna (Chiang et al., 2023);

• *Code models:* CodeGen (Nijkamp et al., 2023) and StarCoder (Li et al., 2023c);

• *Mathematical models:* Llemma (Azerbayev et al., 2024) and DeepSeekMath (Shao et al., 2024).

We also incorporate commercial APIs including OpenAI[3] and Anthropic Claude[4].

### 3.4 Supported Tasks

Currently, LLMBox integrates 18 diverse tasks and corresponding 56 datasets with hundreds of subsets. The broad range of supported datasets within LLMBox enables to evaluate various models. For instance, users can employ English benchmarks, language modeling, and knowledge reasoning datasets for evaluating foundational pre-trained LLMs. In the case of chat-based models, users can utilize datasets focused on open-ended dialogue, human alignment, and instruction following. We list some included tasks and datasets as follows:

[3] https://openai.com/

[4] https://www.anthropic.com/

- *English benchmarks:* MMLU (Hendrycks et al., 2021) and BBH (Srivastava et al., 2023);
- *Chinese benchmarks:* CMMLU (Li et al., 2023a) and C-Eval (Huang et al., 2023);
- *Multilingual benchmarks:* TyDi QA (Clark et al., 2020) and MGSM (Shi et al., 2023);
- *Language modeling:* LAMBADA (Paperno et al., 2016);
- *Open-ended dialogue:* MT-Bench (Zheng et al., 2023) and AlpacaEval (Li et al., 2023d);
- *Machine translation:* general translation task in WMT[5] of every year and Flores-200 (Costa-jussà et al., 2022); 8
- *Text summarization:* CNN/Daily Mail (See et al., 2017) and XSum (Narayan et al., 2018);
- *Code synthesis:* HumanEval (Chen et al., 2021) and MBPP (Austin et al., 2021);
- *Closed-book question answering:* Natural Questions (Kwiatkowski et al., 2019) and TriviaQA (Joshi et al., 2017);
- *Reading comprehension:* SQuAD 2.0 (Rajpurkar et al., 2018) and RACE (Lai et al., 2017);
- *Knowledge reasoning:* HellaSwag (Zellers et al., 2019) and ARC (Clark et al., 2018);
- *Symbolic reasoning:* Tables of Penguins (Herzig et al., 2020) and Colored Objects (Srivastava et al., 2023);
- *Mathematical reasoning:* GSM8K (Cobbe et al., 2021) and MATH (Hendrycks et al., 2021);
- *Human Alignment:* TruthfulQA (Lin et al., 2022) and CrowS Pairs (Nangia et al., 2020);
- *Hallucination detection:* HaluEval (Li et al., 2023b);
- *Instruction following:* IFEval (Zhou et al., 2023b);
- *Environment Interaction:* ALFWorld (Shridhar et al., 2021) and WebShop (Yao et al., 2022);
- *Tool Manipulation:* Gorilla (Patil et al., 2023).

## 4 Library Usage

In this section, we present the application of our library across four distinct research scenarios, illustrated through example code snippets.

**Continually Pre-Training Language-Specific Models.** As introduced in Section 2, we facilitate the continual pre-training of existing English-based LLMs for quick acquisition of new languages. Figure 2 (a) illustrates the process of tuning a Chinese LLM from LLaMA-2. Users are required only to prepare Chinese plain texts, such as those from Wikipedia, into a file named `chinese.txt`. Subsequently, LLMBox integrates new Chinese tokens into the vocabulary and trains the model.

[5]`https://www2.statmt.org/`

- *(a) Continually pre-training Chinese LLM:*

```
python merge_tokenizer.py --input chinese.txt
torchrun --nproc_per_node=8 train.py \
    --model Llama-2-7b --dataset chinese.txt
```

- *(b) Training medical LLM:*

```
torchrun --nproc_per_node=8 train.py \
    --model Llama-2-7b \
    --dataset_ratio 0.3 0.5 0.2 \
    --dataset pubmed.txt medmcqa.json sharegpt.json
```

- *(c) Evaluating davinci-002 on HellaSwag:*

```
python inference.py -m davinci-002 -d hellaswag
```

- *(d) Evaluating Gemma on MMLU:*

```
python inference.py -m gemma-7b -d mmlu -shots 5
```

- *(e) Evaluating Phi-2 on GSM8k using self-consistency and 4-bit quantization:*

```
python inference.py -m microsoft/phi-2 -d gsm8k \
    -shots 8 --sample_num 100 --load_in_4bit
```

- *(f) Designing prompting methods for a new dataset:*

```
def NewDataset(GenerationDataset):
    def load_dataset(self):
        self.exam_data = load(self.dataset, "exam")
        self.eval_data = load(self.dataset, "eval")
    def format_instance(self, instance):
        src, tgt = func(instance, self.exam_data)
        return dict(source=src, target=tgt)
    def reference(self):
        return [i["answer"] for i in self.eval_data]
```

Figure 2: Usage examples of our LLMBox library on six representative tasks.

**Adapting LLMs to Specialized Domains.** LLMBox facilitates the adaptation of LLMs to various specialized domains via instruction tuning, covering domains such as medicine, law, and finance. We present a script in Figure 2 (b) to train a medical LLM. We implement a convenient dataset mixture approach to sample instances from raw medical texts, medical instruction data, and general conversation data. This enables users to adjust the proportion to make a balance between medical knowledge, medical tasks, and conversational skills, thereby crafting an effective medical assistant.

**Comprehensively Evaluating LLMs.** We cover a broad range of tasks and various models within LLMBox to implement comprehensive evaluation. As illustrated in Figure 2 (c), (d), and (e), we present three exemplary command lines. Users are only required to designate the model and dataset names via the `-m` and `-d` options to achieve an efficient and accurate assessment of model performance. Furthermore, LLMBox supports multiple utilization methods, such as in-context learning (`-shots`), self-consistency (`--sample_num`), and quantitation (`--load_in_4bit`).

| LLaMA-2 | | MMLU | BBH | HumanEval | NQs | HellaSwag | ARC-C | WinoGrande | BoolQ | GSM8K |
|---|---|---|---|---|---|---|---|---|---|---|
| 7B | Paper | 45.3 | 32.6 | 12.8 | 25.7 | 77.2 | 45.9 | 69.2 | 77.4 | 14.6 |
| | LLMBox | 46.5 | 33.2 | 13.6 | 25.5 | 75.6 | 49.6 | 69.6 | 78.5 | 14.6 |
| 70B | Paper | 68.9 | 51.2 | 29.9 | 39.5 | 85.3 | 57.4 | 80.2 | 85.0 | 56.8 |
| | LLMBox | 69.5 | 54.8 | 29.2 | 40.3 | 83.3 | 57.8 | 80.7 | 85.6 | 56.6 |

Table 2: The results of different tasks on LLaMA-2 (7B) and (70B).

| Proportion FLAN / Alpaca | MMLU | Alpaca-Eval |
|---|---|---|
| 100 / 0 | 50.6 | 15.0 |
| 50 / 50 | 50.5 | 44.4 |
| 0 / 100 | 47.5 | 47.2 |
| LLaMA-2 (7B) | 46.5 | 23.0 |

Table 3: The performance of base LLaMA-2 (7B) and instruction tuned results using different data mixture.

| Models | HellaSwag | MMLU | GSM8K |
|---|---|---|---|
| **GPT-NeoX** (20B) | 71.4 | 26.4 | 7.1 |
| **OPT** (66B) | 73.5 | 27.3 | 2.2 |
| **BLOOM** (7.1B) | 61.1 | 26.0 | 4.2 |
| **LLaMA-2** (70B) | 83.4 | 69.5 | 56.7 |
| **Pythia** (12B) | 67.2 | 25.1 | 4.6 |
| **MPT** (30B) | 79.8 | 45.4 | 21.5 |
| **Phi-2** (2.7B) | 73.1 | 57.7 | 55.5 |
| **Mistral** (7B) | 80.2 | 63.8 | 43.6 |
| **Falcon** (40B) | 82.5 | 56.4 | 27.1 |
| **Gemma** (7B) | 79.2 | 65.3 | 52.3 |

Table 4: The results of different English LLMs using our developed LLMBox.

**Designing Novel Prompting Methods.** Since the implementation of each dataset in LLMBox is unified, it offers the flexibility to add new datasets or design various prompting methods without affecting other modules. Figure 2 (f) overviews the design of our `Dataset` class. When adding a new dataset, users are only required to implement three functions: `load_dataset` to load evaluation and example datasets; `format_instance` to format each instance with instruction or few-shot examples; and `reference` to define the ground truth. In the core function `format_instance`, users can develop innovative prompting methods tailored for each evaluation instance using example datasets.

## 5 Experiment

In the section, we conduct extensive experiments to verify the effectiveness and efficiency.

### 5.1 Effectiveness Evaluation

The essential attribute of an open-source library is its ability to reproduce results effectively. To confirm this, we choose several representative training and utilization scenarios for testing the outcomes derived from LLMBox.

**Training results.** We train LLaMA-2 (Touvron et al., 2023b) with the mixture of instruction tuning data FLAN (Chung et al., 2022) and Alpaca-52K (Taori et al., 2023) and evaluate its performance. We adjust the proportions of these datasets and assess the impact on performance using the MMLU benchmark (Hendrycks et al., 2021) and the chat-oriented AlpacaEval (Dubois et al., 2023). The experiments are conducted with a batch size of 128 and a constant learning rate of $1 \times 10^{-5}$. The model undergoes training for a total of 1200 steps, and we report the peak performance observed on the evaluation datasets. The results in Table 3 indicate that FLAN improves the model's performance on NLP tasks, whereas Alpaca-52K significantly enhances its performance in daily chat. Moreover, when mixing both instruction datasets yields a balanced improvement across both tasks, aligning with findings from prior research (Wang et al., 2023b).

**Utilization results.** Firstly, we examine the performance of LLaMA-2 (Touvron et al., 2023b) across various supported tasks. We totally evaluate nine tasks, including MMLU (5-shot, accuracy) (Hendrycks et al., 2021), BBH (3-shot, accuracy) (Srivastava et al., 2023), HumanEval (0-shot, pass1) (Chen et al., 2021), Natural Questions (NQs, 5-shot, EM) (Kwiatkowski et al., 2019), HellaSwag (0-shot, accuracy) (Zellers et al., 2019), ARC-Chanllge (ARC-C, 0-shot, accuracy) (Clark et al., 2018), WinoGrande (0-shot, accuracy) (Sakaguchi et al., 2021), BoolQ (0-shot, accuracy) (Clark et al., 2019), and GSM8K (8-shot, accuracy) (Cobbe et al., 2021). The results in Table 2 demonstrates that our LLMBox library faithfully reproduces the results reported in their original papers. Furthermore, we verify the performance of LLMBox across a variety of models. We utilize HellaSwag, MMLU, and GSM8K to evaluate the per-

| Models | HellaSwag | C-Eval | GSM8K |
|---|---|---|---|
| **ChatGLM-3** (6B) | 63.6 | 53.0 | 48.5 |
| **C-LLaMA-2** (13B) | 76.4 | 41.8 | 18.6 |
| **InternLM-2** (20B) | 82.5 | 69.5 | 74.4 |
| **Baichuan-2** (13B) | 74.7 | 59.2 | 42.8 |
| **Qwen-1.5** (72B) | 83.8 | 83.5 | 78.2 |
| **Aquila-2** (34B) | 78.8 | 98.6 | 2.0 |
| **Deepseek** (67B) | 83.4 | 65.9 | 64.1 |
| **Yi** (34B) | 83.2 | 81.4 | 5.4 |

Table 5: The experimental results of different Chinese LLMs and APIs using our developed LLMBox. C-LLaMA-2 is short for Chinese-LLaMA-2.

formance of ten English LLMs, including GPT-NeoX (Black et al., 2022), OPT (Zhang et al., 2022), BLOOM (Le Scao et al., 2022), LLaMA-2 (Touvron et al., 2023b), Pythia (Biderman et al., 2023), MPT (Team, 2023b), Phi-2 (Javaheripi et al., 2023), Mistral (Jiang et al., 2023), Falcon (Almazrouei et al., 2023), Gemma (Google, 2024). We employ HellaSwag, C-Eval (Huang et al., 2023), and GSM8K to evaluate the performance of eight Chinese LLMs, including ChatGLM3 (Zeng et al., 2022), Chinese-LLaMA-2 (Cui et al., 2023), InternLM-2 (Team, 2023a), Baichuan-2 (Baichuan, 2023), Qwen-1.5 (Bai et al., 2023), Aquila-2 (BAAI, 2023), Deepseek (DeepSeek-AI, 2024), Yi (Young et al., 2024). The results of these evaluations are detailed in Tables 4 and 5. We can find that our LLMBox is also compatible with various English and Chinese LLMs.

### 5.2 Efficiency Evaluation

The implementation efficiency is also a key factor to deploy LLMs. In addition to accurately reproducing results, we have optimized LLMBox for training and utilization efficiency. From the results in Table 6, it is evident that our prefix caching approach substantially decreases the inference time compared to the traditional Transformers implementation. As the number of examples increases (from 5-shot setting in MMLU to 8-shot setting in GSM8K), the efficiency gains from our method become increasingly pronounced. Remarkably, with the application of our prefix caching technique to the MMLU benchmark, LLMBox requires merely six minutes to process over ten thousand instances, achieving a 60% reduction in processing time compared to the vLLM toolkit. In the future, we aim to incorporate this prefix caching strategy into vLLM to further enhance the inference efficiency.

| Strategies | HellaSwag | MMLU | GSM8K |
|---|---|---|---|
| **Transformers** | 5.5 | 18.5 | 130.5 |
| **Transformers+PC** | 6.1 | 6.0 | 23.3 |
| **vLLM** | 6.6 | 14.9 | 3.6 |

Table 6: The execution time of different implementation methods on LLaMA-2 (7B) using one A800 (80G) GPU. PC is short for the proposed novel prefix caching mechanism in our developed LLMBox.

## 6 Conclusion

This paper presented **LLMBox**, a comprehensive library for conducting research on training, utilizing, and evaluating large language models. For training, we designed a unified data interface to support the implementation of various training strategies. For utilization and evaluation, we implemented typical approaches to use LLMs (including quantization, ICL, and CoT prompting), covered 18 tasks and 56 datasets, and included a number of popular open-sourced LLMs and closed-source APIs. We further conducted extensive experiments to verify the effectiveness and efficiency of LLMBox. Our library provides a unified framework to compare, reproduce, and develop LLMs and supporting methods for academic purposes, which would be of important value to promote the research on LLMs.

## Acknowledgement

This work was partially supported by National Natural Science Foundation of China under Grant No. 62222215, Beijing Natural Science Foundation under Grant No.4222027 and L233008. Xin Zhao is the corresponding author.

## References

Ebtesam Almazrouei, Hamza Alobeidli, Abdulaziz Alshamsi, Alessandro Cappelli, Ruxandra Cojocaru, Merouane Debbah, Etienne Goffinet, Daniel Heslow, Julien Launay, Quentin Malartic, Badreddine Noune, Baptiste Pannier, and Guilherme Penedo. 2023. Falcon-40B: an open large language model with state-of-the-art performance.

Jacob Austin, Augustus Odena, Maxwell Nye, Maarten Bosma, Henryk Michalewski, David Dohan, Ellen Jiang, Carrie Cai, Michael Terry, Quoc Le, et al. 2021. Program synthesis with large language models. *arXiv preprint arXiv:2108.07732*.

Zhangir Azerbayev, Hailey Schoelkopf, Keiran Paster, Marco Dos Santos, Stephen Marcus McAleer, Albert Q. Jiang, Jia Deng, Stella Biderman, and Sean Welleck. 2024. Llemma: An open language model for mathematics. In *The Twelfth International Conference on Learning Representations*.

BAAI. 2023. Aquila2.

Jinze Bai, Shuai Bai, Yunfei Chu, Zeyu Cui, Kai Dang, Xiaodong Deng, Yang Fan, Wenbin Ge, Yu Han, Fei Huang, et al. 2023. Qwen technical report. *arXiv preprint arXiv:2309.16609*.

Yuntao Bai, Andy Jones, Kamal Ndousse, Amanda Askell, Anna Chen, Nova DasSarma, Dawn Drain, Stanislav Fort, Deep Ganguli, Tom Henighan, et al. 2022. Training a helpful and harmless assistant with reinforcement learning from human feedback. *arXiv preprint arXiv:2204.05862*.

Baichuan. 2023. Baichuan 2: Open large-scale language models. *arXiv preprint arXiv:2309.10305*.

Stella Biderman, Hailey Schoelkopf, Quentin Gregory Anthony, Herbie Bradley, Kyle O'Brien, Eric Hallahan, Mohammad Aflah Khan, Shivanshu Purohit, Usvsn Sai Prashanth, Edward Raff, Aviya Skowron, Lintang Sutawika, and Oskar Van Der Wal. 2023. Pythia: A suite for analyzing large language models across training and scaling. In *Proceedings of the 40th International Conference on Machine Learning*, volume 202 of *Proceedings of Machine Learning Research*, pages 2397–2430. PMLR.

Sidney Black, Stella Biderman, Eric Hallahan, Quentin Anthony, Leo Gao, Laurence Golding, Horace He, Connor Leahy, Kyle McDonell, Jason Phang, Michael Pieler, Usvsn Sai Prashanth, Shivanshu Purohit, Laria Reynolds, Jonathan Tow, Ben Wang, and Samuel Weinbach. 2022. GPT-NeoX-20B: An open-source autoregressive language model. In *Proceedings of BigScience Episode #5 – Workshop on Challenges & Perspectives in Creating Large Language Models*, pages 95–136, virtual+Dublin. Association for Computational Linguistics.

Tom Brown, Benjamin Mann, Nick Ryder, Melanie Subbiah, Jared D Kaplan, Prafulla Dhariwal, Arvind Neelakantan, Pranav Shyam, Girish Sastry, Amanda Askell, Sandhini Agarwal, Ariel Herbert-Voss, Gretchen Krueger, Tom Henighan, Rewon Child, Aditya Ramesh, Daniel Ziegler, Jeffrey Wu, Clemens Winter, Chris Hesse, Mark Chen, Eric Sigler, Mateusz Litwin, Scott Gray, Benjamin Chess, Jack Clark, Christopher Berner, Sam McCandlish, Alec Radford, Ilya Sutskever, and Dario Amodei. 2020. Language models are few-shot learners. In *Advances in Neural Information Processing Systems*, volume 33, pages 1877–1901. Curran Associates, Inc.

Mark Chen, Jerry Tworek, Heewoo Jun, Qiming Yuan, Henrique Ponde de Oliveira Pinto, Jared Kaplan, Harri Edwards, Yuri Burda, Nicholas Joseph, Greg Brockman, et al. 2021. Evaluating large language models trained on code. *arXiv preprint arXiv:2107.03374*.

Tianqi Chen, Bing Xu, Chiyuan Zhang, and Carlos Guestrin. 2016. Training deep nets with sublinear memory cost. *arXiv preprint arXiv:1604.06174*.

Wei-Lin Chiang, Zhuohan Li, Zi Lin, Ying Sheng, Zhanghao Wu, Hao Zhang, Lianmin Zheng, Siyuan Zhuang, Yonghao Zhuang, Joseph E. Gonzalez, Ion Stoica, and Eric P. Xing. 2023. Vicuna: An open-source chatbot impressing gpt-4 with 90%* chatgpt quality.

Hyung Won Chung, Le Hou, Shayne Longpre, Barret Zoph, Yi Tay, William Fedus, Yunxuan Li, Xuezhi Wang, Mostafa Dehghani, Siddhartha Brahma, et al. 2022. Scaling instruction-finetuned language models. *arXiv preprint arXiv:2210.11416*.

Christopher Clark, Kenton Lee, Ming-Wei Chang, Tom Kwiatkowski, Michael Collins, and Kristina Toutanova. 2019. BoolQ: Exploring the surprising difficulty of natural yes/no questions. In *Proceedings of the 2019 Conference of the North American Chapter of the Association for Computational Linguistics: Human Language Technologies, Volume 1 (Long and Short Papers)*, pages 2924–2936, Minneapolis, Minnesota. Association for Computational Linguistics.

Jonathan H. Clark, Eunsol Choi, Michael Collins, Dan Garrette, Tom Kwiatkowski, Vitaly Nikolaev, and Jennimaria Palomaki. 2020. TyDi QA: A benchmark for information-seeking question answering in typologically diverse languages. *Transactions of the Association for Computational Linguistics*, 8:454–470.

Peter Clark, Isaac Cowhey, Oren Etzioni, Tushar Khot, Ashish Sabharwal, Carissa Schoenick, and Oyvind Tafjord. 2018. Think you have solved question answering? try arc, the ai2 reasoning challenge. *arXiv preprint arXiv:1803.05457*.

Karl Cobbe, Vineet Kosaraju, Mohammad Bavarian, Mark Chen, Heewoo Jun, Lukasz Kaiser, Matthias Plappert, Jerry Tworek, Jacob Hilton, Reiichiro Nakano, et al. 2021. Training verifiers to solve math word problems. *arXiv preprint arXiv:2110.14168*.

Marta R Costa-jussà, James Cross, Onur Çelebi, Maha Elbayad, Kenneth Heafield, Kevin Heffernan, Elahe Kalbassi, Janice Lam, Daniel Licht, Jean Maillard, et al. 2022. No language left behind: Scaling human-centered machine translation. *arXiv preprint arXiv:2207.04672*.

Yiming Cui, Ziqing Yang, and Xin Yao. 2023. Efficient and effective text encoding for chinese llama and alpaca. *arXiv preprint arXiv:2304.08177*.

Tri Dao, Dan Fu, Stefano Ermon, Atri Rudra, and Christopher Ré. 2022. Flashattention: Fast and memory-efficient exact attention with io-awareness. In *Advances in Neural Information Processing Systems*, volume 35, pages 16344–16359. Curran Associates, Inc.

DeepSeek-AI. 2024. Deepseek llm: Scaling open-source language models with longtermism. *arXiv preprint arXiv:2401.02954*.

Tim Dettmers, Mike Lewis, Sam Shleifer, and Luke Zettlemoyer. 2022. 8-bit optimizers via block-wise quantization. In *International Conference on Learning Representations*.

Tim Dettmers, Artidoro Pagnoni, Ari Holtzman, and Luke Zettlemoyer. 2023. Qlora: Efficient finetuning of quantized llms. In *Advances in Neural Information Processing Systems*, volume 36, pages 10088–10115. Curran Associates, Inc.

Yann Dubois, Chen Xuechen Li, Rohan Taori, Tianyi Zhang, Ishaan Gulrajani, Jimmy Ba, Carlos Guestrin, Percy S Liang, and Tatsunori B Hashimoto. 2023. Alpacafarm: A simulation framework for methods that learn from human feedback. In *Advances in Neural Information Processing Systems*, volume 36, pages 30039–30069. Curran Associates, Inc.

Dom Eccleston. 2023. Sharegpt. `https://sharegpt.com/`.

Kawin Ethayarajh, Yejin Choi, and Swabha Swayamdipta. 2022. Understanding dataset difficulty with $\mathcal{V}$-usable information. In *Proceedings of the 39th International Conference on Machine Learning*, volume 162 of *Proceedings of Machine Learning Research*, pages 5988–6008. PMLR.

Elias Frantar, Saleh Ashkboos, Torsten Hoefler, and Dan Alistarh. 2023. OPTQ: Accurate quantization for generative pre-trained transformers. In *The Eleventh International Conference on Learning Representations*.

Leo Gao, Jonathan Tow, Baber Abbasi, Stella Biderman, Sid Black, Anthony DiPofi, Charles Foster, Laurence Golding, Jeffrey Hsu, Alain Le Noac'h, Haonan Li, Kyle McDonell, Niklas Muennighoff, Chris Ociepa, Jason Phang, Laria Reynolds, Hailey Schoelkopf, Aviya Skowron, Lintang Sutawika, Eric Tang, Anish Thite, Ben Wang, Kevin Wang, and Andy Zou. 2023a. A framework for few-shot language model evaluation.

Luyu Gao, Aman Madaan, Shuyan Zhou, Uri Alon, Pengfei Liu, Yiming Yang, Jamie Callan, and Graham Neubig. 2023b. PAL: Program-aided language models. In *Proceedings of the 40th International Conference on Machine Learning*, volume 202 of *Proceedings of Machine Learning Research*, pages 10764–10799. PMLR.

Team Google. 2024. Gemma.

Dan Hendrycks, Collin Burns, Steven Basart, Andy Zou, Mantas Mazeika, Dawn Song, and Jacob Steinhardt. 2021. Measuring massive multitask language understanding. In *International Conference on Learning Representations*.

Jonathan Herzig, Pawel Krzysztof Nowak, Thomas Müller, Francesco Piccinno, and Julian Eisenschlos. 2020. TaPas: Weakly supervised table parsing via pre-training. In *Proceedings of the 58th Annual Meeting of the Association for Computational Linguistics*, pages 4320–4333, Online. Association for Computational Linguistics.

hiyouga. 2023. Llama factory. `https://github.com/hiyouga/LLaMA-Factory`.

Edward J Hu, yelong shen, Phillip Wallis, Zeyuan Allen-Zhu, Yuanzhi Li, Shean Wang, Lu Wang, and Weizhu Chen. 2022. LoRA: Low-rank adaptation of large language models. In *International Conference on Learning Representations*.

Yuzhen Huang, Yuzhuo Bai, Zhihao Zhu, Junlei Zhang, Jinghan Zhang, Tangjun Su, Junteng Liu, Chuancheng Lv, Yikai Zhang, jiayi lei, Yao Fu, Maosong Sun, and Junxian He. 2023. C-eval: A multi-level multi-discipline chinese evaluation suite for foundation models. In *Advances in Neural Information Processing Systems*, volume 36, pages 62991–63010. Curran Associates, Inc.

Mojan Javaheripi, Sébastien Bubeck, Marah Abdin, Jyoti Aneja, Sebastien Bubeck, Caio César Teodoro Mendes, Weizhu Chen, Allie Del Giorno, Ronen Eldan, Sivakanth Gopi, et al. 2023. Phi-2: The surprising power of small language models. *Microsoft Research Blog*.

Albert Q Jiang, Alexandre Sablayrolles, Arthur Mensch, Chris Bamford, Devendra Singh Chaplot, Diego de las Casas, Florian Bressand, Gianna Lengyel, Guillaume Lample, Lucile Saulnier, et al. 2023. Mistral 7b. *arXiv preprint arXiv:2310.06825*.

Mandar Joshi, Eunsol Choi, Daniel Weld, and Luke Zettlemoyer. 2017. TriviaQA: A large scale distantly supervised challenge dataset for reading comprehension. In *Proceedings of the 55th Annual Meeting of the Association for Computational Linguistics (Volume 1: Long Papers)*, pages 1601–1611, Vancouver, Canada. Association for Computational Linguistics.

Vijay Anand Korthikanti, Jared Casper, Sangkug Lym, Lawrence McAfee, Michael Andersch, Mohammad Shoeybi, and Bryan Catanzaro. 2023. Reducing activation recomputation in large transformer models. *Proceedings of Machine Learning and Systems*, 5.

Tom Kwiatkowski, Jennimaria Palomaki, Olivia Redfield, Michael Collins, Ankur Parikh, Chris Alberti, Danielle Epstein, Illia Polosukhin, Jacob Devlin, Kenton Lee, Kristina Toutanova, Llion Jones, Matthew Kelcey, Ming-Wei Chang, Andrew M. Dai, Jakob Uszkoreit, Quoc Le, and Slav Petrov. 2019. Natural questions: A benchmark for question answering research. *Transactions of the Association for Computational Linguistics*, 7:452–466.

Woosuk Kwon, Zhuohan Li, Siyuan Zhuang, Ying Sheng, Lianmin Zheng, Cody Hao Yu, Joseph Gonzalez, Hao Zhang, and Ion Stoica. 2023. Efficient memory management for large language model serving with pagedattention. In *Proceedings of the 29th Symposium on Operating Systems Principles*, SOSP '23, page 611–626, New York, NY, USA. Association for Computing Machinery.

Guokun Lai, Qizhe Xie, Hanxiao Liu, Yiming Yang, and Eduard Hovy. 2017. RACE: Large-scale ReAding comprehension dataset from examinations. In *Proceedings of the 2017 Conference on Empirical Methods in Natural Language Processing*, pages 785–794, Copenhagen, Denmark. Association for Computational Linguistics.

Teven Le Scao, Angela Fan, Christopher Akiki, Ellie Pavlick, Suzana Ilić, Daniel Hesslow, Roman Castagné, Alexandra Sasha Luccioni, François Yvon, Matthias Gallé, et al. 2022. Bloom: A 176b-parameter open-access multilingual language model.

Haonan Li, Yixuan Zhang, Fajri Koto, Yifei Yang, Hai Zhao, Yeyun Gong, Nan Duan, and Timothy Baldwin. 2023a. Cmmlu: Measuring massive multitask language understanding in chinese. *arXiv preprint arXiv:2306.09212*.

Junyi Li, Xiaoxue Cheng, Xin Zhao, Jian-Yun Nie, and Ji-Rong Wen. 2023b. HaluEval: A large-scale hallucination evaluation benchmark for large language models. In *Proceedings of the 2023 Conference on Empirical Methods in Natural Language Processing*, pages 6449–6464, Singapore. Association for Computational Linguistics.

Raymond Li, Loubna Ben allal, Yangtian Zi, Niklas Muennighoff, Denis Kocetkov, Chenghao Mou, Marc Marone, Christopher Akiki, Jia LI, Jenny Chim, Qian Liu, Evgenii Zheltonozhskii, Terry Yue Zhuo, Thomas Wang, Olivier Dehaene, Joel Lamy-Poirier, Joao Monteiro, Nicolas Gontier, Ming-Ho Yee, Logesh Kumar Umapathi, Jian Zhu, Ben Lipkin, Muhtasham Oblokulov, Zhiruo Wang, Rudra Murthy, Jason T Stillerman, Siva Sankalp Patel, Dmitry Abulkhanov, Marco Zocca, Manan Dey, Zhihan Zhang, Urvashi Bhattacharyya, Wenhao Yu, Sasha Luccioni, Paulo Villegas, Fedor Zhdanov, Tony Lee, Nadav Timor, Jennifer Ding, Claire S Schlesinger, Hailey Schoelkopf, Jan Ebert, Tri Dao, Mayank Mishra, Alex Gu, Carolyn Jane Anderson, Brendan Dolan-Gavitt, Danish Contractor, Siva Reddy, Daniel Fried, Dzmitry Bahdanau, Yacine Jernite, Carlos Muñoz Ferrandis, Sean Hughes, Thomas Wolf, Arjun Guha, Leandro Von Werra, and Harm de Vries. 2023c. Starcoder: may the source be with you! *Transactions on Machine Learning Research*. Reproducibility Certification.

Xuechen Li, Tianyi Zhang, Yann Dubois, Rohan Taori, Ishaan Gulrajani, Carlos Guestrin, Percy Liang, and Tatsunori B. Hashimoto. 2023d. Alpacaeval: An automatic evaluator of instruction-following models. `https://github.com/tatsu-lab/alpaca_eval`.

Stephanie Lin, Jacob Hilton, and Owain Evans. 2022. TruthfulQA: Measuring how models mimic human falsehoods. In *Proceedings of the 60th Annual Meeting of the Association for Computational Linguistics (Volume 1: Long Papers)*, pages 3214–3252, Dublin, Ireland. Association for Computational Linguistics.

Jiachang Liu, Dinghan Shen, Yizhe Zhang, Bill Dolan, Lawrence Carin, and Weizhu Chen. 2022. What makes good in-context examples for GPT-3? In *Proceedings of Deep Learning Inside Out (DeeLIO 2022): The 3rd Workshop on Knowledge Extraction and Integration for Deep Learning Architectures*, pages 100–114, Dublin, Ireland and Online. Association for Computational Linguistics.

Yao Lu, Max Bartolo, Alastair Moore, Sebastian Riedel, and Pontus Stenetorp. 2022. Fantastically ordered prompts and where to find them: Overcoming few-shot prompt order sensitivity. In *Proceedings of the 60th Annual Meeting of the Association for Computational Linguistics (Volume 1: Long Papers)*, pages 8086–8098, Dublin, Ireland. Association for Computational Linguistics.

Nikita Nangia, Clara Vania, Rasika Bhalerao, and Samuel R. Bowman. 2020. CrowS-pairs: A challenge dataset for measuring social biases in masked language models. In *Proceedings of the 2020 Conference on Empirical Methods in Natural Language Processing (EMNLP)*, pages 1953–1967, Online. Association for Computational Linguistics.

Shashi Narayan, Shay B. Cohen, and Mirella Lapata. 2018. Don't give me the details, just the summary! topic-aware convolutional neural networks for extreme summarization. In *Proceedings of the 2018 Conference on Empirical Methods in Natural Language Processing*, pages 1797–1807, Brussels, Belgium. Association for Computational Linguistics.

Erik Nijkamp, Bo Pang, Hiroaki Hayashi, Lifu Tu, Huan Wang, Yingbo Zhou, Silvio Savarese, and Caiming Xiong. 2023. Codegen: An open large language model for code with multi-turn program synthesis. In *The Eleventh International Conference on Learning Representations*.

Denis Paperno, Germán Kruszewski, Angeliki Lazaridou, Ngoc Quan Pham, Raffaella Bernardi, Sandro Pezzelle, Marco Baroni, Gemma Boleda, and Raquel Fernández. 2016. The LAMBADA dataset: Word prediction requiring a broad discourse context. In *Proceedings of the 54th Annual Meeting of the Association for Computational Linguistics (Volume 1: Long Papers)*, pages 1525–1534, Berlin, Germany. Association for Computational Linguistics.

Shishir G Patil, Tianjun Zhang, Xin Wang, and Joseph E Gonzalez. 2023. Gorilla: Large language model connected with massive apis. *arXiv preprint arXiv:2305.15334*.

Rafael Rafailov, Archit Sharma, Eric Mitchell, Christopher D Manning, Stefano Ermon, and Chelsea Finn. 2023. Direct preference optimization: Your language model is secretly a reward model. In *Advances in Neural Information Processing Systems*, volume 36, pages 53728–53741. Curran Associates, Inc.

Colin Raffel, Noam Shazeer, Adam Roberts, Katherine Lee, Sharan Narang, Michael Matena, Yanqi Zhou, Wei Li, and Peter J. Liu. 2020. Exploring the limits of transfer learning with a unified text-to-text transformer. *Journal of Machine Learning Research*, 21(140):1–67.

Samyam Rajbhandari, Jeff Rasley, Olatunji Ruwase, and Yuxiong He. 2020. Zero: Memory optimizations toward training trillion parameter models. In *SC20: International Conference for High Performance Computing, Networking, Storage and Analysis*, pages 1–16. IEEE.

Pranav Rajpurkar, Robin Jia, and Percy Liang. 2018. Know what you don't know: Unanswerable questions for SQuAD. In *Proceedings of the 56th Annual Meeting of the Association for Computational Linguistics (Volume 2: Short Papers)*, pages 784–789, Melbourne, Australia. Association for Computational Linguistics.

Jeff Rasley, Samyam Rajbhandari, Olatunji Ruwase, and Yuxiong He. 2020. Deepspeed: System optimizations enable training deep learning models with over 100 billion parameters. In *Proceedings of the 26th ACM SIGKDD International Conference on Knowledge Discovery & Data Mining*, KDD '20, page 3505–3506, New York, NY, USA. Association for Computing Machinery.

Jie Ren, Samyam Rajbhandari, Reza Yazdani Aminabadi, Olatunji Ruwase, Shuangyan Yang, Minjia Zhang, Dong Li, and Yuxiong He. 2021. {Zero-offload}: Democratizing {billion-scale} model training. In *2021 USENIX Annual Technical Conference (USENIX ATC 21)*, pages 551–564.

Keisuke Sakaguchi, Ronan Le Bras, Chandra Bhagavatula, and Yejin Choi. 2021. Winogrande: an adversarial winograd schema challenge at scale. *Commun. ACM*, 64(9):99–106.

John Schulman, Filip Wolski, Prafulla Dhariwal, Alec Radford, and Oleg Klimov. 2017. Proximal policy optimization algorithms. *arXiv preprint arXiv:1707.06347*.

Abigail See, Peter J. Liu, and Christopher D. Manning. 2017. Get to the point: Summarization with pointer-generator networks. In *Proceedings of the 55th Annual Meeting of the Association for Computational Linguistics (Volume 1: Long Papers)*, pages 1073–1083, Vancouver, Canada. Association for Computational Linguistics.

Zhihong Shao, Peiyi Wang, Qihao Zhu, Runxin Xu, Junxiao Song, Mingchuan Zhang, YK Li, Y Wu, and Daya Guo. 2024. Deepseekmath: Pushing the limits of mathematical reasoning in open language models. *arXiv preprint arXiv:2402.03300*.

Freda Shi, Mirac Suzgun, Markus Freitag, Xuezhi Wang, Suraj Srivats, Soroush Vosoughi, Hyung Won Chung, Yi Tay, Sebastian Ruder, Denny Zhou, Dipanjan Das, and Jason Wei. 2023. Language models are multilingual chain-of-thought reasoners. In *The Eleventh International Conference on Learning Representations*.

Mohit Shridhar, Xingdi Yuan, Marc-Alexandre Cote, Yonatan Bisk, Adam Trischler, and Matthew Hausknecht. 2021. {ALFW}orld: Aligning text and embodied environments for interactive learning. In *International Conference on Learning Representations*.

Aarohi Srivastava, Abhinav Rastogi, Abhishek Rao, Abu Awal Md Shoeb, Abubakar Abid, Adam Fisch, Adam R Brown, Adam Santoro, Aditya Gupta, Adrià Garriga-Alonso, et al. 2023. Beyond the imitation game: Quantifying and extrapolating the capabilities of language models. *Transactions on Machine Learning Research*.

Rohan Taori, Ishaan Gulrajani, Tianyi Zhang, Yann Dubois, Xuechen Li, Carlos Guestrin, Percy Liang, and Tatsunori B. Hashimoto. 2023. Stanford alpaca: An instruction-following llama model. `https://github.com/tatsu-lab/stanford_alpaca`.

InternLM Team. 2023a. Internlm: A multilingual language model with progressively enhanced capabilities. `https://github.com/InternLM/InternLM`.

MosaicML NLP Team. 2023b. Introducing mpt-7b: A new standard for open-source, commercially usable llms. Accessed: 2023-05-05.

Hugo Touvron, Thibaut Lavril, Gautier Izacard, Xavier Martinet, Marie-Anne Lachaux, Timothée Lacroix, Baptiste Rozière, Naman Goyal, Eric Hambro, Faisal Azhar, et al. 2023a. Llama: Open and efficient foundation language models. *arXiv preprint arXiv:2302.13971*.

Hugo Touvron, Louis Martin, Kevin Stone, Peter Albert, Amjad Almahairi, Yasmine Babaei, Nikolay Bashlykov, Soumya Batra, Prajjwal Bhargava, Shruti Bhosale, et al. 2023b. Llama 2: Open foundation and fine-tuned chat models. *arXiv preprint arXiv:2307.09288*.

Xuezhi Wang, Jason Wei, Dale Schuurmans, Quoc V Le, Ed H. Chi, Sharan Narang, Aakanksha Chowdhery, and Denny Zhou. 2023a. Self-consistency improves chain of thought reasoning in language models. In *The Eleventh International Conference on Learning Representations*.

Yizhong Wang, Hamish Ivison, Pradeep Dasigi, Jack Hessel, Tushar Khot, Khyathi Chandu, David Wadden, Kelsey MacMillan, Noah A. Smith, Iz Beltagy, and Hannaneh Hajishirzi. 2023b. How far can camels go? exploring the state of instruction tuning on open resources. In *Thirty-seventh Conference on Neural Information Processing Systems Datasets and Benchmarks Track*.

Thomas Wolf, Lysandre Debut, Victor Sanh, Julien Chaumond, Clement Delangue, Anthony Moi, Pierric Cistac, Tim Rault, Rémi Louf, Morgan Funtowicz, Joe Davison, Sam Shleifer, Patrick von Platen, Clara Ma, Yacine Jernite, Julien Plu, Canwen Xu, Teven Le Scao, Sylvain Gugger, Mariama Drame, Quentin

Lhoest, and Alexander M. Rush. 2020. Transformers: State-of-the-art natural language processing. In *Proceedings of the 2020 Conference on Empirical Methods in Natural Language Processing: System Demonstrations*, pages 38–45, Online. Association for Computational Linguistics.

Sang Michael Xie, Hieu Pham, Xuanyi Dong, Nan Du, Hanxiao Liu, Yifeng Lu, Percy S Liang, Quoc V Le, Tengyu Ma, and Adams Wei Yu. 2023. Doremi: Optimizing data mixtures speeds up language model pretraining. In *Advances in Neural Information Processing Systems*, volume 36, pages 69798–69818. Curran Associates, Inc.

Can Xu, Qingfeng Sun, Kai Zheng, Xiubo Geng, Pu Zhao, Jiazhan Feng, Chongyang Tao, Qingwei Lin, and Daxin Jiang. 2023. Wizardlm: Empowering large pre-trained language models to follow complex instructions. In *The Twelfth International Conference on Learning Representations*.

Aiyuan Yang, Bin Xiao, Bingning Wang, Borong Zhang, Ce Bian, Chao Yin, Chenxu Lv, Da Pan, Dian Wang, Dong Yan, et al. 2023. Baichuan 2: Open large-scale language models. *arXiv preprint arXiv:2309.10305*.

Shunyu Yao, Howard Chen, John Yang, and Karthik Narasimhan. 2022. Webshop: Towards scalable real-world web interaction with grounded language agents. In *Advances in Neural Information Processing Systems*, volume 35, pages 20744–20757. Curran Associates, Inc.

Alex Young, Bei Chen, Chao Li, Chengen Huang, Ge Zhang, Guanwei Zhang, Heng Li, Jiangcheng Zhu, Jianqun Chen, Jing Chang, et al. 2024. Yi: Open foundation models by 01. ai. *arXiv preprint arXiv:2403.04652*.

YuLan-Team. 2023. Yulan-chat: An open-source bilingual chatbot. `https://github.com/RUC-GSAI/YuLan-Chat`.

Rowan Zellers, Ari Holtzman, Yonatan Bisk, Ali Farhadi, and Yejin Choi. 2019. HellaSwag: Can a machine really finish your sentence? In *Proceedings of the 57th Annual Meeting of the Association for Computational Linguistics*, pages 4791–4800, Florence, Italy. Association for Computational Linguistics.

Aohan Zeng, Xiao Liu, Zhengxiao Du, Zihan Wang, Hanyu Lai, Ming Ding, Zhuoyi Yang, Yifan Xu, Wendi Zheng, Xiao Xia, et al. 2022. Glm-130b: An open bilingual pre-trained model. *arXiv preprint arXiv:2210.02414*.

Susan Zhang, Stephen Roller, Naman Goyal, Mikel Artetxe, Moya Chen, Shuohui Chen, Christopher Dewan, Mona Diab, Xian Li, Xi Victoria Lin, et al. 2022. Opt: Open pre-trained transformer language models. *arXiv preprint arXiv:2205.01068*.

Wayne Xin Zhao, Kun Zhou, Junyi Li, Tianyi Tang, Xiaolei Wang, Yupeng Hou, Yingqian Min, Beichen Zhang, Junjie Zhang, Zican Dong, et al. 2023. A survey of large language models. *arXiv preprint arXiv:2303.18223*.

Lianmin Zheng, Wei-Lin Chiang, Ying Sheng, Siyuan Zhuang, Zhanghao Wu, Yonghao Zhuang, Zi Lin, Zhuohan Li, Dacheng Li, Eric Xing, Hao Zhang, Joseph E Gonzalez, and Ion Stoica. 2023. Judging llm-as-a-judge with mt-bench and chatbot arena. In *Advances in Neural Information Processing Systems*, volume 36, pages 46595–46623. Curran Associates, Inc.

Denny Zhou, Nathanael Schärli, Le Hou, Jason Wei, Nathan Scales, Xuezhi Wang, Dale Schuurmans, Claire Cui, Olivier Bousquet, Quoc V Le, and Ed H. Chi. 2023a. Least-to-most prompting enables complex reasoning in large language models. In *The Eleventh International Conference on Learning Representations*.

Jeffrey Zhou, Tianjian Lu, Swaroop Mishra, Siddhartha Brahma, Sujoy Basu, Yi Luan, Denny Zhou, and Le Hou. 2023b. Instruction-following evaluation for large language models. *arXiv preprint arXiv:2311.07911*.

Yongchao Zhou, Andrei Ioan Muresanu, Ziwen Han, Keiran Paster, Silviu Pitis, Harris Chan, and Jimmy Ba. 2023c. Large language models are human-level prompt engineers. In *The Eleventh International Conference on Learning Representations*.

# LlamaFactory: Unified Efficient Fine-Tuning of 100+ Language Models

**Yaowei Zheng, Richong Zhang***, **Junhao Zhang, Yanhan Ye, Zheyan Luo**
School of Computer Science and Engineering, Beihang University
Open-source repository: **https://github.com/hiyouga/LLaMA-Factory**
Demonstration video: **https://youtu.be/W29FgeZEpus**

## Abstract

Efficient fine-tuning is vital for adapting large language models (LLMs) to downstream tasks. However, it requires non-trivial efforts to implement these methods on different models. We present LlamaFactory, a unified framework that integrates a suite of cutting-edge efficient training methods. It provides a solution for flexibly customizing the fine-tuning of 100+ LLMs without the need for coding through the built-in web UI LlamaBoard. We empirically validate the efficiency and effectiveness of our framework on language modeling and text generation tasks. It has been released at https://github.com/hiyouga/LLaMA-Factory and received over 25,000 stars and 3,000 forks.

## 1 Introduction

Large language models (LLMs) (Zhao et al., 2023) present remarkable reasoning capabilities and empower a wide range of applications, such as question answering (Jiang et al., 2023b), machine translation (Wang et al., 2023b; Jiao et al., 2023a), and information extraction (Jiao et al., 2023b). Subsequently, a substantial number of LLMs are developed and accessible through open-source communities. For example, Hugging Face's open LLM leaderboard (Beeching et al., 2023) boasts over 5,000 models, offering convenience for individuals seeking to leverage the power of LLMs.

Fine-tuning extremely large number of parameters with limited resources becomes the main challenge of adapting LLM to downstream tasks. A popular solution is efficient fine-tuning (Houlsby et al., 2019; Hu et al., 2022; Dettmers et al., 2023), which reduces the training cost of LLMs when adapting to various tasks. However, the community contributes various methods for efficient fine-tuning, lacking a systematic framework that adapts and unifies these methods to different LLMs and provides a friendly interface for user customization.

To address the above problems, we develop LlamaFactory, a framework that democratizes the fine-tuning of LLMs. It unifies a variety of efficient fine-tuning methods through scalable modules, enabling the fine-tuning of hundreds of LLMs with minimal resources and high throughput. In addition, it streamlines commonly used training approaches, including generative pre-training (Radford et al., 2018), supervised fine-tuning (SFT) (Wei et al., 2022), reinforcement learning from human feedback (RLHF) (Ouyang et al., 2022), and direct preference optimization (DPO) (Rafailov et al., 2023). Users can leverage command-line or web interfaces to customize and fine-tune their LLMs with minimal or no coding effort.

LlamaFactory consists of three main modules: ***Model Loader***, ***Data Worker*** and ***Trainer***. We minimize the dependencies of these modules on specific models and datasets, allowing the framework to flexibly scale to hundreds of models and datasets. Concretely, we first establish a model registry where the *Model Loader* can precisely attach adapters to the pre-trained models by identifying exact layers. Then we develop a data description specification that allows the *Data Worker* to gather datasets by aligning corresponding columns. Furthermore, we provide plug-and-play implementations of state-of-the-art efficient fine-tuning methods that enable the *Trainer* to activate by replacing default ones. Our design allows these modules to be reused across different training approaches, significantly reducing the integration costs.

LlamaFactory is implemented with PyTorch (Paszke et al., 2019) and significantly benefits from open-source libraries, such as Transformers (Wolf et al., 2020), PEFT (Mangrulkar et al., 2022), and TRL (von Werra et al., 2020). On the basis, we provide an out-of-the-box framework with a higher level of abstraction. Additionally, we build LlamaBoard with Gradio (Abid et al., 2019), enabling fine-tuning LLMs with no coding efforts required.

*Corresponding author



*Proceedings of the 62nd Annual Meeting of the Association for Computational Linguistics (Volume 3: System Demonstrations)*, pages 400–410
August 11-16, 2024 

| | LLAMAFACTORY | FastChat | LitGPT | LMFlow | Open-Instruct |
|---|---|---|---|---|---|
| LoRA | ✓ | ✓ | ✓ | ✓ | ✓ |
| QLoRA | ✓ | ✓ | ✓ | ✓ | ✓ |
| DoRA | ✓ | | | | |
| LoRA+ | ✓ | | | | |
| PiSSA | ✓ | | | | |
| GaLore | ✓ | ✓ | | ✓ | ✓ |
| BAdam | ✓ | | | | |
| Flash attention | ✓ | ✓ | ✓ | ✓ | ✓ |
| $S^2$ attention | ✓ | | | | |
| Unsloth | ✓ | | ✓ | | |
| DeepSpeed | ✓ | ✓ | ✓ | ✓ | ✓ |
| SFT | ✓ | ✓ | ✓ | ✓ | ✓ |
| RLHF | ✓ | | | ✓ | |
| DPO | ✓ | | | | ✓ |
| KTO | ✓ | | | | |
| ORPO | ✓ | | | | |

Table 1: Comparison of features in LLAMAFACTORY with popular frameworks of fine-tuning LLMs.

LLAMAFACTORY is open-sourced under the Apache-2.0 license. It has already garnered over 25,000 stars and 3,000 forks on the GitHub, and hundreds of open-source models have been built upon LLAMAFACTORY on the Hugging Face Hub[1]. For example, Truong et al. (2024) build GemSUra-7B based on LLAMAFACTORY, revealing the cross-lingual abilities of Gemma (Mesnard et al., 2024). Furthermore, dozens of studies have utilized our framework to explore LLMs (Wang et al., 2023a; Yu et al., 2023; Bhardwaj et al., 2024).

## 2 Related Work

With the rapid increase in demand for fine-tuning LLMs, numerous frameworks for adapting LLMs to specific purposes have been developed. LLaMA-Adapter (Zhang et al., 2024) efficiently fine-tunes the Llama model (Touvron et al., 2023a) using a zero-initialized attention. FastChat (Zheng et al., 2023) is a framework focused on training and evaluating LLMs for chat completion purposes. LitGPT (AI, 2023) provides the implementation of generative models and supports various training methods. Open-Instruct (Wang et al., 2023c) provides recipes for training instruct models. Colossal AI (Li et al., 2023b) takes advanced parallelism strategies for distributed training. LMFlow (Diao et al., 2024) supports training LLMs for specialized domains or tasks. GPT4All (Anand et al., 2023) allows LLMs to run on consumer devices, while also providing fine-tuning capabilities. Compared with existing competitive frameworks, LLAMAFACTORY supports a broader range of efficient fine-tuning techniques and training approaches. We list the features among representative frameworks in Table 1.

[1]https://huggingface.co/models?other=llama-factory

| | Freeze-tuning | GaLore | LoRA | DoRA | LoRA+ | PiSSA |
|---|---|---|---|---|---|---|
| Mixed precision | ✓ | ✓ | ✓ | ✓ | ✓ | ✓ |
| Checkpointing | ✓ | ✓ | ✓ | ✓ | ✓ | ✓ |
| Flash attention | ✓ | ✓ | ✓ | ✓ | ✓ | ✓ |
| $S^2$ attention | ✓ | ✓ | ✓ | ✓ | ✓ | ✓ |
| Quantization | ✗ | ✗ | ✓ | ✓ | ✓ | ✓ |
| Unsloth | ✗ | ✗ | ✓ | ✓ | ✓ | ✓ |

Table 2: Compatibility between the fine-tuning techniques featured in LLAMAFACTORY.

## 3 Efficient Fine-Tuning Techniques

Efficient LLM fine-tuning techniques can be divided into two main categories: those focused on optimization and those aimed at computation. The primary objective of efficient optimization techniques is to fine-tune the parameters of LLMs while keeping costs to a minimum. On the other hand, efficient computation methods seek to decrease the time or space for the required computation in LLMs. The methods included in LLAMAFACTORY are listed in Table 2. We will present these efficient fine-tuning techniques and show the substantial efficiency improvement achieved by incorporating them into our framework in the following sections.

### 3.1 Efficient Optimization

Firstly, we provide an overview of the efficient optimization techniques utilized in LLAMAFACTORY. The freeze-tuning method (Houlsby et al., 2019) involves freezing a majority of parameters while fine-tuning the remaining parameters in a small subset of decoder layers. Another method called gradient low-rank projection (GaLore) (Zhao et al., 2024) projects gradients into a lower-dimensional space, facilitating full-parameter learning in a memory-efficient manner. Similarly, BAdam (Luo et al., 2024) leverages block coordinate descent (BCD) to efficiently optimize the extensive parameters. On the contrary, the low-rank adaptation (LoRA) (Hu et al., 2022) method freezes all pre-trained weights and introduces a pair of trainable low-rank matrices to the designated layer. When combined with quantization, this approach is referred to as QLoRA (Dettmers et al., 2023), which additionally reduces the memory usage. DoRA (Liu et al., 2024) breaks down pre-trained weights into magnitude and direction components and updates directional components for enhanced performance. LoRA+ (Hayou et al., 2024) is proposed to overcome the sub-optimality of LoRA. PiSSA (Meng et al., 2024) initializes adapters with the principal components of the pre-trained weights for faster convergence.

### 3.2 Efficient Computation

In LLAMAFACTORY, we integrate a range of techniques for efficient computation. Commonly utilized techniques encompass mixed precision training (Micikevicius et al., 2018) and activation checkpointing (Chen et al., 2016). Drawing insights from the examination of the input-output (IO) expenses of the attention layer, flash attention (Dao et al., 2022) introduces a hardware-friendly approach to enhance attention computation. $S^2$ attention (Chen et al., 2024a) tackles the challenge of extended context with shifted sparse attention, thereby diminishing memory usage in fine-tuning long-context LLMs. Various quantization strategies (Dettmers et al., 2022a; Frantar et al., 2023; Lin et al., 2023; Egiazarian et al., 2024) decrease memory requirements in large language models (LLMs) by utilizing lower-precision representations for weights. Nevertheless, the fine-tuning of quantized models is restricted to the adapter-based techniques like LoRA (Hu et al., 2022). Unsloth (Han and Han, 2023) incorporates Triton (Tillet et al., 2019) for implementing the backward propagation of LoRA, which reduces floating-point operations (FLOPs) during gradient descent and leads to expedited LoRA training.

LLAMAFACTORY seamlessly combines these techniques into a cohesive structure to enhance the efficiency of LLM fine-tuning. This results in a reduction of the memory footprint from 18 bytes per parameter during mixed precision training (Micikevicius et al., 2018) or 8 bytes per parameter in half precision training (Le Scao et al., 2022) to only 0.6 bytes per parameter. Further elaboration on the components in LLAMAFACTORY will be provided in the subsequent section.

## 4 LLAMAFACTORY Framework

LLAMAFACTORY consists of three main modules: *Model Loader*, *Data Worker*, and *Trainer*. The *Model Loader* manipulates various model architectures for fine-tuning, supporting both large language models (LLMs) and vision language models (VLMs). The *Data Worker* processes data from different tasks through a well-designed pipeline, supporting both single-turn and multi-turn dialogues. The *Trainer* applies efficient fine-tuning techniques to different training approaches, supporting pre-training, instruction tuning and preference optimization. Beyond that, LLAMABOARD provides a friendly visual interface to access these modules, enabling users to configure and launch individual LLM fine-tuning instance codelessly and monitor the training status synchronously. We illustrate the relationships between these modules and the overall architecture of LLAMAFACTORY in Figure 1.

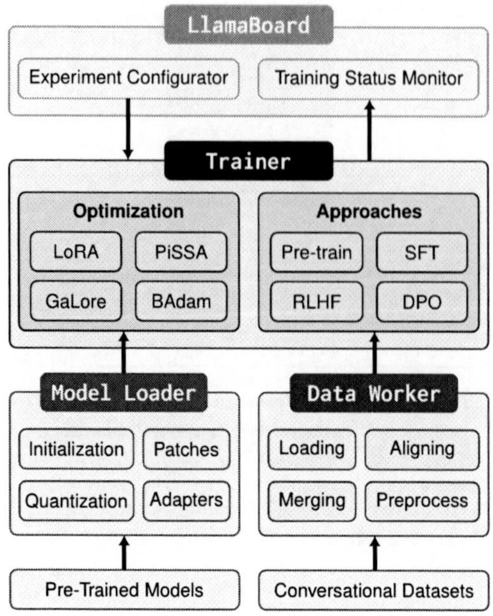


Figure 1: The architecture of LLAMAFACTORY.

### 4.1 Model Loader

This section initially presents the four components in *Model Loader*: model initialization, model patching, model quantization, and adapter attaching, followed by a description of our approach of adapting to a wide range of devices by handling the parameter floating-point precision during fine-tuning.

**Model Initialization** We utilize the *Auto Classes* of Transformers (Wolf et al., 2020) to load pre-trained models and initialize parameters. Specifically, we load the vision language models using the `AutoModelForVision2Seq` class while the rest are loaded using the `AutoModelForCausalLM` class. The tokenizer is loaded using the `AutoTokenizer` class along with the model. In cases where the vocabulary size of the tokenizer exceeds the capacity of the embedding layer, we resize the layer and initialize new parameters with noisy mean initialization. To determine the scaling factor for RoPE scaling (Chen et al., 2023), we compute it as the ratio of the maximum input sequence length to the context length of the model.

**Model Patching** To enable the $S^2$ attention, we employ a monkey patch to replace the forward computation of models. However, we use the native class to enable flash attention as it has been widely supported since Transformers 4.34.0. To prevent excessive partitioning of the dynamic layers, we set the mixture-of-experts (MoE) blocks as leaf modules when we optimize the MoE models under DeepSpeed ZeRO stage-3 (Rasley et al., 2020).

**Model Quantization** Dynamically quantizing models to 8 bits or 4 bits with LLM.int8 (Dettmers et al., 2022a) can be performed through the bitsandbytes library (Dettmers, 2021). For 4-bit quantization, we utilize the double quantization and 4-bit normal float as QLoRA (Dettmers et al., 2023). We also support fine-tuning the models quantized by the post-training quantization (PTQ) methods, including GPTQ (Frantar et al., 2023), AWQ (Lin et al., 2023), and AQLM (Egiazarian et al., 2024). Note that we cannot directly fine-tune the quantized weights; thus, the quantized models are only compatible with adapter-based methods.

**Adapter Attaching** We automatically identify the appropriate layers to attach adapters through traversing the model layers. The low-rank adapters are attached to all the linear layers for a better convergence as suggested by (Dettmers et al., 2023). The PEFT (Mangrulkar et al., 2022) library provides an extremely convenient way to implement the adapter-based methods such as LoRA (Hu et al., 2022), rsLoRA (Kalajdzievski, 2023), DoRA (Liu et al., 2024) and PiSSA (Meng et al., 2024). We replace the backward computation with the one of Unsloth (Han and Han, 2023) to accelerate the training. To perform reinforcement learning from human feedback (RLHF), a value head layer is appended on the top of the transformer model, mapping the representation of each token to a scalar.

**Precision Adaptation** We handle the floating-point precision of pre-trained models based on the capabilities of computing devices. For NVIDIA GPUs, we adopt bfloat16 precision if the computation capability is 8.0 or higher. Otherwise, float16 is adopted. Besides, we adopt float16 for Ascend NPUs and AMD GPUs and float32 for non-CUDA devices. In mixed precision training, we set all trainable parameters to float32 for training stability. Nevertheless, we retain the trainable parameters as bfloat16 in half precision training.

| | |
|---|---|
| Plain text | [{"text": "..."}, {"text": "..."}] |
| Alpaca-like data | [{"instruction": "...", "input": "...", "output": "..."}] |
| ShareGPT-like data | [{"conversations": [{"from": "human", "value": "..."}, {"from": "gpt", "value": "..."}]}] |
| Preference data | [{"instruction": "...", "input": "...", "output": ["...", "..."]}] |
| Standardized data | {"prompt": [{"role": "...", "content": "..."}], "response": [{"role": "...", "content": "..."}], "system": "...", "tools": "...", "images": ["..."]} |

Table 3: Dataset structures in LLAMAFACTORY.

### 4.2 Data Worker

We develop a data processing pipeline, including dataset loading, dataset aligning, dataset merging and dataset pre-processing. It standardizes datasets of different tasks into a unified format, enabling us to fine-tune models on datasets in various formats.

**Dataset Loading** We utilize the Datasets (Lhoest et al., 2021) library to load the data, which allows the users to load remote datasets from the Hugging Face Hub or read local datasets via scripts or through files. The Datasets library significantly reduces memory overhead during data processing and accelerates sample querying using Arrow (Apache, 2016). By default, the whole dataset is downloaded to local disk. However, if a dataset is too large to be stored, our framework provides dataset streaming to iterate over it without downloading.

**Dataset Aligning** To unify the dataset format, we design a data description specification to characterize the structure of datasets. For example, the alpaca dataset has three columns: instruction, input and output (Taori et al., 2023). We convert the dataset into a standard structure that is compatible with various tasks according to the data description specification. Some examples of dataset structures are shown in Table 3.

**Dataset Merging** The unified dataset structure provides an efficient approach for merging multiple datasets. For the datasets in non-streaming mode, we simply concatenate them before the datasets are shuffled during training. However, in streaming mode, simply concatenating the datasets impedes data shuffling. Therefore, we offer methods to alternately read the data from different datasets.

**Dataset Pre-processing** LLAMAFACTORY is designed for fine-tuning the text generative models, which is primarily used in chat completion. Chat template is a crucial component in these models, because it is highly related to the instruction-following abilities of these models. Therefore, we provide dozens of chat templates that can be automatically chosen according to the model type. We encode the sentence after applying the chat template using the tokenizer. By default, we only compute loss on the completions, while the prompts are disregarded (Taori et al., 2023). Optionally, we can utilize sequence packing (Krell et al., 2021) to reduce the training time, which is automatically enabled when performing generative pre-training.

### 4.3 Trainer

**Efficient Training** We integrate state-of-the-art efficient fine-tuning methods, including LoRA+ (Hayou et al., 2024), GaLore (Zhao et al., 2024) and BAdam (Luo et al., 2024) to the *Trainer* by replacing the default components. These fine-tuning methods are independent of the *Trainer*, making them easily applicable to various tasks. We utilize the trainers of Transformers (Wolf et al., 2020) for pre-training and SFT, while adopting the trainers of TRL (von Werra et al., 2020) for RLHF and DPO. We also include trainers of the advanced preference optimization methods such as KTO (Ethayarajh et al., 2024) and ORPO (Hong et al., 2024) from the TRL library. The tailored data collators are leveraged to differentiate trainers of various training approaches. To match the input format of the trainers for preference data, we build $2n$ samples in a batch where the first $n$ samples are chosen examples and the last $n$ samples are rejected examples.

**Model-Sharing RLHF** Allowing RLHF training on consumer devices is crucial for democratizing LLM fine-tuning. However, it is difficult because RLHF training requires four different models. To address this problem, we propose model-sharing RLHF, enabling entire RLHF training with no more than one pre-trained model. Concretely, we first train an adapter and a value head with the objective function for reward modeling, allowing the model to compute reward scores. Then we initialize another adapter and value head and train them with the PPO algorithm (Ouyang et al., 2022). The adapters and value heads are dynamically switched through the `set_adapter` and `disable_adapter` methods of PEFT (Mangrulkar et al., 2022) during training, allowing a single pre-trained model to serve as policy model, value model, reference model, and reward model simultaneously. To the best of our knowledge, this is the first method that supports RLHF training on consumer devices.

**Distributed Training** We can combine the above trainers with DeepSpeed (Rasley et al., 2020; Ren et al., 2021) for distributed training. We adopt data parallelism to fully exploit the ability of computing devices. Leveraging the DeepSpeed ZeRO optimizer, the memory consumption can be further reduced via partitioning or offloading.

### 4.4 Utilities

**Model Inference** During inference time, we reuse the chat template from the *Data Worker* to build the model inputs. We offer support for sampling the model outputs using Transformers (Wolf et al., 2020) and vLLM (Kwon et al., 2023), both of which support stream decoding. Additionally, we implement an OpenAI-style API that utilizes the asynchronous LLM engine and paged attention of vLLM, to provide high-throughput concurrent inference services, facilitating the deployment of fine-tuned LLMs into various applications.

**Model Evaluation** We include several metrics for evaluating LLMs, including multiple-choice tasks such as MMLU (Hendrycks et al., 2021), CMMLU (Li et al., 2023a), and C-Eval (Huang et al., 2023), as well as calculating text similarity scores like BLEU-4 (Papineni et al., 2002) and ROUGE (Lin, 2004). This feature facilitates users to measure the abilities of the fine-tuned models.

### 4.5 LlamaBoard: A Unified Interface for LlamaFactory

LlamaBoard is a unified user interface based on Gradio (Abid et al., 2019) that allows users to customize the fine-tuning of LLMs without writing any code. It offers a streamlined model fine-tuning and inference service, enabling users to easily explore the potential of LLMs in their environments. LlamaBoard has the following notable features.

**Easy Configuration** LlamaBoard allows us to customize the fine-tuning arguments through interaction with the web interface. We provide default values for a majority of arguments that are recommended for most users, simplifying the configuration process. Moreover, users can preview the datasets on the web UI to validate them.

**Monitorable Training** During the training process, the training logs and loss curves are visualized and updated in real time, allowing users to monitor the training progress. This feature provides valuable insights to analyze the fine-tuning process.

| Method | Gemma-2B | | | | Llama2-7B | | | | Llama2-13B | | | |
|---|---|---|---|---|---|---|---|---|---|---|---|---|
| | Trainable Params | Memory (GB) | Throughput (Tokens/s) | PPL | Trainable Params | Memory (GB) | Throughput (Tokens/s) | PPL | Trainable Params | Memory (GB) | Throughput (Tokens/s) | PPL |
| Baseline | / | / | / | 11.83 | / | / | / | 7.53 | / | / | / | 6.66 |
| Full-tuning | 2.51B | 17.06 | 3090.42 | 10.34 | 6.74B | 38.72 | 1334.72 | 5.56 | / | / | / | / |
| Freeze-tuning | 0.33B | 8.10 | 5608.49 | 11.33 | 0.61B | 15.69 | 2904.98 | 6.59 | 0.95B | 29.02 | 1841.46 | 6.56 |
| GaLore | 2.51B | 10.16 | 2483.05 | 10.38 | 6.74B | 15.43 | 1583.77 | 5.88 | 13.02B | 28.91 | 956.39 | **5.72** |
| LoRA | 0.16B | 7.91 | **3521.05** | **10.19** | 0.32B | 16.32 | **1954.07** | **5.81** | 0.50B | 30.09 | **1468.19** | 5.75 |
| QLoRA | 0.16B | **5.21** | 3158.59 | 10.46 | 0.32B | **7.52** | 1579.16 | 5.91 | 0.50B | **12.61** | 973.53 | 5.81 |

Table 4: Comparison of the training efficiency using different fine-tuning methods in LlamaFactory. The best result among GaLore, LoRA and QLoRA of each model is in **bold**.

**Flexible Evaluation** LlamaBoard supports calculating the text similarity scores on the datasets to automatically evaluate models or performing human evaluation by chatting with them.

**Multilingual Support** LlamaBoard provides localization files, facilitating the integration of new languages for rendering the interface. Currently we support three languages: English, Russian and Chinese, which allows a broader range of users to utilize LlamaBoard for fine-tuning LLMs.

## 5 Empirical Study

We systematically evaluate LlamaFactory from two perspectives: 1) the training efficiency in terms of memory usage, throughput and perplexity. 2) the effectiveness of adaptation to downstream tasks.

### 5.1 Training Efficiency

**Experimental Setup** We utilize the PubMed dataset (Canese and Weis, 2013), which comprises over 36 million records of biomedical literature. We extract around 400K tokens from the abstract of the literature to construct the training corpus. Then we fine-tune the Gemma-2B (Mesnard et al., 2024), Llama2-7B and Llama2-13B (Touvron et al., 2023b) models using the generative pre-training objective with various efficient fine-tuning methods. We compare the results of full-tuning, freeze-tuning, GaLore, LoRA and 4-bit QLoRA. After fine-tuning, we calculate the perplexity on the training corpus to evaluate the efficiency of different methods. We also incorporate the perplexities of the pre-trained models as baselines.

In this experiment, we adopt a learning rate of $10^{-5}$, a token batch size of 512. We fine-tune these models using the 8-bit AdamW optimizer (Dettmers et al., 2022b) in bfloat16 precision with activation checkpointing to reduce the memory footprint. In freeze-tuning, we only fine-tune the last 3 decoder layers of the model. For GaLore, we set the rank and scale to 128 and 2.0, respectively. For LoRA and QLoRA, we attach adapters to all linear layers and set the rank and alpha to 128 and 256, respectively. All the experiments are conducted on a single NVIDIA A100 40GB GPU. We enable flash attention in all experiments and Unsloth for LoRA and QLoRA experiments.

**Results** The results about the training efficiency are presented in Table 4, where memory refers to the peak memory consumed during training, throughput is calculated as the number of tokens trained per second, and PPL represents the perplexity of the model on the training corpus. Since full-tuning Llama2-13B lead to a memory overflow, the results are not recorded. We observe that QLoRA consistently has the lowest memory footprint because the pre-trained weights are represented in lower precision. LoRA exhibits higher throughput leveraging the optimization in LoRA layers by Unsloth. GaLore achieves lower PPL on large models while LoRA advantages on smaller ones.

### 5.2 Fine-Tuning on Downstream Tasks

**Experimental Setup** To evaluate the effectiveness of different efficient fine-tuning methods, we compare the performance of various models after fine-tuning on downstream tasks. We construct non-overlapping training set and test set using 2,000 examples and 1,000 examples from three representative text generation tasks, including CNN/DM (Nallapati et al., 2016), XSum (Narayan et al., 2018) and AdGen (Shao et al., 2019), respectively. We select several instruction-tuned models and fine-tune them following the sequence-to-sequence task using different fine-tuning methods. Then we compare the results of full-tuning (FT), GaLore, LoRA and 4-bit QLoRA. After fine-tuning, we calculate the ROUGE score (Lin, 2004) on the test set of each task. We also incorporate the scores of the original instruction-tuned models as baselines.

| Model | CNN / DM | | | | | XSum | | | | | AdGen | | | | |
|---|---|---|---|---|---|---|---|---|---|---|---|---|---|---|---|
| | Baseline | FT | GaLore | LoRA | QLoRA | Baseline | FT | GaLore | LoRA | QLoRA | Baseline | FT | GaLore | LoRA | QLoRA |
| ChatGLM3-6B | 18.51 | 22.00 | 22.16 | 21.68 | 21.70 | 16.14 | 26.25 | 26.34 | 26.50 | 26.78 | 14.53 | 19.91 | 20.57 | 20.47 | 20.49 |
| Yi-6B | 16.85 | 22.40 | 22.68 | 22.98 | 22.97 | 18.24 | 27.09 | 28.25 | 28.71 | 29.21 | 13.34 | 19.68 | 20.06 | 20.97 | 20.31 |
| Llama2-7B | 12.94 | 22.87 | 22.40 | 22.70 | 22.61 | 13.89 | 27.69 | 27.64 | 28.80 | 28.05 | 0.61 | 20.51 | 19.61 | 20.29 | 20.45 |
| Mistral-7B | 14.39 | 22.03 | 22.99 | 23.47 | 23.28 | 15.87 | 23.57 | 28.00 | 30.41 | 30.44 | 7.82 | 20.14 | 20.90 | 20.99 | 20.56 |
| Gemma-7B | 15.97 | 22.07 | / | 22.41 | 22.44 | 15.31 | 25.13 | / | 28.67 | 29.02 | 11.57 | 19.99 | / | 20.62 | 19.81 |
| Qwen1.5-7B | 15.40 | 22.46 | 21.76 | 22.71 | 22.52 | 19.27 | 26.68 | 26.64 | 27.77 | 27.60 | 14.49 | 20.42 | 21.08 | 21.31 | 21.34 |
| Qwen2-7B | 16.46 | 23.20 | / | 23.29 | 23.66 | 19.76 | 26.94 | / | 28.92 | 28.94 | 12.89 | 19.83 | / | 20.96 | 20.86 |
| Llama3-8B | 15.19 | 23.36 | 23.57 | 23.48 | **24.12** | 17.83 | 26.21 | 30.45 | 30.63 | **30.94** | 0.22 | 20.28 | 21.27 | **21.44** | 21.20 |

Table 5: Comparison of the performance (in terms of ROUGE) on specific tasks using different fine-tuning methods in LLAMAFACTORY. The best result of each model is underlined, and the best result of each task is in **bold**.

In this experiment, we set learning rate to $10^{-5}$, batch size to 4 and maximum input length to 2048. We fine-tune these models using the 8-bit AdamW optimizer (Dettmers et al., 2022b) in bfloat16 precision with activation checkpointing. For GaLore, we set the rank and scale to 128 and 2.0, respectively. For LoRA and QLoRA, we attach adapters to all linear layers and set the rank and alpha to 128 and 256, respectively. All the experiments are conducted on NVIDIA A100 40GB GPUs.

**Results** The evaluation results on downstream tasks are shown in Table 5. We report the averaged scores over ROUGE-1, ROUGE-2 and ROUGE-L. Some results of the Gemma-7B and Qwen2-7B (Bai et al., 2023) models are not included in the table because the GaLore method may not be applicable to them. An interesting finding from the results is that LoRA and QLoRA achieve the best performance in most cases, except for the ChatGLM3-6B (Zeng et al., 2024) and Llama2-7B models on the CNN/DM and AdGen datasets. This phenomenon highlights the effectiveness of these efficient fine-tuning methods in adapting LLMs to specific tasks. Additionally, we observe that Llama3-8B achieves the best performance among these models, while Yi-6B (Young et al., 2024) and Mistral-7B (Jiang et al., 2023a) exhibit competitive performance among models of the same size.

## 6 Conclusion and Future Work

In this paper, we demonstrate LLAMAFACTORY, a unified framework for the efficient fine-tuning of LLMs. Through a modular design, we minimize dependencies between the models, datasets and training methods and provide an integrated approach to fine-tune over 100 LLMs with a diverse range of efficient fine-tuning techniques. Additionally, we offer a flexible web UI LLAMABOARD, enabling customized fine-tuning and evaluation of LLMs without coding efforts. We empirically validate the efficiency and effectiveness of our framework on language modeling and text generation tasks.

We will consistently keep LLAMAFACTORY synchronous with the state-of-the-art models and efficient fine-tuning techniques. We also welcome contributions from the open-source community. The road map of LLAMAFACTORY including:

(1) Enabling fine-tuning for models that supports a wider range of modalities, *e.g.*, the audio and video modalities (Zhu et al., 2024).

(2) Integrating more parallel training strategies, *e.g.*, sequence parallelism (Jacobs et al., 2023) and tensor parallelism (Shoeybi et al., 2019).

(3) Exploring stronger fine-tuning methods for conversational models, *e.g.*, self-play (Chen et al., 2024b; Yuan et al., 2024).

## 7 Broader Impact and Responsible Use

LLAMAFACTORY has attracted a large number of individuals interested in LLMs to explore the possibility of customizing models. This contributes significantly to the growth of the open-source communities. It is gaining increasing attention and is being featured in Awesome Transformers[2] as a representative of efficient fine-tuning frameworks for LLMs. We anticipate that practitioners build their LLMs upon our framework that bring benefits to society. Adherence to the model license is mandatory when using LLAMAFACTORY for fine-tuning LLMs, thus preventing from any potential misuse.

## Acknowledgements

This work is supported partly by the National Science and Technology Major Project under Grant 2022ZD0120202, by the National Natural Science Foundation of China (No. U23B2056), by the Fundamental Research Funds for the Central Universities, and by the State Key Laboratory of Complex & Critical Software Environment.

[2]https://github.com/huggingface/transformers/blob/v4.40.0/awesome-transformers.md#llama-factory

## References


Abubakar Abid, Ali Abdalla, Ali Abid, Dawood Khan, Abdulrahman Alfozan, and James Zou. 2019. Gradio: Hassle-free sharing and testing of ml models in the wild. In *ICML Workshop on Human in the Loop Learning*, Long Beach, USA.

Lightning AI. 2023. Lit-gpt.

Yuvanesh Anand, Zach Nussbaum, Brandon Duderstadt, Benjamin Schmidt, and Andriy Mulyar. 2023. GPT4All: Training an assistant-style chatbot with large scale data distillation from GPT-3.5-turbo.

Apache. 2016. Arrow.

Jinze Bai, Shuai Bai, Yunfei Chu, Zeyu Cui, Kai Dang, Xiaodong Deng, Yang Fan, Wenbin Ge, Yu Han, Fei Huang, et al. 2023. Qwen technical report. *arXiv preprint arXiv:2309.16609*.

Edward Beeching, Clémentine Fourrier, Nathan Habib, Sheon Han, Nathan Lambert, Nazneen Rajani, Omar Sanseviero, Lewis Tunstall, and Thomas Wolf. 2023. Open LLM leaderboard.

Rishabh Bhardwaj, Do Duc Anh, and Soujanya Poria. 2024. Language models are homer simpson! safety re-alignment of fine-tuned language models through task arithmetic. *arXiv preprint arXiv:2402.11746*.

Kathi Canese and Sarah Weis. 2013. PubMed: the bibliographic database. *The NCBI handbook*, 2(1).

Shouyuan Chen, Sherman Wong, Liangjian Chen, and Yuandong Tian. 2023. Extending context window of large language models via positional interpolation. *arXiv preprint arXiv:2306.15595*.

Tianqi Chen, Bing Xu, Chiyuan Zhang, and Carlos Guestrin. 2016. Training deep nets with sublinear memory cost. *arXiv preprint arXiv:1604.06174*.

Yukang Chen, Shengju Qian, Haotian Tang, Xin Lai, Zhijian Liu, Song Han, and Jiaya Jia. 2024a. LongLoRA: Efficient fine-tuning of long-context large language models. In *International Conference on Learning Representations*.

Zixiang Chen, Yihe Deng, Huizhuo Yuan, Kaixuan Ji, and Quanquan Gu. 2024b. Self-play fine-tuning converts weak language models to strong language models. *arXiv preprint arXiv:2401.01335*.

Tri Dao, Dan Fu, Stefano Ermon, Atri Rudra, and Christopher Ré. 2022. FlashAttention: Fast and memory-efficient exact attention with io-awareness. *Advances in Neural Information Processing Systems*, 35:16344–16359.

Tim Dettmers. 2021. Bitsandbytes.

Tim Dettmers, Mike Lewis, Younes Belkada, and Luke Zettlemoyer. 2022a. GPT3.int8(): 8-bit matrix multiplication for transformers at scale. *Advances in Neural Information Processing Systems*, 35:30318–30332.

Tim Dettmers, Mike Lewis, Sam Shleifer, and Luke Zettlemoyer. 2022b. 8-bit optimizers via block-wise quantization. In *International Conference on Learning Representations*.

Tim Dettmers, Artidoro Pagnoni, Ari Holtzman, and Luke Zettlemoyer. 2023. QLoRA: Efficient finetuning of quantized llms. *Advances in Neural Information Processing Systems*, 36:10088–10115.

Shizhe Diao, Rui Pan, Hanze Dong, KaShun Shum, Jipeng Zhang, Wei Xiong, and Tong Zhang. 2024. LMFlow: An extensible toolkit for finetuning and inference of large foundation models. In *Proceedings of the 2024 Conference of the North American Chapter of the Association for Computational Linguistics: Human Language Technologies (Volume 3: System Demonstrations)*, pages 116–127, Mexico City, Mexico. Association for Computational Linguistics.

Vage Egiazarian, Andrei Panferov, Denis Kuznedelev, Elias Frantar, Artem Babenko, and Dan Alistarh. 2024. Extreme compression of large language models via additive quantization. *arXiv preprint arXiv:2401.06118*.

Kawin Ethayarajh, Winnie Xu, Niklas Muennighoff, Dan Jurafsky, and Douwe Kiela. 2024. KTO: Model alignment as prospect theoretic optimization. In *International Conference on Machine Learning*, Vienna, Austria. PMLR.

Elias Frantar, Saleh Ashkboos, Torsten Hoefler, and Dan Alistarh. 2023. GPTQ: Accurate post-training quantization for generative pre-trained transformers. In *International Conference on Learning Representations*.

Daniel Han and Michael Han. 2023. unsloth.

Soufiane Hayou, Nikhil Ghosh, and Bin Yu. 2024. LoRA+: Efficient low rank adaptation of large models. In *International Conference on Machine Learning*, Vienna, Austria. PMLR.

Dan Hendrycks, Collin Burns, Steven Basart, Andy Zou, Mantas Mazeika, Dawn Song, and Jacob Steinhardt. 2021. Measuring massive multitask language understanding. In *International Conference on Learning Representations*.

Jiwoo Hong, Noah Lee, and James Thorne. 2024. ORPO: Monolithic preference optimization without reference model. *arXiv preprint arXiv:2403.07691*.

Neil Houlsby, Andrei Giurgiu, Stanislaw Jastrzebski, Bruna Morrone, Quentin De Laroussilhe, Andrea Gesmundo, Mona Attariyan, and Sylvain Gelly. 2019. Parameter-efficient transfer learning for NLP. In *International Conference on Machine Learning*, pages 2790–2799. PMLR.

Edward J Hu, Phillip Wallis, Zeyuan Allen-Zhu, Yuanzhi Li, Shean Wang, Lu Wang, Weizhu Chen, et al. 2022. LoRA: Low-rank adaptation of large language models. In *International Conference on Learning Representations*.

Yuzhen Huang, Yuzhuo Bai, Zhihao Zhu, Junlei Zhang, Jinghan Zhang, Tangjun Su, Junteng Liu, Chuancheng Lv, Yikai Zhang, Yao Fu, et al. 2023. C-Eval: A multi-level multi-discipline chinese evaluation suite for foundation models. *Advances in Neural Information Processing Systems*, 36.

Sam Ade Jacobs, Masahiro Tanaka, Chengming Zhang, Minjia Zhang, Leon Song, Samyam Rajbhandari, and Yuxiong He. 2023. Deepspeed ulysses: System optimizations for enabling training of extreme long sequence transformer models. *arXiv preprint arXiv:2309.14509*.

Albert Q Jiang, Alexandre Sablayrolles, Arthur Mensch, Chris Bamford, Devendra Singh Chaplot, Diego de las Casas, Florian Bressand, Gianna Lengyel, Guillaume Lample, Lucile Saulnier, et al. 2023a. Mistral 7b. *arXiv preprint arXiv:2310.06825*.

Jinhao Jiang, Kun Zhou, Wayne Xin Zhao, Yaliang Li, and Ji-Rong Wen. 2023b. ReasoningLM: Enabling structural subgraph reasoning in pre-trained language models for question answering over knowledge graph. In *Proceedings of the 2023 Conference on Empirical Methods in Natural Language Processing*, pages 3721–3735, Singapore. Association for Computational Linguistics.

Wenxiang Jiao, Jen-tse Huang, Wenxuan Wang, Zhiwei He, Tian Liang, Xing Wang, Shuming Shi, and Zhaopeng Tu. 2023a. ParroT: Translating during chat using large language models tuned with human translation and feedback. In *Findings of the Association for Computational Linguistics: EMNLP 2023*, pages 15009–15020, Singapore. Association for Computational Linguistics.

Yizhu Jiao, Ming Zhong, Sha Li, Ruining Zhao, Siru Ouyang, Heng Ji, and Jiawei Han. 2023b. Instruct and extract: Instruction tuning for on-demand information extraction. In *Proceedings of the 2023 Conference on Empirical Methods in Natural Language Processing*, pages 10030–10051, Singapore. Association for Computational Linguistics.

Damjan Kalajdzievski. 2023. A rank stabilization scaling factor for fine-tuning with LoRA. *arXiv preprint arXiv:2312.03732*.

Mario Michael Krell, Matej Kosec, Sergio P Perez, and Andrew Fitzgibbon. 2021. Efficient sequence packing without cross-contamination: Accelerating large language models without impacting performance. *arXiv preprint arXiv:2107.02027*.

Woosuk Kwon, Zhuohan Li, Siyuan Zhuang, Ying Sheng, Lianmin Zheng, Cody Hao Yu, Joseph Gonzalez, Hao Zhang, and Ion Stoica. 2023. Efficient memory management for large language model serving with PagedAttention. In *Proceedings of the 29th Symposium on Operating Systems Principles*, pages 611–626.

Teven Le Scao, Angela Fan, Christopher Akiki, Ellie Pavlick, Suzana Ilić, Daniel Hesslow, Roman Castagné, Alexandra Sasha Luccioni, François Yvon, Matthias Gallé, et al. 2022. BLOOM: A 176b-parameter open-access multilingual language model. *arXiv preprint arXiv:2211.05100*.

Quentin Lhoest, Albert Villanova del Moral, Yacine Jernite, Abhishek Thakur, Patrick von Platen, Suraj Patil, Julien Chaumond, Mariama Drame, Julien Plu, Lewis Tunstall, et al. 2021. Datasets: A community library for natural language processing. In *Proceedings of the 2021 Conference on Empirical Methods in Natural Language Processing: System Demonstrations*, pages 175–184.

Haonan Li, Yixuan Zhang, Fajri Koto, Yifei Yang, Hai Zhao, Yeyun Gong, Nan Duan, and Timothy Baldwin. 2023a. CMMLU: Measuring massive multitask language understanding in chinese. *arXiv preprint arXiv:2306.09212*.

Shenggui Li, Hongxin Liu, Zhengda Bian, Jiarui Fang, Haichen Huang, Yuliang Liu, Boxiang Wang, and Yang You. 2023b. Colossal-AI: A unified deep learning system for large-scale parallel training. In *Proceedings of the 52nd International Conference on Parallel Processing*, pages 766–775.

Chin-Yew Lin. 2004. ROUGE: A package for automatic evaluation of summaries. In *Text Summarization Branches Out*, pages 74–81, Barcelona, Spain. Association for Computational Linguistics.

Ji Lin, Jiaming Tang, Haotian Tang, Shang Yang, Xingyu Dang, and Song Han. 2023. AWQ: Activation-aware weight quantization for llm compression and acceleration. *arXiv preprint arXiv:2306.00978*.

Shih-Yang Liu, Chien-Yi Wang, Hongxu Yin, Pavlo Molchanov, Yu-Chiang Frank Wang, Kwang-Ting Cheng, and Min-Hung Chen. 2024. DoRA: Weight-decomposed low-rank adaptation. In *International Conference on Machine Learning*, Vienna, Austria. PMLR.

Qijun Luo, Hengxu Yu, and Xiao Li. 2024. BAdam: A memory efficient full parameter training method for large language models. *arXiv preprint arXiv:2404.02827*.

Sourab Mangrulkar, Sylvain Gugger, Lysandre Debut, Younes Belkada, Sayak Paul, and Benjamin Bossan. 2022. PEFT: State-of-the-art parameter-efficient fine-tuning methods.

Fanxu Meng, Zhaohui Wang, and Muhan Zhang. 2024. PiSSA: Principal singular values and singular vectors adaptation of large language models. *arXiv preprint arXiv:2404.02948*.

Thomas Mesnard, Cassidy Hardin, Robert Dadashi, Surya Bhupatiraju, Shreya Pathak, Laurent Sifre, Morgane Rivière, Mihir Sanjay Kale, Juliette Love, et al. 2024. Gemma: Open models based on gemini research and technology. *arXiv preprint arXiv:2403.08295*.

Paulius Micikevicius, Sharan Narang, Jonah Alben, Gregory Diamos, Erich Elsen, David Garcia, Boris Ginsburg, Michael Houston, Oleksii Kuchaiev, Ganesh Venkatesh, et al. 2018. Mixed precision training. In *International Conference on Learning Representations*.

Ramesh Nallapati, Bowen Zhou, Cicero dos Santos, Caglar Gulcehre, and Bing Xiang. 2016. Abstractive text summarization using sequence-to-sequence rnns and beyond. In *Proceedings of the 20th SIGNLL Conference on Computational Natural Language Learning*, pages 280–290.

Shashi Narayan, Shay B. Cohen, and Mirella Lapata. 2018. Don't give me the details, just the summary! topic-aware convolutional neural networks for extreme summarization. In *Proceedings of the 2018 Conference on Empirical Methods in Natural Language Processing*, pages 1797–1807, Brussels, Belgium. Association for Computational Linguistics.

Long Ouyang, Jeffrey Wu, Xu Jiang, Diogo Almeida, Carroll Wainwright, Pamela Mishkin, Chong Zhang, Sandhini Agarwal, Katarina Slama, Alex Ray, et al. 2022. Training language models to follow instructions with human feedback. *Advances in Neural Information Processing Systems*, 35:27730–27744.

Kishore Papineni, Salim Roukos, Todd Ward, and Wei-Jing Zhu. 2002. BLEU: a method for automatic evaluation of machine translation. In *Proceedings of the 40th annual meeting of the Association for Computational Linguistics*, pages 311–318, Philadelphia, Pennsylvania, USA. Association for Computational Linguistics.

Adam Paszke, Sam Gross, Francisco Massa, Adam Lerer, James Bradbury, Gregory Chanan, Trevor Killeen, Zeming Lin, Natalia Gimelshein, Luca Antiga, et al. 2019. PyTorch: An imperative style, high-performance deep learning library. *Advances in Neural Information Processing Systems*, 32.

Alec Radford, Karthik Narasimhan, Tim Salimans, Ilya Sutskever, et al. 2018. Improving language understanding by generative pre-training. *OpenAI blog*.

Rafael Rafailov, Archit Sharma, Eric Mitchell, Stefano Ermon, Christopher D Manning, and Chelsea Finn. 2023. Direct preference optimization: Your language model is secretly a reward model. *Advances in Neural Information Processing Systems*, 37.

Jeff Rasley, Samyam Rajbhandari, Olatunji Ruwase, and Yuxiong He. 2020. DeepSpeed: System optimizations enable training deep learning models with over 100 billion parameters. In *Proceedings of the 26th ACM SIGKDD International Conference on Knowledge Discovery & Data Mining*, pages 3505–3506.

Jie Ren, Samyam Rajbhandari, Reza Yazdani Aminabadi, Olatunji Ruwase, Shuangyan Yang, Minjia Zhang, Dong Li, and Yuxiong He. 2021. ZeRO-offload: Democratizing billion-scale model training. In *USENIX Annual Technical Conference*, pages 551–564.

Zhihong Shao, Minlie Huang, Jiangtao Wen, Wenfei Xu, and Xiaoyan Zhu. 2019. Long and diverse text generation with planning-based hierarchical variational model. In *Proceedings of the 2019 Conference on Empirical Methods in Natural Language Processing and the 9th International Joint Conference on Natural Language Processing (EMNLP-IJCNLP)*, pages 3257–3268, Hong Kong, China. Association for Computational Linguistics.

Mohammad Shoeybi, Mostofa Patwary, Raul Puri, Patrick LeGresley, Jared Casper, and Bryan Catanzaro. 2019. Megatron-LM: Training multi-billion parameter language models using model parallelism. *arXiv preprint arXiv:1909.08053*.

Rohan Taori, Ishaan Gulrajani, Tianyi Zhang, Yann Dubois, Xuechen Li, Carlos Guestrin, Percy Liang, and Tatsunori B. Hashimoto. 2023. Stanford alpaca: An instruction-following llama model.

Philippe Tillet, Hsiang-Tsung Kung, and David Cox. 2019. Triton: An intermediate language and compiler for tiled neural network computations. In *Proceedings of the 3rd ACM SIGPLAN International Workshop on Machine Learning and Programming Languages*, pages 10–19.

Hugo Touvron, Thibaut Lavril, Gautier Izacard, Xavier Martinet, Marie-Anne Lachaux, Timothée Lacroix, Baptiste Rozière, Naman Goyal, Eric Hambro, Faisal Azhar, et al. 2023a. LLaMA: Open and efficient foundation language models. *arXiv preprint arXiv:2302.13971*.

Hugo Touvron, Louis Martin, Kevin Stone, Peter Albert, Amjad Almahairi, Yasmine Babaei, Nikolay Bashlykov, Soumya Batra, Prajjwal Bhargava, Shruti Bhosale, et al. 2023b. Llama 2: Open foundation and fine-tuned chat models. *arXiv preprint arXiv:2307.09288*.

Sang Truong, Duc Nguyen, Toan Nguyen, Dong Le, Nhi Truong, Tho Quan, and Sanmi Koyejo. 2024. Crossing linguistic horizons: Finetuning and comprehensive evaluation of Vietnamese large language models. In *Findings of the Association for Computational Linguistics: NAACL 2024*, pages 2849–2900, Mexico City, Mexico. Association for Computational Linguistics.

Leandro von Werra, Younes Belkada, Lewis Tunstall, Edward Beeching, Tristan Thrush, Nathan Lambert, and Shengyi Huang. 2020. TRL: Transformer reinforcement learning.

Chenglong Wang, Hang Zhou, Yimin Hu, Yifu Huo, Bei Li, Tongran Liu, Tong Xiao, and Jingbo Zhu. 2023a. ESRL: Efficient sampling-based reinforcement learning for sequence generation. *arXiv preprint arXiv:2308.02223*.

Longyue Wang, Chenyang Lyu, Tianbo Ji, Zhirui Zhang, Dian Yu, Shuming Shi, and Zhaopeng Tu. 2023b.

Document-level machine translation with large language models. In *Proceedings of the 2023 Conference on Empirical Methods in Natural Language Processing*, pages 16646–16661, Singapore. Association for Computational Linguistics.

Yizhong Wang, Hamish Ivison, Pradeep Dasigi, Jack Hessel, Tushar Khot, Khyathi Chandu, David Wadden, Kelsey MacMillan, Noah A Smith, Iz Beltagy, et al. 2023c. How far can camels go? exploring the state of instruction tuning on open resources. *Advances in Neural Information Processing Systems*, 36.

Jason Wei, Maarten Bosma, Vincent Zhao, Kelvin Guu, Adams Wei Yu, Brian Lester, Nan Du, Andrew M Dai, and Quoc V Le. 2022. Finetuned language models are zero-shot learners. In *International Conference on Learning Representations.*

Thomas Wolf, Lysandre Debut, Victor Sanh, Julien Chaumond, Clement Delangue, Anthony Moi, Pierric Cistac, Tim Rault, Rémi Louf, Morgan Funtowicz, Joe Davison, Sam Shleifer, Patrick von Platen, Clara Ma, Yacine Jernite, Julien Plu, Canwen Xu, Teven Le Scao, Sylvain Gugger, Mariama Drame, Quentin Lhoest, and Alexander Rush. 2020. Transformers: State-of-the-art natural language processing. In *Proceedings of the 2020 Conference on Empirical Methods in Natural Language Processing: System Demonstrations*, pages 38–45, Online. Association for Computational Linguistics.

Alex Young, Bei Chen, Chao Li, Chengen Huang, Ge Zhang, Guanwei Zhang, Heng Li, Jiangcheng Zhu, Jianqun Chen, Jing Chang, et al. 2024. Yi: Open foundation models by 01.ai. *arXiv preprint arXiv:2403.04652.*

Hao Yu, Zachary Yang, Kellin Pelrine, Jean Francois Godbout, and Reihaneh Rabbany. 2023. Open, closed, or small language models for text classification? *arXiv preprint arXiv:2308.10092.*

Weizhe Yuan, Richard Yuanzhe Pang, Kyunghyun Cho, Sainbayar Sukhbaatar, Jing Xu, and Jason Weston. 2024. Self-rewarding language models. *arXiv preprint arXiv:2401.10020.*

Aohan Zeng, Bin Xu, Bowen Wang, Chenhui Zhang, Da Yin, Diego Rojas, Guanyu Feng, Hanlin Zhao, Hanyu Lai, Hao Yu, Hongning Wang, Jiadai Sun, Jiajie Zhang, Jiale Cheng, Jiayi Gui, Jie Tang, et al. 2024. ChatGLM: A family of large language models from GLM-130b to GLM-4 all tools. *arXiv preprint arXiv:2406.12793.*

Renrui Zhang, Jiaming Han, Aojun Zhou, Xiangfei Hu, Shilin Yan, Pan Lu, Hongsheng Li, Peng Gao, and Yu Qiao. 2024. LLaMA-adapter: Efficient finetuning of language models with zero-init attention. In *International Conference on Learning Representations.*

Jiawei Zhao, Zhenyu Zhang, Beidi Chen, Zhangyang Wang, Anima Anandkumar, and Yuandong Tian. 2024. GaLore: Memory-efficient llm training by gradient low-rank projection. In *International Conference on Machine Learning*, Vienna, Austria. PMLR.

Wayne Xin Zhao, Kun Zhou, Junyi Li, Tianyi Tang, Xiaolei Wang, Yupeng Hou, Yingqian Min, Beichen Zhang, Junjie Zhang, Zican Dong, Yifan Du, Chen Yang, Yushuo Chen, Zhipeng Chen, Jinhao Jiang, Ruiyang Ren, Yifan Li, Xinyu Tang, Zikang Liu, Peiyu Liu, Jian-Yun Nie, and Ji-Rong Wen. 2023. A survey of large language models. *arXiv preprint arXiv:2303.18223.*

Lianmin Zheng, Wei-Lin Chiang, Ying Sheng, Siyuan Zhuang, Zhanghao Wu, Yonghao Zhuang, Zi Lin, Zhuohan Li, Dacheng Li, Eric Xing, et al. 2023. Judging LLM-as-a-judge with MT-bench and chatbot arena. *Advances in Neural Information Processing Systems*, 36.

Bin Zhu, Bin Lin, Munan Ning, Yang Yan, Jiaxi Cui, WANG HongFa, Yatian Pang, Wenhao Jiang, Junwu Zhang, Zongwei Li, et al. 2024. LanguageBind: Extending video-language pretraining to N-modality by language-based semantic alignment. In *International Conference on Learning Representations.*

# Author Index

**Association for Computational Linguistics**
209 N. Eighth Street
Stroudsburg, Pennsylvania 18360

ISBN 979-8-3313-0150-7

CURRAN ASSOCIATES INC.
proceedings.com